KU-474-896

# Pettet, Lowry & Reisberg's Company Law

346.
066

REI

LIVERPOOL
JOHN MOORES
UNIVERSITY

Library Services

| Accession No | 1889854 | |
| Supplier | PQ | Invoice Date |
| Class No | | |
| Site | A | Fund Code LAW1 |

WITHDRAWN

LIVERPOOL JMU LIBRARY

3 1111 01518 9788

# Pearson

At Pearson, we have a simple mission: to help people
make more of their lives through learning.

We combine innovative learning technology with trusted
content and educational expertise to provide engaging
and effective learning experiences that serve people
wherever and whenever they are learning.

From classroom to boardroom, our curriculum materials, digital
learning tools and testing programmes help to educate millions
of people worldwide – more than any other private enterprise.

Every day our work helps learning flourish, and
wherever learning flourishes, so do people.

To learn more, please visit us at **www.pearson.com/uk**

# Pettet, Lowry & Reisberg's Company Law

Fifth Edition

Arad Reisberg

Anna Donovan

 **Pearson**

Harlow, England • London • New York • Boston • San Francisco • Toronto • Sydney
Dubai • Singapore • Hong Kong • Tokyo • Seoul • Taipei • New Delhi
Cape Town • São Paulo • Mexico City • Madrid • Amsterdam • Munich • Paris • Milan

**PEARSON EDUCATION LIMITED**
KAO Two
KAO Park
Harlow CM17 9NA
United Kingdom
Tel: +44 (0)1279 623623
Web: www.pearson.com/uk

First published 2001 (print)
Second edition published 2005 (print)
Third edition published 2009 (print)
Fourth edition published 2012 (print and electronic)
**Fifth edition published 2018** (print and electronic)

© Pearson Education Limited 2001, 2005, 2009 (print)
© Pearson Education Limited  2012, 2018 (print and electronic)

The rights of John Lowry, Arad Reisberg and Anna Donovan to be identified as authors of this work have been asserted by them in accordance with the Copyright, Designs and Patents Act 1988.

The print publication is protected by copyright. Prior to any prohibited reproduction, storage in a retrieval system, distribution or transmission in any form or by any means, electronic, mechanical, recording or otherwise, permission should be obtained from the publisher or, where applicable, a licence permitting restricted copying in the United Kingdom should be obtained from the Copyright Licensing Agency Ltd, Barnard's Inn, 86 Fetter Lane, London EC4A 1EN.

The ePublication is protected by copyright and must not be copied, reproduced, transferred, distributed, leased, licensed or publicly performed or used in any way except as specifically permitted in writing by the publishers, as allowed under the terms and conditions under which it was purchased, or as strictly permitted by applicable copyright law. Any unauthorised distribution or use of this text may be a direct infringement of the authors' and the publisher's rights and those responsible may be liable in law accordingly.

All trademarks used herein are the property of their respective owners. The use of any trademark in this text does not vest in the authors or publisher any trademark ownership rights in such trademarks, nor does the use of such trademarks imply any affiliation with or endorsement of this book by such owners.

Contains public sector information licensed under the Open Government Licence (OGL) v3.0.
http://www.nationalarchives.gov.uk/doc/open-government-licence/version/3/.

Pearson Education is not responsible for the content of third-party internet sites.

ISBN: 978-1-292-07863-2 (print)
        978-1-292-07864-9 (PDF)
        978-1-292-07866-3 (ePub)

**British Library Cataloguing-in-Publication Data**
A catalogue record for the print edition is available from the British Library

**Library of Congress Cataloging-in-Publication Data**
A catalog record for the print edition is available from the Library of Congress
Names: Pettet, B. G., author. | Donovan, Anna H.L.P., author. | Reisberg,
    Arad, 1971- author. | Lowry, John P., author.
Title: Pettet, Lowry & Reisberg's Company Law / Arad Reisberg, Anna Donovan.
Description: Fifth edition. | Harlow, England ; New York : Pearson, 2018.
Identifiers: LCCN 2018025579 | ISBN 9781292078632 (print) | ISBN 9781292078649
    (pdf) | ISBN 9781292078663 (epub)
Subjects: LCSH: Corporation law—Great Britain.
Classification: LCC KD2079 .P48 2018 | DDC 346.41/066—dc23
LC record available at https://urldefense.proofpoint.com/v2/url?u=https-3A__lccn.loc.gov_2018025579&d=DwIFAg
    &c=0YLnzTkWOdJlub_y7qAx8Q&r=eK0q0-QqUPIJD1OLTc7YiWdHxmNowNBMcvK9N3XeA-U&m=ilZC0xYSILfc
    L04r8IhHW6vjdIgw0UwL80Twr36-pK0&s=-DTgMw7_s48bJJu-9sonvXPb-V8cL20oebCdezBgN7c&e=

10 9 8 7 6 5 4 3 2 1
22 21 20 19 18

Front cover image @ Leontura/DigitalVision Vectors/Getty Images

Print edition typeset in 10/12.5, Times LT Pro by iEnergizer, Aptara® Ltd.

Printed by Ashford Colour Press Ltd., Gosport

NOTE THAT ANY PAGE CROSS REFERENCES REFER TO THE PRINT EDITION

# Contents in brief

# Contents in detail

# Preface to the fifth edition

This is the third edition of *Pettet, Lowry & Reisberg's Company Law* since the passing of Ben Pettet in 2005 and the first since John Lowry has retired. We thought it would be fitting to acknowledge John's immense contribution to corporate law scholarship generally, and this text in particular, by adding his name to the title. As with the previous edition, we continue to carry forward the emphasis he placed on financial markets law and corporate finance not as mere bolt-on topics to company law, but as integral parts of the whole.

Given the last edition was published over five years ago and fundamental legislative changes have occurred across the board since then, the exercise of updating this new edition was not an easy one. In preparing it we have tried to respond to this challenge by including the most significant changes and by bringing the reader up to date with the policy implications of these in the wider context. For example, Chapters 16 and 18 discuss the statutory objectives of the Financial Services Act 2012, the Banking Reform Act 2013 and the Bank of England and Financial Services Act 2016. The first two are the major pieces of legislation that the Government has taken through Parliament to fundamentally reform the financial sector, given it was found to be lacking in effectiveness. The new Directive on Markets in Financial Instruments and the new Regulation on Markets in Financial Instruments, commonly referred to as 'MiFIDII' and 'MiFIR', are likewise considered.

Chapter 9 is a new addition to the text, exploring the specific duties to which directors are subject (with Chapter 8 providing a detailed examination of directors' general duties). Chapter 10 brings the reader up to date with several major consultations relating to corporate governance which were published in the UK in 2015–2017, the current version of the UK Corporate Governance Code, and there is an illuminating discussion of the new proposed revised Code. Chapter 11 includes discussion of new double derivative action cases as well as new derivative suit cases in other jurisdictions.

There is an in-depth analysis of the new regulatory framework of Credit Rating Agencies ('CRAs') in Chapter 17, focused on enhancing competition in the credit rating market and including rules aimed at reducing over-reliance on credit ratings. The regulatory technical standards introduced by the European Commission to strengthened regulatory control of CRAs are likewise examined, as well as recent policy studies conducted by the International Organization of Securities Commissions, the European Commission and the European Securities and Markets Authority.

Chapter 18 deals with important new case law on the Financial Services and Markets Act 2000 ('FSMA 2000') and the recent decision of the Supreme Court in *Asset Land*. The new Prospectus Regulation 2017 and the very recent review of the UK listing regime are both analysed in Chapter 19, and there is an in-depth analysis in Chapter 20 of the new EU

Market Abuse Regulation ('MAR') and a number of new insider dealing cases. Chapters 22 and 23 (insolvency and directors' disqualification respectively) address the important changes that have been made to enhance the company insolvency regime, supported by a robust but fair disqualification procedure. In particular, these chapters look at the changes introduced by the Small Business, Enterprise and Employment Act 2015, the recommendations of the Graham Report and the Insolvency (England and Wales) Rules 2016.

As ever, we owe a debt of gratitude to a number of research assistants: Peter O'Loughlin, Eleanore Hickman who in 2016 reviewed a number of chapters, and Francisco de la Pena, who picked up from there and completed the task. Arad Reisberg thanks, in particular, his students at UCL and Brunel Law School, Dan Prentice and Brian Halliday. Anna Donovan thanks, in particular, her students at UCL, Marc Moore, Jonathan Donovan and Jean and David Pope. Anna wishes to make special mention to Freya Pope, Alba Zunino and Benjamin Ruddlesden. We also thank everyone at Pearson for their forbearance.

*Arad Reisberg and Anna Donovan*
*January 2018*

# Preface to the first edition

In writing this book I have three aims. The first is to move the subject of company law closer to what is usually called securities regulation (or capital markets law). I have become ever more convinced in recent years that one cannot understand company law from a practical or theoretical angle without a clear perception of the principles and aims of securities regulation. As an academic and practical subject, company law needs to include securities regulation, and I have tried to demonstrate that in this work.

My second purpose is to provide a lively and thought-provoking analysis of the main legal rules of company law. Readers will find that I have departed somewhat from the list of topics often contained in company law texts, and so some areas have a much lower profile in this book than they have received elsewhere. It has also been necessary to vary the depth of coverage in order for the book to remain short enough for it to claim to be a student textbook. On the other hand, I have given special attention to areas which I have seen students struggle with over the years, and in some chapters I have picked on the facts of seminal cases, or constructed examples, which have then been used to illustrate at length the ideas which I have wished to convey. As far as I am able, and where relevant, I have tried to present the rules in the social and practical context in which they operate, both as a means of making the subject of more interest and to enhance understanding.

My third aim is to give an account of, and assessment of, the important theoretical or jurisprudential issues which are current in this field, with a view to enabling the reader to develop views on the appropriate direction of future reforms. In this regard, it is an exciting time to be considering company law reform, because the DTI's Company Law Review is currently questioning the rationale of many areas, and because a substantially new system of securities regulation is coming into being as a result of the passing of the Financial Services and Markets Act 2000. Also, national and international scholarship on fundamental theoretical issues has continued unabated into the new millennium, spurred both by scholarly interest and by the competitive pressures between different systems of company law created by the global market for capital.

This book is arranged in six Parts: Foundation and Theory, The Constitution of the Company, Corporate Governance, Corporate Finance Law, Securities Regulation, Insolvency and Liquidation. An explanation of the contents of these Parts and the reasons for organising the book in this way are set out in Chapter 1. It has of course been necessary to draw a line under the inclusion of material, and I have endeavoured to present the law and developments as they stand at 1 August 2000. With respect to the Financial Services and Markets Act 2000, the account assumes that the Act is in force, which is very likely to be the case by the time this book is published. As regards my very occasional references to the secondary legislation in that area, I have written on the basis of the draft orders and made this clear in the footnotes, since the finalised versions are unlikely to be available before about autumn 2001. This book has its own companion website and the reader will find on it material which supports the book: http://www.mylawchamber.co.uk/pettet.

I wish to thank Professor Roger Rideout and the other editors, for first encouraging me to write a text on company law, so many years ago, and Pearson Education Ltd for their patience in waiting for it; also Pat Bond, of Pearson Education, who has been a pleasure to work with and a source of helpful advice. Credit is also due to Pearson Education's efficient production team, in particular Anita Atkinson, Kathryn Swift and Sarah Phillipson. I owe much to a generation of students for their enthusiastic criticism and probing of some of my ideas, and of course the debt of any author to past and present scholars and lawyers in the field is immense. In this regard I wish to record special thanks to Guido Ferrarini, Jim Fishman, David Sugarman, Jim Wickenden and others, who have read and commented on some of the material in draft form. Needless to say, the responsibility for the views expressed here and for errors and omissions remains mine, and mine alone.

This book is dedicated to my wife, Corry, and to my children, Emily, Roland and Florence, in grateful recognition of their loving support and encouragement in the years I was writing, particularly during that lost summer of 2000.

*Ben Pettet*
*Faculty of Laws*
*University College London*
*September 2000*

# Foreword to the fourth edition

Writing a book on Company Law at this juncture in the development of the subject is a daunting undertaking. There is the Companies Act 2006, the largest statute on the statute book, 1300 sections and 16 schedules (with of course the supporting secondary legislation). The satellite legislation (if it may be called that) the Financial Services and Markets Act 2000 and the Insolvency Act 1986 also, as this text shows, cast a long shadow over the subject. Added to this, the volume of reported case law has developed dramatically. A small, but important example of this, is the Company Directors Disqualification Act 1986 which has resulted in a number of important decisions having a direct bearing on the substantive duties of directors. John Lowry and Arad Reisberg rise more than admirably to the task of assimilating, explaining and analysing this vast corpus of legal material. The text is pellucidly clear, analytically précis, judicious in its balance in dealing with the various topics, comprehensive, and always cognisant of the policy issues. The contributors have done justice to the legacy of Pettet's previous editions.

*Professor Dan Prentice,*
*Oxford, UCL and Erskine Chambers*
*December 2008*

Dan Prentice held the Allen & Overy Professorship of Corporate Law at the Faculty of Law, University of Oxford, providing leadership in teaching and research at the highest level in the law governing corporate associations. Professor Prentice has been teaching Company Law, Corporate Insolvency and Corporate Finance; he combines this with a mainly advisory practice at Erskine Chambers. He is a member of both the Law Society's Committee on Company Law and the Law Society's Committee on Insolvency Law.

# Table of cases

# Table of statutes

# Table of statutory instruments

# Table of European legislation

# Part I
# Foundation and theory

# 1

# The nature of company law

## 1.1 Preliminary

At the heart of the UK capitalist system, the free market economy, lies company law. Its web of rules establishes the parameters within which the process of bringing together and organising the factors of production can take place. Company law does this by setting up or regulating two environments: the company, which is the organisational structure within which the production takes place, and the capital market through which the money is raised to finance the production process.

In the capital market, people will supply the company with its capital by taking up securities when the company issues them. These will usually be either share capital or debt. The securities will give the holders claims against the company. In the case of shares, it will usually give rights to assets remaining in a future liquidation after the holders of debt securities and other creditors have been paid; they are residual rights. The shareholders will also usually have the right to elect the managers of the company, the board of directors. These managers will buy in the factors of production, consisting of assets and labour. The company will then exchange the goods and/or services which it produces in return for money or other assets. If over a period of time the company receives more back from its activities than it has received from those who have supplied capital, then wealth will have been created for the shareholders. This wealth will usually find its way back to the shareholders either by way of small periodic payments called 'dividends' and/or by a rise in the share price on the market reflecting the fact that the company's assets have increased. Alternatively, though rarely, it may be distributed to the shareholders in a liquidation. More usually, a liquidation marks the end of the company's useful life as a business organisation and will be an insolvent liquidation where the assets are insufficient to pay the creditors all that they are owed.

This analysis relates to what in this text will be described as the 'dispersed-ownership' company, which is a company where its shares are widely held by the public, and where the management have a relatively small or insignificant shareholding, leading to some degree of what is often called 'separation of ownership and control'. Such companies exhibit very different characteristics and face very different problems from companies which in this text will be described as 'small closely-held' companies, where the managers own all or most of the shares and where there is no substantial separation of ownership and control.[1]

---

[1] These definitions, the significance of them and their relationship to legal terms of art such as 'public' company and 'private' company, are explored in more detail below.

## 1.2 Rationale, abstract and agenda

The first Part of this text, 'Foundation and theory', introduces some of the main doctrines of company law, and explores past and current theoretical and practical challenges and the way attempts are being made to resolve them. Company law draws various technical distinctions between different types of companies and there are various types of business vehicle in existence, but the focus of the subject can initially be narrowed down to a consideration of public and private companies limited by shares and created by registration.[2] Companies are treated by the law as having legal personality, as being separate from the shareholders, which means, for instance, that the company, and not the shareholders, is the owner of its property. In most situations there is a related doctrine of limited liability, under which the maximum amount which the shareholders stand to lose is the amount which they have invested or agreed to invest. Thus, if the company goes into insolvent liquidation, the shareholders will not be required to make good the shortfall. The doctrine of limited liability has many effects but in particular it plays an important role in enabling companies to raise capital from the public because it enables individuals to invest small amounts in the shares of a company without risking personal insolvency if the company goes into insolvent liquidation.[3] Jurisprudential writings on company law have produced a rich body of legal theory which both seeks to describe the impact produced by the operation of the rules of company law and to prescribe what those rules should be. Of particular current interest is the impact of economic analysis of law and the continuing challenges of stakeholder company law.[4] The Company Law Review, under the auspices of the Department for Business, Energy & Industrial Strategy (hereafter referred to as DBEIS, formerly the Department of Trade and Industry (DTI)), has undertaken a comprehensive investigation into the purposes and effectiveness of company law. The results of this prolonged process led to what is the longest statute in the history of Parliament: the Companies Act 2006 (CA 2006).[5]

'The constitution of the company' is the subject of Part II of this text, dealing with the ways in which provisions in the constitution of the company affect the contractual rights of various persons dealing with it, and broadly, the way in which functions are divided among the shareholders and directors. The statutory parts of the constitution of a company permit shareholders to entrench rights subject to alteration by prescribed statutory procedures designed to produce a system of checks and balances. Additionally, by means of contractual arrangements called 'shareholder agreements', it is sometimes possible to entrench rights and make detailed provision for an almost unlimited variety of contingencies.[6] The constitution normally vests the power to manage the business of the company in the board of directors, although subject to interference by the shareholders in certain circumstances. Historically, under what is termed the *ultra vires* doctrine, the powers of the company have been limited by the constitution with the result that acts beyond those powers have been regarded as ineffective; this has been curtailed by statute but still

---

[2] These matters are dealt with in this chapter.
[3] See Chapter 2 below.
[4] See Chapter 3 below.
[5] See 1.10 below.
[6] See Chapter 4 below.

continues to give rise to analytical difficulties if the powers of the directors to bind the company are similarly limited.[7] The related question of how a company enters into contractual relations with other legal persons is largely determined by the law of agency. In company law, the area has been made unnecessarily obscure by the development of a doctrine known as the 'indoor management rule' and by the effect of limitations on the powers of directors and other agents contained in the constitution.[8]

'Corporate governance' is dealt with in Part III of the book. The term corporate governance denotes the system by which the company is controlled and governed, but in dispersed-ownership companies it carries the additional connotation that the managers will need to be controlled, otherwise they will be likely to pursue their own interests. So, broadly, it involves an analysis of the ways in which the law seeks to align the interests of the managers with those of the shareholders. The relationship between the board of directors and the shareholders is largely delineated by the provisions in the legislation regulating the calling of meetings and passing of resolutions which are supplemented by provisions contained in the constitution of the company. In dispersed-ownership companies, the realities of the situation make it difficult for the meeting structure to be an effective control mechanism.[9] As a primary alignment mechanism, the law casts duties of care and skill on directors and fiduciary duties of good faith. However, these duties are owed to the company, rather than the shareholders as individuals, which by reason of case law makes litigation for breach of them difficult.[10] Other constraints on directors' powers come about by provisions which enable the shareholders to dismiss the directors, and by statutory provisions which seek to enforce fair dealing by directors and so restrict the extent to which directors are able to benefit from transactions with the company. Also relevant here are rules which require disclosure of financial and other information.[11] Insufficiencies in corporate governance mechanisms have resulted in the appearance of codes of corporate governance, supplementing the legal requirements and relying on elements of self-regulation for compliance.[12] Litigation by shareholders is a last resort and historically the common law has discouraged it, in particular by developing doctrines which restrict the standing of shareholders to bring proceedings.[13] It appears that the recent statutory developments have not, in practice, resulted in material changes in this respect. By comparison, the fairly recent development of litigation based on standing given by the Companies Act 2006 (and its immediate predecessor) to redress conduct which is 'unfairly prejudicial' has resulted in very significant developments in the remedies available to shareholders. However, the increased possibility of litigating matters has, not surprisingly, been of little interest to shareholders in dispersed-ownership companies who have little economic incentive to fight issues of principle through the courts and who will normally 'exit' by sale on the market.[14]

---

[7] See Chapter 5 below.
[8] See Chapter 6 below.
[9] See Chapter 7 below.
[10] See Chapter 8 below.
[11] See Chapter 9 below.
[12] See Chapter 10 below.
[13] See Chapter 11 below.
[14] See Chapter 12 below.

'Corporate finance law' is the subject of Part IV. This is concerned with basic doctrines of corporate finance and the techniques by which companies raise capital as well as the rules which apply to restrict the situations in which the capital raised can be returned to the shareholders. Techniques of corporate finance range from the entrepreneur using his savings to subscribe for shares in his newly formed business, through to venture capital, and on to an initial public offering and flotation on the Stock Exchange. These and other techniques are made possible by the ability of the company to issue shares and to borrow in various ways.[15] Company law has developed a doctrine of nominal value of shares under which the share is given a fixed value at the time of its issue and it retains that nominal value even though the actual market value may later have changed. From this concept rules have been developed which govern the payment for shares when issued. Subsequently, the company comes under restrictions, known as the doctrine of maintenance of capital, regulating how and when it can return capital to the shareholders and related matters.[16] A particular problem developed early in the last century in which a company's assets were used to enable a syndicate to purchase the shares in it. This led to legislation to prohibit what became known as financial assistance for the acquisition of shares. The legislation and related case law have raised problems ever since.[17]

'Securities regulation' is covered in Part V of this text and its inclusion in a text on company law is probably the most controversial topic considered here. Securities regulation, or as it is sometimes called, 'capital markets law', is often thought to be a discrete field, separate and distinct from company law. Culturally it seems different: the state has a high profile through the presence of a powerful regulatory authority as opposed to the often permissive nature of company law rules and low profile presence of the state. It seems more part of public law, and alien to the mainly private law feel of company law with its emphasis on entrepreneurs and common law concepts of property and contract. And yet investor protection has been a major theme of company law texts for many years and company law books almost invariably give some coverage to some of the central areas of securities regulation, such as takeovers, insider dealing and public offerings of shares, but it is usually approached from the perspective of the managers and others trying to get a result, by carrying out the takeover or, for instance, getting through the regulatory hurdles involved in a public offering. Part of the reason for this approach perhaps lies in the fact that the UK has only had a comprehensive system of securities regulation since 1986 and the challenge, as to whether securities regulation should be seen as an indispensable part of the overall picture of what we call company law, is a relatively new one. But there is an important theoretical reason as to why securities regulation/capital markets law is part of company law.[18] A traditional analysis of the human participants in a company involves seeing it as comprised of the directors and the shareholders. They are both 'in' the company, in the sense of being indispensable to its functioning in the manner prescribed by the companies legislation, even if those functions are carried out by the same people. Historically, the legislation contemplates the running of the company

---

[15] See Chapter 13 below.
[16] See Chapter 14 below.
[17] See Chapter 15 below.
[18] These arguments are taken up again in Chapter 16 below and amplified by practical and other perspectives.

through meetings in which people will be present in the room, either in shareholder meetings, voting to elect or remove directors, or in board meetings as directors. It perhaps draws on the concepts of government from the Ancient World in which all the involved parties can and will turn up at a meeting, albeit a large one. Lastly, the shareholders are 'in' the company in the sense that they are committed to it emotionally and financially, and if it is not running properly they will often want to litigate, as the exponential growth in often bitterly contested shareholder litigation in recent decades testifies. Thus, securities regulation, with its emphasis on what happens on capital markets, seems to be outside company law. The shareholders are clearly 'in' the company. But this picture of being bound up with the company in all these ways and so 'in' the company is only true of the small closely-held company. In dispersed-ownership companies, it is a mistaken analysis to regard the shareholders as being 'in' the company in any of the above senses. Typically in dispersed-ownership companies shareholders will not vote; there is little point since their relatively small overall stake (perhaps 1%) will give them very little influence over any outcome. If they do vote, it will usually be by filling in a proxy form; they will not be 'in' the meeting listening to arguments and explanation. Nor will they be sufficiently committed to the company's fortunes, either financially or emotionally, to want to litigate disputes. If they do not like what seems to be happening in the company they will 'exit' by selling their shares on a liquid market, and reinvest in something else. So if the shareholders in dispersed-ownership companies are not 'in' the company, then where are they? They are in the market. But we obviously have to study their position. It cannot be left out – as not really part of 'company law'; the rights and concerns and position of shareholders of dispersed-ownership companies are part of company law. And so, if we are to get a proper perspective of these matters, and the way the law protects their position, it is necessary to study that part of company law which is called 'securities regulation' or 'capital markets law'.[19]

Policy and theory in securities regulation differs from traditional company law theory in a number of respects. The most striking feature is perhaps the cultural differences which arise from the high profile role of the state, making its pervasive presence felt through the agency of the regulator. The main goal of securities regulation is investor protection and much of the policy and theoretical writing is concerned with the different techniques employed by the regulator to achieve an adequate level of protection on the one hand, but on the other, to ensure that the financial services industry, or parts of it, are not made uncompetitive by overheavy regulation.[20] The legislation sets up a comprehensive system under which people offering financial services are usually required to seek authorisation from the regulator, the Financial Conduct Authority (FCA).[21] Authorisation will bring with it responsibilities to comply with detailed rules regulating how their business is to be carried out.[22] During the last decade or so, the activities of credit rating agencies (CRAs) have come under scrutiny. This is, in many ways, a reflection of the prominent role these

---

[19] The terms are used interchangeably in this text, although with the preference towards the longstanding American expression, 'securities regulation'.
[20] See Chapter 16 below.
[21] Or before 2013 its predecessor, the Financial Services Authority (FSA).
[22] See Chapter 18 below.

agencies play in the capital/securities markets.[23] Their emergence has been driven partly by new debt issues and the advent of new structured finance products. As a consequence of the global financial crisis, CRAs have been subject to fierce criticism, particularly in the US, for failing to assess adequately the risk associated with securities backed by sub-prime mortgages.[24] When shares are offered to the public, there is a high risk of fraud if the offer documents are not carefully regulated. Thus, one of the oldest forms of securities regulation is the requirement for adequate disclosure of information about the issuer and the securities in a prospectus.[25] Insider dealing broadly involves the use of inside information by a party to a transaction on a stock exchange which the other party does not have and which enables him to make a profit or avoid a loss. Although the matter is not entirely free from controversy, it has long been felt by regulatory authorities that insider dealing damages investor confidence in markets and for this reason, and others, it falls to be regulated along with other forms of market abuse.[26] Hostile takeovers can easily produce unfairness for shareholders of the target company and for this reason takeovers are subjected to time-table requirements and many other rules designed to ensure that the shareholders are treated equally.[27]

'Insolvency and liquidation' is the final Part. It contains a brief account of the processes which are available to deal with corporate insolvency and winding up generally. The legislation contains complex procedures for the winding up of solvent and insolvent companies and eventual dissolution of the corporate entity.[28] A remarkable feature of company law has been its development of a facility for expulsion of directors from its world, the corporate world. In the last two decades, there have probably been more reported cases on disqualification of directors than any other single aspect of company law. Whether the law has got the balance right between protecting the public from abuses of limited liability and not creating unnecessary deterrents to enterprise is open to question.[29]

## 1.3 Scope of this work

It is clear that this text marks out a conceptually broader field than usual for core company law. On the other hand, it is possible to exaggerate the practical effect of this. Most company law texts will usually give some attention to most of the main areas of securities regulation, insider dealing, public offerings of shares and takeovers. This text differs, since in doing this it places the emphasis on the regulatory aspect of these areas, and sets them in the context of the policy and theory of securities regulation. More generally, in order for the textto remain short enough to claim to be one for use by students, it has been necessary to vary the depth of coverage. It is felt that this is preferable to an artificial restriction of a subject area which for good theoretical and practical reasons needs to be seen as a unified whole. Even so, the text leaves out altogether a whole range of subjects which undoubtedly affect the way companies are structured and how they go about their business; among these

---

[23] See Chapter 17 below.
[24] *Ibid.*
[25] See Chapter 19 below.
[26] See Chapter 20 below.
[27] See Chapter 21 below.
[28] See Chapter 22 below.
[29] See Chapter 23 below.

are revenue law, competition law, environmental law, health and safety law, labour law and consumer law. It is not felt that these areas can be covered in sufficient depth to be meaningful, and they are best left to specialist texts. Although this work is primarily for the student market, it is hoped that practitioners will also find it of use and interest.

## 1.4 The genesis of company law

English company law is mainly concerned with the creation and operation of registered companies, that is, companies with separate legal personality created by the process of registering them with the Registrar of Companies under the Companies Act 2006. This facility of creating companies simply by registration has been available in England since the Joint Stock Companies Act 1844.

Prior to that time companies were created by Royal Charter (a special authorisation from the Crown) or by a special Act of Parliament. These forms of company became common in the sixteenth century and were called 'joint stock' companies because the members of it contributed merchandise or money, and the company traded with the outside world as an entity distinct from the members. At first these companies were colonial companies, formed mainly to open up trade with new colonies, but by the late seventeenth century most of the new companies were created for domestic enterprises. At this time, there was also considerable growth in the numbers of large partnerships which were using various legal devices to make them as much like the chartered and statutory companies as possible. In the early eighteenth century, there were many speculative flotations of various types of company and a stock market collapse. This reached a climax in 1720 when the share price of the South Sea Company collapsed; this event was known as the South Sea 'Bubble' because once it burst, there was nothing (no assets) there. Legislation was then passed which was designed to prevent the large partnerships from acting as though they were companies. Known as the Bubble Act, it was not repealed until 1825, by which time it had been realised that it was economically desirable to permit the easy creation of companies. It also soon became necessary to clarify the status of the many partnerships which had now begun to flourish. In England, legislation in 1844 permitted incorporation by registration for the first time and limited liability was made available in 1855. These provisions were then re-enacted in the Joint Stock Companies Act 1856. In 1862 this and other subsequent legislation was consolidated in the Companies Act 1862. Thereafter, the growth of company law followed a pattern which continues to the present day. In the years following a consolidating Act more reforms are conceived, either as a result of an inquiry into company law by an expert outside committee appointed by the government department responsible for companies, now called the Department for Business, Energy & Industrial Strategy (DBEIS, , formerly the Department of Trade and Industry or DTI), or, as is more common these days, as a result of policy decided by the DBEIS itself. The proposed reforms then become legislation and after many years of this process, another consolidating Act was passed and for a few years thereafter all the statutory material on company law was available in one consolidated Act. A distinguishing feature of the Companies Act 2006, however, is that its reforms do not stop at merely consolidating previous companies' legislation.[30]

---

[30] See 1.5 and 1.10 below.

The facility of creating companies by registration was widely used in the second half of the nineteenth century not only by those wishing to operate a large company with an offer of shares to the public, but also by many who ran small businesses either as single traders or in partnership who now wanted the advantages of limited liability and the corporate form. Partnership law ceased to be the focus of concern by the legislature and, following the Partnership Act 1890 and the Limited Partnership Act 1907 (both of which are currently in force), there was little interest by the legislature in the subject[31] until the closing years of the twentieth century, when it became clear that a new business vehicle combining aspects of partnership law with company law might be desirable. In due course the Limited Liability Partnerships Act 2000 was passed.[32]

## 1.5 The present companies legislation

The present primary legislation relating to companies is the Companies Act 2006. This is both a reforming and a consolidating statute and was brought into force in phases. This began in January 2007 and ended in October 2009. In 1986 a consolidation of insolvency law into the Insolvency Act 1986,[33] which now includes the law on all company liquidations (not just insolvent ones as the Act's name might suggest), led to a repeal of those parts of the Companies Act 1985 which had dealt with company liquidations. Also in 1986 was the Company Directors Disqualification Act into which was consolidated the various scattered provisions relating to the disqualification of directors. Companies were further affected by the Financial Services Act 1986 which amended, repealed and replaced various parts of the Companies Act 1985.[34] Then three years later the Companies Act 1989 was passed, some of which still stands on its own and other parts of which amended earlier legislation which, subsequently, were repealed. Subsequently, the Financial Services and Markets Act 2000 completely restructured the securities regulation aspects of company law and so replaced the Financial Services Act 1986.[35] Thus there is no effective consolidation at the present day. The legislation on company law is spread out between various statutes, not to mention the mass of statutory instruments which the main Acts have spawned. Nevertheless, in a broad sense, the basic Act is the Companies Act 2006.[36]

---

[31] Although the courts continued to develop some aspects of partnership law.

[32] See further 1.9C below.

[33] Amended subsequently by the Insolvency Act 2000 and the Enterprise Act 2002.

[34] The Companies (Audit, Investigations and Community Enterprise) Act 2004 also amended more recently the Companies Act 1985.

[35] The Financial Services Act 2010 amended the Financial Services and Markets Act 2000 (FSMA 2000), including provision about financial education, and other provision about financial services and markets. Following the financial crisis, the Financial Services Act 2012 (FSA 2012) came into force on 19 December 2012 and amended FSMA 2000. This is discussed in the relevant chapters below.

[36] As will be seen in various parts of this text, when the 2006 Act received Royal Assent some areas were nonetheless left behind in the 1985 Act (company investigations; orders imposing restrictions on shares following an investigation; and provisions about Scottish floating charges and receivers); the 1989 Act (powers to require information and documents to assist overseas regulatory authorities; provisions about Scottish incorporated charities; amendments and savings consequential upon the changes in the law made by the 1989 Act; and provisions about financial markets and insolvency); and the 2004 Act (provisions extending the functions of the Financial Reporting Review Panel (FRRP) to interim accounts and reports; provisions about the financing and liability of the Financial Reporting Council (FRC) and its subsidiary bodies; and community interest companies).

References in this text will be to sections in this Act, unless the context makes it clear that some other statute is intended. It will be seen that in addition to copious statute law, case law features in many areas of company law, either as interpretation or application of statutory provisions, or as a result of remedies given in the statutes, or, some areas, entirely independently of statute. Unless otherwise stated or clear from the context, the law described in this text is the English law.[37]

## 1.6 European community legislation

### A The harmonisation programme[38]

As part of the process of creating the common market with free movement of goods, persons, services and capital, the European Community has felt it necessary to attempt to coordinate the laws affecting companies in the various member states. There is to be approximation of laws, not in the sense of making them exactly the same, but similar in their main characteristics, making the safeguards for members and others 'equivalent throughout the Community'.[39] The company law[40] harmonisation policy is based on the EC Treaty, art. 44 (2) (g). The usual pattern has been for the European Commission to make proposals for Directives[41] which, after various subsequent stages, are finally adopted by the Council of Ministers and the European Parliament. Unlike a Regulation, which automatically becomes law in the member states, a Directive is usually a set of principles[42] which the individual member states are required to enact into their own law, making whatever adaptations are necessary to key it in with their domestic law. The Directives are to be binding only as to the result to be achieved. In some limited circumstances, they do have direct effect on the domestic law of the member states. It has been made clear that a national court which hears a case falling within the scope of an EC Directive is required to interpret its national law in the light of the wording and purpose of that Directive.[43]

---

[37] I.e. England and Wales. As regards Northern Ireland, before the Companies Act 2006, the provisions of Great Britain (GB) company law were generally replicated, some time later, in separate Northern Ireland legislation. The 2006 Act provides for a single company law regime applying to the whole of the UK, so that companies are UK companies rather than GB companies or Northern Ireland companies. As regards Scotland, company law is a reserved matter and Companies Acts extend to the whole of GB. However, a legislative consent motion agreed to by the Scottish Parliament on 16 March 2006 means that there are several areas where, in legislating about companies, the 2006 Act deals with matters that are devolved: changes (in Part 41) to the regulation of business names – these correspond to changes (in Part 5) to the regulation of company names; statutory guidance to prosecutors and other enforcement authorities in relation to a new offence of knowingly or recklessly causing an audit report to be misleading, false or deceptive – although the offence itself is a reserved matter, guidance is to be issued by the Lord Advocate in Scotland (see section 509); changes relating to exemptions from audit requirements for companies that are charities (see section 1175); conferral of a power on the Auditor General for Scotland to specify public bodies for his audit (see section 483). In other areas, such as insolvency, there are major differences.
[38] For a detailed account of this, see V. Edwards *EC Company Law* (Oxford: OUP, 1999). See also the EU website http://europa.eu/index_en.htm.
[39] See EC Treaty, art. 44 (2) (g) (art. 54 (3) (g), pre-Amsterdam).
[40] Capital markets harmonisation is dealt with at Chapter 16, 16.5E below.
[41] Occasionally a Regulation has been used.
[42] In practice these have often been very detailed.
[43] See Case C-106/89 *Marleasing SA* v *La Comercial SA* [1993] BCC 421, ECJ.

## B The company law programme: UK implementation

The UK entered the European Community by the European Communities Act 1972. Section 9 of the 1972 Act was an attempt to translate into UK law the relevant provisions of the First Company Law Directive.[44] The main changes necessary in the UK related to doctrines under which persons dealing with companies could find themselves unable to enforce the contracts they had entered into, by virtue of being given 'constructive notice' of constitutional limitations on the power of the company, or its officers and agents, to enter into the contracts. Section 9 was not well drafted to achieve the stated aims of the Directive and further measures were brought in by the Companies Act 1989.[45] Other provisions of the First Directive related to publicity and to the doctrine of nullity.[46]

The Second Directive[47] set out minimum requirements relating to the raising and maintenance of capital and the formation of companies. These were implemented by the Companies Act 1980[48] and although it was not necessary to make very radical changes to the existing UK rules on capital, the Directive did require more legal distinctions to be drawn between public and private companies than had formerly been the case. In particular, since 1980, the end name 'Limited' or 'Ltd' has been applicable only to a private limited company, while public company names must end with the words 'public limited company' or 'plc'.

The Third Directive[49] was implemented by the Companies (Mergers and Divisions) Regulations 1987.[50] Because takeovers in the UK are usually carried out by share exchange, the Third Directive, which relates to mergers by transfers of assets, is not of very great significance.

The Fourth Directive[51] related to the annual accounts of companies, prescribing in detail how those should be presented. It was implemented by the Companies Act 1981 (now contained in the Companies Act 1985).[52]

The Sixth Directive[53] is concerned with demergers of public companies, termed 'scissions' or 'divisions'. It was implemented, along with the Third Directive, by the Companies (Mergers and Divisions) Regulations 1987.[54]

The Seventh Directive[55] is supplementary to the Fourth Directive and makes provision for the regime governing group accounts. It was implemented by the Companies Act 1989.

The Eighth Directive[56] relates to the qualifications and independence of auditors. It was implemented by the Companies Act 1989. The substantive law in this area already

---

[44] Which had been adopted by the European Council on 9 March 1968; Directive 68/151/EEC.
[45] See Chapter 5, 5.3F below.
[46] Nullity was a doctrine unknown to UK law.
[47] 79/91/EEC.
[48] And are now contained in the Companies Act 2006.
[49] 78/855/EEC.
[50] SI 1987 No. 1991.
[51] 78/660/EEC.
[52] The Fourth Directive, and its counterpart the Seventh Directive, have both been amended by many subsequent Directives. There is now also Regulation (EC)1606/2002 on the application of International Accounting Standards; this is dealt with at Chapter 8 below.
[53] 82/891/EEC.
[54] SI 1987 No. 1991.
[55] 83/349/EEC.
[56] 84/253/EEC.

required high standards and not much change was required to comply with the Directive, although a new supervisory structure was created.

The Eleventh Directive on the disclosure requirements of branches of certain types of company[57] was implemented by the Oversea Companies and Credit and Financial Institutions (Branch Disclosure) Regulations 1992.[58]

The Twelfth Directive[59] on single member private limited companies was implemented by the Companies (Single Member Private Limited Companies) Regulations 1992.[60]

The Directive on Takeover Bids[61] (formerly called the Thirteenth Directive on Takeover Bids) was adopted on 21 April 2004[62] after a 15-year struggle. It will have many long-term implications for Europe's capital markets and corporate governance. The European Company Statute (the '*Societas Europaea*' or '*SE*') was enacted by EC Regulation in 2001.[63] It allows companies with operations in more than one member state to operate voluntarily as European companies, that is, European corporate entities, governed by a single law applicable in all member states.[64] In order to enable member states to take account of differences between national systems, the politically sensitive area of the involvement of employees has been dealt with by a Directive.[65]

In June 2008, the European Commission published a proposal that would create a new type of European private company to be known as an SPE (Societas Privata Europaea).[66] This new company form will enable small and medium-sized enterprises (SMEs) to do business throughout the EU, with the aim of cutting costs and encouraging growth in this area. The SPE has been designed to address the current onerous obligations on SMEs operating across borders and which need to set up subsidiaries in different company forms in the member states in which they want to do business.[67] In practical terms, the SPE would mean that SMEs can set up their company in the same form, no matter if they do business in their own member state or in another. Opting for the SPE will save entrepreneurs time and money on legal advice, management and administration. The proposal takes the form of a directly applicable Regulation that was originally intended to come into effect on 1 July 2010. However, political disagreement between member states on its draft regulation eventually postponed its implementation.

On 30 May 2011, the Hungarian presidency presented to the Competitiveness Council a *compromise proposal* to the outstanding issues with a view to reaching political agreement on the draft regulation. Sweden opposed the threshold of 500 employees for employee participation observing that the threshold in Swedish national law is much lower. Germany observed that an SPE should not be allowed to have its registered office

---

[57] Directive 89/666/EEC.
[58] SI 1992 No. 3179. This also implemented the 'Bank Branches' Directive 89/117/EEC.
[59] 89/667/EEC.
[60] SI 1992 No. 1699.
[61] 2004/25/EC.
[62] For a detailed analysis of this see Chapter 21 below.
[63] Regulation (EC) 2157/2001.
[64] However, in many circumstances, some of the applicable corporate laws will be those operating in the member state in which it has its registered office, in respect of public limited liability companies.
[65] Directive 2001/86/EC, implemented in the UK by the European Public Limited-Liability Company Regulations 2004 (SI 2004 No. 2326), which also have relevance for certain aspects of the EC Regulation.
[66] See, http://ec.europa.eu/internal_market/company/docs/epc/proposal_en.pdf.
[67] *Ibid.*

and central administration in different member states. Although it will require local law in each member state to supplement the final version of the Regulation, the features of the SPE are generally more attractive than those of its older brother, the Societas Europaea (SE), which has been in force since 2004 but which has had very little take-up in the UK. As an SPE will have a legal form that is recognised throughout the EU, it has obvious attractions for multinational groups and could in time become the blueprint for European companies. On 9 April 2014, the European Commission published a proposal for a single member SPE as a new way to simplify the creation of companies with a single shareholder across the EU. The Directive aims to make it easier for businesses to establish subsidiaries in other member states as subsidiaries often tend to have only one single shareholder.[68] On 28 May 2015, the Council under Latvian Presidency agreed on a general approach for SPEs. The major innovation is the online-registration.[69]

Unlike the SE, the SPE would not require any cross-border element. According to the proposal, its main features would include a minimum share capital of €1, uniform rules on distributions (and the option of a solvency certificate to be issued before a distribution), a registered share system for shareholders, corporate governance using a one-tier or two-tier system of management and procedure for registered office to be transferred to another member state.

## C The EC Commission's company law action plan[70]

On 21 May 2003, the European Commission published a communication: *Modernising Company Law and Enhancing Corporate Governance in the European Union – A Plan to Move Forward*[71] containing an 'action plan' for the development of company law in Europe for many years to come. The plan envisages 15 new Directives, and several EC Regulations and Commission Communications with a view to enhancing corporate governance and modernising company law.

The detailed plans involve increases in corporate governance disclosure, electronic access to information, recommendations about board conduct in conflict of interest situations, strict rules on the collective responsibility of directors for financial statements,[72] the introduction of a version of the UK's successful wrongful trading law, new ideas and rules on groups[73] of

---

[68] See, http://www.europeanprivatecompany.eu/news/.

[69] *Ibid.*

[70] Discussed further below in Chapter 16, 16.5E 3.

[71] COM (2003) 284 final. This action plan was a response to an earlier report of a group of eminent company law experts chaired by Professor Jaap Winter: *Report of the High Level Group of Company Law Experts on a Modern Regulatory Framework for Company Law in Europe* (Brussels: CEC, 2002).

[72] In this the Commission is therefore not planning to take Europe down the American road adopted in their Sarbanes–Oxley Act of 2002 whereby the Chief Executive Officer (CEO) and the Chief Finance Officer (CFO) are fixed with an enhanced responsibility for the financial statements of their company.

[73] They were not planning to reintroduce the proposal for a Ninth Directive which in some circumstances would have resulted in the group or the dominant undertaking in the group having liability for the debts of subsidiaries, although it may be that some detailed new ideas will emerge along these lines; if so, they would prove controversial in the UK. See generally K. Hopt 'Common Principles of Corporate Governance in Europe?' in B. Markesinis (ed.) *The Clifford Chance Millennium Lectures: The Coming Together of the Common Law and the Civil Law* (Oxford: Hart Publishing, 2000) p. 126.

companies and many other matters.[74] As part of the plan, the Commission initially pressed ahead with new proposals for two previously planned Directives relating to corporate mobility and restructuring.[75] However, the former European Commissioner for Internal Markets and Services, Charlie McCreevy, confirmed in October 2007 some revised plans.[76] First, on shareholder democracy, the Commission decided not to take any action on the concept of 'one share one vote' in light of existing Directives and the domestic laws of member states. Secondly, the proposal for a Fourteenth Company Law Directive, on the transfer of a company registered in the European Union, did not go ahead because it is expected the Cross-border Mergers Directive will give all limited companies the option to transfer their registered offices (e.g. by setting up a subsidiary in the member state to which they want to move and then merging the existing company into this subsidiary). Only if this framework is found wanting would further legislative action in the shape of a Fourteenth Company Law Directive be justified. Finally, a contractor was appointed to determine the feasibility for a European Foundation Statute.

On 3 December 2015, the Commission adopted a proposal to codify and merge a number of existing company law Directives.[77] The aim of this proposal is to make EU company law more reader-friendly and to reduce the risk of future inconsistencies.[78] It does not involve any change to the substance of these Directives. The proposal follows the announcement made in the 2012 action plan on company law and corporate governance. It was to be examined in the Council and the European Parliament according to an accelerated procedure for codification proposals.[79]

In May 2017, the Commission invited external stakeholders to provide inputs to its consultation: *EU Company Law Upgraded: Rules on Digital Solutions and Efficient Cross-border Operations*.[80] The consultation addresses important gaps remaining in the area of law applicable to companies and aims to gather evidence and views on online tools throughout the companies' lifecycle including cross-border mobility (mergers, divisions, conversions).[81] The deadline for the submission of inputs was 6 August 2017. It was thought that the responses would be taken into account in the Commission's impact assessment report in parallel with the results of external studies carried out for the Commission and other available information.[82]

---

[74] In the light of the proposed reforms of corporate governance and the board in the action plan, it is clear that there is no longer any intention to revive the earlier proposal for a Fifth Directive which foundered on the rock of trying to impose some form of structured worker participation in corporate decision-making. For the history of the various versions of the proposals see: A. Boyle 'Draft Fifth Directive: Implications for Directors' Duties, Board Structure and Employee Participation' (1992) 13 Co. Law. 6; J. Du Plessis and J. Dine 'The Fate of the Draft Fifth Directive on Company Law: Accommodation Instead of Harmonisation' [1997] JBL 23.

[75] Proposal for a Tenth Company Law Directive on Cross-border Mergers, and the proposal for a Fourteenth Company Law Directive on the transfer of seat from one member state to another.

[76] Speech by Commissioner McCreevy at the European Parliament's Legal Affairs Committee, SPEECH 07/592.

[77] See, http://eur-lex.europa.eu/legal-content/EN/TXT/?qid=1449665429348&uri=CELEX:52015PC0616.

[78] See, http://ec.europa.eu/justice/civil/company-law/index_en.htm.

[79] *Ibid.*

[80] See, http://ec.europa.eu/newsroom/just/item-detail.cfm?item_id=58190.

[81] See, http://ec.europa.eu/justice/civil/company-law/index_en.htm.

[82] *Ibid.*

## 1.7 Company law, corporate law or corporations law?

It has become quite common in 'the UK' in recent years to see the American term 'corporation' used instead of 'company'. Some universities have chairs of 'corporate' law.[83] Courses on company law in American universities are usually called 'Corporations Law' and their legislation, state 'corporations' statutes. Over the years, the word 'company' has been used in the UK instead of 'corporation' probably mainly for historical reasons. The early joint stock companies used 'company' rather than 'corporation' and the word became part of the title of the statute which was the foundation of modern company law, the Joint Stock Companies Act 1844. Since 1862 the statutes have been entitled 'Companies Act' and their provisions invariably refer to 'company' and 'companies'. Nearly all the textbooks speak of 'company law' and university courses are usually similarly titled. However, the Companies Act makes it clear that a company is a corporation, and, for example, s. 16 (2) of the Companies Act 2006 provides that the effect of registration under the Act is that from the date of 'incorporation' the members of the company 'shall be a body corporate'.

The problem with using the word 'corporations' instead of companies in English law is that, even at the present day, 'corporations' is a wider concept than 'companies'. There are two main types of corporations – corporations 'sole' and corporations 'aggregate'. A corporation sole is basically an office or public appointment that is deemed to be independent of the human being who happens to fill the office from time to time. Originally most corporations sole were of an ecclesiastical nature so that archbishops, bishops, canons, vicars and so on were, and still are, corporations sole. But there are also many lay corporations sole, such as the Sovereign, government ministers (e.g. the Secretary of State for Defence) and non-ministerial offices such as the Treasury Solicitor. A corporation sole will have the normal incidents of corporateness such as perpetual succession, so that when the individual occupying the office dies, the corporation sole, unchanged, is still there and can be filled by someone else, either immediately or at some later point in time. It is clear from all this that a company is not a corporation sole, hence, perhaps, the historical English law reluctance to use 'corporation' as a synonym for 'company', for while all companies are corporations, not all corporations are companies. Thus a company is a corporation aggregate, a corporation made up from a totality of individuals.[84]

## 1.8 Focus – the main business vehicle

### A Company limited by shares

The main business vehicle through which most economic activity is carried on in the UK is the company limited by shares and created by registration under the Companies Act 2006. It is a corporate body, having legal personality separate from its members, and the liability of the members to contribute to its assets in an insolvent liquidation is limited to

---

[83]The 'corporate' title perhaps deriving from the use of the term by City law firms which endow the chairs.

[84]It is not proposed to explore here all the incidents of corporateness. These are dealt with in Chapter 2 below.

the amount unpaid on any shares held by them.[85] Within the legislation, there are two technically separate forms of it, the public company, and the private company. It will be seen below that there are many other types of company[86] and organisation, but these will not generally be covered in this text other than in this chapter below, for comparative purposes and perspective.[87]

## B Public or private

The registered company limited by shares can be formed either as a private company or as a public company. Most, in fact, begin life as private companies and then convert to public companies when they have grown large enough for the managers and share-holders to feel that they can benefit from being able to raise large sums of capital by an offering of their shares to the public. They will also usually want to be a quoted com-pany, that is, for their shares to be quoted on the London Stock Exchange (either as a listed company on the Main Market, or unlisted but quoted on the Alternative Investment Market (AIM))[88] which, of course, has the advantage that investors can feel confident of being able to sell their holdings if they wish, thus making them a more attractive and liquid investment. It is important to realise that being a public company does not automatically mean that prices on its shares are quoted in that way. Many public companies are unquoted.[89] Also, it should be realised that in economic terms some public companies are quite small, smaller perhaps than some of the larger private companies. The mere fact that its legal type is 'public' does not of itself guarantee economic size.

In recent years, partly (though not entirely) due to the influence of the EC Harmonisation Directives, there has been an increase in the differences between the legal rules affecting public and private companies, though much of company law still continues to apply to both types. The main technical legal differences between public and private companies are as follows:

(1) The name endings are different; the public company name must end with 'public lim-ited company' which can be abbreviated to 'plc' and a private limited company must end its name with the word 'limited' which can be abbreviated to 'Ltd'.[90]

---

[85]See Companies Act 2006, s. 3 (2).

[86] There are sometimes various methods available of converting one type to another; see Companies Act 2006, ss. 90–96 and 102–107.

[87] Thus, to avoid confusion, unless the context shows otherwise, the company which is being referred to will be the company limited by shares, created by registration and either public or private.

[88] See further Chapter 19 below.

[89] The majority in fact; there are over 1,300 large companies from 60 different countries on the Main Market of the London Stock Exchange, and since its launch in 1995 some 2,500 companies have joined AIM; see generally Chapter 19 below. It is also worth noting that there are many more private companies than public: as much as 99.6 per cent of the companies on the register in the UK in 2008/9 are, in fact, private companies, although their significance for the economy in terms of economic size is arguably less. On 31 March 2017 there were 3,737,487 private companies on the register; see Companies House, Official Statistics Companies Register Activities 2016–2017.

[90] See Companies Act 2006, ss. 58–59.

(2) A public company may offer its shares to the public; a private company may not do this.[91]

(3) There is a minimum capital requirement ('the authorised minimum') of £50,000 that a public company must have.[92]

(4) A public company must have at least two directors, but a private company need have only one.[93]

(5) A public company must ensure that its company secretary is properly qualified whereas a private company has no statutory obligation to do this.[94]

(6) Public companies are often required by the statutes to go through more onerous procedures than private companies.[95]

(7) In the past, a public company had to have at least two members, whereas a private company only needed one member, but this is no longer the case.[96]

## C Small closely-held and dispersed-ownership companies

As a means of classifying companies in a meaningful way, the technical legal 'public and private' distinction has its limitations. In company law theory, the really important distinction to be made is between those companies which are wholly or substantially owner managed and controlled, and those where there is a major separation of ownership and control. The reasons for this have already been explained,[97] but, in a nutshell, the point is that those two types of companies raise very different problems of corporate governance.[98] In the former type, the owners will be in charge and if things go wrong, that is largely their own problem; they have lost their own money and wasted their own time. In the latter type of company, the shareholders are confronted with the difficulty of trying to ensure that the managers are motivated to act in the interests of the shareholders.

There is a need to identify an expression which conveys accurately these two paradigms. The terms public and private are only partially useful because many public companies are not companies which have dispersed ownership of shares. Fewer than 2,000 of the

---

[91] Companies Act 2006, ss. 755(1) and 760.

[92] *Ibid.* s. 763.

[93] *Ibid.* s. 154.

[94] *Ibid.* s. 273. Directors' common law or fiduciary duties might import such a requirement in certain circumstances.

[95] Private companies have historically been able to adopt an elective regime under the Companies Act 1985, s. 379A which recognised that often in private companies the directors and the members of the company are one and the same and so requirements for meetings, timing of meetings and laying of accounts can be suspended to streamline the operation of the private company. Furthermore, the old Table A articles, art. 53 allowed a more informal decision-making process. The Companies Act 2006's main impact has been in reforming company law to suit small private companies and so many of the problematic requirements for private companies to hold meetings etc. has been done away with in the 2006 Act (the AGM requirement does not apply to private companies– see CA 2006 Part 13 Chapter 14, and CA 2006 s. 288 provides for an expanded written resolution regime for private companies).

[96] Companies Act 1985, s. 1 (1) (3A). Companies Act 2006 s. 7 now provides for single-person private and public companies.

[97] See 1.2 above.

[98] Corporate governance is the system by which the company is managed and controlled; see further Part III of the book.

12,000 or so public companies on the register are quoted on the Stock Exchange.[99] The remaining are in many cases owner managed and controlled. Various expressions are commonly used by company lawyers to refer to companies which are managed and controlled by their owners: small private companies, close companies, companies with concentrated ownership of shares, quasi-partnership companies, small and closely-held companies, SMEs,[100] owner-managed companies, micro companies. Similarly, there are those which are used to describe the companies which have dispersed ownership of shares: large public companies, quoted companies, companies with fragmented ownership of shares, Berle and Means companies,[101] 'public and listed and other very large companies with real economic power'. These expressions all have varying degrees of accuracy and some have potential for confusion; some are cumbersome. As stated earlier, the expressions which will be adopted in this book are: 'small closely-held' companies[102] and 'dispersed-ownership' companies.[103] These expressions are pithy, and more or less accurate for the situations in which they will be used.

## D The Company Law Review and law reform

One of the key areas identified by the Company Law Review[104] as needing reform was 'small companies'.[105] Subsequently, the Review developed a major 'think small first' strategy,[106] which involves simplifying the law for all private companies and especially for small private companies.[107] Many of the complex procedural requirements which currently apply to companies, public and private, would no longer apply to private companies. The idea was therefore that future companies legislation would set out the law relating to private companies first and then build in extra requirements relating to public companies and public companies which are listed on the Stock Exchange. In the Company Law Review Final Report some of these ideas were reiterated, along with various technical recommendations concerning registration of companies and provision of information.[108]

---

[99]See n. 89 above.

[100]Small and medium-sized enterprises; the expression comes from the EC Directive which created exemptions from certain reporting requirements.

[101]See Chapter 3, 3.3 below.

[102]These will, in fact, usually be companies which are private, small in the sense of few shareholders, and of relatively minor economic significance.

[103]These will usually be public, quoted (either on the Main Market or on AIM), with very many shareholders, and of relatively large economic significance.

[104]See generally 1.10 below.

[105]DTI Consultation Document (February 1999) *The Strategic Framework*, paras 2.31, 5.2.33. The subject of the appropriateness of the private company form had been under academic scrutiny for some years; see e.g. J. Freedman 'Small Businesses and the Corporate Form: Burden or Privilege?' (1994) 57 MLR 555; A. Hicks 'Corporate Form: Questioning the Unsung Hero' [1997] JBL 306.

[106]DTI Consultation Document (March 2000) *Developing the Framework*, paras 6.5 *et seq.*

[107]*Ibid.* paras 6.22 *et seq.*

[108]See *Modern Company Law for a Competitive Economy Final Report* (London: DTI, 2001), paras 2.1–2.37, 4.1–4.62. See also the subsequent government White Paper *Modernising Company Law* July 2002, Cmnd 5553.

### 1.9 Other business vehicles[109]

#### A Other types of companies

The other types of companies which can be formed by registration under the Companies Act 2006 are the company limited by guarantee[110] and the unlimited company.[111] The first of these is not commonly used for trading, since it cannot be formed with any share capital and is not appropriate for raising any capital from the members. Its use is therefore mainly confined to clubs, societies and charitable institutions such as schools. The unlimited company has corporate personality but, as the name suggests, the members' liability for debts is not limited. Not surprisingly, the unlimited company is not a very common vehicle through which to do business, although in earlier times it may have provided a useful alternative to large partnerships which were prohibited by s. 716 of the Companies Act 1985 until the removal of limits in 2002.[112]

Sometimes companies which are formed under the Companies Act also attract detailed statutory regulation by other legislation if the company is carrying on a specialised type of business. Thus, for instance, registered companies which are banks will need to comply with the Banking Act 1987 and insurance companies with the Insurance Companies Act 1982. Sometimes, as with investment companies and shipping companies, there are special provisions within the Companies Act itself.

Companies formed by Act of Parliament (other than the Companies Act) are usually referred to as 'statutory companies'. There are various (General) Public Acts[113] under which corporate bodies may be formed for special purposes. Additionally, they can individually be formed by Private Act, as were most of the early canal companies, or by (Special) Public Act, as where a nationalised industry is set up. Common form provisions set out in the Companies Clauses Consolidation Act 1845 will apply unless the creating Act specifically excludes them and creates its own.

Chartered companies are those formed by a charter from the Crown, either under the Royal Prerogative or specific statutory powers. In the Companies Act, these are referred to as companies 'formed ... in pursuance ... of letters patent'.[114] At the present day companies are usually only created by charter if they have a broadly charitable or public service character, although a few of the old chartered trading companies still remain.

Generally speaking, statutory companies and chartered companies are regulated by the law contained in their statute or creating charter, but subject to that will be governed by general principles of company law built up by case law over the last century or so. They will be covered in this text only in so far as they are relevant to the registered company limited by shares.

---

[109] This text will not have any further focus on these except to the extent that they become relevant from time to time in Chapter 18.
[110] Companies Act 2006, s. 3 (3).
[111] *Ibid.* s. 3 (4).
[112] See further below.
[113] Such as the Industrial and Provident Societies Acts 1965–1978, the Credit Unions Act 1979 and the Building Societies Act 1986.
[114] Companies Act 2006, s. 1040 (1).

The European Economic Interest Grouping (EEIG) is a relatively new type of what can probably be called a company, which can be formed in the UK under the European Economic Interest Grouping Regulations 1989.[115] It is a non-profit-making joint venture organisation which, although not giving limited liability to its members, does have corporate personality.

The European Company ('*Societas Europaea*' or '*SE*') is a concept that has been worked on for a long time. It can be used as a corporate vehicle in various cross-border situations.[116] The concept has recently been taken further, into the non-profit area by permitting the creation of an entity called the European Cooperative Society ('*Societas Cooperativa Europaea*' or '*SCE*').[117]

Lastly, it should be mentioned that there is in existence a new legal entity in the form of the Community Interest Company (CIC) which has been specially created for use by not-for-profit organisations pursuing community benefit.[118]

The open-ended investment company (OEIC) is a new type of company which can be formed to operate collective investment schemes. The role and structure of these is considered below.[119] In some situations, companies will fall to be regulated by the Companies Act even though they are not formed under it. Since the UK is an open economy, many foreign companies do business here and will find that they are subjected to various requirements in the Companies Act under the 'overseas companies' regime and/or under the 'branch' regime.[120] There is a single framework for registration by overseas companies (wherever incorporated) under the Companies Act 2006.[121]

## B Other organisations and bodies

There are various other types of organisations within English law. Some of these are unincorporated associations and thus not corporate bodies, while others have a status which while closely resembling corporate bodies fall some way short of that.

Examples of unincorporated associations are:[122] clubs and societies, where the members are bound to each other contractually by the club rules and the club property is vested in trustees; syndicates, where, unlike partnerships, the members put a limit on their liability when they make contracts with third parties. There are also various organisations whose legal status is difficult to classify in any very satisfactory way.[123] Unit trusts, for instance,

---

[115] SI 1989 No. 638; and Regulation (EEC) 2131/85.
[116] For more detail and legislative background see 1.6C above.
[117] Regulation (EC) 1435/2003, OJ 2003, L 207/1.
[118] These are a new legal creature contained in the Companies (Audit, Investigations and Community Enterprise) Act 2004; this is achieved by a 'community interest test' and 'asset lock', which ensure that the CIC is established for community purposes and the assets and profits are dedicated to these purposes. Registration of a company as a CIC has to be approved by the Regulator (the Companies (Audit, Investigations and Community Enterprise) Act 2004 established the Regulator as an independent public office holder appointed by the Secretary of State for Trade and Industry) who also has a continuing monitoring and enforcement role. See http://www.cicregulator.gov.uk/.
[119] At Chapter 18, 18.6.
[120] See Companies Act 2006, Part 34 and ss. 129–135 will also sometimes have the effect of subjecting companies to the Companies Act regimes.
[121] The Overseas Companies Regulations 2009 No. 1801 available at: http://www.legislation.gov.uk/ukdsi/2009/9780111479476/contents.
[122] The case of partnerships is dealt with below.
[123] The new limited liability partnership (LLP) is probably a new example of this; see below.

resemble unincorporated associations, but it was held in *Smith* v *Anderson*[124] that they are not unincorporated associations but that the investors in a unit trust are in legal terms merely beneficiaries under a trust and do not 'associate' with one another. Trade unions have many of the attributes of corporations but it is expressly provided that they are not corporate bodies.[125] The separate legal personality concept is probably the main basis of distinction between unincorporated associations and corporations. However, it should be noticed that occasionally the courts have been prepared to hold that in some situations unincorporated associations have legal personality separate and distinct from their members but not so as to make them corporate bodies.[126] These rather hybrid associations are sometimes referred to as quasi-corporations or near-corporations.

## C Partnerships

There are currently three types of partnership available as business vehicles in English law: the partnership,[127] the limited partnership and the new, limited liability partnership (LLP). It has been estimated that there are around 600,000 general partnerships.[128]

The partnership is governed by the Partnership Act 1890,[129] the common law, in so far as it is not inconsistent with the Act, and the terms of any partnership agreement, again, in so far as they do not conflict with the Act. Partnership is defined as 'the relation which subsists between persons carrying on business in common with a view of profit'.[130] No formalities are necessary for the creation of a partnership;[131] it will exist if the definition is satisfied.[132] The partners will have unlimited liability for the debts of the firm, arising in various circumstances.[133] Broadly speaking, and usually in the absence of contrary provision, partners will share profits equally,[134] be entitled to take part in the management of the firm,[135] and be able to bind the firm within the scope of the partnership business.[136]

---

[124] (1880) 15 Ch D 247.

[125] Trade Union and Labour Relations (Consolidation) Act 1992, s. 10.

[126] See e.g. *Willis* v *British Commonwealth Association of Universities* [1965] 1 QB 140, where an unincorporated association, the Universities Central Council on Admissions (UCCA), was regarded by Lord Denning MR as a body with a distinct legal personality, although it did not (apparently) amount to a body corporate.

[127] Often referred to as the 'general' partnership. The government is keen to reform partnership law to make it more attractive to small businesses. See, DTI Consultation Document of April 2004, *Reform of Partnership Law: The Economic Impact*.

[128] Within the UK. This is a DBEIS estimate; there are no precise statistics available because there is no registration requirement for the formation of an ordinary business partnership. Additionally, there are estimated to be around 400,000 sole traders, so that the combined figure for unincorporated business enterprises in the UK (600,000 partnerships and 400,000 sole traders) is around the million mark. As regards limited partnerships, on 31 March 2017 there was a total of 45,250 limited partnerships registered; see Companies House, Official Statistics Companies Register Activities 2016–2017.

[129] Which codified and amended aspects of the pre-existing common law.

[130] Partnership Act 1890, s. 1.

[131] Although the law may impose other formalities as to how they go about business; see e.g. the Business Names Act 1985.

[132] See also Partnership Act 1890, s. 2. Until recently the Companies Act 1985 required incorporation if the maximum number of partners was more than 20 (although subject to exceptions). This requirement was removed by the Regulatory Reform (Removal of 20 Member Limit in Partnerships etc.) Order 2002 (SI 2002, No. 3203).

[133] See Partnership Act 1890, ss. 9, 10, 12.

[134] *Ibid*. s. 24.

[135] *Ibid*. s. 24 (5).

[136] Subject to *ibid*. ss. 5, 8.

Limited partnerships are under the same regime as general or ordinary partnerships except that they are also subject to the Limited Partnerships Act 1907.[137] The limited partnership provides a vehicle by which one or more partners can have limited liability so long as certain conditions are fulfilled. However, the partnership must also consist of one or more persons who have no limitation of liability. Most limited partnerships are used in tax avoidance schemes or venture capital structures rather than as trading partnerships. Reforms are being worked on at the moment with respect to limited partnerships.[138]

Limited liability partnerships (LLPs) were originally conceived as a new business vehicle for professionals designed to ameliorate the problems being faced, in particular, by audit firms who were finding that litigation for negligence was placing partners in danger of liability well above the limits covered by their professional indemnity insurance policy. The government also feared that accountancy firms would be tempted to relocate to Jersey, where more attractive forms of partnership had been developed. Under that spur, the UK developed one of its first new business forms[139] since the Limited Partnerships Act 1907. The Limited Liability Partnerships Act 2000 introduces a new type of business association, an interesting hybrid entity which possesses some characteristics which derive from company law and some from partnership law. Although originally conceived as a business vehicle for professionals, in its current form it is available to any two or more persons carrying on a lawful business with a view to profit.[140] The Act provides that there shall be a new entity called a limited liability partnership.[141] It provides that the LLP is a body corporate[142] to be created by registration with the Registrar of Companies.[143] There are to be no problems with the *ultra vires* doctrine since it will have unlimited capacity.[144] It must have a minimum of two members.[145] Membership of the LLP comes about by subscribing the incorporation document or by agreement with the existing members.[146] The constitution of the LLP is derived from the agreement between the members, or between the

---

[137] And various statutory instruments.

[138] In November 1997, the DTI requested the Law Commission and the Scottish Law Commission to undertake jointly a review of partnership law. In September 2000, the two Commissions issued a Joint Consultation Paper on partnership law. The Paper set out proposals for the reform of the Partnership Act 1890. In October 2001, the two Commissions issued a further Joint Consultation Paper on proposals to reform the Limited Partnerships Act 1907. The two Commissions published their joint report on partnership law in November 2003. The report included a draft bill. In April 2004, the Department invited interested parties to provide information on the possible economic benefits and costs of the Law Commissions' proposals. In July 2006, the Labour Government announced its decision to implement the limited partnership law reforms recommended by the Law Commissions in their joint report. It was decided that the recommendations in respect of general partnership law reform would not be taken forward. The Labour Government intended to take forward the reforms to limited partnership law by means of a Regulatory Reform Order when Parliamentary time allowed, and published a consultation document containing draft clauses (see, http://bis.ecgroup.net/Publications/BusinessLaw/PartnershipLaw.aspx), but that did not materialise.

[139] The other was the introduction of open-ended investment companies (OEICs) in 1996. See Chapter 18, 18.6 below.

[140] Limited Liability Partnerships Act 2000, s. 2 (1) (a). Academics had criticised the earlier restrictive concept, see J. Freedman and V. Finch 'Limited Liability Partnerships: Have Accountants Sewn up the "Deep Pockets" Debate?' [1997] JBL 387.

[141] Limited Liability Partnerships Act 2000, s. 1 (1).

[142] *Ibid.* s. 1 (2).

[143] *Ibid.* s. 3.

[144] *Ibid.* s. 1 (3).

[145] *Ibid.* s. 2 (1) (a).

[146] *Ibid.* s. 4 (1), (2).

limited liability partnership and its members.[147] Pre-incorporation agreements between the members may carry over into the LLP to some extent.[148] It is provided that every member of an LLP is the agent of it.[149] On the matter of limited liability, the legislation provides that the members of an LLP have 'such liability to contribute to its assets in the event of its being wound up as is provided for by virtue of this Act'.[150]

With their new entity DBIS (as it was) seems to have met a commercial need that was actually there; the LLP is being used.[151] It takes the advantage of limited liability from company law and combines it with what some will regard as advantageous aspects of partnerships, namely partnership taxation. On the important question of disclosure, it much resembles a company in that it must file annual reports and accounts,[152] so in respect of disclosure it looks as though there is going to be little advantage over an ordinary private company.

## 1.10 Reform mechanisms

### A Modern company law

There could not be a more exciting time to be writing and thinking about company law. Early in the new century and the new millennium, we find ourselves dealing with a complete programme of reform of company law. In March 1998, the Department of Trade and Industry (now renamed the Department for Business, Energy & Industrial Strategy) published a Consultation Paper entitled *Modern Company Law – for a Competitive Economy*,[153] the effect of which was to launch a fundamental review which spanned several years. Needless to say, the outcomes of this reform exercise are explored throughout the text. It was the first fundamental reform programme to take place in the 150 years or so of modern company law.

### B The agencies of company law reform

#### 1 *The Department for Business, Energy & Industrial Strategy (DBEIS)*[154]

The basic structure of UK company law, which can be traced to the Joint Stock Companies Act 1844 and its successors, created the facility of incorporation by registration. This in itself was the product of parliamentary reform mechanisms and of political and commercial pressure groups. It was not the product of the judge-made common law. Although

---

[147] *Ibid.* s. 5.
[148] *Ibid.* s. 5 (2).
[149] *Ibid.* s. 6 (1). Although in some circumstances a member without actual authority to act will not be able to bind the partnership to a third party: s. 6 (2).
[150] *Ibid.* s. 1 (4). The Limited Liability Partnerships Regulations 2001 (SI 2001 No. 1090), reg. 5, apply the provisions of the Insolvency Act 1986 so as to bring about limited liability (i.e. s. 74 thereof).
[151] At 31 March 2004 there were 7,396 on the register (Great Britain); source *Companies in 2003–2004* (London: DTI, 2004) p. 50.
[152] See reg. 3 of the LLP Regulations.
[153] To avoid confusion with an earlier less ambitious review launched in 1992, it will be referred to in this text as the 'Company Law Review'.
[154] Formerly the Department for Business, Innovation and Skills (DBIS) and, prior to that, the Department of Trade and Industry (DTI).

judges have had a major influence on the incremental development of company law, it should be borne in mind that this has been in the wake of the legislative framework.

From the earliest pre-1844 days, the DBEIS or its predecessors, the Department for Business, Innovation and Skills, the Department for Business, Enterprise and Regulatory Reform, the Department of Trade and Industry and the Board of Trade, has had a dominant role in the process of company law reform. It was the trenchant energy of William Ewart Gladstone, as President of the Board of Trade, which saw through the passage of the 1844 Act which gave birth to the UK company law system. Thereafter, although the DTI would periodically produce its own agenda derived from difficulties which had been brought to its attention or which it had come across, company law reform was often the product of recommendations of committees set up to inquire into particular problems or simply to rove through known problem areas.

If a major reform has been in contemplation, then the input of time and care is apparent from a reading of the committee reports, which remain fascinating sources of company law history. For instance, there were four inquiries in which the matter of limited liability was canvassed:[155] Bellenden Ker's Report (on limited partnerships) in 1837,[156] the Select Committee on Investments for the Savings of the Middle and Working Classes 1850,[157] the Select Committee on the Law of Partnership 1851,[158] and the Royal Mercantile Law Commission 1854.[159] Eventually, Parliament took the plunge and enacted the controversial Limited Liability Act 1855, which added the facility of limited liability to the 1844 Act's facility of incorporation by registration.

In the twentieth century, the usual pattern was that a committee would be set up periodically under the chairmanship of a member of the judiciary distinguished in company law. The Loreburn Committee of 1906 led to the introduction of the distinction between public and private companies. Other reforms, of a wide-ranging nature, were instituted as a result of the Wrenbury Committee (1918). The Greene Committee (1926) left its mark on company law by[160] the introduction of the first legislation against financial assistance for the purchase of shares. The Cohen Committee (1945) was responsible for the introduction of legislation against directors' loans, and for the 1948 consolidation. The last such committee was chaired by Lord Jenkins. Its report in 1962 was full of recommendations. Many of these never reached the statute book but one that did changed UK company law forever, for it was the Jenkins Committee which recommended the introduction of the unfair prejudice remedy. Although these committees were given wide terms of reference, they generally remained focused on specific problems which had become apparent to practitioners generally or to the DTI. They were not committees which embarked on a wholesale reassessment of fundamental principles.

The Jenkins Committee was the last of its type. For some years thereafter, the DTI adopted the policy of securing the appointment of committees to look into specific areas of malfunction, such as the Cork Report[161] which led to reforms in the Insolvency Act

---

[155] Although no significant weight of opinion in favour of the principle emerged.
[156] BPP Vol. XLIV.
[157] BPP Vol. XIX.
[158] BPP Vol. XVII.
[159] BPP Vol. XXVII.
[160] Among other things.
[161] Sir Kenneth Cork *Report of the Review Committee on Insolvency Law and Practice* (London: Cmnd 8558, 1982); also the White Paper *A Revised Framework for Insolvency Law* (Cmnd 9175, 1984).

1985. Another technique was to secure the appointment of a distinguished academic to look into a matter and report. In this way, the appointment of Professor Jim Gower produced the Gower Report[162] and ultimately led to the Financial Services Act 1986 which set up the first comprehensive system for the regulation of financial services in the UK. Other academics were asked to take on the task of inquiring into particularly knotty academic problems, such as *ultra vires*[163] and company charges.[164]

In November 1992, the DTI announced that it was launching a 'Company Law Review'.[165] This turned out to be a series of consultation documents on various problem areas. Although it covered a broad range of topics, it was clear that this 'Review' was not intended to be a thorough re-examination of basic principles. By the beginning of 1995, the DTI had produced detailed consultation papers and proposals covering such topics as: financial assistance for the purchase of shares; shareholders' written resolutions; simplifying accounts; simplifying disclosure of interests in shares; a new company voluntary arrangements procedure; partnership companies; simpler summary financial statements; late payment of commercial debts; draft uncertificated securities regulations for CREST; registration of charges; and model articles of association for partnership companies. Many of these led to legislation[166] and others will in time. Some proposals have been undergoing further refinement.[167] It seems that the 1992 Company Law Review ended around 1994–95. Thereafter, the DTI simply continued its work of reform by producing consultation documents[168] and they no longer bore the legend 'Company Law Review', but merely 'Company Law Reform'.

The post-1995 consultation documents on 'Company Law Reform' covered a similarly diverse range of matters: Disclosure of Directors' Emoluments Draft Regulations;[169] Shareholder Communications at the Annual General Meeting;[170] Private Shareholders: Corporate Governance Rights;[171] Disclosure of Directors' and Company Secretaries' Particulars;[172] Share Buybacks;[173] Investment Companies Share Repurchases using Capital Profits;[174] Political Donations by Companies;[175] Directors' Remuneration.[176] A good number of the issues dealt with in these consultation papers are unresolved and some have found their way on to the agendas of the 1998 Company Law Review described below.

---

[162]See L. C. B. Gower *Review of Investor Protection: A Discussion Document* (HMSO, January 1982) and Final Report Cmnd 9125 (1984) discussed below in Chapter 16, 16.4A.

[163]Professor D. Prentice produced a report on the *ultra vires* doctrine in 1986.

[164]Professor A. Diamond produced a report into company charges in 1989. See Chapter 12[check] below.

[165]This is not to be confused with the later Company Law Review launched in March 1998. They are very different creatures.

[166]E.g. the consultation letter of August 1993 on the problems with the new written resolution procedure in the Companies Act 1989 led to the Deregulation (Resolutions of Private Companies) Order 1996 (SI 1996 No. 1471).

[167]E.g. the well-known difficulties with the area of financial assistance for the purchase of shares were examined in Consultation Document (October 1993) *Proposals for the Reform of Sections 151–158 of the Companies Act 1985*, but there was subsequent output on this in September 1994, November 1996, and April 1997. The matter has since been taken up in the 1998 Company Law Review (see below).

[168]And prepared to conduct a Review of far greater magnitude.

[169]January 1996.

[170]April 1996.

[171]November 1996.

[172]February 1997.

[173]May 1998.

[174]March 1999.

[175]March 1999.

[176]July 1999.

Additionally, there have been two big projects on shareholder remedies and limited liability partnerships. The first of these had largely been a Law Commission venture[177] but the DTI later produced its own consultation document.[178] For the second of them the DTI produced three consultation documents, and this work has recently found fruition in the passing of the Limited Liability Partnerships Act 2000.[179]

As has been seen above, the DTI has also been responsible for the sometimes awesome task of implementing the EC Directives on company law and financial services, although since 1992 the Treasury has had responsibility for such matters relating to financial services.

## 2 *The Law Commission*

Since 1994 the Law Commission[180] has been making a significant input into company law reform. It has investigated various matters which have been referred to it by DBEIS (and its predecessors) and has produced consultation papers, reports and draft legislation. Its investigations have ranged across company law, covering such matters as alternatives to small private companies, the offence of corporate killing, review of partnership law, codification and review of directors' duties, execution of documents and shareholder litigation. In addition, the Law Commissioners have given unstinting leadership to the academic and practitioner communities with the intention of widening the constituency of input into the inquiry and reform process. The work of the Law Commission will have done much to assist the task of the 1998 Review in some areas.

## 3 *City and institutional input*

In recent years it has become apparent[181] that the City, its institutions and professions are willing to participate in the reform process. The example of the work of the Cadbury, Greenbury and Hampel committees on corporate governance, in conjunction with the Stock Exchange, spanning nearly a decade, has shown the innovative possibilities of self-regulation.

Also looking at company law reform has been the Law Society's Standing Committee on Company Law. Comprising leading practitioners and academics, this group has taken a keen interest in reform. In 1991 they produced a memorandum document called 'The Reform of Company Law' which critically considered the adequacy of the present structures of company law and recommended the establishment of an independent standing Company Law Commission which would harness the experience of civil servants, practitioners and academics. It would publish draft legislation well in advance of enactment so that it could be scrutinised publicly. The Law Society's Standing Committee has also been performing the useful function of responding to the output of DTI and Law Commission consultation material.[182]

---

[177] See Law Com. Consultation Paper No. 142 and the Law Com. Report No. 246 on *Shareholder Remedies*.
[178] *Shareholder Remedies* (November 1998).
[179] See further above 1.9C.
[180] On some projects, such as the investigation into shareholder remedies, the Scottish Law Commission also was involved.
[181] See Chapter 10 below.
[182] The Financial Law Steering Group has made similar inputs.

The Institute of Chartered Accountants of England and Wales (ICAEW) has also made considered responses on matters which would affect the interests of those engaged in the financial reporting industry. They have been particularly active in recent years in trying get something done about what is widely seen as the over-exposure of accountants to litigation in respect of their audit functions. Other accountancy bodies have from time to time also joined the debate.

## 4 *Academics*

Down the years the academics have also contributed, not only through the traditional forms of academic output, of writing articles and books, but also through undertaking investigations into problem areas, through sitting on reform committees, editing journals and collections, or generally getting involved in the reform process.[183]

## 5 *European Commission*

The input made to company law by the EC harmonisation programme has already been described, as have the major new initiatives set out in the Commission's action plan for Company Law.[184] As will be seen later, there has been a similar, but more radical, programme in the field of capital markets law, designed to create a single market in financial services within the EU.[185]

## C The 1998 review

### 1 *Structure*

The Consultation Paper *Modern Company Law – For a Competitive Economy* set out the mechanisms and the timetable for the running of the Company Law Review. It seemed that the Review was to be substantially a DTI project. The structure of the mechanisms for bringing about the Review preserve the historical primacy of the role of the DTI in company law reform. Overseeing the management of the project was the Steering Group, and this was chaired by the Director of the Company Law and Investigations Directorate of the DTI. There was also a Consultative Committee chaired by the DTI's Director General, Competition and Markets. The Project Director was Jonathan Rickford.

The Steering Group was a small committee made up of senior lawyers, representatives of large and small businesses, the chairpersons of the various Working Groups, a Scottish representative and the Project Director. The role of the Steering Group was to ensure that the outcome was clear in concept, well-expressed, internally coherent and workable. The Consultative Committee included representatives from key groups such as the accountancy bodies, the Law Society, the CBI, the TUC, and other government departments. Wider interests were also represented including those of small business and shareholders. In addition to

---

[183] See e.g. the story of Professor Gower's role in creating the UK's first comprehensive system of securities regulation in Chapter 16, 16.4A below.

[184] At 1.6C above.

[185] See further Chapter 16, 16.5E 3 below.

the Steering Group and the Consultative Committee, there were Working Groups which did much of the work of analysis of policy and problems and producing draft proposals under the overview of the Steering Committee. At the outset of the Review it was intended that the Final Report would be published in conjunction with a White Paper by March 2001.

## 2 *Guiding principles*

It was clear from the objectives and terms of reference set out in the Consultation Paper[186] that the primary guiding principle is intended to be the competitiveness of British companies. The objectives and terms of reference overlapped to some extent but several clear themes emerged. The Review was to help achieve a company law which was competitive in the sense of helping to provide a framework within which British businesses can grow and compete effectively in an economic sense. But the DTI also had in mind what is sometimes referred to as the 'Delaware effect', under which a legal system which has a desirable framework of company law will attract businesses to it with all the benefits to the economy which that brings in terms of employment and investment.

Another theme was the need for company law to embrace a basic *laissez-faire* approach to the regulation of the business world, giving maximum choice and freedom of action to the managers of the business and yet square this with the need to secure the interests of others who have contact with or are in some way involved with the business. This is expressed to include not only those who provide the working capital of the business, shareholders and creditors, but also the employees and possibly others. Essentially here, the Review was to be required to investigate whether company law strikes the right balance between these interests, and the language used was sufficiently wide arguably to require a consideration of the desirability of concepts of stakeholder company law. The promotion of proper standards of corporate governance was another area for investigation and in particular here, the pros and cons of the use of self-regulation needed to be considered.

Accessibility of the law was another main focus. Over the years, company law has acquired a reputation as a field of law known only to lawyers, and even then yielding up its secrets only after painstaking analysis. The Review was required to consider how the drafting of company law can be modernised, so as to ensure that it can be understood by the people in the business world who are going to have to use it.

## 3 *Swift progress*

The Company Law Review speedily produced a series of high quality and very clearly written consultation documents.[187] The first of these, *The Strategic Framework*,[188] described the way in which the Review had started its work and the future arrangements

---

[186] See generally, *Modern Company Law for a Competitive Economy* (London: Department of Trade and Industry, 1998), paras 5.1–5.2.
[187] The Review has also produced a number of other useful background documents, such as: C. Jordan *International Survey of Company Law* and Centre for Law and Business, Faculty of Law, University of Manchester *Company Law in Europe: Recent Developments*.
[188] DTI Consultation Document (February 1999).

for the process. The document discussed the objectives of the Review:[189] the predominant objective was law for a competitive economy, and modern law, in the sense of being well fitted to meet current and foreseeable future needs; with an optimal balance between freedom for management and risk of abuse; the reforms should be coherent and comprehensive; and take account of key trends such as globalisation, Europeanisation, other regulators, information technologies, changing patterns of share ownership and the increasing importance of human resources; small private companies were particularly important in job creation and needed an optimal legal climate. With the objectives in mind, the Review sought to develop Guiding Principles: facilitation of transactions, with a presumption against prescription; accessibility, ease of use and identification of the law; observance of regulatory boundaries.

Eight key issues were then identified as priorities for early work.[190] Seen as of paramount importance were 'the scope of company law' (i.e. the stakeholder issue) and the 'problems of the small, or closely-held company'. Also key issues were the questions of the boundaries of regulatory and self-regulatory bodies, and international aspects of law. Finally, also chosen as 'key' were company formation, company powers, capital maintenance, and electronic communications and information.

The later consultation documents obviously reflected the choice of these key issues and contained ideas and sought views on specific matters. The second consultation document *Company General Meetings and Shareholder Communication*[191] raised the question of whether the law should abandon the requirement for public companies to hold an annual general meeting and considered the use of electronic communication. The third consultation document *Company Formation and Capital Maintenance*[192] contained radical proposals for the restructuring of the constitution of the company, and relaxations of the capital maintenance doctrine. *Reforming the Law Concerning Overseas Companies*[193] reviewed the legal treatment of companies which are incorporated overseas and which operate in the UK without incorporating there. The fifth consultation document *Developing the Framework*[194] dealt with corporate governance and the policies for the legislative treatment of small private companies. This document was also described as the second 'strategic' document since it contained plans for how the remainder of the work of the Review should proceed. Subsequently there has been a further document *Capital Maintenance: Other Issues*[195] focusing on a small number of residual technical issues. Then a consultation document called *Registration of Company Charges*[196] and lastly, drawing together many of the previous issues, came *Completing the Structure*[197] which prepared the way for the Final Report.

---

[189] DTI Consultation Document *The Strategic Framework* pp. 8 *et seq.*
[190] *Ibid.* p. 19.
[191] DTI Consultation Document (October 1999).
[192] *Ibid.*
[193] DTI Consultation Document (October 1999).
[194] DTI Consultation Document (March 2000).
[195] DTI Consultation Document (June 2000).
[196] DTI Consultation Document (October 2000).
[197] DTI Consultation Document (November 2000).

## 4 *The Final Report and subsequent developments*

The Review Steering Group presented the Final Report (*Modern Company Law for a Competitive Economy Final Report*) to the Secretary of State in June 2001. The Report is in three parts, Part I consisting of an overview of the objectives and core proposals. Part II goes into the recommendations in more detail and Part III contains examples of how parts of the legislation might be drafted. As would be expected, it is a final gathering together of the ideas which were the subject of extensive discussion and consultation during the Review years. The Report identifies three core policies which are at the heart of the Review: (1) the 'think small first' strategy for small and private companies, (2) an open, inclusive and flexible regime for company governance, (3) an appropriate institutional structure for law reform, enforcement and related matters.

Further references are made to some of the detail of the Final Report's recommendations in chapters throughout this text.

Finally, two White Papers were issued by the DTI. The first, which was published in July 2002, was in two volumes, *Modernising Company Law* (Cm 5553-I) and *Modernising Company Law – Draft Clauses* (Cm 5553-II). In it the Government set out some of its proposals. It did not accept all the recommendations of the Review. However a 'mini' Bill, the Companies (Audit, Investigations and Community Enterprise) Bill, was introduced in the House of Lords on 3 December 2003 and passed into legislation the following year. The Act seeks to strengthen several regimes: the regulation of auditors; the enforcement of accounting and reporting requirements; and company investigations. It also makes provision for the setting up of Community Interest Companies (CICs). Its provisions are dealt with at appropriate places in this text.[198] The second White Paper appeared in March 2005,[199] setting out a list of the key legislative changes, which, subsequently, formed the basis for the Companies Act 2006, discussed in the next section.

## D The Companies Act 2006

### 1 *Background*

As commented on above, the reform of UK company law announced by the Government in March 1998 spawned a range of consultation papers issued by the Company Law Reform Steering Group which was charged by the Department of Trade and Industry (DTI), now DBEIS, with undertaking the reform process. The results of this process led to what was, at the time, the longest statute in the history of Parliament: the Companies Act 2006 (CA 2006), which received Royal Assent in November of that year.[200] This is both a reforming and a consolidating statute and was being brought into force in phases which

---

[198] Also dealt with in appropriate places are the relevant provisions of the Enterprise Act 2002, the provisions of which mainly relate to insolvency law.
[199] Department of Trade and Industry, *Company Law Reform* (White Paper, Cm 6456, 2005).
[200] A number of documents relating to the Act are available on the DBEIS website, including the Act itself, supporting secondary legislation and explanatory notes and briefing on latest developments: http://www.bis.gov.uk/policies/business-law/company-and-partnership-law/company-law.

lasted short of three years. This began in January 2007 and ended in October 2009. It is noteworthy that the original view that the Companies Act 1985 would be retained except insofar as it was reformed by the Company Law Reform Bill was jettisoned in favour of a single statute. The result is that the CA 2006 contains 47 Parts with 1,300 sections and is followed by 16 Schedules. There are also over 70 statutory instruments made under the 2006 Act. The key objectives of the CA 2006 are:

- to simplify the administrative burdens on small private companies;
- to facilitate shareholder engagement, particularly in quoted companies; and
- to update and clarify the law, particularly in relation to directors' duties.

## 2 *Treatment in this text*

Thus far we have largely confined ourselves to illustrating the mechanisms at work in the reform process. We have not considered the substantive reforms introduced by the Companies Act 2006.[201] Rather, the provisions of the new Act and the policy objectives underlying the reforms contained therein are considered in the following chapters.

## 1.11 Brexit

This jurisdiction is, of course, facing unprecedented times following the referendum to leave the European Union and the subsequent trigger of Article 50. The impact of the decision to leave the EU will have a potentially significant impact on our company law and financial services framework (as will be clear from discussions throughout this text that demonstrate the impact that our membership of the EU has had on our domestic company law). Conversely, the EU is preparing to adapt to the departure of the UK by reviewing its regulation of financial services. It is considered problematic that such a significant volume of financial services would then be conducted outside the EU and not subject to regulatory supervision within the EU. For example, the Commission has proposed to amend the ESMA Regulation so that the clearing of Euro-denominated securities be brought under the control of ESMA (the European Securities and Markets Authority, see Chapter 16 below). However, this met opposition from some member states who are insisting that member state regulatory authorities remain competent.[202] European financial authorities (including ESMA) have published various papers setting out principles on their post-Brexit supervisory approach, including relocations. That said, these are subject to further discussions and negotiations.

---

[201] For an assessment of whether the CA 2006 has met its objectives see, A. Reisberg, 'Corporate Law in the UK after Recent Reforms: The Good, the Bad and the Ugly' *Current Legal Problems* (Oxford: OUP, 2010) 315, available at: http://papers.ssrn.com/sol3/papers.cfm?abstract_id=1635732.
[202] H. Smith Freehills, 'The View from Brussels – Developments in November and December' (19 December 2017), 3.

It is clear from the above that given that the precise nature, extent and timing of such changes are not yet clear, this text does not address any speculation in this regard. Rather, any such impact will be addressed in subsequent editions (or by online updates) as and when we have greater clarity on this issue.

## Further reading

A. Reisberg, 'Corporate Law in the UK after Recent Reforms: The Good, the Bad and the Ugly' *Current Legal Problems* (Oxford: OUP, 2010) 315, available at: http://papers.ssrn.com/sol3/papers.cfm?abstract_id=1635732.

# 2

# Corporate entity, limited liability and incorporation

## 2.1 Corporate entity

### A The *'Salomon'* doctrine

Incorporation by registration was introduced in 1844 and the doctrine of limited liability followed in 1855.[1] Subsequently, in 1897, in *Salomon* v *Salomon & Co*[2] the House of Lords explored the effects of these enactments and cemented into English law the twin concepts of corporate entity and limited liability. Incorporation gives the company legal personality, separate from its members, with the result that a company may own property, sue and be sued in its own corporate name. It will not die when its members die. In many areas of company law, the legal rules are shaped by and to some extent flow from the concept of separate personality. Thus, the share capital, once subscribed must be maintained by the company, it no longer belongs to the members and cannot be returned to them except subject to stringent safeguards.[3] Similarly, the rule that for a wrong done to the company the proper claimant is the company itself, is largely the result of this principle.[4] The separate personality concept is often spoken of as though it also necessarily involves the idea that the liability of the company's members is limited but of course this is not always so; it is perfectly possible to form an unlimited company under s. 3 (4) of the Companies Act 2006. In this case, there is no limited liability, but under the corporate entity doctrine the company will have separate legal personality. In practice, most companies are limited companies and so corporate personality and limited liability[5] tend to go hand in hand.

The corporate entity principle was firmly settled at the end of the nineteenth century in the *Salomon* case.[6] It concerned a common business manoeuvre whereby Aron Salomon, the owner of a boot and leather business, sold the business to a company he formed (Aron Salomon and Company Limited), in return for fully paid-up shares in it, allotted to him and members of his family. Following an initial allotment of additional shares Aron Salomon held 20,001 shares in the company whilst his wife, daughter and four sons held

---

[1] Joint Stock Companies Act 1844; Limited Liability Act 1855. For a more detailed account of these events and related matters, see B. Pettet 'Limited Liability – A Principle for the 21st Century?' (1995) 48 *Current Legal Problems* (Part 2) 125 at pp. 128–132.
[2] [1897] AC 22.
[3] See further Parts 17, 18 and 23 of the Companies Act 2006, considered in Part IV.
[4] This was part of the rule in *Foss* v *Harbottle*; see further Chapter 12 below.
[5] Limited liability is discussed under 2.2 below.
[6] [1897] AC 22.

one share each. Salomon also received an acknowledgement of the compa'
ness to him, in the form of secured debentures. These were later mortgaged to
Soon after formation, the company went into liquidation at the behest of unpaid
creditors. The debentures, being secured by a charge on the company's assets ranked in
priority to the trade creditors and so the mortgage to the outsider was paid off. About
£1,000 remained and Aron Salomon, now as unencumbered owner of the debentures,
claimed this in priority to the trade creditors. In deciding the claim, the critical question
before the court was whether the company had been validly constituted or whether the
incorporation was contrary to the true intention of the Act. The Companies Act 1862 (the
relevant incorporation statute at the time) mandated that a company be incorporated with
seven members;[7] a requirement that had, technically, been complied with in Salomon's
case. Nevertheless, doubts arose as to the legitimacy of the incorporation. Here, the company was a so-called 'one-man company' as six of the seven shareholders were mere
nominees, each holding a single share. Thus, the issue before the court was whether the
Act required seven shareholders of substance or whether strict compliance with the Act (as
in this case) was sufficient to bestow separate personality.

At first instance, the court found against Salomon.[8] Vaughan Williams J held that Aron
Salomon (the individual) was simply carrying 'on business under another name' and that
there must have been an 'implied agreement by [Aron Salomon] to indemnify the company'.[9] Perhaps unsurprisingly, Vaughan Williams J applied principles of individual bankruptcy to the facts before him and described the company as a mere alias or agent of Aron
Salomon. As a consequence he held that the company (as agent) was entitled to an indemnity from its principal (Aron Salomon).

Aron Salomon appealed arguing, *inter alia*, that the incorporation statute did not require
that a company be incorporated with seven shareholders of substance. He claimed that to
read a materiality requirement into the Act in this way would only serve to introduce
uncertainty into what was otherwise a clear legislative provision. In response, it was
argued that the company was a 'sham' and, reiterating the judgment of Vaughan Williams
J, an agent of Aron Salomon. Reflecting the prevailing view of the time, namely that incorporation was a privilege for economically significant businesses,[10] counsel for the company suggested that it would be 'most unfortunate . . . if a trader could limit his liability
by the device of using the name of a limited company'.[11]

Adopting a purposive approach, the Court of Appeal upheld the decision of the lower
court (albeit finding the company to be a trustee, rather than agent, of Aron Salomon).
Lindley LJ held that there could be 'no doubt' that this was an attempt to use the
Companies Act 1862 for a 'purpose for which it never was intended'.[12] Lopes LJ observed
that the Act was not intended to apply to incorporation by 'one substantial person and six

---

[7] The Limited Liability Act 1855 had previously required that a company be incorporated with 25 shareholders.
This figure was reduced to seven by the Joint Stock Companies Act 1856.
[8] *Broderip v Salomon* [1895] 2 Ch 323.
[9] [1895] 2 Ch 323, 331.
[10] For a more detailed discussion of this perspective and of the historical development of the classification of
business forms see: P.W. Ireland, 'The Rise of the Limited Liability Company,' (1984) 12 *International Journal
of the Sociology of Law* 239.
[11] [1895] 2 Ch 323 334.
[12] [1895] 2 Ch 323 337.

mere dummies',[13] and that the 'scheme' before the court was a 'perversion'[14] of the Acts. Upholding the first instance decision, the Court of Appeal found Aron Salomon liable to indemnify the company.

Undeterred, Aron Salomon again appealed and the matter came before the House of Lords. In a stark departure from the lower courts, the House of Lords found in favour of Aron Salomon. The House of Lords affirmed the principle that the company was a separate legal person from its controlling shareholder, and that it was not to be regarded as his agent or trustee (even in cases of so-called one-man companies).[15] As such, Aron Salomon was not liable to indemnify the company's creditors, thus giving effect to the limited liability doctrine.

In reaching this decision, Lord Halsbury noted that to determine whether the company was validly incorporated he could only look to the words of the statute. The Companies Act 1862 was silent as to the motive or materiality of the company's shareholders and he was not permitted to imply any such requirement. Indeed, in addressing the allegation of the lower courts that Aron Salomon had simply incorporated the company to limit his liability, Lord Herschell observed that the very object of incorporation was limited liability.[16]

In delivering his judgment, Lord MacNaghten suggested that Aron Salomon had been 'dealt with somewhat hardly'[17] in the case. He noted that the Act simply required seven shareholders and did not impose a condition that a company's shareholders be independent or that there be a balance of power between them. Rather, provided there were seven sub-scribers to the memorandum the company 'attains maturity at birth'[18] and separate person-ality will not be lost by the existence of a majority shareholder. In affirming this fundamental feature of modern company law, Lord MacNaghten observed that once incorporated 'the company is at law a different person altogether from the subscribers to the memorandum; and, though it may be that after incorporation the business is precisely the same as it was before . . . the company is not in law the agent of the subscribers or trustee for them. Nor are the subscribers as members liable, in any shape or form.'[19]

The consequences of the House of Lords' judgment in *Salomon* should not be underes-timated. The corporate entity principle, often now referred to as the '*Salomon*' principle, is applied systematically in most cases and these have gradually built up a picture of its ramifications.[20] It was held that it was possible to regard a shareholder who was employed

---

[13] [1895] 2 Ch 323, 341.

[14] [1895] 2 Ch 323 341.

[15] This was necessary to the result reached, for if the company had been Salomon's agent, he would have been liable to the creditors, as principal, on the contracts he had made; on agency generally, see further Chapter 6. For a trenchant critique of the decision, see O. Kahn-Freund 'Some Reflections on Company Law Reform' [1944] MLR 54.

[16] [1897] AC 22, 44.

[17] [1897] AC 22, 47.

[18] [1897] AC 22, 51.

[19] *Ibid.*

[20] It continues to stimulate academic interest, particularly on the question of piercing the corporate veil, as the undiminishing flow of scholarship testifies; see e.g. R. Grantham and C. Rickett (eds) *Corporate Personality in the 20th Century* (Oxford: Hart Publishing, 1998); H. Rajak 'The Legal Personality of Associations' in F. Patfield (ed.) *Perspectives on Company Law: 1* (London: Kluwer, 1995) p. 63; L. Sealy 'Perception and Policy in Company Law Reform' in D. Feldman and F. Meisel (eds) *Corporate and Commercial Law: Modern Developments* (London: LLP, 1996) 11. And on 'piercing the veil' (see below): S. Ottolenghi 'From Peeping Behind the Veil, To Ignoring it Completely' (1990) 53 MLR 338; J. Gray 'How Regulation Finds its Way through the Corporate Veil' in B. Rider (ed.) *The Corporate Dimension* (Bristol: Jordans, 1998) p. 255; C. Mitchell 'Lifting the Corporate Veil in the English Courts: an Empirical Study' [1999] CFILR 15.

as a pilot by the company as a 'worker' (within the meaning of a statute) even though he controlled the company and was its chief executive.[21] Another case quite logically confirmed that the shareholder was not the owner of the property of the company.[22]

## B Piercing the corporate veil

At times, the *Salomon* principle produces what appear to be unfair or purely technical results and in such circumstances judges[23] come under a moral and/or intellectual pressure to sidestep the *Salomon* principle and produce a result that seems more 'just'. This necessarily gives rise to the question as to when (if at all) the court would be willing to 'pierce the corporate veil'. That is, when would the court be willing to disregard the separate personality of the corporation and treat certain liabilities of the company as the liabilities of its members?[24] There are many reported examples of the courts having to grapple with this question and their approach has not always been clear or consistent. Indeed, Lord Sumption recently suggested that case law on piercing the veil was 'characterised by incautious dicta and inadequate reasoning'.[25] To understand why this might be the case, and the difficulties faced by the courts in deciding whether to pierce the veil or not, it is helpful to briefly reflect on these earlier decisions before considering the recent Supreme Court decision of *Prest* v *Petrodel Resources Ltd.*[26]

## 1 *Single economic unit*

Commonly, although not exclusively, the issue before the court involves a group of companies and whether a parent should be liable for (or, as we shall see, benefit from) the conduct or business of its subsidiaries. For instance, a number of cases have revolved around versions of this problem: Company A has a subsidiary, Company B. Company A owns land on which stands a factory. Its subsidiary Company B operates the factory business. A local government authority makes a compulsory purchase of the land. The statute under which it does this provides for compensation for the landowner in respect of disturbance to a business carried on by him on the land. In our problem, applying the *Salomon* doctrine strictly, Company A cannot claim, since it has no business which is disturbed (it is simply a landowner), nor can Company B since although it does have a business which has been disturbed, it has no land. Obviously in reality the two companies function as a single unit, but in law (and on a strict application of *Salomon*) they are separate.

---

[21] *Lee* v *Lee's Air Farming* [1961] AC 12, PC. See also, *Clark* v *Clark Construction Initiatives* [2008] All ER (D) 440 (Feb).
[22] *Macaura* v *Northern Assurance Co.* [1925] AC 619, where the beneficial owner of all the shares in a company did not realise that he was not owner of the company's property and so when he insured that property by policies in his own name and the property was later damaged by fire, he failed to recover. Similarly, it has been held that it is possible for the sole shareholders and directors to steal from their company: *R* v *Philippou* (1989) 5 BCC 665.
[23] In some circumstances the corporate entity principle will be set aside by statute, as is common in taxation legislation. From the perspective of company law, s. 399 of the Companies Act 2006 provides that parent companies are under a duty to produce group accounts.
[24] *Atlas Maritime Co. SA* v *Avalon Maritime Ltd (No. 1)* [1991] 4 All ER 769, 779.
[25] *Prest* v *Petrodel Resources Ltd* [2013] UKSC 34, [19].
[26] [2013] UKSC 34.

In *DHN Ltd* v *Tower Hamlets*,[27] Lord Denning MR[28] considered a variant of this issue, which concerned three companies operating a wholesale grocery business. Here, the parent company DHN Food Distributors Limited ('DHN') ran the grocery business and had two wholly-owned subsidiaries: Bronze Investments Limited ('Bronze'), the sole business of which was owning premises that it licensed to DHN, and DHN Food Transport Ltd that owned (and similarly licensed to DHN) the vehicles required by the business. When the local authority made a compulsory acquisition of the premises owned by Bronze, DHN argued that, notwithstanding its separate personality at law, it should receive compensation for the disruption to its business. In his judgment, Lord Denning MR found in favour of the company and held that the corporate veil should be pierced.[29] In doing so, Lord Denning MR explained that the companies were in reality a 'single economic unit', and so compensation was payable for the loss of business. Describing the case as the 'three in one'[30] Lord Denning MR noted, *inter alia*, that prior to the compulsory acquisition DHN had the power to procure the transfer of the property from Bronze. As such, and regardless of the fact that DHN did not in fact procure such a transfer, Lord Denning held that DHN should nevertheless be compensated in full. Given this departure from *Salomon* it is perhaps not surprising that when the House of Lords considered an analogous fact pattern shortly after *DHN* was decided, Lord Keith of Kinkel expressed 'some doubts whether in this respect the Court of Appeal [in *DHN*] properly applied the principle that it is appropriate to pierce the veil only where special circumstances exist indicating that [the company] is a mere façade concealing the true facts'.[31] Lord Keith of Kinkel's reasoning was subsequently followed in *Adams* v *Cape Industries plc*[32] where the Court of Appeal, rejecting a single economic unit argument, noted that 'our law, for better or worse, recognises the creation of subsidiary companies, which though in one sense the creature of their parent companies, will nevertheless under the general law fall to be treated as separate legal entities'.[33]

## 2 Sham or façade

Both *Woolfson* v *Strathclyde* and *Adams* v *Cape* made it clear that the court would only be permitted to pierce the veil when a company is a mere façade concealing the true facts. However, this naturally raises the question as to what constitutes 'a façade' for this purpose. There is already a little guidance. In *Adams* v *Cape*, it was felt that the motive of the person using the company would sometimes be highly material and the Court of Appeal clearly felt that *Jones* v *Lipman*[34] was a good example of a case that would satisfy the façade test (and that as a consequence the judge there was right to pierce the corporate veil). The first defendant, Lipman, had agreed to sell some land to the claimants, but after entering into the contract he changed his mind. So he sold it to a company of which he owned nearly all the shares. The judge made an order for specific performance against

---

[27] [1976] 1 WLR 852.
[28] Although the remainder of the Court of Appeal adopted a more orthodox analysis.
[29] This was followed by the Northern Ireland Court of Appeal in *Munton Bros* v *Sect of State* [1983] NI 369.
[30] [1976] 1 WLR 852, 857.
[31] *Woolfson* v *Strathclyde Regional Council* [1978] SC (HL) 90, 96.
[32] [1990] BCC 786.
[33] [1990] BCC 786, [820] (Slade LJ).
[34] [1962] 1 WLR 832.

Lipman and the company. The Court of Appeal approved[35] of the judge's description of the company as 'the creature of the first defendant, a device and a sham, a mask which he holds before his face in an attempt to avoid recognition by the eye of equity'. Similarly, in *Gilford Motor Company Limited* v *Horne*[36] the defendant had incorporated a company to conduct business that he was prohibited from undertaking personally due to the restrictive covenants that applied to him as the former managing director of the plaintiff. In this instance, Lord Hanworth MR held that the purpose of the company was to enable the defendant 'under what is a cloak or sham, to engage in business which, on consideration of the [restrictive covenants] . . . was a business in which he had a fear that the plaints might intervene and object'[37] and that as such the court was entitled to pierce the veil.

In *Trustor AB* v *Smallbone and others (No. 3),*[38] the managing director of Trustor had transferred money to Introcom, a company which he controlled, and one of the issues which arose was whether the corporate veil of Introcom could be pierced so as to treat receipt by Introcom as receipt by him. Morritt V-C held that the court would be 'entitled to pierce the corporate veil and recognise the receipt by a company as that of the individual(s) in control of it if the company was used as a device or façade to conceal the true facts thereby avoiding or concealing any liability of those individual(s)'[39] and that on the facts this was satisfied. Of note, in *Trustor* the court made it clear that mere impropriety is not enough to pierce the veil as 'companies are often involved in improprieties'.[40] Rather, what is required is impropriety 'linked to the use of the company structure to avoid or conceal liability'.[41] It is implicit within this decision, and others concerning the corporation as a mere façade, that to pierce the veil the company must be being used to avoid an existing obligation or liability.[42] The court will not pierce the veil where the corporate form is being used to manage or mitigate future liabilities, as this is a right that 'is inherent in our corporate law'.[43] Thus, it is perhaps of little surprise that the court in *Ord* v *Belhaven Pubs Ltd*[44] did not pierce the veil having found that 'the companies were operating at material times as trading companies and they were not being interposed as shams or for some ulterior motive . . . it was just the ordinary trading of a group of companies under circumstances where . . . the company is in law entitled to organise the group's affairs in the manner that it does'.[45]

## 3 *Interests of justice*

The difficulty with the 'façade' test is that it may preclude the court from piercing the veil in cases where broader notions of fairness or justice may otherwise suggest that it would

---

[35] *Ibid.* at p. 825.
[36] [1933] Ch 935.
[37] [1933] Ch 935, 956.
[38] [2002] BCC 795.
[39] *Ibid.* at p. 801.
[40] [2001] 1 WLR 1177, 1185.
[41] *Ibid.*
[42] See e.g. *Jones* v *Lipman* [1962] 1 WLR 832; *Gilford Motor Company Limited* v *Horne* [1993] 1 Ch 935.
[43] *Adams* v *Cape Industries plc* [1990] BCLC 479, 520.
[44] [1998] BCC 607.
[45] *Ibid.*

be appropriate to do so. Indeed, in several cases the judges have openly stated that if justice requires it then the precedent of *Salomon* can be by-passed. Thus in *Re A Company*[46] the Court of Appeal seemed to be taking the view that *Salomon* was of *prima facie* application only: 'In our view, the cases . . . show that the court will use its powers to pierce the corporate veil if it is necessary to achieve justice . . .'[47] and in *Creasey* v *Breachwood Motors Ltd*[48] it was held that the court had power to lift the veil 'to achieve justice where its exercise is necessary for that purpose'.[49] However, the judicial movement in support of piercing the corporate veil to 'achieve justice' has been firmly suppressed in several influential Court of Appeal cases concerned with how the *Salomon* doctrine should be applied to the way in which group structures are organised (an approach that has now been upheld by the Supreme Court in *Prest* v *Petrodel*) in *Adams* v *Cape Industries plc,*[50] the idea that a court was free to disregard *Salomon* merely because it considered that justice so required was firmly rejected and the court gave strong support to the idea[51] that the existence of the company as a façade concealing the true facts is really the only well-recognised exception to the rule prohibiting the piercing of the corporate veil.[52] A number of subsequent cases have generally followed the *Adams* v *Cape* approach as to the impermissibility of the 'interests of justice' as a basis for piercing the veil,[53] and *Creasey* v *Breachwood Motors,* which did not, was flatly overruled by the Court of Appeal in *Ord* v *Belhaven Pubs Ltd.*[54] In *Ord* v *Belhaven Pubs Ltd,* the claimants had taken a 20-year lease of a pub from the defendant company in 1989 and were later claiming damages for misrepresentation. The claimants became worried that the restructuring of assets between 1992 and 1995 within the group of companies, which the defendant was a part of, had left the defendant company without sufficient assets to pay their claim if it was eventually successful. The claimants applied to substitute the defendant's holding company and/or another company in its group for the defendant. Although the claim was successful at first instance, the Court of Appeal reversed this and delivered a resounding affirmation of the *Salomon* doctrine:

> In the course of its judgment [in *Adams* v *Cape*] the Court of Appeal considered both what is described as the single economic unit argument of groups of [companies] and . . . piercing the corporate veil. They discussed the authorities and clearly recognised that the concepts were extremely limited indeed . . . The approach of the judge in the present case was simply to look at the economic unit, to disregard the distinction between the legal entities that were involved and then to say: since the company cannot pay, the shareholders who are the people financially interested should be made to pay instead. That of course is radically at odds with the whole concept of corporate personality and limited liability and the decision of the House of Lords in *Salomon* . . . On the question of lifting the corporate veil, they expressed themselves similarly . . . but it is clear that they were of the view that there must be some impropriety before the corporate veil can be pierced. It is not necessary to examine the extent of the limitation of the principle because, in

---

[46] (1985) 1 BCC 99, 421.
[47] *Ibid.* at p. 99, 425.
[48] [1992] BCC 638; noted by J. Lowry, [1993] JBL 41.
[49] *Ibid.* at p. 647, *per* Judge Southwood QC.
[50] [1990] BCC 786.
[51] Which had been developing in *Woolfson* v *Strathclyde DC* (1979) 38 P & CR 521.
[52] [1990] BCC 786 at p. 822.
[53] E.g. *Re Polly Peck plc* [1996] BCC 486; *Re H Ltd* [1996] 2 All ER 391; *Yukong Lines Ltd of Korea* v *Rendsberg Investments Corp* [1998] BCC 870; *Raja* v *Van Hoogstraten, The Times,* 23 August 2007.
[54] [1998] BCC 607.

the present case, no impropriety is alleged. [The Court of Appeal] quoted what was said by Lord Keith in *Woolfson* . . . [that] it is appropriate to pierce the corporate veil only where special circumstances exist, indicating that it is a mere facade concealing the true facts . . . The plaintiffs in the present case cannot bring themselves within any such principle. There is no facade that was adopted at any stage; there was [no] concealment of the true facts . . . it was just the ordinary trading of a group of companies under circumstances where, as was said in [*Adams* v *Cape*] the company is in law entitled to organise the group's affairs in the manner that it does, and to expect that the court should apply the principles of [*Salomon*] in the ordinary way . . .[55]

Thus, after a period of oscillation and intervention, the courts had seemingly settled on the circumstances in which the corporate veil may be pierced. In reviewing the authorities, Munby J in *Ben Hashem* v *Ali Shayif and ors*[56] held that the veil may only be pierced when the company is a façade concealing the true facts and distilled the following principles that apply:

In the first place, ownership and control of a company are not of themselves sufficient . . . Secondly, the court cannot pierce the corporate veil . . . merely because it is thought to be necessary in the interests of justice . . . Thirdly, the corporate veil can be pierced only if there is some 'impropriety' . . . Fourthly, . . . the impropriety must be linked to the use of the company structure to avoid or conceal liability . . . Fifthly, it follows from all this that if the court is to pierce the veil it is necessary to show both control of the company by the wrongdoer(s) and impropriety . . . Finally, and flowing from all this, a company can be a façade even though it was not incorporated with any deceptive intent. The question is whether it is being used as a façade at the time of the relevant transaction(s).[57]

Nevertheless, the doctrine remained one that was arguably characterised by a (perceived, if not actual) lack of clarity, due in part to the tension between commercial certainty and the desire to achieve a 'just' result. This uncertainty was highlighted in the first of two cases before the Supreme Court in 2013, which raised the question of the court's jurisdiction to pierce the corporate veil. In *VTB Capital plc* v *Nutritek International Corp and ors,*[58] the Supreme Court declined to pierce the corporate veil in order to treat the alleged principal beneficial owner and controller of a company as jointly and severally liable for the breach of a facility agreement entered into by it, which would have made him liable as if he were a co-contracting party even though neither he nor any other party intended him to be such. The Supreme Court took the view that it would be an extension of the circumstances in which this had been done previously. Further, the facts did not involve the company being used as a façade concealing the true facts.

When giving his judgment in *VTB Capital* Lord Neuberger observed that 'the notion that there is no principled basis upon which it can be said that one can pierce the veil of incorporation receives some support from the fact that the precise nature, basis and meaning of the principle are all somewhat obscure, as are the precise nature of circumstances in which the principle can apply.'[59] In making these observations, there was once again a

---

[55] *Ibid*. at p. 615, *per* Hobhouse LJ (Brooke and Balcombe LJJ agreeing). For an example of 'impropriety' see *Kensington International Ltd* v *Congo* [2007] EWCA Civ 1128, where the court lifted the veil to reveal that dishonest transactions between related companies were designed to avoid existing liabilities.
[56] [2008] EWHC 2380 (Fam).
[57] *Ibid,* [159]–[164].
[58] [2013] UKSC 5.
[59] *Ibid.* [123].

renewed focus on the circumstances in which the court might pierce the veil and whether or not the current doctrine had achieved the right balance between commercial certainty (predicated on the sanctity of *Salomon*) and wider concerns of justice. Indeed, it was questioned in *VTB* whether the court had jurisdiction to pierce the veil at all.[60]

## 4 *Prest v Petrodel Resources Ltd*

The question of the court's power to pierce the veil, and the circumstances (if any) in which it would be permissible to do, so came before the Supreme Court for a second time in 2013 in the case of *Prest v Petrodel Resources Limited*.[61] This was a matrimonial dispute where the wife claimed an entitlement to properties held by companies that were (directly or indirectly) wholly owned or controlled by her husband. The Supreme Court found in favour of the wife, not by piercing the veil of the relevant companies, but by finding that on the particular circumstances of the case the companies held the properties on resulting trust for the husband and were therefore subject to an order (in favour of the wife) pursuant to the Matrimonial Causes Act 1973.

Notwithstanding the basis on which the case was decided, the Supreme Court in *Prest* v *Petrodel* did address the doctrine of piercing the veil. In giving the leading judgment, Lord Sumption observed that the 'principle that the court may be justified in piercing the corporate veil if the company's separate legal personality is being abused for the purpose of some relevant wrongdoing is well established in the authorities.'[62] Nevertheless, Lord Sumption was clear that this power to pierce the veil only arises in a limited range of cases where the separate personality of the company is disregarded.[63] It does not, contrary to the fairly indiscriminate use of the term, apply in cases where the law attributes liability without disregarding separate personality, for example where a genuine agency relationship arises.[64]

Against that definition, Lord Sumption found that the court had scope to pierce the veil 'when a person is under an existing legal obligation or liability or subject to an existing legal restriction which he deliberately evades or whose enforcement he deliberately frustrates by interposing a company under his control.'[65] In this regard, this formulation of the principle of piercing the corporate veil is consistent with authority (e.g. *Jones* v *Lipman*) and well-established legal principles that the corporate structure should not be abused for the purpose of some relevant wrongdoing.

Whilst Lord Sumption agreed with the Court of Appeal that the veil can be pierced where there is a relevant impropriety he distinguished and categorised two types of wrongdoing. The first is concealment and the second is evasion. The concealment principle is 'legally banal and does not involve piercing the corporate veil at all.'[66] Rather, this principle applies where a company is used to 'conceal the identity of the real actors'[67] and in

---

[60] *Ibid.* [121].
[61] [2013] UKSC 34.
[62] *Ibid.* [27].
[63] *Ibid.* [16].
[64] *Ibid.* As to cases where agency was found see: *Smith, Stone & Knight Ltd* v *Birmingham Corp* [1939] 4 All ER 116; *FG (Films) Ltd* [1953] 1 WLR 483.
[65] *Ibid.* [35].
[66] *Ibid.* [28].
[67] *Ibid.*

this case the court may lift the veil to identify the true facts. In contrast, the evasion principle applies where there is a 'legal right against the person in control of [the company] which exists independently of the company's involvement, and a company is interposed so that the separate legal personality of the company will defeat the right.'[68] It is in cases of evasion that the court may pierce the corporate veil. In distilling these principles, Lord Sumption made clear that the corporate veil may 'only be pierced to prevent the abuse of corporate legal personality' and, reflecting the earlier decision of *Adams* v *Cape*, that '[i]t is not an abuse to cause a legal liability to be incurred by the company in the first place'.[69]

Lord Sumption's concealment and evasion principles, although *obiter*, have been applied in subsequent decisions.[70] However, as recognised in *Akzo Nobel* v *Competition Commission*,[71] the majority of the Supreme Court in *Prest* were not willing to hold that there could not be a future extension of the circumstances in which the corporate veil may be pierced,[72] although it was acknowledged that any such expansion would be difficult to establish.[73] As such, whilst *Prest* v *Petrodel* has almost certainly brought clarity (and certainty) to this issue it may nevertheless be subject to further development.

## C Corporate liability for torts and crimes

### 1 *The problem of the corporate mind*

The doctrine of separate legal personality of companies runs into problems as soon as it meets those parts of the general law which apply to natural persons and which involve assessing the mental state of the person for the purpose of imposing liability. In these circumstances, the courts have recourse to the expedient[74] of treating the state of mind of the senior officers of the company as being the state of mind of the company.[75] The idea was put nicely by Denning LJ in *Bolton Engineering* v *Graham*,[76] where a landlord company opposed the grant of a new tenancy on the ground that it intended to occupy the land for its own business. There had been no formal board meeting or other collective decision which could be said to show the company's intention, but it was argued that in a managerial capacity, the directors simply had that intention. The Court of Appeal held that the intention of the company could be derived from the intention of its officers and agents. Denning LJ said in his graphic prose which was to become so familiar in subsequent years:

> A company may in many ways be likened to a human body. It has a brain and a nerve centre which controls what it does. It also has hands which hold the tools and act in accordance with directions from the centre. Some of the people in the company are mere servants or agents who

---

[68] *Ibid.*

[69] *Ibid.* [34].

[70] *Pennyfeathers Ltd* v *Pennyfeathers Property Co. Ltd* [2013] EWHC 3530.

[71] [2013] CAT 14, [95].

[72] [2013] UKSC 34. See the judgments of Lady Hale [92], Lord Mance [100], Lord Clarke [102], and Lord Walker [106].

[73] [2013] UKSC 34, [102].

[74] In a jurisprudential sense it tends to suggest that the fictional entity theory (see the discussion in Chapter 3 below) is not a sufficient explanation of the phenomenon of corporate personality and that, to some extent, the company soon has to be regarded in law as the people in it, thus lending support to the real entity theory of incorporation.

[75] See e.g. *Lennard's Carrying Company Ltd* v *Asiatic Petroleum Co. Ltd* [1915] AC 705.

[76] [1957] 1 QB 159.

are nothing more than the hands to do the work and cannot be said to represent the mind or will. Others are directors and managers who represent the directing mind and will of the company and control what it does. The state of mind of these managers is the state of mind of the company and is treated by the law as such.[77]

It has become clear that in special circumstances, persons lower down the managerial hierarchy might be regarded as the 'directing mind and will' or the persons whose state of mind should be attributed to the company. In *Meridian* v *Securities Commission,*[78] the Privy Council held that a company's chief investment officer and a senior portfolio manager were the persons whose knowledge was to count as the knowledge or state of mind of the company for the purposes of the application of a New Zealand Securities Act. They were not board members, but unless they were held to be the directing mind and will in the context of a duty to notify an acquisition of shares, then the purposes of the Act would be defeated.

The problem of the corporate mind has often become relevant in relation to the company's tortious and criminal liability.

## 2 Corporate liability for torts

A company acts through its servants or agents and, in the context of tortious liability, it is well established that it is vicariously liable for torts committed by its servants or agents acting in the course of their employment, just as any other principal or employer would be vicariously liable. Companies are sued on this basis all the time.[79]

The employee who actually commits the act will also be liable as the primary tortfeasor. So if an employee of a bus company drives a bus negligently and injures someone, in addition to creating vicarious liability for his employer company, he will himself be liable as the individual primary tortfeasor. This aspect of tortious liability has recently been giving rise to problems. Suppose the controlling shareholder and managing director of a company sets in motion all the events which produce a tort committed against a third party. It would seem under the above principles that he would be personally liable. Apart from the obvious situation of his driving the bus, where causation is not in doubt, in many cases his liability will depend on his having done enough to set the events in motion to be able to regard him as the primary tortfeasor. In the past, the test adopted has sometimes been whether he has acted in such a way as to 'make the tort his own'.[80] Of course, in a situation where he is

---

[77] *Ibid.* at p. 172. On this kind of basis, the knowledge of a director can sometimes be imputed to a company so as to make it liable for knowing receipt of trust property; see *Trustor AB* v *Smallbone and others* [2002] BCC 795. Other aspects of this case are discussed above.

[78] [1995] BCC 942.

[79] The argument that a company could not be liable for an *ultra vires* tort has never been generally accepted by the courts (see e.g. *Campbell* v *Paddington Corporation* [1911] 1 KB 869). On *ultra vires* generally, which is now of less importance in company law, see further Chapter 5 below. An interesting use of tort principles to try (in effect) to circumvent the separate entity doctrine of *Salomon*, occurred in *Lubbe* v *Cape (No. 2)* [2000] 4 All ER 268, HL, where, in circumstances where injury had been negligently caused by a subsidiary company, it was argued against the holding company that it had exercised de facto control over the subsidiary and therefore owed a duty of care to those injured, in relation to its control of and advice to its subsidiary. The proceedings were eventually settled without this issue having been the subject of judicial decision.

[80] *Fairline Shipping Corp* v *Adamson* [1975] QB 180; *Trevor Ivory Ltd* v *Anderson* [1992] 2 NZLR 517, Cooke P; *Evans* v *Spritebrand* [1985] BCLC 105; *Mancetter Developments Ltd* v *Garmanson Ltd* [1986] 1 All ER 449, (1986) 2 BCC 98,924; *Attorney General of Tuvalu* v *Philatelic Ltd* [1990] BCC 30; *Noel* v *Poland* [2001] 2 BCLC 645.

the major shareholder and managing director, the practical effect of holding him liable as primary tortfeasor will be, in effect, to strip him of the protection generally assumed to be afforded to incorporators by the *Salomon* doctrine.

In *Williams* v *Natural Life Health Foods*,[81] the House of Lords had to grapple with these issues in a situation where the claimant was seeking damages under the *Hedley Byrne* principle for negligent misrepresentation. The company had become insolvent, and so the claimant was seeking to make the major shareholder and managing director liable. The question arose of whether there was the necessary special relationship for the purposes of his liability for negligent misstatement. The House of Lords took the view that the manager would not be liable unless it could be shown that there was an assumption of responsibility by him, sufficient to create the necessary special relationship, and here there was no such assumption, particularly since he had chosen to conduct his business through the medium of a limited liability company.[82] On the other hand, in *Chandler* v *Cape plc*,[83] Lady Justice Arden held that a parent company, Cape plc, owed a duty of care to the claimant, an employee of its wholly-owned subsidiary company Cape Building Products Limited ('Cape Products'), where the claimant had been exposed to asbestos and subsequently suffered asbestosis. In so finding, Lady Justice Arden agreed with the approach of the High Court in applying the tripartite test of foreseeability, proximity and whether it was fair, just and reasonable for a duty to exist as laid down in *Caparo Industries plc* v *Dickman*[84] and found that Cape plc had assumed responsibility for the safety of the employees of its subsidiary.[85] In coming to this decision, the Court of Appeal set out four circumstances where the law may impose liability on a parent company for the health and safety of its subsidiary's employees. Those circumstances include:

> a situation where, as in the present case, (1) the business of the parent and subsidiary are in a relevant respect the same; (2) the parent has, or ought to have, superior knowledge on some relevant aspect of health and safety in the industry; (3) the subsidiary's system of work is unsafe as the parent company knew, or ought to have known; and (4) the parent knew or ought to have foreseen that the subsidiary or its employees would rely on it using that superior knowledge for the employees' protection.[86]

The judge found that Cape had actual knowledge of the claimant's working conditions and the risk of an asbestos-related disease from exposure to asbestos dust was obvious. While Cape employed a scientific officer and a medical officer who were responsible for health and safety issues, it nevertheless retained responsibility for ensuring that its employees and those of its subsidiaries were not exposed to harm. The claimant had therefore established a sufficient degree of proximity between Cape and himself in accordance with the *Caparo* test.

---

[81] [1998] 1 BCLC 689. See J.H. Farrar 'The Personal Liability of Directors for Corporate Acts' [1997] Bond L R 102; J. Lowry and R. Edmunds 'Holding the Tension between *Salomon* and the Personal Liability of Directors' [1998] Can Bar Rev 467; N. Campbell and J. Armour 'Demystifying the Civil Liability of Corporate Agents' [2003] CLJ 290.

[82] The further argument that the managing director and the company could be joint tortfeasors was disposed of on the policy grounds that it would 'expose directors, officers and employees . . . to a plethora of new tort claims' ([1998] 1 BCLC 689 at p. 698).

[83] [2012] EWCA Civ 525.

[84] [1990] 2 AC 605.

[85] [2012] EWCA Civ 525, [62]–[68] and [80].

[86] [2012] EWCA Civ 525, [80].

In finding Cape plc liable, Lady Justice Arden was clear that liability did not arise merely due to Cape's position as the parent company of Cape Products and nor did the facts justify piercing the corporate veil.[87] On the contrary, by finding liability in this way, the court was reinforcing the sanctity of *Salomon* and the existence of two legal personalities. Rather, liability was founded upon the fact that the conduct giving rise to the breach of duty was under the direct control of Cape.[88] The significance of this decision is that the court was prepared to abrogate the harshness of *Adams* v *Cape Industries* so as to favour the claimant-employee, and as such it may be a turning point as far as involuntary creditors are concerned (although as we shall see recent cases have demonstrated that a duty of care will not necessarily be easily imposed on a parent company).

The application of *Chandler* v *Cape* was considered by the court in *HRH Emere Godwin Bebe Okpabi & Ors* v *Royal Dutch Shell plc & Anor*.[89] Here, Fraser J held that a two-stage approach should be taken when applying the four indicators of potential liability set out by Arden LJ. First, the court should consider whether the parent company (due to superior knowledge or expertise) was better placed to protect the employees of the subsidiary and, secondly, as a result of so being, is it fair to infer that the subsidiary will rely upon the parent deploying that superior knowledge?[90] In applying this approach, and reiterating the fact that liability does not attach merely as a result of a company being the ultimate holding company of a group,[91] Fraser J held that in this instance the parent company had not assumed a duty of care. There was insufficient proximity between the companies and nor was it fair, just and reasonable to impose such a duty. Moreover, on the facts, the parent company (RDS) was not better placed than its subsidiary to protect against the harm complained of. Here, RDS was based in the UK and the harm complained of concerned the damage caused by oil operations in Nigeria, an activity that the parent (unlike it subsidiary) had no experience of.[92]

Different issues arose in *Standard Chartered Bank* v *Pakistan National Shipping Corporation (No. 2)*,[93] where the managing director had made a fraudulent misrepresentation. He was held liable in the tort of deceit for which it was not necessary to establish a duty of care. All the elements of the tort were proved against him. It was irrelevant that he made the representation on behalf of the company or that it was relied on as such. Lord Hoffmann stressed that the director was liable not because he was a director but because

---

[87] *Ibid*, [69].

[88] At first instance, the judge was able to call in aid the dicta of Lord Goff in *Smith* v *Littlewoods Organisation Ltd* [1987] AC 241. Wyn Williams J noted, at [71], that: 'It is true that generally the law imposes no duty upon a party to prevent a third party from causing damage to another. That emerges clearly from *Smith* v *Littlewoods Organisation Ltd* . . . However, that same case makes it clear that there are exceptions to the general rule. In his speech Lord Goff identified the circumstances in which a duty might arise. They were a) where there was a special relationship between the Defendant and Claimant based on an assumption of responsibility by the Defendant; b) where there is a special relationship between the Defendant and the third party based on control by the Defendant; c) where the Defendant is responsible for a state of danger which may be exploited by a third party; and d) where the Defendant is responsible for property which may be used by a third party to cause damage . . .'

[89] 2017 EWHC 89.

[90] *Ibid*. [79].

[91] *Ibid*. [92].

[92] *Ibid*. [117].

[93] [2003] 1 BCLC 244, HL. See also *Koninklijke Philips Electronics NV* v *Princo Digital Disc GmbH* [2004] 2 BCLC 50.

he committed a fraud, '[n]o one can escape liability for fraud by saying "I wish to make it clear that I am committing this fraud on behalf of someone else and I am not to be personally liable."'[94] In a similar vein, Lord Rodger noted, 'the maxim *culpa tenet suos auctores* may not be the end, but it is the beginning of wisdom in these matters. Where someone commits a tortious act, he at least will be liable for the consequences; whether others are liable also [for example, the company] depends on the circumstances.'[95]

## 3 *Corporate liability for crimes*

Until 1944, companies had no general common law liability for crimes,[96] although the principle of vicarious liability had been used to make companies liable for certain 'strict liability' offences, where *mens rea* was not a required element of the offence. In *DPP* v *Kent and Sussex Contractors Ltd,*[97] it was decided that the state of mind of the officers of the company could be imputed to it for the purpose of establishing 'intent' to deceive. Companies can therefore now have direct criminal liability imposed on them[98] by the use of this technique of 'identifying' senior individuals whose state of mind can be regarded as that of the company for the purposes of establishing *mens rea*.

Corporate liability for manslaughter highlighted some of the limitations of this approach. It was established in *R* v *P & O European Ferries (Dover) Ltd*[99] that a company could be indicted for manslaughter but that it was necessary to be able to identify one individual who had the necessary degree of *mens rea* for manslaughter, and so the prosecution against the company failed.[100] Subsequently, the Law Commission made recommendations for the introduction of a new offence of corporate killing where the conduct of the company falls below what could reasonably be expected, and death will be regarded as having been caused by the conduct of the company if it is caused by a failure in the way the company's activities are managed and organised.[101] The Law Commission's proposals were broadly implemented by the Corporate Manslaughter and Corporate Homicide Act

---

[94] *Ibid*. at 252.
[95] *Ibid*. at 257. See, *MCA Records Inc.* v *Charly Records Ltd* (No. 5) [2003] 1 BCLC 93, CA, where the company had infringed the copyright vested in the claimants over certain recordings. Chadwick LJ, delivering the judgment of the Court of Appeal, sought to explain the circumstances in which liability as a joint tortfeasor may arise: 'if all that a director is doing is carrying out the duties entrusted to him as such by the company under its constitution, the circumstances in which it would be right to hold him liable as a joint tortfeasor with the company would be rare indeed . . . [however] there is no reason why a person who happens to be a director or controlling shareholder of a company should not be liable with the company as a joint tortfeasor if he is not exercising control through the constitutional organs of the company and the circumstances are such that he would be so liable if he were not a director or controlling shareholder.' He stressed that such liability arises from his participation or involvement in the wrongdoing in ways which go beyond the exercise of constitutional control.
[96] Subject to certain exceptions.
[97] [1944] KB 146.
[98] Obviously there is a wide range of crimes that it is impossible for the company to commit.
[99] (1990) 93 Cr App R 72.
[100] A successful prosecution for corporate manslaughter was subsequently brought against a company where the managing director himself had been convicted of manslaughter; see *R* v *OLL Ltd* (1994) unreported but noted by G. Slapper in 144 NLJ 1735.
[101] Law Com. Report No. 237 *Legislating the Criminal Code: Involuntary Manslaughter* (1996). The area was subject to further consultation; see Home Office Consultation Paper (23 May 2000) *Reforming the Law on Involuntary Manslaughter: The Government's Proposals* and a draft Bill was published in the White Paper, *Corporate Manslaughter: The Government's Draft Bill for Reform* (Cm 6498, 2005). See G.R. Sullivan 'The Attribution of Culpability to Limited Companies' [1996] CLJ 515.

2007, which came into force on 6 April 2008. The Act creates a dedicated offence of corporate manslaughter and a company convicted of the offence will face an unlimited fine.[102]

## 2.2 Limited liability

### A The meaning of limited liability

Eleven years after the passing of the Joint Stock Companies Act 1844, which for the first time permitted the creation of companies by registration, limited liability became generally[103] available in the Limited Liability Act 1855. By 1855 it was felt by the legislature that limited liability was a necessary addition to the facility of incorporation by registration.[104] The contemporary reports of the debate during the passage of the Limited Liability Bill illustrate the polarisation of views on the issue. The *Law Times* was moved to describe the Bill as a 'Rogues' Charter'.[105] On the other hand, those who defended its introduction gave it vigorous support. *The Economist* of 18 December 1926 pleaded that:

> [t]he economic historian of the future may assign to the nameless inventor of the principle of limited liability, as applied to trading corporations, a place of honour with Watt and Stephenson, and other pioneers of the Industrial Revolution. The genius of these men produced the means by which man's command of natural resources was multiplied many times over; the limited liability company the means by which huge aggregations of capital required to give effect to their discoveries were collected, organised and efficiently administered.[106]

Outside company law, 'limited liability' is not a term with any very precise meaning and is commonly used to describe the situation where a person has done an act which under the generally prevailing rules of the legal system would incur a liability to pay money but is excused, wholly or partly, from incurring that liability. Within company law, the notion of limited liability is very technical and often misunderstood. Sometimes wrongly referred to as 'corporate' limited liability,[107] it is the principle or principles as a result of which the members of an insolvent company do not have to contribute their own

---

[102] In the first prosecution brought under the 2007 Act, the defendant company was convicted of manslaughter following the death of D, an employee, who had, in the course of his employment, entered a pit that was entirely unsupported and which collapsed on him. The company was fined £385,000, to be paid over ten years, notwithstanding the fact that the fine resulted in the company going into liquidation: see R v *Cotswold Geotechnical Holdings Ltd* 2011 WL 2649504; leave to appeal to the Court of Appeal was refused: see [2011] EWCA Crim 1337.

[103] Prior to this, limited liability could be secured on an ad hoc basis by the creation of a company by statute or by the grant of a charter of incorporation. However, obtaining legislative incorporation was difficult and charters granted sparingly.

[104] About half a century of public debate and argument had preceded it.

[105] See (1854) 24 LT 142; (1855) 25 LT 116 and 210; (1856) 26 LT 230; and (1858) 31 LT 14.

[106] Cited by Hunt, *The Development of the Business Corporation in England 1800–1867* (1936) at 116. Similarly, at an address in 1911, the President of Columbia University was moved to say that: 'I weigh my words when I say that in my judgment the limited liability corporation is the greatest single discovery of modern times . . . Even steam and electricity are far less important than the limited liability corporation, and they would be reduced to comparative impotence without it' Nicholas Murray Butler, President, Columbia University; W. Fletcher, 1 *Cyclopedia of The Law of Private Corporations* §21 (1917). See further, Meiners, Mofsky and Tollison, 'Piercing the Veil of Limited Liability' [1979] Del J of Corp L 351.

[107] The liability of the company for its various debts is unlimited; in an insolvent liquidation, where the debts over-top the assets available, all of the assets will be used up in satisfying the claims of creditors and not all creditors will be paid in full. There is no point at which, prior to exhaustion of its assets, the company is relieved of its liability; it is emptied.

money to the assets in the liquidation to meet the debts of the company.[108] Under the Insolvency Act 1986, the members have a liability to contribute to the assets of the company in the event of its assets in the liquidation being insufficient to meet the claims of the creditors.[109] It is this liability which is limited.[110]

## B The continuing debate about the desirability of limited liability

When limited liability was introduced in 1855, the preceding public debate had been about whether it was morally justified and efficient. However, owing to the relatively undeveloped nature of tort law at that time, no consideration was given to how limited liability would impact on someone who was a tort creditor as opposed to a contract creditor.

As regards contract creditors, the essence of the argument in favour of permitting limited liability is along the lines that manufacturing, trade and economic activities generally are good for us because they create the goods and services which we like having around us and which enrich our lives. Thus, a business form which is conducive to economic activity is preferable to one which is not and limited liability is needed because it encourages the channelling of resources into productive businesses. The encouragement is given by enabling the investor who has capital to invest it in the company without having to worry much about the liabilities being incurred by the company. The main argument against this is that limited liability encourages recklessness in business ventures and innocent creditors have to bear the loss.

It is clear that the arguments in favour of limited liability for contract debts have won the day. Limited liability for contract debt is here to stay and there is no great movement for its abolition. On the contrary, it is usually regarded as one of the main pillars of company law and our economic system and in addition to the usual intuitive arguments of lawyers and politicians the copious literature dealing with economic analysis[111] of limited liability is generally in favour of it. The economists lay stress on the idea that the creditor chooses to give credit and when he enters into the agreement he can compensate himself for the risk he runs that his debt will not be paid. Thus a bank will charge a higher interest rate if the loan is unsecured or is otherwise deemed risky, or it can bargain around the limitation of liability by requiring a personal guarantee from the incorporators, or a trade creditor can raise the price of his goods to compensate for the fact that during the course of the year he knows he will probably encounter some bad debts. Seen in this way, the limited liability doctrine does not empower the company to cause harm to the contract creditor; he is a voluntary creditor and is in a position to look after himself.

---

[108] It is often said that their liability for the company's debts is limited, but this is wrong; they are not liable at all for the company's debts.

[109] Insolvency Act 1986, s. 74.

[110] Limited to the amount 'unpaid' on the shares (Insolvency Act 1986, s. 74 (2) (d)), called a 'company limited by shares', or limited to the amount which the members have undertaken to contribute to the assets of the company in the event of its being wound up (s. 74 (3)), called a 'company limited by guarantee'. There is also the possibility of forming a company which does not have any limit on the liability of its members, called 'an unlimited company'. In each case, the names given to the company by the Companies Act 2006 in s. 3 (4) are misleading; the *company* is not limited by shares nor by guarantee, and all these companies are unlimited in the sense just described. The names only make any sense if they are taken to refer to the financial backup that is ultimately available in a liquidation, so that 'company limited by shares' really means 'company where shareholder backup is limited to the amount unpaid on their shares'.

[111] On economic analysis of company law generally, see Chapter 3 below.

It is highly arguable that it is different with a tort creditor because tort creditors are involuntary creditors. Suppose, for instance, the company's factory emits poisons which afflict the surrounding population. They have not been in a position to bargain with the company. As a result the company may not have bothered to ascertain whether appropriate care had been taken by it, for it knew that any loss arising from failure to take care would be borne by the local people and not by the shareholders. The risk has been shifted away from the company and may well have enabled it to take decisions which are inefficient for society as a whole. Such effects are described by economists as 'third party effects' or 'externalities'. These issues have been the subject of considerable academic debate which has not closed. Professor Pettet's particular views to the effect that an insurance solution is desirable have been expressed elsewhere and the reader wishing to pursue the debate is referred there.[112]

## C Fraudulent trading and wrongful trading

Within the field of company law, there have been two major attempts to curb situations in which it is arguable that limited liability[113] is being abused. These are fraudulent trading and wrongful trading.

The fraudulent trading provisions were first introduced in 1929.[114] Under the present form of the provisions, the court has power to declare that persons who have carried on a company with intent to defraud creditors are liable to make contributions to the company's assets. There is also the possibility of criminal liability which can attract up to ten years' imprisonment.[115] The provisions have not been much used; the main problem being that because criminal liability was in issue the courts developed a test for intent which was in practice difficult to satisfy. In *Re Patrick & Lyon Ltd*,[116] it was held that what was necessary was 'actual dishonesty, involving, according to current notions of fair trading among commercial men, real moral blame'. However, despite their shortcomings the provisions are by no means a dead letter and are still used in cases where the necessary intent can be established. For example, in *Re Todd Ltd*,[117] the director was liable for debts of the company amounting to £70,401. Moreover, in clear cases of fraud the criminal offence of fraudulent trading is frequently used.

---

[112] B. Pettet 'Limited Liability – A Principle for the 21st Century?' (1995) 48 *Current Legal Problems* (Part 2) 125 at pp. 152–159.

[113] Technically it is arguable that they merely impose penalties on managers and do not seek to remove limited liability from shareholders. However, the reality is that most of the situations in which they are used concern small private companies where the managers are the major shareholders, and thus the effect is to create a kind of removal of limited liability.

[114] Amended since, the provisions are now contained in s. 213 of the Insolvency Act 1986 and s. 993 of the Companies Act 2006. Section 213 provides: '(1) If in the course of the winding up of a company it appears that any business of the company has been carried on with intent to defraud creditors of the company or creditors of any other person, or for any fraudulent purpose, the following has effect. (2) The court, on the application of the liquidator may declare that any persons who were knowingly parties to the carrying on of the business in the manner above-mentioned are to be liable to make such contributions (if any) to the company's assets as the court thinks proper.' Criminal liability is added by s. 993 of the 2006 Act, which applies whether or not the company has been, or is in the course of being wound up. Since 1986 the court has had the additional power to defer debts owed by the company to persons who have carried on fraudulent trading: Insolvency Act 1986, s. 215 (4).

[115] See Companies Act 2006, s. 993 (3).

[116] [1933] Ch 786, 790.

[117] [1990] BCLC 454.

Wrongful trading liability was conceived as an attempt to discourage and penalise abuses of limited liability which stemmed from negligent rather than fraudulent conduct.[118] If the requisite conditions set out in s. 214 of the Insolvency Act 1986 are satisfied, the court may declare that the director is liable to make such contribution to the company's assets as the court thinks proper. Liability will arise where the company has gone into insolvent liquidation and at some time before commencement of the winding up, the director: '. . . knew or ought to have concluded that there was no reasonable prospect that the company would avoid going into insolvent liquidation . . .'[119] The provision is not designed to remove limited liability altogether the instant that a company becomes insolvent. It is perfectly possible for some companies to trade out of a position of insolvency and so avoid going into insolvent liquidation. Many directors of insolvent companies doubtless carry on with this hope in mind. What the statute is saying is that there may however come a 'moment of truth' when the reasonable[120] director should realise that the company cannot recover. If he carries on[121] trading thereafter, he does so with the risk that in the subsequent insolvent liquidation the court will order him to make a contribution and the case law shows that he is likely to have to shoulder any worsening in the company's position after the moment of truth.[122]

The first reported case on the new provisions was a strong one in the sense that it involved no deliberate course of wrongdoing but had severe consequences for the directors involved. This was *Re Produce Marketing Consortium Ltd (No. 2)*[123] in 1989, where the company was operating a fruit importing business. From a relatively healthy position of solvency in 1980, it gradually drifted into a position of insolvency with losses amounting to £317,694 in 1987. The business was mainly run by the two directors who worked full time in the company and at no time did they stand to get much out of it; their remuneration for the last three years being around £20,000 per annum.[124] For various reasons it was held that they should have put the company into creditors' voluntary liquidation earlier than they did and were jointly ordered to pay the liquidator £75,000.[125] Subsequent cases have shown that the directors will not always lose. In *Re Sherborne Ltd*,[126] the company was formed with a paid-up capital of £36,000. The first year trading loss was of £78,904 and then the directors injected more of their own funds into it so that the capital was increased

---

[118] Sir Kenneth Cork *Report of the Review Committee on Insolvency Law and Practice* (the Cork Report) (London: HMSO, Cmnd 8558, 1982) Chapter 44 had recommended the creation of civil liability without need for proof of dishonesty. This led to the introduction in 1985 of liability for what has generally become known as 'wrongful trading'; the provisions are now in the Insolvency Act 1986, s. 214.

[119] Insolvency Act 1986, s. 214 (2) (b).

[120] *Ibid*. s. 214 (4).

[121] The Insolvency Act 1986 also gives a defence if the director can show that, after he should have realised that there was no reasonable prospect that the company would avoid going into insolvent liquidation, he took every step that he ought with a view to minimising the potential loss to the company's creditors: s. 214 (3). In practice this will often mean that he must speedily take steps to put the company into creditors' voluntary liquidation.

[122] See *Re Produce Marketing Consortium Ltd (No. 2)* (1989) 5 BCC 569 at p. 597, per Knox J. 'Prima facie the appropriate amount that a director is declared to be liable to contribute is the amount by which the company's assets can be discerned to have been depleted by the director's conduct which caused the discretion under s. 214 (1) to arise.'

[123] (1989) 5 BCC 569.

[124] *Ibid*. at p. 589.

[125] For an example of liability and where the defences failed, see *Re Brian D Pierson (Contractors) Ltd* [1999] BCC 26.

[126] [1995] BCC 40.

to £68,000. The final deficiency was £109,237. The directors were not regarded as having acted unreasonably in all the circumstances and escaped liability. Judge Jack QC counselled against '. . . [T]he danger of assuming that what has in fact happened was always bound to happen and was apparent.'[127]

Later cases have contained extremely important developments for groups of companies. In *Re Hydrodam Ltd,*[128] the question arose as to whether a holding company could be liable for wrongful trading in respect of its subsidiary company.[129] The legislation is clear in principle that in appropriate circumstances this could happen, since by virtue of s. 214 (7), director is defined so as to include 'shadow director'. The Insolvency Act definition of shadow director is 'a person in accordance with whose directions or instructions the directors of the company are accustomed to act'.[130] Thus the question arises as to what level of interference by the holding company, or by its individual directors, could make it (and/or those individual directors)[131] liable as shadow directors. In *Hydrodam,* a decision had been taken to dispose of a company's business and the question for consideration was whether the holding company (or its directors) had been sufficiently implicated so as to make them into shadow directors. Millett J said:

> It is a commonplace that the disposal of a subsidiary or a subsidiary's business by its directors would require the sanction or approval of the parent, acting in this instance as the shareholder. Provided that the decision is made by the directors of the subsidiary, exercising their own independent discretion and judgment whether or not to dispose of the assets in question, and that the parent company only approves or authorises the decision, then in my judgment there is nothing which exposes the parent to liability for the decision or which constitutes it a shadow director of the subsidiary.[132]

A later case gave further guidance on the problem: in *Re PFTZM Ltd,*[133] the holding company had lent money to the subsidiary and the holding company directors were in the habit of attending weekly management meetings. On the point whether the holding company might be liable as shadow director, Judge Paul Baker said:

> [The definition of shadow director] is directed to the case where nominees are put up but in fact behind them strings are being pulled by some other persons who do not put themselves forward as appointed directors. In this case, the involvement of the [holding company directors] here was thrust upon them by the insolvency of the [subsidiary] company. They were not accustomed to give directions. The actions they took, as I see it, were simply directed to trying to rescue what they could out of the company using their undoubted rights as secured creditors. It was submitted to me that it was a prima facie case of shadow directors, but I am bound to say that this is far from obvious . . . The central point, as I see it, is that they were not acting as directors of the company;

---

[127] *Ibid.* at p. 54.
[128] [1994] 2 BCLC 180. See further generally the analysis by G. Morse 'Shadow and de facto Directors in the Context of Proceedings for Disqualification on the Grounds of Unfitness and Wrongful Trading' in B. Rider (ed.) *The Corporate Dimension* (Bristol: Jordans, 1998) p. 115.
[129] Actually a sub-sub-subsidiary on the facts of the case.
[130] Insolvency Act 1986, s. 251.
[131] Liability of the individual directors is very unlikely because in most situations they will be acting on behalf of the holding company rather than on their own behalf, and the pressure on the subsidiary to abide by their suggestions will come about as a result of the fact that the holding company holds a controlling interest in the subsidiary rather than by virtue of any special charisma of the individual holding company directors.
[132] [1994] 2 BCLC 180 at p. 185.
[133] [1995] BCC 280.

they were acting in defence of their own interests. This is not a case where the directors of the company . . . were accustomed to act in accordance with the directions of others i.e. the [holding company directors] here. It is a case where the creditor made terms for the continuation of credit in the light of threatened default. The directors of the company were quite free to take the offer or leave it.[134]

Although these two cases turn on their own facts, it is perhaps clear from the tenor of the judgments that a considerable level of involvement by holding company directors in the affairs of the subsidiary is likely to be required before a holding company will be held to be a shadow director.[135] Nevertheless, in structuring and operating the control relationships between companies in a group, incorporators need to have regard to the shadow director problem if they are to preserve the limited liability doctrine within the group.

Other interesting effects may arise from s. 214 of the Insolvency Act 1986. English company law has no doctrine of adequacy of capital[136] under which the company, when first incorporated, must have capital sufficient to enable it to be likely to meet its business obligations, otherwise the law will not accord to it the advantages of incorporation, in particular limited liability. However, in *Re Purpoint Ltd,*[137] Vinelott J expressed the view that arguably the company being dealt with in the case was, at the outset, so undercapitalised in relation to its business undertakings that it might have been insolvent from the moment of commencement of business.[138] If so, the implication was that wrongful trading liability would have been present throughout the life of the company and, presumably, would have covered the whole of the shortfall between assets and debts. It remains to be seen whether a doctrine of adequacy of capital will grow from these ideas.

There are different views about the extent to which s. 214 has been a success. It is clear that, in many cases, liquidators will not want to risk incurring the costs of bringing the proceedings against the directors, since the prospect of a successful outcome is uncertain[139] and all that happens is that the assets which might otherwise have been available for the creditors in the liquidation are wasted on legal proceedings. Thus, wrongful trading proceedings are a rarity compared, say, to proceedings for the disqualification of directors.[140]

On the other hand, the infrequency of proceedings is probably not an accurate pointer to the effectiveness of the provisions. In many situations the wrongful trading provisions are

---

[134]*Ibid.* at pp. 291–292. See further, *Ultraframe (UK) Ltd* v *Fielding* [2005] EWHC 1638, Lewison J.

[135]Although concerned with disqualification proceedings against individuals, some of the more general statements made by the Court of Appeal in *Secretary of State for Trade and Industry* v *Deverell* [2000] BCC 1057 may have some bearing on the liability of holding companies as shadow directors. In particular, the court cautioned against the use of epithets or graphic descriptions such as 'puppet' in place of the actual words of the statute; *per* Morritt LJ at p. 1,068. It was also stressed that the directions or instructions given by the shadow director do not have to extend over all or most of the corporate activities of the company; *ibid.*

[136]Public companies must have a nominal capital at or above the minimum of £50,000 but this is a different concept; see Chapter 1 above.

[137][1991] BCC 121.

[138]'I have felt some doubt whether a reasonably prudent director would have allowed the company to commence trading at all. It had no capital base. Its only assets were purchased by bank borrowing or acquired by hire purchase . . .' [1991] BCC 121 at p. 127. Ultimately, he took the view that this was not the position on the facts: 'However, I do not think it would be right to conclude that . . . [the director] ought to have known that the company was doomed to end in an insolvent winding up from the moment it started to trade'; *ibid.*

[139]Also, in many cases, even if the case against the directors is clear, they may not have any money since they will have given personal guarantees to banks and others and will often be facing personal insolvency.

[140]See Chapter 23 below.

ably operating on the minds of directors, who will have been warned by their legal sers about the dangers they face once the company becomes insolvent and it will have been put to them that they should consider putting the company into creditors' voluntary liquidation.[141] But, as suggested above,[142] directors of small businesses which are sinking will already be facing personal insolvency and in such cases the threat of wrongful trading liability will hardly make matters seem any worse. In any event, the legislation represents an important theoretical limitation on the doctrine of limited liability. However, if limited liability (for contract debts) is seen as a morally desirable and efficient doctrine, then the question does of course arise as to whether the wrongful trading provisions are misconceived. Intuitively, the answer which can be given is that in most situations they remove the protection of limited liability at more or less the time when the contract creditors (in particular the trade creditors) cease to be able to influence the extent to which the company is now shifting its losses on to them, for they will usually lack the detailed information about the week to week trading position of the company such as might enable them to protect themselves by refusing further credit. They are, so to speak, 'sitting ducks',[143] and legal provisions designed to discourage and compensate for this must therefore be appropriate.[144]

## 2.3 Groups of companies

Behind the apparent simplicity of the *Salomon* doctrine, with its shareholders separate from the company and its emphasis on business carried on by small private companies, lies the more complex reality that most large businesses are carried on through the medium of groups of companies. A listed public company will often have hundreds of private company subsidiaries. The reasons for this are many and various. Often there are taxation advantages. In other situations, the holding company is deliberately running a risky business through a subsidiary in order to avoid liability for its activities. Sometimes companies are arranged in a pyramid structure which can have the effect of enabling those who own a majority of shares of the holding company to control a large amount of capital.[145]

English company law is remarkably unreactive to the phenomenon of corporate groups[146] and almost invariably proceeds to apply the *Salomon* entity concept separately

---

[141] On which, see Chapter 22 below.

[142] See section 2.2 B.

[143] Put in the language of economic analysis, one might say that the wrongful trading provisions remove the protection of limited liability at more or less the precise moment when the business starts to make a negative social input and survives only by externalising its losses on to the creditors.

[144] The same justifications would broadly apply to liability for fraudulent trading.

[145] For a further explanation of pyramiding, see Chapter 3, 3.3. For an interesting analysis of group structures and policy implications, see T. Hadden 'Regulation of Corporate Groups: An International Perspective' in J. McCahery, S. Picciotto and C. Scott (eds) *Corporate Control and Accountability: Changing Structures and the Dynamics of Regulation* (Oxford: Clarendon Press, 1993) p. 343 and D. Milman 'Groups of Companies: The Path Towards Discrete Regulation' in Milman (ed.) *Regulating Enterprise: Law and Business Organisations in the UK* (Oxford: Hart Publishing, 1999) p. 219. Where the group operates on a transnational basis the economic power that it exercises will often raise issues for the development of economic policy in the states in which it operates: see generally T. Muchlinski *Multinational Enterprises and the Law* (Oxford: Blackwell, 1995). Some restriction is placed on the arrangement of group structures by the Companies Act 2006, s. 136 (1), which provides that a company may not hold shares in its holding company.

[146] The policy issues in developing a group law are complex and the legislature has been largely silent. Recent attempts at imposing parent company liability in tort are very fact specific and do not introduce a general concept of group liability; see *Chandler* v *Cape plc* [2012] EWCA Civ 525.

to each company in the group. As Roskill LJ observed in *The Albazero* (and in doing so alluded to concerns that arise from limited liability in a group context):[147]

> each company in a group of companies (a relatively modern concept) is a separate legal entity possessed of separate legal rights and liabilities so that the rights of one company in a group cannot be exercised by another company in that group even though the ultimate benefit of the exercise of those rights would enure beneficially to the same person or corporate body irrespective of the person or body in whom those rights were vested in law. It is perhaps permissible under modern commercial conditions to regret the existence of these principles. But it is impossible to deny, ignore or disobey them.[148]

Thus, limited liability for corporate debts is the automatic right of the holding company. It was put clearly by Templeman LJ in *Re Southard Ltd*:[149]

> English company law possesses some curious features, which may generate curious results. A parent company may spawn a number of subsidiary companies, all controlled directly or indirectly by the shareholders of the parent company. If one of the subsidiary companies, to change the metaphor, turns out to be the runt of the litter and declines into insolvency to the dismay of its creditors, the parent company and the other subsidiary companies may prosper to the joy of the shareholders without any liability for the debts of the insolvent subsidiary.[150]

Similarly, the holding company has a right to deliberately set about creating structures which minimise its own liability. In *Adams* v *Cape Industries plc*,[151] this right was expressly recognised by Slade LJ in this way:

> . . . [W]e do not accept as a matter of law that the court is entitled to lift the corporate veil as against a defendant company which is a member of a corporate group merely because the corporate structure has been used to ensure that the legal liability (if any) in respect of future activities of the group . . . will fall on another member of the group rather than the defendant company. Whether or not this is desirable, the right to use a corporate structure in this manner is inherent in our corporate law. [Counsel] urged on us that the purpose of the operation was in substance that [Cape Industries plc] would have the practical benefit of the group's asbestos trade in the US, without the risks of tortious liability. This may be so. However, in our judgment [Cape Industries plc] was entitled to organise the group's affairs in that manner and . . . to expect that the court would apply the principle of *Salomon* v *Salomon* in the ordinary way.[152]

Other areas of company law proceed in a similar way, and thus directors of a company owe their duties to the individual company which they happen to be directors of, rather than to the group as a whole.[153] Occasionally, company law does bend to the group reality. The main example of this is in relation to the rules on financial reporting; group accounts are required showing the position for the group as a whole in a consolidated balance sheet and profit and loss account.[154] Not all countries have been content to follow the English

---

[147] [1977] AC 774.
[148] *Ibid*. at [807].
[149] [1979] 3 All ER 556.
[150] *Ibid*. at p. 565.
[151] [1990] BCC 786.
[152] *Ibid*. at p. 826.
[153] *Pergamon Press* v *Maxwell* [1970] 1 WLR 1167; *Charterbridge Corp* v *Lloyds Bank* [1970] Ch 62; *Lonhro* v *Shell Petroleum* [1981] 2 All ER 456.
[154] See Chapter 10 below.

approach. Germany, for example, has had special rules governing groups of companies since 1965, the 'Konzernrecht', in which the parent company will be liable to make good the losses of the subsidiary in certain circumstances.[155] Within the EU, it is possible that member states may eventually find that they have to review this question if the draft Ninth Directive is ever adopted, although this seems highly unlikely at present.[156]

The Companies Act 2006 contains definitions of the various terms used to describe companies in groups. These are technical and somewhat at odds with the way in which the terms are used in common parlance. The main general distinction in the Act is between 'holding company' and 'subsidiary'. This is confusing, since people will generally talk about 'parent' and subsidiary whereas the term 'parent company' is very technical[157] and confined to the areas of legislation which deal with the duty to prepare group accounts and matters incidental thereto.[158]

The general definition is contained in s. 1159 (1):

A company is a 'subsidiary' of another company, its 'holding company', if that other company –

(a) holds a majority of the voting rights in it, or
(b) is a member of it and has the right to appoint or remove a majority of its board of directors, or
(c) is a member of it and controls alone, pursuant to an agreement with other shareholders or members, a majority of the voting rights in it, or if it is a subsidiary of a company which is itself a subsidiary of that other company.

Various expressions in s. 1159 are supplemented and explained by lengthy provisions in s. 1159 (3), incorporating Sch. 6 to the Act.[159] No doubt people will continue to use the expressions 'holding company' and 'parent company' as if they were completely interchangeable and most of the time this will probably not give rise to misunderstandings.

## 2.4 Incorporation

### A Formal requirements

Forming a company by registration is relatively simple[160] and costs very little. All that is necessary is for certain documents to be delivered to the Registrar of Companies along with the registration fee. Often the layperson will choose to purchase from his solicitors, or accountant or other commercial supplier, a company which has already been formed (an 'off-the-shelf' company) and then change its name and constitution to suit him or herself. However, the ease of formation can create the wrong impression, for as will gradually become clear throughout this text, and not least in the last chapter,[161] the use of the legal

---

[155] See J. Peter 'Parent Liability in German and British Law: Too Far Apart for EU Legislation' [1999] *European Business Law Review* 440.
[156] See Chapter 1, 1.6 above.
[157] In essence, as one would expect, it is similar to the definition of holding company, but it is wider since it is being used in legislation designed to curb off-balance-sheet financing; see Companies Act 2006, ss. 1161–1162 and Sch. 7.
[158] Namely, Part 15 of the 2006 Act.
[159] The expression 'wholly-owned subsidiary' is defined in the Companies Act 2006, s. 1159 (2) as follows: 'A company is a "wholly-owned subsidiary" of another company if it has no members except that other and that other's wholly-owned subsidiaries or persons acting on behalf of that other or its wholly-owned subsidiaries.'
[160] Compared, say, to trying to get incorporation by Royal Charter or private Act of Parliament.
[161] On disqualification of directors.

facilities provided by the corporate form brings with it many obligations, liabilities and pitfalls.

While the Companies Act 2006 makes little substantive change to the pre-existing regime governing company formations the relevant provisions are drafted in less technical language in line with the over-arching objective of making the statute accessible. Sections 7–13 lay down the requirements for registering a company. There are a number of documents which may need to be delivered to the Registrar of Companies prior to registration, depending on the type of company being formed and the circumstances. First, it should be noted that the memorandum of association no longer has the significance it had under the Companies Act 1985. Under the previous law it was a key constitutional document; it now has merely a residual role.[162] Section 8 (1) defines the memorandum of association as a memorandum stating that the subscribers wish to form a company under the Act and agree to become members of the company and, in the case of a company that is to have a share capital, to take at least one share each. Section 9 (1) then goes on to add that together with the memorandum, an application for registration of the company must be delivered to the Registrar of Companies with the documents required by the section together with a statement of compliance.

The application for registration must state: (a) the company's proposed name; (b) whether its registered office is to be situated in England and Wales (or in Wales), in Scotland or in Northern Ireland; (c) whether the liability of the members is to be limited, and if so whether it is to be limited by shares or by guarantee and (d) whether the company is to be a private or a public company. For a company with a share capital, s. 9 (4) goes on to provide that the application must also contain a statement of capital and initial shareholdings. Under the pre-existing law, it was a requirement that the memorandum of association would state the amount of the company's 'authorised' share capital. However, the Companies Act 2006 abolished the requirement of authorised share capital and by s. 10 (2) the statement must declare, amongst other things, the total number of shares of the company to be taken on formation by the subscribers to the memorandum together with the aggregate nominal value of those shares. For each class of share it must state: (i) prescribed particulars of the rights attached to the shares; (ii) the total number of shares of that class; (iii) the aggregate nominal value of shares of that class; and (iv) the amount to be paid up and the amount (if any) to be unpaid on each share (whether on account of the nominal value of the shares or by way of premium). It must also contain information to be prescribed for the purpose of identifying the subscribers to the memorandum and must also disclose, by reference to the above, information with respect to each subscriber.[163]

The application must contain a statement of the company's proposed officers,[164] which by s. 12 (1) will give particulars of the first director or directors of the company and, in the case of a public company and a private company that opts to have a secretary, or the first secretary or joint secretaries of the company.[165] Section 13 requires a statement of

---

[162] See below, and Chapter 4.
[163] See ss. 10 (3) and (4).
[164] Section 9 (4) (c).
[165] See also, ss. 162–166 and ss. 277–279 of the Companies Act 2006. Because of abuses of such publicly available information, ss. 165–166 permits directors to have only a service address, for example the company's registered office, on the public record instead of his or her residential address.

compliance to be delivered to the Registrar to the effect that the registration requirements have been complied with this may be accepted by the Registrar as sufficient evidence of compliance. The provisions relating to company names are contained, in the main, in ss. 53–81 of the Companies Act 2006. The public company name must[166] end with 'public limited company' which can be abbreviated to 'plc' and a private limited company must end its name with the word 'limited' which can be abbreviated to 'Ltd'.[167] Subject to this, and to various statutory prohibitions, a company can have any name. It is clear that a company will not be registered with a name which is the same as a name already appearing in the Registrar's index of company names, so a search of the register is one of the steps to take in the formation of a company.[168] There are certain rules of construction for helping to determine when the names are the same[169] and there are guidance notes issued by DBEIS.[170] There are various other prohibitions[171] such as use of a name which would, in the opinion of the Secretary of State (in effect, DBEIS), constitute a criminal offence,[172] or be offensive; nor is it possible[173] to use names which would be likely to give a misleading indication of the nature of the company's activities, for example that the business is connected with the government.[174] Section 69 is a new provision introduced to implement the recommendations of the Company Law Review.[175] It provides that a person (the applicant) may object to the 'company names adjudicator'[176] if a company's name is (a) similar to a name in which the applicant has goodwill or (b) it is sufficiently similar to such a name that its use in the UK would be likely to mislead by suggesting a connection between the company and the applicant. If one of these grounds is established the company, as primary respondent, must show that the name was adopted on legitimate grounds,[177] otherwise the objection will be upheld.

It is relatively easy for a company to change its name. All that is needed is a special resolution[178] and compliance with the above provisions. The Companies Act 2006 introduces two additional procedures for effecting a change of name. First, by the means provided for in the company's articles of association.[179] Or, secondly, by order of the company names adjudicator.[180] Sections 82–85 provide for trading disclosures. The Secretary of

---

[166] Companies Act 2006, s. 58 (1).

[167] Section 59 (1). Welsh equivalents are permitted; see ss. 58 (2) and 59 (2).

[168] *Ibid.* s. 66.

[169] *Ibid.* s. 66 (2) and (3).

[170] Using a name or similar name is unwise, in any event, since it could make the company liable at common law for the tort of passing off (see e.g. *Erven Warnink BV* v *Townend (J) & Sons (Hull) Ltd (No. 1)* [1979] AC 731, HL), or it may infringe a registered trade mark; see Trade Marks Act 1994.

[171] See the Companies Act 2006, s. 76.

[172] Section 53.

[173] Except with the consent of the Secretary of State.

[174] Section 54. Certain companies are, by s. 60, exempt from having to use the word 'limited' as part of their name; the main requirement being that the objects of the companies will be the promotion of commerce, art, science, charity etc.

[175] See *Modern Company Law for a Competitive Economy Final Report* para. 11.50.

[176] See s. 70.

[177] The grounds are listed in s. 69 (4).

[178] Sections 77–78. Broadly, three-quarters of members present and voting, or voting by proxy; see Chapter 7 below.

[179] Section 77. Section 79 (1) requires the company to provide the Registrar with a notice of the name change and a statement that the change has been made by the means provided for in the articles.

[180] Section 77 (2). See s. 69, above.

State has power to make regulations requiring companies to display its name or other prescribed information at specified locations and on documents and communications and to provide specified information on request to those they deal with in the course of business.[181] Failure to comply with the regulations laid down under s. 82 can result in both civil and criminal sanctions.[182]

The articles of association is now the key constitutional document.[183] It sets out the internal rules as to the running of the company and covers such matters as appointment and removal of directors, quorum and frequency of meetings. The Companies Act 2006, s. 19 confers on the Secretary of State the power to prescribe articles. This has long been the case so that companies have typically adopted the model articles contained in Table A of 1985 which automatically applied to a company limited by shares unless, and to the extent that, it is excluded.[184] Under the 2006 Act there are two sets of model articles for companies limited by shares: one for private companies[185] and one for public companies,[186] and s. 20 makes clear that on the formation of a limited company it will be treated as having adopted the relevant model articles except to the extent that they are excluded or modified. It is noteworthy that s. 20 (2) provides that the 'relevant model articles' means the set prescribed for a company, unless excluded, as in force at the date on which the company is registered. Accordingly, the model articles prescribed under s. 19 will not affect companies registered under earlier companies statutes.[187] The constitutional significance of the articles of association is dealt with in Chapter 4 below, and various other aspects are considered throughout the text.[188]

Commencement of business[189] is not permitted in the case of a public company unless the Registrar has issued it with a trading certificate under s. 761 (4) of the 2006 Act. He can only issue the certificate if, on an application made to him in the prescribed form,[190] he is satisfied that the nominal value of the company's allotted share capital is not less than the 'authorised minimum'.[191] The 'authorised minimum' is a minimum capital requirement of £50,000[192] or prescribed euro equivalent (which has been fixed by regulations at €65,000) for public companies as originally set by the Second Directive[193] (as was the case under the pre-existing law, no minimum capital is prescribed for private companies).

---

[181] Section 82 (1).

[182] Sections 83–84.

[183] Section 17. Under the pre-existing law the memorandum was also a key constitutional document but, as noted above, its role has been significantly reduced by s. 8. The reasons underlying this decision were explained by the Under Secretary of State during the parliamentary debates on the Companies Bill. He said that the CLR was 'keen to see the company's internal rules as far as possible set out logically in one place and pointed out the potential for overlap under current arrangements between a company's memorandum and its articles. In taking forward those valuable suggestions, we wanted to do away with any scope for confusion between the memorandum and the articles, and introduce a clear distinction between the information in the memorandum, which will be in effect an historical snapshot, which, once provided, has no continuing relevance, and the constitution of the company properly so-called, as contained essentially in its articles . . .': Hansard Vol. 678 No. 96 Col. GC3.

[184] As set out in the Companies (Tables A to F) Regulations 1985 (SI 1985 No. 805).

[185] See the Companies (Model Articles) Regulations 2008.

[186] See the Companies (Model Articles) Regulations 2008.

[187] The relevant provisions of the 2006 Act concerning the constitution of companies came into force on 1 October 2009.

[188] See index.

[189] Or exercise of any borrowing powers.

[190] Section 762.

[191] And a statutory declaration in accordance with s. 762 is also delivered to him.

[192] It can be increased by statutory instrument.

[193] See s. 763 of the Companies Act 2006.

## B Certificate of incorporation

Once the documents have been delivered to the Registrar of Companies and the Registrar is satisfied that the legal formalities have been complied with, then the Registrar registers the documents and issues a certificate of incorporation.[194] From the date of incorporation mentioned in the certificate, the subscribers of the memorandum, together with such other persons as may from time to time become members of the company, 'shall be a body corporate by the name contained in the memorandum . . .'[195] The presence of the word 'shall' in ss. 14 and 15 of the Companies Act 2006 makes it clear that, provided that the Act has been complied with, the Registrar has no discretion as to whether to register the company and if the Registrar refuses, proceedings can be brought by the promoters to compel the Registrar to register.[196]

The certificate of incorporation is 'conclusive evidence' that the requirements of the Act as to registration have been complied with, and that the company is duly registered.[197] The effect of this is generally thought to be to preclude the existence of any doctrine of nullity in UK law (under which a company might be regarded as defectively incorporated with consequent complications for persons who might have acquired rights against it). It was against this problem that articles 11 and 12 were included in the First Directive[198] under which persons who have dealt with the defective company would be protected if it was later annulled in court proceedings. No steps have been taken to implement these provisions of the Directive in the UK.

If a company is incorporated for what turns out to be an unlawful object then it can be wound up.[199] It has been suggested that the Attorney General can initiate proceedings to get the certificate of incorporation cancelled or revoked.[200] If this were to become a frequent occurrence it might raise problems which fall within the ambit of articles 11 and 12 of the First Directive, and then a court might be faced with the argument that even though it had not been implemented in a UK statute, the parties could nevertheless perhaps rely on it under the doctrine of direct effect.

## C Publicity and the continuing role of the Registrar

On receipt of the incorporation documents, the Registrar of Companies will open a file on the company which is then open to inspection.[201] Thereafter, more information will appear on the file from time to time in pursuance of the Companies Act provisions relating to annual returns and accounts.[202] Also, 'Official Notification' is necessary under which the Registrar must publish in the *Gazette* notice of the issue of receipt by him of various documents, one of which is the issue of any certificate of incorporation.[203]

---

[194] Companies Act 2006, ss. 14–15.
[195] *Ibid.* ss. 16 (1) and (2).
[196] *R* v *Registrar of Companies, ex parte Bowen* [1914] 3 KB 1161.
[197] Section 15 (4).
[198] 68/151/EEC.
[199] Under Insolvency Act 1986, s. 122 (1) (g); see also *Princess of Reuss* v *Bos* (1871) LR 5 HL 176.
[200] *R* v *Registrar of Companies, ex parte Central Bank of India* [1986] QB 1114 at pp. 1169 (Lawton LJ) and 1177 (Slade LJ).
[201] Companies Act 2006, s. 1085.
[202] See Chapter 10 below.
[203] Companies Act 1985, s. 1064 (1). Failure to comply with official notification by the Registrar (which is unlikely) might have adverse consequences under s. 1079, for it provides that a company is not entitled to rely against other persons on the happening of certain events (such as the alteration of the articles) if the event had not been officially notified at the material time (and certain other conditions are satisfied). The issue of the certificate of incorporation is not one of the matters referred to in s. 1079 which, in this respect, can therefore produce difficulties.

# D Promoters and pre-incorporation contracts

Those who set up a company will, in addition to all the legal duties that descend on them after incorporation, usually find that they owe a fiduciary duty to the company covering matters relating to the setting up of it. These are known as promoters' duties. The term 'promoter' has accordingly acquired a fairly specific meaning, expressed in the language of Lord Cockburn CJ as '[O]ne who undertakes to form a company with reference to a given project and to set it going, and who takes the necessary steps to accomplish that purpose'.[204] On the other hand, people who act merely in a professional capacity such as solicitors and accountants will not be promoters unless they step outside their professional sphere of activity and become involved in the business side of formation.[205]

Cases on the duties of promoters have been very rare over the last 100 years for two reasons. First, most companies start life as small private companies where the promoters immediately become the shareholders and first directors, and not surprisingly they are not in a hurry to raise legal complaints against the promoters. No one else is involved for many years until the company starts to expand and seeks more shareholders, by which time the possible wrongdoing of the company's founders many years earlier is of little interest to the new shareholders in a thriving and expanding business. Secondly, if a public offering of shares is to have any chance of being fully subscribed for by the public it will need to be underwritten by an investment bank and such institutions will usually find it in their commercial interests to ensure that problems about promoters breaching their legal duties do not arise, and if they do arise, are probably quickly and quietly settled.

The ideas are established by the (mainly) nineteenth-century cases. Promoters are regarded as standing in a fiduciary relationship[206] to the company. It is entirely in their hands, they create it and shape it, and because of this they owe it fiduciary duties. Most of the cases involve the promoters selling some item of their own property to the newly formed company which only later finds out that it was their property, or that the property was worth a good deal less than the price the company paid, or that, whatever the value of the property, the promoters had sold it to the company at a higher price than they had paid. The case law is confused at times and overlapping, but the following two principles seem to be supportable. First, promoters must disclose to the company any interest which they have in the property they are selling to the company, and furthermore the disclosure must be made to a board of directors (or group of shareholders) who are truly independent so that they can decide on the company's behalf, whether the terms of the contract are prudent or not. It the directors are not independent, the disclosure is obviously useless.[207] Failure to make disclosure in this way will entitle the company to rescind the contract once an independent board does discover the true facts, provided both that it is reasonably possible to put the contracting parties back into the position they were in before the contract was entered into and that there has not been sufficient delay to amount to acquiescence. Thus, in *Erlanger* v *New Sombrero Phosphate Co.*,[208] the promoters had sold an island to the company in breach of these principles and

---

[204] *Twycross* v *Grant* (1877) 2 CPD 469 at p. 541.
[205] *Re Great Wheal Polgooth Ltd* (1883) 53 LJ Ch. 42.
[206] On this concept in relation to directors, see Chapter 8 below.
[207] See *Erlanger* v *New Sombrero Phosphate Co.* (1878) 3 App Cas 1218 at pp. 1236, 1239, *per* Lord Cairns LC referring to the need for 'the intelligent judgment of an independent executive'.
[208] (1878) 3 App Cas 1218.

ended up getting it back and having to return the money and shares they had received for it. Secondly, promoters who make a profit by selling to the company for a higher price than they themselves paid will be liable to hand that over (i.e. account to the company) if, at the time when they purchased it, they had already become promoters to the extent that it is possible to regard them as trustees who at the time should have been trying to make a profit for the trust (i.e. the company) rather than themselves.[209]

Pre-incorporation contracts are another feature of incorporation procedure which has occasionally given rise to legal difficulties.[210] If a promoter makes a contract purportedly on behalf of the company but prior to its incorporation, it is well established that, as regards the company, the contract is a nullity, since the company was not in existence at the time when the contract was entered into.[211] However, the promoter who enters into such a void contract may find himself personally liable on it, for s. 51 (1) of the Companies Act 2006 provides:

> A contract which purports to be made by or on behalf of a company at a time when the company has not been formed has effect, subject to any agreement to the contrary, as one made with the person purporting to act for the company or as agent for it, and he is personally liable on the contract accordingly.

The words 'subject to any agreement to the contrary' have been held to mean 'unless otherwise agreed' and it has been held that it is not sufficient in this regard merely for the promoter to sign 'as agent for' the company.[212] In *Braymist Ltd* v *Wise Finance Co Ltd*,[213] a firm of solicitors entered into a contract as agents on behalf of a company which was not yet formed, in which the company agreed to sell some land to some developers. Later the developers changed their minds and the solicitors sought to enforce the contract against them under s. 51 (36C of the Companies Act 1985). The Court of Appeal held that the words of the section did not merely create an option enabling the developers to sue the agent if they so wished, but specified that the contract had 'effect', and thus the contract was enforceable by the agent.

## E Right of establishment

As part of the process of creating the common market with free movement of goods, persons, services and capital, the EC Treaty[214] gives a right of establishment to natural persons to carry out business in any member state.[215] Similarly, a right of establishment is given to companies by the provision that companies shall be treated in the same way as natural persons, provided that they have been formed in accordance with the law of a member state

---

[209] *Re Cape Breton Co.* (1885) 29 Ch D 795 at pp. 801–805 *passim, per* Cotton LJ; *Erlanger* v *New Sombrero Phosphate Co.* (1873) 3 App Cas 1218 at pp. 1234–1235, *per* Lord Cairns LC.

[210] A related problem concerns the question of how promoters go about getting compensated for expenses incurred or remunerated for work done in promoting the company. In most cases this raises no practical difficulty and the method adopted is to put a power into the company's articles enabling the first directors of the newly formed company to pay promoters' expenses and remuneration.

[211] Nor is it possible for the company once formed to ratify a pre-incorporation contract or to purport to adopt it merely by ratification; it is necessary to enter into a new contract: *Natal Land Co.* v *Pauline Syndicate* [1904] AC 120.

[212] *Phonogram* v *Lane* [1982] QB 938 at p. 944, *per* Lord Denning MR.

[213] [2002] BCC 514.

[214] The Treaty of Rome.

[215] EC Treaty, art. 43 (art. 52, pre-Amsterdam).

and that they have their registered office, or central administration or princ
business within the European Community.[216] The principle was tested in the
and the European Court of Justice gave a ruling firmly upholding the doctrine

## Further reading

O. Kahn-Freund 'Some Reflections on Company Law Reform' [1944] *MLR* 54.

B. Pettet 'Limited Liability – A Principle for the 21st Century?' (1995) 48 *Current Legal Problems* (Part 2) 125.

R. Grantham and C. Rickett (eds) *Corporate Personality in the 20th Century* (Oxford: Hart Publishing, 1998).

L. Sealy 'Perception and Policy in Company Law Reform' in D. Feldman and F. Meisel (eds) *Corporate and Commercial Law: Modern Developments* (London: LLP, 1996) 11.

S. Ottolenghi 'From Peeping Behind the Veil, To Ignoring it Completely' (1990) 53 *MLR* 338.

C. Mitchell 'Lifting the Corporate Veil in the English Courts: an Empirical Study' [1999] *CFILR* 15.

J. Lowry and R. Edmunds 'Holding the Tension between *Salomon* and the Personal Liability of Directors' [1998] *Can Bar Rev* 467.

Home Office Consultation Paper (23 May 2000) *Reforming the Law on Involuntary Manslaughter*.

White Paper, *Corporate Manslaughter: The Government's Draft Bill for Reform* (Cm 6498, 2005).

G.R. Sullivan 'The Attribution of Culpability to Limited Companies' [1996] *CLJ* 515.

G. Morse 'Shadow and de facto Directors in the Context of Proceedings for Disqualification on the Grounds of Unfitness and Wrongful Trading' in B. Rider (ed.) *The Corporate Dimension* (Bristol: Jordans, 1998) p. 115.

D. Milman 'Groups of Companies: The Path Towards Discrete Regulation' in Milman (ed.) *Regulating Enterprise: Law and Business Organisations in the UK* (Oxford: Hart Publishing, 1999) p. 219.

---

[216] By EC Treaty, art. 48 (art. 58, pre-Amsterdam).
[217] Case C-212/97 *Centros Ltd* v *Erhvervsog Selskabsstyrelsen* [1999] BCC 983. The doctrine has been emphatically confirmed in several subsequent ECJ cases: see, e.g. Case C-208/00 *Überseering BV* v *Nordic Construction Co Baumanagement GmbH* [2002] ECR I-9919; and Case C-167/01 *Kamer van Koophandel en Fabrieken voor Amsterdam* v *Inspire Art Ltd* [2003] ECR I-10155 (*cf Cartesio Okató Es Szolgáltató bt* Case C-210/06 (2009)). For analysis of the interesting issues raised by *Centros*, see E. Micheler 'The Impact of the Centros Case on Europe's Company Laws' (2000) 21 Co Law 179; J. Lowry 'Eliminating Obstacles to Freedom of Establishment: The Competitive Edge of UK Company Law' (2004) 63 CLJ 331; J. Armour 'Who Should Make Corporate Law? EC Legislation *versus* Regulatory Competition' (2005) 58 *Current Legal Problems* 369.

# 3

# Legal theory and company law

## 3.1 The role of theory in company law

Company law 'theory', is a body of writing that has expanded over the years and normally has two components: a descriptive aspect and a normative aspect. It does not concern itself with the exposition of legal rules themselves. The descriptive aspect of theoretical writing typically involves examining the operation of legal rules and the structures produced by them in an objective and contextual way; it will often involve the writer in spotting an underlying rationale or illogicality contained in the rules. The normative aspect involves the writer in making propositions as to how something should be. This will usually be either that the structures or individual legal rules ought to change, in other words that they are not morally justified, or, that they ought to remain as they are, in other words, that they are morally justified. Recent and contemporary writings use the expression moral 'legitimacy' instead of moral 'justification'. In practice the distinction between descriptive writing and normative writing is rarely clear cut, not least because the way in which a descriptive writer sees and interprets a situation is value laden and subjective, in the sense that he or she is not always aware that their selection of material will influence people's conclusions about the moral legitimacy of the structure being described.

It is the normative aspect which lends dynamism and force to legal theory, because, essentially, we are looking at arguments about the way we should be living; arguments which are of fundamental social and political importance. In the context of company law, legal theory will be trying to tell us what sort of company law we have, and what sort of company law we should have.

This chapter analyses the main issues which have emerged in the last century or so. The focus is primarily on the Anglo-American writing although occasional reference is made to theory emanating from continental Europe. Theoretical issues relating to securities regulation are dealt with in a separate chapter, largely because the subject has developed independently of mainstream company law.[1] The areas covered here overlap, and are interwoven in countless ways. Nevertheless, for the sake of convenience they are grouped under headings as follows: the nature and origins of the corporation, managerialism, corporate governance, stakeholder company law (including social responsibility and industrial democracy), and economic analysis of corporate law.

---

[1] Chapter 16 below.

## 3.2 The nature and origins of the corporation

### A The theories

The industrial revolution in Europe and America coupled with increased legal facilities for incorporation in some of the world's major legal systems[2] fuelled a juristic interest in the phenomenon of the corporation. The nature of the corporation, particularly its corporate personality, became the focus of thought. It is possible to identify two main and distinct theories: the fiction theory and the real entity theory.[3]

The fiction theory[4] asserts that the legal person has no substantial reality, no mind, no will; it exists only in law. The corporation is 'an artificial being, invisible, intangible, and existing only in contemplation of law'.[5] It is a theory which asserts that the corporate body is merely a creature of the intellect.[6] It seems that it can be traced to the canon law of the Roman church of the thirteenth century and earlier.[7] The real entity theory is of later origin and is generally regarded as the work of nineteenth-century German realists, particularly Gierke.[8] Gierke saw corporate personality not merely as a juristic conception, but as a social fact with an actual living nature. It is a living organism, for when individuals associate together, a new personality arises which has a distinctive sphere of existence and will of its own. The function of the law is to recognise and declare the existence of the personality.[9]

The arguments about the nature of the corporation became linked and at times confused with a separate issue, namely the origins of the corporation. Two main theories were developed to explain the origins of the corporation: the concession theory and the contract theory. The essence of the concession theory is that the corporation's legal power is derived from the state. The idea seems to have emerged as a state response to the problem of how to check the power of groups arising within it; the answer being that a corporation could only achieve recognition and acceptability through a validation process emanating from the state, whether a grant by Royal Charter or registration under some state-created system.[10]

The contract theory essentially ran counter to the thrust of the concession theory, and sought to show that companies were associations formed by the agreement of the shareholders.[11] The corporate structure was in substance the outcome of a series of contracts

---

[2] E.g. Joint Stock Companies Act 1844 in the UK, various state incorporation statutes in the USA dating from early in the century such as 1811 in New York.

[3] The latter is sometimes referred to as the 'natural entity' theory or 'organic' theory.

[4] It is sometimes suggested that there is separate theory which sees the company merely as an aggregate of individuals; but this is really the corollary of the fiction theory, for if the company is a legal fiction, that will leave the people involved with it as merely an aggregate of individuals.

[5] *Trustees of Dartmouth College* v *Woodward* (17 US) 4 Wheat 518 at p. 636, *per* Marshall CJ.

[6] See J. Dewey 'The Historic Background of Corporate Legal Personality' 35 Yale LJ 655 (1926) at p. 669.

[7] Dewey, n. 6 above, at pp. 667–668. It is possible that the fiction theory was in the minds of the Roman jurists as Savigny has claimed; see F. Hallis *Corporate Personality: A Study in Jurisprudence* (London: OUP, 1930) p. 6, n. 3.

[8] Das Deutsche Genossenschaftsrecht (1887), translated in O. Gierke *Political Theories of the Middle Age* (F.W. Maitland (ed.), 1900).

[9] See generally the summaries in Hallis, n. 7 above, at p. 150 and E. Freund *The Legal Nature of Corporations* (Chicago, IL: University of Chicago Press, 1897) at p. 13.

[10] See generally Dewey, n. 6 above, at p. 668. It seems that the choice of the word 'concession' was influenced by Roman law; *ibid*.

[11] M. Horwitz in '*Santa Clara* Revisited: The Development of Corporate Theory' 88 W Va L Rev 173 (1985) at p. 203 attributes the theory to a work by V. Morawetz *A Treatise on the Law of Private Corporations* 2nd edn (Boston, MA: Little, Brown, 1886).

between the shareholders and the managers and so was really hardly any different from a partnership. It followed that there was no reason why individuals should need to obtain permission from the legislature in order to form a company. This, while being a theory about the origins of the company, also has implications for the nature of the company. The idea of the company as a contract, or as a nexus of contracts, has undergone a renaissance with the development in the 1970s of the economic theory about the nature of the firm.[12]

## B Rationale and application of the theories

The above ideas have been presented as analytically separate and distinct, but in many of the writings they were linked together in various ways. The way they were linked seems to have varied depending on the social or political agenda possessed by those advancing the theories. The fiction theory about the nature of the corporation was often run alongside the concession theory[13] and so the proposition became that a company was a fictional entity created by the exercise of state power. In this form, the proposition reflected nine-teenth-century political theory based on liberal individualism: state consent was needed for the formation of a group and even then the 'groupness' was fictional, the company was merely an aggregate of individuals. The proposition in this form also provided a justifica-tion for state regulation of companies, for in giving the concession, the state had done something gratuitous or special, in return for which it could expect that its right to regulate companies had been acknowledged. By contrast, the real entity theory of Gierke and others clearly had logical links with the contract theory of creation of the corporation, which stressed the underlying reality of the contractual organisation and denied that the state had a major role in creating it, or therefore, in regulating it. Historically, the realist theory, with its emphasis on the reality of groups can be seen[14] as part of the challenge to individualist political theory and its associated fiction theory of incorporation posed by the emergence by the late nineteenth century of powerful groups such as corporations.

The question of whether these theories have had or still have any useful role has attracted a lively debate which has simmered on into modern times. In his article in 1926,[15] Dewey mounted a powerful legal realist diatribe against the usefulness of theorising about the nature of the corporation, arguing that the theories have been used variously to serve opposing ends[16] and that the discussion was needlessly encumbered with traditional doc-trines and old issues.[17] By the early 1930s, jurisprudence in company law was pursuing different paths and theorising about the nature and origins of the corporation dried up.[18] The area has been revisited more recently. Professor Horwitz, taking a stance against the Critical Legal Studies position that legal conceptions have little or no influence in deter-mining outcomes, argued[19] that in specific historical settings legal theory can influence the

---

[12] See further, 3.6 below.
[13] Dewey, n. 6 above, at p. 670.
[14] For this view, see Horwitz, n. 11 above, at pp. 180–181.
[15] See n. 6 above.
[16] Dewey, n. 6 above, at p. 671.
[17] *Ibid.* at p. 675.
[18] See below.
[19] See Horwitz, n. 11 above.

direction of legal understanding and in particular sought to show that the rise of the natural (i.e. real) entity theory was a significant factor in legitimating the concept of the large business enterprise. In a subsequent critique of this approach, Millon argued that at the same time that theory is influencing legal doctrine, it in turn is being influenced by legal doctrine.[20] It is clear that to some extent the relevance of theory as providing justification for state intervention has been overtaken by events. The state has largely won the battle, in the UK certainly, and elsewhere. The corporation is the plaything of the state and has been subjected to an elaborate apparatus of regulation, both from Westminster and Brussels, and in the UK the new superpowerful Financial Conduct Authority has been created to watch over investment business. Almost as a faint echo of *laissez-faire*, the individual interest, the principle of freedom from state intervention is now represented by human rights legislation which puts down markers as to the limits of state intervention.[21] But state intervention itself is not in doubt. Having said this, though, it is clear from the 'stakeholder' debate[22] that the extent of state intervention is very much a live issue; and it will be for legislators of the future to decide the extent to which company law must facilitate the representation of interests in corporate governance, beyond merely the shareholders. Here lies the current interest in what the corporation actually is. There has been renewed interest in these early writings as modern juristic activity strives to find a sound philosophical basis for the new 'stakeholder' ideas. In particular, some of the ideas about the company's 'social conscience' can be seen as developments of the real entity theory.[23]

## 3.3 Managerialism

The publication in 1932 of *The Modern Corporation and Private Property* by Adolf Berle and Gardiner Means[24] changed the focus of theoretical scholarship in corporate law for many decades and the central thrust of their thesis continues to be an axiom in modern times.[25] They adopted[26] the broad notion that control of a company resides in the hands of the individual or group who have the power to select the board of directors[27] and proceeded[28] to identify five types of control: control through almost complete ownership (where the corporation might well be described as private); majority control (which will usually give the power to select the board); control through legal device without majority ownership (e.g. by 'pyramiding');[29] minority control (less than 50.1% will often

---

[20] D. Millon 'Theories of the Corporation' (1990) Duke LJ 201. He also takes issue with Horwitz's stance on the meaning of legal concepts.
[21] See further Chapter 23, 23.5 below.
[22] See 3.5 below.
[23] See further 3.5 below.
[24] New York: Harcourt, rev. edn 1968. First published in 1932.
[25] See e.g. E. Herman *Corporate Control, Corporate Power* (New York: CUP, 1981) p. 14, who expressed the view that control of large corporations generally by top management is an 'established truth'. See also the discussion of convergence at 3.4C below.
[26] A. Berle and G. Means *The Modern Corporation and Private Property* (New York: Harcourt, rev. edn 1968) p. 66.
[27] The directors of course usually having control over the day-to-day activities of a company.
[28] Berle and Means, n. 26 above, at pp. 66–84.
[29] Pyramiding involves owning the majority of the shares of one corporation which in turn holds the majority of another, and so on. The effect is to create a situation where the majority at the top of the pyramid control a huge business concern even though the overall wealth they have invested is but a small percentage of the total: Berle and Means, n. 26 above, at p. 69.

give working control in the absence of organised opposition from the remainder); and management control. It is in 'management control' that the kernel of their thesis resided. They defined management control as where ownership is so widely distributed that no individual or small group has an interest large enough to dominate the affairs of the company and so the existing management will be in a position to become a self-perpetuating body.[30] They then sought to discover the extent to which each type of control existed among the largest US non-banking[31] companies. In spite of the necessity of a certain amount of guesswork, the clarity of the results was startling.[32] They found that 44% of companies by number and 58% by wealth[33] were subject to management control and that 21% by number and 22% by wealth were controlled by legal device involving only a small proportion of the ownership. They concluded that the fact that 65% of the companies and 80% of their combined wealth should be controlled by management or legal device showed clearly the extent to which ownership and control of companies had become separate.[34] One of the main effects of this separation of ownership and control was, they argued, that management might pursue their own goals of personal profit, prestige or power.[35]

Although later studies have criticised their empirical methods and definitions and lack of sophistication,[36] the essence of the Berle and Means' thesis remains a central fact of company law theory: dispersed ownership, combined with shareholder passivity, leads to a separation of ownership and control, with control substantially residing in the managers. This management control premise is what is meant by the term 'managerialism'.[37]

There is an important caveat, necessary to an understanding of the significance of managerialism in its worldwide setting, namely that it needs to be emphasised that it is a thesis about the effects of dispersed ownership on corporate control. It is a thesis about patterns of ownership then, and largely still, pertaining in the US. It has similar relevance in the UK which has dispersed ownership patterns. It has very little application to most of the other countries of the developed world, for these have concentrated ownership patterns. These different ownership patterns and the different systems of corporate governance which exist under them has, in the last decade, become the fascinating focus of what might be termed 'convergence' scholarship.[38]

The research by Herman published in 1981[39] was essentially a re-examination and re-assessment of the phenomenon of managerialism in the light of developments in the

---

[30] The background being that when they receive the proxy forms for the election of the board, most of the individual shareholders (having insignificant stakes in the company) will either not bother to vote, or will sign the proxy form giving their vote to the proxy committee, which itself will have been nominated by the management; it will then reappoint the management: Berle and Means, n. 26 above, at pp. 80–81.

[31] I.e. non-financial: Berle and Means, n. 26 above, at p. 18, n. 2.

[32] Although not altogether surprising, for the phenomenon had not gone unnoticed, even if the evidence for it tended to be anecdotal; see Herman, n. 25 above, at pp. 6–8.

[33] I.e. 58% of the total wealth of the largest 200 companies.

[34] Berle and Means, n. 26 above, at p. 110.

[35] *Ibid.* at pp. 112–116.

[36] See e.g. the list in Herman, n. 25 above, at pp. 11–14.

[37] See Herman, n. 25 above, at p. 9.

[38] This is discussed at 3.4C below.

[39] E. Herman *Corporate Control, Corporate Power* (New York: CUP, 1981).

half-century or so since Berle and Means. Herman was careful to stress that managerial discretion and power are realities and not seriously open to question.[40] However, he criticised Berle and Means on the basis that they had failed to explore the limits and constraints on managerial power and, in essence, he argued that their position on control was unsophisticated, that they took the view that either there was control, or there was not. Herman put forward a theory of constrained managerial control. He argued that 'strategic position' in the sense of occupancy of high office in the company was the source of control[41] (although ownership should be seen as an important basis for obtaining strategic position).[42] By 'control', Herman meant the power to make the key decisions of a company and he contrasted this with 'constraint', which he said was a form of control, but was merely a power to limit certain choices or involved power over only a narrow range of corporate activities.[43] Thus, whilst he found a huge decline in the exercise by financial institutions of direct control[44] he maintained that they still exercised powerful constraints over management.[45]

Interestingly, whilst Herman found the impact of the managerialist phenomenon on corporate performance difficult to assess (in view of all the other occurrences which might have had an influence),[46] he ultimately reached a conclusion at odds with the fears expressed by Berle and Means that management would eschew the profit maximisation objective required by the stockholders in favour of goals of their own. Herman's view was that companies with management control seemed as committed to profitable growth as companies dominated by shareholder owners and that this was partly due to an internalisation of profit maximisation criteria in corporate culture and internal operating rules.[47] Herman's empirical data and thoughtful reasoning made an important contribution to our understanding of the phenomenon of managerialism.

The fact of managerialism is linked to other major issues in the theory of company law. The separation of ownership and control has been seen as raising an inquiry into the legitimacy of corporate power. It is clear that large public corporations have colossal economic strength. The power that these kinds of companies can wield over the lives of ordinary people is very significant. In democratic countries we expect power, political or otherwise, to be subject to controls and constraints. Uncontrolled power is seen as lacking moral legitimacy and thus the separation of ownership and control raises important questions as to whether there are sufficient controls on managerial power.[48] Two major issues in company law theory bear on this question. The first is what has come to be called the corporate governance debate, the second being the social responsibility debate. The

---

[40] *Ibid.* p. 14.
[41] *Ibid.* p. 26.
[42] *Ibid.* p. 27.
[43] *Ibid.* p. 19.
[44] *Ibid.* p. 157.
[45] *Ibid.* p. 153.
[46] *Ibid.* pp. 106–107.
[47] *Ibid.* p. 113.
[48] See e.g. M. Stokes 'Company Law and Legal Theory' in W. Twining (ed.) *Legal Theory and Common Law* (Oxford: Blackwell, 1986) p. 155.

corporate governance debate[49] is principally concerned with whether there are, as a matter of fact, sufficient controls, legal or otherwise, on boards of directors, to ensure that their powers are exercised for the benefit of stockholders. The social responsibility debate has origins which are broader than the legitimacy question but to some extent it can be seen as a response to the legitimacy deficiency in terms of trying to change, to broaden out the goals of corporate life,[50] to give managerial power legitimacy by ensuring it is exercised responsibly, and of direct benefit to a wider range of people than merely the shareholders and creditors. The second issue has often been referred to as the social responsibility debate or social enterprise theory but recent developments have given us another name: stakeholder company law. These two issues will now be considered.

## 3.4 Corporate governance

### A Alignment

The term 'corporate governance' is essentially a reference to a system. What system is there to ensure that the providers of capital get any return on their investment? To a large extent, the company is, after all, a collection of assets which fall under the control of the managers. The assets have arisen from capital contributions from the shareholders and retained profits arising from the trading activities of the company. Of course, the assets may also have arisen from inputs made by creditors, whose interests are clearly also part of the corporate governance picture.[51] And so corporate governance is about alignment; that is, it is about what system of legal or other mechanisms exist to ensure that the interests of the managers of the company are aligned with those of the shareholders:[52] to ensure that the managers do not pursue their own interests which might embrace anything, from, on the one hand, doing as little as possible in return for their remuneration, to, on the other, walking away with the money.

Corporate governance systems contain both internal and external mechanisms. The internal elements will involve the extent to which the law puts in the hands of shareholders

---

[49] Some writers use the term 'corporate governance' to include what is here characterised as the second branch. See e.g. IPPR Report *Promoting Prosperity: A Business Agenda for Britain* (London: Vintage, 1997) p. 103. The IPPR Report argues that corporate governance is the system whereby managers are ultimately held accountable to all stakeholders for their stewardship. In view of the fact that the UK committees on corporate governance said very little about the wider 'stakeholder' constituency, it is probably in the interests of clarity if the term 'corporate governance' continues to exclude the 'stakeholder' debate. There are very different institutions and interest groups involved in each field. This will not affect the outcome of that debate because there is no great advantage anyway in calling it 'corporate governance' but it will avoid confusion. Eventually, if the wider constituencies become part of our company 'law' (whether as codes or otherwise) then the fields will probably merge and the IPPR Report description of the term 'corporate governance' will be appropriate; at the moment, it is not.
[50] An approach described by Stokes as the corporatist countervision; see n. 48 above, at p. 178.
[51] In some circumstances, there is even legal recognition that the company must be run in the interests of the creditors; see *Winkworth* v *Baron* [1987] 1 All ER 114; *West Mercia Safety Wear* v *Dodd* [1988] BCLC 250. The doctrine was put thus by Leslie Kosmin QC in *Colin Gwyer & Associates Ltd* v *London Wharf (Limehouse) Ltd* [2003] BCC 885 at p. 906: 'Where a company is insolvent or of doubtful solvency or on the verge of insolvency and it is the creditors' money which is at risk the directors, when carrying out their duty to the company, must consider the interest of the creditors as paramount and take those into account when exercising their discretion.'
[52] The point has already been made (n. 49 above) that the discussion of corporate governance will proceed here on the orthodox basis that the only stakeholders are the shareholders; the issues relating to widening this constituency are considered below under the heading 'Stakeholder company law'.

the ability to control or influence the board of directors, through voting in meetings, or perhaps by the use of litigation to enforce the legal duties owed by directors. The external mechanisms are to be found in the regulatory environment in which the company operates, for instance, the existence of facilities for the detection and prosecution of corporate fraud, or the existence of rigorous corporate insolvency procedures. In recent years, great interest has been shown in the idea that the stock markets play an important part in providing mechanisms of corporate governance. This comes about through the idea that the price of a company's share can influence the managers. If confidence in their abilities is low, then this will be reflected in a relatively low price for the company's stock, resulting in criticism in the financial press, or in company meetings. Additionally, if management have been given share options, then a fall or rise in the company's share price will have a direct bearing on the personal wealth of the directors. In countries where companies are susceptible to being taken over by hostile takeover bid, then the existence of this 'market for corporate control' is thought to provide a powerful mechanism for disciplining management. The idea being that, if management are underperforming, then the share price will be lower than those of other companies in that sector of industry. This will make the company vulnerable to a hostile bid which if successful will usually result in the dismissal of the directors.[53]

## B The Cadbury Report and self-regulation

The last two decades of the twentieth century saw an upsurge in public and political interest in corporate governance in the UK.[54] Corporate scandals and frauds were not an invention of the 1980s but that decade saw a series of very high profile scandals involving very large companies. These pointed to failures in the way companies were being run, and exposed failures in the response of the regulatory system.[55] It became common to sue the auditors of a company which had collapsed in circumstances where it was at least arguable that the auditors should have spotted the problems earlier. Accountancy firms are not usually limited liability companies[56] and so, under partnership law, the partners of these firms were personally liable for the debts of the partnership. Additionally, the size of the claims often exceeded the amounts covered by professional indemnity insurance policies. Accountancy firms took a variety of steps to improve their position. The most significant in terms of the overall development of company law was their role, along with the

---

[53] The effectiveness or otherwise of these mechanisms is the subject of much research and argument: see e.g. J. Franks and C. Mayer 'Hostile Takeovers and the Correction of Managerial Failure' (1996) 40 J Finan Econ 163, arguing that there was little evidence of poor performance prior to bids and hostile takeovers do not therefore perform a disciplining function. See also A. Agrawal and J.F. Jaffe 'Do Takeover Targets Underperform? Evidence from Operating and Stock Returns' (2002) 38 *Journal of Financial and Quantitative Analysis* 721. It has been argued that, in fact, takeovers are often simply the result of irrational and self-interested managerial decision-making: M. Martynova and L. Renneboog 'A Century of Corporate Takeovers: What Have We Learned and Where Do We Stand?' (2008) 32 *Journal of Banking & Finance* 2148. Also under scrutiny is the issue of whether good corporate governance can be linked with strong performance: see J. Millstein and P. MacAvoy 'The Active Board of Directors and the Performance of the Large Publicly Traded Corporation' (1998) 98 Col LR 1283.

[54] And elsewhere; the corporate governance movement is worldwide.

[55] See further Chapter 21 below.

[56] Incorporation of audit firms was not permitted until the passing of the Companies Act 1989.

Financial Reporting Council and the London Stock Exchange, in setting up in May 1991 the Committee on the Financial Aspects of Corporate Governance, to be chaired by Sir Adrian Cadbury. This led to the famous 'Cadbury' Report with its controversial emphasis on the role of self-regulation in corporate governance. These issues are taken up below.[57]

## C Global convergence in corporate governance

### 1 *Two patterns of share ownership and two systems of corporate governance*

During the 1990s in the US, there emerged an important sequel to the Berle and Means thesis of separation of ownership and control, dispersed ownership and shareholder passivity; a focus of scholarship which remains very alive. It had become very clear that the world seemed to have divided itself broadly into two patterns of share ownership: countries like the US and UK which have dispersed ownership of shares, with small stakes in the company being held widely by many shareholders, and most other countries where there is concentrated ownership of shares.[58] The differences in ownership patterns produce different background systems of corporate governance. In countries with dispersed ownership of shares, individual shareholders will often have little incentive to monitor management because their small stakes in the company give them very little power to do so. On the other hand, this is counterbalanced by the presence of highly developed and liquid equity markets that enable the minority shareholder to exit from the company and, furthermore, the presence of large numbers of small shareholders also makes the company vulnerable to takeover offers, the possibility of which has the effect of disciplining management.[59] In countries with concentrated ownership of shares, the corporate governance systems are different. In these countries, large blocks of shares are held by families or by banks or by other companies under cross-holding arrangements; and these are sometimes described as 'networked' systems because of the link-ups between the shareholders. The result is that the shareholders are often in a position to exercise quite direct controls over management. Conversely, such systems are usually characterised by relatively undeveloped stock markets and little possibility of effective takeover bids; hence their stock markets provide little in the way of controls on management via takeover bids. The current academic debate largely centres around the question of what causes these two patterns of ownership and resultant systems of corporate governance and whether they will 'converge', in the sense that one or other will become the sole pattern and the other will change.[60]

---

[57] See further Chapter 10 below for discussion of these issues and subsequent developments.

[58] See generally the reference in n. 60 below.

[59] See further Chapter 21 below.

[60] See Coffee Jr, John C. 'Future as History: The Prospects for Global Convergence in Corporate Governance and its Implications' (1998) 93 Nw UL Rev. 641 and, for a discussion of empirical evidence of European convergence towards Anglo-American systems of corporate governance see: M. Goergen, M. Martynova and L. Renneboog 'Corporate Governance Convergence: Evidence from Takeover Regulation Reforms in Europe' (2005) 21 *Oxford Review of Economic Policy* 243. A similar debate has been going on in the EU about the harmonisation of capital markets and corporate governance systems; see generally K.J. Hopt, H. Kanda, M.J. Roe and E. Wymeersch (eds) *Comparative Corporate Governance – The State of the Art and Emerging Research* (Oxford: Clarendon Press, 1998).

## 2 *Causes of dispersed share ownership*

There are three discernible trends of thought about the causes of dispersed share ownership which can conveniently be labelled as: the efficiency approach, the politics and path dependency approach, and legal protection of minority approach. The first of these derives from traditional economic theory that corporate law and corporate structures will come to assume the form which is most efficient in the sense of producing the greatest profit for the shareholders.[61] Under this approach, the large public firm with dispersed ownership evolved as an efficient response to the needs of industry for large-scale organisations which could only be created by the aggregation of share capital from very many shareholders.

This view has been challenged, principally in the work of Professor Mark Roe,[62] who argued that politics played a major part in the evolution of the large public corporation. He observed that in other countries the large companies have concentrated institutional ownership and maintained that as well as the usual efficiency considerations, the reason for the development and retention of fragmented ownership in the US was that politicians (and the electorate) did not want the Wall Street institutions to have the power to control large corporations. This therefore led to legal constraints which prohibited or raised the costs of banks and other institutions holding large blocks of shares.[63] Roe's conclusion was that politics confined the terrain on which the large public corporation evolved, with the result that the corporation with fragmented ownership evolved and survived rather than some other organisation (e.g. with concentrated ownership).[64] In his later work, Roe developed a theory of 'path dependency', which seeks to explain observed persistent differences in the world's corporate ownership structures: dispersed, on the one hand, concentrated on the other.[65] Under the idea of 'path dependence' current circumstances are ascribed partly to the circumstances which existed in earlier times.[66] Thus it is argued[67] that initial ownership structures have an effect on subsequent ownership structures[68] and further that initial ownership structures can have an influence on legal rules[69] which in turn will influence the way subsequent structures are chosen.

The third approach to the problem of explaining different patterns of corporate ownership emphasises the role of law. Professor Coffee has argued[70] that dispersed share ownership may be the result of giving strong legal protection to minority shareholders. This

---

[61] See generally F. Easterbrook and D. Fischel *The Economic Structure of Corporate Law* (Cambridge, MA: HUP, 1991) pp. 1–39 and 212–218. According to Easterbrook and Fischel, corporate law works and should work like a standard form contract, containing the terms investors would have negotiated if the costs of negotiating were sufficiently low.
[62] M. Roe 'A Political Theory of American Corporate Finance' (1991) 91 Col LR 10.
[63] E.g. the prohibition on bank ownership of equity in the US Glass–Steagall Act 1933 (now partially repealed).
[64] Roe, n. 62 above, at p. 65.
[65] M. Roe 'Chaos and Evolution in Law and Economics' (1996) 109 Harv LR 641.
[66] Roe gives the example of the winding road which was originally constructed to avoid dangerous areas. Once the dangers have disappeared there is no need for the road to wind and bend; a straight road could be put through. And yet, it may not be economically efficient to build a completely new straight road, and so the old remains; see Roe, n. 65 above, at p. 643.
[67] See L. Bebchuk and M. Roe 'A Theory of Path Dependence in Corporate Ownership and Governance' (1999) 52 Stan LR 127.
[68] Described as 'structure-driven path dependence'.
[69] Called 'rule-driven path dependence'.
[70] J. Coffee 'The Future as History: The Prospects for Global Convergence in Corporate Governance and its Implications' (1999) 93 Nw UL Rev. 654.

means that they are content with being minority shareholders in corporations and do not feel that they have to network themselves into the controlling group in order to avoid being expropriated or otherwise badly treated. Their strong legal position protects them, with the result that corporate ownership remains dispersed into small fractional holdings.

## 3 Prospects for convergence

The fascinating question arising out of the existence of the two patterns of corporate ownership is 'What will happen in the future'? Faced with global competition between companies in markets for products, it is interesting to speculate as to the effects of competition between the dispersed and concentrated systems of corporate governance. If one system is inherently better than the other, it is arguable that companies in the weaker system will ultimately be forced either to join the stronger system by obtaining a stock exchange listing there, or seek to change their weaker system.

The three trends of thought discussed above all have interesting angles on the convergence question. The efficiency approach tends towards the idea that the two rival systems of corporate governance have, through globalisation, been put into competition with one another and the most efficient will ultimately win.[71] For instance, it is sometimes argued that the US/UK system of corporate governance is more efficient than European systems[72] because the former have a developed and liquid market for corporate control which enables companies to make share for share takeover offers and grow in size. The politics and path dependency approach stresses that politics and path dependency factors will constrain convergence and so, broadly, the two systems will continue to exist alongside each other. As regards the legal protection of minority approach Coffee stresses the need for regulators to address the policy question of whether the Anglo-American approach should be adopted[73] and argues that some degree of convergence can and will be brought about on a voluntary basis by companies electing to join the US corporate governance system by obtaining a listing in the US. This will then enable them to use the capital raising and takeover mechanisms of the US markets to grow to global scale.

## 4 Conclusions

It seems clear that each of the approaches discussed above brings a valuable insight to the complex problem of trying to identify the forces which are responsible for shaping corporate structure. It is also becoming clear that convergence is coming about in a practical sense in two ways.[74] First, there have been examples of European companies seeking

---

[71] See the analysis in Coffee, n. 70 above, at pp. 645–646.

[72] For a trenchant European view of this see: K. Hopt 'Corporate Governance in Germany' in K. Hopt and E. Wymeersch (eds) *Capital Markets and Company Law* (Oxford: OUP, 2003) p. 289.

[73] Coffee, n. 70 above, at pp. 649–650.

[74] For a more detailed analysis of these and related issues, see K. Hopt 'Common Principles of Corporate Governance in Europe' in B. Markesinis (ed.) *The Clifford Chance Millennium Lectures: The Coming Together of the Common Law and the Civil Law* (Oxford: Hart Publishing, 2000) p. 105. See also K. Hopt 'Modern Company and Capital Markets Problems: Improving European Corporate Governance after Enron' (2003) 3 JCLS 2001.

listings in the US; the most significant of these in recent years being that of the German company Daimler getting a listing on the New York Stock Exchange in 1993 and subsequently being able to make a successful share for share takeover offer for the US company Chrysler.[75] Secondly, it seems that back in continental Europe, things are changing, and the market for corporate control is beginning to look more open.[76] The European Commission sought to chivy this process along through its European Directive on Takeover Bids.[77]

## 3.5 Stakeholder company law

### A Social responsibility

As well as the Berle and Means' thesis on the separation of ownership and control,[78] the early 1930s also saw the famous Berle and Dodd debate on the question 'For whom are corporate managers trustees?'[79] Dodd argued that the existence of the corporation as an entity separate from the individuals who compose it meant that it could be conceived as a person imbued with a sense of social responsibility.[80] Berle himself, although originally in favour of a narrow interpretation of the company's responsibilities, later explored the idea that the company had a 'conscience' which could lead it to assume wider responsibilities to society than merely profit maximisation within the law. Berle saw conscience as something which must be built into institutions so that it could be invoked as a right by the individuals and interests subject to the corporate power.[81] The conscience was the existence of a set of ideas, widely held by the community, and often by the organisation itself and the people who direct it, that certain uses of power were contrary to the established interest and value system of the community.[82] Some aspects of the conscience idea are more than just saying that a company owes a duty to society to behave responsibly. There is also an element of realist jurisprudence, strongly evocative of the real entity theory.[83] The corporation is seen not as a mere fiction of law, but existing in a real sense; the real sense of social reality.[84]

---

[75] For other examples, see Coffee, n. 70 above, at n. 129.

[76] See L. Enriques and P. Volpin 'Corporate Governance Reforms in Continental Europe' (2007) 21 *The Journal of Economic Perspectives* 117.

[77] See further Chapter 21, 21.6 below.

[78] In addition to their managerialist thesis, Berle and Means developed ideas on social responsibility; see n. 26 above, especially at pp. 219–243, 293–313.

[79] A. Berle 'Corporate Powers as Powers in Trust' (1931) 44 Harv LR 1049 and M. Dodd 'For Whom are Corporate Managers Trustees?' (1932) 45 Harv LR 1145. For a detailed analysis of the debate and the later literature, see: S. Sheikh *Corporate Social Responsibilities: Law and Practice* (London: Cavendish, 1996) pp. 153–157.

[80] Dodd, n. 78 above, at p. 1161.

[81] A. Berle *The Twentieth Century Capitalist Revolution* (London: Macmillan, 1955) pp. 89–90.

[82] A. Berle *Power Without Property* (New York: Harcourt Brace, 1959) p. 90.

[83] See 3.2A above.

[84] Such themes have been developed by German social systems theorists. Teubner has referred to academic views about the nature of the legal person that stress its 'dynamic social reality'. See G. Teubner 'Enterprise Corporatism: New Industrial Policy and the Essence of the Legal Person' (1988) 36 *American Journal of Comparative Law* 130–155.

The development of social responsibility within the UK was comprehensively stunted by legal doctrine, which not only enshrined profit maximisation as a major corporate goal, but made it clear that it was the only permissible goal. It was the decision in *Hutton v West Cork Railway Company*[85] which held up the development of corporate social responsibility in the UK. The company was in the process of being wound up when a general meeting endorsed a proposal of the directors to compensate corporate officers for the loss of their employment, not because of any legal claim for salary that they then had but as a gratuity.[86] It was held that the payments would be *ultra vires* the company. *Hutton* enshrined the profit driven mechanism of our capitalist system – it is unlawful to give the workers anything unless it is good for the shareholders; meaning, unless it increases efficiency and therefore increases profits. *Hutton* cemented the shareholders' legal rights to the efficient use of resources at the disposal of the board of directors. Because of this use of the *ultra vires* doctrine to block corporate giving, future developments in the arena of corporate social responsibility tended to concentrate on finding ways of circumventing the doctrine so as to at least make it lawful for companies to make gratuitous distributions for philanthropic reasons if they wanted to. The *ultra vires* doctrine has been eroded by statute and common law doctrine.[87] From the beginning of the 1980s, Great Britain has seen a significant increase in corporate giving to the wider community.[88] The Annual Reports of many large companies reveal the high profile which they accord to their philanthropic activities. Many companies give contributions to political parties; historically, mainly the Conservative Party.[89]

## B Industrial democracy

Industrial democracy, participation of the workforce in corporate decision making, has in recent years formed a major part of the social responsibility debate in the UK. By the late 1970s it had acquired a high public profile, when the majority report of the Bullock Committee recommended having worker representation on company boards.[90] In 1980 Parliament enacted that boards of directors must have regard to the interests of their employees as well as their members.[91] In broadening the constituency in this way company law had taken a great leap, even though the technicalities ensured that it would be virtually

---

[85] (1883) 23 Ch D 654.
[86] Also to apply about £1,500 in remuneration for the past services of the directors, who had never received any remuneration.
[87] See Chapter 5, 5.3B below. *Hutton* was overturned in the Companies Act 1980 so that in circumstances of cessation of business a company can make provision for employees, even if it will not promote the success of the company; see now Companies Act 2006, s. 247 (2).
[88] Sheikh, n. 78 above, at p. 45 and n. 22, cites statistics showing a substantial rise during the 1980s. Since then that picture has continued and statistics from Reynolds, Huyton and Hobson, *The Guide to UK Company Giving 2017/2018* (11th edn, Directory of Social Change) shows that the top ten 'corporate givers' donated in excess of £212m during the relevant financial year.
[89] Corporate donations to political parties are now subject to controls contained in the Companies Act 2006, Part 14 (previously Companies Act 1985, ss. 347A–K, which were inserted by the Political Parties, Elections and Referendums Act 2000). These prohibit donations and political expenditure by companies unless the donation or expenditure has been authorised by an approval resolution. There are special rules for subsidiaries. Certain procedures are specified and there are various exemptions.
[90] Report of the Committee of Inquiry on Industrial Democracy (London: HMSO, Cmnd 6706, 1977).
[91] Companies Act 1980, s. 46; now Companies Act 2006, s. 172 (1). See further Chapter 10, 10.3C below.

impossible for employees to get any legal remedies.[92] During the 1980s, numerous academics emphasised the challenges posed for company law by industrial democracy.[93] In his influential article 'The Legal Development of Corporate Responsibility: For Whom Will Corporate Managers be Trustees?'[94] Lord Wedderburn argued that no solution for managerial authority would be found without some renegotiation of the legitimacy on which corporate government rests and that that could not be accomplished without the acceptance of the workers as an integral constituent, albeit a conflictual constituent, in the business corporation.[95]

In the 1990s, the movement towards industrial democracy made some progress. In the face of opposition from the UK, little satisfactory progress was made with the draft EC Fifth Directive, the earliest draft of which would have required larger companies to have a two-tier board structure, consisting of a top-tier supervisory board and an executive, management board and some form of worker representation.[96] Work on the earlier Vredeling Directive[97] and on the European Company Statute had a similar history.[98] However, the 1992 Maastricht Treaty on European Union and its annexed Protocol and Agreement on Social Policy authorised the member states to adopt Directives for the information and consultation of employees, and so, despite earlier UK opposition, the European Works Council Directive[99] was adopted in 1994. It covered about 1,500 or so European companies (namely those employing over 1,000 workers with more than 150 in at least two member states)[100] and required them to establish company-wide information and consultation committees for their employees.[101] Subsequently, there has been a further

---

[92] See B. Pettet 'Duties in Respect of Employees under the Companies Act 1980' (1981) 34 *Current Legal Problems* 199, at pp. 200–204. Conservative government policy remained one of promoting employee involvement voluntarily; an example of this being the statement about employee involvement required in the Directors' Report by what is now s. 416 (4) Companies Act 2006 which gives the Secretary of State power to make provisions by regulations as to other matters that must be disclosed in the directors' report. These regulations replace the provision formerly made by Sch. 7 to the 1985 Act.

[93] Wedderburn 'The Legal Development of Corporate Responsibility: For Whom Will Corporate Managers be Trustees?' in K. Hopt and G. Teubner (eds) *Corporate Governance and Directors' Liability: Legal, Economic and Sociological Analyses of Corporate Social Responsibility* (Berlin: de Gruyter, 1985); Wedderburn 'The Social Responsibility of Companies' (1985) 15 *Melbourne University Law Review* 1; Wedderburn 'Trust, Corporation and the Worker' (1985) 23 *Osgoode Hall Law Journal* 203; G. Teubner 'Corporate Fiduciary Duties and their Beneficiaries: A Functional Approach to the Legal Institutionalisation of Corporate Responsibility' in K. Hopt and G. Teubner (eds) *Corporate Governance and Directors' Liability: Legal, Economic and Sociological Analyses of Corporate Social Responsibility* (Berlin: de Gruyter, 1985); Sealy 'Directors Wider Responsibilities – Problems Conceptual, Practical and Procedural' (1987) 13 Mon LR 164; P. Xuereb 'The Juridification of Industrial Relations through Company Law Reform' (1988) 51 MLR 156; Wedderburn 'Companies and Employees: Common Law or Social Dimension' (1993) LQR 220.

[94] See n. 91 above.

[95] Wedderburn, 'The Legal Development of Corporate Responsibility: For Whom Will Corporate Managers be Trustees?' n. 92 above, at p. 43.

[96] The full story of the subsequent drafts is analysed in detail in J. Du Plessis and J. Dine 'The Fate of the Draft Fifth Directive on Company Law: Accommodation Instead of Harmonisation' [1997] *JBL* 23.

[97] OJ 1983 C217.

[98] For detail of the proposals, see J. Dine 'The European Company Statute' (1990) 11 Co Law 208; A. Burnside 'The European Company Re-proposed' (1991) 12 Co Law 216.

[99] Council Directive 94/45/EEC on the establishment of a European Works Council or other procedure in Community-scale undertakings or Community-scale groups of undertakings for the purposes of informing and consulting employees, OJ 1994 L254/64.

[100] Council Directive 94/45/EEC, art. 2.

[101] With the coming to power of the Blair 'New Labour' Government, policy towards Europe changed, and the UK signed the Protocol, with the result that UK implementation of the Directive became required.

Directive of more general application, namely the Directive Establishing a General Framework for Informing and Consulting Employees in the European Community.[102] In the long run, this legislation might prove to be a catalyst for a major change in corporate culture.

## C Stakeholder company law

During the 1990s, the social responsibility debate broadened into philosophical and political arguments about creating a 'stakeholder' society. Although the roots go back further, much of the basic ideology stems from communitarian[103] philosophy which became a quasi-political movement in the US in the early 1990s. The electoral success of the Democratic Party in the US may well have inspired an infusion of elements of communitarian ideology into the British Labour Party – which at one stage[104] appeared to endorse the stakeholder concept, although it has since backpedalled somewhat – to produce a call for cultural changes in companies.[105] Nevertheless, the genuine public interest in the stakeholder debate in Britain represented a natural desire to search for social consensus, for community. In the UK, the stakeholder philosophy and agenda has been set out in books and articles which appeared spontaneously in a burst of activity in the mid 1990s. Hutton's influential work *The State We're In*[106] argued that the financial system needed to be comprehensively republicanised. Plender's *A Stake in the Future – The Stakeholding Solution*[107] took a milder line than Hutton, setting out the theoretical basis of the doctrine as he saw it.[108]

---

[102] 2002/14/EC, as amended by Directive 2015/1794/EC.

[103] On communitarianism the main source is A. Etzioni *The Spirit of Community – Rights, Responsibilities and the Communitarian Agenda* (USA: Crown, 1993) (reprinted in the UK by Fontana, 1995). Recent journal sources on corporate responsibility are: A. Sommer 'Whom Should the Corporation Serve? The Berle–Dodd Debate Revisited Sixty Years Later' (1991) 16 *Delaware Journal of Corporate Law* 33; A. Fejfar 'Corporate Voluntarism: Panacea or Plague? A Question of Horizon' (1992) 17 *Delaware Journal of Corporate Law* 859; M. De Bow and D. Lee 'Shareholders, Nonshareholders and Corporate Law: Communitarianism and Resource Allocation' (1993) 18 *Delaware Journal of Corporate Law* 393. There are also distinguished collections in Volume 50 of the *Washington and Lee Law Review* 1373–1723 (1993) and in Volume 43 of the *University of Toronto Law Journal* 297–796 (1993). For earlier material see the extensive bibliography in J.E. Parkinson *Corporate Power and Responsibility: Issues in the Theory of Company Law* (Oxford: Clarendon Press, 1993).

[104] This is widely attributed to Tony Blair's stakeholder speech in Singapore; see *Financial Times*, 9 January 1996. Labour Party thinking in this area was set out in *Vision for Growth: A New Industrial Strategy for Britain* (London: Labour Party, 1996).

[105] See *Financial Times* 26 June 1996.

[106] London: Vintage, 1996 (first published in 1995 by Jonathan Cape).

[107] London: Brealey Publishing, 1997.

[108] The literature is immense. See also e.g.: *Your Stake at Work: TUC Proposals for a Stakeholding Economy* (London: TUC, 1996); Report of the *Tomorrow's Company* inquiry from the Royal Society of Arts (Royal Society for the Encouragement of Arts, Manufactures and Commerce, 1995); J. Kay and A. Silberstone 'Corporate Governance' *NIESR Review, August 1995* (National Institute of Economic and Social Research Review) p. 84; A. Alcock 'The Case Against the Concept of Stakeholders' (1996) 17 Co Law 177; P. Ireland 'Corporate Governance, Stakeholding, and the Company: Towards a Less Degenerate Capitalism?' (1996) 23 *Journal of Law and Society* 287; P. Ireland 'Company Law and the Myth of Shareholder Ownership' (1999) 62 MLR 32; S. Leader 'Private Property and Corporate Governance Part I: Defining the Interests' and J. Dine 'Private Property and Corporate Governance Part II: Content of Directors' Duties and Remedies' and F. Patfield 'Challenges for Company Law' in F. Patfield (ed.) *Perspectives on Company Law: 1* (London: Kluwer, 1995) pp. 1, 85, 115; J. Dine 'Companies and Regulations: Theories, Justifications and Policing' in D. Milman (ed.) *Regulating Enterprise: Law and Business Organisations in the UK* (Oxford: Hart Publishing, 1999) p. 291.

The word 'stakeholders' originated in the US and it has been argued that it developed as a deliberate play on the American word for 'shareholders', namely 'stockholders'.[109] Arguably it was less subtle than that, and perhaps was adopted because it had a deep historical appeal to the American psyche, carrying the connotation of the hardworking and deserving settler 'staking a claim' by ringfencing a plot of land and thus acquiring it; it denotes a moral claim for participation and for rights not yet recognised by the law.

Plender argued that a stakeholder economy is one which derives competitive strength from a cohesive national culture, in which the exercise of property rights is conditioned by shared values and cooperative behaviour.[110] As a result, not only do people have a greater sense of worth and well-being, but the economy becomes more efficient and grows faster. Some of the efficiency is said by economists to come from lower transaction costs[111] because fewer monitors are needed in the workplace, commercial contracting is simpler and cheaper because of a higher level of trust and shared values between the parties, and less state legislation and costly regulation is needed.[112] Stakeholder theory emphasises the importance of inclusion, the role of intermediate institutions, companies, unions, churches, clubs, campaigning groups.[113]

The agenda produced by stakeholder theory for the reform of company law is difficult to pin down, but at present it involves participation of employees and other constituencies in corporate decision-making structures, varying the scope of directors' duties, either by including the wider constituencies as the subjects of the duty or redefining the company so as to include them. There are many other suggestions; ranging from rights to training, to requirements for companies to produce a social audit.[114]

Most stakeholder proposals involve a greater or lesser degree of what may broadly be called corporate voluntarism[115] or profit-sacrificing social responsibility;[116] that is, some level of departure from the principle of running the company for the sole benefit of the shareholders. Over the years corporate voluntarism has been subjected to a great deal of theoretical analysis and criticism. The debate revolves around three main criticisms, although these are overlapping and linked and there are many other angles.[117] It is argued, first, that the pursuit of corporate goals other than profit is inefficient and so in the long run we would all be worse off for it. Further it is said that the company and its shares are private accumulations of capital, and any goal other than profit for shareholders is an infringement of private property, a naked redistribution of wealth; sometimes called the

---

[109] See P. Ireland 'Corporate Governance, Stakeholding and the Company: Towards a Less Degenerate Capitalism?' (1996) 23 *Journal of Law and Society* 287 at p. 295 and n. 47.
[110] J. Plender *A Stake in the Future – The Stakeholding Solution* (London: Brealey Publishing, 1997) at p. 23.
[111] For this concept, see 3.6B below.
[112] See e.g. Plender, n. 110 above, at p. 24 arguing that the historic success of stakeholder economies such as Germany, Switzerland or Japan is partly explained by their lower transaction costs, both inside and outside the firm.
[113] *Ibid.* at p. 256.
[114] See *Your Stake at Work: TUC Proposals for a Stakeholding Economy* (London: TUC, 1996). In fact, in view of the TUC's enthusiasm for their interpretation of stakeholder ideals, it is difficult to see whether the industrial democracy debate survives as a separate issue.
[115] E.g. as in A. Fejfar 'Corporate Voluntarism: Panacea or Plague? A Question of Horizon' 17 *Delaware Journal of Corporate Law* 859 (1992).
[116] J.E. Parkinson *Corporate Power and Responsibility: Issues in the Theory of Company Law* (Oxford: Clarendon Press, 1993) at p. 304.
[117] For a more detailed analysis see Parkinson, n. 116 above, at pp. 304–346.

shareholders' money argument. Thirdly and alternatively, boards of directors are the wrong people to be making decisions about the distribution of wealth, they are not elected by or accountable to the populace, and it extends their already overlarge powers; it is a state function and they should defer to the state which can make appropriate redistributions through the taxation system. This is sometimes called the deference argument.

Various replies could be mounted. The efficiency argument can be met head on by pointing to the counter efficiencies produced by the reduction of social friction which stakeholder policies would produce. Germany and Japan have forms of worker involvement in larger companies and have clearly been doing better than many countries in recent decades. In his book *Competitive Advantage Through People*,[118] Jeffrey Pfeffer, Professor of Organisational Behaviour at Stanford Graduate School of Business, used the example of the five top performing US companies between 1972 and 1992.[119] The factor they had in common was the way in which they managed their workforce. Employment security, high wages and greater employee share ownership can all produce efficiencies and so enhance competitiveness.[120] The shareholders' money argument is arguably diminished by the legitimacy problem created by the immense power that companies in fact exercise over the lives of individuals and in the lack of sufficient controls on that power.[121] The deference argument is challenging but its strength can be diminished by the argument that the general cultural improvement in society resulting from stakeholder policies diminishes the need for strict adherence to democratic theory.[122]

## D The Company Law Review and stakeholders

At an early stage, the Company Law Review[123] recognised that the stakeholder issue was of great importance; it was picked out as one of the key issues for attention.[124] Although, at the end of the day, the prominence of 'enlightened shareholder value', discussed below, prevailed in the Companies Act 2006.[125] The stakeholder issue was, quite properly, linked to the question of identifying the proper scope of company law, meaning, whose interests it should be designed to serve.[126] It was observed that the Review was essentially concerned with law reform and was not concerned with wider ethical issues about the behaviour of participants in companies except to the extent that it was appropriate to reflect them in the law. However, it was made clear the behaviour could be influenced by a wide range of non-legal factors and that the design of the law needed to recognise the importance of these.[127]

---

[118] Boston, MA: Harvard Business School Press, 1994.
[119] J. Pfeffer *Competitive Advantage Through People* (Boston, MA: Harvard Business School Press, 1994) at p. 5. Top performing in terms of the percentage returns on their shares. They were South West Airlines, Tyson Foods, Circuit City and Plenum Publishing.
[120] Pfeffer, n. 119 above, at p. 4.
[121] See e.g. *Your Stake at Work*, n. 113 above, at p. 14 with the observation that less than 15% of the votes of pension funds are cast at AGMs.
[122] E.g. Plender, n. 110 above, at p. 256 arguing that by emphasising the role of intermediate institutions the stakeholding concept consciously downgrades the role of the state.
[123] For an account of the mechanisms of this, see Chapter 1.
[124] DTI Consultation Document (February 1999) *The Strategic Framework*.
[125] In the form of section 172 discussed below in Chapter 8, 8.2B.
[126] DTI Consultation Document (February 1999) *The Strategic Framework* para. 5.1.1.
[127] *Ibid.* para. 5.1.2.

The Review identified two broad approaches; 'enlightened shareholder value', and 'pluralist'. The first of these is that the ultimate objective of companies is that which is currently reflected in the law, namely to generate maximum value for shareholders.[128] But that this approach is to be 'enlightened' by the recognition that a wider range of interests can be served as subordinate to the overall aim of achieving shareholder value and indeed will probably need to be so as to avoid short-term concentration on profit levels, and instead have regard to the fostering of cooperative relationships which will bring greater benefits in the longer term.[129] The pluralist approach is that company law should be modified to include other objectives so that a company should be required to serve a range of other interests in their own right and not merely as a means of attaining shareholder value.[130] It was observed that because the enlightened shareholder value approach was not dependent on any change in the ultimate objective of companies, then there would be no need substantially to reform directors' duties.[131]

The Review returned to the issue in a later document.[132] The responses to the consultation showed that there was strong support for retaining the objective of shareholder value, but that it should be framed in an inclusive way[133] and that due recognition was needed of the importance in modern business of developing effective long-term relationships with employees, customers and suppliers, and in the community more widely.[134]

The later Review document also considered the difficulties with implementing the pluralist approach and noted recent trends in continental systems away from 'enterprise law'[135] and towards the primacy of shareholder value.[136] The Final Report contained recommendations along these lines.[137] The eventual outcome is a codification of directors' duties framed so as to include an obligation to achieve the success of the company for the benefit of shareholders by taking proper account of all the relevant considerations,[138] but that this involves a balanced view of the short and long term, the need to sustain ongoing relationships with employees, customers, suppliers and others, the need to maintain the company's business reputation and to consider the impact of its operations on the community and the environment.[139] In the subsequent government White Paper *Modernising Company Law*, the draft Bill codifying directors' duties adopted this kind of approach.[140]

---

[128] This means shareholder wealth maximisation; *ibid.* para. 5.1.17 and is similar to the concept as used in corporate finance; see Chapter 13, 13.1B below.

[129] *Ibid.* para. 5.1.12.

[130] *Ibid.* para. 5.1.13.

[131] *Ibid.* para. 5.1.17.

[132] DTI Consultative Document (March 2000) *Developing the Framework*.

[133] I.e. made clear that it was to be 'enlightened'.

[134] DTI Consultation Document (March 2000) *Developing the Framework* para. 2.11.

[135] I.e. a system under which concepts like the character or integrity of the company can be seen as legally paramount to the wishes or needs of the shareholders.

[136] DTI Consultation Document (March 2000) *Developing the Framework* paras 3.26–3.36.

[137] *Modern Company Law for a Competitive Economy Final Report* (June 2001), paras. 3.4–3.20.

[138] This is to be coupled with enhanced disclosure and consequent public accountability.

[139] DTI Consultation Document (March 2000) *Developing the Framework* summarised at para. 2.19; the Review later sets out a trial draft of the directors' duties reflecting these ideas; *ibid.* at para. 3.40. See now s. 172 CA 2006, discussed in Chapter 8 below.

[140] July 2002, Cmnd 5553. See also *Company Law. Flexibility and Accessibility: A Consultative Document* (London: DTI, 2004).

The reality is that this was probably the right thing to do for the time being.[141] There did not seem to be any political consensus for the enforcement[142] of the representation of wider interests in companies and nor were the mechanisms through which this might usefully be achieved very obvious. It is true that, with regard to employee participation, continental systems of law have tried and tested structures[143] but it is also true that many people in those systems are increasingly worried about the ability of their companies to attract international capital unless shareholder value is given legal primacy. Furthermore, the absence of employee participation in board structure in the UK might be partially offset by the developments in European Works Councils.[144] In many ways, the Review proposals on the stakeholder issue were exciting and forward looking, and could be said to represent a partial triumph for the stakeholder doctrine having made its mark on the law.[145]

## 3.6 Law and economics

### A Efficiency as a moral value

Lawyers and the public at large have an inbuilt resistance to the notion that economics can have any relevance to law. Justice is what lawyers like to feel they are about, and however cynical or disillusioned the experienced lawyer can get about the ability of the system to deliver justice, he or she will usually strive to ensure that they are involved in a system that does or should deliver justice. The same is true of the public perception of law. After all, are not the television channels filled with dramas based on people who one way or another are getting justice or just deserts from the legal system, or, if the scriptwriter has really excelled himself, a tale with a difference: injustice? Either way, law is seen as being about justice, and if it is not about justice, then it is not about law.

Anathema then, that economists, with their focus on 'efficiency',[146] could be seen as having anything to say about law or legal systems. Surely it is obvious that efficiency should be irrelevant where matters of justice are concerned? And yet efficiency is not always so. Suppose on a workers' cooperative fish farm it is one day discovered that if the fish in the lakes are fed at sunrise instead of at sunset (as is currently the practice) then the number of fish which can be produced annually is doubled. Suppose also, that no one minds whether they do their feeding duty at sunrise or sunset, that no more food is

---

[141] Interestingly, the EC Commission has adopted a definition of Corporate Social Responsibility (CSR) and an approach to CSR which stresses what it regards as its voluntary nature: see the communication *Corporate Social Responsibility: A Business Contribution to Sustainable Development* (COM 2002, 347 final).

[142] Initially the UK government appeared to be actively fostering the voluntary approach through its appointment of a Minister for Corporate Social Responsibility. However, the vacancy that arose for the ministerial position upon change of government has never been re-filled.

[143] E.g. the German system of co-determination (mitbestimmung) under which the executive board (Vorstand) is elected by a supervisory board (Aufsichtsrat) made up of shareholder and worker representatives.

[144] The Transnational Information and Consultation of Employees Regulation 1999 (as amended in 2010).

[145] Whether or not the enlightened shareholder value principle has had any impact is still a matter of debate. See A. Keay 'Tackling the Issue of the Corporate Objective: An Analysis of the United Kingdom's Enlightened Shareholder Value Approach' (2007) 29 Sydney L Rev, 577.

[146] Economists make technical distinctions between different types of efficiency; see B. Cheffins *Company Law: Theory, Structure and Operation* (Oxford: OUP, 1997) at pp. 14–16.

required, and that no other effects result from changing to the sunrise feeding routine. In these circumstances, a change to sunrise feeding seems a rational course of action. It is clearly more efficient. Doubling the output would make the farm more wealthy and so improve the lot of everyone on it. So it is not difficult to see how arguments about the change in routine could acquire a moral quality. It is not only rational to change to sunrise feeding; it is stupid not to. Perhaps then, even, it is wicked not to; almost deliberatively destructive of ideas of human growth and advancement.

Efficiency will therefore sometimes be seen as an important moral value. We live in a world of scarce resources. We strive to produce goods and services; we need them and we like them. Waste is usually seen as immoral and wasteful ways of doing things will sometimes attract moral condemnation. Nevertheless, efficiency will, in many situations, be trumped by other moral values, and human beings will often regard an inefficient course of action as desirable.[147] Sometimes, then, arguments based on whether the law is efficient, in the sense of producing an optimal use of resources, may not be determinative of the weight of the moral argument on one side or the other. On the other hand, given that efficiency is so fundamental to our values, it is nevertheless useful to know whether a particular legal rule will produce an efficient outcome or not.

Economic analysis of legal rules can sometimes shed light on the values inherent in those rules. It will often show that there is a much closer link between efficiency and legal rules than lawyers, with their lofty notions of 'justice', would like to imagine. Of particular relevance to company law have been the economic theories which try to elucidate the nature of the firm,[148] or which try to explain in economic terms, the operation of concepts or structures produced by company law such as limited liability, or the market for corporate control. The analysis which follows will mainly concentrate on the theories relating to the nature of the firm which will serve to give the reader a picture of the kind of issues which economic analysis of company law raises and from which come many of the basic concepts used in the economic analysis of corporation law.[149] The economic analysis of limited liability has already been discussed[150] and economic aspects of takeovers and the market for corporate control are dealt with below.[151]

---

[147] For example, it would be far more efficient for there to be a market in human organs but most people would agree that the immorality of such a market trumps any efficiency related benefits.

[148] 'Firm' in economic theory loosely means business organisation. It is a wider use than the English lawyer's term of art for partnership.

[149] For a work which deals with the whole picture of company law from the economic angle, see: F. Easterbrook and D. Fischel *The Economic Structure of Corporate Law* (Cambridge, MA: Harvard University Press, 1991) arguing that corporation law is a sort of common form contract which should and in fact does supply the rules that investors would contract for if it were easy to contract sufficiently fully. For an interesting example of the counterview that company law is public regulation arising from a choice among policies, see: D. Sugarman 'Is Company Law Founded on Contract or Public Regulation? The Law Commission's Paper on Company Directors' (1999) 20 Co. Law 162; D. Sugarman 'Reconceptualising Company Law: Reflections on the Law Commission's Consultation Paper on Shareholder Remedies: Part 1' (1997) 18 Co. Law 226, and Part 2, *ibid*. 274.

[150] See Chapter 2, 2.2 C, above.

[151] See Chapter 21, 21.2, below. For the 'Efficient Capital Markets Hypothesis' and other economic aspects of the theory of securities regulation, see Chapter 16, 16.5 below.

## B The theory of the firm

### 1 *Transaction cost economics*

The 'theory' of the firm is perhaps best seen as a group of closely related writings by economists about various aspects of the firm; about why it exists and about what goes on inside it. Economic scholarship about why the firm exists[152] is generally regarded as having taken a quantum leap forward[153] with the publication in 1937 of an article by Ronald Coase.[154]

Coase sought to explain why production is sometimes coordinated by price movements on the market and why it is sometimes coordinated by an entrepreneur within the organisation of a firm. Thus, he sought to show why firms exist in an exchange economy in which it is generally assumed that the distribution of resources is organised by the price mechanism,[155] in other words, why organisations exist if production is regulated by price movements and could be carried on without any organisation at all.[156] Coase observed that the main reason why it is profitable to establish a firm would seem to be that there is a cost of using the price mechanism.[157] If there were zero transaction costs associated with transacting, the market mechanism would always be the most efficient way of transacting. But there are always costs, such as the costs of negotiating and concluding contracts for each exchange transaction on the market.[158] In particular he argued that a firm would be likely to emerge in cases where a short-term market contract would be unsatisfactory; such as where it was for the supply of a service and where the details of what the supplier is expected to do are left to be decided on later by the purchaser.[159] Thus he argued that by forming an organisation and allowing an entrepreneur to direct the resources, certain marketing costs are saved[160] and so a firm, therefore, consists of the system of relationships which comes into existence when the direction of resources is dependent on an entrepreneur.[161] Then, approaching the problem from the other end, he considered why there are any market transactions at all, given that transaction costs are never zero and if, through organising, one can eliminate certain costs and thereby reduce the cost of production. In other words, why is production not carried on by one big firm?[162] Coase found the answer to be that a firm will expand until the costs of organising an extra transaction within the firm become equal to the costs of carrying out the same transaction by means of an exchange on the open market.[163]

---

[152] This term embraces both companies and partnerships in this context.
[153] Prior to that, the neoclassical approach was the dominant analysis; and it continues to survive. Neoclassical theory views the firm as a set of feasible production plans presided over by a manager who buys and sells assets with a view to maximising the welfare of the owners; see O. Hart 'An Economist's Perspective on the Theory of the Firm' in P. Buckley and J. Michie (eds) *Firms, Organizations and Contracts: A Reader in Industrial Organization* (Oxford: OUP, 1996) pp. 199, 200.
[154] R. Coase 'The Nature of the Firm' *Economica*, New Series, IV, 386 (1937).
[155] *Ibid.* at p. 393.
[156] *Ibid.* at p. 388.
[157] *Ibid.* at p. 391.
[158] Usually referred to by later economists as the costs of 'writing contracts'.
[159] Coase, n. 154 above, at pp. 391–392 *passim*.
[160] *Ibid.* at p. 392.
[161] *Ibid.* at p. 393.
[162] *Ibid.* at p. 394.
[163] Or the costs of organising in another firm; *ibid.* at p. 395.

The emphasis given to the costs of transacting on the market as compared with the costs of organising within a firm has resulted in this kind of analysis being referred to as 'transaction cost' economics. Many later writers have developed aspects of Coase's theory; in particular, Oliver Williamson, a major exponent of the transaction cost approach, has argued that the modern corporation is mainly to be understood as the product of a series of organisational innovations that have had the purpose and effect of economising on transaction costs,[164] and so transactions will be organised by markets unless market exchange gives rise to substantial transaction costs.[165] Williamson considered in detail where these costs can arise, focusing especially on the costs associated with opportunism and bounded rationality on the part of the transacting parties which serve to make comprehensive contracting impossible.[166] Furthermore, for Williamson, the reduction in transaction costs achieved by the use of the firm in some situations provides a moral justification for allowing firms to exist, on the basis that since transaction cost economising is socially valued, then it follows that the modern corporation serves affirmative economic purposes.[167] This is a crucial insight, for it encapsulates one of the main tenets of the economic analysis of corporation law, that one of the reasons for the existence of corporation law is the reduction of transaction costs.

## 2 Shirking, agency costs and nexus of contracts

Other economic theorists have concentrated more on what goes on inside a firm (rather than how and why it comes into existence) and provided some important perspectives. Alchian and Demsetz[168] maintained in 1972 that their view of the firm was not necessarily inconsistent with Coase's observation that the higher the cost of transacting across the markets the greater will be the comparative advantage of organising resources within the firm.[169] However, in order to move the theory forward, they argued that it was necessary to know what is meant by a firm and to explain the circumstances under which the cost of managing resources is low relative to the cost of allocating resources through market transaction.[170] Their approach stresses that a firm should not be characterised by the existence of authoritarian power and argued that a firm has no power of fiat, or authority or disciplinary action any different from ordinary market contracting between any two people[171] and therefore that the employee 'orders' the owner of the team to pay him money in the same sense that the employer directs the team member to perform certain acts.[172] They thus placed their focus on contract, as the mechanism which brings about exchange, and locate the firm in circumstances which they describe as the team use of inputs and a centralised position of some

[164] O. Williamson 'The Modern Corporation: Origins, Evolution, Attributes' (1981) 19 *Journal of Economic Literature* 1537.

[165] Williamson, n. 164 above, at p. 15

[166] O. Williamson *The Economic Institutions of Capitalism* (New York: The Free Press, 1985).

[167] *Ibid.* at p. 1538.

[168] See A. Alchian and H. Demsetz 'Production, Information Costs, and Economic Organisation' (1972) 62 *American Economic Review* 777.

[169] *Ibid.* at p. 783.

[170] *Ibid.* at pp. 783–784.

[171] *Ibid.* at p. 777.

[172] *Ibid.* at p. 783.

party in the contractual arrangements of all other inputs.[173] They described the need for the firm to monitor carefully who is doing what and to reward those who deserve it, referring to this process as 'metering'.[174] In relation to this they identify the problem of what they term 'shirking' and argue that there is a higher incentive for people to shirk when they are part of a team (because it is more difficult to monitor than if they work singly).[175] They therefore move to the position that because it involves team production, one of the firm's chief difficulties is the monitoring of shirking.[176] In identifying how the firm structure seeks to provide the monitor[177] they raise what at first sight looks like a red herring but in fact provides a powerful insight into the firm's organisational structure. They raise the question of who will monitor the monitor[178] and in considering this they see the point that the firm structure has a particular answer to this, to be found in the concept of the residual claimant (i.e. the equity shareholder(s)) because if you give someone the title to the net earnings of the team then they have an incentive not to shirk as a monitor.[179] Ultimately, they summarise the bundle of rights possessed by the equity shareholder,[180] and conclude that the coming together of them has arisen because it resolves the shirking-information problem of team production better than the non-centralised contractual arrangement.[181]

The Alchian–Demsetz analysis is an important elucidation of the problem of aligning the interests of the various participants in corporations towards an efficient outcome. In this respect, their analysis is closely related to Jensen and Meckling's influential work on agency costs to which it is now necessary to turn.

Jensen and Meckling bring a wide range of perspectives to the theory of the firm.[182] Perhaps the most influential aspects are those which derive from their analysis of the firm as a 'nexus'[183] of contracts, and their analysis of the role of agency costs.[184] They define the firm as simply one form of legal fiction[185] which serves as a nexus for contracting

---

[173] *Ibid.* at p. 778.

[174] Metering is seen as important because if the economic organisation meters poorly, with rewards and productivity only loosely correlated, then productivity will be smaller: *ibid.* at p. 779.

[175] *Ibid.* at p. 779.

[176] The shirking-information problem.

[177] Alchian and Demsetz use the term monitor to connote activities such as measuring output performance, apportioning rewards, and giving assignments or instructions in what to do and how to do it (in addition to its normal disciplinary connotation): Alchian and Demsetz, n. 163 above, at p. 782.

[178] *Ibid.* at p. 782.

[179] *Ibid.*

[180] To be a residual claimant; to observe input behaviour; to be the central party common to all contracts with inputs; to alter the membership of the team; to sell these rights.

[181] *Ibid.*

[182] See M. Jensen and W. Meckling, 'Theory of the Firm: Managerial Behaviour, Agency Costs and Ownership Structure' (1976) 3 *Journal of Financial Economics* 305.

[183] 'Nexus' has the dictionary meaning of 'bond, link or connection'.

[184] The term 'agency costs' is used here to denote the costs of organising resources within firms, as opposed to the term 'transaction costs' which is generally used to denote the costs of organising across markets. This perhaps is in keeping with the approach originally used by the writers and may help to avoid confusion; see e.g. H. Demsetz 'Theory of the Firm Revisited' in O. Williamson and S. Winter (eds) *The Nature of the Firm: Origins, Evolution, and Development* (New York, Oxford: OUP, 1993) at pp. 161–162 referring to the terminology problem arising if the term 'transaction costs' is used to cover both. (Demsetz also preferred the term 'management costs' instead of 'agency costs'.) However, quite often agency costs are equated with and are regarded as a species of transaction cost; see e.g. S. Deakin and A. Hughes 'Economics and Company Law Reform: A Fruitful Partnership' (1999) 20 Co. Law 212.

[185] 'Legal fiction' is earlier defined as the artificial construct under the law which allows certain organisations to be treated as individuals: Jensen and Meckling, n. 182 above, at n. 12.

relationships. It is also characterised by the existence of divisible residual claims on the assets and cash flows of the organisation which can generally be sold without permission of the other contracting individuals.[186] One of the claims which they make for this approach is that it serves to make it clear that it is seriously misleading to personalise the firm by reference to its social responsibility. The firm is not an individual, it is a legal fiction which serves as a focus for a complex process in which the conflicting objectives of individuals are brought into equilibrium within a framework of contractual relations.[187]

In their paper, Jensen and Meckling focus on an analysis of agency costs generated by the contractual arrangements between the owners and the top management of the corporation. They define an agency relationship as a contract under which one or more persons (the principal(s)) engage another person (the agent) to perform some service on their behalf which involves delegating some decision-making authority to the agent.[188] They argue that agency costs come about because if both parties to the relationship are utility maximisers there is good reason to believe the agent will not always act in the best interests of the principal[189] and trying to align the interests of the agent and the principal gives rise to costs.

These 'agency costs' are defined as the sum of (1) the monitoring expenditures by the principal,[190] (2) the bonding expenditures by the agent[191] and (3) the residual loss.[192] The core of Jensen and Meckling's paper consists of formal mathematical economic analysis of the effect of outside equity on agency costs by comparing the behaviour of a manager when he owns 100% of the residual claims on a firm to his behaviour when he sells off a portion of those claims to outsiders. Their general concluding observations are that agency costs are as real as any other costs and the level of agency costs depends among other things on statutory and common law and human ingenuity in devising contracts and that whatever its shortcomings, the corporation has thus far survived the market test against potential alternative forms of organisation.[193]

## 3 *Property rights theory*

Subsequently, a 'property rights' approach has been developed, initially in an article by Sanford Grossman and Oliver Hart.[194] This seeks to take further Coase's observation that

---

[186] *Ibid.* at p. 311.
[187] *Ibid.* It is interesting to compare this claim, which makes little allowance for realist theory, with writings about social responsibility; see 3.5A above.
[188] Jensen and Meckling, n. 182 above, at p. 308.
[189] *Ibid.*
[190] 'Monitoring' here includes any rules designed to control the behaviour of the agent; see Jensen and Meckling, n. 182 above, at n. 9.
[191] 'Bonding' refers to situations where it will pay the agent to enter into arrangements which guarantee that he will act in the principal's interests.
[192] Jensen and Meckling, n. 182 above. 'Residual loss' means that even given optimal monitoring and bonding activities between principal and agent, there will still be some divergence between the agent's decisions and those decisions which would maximise the welfare of the principal.
[193] Jensen and Meckling, n. 182 above, at p. 357. For an agency costs analysis in the context of derivative actions see, A. Reisberg, *Derivative Actions and Corporate Governance: Theory and Operation* (Oxford: Oxford University Press, 2007) Chapter 1.
[194] S. Grossman and O. Hart 'The Costs and Benefits of Ownership: A Theory of Vertical and Lateral Integration' (1986) 94 J Pol Econ 691; O. Hart *Firms, Contracts and Financial Structure* (Oxford: Clarendon Press, 1995).

transactions will be organised in the firm[195] when the cost of doing this is lower than the cost of using the market[196] by exploring the content of the idea that there are benefits of organising the transaction within the firm.

The background to the property rights approach, and the platform from which it moves forward, lies in the development of transaction cost theory subsequent to Coase, largely by Williamson.[197] It is useful to start[198] with the observation that contracts are 'incomplete' in the sense that the parties will not provide for every single contingency in their contracts.[199] The result of this is that as their business relationship progresses the parties will seek to 'renegotiate' the contract. This renegotiation process will involve costs; for example, because the parties will haggle over the new terms. The costs may be so high that it becomes worth the while of the parties to go their separate ways and find other partners. However, they will be deterred from doing this, and will be willing to put up with quite a lot of renegotiation costs if they have already put a lot of work or money (i.e. investment) into preparations for the business relationship – this is referred to as an '*ex ante* relationship-specific investment'. This puts us into a position to comprehend one other renegotiation cost which may arise. Prior to the parties' entering into a contract setting up a relationship-specific investment, they will tend to look ahead, and may well anticipate that the incomplete contract governing it will sooner or later need to be renegotiated and that they could then find that the trading gains which they hope to make from it will be eaten up by the other party being difficult[200] in those renegotiations. This fear might well be so significant that it causes them never to enter into the contract for the relationship-specific investment in the first place, even though that would have been their best option in efficiency and trading terms. Instead, they decide to opt for a less relationship-specific investment which will sacrifice some of the efficiency benefits[201] which the more specific investment would have brought, but avoids the risks arising from the incomplete contract and potential hold-up behaviour. Thus we have been examining the transaction costs which are potentially present in transactions between separate firms (i.e. firms which are non-integrated). It is part of transaction cost theory (stemming from Coase) that in some circumstances these costs will be less within an integrated firm.[202] Hart argues that transaction cost theory does not tell us why, but that property rights theory does.[203]

Hart starts his explanation[204] by focusing on the effect of an acquisition by firm A of firm B, and argues that what A actually gets out of it is that it becomes owner of firm B's

---

[195] I.e. there will be integration.

[196] Grossman and Hart, n. 194 above, at p. 692.

[197] See generally O. Williamson *The Economic Institutions of Capitalism* (New York: Free Press, 1985).

[198] This summary is largely derived from Chapters 1 and 2 *passim* of O. Hart *Firms, Contracts and Financial Structure* (Oxford: Clarendon Press, 1995).

[199] The incompleteness comes about largely as a result of difficulties in seeing all the contingencies and of 'writing' them into the contract.

[200] This 'being difficult' is often referred to as 'hold-up' behaviour.

[201] The loss of the efficiency benefits is thus the cost.

[202] I.e. if the transaction is being carried out within a firm (the integrated situation) rather than across a market (i.e. between two non-integrated firms).

[203] See O. Hart *Firms, Contracts, and Financial Structure* (Oxford: Clarendon Press, 1995) at p. 28. He later makes it clear that the theory applies most directly to owner-managed firms, but that the main insights of the property rights approach continue to be relevant to the large company cases; see *ibid.* pp. 61–62 and Chapters 6–8.

[204] Hart, *Ibid.* pp. 30–32 *passim*.

assets. He uses the phrase 'nonhuman assets' to take in the point that the firm does not own the people employed by it.[205] He then observes that because contracts are incomplete, they will not specify all aspects of the use of the asset, there will be gaps, and so the question will arise of which party has the right to decide about the gaps. Hart takes the view that the owner of the asset has the residual control right.[206] The core of the theory is that in view of the incompleteness of contracts, this residual control will affect bargaining power during the renegotiation of incomplete contracts. Hart summarises that the benefit of integration is that the acquiring firm's incentive to make relationship-specific investments increases since, given that it has more residual control rights, it will receive a greater fraction of the *ex post* surplus[207] created by such investments. On the other hand, the cost of integration is that the acquired firm's incentive to make relationship-specific investments decreases since, given that it has fewer residual control rights, it will receive a smaller fraction of the incremental *ex post* surplus created by its own investments.[208]

This proposition is then formalised in mathematical models.[209] The essence of the theory is that changes in ownership[210] can affect the severity of the hold-up problem that arises owing to the incompleteness of contracts for relationship-specific investments.[211] It remains to be seen whether the difficult insights of this theory will become as influential as those provided by the earlier transaction cost and agency cost analyses.

## 4 *Assessment*

How should we assess the relevance of these economic writings on the nature of the firm for the study of company law? First, it needs to be said that, famous though they are, there is a danger in presenting the above[212] theories as if they represented some settled orthodoxy within the discipline of economics. This is not the case. Work on the theory of the firm has evolved over many years and continues to do so both in terms of criticism of the existing theories and in the evolution of new theory.[213] Even self-criticism is not lacking. For instance, Demsetz later felt able to observe that the Alchian and Demsetz analysis of abating the cost of shirking

---

[205] Although obviously it will be the owner of any rights (choses in action) which it has against those people by virtue, e.g. of their employment contracts.

[206] Hart argues (citing Oliver Wendell Holmes Jr) that this view of ownership seems consistent with the standard view of ownership adopted by lawyers and seems to accord with common sense: Hart, n. 198 above, at p. 30.

[207] '*Ex post* surplus' broadly means the trading gains accruing to the parties after the contract has been entered into.

[208] Hart, n. 203 above, at p. 33.

[209] *Ibid.* at pp. 33 *et seq.* The theory seems to be assuming that the acquired firm retains considerable rights of autonomy as regards how it continues to undertake business.

[210] Meaning, changes in the boundaries of firms (i.e. the integration of non-integrated firms).

[211] This is paraphrased from Hart, n. 203 above, at p. 87. Hart uses the hold-up example, but points out (*ibid.*) that although the hold-up problem is a useful vehicle for developing the property rights approach, it is not an essential part of the approach. That is, even in the absence of a hold-up problem, asset ownership would still generally matter and what is required for a theory of asset ownership is that there is some inefficiency in the economic relationship, which the allocation of residual control rights can influence.

[212] Or others.

[213] See M. Dietrich Tr*ansaction Cost Economics and Beyond: Toward a New Economics of the Firm* (London: Routledge, 2008) and L. Poppo, and T. Zenger 'Testing Alternative Theories of the Firm: Transaction Cost, Knowledge Based, and Measurement Explanations for Make or Buy Decisions in Information Services' (1998) 19 *Strategic Management Journal*, 853.

helped to explain the firm's inner organisation but provided no rationale for the firm's existence.[214] Others have mounted sharp critiques of the theories; thus, in 1993, Winter, when considering the explanations offered by economics of the role of the business firm in a market economy, wrote of a state of incoherence, of significantly conflicting answers, of an interesting babble.[215] In recent years, many new theories, ideas and approaches have emerged.[216] Hart makes reference to the vast literature on aspects of agency theory.[217]

How relevant are these theories to an understanding of company law? The question is difficult to answer with any precision. Roberta Romano, in 1993, expressed the enthusiastic view that corporate law has undergone a revolution and that legal scholarship has been transformed by the use of the new analytical apparatus of the economics of organisation.[218] There is obviously much truth in this in the sense, at least, that legal academics have continued to develop a respectful interest in the economic analysis of law. And certainly, some of the economic concepts have become common parlance among legal teachers and students. 'Reduction of agency costs' is a phrase which would be used freely in any discussion of laws dealing with the alignment of management with shareholder interests and people would share the connotations which it carried in respect of the function and policy of the law. But most lawyers are not economists, and whilst, with effort, they can get on top of the broad thrust of an economist's explanation of his or her theory, most will stop well short of being able to comprehend the formal mathematical proofs which are so important to many economists.

Perhaps a better approach is to ask how relevant is economic theory to the reform of company law and how relevant should it be? Is this not the litmus test? If economic analysis could identify absurdities in the policies currently enforced by the law and then point the way to the socially optimal policy, it would be the indispensable tool of the law reformer and politician. Interest in economic analysis from law reform agencies has not been absent.[219] But the reliance on economic analysis seems very much patchy at this

---

[214] S. Winter 'The Theory of the Firm Revisited' in O. Williamson and S. Winter (eds) *The Nature of the Firm: Origins, Evolution, and Development* (New York, Oxford: OUP, 1993) pp. 159, 168.

[215] 'On Coase, Competence, and the Corporation' in O. Williamson and S. Winter (eds) *The Nature of the Firm: Origins, Evolution, and Development* (New York, Oxford: OUP, 1993) p. 179. Also somewhat sceptical is C. Goodhart 'Economics and the Law: Too Much One-Way Traffic?' (1997) 60 MLR 1.

[216] See generally the collection in M. Casson (ed.) *The Theory of the Firm* (Cheltenham: Elgar, 1996) and the survey in P. Milgrom and J. Roberts 'Economic Theories of the Firm: Past, Present and Future' in P. Buckley and J. Michie (eds) *Firms, Organizations and Contracts: A Reader in Industrial Organization* (New York: OUP, 1996). For a fascinating analysis of corporate law which seeks to identify the common structure of corporate law across national boundaries, see R. Kraakman *et al.*, *The Anatomy of Corporate Law: A Comparative and Functional Approach* (Oxford: OUP, 2004). Other writings include: S. Deakin and A. Hughes 'Economic Efficiency and the Proceduralisation of Company Law' [1999] CFILR 169; M. Whincop 'Painting the Corporate Cathedral: The Protection of Entitlements in Corporate Law' (1999) 19 OJLS 19; S. Copp 'Company Law Reform and Economic Analysis: Establishing Boundaries' (2001) 1 JCLS 1; A. Macneil 'Company Law Rules: An Assessment from the Perspective of Incomplete Contract Theory' (2001) 1 JCLS 401; B. Maughan and M. McGuinness 'Towards an Economic Theory of the Corporation' (2001) 1 JCLS 141; J. Armour and M.J. Whincop 'The Proprietary Foundations of Corporate Law' (2007) 27 *Oxford Journal of Legal Studies*, 429.

[217] Hart, n. 203 above, p. 19.

[218] R. Romano *Foundations of Corporate Law* (New York: OUP, 1993) Preface.

[219] The Law Commission's efforts to involve economic analysis in the reform of directors' duties quickly stimulated a sharp and lively debate: see Law Com. Consultation Paper No. 153, Scottish Law Commission Consultation Paper No. 105 *Company Directors: Regulating Conflicts of Interests and Formulating a Statement of Duties* (1998) and the Report of the same name (1999). See e.g.: C. Maughan and S. Copp 'The Law Commission and Economic Methodology: Values, Efficiency and Directors' Duties' (1999) 20 Co Law 109; S. Deakin and A. Hughes 'Economics and Company Law Reform: A Fruitful Partnership?' (1999) 20 Co Law 212; C. Maughan and S. Copp 'Company Law Reform and Economic Methodology Revisited' (2000) 21 Co Law 14.

stage[220] and it seems that, in the UK at any rate, most reforms in corporate law proceed on the basis that the arguments are still lost and won by intuitive moral reasoning, the lawyers' and politicians' traditional chosen field of battle.

Much of the problem with economic analysis of corporate law really stems from the fact that it does not tell us much more than our vague orthodox processes based on moral reasoning. Reference has been made to economic analysis of the concept of limited liability and yet it is clear that on careful examination, the ideas and analyses which the economists of the late-twentieth century expounded were already present in the committee reports and parliamentary debates of the mid-nineteenth century.[221] This is largely because corporate law is founded on the intuitive concepts of efficiency embraced by the *laissez-faire* economic systems of the nineteenth century.[222] Neither the mid-nineteenth century reformers nor the late-twentieth century economists were able to demonstrate a conclusive scientific case for having limited liability; the arguments run either way and the balance of them falls broadly in favour of limited liability.[223] The nineteenth-century reformers stumbled towards having limited liability and the twentieth-century economic justifications chart a similarly erratic path.

Part of the difficulty lies with the complexity of the problems which confront any reformers. Many of the economists' articles recognise the need to try to produce formal models of the theories.[224] But formal models tend to be a simplification of the real world. If it tries to embrace all the considerations needed, the model loses its force. As Hanson and Hart have pointed out, the most common and potent criticisms of law and economics are either that its models are indefensibly unrealistic or that the analysis is insufficiently scientific.[225] However, we should not lose sight of three important facts. First, that an economic analysis of a problem will often throw up useful perspectives which can then be assessed using the normal intuitive processes which lawyers and law reformers usually use. Although the economic perspective will be geared towards showing whether the outcome is efficient or not, this will often be of interest to the reformer, since in the absence of some other moral value which is felt should govern the situation and therefore trumps efficiency, the reformer will probably be morally right to opt for a law which produces an efficient outcome. Secondly, that in some situations the economist will have empirical research behind his analysis which will tend to show how the existing law or an existing problem is actually affecting matters and so it is possible that there are occasions when the input of law and economics will tend towards being conclusive of a policy discussion which may have been going on for years on an intuitive basis. Finally, like all fields of

---

[220] See, for example, B. Cheffins *Company Law: Theory, Structure and Operation* (Oxford: OUP, 1997) which provides an analysis of UK company law utilising economic theory to provide a conceptual framework. Likewise, the Court of Appeal utilised economic analysis of the law in 2004 in deciding *Item Software (UK) Ltd v Fassihi* [2004] EWCA Civ 1244, but this remains, to date, an isolated case. For a discussion of the judgment in this case see J. Lowry 'The Duty of Loyalty of Company Directors: Bridging the Accountability Gap Through Efficient Disclosure' (2009) 68 *Cambridge Law Journal*, 607.

[221] This is demonstrated in detail in B. Pettet 'Limited Liability – A Principle for the 21st Century' (1995) 48 *Current Legal Problems* (Part 2) 125 at pp. 143–150.

[222] See, in particular, Posner's comments; cited in Pettet, n. *ibid.* 215 above, at p. 143.

[223] See Pettet, n. 221 above, pp. 141–157.

[224] *Ibid.* at p. 156, nn. 142, 153.

[225] J. Hanson and M. Hart 'Law and Economics' in D. Patterson (ed.) *A Companion to Philosophy of Law and Legal Theory* (Oxford: Blackwell, 1996) p. 329.

research, law and economics continues to progress and, at times, reconsiders, reassesses, and as a result, refines old premises. For example, according to the classical rational choice theory any behaviour that does not directly maximise an actor's financial wealth is irrational. But over the last decade or so, numerous legal scholars have acknowledged that some of the foundational assumptions behind the classical rational choice theory may reflect an unrealistic picture of human behaviour. Not surprisingly, models based on these assumptions sometimes yield erroneous predictions. This has led to the development of the field of behavioural law and economics which attempts to improve the predictive power of law and economics by building in more realistic accounts of actors' behaviour.[226] This field of research has been widely popularised and led to a large array of books on the subject of human behavior and its linkages with law and economics reaching the mainstream.[227]

## 3.7 Future issues

It is interesting to speculate as to the path of future scholarship in the legal theory of company law. First, it is clear that what might be called 'technical' improvements will continue to be made as a result of law reform agencies and scholars identifying areas of law which are not working in the way that people feel they should. Many of the thoughtful recommendations of the Company Law Review which is discussed in the first chapter are of this quality. Certain procedural requirements have been removed, others have been introduced; and unless there is some overriding moral reason, all changes are, usually, made in order to enable the corporate law system to function more efficiently, or to put it in economic terms, to reduce transaction costs.

Secondly, globalisation will continue to provide a fertile area for research and interest not only by scholars but also by companies themselves who will increasingly be forced to consider whether it is worth their while getting a listing on a stock market other than that operated by their own country. The clash between the two rival systems of corporate governance, dispersed ownership and concentrated ownership, is only just beginning.

Finally, the stakeholder debate will not go away. It will survive at two levels. First, if stakeholder policies do in fact produce more efficient firms, and more efficient economies, then, in the course of time, this will become painfully apparent to countries which have not developed such systems and it will be difficult for them to compete successfully in international markets. Secondly, even if the pursuit of stakeholder policies is in fact either not proven to be more efficient or is even seen to damage corporate performance at the margin, it may well nevertheless come to be seen as one of those areas of corporate law where our usual striving to produce an efficient system needs to be trumped by the moral imperative of adopting corporate structures which ensure a humanisation of corporate power.

---

[226] C.R. Sunstein (ed.) *Behavioral Law and Economics* (Cambridge: Cambridge University Press, 2000).
[227] For example, D. Kahneman *Thinking, Fast and Slow* (London: Macmillan, 2011), G. Akerlof, and R.J. Shiller *Animal Spirits: How Human Psychology Drives the Economy, and Why It Matters for Global Capitalism* (New Jersey: Princeton University Press, 2010), D. Ariely 'Predictably irrational: The Hidden Forces That Shape Our Decisions' (New York, HarperCollins Publishers, 2008).

## Further reading

D. Millon 'Theories of the Corporation' (1990) *Duke LJ* 201.

E. Herman *Corporate Control, Corporate Power* (New York: CUP, 1981).

M. Stokes 'Company Law and Legal Theory' in W. Twining (ed.) *Legal Theory and Common Law* (Oxford: Blackwell, 1986).

F. Easterbrook and D. Fischel *The Economic Structure of Corporate Law* (Cambridge, MA: HUP, 1991) pp. 1–39 and 212–218.

L. Bebchuk and M. Roe 'A Theory of Path Dependence in Corporate Ownership and Governance' (1999) 52 *Stan LR* 127.

A. Berle 'Corporate Powers as Powers in Trust' (1931) 44 *Harv LR* 1049.

M. Dodd 'For Whom are Corporate Managers Trustees?' (1932) 45 *Harv LR* 1145.

G. Teubner 'Enterprise Corporatism: New Industrial Policy and the Essence of the Legal Person' (1988) 36 *American Journal of Comparative Law* 130.

B. Pettet 'Duties in Respect of Employees under the Companies Act 1980' (1981) 34 *Current Legal Problems* 199.

Lord Wedderburn 'The Legal Development of Corporate Responsibility: For Whom Will Corporate Managers be Trustees?' in K. Hopt and G. Teubner (eds) *Corporate Governance and Directors' Liability: Legal, Economic and Sociological Analyses of Corporate Social Responsibility* (Berlin: de Gruyter, 1985).

P. Ireland 'Company Law and the Myth of Shareholder Ownership' (1999) 62 *MLR* 32.

P. Ireland 'Corporate Governance, Stakeholding and the Company: Towards a Less Degenerate Capitalism?' (1996) 23 *Journal of Law and Society* 287.

B. Cheffins *Company Law: Theory, Structure and Operation* (Oxford: OUP, 1997).

H. Demsetz 'Theory of the Firm Revisited' in O. Williamson and S. Winter (eds) *The Nature of the Firm: Origins, Evolution, and Development* (New York, Oxford: OUP, 1993).

S. Winter 'The Theory of the Firm Revisited' in O. Williamson and S. Winter (eds) *The Nature of the Firm: Origins, Evolution, and Development* (New York, Oxford: OUP, 1993).

J. Armour and M. Whincop 'The Proprietary Foundations of Corporate Law' (version 12 September 2004) available at SSRN: http://www.ssrn.com/abstract=665186.

S. Deakin and A. Hughes 'Economics and Company Law Reform: A Fruitful Partnership?' (1999) 20 *Co Law* 212.

C. Maughan and S. Copp 'Company Law Reform and Economic Methodology Revisited' (2000) 21 *Co Law* 14.

# Part II
# The constitution of the company

# 4

# Entrenchment of rights

## 4.1 Entrenchment of expectation versus flexibility

When the promoters incorporate a company, they usually have in mind that the company will grow and that they will all make a great deal of money out of it. The other major concern that they have will be how much influence and power each will have over the company's operations. The legal rules relating to shares go some way towards settling these two related issues. However, it is the organisation of the constitution of the company that largely completes the picture. This chapter is concerned with the way company law attempts to resolve the tension which arises between, on the one hand, the promoters' desire to secure firmly entrenched rights for themselves and, on the other hand, their realisation that if the company is to grow and respond to business opportunities, it will sometimes be necessary for those entrenched rights to give way to change. This chapter looks first at the way in which the constitution of a company is organised and then explores the range of processes by which the various rights enshrined in the constitution can be altered. Thereafter, Chapter 5 examines the way in which the constitution organises the key constituents of the company and considers the difficult question of the impact of any limitations on corporate power contained in the constitution. Chapter 6 then investigates how the constitution may potentially constrain the authority of individuals to bind the company to contractual relations with third parties and the ways in which the Companies Act 2006 has responded to this concern.

## 4.2 Articles of association

The key constitutional document of a company is the articles of association as supplemented by any resolutions and shareholders' agreements.[1] As we have seen, as part of the incorporation process the articles must be delivered to the Registrar in the application for registration of the company.[2] If articles are not so delivered then the relevant model

---

[1] Sections 17 and 29 of the Companies Act 2006. As commented on in Chapter 2, under the pre-existing law the memorandum of association was seen as the 'senior' constitutional document as compared to the articles. The seniority idea had some significance when it came to construing the constitution as a totality. In *Re Duncan Gilmour* [1952] 2 All ER 871, there was a discrepancy between the rights given by the memorandum and those given by the articles. The articles gave more extensive rights to preference shareholders and they were arguing that they were entitled to these. It was held that the memorandum was the primary document and that if it was clear on its face, then doubts could not be raised as to its meaning by reference to the articles. If, however, the memorandum was on its face ambiguous, and posing difficulties of construction, reference to the articles is possible to help resolve the doubt. In the circumstances the memorandum was unambiguous and so the preference shareholders were disappointed.

[2] Section 9 (5) (b). See further, Chapter 2.

articles of association will apply as a matter of default (s. 20).[3] In practice, most private companies limited by shares will adopt the model articles, subject to a small number of specific amendments that are drafted to address their particular business or strategic needs. Ordinarily, it is where a company has secured significant third party investment (from a venture capitalist, for example) where significant amendments are made (to provide for that investor's conditions of investment, e.g. concerning voting and dividend rights). Section 18 (1) lays down the requirement that a company must have articles of association prescribing its regulations which, according to s. 18 (3), must be contained in a single document divided into paragraphs numbered consecutively. As has long been the case, the 2006 Act continues to give the Secretary of State the power to prescribe model articles,[4] and different articles may be prescribed for different types of company.[5] Following consultation exercises during 2007, a set of model articles for private companies limited by shares, private companies limited by guarantee and public companies limited by shares are now available as the default rules for companies incorporated on or after 1 October 2009.[6] The articles of association set out the internal rules governing the operation of the company and, for example, cover matters relating to meetings, such as quorum, length of notice, voting and matters relating to directors such as their general authority, appointment and retirement, and remuneration. For companies registered under the Companies Act 1985, the Companies (Tables A to F) Regulations 1985[7] contain a common form list (Table A) of the sort of provisions that most companies require. In practice most companies adopted Table A, making modifications which are necessary in their particular case. Table A has been modified by, what is now, DBEIS so as to be compatible with the 2006 Act. Given the number of companies registered under the 1985 Act and, indeed, its predecessors, the 'old' style model articles will continue to be of relevance for years to come.

## A The company's objects

Under the pre-existing law every company was required to include in its memorandum of association a statement of its objects, i.e. a statement setting out the business activities that the company had been incorporated to pursue, for example, 'to operate trains and bus services'. The policy here was aimed at protecting shareholders and creditors who would thereby know for what purposes their investment or loan would be used. It also set limits on the authority of directors. If they committed the company to an activity beyond its objects the effect was that it was *ultra vires* (namely, beyond the company's powers) and void. As a consequence, and as discussed further in Chapter 5, third parties contracting with the company in good faith were particularly vulnerable as they were at risk of their contract being unenforceable through no fault of their own. To mitigate this impact on

---

[3] For companies registered before 1 July 1985, see Table A, Sch. 1 to the Companies Act 1948 (as amended). For companies registered under the Companies Act 1985, see the Companies (Tables A to F) Regulations 1985, SI 1985/805.
[4] Section 19 (1).
[5] Section 19 (2).
[6] See the Companies (Model Articles) Regulations 2008 (SI 2008/3229), Schedules 1 and 3, respectively.
[7] SI 1985 No. 805.

third parties, the Companies Act 2006 introduced a suite of provisions designed to protect third parties and re-allocate risk to the individual directors that acted outside of the company's powers.[8] The Companies Act 2006 removes the requirement for an objects clause. Section 31 (1) provides that unless the company's articles specifically restrict the company's objects, its objects are unrestricted. The default position therefore is that a company has unlimited capacity unless it decides otherwise. If, however, a restriction is made, directors who cause the company to act beyond its objects will be in breach of their duty to act in accordance with the company's constitution as laid down by s. 171.[9]

One would have thought that the law would provide that the members would be able to enforce the articles. There would not, it might be thought, be much point in calling them articles of *association* if they were not meant to govern the way in which the members thereafter *associate*. Unfortunately, for those of this mind, UK case law has prepared a disappointment. The mechanism adopted by the draftsmen of the legislation was, ostensibly, simple enough. They must have instinctively turned to the idea which was in use for pre-1844 deed of settlement companies that, being essentially partnerships by nature, linked their members to one another by the use of contractual obligations.[10] The result, which then passed down through successive Companies Acts, is what is now s. 33 (1) of the 2006 Act (replacing s. 14 (1) of the Companies Act 1985), which provides:

> The provisions of a company's constitution bind the company and its members to the same extent as if there were covenants on the part of the company and of each member to observe those provisions.

Against this path dependency of partnership law, a problem that arose with s. 14 of the 1985 Act (which stated that the articles bound the company and its members to the same extent as if they respectively had been signed and sealed by each member) was whether the company itself was a party to the contract. Section 33 (1) now addresses this by clearly stating that it is.[11] Apart from this, the drafting of the new provision is very similar to its predecessor and so much of the case law continues to be relevant. In this regard, the courts have admitted a certain, but not unlimited, level of enforceability. The rules of enforcement (or otherwise) are considered next.

First, and again not surprisingly given the background analogy with partnerships inherent in s. 33, it has been held that the members can enforce the articles against each other. This is apparent from the somewhat difficult case of *Rayfield* v *Hands*.[12] Here, article 11 of the articles of association provided that a member who wished to transfer his shares should inform the directors (who were also shareholders) of that intention and the said 'directors . . .

---

[8] See Chapters 5 and 6. Also see: the Companies Act 1985, s. 35. For the common law position see *Ashbury Railway Carriage and Iron Co Ltd* v *Riche* (1875) LR 7 HL 653; *Cotman* v *Brougham* [1918] AC 514; *Re Jon Beauforte (London) Ltd* [1953] Ch 131; *Re Introductions Ltd* [1970] Ch 199.

[9] See Chapter 8.

[10] Thus, in *Re Tavarone Mining Co., Pritchard's Case* (1873) LR 8 Ch App 956, Mellish LJ observed, at p. 960: 'the articles of association are simply a contract as between the shareholders *inter se* in respect of their rights as shareholders. They are the deed of partnership by which the shareholders agree *inter se*.'

[11] Section 14 of the 1985 Act made no mention of the company being bound by the articles. The problem was considered by Astbury J in *Hickman* v *Kent or Romney Marsh Sheepbreeders Association* [1915] 1 Ch 881 and his solution, which seems sensible, was that 'the section cannot mean that the company is not to be bound when it says that it is to be bound.' Section 33, therefore, gives this reasoning the force of statute.

[12] [1958] 2 All ER 194.

will take the said shares equally between them at a fair value'. This was probably meant to be a kind of pre-emption clause designed to give the directors and shareholders a method of preventing transfer to an outsider who they would not want to work with. But the wording, far from giving the directors a mere right of pre-emption, actually cast an obligation upon them to buy the shares. Rayfield had spotted this and argued that the directors should take his shares. Vaisey J, whilst lamenting that the articles were 'very inarticulately drawn by a person who was not legally expert', nevertheless upheld his claim. In coming to this decision, Vaisey J held that, notwithstanding that article 11 was seemingly written to impose an obligation on the company's directors, the article was actually concerned with the relationship between the plaintiff as a member and the defendants, not as directors, but as members.[13] Having characterised the directors as 'member-directors,'[14] Vaisey J then held that the articles could be enforced between the members *inter se*. Whilst the reasoning in this decision can be challenging to follow, the case is an example of the powerful contractual effect that the articles can have between the members.

Secondly, it has been established that a member may enforce membership rights contained in the articles against the company. In *Wood* v *Odessa Waterworks Co.*,[15] the articles empowered the directors to declare a dividend 'to be paid' to the shareholder. Wood was a shareholder who objected to the directors' plan to pay a dividend in debentures rather than cash. He successfully obtained an injunction to prevent payment by the issue of debentures since the court accepted his argument that 'to be paid' *prima facie* meant paid in 'cash'. Wood was able to enforce the articles against the company here, even though the shareholders in general meeting had resolved, by ordinary resolution, to carry out the directors' idea. The case is a very important example of the limited instances of the principle of majority rule,[16] which normally ascribes a binding effect to a decision of the majority of shareholders in general meeting, giving way to the principle that a shareholder can enforce their rights *qua* shareholder set out in the constitution.

Thirdly, as the converse of the second situation, it has been held that a company can enforce the articles against the members. This is clear from the seminal case, *Borland's Trustee* v *Steel Brothers & Co Ltd*,[17] and was seen in the decision of *Hickman* v *Kent or Romney Marsh Sheepbreeders' Association*.[18] Here, the court held that article 49 of the company's articles that required any dispute concerning the articles be referred to arbitration, bound both the company and the members. In coming to this decision, Lord Astbury observed that:

> s [33 CA 2006] cannot mean that a company is not to be bound, when it says it is to be bound . . . nor can the section means that the members are to be under no obligation to the company under the articles in which their rights and duties are . . . to be found . . .[19]

However, these three situations are subject to two doctrines that will, in some circumstances, deprive the member of the chance of enforcing the article. One doctrine is

---

[13] [1958] 2 All ER 194, [6].
[14] [1958] 2 All ER 194, [9].
[15] (1889) 42 Ch D 636.
[16] See further, at Chapter 11 below.
[17] [1901] 1 Ch 279.
[18] [1915] 1 Ch 881.
[19] [1915] 1 Ch 881, 896–897.

connected with the 'rule' in *Foss* v *Harbottle*,[20] which in some situations will maintain that matters of internal management, or internal disputes between the shareholders, cannot be litigated (when the majority have approved the act or omission in question). In at least one case,[21] the courts have used this principle to prevent a member from being able to insist that the management or conduct of the company be conducted in accordance with the articles. This whole topic is explored later in this text.[22] The other doctrine, which will be examined in detail here, is that of insider and outsider rights.

Broadly, the idea is that, under s. 33, a member may only enforce those rights which affect him in his capacity as a member (an insider) and that he may not enforce rights which affect him in some other capacity, such as a solicitor[23] or a director (an outsider). It may seem strange to refer to a director as an outsider in this context, since in a very obvious sense he or she is intimately connected with the company, but what is meant is that the director is, *in that capacity*, a stranger to the membership contract and all its mutual obligations. The doctrine was first set out in authoritative form in 1915 by Astbury J in *Hickman* v *Kent or Romney Marsh Sheepbreeders Association*.[24] He reviewed the case law and concluded that:

> . . . No right merely purporting to be given by an article to a person, whether a member or not, in a capacity other than that of a member, as, for instance, as solicitor, promoter, director, can be enforced against the company.[25]

The effects of the doctrine are quite dramatic, so that, for instance, if the articles provide for a salary for a director, he will not be able to rely on s. 33 to sue for it.[26]

The doctrine was taken up by the Court of Appeal in 1938 in *Beattie* v *E. Beattie Ltd*,[27] where the issues were subtle but the result was a clear enunciation and application of the doctrine. In *Beattie* the issue arose as to whether part of an action could be stayed pursuant to an arbitration clause contained in the articles. The action was being brought by a shareholder against one of the directors, Ernest Beattie (who was also a shareholder), and the part of the action which formed the subject matter of these proceedings was brought in respect of alleged improper payments of remuneration by him. Ernest Beattie applied to have this part of the action stayed on the basis of an arbitration clause contained in clause 133 of the articles which provided that disputes arising between the company and any member or members (concerning various matters) should be referred to arbitration. In order to bring himself within the Arbitration Act then governing the situation it was necessary for Ernest Beattie to be able to point to a written agreement (i.e. contract) for

---

[20] (1843) 2 Hare 461. See Chapter 11, below.
[21] *McDougall* v *Gardiner (No. 2)* (1875) 1 Ch D 13, CA.
[22] See Chapter 11.
[23] *Eley* v *Positive Government Security Life Assurance Co. Ltd* (1876) 1 Ex D 88.
[24] [1915] 1 Ch 881. An earlier example is said to be *Eley* v *Positive Government Security Life Co.* (1876) 1 Ex D 88 but this is the explanation offered in *Hickman* although it is difficult to discern the principle in the case itself.
[25] [1915] 1 Ch 881 at p. 900.
[26] This is the effect of *Eley*, n. 20 above, as explained in *Hickman*. The director may, however, be able to rely on the doctrine of implied contract under which the courts will infer the existence of a contract from the course of dealing between the parties and obtain the detailed terms by reference to the articles; see *Swabey* v *Port Darwin Gold Mining Co.* (1889) 1 Meg 385; *Re New British Iron Co., ex parte Beckwith* [1898] 1 Ch 324. In practice, a written employment contract is used to avoid these problems.
[27] [1938] 1 Ch 708.

submission to arbitration. There was nothing except the articles, and so it became necessary for Ernest Beattie to establish that clause 133 of the articles constituted a contract to submit to arbitration. This threw the spotlight on to the contractual effect of what is now s. 33.[28] Sir Wilfred Greene MR delivered the judgment of the court[29] holding that:

> . . . Ernest Beattie is, and was at all material times, a director of the company and it is against him, in his capacity as director that these claims are made. It is as a director in charge of the company's funds that he is responsible for their proper application, in accordance with the regulations which govern the company . . . [T]he contractual force given to the articles of association by the section is limited to such provisions of the articles as apply to the relationship of the members in their capacity as members . . . the real matter which is here being litigated is a dispute between the company and the appellant in his capacity as a director . . . and by seeking to have it referred [to arbitration] he is not, in my judgment, seeking to enforce a right which is common to himself and all other members . . . He is not seeking to enforce a right to call on the company to arbitrate a dispute which is only accidentally a dispute with himself. He is seeking, as a disputant, to have the dispute to which he is a party referred. That is sufficient to differentiate it from the right which is common to all the other members of the company under this article.[30]

It is clear from this passage that a major part of the underlying rationale of the insider/outsider doctrine is the notion that insider rights are those which are common between the shareholders. Returning to *Rayfield* v *Hands*,[31] it is this idea that seemed to have helped Vaisey J reach his decision in that case, for a possible objection to his conclusion was that the action was being brought against the directors (i.e. outsiders). On the other hand, the right to have their shares purchased was common to all the members and Vaisey J laid stress on the idea that the articles were 'a contract between a member and member-directors in relation to their holdings of the company's shares'.[32] It is of note, reflecting the partnership roots of s. 33 as it now is, that Vaisey J also placed emphasis on the fact that the company in question 'bears close analogy to a partnership . . . [and that] . . . nobody, I suppose, would doubt that a partnership deed might validly and properly provide for the acquisition of the share of one partner by another partner on terms identical with those set out in the present case.'[33]

Not surprisingly, this area of law has been the subject of steady academic scrutiny spanning many decades. The literature has variously questioned the wisdom of the doctrine, puzzled to find a rationale, and struggled with cases that seem out of line. Writing in 1957,[34] Lord Wedderburn developed the idea that a member would sometimes be able to enforce indirectly an outsider right as long as he made it clear that he was suing in his capacity as a member. Using this concept, he sought to explain the House of Lords'

---

[28] Actually then, s. 20 of the Companies Act 1929. There was also another issue in the case, namely whether clause 133 of the articles, on its true construction, actually applied to the present dispute. It had been held at first instance that it did not apply, but the Court of Appeal did not 'find it necessary to resolve' that matter: [1938] 1 Ch 708 at p. 719.

[29] Scott and Clauson LJJ concurring.

[30] [1938] 1 Ch 708 at pp. 718–722 *passim*.

[31] [1958] 2 All ER 194.

[32] [1958] 2 All ER 194 at p. 199. Subsequently, the doctrine has received tacit support in the House of Lords in *Soden* v *British and Commonwealth Holdings plc* [1997] BCC 952.

[33] [1958] 2 All ER 194, [9].

[34] 'Shareholders' Rights and the Rule in *Foss* v *Harbottle*' [1957] CLJ 194 at p. 212 and [1958] CLJ 93.

decision in *Salmon v Quinn & Axtens*,[35] where one of two managing directors (who was also a shareholder) was entitled to an injunction to enforce a veto over a board decision, which had been given to him in the articles (seemingly enforcing, via the articles, an 'outsider' right). In 1972,[36] Goldberg endeavoured to enunciate a new explanation of what was really going on in the cases. He argued that the true position was that a member would be able to enforce any clause in the articles provided that the clause was ascribing a function to a particular organ of the company. Thus, he explained the *Salmon* case on the basis that the organ prescribed by the articles for the particular board action was the board and two managing directors. Salmon's action was designed to ensure that this organ was indeed the one which carried out that function, and so succeeded. One of the difficulties with this thesis is that the cases do not purport to be decided on this basis. Drury, writing in 1986,[37] argued that this area had to be looked at in the light of the fact that the articles were a long-term contract and therefore it was inappropriate that a party could point to particular clauses and demand that they be enforced. The difficulty with this is that, as will be seen below, the legislation contains detailed provisions under which the articles and class rights can be altered, with the obvious purpose of providing long-term flexibility, but with built in safeguards of checks and balances so as to give a measure of protection to settled expectations and bargains.

Gregory, writing in 1981,[38] adopted a somewhat different approach, but one which has much to commend it. His view was that, contrary to what Astbury J claimed, the analysis in *Hickman* was wrong and that prior to *Hickman* the courts were in the habit of enforcing the articles without limitation. One of the great strengths of this approach is that it gives effect to the wording of the statute. The gloss put upon it by the *Hickman* case is not justified by any established principle of statutory interpretation and the result is hardly edifying.

In fact, it is possible to construct two quite fundamental objections to the *Hickman* doctrine, both deriving from very significant but relatively recent developments in other areas of company law.

First, the developments in the case law on unfair prejudice[39] have taken the opposite direction to *Hickman* to such an extent as to make it highly arguable that it no longer represents the law, even if it ever really did. Under the unfair prejudice case law the courts will often give effect to equitable expectations which go *beyond* the express terms of the articles. These expectations will often include matters which under the *Hickman* approach would probably be regarded as outsider rights. Early case law in this field had a similar attitude, so that in *Re Lundie Bros*[40] the removal of a director in a small partnership style company (a so-called quasi-partnership company) was held not to amount to 'oppression' under the then prevailing legislation because it affected the petitioner in his capacity as a director and not (as the statute required) as a member. Under the unfair prejudice

---

[35] [1909] AC 442. It is noteworthy that the decision pre-dated the high level of articulation given to the doctrine in *Hickman*.
[36] 'The Enforcement of Outsider-Rights under s. 20 (1) of the Companies Act 1948' (1972) 35 MLR 362.
[37] 'The Relative Nature of a Shareholder's Right to Enforce the Company Contract' [1986] CLJ 219.
[38] 'The Section 20 Contract' (1981) 44 MLR 526.
[39] See generally Chapter 12 below.
[40] [1965] 1 WLR 1051; a case on the old s. 210 of the Companies Act 1948.

legislation which replaced the oppression remedy in 1980,[41] the principle that the prejudice had to affect the member in his capacity as a member was reiterated,[42] but tempered by the idea that in appropriate circumstances his membership rights might well include expectations of management, directorship and accompanying financial rewards. These kinds of matters would have been regarded as 'outsider' or non-membership rights in the *Lundie Bros* era. They are no longer so regarded. What matters now is not any rigid classification based on narrow notions of what the membership contract involves, but what the justice of the situation demands. It is therefore perhaps arguable that the current position with the s. 33 contract is that all the terms of the articles are *prima facie* enforceable.[43]

Secondly, there has been a substantial growth in the use by small companies of complex written shareholders' agreements.[44] As we have seen, s. 17 defines the company's constitution as including such agreements and copies are required to be sent to the Registrar.[45] Shareholders' agreements are enforceable by dint of the common law, of contract, and are not dependent on s. 33. For this reason, they are often used by practitioners to secure the enforcement of rights which would otherwise be in danger of being unenforceable under the *Hickman* doctrine. To some extent, the development of shareholders' agreements illustrates the practical challenge of the law in s. 33. Promoters who wish to define the terms on which they are going to associate must be careful not to put certain matters into the articles of *association*, for these will possibly not, in fact, regulate how they are required to associate. Instead, they must put the terms into a document which is enforceable by the law of contract, even though the section in the Companies Act which it has become necessary to avoid says, in effect, that the articles are to be enforceable contractually.

The Law Commission in its report *Shareholder Remedies*,[46] after consultation, took the view that this area was not in need of reform because it was not a problem in practice.[47] It may well be that whilst practitioners nearly always avoid difficulty, the *Hickman* doctrine remains challenging. Nevertheless, although the matter was looked at by the Company Law Review, the subsequent White Paper *Modernising Company Law* contained no commitment to deal with the problem.[48]

## 4.3 Shareholders' agreements

It is common in small private companies, for the articles to be supplemented by a shareholders' agreement.[49] Theoretically, since they operate under normal contract law, it is not necessary for them to be put in writing and there are situations where an oral shareholders'

---

[41] Now s. 994 of the Companies Act 2006.
[42] *Re a Company 00477/86* (1986) 2 BCC 99, 171.
[43] In some circumstances it will no doubt be unfairly prejudicial to rely on the article, or a particular article.
[44] See further 4.3 below.
[45] See s. 30 of the Companies Act 2006. See also, ss. 32 and 36.
[46] Law Com. Report No. 246. See further Chapter 11 below.
[47] *Ibid.* para. 7.11.
[48] London: DTI, 2002.
[49] For a detailed treatment of the subject, see G. Stedman and J. Jones *Shareholder Agreements* 3rd edn (London: Sweet & Maxwell, 1998); see also, P. Finn 'Shareholder Agreements' (1978) 6 ABL Rev. 97. Shareholders' agreements are very common in small (close) companies in North America. They are becoming increasingly popular in small UK companies and, as we have seen, reference is made to them as forming a part of the company's constitution in the Companies Act 2006.

agreement will be enforceable. Sometimes the courts have even been prepared to imply the existence of a shareholders' agreement arising from the course of dealing between the parties.[50] However, it is obviously preferable for the agreement to be in writing[51] and the complexity of modern ones normally makes this essential.

At the outset, it is clear that shareholders' agreements have some significant disadvantages, which will need to be overcome if the agreement is to be effective. The most obvious point is that if they are going to be used to create what is in effect a third part of the constitution of the company,[52] then they are really only suitable for small companies, since the agreement of all the members will be necessary if the mechanism is to be effective.[53] Furthermore, the transfer of a share by a member will pose a challenge for the draftsperson of a shareholders' agreement. The transferee of a share will not be bound by the shareholders' agreement unless she expressly agrees to be bound (by executing a deed of adherence or by all parties executing a new shareholders' agreement with the new shareholder being included as a party). She will, however, be bound by the terms of the articles, since this is the statutory effect of s. 33 of the Companies Act 2006. The statute operates so that the transferee automatically steps into the shoes of the transferor as regards the rights and obligations arising under the articles. Conversely, if the parties to a shareholders' agreement want it to have some chance of surviving as a document which binds all the members from time to time it will be necessary to make contractual provisions which bring this about. For instance, it is desirable to include a clause which puts an obligation on an intending transferor of shares to oblige her to put a clause into the sale contract which requires the purchaser to enter into the shareholders' agreement.[54]

Why would it ever be desirable to use a shareholders' agreement rather than rely on the facilities provided by the articles? The common law gives freedom. The parties can construct the agreement to suit themselves. A particular head of agreement may be so important to the parties that they do not want it alterable at a later date by less than 100% agreement. If such a clause is put into the articles, it will normally be alterable[55] by a special resolution[56] and this alone may make the articles unacceptable as a constitutional vehicle for carrying out their business plans. Alternatively, the parties may wish that a certain clause or clauses be alterable by a different majority than the 75% of the special resolution, say 90% or 60%; this can easily be done under a shareholders' agreement.[57]

---

[50] See e.g. *Pennell* v *Venida* (unreported) noted by S. Burridge (1981) 40 MLR 40.

[51] There will normally be sufficient mutuality of obligations for the contractual requirement of consideration to be satisfied, but in exceptional circumstances it may be necessary to circumvent the need for consideration by making the agreement a deed, under seal.

[52] See s. 17 of the Companies Act 2006.

[53] However, agreements between small groups of shareholders in a large company are, of course, possible, and in the form of voting agreements are quite common.

[54] Another similar problem would arise if the company were to issue more shares at a future date. It would be necessary to ensure that the subscribers would be bound by the shareholders' agreement. This could perhaps be done by making the company a party to the shareholders' agreement and inserting a clause therein which obliged the company to put a clause into the agreement to subscribe which obliged the subscriber to enter into the shareholders' agreement.

[55] Under Companies Act 2006, s. 21. See further below.

[56] 75% of members voting.

[57] Tampering with the statutory power to alter the articles has not found favour with the courts; see *Allen* v *Gold Reefs of West Africa* [1900] 1 Ch 656; *Southern Foundries (1926) Ltd* v *Shirlaw* [1940] AC 701; *Russell* v *Northern Bank Development Corporation* [1992] 1 WLR 588.

If the constitutional mechanisms offered by company law can be by-passed in this way, it becomes pertinent to consider what view company law will take of a shareholders' agreement. How much of company law can be ignored by use of the mechanisms of a shareholders' agreement?

The first matter is publicity. Legislative policy in this field has been that limited liability comes at a price; the price of publicity. The articles have to be registered with the Registrar of Companies and are on public file, open to inspection. But the effect of this registered constitution may in fact be wholly altered by a third document of the constitution, the shareholders' agreement, making the policy of disclosure in these circumstances at best incomplete and, at worst, positively misleading. Whilst the registration requirements set out in ss. 29 and 30 are broad, in practice shareholders' agreements are not generally filed with the Registrar. As such, the public filings of the shareholders' practical rights and obligations are, arguably, incomplete.

The second issue to consider is what would be the result of a direct clash between, say, a statutory provision of company law and a contrary provision in the shareholders' agreement? This and other issues were explored by the House of Lords in *Russell* v *Northern Bank Development Corp.*[58] The case involved an extensive shareholders' agreement, clause 3 of which provided that 'no further share capital shall be created or issued in the company . . . without the written consent of each of the parties hereto'. Importantly, both the company and its shareholders were a party to the shareholders' agreement. The directors were proposing to issue more shares[59] and the claimant shareholder sought an injunction to restrain this. He was not deeply opposed to their proposal, but wanted to test the efficacy of clause 3 because he feared that the directors might on a future occasion try to issue more shares in circumstances which might lead to his voting power being reduced. The House of Lords held that, in so far as the clause purported to bind the company, it was void as being contrary to statute. In particular, clause 3 was, *inter alia*, a fetter on the company's statutory right to amend its articles by special resolution and accordingly, in so far as it bound the company, then it was void. However, the House of Lords upheld the validity of the clause as regards its enforceability between the shareholders on the basis that, as between the shareholders, it could be interpreted as operating as a voting agreement. It being well established in the case law that a voting agreement was valid, this provided a way of upholding the shareholders' agreement to a considerable extent. Furthermore, the remainder of the shareholders' agreement was not affected by the void aspect of clause 3 which was capable of being severed from the agreement. The claimant succeeded in getting a declaration to the above effect, it having been realised that an injunction was an inappropriate remedy in the circumstances, since he had no real objection to the share issue then under consideration.

The case is significant because it shows a marked lack of judicial hostility to the concept of the complex written shareholders' agreement operating as the third constitutional document of the company. Where the agreement was unavoidably seen to be in direct conflict

---

[58] [1992] 1 WLR 588; [1992] 3 All ER 161. In *Halton International Inc (Holdings) SARL* v *Guernoy Ltd* [2006] 1 BCLC 78, Patten J held that absent an express agreement to the contrary, a voting agreement did not give rise to fiduciary duties on the part of the parties to act in the interests of the other shareholders.
[59] It was actually a capitalisation issue.

with company law then it was, understandably, superseded by the law and void. Nevertheless, the rigours of company law were upheld only to the extent that this was necessary and overall it could be said that the case gives significant recognition to shareholders' agreements, even where their practical effect (operating as a form of voting agreement) is seen to run counter to the intention of the Act.

The third matter for consideration, which is closely linked to the second, is what would be the result of a clash between a principle of company law established by case law, and a shareholders' agreement? There is plenty of scope for this situation to occur and it is clearly something which needs to be borne in mind when drafting a shareholders' agreement. One example which might often be relevant is the director's fiduciary duty to exercise an unfettered discretion.[60] If a shareholders' agreement binds the board of directors to supporting a particular policy over a long period of time, this might put the directors into an impossible position.[61] Other circumstances might make the enforcement of a shareholders' agreement inappropriate. In *Re Blue Arrow*,[62] for example, Vinelott J was unwilling to give effect to an alleged expectation of management, which may have amounted to an informal agreement to that effect,[63] because the policy of the law with regard to publicly quoted companies was that the full extent of the constitution should be publicly available to a would-be investor. As such, a potential investor should not be put in the position of buying shares in a company and then finding that the true constitutional position was subject to understandings of which he could have had no notice.

## 4.4 Changing the constitution and reconstruction

### A Introduction

Sooner or later most companies find that changing business conditions mean that if they are to survive and prosper, they will need to adapt accordingly. In contrast, shareholders with settled interests and expectations will want certain protections from such change. Company law aims to strike a balance between these potentially conflicting needs by providing for the entrenchment of rights within the constitution together with a variety of checks and balances that come into play once an attempt to alter those entrenched rights is made. The analysis here will start by looking at the most simple methods of change and gradually progress to a consideration of the more complex and powerful methods which are needed to deal with high levels of entrenchment or more complicated changes.

### B Contract

As previously mentioned, whilst outside of the strict remit of company law, the company and its members (or the members to the exclusion of the company) may govern their

---

[60] See s. 173 of the Companies Act 2006; Chapter 8 below.
[61] On the other hand, the courts have adopted a very commercially aware approach to this particular duty and if there is a good commercial reason for the directors having fettered their discretion, then this will negate the suggestion that they have broken their fiduciary duty; see *Fulham* v *Cabra Estates Ltd*, discussed in Chapter 8 below.
[62] [1987] BCLC 585.
[63] It is not clear whether it did actually amount to a shareholders' agreement; but, for the sake of example, it might just as well have done.

relationship by way of contract, by entering into a shareholders' agreement. In many business situations this is all that will be required. If a shareholders' agreement governs the matter and change is required, then the agreement itself is often likely to provide a mechanism for effecting the change in question. If the shareholders' agreement makes no provision, change can be effected in accordance with traditional contractual principles, namely by getting all parties to agree to the amendment.

However, contract has its limitations. The most significant being that the agreement of all the parties is needed for change[64] and in a business context unanimity is often an elusive quality. For this reason, as we will see, one of the salient features of company law is collective decision making by the majority. As such, the Companies Act 2006 allows the majority of shareholders to alter the corporation constitution and that alteration will be binding on any minority who disagree.

## C  Alteration of articles

The position as regards alteration of the articles of association is relatively straightforward. Section 21 (1) of the Companies Act 2006 clearly stipulates that:

> A company may amend its articles by special resolution.

The use of the special resolution[65] mechanism enables the majority of shareholders to bind a minority who disapprove of the changes. That said, the requirement of a special resolution provides a distinctly higher level of protection to the minority than if an ordinary resolution[66] had been required. In this way, the legislature seeks to provide a balance between the practical necessity of majority rule and the need for minority shareholder protection. However, the courts have decided that more protection for the minority is required and have claimed a carefully prescribed jurisdiction to review a constitutional alteration. In *Allen v Gold Reefs of West Africa*,[67] Lindley MR held that the power of alteration must be exercised 'bona fide for the benefit of the company as a whole'.[68] The 'company as a whole' in this context is not a reference to the fictional entity but is usually regarded as meaning 'the members'.[69]

---

[64] Absent a shareholder agreement authorising something like majority voting.

[65] A special resolution is one which has been passed by a majority of not less than 75% of such members as (being entitled to do so) vote in person or the persons who vote on the resolution as duly appointed proxies of members entitled to vote on it or, where proxies are allowed by proxy, at a general meeting of which not less than 21 days' notice, specifying the intention to propose the resolution as a special resolution, has been duly given: see the Companies Act 2006, s. 283.

[66] An ordinary resolution is one which is passed by a simple majority of those members who are present and voting at the meeting either in person or by proxy. The ordinary resolution is best thought of as the basic or residual resolution for it can be used in all circumstances unless the legislation or the constitution of the company provides that some other resolution should be used; see Chapter 7 below.

[67] The case also makes it clear that the s. 21 power to alter the articles is a statutory power and cannot be taken away by any provision in the company's constitution. However, although the company cannot be precluded from altering its articles, it may nevertheless find that the alteration causes it to be in breach of contract with some other party. There are many cases involving directors' service contracts; see e.g. *Southern Foundries v Shirlaw* [1940] AC 701, HL.

[68] [1900] 1 Ch 656 at p. 671.

[69] In *Greenhalgh v Arderne Cinemas Ltd* [1950] 2 All ER 1120, Lord Evershed MR took the view that it means 'the corporators as a general body': *ibid.* at p. 1126. In some circumstances it may include the interests of creditors; see Chapter 3, 3.4.

The application of this deceptively simple test has given rise to a divergence of approach. In some cases the approach has been to hold that the term 'bona fide' imports a subjective requirement into the conduct required, so that it is sufficient if the members honestly believe that it is for the benefit of the company as a whole. On this approach, it would not matter if an objective bystander would not have agreed with their view of the situation. Thus the judges have been unwilling to substitute their own views as to what is desirable in place of the views of those actually involved with the company. The policy often appears in cases in other areas of company law. It is felt that it is all too easy to second guess decisions with the benefit of hindsight and in most cases the judges are aware that they would lack the specialist knowledge of that area of commerce which the company was involved in. There are a number of cases which develop this idea but a clear statement of the policy is contained in *Rights and Issues Investment Trust Ltd v Stylo Shoes Ltd*.[70] Here, the court was asked to set aside a resolution for the alteration of articles, where the alteration increased the voting rights of one class of shares, called the 'management shares', with the aim of preserving the voting power held by the directors in circumstances where their power would otherwise have been watered down by new share capital that was being issued. The judge, Pennycuick J, upheld the alteration:

> What has happened is that the members of the company . . . have come to the conclusion that it is for the benefit of this company that the present basis of control should continue to subsist, notwithstanding that the management shares will henceforward represent a smaller proportion of the issued capital than heretofore. That, it seems to me, is a decision on a matter of business policy to which they could properly come and it does not seem to me a matter in which the court can interfere.[71]

In spite of this 'subjective' approach, in other cases the courts found themselves drawn into the question of whether the alteration was in fact for the benefit of the members as a whole. Clearly the alteration is sometimes obviously not for the benefit of some of the members and the courts have had to perform a sort of balancing act, weighing the advantage to the majority against the disadvantage to the minority and perhaps reaching the conclusion that sometimes a group of members can be sacrificed to the greater good of the company as a whole. Thus in *Sidebottom v Kershaw Leese Ltd*[72] the Court of Appeal allowed an alteration of articles under which any member of the company who competed with it was liable to have his shares compulsorily purchased by the directors. This was so even though some of the members were thus liable to have their shares expropriated under the new article.[73]

In considering this test, Scrutton LJ in *Shuttleworth v Cox Bros & Co. (Maidenhead) Ltd*[74] was clear; Allen did not impose a two-stage test as had been suggested in earlier cases (such as *Dafen*).[75] That is, it did not require a consideration of bona fides and then,

---

[70] [1965] 1 Ch 250.
[71] *Ibid.* at pp. 255–256.
[72] [1920] 1 Ch 154.
[73] The balance is a difficult one and other decisions, on similar matters, went the other way; see *Dafen Tinplate Co. Ltd v Llanelly Steel Co. Ltd* [1920] 2 Ch 124; *Brown v British Abrasive Wheel Ltd* [1919] 1 Ch 290.
[74] [1927] 2 KB 9 (CA).
[75] *Dafen Tinplate Co. Ltd v Llanelly Steel Co. Ltd* [1920] 2 Ch 124.

as a separate matter, the 'benefit of the company'. Rather, the 'test is whether the alteration of the articles was in the opinion of the shareholders for the benefit of the company.'[76] Further, that:

> . . . when persons, honestly endeavouring to decide what will be for the benefit of the company and to act accordingly, decide upon a particular course then provided there are grounds on which reasonable men could come to the same decision, it does not matter whether the court would or would not come to the same decision or a different decision. It is not the business of the Court to manage the affairs of the company.[77]

In practical terms, the difference of approach may not be significant, for the simple reason that if a shareholder or group of shareholders wished to attack an alteration of articles they would most likely do so by bringing a petition under s. 994 of the Companies Act 2006, alleging that the alteration was unfairly prejudicial to their interests. In hearing the petition, the court would no doubt pay some regard to the reasoning in the earlier case law but it would not be likely to sidestep the issue by saying that it was a matter of subjective honesty for the shareholders. Honesty, if present, might well be a factor to be taken into account, but so too would the issue of whether there was prejudice to the petitioner's interests and, if so, whether it was, in all the circumstances, *unfair* prejudice; this would involve a balancing act of the sort which the courts have become very familiar with in unfair prejudice cases.

## D Entrenchment provisions in the articles

In contrast to the members' ability to alter the articles of association, historically, the Companies Act 1985 did not provide an overall method for the alteration of the memorandum of association. As such, as a means of making it difficult to alter a constitutional provision (that would typically be included in the articles), companies adopted a practice of inserting it in the memorandum instead. As a result, when it came to varying class rights, for example, the particular procedure that had to be followed depended upon whether the right was contained in the articles or the memorandum. The law was therefore overlaid with complex statutory procedures. As one particular means to simplify the law (and reflecting the reduced role of the memorandum), s. 22 of the 2006 Act now provides for the possibility of articles of association to contain a so-called 'provision for entrenchment.' As we have seen, while a company can generally amend its articles by special resolution under s. 21, an entrenched provision will be subject to more restrictive conditions or procedures than is normally the case with a special resolution.[78] For example, a company may decide to set a higher majority than the 75% required by s. 21 to alter the articles or impose longer notice periods for a meeting to consider such a proposal.

Where a company's articles on formation contain a provision for entrenchment, or are amended so as to include such provision, or are altered by order of the court or other authority so as to restrict or exclude the power of the company to amend its articles, notice

---

[76] [1927] 2 KB 9 (CA), 18.
[77] *Ibid*. [23].
[78] Section 22 (1).

must be given by the company to the Registrar.[79] Conversely, where the articles are amended so as to remove a provision for entrenchment, or by order of the court or other authority such provision or any other restriction on, or exclusion of, the power of the company to alter its articles is removed, the company must also give notice to the Registrar.[80] Where a company's articles contain a provision for entrenchment, or the company is subject to an order which restricts or excludes its power to amend the articles, and the company nevertheless resolves to amend its articles, it will be required to deliver a statement of compliance to the Registrar,[81] together with any documents making or evidencing the amendment.[82]

## E Variation of class rights

### 1 *Meaning of variation of class rights*

Section 21 sets out the statutory mechanisms for the alteration of the company's articles. It is clear that the Act contains checks and balances designed to produce a workable compromise between the need to protect the bargain reached with existing shareholders and the desire to facilitate a constitution that is flexible and can respond to business imperatives. However, there is a further layer of protection for certain types of rights known as shareholders' class rights (defined below).

A company does not have to issue a single 'class' of share. That is, it may issue a variety of shares with different rights attached (such as ordinary shares or preference shares). In this regard, shares are 'of one class if the rights attached to them are in all respects uniform.'[83] If it is sought to alter or vary or remove a right attached to a class of shares, known as a 'class right', then the legislature has produced a further procedure to be complied with: Companies Act 2006, ss. 630–634. Broadly speaking, this will involve the need for the consent of 75% of that class of shareholders at a separate class meeting.[84] Effectively, shareholders of a particular class, having bargained for special rights, are the only ones able to alter or remove those rights and the alteration provisions in the Act mean that any proposals for reform are subject to special scrutiny by the class. These class rights protections can also have the effect of increasing the commercial bargaining power of the class as often the class can block a proposal if more than 25% of them disapprove. As a result, the directors proposing an amendment will have to make sure at the outset that the class is being offered a fair deal.[85] Otherwise, the changes proposed will fail to take effect and the whole exercise will have been a waste of time and money.

There is no statutory definition of a class right. It is usually understood as referring to the special rights that are attached to a particular class of shares. For example, a preference share will fairly typically have attached to it the right to a fixed cumulative preference

---

[79] Section 23 (1).
[80] Section 23 (2).
[81] Section 24 (2).
[82] Section 24 (2) (b).
[83] Section 629 (1).
[84] For the detail and alternatives, see below.
[85] *Re British & Commonwealth Holdings plc* [1992] BCC 58 is an interesting example of this kind of commercial perspective. It is dealt with below.

dividend while the company remains a going concern and a prior right to a return of capital on a winding up. These rights are class rights. However, in 1987 the court arguably widened the concept of a class right in a way that leaves the boundaries vague, whilst illustrating the potential power that class rights can give to even a single shareholder.

*Cumbrian Newspapers Ltd* v *Cumberland & Westmoreland Printing Ltd*[86] concerned a private company (the defendant) that had entered into an agreement with the claimant company under which a number of ordinary shares, amounting to just over 10% of the total share capital, were issued to the claimant. Additionally, and pursuant to the agreement, the articles of the defendant company were altered so as to include various provisions that would enable the claimant to frustrate any attempted takeover of the defendant company. Under these altered articles, the claimant was granted: (1) pre-emption rights over the ordinary shares; (2) various rights in respect of unissued shares; and (3) the right to appoint a director, although this last-mentioned right was subject to the proviso that the claimant retained not less than 10% of the issued ordinary shares. Some years later the board of directors of the defendant wanted to cancel these special rights of the claimant by convening a meeting and getting a special resolution passed altering the articles so as to remove the rights. The claimant sought an injunction to prevent the meeting from being held. It also sought a declaration that its rights under the articles were class rights within s. 630. If they were class rights this would mean that, in the circumstances, they could not be varied or abrogated without the claimant's consent (and the claimant would not be giving consent). The action was successful. It was held that although the claimant's rights were not rights annexed to particular shares in the way that, for instance, preference dividend rights would be clearly annexed to preference shares, they were nevertheless conferred on the claimant in its capacity as a member of the defendant company, and dependent upon it holding a particular number of shares. The court held that these rights were within the wording of s. 630 (1) which provides: 'This section is concerned with the variation of rights attached to a class of shares in a company having a share capital' on the basis that:

> . . . [I]f specific rights are given to certain members in their capacity as members or shareholders, then those members become a class. The shares those members hold for the time being, and without which they would not be members of the class, would represent . . . a 'class of shares' for the purposes of section 125 [now s. 630 of the 2006 Act] . . . [and] . . . the share capital of a company is . . . divided into shares of different classes, if shareholders qua shareholders, enjoy different rights.[87]

On the facts of the case, it resulted in the claimant effectively having a veto over the proposal to alter the articles, a result which is a graphic example of the dynamic effect that these technical constitutional subtleties can have on the relative rights of the shareholders in a company.

The legislation, whilst it gives no help on the definition of 'class right', does make a small contribution as regards the meaning of the term 'variation'. Section 630 (6) provides:

> In this section, and (except where the context otherwise requires) in any provision in a company's articles for the variation of the rights attached to a class of shares, references to the variation of those rights include references to their abrogation.

---

[86] [1987] Ch 1. As regards the parties, the above facts are somewhat simplified.
[87] *Ibid.* at p. 22, *per* Scott J.

This is clear enough. However, the judicial contribution here is less helpful. Some years ago, the courts developed the doctrine that an 'indirect' variation of rights would not amount to a variation of rights within the statute. The leading exponent of this approach is *Greenhalgh* v *Arderne Cinemas Ltd.*[88] The background to the litigation here was that some years earlier the company had been in financial difficulties and Greenhalgh had invested a significant amount of money to put it back on its feet. In return, arrangements were put in hand to give him voting control of the company.[89] Almost immediately the other shareholders set in chain a series of technical manoeuvres aimed at wresting this control from him. Starting in 1941 he waged a 10-year battle against them. It ultimately involved Greenhalgh bringing seven actions, taking five of them to the Court of Appeal and the proceedings in this case occurred about halfway through the struggle. By this stage, there were two types of shares in the company, 2 shilling shares (10p) and 10 shilling (50p) shares. Greenhalgh held most of the 2 shilling shares. The other shareholders had enough votes to pass an ordinary (simple majority) resolution but they ideally wanted[90] to be able to pass a special (75%) resolution, so that they would be in a position to alter the articles of association and further reduce Greenhalgh's position.[91]

The prevailing legislation, the Companies Act 1929,[92] contained a power exercisable by ordinary resolution whereby shares of, say, £1 nominal value could be subdivided into multiple shares of a smaller amount. There is a sound technical reason for having such a facility,[93] but it was not relevant here. Here, that facility was misused to destroy the constitutional protection that the scheme of the Companies Act was supposed to give to Greenhalgh. The other shareholder faction passed an ordinary resolution subdividing each of their 10 shilling shares into five shares, of 2 shillings each, giving them five times as many votes as they had had.[94] As a result, they were then in a position to pass the special resolution and alter the articles. Greenhalgh argued that this amounted to a variation of his class rights[95] that needed the approval of a class meeting.[96] The Court of

---

[88] [1946] 1 All ER 512, CA.

[89] See [1945] 2 All ER 719 at pp. 720–722, Vaisey J.

[90] Presumably; in view of what subsequently happened in *Greenhalgh* v *Arderne Cinemas Ltd* [1950] 2 All ER 1120.

[91] Lord Greene spoke of his shareholding as 'his safeguard against the passing of special resolutions or extraordinary resolutions which might be contrary to his wishes': [1946] 1 All ER 512 at p. 514. They did eventually pass a special resolution, to satisfactory effect; see *Greenhalgh* v *Arderne Cinemas Ltd* [1950] 2 All ER 1120.

[92] The provision was s. 50 (combined with art. 37 of the prevailing Table A).

[93] See Chapter 13 below.

[94] 'It was that remaining measure of control which was attacked and sought to be destroyed by the next manoeuvre, which was the passing of the resolution now in question under which the issued 10s shares were split, with the consequence that the holders of each of those shares had acquired five times as many votes as they originally had': [1946] 1 All ER 512 at p. 514, *per* Lord Greene MR.

[95] The Court of Appeal assumed, without holding, that the 2 shilling shares were a separate class: [1946] 1 All ER 512 at p. 515. Vaisey J at first instance ([1945] 2 All ER 719) adopted a similar approach although he seemed a little more persuaded, referring to *Re United Provident Assurance Co. Ltd* [1910] 2 Ch 477 which had, surely, settled the point.

[96] As stated earlier, the current provision is s. 630 of the Companies Act 2006; in *Greenhalgh*'s case it was a provision in the articles of association.

Appeal held that his rights had not been varied, they were just the same; the enjoyment of them had been affected, but not the rights themselves. Lord Greene spelled out the results of the reasoning:

> Instead of Greenhalgh finding himself in a position of control, he finds himself in a position where the control has gone, and to that extent the rights of the . . . 2 s[hilling] shareholders are affected, as a matter of business.[97]

But nevertheless, he held: 'As a matter of law . . . they remain as they always were – a right to have one vote per share.'[98]

The decision is a challenging one. Voting rights are only a relative concept; no one votes on their own, if they are the only voter in the constituency. The concept only has human meaning when a person is set against others who vote, and then the votes are added to see who wins. If the votes of one side are quintupled, that must vary the rights of the other side. The court conceded that as a matter of business this *was* true, but as a matter of law it was untrue. The reasoning is technical, legalistic and the factual result both in the instant case and in the ten-year saga generally was profoundly unfair.

Even if the case is binding authority on the technical point that an indirect variation of rights is not a variation of rights that could trigger a class meeting,[99] a person in Greenhalgh's position today would be unlikely to be adversely affected by it. Again, such a shareholder would likely bring a petition under s. 994, alleging unfair prejudice. The appearance in 1980 of the unfair prejudice remedy soon spawned a series of cases[100] ending attempts to water down control and voting rights[101] and it is highly unlikely that the subdivision manoeuvre perpetrated on Greenhalgh would survive a petition under s. 994 of the Companies Act 2006.[102]

---

[97] [1946] 1 All ER 512 at p. 518.

[98] *Ibid.* at p. 518. As Lord Greene had earlier observed ' . . . these things are of a technical nature; . . . ': *ibid.* at p. 516.

[99] It cannot be written off lightly; it is a Court of Appeal authority, and the doctrine was given some support in the later Court of Appeal decisions in *White v Bristol Aeroplane Co.* [1953] Ch 65 and *Re John Smith's Tadcaster Brewery* [1953] Ch 308.

[100] *Re Cumana Ltd* [1986] BCLC 430; *Re DR Chemicals Ltd* (1989) 5 BCC 39; *Re Kenyon Swansea Ltd* (1987) 3 BCC 259; *Re a Company 007623/84* (1986) 2 BCC 99,191; *Re a Company 002612/84* (1984) 1 BCC 99,262; *Re a Company 005134/86* [1989] BCLC 383. Also, obviously, s. 561 of the 2006 Act (introduced in 1980) will sometimes be relevant in these kinds of cases; see e.g. the discussion in *Re DR Chemicals* (above) at p. 51.

[101] Even before the appearance of the unfair prejudice remedy, Foster J in *Clemens v Clemens* [1976] 2 All ER 268 was prepared to recognise the element of negative control possessed by a 45% shareholder (in that she could block a special resolution) and an issue of shares to people who would vote with the 55% holder was set aside.

[102] The Court of Appeal decisions in *White v Bristol Aeroplane Co.* [1953] Ch 65 and *Re John Smith's Tadcaster Brewery* [1953] Ch 308 (capitalisation issue of bonus ordinary shares is not a variation of rights of preference shares), although having some similarities with *Greenhalgh*, are also distinguishable in some respects; e.g. they lack the improper motive present in *Greenhalgh*, the long course of unfairly prejudicial conduct, and the liability to watering by bonus issue could be seen as part of the generally understood commercial relationship between preference and ordinary shares. It is not altogether clear that these cases would not be followed at the present day. On the problems in this area generally, see further B. Reynolds 'Shareholders Class Rights: A New Approach' [1996] JBL 554.

## 2 *Variation procedure*

The procedure for the variation of class rights is set out in s. 630 of the Companies Act 2006.[103] It is simpler and more straightforward than its 1985 Act predecessor (contained in s. 125), not least because provision is no longer required for class rights being contained in a company's memorandum of association. In essence, s. 630 provides that rights attached to a class of shares may only be varied:[104]

(a) in accordance with the relevant provisions in the company's articles; or
(b) if no such provision is made in the articles, if the holders of three-quarters in value of the shares of that class consent either in writing or by special resolution passed at a separate meeting of the holders of such shares.[105]

The company must notify the Registrar of any variation of class rights within one month from the date on which the variation is made.[106]

Sections 630 (2)(a) and (3) permit the company's articles to specify either less or more demanding requirements for a variation of class rights than the default provisions laid down in s. 630 (4). In effect, this has two consequences. First, if and to the extent that the company has adopted a more restrictive regime in its articles for the variation of class rights, for example by requiring a higher percentage than the statutory minimum, the company must comply with that requirement. Secondly, if and to the extent that the company has protected class rights by making provision for the entrenchment of those rights in its articles,[107] that protection cannot be avoided by varying the rights under s. 630.

Section 633 gives the holders of not less than 15 per cent of the issued shares of the class in question, the right to apply to the court to have the variation cancelled. The application must be made within 21 days after the date on which the consent was given or the resolution was passed.[108] If such an application is made, the variation has no effect unless and until it is confirmed by the court.[109] The court may disallow or confirm the variation depending on whether it is satisfied, having regard to all the circumstances of the case, that the variation would not unfairly prejudice the shareholders of the class in question.[110] The decision of the court in this regard is final.[111]

## F Compromises and arrangements under s. 895

### 1 *Rationale*

A variety of procedures for altering the constitution of a company have been examined. It will have become apparent that given the balance between entrenchment and flexibility

---

[103] See s. 630 (1).
[104] Section 631 sets out the procedure for varying class rights for companies without a share capital.
[105] See s. 630 (4).
[106] Section 637.
[107] See s. 22 at 4.4D, above.
[108] Section 633 (4).
[109] Section 633 (3).
[110] Section 633 (5). In view of this, it is difficult to see whether the section adds anything to the right of any member to petition under s. 994. It is, however, possible that the effect of s. 633 (5) is to restrict the ability of a class member to rely on s. 994 since the 15% threshold will be meaningless otherwise.
[111] Section 633 (5).

that there are, in the mechanisms looked at above, situations where the entrenchment principle wins. In other words, there are various methods of entrenching rights in such a way that it becomes practically very difficult to alter them.

To deal with such situations, the legislature in partnership with the courts has developed a procedure that balances a significant power to cut through such entrenchment and bind a minority, with important levels of protection for those whose rights are being varied. The current regulatory framework for such a scheme of arrangement is contained in Part 26 of the Companies Act 2006. Section 895 and its accompanying case law sets up both a process of scrutiny by the members of the class being affected, and a process of scrutiny by an outsider to the transaction, namely the court. As will be seen, s. 895 will not always result in the proposals going ahead, and, as will also be seen, the uses of the procedure range well beyond the examples mentioned above. There are many commercial applications.

Section 895 states that the relevant provisions of the Act apply where a compromise or arrangement is proposed between a company and (a) its creditors, or any class of them, or (b) its members, or any class of them. Section 895 (2) provides that the term 'arrangement' includes 'a reorganisation of the company's share capital by the consolidation of shares of different classes or by the division of shares into shares of different classes, or by both of those methods.' The procedure commences[112] with an application to the court to order a meeting (or meetings) of the various classes of members and creditors.[113] If 'three-fourths in value' of the creditors or members present and voting in person or by proxy at the meetings agree to the compromise or arrangement, then, if sanctioned by the court, it will be binding on all of them.[114] It should also be mentioned that the section is not wholly without limit and it has been held that the statutory use of the words 'compromise or arrangement' require that each party should be receiving some benefit under the scheme. If this is not the case, there will be no jurisdiction to sanction the scheme.

> The word 'compromise' implies some element of accommodation on each side. It is not apt to describe total surrender. A claimant who abandons his claim is not compromising it. Similarly, I think that the word 'arrangement' in this section implies some element of give and take. Confiscation is not my idea of an arrangement.[115]

This goes beyond the nominal consideration required in the law of contract, for the loss of the contingent obligation to contribute 5 pence in the liquidation of a company limited by guarantee was held to be *de minimis*.[116]

## 2 *The meetings*

The company (i.e. the board)[117] will be proposing the scheme and it will be its responsibility to decide how the meetings are to be structured. A difficulty that the company will

---

[112] Various other procedural requirements are also contained in the Companies Act 2006, Parts 26–27.
[113] Companies Act 2006, s. 896 (1).
[114] *Ibid.* s. 899 (1).
[115] *Re NFU Development Trust Ltd* [1971] 1 WLR 1548 at p. 1555, *per* Brightman J. The case is explored in further detail below.
[116] [1971] 1 WLR 1548 at p. 1554.
[117] Or liquidator or administrator in some circumstances.

sometimes face is that some of the persons it has selected to go into a particular class are thereby put in a position where there will be a conflict of interest. The meetings must only contain 'those persons whose rights are not so dissimilar as to make it impossible for them to consult together with a view to their common interest'.[118] If this point is not dealt with properly, then, when at a later stage the court is asked to sanction the scheme, it will find that it cannot do so. This is well illustrated by *Re United Provident Assurance Company Ltd*,[119] where after the meetings, the company applied to the court for it to approve the scheme. It was held that the holders of fully paid shares formed a different class from the holders of partly paid shares and that there should have been separate meetings of the classes. Swinfen Eady J held: 'In these circumstance, the objection that there have not been proper class meetings is fatal, and I cannot sanction the scheme.'[120]

If the problem is spotted early enough it is possible to get the guidance of the court.[121] An interesting variation on this problem occurred in *Re British & Commonwealth Holdings plc*,[122] where a scheme of arrangement was being proposed. The holders of subordinated debt knew that they no longer had any financial interest in the company because it was clear that even the unsubordinated creditors were not going to be paid in full. Nevertheless, they were threatening to ruin the s. 895 scheme by voting against it in the meetings, and in doing so were trying to use their right to vote as a bargaining chip to get something out of the scheme of arrangement. The court held that they could be excluded from the meetings.

### 3 *Review by the court*

The court will check that the statutory procedure has been complied with, that the meetings were properly convened and held, and that they were free from conflicts of interest which could vitiate the consent given. In addition to checking these kinds of technical matters, the court has a discretion to take a view as to whether to sanction the scheme or not. The test applied is whether it was an arrangement which 'an intelligent and honest man, considering the interests of the class of which he forms part, might reasonably approve'.[123]

A good example of the court actually refusing to sanction a scheme occurred in *Re NFU Development Trust Ltd*.[124] The company was a company limited by guarantee which had the object of assisting farmers who were involved in fatstock farming and to encourage farming generally. It had about 94,000 farmer members. A scheme of arrangement was proposed for the purpose of reducing administrative expenses. It entailed the farmers losing their membership. Instead, the company would have only seven members some of whom would be nominees of councils of farmers' unions. At the meeting directed by the court 1,439 votes

---

[118] *Sovereign Life Assurance* v *Dodd* [1892] 2 QB 573 at p. 583, *per* Bowen LJ.
[119] [1910] 2 Ch 477.
[120] *Ibid.* p. 481.
[121] And it is possible that the tenor of the judgment of Chadwick LJ in *Re Hawk Insurance Ltd* [2001] 2 BCLC 480 will bring about a change of approach so that the court when ordering the meetings actually also directs its mind to the question of whether they are the right meetings.
[122] [1992] BCC 58.
[123] *Re Dorman Long & Company Ltd* [1934] Ch 635 at p. 657, *per* Maugham J. In *Scottish Lion Insurance Co. Ltd* v *(First) Goodrich Corp* [2010] BCC 650, a decision of the Inner House of the Court of Session, Lord Hamilton, the Lord President, stressed, at [36], that there is no entitlement to the sanction of a scheme.
[124] [1972] 1 WLR 1548.

were cast, seven in person and the remainder by proxy. Of those, 1,211 were in favour of the scheme and 228 against, making a majority in favour of the scheme of nearly 85%. At the hearing of the petition to sanction the scheme five persons appeared to oppose the petition.

Brightman J refused to sanction the scheme and produced two alternative reasons for his decision. The first has been discussed above, namely that the lack of give and take in the scheme meant that it did not fall within the statutory words 'compromise or arrangement' and that accordingly there was no jurisdiction to sanction the scheme.[125] His second and alternative reason was that the scheme was unreasonable in that it was not an arrangement which an intelligent and honest man, considering the interests of the class of which he forms part, might reasonably approve:

> Although, therefore, this scheme has been devised in the sincere belief that it could properly be recommended by the board of directors to members for their approval, I do not think that, even if I considered that I had jurisdiction, I would have been justified in sanctioning it.[126]

It is possible that there was, at the back of the judge's mind, a third reason; namely that there had not been fair representation of the members at the meeting. Fewer than 1,500 of the 94,000 had bothered to vote, and it is possible that he took the view that the meeting had not been an adequate safeguard.

The *NFU* case can perhaps be seen as the high point of judicial scrutiny in this field. But cases where the courts have actually gone as far as to turn down a scheme are rare. The schemes are normally carefully prepared by expert practitioners and they are intended to go smoothly through the various gates of the procedure. Most of the shareholders involved will, these days, be institutional investors and quite capable of looking after their own interests or seeking professional advice.

A passage in the judgment of Harman J in *Re MB Ltd*[127] shows these matters being taken into account and their consequential effect on the level of scrutiny which the court brings to bear. The case concerned an international merger which was going through under s. 895:

> Petitions for approval of schemes of arrangement, even when as complicated, international and substantial as this, are usually matters where the court can sanction the scheme without more than a careful check that all the correct steps have been taken. Although the court must be satisfied that 'the proposal is such that an intelligent and honest man . . . might reasonably approve . . .' yet the underlying commercial purposes need not be investigated by the court since if the persons with whom the scheme is made have been accurately and adequately informed by the explanatory statement and any additional circulars and the requisite majority has approved the scheme, the court will not be concerned with the commercial reasons for approval.

## 4 *Uses of s. 895*

To a large extent, the strength of s. 895 lies in its power to bind the dissenting minority. It is often well-nigh impossible in a commercial situation to get the agreement of all the parties to a dispute or proposal. The section enables that difficulty to be overcome, subject to the various safeguards.

---

[125] See also, *Re La Seda de Barcelona SA* [2011] 1 BCLC 555, Proudman J.
[126] *Ibid.* at p. 1555.
[127] [1989] BCC 684 at p. 686.

The applications of s. 895 are many and various.[128] It was commented at the beginning of this section that the entrenchment provisions of the articles can make it difficult or impossible to alter clauses in the constitution of the company. In those kinds of situation, s. 895 can provide a solution.[129] So, for instance, under the pre-existing law it had been used to alter class rights which were contained in the memorandum.[130] It has been used to reach a compromise between shareholders in dispute about the extent of their class rights as a result of inadequate drafting.[131] The section is quite often used to carry out a takeover; the *MB* case mentioned above was an example of that. It has been held that it is not available for a hostile takeover since the wording of s. 895 (1) envisages that it is the company itself (i.e. its board of directors) that will set the process going and convene the meetings.[132] Some types of takeover find s. 895 particularly appropriate because in some circumstances the powers of s. 900 become available, under which the court can make orders for the transfer of property and liabilities.[133] Section 895 is sometimes used to help a company, in liquidation or otherwise, to reach a compromise with its creditors. A case in 1987 shows it being used another way by liquidators. *Re Exchange Securities Ltd*[134] concerned a large number of commercially interrelated companies which had received money from people to invest in commodities. All the companies were in liquidation and faced terribly complex claims on an intercompany basis. It was going to take years of litigation to sort it out. The liquidator proposed a scheme under s. 895 which involved pooling all the assets and then letting all the outside claimants share in the assets in various percentages to be agreed by them.

## G Other methods of reconstruction

The Insolvency Act 1986 contains other methods of reconstruction which will sometimes be of use. These are reconstruction by voluntary liquidation and by company voluntary arrangements (CVA). Only the former of these will be dealt with here. The CVA is considered later in Part VI of this text, 'Insolvency and liquidation'.

Sections 110–111 of the Insolvency Act 1986 contain a fairly simple reconstruction mechanism not involving any application to the court. The mechanics of it involve a sale in a voluntary liquidation of the business and undertaking of one company to another in return for shares in that other which are then distributed to the shareholders of the company being wound up. Because it involves liquidation,[135] a special resolution is required to operate the mechanism. Dissenters have a right under s. 111 to require the liquidator either to abstain from carrying the resolution into effect or to purchase their shares.

---

[128] See, for example, *Re Uniq plc* [2011] EWHC 749 (Ch), discussed in Chapter 15, below.

[129] But not always; the section is not a panacea. If e.g. the problem stems from the fact that the class which would need to give consent is owned by one person who is implacably opposed to the proposal, then s. 895 will not help. For instance, it would not have helped in *Cumbrian Newspapers Ltd* v *Cumberland & Westmoreland Printing Ltd* [1987] Ch 1 discussed above.

[130] *City Property Trust Ltd, Petitioners* 1951 SLT 371.

[131] *Mercantile Investment and General Trust Co.* v *River Plate Trust Co.* [1894] 1 Ch 578.

[132] See *Re Savoy Hotels Ltd* [1981] 3 All ER 646.

[133] In some circumstances a conflict has arisen between ss. 974–979 and s. 895. Under the former a 10% minority who have refused to take up a takeover offer can be bought out by the bidder. This, although irksome, may be a lot better for them than simply being part of a losing 25% minority in a s. 895 application. If the minority in a takeover would face a disadvantage as a result of s. 895 being used, then the courts have decided that s. 895 is not available and the s. 979 procedure must be used instead: see *Re Hellenic and General Trust* [1976] 1 WLR 123.

[134] [1987] BCLC 425.

[135] See further Chapter 22 below.

It is a mistake to view this procedure as of equal significance with s. 895 of the Companies Act 2006. It is not. Even at a theoretical level its uses are very limited and in practice it has other limitations. In the past it was sometimes used to get around a potential *ultra vires* problem. If the company found that its objects clause did not permit some new activity that it was planning to do, and that the statutory power to alter the memorandum was not extensive enough to produce a solution, then one solution might be to use the s. 110 procedure[136] to roll the business of the old company into a newly formed company. These days this will not be necessary since the Companies Act 1989 created a more extensive power to alter the objects.[137] However, this is now largely academic in the light of s. 31 of the 2006 Act.[138] Another use that has become out of date was to use the mechanisms to vary the class rights of shareholders where the articles of association contained no clause permitting the variation of class rights. Since 1980[139] there has been a statutory procedure for the variation of class rights and thus if the articles lack it, reliance on a reconstruction by voluntary arrangement would not be necessary. There is a further, more general point here, and that is that the s. 110 procedure is often not much practical use for dealing with a situation where there is likely to be any significant dissent, for the simple reason that the liquidator may find that the scheme cannot be carried out without purchasing the shares of the dissenters. This may well be expensive and possibly will neutralise the commercial advantage of what is being proposed. In many situations it will be easier and cheaper to destroy the opposition by using a s. 895 scheme of arrangement.

## Further reading

Lord Wedderburn 'Shareholders' Rights and the Rule in *Foss* v *Harbottle*' [1957] *CLJ* 194 and [1958] *CLJ* 93.

G. Goldberg 'The Enforcement of Outsider-Rights under s. 20 (1) of the Companies Act 1948' (1972) 35 *MLR* 362.

R. Drury 'The Relative Nature of a Shareholder's Right to Enforce the Company Contract' [1986] *CLJ* 219.

R. Gregory 'The Section 20 Contract' (1981) 44 *MLR* 526.

P. Finn 'Shareholder Agreements' (1978) 6 *ABL Rev* 97.

B. Reynolds 'Shareholders Class Rights: A New Approach' [1996] *JBL* 554.

---

[136] Or similar provisions in the articles in the days when there was no statutory power.
[137] Companies Act 1985, s. 4, as inserted by the Companies Act 1989, s. 110 (2).
[138] See 4.2, above.
[139] Now Companies Act 2006, s. 630.

# 5

# Organisation of functions and corporate powers

## 5.1 Introduction

This chapter explores another important area of law that largely flows from a company's constitution. That is, the effect that the constitution has on the organisation of the functions of the key constituents within the company. This chapter first considers the impact that the company's constitution has on the fundamental relationship between the directors and shareholders. Thereafter, it will be seen that the constitution has an effect on the powers of the company and, to some extent, the powers of its officers and agents.

## 5.2 The institutions of the company: the board and the shareholders

English company law facilitates the functioning of companies that have within them two distinct institutions, namely, the board of directors and the shareholders acting in general meeting (or equivalent).[1] These institutions are often referred to by analogy with the human body as the organs of the company. That is, whilst the board and the general meeting each have their own internal rules governing how they function each forms an integral part of the composite whole of the corporation, without which, that whole cannot function.

As has been seen, in small closely-held companies this distinction does not have much practical significance. In these companies the shareholders will often also be the directors and so the two organs, while they exist in law, in practice are wholly overlapping. However, in larger companies, there will be many shareholders only a few of whom will be on the board of directors. In such a situation there is a separation of ownership and control, a phenomenon which has major implications for corporate governance and has been the subject of much theoretical writing.[2] Each of the organs is capable of making decisions which can in some circumstances be regarded as decisions of the company. However, most companies incorporated under the Companies Act 1985 adopted art. 70 of Table A,[3] which allocates the powers of the company between the board of directors and the shareholders in general meeting in such a way that clearly

---

[1] Unlike, e.g. Germany and the Netherlands, Anglo-American companies are wedded to the idea of the unitary board of directors. See Chapter 3 above.
[2] See Chapter 3, 3.3 above and Part III below.
[3] Or an earlier version of it.

makes the board of directors the primary decision-making organ of the company.[4] Article 70 reads as follows:

> Subject to the provisions of the Act, the memorandum and the articles *and to any directions given by special resolution,*[5] the business of the company shall be managed by the directors who may exercise all the powers of the company.[6]

Similarly, the model articles for private companies and for public companies state that:[7]

3. Subject to the articles, the directors are responsible for the management of the company's business, for which purpose they may exercise all the powers of the company.

4. (1) The shareholders/members may, by special resolution, direct the directors to take, or refrain from taking, specified action  . . .

Where the board is deadlocked or for some other reason cannot act, or there are no directors for the time being, case law has established that the powers of the board revert to the shareholders in general meeting.[8] It will be recalled that there was no obligation for a company to adopt Table A, just as there is no obligation to adopt the model articles of association. As such, it is possible for companies to specify some other structure for the exercise of managerial power, such as providing that 'the business of the company shall be managed by a committee consisting of all the shareholders'. In this kind of situation, the shareholders may nevertheless find that the legislation regards them as directors for certain purposes. Section 250 (1) of the Companies Act 2006 provides that 'In the Companies Act "director" includes any person occupying the position of director, by whatever name called' and so the shareholders on their management committee may find that they are subject to the duties that apply to directors.[9]

Both article 70 of Table A and article 4 of the model articles make it clear that the general meeting can give directions to the directors by special resolution. This is a considerable improvement on art. 80 of Table A in the 1948 Act[10] which left it very unclear as to how and to what extent the general meeting could interfere with decisions of the board.[11] Thus art. 70 and the new art. 4 give a residual (or reserve) power to the general meeting to interfere with board decisions by special resolution. It may seem incongruous that it

---

[4] The special case of litigation is dealt with in Chapter 11 where, it will be seen, it is possible that the general meeting and the board share a right to use the company's name in litigation.

[5] Emphasis added.

[6] Article 70 continues: 'No alteration of the memorandum or articles and no such direction shall invalidate any prior act of the directors which would have been valid if that alteration had not been made or that direction had not been given. The powers given by this regulation shall not be limited by any special power given to the directors by the articles and a meeting of directors at which a quorum is present may exercise all powers exercisable by directors.'

[7] The Companies (Model Articles) Regulations 2008 (SI 2008, No. 3229), which came into force on 1 October 2009.

[8] See *Barron* v *Potter* [1914] 1 Ch 895; *Foster* v *Foster* [1916] 1 Ch 532.

[9] See e.g. Chapters 8 and 9 below.

[10] And other even earlier versions.

[11] The case law and academic writings on these earlier versions would still be relevant in respect of companies which have not adopted art. 70 or art. 3 of the model articles for private companies and public companies; see generally G. Goldberg 'Article 80 of Table A of the Companies Act 1948' (1970) 33 MLR 177, G. Sullivan 'The Relationship Between the Board of Directors and the General Meeting in Limited Companies' (1977) 93 LQR 569 and *Breckland Group Ltd* v *London & Suffolk Properties Ltd* (1988) 4 BCC 542.

takes a special (75%) resolution to interfere with a single management decision whereas, as will be seen in Chapter 8, under s. 168 (1) of the 2006 Act only an ordinary resolution (more than 50%) is required for the removal of directors. However, it reveals an unstated policy in the legislation that the normal model of a company under the Companies Act 2006 (and its 1985 predecessor) is one where the management are left free to manage subject to the right of removal.[12]

## 5.3 The *ultra vires* doctrine

### A Introduction

The effects of the company's constitution on the relationship between the directors and the shareholders have been noted. Equally significant, however, is the effect that it has on the *powers* of the company and on the powers of its agents. The first of these matters has given rise to the *ultra vires* doctrine which has bedevilled company law for over a century and continues to do so despite various efforts of the legislature, beginning with the European Communities Act 1972, to ameliorate it. Although the Companies Act 2006 has done much to reduce the impact of the doctrine still further, it has not completely disappeared. The doctrine of *ultra vires* and some of its more obvious ramifications were set out reasonably clearly in the House of Lords case of *Ashbury Railway Carriage and Iron Company* v *Riche*.[13] The company had been carrying on business making railway wagons, carriages, signals and other items for use on railways but had not actually been involved in the construction of the railways themselves in the sense of making cuttings, building tunnels and bridges. The directors decided to expand into this activity and caused the company to purchase a railway concession entitling it to build a railway. The company contracted with the defendant Mr Riche (and, at the time, his brother with whom he was in partnership but who had passed away by the time of the hearing) for him to build a railway and he set about performance under the contract and received some payment. After the work commenced the shareholders became concerned as to the directors' conduct regarding the railway (and other matters). Nevertheless, given the importance of the work, they resolved to settle this dispute with the board so that the work could continue. Notwithstanding this, difficulties about payment to Messrs Riche continued and the company ultimately repudiated its contract with Riche, who then sued for damages. The company claimed the contract was *ultra vires* and therefore void. Thus, the principle at stake was of extraordinary significance; could a company point to an aspect of its constitution and use it to escape liability on a contract with a third party? If something had gone wrong within the company, did company law in some way shift the risk of this on to an outside commercial party? If the directors were acting outside the constitution, who would suffer, the shareholders or a commercial creditor?

The objects clause, which had to be included in the memorandum of association before the reforms introduced by the Companies Act 2006,[14] included the words 'to carry on the

---

[12] In reality the point is not as clear cut as this, since there are often pressures on the shareholders which would discourage them from using s. 168, such as the company having to pay damages to the dismissed directors for breach of their service contracts; see further Chapter 8, below.

[13] (1875) LR 7 HL 653. On the contractual capacity of companies generally, see A. Griffiths *Contracting with Companies* (Oxford: Hart Publishing, 2005).

[14] See further Chapter 4 above.

business of mechanical engineers and general contractors'. The House of Lords held that the contract was beyond the powers of the company (*ultra vires*) and void. They did not think that the words 'mechanical engineers' were apt to cover the activity in question and the expression 'general contractors' should be construed *ejusdem generis*[15] with 'mechanical engineers'. Thus, Riche lost his action for damages for breach of contract. The obvious unfairness of this could be partly mitigated on the basis that because the memorandum was a public document, on file in the Companies Registry, Riche had constructive notice of it.[16] Before contracting, he might thus be expected to inspect the memorandum and also understand the full significance which the objects clause would have for the proposed transaction. The risk of not doing this was on him.

The House of Lords made it clear that the policy behind the *ultra vires* doctrine was to protect shareholders. They had invested money in the company on the basis that it would be applied for certain purposes set out in the objects clause of the memorandum. If the directors applied it for other purposes the *ultra vires* doctrine operated to ensure that the shareholders would not be prejudiced, since those acts would be void.[17] Such protection is of course bought at the expense[18] of third parties who dealt with the company. Third parties effectively have a choice of expending resources on researching whether the proposed contract is within the powers of the company, or conserving those resources and running the risk that the company may resile from the contract with impunity.

## B Reforming the rule: a historical overview

### 1 Background

Despite this policy of shareholder protection, the doctrine was not popular with incorporators, who often felt that it might unduly restrict the future activities of the company. To mitigate the impact of the doctrine it became common practice to insert a very long list of objects into the objects clause of the memorandum, thereby increasing the authorised capacity (or powers) of the company. The effectiveness of this was damaged by the development of a doctrine known as the 'main objects rule' under which the courts would decide that, as a matter of construction, one object in the list was in fact the main object.[19] This meant that unless the main object was being pursued, the trading would be *ultra vires*.[20] However, by 1918 it had been decided that since the main objects rule was no more than a canon of construction, it would yield to an expressed contrary intention, so that a

---

[15] The *ejusdem generis* rule of construction broadly requires that when general words appear at the end of a phrase their meaning is limited by the context in which they appear.
[16] The constructive notice doctrine was enunciated in *Ernest* v *Nicholls* (1857) 6 HLC 407. It is now effectively abolished by s. 40 of the Companies Act 2006, discussed below.
[17] There is possibly also a less policy based and more technical reason for the existence of the *ultra vires* doctrine, along the lines that the creation of the company by the Registrar of Companies is an act of delegated legislation and the corporation which is created by the Registrar's issue of the certificate of incorporation only exists in law to the extent of the purposes set out in the objects clause of the memorandum.
[18] It was also held that an *ultra vires* act was non-ratifiable, on the basis that ratification by the principal of an act done by an agent acting beyond his authority is not appropriate if the act was not one that the principal himself could do. On ratification, see further Chapters 6 and 11.
[19] See *Re German Date Coffee Company* (1882) 20 Ch D 169.
[20] This might also have the effect that the company could be wound up for 'failure of substratum' as was the situation in the *German Date* case.

clause which stated that each object was a separate and independent object and was not ancillary to any other object, would be effective to preclude a court from adopting the main objects rule when construing a memorandum.[21] Between 1918 and 1972 there were several other decisions which helped, by degrees, to diminish the effect of the doctrine.[22] The year 1972 saw the legislature's first attempt to restrict the doctrine and in 1989 a more comprehensive package of reforms was enacted. Before these are examined, it is necessary to introduce some complications, for the above account is a straightforward but somewhat superficial analysis of the rise and fall of the doctrine, and does not take account of the problems underlying some of the basic ideas of the doctrine.

## 2 Underlying complications – objects and powers

The difficulties stem from a distinction between objects and powers, which appears in many of the cases, the broad idea being that a company might have, say, an object to run an airline, but would then need powers to perform all the acts necessary to bring this about, such as power to hold land, to buy, lease and sell aircraft etc. Lawyers drafting an objects clause would commonly insert a list of powers, although the exact status of these could not have been clear, since the then legislation merely required a statement of the objects of the company.[23] Nevertheless, the common law also developed a doctrine of implied powers whereunder a company, in the absence of appropriate express powers in the memorandum, would be deemed to have implied power to carry out any act which was reasonably incidental to its objects.[24] So, for instance, a trading company would have implied power to borrow money for the purposes of its business.[25] This seems reasonably straightforward, but it, in fact, leads into the quagmire that lay at the heart of the concepts which make up the *ultra vires* doctrine.

*Re Introductions Ltd*[26] is a good example of one type of approach to the problem of objects and powers. The company had been formed to provide facilities for the 1951 Festival of Britain. It seems to have become dormant at a later stage of its life, but later still, carried on a pig breeding venture. Debentures had been issued to a bank which had lent money to the company. The bank had been sent a copy of the memorandum and, additionally, was aware that the money was to be used for pig breeding. The company went into insolvent liquidation and the liquidator had rejected the bank's claim on the basis that the borrowing was *ultra vires*. The argument was successful. The Court of Appeal held that since the pig breeding was *ultra vires* then the borrowing for pig breeding was similarly *ultra vires*. This was so, even though the objects clause of the memorandum of association contained an express power to borrow money. A power could not stand on its own, it was necessarily ancillary to an object. Thus, express powers need to be 'read down' by reference to the objects.

---

[21] See *Cotman* v *Brougham* [1918] AC 514.
[22] See *Bell Houses* v *City Wall Properties Ltd* [1966] 2 QB 656; *Re New Finance and Mortgage Company Ltd* [1975] 1 All ER 684; *Newstead* v *Frost* [1980] 1 All ER 373 discussed by B. Pettet in (1981) 97 LQR 15. Also noteworthy is *Re Horsley & Weight* [1982] Ch 442; this is discussed further below.
[23] See the Companies Act 1985, s. 2 (1) (c). As was seen in Chapter 4, s. 31 (1) of the 2006 now provides that unless the company's articles specifically restrict the company's objects, its objects are unrestricted.
[24] *Attorney General* v *Great Eastern Railway* (1880) 5 App Cas 473.
[25] *General Auction Estate* v *Smith* [1891] 3 Ch 432.
[26] [1970] Ch 199.

The case raises some interesting points that are perhaps best illustrated by asking, and attempting to answer, three questions:

(1) Would the result have been different if the bank had not been sent a copy of the memorandum of association, in other words, if it had not had actual notice of the memorandum? The answer here is 'no', for the simple reason that it would anyway have constructive notice under the constructive notice doctrine referred to above.[27]

(2) Would the result have been different if the bank had not had knowledge of the purpose of the loan? There is strong case law authority for the view that the answer here is 'yes'. In *Re Introductions,* the Court of Appeal made it clear that it was significant that the bank had knowledge of the purpose of the loan. Earlier cases had proceeded on a similar basis.[28] The idea is that the exercise of a power to borrow is equivocal; the third party sees[29] the objects clause (Festival of Britain) and is aware of the existence of the power to borrow. Without more, he is not aware of any impropriety. Only when he knows that the loan is being used for an improper purpose (pigs) should the *ultra vires* nature of the transaction (and hence its impropriety) become clear to him.

(3) If *ultra vires* transactions are void, then why, in the situation discussed in question 2 above, should it be relevant that the third party has knowledge of the purpose? In other words, if the doctrine provides that there is no corporate capacity to perform the act, then how does the company suddenly acquire capacity simply by virtue of the fact that the third party has no knowledge of the improper purpose? It is difficult to find an answer to this in the case law. It is probable that in order to protect a third party who is innocent, the courts have allowed an illogicality to creep into the *ultra vires* doctrine.

A later case, *Rolled Steel Products Ltd v British Steel Corporation,*[30] provides a very different (but also somewhat difficult) analysis of the problems posed by the distinction between objects and powers. Here, the claimant company (Rolled Steel Products Ltd) had in its memorandum express power to give guarantees. It gave a guarantee of another company's debt (Scottish Steel Sheet Ltd ('SSS Ltd')) to a third company (Colvilles Ltd ('C Ltd')). In return for the guarantee the claimant received a loan from C Ltd to enable it to pay off the claimant company's existing debt to SSS Ltd. The liability under the guarantee was greater than the debt owed by it and so there was a partly gratuitous element in the giving of the guarantee. In other words, to some extent at least, the guarantee was not being given for a proper commercial purpose. Later, the claimant company ran into financial difficulties and to help alleviate its position it brought an action for a declaration that the guarantee was unenforceable. At first instance Vinelott J held that not all the objects in the memorandum were independent objects and the object concerning the giving of guarantees was merely a power, which was ancillary to the objects of the company. Therefore, if the transaction was for a purpose not authorised by the memorandum it could be *ultra vires* even though it was within the scope of the express powers. Although a third party who did not know of the *ultra vires* purpose would, following *Re Introductions,*

---

[27] Again, it is worth mentioning that this aspect of the analysis has been altered by statute, but this was not operative at the time the case was decided. See below.
[28] *Re David Payne & Co. Ltd* [1904] 2 Ch 608 and *Re Jon Beauforte (London) Ltd* [1953] 2 Ch 131.
[29] Or gets constructive notice.
[30] [1986] Ch 246.

nevertheless be able to enforce it, here, the third party, C Ltd, was aware that the guarantee was partly gratuitous and not for the benefit of the claimant company. As such, it was unenforceable.

An appeal to the Court of Appeal failed, with the result that the guarantee remained unenforceable. However, the reasons that the court gave differed substantially from the analysis adopted at first instance. This approach avoids some of the evident illogicality of the *Re Introductions* analysis but, as will be seen, raises questions of its own. In essence, the Court of Appeal held that where the objects clause of the memorandum contains an express power to carry out an act, then the company has *vires* (power) to do that act. In other words, express[31] powers are not read down or limited by reference to the objects or purposes of the company.[32] As regards corporate capacity, this approach disposed of the problem in *Rolled Steel*: the company had given a guarantee, it had express power to give guarantees, therefore the guarantee was *intra vires*. However, that was not the end of the analysis. When directors purport to exercise a power, that exercise can sometimes be vitiated. For the purposes of this discussion, there are broadly two ways that this can happen.

First, the exercise may be vitiated because the directors were never given such a power by the constitution of the company. In such a case, their action can be said to be an *excess* of power. This is really an aspect of the law of agency. An agent who exceeds her power and acts outside her actual authority may nevertheless bind her principal if she acts within the principal's apparent authority.[33] However, a third party who is seeking to make the company liable on the basis of apparent authority will not be able to do so where he has become aware of facts that make it clear to him that the agent has no actual authority. In this instance, there is no appearance of authority.

The second way in which a power can be vitiated is where it has actually been given to the directors, but is nevertheless exercised for a purpose which is improper. This can be described as an *abuse* of power. The point here is simply is that directors are fiduciaries and are bound to exercise their powers in good faith for the benefit of the company, and for a proper (not collateral) purpose.[34] On this analysis, where directors caused the company to enter into a transaction which did not benefit it in the sense of taking it further down the path described in the objects clause, then this would be an abuse of power. This could occur, for instance, where a power to borrow was exercised for a commercial purpose which was not in the objects clause, such as where it was for a trade not authorised by it, or was given for improper motives such as to help friends of the directors, or where it was gratuitous and given for solely charitable reasons. A third party, who has become aware of facts which make it clear to him that the action of the directors is an abuse of power, will be in the same position as any other person who deals with a fiduciary, knowing that they are acting in breach of trust.[35]

---

[31] It was suggested that the same approach could be adopted for implied powers (*ibid.*, p. 287). Thus, where the common law would, under the doctrine of implied powers, have implied a power, then such a power would not be read down by reference to the objects. This is probably correct in principle and so the power to borrow, which would be implied for a trading company at common law (*General Auction Estate* v *Smith* [1891] 3 Ch 432), would not be read down by reference to purposes expressed in the objects clause.

[32] As they were in the *Re Introductions* approach (above).

[33] On this agency concept, see further below.

[34] See the discussion of s. 171 of the Companies Act 2006 in Chapter 8.

[35] They will hold any property received on a constructive trust for the company; see below, for this result in *Rolled Steel*.

Traces of both these approaches can be found in *Rolled Steel*. The exercise of the power to give guarantees was variously described as an *excess* of power, and as an *abuse* of power.[36] This is not surprising, as it is obvious that many situations could be analysed in either way, and that both ways broadly amount to the same thing which is being looked at differently through the eyes of the Courts of Common Law, and the Courts of Chancery. However, the dominant analysis in *Rolled Steel* seems to have been based on abuse of power. Thus, the giving of the guarantee was an abuse of power. Further, the third party C Ltd was aware of the circumstances that made the giving of the guarantee an abuse of power and therefore held it on constructive trust for the company.[37]

The *Rolled Steel* approach shifts the focus of the analysis away from the problem of the capacity of the company and on to the question of whether the directors have power. In particular, whether they have exercised that power in a way that is consistent with their fiduciary obligations, chief of which in the present context is to advance the company down the path[38] laid out in the objects clause and not some other path of their own choosing. The approach has the merit that it provides a satisfactory answer to question 3 which was discussed above. The explanation is that the situation[39] is not an *ultra vires*[40] problem at all; there is an express power in the constitution and so the company has capacity and if the directors have abused their power, the third party will not be adversely affected by that unless he is aware of the impropriety.

As well as adopting its new approach, the Court of Appeal in *Rolled Steel* made a valiant effort to 're-explain' the older cases, particularly *Re Introductions*, in such a way as to bring them into line with the new approach. The suggestion that the judicial analysis in *Re Introductions* is the same as the new approach in *Rolled Steel* is unconvincing, with the result that under the doctrine in *Young v Bristol Aeroplane Co. Ltd*[41] a later court is free to choose between the two conflicting approaches of the Court of Appeal: on the one hand, the approach in *Re Introductions*[42] and on the other, the analysis in *Rolled Steel*. Subsequent cases have failed to establish any clear preference. The decision of Hoffmann J (as he then was) in *Aveling Barford v Perion*[43] arguably has traces of the *Re Introductions* analysis. In *Halifax Building Society v Meridian Housing Association*,[44] a decision of Arden J (as she then was) contained a clear endorsement and useful example of the *Rolled Steel* approach. Meridian had entered into an agreement to develop a site, consisting of offices and flats.

---

[36] [1986] Ch 246 at pp. 281, 286, 297.

[37] This presumably neutralised it, on the basis that the guarantee, a chose in action, was held on trust for the person it gave an action against. However, a cloud hangs over this analysis, in view of the approach taken by the House of Lords in *Criterion Properties plc v Stratford UK Properties LLC* [2004] BCC 570, and it is likely that in future cases involving an executory contract between two parties, the analysis will focus on agency concepts rather than fiduciary concepts.

[38] Or at any rate, if no 'path' is evident from the objects clause, to observe the limits on the activities of the company, set out there.

[39] Envisaged in question 2 and referred to in question 3, above.

[40] The term '*ultra vires*' is used in this text to denote the situation where the activity is outside the scope of the objects clause (taken together with any implied powers) and hence beyond the capacity of the *company*. It is quite obvious that since the term means (literally) 'beyond the powers', it could also be used to describe the situation where the directors have acted beyond their powers. But to use it in that way is thoroughly confusing in the present context.

[41] [1944] KB 718.

[42] And with it, *Re David Payne & Co. Ltd* [1904] 2 Ch 608 (also Court of Appeal).

[43] (1989) 5 BCC 677.

[44] [1994] 2 BCLC 540.

Meridian was now in receivership and the question had arisen of whether it was within Meridian's capacity to develop the site, for office purposes. The objects clause of Meridian included the following: '2. To carry on the industry business or trade of providing housing or any associated amenities. 3. [Meridian] shall have power to do all things necessary or expedient for the fulfilment of its objects.'

The matter focused on whether the development of the offices *could* ever be performed as reasonably incidental to the pursuit of the objects set out in clause 2. It was held that it clearly could, since it would have been incidental to provide an estate office in connection with residential development. Whether this would have been an improper exercise of power was irrelevant to the question of whether it was within the capacity of Meridian.

It is now necessary to take a closer look at some of the not-so-obvious effects of the *Rolled Steel* approach. The main point really is that the approach had the (probably unintended) effect of abolishing the *ultra vires* doctrine in most situations. It had been common practice for over a century for companies to put a long list of powers into the objects clause, in addition to the long list of objects or purposes. Thus, the objects clause would normally contain, for example, power to borrow, power to give guarantees, power to make contracts, power to hold land etc. Even if certain powers are not present, we have already seen that the common law has a doctrine of implied powers[45] and it seems that *Rolled Steel* applies to implied powers as well as express powers. The effect of the existence of these powers is that in virtually any problem which looks like a classic example of *ultra vires* (lack of corporate capacity) the mere existence of the power will be sufficient to give the company capacity.

The point can be reiterated by looking again at *Ashbury Railway Carriage and Iron Company* v *Riche*.[46] There, it was held that the building of the railway was *ultra vires*, because it was not covered by the phrase in the objects clause 'to carry on the business of mechanical engineers and general contractors'. A *Rolled Steel* analysis of the case would go as follows: the objects clause contained express power, to 'make contracts . . .' or although the objects clause contained no express power for the company to 'enter into contracts . . .'; nevertheless since this was a trading company it would clearly need power 'to enter into contracts' and so such a power would be implied.[47] Having been expressly included or implied, it would not be 'read down' by reference to the objects[48] and so, as a matter of corporate capacity, the situation poses no problems; the contract is *intra vires*. Nevertheless, the directors were abusing their powers in that they were causing the company to enter into a contract knowing that it was outside the scope of the purposes expressed in the objects clause. They were therefore in breach of fiduciary duty.[49] Riche, the third party, was aware of the circumstances which showed that they were in breach of duty, namely, he was aware of the nature of the contract and had actual or constructive notice of the objects clause and therefore he held the benefit of the contract on constructive trust[50] for the company.

---

[45] See further above.

[46] (1875) LR 7 HL 653, see above.

[47] In accordance with the doctrine of implied powers. An objection might be that a power as general as this would never be implied. But, on the other hand, a general 'power to borrow' would normally be implied for a trading company (see *Anglo Overseas Agencies* v *Green* [1961] 1 QB) and objects clauses frequently contain such wide powers.

[48] As *Re Introductions* would require, see above.

[49] See s. 171 of the Companies Act 2006, discussed in Chapter 8.

[50] Or alternatively, following the approach of the House of Lords in *Criterion* (see n. 37 above), the directors had no actual or apparent authority to bind the company.

As will be seen, the 1989 legislative reforms produced a situation similar to that pertaining at common law under the *Rolled Steel* approach. However, the drafting of the Companies Act 1989 did not fully take account of the effects produced by *Rolled Steel*.

## 3 *Shareholder intervention*

Before looking at the 1989 statutory reforms (and, finally, the effect of the Companies Act 2006) on all this, one more aspect of the case law needs to be mentioned. It is clear from a number of cases[51] that a shareholder of a company has a right to seek an injunction to restrain a company and/or its directors from entering into an *ultra vires* act. This has been a well-recognised exception to the principle of *Foss* v *Harbottle*[52] which normally suppresses litigation by shareholders. This aspect of the *ultra vires* doctrine is sometimes referred to as the 'internal' aspect of the doctrine since the action of the directors is restrained before any outside party has become involved and the issue is fought out between the directors and some of the shareholders.

## 4 *The 1989 reforms – background matters and problems*

The Companies Act 1989 contained a package of provisions which were designed to restrict the *ultra vires* doctrine in various ways. To some extent they were intended to implement the First Company Law Directive, which had required the *ultra vires* doctrine to be removed, as against outsiders dealing with the company. The 1989 provisions replaced an earlier attempt contained in the European Communities Act 1972,[53] which had been felt to be deficient. The 1989 provisions present problems, not least because they are overlaid on what Parliament imagined was the common law of *ultra vires*.

Probably the least difficulty is presented by what was s. 4 of the Companies Act 1985.[54] This provided that a company may by special resolution alter the objects clause in its memorandum. The previous provision was limited to certain grounds which seriously impinged on the ability of companies to make much use of it. Less happy was s. 3A of the Companies Act 1985.[55] It was probably intended to reverse the longstanding corporate practice of putting lengthy lists of powers and purposes into the objects clause. But there is a problem with it. Section 3A provided:

> Where the company's memorandum states that the object of the company is to carry on business as a general commercial company –
>
> (a)  the object of the company is to carry on any trade or business whatsoever, and
> (b)  the company has power to do all such things as are incidental or conducive to the carrying on of any trade or business by it.

[51] Examples are *Hutton* v *West Cork Railway Company* (1883) 23 Ch D 654; *Parke* v *Daily News* [1962] Ch 927. To some extent these cases were overturned by statute: see Companies Act 1985, s. 719, now s. 247 of the 2006 Act.
[52] See further Chapter 11 below.
[53] Section 9 (1). This section became s. 35 in the consolidating Companies Act 1985, until its repeal and replacement by new provisions in 1989. It is important to note therefore that between 1972 and 1989 there was a different statutory regime in force which made certain amendments to the common law.
[54] Substituted by Companies Act 1989, s. 110 (2).
[55] Inserted by Companies Act 1989, s. 110 (1).

Paragraph (a) was clearly effective in giving the company discretion to engage in a very wide range of commercial activities. However, it is not possible to say that para. (a) gave the company unlimited objects. For instance, could it have carried on a *profession*, as an incorporated accountancy firm? Maybe this would be a 'business'. Would para. (a) have given the company non-commercial objects, such as to make gratuitous gifts of a charitable or educational or political nature? Probably not; this point is taken up in the next paragraph.

Paragraph (b) raised a problem.[56] Companies often wish to make political or charitable gifts, or make payments which are gratuitous, such as a gift of a pension to a director who is not legally entitled to any pension.[57] The case law shows that arguments that these things are incidental (or conducive or ancillary) to its trade and for its benefit are difficult to maintain (although not impossible).[58] A considerable breakthrough came in 1982 when it was decided by the Court of Appeal in *Re Horsley & Weight*[59] that the objects clause could make it clear that non-commercial purposes (such as charitable or educational purposes) were to be regarded as independent objects of the company sitting alongside its commercial purposes. This had the result that there was no need to show that the pursuit of these non-commercial objects was incidental or conducive to the commercial objects. A company which utilised s. 3A with its para. (b) will have found that its power to make non-commercial payments was considerably more limited than if it had drafted its own objects clause, picking up on the points contained in *Re Horsley & Weight*.

One last point remains. The Companies Act 1989 contained a provision which purported to abolish the constructive notice doctrine; not merely in the context of *ultra vires* and related areas, but generally, for all areas of company law.[60] But it was never brought into force. Section 142 of the 1989 Act would have amended the Companies Act 1985 by inserting a s. 711A. This would have provided:

(1) A person shall not be taken to have notice of any matter merely because of its being disclosed in any document kept by the registrar of companies (and thus available for inspection) or made available by the company for inspection.

(2) This does not affect the question whether a person is affected by notice of any matter by reason of a failure to make such inquiries as ought reasonably to be made.

The drafting of this is unfortunate, because the open-ended provision in subs. (2) cut across the intention of subs. (1), leaving it quite unclear as to when the protection of subs. (1) would be available. Not surprisingly, this was not brought into force.

## C Core provisions of the 2006 reforms: a company's capacity and related matters

As we have seen, drafting techniques had developed to significantly increase the scope of a company's objects and correspondingly reduce the practical impact of the *ultra vires*

---

[56] Although some of that difficulty stems from the limitations of s. 3A (a) of the 1985 Act.

[57] The making of political donations is now subject to procedures contained in the Companies Act 2006, ss. 362–373.

[58] *Re Lee Behrens & Co. Ltd* [1932] 2 Ch 46; *Re W & M Roith* [1967] 1 WLR 432. But, see *Evans* v *Brunner Mond* [1921] 1 Ch 359 where the gift was held to be of sufficient benefit to the company.

[59] [1982] Ch 442.

[60] Although it has little significance in most areas.

doctrine. This, together with the potentially unfair consequences of the doctrine for third parties, meant that it was not surprising that part of the reforms introduced by the Companies Act 2006 stipulated that a company is no longer required to state its objects in a separate clause contained in the constitution.[61] In this regard, s. 31 provides that unless the articles specifically restrict the objects of the company, its objects are unrestricted. Thus, the default position is that companies incorporated under the 2006 Act have unlimited objects.[62] However, this does not render the *ultra vires* doctrine completely redundant. First, a company may still choose to incorporate objects within their articles of association. Secondly, although these are deemed to be included as a provision in their articles of association, companies incorporated under earlier companies legislation will doubtless have an objects clause that will continue to limit their capacity.[63] Moreover, s. 39, which replaces ss. 35 (1) and (4) of the 1985 Act (which made similar provision for restrictions of capacity contained in the memorandum), provides that the validity of a company's acts is not to be questioned on the ground of lack of capacity because of anything in a company's constitution. It is noteworthy that s. 39 does not restate either s. 35 (2) of the 1985 Act which provided for shareholder injunctive relief, or s. 35 (3) which stated that it remains the duty of directors to observe any limitations on their powers contained in the company's memorandum.[64] The reasons for these omissions are set out in the Explanatory Notes to the 2006 Act:

> It is considered that the combination of the fact that under the [2006] Act a company may have unrestricted objects (and where it has restricted objects the directors' powers are correspondingly restricted), and the fact that a specific duty on directors to abide by the company's constitution is provided for in section 171, makes these provisions unnecessary.

It is clear that while s. 39 has removed the problem of corporate capacity, the directors are still subject to limitations on their powers. There is an obvious parallel here with the common law analysis under *Rolled Steel*, which, it will be recalled, in effect removed the problem of corporate capacity by refusing to read down corporate powers by reference to the objects, but retained the problem in a different form by treating the objects as limitations on the powers of the directors (rather than the company), so that an infringement of the limitation would be seen as either an excess or abuse of power. Broadly speaking, the effect of s. 39 is to enact the decision in *Rolled Steel*, although as shall be seen the legislation goes on to give even greater protection to third parties.

Section 40 of the Companies Act 2006 very substantially restricts the extent to which the constitution of the company can affect a third party. Section 40 (1) is a deeming

---

[61] The articles of association.

[62] See *Modern Company Law for a Competitive Economy Final Report* (London: DTI, 2001) para. 9.10.

[63] By s. 28 (1) of the Companies Act 2006 the objects clause will be treated as a provision of the company's articles.

[64] Section 35 (2) and (3) of the Companies Act 1985 provided:

> (2) A member of a company may bring proceedings to restrain the doing of an act which but for subsection (1) would be beyond the company's capacity; but no such proceedings shall lie in respect of an act to be done in fulfilment of a legal obligation arising from a previous act of the company.
>
> (3) It remains the duty of the directors to observe any limitations on their powers flowing from the company's memorandum; and action by the directors which but for subsection (1) would be beyond the company's capacity may only be ratified by the company by special resolution.
>
> A resolution ratifying such action shall not affect any liability incurred by the directors or any other person; relief from any such liability must be agreed to separately by special resolution.

provision, which provides that the power of the directors to bind the company[65] shall be deemed to be free of any limitation under the company's constitution.[66] The deeming effect is expressed to occur only 'in favour of a person dealing[67] with a company in good faith'[68] and the third party is presumed to have acted in good faith unless the contrary is proved.[69] Section 40 (2) (b) (i), replacing s. 35 B of the 1985 Act, in effect abolishes the doctrine of constructive notice in this area by making it clear that the third party 'is not bound to enquire' as to whether the transaction is permitted by the constitution or as to whether there are any limitations on the powers of the board of directors to bind the company (or authorise others to do so).

As well as making it clear that the burden is not on the third party to prove his or her good faith, the legislation deals with another problem which could easily arise at common law, namely that of the unsophisticated third party who has actually been sent the constitution and knows all the facts from which it could reasonably be deduced that the transaction is *ultra vires* or an abuse or excess of power but who actually has no inkling that there is anything wrong, indeed he has probably not thought about it at all. Although it has never really been finally settled, under the common law there was at least a likelihood that such a person would be held to be aware of the problems and thus adversely affected by the *ultra vires* or improper nature of the transaction; their subjective honesty would be irrelevant if objectively they should have realised what was going on.[70] The solution adopted is in s. 40 (2) (b) (iii), which provides a person dealing with a company:

> is not to be regarded as acting in bad faith by reason only of his knowing that an act is beyond the powers of the directors under the company's constitution.

The effect of this is to prevent a court from automatically inferring bad faith (and so depriving the third party of the protection of s. 40 (1)) merely because he has knowledge of the factual technicalities which make the act beyond the powers of the directors. It is easy to exaggerate the effect of the provision. It is clearly not intended to make the knowledge that the act is beyond the powers of the directors into an irrelevance, and it is obvious that anyone who is acting in bad faith will usually have to have such knowledge. Probably all that is really happening here is that the legislation is emphasising the need to prove

---

[65] '[O]r authorise others to do so.' These words have more significance in the context of agency and the *Turquand* rule and are discussed below, see Chapter 7. Also discussed there is s. 40 (3), which has no relevance in the *ultra vires* context.

[66] It is very important to realise that an infringement of a limitation under the constitution can give rise to an *excess* of power, or an *abuse* of power as explained above. Or, to put it the other way round, excess of power or abuse of power situations can both stem from limitations under the company's constitution and are thus capable of being cured by the deeming provision of s. 40 (1); provided of course that the conditions in s. 40 are satisfied.

[67] The word 'dealing' has the meaning given in s. 40 (2) (a): 'a person "deals with" a company if he is a party to any transaction or other act to which the company is a party.' Thus, receiving a gratuitous distribution from the company would fall within the concept of dealing, for while it arguably does not amount to a 'transaction', such a gift would certainly be an 'other act to which the company is a party'.

[68] Section 40 (1).

[69] Section 40 (2) (b) (ii).

[70] E.g., in *Re Jon Beauforte (London) Ltd* [1953] Ch 131 the luckless third party who had supplied coke to the company was expected to have realised from the letterheading that the company was engaged in an *ultra vires* activity. The uncompromising nature of the common law in this field is further revealed by the technical and unrealistic constructive notice doctrine. The imposition of constructive trust liability was similarly rigorous (see *Selangor* v *Cradock*, at least until the advent of *Royal Brunei Airlines Sdn Bhd* v *Tan* discussed below, see Chapter 15).

subjective bad faith, and so where a third party is genuinely unaware of the significance of the technicalities he will not be adversely affected by them. With this background in mind, s. 40 (2) (b) (iii) makes sense.[71]

## D Pulling it together

So how does this all fit together? A useful way of illustrating this is to turn (again) to the facts of *Re Introductions*[72] and consider how a court would decide the case now. The company, which had originally been formed to provide facilities for the Festival of Britain, was now involved in pig breeding and had borrowed from a bank. The memorandum contained an express power to borrow. The bank had actual notice of the contents of the memorandum, having been sent a copy, and was aware that the money was to be used for pig breeding. The liquidator was arguing that the company did not have to pay the bank because the loan was *ultra vires* and void. In the Court of Appeal, this argument succeeded because the express power to borrow was read down by reference to the objects.

At the present day, the argument that the loan was *ultra vires* and void would clearly fail. It would be nullified by s. 39 (1), which provides that the validity of an act done by a company shall not be called into question on the ground of lack of capacity by reason of anything in the company's constitution. Additionally, if the judge used the analysis adopted in *Rolled Steel*[73] there would be no problem of corporate capacity anyway, because of the presence in the constitution of an express power to borrow. Either way, by statute, or by the *Rolled Steel* analysis at common law, the corporate capacity problem is eliminated.[74]

But, as we have seen, s. 39 must be read in conjunction with s. 171 of the Companies Act 2006, which provides that a director must act in accordance with the company's constitution.[75] This would have been the same at common law under a *Rolled Steel* analysis, so here again, it would seem that the legislation more or less enacts *Rolled Steel*. It is clear that by causing the company to borrow money for pig breeding the directors ignored the limitations on their powers flowing from the constitution. The question would then arise of whether the third party, the bank, would be adversely affected by this. Under the present law, the answer to this will depend on whether the bank is in 'good faith' because, if it is in good faith (and s. 40 (2) (b) (ii) makes it very difficult to demonstrate bad faith), then s. 40 (1) will generate a deemed removal of the limitations on the powers of the board contained in the company's constitution. The removal from the factual matrix of the problem of the constitutional limitations effectively removes the existence of any legal principle under which the transaction could be set aside against the third party bank.

So, is the bank in good faith? Would the liquidator have been able to prove that they were in bad faith? We cannot be sure. Bad faith would be something for the trial judge to

---

[71] The approach is in line with the approach of the common law in *Royal Brunei Airlines Sdn Bhd* v *Tan*, under which a constructive trust is not to be imposed unless 'dishonesty' can be proved.
[72] [1970] Ch 199. The facts of the case are given in more detail under B 2 above.
[73] Rather than the 'reading down' approach actually adopted by the Court of Appeal in *Re Introductions*.
[74] The common law position is only mentioned at this point to show the extent to which the legislation follows the path already laid down by *Rolled Steel*. It is not being suggested that the judge has a choice; the statute prevails.
[75] See further Chapter 8.

find as a proven fact from the evidence before him or her. It is clear from s. 40 (2) (b) (iii) that merely showing that the bank knew that the loan was beyond the powers of the directors would not of itself establish bad faith.

## Further reading

G. Goldberg 'Article 80 of Table A of the Companies Act 1948' (1970) 33 *MLR* 177.

G. Sullivan 'The Relationship Between the Board of Directors and the General Meeting in Limited Companies' (1977) 93 *LQR* 569.

# 6

# Relations with third parties: agency and constitutional limitations

## 6.1 Contractual relations with third parties

It has been seen that a company is a person in law, separate from its shareholders. One aspect of the corporate entity doctrine, which has not yet been looked at in any detail, is the question of how the corporate entity enters into contractual relations with other persons (either natural or corporate) in the legal system. This is an area of law that, although potentially very simple, has become characterised over the last 150 years by oftentimes challenging judicial and academic doctrine with, until now,[1] similarly mixed success at statutory attempts at reform. Notwithstanding this historic difficulty, the underlying principles are in fact straightforward and this account will endeavour to chart a path through by starting with first principles. If these first principles are then kept in mind throughout, many of the perceived difficulties disappear.

The essential point to hold in mind is that, subject to certain statutory exceptions,[2] in English law it is not possible for a person to sue, or be sued, on a contract unless that person is a party to it. It is a rule which contract lawyers call *privity of contract* (and which everybody learns when they first start to study law).[3] That said, the common law developed an important exception to this principle, known as the *doctrine of agency*, which provides that, *inter alia*, a principal will be bound by legal obligations created by their duly authorised agent. In a corporate setting, whilst the board as a collective is granted general managerial rights (article 3 of the Model Articles of Association), the question of authority arises when determining whether an individual (either a director or otherwise) has authority to bind the company. Further confusion was then created in the context of company law from the fact that company lawyers thought that they had invented another exception, called the rule in *Royal British Bank v Turquand*,[4] when they had not.

---

[1] Section 40, Companies Act 2006 (which, if nothing else, brings certainty for contractual counterparties).
[2] Mainly now the Contracts (Rights of Third Parties) Act 1999, which gives a person who is not a party to a contract a right to enforce a contractual provision where the contract expressly provides that he or she may or where the provision purports to confer a benefit on him or her. However, this legislation does not generally affect the analysis of agency concepts in this chapter.
[3] See e.g. *Scruttons v Midland Silicones* [1962] AC 446.
[4] (1856) 6 El. & Bl. 327; sometimes also called the 'indoor management rule'.

## 6.2 Agency

In daily corporate life, it is this major exception, the doctrine of agency, which provides the vehicle through which the company carries out most commercial transactions.[5] Without it, all that is left is the insuperable theoretical problem that the company, being a fictional entity, cannot do anything on its own account. The basic idea of agency is that if the agent enters into a contract which is within the scope of the authority given to him by the principal, then the contractual rights and obligations which the agent acquires are transmitted[6] to the principal so that the principal can sue and be sued on the contract. Thus in the context of company law, the company, the principal, finds itself able to sue and be sued on contracts which are made by its agents, such as its directors. In fact, the position is not as simple as this. First, because agency law is more complicated than has been suggested above and secondly because there are difficulties inserted into the company law context by the existence of the constitution of the company and the consequent case law and legislative responses to the agency exception.

There are two types of authority that an agent can have, both of which are predicated on quite distinct ideas and each with a different rationale. The first type is called *actual* authority and the second is called *apparent* authority.[7]

An agent will possess actual authority when acting entirely within the mandate given to him by his principal. Actual authority (which can be express or implied) arises as a result of a consensual relationship between the principal and the agent. The principal has asked the agent to act on his behalf, the agent agrees, and then goes and does it. The contractual rights and obligations that the agent acquires are then transmitted to the principal in accordance with the basic principles of agency.[8] Thus, when looking at relationships of actual authority (whether express or implied) we are concerned with the relationship between the principal and agent; we are not concerned in this scenario with the third party to the contract. Normally, actual authority will be created as a result of an express agreement between the principal and the agent (hence, express actual authority). However, it is now clear that actual authority can come about as a result of a course of dealing between those parties as a result of which the court is able to infer that a contractual relationship exists between

---

[5] Some, however, are made under the company's common seal. It is possible that where the company makes the contract in writing under its common seal, the effect of s. 44 of the Companies Act 2006 (replacing s. 36 (a) of the Companies Act 1985) is that the company thereby enters into a direct privity of contract with the third party and that no agency principle is operating. Section 43 appears to be drawing a distinction between a contract being made (a) *by a company* and (b) *on behalf of a company* by any person acting under its authority.

[6] It is not necessary in this work to explore how this comes about. It can be pragmatically accepted as a long-established reality of the common law.

[7] 'Apparent authority' is the expression used in this text because it best describes the basis on which the principal is held liable. It is in use worldwide, and thus for instance is the term used in the American Restatement of Agency. Other expressions are in use denoting the same concept; of particular currency is the term 'ostensible authority' (see e.g. *Armagas* v *Mundogas* [1986] 2 All ER 385, HL). In the past, other expressions have been common, such as 'agency by estoppel', or 'estoppel authority' (useful as it describes the juridical basis of the authority), 'constructive authority' (confusing; easy to muddle with the constructive notice doctrine), 'implied authority' (very confusing; in view of the fact that modern law contains a subdivision of *actual* authority into 'express' and 'implied'). Obviously the principal will also be bound if he chooses to ratify a contract which is outside the scope of the agent's authority.

[8] Where actual authority is present, it is not necessary for the third party to be aware that he is dealing with an agent; see e.g. *Dyster* v *Randall* [1926] Ch 932.

them. In this text this is described as *implied* actual authority, as opposed to *express* actual authority. Implied actual authority commonly arises from the grant of an executive office to a director, such as Managing Director. The basic notion of implied actual authority was explained by Lord Denning MR in *Hely Hutchinson v Brayhead*.[9] Here, Lord Denning MR held that Mr Richards, the chairman of the board (a non-executive position that does not carry with it authority to execute contracts on the company's behalf), had implied actual authority to act as managing director arising from the fact that the other directors had acquiesced in his acting as chief executive over many months, although he had never been appointed formally as such. It is important to note that in *Hely Hutchinson*, implied actual authority arose as the directors' acquiescence amounted to a finding that Mr Richards was in fact de facto managing director (or chief executive).[10] It was from this executive position that implied actual authority was found to exist. The scope of an agent's actual authority (whether express or implied) is limited to the scope of the principal's actual authority. Thus, if there is a limitation on the principal's capacity then the agent's actual authority will be similarly limited.

Entirely different is apparent (or ostensible) authority. The broad essence of which is that apparent authority will exist where two conditions are satisfied: first, where it *appears* to the third party that the agent has authority to enter into the contract,[11] and secondly, that the appearance has come about through the *fault* of the principal meaning that it is fair[12] for the principal to be estopped from denying that appearance. Thus, in contrast to actual authority, here we are concerned with the relationship between the principal and third party, not the principal and agent. In the context of a principal that is a company, the question of apparent authority can be complicated by the fact that a company will be controlled and represented by various officers, and from the fact that the constitution of the company (which may make prescriptions about the authority of its officers) has traditionally been a public document that third parties have constructive notice of. Thus, the question arises (which we shall return to later) as to whether or not third parties will be bound by provisions in the constitution that impose limits on the agent's actual authority.

The existence of apparent authority was considered by Diplock LJ in *Freeman & Lockyer (a firm) v Buckhurst Park Properties (Mangal) Ltd*.[13] In this case, Mr Kapoor and Mr Horn incorporated Buckhurst Park Properties (Mangal) Ltd ('Buckhurst') to acquire and ultimately resell Buckhurst Park Estate. Both Kapoor and Hoon (together with two nominees) were appointed as directors of the company. Nevertheless, Hoon was, at all material times, out of the country and it was clearly not the intention of the parties that he would be involved in the management of the company. Rather, Kapoor, whilst never

---

[9] [1968] 1 QB 549. For a more recent exploration of these kinds of issues see *SMC Electronics Ltd v Akhter Computers Ltd* [2001] 1 BCLC 433, CA.

[10] [1968] 1 QB 549, 584.

[11] But if a third party knows or is put on enquiry, perhaps by suspicious circumstances, that the individual he is dealing with does not have the authority claimed, the transaction will not bind the company. For example, in *Hopkins v TL Dallas Group Ltd* [2005] 1 BCLC 543, the court held that the signing of an undertaking and acknowledgement of indebtedness by a deputy managing director was sufficiently abnormal to put the other party on enquiry. On the facts, the court held the letters were so abnormal as to allow the inference of actual knowledge (on the part of the other party) of the deputy managing director's breach of duty.

[12] And it would not be 'fair' if the third party had not in fact relied on the appearance.

[13] [1964] 2 QB 480.

appointed as managing director, undertook key managerial functions of the board, including contracting with Freeman & Lockyer (in Buckhurst's name) for the provision of, *inter alia*, architectural services. Freeman & Lockyer were never paid for their services to Buckhurst and the question that came before the court was whether Buckhurst was bound by the actions of Kapoor in engaging them (as Buckhurst denied that Kapoor was authorised to enter into such a contract on its behalf). In finding that Kapoor had apparent authority to bind Buckhurst, Diplock LJ observed that:[14]

> [T]he … law … can be summarised by stating four conditions which must be fulfilled to entitle a contractor to enforce against a company a contract entered into on behalf of the company by an agent who had no actual authority to do so. It must be shown: (1) that a representation that the agent had authority to enter on behalf of the company into a contract of the kind sought to be enforced was made to the contractor; (2) that such representation was made by a person or persons who had 'actual' authority to manage the business of the company either generally or in respect of those matters to which the contract relates; (3) that he (the contractor) was induced by such representation to enter into the contract, that is, that he in fact relied upon it; and (4) that under its memorandum and articles of association the company was not deprived of the capacity either to enter into a contract of the kind sought to be enforced or to delegate authority to enter into a contract of that kind to the agent.

As regards condition (1), it is clear that such representations can take many forms. They can be oral or written, or (as is often the case) they may arise, impliedly, from a state of affairs. Oftentimes the representation will not be specifically about the authority the agent has, but instead arise from the conduct of the company. For example, by allowing the agent to act in a particular way (such as signing contracts) without censure.

Condition (2) is often misunderstood. What Diplock LJ was getting at here is the point that the representation must come from the principal. An agent cannot create the appearance of authority all by himself, the appearance has to be created by acts of the principal; the principal will only be bound if he has made representations that he is then estopped from denying or, to put it another way, which it would be unfair to the third party to now let him deny. So, if the representations have come solely from the 'agent', then there is no basis for holding the principal liable.[15] In many cases, the agent will add his own representation, but it is the representation from the principal that has legal effect. But, of course, in the company law context, that is not straightforward, because the principal, the corporate entity itself, is not able to do anything because it is an inert and fictional entity. So how could it ever be bound by apparent authority? The answer is that the representation must have come from those who are in fact authorised to represent the company, who are, as Diplock LJ says, 'persons who [have] "actual" authority to manage the business of the company'.[16] In most companies, this is the board of directors acting under their general managerial power.

Condition (3) is straightforward. The doctrine of apparent authority rests on fairness. If the third party has not relied on the 'appearance' of authority, then there is no basis for

---

[14] [1964] 2 QB 480, 505.
[15] The point arose in *Armagas* v *Mundogas SA* [1986] 2 All ER 385, HL..
[16] [1964] 2 QB 480, 504–505.

invoking an estoppel against the principal.[17] Thus, at common law,[18] apparent authority can be lost on notice. As Lord Keith observed in *Armagas Ltd* v *Mundogas SA*:[19]

> Ostensible … authority can, however, never arise where the contractor knows that the agent's authority is limited so as to exclude entering into transactions of the type in question, and so cannot have relied on any contrary representation by the principal.

Condition (4) of Diplock LJ's formulation was a significant condition at the time the judgment was given. However, it is no longer of material relevance due to the reforms introduced by the Companies Act 2006.[20]

## 6.3 The *Turquand* doctrine

The impact of the constructive notice doctrine[21] on third parties was somewhat mitigated by the decision in *Royal British Bank* v *Turquand*.[22] Here, the company argued that it was not liable to repay a loan that had been made to it because the board of directors had no power to borrow. The company's argument rested on the fact that the board had not obtained the prior authorisation of the shareholders in general meeting, which was a requirement set out in the company's constitution. In rejecting this claim, the court held that the company was liable. The court acknowledged that (at the time) the third party bank was under a duty to inspect the constitution.[23] However, on finding that the directors could have power to borrow the bank could infer that the general meeting had taken place; in other words, the bank was not adversely affected by mere matters of 'indoor management'.[24]

Various cases then followed this approach,[25] so that where there was a problem involving the company's contractual liability to a third party that was complicated by the presence of clauses in the constitution, *Turquand* became a byword for a quick solution.[26] Whilst the necessity of *Turquand* has been diminished by s. 40 of the Companies Act 2006, its influence had already started to reduce prior to this. For example, as we have seen the approach of the Court of Appeal in *Freeman & Lockyer* was firmly rooted in agency. Whilst English law had, since at least the end of the eighteenth century,[27] a developed doctrine of agency *Freeman & Lockyer* was one of the first cases[28] to analyse that kind of company law problem without resort to the *Turquand* rule as a kind of *tabula in*

---

[17] In contrast to the position with actual authority.
[18] As shall be seen, s. 40 of the Companies Act 2006 (for those who fall within its remit) removes this problem of constructive notice.
[19] [1986] AC 717, 777. See also: *Rolled Steel Products (Holdings) Ltd* v *British Steel Corporation* [1996] Ch 246.
[20] Sections 39 and 40 of the Companies Act 2006.
[21] Namely, that third parties were deemed to have notice of the corporation's public documents, regardless of their actual knowledge. See *Ernest v Nicholls* (1857) 6 HL Cas 401.
[22] (1856) 6 E & B 327.
[23] The constructive notice doctrine.
[24] Although constructive notice is abolished for those seeking to rely on s. 40 of the Companies Act 2006, discussed at 6.5, below, it has not been abolished otherwise. See the Companies Act 2006, s. 1295, Sch. 16.
[25] E.g. *Mahoney* v *East Holyford Mining Company* (1875) LR 7 HL 869; *Liggett* v *Barclays Bank* [1928] 1 KB 48.
[26] It became known as the *Turquand* rule, or the 'indoor management rule'.
[27] See, for example, *Wolf* v *Horncastle* (1798) 1 Bos & P 316.
[28] Although it has to be said that the analysis of Slade J in *Rama Corporation Ltd* v *Proved Tin and General Investments Ltd* [1952] 2 QB 147 was basically an agency approach.

*naufragio*.[29] Indeed, two of the Lord Justices of Appeal[30] did not even mention it. Diplock LJ in particular clearly felt the need to try to explain the older cases and to set out some clear principles in the format that has been discussed above (this in itself is indicative of the confusion that was prevailing in the textbooks at that time).

## 6.4 The 'relationship' between *Turquand* and agency

Does the rule in *Turquand* exist? Exist, that is, in the sense that it brings to company law a principle, or set of principles, that are not simply already present by virtue of the doctrines of agency. It will indeed be argued here that there is little in the *Turquand* rule that cannot be arrived at by a careful application of the agency concept of apparent authority.[31] Further, and equally importantly, that there is nothing in the *Turquand* rule by which a non-party can become entitled to sue on a contract or liable to be sued on it.

To demonstrate this point, it is helpful to consider an example. If the articles contain a restriction that stipulates that a director can only act on a certain transaction with the authority of the shareholders in general meeting, can a third party assume that the permission has been given? Or does he have to inquire? *Turquand*'s answer to this is that whether or not permission has been given is a matter of 'indoor management' and so he need not inquire. However, it is equally arguable that the authority for that step in the argument is simply that it is part of the doctrine of apparent authority. The article is equivocal. It does not negate that appearance of authority, which is the core of the apparent authority doctrine. This is, of course, particularly the case if the board has previously acquiesced and allowed the director in question to act contrary to that restriction. Therefore, it is possible to reach a conclusion about the effect of the article on agency considerations without recourse to any separate principle of law, such as the rule in *Turquand*. The solution here thus lies with a sensible application of the apparent authority doctrine.[32]

What is clear is that the rule in *Turquand* does not provide an independent way for a company (or non-party) to be bound by a contract.[33] Rather, *Turquand* says that a third party dealing with a company is required only to take notice of its external position and

---

[29] A plank in a shipwreck (of the analysis).

[30] Diplock and Pearson LJJ.

[31] The general thrust of this argument is not new; see R. Nock 'The Irrelevance of the Rule of Indoor Management' (1966) 30 Conv (NS) at pp. 123 and 163, arguing that although the earlier cases may have treated the rule in *Turquand*'s case as a special principle of company law, the modern cases show that the rule can be explained entirely through agency concepts. Campbell adopted a similar approach but found a role for *Turquand* as a subordinate stage of an analysis based on agency, arguing that *Turquand* operated as a modification of the doctrine of constructive notice in cases where there is apparent authority; see I. Campbell 'The Contracts with Companies' (1959) 75 LQR 469; (1960) 76 LQR 115.

[32] This is also true when we consider the rule, part of the *Turquand* jurisprudence, that *Turquand* does not apply when the third party is 'put on inquiry'; see e.g. *Liggett* v *Barclays Bank* [1928] 1 KB 48. On this point, Campbell (n. 25 above, at pp. 126–127) gives the example of 'a delegation to the office boy', meaning that if the third party comes across an implausible situation, he would not be able to rely on the indoor management idea. But then, the point here surely is that there really is no appearance of authority in such a situation.

[33] It could be argued that the rule in *Turquand* is really an embryonic and incomplete statement of the application in the company context of the doctrine of agency by apparent authority. If so, then much would have to be added to the traditional statement of it. But even then, there is the problem of deciding whether it actually added anything to the widely accepted concept of agency.

need not inquire into matters of indoor management.[34] As to the relationship between *Turquand* and agency, it is apparent from the discussion above that the role of the 'indoor management' rule (to the extent that it is still required) is necessarily going to be a subordinate one; subordinate to agency, and perhaps only playing a small part in the overall constellation of legal principles which are operating here. Thus, it is possible to see that the rule in *Turquand* was an early example of one tiny facet of the doctrine of apparent authority. *Turquand* adds very little to a careful application of agency doctrine.[35] It has, however, added decades of confusion. It is now likely that company lawyers follow the lead given by Diplock LJ in *Freeman & Lockyer* and solve their problems without citing or making reference to *Turquand*.

## 6.5 Section 40 of the Companies Act 2006

The challenges with establishing individual authority are clear. Even mitigated by *Turquand*, the application of the constructive notice doctrine created uncertainty and inefficiency, as third parties were required to undertake significant due diligence or risk the validity of their contract for a want of authority. To address this concern, the Companies Act 2006 (building on previous legislative efforts) introduced section 40, which provides significant protection to third parties (the legislative history of s. 40[36] and its impact on the *ultra vires* doctrine has previously been discussed).[37] It is worth setting out the full text of the provision at this juncture:

**40 Power of directors to bind the company**

(1) In favour of a person dealing with a company in good faith, the power of the directors to bind the company, or authorise others to do so, is deemed to be free of any limitation under the company's constitution.

(2) For this purpose –
   (a) a person 'deals with' a company if he is a party to any transaction or other act to which the company is a party,
   (b) a person dealing with a company –
      (i) is not bound to enquire as to any limitation on the powers of the directors to bind the company or authorise others to do so,
      (ii) is presumed to have acted in good faith unless the contrary is proved, and
      (iii) is not to be regarded as acting in bad faith by reason only of his knowing that an act is beyond the powers of the directors under the company's constitution.

---

[34] Of note is that, much like the position with apparent authority, *Turquand* does not protect a third party that is on notice of a want of authority (beyond mere constructive notice).

[35] The decision in *Smith* v *Henniker-Major & Co.* [2002] BCC 768, CA, has no bearing on this analysis.

[36] In the account which follows attention will focus on this important provision. Mention should, however, be made of s. 161 of the Companies Act 2006 which provides that a director's acts (or those of a manager) are valid notwithstanding any defect that may afterwards be discovered in his appointment. Over the years, judges have declined to give this provision any great significance and so, e.g. in *Morris* v *Kanssen* [1946] AC 459, it was held that it did not extend to the situation where no appointment had been made at all. Thus it probably merely extends to small technical irregularities relating to appointment formalities and share qualification.

[37] See Chapter 5, 5.3C above.

(3) The references above to limitations on the directors' powers under the company's constitution include limitations deriving –
   (a) from a resolution of the company or of any class of shareholders, or
   (b) from any agreement between the members of the company or of any class of shareholders.
(4) This section does not affect any right of a member of the company to bring proceedings to restrain the doing of an action that is beyond the powers of the directors.
   But no such proceedings lie in respect of an act to be done in fulfilment of a legal obligation arising from a previous act of the company.
(5) This section does not affect any liability incurred by the directors, or any other person, by reason of the directors' exceeding their powers.
(6) This section has effect subject to –
   section 41 (transactions with directors or their associates), and
   section 42 (companies that are charities).

Obviously, in a general sense, the intended effect of the provision is to restrict the extent to which a third party can be adversely affected by limitations on authority contained in the company's constitution. For under the constructive notice doctrine,[38] a third party is deemed to have notice of those matters that are on public file, which would include the constitution of the company.[39] To some extent, therefore, the section will have the effect of suspending the operation of that doctrine, where the third party falls within the remit of the section.[40] Section 40 may, of course, also have effects which are wider than merely suspending that doctrine, but whether or not this is the case, a third party will be protected, in some situations, from having deemed notice of restrictions in the constitution.

Why is such notice thought to be a matter requiring reversal? The point is that, in some circumstances, the deemed notice will cause the third party to be unable to enforce the contract against the company. A good example of this can be found by considering a situation where the articles of association contain a restriction that the third party is indeed aware of, say, a restriction that prohibits branch managers of a car dealership from purchasing cars on behalf of the company. However, such a purchasing contract is one which branch managers in that line of business can normally enter into, but how can *T* (the third party) argue that *A* (the branch manager) has apparent authority to bind the company when this restriction makes it clear that she has no such authority? Thus it can be seen that, in some circumstances, restrictions in the constitution will have an adverse effect on a third party's ability to rely on the apparent authority doctrine. This may not produce an unfair looking result because *T* knew of the clause in the articles (but arguably sought to rely on an industry standard), but it does not look so fair if he is precluded from enforcing the contract by a technical doctrine that deems him to have notice when in fact he had no notice. This is particularly so if, as is often likely in commercial practice, *T* has not actually inspected the registered documents of the company. The unfairness inherent in the constructive notice doctrine led to the enactment of s. 40 (replacing ss. 35A (1) and 35B of the Companies Act 1985).

---

[38] See Chapter 5, 5.3 above.
[39] The articles, and also certain shareholder resolutions and agreements: s. 17. See further Chapter 4 above.
[40] Remember that the general abolition of the constructive notice doctrine was never brought into force; see further Chapter 5, 5.3B above.

To understand the breadth of s. 40 it is necessary to examine its provisions in more detail. First, to fall within the protection of the section, s. 40 (1) requires that a third party is 'a person dealing with a company'. In *Smith v Henniker-Major & Co.*[41] the court accepted that, in ordinary discourse, the term 'person' included a 'director'. Nevertheless, in the exceptional circumstances of this case the director (who was also the company chairman) could not rely on what is now s. 40 CA 2006. Notwithstanding the potential uncertainty in the common law as to the position of corporate insiders,[42] s. 40 does help to bring some clarity. Section 40 (6) expressly states that s. 40 is subject to the application of s. 41, which applies to contracts that otherwise depend on s. 40 for their validity. Section 41 (2) provides that where the counterparty to the contract is a director or their associate then the contract is voidable at the instance of the company. Note that in this instance, s 41 (3) makes clear that the director (or associate) is liable to the company to account for any gain made or indemnify the company for any loss suffered.

When is a person 'dealing with a company'? There is a definition of this in s. 40 (2) (a), to the effect that 'a person "deals with" a company if he is a party to any transaction or other act to which the company is a party'. This looks unhelpful, since the use of the word 'party' might be taken to require that the company has entered into or been involved in some kind of legal relationship with the person, and the whole difficulty here, from the person's point of view, is that unless he can show that this or another section applies to eliminate the effect of the constructive notice doctrine, then he will not, on the facts under discussion, be able to establish that the company is a party so that he can sue it. The basic problem here against which s. 40 (1) is being called in aid, is that very issue, to establish that the company is a party. So it appears that the drafting of s. 40 (1) falls at the first hurdle. The problem can perhaps be overcome if the words 'party ... to' are interpreted in an imprecise non-legal way so as to mean something like 'in some way involved in'. Indeed, this is commonly how the term has been understood but it is likely to exclude gratuitous or unilateral transfers.[43]

It is clear that s. 40, as with previous common law,[44] requires that the third party be acting in good faith to rely on its protection. Whilst this might ostensibly seem like a significant test for the third party seeking to rely on s. 40, the statue actually makes it difficult for a party to be found to be acting in bad faith.[45] First, s. 40 (2) (b) (ii) stipulates that a third party is presumed to have acted in good faith, unless the contrary is proved. Secondly, s. 40 (2) (b) (iii) goes on to say that a person will not be acting in bad faith by reason only of their knowing that an act is beyond the powers of the director in question. Thus, something more (beyond knowledge) is needed for bad faith to be established.[46]

[41] [2002] BCC 768 (CA).
[42] The unusual facts of *Smith v Henniker-Major & Co.* [2002] BCC 768 (CA) show that in circumstances where there is a narrow issue of the legality of procedure within the company (and no third party involved), then it will be difficult to rely on these sections; particularly so for insiders such as directors. As to shareholders, *EIC Services v Phipps* [2003] BCC 931 held in the first instance that shareholders could rely on this provision. This was then overruled on appeal: see [2004] BCC 814.
[43] *EIC Services v Phipps* [2004] BCC 814, [35]: 'the section contemplates a bilateral transaction between the company and the person dealing with the company or an act to which both are parties.'
[44] *EIC Services v Phipps* [2004] BCC 814, [35].
[45] The definition of good faith in s. 40 (2) (b) has been discussed in Chapter 5, 5.3C above.
[46] See *Wrexham Associated Football Club Ltd v Crucialmove Ltd* [2007] BCC 139, [44], where on the 'highly unusual' facts of the case the third party was found to have acted in bad faith. Here, the third party was a solicitor and aware of the fact that the transaction in question was potentially contrary to the interests of the AFC. As such, he was bound to enquire as to whether it had been duly authorised by the company.

Section 40 (2) (b) (i) makes it clear that a third party is not bound to inquire as to any limitation on the powers of the board to bind the company or authorise others to do so. It is not a deeming provision but operates by providing a focused[47] but indirect abolition of the common law constructive notice doctrine. The constructive notice doctrine effectively coerces a third party to 'inquire', in the sense of reading the registered documents of the company, and establishes that if he does not inquire, he will be deemed to have notice of any matters on public file at the Companies Registry. Now, a third party has a valid excuse not to inquire – the statute says he need not, and so his failure to do so can therefore no longer provide a rationale for the law to treat him as if he had inquired; in other words, there is no longer a reason to regard him as having 'constructive' notice.[48]

If a person satisfies the conditions set out in s. 40 (1), what will the section do for him? There are two possibilities envisaged by the provision. The first is that '… the power of the directors to bind the company … is deemed to be free of any limitation under the company's constitution.' The second possibility envisaged by the section is that the power of the directors to 'authorise others to' bind the company is 'deemed to be free of any limitation under the company's constitution'.

There is, however, another – and better – way of looking at this. If the construction of the words of the statute is approached from the perspective of seeing the directors as being the organ responsible for the running of the company (as in art. 70 of Table A and art. 3 of the model articles for private companies limited by shares and for public companies), and as being the organ responsible for binding the company to third parties (as is inherent in art. 70 and art. 3), then it can be seen that a different interpretation is possible.[49] Any specific limitation in the constitution on the powers of any person will in fact be a restriction on the power of the directors to authorise that person to bind the company. Thus, the statute is aiming to preserve the ability of the directors to bind the company and to preserve their discretion to grant authorisation to others in the company, such as agents operating below boardroom level. This, surely, is the better construction of the wording. In our earlier example, where the articles seek to restrict the ability of a branch manager to enter into certain transactions, this is seen as a limitation on the power of the directors to authorise others (i.e. branch managers) to bind the company. Assuming that a third party were to satisfy the various conditions for the applicability of s. 40 (1), the section would operate by deeming away the limitations on the agent's authority contained in that article. This would leave a third party able simply to rely on the agent's apparent authority and thereby enforce the contract against the principal.

It is clear that this field is still complicated and that the statutory intervention has a hit and miss quality to it. The statutory technique is to suppress various bits of the common law in certain situations, and the legislation is at times ill-conceived and not well drafted. It is probable that when faced with the need to make a decision on its meaning, the courts

---

[47] Focused in the sense that it is not a general abolition applying to all areas of company law but instead is focused on the problems arising in the areas of *ultra vires* and agency.

[48] It is worth noting that as regards limitations on the powers of the board to bind the company or authorise others to do so, the exemption from inquiry provided by s. 40 (2) is not limited to the constitution although in most situations this will make little difference.

[49] The wording of art. 9 (2) of the First Directive (68/151/EEC) is also supportive of this: 'The limits on the powers of the organs of the company, arising under the statutes or from a decision of the competent organs, may never be relied on as against third parties, even if they have been disclosed.'

will make the best of it and strive to give effect to the obvious intention of the legislation to diminish the circumstances in which the third party is adversely affected by limitations contained in the constitution.

## Further reading

R. Nock 'The Irrelevance of the Rule of Indoor Management' (1966) 30 *Conv* (NS) 123, 163.

D. Campbell 'The Contracts with Companies' (1959) 75 *LQR* 469; (1960) 76 *LQR* 115.

D. Rice 'The Power of a Director to Bind the Company' [1959] *JBL* 332.

A. Griffiths *Contracting with Companies* (Oxford: Hart Publishing, 2005).

# Part III
# Corporate governance

# 7

# The governance problem and the mechanisms of meetings

## 7.1 Alignment of managerial and shareholder interests

As has been seen,[1] corporate governance is about alignment; that is, it is about the system of legal or other mechanisms which ensure that the interests of the managers of the company are aligned with those of the shareholders.[2] The study of corporate governance is therefore concerned with the analysis of the environment in which the directors/managers operate, with a view to considering the totality of the system which is in place to ensure that managers do not pursue their own interests with the company's money, rather than those of the shareholders.

It will be recalled[3] that corporate governance systems contain mechanisms that are internal to the company and mechanisms that are external to the company. The former are the mechanisms which are put into the hands of shareholders, which give them some level of ability to control or influence the board of directors. The external mechanisms exist in the regulatory environment in which the company operates and will include the existence of state agencies for the detection of fraud or the existence of insolvency procedures as well as the market mechanisms such as the disciplining effect of the possibility of a hostile takeover. In the following chapters, the emphasis will be on consideration of the internal mechanisms of corporate governance[4] for these form an important part of basic company law and it is interesting to consider those fundamental elements of the law in the context of their efficacy as governance mechanisms.[5]

The effectiveness of the system will depend very much on what type of company is under observation. In the small closely-held company, the shareholders will also be the directors and so the problem of alignment is often not present, although if there are shareholders who are not also directors, they may well find that they do have to worry about how they can influence what the directors are doing. If, on the other hand, the 'dispersed-ownership company' is considered, the problem of who controls the managers, and how

---

[1] The theoretical aspects of corporate governance are discussed in more detail in Chapter 3, 3.4 above.

[2] The discussion of corporate governance will proceed here on the orthodox basis that the only stakeholders are the shareholders; the issues relating to widening this constituency have already been considered under the heading 'Stakeholder company law' in Chapter 3, 3.5 above.

[3] See Chapter 3, 3.4B above.

[4] For a discussion on the external mechanisms, see Chapter 3 above and for the explanation of the hostile take-over mechanism see further Chapter 21 below and see generally Chapter 13, 13.2C below (effect of going public).

[5] For an analytical perspective on our system see Lady Justice Arden DBE 'UK Corporate Governance after Enron' (2003) 3 JCLS 269.

will they do it, becomes acute. The shareholders of such companies will have relatively small stakes in it, and therefore little economic incentive to monitor the management or to interfere in what they are doing. Thus the mechanisms of corporate governance will have differing degrees of utility depending on what type of company is under consideration and this needs to be borne in mind in the account which follows.

The approach to the subject in this chapter will be to give an account of the workings of the meeting mechanisms, both in respect of the board of directors and the shareholders in general meetings. In Chapter 8 the general duties which the law imposes on directors will be considered, whilst Chapter 9 examines a range of other, more specific, constraints on the legal and practical position of directors. The input made by the self-regulatory mechanisms developed during the 1990s will be considered in Chapter 10. Chapters 11 and 12 will deal with the ways in which shareholders can bring litigation in respect of failures of corporate governance.

## 7.2 The role and functioning of the board of directors

### A Directors as managers and 'alter ego'

The legislation requires a public company to have at least two directors and a private company to have at least one director.[6] However, the articles of association may require a minimum number greater than these and/or fix a maximum. By s. 250 of the Companies Act 2006 the term 'director' is expressed to include 'any person occupying the position of director, by whatever name called' so if the directors are known by some other title, such as 'the committee of management' they will still be regarded as directors by the legislation. As a result, this will necessitate their compliance with the many statutory[7] obligations which are cast upon directors and thus it is not possible to avoid the obligations of the companies legislation by simply calling the directors something different.[8]

The normal position in a company registered under the Companies Act 1985 is that it will have adopted art. 70 of the 1985 Table A, or for companies registered under the Companies Act 2006, art. 3 of the model articles for private or public companies as the case may be.[9] Both sets of articles ensure that, *prima facie*, the directors are the managers of the business of the company.[10] In practice, it is common in larger companies for managerial power to be devolved to groups or individuals below board level, leaving the board to meet once a month or quarterly.[11]

Because of their managerial role, the directors are sometimes said to be the '*alter ego*' of a company; the word '*alter*' meaning here 'the other' (of two). There are various

---

[6] Companies Act 2006, s. 154.

[7] And in appropriate circumstances, with the obligations created by case law. See e.g. Chapter 8.

[8] On the question of whether or not an individual's conduct is such as to render him or her a de facto director notwithstanding the lack of formal appointment to the board, see *Revenue and Customs Commissioners* v *Holland* [2010] UKSC 5. See further, A. Lowry 'De Facto Directorships: Multiple Tests Prevail' (2011) 8 ICR 194. See also, *Re Mumtaz Properties Ltd* [2011] EWCA Civ 610.

[9] The Companies (Model Articles) Regulations 2008 (SI. 2008 No. 3229), which came into force on 1 October 2009.

[10] These articles are discussed in Chapter 5 above. See further, S. Watson 'The Significance of the Source of the Powers of Boards of Directors in UK Company Law' [2011] JBL 597.

[11] See art. 5 of the Companies (Model Articles) Regulations 2008.

manifestations of this in the case law. One is where the courts are looking for mind of the company. As we have seen,[12] the courts have tended to regard the ⌐ of the directors or managing director as the state of mind of the company. Si⌐ are situations where the directors are actually regarded as the company for some purpo⌐⌐ This was illustrated in *Stanfield* v *National Westminster Bank*,[13] where it was held that the proper person to answer interrogatories served on a company was the director or other similar officer:

> Interrogatories administered to a company have of course the special feature that as the company is an artificial person they must be answered not by the litigant, but by some human being who holds a position in relation to the company which enables him to give the answers, such as a director or [here] a liquidator.[14]

The doctrine is not applied rigidly and the courts will not invariably regard the director as a second defendant or second target in every situation.[15]

## B Appointment and retirement of directors

The appointment and retirement of directors is left, primarily, to the articles, although, as will be seen, the legislation does contain a few provisions that are of relevance and which will override the articles in some circumstances. Companies registered under the Companies Act 2006 typically adopt the model articles, which contain provisions in articles 17–18 for private companies and articles 20–22 for public companies.[16] The broad principle is that directors may be appointed by ordinary resolution of the shareholders or a decision of the directors.[17] Provision is also made for public companies for the appointment of an *alternate* director who is, in essence, someone who stands in for a director who is temporarily absent; but he is not an agent and is not treated as a director for all purposes.[18] Provision is made for the retirement of directors of public companies by rotation. Article 21 of the model articles for public companies similarly provides that all directors must retire from office at the first annual general meeting (AGM). Article 21 (2) goes on to provide that at every subsequent AGM any directors (a) who have been appointed by the directors since the last AGM, or (b) who were not appointed or reappointed at one of the preceding two AGMs, must retire from office and may offer themselves for reappointment by the members.

[12] See Chapter 2, 2.1C, above. See also, *Moore Stephens* v *Stone & Rolls Ltd* [2009] 2 BCLC 563, discussed in Chapter 8.
[13] [1983] 1 WLR 568.
[14] *Ibid.* at p. 570, *per* Megarry J.
[15] *Attorney General of Tuvalu* v *Philatelic Ltd* [1990] BCC 30. The matter has been discussed in Chapter 2 above in relation to the director's liability for torts in the light of the House of Lords' decisions in *Williams* v *Natural Life* [1998] BCC 428 and *Standard Chartered Bank* v *Pakistan National Shipping Corporation (No. 2)* [2003] 1 BCLC 244.
[16] Corresponding articles for companies incorporated under the Companies Act 1985 are articles 73–80 of Table A.
[17] For companies registered under the Companies Act 2006, see art. 17 of the model articles for private companies; art. 20 of the model articles for public companies. For companies registered under the Companies Act 1985, see Table A, art. 78.
[18] Any director may appoint any other director or any other person approved by resolution of the directors to be an alternate director; see model articles of association for public companies articles 25–27; Table A, articles 65–69.

The legislation has a few scattered provisions of relevance. When a company is formed, the statement of the company's first director or directors must be delivered to the Registrar of Companies.[19] Section 157 introduces a minimum age of 16 for appointment as a company director. However, an appointment can be made below the minimum age provided it does not take effect until the person attains the age of 16.[20] Section 160 provides that for public companies the appointment of directors shall be voted on individually unless a block resolution is unanimously agreed.[21] This is to prevent an unpopular or unsuitable candidate being squeezed through the general meeting by putting him into a composite resolution to elect the directors, knowing that the shareholders will probably pass the resolution because they want all the other candidates elected.

The legislative provisions for the removal and disqualification of directors impact very substantially on the extent to which the power of the directors is constrained, and for that reason these matters are dealt with below.[22]

## C Proceedings at directors' meetings

The Companies Act 2006, like its predecessor, is silent on how the directors are to conduct their meetings. However, articles 7–16 of the model articles of association for private companies and articles 7–19 of the model articles of association for public companies lay down details as to the proceedings of directors.[23] Although certain prescriptions are made (e.g. as to quorum) they are permissive in style and leave relative freedom to the board to manage the meeting process.

In the absence of express provisions to the contrary in the articles, the case law establishes a few propositions.[24] Thus, it has been held that notice of meetings must be sent to all those entitled to attend.[25] It has been emphasised that directors act collectively, as a board, and that once decisions have been reached by a majority of those present, they bind the others. This rule can sometimes have a significant effect on the opposition to a proposal, for, as was stated by Millett J in *Re Equiticorp plc*:[26] 'Once a proper resolution of the board has been passed . . . it becomes the duty of all the directors, including those who took no part in the deliberations of the board and those who voted against the resolution, to implement it . . .' As commented on above, the model articles for private companies and public companies each contain provisions covering decision making by directors. For example,

---

[19] Companies Act 2006, s. 12. See also s. 9, discussed in Chapter 2, 2.4,
[20] Section 157 (2).
[21] A resolution moved in contravention of this provision is void.
[22] See Chapter 23.
[23] See articles 88–98 and 100 of Table A.
[24] In *Sneddon v MacCallum* [2011] CSOH 59, it was emphasised by the Court of Session (Outer House) that the case law clearly establishes that where it is suggested in relation to any board meeting that the meeting was not duly held and convened, it is for the person arguing that to prove it; if it is suggested that the minutes are inaccurate in recording the proceedings at the meeting, again the onus lies on the person claiming the inaccuracy to prove it; and where any appointment was made at the meeting, the onus lies on the person disputing its validity to prove this.
[25] *Young v Ladies Club Ltd* [1920] 2 KB 523. It is probable that in the absence of any express provision in the articles, the notice need not state the business or any proposed resolutions; see *La Compagnie de Mayville* v *Whitley* [1896] 1 Ch 788, although there is a dictum to the contrary, in the *Ladies Club* case which suggests that it is necessary to convey to the director what is going to be done.
[26] (1989) 5 BCC 599 at p. 600. See also, *Minmar (929) Ltd v Khalatschi* [2011] EWHC 1159 (Ch).

both provide for collective decision making,[27] though for private companies additional provision is made for companies with one director by disapplying the general rule.

## D Remuneration of directors

The law on remuneration of directors was subjected to a thorough examination by the House of Lords in *Guinness* v *Saunders and another*,[28] a civil case which arose out of the Guinness saga. This difficult case is examined in more detail below. We will also return to the subject of remuneration in the next chapter, for it has considerable significance in the self-regulatory context. Before looking at the detail of *Guinness*, it is worth attempting to summarise the main legal propositions.

As with the previous few topics, much (although not all) depends on what is in the articles. The relatively little legislation on this topic is dealt with below.[29] Directors are fiduciaries[30] and because of this they must not profit from their relationships with the company.[31] Thus, as a *prima facie* rule, it is well established, and reiterated in *Guinness*,[32] that they are not entitled to any remuneration at all. Because of this it is normal for the articles to provide for the award of remuneration. The model articles for private and public companies limited by shares provide that directors are entitled to such remuneration as the directors determine.[33] This should be contrasted with the 1985 Table A which required shareholder approval.[34] Where remuneration is fixed without complying with the articles of association, the directors will not be entitled to any remuneration. Nor will they be able to argue that they should succeed under a *quantum meruit* for the value of their services. This too was established in *Guinness*.[35] The background to these civil proceedings was a takeover battle in which Guinness made a successful bid for the shares of a company called Distillers. Various proceedings were brought against certain officers of Guinness who had been involved with the takeover.[36] Quite early on in the investigation into the matter, it was found that W, an American lawyer who was a director of Guinness, had been paid £5.2m (0.2% of the value of the bid)[37] for acting as a business consultant for advising on the takeover. Guinness immediately brought summary proceedings to recover this sum. Summary proceedings are designed to be used only if there is no arguable defence to the claim and if, during the course of the trial, it becomes clear that there is an issue, then the proceedings will fail and the case will eventually go for trial of the issues. Guinness fought the case to the House of Lords and was in difficulties over its claim that s. 317 of the

---

[27] See art. 7 respectively.

[28] [1990] BCC 205.

[29] See Chapter 8.

[30] For this concept see further Chapter 8 below. Broadly it means that they are like trustees and will owe duties of good faith to the beneficiaries, which in the company law context means the company.

[31] See further Chapter 8 below.

[32] [1990] BCC 205 at p. 211.

[33] Art. 19 in the model articles for private companies; and art. 23 in the model articles for public companies. The exercise of this power is subject to the duty to promote the success of the company contained in s. 172. See further, Chapter 8, below.

[34] Table A, art. 82. Readers should Monitor the website of DBIS because the current government is determined to reform the process for determining directors' renumeration.

[35] See also, *UK Safety Group Ltd* v *Heane* [1998] 2 BCLC 208; and *Re Sunrise Radio Ltd* [2010] 1 BCLC 367.

[36] Leading, in one case, to a successful Human Rights challenge.

[37] Not actually a huge amount by Wall Street standards.

Companies Act 1985 enabled it to recover.[38] However, the company came up with an alternative argument along the lines that the committee of the board of directors which W claimed had agreed to his remuneration had no power under the articles of association to award special remuneration, only the full board could do this, and it had made no such award. This was successful and W was held to be a constructive trustee of the money.[39]

The discussion above refers to the situation where someone is a bare director under the Companies Act and who does not have any full-time contract of employment with the company. However, it is common for directors, especially in the larger companies, to be appointed to paid posts requiring their full-time attention.[40] But here again, their appointments must be properly authorised by the articles or they will not be entitled to any remuneration.

Even if the remuneration is given in accordance with the articles, it will not necessarily follow that all remuneration given to directors will be unimpeachable. It is clear from the decision in *Re Halt Garage Ltd*[41] that if the sums paid to the director are so out of proportion to any possible value to the company attributable to him holding office then the court will treat the payments as gratuitous distributions of capital 'dressed up as remuneration'. In such circumstances they will be recoverable. It has also been held in *Re Cumana Ltd*[42] that excessive remuneration can amount to conduct which is unfairly prejudicial.

Traditionally, legislative provisions concerning directors' remuneration sought to address the traditional agency problem (or risk) of directors favouring their own interests (including those of their fellow directors) over that of their shareholders. In common with this tradition, the Companies Act 2006 (like its predecessors) seeks to mitigate this concern through a suite of provisions that mandate shareholder approval for various aspects of a director's employment relationship with the company. Sections 215–222 of the Companies Act 2006 regulate payments made to directors in respect of loss of office or retirement in situations where conflicts of interest may arise. Section 228 provides that directors' service contracts are open to inspection. Contracts of employment with a guaranteed term (broadly defined) of two years or more (rather than five years as was the requirement under s. 319 of the Companies Act 1985) require shareholder approval pursuant to s. 188. Lastly, s. 412 requires disclosure in the annual accounts of the aggregate amount of directors' emoluments, including present and past directors' pensions and payments received for loss of office.

Against this traditional approach to regulating directors' employment, recent (and widespread) public concern as to the level of directors' remuneration and, in particular, 'rewards for failure' has resulted in increased legislative provisions regarding directors' remuneration. In particular, ss. 79–82 of the Enterprise and Regulatory Reform Act 2013 introduced a new regime for directors' remuneration for listed companies. It applies to financial years ending on or after 30 September 2013 and amends, *inter alia*, ss. 226, 421, 422 and 439 of the Companies Act 2006. Further, the Large and Medium-sized Companies and Groups (Accounts and Reports) (Amendment) Regulations 2013 replaced Sch. 8 to the

---

[38] See now ss. 182–187 of the Companies Act 2006, discussed in Chapter 8 below.
[39] W was later acquitted in criminal proceedings arising out of the takeover.
[40] Sometimes the articles themselves appoint the director to executive office at a salary. In the absence of an express contract outside the articles, this can give rise to enforcement problems; see Chapter 4 above.
[41] [1982] 3 All ER 1016.
[42] [1986] BCLC 430, CA.

Large and Medium-sized Companies and Groups (Accounts and Reports) Regulations 2008 to reform the framework for reporting on and approving directors' remuneration. These provisions apply to UK quoted companies and require the directors' remuneration report of those companies to set out the actual payments made to directors in the previous financial year as well as the company's forward-looking policy on directors' remuneration. The relevant companies are then required to put this forward-looking policy to a binding shareholder vote at least once every three years.[43] Once approved, the company can not make payments outside of that policy without further shareholder approval. The backward-looking report is also subject to a shareholder vote but this is advisory only.[44] Nevertheless, if the advisory vote is not passed, this triggers a requirement for the company to seek a binding shareholder vote on its directors' remuneration policy the following year.[45] Taken together, these reforms seek to increase transparency as to the payments actually made to the board, whilst giving shareholders greater power (through binding votes) to hold companies to account.

## 7.3 The role and functioning of the shareholders in general meeting

### A The general meeting as the residual authority of the company

It is difficult to state concisely what the role of the shareholders in general meeting is. Historically, it was clear that in accordance with art. 70 of Table A of the Companies Act 1985 the scheme of the legislation is that the business of the company is managed by the board, who 'exercise all the powers of the company'. This delegation of power is now found in article 3 of the model articles for private and public companies respectively:

**Directors' general authority**

3.   Subject to the articles, the directors are responsible for the management of the company's business, for which purpose they may exercise all the powers of the company.

The reserve power of shareholders is now found in article 4 of the model articles:

**Shareholders' reserve power**

4. – (1) The shareholders may, by special resolution, direct the directors to take, or refrain from taking, specified action.
(2) No such special resolution invalidates anything which the directors have done before the passing of the resolution.

The role ascribed to the shareholders is, therefore, a residual one. Further, the courts are now clear that having granted general managerial powers to the board pursuant to the articles, shareholders can only revoke (or interfere with) this grant in accordance with the terms of the articles themselves,[46] that is, by special resolution. In some (very limited) circumstances the powers of the board will revert to the shareholders,[47] and it is clear from that by special resolution the shareholders can give directions to the directors.

---

[43] Section 439 (A) (1) Companies Act 2006.
[44] Section 439 Companies Act 2006.
[45] Section 439 (A) (2) Companies Act 2006.
[46] *Automatic Self-Cleansing Filter Syndicate Co.* v *Cunninghame* [1906] 2 Ch 34. This can be contrasted with the earlier decision of *Isle of Wright Railway Company* v *Tahourdin* (1884) 25 Ch D 320.
[47] *Barron* v *Potter* [1914] 1 Ch 895.

There are, however, a number of situations where the shareholders in general meeting are the primary functionaries and are in no sense residual. One is where the Act requires the permission of the shareholders before something can be carried out. An example would be s. 188 (requirement of members' approval of directors' long-term service contracts), referred to above, but there are many, scattered throughout the legislation. For example, the need to approve substantial property transactions with a director,[48] an amendment to the articles of association[49] or a reduction in capital.[50] Another situation, which is the result of case law rather than statute, is where the question to be decided is whether the company name can be used to commence litigation against, say, one of the directors for breach of duty. In this situation, the traditional response of the case law is to regard the matter as one which is to be decided by a majority of shareholders in general meeting. In fact, as we will see when the matter is examined in Chapter 11, the position is rather muddled and one line of authority suggests that the board may have a role here too.

Reading the above makes it possible to forget the traditional paradigm that shareholders are the owners of the company. Nevertheless, in this role shareholders (especially of listed corporations) can be passive for the majority of the time (for a number of reasons).[51] That said, there will also sometimes come a point when the shareholders decide that it is high time they removed the directors and will use their power under s. 168 of the Companies Act 2006 to do this.[52]

## B Resolutions at meetings

The two main types of resolution have already been encountered; these are the ordinary resolution and the special resolution. There is no statutory definition of an ordinary resolution, but it is clear from general usage that an ordinary resolution is one which is passed by a simple majority[53] of those members who are present and voting either in person or by proxy. It can be used in all circumstances unless the legislation or the constitution of the company provide that some other resolution be used. Because of that, it is best thought of as the basic or residual resolution.

A special resolution is one which has been passed by a majority of not less than three-fourths (75%) of such members as, being entitled to do so, vote in person or, where proxies are allowed, by proxy, at a general meeting, where notice specifying the intention to propose the resolution as a special resolution has been duly given.[54] Special resolutions must be used where the legislation or constitution of the company so requires. Special resolutions obviously provide a harder task for the meeting and are used by the legislation as a method of achieving a greater safeguard. Thus, for example, an alteration of articles requires a special resolution because it is of a fundamental nature, being an alteration to the constitution of the company.[55]

---

[48] Section 190 Companies Act 2006.
[49] Section 21 Companies Act 2006.
[50] Section 641 Companies Act 2006.
[51] See generally Chapter 1, 1.2, above.
[52] As will be seen below, their ability to do this is often circumscribed by other considerations; see further Chapter 8, 8.5C.
[53] I.e. by voting power of more than 50%. S. 282 (1).
[54] Companies Act 2006, s. 283 (1) and (4) to (6).
[55] *Ibid.* s. 21 (1).

In the past, there was a third type[56] of resolution, the extraordinary resolution[57] (which differs from the special resolution only in terms of the period of notice required), but these type of resolutions have been abolished by the Companies Act 2006.

## C The shareholders' general meetings

The term 'general meeting' is difficult to define, but in essence it means a meeting of the ordinary shareholders together with any other shareholders who are entitled to attend. The general meeting should be distinguished from the shareholders' class meeting. We have already seen[58] that where the company has issued different classes of shares it will sometimes be necessary for the shareholders of a class to have their own meeting[59] to consider, for example, proposals for variation of rights or a scheme of arrangement.

The Companies Act 1985 established two types of shareholders' general meeting; the annual general meeting (AGM) and the extraordinary general meeting (EGM), but as indicated above, the concept of an EGM has been abolished. The provisions of the Companies Act 2006 refer simply to a general meeting, regardless of the resolution being passed.[60] The main provision on AGMs is s. 336 of the Companies Act 2006, which makes it clear that in addition to any other meetings which it holds a public company[61] must, every year,[62] hold a general meeting as its AGM (again, abolishing the requirement for a private company to convene an AGM). The business of the AGM is whatever is required by the articles as well as any other matters that are being raised. In practice, certain matters are usually dealt with at the AGM, such as the laying of accounts, declaration of dividends, reports of directors and auditors, and election of directors. Minutes must be kept of the proceedings of all general meetings and of meetings of directors (and managers) for at least ten years from the date of the resolution.[63] The minutes must be entered in books kept for that purpose and which are open to inspection by members.[64]

---

[56] In some circumstances a written resolution procedure can be used. This is dealt with at 7.5 below.
[57] Section 378 Companies Act 1985.
[58] In Chapter 4.
[59] The legal rules discussed here in the Companies Acts concerning meetings and the common law rules will apply to class meetings unless they are expressed to apply or can obviously only apply to general meetings. As regards class meetings connected with variation of rights, s. 334 of the Companies Act 2006 makes express provision for the rules of the statutes to apply, subject to modifications.
[60] The Companies (Shareholders' Rights) Regulations 2009 (SI No. 2009 1632), which implements EU Directive 2007/36/EC on the exercise of certain rights of shareholders in listed companies, makes provision for electronic meetings and voting. Regulation 8 (implementing Article 8 (participation in general meetings by electronic means)) inserts s. 360 A into the 2006 Act: '(1) Nothing in this Part is to be taken to preclude the holding and conducting of a meeting in such a way that persons who are not present together at the same place may by electronic means attend and speak and vote at it.'
[61] Private companies which are not listed are no longer required to hold an AGM, so there is no longer any need to pass an elective resolution to dispense with AGMs as was the case under s. 366 A of the Companies Act 1985. However, the Companies (Shareholders' Rights) Regulations 2009, above, n. 59, reg. 15, amends s. 336 of the 2006 Act by inserting, after s. 336 (1): '(1A) Every private company that is a traded company must hold a general meeting as its annual general meeting in each period of 9 months beginning with the day following its accounting reference date (in addition to any other meetings held during that period.' Regulation 15 therefore requires private companies with traded shares to hold AGMs.
[62] Calendar year.
[63] Companies Act 2006, s. 355.
[64] *Ibid.* s. 358.

## D Convening of meetings and notice

Under the Companies Act 2006, s. 302 gives the directors powers to convene[65] general meetings. There are also situations where the members, officers and the Courts have rights in relation to the convening of meetings.[66] For example, article 28 of the model articles for public companies limited by shares makes provision for two or more members to call a general meeting (or instruct the company secretary to do so) for the purpose of appointing one or more directors if: (a) the company has fewer than two directors; and (b) the director (if any) is unable or unwilling to appoint sufficient directors to make up a quorum or to call a general meeting to do so.

As regards notice, s. 307 requires that notice of meetings must be served on every member of the company, unless the articles provide otherwise. On the other hand, if a member has no voting rights, she will have no right actually to attend the meeting.[67] The length of notice required varies. For an AGM in a public company, 21 days' notice in writing is needed whereas for other meetings, the period is 14 days.[68] A general meeting of a private company (other than an adjourned meeting) must be called by notice of at least 14 days.[69] These are minimum prescriptions and the articles may require longer notice.[70] In each case, 'clear days' notice is required, meaning that the notice period is calculated without reference to the date of the notice or the date of the meeting.[71]

In some situations a detailed procedure known as 'special notice' is required.[72] As a result of various provisions scattered throughout the legislation, it is required where certain significant ordinary resolutions are to be passed. That is, where it is proposed to remove a director[73] or auditor[74] against their will.

Section 311 of the Companies Act 2006 provides for the contents of notices. Notice of a general meeting must state the time, date and place of the meeting together with a statement of the general nature of the business to be dealt with. Further, s. 325 (1) specifies that with a company having a share capital, the notice calling the meeting must contain a statement that a member who is entitled to attend and vote is entitled to appoint a proxy to attend and vote instead of him and any more extensive rights conferred by the company's articles to appoint more than one proxy. As elsewhere in the law relating to meetings, the provisions of the legislation is supplemented by the common law of meetings which is created by the case law. In the present context, of content of notices, the effect of the cases is that the substance of any business should be set out in the notice in sufficient detail to enable a member to make a proper decision

---

[65] Meaning 'call'.
[66] See Companies Act 2006, ss. 303, 304 and 306. The Companies (Shareholders' Rights) Regulations 2009, above n. 59, amend s. 303 of the 2006 Act. Shareholders with 5% of voting shares can require directors to call a general meeting (previously a 10% holding was needed).
[67] *Re Mackenzie Ltd* [1916] 2 Ch 450.
[68] *Ibid*. s. 307 (2).
[69] *Ibid*. s. 307 (1). A shorter notice period is permitted if agreed by the majority of members (see ss. 307(4)–(6); but a shorter notice period is not permitted for an AGM of a public company: s. 307 (7). For traded companies, see s. 307 (A1)–(A2), introduced by the Companies (Shareholders' Rights) Regulations 2009, above, n. 59.
[70] *Ibid*. s. 307 (3).
[71] Section 360 (2) Companies Act 2006.
[72] *Ibid*. s. 312.
[73] Section 168 (2) Companies Act 2006.
[74] Section 511 Companies Act 2006.

about whether to attend or not, whilst special resolutions must be set out in full with no variations of substance.[75]

## E Shareholder independence – meetings and resolutions

The legislation contains ways in which the members can seek to act independently of the board in relation to the convening of meetings and passing of resolutions.

Section 303 (1) and (2) gives the members holding at least 5% of the paid-up voting capital the right to require the directors to convene a meeting. The members' 'requisition' must state the object of the meeting.[76] The directors must call a meeting within 21 days from the date on which they become subject to the requirement.[77] The date fixed for the meeting must[78] be within 28 days of the notice calling the meeting, thus precluding directors' historic attempts at frustrating the members' objectives by calling the meeting fairly quickly (i.e. issuing the notices) but fixed for a date many months later.[79] If the directors do not duly convene the meeting within the 21 days of the deposit of the duly signed requisition at the company's registered office, then the requisitionists, or any or them representing more than one half of the total voting rights of all of them, may themselves convene a meeting to be held within three months of the date of the deposit of the requisition, and their reasonable expenses are recoverable from the company.[80]

Resolutions will almost always be proposed and backed by the board of directors. The notice summoning the meeting will have set out the text of the resolution and will usually have been accompanied by a circular explaining the reasons why the directors think that the resolution should be adopted. Sometimes members will feel that simply voting against the board's proposals is too passive a form of opposition. Section 314 provides the means for such members, at their expense, to mount some sort of campaign against the board, by proposing resolutions backed by a carefully argued circular sent out to the members before the meeting happens. This mechanism can be invoked by any number of members representing at least 5% of the total voting rights of all the members who have a relevant right to vote (excluding any voting rights attached to any shares in the company held as treasury shares), or alternatively, by not less than 100 members holding shares in the company, paid up to at least £100 per member.[81]

## F Procedure at meetings

A meeting must be quorate to be valid, that is, it must have the requisite minimum number of shareholders present. This quorum must be present throughout the meeting, which

---

[75] See *Tiessen v Henderson* [1899] 1 Ch 861; *MacConnell v Prill Ltd* [1916] 2 Ch 57; *Choppington Collieries Ltd v Johnson* [1944] 1 All ER 762; *Re Moorgate Mercantile Ltd* [1980] 1 All ER 40. Companies with a Stock Exchange Listing are under further 'continuing' obligations with respect to notices.
[76] Companies Act 2006, s. 303 (4).
[77] *Ibid*. s. 304 (1) (a).
[78] By virtue of an amendment contained in the Companies Act 1989.
[79] Companies Act 2006, s. 304 (1) (b).
[80] *Ibid*. s. 305.
[81] *Ibid*. s. 314 (2). Various other conditions and procedures are set out in ss. 314–317. In practice these provisions are seldom used and the limit of 1,000 words is not always helpful in this regard.

otherwise stands adjourned.[82] Historically, it was not possible to hold a quorate meeting with fewer than two members.[83] However, the Companies Act 2006 expressly provides that whilst ordinarily (for both private and public companies) two members constitute a quorum,[84] where the company is a single member company[85] then of course, only one member is required for the meeting to be quorate.[86] Further, s. 306 enables the court to order a meeting in some situations, and it empowers the court to direct that, even where the company has more than one member, 'one member of the company . . . be deemed to constitute a meeting'.[87] In *Re RMCA Reinsurance Ltd*,[88] the court was prepared to order a meeting of one (to be held in Singapore). Similarly, in *East* v *Bennett*,[89] one member who held all the shares of a particular class could constitute a class 'meeting' on his own. Subject to these exceptions (and the case of single member companies), it is clear that even if there is no quorum requirement, the general rule is that a meeting of one is no meeting.

It is normal for a meeting to take place under the direction of a chair. Indeed, art. 39 of the model articles of association for private companies and art. 31 of the model articles for public companies mandate this.[90] Both articles make provision for this to be the chair of the board of directors, or in her absence, a director or shareholder nominated by the directors present (or the meeting if no directors are present).[91] The chair's function is to see that the business of the meeting is conducted properly and in accordance with the common law of meetings, the articles and the companies legislation.[92]

Voting at meetings[93] usually takes place on a 'show of hands' of the members present.[94] What this means is that it is done without counting up the votes held by each member. The chair would then declare the resolution carried or lost by '28 votes to 19' as the case may be. Voting by a show of hands is thus a convenient way of getting through the uncontentious business of the meeting. However, if someone present wishes to mount a serious challenge to the resolution then, provided they have the requisite shareholding,[95] they will demand a poll, either before or on the declaration of the result by the chair.[96] A poll is a

---

[82] Table A of the Companies Act 1985, art. 41.

[83] *Re London Flats Ltd* [1969] 1 WLR 711.

[84] Section 318(2) Companies Act 2006.

[85] It has been possible since 1992, pursuant to the Companies (Single Member Private Limited Companies) Regulations 1992 (SI 1992 No. 1699), for private companies limited by shares or by guarantee to be formed with only one member.

[86] Section 218 (1) Companies Act 2006.

[87] See *Re Sticky Fingers Restaurant Ltd* [1991] BCC 754.

[88] [1994] BCC 378; applied in *Re Oceanrose Investments Ltd* [2008] EWHC 3475 (Ch).

[89] [1911] 1 Ch 163.

[90] Article 42 is the corresponding provision of Table A.

[91] Companies Act 2006, s. 319 provides that, subject to any contrary provision in the articles, the meeting may be chaired by any member elected by the members present.

[92] See generally *John v Rees* [1970] Ch 345 at p. 382.

[93] See generally, Table A of the Companies Act 1985, articles 46–52, and the model articles for private companies limited by shares, articles 42–47; for public companies, see articles 34–40.

[94] Article 42 of the model articles for private companies limited by shares; article 34 for public companies.

[95] Pursuant to the articles, either two or more shareholders or a person or persons holding at least 10% of the total voting rights of all members having the right to vote on the resolution have the right to demand a poll. See art. 44 (2) of the model articles for private companies limited by shares; article 36 (2) for public companies.

[96] Article 44 of the model articles for private companies limited by shares; article 36 for public companies.

count of the votes held by each shareholder or 'hand'.[97] The demand for a poll nullifies the result reached by the show of hands.

The system of proxy voting is a subject which will be returned to below, for it is one of those areas which in its practical workings has been seen to impact adversely on corporate governance.[98] The basic legal position, however, is relatively straightforward and the legislation and the model articles contain detailed provisions with regard to proxies.[99] A member of a company who is entitled to attend and vote at a meeting is entitled to appoint another person (who may or may not be a member) as his proxy, to exercise all or any of his rights to attend and to speak and vote at a meeting of the company instead of him.[100] If the company is listed on the London Stock Exchange the company must send out what are called 'three-way' proxy forms with any notices calling meetings.[101] These forms have on them a clear direction for the proxy to vote for or against the resolution or a statement that, in the absence of any such direction, the proxy will exercise her discretion as to whether and, if so, how to vote.

## 7.4 Problems with the meeting concept

It is clear from the above fairly detailed examination of the workings of the board and the general meeting that company law is very dependent on the idea of governance through democratic meetings, and particularly through the shareholders' general meeting. Great power is given to the board by art. 3 of the model articles,[102] and yet the general meeting has a measure of control through its ability to, *inter alia*, exercise its reserve right (by special resolution) set out in art. 4, its ability to remove the directors by ordinary resolution,[103] and through its ability to appoint directors.[104]

In practice, the extent to which the shareholders' general meeting can operate as an input to the governance of the company is reduced by two factors. The first is that in many situations, in particular where the company is the size of a listed plc, the shareholders would simply think it not worth their while to bother to attend or vote, on the basis that little or no economic advantage could come from their investment of time. The market capitalisation of the average listed plc is so large that any particular shareholder usually owns only a small proportion of the overall voting shares. In that situation, the chance of being able to influence the outcome is negligible. But the problem is more fundamental than this. The shareholder does not see it in her individual economic interest to even try. Investors tend to follow 'portfolio theory'.[105] This means that shareholders

[97] Companies Act 2006, s. 321 (1) preserves and safeguards the common law right of any member to demand a poll, except in relation to the election of chair or adjournment of the meeting in which cases the right can be restricted by the articles although no further than the extent stated in s. 321 (2). Proxies are also given similar rights to demand a poll: s. 329. Section 323 protects the position of a nominee in some circumstances.

[98] See next section. Note that s. 285 of the Companies Act 2006 is amended by the Companies (Shareholders' Rights) Regulations 2009.

[99] See generally, Companies Act 2006, ss. 324–331; Table A, articles 54–63; the model articles for private companies limited by shares, articles 42–47; and the model articles for public companies, articles 34–40.

[100] Companies Act 2006, s. 324.

[101] FCA Listing Rules, paras 9.3.6 and 9.3.7.

[102] Article 70 of Table A of the Companies Act 1985.

[103] Section 168 Companies Act 2006.

[104] Article 17 model articles of association for private companies; article 20 for public companies.

[105] See further Chapter 18, 18.6, below in the context of collective investment schemes.

will try to reduce their exposure to the risk that an investee company collapse by diversifying their portfolio by holding shares in many different companies. Such an investor will not want to spend time worrying about the outcome of some incident or boardroom battle in any one individual company. If the investor senses trouble in the performance of the company, he or she will sell the shares, and invest the proceeds in another company. In 1999 the DTI found that between 70% and 80% of shares are owned by institutions such as pension funds and unit trusts.[106] There is evidence that some of these in recent years have seen it as worth their while to take an interest in the governance of companies in which they have invested.[107] Due to the scale of these funds, they are in a position to buy sizeable stakes in companies and this may have increased their commitment to intervention. However, it is probable that this is sporadic and it is questionable whether the input to corporate governance is significant. Recent years have seen attempts by the various committees on corporate governance to stir the institutions into more activity in this regard.[108]

The second factor that reduces the effectiveness of the shareholder meeting as an instrument of corporate governance stems from the fact that very few shareholders attend the meetings in person. Instead, if they are minded to take any interest at all, they will appoint a proxy to vote on their behalf. The proxy will usually be one of the directors because if a contentious resolution is coming up at the meeting, the board will have sent out a circular explaining their position and soliciting proxy votes. This means that whatever is said at the meeting will be largely irrelevant because the board will have with them a large pile of proxy votes which will defeat any opposition. If an insurgent shareholder group had mounted an opposition circular it would have arrived after[109] the shareholders had returned their proxy forms, which is a considerable disincentive to voting against[110] the board.[111]

These factors, coupled with the internationalisation of capital markets, with shareholders dispersed all over the world, mean that the input that will be made by individual shareholders in the governance of companies is seriously limited. Rather like the representative governing bodies of ancient republican Rome, the legal mechanism of UK corporate governance is founded on the idea that all the members of the company can gather together in one place and will actually be enthusiastic enough to do

---

[106] See DTI Consultation Document (October 1999) *Company General Meetings and Shareholder Communications* para. 20. More recent statistics show that following a period of continued downward trends in individual share ownership this pattern has now steadied. The Office for National Statistics Share Ownership Survey 2016 states that: 'The proportion of shares held by individuals (see Figure 4) has declined since 1963, when individuals owned approximately 54% of UK quoted shares in terms of total value. In 2014, this same sector's holding in comparison stood at 12.4%. In 2016, individual ownership remained steady at 12.3% of all shares in quoted UK domiciled companies. This long-term reduction in the proportion of shares owned by individuals in part reflects the increasing internationalisation of the London Stock Exchange over the period (individual overseas investors being classified to the "rest of the world" sector).' Available at <https://www.ons.gov.uk/economy/investmentspensionsandtrusts/bulletins/ownershipofukquotedshares/2016#share-held-by-individual-holds-steady-after-years-of-decline>

[107] See J. Farrar *Farrar's Company Law* 4th edn (London: Butterworths, 1998) p. 580.

[108] See further Chapter 10 below.

[109] Unless of course the shareholders are able to spot the contentious issue early enough.

[110] In theory the shareholder could change his mind by revoking the appointment of the proxy.

[111] See further M. Pickering 'Shareholder Votes and Company Control' (1965) 81 LQR 248.

so.[112] And like the Roman bodies, it has found that, in the passage of time, the expansion in size of the human organism to be governed has rendered the governance mechanisms partially obsolete.

## 7.5 Meetings in small closely-held companies

In small closely-held companies, special procedures have been developed over the years to enable the shareholders and directors of small closely-held companies to avoid the necessity of holding formal meetings.

First, the common law has developed a doctrine,[113] often referred to as 'shareholder consent', to the effect that if an act may be done by the shareholders formally in a meeting, then such act may be done informally, without a meeting provided that all the shareholders in the company consent. The doctrine can be used in many ways and its existence can produce some unexpected results in litigation.[114] It seems that even long-term acquiescence (coupled with knowledge of the circumstances) can amount to shareholder consent.[115] The consent doctrine has provided a useful vehicle for many years, by which members and directors of small closely-held companies have been enabled legally to circumvent the necessity to hold some of their meetings. In practice the doctrine is often utilised by formulating a proposal in writing and circulating it for successive signature by all the members. In the past, Article 53 of Table A of the Companies

---

[112] In the course of time the use of internet technology might bring about a solution to the problem of global dispersion of shareholders. With effect from 20 January 2007, provisions linked to implementation of the EU Transparency Obligations Directive (Directive 2004/109/EC [2004] OJ L390/38) commenced. These include provisions on company communications to shareholders and others, which include provisions facilitating electronic communication. The 'communications provisions' are defined by the Companies Act 2006, s. 1143 as ss. 1144–1148 together with Schedules 4 and 5 (of which Sch. 4, para. 3 and Sch. 5, para. 3 in particular relate to electronic communications; s. 1168 under Part 38 provides additional useful definitions). These provisions were brought into force ahead of most other parts of the Act. This was for two reasons: first, to coincide with the implementation of the EU Transparency Obligations Directive; and, secondly, to allow early delivery of the benefits of e-communications – including significant cost savings to business, improved accessibility to information, and enhanced immediacy of dialogue between companies and shareholders. The general principle of the Companies Act 2006 is that companies should, subject to shareholder approval, be able to default to using e-communications. Individuals, however, will retain the right to receive information on paper if they wish. The company communications provisions set out in the Act apply to all companies, public and private.

[113] See generally *Re Duomatic Ltd* [1969] 1 All ER 161; *Atlas Wright (Europe) Ltd* v *Wright* [1999] BCC 163. It has been held in *Re Torvale Group Ltd* [2000] BCC 626 that the shareholder consent doctrine is not limited to situations where all the shareholders of the company are involved, but is also applicable where statute or the constitution of the company enabled certain acts to be done if a particular group consented.

[114] See e.g. *Multinational Gas Ltd* v *Multinational Services Ltd* [1983] 2 All ER 563 where directors escaped the consequences of breach of duty because all the shareholders knew of their actions and acquiesced in them.

[115] *Re Bailey Hay & Co* [1971] 3 All ER 693. In *Schofield* v *Schofield* [2011] EWCA Civ 154, the first defendant, L, had been removed as sole director of a company at a purported extraordinary general meeting. The claimant, S, relying on the principle in *Re Duomatic Ltd*, above n. 105, argued that the EGM was effective to achieve the removal because, although it was not called within the 14 days' notice as required by the Companies Act 2006, s 305 (4) and s 307, he held 99.9% of the shares in the company and L, as the owner of the remaining share, had agreed, or was to be regarded as having agreed, to treat the meeting as valid and effective. The Court of Appeal, upholding the trial judge's finding that the EGM was not properly convened, held that S had to establish an agreement by L to treat the meeting as valid and effective, notwithstanding the lack of the statutory notice period. Although L's agreement could be express or implied, nothing short of unqualified agreement, objectively established, would suffice. On the evidence it was clear that L, as a shareholder, did not treat the meeting and the resolutions passed at it as valid. There was, therefore, no objective agreement by him within the *Duomatic* principle. See also, *Re Stakefield (Midlands) Ltd* [2010] EWHC 3175 (Ch), Newy J at [37]–[45].

Act 1985 enshrined the doctrine in the articles of most companies but, as will be seen, this is no longer necessary.

As part of a package of reforms[116] designed to help small companies operate more efficiently and less burdened with unnecessary procedures by companies legislation, the Companies Act 1989 introduced a statutory procedure whereby written resolutions could be used. Unfortunately, the drafting introduced complications and subsequent amendments were introduced by statutory instrument.[117] The amended provisions, which apply to private companies, were contained in ss. 381 A–381 C of the Companies Act 1985.

As part of its 'think small first' approach, the Companies Act 2006 sought to improve this procedure. For private companies only, resolutions may now be passed either at a members' meeting or by a new, more detailed, written resolution procedure.[118] A private company is not able to opt out of this statutory regime[119] and has no ability to pass a written resolution in accordance with any procedure (e.g. in articles) that does not meet the requirements of the regime.[120] The new written[121] resolution procedure is contained in ss. 288–300 and 502. In short, it requires a simple majority of eligible votes (an ordinary written resolution) or 75% of eligible votes (a special written resolution), rather than unanimity as under the Companies Act 1985. It requires the company to circulate the resolution accompanied by a statement informing members how to signify agreement and the date by which the resolution must be passed. It also specifies that a resolution lapses if not passed before the end of the period specified in the articles (or, absent such provision, 28 days from the circulation date). The procedure likewise specifies that if the company is authorised to use electronic communications under the Companies Act 2006 and sends a written resolution via its website, the resolution must be available on the website throughout the period from the circulation date to the date on which it will lapse if not passed. It goes on to state that a resolution is passed when the required majority has signified agreement and that a member's agreement cannot, once signified, be revoked. A written resolution will still need to be sent to auditors together with any accompanying statement required to be sent to members under ss. 288–300. The written resolution regime can be used for all resolutions save for those concerning the removal of a director or an auditor before the expiry of their office.[122]

It is clear then that the Companies Act 2006 is drafted on the basis that most decision making in private companies will be by written resolution, rather than by general meeting. The Act does not require unanimity on written resolutions, making it easier to pass a written resolution, but the price for this is the mandatory additional, albeit limited, formality regarding circulation and timing.

---

[116] See also the 'elective regime' contained in the past in s. 379 A of the Companies Act 1985.
[117] Deregulation (Resolutions of Private Companies) Order 1996 (SI 1996 No. 1471), now repealed.
[118] Companies Act 2006, ss. 281, 284 and 288–300. The Companies (Shareholders' Rights) Regulations 2009 inserts s. 285 A into the Companies Act 2006 which provides: 'In relation to a resolution required or authorised by an enactment, if a private company's articles provide that a member has a different number of votes in relation to a resolution when it is passed as a written resolution and when it is passed on a poll taken at a meeting . . .' such a provision is void and 'a member has the same number of votes in relation to the resolution when it is passed on a poll as the member has when it is passed as a written resolution.'
[119] *Ibid.* s. 300.
[120] *Ibid.* s. 288.
[121] The word 'written' includes electronic form, including for the purpose of signifying agreement.
[122] Section 288(2) Companies Act 2006.

## Further reading

Lady Justice Arden DBE 'UK Corporate Governance after Enron' (2003) 3 *JCLS* 269.

A.K. Lowry 'De Facto Directorships: Multiple Tests Prevail' (2011) 8 *ICR* 194.

M. Pickering 'Shareholder Votes and Company Control' (1965) 81 *LQR* 248.

# 8

# Duties of directors: general duties

## 8.1 Introduction

The next stage of analysis of the legal constraints on the directors of a company[1] is consideration of directors' duties, which originate in case law and have developed slowly over approximately 150 years, often drawing on even older concepts from the law of trusts and restated by the Companies Act 2006, Part 10. It is helpful to divide the duties into two categories: first, and perhaps most significantly, there are the general duties which form the subject of this chapter. These general duties can be further subdivided into common law duties of care and skill and fiduciary duties. As will be seen, the statutory restatement follows this division. The second category of duty can be referred to as specific duties and they relate to the statutory controls over the conduct of directors in specific situations. These specific duties are considered in the next chapter.

The move towards the Companies Act 2006 restatement was underpinned by three key policy objectives highlighted in a review conducted by the English and Scottish Law Commission and developed by the CLR.[2] These objectives were, first, to 'provide greater clarity on what is expected of directors and make the law more accessible',[3] secondly, to 'enable defects in the . . . law to be corrected' especially 'in relation to the duties of conflicted directors' and finally, to enable the fundamental question of 'scope' (i.e. in whose interests should companies be run) to be addressed 'in a way which reflects modern business needs and wider expectations of responsible business behaviour'.[4]

[1] For a detailed comparative analysis, see B. Butcher *Directors' Duties: A New Millennium, A New Approach?* (Deventer: Kluwer, 2000).
[2] See the Law Commission's and the Scottish Law Commission's joint report, *Company Directors: Regulating Conflicts of Interest and Formulating a Statement of Duties* (Law Com No. 261, Cm 4436, 1999), Part 4. The three core policy proposals that formed the basis of the CLR's recommendations were: 'the "think small first" approach to private company regulation and legislative structure; an inclusive, open and flexible regime for company governance; and a flexible and responsive institutional structure for rule-making and enforcement, with an emphasis on transparency and market enforcement': see *Modern Company Law For a Competitive Economy Final Report* (London: DTI, 2001), para. 1.52.
[3] The Department for Business, Innovation & Skills (DBIS) (as DBEIS was then known) evaluated the outcomes of the main provisions of the Companies Act 2006 and the consequences of the regulatory changes for companies, shareholders and other stakeholders. With respect to Part 10 of the Act, it was found that: 'Although awareness of the codification of directors' duties was high (79%), the proportion of those perceived to have responded was lower at 50%, given the codification did not represent a change in the current law (all must comply with these provisions) but for just under half of companies interviewed, the codification had not prompted a change in how they carry out their duties). Overall, one-fifth of those who had responded agreed the statutory statement had had an impact on the way directors discharged their duties, and almost three-fifths were aware of the changes to the procedure for bringing about a derivative action for breach of duty (59%). Of those companies not initially aware of the changes relating to directors' duties, over one-third indicated that they would now take advice from the company's accountant on the nature of their requirements.' The DBIS findings can be found at http://www.bis.gov.uk/policies/business-law/company-and-partnership-law/evaluation%20of%20companies%20act%202006.
[4] *Ibid.* para. 3.7.

The division between the common law duties of care and skill and fiduciary duties, which is also replicated in the statutory restatement contained in ss. 171–177 of the Companies Act 2006, is the result of the idea that the director has two types of function which are treated separately by the law. From one angle the director can be seen as a trustee, whose role it is to protect and preserve the assets for the beneficiary. From the other angle, she is seen as a dynamic entrepreneur whose job it is to take risks with the subscribed capital and multiply the shareholders' investment. This is clearly a wide spectrum of behaviour to regulate and would pose difficulty for any legal system. In the UK there have been attempts to solve the problem by drawing heavily and easily on pre-existing concepts of the law of trusts and, until recent years, largely ignoring the challenges posed by the entrepreneurial function. As a result this area of law, notwithstanding its codification, has a curious, bifurcated feel, echoing the ancient split between the courts of common law and Chancery.[5]

The enforcement mechanisms for breach of duty present certain practical difficulties, and remain within the grip of the 'rule in *Foss* v *Harbottle*', the shadow of which is discernible in the new statutory procedure introduced by Part 11 of the 2006 Act.[6] This in itself flows directly from the existence of another rule, namely the rule in *Percival* v *Wright*,[7] now given statutory force by virtue of s. 170, which establishes that directors, both collectively and individually,[8] owe their duties to the company of which they are the directors. This means that the shareholders themselves have no cause of action against directors for breach of their duties. Only the company has a cause of action. The ramifications of these rules are explored in Chapter 11. The overall effect, however, is often to make it difficult or impossible for directors to be held accountable. It still remains to be seen how the judges will use their considerable discretion conferred by the new statutory procedure governing the derivative claim, although early indications are that it will be used conservatively.[9] If a more flexible approach is eventually adopted, the hurdles that exist against holding errant directors accountable may yet be overcome. On the other hand, the availability of the unfair prejudice remedy, discussed at Chapter 12, is relatively unrestricted. Briefly, the enactment of the unfair prejudice remedy in 1980, and the subsequent dynamic case law development of the concept, has somewhat challenged established ideas concerning directors' duties. Under the case law on unfair prejudice, there is a range of acts that would probably not cause directors to breach their duties, but will nevertheless be likely to cause them to lose an unfair prejudice petition.[10] This, coupled with the wideness and flexibility of the substantive law of unfair prejudice, means that if directors approach their responsibilities solely through the perspective of the traditional duties restated in Part 10 of the 2006 Act they will be under-informed.

---

[5] See L.S. Sealy 'The Director As Trustee' [1967] CLJ 83.

[6] (1843) 2 Hare 461. This is an important concept in the law of unfair prejudice and the expression is used here loosely to describe both the restrictions inherent in the *Foss* v *Harbottle* doctrine and the gateways created by the recognised exceptions to it. See now the Companies Act 2006, Part 11, discussed in Chapter 11.

[7] [1902] 2 Ch 421. In *Multinational Gas and Petrochemical Co. Ltd* v *Multinational Gas and Petrochemical Services Ltd* [1983] Ch 258, Dillon LJ explained, at 288, that: 'directors indeed stand in a fiduciary relationship to the company, as they are appointed to manage the affairs of the company and they owe fiduciary duties to the company though not to the creditors, present or future, or to individual shareholders.'

[8] *Ross River Ltd & Anor* v *Waverley Commercial Ltd & Ors* [2012] EWCA Civ 1090.

[9] See Chapter 11 below, and the recent decisions discussed at 11.6.

[10] See Chapter 12.

As commented above, Part 10 of the Act sets out the statutory restatement of the general duties of directors.[11] It begins by addressing the scope and nature of the duties in s. 170. It then goes on to lay down the substantive duties owed by directors to the company:

- Duty to act within powers – s. 171.
- Duty to promote the success of the company – s. 172.
- Duty to exercise independent judgment – s. 173.
- Duty to exercise reasonable care, skill and diligence – s. 174.
- Duty to avoid conflicts of interest – s. 175.
- Duty not to accept benefits from third parties – s. 176.
- Duty to declare interest in proposed transaction or arrangement – s. 177 (the duty to declare interest in an existing transaction or arrangement is laid down by s. 182).

In addition, following widespread concern regarding the short-termism of large companies, in 2012 BIS (as it was then) issued additional practical guidance for company directors aimed at promoting more long-termist behaviour.[12]

Before embarking on an examination of the restatement, it is noteworthy that having restated the principle laid down in *Percival* v *Wright* in s. 170 (1),[13] subsection (3) states that the general duties set out in ss. 171 to 174 'are based on certain common law rules and equitable principles . . . and have effect in place of those rules and principles . . .' It is therefore clear that the relevant provisions replace the pre-existing law, although s. 170 (4) directs the courts to have regard to the pre-existing case law when 'interpreting and applying the general duties'.[14] Indeed, ordinary principles of equity regarding fiduciary duties

---

[11] To the extent that they are capable of doing so these duties also apply to shadow directors (Companies Act 2006 s. 170 (5) (substituted by the Small Business, Enterprise and Employment Act 2015 s. 289 (1))).

[12] In November 2012 DBIS (as DBEIS was then known) released its response to the Kay Review on short-termism (see below, Chapter 10) containing at Annex A: A Good Practice Statement for Company Directors. Company directors should (text abridged): 1. Understand their duties under the Companies Act 2006 giving particular consideration to issues of long-termism, including environmental, social and governance issues, amongst others; 2. Acknowledge that long-term value creation requires strategies for sustainable performance; 3. Ensure intermediation costs are kept to a minimum; 4. Ensure that corporate reporting includes a focus on forward-looking strategy; 5. Facilitate engagement with shareholders, particularly institutional shareholders; 6. Ensure corporate reporting and shareholder engagement provides information which supports shareholders' understanding of company strategy and likely long-term creation of value; 7. Communicate information to shareholders which aids understanding of the future prospects of the company; 8. Not allow expectations of market reaction to particular short-term performance metrics to significantly influence company strategy; 9. Refrain from publishing or highlighting inappropriate metrics; 10. Structure payments in a way which incentivises sustainable long-term business performance; 11. Consult their major long-term investors over major board appointments; and 12. Seek to disengage from the process of managing short-term earnings expectations and announcements. (See http://www.bis.gov.uk/kayreview.)

[13] [1902] 2 Ch 421. It should be noted, however, that in some circumstances it has been found that a duty is owed to the shareholders personally. For instance, where the directors have held themselves out as negotiating on behalf of the shareholders, they will owe their duties to them; see *Allen* v *Hyatt* [1914] 30 TLR 444. In a takeover bid, the directors of the offeree company will owe a duty to the shareholders not to mislead them: *Heron International* v *Lord Grade* [1983] BCLC 244. In *Peskin* v *Anderson* [2001] BCC 874, CA, it was held that in order for directors to owe fiduciary duties to shareholders it was necessary to establish a special factual relationship between the directors and the shareholders in the particular case. They do not simply arise from the legal relationship that existed between the company and its directors.

[14] In *Eastford Ltd* v *Gillespie* [2010] CSOH 132, at [13], Lord Hodge, considering s. 170(4), observed that it 'seeks to address the challenge which the Law Commissions and the Company Law Review had identified, namely of avoiding the danger that a statutory statement of general duties would make the law inflexible and incapable of development by judges to deal with changing commercial circumstances. Parliament has directed the courts not only to treat the general duties in the same way as the pre-existing rules and principles but also to have regard to the continued development of the non-statutory law in relation to the duties of other fiduciaries when interpreting and applying the statutory statements. The interpretation of the statements will therefore be able to evolve.'

must be applied when considering directors' fiduciary duties.[15] However, there are two areas where the statutory statement departs from the old law. These both relate to the regulation of conflicts of interest and are explored further below.[16] More generally, the provisions are drafted so as to maintain flexibility while facilitating judicial development and it is clear that, s. 174 excepted (duty to exercise reasonable care, skill and diligence), the statutory duties are fiduciary in nature. Part 10 is not intended to form a comprehensive code of directors' duties and so other duties are to be found elsewhere in the statute (e.g. the duty to prepare a directors' report contained in s. 415), while other duties such as the requirement to consider the interests of creditors when the company is insolvent remain uncodified by Part 10.

## 8.2 The general duties of directors under Part 10

### A The duty to act within powers

The common law position is that directors owe a duty of 'good faith' to the company and that one of the facets of this equitable obligation is that directors must exercise their powers bona fide for the benefit of the company and must not seek any collateral advantage for themselves when doing this.[17] The statutory restatement in s. 171 sets the duty to act within powers as a separate obligation and the more general duty to act in good faith to promote the success of the company is now encompassed in s. 172, though, as is made clear by s. 179, the general duties overlap so that '[e]xcept as otherwise provided, more than one of the general duties may apply in any given case'.

Section 171 is structured in two parts. First, it requires a director to act in accordance with the company's constitution and, secondly, to exercise powers only for the purposes for which they are conferred (this became known as the 'proper purposes doctrine' at common law and originates from Lord Greene MR's formulation of the good faith duty in *Re Smith & Fawcett Ltd*). The duty to abide by the constitution has generated very little case law. It is linked to what was s. 35 of the Companies Act 1985 under which directors who caused the company to enter into an *ultra vires* contract were personally liable.[18]

It is the second limb of the duty restated in s. 171 that generates more interest. The importance of the duty has recently been described by Lord Sumption as follows:

'The rule that the fiduciary powers of directors may be exercised only for the purposes for which they were conferred is one of the main means by which equity enforces the proper conduct of directors. It is also fundamental to the constitutional distinction between the respective domains of the board and the shareholders. These considerations are particularly important when the company is in play between competing groups seeking to control or influence its affairs.[19]

The duty most frequently arises in connection with the issue of shares, a power given to the directors to enable them to raise capital.[20] In some situations, typically where a

[15] *Towers v Premier Waste Management Ltd* [2011] EWCA Civ 923.
[16] See below, 8.2E.
[17] See *Re Smith & Fawcett Ltd* [1942] Ch 304, Lord Greene MR's formulation of the good faith duty.
[18] See Chapter 5.
[19] *Eclairs Group Ltd and Glengary Overseas Ltd v JKX Oil & Gas plc* [2015] UKSC 71.
[20] It is settled law that the duty applies to the exercise of all powers conferred on directors. See *Darvall v North Sydney Brick and Tile Co. Ltd* (1989) 16 NSWLR 260. See further, *Extrasure Travel Insurances Ltd v Scattergood* [2003] 1 BCLC 598, Ch D, discussed below.

takeover bid is about to be launched, directors have sought to further their own interests (and secure their jobs) by issuing shares to an individual (sometimes called a 'white knight') who supports them. This will have the effect of diluting the voting power of those existing shareholders who might support the takeover offer.[21] Thus in *Punt v Symons*,[22] an issue of shares was set aside because it had been done with a view to creating voting power to enable the directors to make their own position more secure. In *Howard Smith v Ampol Petroleum*,[23] an issue of shares was set aside because it had been done to enable a takeover bid to go the way the directors wanted. Lord Wilberforce explained that:

> Just as it is established that directors, within their management powers, may take decisions against the wishes of the majority of shareholders, and indeed that the majority of shareholders cannot control them in the exercise of these powers while they remain in office . . . so it must be unconstitutional for directors to use their fiduciary powers over the shares in the company purely for the purpose of destroying an existing majority, or creating a new majority which did not previously exist.[24]

More recently, the issue has arisen where directors have misused corporate assets for an improper purpose. In *Extrasure Travel Insurances Ltd v Scattergood*,[25] the directors of Extrasure transferred company funds, some £200,000, to another company in the group in order to enable it to meet its liabilities. The judge, finding this was an improper exercise of power insofar as it was not exercised to promote the interests of Extrasure, stated that a claimant is not bound to prove that a director was dishonest, or that he knew he was pursuing a collateral purpose. Rather, liability is to be determined by reference to a four-part test:

(i)   identify the power whose exercise is in question;
(ii)  identify the proper purpose for which that power was delegated to the directors;
(iii) identify the substantial purpose for which the power was in fact exercised; and
(iv)  decide whether that purpose was proper.

The nature of the 'proper purposes' doctrine was explained by Ungoed-Thomas J in *Selangor United Rubber Estates Ltd v Cradock (No. 3)*,[26] where he noted that directors and trustees have this in common:

> that the property in their hands or under their control must be applied for the specified purposes of the company or the settlement; and to apply it otherwise is to misapply it in breach of the

---

[21] See e.g. *Hogg v Cramphorn Ltd* [1967] Ch 254; and *Whitehouse v Carlton Hotel Property Ltd* (1987) 162 CLR 285. In *Piercy v S Mills & Co. Ltd* [1920] 1 Ch 77 the court set aside a share issue on the basis that this was done 'simply and solely for the purpose of retaining control in the hands of the existing directors'. The drafting of s. 171 reflects the approach taken in these decisions of treating proper purposes and bona fides (see s. 172, below) as distinct issues.

[22] [1903] 2 Ch 506. There are now further statutory controls on the issue of shares; see Chapter 13, below.

[23] [1974] AC 821.

[24] *Ibid.* at p. 837. As indicated above, the unfair prejudice provision, s. 994 of the Act (discussed in Chapter 12 below), is commonly enlisted to pursue claims against directors of private companies for breach of fiduciary duty, including allegations of an improper share allotment which results in the dilution of the petitioner's shareholding: see, for example, *Re Sunrise Radio Ltd* [2010] 1 BCLC 367.

[25] [2003] 1 BCLC 598. A rarer example is afforded by *Criterion Properties plc v Stratford UK Properties LLC* [2004] UKHL 28, which concerned a 'poison pill' arrangement that was held by the Court of Appeal to amount to a gratuitous disposition of the company's assets. The House of Lords approached the issue on the basis of directors' authority, i.e. whether the directors had actual, apparent, or ostensible authority to sign the agreement. Since this could not be decided on the evidence available, the case was remitted for trial.

[26] [1968] 1 WLR 1555, at p. 1578.

obligation to apply it to those purposes for the company or the settlement beneficiaries. So, even though the scope and operation of such obligation differs in the case of directors and strict settlement trustees, the nature of the obligation with regard to property in their hands or under their control is identical, namely, to apply it to specified purposes for others beneficially.

## B Duty to promote the success of the company

Directors have in their hands the control of the assets of the company and by analogy with the law of trusts, they are regarded as owing fiduciary duties in respect of those assets. We have already seen that the duty is owed to the company rather than the individual shareholders.[27] The courts have described the fiduciary duty as fundamentally being that of 'good faith' or 'loyalty' and the duty is now restated in s. 172.

In *Re Smith & Fawcett Ltd*,[28] Lord Greene MR said that directors should exercise their powers 'bona fide in what they consider – not what a court may consider – is in the best interests of the company,[29] and not for any collateral purpose,'[30] itself being a term that has received judicial consideration.[31] Similarly, in *Dorchester Finance v Stebbing*,[32] Foster J stated: 'A director must exercise any power vested in him as such, honestly, in good faith and in the interests of the company . . .'[33] It is important to realise that the expression 'good faith' in the context of the duty of loyalty is used by the courts as a kind of shorthand to describe the range of obligations which attach to the directors as fiduciaries. They are not 'trustees' in the technical sense of the word because they are not holding the legal title to the property of the company as a beneficiary holds the equitable title. However, they are similar to trustees in the sense that the company's assets are under their close control and they will usually be liable as constructive trustees if they misapply the assets. They are certainly fiduciaries, however,[34] and in that capacity will owe their duty of good faith. Broadly, good faith in this context means that they must be fair. But 'fair' in this context is a word with wide connotations. In the context of directors it means that they are charged by the law to deal with property for the benefit of another. Directors obviously have to carry out the business of the company which will involve the assets of the company in business risks,[35] but subject to this, they have

---

[27] *Percival* v *Wright* [1902] 2 Ch 421.

[28] [1942] Ch 304.

[29] The 'company' in this context is not usually construed as meaning the company as a detached legal entity and the courts look for some humans by which to gauge it. Thus in *Gaiman* v *Association for Mental Health* [1971] Ch 317 at p. 330 Megarry J said, 'I would accept the interests of both present and future members of the company as a whole, as being a helpful expression of a human equivalent.' A similar statement has been noted above in relation to the alteration of articles; see Chapter 4. It is clear that when faced with the task of assessing the behaviour of the directors or shareholders in the context of a duty of good faith towards the company as a whole, the *Salomon* concept of the detached legal entity is temporarily put aside in favour of a pragmatic reckoning based on the social reality of the company, namely the shareholders as a group. In some circumstances the interests of the creditors can take the place of those of the shareholders in assessing the nature of the interests of the company; see the discussion at Chapter 3, above.

[30] [1942] Ch 304 at p. 306.

[31] For the 'collateral purpose' element of this formulation, see the discussion above, text to notes 23–28.

[32] [1989] BCLC 498.

[33] *Ibid*. at pp. 501–502.

[34] *Aberdeen Railway* v *Blaikie* (1854) 1 Macq 461, HL.

[35] For which they may face liability if their conduct has fallen short of the common law duties of care and skill, see s. 174 discussed below.

a duty to preserve the assets of the company, not to harm the assets and therefore not to detract from the business of the company. These basic ideas will affect how the directors must go about their conduct of the business of the company. Business decisions taken on behalf of the company must be taken solely for its benefit. They must not be taken with a view to getting some personal benefit or advantage for the directors. The case law contains various illustrations of these ideas being applied in different business contexts.

The most obvious and fundamental breach of a trustee's duty is for she or he to make off with the trust property.[36] Similarly, directors who take the company's assets will be liable as constructive trustees of any property they take, as will any third parties who take the assets with notice of the breach of duty.[37] If the company is in liquidation the matter is often raised against the directors by what are known as 'misfeasance proceedings', brought under s. 212 of the Insolvency Act 1986.[38] Directors who take the assets of the company may also find themselves liable to criminal proceedings for theft or related offences.[39]

It has long been settled that the court will not substitute its own view about which course of action the directors should have taken in place of the board's own judgment,[40] although this is subject to the overriding jurisdiction of the courts to assess objectively the conduct in question. It was stressed by Arden LJ in *Item Software (UK) Ltd* v *Fassihi*[41] that if a director embarks on a course of action without considering the interests of the company and there is no basis on which he or she could reasonably have come to the conclusion that it was in the interests of the company, the director will be in breach.

Although the statutory manifestation of Lord Greene MR's formulation of the good faith duty reaffirms the primacy of shareholders, it also gives prominence to the notion of 'enlightened shareholder value' which, in the opinion of the Company Law Review Steering Group, 'is more likely to drive long-term company performance and maximize

---

[36] Property is a broad notion and can include confidential information in some circumstances; see *Seager* v *Copydex* [1967] 2 All ER 415; *Scherring Chemicals* v *Falkman* [1981] 2 All ER 321. See further the discussion below on the matter of whether a business opportunity can constitute property. It has recently been held that the good faith duty also encompasses the duty to disclose misconduct by the director to the company: see the judgment of Arden LJ in *Item Software (UK) Ltd* v *Fassihi* [2005] 2 BCLC 91. See also, *Midland Tool Ltd* v *Midland International Tooling Ltd* [2003] 2 BCLC 523; and *Lexi Holdings plc* v *Luqman* [2008] 2 BCLC 725.

[37] *Cook* v *Deeks* [1916] 1 AC 554; *Rolled Steel Products Ltd* v *BSC* [1985] 3 All ER 52; *Aveling Barford Ltd* v *Perion* (1989) 5 BCC 677. On bribes, see *Boston Deep Sea Fishing Co.* v *Ansell* (1888) 39 Ch D 399; *Hannibal* v *Frost* (1988) 4 BCC 3 and, s. 176, below.

[38] Although s. 212 is not restricted to the taking of corporate assets.

[39] See e.g. *Attorney General's Reference (No. 2 of 1982)* [1984] 2 All ER 216; *R* v *Rozeik* [1996] BCC 271.

[40] This non-interventionist policy (the internal management rule) was explained by Lord Eldon LC in *Carlen* v *Drury* (1812) 1 Ves & B 154, who said: 'This Court is not required on every Occasion to take the Management of every Playhouse and Brewhouse in the Kingdom.' See further, *Howard Smith Ltd* v *Ampol Petroleum Ltd* [1974] AC 82, PC; and *Re Southern Counties Fresh Foods Ltd, sub nom. Cobden Investments Ltd* v *RWM Langport Ltd and others* [2008] EWHC 2810 (Ch). In *Regentcrest plc* v *Cohen* [2001] 2 BCLC 80, Jonathan Parker J, at p. 105, explained that the duty to act *bona fide* in the interests of a company is a subjective one: 'The question is not whether, viewed objectively by the court, the particular act or omission which is challenged was in fact in the interests of the company; still less is the question whether the court, had it been in the position of the director at the relevant time, might have acted differently. Rather, the question is whether the director honestly believed that his act or omission was in the interests of the company. The issue is as to the director's state of mind . . .' See also, *Knight* v *Frost* [1999] 1 BCLC 364.

[41] [2005] 2 BCLC 91. See J. Lowry 'The Duty of Loyalty of Company Directors: Bridging the Accountability Gap Through Efficient Disclosure' [2009] CLJ 607.

overall competitiveness and wealth and welfare for all'.[42] Section 172 (1) thus requires a director:

> to act in the way he considers, in good faith, would be most likely to promote the success of the company for the benefit of its members as a whole, and in doing so, have regard (amongst other matters) to –
> (a) the likely consequences of any decision in the long term,
> (b) the interests of the company's employees,
> (c) the need to foster the company's business relationships with suppliers, customers and others,
> (d) the impact of the company's operations on the community and the environment,
> (e) the desirability of the company maintaining a reputation for high standards of business conduct, and
> (f) the need to act fairly as between members of the company.

The phrase 'have regard to' was explained by Margaret Hodge, then Minister of State for Industry and the Regions:

> The words 'have regard to' means 'think about'; they are absolutely not about just ticking boxes. If 'thinking about' leads to the conclusion, as we believe it will in many cases, that the proper course is to act positively to achieve the objects in the [provision], that will be what the director's duty is. In other words 'have regard to' means 'give proper consideration to' . . .[43]

The factors listed in subsection (1) are not intended to be exhaustive. Rather, it is designed to give emphasis to factors that reflect wider expectations of responsible business behaviour.[44] In this regard, factor (b) carries forward the requirement to have regard to the interests of employees that was laid down in s. 309 of the Companies Act 1985.[45] That said, it remains the case that, as under the pre-existing law, the 'interests of the company' are of overriding importance. Nevertheless, the list mirrors the government's thinking that such matters embrace the 'wider social responsibilities' of companies,[46] and the provision is reinforced by the requirement laid down in s. 417 (2) that the directors' business review should inform members of the company and help them assess how the directors have performed their duty under section 172.[47] Whether or not the statutory

---

[42] White Paper, 2005, para 3.3. Available at <http://webarchive.nationalarchives.gov.uk/20070603185140/http://www.dti.gov.uk/bbf/co-act-2006/white-paper/page22800.html>.

[43] Hansard, HC, vol. 450, col. 789 (17 October 2006).

[44] See the Explanatory Notes to the Act. In a prescient judgment delivered in *Teck Corporation* v *Millar* (1972) 33 DLR (3d) 288 at p. 314, Berger J recognised that: 'If today the directors of a company were to consider the interests of its employees no one would argue that in doing so they were not acting bona fide in the interests of the company itself. Similarly, if the directors were to consider the consequences to the community of any policy that the company intended to pursue, and were deflected in their commitment to that policy as a result, it could not be said that they had not considered bona fide the interests of the shareholders.' In *Re West Coast Capital (Lios) Ltd* [2008] CSOH 72, a Court of Session decision, Lord Glennie expressed the view that although there was no equivalent in the earlier Companies Acts, this section does 'little more than set out the pre-existing law on the subject' (at para. [21]). It will be interesting to see whether this interpretation is followed, because the provision sets out, for the first time in the companies legislation, certain factors that directors are required to consider. See also, *Re Southern Counties Fresh Foods Ltd, sub nom. Cobden Investments Ltd* v *RWM Langport Ltd and others* [2008] EWHC 2810 (Ch), at [52].

[45] The decisions in *Parke* v *Daily News Ltd* [1962] Ch 927 and *Hutton* v *West Cork Railway Co.* (1883) 23 Ch D 654 are now only of historical interest. In this respect, see also s. 247 of the Companies Act 2006 (power to make provision for employees on cessation or transfer of business).

[46] See *Duties of company directors: Ministerial Statements* (London: DTI, 2007).

[47] See further, J. Lowry 'The Duty of Loyalty of Company Directors: Bridging the Accountability Gap Through Efficient Disclosure' [2009] CLJ 607.

statement of these considerations will impact upon directorial decision making has been the subject of debate.[48]

Indeed, the fear that s. 172 holds the potential to open the commercial decision making of directors to judicial challenge seems ill-founded in the light of the reasoning of Mr Justice Sales in *R (on the application of People & Planet)* v *HM Treasury*.[49] The case arose by way of an application for permission to bring judicial review proceedings. People & Planet objected to HM Treasury's policy in relation to the management of the Royal Bank of Scotland (RBS) by UK Financial Investments Ltd (UKFI), the company through which the Government owns RBS. The claimant argued that HM Treasury acted unlawfully in adopting the policy it promulgated relating to how UKFI should manage the investment in RBS. The policy it adopted calls for a commercial approach on the part of UKFI. The claimant objected to this on the basis that UKFI should be promoting a more intervention- ist approach as a major shareholder in RBS, and seek to persuade or require RBS to change its current commercial lending practices and adopt instead lending policies which did not support ventures or businesses which might be said to be harmful to the environment by reason of their carbon emissions or be said to be insufficiently respectful of human rights. One of the lines of attack made by the claimant was that there was a misdirection of law by HM Treasury as to the effect of s 172. The application was refused. The judge held that in evaluating the policy with reference to the Green Book (which set out guidance for decision making in central government), officials correctly identified the proper way in which social and environmental considerations may be taken into account by the directors of RBS in the context of the duties of those directors under s 172. He noted that the ques- tion then was whether HM Treasury should have sought to go further, so as in effect to seek to impose its own policy in relation to combating climate change and promoting human rights on the board of RBS, contrary to the judgment of the directors:

> In my view, that clearly would have a tendency to come into conflict with, and hence would cut across, the duties of the RBS Board as set out in section 172(1). It would also have given rise to a real risk of litigation by minority shareholders seeking to complain that the value of their shares had been detrimentally affected by the Government seeking to impose its policy on RBS, as was identified in the background document which accompanied the Green Book assessment.[50]

Mr Justice Sales went on to state that decisions regarding the management of RBS will be matters for the judgment of the directors of RBS:

> The policy adopted by HM Treasury is that UKFI can properly seek to influence the Board of RBS to have regard to environmental and human rights considerations in accordance with the RBS Board's duty under s 172 . . . It was a legitimate argument against going further than that that there would be a risk of trying to press the RBS Board beyond the limits of their own duties, and in my view that is all that has been said in paragraph 13(e) of the Green Book assessment, read in its proper

---

[48] Fisher, D. 'The Enlightened Shareholder: Leaving Stakeholders in the Dark -- Will Section 172 (1) of the Companies Act 2006 Make Directors Consider the Impact of their Decisions on Third Parties?' *International Company and Commercial Law Review* 20(1) 2009: 10; Keay, A. 'Section 172 (1) of the Companies Act 2006: An interpretation and assessment' Comp Law 28.4 (2007): 106–110.

[49] [2009] EWHC 3020 (Admin), See, S.F. Copp 'S. 172 of the Companies Act 2006 Fails People and Planet' [2010] Comp Law 406. The Law Society had raised a concern that the provision could raise the spectre of courts reviewing business decisions taken in good faith by subjecting such decisions to objective tests, with serious resulting implications for the management of companies by their directors. See, the Law Society's 'Proposed Amendments and Briefing for Parts 10 & 11' (issued 23 January 2006).

[50] *Ibid.* [34].

context as one reason among others. In my view, on a fair reading of that document, it was not being said that there was an absolute legal bar to the introduction of a different policy, but rather that was a good reason for not pressing the RBS Board by means of a more interventionist policy for UKFI.[51]

The decision certainly seems to accord with the legislative intention underlying s. 172. In the Lords Grand Committee,[52] Lord Goldsmith summarised the scope of the provision in the following terms: 'it is for the directors, by reference to those things we are talking about – the objective of the company – to judge and form a good faith judgment about what is to be regarded as success for the members as a whole . . . the duty is to promote the success for the benefit of the members as a whole – that is, for the members as a collective body – not only to benefit the majority shareholders, or any particular shareholder or section of shareholders, still less the interests of directors who might happen to be shareholders themselves.' However, it will not be enough to simply assert that their motivations, as directors, were in good faith; the court will have to determine the credibility of those assertions.[53]

Section 172 (3), while not codifying as such the case law in which the courts have recognised that directors in discharging their good faith duty to the company must have regard to the interests of creditors where the business is insolvent or of doubtful solvency, nevertheless provides that the duty in s. 172 (1) is subject to any enactment or rule of law requiring directors, in certain circumstances, to consider or act in the interests of creditors. The reference to 'any enactment' no doubt refers to provisions such as s. 214 of the Insolvency Act 1986.[54] With respect to the common law, the position was summarised by Richard Reid QC, sitting as a deputy judge in the High Court, in *Re Pantone 485 Ltd*:[55]

In my view, where the company is insolvent, the human equivalent of the company for the purposes of the directors' fiduciary duties is the company's creditors as a whole, *ie* its general creditors. It follows that if the directors act consistently with the interests of the general creditors but inconsistently with the interest of a creditor or section of creditors with special rights in a winding-up, they do not act in breach of duty to the company.[56]

---

[51] *Ibid.* at [35].
[52] 6 February 2006 (col. 256).
[53] See *Roberts* v *Frohlich* [2011] EWHC 257 (Ch).
[54] Discussed below under D. Commenting on the language of subs (3) and its interrelationship with subsection (1), Lord Mance, dissenting, in *Stone & Rolls Ltd* v *Moore Stephens* [2009] UKHL 39, [224], noted that: 'Section 172(1) of the Companies Act 2006 now states the duty, in terms expressly based on common law rules and equitable principles (see s 170(3)), as being to "act in the way he considers, in good faith, would be most likely to promote the success of the company for the benefit of its members as a whole" – a duty made expressly "subject to any enactment or rule of law requiring directors, in certain circumstances, to consider or act in the interests of creditors of the company" (see s 172(3)).'
[55] [2002] 1 BCLC 266. See also, *West Mercia Safetywear Ltd (in liq.)* v *Dodd* [1988] BCLC 250 and *Winkworth* v *Edward Baron Development Co. Ltd* [1987] BCLC 193, HL.
[56] *Ibid.* at pp. 286–287. In *Colin Gwyer and Associates Ltd* v *London Wharf (Limehouse) Ltd* [2003] 2 BCLC 153, at [87], it was held that a resolution of the board of directors passed without proper consideration being given by certain directors to the interests of creditors would be open to challenge if the company had been insolvent at the date of the resolution. Leslie Kosmin QC, sitting as a deputy judge in the High Court, observed: 'In relation to an insolvent company, the directors when considering the company's interests must have regard to the interests of the creditors. If they fail to do so, and therefore ignore the relevant question, the *Charterbridge Corpn Ltd* v *Lloyds Bank Ltd* [1970] Ch 62 test can be applied with the modification that in considering the interests of the company the honest and intelligent director must have been capable of believing that the decision was for the benefit of the creditors. In my view the *Charterbridge Corporation* test is of general application.' In *Roberts* v *Frohlich* [2011] EWHC 257 (Ch), Norris J, citing this passage, held that if there is no reasonable prospect of the company avoiding an insolvent liquidation, the directors have a duty to minimise potential loss to the company's creditors.

In *Re HLC Environmental Projects Ltd*,[57] the court heard an application by the company's liquidators under s. 212 of the Insolvency Act 1986 for financial relief against the defendant director in respect of certain payments he had caused the company to make. It was alleged that the defendant had made those payments despite knowing that the company was in financial difficulties and were therefore made in breach of s. 172 and in breach of the duty to act in creditors' interests under s. 172(3). The judge, granting the application (*West Mercia Safetywear Ltd (in liq.)* v *Dodd*, followed), observed that directors were not free to put the interests of the company ahead of creditors' prospects of being paid. He said that the duties under s. 172 were generally subjective (see *LNOC Ltd* v *Watford AFC Ltd*),[58] however an objective test would apply (a) in considering whether creditors' interests were paramount; (b) where there was no evidence of actual consideration: the test was then whether an intelligent and honest man in the director's position could have reasonably believed that the transaction was for the company's benefit; and (c) where a large creditor's interest was overlooked.

## C  Duty to exercise independent judgment

Section 173 encapsulates another aspect of the duty of good faith, namely that directors must exercise an 'unfettered discretion'. Section 173(1) provides that: 'A director of a company must exercise independent judgment'; however, subsection (2) goes on to add that:

This duty is not infringed by his acting –
(a) in accordance with an agreement duly entered into by the company that restricts the future exercise of discretion by its directors, or
(b) in a way authorised by the company's constitution.

What this means is that the company, the beneficiary, is entitled to have a decision on a business matter reached solely on its commercial merits pertaining at the time the decision is taken. Thus, a director who undertakes to vote in a particular way on some issue will be in breach of duty unless that commitment was itself undertaken for genuine commercial reasons. These kinds of issues were discussed in *Fulham BC* v *Cabra Estates*,[59] where it was held that, in the circumstances the directors were not in breach of their duty because they had committed themselves to a long-term policy for commercial reasons. Neill LJ explained that:

It is trite law that directors are under a duty to act *bona fide* in the interests of their company. However, it does not follow from that proposition that directors can never make a contract by which they bind themselves to the future exercise of their powers in a particular manner, even though the contract taken as a whole is manifestly for the benefit of the company. Such a rule could well prevent companies from entering into contracts which were commercially beneficial to them.[60]

---

[57] [2013] EWHC 2876 (Ch).
[58] [2013] EWHC 3615 (Comm), at [64].
[59] [1992] BCC 863.
[60] [1992] BCC 863, 875. Neil LJ endorsed the view of Kitto J in the Australian case *Thorby* v *Goldberg* (1964) 112 CLR 597, 605–606, who had stated that: 'There are many kinds of transaction in which the proper time for the exercise of the directors' discretion is the time of the negotiation of a contract and not the time at which the contract is to be performed . . . If at the former time they are *bona fide* of opinion that it is in the interests of the company that the transaction should be entered into and carried into effect I see no reason in law why they should not bind themselves to do whatever under the transaction is to be done by the board.'

The duty to exercise independent judgment has also come to the fore in relation to nominee directors (e.g. where a parent company appoints a nominee to the board of its subsidiary). It is settled that they cannot be the mere puppets of those who appoint them.[61] During the passage of the Bill through Parliament, the Solicitor General explained that:

> Subsection (2) (b) will allow the status of the nominee director to be enshrined in the company's constitution so that the nominee is able to follow the instructions of the person who appointed him without breaching that duty. The extent to which that is possible under the existing law was unclear, but we have now made it clear. However, even where a nominee follows instructions, he must still comply with all his other duties – there may well be other duties – such as a duty to act broadly in the interests of the company.[62]

The intent, therefore, is that the constitution can alleviate the duty laid down in subsection (1) for nominee directors, though they will continue to be subject to the other duties.

More generally, directors are not permitted to delegate their powers unless the company's constitution provides otherwise.[63] Where delegation is permitted, a director must exercise reasonable care and skill in deciding to whom to delegate particular functions. In *Re Westmid Packing Services Ltd*,[64] Lord Woolf took a realistic view of the duty:

> A proper degree of delegation and division of responsibility is of course permissible, and often necessary, but total abrogation of responsibility is not. A board of directors must not permit one individual to dominate them and use them . . .[65]

It has been suggested that s. 173 casts doubt on the extent to which directors can rely on their colleagues (e.g. a managing director or a director with specialist expertise in relation to a matter requiring a decision of the board) or external advisers.[66] Responding to this anxiety, Lord Goldsmith, in the Lords Grand Committee, explained that:

> The duty does not prevent a director from relying on the advice or work of others, but the final judgment must be his responsibility. He clearly cannot be expected to do everything himself. Indeed, in certain circumstances directors may be in breach of their duty if they fail to take appropriate advice – for example, legal advice. As with all advice, slavish reliance is not acceptable,

---

[61] *Scottish Co-operative Wholesale Society Ltd* v *Meyer* [1959] AC 324. See also, *Re Neath Rugby Club Ltd* [2008] BCLC 527, at [26]–[27], HHJ Havelock-Allan QC (reversed in part by the Court of Appeal, reported as *Hawkes* v *Cuddy* [2009] 2 BCLC 427, although the judge's reasoning set out in [26]–[27] was not in issue on appeal). Here a director had been nominated by a shareholder. Stanley Burnton LJ said, at [32]: 'the fact that a director of a company has been nominated to that office by a shareholder does not, of itself, impose any duty on the director owed to his nominator. The director may owe duties to his nominator if he is an employee or officer of the nominator, but such duties do not arise out of his nomination, but out of a separate agreement or office. Such duties cannot however, detract from his duty to the company of which he is a director when he is acting as such . . .' We return to the topic of nominee directors below in relation to s. 175 (duty to avoid conflicts of interest).
[62] See the answer by the Solicitor General, HC Official Report, SC D (Company Law Reform Bill), 11 July 2006, col. 601.
[63] Table A, art 72 (Companies (Tables A to F) Regulations 1985 (SI 1985/805)) provides for the delegation of functions by directors. See also, the Companies (Model Articles) Regulations 2008 (SI 2008/3229) for private companies limited by shares (Sch. 1) and public companies (Sch. 3), art. 5, respectively.
[64] [1998] 2 BCLC 646, CA.
[65] *Ibid*. 653. See also, *Re Barings plc (No. 5) Secretary of State for Trade and Industry* v *Baker (No. 5)* [2000] 1 BCLC 523, CA, at 536.
[66] See the Law Society's 'Proposed Amendments and Briefing for Parts 10 & 11' (issued 23 January 2006) 11.

and the obtaining of outside advice does not absolve directors from exercising their judgment on the basis of such advice.[67]

In this respect, a decision of the Federal Court of Australia contains some important lessons for directors (particularly non-executive directors) who, in defending a claim for breach of duty, argue they relied on expert advice. In *Australian Securities and Investments Commission* v *Healey*,[68] the court found the CEO, the CFO, the non-executive chair and five other non-executive directors of the Centro group of companies in breach of their duties in failing to notice multi-billion Australian and US dollar errors in the group's financial statements.[69] In his reasoning, his Honour Justice Middleton stressed the importance of financial statements and the critical role of a director as the 'final filter' in checking corporate financial accounting.[70] The directors argued that they had proper safeguards in place, including receiving professional advice from PricewaterhouseCoopers, and so their responsibilities had been discharged. Rejecting this contention, the court found that the fact that those advising the directors were themselves in error was irrelevant to the determination of the directors' conduct. The judge observed:

> Nothing I decide in this case should indicate that directors are required to have infinite knowledge or ability. Directors are entitled to delegate to others the preparation of books and accounts and the carrying on of the day-to-day affairs of the company. What each director is expected to do is to take a diligent and intelligent interest in the information available to him or her, to understand that information, and apply an enquiring mind to the responsibilities placed upon him or her . . .[71]

## D Duty to exercise reasonable care, skill and diligence

The common law duties of care and skill represent the courts' attempts to regulate the entrepreneurial side of the director's activities. Until relatively recently, the legal position tended towards regarding holding a directorship as a gracious activity where some gentle coaxing from the courts was sometimes appropriate.[72] Thus, judicial expressions of the duty of care were couched in subjective terms,[73] careful not to require anything approaching the objective concept of reasonable care inherent in the tortious 'neighbour test'. For instance, in *Dorchester Finance Co. Ltd* v *Stebbing*,[74] Foster J regarded the law as being that: 'A director is required to take in the performance of his duties such care

---

[67] Lords Grand Committee, 6 February 2006 (col. 282). See, *Re Brian D Pierson (Contractors) Ltd* [2001] 1 BCLC 275.

[68] [2011] FCA 717. See J. Lowry 'The Irreducible Core of the Duty of Care, Skill and Diligence of Company Directors' [2012] MLR 249.

[69] Taken together, ss. 180 and 344 of the (Australian) Corporations Act 2001 require directors to be diligent and careful in their consideration of the resolution to approve the accounts and reports and to take all reasonable steps to secure compliance with the statutory requirements, and to inquire about any potential deficiency in the accounts and reports that they observed.

[70] Above, n. 70, at para 582.

[71] *Ibid.* at para. 20.

[72] This refers to the non-executive director. Directors with full-time service contracts will normally owe duties of reasonable care in accordance with those contracts.

[73] See Romer J's consideration of the earlier authorities in *Re City Equitable Fire Insurance Co. Ltd* [1925] Ch 407. See V. Finch 'Company Directors: Who Cares about Skill and Care' (1992) 55 MLR 179.

[74] [1989] BCLC 498.

as an ordinary man might be expected to take on his own behalf.'[75] There was a similar subjective duty of skill: 'A director is required to exhibit in the performance of his duties such degree of skill as may reasonably be required from a person with his knowledge and experience.'[76] Due to the approach taken by Lord Hoffmann in *Norman* v *Theordore Goddard*,[77] and *Re D'Jan of London Ltd*,[78] the standard of care laid down in s. 214 (4) of the Insolvency Act 1986 (the 'wrongful trading' provision)[79] was imported into the more general realms of directors' common law duties of care and skill. By s. 214 (4), the director was required to behave as:

a reasonably diligent person having both –
(a)  the general knowledge, skill and experience that may reasonably be expected of a person carrying out the same functions as are carried out[80] by that director in relation to the company, and
(b)  the general knowledge, skill and experience that that director has.

This had the effect of combining the objective standards in para. (a) with the 'sting' apparent in the *Dorchester Finance* case in the subjective standard in para. (b). Section 174 (1) and (2) of the Companies Act 2006 is closely modelled on this provision. However, in addition to the objectivity requirement, in order to establish liability it will also be necessary to show a causal link between the loss suffered by the company and the alleged breach of duty.[81]

Claims for breach of the duty will generally be assessed on the basis of expert evidence. In *Abbey Forwarding Ltd* v *Hone*,[82] a number of allegations were made against four directors, including that they had breached the duty to exercise reasonable care, skill and diligence under s. 174 by allowing the company to become increasingly indebted to HMRC. Lewison J, holding that the directors were not in breach of the duty, explained that:

In deciding whether directors have fallen short of their duty of skill and care, particularly where the breach of duty concerns the precise way in which the business is run, evidence of what is normal in the field of commerce in which the company operates is of considerable relevance.[83]

In his reasoning, the judge went on to note:

Although it is only an analogy, in *Sansom* v *Metcalfe Hambleton & Co* [1998] 2 EGLR 103 (which was a case of alleged professional negligence) Butler-Sloss LJ said:
'In my judgment, it is clear, from both lines of authority to which I have referred, that a court should be slow to find a professionally qualified man guilty of a breach of his duty of skill and care towards a client (or third party) without evidence from those within the same profession as to the standard expected on the facts of the case and the failure of the professionally qualified man

---

[75] *Ibid.* at pp. 501–502.
[76] *Ibid.*
[77] [1991] BCLC 1028 at pp. 1030–1031, Hoffmann J, as he then was.
[78] [1993] BCC 646 at p. 648, Hoffmann LJ, as he then was.
[79] See below.
[80] Or are entrusted to him; see Insolvency Act 1986, s. 214 (5).
[81] *Weavering Capital (UK) Ltd & Anor* v *Peterson & Ors* [2012] EWHC 1480 (Ch), where it was shown that the directors were liable because allowing the business to continue had been the direct cause of the loss to the company.
[82] [2010] EWHC 2029 (Ch).
[83] *Ibid.* at [198].

to measure up to that standard. It is not an absolute rule, as Sachs LJ indicated by his example, but, unless it is an obvious case, in the absence of the relevant expert evidence the claim will not be proved.'[84]

The move towards adopting greater objectivity in assessing the standard of care and skill expected of the modern director can be seen in the judicial recognition that it is no longer possible to make symbolic appointments to boards of directors on the basis of social standing or merely to maintain a family connection.[85] For example, in *Francis v United Jersey Bank*,[86] the business of the company had been conducted for many years with the husband and wife, and their sons, as directors. The husband died and the sons carried on running the business. The wife remained a director but had become ill after her husband's death and took no part in the running of the business. The sons perpetrated a fraud that damaged the company, and it was later sought to make the wife liable for breach of her duties as director.[87] The argument that she did not bear the full responsibility of a director was rejected by the New Jersey Court of Appeal on the basis that if a person sat on a board it was a representation to the shareholders and creditors that she or he was making an input in the normal way and that it was not possible, when in breach of duty, to 'point to a sign saying "dummy director"'.[88]

Section 174, while settling the matter once and for all that directors will be judged according to mixed objective/subjective tests as first laid down in the 'wrongful trading' provision,[89] nevertheless leaves open another problem that the courts will need to confront. That is, the argument that in modern companies carrying out very many transactions in dispersed geographical locations, it is often going to be very difficult even for the most diligent director to keep track of what is going on.[90] If the courts are too severe here in their interpretation of what reasonableness requires, they will make it difficult for

---

[84] *Ibid.*

[85] For an example of the appointment of a director on the basis of social standing, see *Re Cardiff Savings Bank* [1892] 2 Ch 100.

[86] 87 NJ 15, 432 A 2d 814 (1981). See L. Griggs and J. Lowry 'Minority Shareholder Rights in England, Canada, Australia and the USA' [1994] JBL 463. In *Australian Securities and Investments Commission v Healey*, above n. 70, at para. 19, the judge noted that: 'The words of Pollock J in the case of *Francis v United Jersey Bank . . .* quoted with approval by Clarke and Sheller JJA in *Daniels v Anderson* (1995) 37 NSWLR 438, make it clear that more than a mere "going through the paces" is required for directors. As Pollock J noted, a director is not an ornament, but an essential component of corporate governance.' His Honour Justice Middleton also observed, at para. 16, that: 'The case law indicates that there is a core, irreducible requirement of directors to be involved in the management of the company and to take all reasonable steps to be in a position to guide and monitor.'

[87] By then she had died and the action was actually against her estate.

[88] 432 A 2d 814 (1981). See also, *Re Brian D Pierson (Contractors) Ltd* [2001] 1 BCLC 275 at pp. 309–310, where Hazel Williamson QC, sitting as a deputy judge of the High Court, refused to countenance symbolic roles for directors: 'The office of director has certain minimum responsibilities and functions, which are not simply discharged by leaving all management functions, and consideration of the company's affairs to another director without question, even in the case of a family company . . . One cannot be a "sleeping" director; the function of "directing" on its own requires some consideration of the company's affairs to be exercised.' See also, *Daniels v Anderson* (1995) 37 NSWLR 438, which suggests that financial competence and knowledge of the business is the minimum to be expected of directors in terms of skill.

[89] Recently, in the case of *Richmond Pharmacology Ltd v Chester Overseas Ltd & Ors* [2014] EWHC 2692, the mixed objective/subjective test was described as the objective test. However, in the majority of cases, the test is described as dual in nature.

[90] As will be seen, this issue frequently arises in the context of applications for the disqualification of directors for unfitness under the Company Directors Disqualification Act 1986, s. 6. See, *Re Barings plc (No. 5)* [1999] 1 BCLC 433; *Re Westmid Packing Services Ltd* [1998] 2 BCLC 646; and *Re London Citylink Ltd* [2005] EWHC 2875 (Ch).

boards to find directors. This complexity, combined with a move towards reducing the court's requirement to be explicit in its statements of the duty and the standards of care considered breach, may cause significant concern for potential directors.[91] Indemnity insurance will not solve the problem indefinitely because if claims were too high it would eventually become difficult to obtain. Here then lies a practical problem in corporate governance. How can directors keep track of the business[92] of their companies in a way sufficient to meet their legal liabilities? Non-executive directors have been given some guidance (issued by the ICSA in January 2013) in this regard. The guidance suggests ways in which non-executive directors can approach their work to allow them to demonstrate to a regulator or court, if necessary, that they had taken appropriate steps to exercise reasonable care, skill and diligence in their role.[93] However, executive directors will be aware that there have been very few cases brought under s. 174 since the codification and only one finding of breach, raising that question as to whether, in practice, this issue may easily be overstated.[94]

## E Duty to avoid conflicts of interest

### 1 *Rationale of the rule*

Section 175 of the Companies Act 2006 seeks to restate the core fiduciary duty of a director to avoid a conflict between his or her own personal interest with the interests of the company, albeit with some modification. The policy underlying equity's anxiety in this regard was explained by Lord Herschell in *Bray* v *Ford*:[95]

> It is an inflexible rule of a court of equity that a person in a fiduciary position . . . is not, unless otherwise expressly provided . . . allowed to put himself in a position where his interest and duty conflict. It does not appear to me that this rule is . . . founded upon principles of morality. I regard it rather as based on the consideration that, human nature being what it is, there is a danger, in such circumstances, of the person holding a fiduciary position being swayed by interest rather than by duty, and thus prejudicing those whom he was bound to protect.[96]

---

[91] In *Weavering Capital (UK) Ltd (in liq.)* v *Dabhia* [2013] EWCA Civ 71, McCombe LJ noted that 'provided a judge recognises the law's requirements as to the duties placed upon directors and, having reviewed the facts, considers that the relevant duty has been broken, it is not necessary to spell out any further what the duty is or the standard of care to be exercised by the particular director whose conduct is being called into question.'

[92] The problem is particularly acute for non-executive directors, who, by definition, are not required to give all their time or attention to the company. For recent preliminary issue litigation on the extent of the duties owed by NEDs, see *Equitable Life Assurance Society* v *Bowley* [2003] BCC 829.

[93] In summary the guidance suggests that non-executive directors should: understand that more is expected from a non-executive director with a specific skill or specific experience; recognise that part of their role is to uphold high standards of integrity and probity, and to support the chair and executive directors in instilling the appropriate culture, values and behaviours in the boardroom; understand the requirements of the Companies Act 2006 in relation to conflicts of interest, gifts and hospitality and familiarise themselves with the company's policies on the same; insist on receiving high-quality information sufficiently in advance of meetings, which is accurate, clear, comprehensive, up-to-date and timely; and speak to the company's advisers (e.g. the external auditor) if they consider it necessary.

[94] The breach was found in *Weavering Capital (UK) Ltd & Anor* v *Peterson & Ors* [2012] EWHC 1480 (Ch).

[95] In *Bray* v *Ford* [1896] AC 44.

[96] *Ibid.* at p. 47. In *Boardman* v *Phipps* [1967] 2 AC 46 at p. 123, Lord Upjohn stated: 'The fundamental rule of equity [is] that a person in a fiduciary capacity must not make a profit out of his trust which is part of the wider rule that a trustee must not place himself in a position where his duty and his interest may conflict.'

Section 175 (1) provides that a director must avoid a situation in which he has, or can have, a direct or indirect interest that conflicts, or possibly may conflict,[97] with the interests of the company.[98] Section 175 (2) elaborates further on the contours of the duty as calibrated by the courts (particularly in relation to the application of the duty to directors), by providing that it applies in particular 'to the exploitation of any property, information or opportunity (and it is immaterial whether the company could take advantage of the property, information or opportunity)'. However, some limit is placed on the duty by s. 175 (3) which excludes from its ambit conflicts arising in relation to a transaction or arrangement with the company. These must be declared under s. 177 in the case of proposed transactions or under s. 182 in the case of existing transactions.[99]

The duty came to the fore in the eighteenth century with the emergence of the family trust,[100] and was applied to commercial relationships where fiduciary obligations were found to exist. When adjudicating on an alleged breach of fiduciary duty, by a director, or trustee, the courts are faced with a problem which they have long recognised. The beneficiary is at an almost impossible disadvantage when it comes to proving that there has been a breach of duty. This is particularly true if the beneficiary under a trust is a minor. But the problem is there even if she or he is of full age. And the problem is there in companies. The disadvantage stems from the fact that the directors (or trustee, if a trust) often have in their hands the ability to ensure that the facts appear as they would wish them to appear. This is obviously not always possible. If, for instance, assets have been taken from a trust or from the company's bank account, there may well be independent evidence of this in the hands of the beneficiary or coming into the hands of the court. But where the breach being complained of relates to an exercise of discretion or a decision on a course of action, the problem is almost insurmountable. Suppose the directors of a company have turned down some business offer from a third party with the intention of secretly taking up the offer themselves in their private capacity. They have in their hands the ability to make it appear that their decision was properly reached. They will ensure that there are fictitious minutes of the board meeting showing that the business proposition was discussed carefully, but then rejected, on the perfectly proper grounds that the company did not have enough capital for the project, and also there were worries expressed about the compatibility of the proposed project with the company's existing commitments etc. Faced with this, how is a suspicious shareholder to prove that they were in breach of duty and that the board decision was reached, not on a commercial basis as appeared from the minutes, but for reasons of personal advancement?

For hundreds of years, the courts have had a solution to this problem. Any situation which ostensibly gives rise to a conflict between the director's personal interests, and his duty to the company, is treated as a situation from which the director cannot benefit; or can

---

[97] In *Boardman* v *Phipps*, *ibid.* at p. 124, Lord Upjohn observed that 'The phrase "possibly may conflict" requires consideration. In my view it means that the reasonable man looking at the relevant facts and circumstances of the particular case would think that there was a real sensible possibility of conflict; not that you could imagine some situation arising which might, in some conceivable possibility in events not contemplated as real sensible possibilities by any reasonable person, result in a conflict.'

[98] The provision thus encapsulates the various formulations of the duty delivered by, for example, Lord Cranworth LC in *Aberdeen Railway* v *Blaikie* (1854) 1 Macq 461 at pp. 471–472; by Lord Herschell in *Bray* v *Ford* [1896] AC 44 at p. 44; and by Lord Upjohn in *Boardman* v *Phipps*.

[99] A specific duty, discussed in Chapter 9.

[100] See e.g. *Keech* v *Sandford* (1726) Sel Cas Chapter 61.

only benefit after protective procedures have been complied with. In a sense, the courts are applying a presumption that the fiduciary duty has been broken, and taking action accordingly. The policy was clearly enunciated in the eighteenth-century case of *Keech* v *Sandford*.[101] Here, the court was being asked to allow a trustee (who was holding a lease as trust property) to renew the lease for his own benefit, on the genuine basis that the lessor had refused to renew it for the trust. The situation elicited Lord King LC's cynical observation: 'If a trustee, on the refusal to renew, might have a lease to himself, few trust estates would be renewed [for the benefit of the trust].'[102] Translated into the company law situation, the doctrine holds that any situation which is inherently likely to lead to a breach of the duty of good faith should automatically be treated as if the breach had occurred. In such cases therefore, whether the directors are actually in good faith or not, is not in issue.

In *Sharma* v *Sharma*,[103] Jackson LJ took the opportunity to summarise the case law which s. 175 restates. He said:

> I must apply the following principles in resolving the issues in the present appeal . . .
>
> (i)   A company director is in breach of his fiduciary or statutory duty if he exploits for his personal gain (a) opportunities which come to his attention through his role as director or (b) any other opportunities which he could and should exploit for the benefit of the company.
>
> (ii)  If the shareholders with full knowledge of the relevant facts consent to the director exploiting those opportunities for his own personal gain, then that conduct is not a breach of the fiduciary or statutory duty.
>
> (iii) If the shareholders with full knowledge of the relevant facts acquiesce in the director's proposed conduct, then that may constitute consent. However, consent cannot be inferred from silence unless:
>
>   (a)  The shareholders know that their consent is required, or
>
>   (b)  The circumstances are such that it would be unconscionable for the shareholders to remain silent at the time and object after the event.
>
> (iv)  For the purposes of propositions (ii) and (iii) full knowledge of the relevant facts does not entail an understanding of their legal incidents. In other words the shareholders need not appreciate that the proposed action would be characterised as a breach of fiduciary or statutory duty.[104]

The difficulty that the courts have faced, in this field, is, as in so many others: 'Where to draw the line?' It is easy to say that a director must not put himself into a position where his duty and interest conflict, but how much of a conflict does there have to be before it will trigger the presumption that a breach of fiduciary duty has occurred? We will see that in recent years the courts have become uncomfortable with the severity of the approach normally adopted towards directors who have business interests of their own, and have tried to strike what they see as a fairer balance between the likelihood of damage to the company and the likelihood of damage to the director's own legitimate business interests or career aims. The case law in this respect will continue to be of relevance. It will be recalled that s. 170 (4) directs the courts to have regard to the corresponding common law rules and equitable principles in interpreting and applying the general duties.

[101] *Ibid*.
[102] *Ibid*.
[103] [2013] EWCA Civ 1287, at [52].
[104] See also *Safetynet Security* v *Coppage* [2013] EWCA Civ 1176, at [27]–[29], Rix LJ.

## 2 Business opportunities

The question of how to handle directors who take up a business opportunity while they are directors is apparently not easy to answer. There are, however, several ways of looking at the problem.

One view is to see business opportunities coming to the company as the property of the company. In which case, in order to make the directors liable for breach of duty, all that has to be shown is that they have taken up the opportunity themselves.[105] It is arguable that this is what happened in *Cook v Deeks*.[106] Here, the defendant directors on behalf of the company negotiated a contract with a third party just as they had done on previous occasions, but when the agreement was formalised, they took the contract in their own names. Although in a sense the contract had not yet come to the company, the court took the view that the contract 'belonged in equity to the company and ought to have been dealt with as an asset of the company'.[107] There are difficulties with this view. It is not really clear whether it is being held there that a mere business opportunity is a property right, and the case can perhaps be explained on the basis that the contract had actually been negotiated for the company and taken up by it, and that the directors had merely put what was by then an asset of the company in their own names. It is perhaps not authority on the wider, and more frequently occurring, question which arises where the business opportunity is not in any way taken up on behalf of the company, but is rejected[108] on behalf of the company and then taken up by the directors personally. If the opportunity is property, then it is pertinent to inquire as to the scope of the property right. It is easy to make the assumption that the profits made by the directors are within the scope of the property right, but this is to forget that the directors could have bona fide rejected the opportunity and then not taken it up themselves. A further and perhaps more significant difficulty comes from the fact that it has been held by the House of Lords in *Regal (Hastings) Ltd v Gulliver*[109] that the directors can be liable for breach of duty in relation to the opportunity even though it was established that the company itself was not in a position to take up the opportunity (in this regard it should be noted that s. 175 (2) expressly states that 'it is immaterial' whether the company could take advantage of the opportunity). This suggests that perhaps the opportunity was not there seen as an asset of the company[110] and means that there is another principle of liability at work here.

In *Regal (Hastings) Ltd v Gulliver*,[111] the company owned a cinema and the directors thought it beneficial for the company to acquire two other nearby cinemas. They formed a subsidiary company to hold the leases of these two new cinemas but the lessor required

---

[105] One basis for the idea is that the directors should have decided to take the opportunity for the company (although they could have bona fide rejected it, they can hardly deny this if they did it themselves) and are treated as carrying it out on the company's behalf. The law on promoters reaches a similar position in some situations; see Chapter 2 above.

[106] [1916] 1 AC 554, PC.

[107] *Ibid.* at p. 564, *per* Lord Buckmaster.

[108] It will not always be clear whether the appropriate organ to do this will be the board, or the general meeting.

[109] [1967] 2 AC 134, [1942] 1 All ER 378.

[110] Even if it was an asset, it would presumably have a negligible value if the company was unable to take it up. Nor, in the circumstances, would they have been able to assign it for value.

[111] [1967] 2 AC 134, [1942] 1 All ER 378.

either a personal guarantee from the directors or that the subsidiary should have a paid-up capital of £5,000.[112] The directors were unwilling to give the guarantees and in the circumstances the company was unable to afford to put more than £2,000 into the subsidiary. To enable the deal to go ahead, the directors and some of their business contacts put the money in themselves, taking shares in return. Eventually, the three cinemas were sold as a group, the purchaser agreeing to take all the shares in the two companies, instead of taking the cinemas on their own. The directors and other shareholders made a profit of nearly £3 per share. Thus Regal and its subsidiary passed under different control, that of the purchaser, who then caused Regal to commence an action to recover the profit that the directors had made on their shares. The action against the directors was successful (although the others involved who were not directors were not liable in the circumstances).[113] Citing *Keech* v *Sanford*, the House of Lords held the directors liable to account because by reason and in the course of their fiduciary relationship, they had made a profit. That was sufficient for liability under the 'no-conflict' rule. They had a fiduciary relationship with the company, and had made a profit out of an opportunity which had come to the company. The House of Lords stressed that liability here in no way depended on absence of good faith. It was also apparent that the company itself could not have taken advantage of the chance to buy the shares which the directors and others purchased, since the company was unable to afford more than £2,000.[114] So why was there liability?

To understand how the no-conflict rule is working it is necessary to see it from the cynical perspective of Lord King LC in *Keech* v *Sandford*.[115] The directors were held to be in good faith because there was no evidence of bad faith. They may well have made sure that no such evidence existed. Similarly, there is cause for scepticism as to the fact that the company could not find more than £2,000, thus opening the way for the directors nobly to step in and save the deal. Who said it could not find more than £2,000? What steps had the board taken to raise more loan or equity capital for Regal so that it would have the money? Since the *Regal* case,[116] other decisions have followed and enshrined the hard line taken there: *Boardman* v *Phipps*;[117] *IDC* v *Cooley*;[118] *Carlton* v *Halestrap*;[119] *Attorney General for Hong Kong* v *Reid*;[120] *Bhullar* v *Bhullar*;[121] and, most recently, *O'Donnell* v

---

[112] As to 'paid-up capital', see Chapter 14.

[113] The action had little moral merit; in effect it was producing a clawback of part of the purchase price.

[114] See also *IDC* v *Cooley* [1972] 1 WLR 443, where the defendant, the managing director of the claimant company, took in his own name a contract which Roskill J found was not likely to be coming to the company. The judge thought that at most there was a 10% chance that the company might get it (at p. 454). The defendant was nevertheless held liable to account for the profit he made from the contract. Commenting on the decision in *Cooley*, Professor Birks notes that: 'in such a case the defendant's liability can be said to be based on an anti-enrichment wrong' so that the no-conflict duty seen operating here means that '[t]he fiduciary must use all his efforts for his beneficiary and must not turn aside to enrich himself while there is the least possibility of enriching the beneficiary.' See P. Birks *An Introduction to the Law of Restitution* (Oxford: OUP, 1989) at p. 340.

[115] See the quotation at E1 above.

[116] Which was actually decided in 1942 although not fully reported until 1967.

[117] [1967] 2 AC 46.

[118] [1972] 1 WLR 443.

[119] (1988) 4 BCC 538.

[120] [1994] 1 AC 324; and see A. J. Boyle '*Attorney-General* v *Reid*: The Company Law Implications' (1995) 16 Co Law 131.

[121] [2003] 2 BCLC 241, CA.

*Shanahan*.[122] Reviewing the cases in which the fiduciary was found not to be acting in bad faith, Professor Birks observes:

> All cases in which such fiduciaries have to make restitution of benefits acquired in breach of this duty can be explained by reference to the policy of prophylaxis. Equity does not wait to see whether the beneficiary has actually suffered and it cannot, therefore, sanction the duty by compelling the fiduciary to repair a loss. Instead the question is whether, in the given circumstances, the fiduciary *might have been* tempted to sacrifice the interests of the beneficiary. The only available sanction, once the fiduciary has actually made the acquisition in question, is therefore restitution.[123]

There is some evidence of a change of approach in cases where the allegation is based on a director's post-resignation breach of duty. In *Island Export Finance Ltd* v *Umunna*[124] the director won. The company, IEF Ltd, had a contract with the Cameroonian government to supply it with post boxes. Umunna was the managing director. After the contract was ended, he resigned. Later he obtained a new contract in his own capacity.[125] IEF Ltd, perhaps not surprisingly, brought an action for breach of fiduciary obligation. The judge held that the director's fiduciary obligation did not necessarily come to an end when he left the company[126] and that a director was not permitted to divert to himself a maturing business opportunity which the company was actively pursuing. However, he found as a fact that the company was not actively pursuing it at the time Umunna took up the opportunity for himself. Moreover, the knowledge that the market existed was part of Umunna's stock in trade and know-how, and it would be against public policy and in restraint of trade to prevent him using this knowledge. The action failed.

The decision is in line with the no-conflict rule, because even under that rule there will come a point when the business opportunity which is taken up by the director is so remote from what the company does or plans to do that there is essentially no conflict. It all comes down to what the business of the company is.[127] The *Umunna* case breaks new ground by being quite lenient towards the director in its definition of what the business of the company was. But it is lenient in another way, also related to the definition of the business of the company, because in assessing what that business is, *Umunna* also requires us to have

---

[122] [2009] 2 BCLC 666, CA; noted by D. Ahern [2011] *MLR* 596. The case came before the courts via an unfair prejudice petition, as to which see below, 8.4 and Chapter 12. The inflexibility of the no-conflict duty as envisioned in the early trusts cases such as *Keech* v *Sandford* was roundly endorsed by Rimer LJ in *O'Donnell*, who said, at [55]: 'the rationale of the "no conflict" and "no profit" rules is to underpin the fiduciary's duty of undivided loyalty to his beneficiary. If an opportunity comes to him in his capacity as a fiduciary, his principal is entitled to know about it. The director cannot be left to make the decision as to whether he is allowed to help himself to its benefit.' See also, *Towers* v *Premier Waste Management Ltd* [2011] EWCA Civ 923. In *Item Software Ltd* v *Fassihi* [2003] 2 BCLC 1 it was even held that a director would owe a duty to disclose his own misconduct in some circumstances. This was what was described as a 'superadded' duty of disclosure.

[123] P. Birks *An Introduction to the Law of Restitution* (Oxford: OUP, 1989) at p. 339.

[124] [1986] BCLC 460. See also, *Balston Ltd* v *Headline Filters Ltd* [1990] FSR 385.

[125] Actually for a company he then owned.

[126] A similar conclusion had been reached in the earlier case of *IDC* v *Cooley* [1972] 1 WLR 443, where Cooley had resigned on the fictitious grounds of ill-health in order to take up a contract which the company he worked for would have been pleased to obtain. Thus, s. 170 (2) provides that the duty under s. 175 applies to a former director as regards the exploitation of any property, information or opportunity of which he became aware at a time when he was a director.

[127] In *O'Donnell* v *Shanahan* [2009] 2 BCLC 666 it was held on appeal that whether or not the corporate opportunity fell outside the scope of the business of the claimant company was irrelevant. The key difference in the Umunna case is the retirement of the director in question.

regard to what the business of the director is. If he has a lifetime of general entrepreneurial activity in various markets, it will not be possible for a company which hires him for a few years of that lifetime to argue that all future business in that area becomes the business of the company.

Most certainly, Rix LJ's judgment in the recent case of *Foster Bryant Surveying Ltd* v *Bryant*,[128] holds important lessons for future courts in this regard. Having subjected *Umunna* to close scrutiny, he stressed that there must be 'some relevant connection or link between the resignation and the obtaining of the business'.[129] He emphasised the need to demonstrate both lack of good faith with which the future exploitation was planned while still a director, and the need to show that the resignation was an integral part of the dishonest plan. Thus, in cases where liability for post-resignation breach of duty had been found, there was, he noted, a causal connection between the resignation and the subsequent diversion of the opportunity to the director's new enterprise.[130] However, Rix LJ recognised the difficulties of accurately summarising the circumstances in which retiring directors may or may not be held to have breached their fiduciary duties because the issue is necessarily 'fact sensitive'.[131]

In post-resignation cases,[132] it seems that the courts are now sometimes prepared to consider an application of the duty which seeks to strike a balance that is considerably more in favour of directors than hitherto. Nevertheless, the position has not been reached as in other jurisdictions[133] where the courts are prepared to go behind the no-conflict duty and to try to make some assessment of whether or not the directors are in good faith. This takes them down the path, forbidden to the English courts by *Regal*, that involves looking at the evidence which the directors may themselves have so carefully manufactured in order for it to give the appearance of their bona fides.

Typical of this approach, which is current in some[134] American states as well as Commonwealth jurisdictions, is the decision of the Minnesota Court of Appeal in *Miller* v *Miller Waste Co.*[135] An action had been brought against the directors on the basis that they had taken the business opportunities of the company by setting up a web of companies around it which were supposedly supporting its business activities, but in reality were siphoning its business away. The court adopted a two-stage test for dealing with the situation. The first stage was the question, 'Was the opportunity a *corporate* opportunity?' – the scope of the inquiry here being whether the business opportunity could properly be regarded as one which the company could claim as against any personal claim the directors

---

[128] [2007] EWCA Civ 200; see J. Lowry 'Judicial Pragmatism: Directors' Duties and Post-Resignation Conflicts of Duty' [2008] JBL 83. See also, *Framlington Group plc* v *Anderson* [1995] BCC 611. See further, *CMS Dolphin Ltd* v *Simonet* [2002] BCC 600, where the judgment contained a careful analysis of the balance to be struck when a director has resigned his office and thereafter taken up what the company alleges is a corporate opportunity.

[129] *Ibid*. at [91].

[130] *Ibid*. at [69], citing the Court of Appeal decision in *In Plus Group Ltd* v *Pyke* [2002] 2 BCLC 201.

[131] *Ibid*. at [76].

[132] See further, J. Lowry 'Regal (Hastings) Fifty Years On: Breaking the Bonds of the Ancien Régime' [1994] NILQ 1.

[133] For a comparative examination of this area, see, J. Lowry and R. Edmunds 'The Corporate Opportunity Doctrine: The Shifting Boundaries of the Duty and its Remedies' (1998) 61 MLR 515. See also, D. Kershaw 'Lost in Translation: Corporate Opportunities in Comparative Perspective' (2005) 25 OJLS 603.

[134] But not all; versions of the *Regal* approach are to be found in some states.

[135] 301 Minn 207, 222 NW 2d 71.

might have by virtue of their own legitimate business activities. In deciding whether the opportunity was '*corporate*', the court would apply the 'line of business test', which basically meant that it would ask whether it was the sort of thing the company would normally do, or perhaps was currently planning to do. The court would also look at matters such as whether the company realistically had the financial resources to undertake the activity in question. All these matters related to the first stage of the two-stage test. If the court reached the conclusion that the opportunity was non-corporate, then the directors would be free to take it up themselves. If they concluded that it was a corporate opportunity, then the court would proceed to the second stage of the test. This involved answering the question: 'Even if it is a corporate opportunity, would it be fair, in all the circumstances, to allow the directors to take up the opportunity?'[136] Here, the court would hear evidence presented as to why the directors decided that it was not a good idea for the company to take up the opportunity, their good faith, and any other relevant matters. The actual result in the case was that very few of the opportunities were held to be corporate, and those that were, were fairly taken up by the directors.

In the first stage of the test here, there are obviously parallels with the UK approach, in the sense that the question 'was it a corporate opportunity?' is a similar inquiry to whether a conflict exists. If the business opportunity is non-corporate (under the *Miller* test), there will probably be no 'conflict of interest' under the English approach. However, the second stage of the test, the inquiry into the fairness of letting the directors take the opportunity and their good faith, is largely anathema to the rigid stance taken in *Keech* and *Regal* which embody a resolute refusal to regard the good faith of the directors as a relevant factor[137] and see the inquiry into it as a trap, in which '. . . few trust estates would be renewed . . .'[138]

A few final thoughts are pertinent with regard to the difficult issues raised by business opportunities. When a company receives a business opportunity, what is the fiduciary duty of the directors in relation to that? It is clear that the duty of care and skill now encapsulated in s. 174 would require some level of proper assessment of the commercial merits of the situation; we need not discuss that further here. The fiduciary duty requires, as it always will, that the board decision to accept or reject the opportunity is made in a fashion which is wholly consistent, and *exclusively* consistent, with the interests of the company. In particular this will mean that if the opportunity is rejected it is not being rejected so that the directors can then take it up themselves.

Suppose then that the board of directors can be proved to be grossly in breach of this fiduciary duty and that, for instance, documents show that they had rejected the opportunity because 'our formal remuneration is rubbish and it's about time we took the chance to make a bit on the side'. If they then make a profit, on what legal basis does the company litigate this? Presumably it can just go ahead[139] and make the claim for breach of fiduciary duty under Part 10 of the 2006 Act. The breach alleged is that the directors failed to

---

[136] Or keep the profits if they have already taken it up.
[137] It was not relevant in *Boardman* v *Phipps* [1966] 3 All ER 721, either, although their good faith obviously helped the court's conclusion that they should receive remuneration 'on a liberal scale'.
[138] See *Keech* v *Sandford* (1726) 25 ER 223, *per* Lord King LC, see pp. 170–172 above and the explanation there.
[139] Assuming there are no problems with launching a derivative claim, as discussed in Chapter 11.

consider the opportunity in the way their fiduciary duty required, i.e. wholly and exclusively consistent with the interests of the company. On the evidence, the action is going to be successful and the court will then decide what damage the company has suffered as a result of the breach of duty. It is probable that the court will take the profit made by the directors as being the amount recoverable.[140]

Although s. 175 encapsulates the classic decisions handed down on the no-conflict duty, it does, however, modify the position established by the case law. Under the common law a director could avoid liability by disclosing the breach to, and obtaining the consent of, the company in general meeting.[141] Typically the articles of association replaced this by requiring disclosure to the board of directors.[142] By s. 175 (5) this is now made the default position for private companies. Public companies require express authorisation in their articles of association. Section 175 (6) goes on to provide that such authorisation is effective only if (a) any requirement as to quorum at the board meeting at which the matter is considered is satisfied without counting the director in question or any other interested director; and (b) the matter is agreed to without their voting or would have been agreed to if their votes had not been counted. In this regard, s. 180 (1) provides that if authorisation of the directors is obtained, the transaction or arrangement in question is not liable to be set aside by virtue of any common law rule or equitable principle requiring the consent or approval of the general meeting. However, where the conditions laid down in s. 175 (6) cannot be satisfied, the common law position applies so that disclosure will need to be made to the company in general meeting.[143]

## 3 Competing directors

Section 175 (7) of the Companies Act 2006 states in clear terms that any reference in s. 175 to a conflict of interest includes a conflict of interest and duty and a conflict of duties. It has long been common for people who hold bare or non-executive directorships[144] to hold directorships in more than one company. Normally this will not, of itself, give rise to a breach of duty to either of the companies. However, if the director holds a directorship in each of two competing companies, there is a danger that he is in a situation where his duty to one will conflict with his duty to the other, and he will possess inside knowledge of both.

The older case law makes light of the problem and suggests that a director is free to direct a competing company. In *London & Mashonaland Ltd* v *New Mashonaland Ltd*,[145] Chitty J refused an injunction to restrain the director of one company from becoming a director of a rival company on the basis that a director was not required to give the whole of his time to the company. This does not address the issue of the possible application of

---

[140] In *Regal*, the sum recovered was the profit made. See further, P. Birks *An Introduction to the Law of Restitution* (Oxford, OUP, 1989), Chapter 10.

[141] See *Regal Ltd* v *Gulliver* [1967] 2 AC 134; *Gwembe Valley Development Co. Ltd* v *Koshy* [2004] 1 BCLC 131; and *O'Donnell* v *Shanahan* [2009] 2 BCLC 666.

[142] See Table A, art. 85 (to the Companies Act 1985).

[143] Section 180 (4). See generally, J. Lowry 'Self-Dealing Directors – Constructing A Regime of Accountability' [1997] NILQ 211.

[144] In other words, directorships where the holder does not also have an employment contract requiring full-time attention to some executive role in the company.

[145] [1891] WN 165. See also the dictum of Lord Blanesburgh in *Bell* v *Lever Bros* [1932] AC 161 at p. 195.

the no-conflict rule in this situation and pre-dates the high profile given to that rule in *Regal* and subsequent decisions. This field of company law often draws an analogy with the law of trusts where trustees may not compete with the trust.[146]

Thus from general principle it seems that a director who competes with the company, either in business on his own account, or by being director of a rival company, will run the risk of being found to be in breach of fiduciary duty. Good faith requires loyalty, and would require him to abstain from behaviour that deliberately damages the company.[147] Furthermore, it is an area where the no-conflict duty is likely to become relevant making it unnecessary to prove actual harm. The mere holding of the office of director in each of two competing companies could be sufficient to trigger a remedy in an appropriate case. Where the line would be drawn remains to be seen. How much of an element of competition would there have to be? If the approach adopted in *Umunna* and its progeny is going to be followed, it is likely that the courts would require a very high degree of overlap in what the companies were doing, before they were prepared to invoke the no-conflict duty under s. 175 (1) and (2).[148]

## 4 Nominee directors

Another area which is a good candidate for infringing s. 175 is the practice of appointing 'nominee' directors. A nominee director is a director who has been appointed specifically to represent and protect the interests of some outside party,[149] perhaps a venture capital company which has agreed to lend or subscribe capital only on condition that it can 'keep an eye' on the company by having its nominee on the board.[150] The practice of appointing nominees is well recognised in the case law as are the dangers they face from a position which involves a potential conflict of interest.

It is clear that nominees must be careful not to get themselves into difficulties with conflicts of interest. Lord Denning gave this warning:

> It seems to me that no one who has duties of a fiduciary nature to discharge can be allowed to enter into an engagement by which he binds himself to disregard those duties or to act inconsistently with them . . . take a nominee director . . . There is nothing wrong in it . . . so long as the director is left free to exercise his best judgment in the interests of the company which he serves. But if he is put upon terms that he is bound to act in the affairs of the company in accordance with the directions of his patron, it is beyond doubt unlawful.[151]

---

[146] *Re Thompson* [1930] 1 Ch 203.

[147] Excepting negligent breaches of his or her common law duties restated in s. 174.

[148] For instance, in *In Plus Group Ltd* v *Pyke* [2002] 2 BCLC 201, the Court of Appeal held that there was no completely rigid rule that a director could not be involved in the business of another company which was in competition with a company of which he was a director, and they stressed that every situation was 'fact-specific'. A much stricter view was, however, put forward by Millett LJ in *Bristol and West BS* v *Mothew* [1998] Ch 1, CA, at p. 18: 'A fiduciary who acts for two principals with potentially conflicting interests without the informed consent of both is in breach of the obligation of undivided loyalty; he puts himself in a position where his duty to one principal may conflict with his duty to the other . . . This is sometimes described as "the double employment rule." Breach of the rule automatically constitutes a breach of fiduciary duty.'

[149] Sometimes called the 'patron' or the 'nominator'.

[150] The term 'nominee' director needs to be distinguished from a 'shadow director'. A shadow director is a statutory concept, which was first introduced in the Companies Act 1980, so that the various statutory provisions regulating directors' activities could be made to have a wider impact. The concept is explored with reference to its operation in the field of wrongful trading in Chapter 2, 2.2 above.

[151] *Boulting* v *ACTT* [1963] 2 QB 606 at p. 626.

The matter was explored in *Kuwait Bank* v *National Mutual Life*.[152] By virtue of a 40% shareholding, the bank had nominated two directors to the board of a company which was a money broker involved in deposit-taking activities. The company had gone into insolvent liquidation and the depositors lost money. The question arose as to whether the bank, the nominator, could be held liable for the negligence of its nominees. In the process of trying to establish this, it was argued that the bank was vicariously liable because the nominees were appointed by the bank, were employed by it and carried out their duties as directors in the course of their employment by it. It was held that the bank was not vicariously liable because the nominee directors were bound (because of their fiduciary duty to the company) to ignore the wishes of their employer, the bank. An argument that the nominees were agents of the bank similarly failed; they were agents of the company.

The case shows the court applying quite a robust presumption that the nominee directors were obeying the precepts of company law and to that extent it gives strong judicial support to the general practice of appointing nominees. If it becomes clear that they are not complying with their duties, then they are in difficulties. This could arise by gradually drifting into a situation which is legally untenable or by deliberate fraud. In *SCWS* v *Meyer*,[153] the articles of association of company A permitted company B to nominate three out of its five directors, which company B proceeded to do. Later, the directors stood accused of failing to defend the interests of company A against the depredations of company B. Lord Denning put the problem in this way:

> So long as the interests of all concerned were in harmony, there was no difficulty. The nominee directors could do their duty by both companies without embarrassment. But as soon as the interests of the two companies were in conflict, the nominee directors were placed in an impossible position . . .[154]

In *Selangor United Rubber Co. Ltd* v *Cradock (No. 3)*,[155] the two nominee directors, L and J, were involved in causing the company to provide funds to Cradock to enable him to purchase shares of the company contrary to what was a prohibition against private companies providing financial assistance for the acquisition of their shares (s. 151 of the Companies Act 1985; the prohibition now only extends to public companies).[156] Ungoed-Thomas J held the directors liable for the misapplication of the company's funds:

> It seems to me, however, that both L and J were nominated as directors . . . to do exactly what they were told by Cradock, and that is in fact what they did. They exercised no discretion or volition of their own and they behaved in utter disregard of their duties as directors . . . They put themselves in [Cradock's] hands . . . as their controller.[157]

The *Selangor* case is an example of nominee directors who committed a clear breach of their basic fiduciary duty. *SCWS* v *Meyer* also involved the situation where the breach of duty was evidentially established, although the circumstances were less deliberate than *Selangor*.

---

[152] [1990] 3 All ER 404, PC.
[153] [1959] AC 324.
[154] *Ibid.* at p. 366.
[155] [1968] 1 WLR 1555.
[156] See generally Chapter 15.
[157] [1968] 1 WLR 1555 at p. 1613.

However, there is then the question as to whether the nominee director phenomenon is one which inherently infringes the no-conflict duty as applied in *Regal (Hastings) Ltd* v *Gulliver* and *Keech* v *Sandford*.[158] In other words, the position of the nominee is highly likely to lead to a situation where he covertly prefers the interests of his nominator to those of the company. It would usually be impossible to prove. Just the kind of situation to attract the no-conflict duty. The courts, however, seem disinclined to take this approach.[159] On the contrary, the decision in *Kuwait Bank* v *National Mutual Life* seems to be operating a presumption which is almost the opposite of the no-conflict duty, namely that the nominator could not be vicariously liable, because the nominees owed a duty to ignore the bank's instructions by virtue of their paramount duty to the company.[160]

It would perhaps be unwise to rule out the application of the no-conflict duty in all cases. The practice of appointing nominees is so well established in commercial practice that the approach of the courts seems to be to make a finding against the nominees if, but only if, it can be shown that they are actually in breach of fiduciary duty.

## F Duty not to accept benefits from third parties

Section 176 (1) replaces the equitable prohibition against fiduciaries accepting bribes or secret commissions conferred by reason of '(a) his being a director or (b) his doing (or not doing) anything as director',[161] received in their capacity as director.[162] This is an element of the 'no-profit' rule which is a part of the no-conflict duty falling within s. 175 and liability for breach, therefore, will arise under both provisions. In language similar to s. 175 (4) (a), the duty is not infringed if the acceptance of the benefit cannot reasonably be regarded as likely to give rise to a conflict of interest,[163] and benefits conferred by the company, including its holding company or subsidiaries, do not fall within the duty because it is restricted to benefits received from 'a third party'.[164] In this regard, s. 176 (3) also excludes from the duty benefits received by the director by way of salary. The term 'benefit' is not defined in the 2006 Act, although Lord Goldsmith explained during the parliamentary debates on the Bill that it bears its ordinary meaning taken from the *Oxford English Dictionary* which defines it as 'a favourable or helpful factor, circumstance, advantage or profit'.[165]

In contrast to s. 175, the duty is not subject to any provision permitting authorisation by the board although s. 180 (4) (a), which provides for the members of the company to authorise a breach of duty (other than the duties laid down in ss. 175 and 177), may apply. Further, in theory at least, the articles of association could contain relieving provisions.

---

[158] Above.
[159] See *FHR European Ventures LLP* v *Mankarious & Ors* [2013] EWCA Civ 17 and *Boulting* v *ACTT* [1963] 2 QB 606 at p. 618, *per* Lord Denning 'There is nothing wrong in it . . .' (see above).
[160] See also, *Hawkes* v *Cuddy* [2009] 2 BCLC 427; *cf Cobden Investments Ltd* v *RWM Langport Ltd* [2008] EWHC 2810 (Ch).
[161] See e.g. *Attorney-General for Hong Kong* v *Reid* [1994] 1 AC 324, PC. See also, *Mahesan S/O Thambiah* v *Malaysia Government Officers' Cooperative Housing Society* [1979] AC 374; [1978] 2 WLR 444.
[162] *Pullan* v *Wilson & Ors* [2014] EWHC 126 (Ch) held that benefits received by a non-executive director were not a breach of s. 176 because they were received in his capacity as a trustee, not as director.
[163] Section 176 (4).
[164] Section 176 (2).
[165] HC Comm D, 11/7/06 Cols 621–622.

## G Duty to declare interest in a proposed or existing transaction or arrangement

The law has not always sought to regulate directors' conflicts of interest by requiring the director to hand over his profit to the company. A less severe technique would be to set up some procedure which would go some way towards providing a safeguard against a director breaching his duty. This approach has been adopted for many years where the conflict situation is that the director has a personal interest in some contract that he is making with the company, perhaps because he is selling an item of his own property to the company, or because he is negotiating a contract with the company under which the company will supply him with goods. In recent years, the American expression 'self-dealing' is sometimes used to describe this kind of situation.

At first, the case law required disclosure to the general meeting and approval by it. In default of this, the contract was voidable at the option of the company.[166] Then it became common for the articles of association to require disclosure to the board (see art. 85 of the 1985 Table A) – an easier process than disclosure to the general meeting. The legislature became concerned to ensure that the articles did not dispense with the disclosure requirement altogether and enacted s. 317 of the Companies Act 1985. The effect of s. 317 was to make disclosure to the board a *minimum* duty and to prevent the articles from dispensing with it, but it did not authorise disclosure to the board instead of the general meeting and unless the articles gave permission for disclosure to the board, then the basic case law duty of disclosure to the general meeting governed the situation.

Section 177 of the Companies Act 2006 dispenses with the equitable rule and requires a director to disclose any interest, whether direct or indirect, that he has in a proposed transaction or arrangement with the company to the other directors. The reference to an 'indirect' interest means that a director need not be a party to the transaction for the duty to apply. As we have seen, the duty is supplemented by s. 180 (1) which states that provided s. 177 is complied with (in this regard, see also s. 175 (5)), any transaction or arrangement is not liable to be set aside by virtue of any common law rule or equitable principle requiring the consent or approval of the members of the company in general meeting.

Section 177 (4) makes it clear that the duty to declare an interest must be performed before the company enters into the transaction or arrangement, and s. 177 (2) allows the disclosure to be made at a meeting of directors or by written notice or general notice (see ss. 184 and 185 respectively). Directors must disclose 'the nature and extent' of their interest. It is not sufficient for a director to merely state that he has an interest.[167] However, the disclosure duty is expressed to be 'to the other directors' and so it does not apply where the company has only one director.[168] The limits of the duty are laid down

---

[166] *Aberdeen Railway Co.* v *Blaikie* (1854) 1 Macq 461, HL; *North-West Transportation Co.* v *Beatty* (1887) 12 AC 589.

[167] In *FursLtd* v *Tomkies* (1936) 54 CLR 583 at p. 602, Starke J explained that disclosure 'requires [the director] to make a full disclosure of all information which is then or may thereafter during the currency of the agreement be within his knowledge or power.' On the disclosure standard see also, *Gwembe Valley Development Co. Ltd* v *Koshy* [1999] 2 BCLC 613; and *EIC Services Ltd* v *Phipps* [2004] 2 BCLC 589.

[168] See s. 186; although the terms of the transaction must be in writing or recorded in the minutes (s. 231). See further e.g. *MacPherson* v *European Strategic Bureau Ltd* [2002] BCC 39.

by s. 177 (6). There is no need to disclose an interest the other directors already know about or ought reasonably to have known. Nor is there a duty to declare an interest in a service contract that has been considered by the board or by a committee of the board appointed for the purpose under the company's constitution.[169] As under the common law, no declaration of interest is required if it cannot reasonably be regarded as likely to give rise to a conflict of interest.[170]

The failure to comply with s. 177 is a breach of duty and civil remedies apply.[171] The transaction is voidable at the option of the company.[172] As such, general contractual principles will apply.[173] Thus the company will not be able to rescind if it affirms the contract; or unreasonably delays avoidance; or the rights of a bona fide third party intervenes. Further, once the transaction is entered into the director will be under the duty to disclose his interest by virtue of s. 182. Breach of this duty carries criminal penalties for breach.[174]

## H Ratification of acts giving rise to liability

It was noted above that under the common law a director could avoid liability by disclosing the breach to, and obtaining the consent, by ordinary resolution, of, the company in general meeting.[175] The Companies Act 2006 maintains this rule, albeit subject to one major change. Section 239 (1) states that the provision applies to the ratification by a company of conduct by a director 'amounting to negligence, default, breach of duty or breach of trust in relation to the company'. It thus extends the ratification process to all breaches of the duties set out in the statutory restatement in Part 10 of the Act. The common law is modified by ss. 239 (3) and (4) which provide that the ratification is effective only if the votes of the director in breach (and any member connected with him) are disregarded. The effect therefore is to disenfranchise the defaulting director and this includes directors acting in their capacity as shareholder.[176]

Section 239 (6) (a) goes on to provide that nothing in the section affects the validity of a decision taken by the unanimous consent of the members of the company. This appears to mean that the restrictions contained in ss. 239 (3)–(4) on who may vote on a resolution will not apply when every member, including the director qua shareholder, agrees to condone the breach of duty. This places on a statutory footing the common law principle that a breach of duty is ratifiable by obtaining the informal approval of every member who has a right to vote on such a resolution.[177]

---

[169] *Runciman* v *Walter Runciman plc* [1992] BCLC 1084.
[170] Section 176(4); see *Cowan de Groot Properties Ltd* v *Eagle Trust plc* [1992] 4 All ER 700.
[171] Section 178.
[172] *Hely-Hutchinson & Co. Ltd* v *Brayhead* [1968] 1 QB 549, CA; and *Cowan de Groot Properties Ltd* v *Eagle Trust plc, ibid.*
[173] See R. Halson *Contract Law* (Harlow: Longman, 2001), pp. 43–52.
[174] Section 183.
[175] See *Regal Ltd* v *Gulliver* [1967] 2 AC 134; and *Gwembe Valley Development Co. Ltd* v *Koshy* [2004] 1 BCLC 131.
[176] In *Goldtrail Travel Ltd* v *Aydin & Ors* [2014] EWHC 1587 (Ch), it was held that the sole shareholder, who was also sole director, could not ratify the directorial misconduct in either capacity.
[177] See e.g. *Re Duomatic Ltd* [1969] 2 Ch 365. See also, *Parker & Cooper Ltd* v *Reading* [1926] Ch 975; *EIC Services Ltd* v *Phipps* [2003] 1 WLR 2360; *Euro Brokers Holdings Ltd* v *Monecor (London) Ltd* [2003] 1 BCLC 506, CA.

## I Remedies for breach of duty

Section 178 provides that the consequences of breach (or threatened breach) of ss. 171–177 are the same as would apply if the corresponding common law rule or equitable principle applied. The provision therefore preserves the civil consequences of breach (or threatened breach) of any of the general duties. Although an attempt was made to codify the remedies available for breach of directors' duties, this proved to be 'too difficult to pursue'.[178] In general, the remedies available to the company for breach of fiduciary duty are:[179] (i) damages or compensation where the company has suffered loss; (ii) restoration of the company's property;[180] (iii) an account of profits made by the director;[181] (iv) injunction or declaration;[182] and (v) rescission of a contract where the director failed to disclose an interest.[183] The consequences of a breach of the duty of care and skill may include the court awarding compensation or damages[184] in addition to any misapplied money or property being accounted for and made good.[185]

Although s. 178 therefore offers little guidance on the remedial consequences of a director's breach of fiduciary duty, the Court of Appeal in *Sinclair Investments (UK) Ltd v Versailles Trading Finance Ltd*[186] took the opportunity to consider in some detail what relief is available. In this landmark decision, the Master of the Rolls, delivering the leading judgment, held that a beneficiary of a fiduciary's duties has no proprietary interest in any money or asset acquired by the fiduciary in breach of his duties, 'unless the asset or money is or has been beneficially the property of the beneficiary or the trustee acquired the asset or money by taking advantage of an opportunity or right which was properly that of the beneficiary',[187] even if the fiduciary could not have acquired the asset had he not been a fiduciary. In holding that the appropriate remedy is an equitable account, the Court of Appeal expressly disapproved the decision of the Privy Council in *Attorney-General for Hong Kong v Reid*,[188] preferring its own decision in *Lister & Co. v Stubbs*.[189] Lord

---

[178] See Official Report, 9/2/2006; col. GC335 (Lord Goldsmith).

[179] For a full discussion of the remedies, see S. Worthington 'Corporate Governance: Remedying and Ratifying Directors' Breaches' [2000] LQR 638, at 659–674.

[180] *Re Forest of Dean Coal Co.* (1879) 10 Ch D 450; *JJ Harrison (Properties) Ltd v Harrison* [2002] 1 BCLC 162, CA.

[181] This liability may arise either out of a contract between a director and the company (see e.g., *Imperial Mercantile Credit Association v Coleman* (1873) LR 6 HL 189) or as a result of some contract or arrangement between the director and a third person (see e.g. *Burland v Earle* [1902] AC 83).

[182] In case the breach is threatened but has not yet occurred. An injunction may also be suitable where the breach has already occurred but is likely to continue or if some of its consequences can be avoided. See e.g. *Cranleigh Precision Engineering Ltd v Bryant* [1965] 1 WLR 1293.

[183] See e.g. *Transvaal Lands Co. v New Belgium (Transvaal) Land & Development Co* [1914] 2 Ch 488, CA.

[184] See, for example, *Dorchester Finance Co. v Stebbing* [1989] BCLC 498; and *Re D'Jan of London* [1994] 1 BCLC 561.

[185] See *CMS Dolphin Ltd v Simonet & Anr* [2001] EWHC Ch 415 and *Access Bank Plc v Akingbola & Ors* [2012] EWHC 2148 (Comm). Even when there is no evidence of loss to the company, any profits made by the director due to his breach must be accounted for: *Towers v Premier Waste Management Ltd* [2011] EWCA Civ 923.

[186] [2011] EWCA Civ 347.

[187] *Ibid.* at [88].

[188] [1994] 1 AC 324.

[189] (1890) LR 45 Ch D 1. Lord Neuberger MR also noted that *Lister* had been followed in two recent Court of Appeal decisions, namely *Gwembe Valley Development Co. Ltd v Koshy (No. 3)* [2004] 1 BCLC 131 and *Halton International Inc. v Guernoy* [2006] EWCA Civ 801. The reasoning in *Lister* is supported by numerous academic commentators including: R.M. Goode 'Ownership and Obligation in Commercial Transactions' [1997] *LQR* 433; and P. Watts 'Bribes and Constructive Trusts' [1994] LQR 178. See also, P. Birks *Introduction to the Law of Restitution* (Oxford: OUP, 1989), pp. 386–9.

Neuberger MR added that if it is a matter of equitable policy that a fiduciary should not be allowed to profit from his breach of duties, that can be achieved by extending or adjusting the rules relating to equitable compensation rather than those relating to proprietary interests.[190]

## 8.3 Relief for directors

### A Ought fairly to be excused

Section 1157 of the Companies Act 2006 will sometimes be of assistance to a director[191] who has been subjected to proceedings for breach of duty, negligence, default etc. Under it, directors may seek relief, on the basis that although they may be liable, they nevertheless have acted honestly and reasonably and 'ought fairly to be excused'. It will often cover the situation where they have committed merely a technical breach of duty, although it is wider than that. However, it is clear that inactivity of directors that amounted to a breach will not attract relief from liability any more than actions in breach will.[192] Relief under s. 1157 is often claimed by directors but in most cases, especially where the breach of duty is substantial, the application for relief is given fairly short shrift.[193] Thus, in *Dorchester Finance Ltd* v *Stebbing*,[194] Foster J said: '. . . I have no hesitation in concluding that they should not be relieved under the provisions of this section.'[195]

### B Exemption and insurance

In view of concerns that potential liabilities of directors have increased to the extent that able people are being deterred from holding office as directors, the Company (Audit, Investigations and Community Enterprise) Act 2004 introduced new provisions into the Companies Act 1985 designed to ameliorate the position of directors of the company. These have been re-enacted in the Companies Act 2006.

Section 232 (1) provides that any provision purporting to exempt a director from liability attaching to him in connection with any negligence, default, breach of duty or breach of trust in relation to the company is void. Furthermore, any provision by which a company provides an indemnity for a director of the company or associated company against such liability is void.[196] However, under ss. 232–233, the company may purchase and maintain insurance against such liability, in respect of a director of the company or associated company (as defined); and by virtue of s. 234, the prohibition against

---

[190] [2011] EWCA Civ 347, at [90]. In *FHR European Ventures LLP* v *Mankarious* [2013] EWCA Civ 17, the Court of Appeal followed *Sinclair*, but on the facts concluded that the appropriate remedy was proprietary.
[191] Or auditor or officer.
[192] *Finch (UK) plc & Ors* v *Finch & Anor* [2015] EWHC 2430 (Ch).
[193] In *Towers* v *Premier Waste Management Ltd* [2011] EWCA Civ 923, Mummery LJ said, at [56], that the absence of any finding of bad faith or actual conflict and the absence of quantifiable loss by the company, or the negligible profit to the defendant director, did not justify relieving him from the consequences of his breach of duty.
[194] [1989] BCLC 498 at p. 506. See J. Lowry and R. Edmunds 'The Continuing Value of Relief for Director's Breach of Duty' (2003) 66 MLR 195.
[195] See also *Bairstow* v *Queens Moat Houses plc* [2002] BCLC 91, CA.
[196] Section 232 (2).

indemnifying a director does not apply to a 'qualifying third party indemnity' provision. Lastly, it should be mentioned that the position as regards the company's funding of directors' expenditure on defending proceedings has been ameliorated in certain circumstances by s. 205.

## 8.4 Duty not to commit an unfair prejudice

Unfair prejudice is a concept which is usually seen as a liability, namely a liability that a member will petition under s. 994 of the 2006 Act 'on the ground that the company's affairs . . . have been conducted in a manner which is unfairly prejudicial to the interests of its members generally or of some part of its members . . .' On the other hand, when the unfair prejudice jurisdiction was first created in 1980, there seemed to be more litigation against directors in the first few years under those provisions than there had been in the previous 100 years under the general law. It is true that some of the points raised in that litigation added nothing substantive[197] to the existing liability of directors, because they were merely references to the existing common law or fiduciary duties. On the other hand, the unfair prejudice cases may sometimes contain instances where the directors would have probably escaped any liability under their common law or fiduciary duties, but find that the case goes against them because they infringed some aspect of the wider concept of unfair prejudice. These cannot be examined in detail here, but should be borne in mind when studying the concept of unfair prejudice in Chapter 12. An important note of caution here is that there is an artificiality and an insufficiency in seeing directors' duties solely from the traditional angle of common law and fiduciary duties. Because of the unfair prejudice jurisdiction, the liability of directors is wider and more subtle than will be suggested solely by an examination of those traditional duties.

## 8.5 Other legal constraints on directors' powers

Aside from directors' duties now restated in Part 10 of the Companies Act 2006, the law has also sought to constrain the power of the directors in other ways. Some of the rules are flat prohibitions on certain types of transactions which are thought to be unacceptable. Other rules are gateway provisions which seek to prevent an unfairness coming into the situation by establishing a procedure to be followed.[198] Other types of rules seek to operate, as it were, *in terrorem*, and enable another party to set in motion something that the directors will find adverse, such as removal under s. 168, or wrongful trading proceedings. In addition to all these, there is another group of rules that can be seen as setting up structures that will have, *inter alia*, a monitoring function in regard to the directors. These rules and constraints are examined in the next chapter under the categorisation of directors' specific duties.

---

[197] They often added liability at a procedural level because the rule in *Foss* v *Harbottle* was generally not available to prevent the bringing of proceedings based on conduct that is alleged to be unfairly prejudicial, whereas it is available to stifle proceedings based on breach of common law or fiduciary duties. See now Part 11 of the 2006 Act, considered in Chapter 11. See further *O'Donnell* v *Shanathan* [2009] 2 BCLC 666; and *Franbar Holdings Ltd* v *Patel* [2008] EWHC 1534 (Ch).
[198] Such as Companies Act 2006, ss. 177 and 180.

## Further reading

DTI *Modern Company Law For a Competitive Economy Final Report* (London, 2001).

L.S. Sealy 'The Director As Trustee' [1967] *CLJ* 83.

J. Lowry 'The Duty of Loyalty of Company Directors: Bridging the Accountability Gap Through Efficient Disclosure' [2009] *CLJ* 607.

J. Loughrey, A. Keay, and L. Cerioni 'Legal Practitioners, Enlightened Shareholder Value and the Shaping of Corporate Governance' (2008) *Journal of Corporate Law Studies* 8: 79.

V. Finch 'Company Directors: Who Cares about Skill and Care' (1992) 55 *MLR* 179.

A.J. Boyle '*Attorney-General* v *Reid*: The Company Law Implications' (1995) 16 *Co Law* 131.

J. Lowry 'Judicial Pragmatism: Directors' Duties and Post-Resignation Conflicts of Duty' [2008] *JBL* 83.

J. Lowry 'Regal (Hastings) Fifty Years On: Breaking the Bonds of the Ancien Régime' [1994] *NILQ* 1.

J. Lowry and R. Edmunds 'The Corporate Opportunity Doctrine: The Shifting Boundaries of the Duty and its Remedies' (1998) 61 *MLR* 515.

D. Kershaw 'Lost in Translation: Corporate Opportunities in Comparative Perspective' (2005) 25 *OJLS* 603.

J. Lowry 'Self-Dealing Directors – Constructing A Regime of Accountability' [1997] *NILQ* 211.

S. Worthington, 'Corporate Governance: Remedying and Ratifying Directors' Breaches' [2000] *LQR* 638.

J. Lowry and R. Edmunds 'The Continuing Value of Relief for Director's Breach of Duty' (2003) 66 *MLR* 195.

D. Ahern 'Guiding Principles for Directorial Conflicts of Interest: Re Allied Business and Financial Consultants Ltd; O'Donnell v Shanahan' *The Modern Law Review* (2011) 74.4: 596–607.

J. Farrar and S. Watson 'Self-Dealing, Fair Dealing and Related Party Transactions – History, Policy and Reform' *Journal of Corporate Law Studies* (2011) 11.2: 495–523.

# 9

# Duties of directors: specific duties and controls

## 9.1 Introduction

The Companies Act 2006 contains a number of provisions that supplement the general duties in Part 10 by regulating the conduct of directors in specific situations. They mainly relate to transactions that have been seen, over the years, to give rise to abuses predicated on the classic agency problem that arises between the shareholders and the board. Here they are considered in two parts; first, those provisions that control the actions of directors and, secondly, those provisions that provide a monitoring function.

To some extent the specific provisions overlap with the general duties in that, if the statutory provisions were not there, it might be possible to attack the transaction on the basis that it was a breach of duty in some respect or other, typically on the basis that the director was in breach of the duty to avoid a conflict of interest.[1]

## 9.2 Director controls

The provisions that seek to control specific behaviour (or behaviour in specific situations) can be sub-categorised as those that:

(a) regulate transactions;
(b) control the issuance of shares; and
(c) deter or discipline errant behaviour.

### A Regulating specific contract transactions

Chapters 4 and 5 of Part 10 of the Companies Act 2006, replace Part 10 of the 1985 Act, which contained a range of provisions designed to enforce fair dealing. The 2006 reforms originate from the recommendations of the Law Commissions, which were adopted by the CLR.[2] The objective of the reforms was to improve accessibility and consistency to the fair dealing regime since the 1985 Act was found to be excessively detailed and lacking in coherence. In essence, the new regime is structured so as to require that certain

---

[1] Section 175.
[2] See the English and Scottish Law Commissions joint report *Company Directors: Regulating Conflicts of Interest and Formulating a Statement of Duties*, above, n. 2. See also, the CLR's *Modern Company Law For a Competitive Economy Final Report* (London, DTI, 2001), Chapter 6; and the subsequent government White Paper, *Modernising Company Law* (July 2002, Cmnd 5553).

conflict-transactions be disclosed to the members of the company whilst others require shareholder approval.[3] In this regard, chapter 4 requires shareholder approval in respect of the following transactions with directors:

- long-term service contracts;
- substantial property transactions;
- loans, quasi-loans and credit transactions; and
- payments for loss of office.

Chapter 5 requires disclosure to shareholders in relation to directors' service contracts. It is noteworthy that the criminal penalties for breach of the requirements relating to the Chapter 4 transactions, which were laid down in the 1985 Act, have been removed.

## 1 *Directors' service contracts*

To regulate the extent to which directors can use fixed term contracts to entrench themselves with the company (which carried generous compensation payments, termed 'golden parachute' provisions, in the event of early termination of employment) s. 188 of the Companies Act 2006 requires shareholder approval to a 'guaranteed term' contained in a director's service contract that 'is, or may be, longer than two years'. A director's 'service contract' is defined by s. 227 as including a contract of service, a contract for services and a letter of appointment as director. By s. 223 (1) (a) the requirement also applies to engagements with shadow directors. However, it is important to remember that these provisions should not be viewed in isolation, but rather as supplementing the general duties in Part 10; more particularly, the duty to act within powers (s. 171) and the duty to promote the success of the company (s. 172) in agreeing to service contract terms.[4] The failure to obtain the approval of members renders the relevant provision void, and the contract is deemed to contain a term entitling the company to terminate it at any time by the giving of reasonable notice.[5]

The approval principle laid down by ss. 188–189 is reinforced by ss. 227–230 that require directors' service contracts to be open to inspection by members. Further, by virtue of s. 412, companies must disclose, by way of notes to the annual accounts, information about aggregate directors' remuneration (there are exemption provisions for small companies, unquoted and unlisted companies).

## 2 *Substantial property transactions*

Sections 190–196, replacing ss. 320–322 of the Companies Act 1985, require substantial property transactions (namely, transactions where the company buys or sells a non-cash asset from or to a director, including a director of its holding company, and including a person connected with the director) to be approved by the company's

---

[3] The requirements in the Companies Act 1985, Part 10 relating to share dealings by directors are repealed.
[4] See the judgment of Scott J in *Wilton Group plc* v *Abrams* [1991] BCLC 315 at pp. 322–323.
[5] Section 189.

members.[6] The provision also applies to shadow directors (s. 223 (1) (b)). By s. 191 (2) an asset is 'substantial' if its value:

(a) exceeds 10% of the company's asset value and is more than £5,000, or
(b) exceeds £100,000.

Therefore, approval is not required if the value of the asset is less than £5,000. The policy underlying the approval requirement was explained by Nourse LJ in *Re Duckwari plc*,[7] who stated that the purpose of the provision is 'to give shareholders specific protection in respect of arrangements and transactions which will or may benefit directors to the detriment of the company'.[8]

There are a number of exceptions to the s. 190 requirement. Approval is not required for a transaction between a company and a person in his character as a member of that company or for a transaction between a holding company and its wholly-owned subsidiary or two wholly-owned subsidiaries of the same holding company.[9] Section 193 provides an exception in the case of a company in winding up or administration. Nor is approval required for a transaction on a recognised investment exchange.[10] Payments under directors' service contracts and payments for loss of office are excluded by s. 190 (5).

Section 195 sets out the civil consequences of contravening s. 190. They are broader than the equitable remedies for breaching the no-conflict duty. In essence, any arrangement or transaction entered into in breach of s. 190 is voidable at the instance of the company. The right to avoid will be lost, however, if restitution is no longer possible if the company has been indemnified for the loss or damage it has suffered; or if rights acquired in good faith, for value and without actual notice of the contravention by a person who is not a party to the arrangement or transaction would be affected by the avoidance. On the other hand, where a transaction or arrangement is entered into by a company in contravention of s. 190 but, within a reasonable period, it is affirmed by the members of the company, the right of avoidance under s. 195 will be lost.

## 3 *Loans, quasi-loans and credit transactions*

The making of a loan by the company to a director is a situation which is open to abuse in a number of ways.[11] The loan may be at an unrealistically low rate of interest and therefore be disguised remuneration. If the loan is not repaid over a long period of time, it can be a form of disguised gift. The Companies Act 1948 contained provisions to regulate loans to directors which eventually came to be seen as inadequate and widely circumvented. The Companies Acts 1980 and 1985 set out to rectify this by prohibiting directors obtaining benefits from the company by way of loan, property transfers or by 'quasi-loans', 'credit transactions' and 'assignments' and 'arrangements'.

---

[6] Transactions that remain uncertain regarding whether or not the property will be acquired will not attract liability (*Smithton Ltd* v *Naggar* [2014] EWCA Civ 939).
[7] [1998] 2 BCLC 315, CA.
[8] *Ibid.* at p. 324.
[9] Section 192.
[10] Section 194.
[11] See the White Paper, *The Conduct of Company Directors* (Cmnd 7037, 1977).

These prohibitions on loans, quasi-loans and credit-transactions were retained by the Companies Act 2006 subject to several important changes. That is, ss. 197–214 stipulate that loans to directors, including shadow directors,[12] and connected persons are no longer prohibited but are subject to the approval of the members of the company.[13] The provisions relating to quasi-loans and credit transactions apply only to public companies and to companies associated with public companies.[14] There are a number of exceptions where approval under s. 197 is not required. These cover situations where a company provides a director with funds to meet expenditure incurred on company business;[15] expenditure incurred in defending criminal or civil proceedings in connection with a regulatory action or investigation or in connection with, for example, an application for relief under s. 1157 (although the loan will need to be repaid in the event of the director being convicted or judgment being given against him or her or where the court refuses relief);[16] expenditure for minor and business transactions where the value of the loan is less than £10,000, or in the case of credit transactions less than £15,000;[17] expenditure for intra-group transactions;[18] and expenditure for money lending companies.

A transaction or arrangement entered into in contravention of any of these provisions is voidable at the instance of the company, subject to the same conditions we saw in relation to substantial property transactions.[19] Section 213 (8) provides that nothing in this section shall be read as excluding the operation of any other enactment or rule of law by virtue of which the transaction or arrangement may be called in question or any liability to the company may arise. In this regard, it is noteworthy that in *Currencies Direct Ltd* v *Ellis*,[20] it was held that the relevant provisions did not have the effect of rendering a loan made to the director unenforceable because the effect of s. 213 is that the loan is voidable at the instance of the company. Gage J concluded that this implied that public policy did not prevent a company from recovering a loan made to a director in contravention of ss. 197, 198, 200, 201 or 203.[21] Further, it has been held that a director who receives a loan in contravention of s. 197 is liable for misfeasance and to compensate the company for any losses it suffers.[22]

## 4 *Payments for loss of office*

Sections 215–222 and 226 C of the Companies Act 2006 regulate payments made by a company to a director, including a director of its holding company, in respect of loss of office or in connection with the director's retirement. The rules are complex and do not apply to payments which the company is bound to make by virtue of a contractual obliga-

---

[12]Section 223 (1) (c).
[13]Section 197 (1).
[14]Sections 198 and 201.
[15]Section 204.
[16]Sections 205 and 206.
[17]Section 207.
[18]Section 208.
[19]Section 213. See s. 195 above. Similarly, s. 214 allows for affirmation by the members within a reasonable time.
[20][2002] 1 BCLC 193; the trial judge's decision was upheld on other grounds: see [2002] 2 BCLC 482, CA.
[21]*Ibid.* at p. 208.
[22]*Wallersteiner* v *Moir (No. 1)* [1974] 1 WLR 991.

tion.[23] In essence, s. 217 requires member approval to non-contractual payments made to directors for loss of office.[24] Their approval is also required where the loss of office arises in connection with the transfer of the whole or any part of the company's undertaking, namely an asset transfer, or as a result of a takeover, namely a share transfer.[25] However, s. 226 C permits payment upon loss of office where such payment is consistent with the approved director's remuneration policy.[26]

The remedies for breach of these provisions are laid down in s. 222. If a payment is made in breach of s. 217, it is held by the recipient on trust for the company and any director who authorised the payment is jointly and severally liable to indemnify the company for any resulting loss.[27] If a payment is made in contravention of s. 218 (payment made in connection with transfer of undertaking), section 222(2) stipulates that it is held by the recipient on trust for the company whose assets are or are proposed to be transferred.[28] If a payment is made in contravention of s. 219 (payment in connection with share transfer), section 222(3) provides that it is held by the recipient on trust for the persons who have sold their shares as a result of the offer and the recipient will bear the expenses of distributing the sum (that is, the costs of distribution will not be borne out of the sum so distributed).[29] Where a payment is made which contravenes both ss. 217 and 218, the remedy laid down by s. 222 (2) (above) applies. But where a payment is made in contravention of both ss. 217 and 219, the remedy laid down in subsection (3) applies, unless the court directs otherwise.

## B Controls over the issue of shares

The power to issue shares is obviously one that is open to abuse by directors. Past examples[30] include issuing shares to themselves: to water down the voting rights of another so as to assist them in a battle for control within the company;[31] or to make them less vulnerable to removal;[32] or issuing shares to the bidder in a takeover to help produce what they saw as a favourable outcome.[33] Prior to 1980 there was no statutory regulation of the power to issue shares. The power was generally assumed to reside in the directors by virtue of art. 80[34] of the 1948 Act's Table A. The Companies Act 1980 tightened up on

---

[23]See s. 220.
[24]The requirements also extend to payments made to connected persons (s. 215 (3)).
[25]Sections 218 and 219.
[26]Section 226 C inserted into the Companies Act 2006 by s. 80 of the Enterprise and Regulatory Reform Act 2013.
[27]Section 222 (1).
[28]Section 222 (2).
[29]Section 222 (3).
[30]The directors' efforts in these cases were unsuccessful and the share issues were set aside. The unfair prejudice jurisdiction has uncovered similar ingenuity and reacted against it; see *Re Cumana Ltd* [1986] BCLC 430; *Re DR Chemicals Ltd* (1989) 5 BCC 39; *Re Kenyon Swansea Ltd* (1987) 3 BCC 259; *Re a Company 007623/84* (1986) 2 BCC 99, 191; *Re a Company 002612/84* (1984) 1 BCC 92, 262; *Re a Company 005134/86* [1989] BCLC 383 and see generally Chapter 13 below.
[31]*Piercy v Mills* [1920] 1 Ch 77. See further s. 171 of the Companies Act 2006 and the discussion on the proper purposes doctrine above.
[32]*Punt v Symons* [1903] 2 Ch 506.
[33]*Howard Smith v Ampol Petroleum* [1974] AC 821; see n. 19 above, and text thereto.
[34]Similar to art. 70 of the 1985 Table A and art. 3 Model Articles in the sense that it vested the power to manage the business of the company in the board; there are important differences.

the provisions by introducing what were ss. 80 and 89–96 of the Companies Act 1985. The Companies Act 2006 introduces further safeguards against directors abusing their power.

Sections 549–551 of the 2006 Act limit the power of directors to allot shares in the company or grant rights to subscribe for, or to convert any security into, shares in the company unless they have the authority of the members granted either in the articles of association or by an ordinary resolution. The authority of the members may be given for a particular exercise of the power or for its exercise generally, and may be unconditional or subject to conditions. In any case, it must be renewed every five years.

There are exceptions to the authorisation requirement. Thus, s. 549 excludes issues of shares to the original subscribers, to an employees' share scheme, or to existing holders of rights to acquire or convert their shares.[35] Further, s. 550 provides that in the case of a private company with only one class of shares, the directors may, without obtaining further authorisation, allot shares of that class or grant rights to subscribe for or to convert any security into such shares. This is made subject to any provision in the articles that may limit the power of directors in this respect.

Since the 2006 Act abolishes the requirement of authorised share capital,[36] the company's constitution will no longer need to contain an upper limit on the number of shares that directors are authorised to allot. One consequence of this is that any changes to a company's issued share capital must be notified to the Registrar of Companies every time a new allotment is issued.[37]

## C  Deterrent and disciplinary provisions

This *in terrorem* categorisation gathers together a group of statutory provisions that might have a salutary influence on the behaviour of directors. Each one of them is a drastic measure and typically will only come into effect after the undesirable behaviour has occurred. Nevertheless, their existence will sometimes help to deter directors from wrongdoing by conveying in advance the message that such actions may carry adverse consequences. The list below is not exhaustive; although these are the main provisions of this nature.

## 1 *Removal of directors*

Under s. 168 of the Companies Act 2006, a company may remove a director before the expiration of his period of office. The power is exercisable by ordinary resolution and cannot be taken away by anything in the articles or in any agreement.[38] The power to remove directors merely by passing an ordinary resolution is an important shareholder right. This is particularly so in view of the fact that it is not necessary to show any wrongdoing. The director is liable to removal 'without cause', although presumably in general meeting it will often be tactically necessary to produce some reasons.

---

[35]See Allotment of Shares and Rights of Pre-Emption (Amendment) Regulations 2009 (SI 2009/2561).
[36]Section 542.
[37]Section 555.
[38]Section 168 (1). Special notice is required (s. 168 (2)); see further Chapter 7 above.

Section 168 will sometimes have an effect on directors' behaviour by deterring wrong-doing which, if discovered, would lead to their removal. It is also an important adjunct to the operation of an efficient takeover market in which boards of directors who underperform (in the sense of getting a poor return on the resources at their disposal) may find that they become the target of a takeover bid. Once control has passed to the bidder, it will be in a position to remove the target board under s. 168. The threat of this can operate as a spur to incumbent management to improve their performance.[39]

In some situations there will be significant restrictions on the use of s. 168. These can come about in a number of ways. In a large public company, one practical reason might be the political necessity to keep the director reasonably well disposed towards the company, especially if he is the only one being removed. He may well be aware of wrongdoing by other directors which they would rather not have mentioned. In such a situation, the likely outcome might be for the company to pay him off with a huge financial settlement; confidentiality comes at a price. The public are regularly baffled when they read in the financial press that a director has been found to have been implicated in the incompetent running of the company and its subsequent poor performance, and then paid off with a settlement running into millions.[40]

Another factor restricting the use of s. 168 is that, in the case of an executive director who has a fixed term employment contract, removal may be a breach of that contract, giving rise to substantial damages. The company's liability is expressly preserved by s. 168 (5) (a).

Use of s. 168 runs another risk, particularly in small partnership style companies. The removal of a director will often give him the right to petition the court under s. 994 to complain of unfairly prejudicial conduct. This may involve the other shareholders or directors in having to find the money to purchase his shares. Alternatively, in rare circumstances, a director excluded from management could seek to have the company wound up under s. 122 (1) (g) of the Insolvency Act 1986.[41] This kind of litigation is often catastrophic for those involved in a small company.[42]

The last problem sometimes arising with s. 168 is that, in some situations, the company's articles will have effectively excluded its use. The effectiveness of such provisions was tested in *Bushell* v *Faith*.[43] Faith and his two sisters each had 100 £1 shares. The sisters tried to remove him under s. 168 (s. 303 of the 1985 Act) but failed because of a clause in the articles which uplifted his voting power by three votes per share on a resolution to remove a director. He thus polled 300 votes on the resolution against their 200. The argument that the voting uplift was void as being contrary to statute was not accepted by the House of Lords who took the view that the clause was really in the

---

[39]On the theoretical aspects of the market for corporate control, see further Chapter 21. Section 168 also becomes significant in a proxy battle.

[40]For example, the chief executive of Barclays, removed from office in July 2015, was due to receive a £28m 'golden goodbye' despite his failure to deliver on company objectives. See Aimee Donnellan, 'Sacked Barclays Boss Jenkins to Leave with £28m Package', *The Sunday Times* (12 July 2015) <http://www.thesundaytimes.co.uk/sto/business/Finance/article1580130.ece>.

[41]See *Ebrahimi* v *Westbourne Galleries* [1972] 2 All ER 492.

[42]See further Chapter 12.

[43][1970] AC 1099.

nature of a voting agreement and the legality of such had long been recognised.[44] Voting agreements of this nature can therefore create a high degree of entrenchment, but are probably limited to small and medium-sized companies for it is unlikely that the Stock Exchange or the FCA would permit the listing of a company which had such a clause in its articles.

## 2 Wrongful trading

Section 214 of the Insolvency Act 1986 contains provisions under which, in some circumstances, directors of an insolvent company will become liable to contribute to the assets of the company in the liquidation.[45] Their liability will in no way depend on fraud being proved or a dishonest state of mind. Conduct, which could be loosely described as being 'negligent',[46] is sufficient to trigger this liability. Thus, directors may find that if they carry on trading when the company is in financial difficulties and when insolvency is looming, then money will have to be found from their own pockets. In the first reported case on wrongful trading, the directors were required to pay £75,000 to the liquidator because they struggled on trading for longer than they should have.[47] It was a huge sum when compared to the amounts that they had been drawing from the company over the years. It is highly probable that the section has had a significant effect on boards of directors[48] and their advisers.[49]

## 3 Disqualification

Under the Company Directors Disqualification Act 1986, the court can disqualify persons from acting as directors.[50] In the year 2014–15, a total of 1,209 directors were disqualified, with an average disqualification term of six years. Although orders for disqualification are made in civil proceedings, rather than criminal proceedings, the process must inevitably be extremely unpleasant for the director at the receiving end. He is being put through a trial of his competence as a professional director, a trial which will examine a significant part of his past business conduct.[51] At the end of it, if he is unsuccessful in defending his position, he will be disqualified from carrying on as a director for at least two years. This may well destroy permanently or temporarily his ability to earn a living. Most of the cases brought seem to relate to small businesses where the management were usually basically honest but found themselves in difficult situations which gradually slipped out of control. However, such an order can be necessary protection for unwitting creditors against errant

[44]For a similar approach in a different context, see *Russell v Northern Bank Development Corp* [1992] BCC 578, HL, discussed in Chapter 4.
[45]See further Chapter 2, 2.2C.
[46]In fact, some quite specific standards are laid down in s. 214 (2)–(5); see further Chapter 2, 2.2C.
[47]*Re Produce Marketing Consortium Ltd (No. 2)* (1989) 5 BCC 569.
[48]See further Chapter 2.
[49]The Insolvency Service Annual Report and Accounts 2014–15.
[50]And from holding other positions. On this, see Chapter 23.
[51]Unless the summary procedure is being used; see Chapter 23.

directors.[52] In fact, the Insolvency Service estimated that in 2014–15, creditor damage of £100,000 was prevented for each director disqualified during that period.[53] In any event, it is clear that disqualification proceedings form a major part of the depressing vista which the law creates for businesspeople who fail to live up to the standards which are now thought to be necessary.

## 4 *Other insolvency provisions*

Insolvency proceedings can involve a wide range of remedies and processes which will subject the director to investigation, and possible disgorgement of assets, in addition to the danger of wrongful trading liability and disqualification.[54]

## 9.3 Monitoring of directors

Part of the picture of the legal regulation of the environment in which directors operate are mechanisms which result in the directors being monitored. Sometimes, the monitoring will then produce a reaction from another organisation, which will impact on the directors.

## A The policy of disclosure of the financial affairs of the company

Disclosure is a fundamental regulatory tool,[55] which is as old as UK company law itself. The Joint Stock Companies Act 1844 had contained a requirement for companies to publish their annual balance sheet and in later years the extent of disclosure required was increased and made more complex, although periodically the legislature has exhibited a change of heart and produced measures which for a time have required less disclosure than before; so the growth in the requirements has not been steady. It continues to fluctuate as the legislature strives to find a balance between protecting those who deal with companies on the one hand, and the needs of commerce to be free of unnecessary burdens, on the other.[56]

Disclosure is a fundamental technique of that area of company law known as capital markets law, or securities regulation. Disclosure of financial information is merely one aspect of disclosure technique, although an important one nevertheless. Not only does it provide information about the performance of the company but it also helps to prevent fraud. Similarly, disclosure is also of great significance in the area of company law known as corporate governance because by providing public information about the affairs of the

---

[52]For example, in *Feld* v *The Secretary of State for Business, Innovation And Skills* [2014] EWHC 1383 (Ch), a disqualification period of 12 years was upheld on the basis that the director in question had, after being disqualified from directorial positions following one example of unfitness to be a director, applied for permission to act as director again, was granted that permission and then proceeded to rack up large debts which the new company became unable to service.

[53]Insolvency Service Annual Report and Accounts 2014–15.

[54]See Chapter 22.4 below.

[55]For a wider analysis of the role of disclosure in company law and securities regulation, see generally, Chapter 16.

[56]See Impact Assessment for the Companies Act 2006 (Strategic Report and Directors' Report) Regulations 2013 (SI 2013/1970) for an example of the way in which government tries to find a balance.

company, it enhances the ability of the markets to monitor the performance of management.[57] It is probable that Orders, which may be made under the Electronic Communications Act 2000, will enhance the ability of shareholders to monitor management by enabling them to access annual reports and other information through electronic means. It is difficult to be precise about whether disclosure of financial information by a company should be considered as part of company law or part of the law of securities regulation; it clearly belongs to both, and provides further illustration of the artificiality of the boundaries between company law and capital markets law.

## 1 *Accounts and reports*

The Companies Act 2006[58] casts the main responsibility for financial reporting[59] firmly on the board of directors. It is they who have to ensure that accounting records are kept, that these are sufficient to show and explain the company's transactions, and disclose with reasonable accuracy the financial position of the company, and enable the proper preparation of the balance sheet and the profit and loss account.[60] Accordingly, the directors 'must prepare' a balance sheet and a profit and loss account[61] for each financial year[62] of the company. The company's annual accounts need to be approved by the board of directors and duly signed by a director on behalf of the board.[63]

The Large and Medium-sized Companies and Groups (Accounts and Reports) Regulations 2008[64] set out the detailed format and content for the accounts of large and medium-sized companies, as part of the reforms introduced by the Companies Act 2006. Small companies are now the subject of separate regulations.[65] Section 396 contains, *inter alia*, a statement of accounting principles and rules but departure from these is allowed where this is necessary to show what the legislation calls a 'true and fair view'.[66] Behind this lies the more detailed Financial Reporting Standards issued by the FRC Board.[67] In

[57]See Chapter 3 under 3.4.

[58]In addition to the statutory requirements and the accounting standards that are mentioned in this chapter, a listed plc will need to comply with the relevant requirements of the FCA Listing Rules.

[59]Many matters in relation to financial reporting are the responsibility of the Financial Reporting Council (FRC) and its 'subsidiary' bodies. Descriptions of these important bodies and their very important work are available on http://www.frc.org.uk.

[60]Companies Act 2006, ss. 386–389. See the decision in *Australian Securities and Investments Commission*, above n. 60 (and text thereto), where the Federal Court of Australia discussed the nature and the content of the duties of directors as the 'final filter' of corporate financial accounting.

[61]*Ibid.* ss. 394 and 396. If the company is a parent company, group accounts will sometimes be required as well as the company's individual accounts: ss. 398–408 (the accounts are referred to in s. 394 as the company's 'individual' accounts to distinguish them from group accounts).

[62]Defined in ss. 390–392.

[63]Companies Act 2006, s. 414 (1).

[64](2008) No. 410.

[65]The Small Companies and Groups (Accounts and Directors' Report) Regulations 2008 were made on 19 February and came into force on 6 April 2008, (2008) No. 409.

[66]S. 396 (5). The duty for accounts to give true and fair view is found in s. 393.

[67]In some circumstances Urgent Issues Task Force (UITF) Abstracts will also be relevant. Certain small companies or groups can choose to apply the Financial Reporting Standards for Smaller Entities (FRSSE). Previously there were also Statements of Standard Accounting Practice (SSAPs) but most have been superseded by FRSs although some are still in force.

practice these FRSs are usually followed by accountants, for although they are not given the force of law by the Companies Act, there is a requirement for it to be stated whether the accounts have been prepared in accordance with applicable accounting standards and any material departures from the standards must be mentioned and reasons given.[68] If the company is a parent company within the meaning of the Act, then as well as preparing individual accounts, the directors must prepare group accounts that comprise a consolidated balance sheet dealing with the state of affairs of the parent company and its subsidiary undertakings and a similar profit and loss account.[69]

International Accounting Standards (IAS)[70] have been developed and issued by the International Accounting Standards Board (IASB) with a view to setting and encouraging the use of global standards.[71] These have now been adopted as law in the EU, and so EU companies which are traded publicly must prepare their consolidated accounts in line with IAS.[72] The UK government policy is to permit the use of IAS in other situations also.[73] In May 2008, the Financial Reporting Council (FRC) published an opinion from Martin Moore QC regarding the continued relevance of the 'true and fair view' concept to company accounts. This was considered necessary because of the uncertainty about the continuing relevance of 'true and fair' in the context of International Financial Reporting Standards (IFRS) and the reformulation of the 'true and fair' concept in s. 393 of the Companies Act 2006. The opinion confirms the centrality of the true and fair requirement to the preparation of financial statements in the UK, whether they are prepared in accordance with international or UK accounting standards. It also emphasises that the application of the standards is not merely a mechanical exercise and directors cannot conclude that the financial statements they approve are 'true and fair' simply because they were prepared in accordance with applicable accounting standards.[74]

[68]*Ibid*. s. 396 (5).
[69]Ss. 398–408.
[70]Standards which were issued on 6 April 2004 and thereafter referred to as International Financial Reporting Standards (IFRS). Standards issued prior to that date will continue to be referred to as IAS.
[71]At a global level their main rivals are the Americans who have developed and continue to hold to US GAAP (US Generally Accepted Accounting Principles).
[72]Effective since 1 January 2005. This is as a result of the EC Regulation of July 2002. For further details of this, see Chapter 1, 1.6 above. New accounting standards were issued by the IASB in May 2011 by way of response to calls by the G20 for changes to accounting standards following the global financial crisis. The standards came into effect for accounting periods beginning on or after 1 January 2013.
[73]I.e. in the individual accounts of publicly traded companies and in the individual and consolidated accounts of most other companies.
[74]Counsel's opinion provides an update on the previous opinions from Leonard Hoffmann QC and Mary Arden QC obtained in 1983, 1984 and 1993 on the 'true and fair view' concept and the connection between the concept and accounting standards, which continue to apply. It also considers the impact of the Companies Act 2006, EU Directives and Regulations, IFRS and decisions from national Courts and the European Court of Justice. All of the opinions, when taken together, offer useful guidance as to when the courts might consider a departure by a company from the use of the 'true and fair view' concept as being appropriate. The FRC Press Notice, the FRC statement and both the new and older opinions can be found on the FRC website at http://www.frc.org.uk/about/trueandfair.cfm. In June 2014 the FRC published a statement, 'True and Fair', confirming the fundamental importance of the true and fair concept for the preparation of accounts: see https://www.frc.org.uk/getattachment/f08eecd2-6e3a-46d9-a3f8-73f82c09f624/True-and-fair-June-2014.pdf.

In addition to the accounts, the directors are required to prepare a directors' report[75] containing a 'fair review'[76] of the development of the business of the company and its subsidiary undertakings during the financial year and of their position at the end of it' and also a statement as to the amount of dividend which they are recommending. Additionally, the directors' report must contain the matters required by section 992 of the Companies Act 2006. Since 20 May 2006, all companies whose shares are admitted to trading on an EU regulated market have been required to include in their directors' report the information set out in s. 992. The disclosures focus on the company's share and control structures and the aim is to provide greater transparency to the market. Although the requirements originate from the EU Takeovers Directive, it is irrelevant whether the company is, or has been, involved in a takeover. Section 992[77] contains a prescriptive list of what needs to be disclosed, including information on the company's capital structure, details of its major shareholders, any restrictions on the transfer of shares or on voting rights and the powers of the directors. There is also a requirement that any agreements providing for compensation to board members or employees resulting from resignations or redundancies following a takeover bid be disclosed. The most interesting of these requirements is the need to disclose significant agreements that take effect, alter or terminate upon a change of control of the company following a takeover bid.

Section 414 A–E requires certain publicly listed companies to produce an annual report called a 'Strategic Report', which replaced the 'Business Review' in 2013.[78] The Report is intended to provide shareholders with a better understanding of the operation of the business and its future prospects.[79] The Report should contain detail about the principal risks and uncertainties that the company is facing, as well as analysis of the company's development and performance. It must also disclose information relating to Key Performance Indicators, which are to include matters relating to the environment and employees. Quoted companies are required to provide an enhanced level of detail.[80]

Put simply, the Strategic Report requires a narrative about the business of the company that can accompany the figures as shown in the annual accounts. The section is the product

[75]Companies Act 2006, s. 415.
[76]The requirements for the contents of the directors' report has changed in accordance with the Modernisation Directive (2003/51/EC). The Directive defines the 'fair review' as 'a balanced and comprehensive analysis of the development and performance of the company's business and of its position, consistent with the size and complexity of the business.' These requirements are found in ss. 415–419, which collectively concern the duty to prepare a directors' report, its content, approval and signature.
[77]Which amends Sch. 7 of the 1985 Act.
[78]Companies Act 2006 (Strategic Report and Directors' Report) Regulation 2013.
[79]Detailed guidance on what is required by the Strategic Report has been provided by the FRC, in its June 2014 publication 'Guidance on the Strategic Report',
[80]Quoted companies are those that are listed on the main market of the London Stock Exchange and a few others. The definition of which companies are included and which are not is quite complicated. According to s. 385 of the Act, a 'quoted company' means a company whose equity share capital either: (a) has been included in the official list in accordance with the provisions of Part 6 of the Financial Services and Markets Act 2000 (c. 8); or (b) is officially listed in an EEA State; or (c) is admitted to dealing on either the New York Stock Exchange or the exchange known as Nasdaq (www.opsi.gov.uk/ACTS/acts2006/60046-p.htm). This includes the FTSE 100 Index (including HSBC, BP and Vodafone). These publicly trading companies may have thousands of shareholders, from large institutional investors who manage shares on behalf of groups such as pension funds or the insurance sector, to individuals. Some sub-markets of the London Stock Exchange will not have to produce a report (e.g. those listed on the Alternative Investment Market (AIM) which includes Domino's Pizza and M&C Saatchi). Neither will privately-owned companies such as Virgin Airlines and Asda.

of much development regarding the way in which the requirement for such a report is articulated. It arises not only out of the ashes of the Business Review but is also the product of the debate about narrative reporting conducted by the Company Law Review and subsequently by the Department of Trade and Industry (now DBEIS), including on the occasion of the repeal of the short-lived statutory Operating and Financial Review (OFR), and from requirements of the so-called EC Modernisation Directive, mentioned above.[81]

Of special note is the fact that the statutory responsibilities for the preparation of the accounts and directors' report cannot be shifted on to the auditors, even if they are retained as the accountants to the company and so, in fact, are the people most directly involved in the actual work of preparing the figures out of the mass of internal documentation which the directors have handed over to them. This point has become particularly apparent in relation to wrongful trading cases where it has been held that the directors cannot escape liability by arguing that they were unaware of the financial state of the business because the accounts were not ready in time.[82]

Companies are also obliged to deliver[83] an annual return to the Registrar in the prescribed form,[84] which must contain information[85] such as the address of the company's registered office, the names and addresses of every director and various other details. Much of this information remains the same each year and the procedure has been made more efficient by the introduction of a 'confirmation' system whereby a document is sent from the Registrar containing the previous year's information and requiring only necessary amendments to the document which is then returned.

## 2 *Publicity*

The legislation contains a range of processes and requirements designed mainly with a view to getting the accounts and reports thoroughly publicised throughout the company and put on public file. The accounts in respect of each financial year must be laid before the company in general meeting within the periods prescribed.[86] Additionally, the accounts must be delivered to the Registrar of Companies where they will be placed on public file.[87] A copy of the annual accounts must be sent to every member, debenture holder and any other person entitled to receive notice of general meetings, within prescribed time limits.[88] Furthermore, any member or debenture holder is entitled to demand a copy of the

---

[81]Directive 2003/51/EC at [2003] OJ/L178/16. This directive amended various accounting directives that, *inter alia*, set the requirement, in European legislation, for the directors' report (e.g. the EC Fourth Company Law Directive, 78/660/EEC at [1978] OJ/L222/11, as amended).

[82]*Re Brian D Pierson (Contractors) Ltd* [1999] BCC 26; see also *Re Produce Marketing Consortium Ltd (No. 2)* (1989) 5 BCC 569.

[83]Within certain time periods.

[84]Companies Act 2006, ss. 854 and 858.

[85]Set out in ss. 855 and 856.

[86]Companies Act 2006, ss. 437, 438.

[87]*Ibid.* s. 441. Sections 444–448 contain provisions enabling companies and groups which qualify as 'small' to file with the Registrar accounts which contain less information than those which they must circulate to the shareholders, sometimes referred to as 'modified accounts' or 'abbreviated accounts'. Thus, the medium-sized group exemption from preparing consolidated accounts (contained in ss. 246–249 Companies Act 1985) has been removed.

[88]Companies Act 2006, ss. 423–425; there are certain exceptions.

company's last annual accounts.[89] If a company publishes its accounts, then there are various prescriptions designed to ensure that they are complete and that certain misleading impressions are not created.[90] In recognition of the abolition of the requirement for private companies to hold an AGM, under the Companies Act 2006, private companies are no longer required to send out their annual accounts prior to a general meeting. Instead, the annual accounts, or summary financial statements if appropriate, must be sent to members by the time they are due to be filed with the Registrar of Companies.

## 3 *Non-statutory reports*

Accounts usually contain more than the balance sheet and profit and loss account required by the legislation. In particular, accounting standards require a cash flow statement.[91] Often also there are reports containing a review of the company's financial needs, resources and treasury management, a report on operations, on community programmes. For many years, listed plcs have used the need to circulate annual accounts to shareholders as a way of promoting the image of the company and so the accounts and related non-statutory reports are presented in a glossy magazine format designed to present the company in its best light.[92]

## 4 *The role of the auditors*

The auditors are a significant part of the overall mechanism for the protection of shareholders and the corporate governance process generally. They have an important statutory function which establishes them as a kind of independent checking mechanism. This comes about through the operation of s. 495 of the Companies Act 2006, which requires that the auditors must make a report to the company's members on all annual accounts of the company of which copies are to be laid[93] before the company in general meeting during their tenure of office. This auditors' report must state whether in the opinion of the auditors the annual accounts have been properly prepared in accordance with the 2006 Act and whether a true and fair view is given. They must also consider whether the information given in the directors' report is consistent with the accounts, and if not, they must state that in their report.[94] The auditors have a duty to carry out sufficient investigations to enable them to form an opinion as to whether proper accounting records have been kept by the company and proper returns adequate for their audit have been received from branches not visited by them and also whether the company's individual accounts are in agreement with the accounting records and returns.[95] If these or any of the other matters are not satisfactory,

---

[89] *Ibid.* ss. 431–432; the company must comply within seven days.
[90] *Ibid.* ss. 434–436.
[91] FRS 1.
[92] On the importance of annual reports generally, see S. Bartlett and R. Chandler 'The Private Shareholder, Corporate Governance, and the Role of the Annual Report' [1999] JBL 415. In relation to accounting narratives, see M. Clatworthy and M.J. Jones 'Financial Reporting of Good News and Bad News: Evidence from Accounting Narratives' (2003) *Accounting and Business Research* 33(3) at pp.171–185.
[93] On the laying process, see Chapter 7, 7.3(D) and 9.3(D) above.
[94] Companies Act 2006, s. 496.
[95] *Ibid.* s. 498.

the auditors must state that in their report. In a listed company an adverse report by the auditors can lead to a DBEIS investigation.

Events in the last three decades have turned a spotlight on the liability of auditors for their audit reports. Although the House of Lords' decision in *Caparo plc* v *Dickman*[96] provided some amelioration for them by limiting the scope of their liability for negligent mis-statement in tort, their contractual liability to the company was more than sufficient to give rise to a plethora of claims against them where the standard of their efforts had arguably fallen below the reasonable care implied in their contracts. The claims were brought by the liquidator or administrator of the failed company and since these were usually partners from the top accountancy firms the result was that most of the firms found themselves pitted against each other in what in financial terms were life or death struggles.[97] There were plenty of corporate scandals around to provide the basis for actions: Barlow Clowes, Maxwell, Polly Peck to name but a few. Some of the claims were huge; the largest was probably the action brought by the liquidators of Bank of Credit and Commerce International (BCCI) against Price Waterhouse and Ernst & Whinney,[98] claiming £5.2bn.[99]

The decision of the House of Lords in *Moore Stephens* v *Stone & Rolls Ltd*,[100] will give comfort to auditors (and their liability insurers) who find themselves defending a claim for breach of duty in failing to detect fraud. Stone & Rolls Limited (hereafter, 'SR') was a 'one-man company' which was used by its sole director and shareholder to facilitate a massive bank fraud. The bank obtained judgment against SR and its controller but neither of the defendants were able to satisfy the judgment. The liquidators claimed against its auditors, Moore Stephens (hereafter, 'MS') on the basis that they should have detected that SR was being used by its controller for fraudulent activities. MS applied to strike out the claim on the basis of *ex turpi causa non oritur actio* (i.e., a claim cannot be based on the illegal actions of the claimant). The auditors contended that the fraud of the controller was essentially the same as a fraud by the company.

By a majority of three to two, the House of Lords upheld the Court of Appeal decision that the claim should be struck out. The majority of their Lordships found that the fraud could be attributed to SR since it was a 'one-man company'. It was not, therefore, possible to interpret the actions of the company as anything but the actions of the controller. Further, given that a sole shareholder had committed the fraud, there were no innocent parties within the company who did not share the guilty knowledge. Therefore, there was no merit in the claim that the company was not a fraudster but a secondary victim. Lord Mance, dissenting, thought that numerous 'Ponzi' style fraud schemes were operated by 'one-man companies' and that to absolve auditors from all responsibilities in these circumstances would be questionable policy.

---

[96][1990] 2 AC 605. However, if the auditors have 'assumed a duty of care' to the claimants, this may lead to liability: see *Henderson* v *Merrett Syndicates* [1995] 2 AC 145, HL; *ADT* v *BDO Binder Hamlyn* [1996] BCC 808; *Electra Private Equity Partners* v *KPMG Peat Marwick* [2000] BCC 368, CA.
[97]In the Barings Bank collapse, the administrators were the accountancy firm Ernst & Young and the defendants were Coopers & Lybrand (London and Singapore) and Deloitte Touch (Singapore).
[98]Later called Ernst & Young.
[99]*Financial Times*, 5 August 1994. It was eventually drastically scaled down (to around £250m) and settled.
[100][2009] 2 BCLC 563.

Their Lordships also considered the nature of the duties owed by auditors. The majority held that MS did not owe a duty to protect those whom SR may defraud, but rather, MS only had a duty to protect directors and those who had a proprietary interest in the company. In this case, as the controller was the sole director and shareholder, MS's duty only extended to the controller. As the controller was the fraudster, *ex turpi causa* gave MS a defence against this claim. Lords Mance and Scott, dissenting, argued that MS owed a duty to innocent creditors when the company was insolvent or under the threat of insolvency. In such a case, *ex turpi causa* should not defeat the claim.

Accountants had traditionally pursued their professional activities as partnerships and those who are partners are jointly liable for the contract debts of the firm.[101] Professional indemnity insurance provided protection only to a certain level. Beyond that, the partners were personally liable. The accountancy profession developed various ideas on how their problems might be mitigated.[102] They were largely instrumental in setting up the Cadbury Committee on the Financial Aspects of Corporate Governance, the Report of which produced a revolution in the self-regulatory aspects of corporate governance.[103] The problems faced by the accountancy profession were the initial incentive for the development of the Limited Liability Partnership.[104] To some extent, provisions in the Companies (Audit, Investigations and Community Enterprise) Act 2004 (largely incorporated into the Companies Act 2006) improved their position.[105] This Act gives auditors rights to require information from a wider group of people than previously, and introduces a new offence for failing to provide information or explain. There is also a duty cast upon directors to consider whether they have supplied the information necessary for a successful audit, and the accounts contain a statement certifying that the directors have not withheld information necessary for the auditors to form their opinion.[106]

Finally, it should be noted that the Companies Act 2006 introduced new rules allowing auditors and companies to agree limitations of the auditors' liability subject to certain conditions.[107] Companies are now permitted to enter into auditor limitation liability

---

[101] And jointly and severally liable for tort debts; see Partnership Act 1890, ss. 9, 10 and 12.

[102] Besides improving their own internal procedures. One proposal was to put a 'cap' on their liability to clients, based on a multiple of their audit fee.

[103] See Chapter 10.

[104] See Chapter 1, 1.9C.

[105] This Act received Royal Assent on 28 October 2004 and its provisions came into force on 6 April 2005. The company law provisions of the 2006 Act restated almost all of the provisions of the Companies (Audit, Investigations and Community Enterprise) Act 2004 with minor amendments to ss. 14 and 15 of the 2004 Act (the amendments mean that periodic accounts and reports of issuers required under corporate governance rules or transparency rules may be examined by the Financial Reporting Review Panel). The 2006 Act also provides power to designate a competent authority for reporting framework purposes by amending the Companies (Audit, Investigations and Community Enterprise) Act 2004. See Sch. 15 (Part 2) of the 2006 Act.

[106] See ss. 8–18. The Act also seeks to strengthen auditor independence by requiring companies to publish detailed information in their annual accounts as to the non-audit services which their auditor has provided. The idea being that shareholders will be able to judge from this whether the auditor is subject to conflicts of interest which may affect the objectivity of the audit.

[107] See ss. 532–538 Companies Act 2006. The Companies (Disclosure of Auditor Remuneration and Liability Limitation Agreements) Regulations 2008 SI 2008/489. These Regulations replaced the former Companies (Disclosure of Auditor Remuneration) Regulations 2005 (SI 2005/2417).

agreements (LLA) subject to gaining shareholder approval.[108] An LLA may cover negligence, default, breach of duty or breach of trust on the part of the auditor to the company occurring in the course of the audit of accounts. Sections 532–538 of the 2006 Act provide the framework governing provisions exempting auditors from liability. More specifically, s. 534 permits auditors to enter into an agreement 'that purports to limit the liability owed to a company by its auditor in respect of any negligence, default, breach of duty or breach of trust, occurring in the course of the audit of accounts, of which the auditor may be guilty in relation to the company.' To be valid, such agreements must comply with s. 535 and must be authorised by the company's shareholders by an ordinary resolution under s. 536.[109] It remains to be seen how and to what extent these LLAs will become a common practice.[110]

## 5 *Company secretary*

The existence of other officers of the company, such as the company secretary,[111] could in some circumstances help to provide a check on the activities of directors. Every public company must have a secretary.[112] The legislation has prohibitions on who can be a secretary in certain situations.[113] Since the Companies Act 1980, the rules on who can be the secretary of a public company have been tightened up with the overall aim of ensuring that the secretary of a public company is, broadly, a 'professional'. The statute provides that it is the duty of the directors to take all reasonable steps to secure that the secretary[114] is a person who appears to them to have the requisite knowledge and experience to discharge

---

[108] The Companies (Disclosure of Auditor Remuneration and Liability Limitation Agreements) Regulations 2008 require a company to disclose the principal terms of an LLA and the date of the approval resolution (or resolution waiving the need for approval in the case of a private company) in a note to the company's accounts; in addition it must provide details of auditor's remuneration for services not limited to the audit (see The Companies (Disclosure of Auditor Remuneration and Liability Limitation Agreements) Amendment Regulations 2011 (SI 2011/2198)). Guidance on limited liability agreements, and the framework introduced by the Act, was published by the Financial Reporting Council (FRC). The guidance explains what is and is not allowed under the Act; several factors to consider when considering the case for an agreement; what should be included in the agreement including example clauses; and the shareholder approval process including example wording for inclusion in shareholder resolutions. This FRC guidance is available on the FRC website.

[109] Unless the articles specify a higher threshold by public and private companies either before or after they enter into it (although private companies can resolve to waive the need for approval).

[110] In response to their introduction, the Association of British Insurers (ABI) has warned that it will 'red top' any listed company that agrees a fixed financial cap for their auditor's liability rather than a proportional cap based on the extent of the auditor's role and responsibility, and does not provide assurances as to the appropriateness of an LLA. The ABI also recommends that LLAs should be made available for shareholder inspection. Likewise, the Pensions and Lifetime Savings Association has stated that investors should consider voting against resolutions which propose any form of liability limitation other than proportional liability, unless there are compelling reasons why that is not appropriate and why another form of liability limitation is 'fair and reasonable'.

[111] Section 271 Companies Act 2006. See also the definition in s. 1121 of the Companies Act 2006: 'officer . . . includes (a) any director, manager, or secretary'.

[112] Section 272 Companies Act 2006. Since 6 April 2008, private companies are no longer obliged to have a company secretary, although they may continue to have one if they wish. If they no longer wish to have a secretary they need do nothing, apart from the secretary resigning or his or her appointment being terminated. Section 274 (b) of the Companies Act says that a director or person authorised by the directors can do anything required to be done by or to the secretary. If a private company does continue to have, or appoints, a secretary then he or she will have the same status as previously.

[113] Section 273 Companies Act 2006.

[114] And each joint secretary.

the functions of secretary.[115] Additionally, they must also satisfy one of the detailed requirements set out in s. 273 of the Companies Act 2006.[116] The terms of appointment of the secretary are usually governed by the articles in respect of issues such as appointment and remuneration (removal of a secretary is in the hands of the directors). The company secretary may sometimes become liable for failures to perform his duties. Often the legislation penalises the 'officers' of the company for, for instance, failing to deliver a document to the Registrar of Companies. As we have seen, the secretary is an officer by virtue of the definition in s. 1121. In some circumstances he might become personally liable for debts and other payments.[117] Disqualification of a company secretary is also possible in certain limited circumstances.[118]

It is difficult to be precise about the nature of the duties and role of the company secretary. Much will depend on the contractual terms of his employment and the size of the company involved. Usually the company secretary will be expected to ensure that the company complies with all the 'disclosure' requirements in the legislation so that, for instance, he will be responsible for the operation of the various registers, books and particulars required to be kept at the company's registered office. The summoning and arranging of meetings and other legislative requirements like the annual return will also usually fall to him. He may also find that extensive liaison with the auditors is necessary, particularly if they are being dilatory about preparing the annual audit, delay with which can now attract severe penalties. In smaller companies in particular, the company secretary may often be required to provide a legal service also, dealing with matters like drafting of contracts and employment law. Sometimes he will have an executive or commercial function and may have actual or apparent authority to bind the company in contracts.[119]

## 6 *Government and other agencies*

The activities of companies are monitored in various ways by a number of government and non-governmental agencies and organisations; these include the Department for Business, Energy & Industrial Strategy, the London Stock Exchange, the Financial Conduct Authority, the Insolvency Service, as well as the police, the Serious Fraud Office and the Crown Prosecution Service.[120] General monitoring of the management and affairs of companies is

---

[115] Section 273 (1).
[116] Section 273 Companies Act 2006 updates s. 286 of the 1985 Act. It makes it the duty of the directors of a public company to ensure that the secretary has both the necessary knowledge and experience and one of the following qualifications (listed in subsection (2)): to have been secretary for a public company for at least three of the five years preceding the appointment, be a member of a specified body (listed in subsection (3) and including the Institute of Chartered Accountants in England and Wales, the Institute of Chartered Secretaries and Administrators and the Chartered Institute of Management Accountants), be a barrister, advocate or solicitor in any part of the UK or someone who appears, by virtue of experience or qualifications, to be capable of discharging the duties. There is no requirement for the company secretary to be a natural person (compare the requirement in s. 155 Companies Act 2006 that a company must have at least one director who is a natural person).
[117] See e.g. Companies Act 2006, s. 1121.
[118] See e.g. Company Directors Disqualification Act 1986, ss. 4 (1) (b), 22 (6).
[119] See e.g. *Panorama Developments Ltd* v *Fidelis Furnishing Fabrics Ltd* [1971] 3 All ER 16.
[120] See generally Chapters 17–23.

carried out by the DBEIS, which has various statutory powers of investigation.[121] It should be noted that the area of company investigations is one of the very few areas that were left behind in the 1985 Act with the introduction of the Companies Act 2006.[122]

There are two main types of DBEIS investigation – s. 447 of the Companies Act 1985 requisitions and s. 432 of the Companies Act 1985 investigations.[123] Under s. 447 of the Companies Act 1985, the Secretary of State has power to require the production of documents if he thinks that there is good reason to do so. A s. 447 inquiry is unannounced and, for those on the receiving end, sudden. It enables DBEIS to get enough information[124] to decide whether to do anything further. In the year ending 31 March 2015 there were 150 such investigations,[125] some as a result of requests from the public, some on the DTI's (as it was then known) own initiative, and some as a result of a request from a variety of other sources such as other regulators. Many such investigations lead no further. Some do, however, and may result in criminal investigations and proceedings, or perhaps winding up.[126] Occasionally such an investigation is a preliminary to a s. 432 investigation.

Section 432 provides various grounds for the DBEIS to appoint inspectors to investigate a company. These are generally carried out by outside inspectors, often a Queen's Counsel and an accountant, and lead to a detailed report which is usually published. The investigations are very rare events.

As noted above, Part 32 of the Companies Act 2006 introduces some amendments to the previous regime on company investigations.[127] It gives the Secretary of State the power to take appropriate action in cases where the investigation appears to be taking too long. The Act also deals with situations that were previously not dealt with.[128] The Act confers new powers upon the Secretary of State to give directions to company investigators.[129] The Secretary of State may give a company investigator a direction: as to the subject matter of his investigation (whether by reference to a specified transaction, a specified area of a company's activities or a specified period of time); or requiring an inspector to take (or not take, as the case may be) a specified step in his investigation. The Secretary of State may

---

[121] These are contained in the Companies Act 2006, Part 32 and make detailed provision for the investigation of companies. DBEIS also has powers in relation to insider dealing offences; these are dealt with in Chapter 20 under 20.4.

[122] But as will be seen below, Part 32 of the Companies Act 2006 introduces some amendments to the regime on company investigations.

[123] As amended by s. 1038 and s. 1035 Companies Act 2006 respectively. It should also be mentioned that under s. 442 inspectors may be appointed by the DBEIS to investigate the ownership of a company's shares. Also under s. 431 inspectors may be appointed at the formal request of the company in certain circumstances, although this power is very rarely used.

[124] The Companies (Audit, Investigations and Community Enterprise) Act 2004 seeks to strengthen the investigations regime by increasing the DBEIS's powers in relation to obtaining information and increasing remedies available against people who fail to provide information.

[125] See Insolvency Service Annual Report and Accounts 2014–15, 15.

[126] Under s. 124 A of the Insolvency Act 1986. It is not uncommon for disqualification proceedings against directors to be brought in the wake of a DBEIS investigation: see, for example, *Secretary of State for Business, Enterprise and Regulatory Reform* v *Sullman* [2009] 1 BCLC 397.

[127] These changes introduced by the Act took effect by way of amendments to the existing Companies Act 1985 and came into force on 1 October 2007.

[128] For example, the resignation or death of inspectors and the ability to appoint replacement inspectors.

[129] Section 1035 inserting s. 446 A in the Companies Act 1985.

direct an investigator to terminate an investigation.[130] However, in relation to those company investigations that have been initiated by the company itself, by its members or by a court order, such a direction can only be given where matters have come to light during the investigation that a criminal offence has been committed and those matters have been referred to the appropriate prosecuting authorities.[131]

The 2006 Act provides that an inspector may resign his position by notice in writing to the Secretary of State.[132] The Act also provides that the Secretary of State may remove an inspector by notice in writing to the inspector.[133] In cases where an inspector dies, resigns or has his appointment revoked, the Secretary of State has the power to appoint alternative investigators.[134]

## Concluding remarks

This part of the chapter has provided a résumé of the legal constraints which constitute the environment in which directors operate. It hardly seems possible to conclude that the law is 'woefully inadequate' or some similar epithet; indeed, as it currently stands, it is not inadequate. The scandals of the 1980s were largely the product of a very different legal regime; a regime formed in the 1960s and 1970s, and earlier. Much of the law changed in the 1980s, and the way in which it was operated by the regulators changed too.

The unfair prejudice remedy dates from 1980 but took some years to develop, by which time it had become clear that it had revolutionised shareholder litigation to the extent that, far from being almost impossible to set up, it had by the 1990s become almost a crippling nuisance.[135] Most of the insolvency law reforms date from 1985 and they also took a while to impact; but eventually it became clear that the environment had changed. Wrongful trading cases became a more frequent sight in the law reports and a jurisprudence developed on the issue of the liability of a parent company for wrongful trading through its subsidiary.[136] Disqualification cases became more common in the late 1980s after the passing of the Company Directors Disqualification Act 1986 and these have steadily grown. The system for filing of accounts had become notorious due to accounts being years out of date but the introduction of substantial civil fines has largely succeeded in changing this. The regulatory climate was changing. As regards the regulators themselves, the scene changed out of all recognition from 1986 onwards. The old DTI-operated system of licensing of share dealers under the Prevention of Fraud (Investments) Act 1958 gave way to comparatively ferocious regulation of the wider financial services industry under the Securities and Investments Board,[137] replaced by the Financial Services Authority (FSA) and since divided into the Financial Conduct Authority (FCA) and the Prudential Regulation Authority (PRA). This and other changes[138] produced a marked shift in the

---

[130] Section 1035 inserting s. 446 B in the Companies Act 1985.
[131] Section 1035 inserting s. 446 B (2) in the Companies Act 1985.
[132] Section 1035 inserting s. 446 C (1) in the Companies Act 1985.
[133] Section 1035 inserting s. 446 C (2) in the Companies Act 1985.
[134] Section 1035 inserting s. 446 D in the Companies Act 1985.
[135] See further Chapter 12 under 12.2 below on judicial efforts to contain unfair prejudice litigation.
[136] See further Chapter 2, 2.2C above.
[137] Set up by the Financial Services Act 1986.
[138] E.g. the enhanced enforcement of insider dealing law.

culture of the business industry. Businesspeople had not grown to like business law, but they had certainly begun to realise that it could not be ignored without undesirable results.

Many of these matters will be taken up later in this text. But this much is clear. It is important not to assess the UK system of corporate governance by reference to the past, looking at past scandals and at a legal climate which has since moved on. We will see in the Chapter 10 that for larger companies, there is also now a substantial layer of regulation emanating from the Corporate governance committees. This too has had its impact.

## Further reading

J. Lowry 'Self-Dealing Directors – Constructing a Regime of Accountability' [1997] *NILQ* 211.

S. Worthington, 'Corporate Governance: Remedying and Ratifying Directors' Breaches' [2000] *LQR* 638.

L. West 'Challenging the "Golden Goodbye"' [2009] *JBL* 447.

A. Keay 'Company Directors Behaving Poorly: Disciplinary Options for Shareholders' [2007] *JBL* 656.

R. Williams 'Disqualifying Directors: A Remedy Worse Than the Disease?' [2007] *Journal of Corporate Law Studies* 213.

# 10
# Role of self-regulation

## 10.1 Reliance on self-regulation

It has been seen[1] how the corporate scandals of the 1980s and the exposed legal position of statutory auditors prompted a reconsideration of the adequacy of corporate governance mechanisms and that the Cadbury Committee was set up in May 1991 by the Financial Reporting Council ('FRC'), the London Stock Exchange ('LSE') and the accountancy profession to examine the financial aspects of corporate governance. The resultant Cadbury Report,[2] issued in 1992, reviewed the structure and responsibilities of boards of directors, the role of auditors and the rights and responsibilities of shareholders. The recommendations as regards directors were summarised in a 'Code of Best Practice'. Although the report intended to focus on those aspects of corporate governance specifically related to financial reporting and accountability, the committee intended that their ideas would seek to contribute to the promotion of good corporate governance as a whole.[3]

The chief distinguishing feature of the Cadbury Report was its reliance mainly on self-regulation. It was not a report which produced a long list of recommended changes to the law[4] and which thereby postponed the resultant hoped-for improvements until some remote future date after the legislature had acted on the recommendations. The Cadbury Report took effect swiftly and without reliance on the law.[5] Sometime after it was issued the LSE added force to the recommendations of the report by amending the listing rules so as to require listed companies to make a statement about their level of compliance with the Cadbury Code of Best Practice and give reasons for non-compliance. The Cadbury Report also made the point, as is often done by regulators in the context of self-regulation, that if the self-regulatory mechanisms were seen not to be working, then legislation would become inevitable.[6]

---

[1] See chapter 3 3.4 B above.

[2] *Report of the Committee on the Financial Aspects of Corporate Governance* (London: Gee, 1992).

[3] The literature is immense. See e.g. D. Prentice and P. Holland (eds) *Contemporary Issues in Corporate Governance* (Oxford: Clarendon Press, 1993); N. Maw, P. Lane and M. Craig-Cooper *Maw on Corporate Governance* (Aldershot: Dartmouth Publishing, 1994); S. Sheikh and W. Rees (eds) *Corporate Governance and Corporate Control* (London: Cavendish, 1995); G. Stapledon *Institutional Shareholders and Corporate Governance* (Oxford: Clarendon Press, 1996); K. Hopt and E. Wymeersch (eds) *Comparative Corporate Governance* (Berlin: de Gruyter, 1997); J. Kay and A. Silberston 'Corporate Governance' in F. Patfield (ed.) *Perspectives on Company Law: 2* (Deventer: Kluwer, 1997) p. 49. See also the footnote references in Chapter 3 above, under 3.4.

[4] There were some, but these formed a minor aspect of the Cadbury Report's overall approach (see e.g. para. 4.41 (Companies Act to be amended to require shareholder approval for directors' service contracts exceeding three years)).

[5] Although it was mindful of the legal background.

[6] Cadbury Report, paras 1.10, 3.6.

The Cadbury Report gave renewed impetus to the debate about the merits or demerits of self-regulation for a similar controversy had already surrounded the self-regulatory Code on Takeovers and Mergers.[7] Much of the early public reception given to the Cadbury Report and the idea of self-regulation in corporate governance was sceptical.[8] Self-regulation has its disadvantages, chiefly in relation to enforceability, and there is an obvious theoretical objection to allowing those who are likely to benefit most from a weakly regulated regime to be responsible for regulating it. And yet, by 1995, evidence was beginning to emerge of significant levels of compliance with the Cadbury Code, albeit with lower levels among smaller companies.[9] The Company Law Review expressed the view that the evidence[10] suggested a fairly high level of compliance with the Combined Code and that it was increasing.[11] The Review cited a survey by PIRC[12] which shows that 93% of a sample of FTSE All Share Index companies had a board made up of one-third or more non-executive directors.[13] It is arguable that self-regulation is superior in some respects to regulation by statute: its potential for cultural change is likely to be greater because, deriving from public debate and perceived consensus within the sector to be regulated, it commands greater respect within that sector than rules imposed by an external lawgiver. It is also more flexible and can respond more quickly to change. Enforcement mechanisms, while not as final and crushing as legal enforcement, can nevertheless be very varied and create a supportive environment for a self-regulatory code.[14] The use of self-regulatory codes is widespread, and, while it could be a grand exercise in self-deception, it is more likely that the public enthusiasm for them is based on a shared intuitive perception that they have a contribution to make. As a *caveat* to this, it is worth observing that there may be some matters that are not amenable to self-regulation and where legislation may be needed, particularly where there is no consensus on the matter within the sector being regulated. Indeed, as will be seen below, one of the lessons of the financial crisis of 2007–2008 is that corporate governance, mostly based on self-regulation, was not always as effective as it could have been.[15]

---

[7] Cadbury Report, paras 1.10, 3.6.

[8] In its Lex column the *Financial Times*, 28 May 1992, swung its weight against the idea with a piece entitled 'Cadbury's Soft Centre'. Doubts were expressed by both academics and practitioners: see e.g. Finch 'Board Performance and Cadbury on Corporate Governance' [1992] JBL 581 at p. 595; N. Maw, P. Lane and M. Craig-Cooper *Maw on Corporate Governance* (Aldershot: Dartmouth Publishing, 1994).

[9] See the 1994 Report of the Cadbury Committee's Monitoring Sub-Committee. For further empirical analysis in this area, see A. Belcher 'Regulation by the Market: The Case of the Cadbury Code and Compliance Statement' [1995] JBL 321; A. Belcher 'Compliance with the Cadbury Code and the Reporting of Corporate Governance' (1996) 17 *Company Lawyer* 11.

[10] By March 2000.

[11] See the Department of Trade and Industry (DTI) Consultation Document (March 2000) *Developing the Framework* para. 3.129.

[12] Pensions Investment Research Consultants.

[13] Although there are gaps in compliance in other respects.

[14] The Cadbury Report stressed the role to be played by financial institutions, and a wide range of public bodies; also the role of the media in drawing attention to governance issues of public or shareholder concern: Cadbury Report, para. 3.14.

[15] Below, under 10.8.

## 10.2 Techniques of Cadbury

### A Different approaches

In order to achieve its aim of an improvement in the quality of corporate governance, the Cadbury Report tackled the problems from different angles, with the overall intention of changing the environment in which companies operate. The following three approaches can be identified:

(1) structural and functional alterations designed to spread the balance of power;
(2) increases in assumptions of responsibility; and
(3) enhanced quality of disclosure.

These will now be examined below.

### B Structural and functional alterations

Some of the Cadbury Report's key recommendations were designed to ensure that power is spread around within the governance structure and not concentrated in one person, or in one small group. It was seen as important to get the structure working; in particular, to get the board working as a group and to provide proper checks and balances[16] so that the board does not simply agree to do whatever the chief executive wants and does not have too much power. The Cadbury Committee evolved an enhanced status and function for non-executive directors (NEDs), of whom there had to be at least three.[17] The idea, broadly, is that the NED is someone who is not involved on a full-time basis in the running of the company.[18] Accordingly, he is not dependent on it for his livelihood, and he is not going to be in the pocket of the chief executive or the rest of the board. Because he derives only a small part of his overall income from the company (he might be a NED on several boards), he will not risk his reputation and overall earning capacity by getting involved in corporate malpractices. In short, he is independent. As such, he is in a position to carry out the task assigned by the Cadbury Report, which is to bring an 'independent judgment to bear on issues of strategy, performance, resources, including key appointments, and standards of conduct'.[19] Thus the NEDs would form an independent element within the board, playing a normal directorial role in the leadership of the company but also exercising a kind of monitoring and control function. Additionally, the report envisaged the NEDs playing an important role on sub-committees of the board.[20]

Spreading of power was enhanced by the recommendation that there should be a division of responsibilities at the head of the company, that the role of the chair of the board should, in principle, be separate from that of the chief executive.[21] It had been found that in companies where corporate governance had gone badly wrong, it was common to find

[16] Cadbury Report, para. 4.2.
[17] *Ibid*. para. 4.11. There was no definition of 'non-executive director'.
[18] In other words, he or she is not an executive director on a full-time employment contract.
[19] Cadbury Report, para. 4.11.
[20] *Ibid*. paras 4.35 (b) and 4.42.
[21] *Ibid*. para. 4.9.

that the powerful positions of chair and chief executive had been combined in one person, who was thus in a position to stifle board discussion.

The establishment of sub-committees of the board was another area explored by the Cadbury Committee, which came to the conclusion that boards should appoint 'audit committees'. This would enable a board to delegate to such a committee, a thorough review of audit matters. It would enable NEDs to play a positive role in audit matters and also offer auditors a direct link with the NEDs.[22] Additionally, it was recommended that boards should appoint 'remuneration committees', consisting wholly or mainly of NEDs, to make recommendations as to the level of remuneration of the board. Thus, executive directors should play no part in deciding what their remuneration should be.[23]

The role of the company secretary was given an enhanced status, with responsibilities for ensuring that board procedures are both followed and regularly reviewed and that all directors have access to the company secretary's advice and services.[24]

## C Assumptions of responsibility

The Cadbury Committee was concerned to ensure that people within the governance structure knew where their responsibilities began and ended, and also concerned that people assumed those responsibilities and got on and discharged them properly. Various provisions within the report were geared to bringing this about. Thus it was recommended that there should be a statement of directors' responsibilities for the accounts and a counterpart statement by the auditors about their auditing responsibilities.[25] In a similar vein, the responsibility of the board to ensure that a proper system of control over the financial management of the company was highlighted, by recommending that the directors should make a statement about it in the report and accounts.[26] Institutional investors were to be encouraged to make greater use of their voting rights (and hence exercise more responsibility for the monitoring of board performance) by requiring them to make a policy statement about their use of their voting power.[27]

## D Enhanced quality of disclosure

Much of the Cadbury Report was geared to enhancing the quality of financial information being disclosed by companies. The disclosure of financial information is an important regulatory tool. If the information is accurate, it enables the market to react appropriately and is thought to result in an accurate valuation of the company's securities.[28] Accordingly, the Report's recommendations were directed towards ensuring that the system of financial reporting and the audit function were working well.[29] In particular, the report addressed

---

[22] *Ibid.* para. 4.36.
[23] *Ibid.* para. 4.42.
[24] *Ibid.* paras 4.25–4.27.
[25] *Ibid.* para. 4.28.
[26] *Ibid.* para. 4.32.
[27] *Ibid.* paras 6.9–6.12.
[28] *Ibid.* para. 4.48.
[29] *Ibid.* paras 4.47–4.59, 5.1–5.37.

the problem of different accounting treatments being applied to essentially the same facts. It also supported and proposed measures to increase the effectiveness and objectivity of the audit, which it saw as an important external check on the way in which financial statements are prepared and presented, and regarded the annual audit as one of the cornerstones of corporate governance, an essential part of the checks and balances required.[30]

## 10.3 The Greenbury Report

The next self-regulatory initiative on corporate governance occurred in January 1995 when, in response to a public debate fuelled by media stories of excessive remuneration of directors, the Confederation of British Industry set up the Study Group on Directors' Remuneration chaired by Sir Richard Greenbury. The resultant 'Greenbury Report' in July that year contained a Code of Best Practice for Directors' Remuneration. The Code reinforced the Cadbury Committee's ideas relating to the establishment of remuneration committees and contained a requirement for the audit committee to submit a full report to shareholders each year, explaining the company's approach to remuneration. It also required much more detail about the remuneration package of each director than was required by the law existing at that time.[31]

## 10.4 The Hampel Report: evolution of the Combined Code 1998

The Cadbury Report had recommended the appointment of a new committee by the end of June 1995 to examine compliance, and to update the Cadbury Code.[32] The Greenbury Committee expressed similar sentiments as to a successor body.[33] In the event, this took the form of the 'Committee on Corporate Governance' chaired by Sir Ronald Hampel. It was established in November 1995 on the initiative of the Chairman of the FRC. It produced a preliminary report in August 1997 and a final report in January 1998. The Hampel Committee then produced a draft document, which was a set of principles and a code which embraced Cadbury, Greenbury and their own work. The document was passed to the LSE, which then published, in March 1998, a consultation document setting out the draft Combined Code[34] and the proposed related changes to the listing rules. Consequent upon consultation, the LSE made a number of changes to the draft.[35]

The Combined Code was issued by the LSE on 25 June 1998. Its status was that of an appendix to what are now the FCA Listing Rules,[36] and it did not form part of the rules. Subtitled 'Principles of Good Governance and Code of Best Practice', it brought together the work of the Cadbury, Greenbury and Hampel Committees on corporate governance.

---

[30] *Ibid.* para. 5.1.
[31] Greenbury Report, Section 2, Code Provisions A1–A9, B1–B12. Other parts of the Code contained guidelines and advice on company remuneration policy and directors' service contracts and compensation for dismissal; *ibid.* C1–C12, D1–D6.
[32] Cadbury Report, para. 3.12.
[33] Greenbury Report, para. 3.11.
[34] Also, an annotated version of the Code prepared by the Hampel Committee, showing derivations.
[35] With the Hampel Committee's agreement.
[36] Available at https://www.handbook.fca.org.uk/handbook/LR/.

The Combined Code is a consolidation of the work of those committees and was not a new departure.[37]

The basic feature of the Combined Code that distinguished it from the Cadbury and Greenbury Codes was the emphasis on the desirability of complying with broad principles and, in addition, complying with more specific provisions contained in a code of best practice. This feature came about as a result of the Hampel Committee's disapproval of what they called 'box ticking'. They recounted how the actual experience of many companies with regard to implementation of the Cadbury and Greenbury Codes was that the codes had been treated as sets of prescriptive rules, and that the focus of interest had narrowed to the simple question of whether the letter of the rule had been complied with, if yes, then the 'box' on a checklist[38] would receive a tick. The Hampel Committee deprecated box ticking on the basis that it took no account of the diversity of circumstances and experience among companies and on the further basis that it could lead to arrangements whereby the letter of the rule is complied with, but not the substance. Their conclusion was that good corporate governance was not just a matter of prescribing structures and rules, but there was also a need for broad principles.[39] Thus, it helped with understanding the name 'Combined Code' if the name is seen as signalling that it is a *package* consisting of principles *and* code (although the other meaning of the name is that it is derived from and is a consolidation of the work of past committees and the existing codes). It is clear that much of the Cadbury 'Code of Best Practice' was subsumed into the provisions of the Combined Code, but it is worth observing that, less obviously, many of the principles and code provisions in the Combined Code were derived from recommendations or suggestions in the text of the Cadbury Report, which did not find their way into the Cadbury Code of Best Practice.[40]

## 10.5 The Higgs Review and the Combined Code 2003

In 2002, the UK Government commissioned Sir Derek Higgs (as a senior independent figure from the business world) to lead a short independent review of the role and effectiveness of non-executive directors in the UK. On 7 June 2002, a Consultation Paper was published entitled 'A Review of the Role and Effectiveness of Non-Executive Directors'. A final report was published on 20 January 2003.[41] Consequent upon the Higgs Review,[42] on widespread public comment, and on further work by various groups, a new version of the *Combined Code on Corporate Governance* was issued by the FRC[43] on 23 July 2003.

---

[37] Combined Code, Preamble, para. 7.

[38] See generally Hampel Report, paras 1.11–1.14.

[39] The broad principles needed to be applied flexibly and with common sense to the varying circumstances of individual companies and this was how the Cadbury and Greenbury Committees intended their ideas to be implemented.

[40] Although some of them were code provisions in Cadbury that are elevated to the status of principles in the Combined Code; *e.g.* Cadbury Code of Best Practice, para. 1.2 becomes part of Combined Code, Principle A.2.

[41] Available at http://www.ecgi.org/codes/documents/higgsreport.pdf.

[42] And also consequent upon the Smith Report on Audit Committees; available at http://www.frc.org.uk/publications.

[43] The FRC has responsibility for the contents of the Code and for updating it.

The Higgs Review followed the tradition of recent developments in UK corporate governance under which self-regulation in the application of governance codes forms a major part and most of his recommendations were presented as modifications of the existing Combined Code 1998. On the important matter of the role of the board, the review saw no case for abandoning the unitary board structure in favour of a continental-style supervisory board and executive board, and saw benefit in the unitary board having executive knowledge within the board, alongside non-executive directors who can bring in wider experience.[44] The role of the Chairman was seen as 'pivotal' in creating board effectiveness and lent support to the idea that the roles of the Chairman and Chief Executive should be separate.[45] A more controversial proposal was that the Code should provide that a chief executive should not thereafter become chairman of the same company.[46] As regards non-executive directors, the Review felt that there was no essential contradiction between the monitoring role and the strategic role; both needed to be present.[47] However, concerned to strengthen independence on the board, the review recommended that at least half the members of the board[48] should be independent[49]non-executive directors,[50] although it was recognised that widespread compliance might take time to achieve. The procedures relating to recruitment and appointment of non-executives to the board were seen as being in need of formalising[51] and nomination committees should consist of a majority of independent non-executives.[52] New non-executives needed an induction process.[53] The Review welcomed the report by Sir Robert Smith, recommending that the audit committee needed to include at least three members, all independent non-executives. The remuneration committee needed to work closely with the nomination committee so as to ensure that incentives are appropriately structured.[54] Guidance was formulated on the difficult matter of the legal liability of NEDs.[55] Support was voiced for the Institutional Shareholders' Committee's Code of Activism.[56] In relation to smaller listed companies,[57] it was recognised that it may take more time for compliance and some of the Code's provisions may be less relevant, although the review stopped short of differentiating Code provisions for different sizes of companies.[58] It will be apparent from the summary of the Combined Code in the next section, that many of the ideas and concerns espoused in the Higgs Review have found their way into the Combined Code 2003 which formed the basis for the 2006 and June 2008 versions.[59]

---

[44] Higgs Review, para. 4.2.
[45] *Ibid.* paras 5.1–5.2.
[46] *Ibid.* para. 5.7.
[47] *Ibid.* para. 6.2.
[48] Excluding the chairman.
[49] The Review formulated a detailed definition of independence; *ibid.* para. 9.11.
[50] *Ibid.* para. 9.5.
[51] *Ibid.* para. 10.9.
[52] *Ibid.* para. 10.9ff.
[53] *Ibid.* para. 11.1.
[54] *Ibid.* para. 13.10ff.
[55] *Ibid.* draft guidance statement, Annex A.
[56] *Ibid.* para. 15.24.
[57] I.e., listed companies outside the FTSE 350.
[58] *Ibid.* para. 16.8.
[59] Also emanating from the Higgs Review was the increased use of suggestions for good practice. These were set out in the Combined Code pp. 59–79 and provided a range of useful items such as summaries of duties of committees, checklists and guidance.

## 10.6 The Combined Code (2006 and June 2008)

Following a review of the implementation of the Combined Code in 2005, the FRC consulted on a small number of changes to the Code. These changes were incorporated in an updated version of the Code published in June 2006 to apply to reporting years beginning on or after 1 November 2006. The main changes made to the 2003 Combined Code include:

- amendments to the restriction on the company Chairman serving on the remuneration committee to enable him or her to do so where considered independent on appointment as Chairman (although it is recommended that he or she should not also chair the committee);
- providing a 'vote withheld' option on proxy appointment forms to enable shareholders to indicate if they have reservations on a resolution but do not wish to vote against. A 'vote withheld' is not a vote in law and is not counted in the calculation of the proportion of the votes for and against the resolution; and
- a recommendation that companies publish on their website the details of proxies lodged at a general meeting where votes are taken on a show of hands.

In October 2007, the FRC announced that its latest review of the Combined Code on Corporate Governance had concluded that the Code was working reasonably well and no major changes were planned. The FRC did, however, emphasise that there was room for improvement in the way the Code was applied by companies, investors and intermediaries, and proposed two further amendments to the Code.[60] Consultation on the text of the proposed amendments then began in November 2007 and a revised Code came into effect in June 2008.[61] For a short period, two versions were in effect: the 2006 edition, which applied to accounting periods beginning on or after 1 November 2006; and the June 2008 edition which applied to accounting periods beginning on or after 29 June 2008. As has been seen above, the Code itself is subject to periodic reviews by the FRC. Following a review of the Code carried out during 2009 (in light of the financial crisis) and consultation on a draft of the revised Code that ended in March 2010,[62] a new version was issued in May 2010. This is explored in detail next.

In May 2010, the FRC issued a new edition of the UK Corporate Governance Code which applied to financial years beginning on or after 29 June 2010 and would in future

---

[60] Namely, to remove the restriction on an individual chairing more than one FTSE100 company; and to allow the chairman of a smaller listed company to be a member of the audit committee where (s)he was considered independent on appointment.

[61] The June 2008 edition of the Code took effect at the same time as new FSA Corporate Governance Rules implementing EU requirements relating to corporate governance statements and audit committees. In particular, the Financial Services Authority Pt 6 Rules (including the listing rules) implemented new EU requirements on corporate governance included in the revised Fourth Company Law Directive to provide a requirement for a 'comply or explain' report for a compulsory corporate governance statement by listed companies. There is some overlap between the Rules and the Code, which is summarised in the Schedule to the Code.

[62] In March 2009 the FRC launched the review with a call for evidence inviting views on these questions: Which parts of the Code have worked well? Do any of them need further reinforcement? Have any parts of the Code inadvertently reduced the effectiveness of the board? Are there any aspects of good governance practice not currently addressed by the Code or its related guidance that should be? Is the 'comply or explain' mechanism operating effectively and, if not, how might its operation be improved?.

be known as the UK Corporate Governance Code, in order to make the Code's status as the UK's recognised corporate governance standard clearer to foreign investors, and to foreign companies listed in the UK. These, as a result of changes to the FCA's listing regime, now needed to report on how they have applied the Code if they have a premium listing of equity shares.

## 10.7 The UK Corporate Governance Code (June 2010)

### A Background

The financial crisis which came to a head in 2008–2009 triggered widespread reappraisal, both nationally and internationally, of the corporate governance systems which were seen as having failed to alleviate it. In the UK, Sir David Walker was charged with reviewing the governance of banks and other financial institutions. The FRC also decided to bring forward the Code review scheduled for 2010 so that corporate governance in other listed companies could be assessed at the same time.[63] When Sir David Walker's report was published in November 2009 it contained a number of recommendations, which the FRC agreed to implement and apply to all listed companies. Further details were set out in the FRC's report on its own review of the Combined Code that concluded in December 2009.[64] Two principal conclusions were drawn in its review.[65] First, much more attention needed to be paid to follow the spirit of the Code as well as its letter. Secondly, the impact of shareholders in monitoring the Code could and should be enhanced by better interaction between the boards of listed companies and their shareholders. To this end, the FRC assumed responsibility for a new Stewardship Code, which was issued in July 2010 (discussed below under 10.8) that provides guidance on good practice for investors. Two months earlier, in May 2010, the FRC issued a new edition of the UK Code, which would apply to financial years beginning on or after 29 June 2010. The FRC announced that the Code would be known as the UK Corporate Governance Code, in order to make the its status as the UK's recognised corporate governance standard clearer to foreign investors, and to foreign companies listed in the UK.

### B Disclosure of corporate governance arrangements and listing rules

Corporate governance disclosure requirements are set out in three places:

(1) FCA Disclosure Guidance and Transparency Rules (which set out certain mandatory disclosures).[66]

---

[63] See UK Corporate Governance Code (June 201), Preface, para. 1.
[64] Some of the report recommendations were implemented through revisions to the renamed UK Corporate Governance Code.
[65] See UK Corporate Governance Code (June 2010), Preface, para. 2.
[66] Available at https://www.handbook.fca.org.uk/handbook/DTR.pdf.

(2) FCA Listing Rules 9.8.6 R, 9.8.7 R and 9.8.7A R (which includes the 'comply or explain' requirement).

(3) The UK Corporate Governance Code.[67]

There is some overlap between the mandatory disclosures required under the disclosure and transparency rules and those expected under the UK Corporate Governance Code.[68] In respect of disclosures relating to the audit committee and the composition and operation of the board and its committees, compliance with the relevant provisions of the Code will result in compliance with the relevant rules.[69]

Paragraph 9.8.6 R of the Listing Rules states that in the case of a *listed company* incorporated in the *United Kingdom*, the following additional items must be included in its annual financial report:[70]

- a statement of how the listed company has applied the main principles of the UK Corporate Governance Code, in a manner that would enable shareholders to evaluate how the principles have been applied;
- a statement as to whether the listed company has:

    (a) complied throughout the accounting period with all relevant provisions set out in the UK Corporate Governance Code; or
    (b) not complied throughout the accounting period with all relevant provisions set out in the UK Corporate Governance Code and if so, setting out:
        (i) those provisions, if any, it has not complied with;
        (ii) in the case of provisions whose requirements are of a continuing nature, the period within which, if any, it did not comply with some or all of those provisions; and
        (iii) the company's reasons for non-compliance.

It is important to note that the compliance statements required by the paragraphs above relate only to compliance with what is described as the main principles of the UK Corporate Governance Code. The Code consists of principles (main and supporting) and provisions.

The principles are the core of the Code and the way in which they are applied should be the central question for a board as it determines how it is to operate according to the Code. These principles are now in sections A, B, C, D and E.[71]

---

[67] In addition to providing an explanation where they choose not to comply with a provision, companies must disclose specified information in order to comply with certain provisions.

[68] Areas of overlap are summarised in the Appendix to Schedule B of the UK Corporate Governance Code (June 2010). The Disclosure and Transparency Rules sub-chapters 7.1 and 7.2 apply to issuers whose securities are admitted to trading on a regulated market (this includes all issuers with a premium or standard listing). The Listing Rules 9.8.6 R, 9.8.7 R and 9.8.7A R and UK Corporate Governance Code apply to issuers of premium listed equity shares only.

[69] *Ibid.*, Schedule B.

[70] The FRC decided not to proceed with the suggestion in its 2009 consultation paper that companies be allowed to disclose information for Code purposes in the annual report or on a website. It stated that the FRC would consider this further as part of its wider project to reduce the complexity of annual reports.

[71] The format in the 2008 Combined Code separated requirements in section 1 for listed companies and in section 2 for institutional shareholders. This can be traced back to the Hampel Committee, which had felt that it was inappropriate to include matters in section 2 within the listing requirement. It is to be noted that when the Code was published in May 2010 it included in Schedule C some engagement principles for institutional investors. This Schedule has now been superseded by the UK Stewardship Code and has therefore been deleted from the Code with effect from 1 August 2010.

## C Excerpts and summary of the main provisions

### 1 *General format of the Code*

The Code is divided into five sections (the main principles of the Code A–E): A: Leadership; B: Effectiveness; C: Accountability; D: Remuneration; E: Relation with shareholders and two schedules. These will now be examined. At the outset, it is worth observing that the UK Corporate Governance Code keeps within each section the distinction between main principle and supporting principles. One of the main innovations in the 2008 format compared to the Combined Code of 1998 was the division of 'principles' into 'main principles' and 'supporting principles'. The FRC changed the structure of the Code to emphasise its underlying principles. The main principles are now listed separately at the front of the Code. A number of previous supporting principles have been upgraded to main principles so that the company must report how they have been applied. There is a new section on 'comply or explain' at the beginning of the Code, which recognises that non-compliance may be justified if good governance could be achieved in other ways. The company should 'clearly and carefully' explain its reasons for non-compliance to shareholders and should aim to illustrate how its practices are consistent with the principle to which the particular provision relates and contribute to good governance. Interestingly, in the preface to the Code, the FRC encourages chairmen 'to report personally in their annual statements on how the principles relating to the role and effectiveness of the board . . . have been applied'.[72] In relation to the new annual re-election requirements (see below), the FRC points out that companies are free to explain rather than comply if they believe that their existing arrangements ensure proper accountability and underpin board effectiveness, or that a transitional period is needed before they comply.[73] The sub-sections below include regular updates and tweaking of the Code in 2012, 2014 and 2016.

### 2 *Leadership*

**A.1 The role of the Board**
**Main Principle: Every company should be headed by an effective board which is collectively responsible for the long-term[74] success of the company.**
Supporting Principles: see text at http://www.frc.org.uk/corporate/ukcgcode.cfm.
**Code Provisions** A.1.1, A.1.2[75], A.1.3 (see text at http://www.frc.org.uk/corporate/ukcgcode.cfm).

The relationship between the *principles* and the *Code provisions* which go with it (both here and elsewhere in the UK Corporate Governance Code) is not entirely clear. Presumably Code provisions A.1.1–A.1.3 are not meant to be exhaustive in the sense that they are the only things necessary to achieve a successful application of the principles. But if they are not exhaustive, then what are they? Presumably they are a list of the main

---

[72] Preface, para. 7.
[73] Preface, para. 8.
[74] The phrase 'long-term' was added. It was not part of the 2008 version.
[75] This is an expanded Code provision. The annual report should identify members of all board committees, not just the nomination, audit and remuneration committees. Provisions A.1.1 and A.1.2 overlap with FCA Rule DTR 7.2.7 R; provision A.1.2 also overlaps with DTR 7.1.5 R (see Schedule B).

specific things which are thought to be needed in order to help bring about the broader goals set out in the principle – things which the various committees had noticed as being areas where things had gone wrong in the past. But, obviously, a whole host of other things might be necessary in various circumstances in order to secure good corporate governance. And to emphasise the need to keep an eye on the background, it is only necessary to recall that there are various statute and case law principles which set out the legal duties of directors and govern the way companies are run. Thus, whatever the second supporting principle A.1 rather vaguely says about directors having to take decisions 'for the long-term success of the company', they will obviously have to take pains to do this in such a way as to discharge their duties of care and skill to the standards set by law (s. 174 of the Companies Act 2006) as well as the same corresponding duty to promote the success of the company under s. 172 of the Companies Act 2006.[76]

The linking of the role of chair and chief executive has long been identified as a potential source of trouble in companies. The Cadbury Committee had felt that if the two roles were combined in one person it represented a considerable concentration of power and recommended that there should be a clearly accepted division of authority, although if the roles were combined, then there needed to be a strong and independent element on the board.[77] A similar attitude has been taken by the subsequent reports and this is reflected in the provisions in A.2 below. Perhaps one slightly strange feature is the requirement that the chair should 'ensure that the directors receive accurate, timely and clear information' because the companies legislation clearly casts on to the board of directors the duty to prepare reports and accounts, and so presumably with it the ancillary duty to themselves to make sure that they get proper information.[78]

### A.2 Division of Responsibilities

**Main Principle: There should be a clear division of responsibilities at the head of the company between the running of the board and the executive responsibility for the running of the company's business. No one individual should have unfettered powers of decision.**

**Code Provision** A.2.1 (see text at http://www.frc.org.uk/corporate/ukcgcode.cfm).

### A.3 The Chairman[79]

**Main Principle: The chairman is responsible for leadership of the board and ensuring its effectiveness on all aspects of its role.**

Supporting Principle: see text at http://www.frc.org.uk/corporate/ukcgcode.cfm.

**Code Provision A.3.1**[80] (see text at http://www.frc.org.uk/corporate/ukcgcode.cfm).

It is clear then that the new Code has added additional responsibility to and emphasis on the role of the chair: he or she is responsible for leadership of the board and ensuring its effectiveness, for achieving the requisite culture of constructive challenge by non-executives to the executives, and a particular responsibility for training, evaluation and board composition.

---

[76] This is explored further in Chapter 8 under 8.2B.
[77] Cadbury Report, para. 4.9.
[78] Companies Act 2006, ss. 386–389, 394–395, 409–412, 414, 433–436, 444–447, 450.
[79] This is a new main principle upgraded from a supporting principle.
[80] Compliance or otherwise with this provision need only be reported for the year in which the appointment is made.

When the Cadbury Committee delivered its Report in 1992, the single most significant (and controversial) element of it was the enhanced and pivotal role given to non-executive directors (NEDs).[81] In the years that followed, much public debate became centered around the question of the extent to which such NEDs should be independent. Progress on this issue is now reflected in the latest version of the provisions dealing with non-executive directors in section A and section B Effectiveness (see below). A new main principle – A4 – upgraded from a supporting principle now says that NEDs should *constructively challenge* and help develop proposals on strategy.

### A.4 Non-executive Directors

**Main Principle: As part of their role as members of a unitary board, non-executive directors should constructively challenge and help develop proposals on strategy.**
Supporting Principle: see text at http://www.frc.org.uk/corporate/ukcgcode.cfm.
**Code Provisions** A.4.1, A.4.2, A.4.3 (see text at http://www.frc.org.uk/corporate/ukcgcode.cfm).

The latest version of this Code recommends regular board meetings and distinct and separate roles for the chair and chief executive. It also advocates for NEDs to apply scepticism in order to challenge and scrutinise management effectively.

## 3 *Effectiveness*[82]

### B.1 The Composition of the Board

**Main Principle: The board and its committees should have the appropriate balance of skills, experience, independence and knowledge of the company to enable them to discharge their respective duties and responsibilities effectively.**[83]
Supporting Principles: see text at http://www.frc.org.uk/corporate/ukcgcode.cfm.
**Code Provisions** B.1.1[84], B.1.2[85] (see text at http://www.frc.org.uk/corporate/ukcgcode.cfm).

It is noteworthy that in addition to the above a new main principle (B.3 Commitment – upgraded from a supporting principle) emphasises that all directors should be able to allocate sufficient time to the company to perform their responsibilities effectively. The FRC has not specified minimum time commitments.

The remaining matters dealt with by the UK Corporate Governance Code under the heading 'Effectiveness' relate to appointments to the board, commitment, development,

---

[81] Cadbury Report, paras 4.1–4.6, 4.10–4.17.
[82] It should be noted that in March 2010 the FRC published new guidance entitled 'Guidance on Board Effectiveness', which relates primarily to Sections A and B of the Code on the leadership and effectiveness of the board. The guidance was developed by the Institute of Chartered Secretaries and Administrators on the FRC's behalf, and replaces 'Suggestions for Good Practice from the Higgs Report' (known as the Higgs guidance), which has been withdrawn.
[83] This version appears more general than the 2008 one, which referred to appropriate balance of executive and non-executive directors. In the 2010 version this was moved to supporting principles.
[84] The board should identify in the annual report each non-executive director it considers to be independent. The UK Corporate Governance Code by footnote here provides that: 'A.3.1 states that the chairman should on appointment, meet the independence criteria set out in this provision, but thereafter the test of independence is not appropriate in relation to the chairman.'
[85] This provision does not apply to 'smaller companies'. The UK Corporate Governance Code by footnote provides: 'A smaller company is one that is below the FTSE 350 throughout the year immediately prior to the reporting year.'

information and support, evaluation, and re-election. Here again, the pattern is repeated: suggestions and Code provisions originally in Cadbury, followed by approval and amendments from Hampel, followed by amendments, new ideas and amplification from the Higgs Review. The principles and Code provisions in the UK Corporate Governance Code relating to these matters are as follows:

### B.2 Appointments to the Board

**Main Principle: There should be a formal, rigorous and transparent procedure for the appointment of new directors to the board.**

Supporting Principles: see text at http://www.frc.org.uk/corporate/ukcgcode.cfm.

The Code then sets out Code provisions B.2.1–B.2.4 relating to these principles, and covering such matters as the role of the nomination committee, job specifications and terms of appointment.

**Code Provisions** B.2.1, B.2.2, B.2.3, B.2.4 (see text at http://www.frc.org.uk/corporate/ukcgcode.cfm).

### B.3 Commitment

**Main Principle: All directors should be able to allocate sufficient time to the company to discharge their responsibilities effectively.**

**Code Provisions** B.3.1, B.3.2, B.3.3 (see text at http://www.frc.org.uk/corporate/ukcgcode.cfm).

### B.4 Development

**Main Principle: All directors should receive induction on joining the board and should regularly update and refresh their skills and knowledge.**

Supporting Principles: see text at http://www.frc.org.uk/corporate/ukcgcode.cfm.

**Code Provisions** B.4.1, B.4.2 (see text at http://www.frc.org.uk/corporate/ukcgcode.cfm).

### B.5 Information and Support

**Main Principle: The board should be supplied in a timely manner with information in a form and of a quality appropriate to enable it to discharge its duties.**

Supporting Principles: see text at http://www.frc.org.uk/corporate/ukcgcode.cfm.

The Code then sets out Code provisions B.5.1–B.5.2 relating to these principles, covering professional advice, and role and appointment of the company secretary.

### B.6 Performance evaluation

**Main Principle: The board should undertake a formal and rigorous annual evaluation of its own performance and that of its committees and individual directors.**

The Code then here sets out a supporting principle and Code provisions B.6.1–B.6.3.

**Code Provisions** B.6.1, B.6.2, B.6.3 (see text at http://www.frc.org.uk/corporate/ukcgcode.cfm).

### B.7 Re-election

**Main Principle: All directors should be submitted for re-election at regular intervals, subject to continued satisfactory performance.**

**Code Provisions**[86] B.7.1, B.7.2.

---

[86] These are all new and were not part of the 2008 version. See commentary below.

The changes introduced above to the new edition of the Code are designed to respond to what have been perceived to be shortcomings in the pre-financial crisis era of corporate governance. The key focus is on increased board effectiveness and accountability to shareholders. Probably the most controversial, and certainly the most discussed, example of the focus on increased effectiveness and accountability is the introduction of a recommendation that all directors of FTSE 350 companies be put up for re-election every year. This reflects the preference of institutional shareholders and is seen as key to improving shareholder engagement.[87] The introduction of this provision has received particular criticism from the Institute of Directors.[88]

The size, skills, experience and balance of non-executive and executive directors should be adequate to deal with the complexity of the business and its industry. NEDs should be independent. Board appointment, evaluation and re-selection procedures should be transparent. All directors, especially NEDs, ought to demonstrate commitment whilst getting support from management to develop an understanding of the business and its industry.

## 4 Accountability

Here again, the picture is one of ideas in the Cadbury Report being supplemented by further thoughts and refinement in the later reports. Many of the points were already in the Cadbury Code and the current position in the Code is as follows:

> **C.1 Financial and Business Reporting**
> **Main Principle: The board should present a balanced and understandable assessment of the company's position and prospects.**
> Supporting Principle: see text at http://www.frc.org.uk/corporate/ukcgcode.cfm.

This is supplemented by further details in Code provisions C.1.1,[89] C.1.2,[90] C.1.3[91].

The Code then turns to deal with risk management and internal control. There is a new main principle (C.2, below) that the board is responsible for determining the nature and

---

[87] While the majority of corporate responses to the review argued for the previous three-year rotation, those companies that have already adopted annual re-election of the entire board were reported as not having identified any change to voting patterns.

[88] In a letter to the FRC sent on 24 February 2010 it states (in p. 4): 'We do not agree with the introduction of an annual vote for each of the directors. The board is a collective decision-making body. A separate vote on individual directors implies that the responsibility for specific decisions can be attributed to specific individuals. This is not the case, and serves to undermine the integrity of collective decision-making. The board is collectively responsible for all key decisions, regardless of whether individual board members or board committees are particularly involved in deliberations on specific issues. In addition, an annual vote on individual directors creates a risk that individuals become targeted with respect to matters for which they are not fully responsible. In those unusual cases where a board is unwilling to deal with issues relating to individual directors, shareholders already have sufficient weapons at their disposal, e.g. the right to call a General Meeting and remove the director through an ordinary resolution of members.'

[89] This provides clarification on previous Code provision. It is now clear that the directors should explain in the annual report their responsibility for preparing the annual report as well as (as previously provided) the accounts.

[90] This is a new provision. The wording has been amended in the final version of the Code to mirror the Accounting Standard Board's (ASB) voluntary Reporting Statement on the Operating and Financial Review, to which the FRC refers companies for guidance. The FRC recommends that the explanation appear in the same part of the annual report as the business review required by s. 417 of the Companies Act 2006.

[91] This is an expanded Code provision. It is now clear that the directors should report on going concern in annual and half-yearly financial statements. Previously the Code specified no place for the going concern report.

extent of the significant risks it is willing to take in achieving its strategic objectives. Interestingly, the main principle that requires a sound system of internal control has been expanded to cover risk management. The requirement for formal and transparent arrangements for considering how the board should apply the internal control principles also now applies to risk management under C.3 (see below).

### C.2 Internal[92]
**Main Principle: The board is responsible for determining the nature and extent of the significant risks it is willing to take in achieving its strategic objectives. The board should maintain sound risk management and internal control systems.**

This is supplemented by Code provision C.2.1.[93]

### C.3 Audit Committee and Auditors[94]
**Main Principle: The board should establish formal and transparent arrangements for considering how they should apply the corporate reporting and risk management and internal control principles and for maintaining an appropriate relationship with the company's auditor.**

Code provisions C.3.1–C.3.7[95] require the board to establish an audit committee and set out some of its duties.

The board should present a fair, balanced and understandable assessment of the company's position and prospects in its annual report. The directors should state in annual and half-yearly financial statements whether they consider it appropriate to adopt the going concern basis of accounting in preparing them, and identify any material uncertainties as to the company's ability to continue to do so over a period of at least 12 months from the date of approval of the financial statements.

In addition to a statement that the business is a going concern, the directors should make a statement indicating (i) that they have a reasonable expectation that the company will be able to continue in operation and meet its liabilities as they fall due over an assessed period, the length of which must also be disclosed; and (ii) the principal risks facing the company, having a specific responsibility for monitoring the company's risk management and internal control systems, and ensuring these are sound whilst also maintaining an appropriate relationship with the company's auditors. The audit committee, a sub-committee of the board, should also look after financial reporting matters and the workings of both internal and external auditors. At least one member of the audit committee must be a qualified accountant.

---

[92] This should be read in conjunction with the Turnbull Guidance on Internal Control which sets out best practice on internal control for UK listed companies, and assists them in applying this section. The Turnbull guidance was originally published in 1999. In 2004 the FRC set up a group chaired by Douglas Flint (then Group Finance Director, HSBC Holdings plc) to review the guidance and update it where necessary, in the light of experience in implementing the guidance and developments in the UK and internationally since 1999.

[93] In addition to Code provision C.2.1, FCA rule DTR 7.2.5 R requires companies to describe the main features of the internal control and risk management systems in relation to the financial reporting process.

[94] Guidance on Audit Committees (formerly known as the Smith Guidance), which provides guidance on this section of the Code, can be found at https://www.frc.org.uk/getattachment/6b0ace1d-1d70-4678-9c41-0b44a62f0a0d/Guidance-on-Audit-Committees-April-2016.pdf.

[95] Again, there is some overlap between these Code provisions and FCA rule DTR 7.1.1 R (with C.3.1) and rule DTR 7.1.3 R (with C.3.2).

## 5 *Remuneration*

Section D of the UK Corporate governance Code is taken up with remuneration. The Hampel Committee had earlier made it clear that directors' remuneration should be embraced in the corporate governance process since the handling of remuneration can damage a company's public image and have an adverse effect on morale within the company.[96] The Code provisions relating to the principles in this field are long and complex and it is not practicable to set them out in full here. Instead, it is proposed to look briefly at the principles and include references to the Code provisions. The principles relating to remuneration are as follows.

**D.1 The Level and Make-up of Remuneration**
**Main Principles: Levels of remuneration should be sufficient to attract, retain and motivate directors of the quality required to run the company successfully, but a company should avoid paying more than is necessary for this purpose. A significant proportion of executive directors' remuneration should be structured so as to link rewards to corporate and individual performance.**

Principle D.1, Code provisions D.1.1–D.1.3, and also Schedule A to the Code, then refer to the design of performance-related remuneration for executive directors.

**D.2 Procedure**
**Main Principle: There should be a formal and transparent procedure for developing policy on executive remuneration and for fixing the remuneration packages of individual directors. No director should be involved in deciding his or her own remuneration.**

Here again the supporting principles and Code provisions D.2.1[97]–D.2.4 make detailed prescription about the role of remuneration committees. A number of key changes in the new Code should be noted. First, a new supporting principle to the main principle D.1 states that the performance-related elements of executive directors' remuneration should be designed to promote the long-term success of the company (again see s. 172 of the Companies Act 2006) as well as being flexible. Secondly, Code Provision D.1.3 discourages all forms of performance-related remuneration for NEDs, not only share options. Finally, the performance-related remuneration provisions have been amended in Schedule A.[98] The main changes are as follows: performance conditions should be designed to promote the long-term success of the company; non-financial performance metrics should be reflected in performance criteria where appropriate; the company should consider using provisions that permit the company to reclaim variable components in exceptional circumstances of misstatement or misconduct; and remuneration incentives should be compatible with risk policies and systems.

The Code sets out expectations for the remuneration of the executive directors in Main Principle D.1, which states that: '[. . .] remuneration should be designed to promote the

---

[96] Hampel Report, para. 2.9.
[97] This specific provision overlaps with FCA rule DTR 7.2.7 R.
[98] The Remuneration Consultants Group has published in June 2011 a consultation on its 2009 Code of Conduct for remuneration consultants. It can be accessed at http://www.remunerationconsultantsgroup.com/assets/Docs/Consultation%20on%20the%20Code%20of%20Conduct%20June%202011.pdf.

long-term success of the company. Performance-related elements should be transparent, stretching and rigorously applied.'

## 6 Relations with shareholders

The importance of the shareholder input to corporate governance was recognised by the Cadbury Committee[99] although none of their ideas made it into the Cadbury Code. It has been taken further by subsequent reports, although it is fair to say these have not seen the shareholder input as a panacea and place their main emphasis in corporate governance in getting the board to function properly of its own accord.

> **E.1 Dialogue with Institutional Shareholders**
>
> **Main Principle: There should be a dialogue with shareholders based on the mutual under- standing of objectives. The board as a whole has responsibility for ensuring that a satis- factory dialogue with shareholders takes place.**[100]
>
> Supporting Principles:[101] see text at http://www.frc.org.uk/corporate/ukcgcode.cfm.

The Code provisions relating to this are E.1.1–E.1.2.

There is considerable activity developing in this regard.[102] It is well known that the majority of shares in public listed companies are held by financial institutions.[103] The Company Law Review has described[104] that these institutions exercise their membership rights, not through attendance at the shareholders' meeting, but through a process of meet- ing and dialogue with the management. This process usually takes place in the interval between the company publishing its preliminary results and its full accounts. Quite often the institutions are represented by financial analysts. Searching questions are asked and a considerable amount of information[105] is obtained about the company's performance and prospects. There is considerable anecdotal evidence available that this is becoming very common.

> **E.2 Constructive Use of the AGM**
>
> **Main Principle: The board should use the AGM to communicate with investors and to encourage their participation.**

---

[99] Cadbury Report, paras 6.1–6.16.

[100] The UK Corporate Governance Code by footnote here provides that: 'Nothing in these principles or provisions should be taken to override the general requirements of law to treat shareholders equally in access to informa- tion.'

[101] This is an expanded supporting principle. Previously, the chair, senior independent director and 'other directors as appropriate' were required to maintain contact with major shareholders. Whilst recognising that most share- holder contact is with the chief executive and finance director, the chair should ensure that all directors are made aware of their major shareholders' issues and concerns. The board should keep in touch with shareholder opinion in whatever ways are most practical and efficient.

[102] For a picture of the wide range of monitoring activity and involvement by institutions, see the websites of Pensions Investment Research Consultants (PIRC) and Hermès™. These, respectively, are: http://www.pirc. co.uk and http://www.hermes.co.uk.

[103] Between 70% and 80%. See DTI Consultation Document (October 1999) *Company General Meetings and Shareholder Communications* para. 20.

[104] See previous note.

[105] Participants have to be careful not to get involved in insider dealing or market abuse in this situation. The US SEC have adopted (on 21/8/2000) the solution of requiring contemporaneous disclosure of any non-public infor- mation which is given by the board; see SEC Regulation FD (Fair Dealing), rule 100: http://www.sec.gov.

Going with this are Code Provisions E.2.1–E.2.4, which make prescription with regard to procedures at and prior to meetings, and the new Stewardship Code discussed below.[106] Voting is central to the exercise of ownership control. However, the ability of ultimate beneficiaries (e.g. members of a pension fund) to monitor the way in which institutional investors exercise voting rights is limited in practice. The CLR[107] concluded that disclosure of voting by institutional shareholders was a desirable objective. There has been a growing trend internationally to require disclosure. There has also been an increasing trend by UK fund managers towards voluntary disclosure.[108] So it should come as no surprise that the exercise of voting rights by institutional investors is now also the subject of provisions in the Companies Act 2006.[109]

It is to be noted that when the Code was published in May 2010 it included in Schedule C some engagement principles for institutional investors. This Schedule has now been superseded by the UK Stewardship Code (discussed below under 10.8) and has therefore been deleted from the Code with effect from 1 August 2010.

In 2014, Code Provision E.2.2 was introduced to require companies to explain, when publishing meeting results, how they intend to engage with shareholders when a significant percentage of them have voted against a resolution. The purpose is to encourage companies to detail the process they will undertake to assess the concerns of shareholders, as well as setting out how they intend to respond to those concerns, although reporting on these may occur at different times.

## 7 Gender diversity

In May 2011, the FRC began consultation on possible amendments to the Code that would require companies to publish their policy on gender diversity in the boardroom and report against it annually. The consultation followed a report by Lord Davies, 'Women on Boards',[110] which was published in February 2011 and called on the FRC to amend the Code to require listed companies to establish a policy concerning boardroom diversity (including how they would implement such a policy, and disclose annually a summary of the progress made). Lord Davies also recommended that UK listed companies in the FTSE 100 should be aiming for a minimum of 25% female board member representation by 2015 and that FTSE 350 companies should be setting their own, challenging, targets, and expects that many will achieve a much higher figure than this minimum. The report recommended that companies should set targets for 2013 and 2015 to ensure that more talented

---

[106] To this should be added the new provisions 1277–1280 in the Companies Act 2006 discussed in n. 113 below.
[107] In its Final Report, para. 6.39.
[108] See Explanatory Notes on the Companies Act 2006, para. 1687.
[109] Ss. 1277–1280. Section 1277 confers a power on the Secretary of State and the Treasury to make regulations requiring certain categories of institutional investor to provide information about the exercise of their voting rights. The power is drawn intentionally widely to enable any mandatory disclosure regime to respond to varied corporate governance arrangements and to capture a range of institutions investing in different markets. Exercise of the power is subject to the affirmative resolution procedure. See Explanatory Notes on the Companies Act 2006, para. 1688. Sections 1278–1280 deal with the categories of institutions in relation to which the power conferred by s. 1277 is exercisable, power to specify by regulations the descriptions of shares in relation to which the information provisions apply and specifies the information that can be required, respectively.
[110] http://www.bis.gov.uk/assets/biscore/business-law/docs/w/11-745-women-on-boards.pdf.

and gifted women can get into the top jobs in companies across the UK. As part of the report Lord Davies also stated that companies should fully disclose the number of women sitting on their boards and working in their organisations as a whole, to drive up the numbers of women with top jobs in business.

Amendments to the 2010 Code introduced a reference to diversity in the Code for the first time. Subsequently, in 2014, on the occasion of the issue of an updated version of the Code, the FRC emphasised that one of the ways in which a constructive and challenging debate could be encouraged to ensure effective board functioning was through having sufficient diversity on the board, including gender and race.[111] Nevertheless, it also stressed that diverse board composition in these respects was not on its own a guarantee and could be just as much about difference of approach and experience, which must be right.

## 8 *Enhancing corporate reporting and audit*

On 7 January 2011, the FRC published its report 'Effective Company Stewardship: Enhancing Corporate Reporting and Audit'[112] aimed at improving the dialogue between company boards and their shareholders. It responds to lessons of the financial crisis and builds on changes already made, such as the new UK Corporate Governance Code and the introduction of the Stewardship Code for institutional investors, discussed below. The report proposes that the whole of the annual report and accounts should be balanced and fair, including the chair and chief executive reports, rather than just specific parts of it as it is currently required to be. While the best annual reports continue to improve, research by the FRC shows that some companies fall short of fulfilling their Companies Act requirements. Of 50 companies studied, a half to two-thirds fell short in some areas, including in their reporting of principal risks.

While the Code was already consistent with the majority of Regulation EU/537/2014, covering specific requirements regarding statutory audit of public interest entities, and Directive 2014/56/EU, covering the statutory audit of annual accounts and consolidated accounts, the following minimal changes to provision C.3 were made in 2016 following a public consultation: new wording was added to C.3.1 to require the audit committee, as a whole, to have competence relevant to the sector in which the company operates. The requirement in C.3.7 for FTSE 350 companies to put the external audit contract out to tender at least every ten years has been deleted following its inclusion in the Companies Act 2016 in light of the implementation of the Directive and Regulation. Wording has been added to C.3.8, which sets out what the audit committee's report in the annual report should include, to specify that the audit committee should give advance notice of any audit re-tendering plans.

It is worth noting that the Guidance on Audit Committees was also revised to take account of the changes to the Code and the regulatory framework in light of the implementation of the above Regulation and Directive. It also reflected other market developments, such as the Recommendations and Orders of the Competition and Markets Authority in relation to audit engagements.

---

[111] See https://www.frc.org.uk/news/september-2014/frc-updates-uk-corporate-governance-code.
[112] https://frc.org.uk/getattachment/e36f77b4-60d2-4f70-a90c-c31f95790985/;.aspx.

### 9 *Risk management and internal control*

Amendments to the Code in 2014 introduced reporting of a longer-term view of a company's prospects in the form of a viability statement. Companies have since then been expected to consider how solvency, liquidity or other risks may impact the long-term viability of the business. In identifying the material risks and uncertainties a company faces, directors should consider a wide range of factors from operational and financial considerations, to risks in the broader environment in which it operates, such as cyber security and climate change.

## 10.8 The UK Stewardship Code (July 2010)

## A Background

Side by side with the UK Corporate Governance Code the UK Stewardship Code was published in July 2010.[113] The Stewardship Code, the first of its kind for the FRC, 'aims to enhance the quality of engagement between institutional investors and companies to help improve long-term returns to shareholders and the efficient exercise of governance responsibilities'.[114] The UK Corporate Governance Code has traditionally emphasised the value of a constructive dialogue between institutional shareholders and companies based on a 'mutual understanding of objectives'. In the Stewardship Code, the FRC sets out the good practice on engagement with investee companies which it believes institutional shareholders should aspire to. The FRC has hoped that the Stewardship Code will create a stronger link between the governance and investment process and said that it expects the Code to evolve over time as the industry learns from the experience. But this Code has raised concerns, for example, as to how to treat non-UK investors who collectively now hold upwards of 40% of the country's equity market. Would they voluntarily adhere to a stewardship code, and, if not, how relevant or effective would the code be? And would adoption of the code result in a non-UK investor being subject to any FRC rules?[115]

When the Stewardship Code was finalised, it was the culmination of months of wrangling between regulators, politicians and institutional shareholders over a newly defined role for investors as stewards of companies.[116] Heightened scrutiny of the role of investors in the banking crisis led to a realisation that perhaps institutional fund management groups – pension funds, insurance companies and mutual fund groups managing assets for individual investors – were in part to blame for not calling boards to account and halting some of the worst excesses. So regulators and politicians began to worry about the 'considered use of votes' by shareholders and whether they engaged with companies sufficiently.[117]

---

[113] For an in-depth analysis of the Stewardship Code and the challenges in implementing it see A. Reisberg 'The Notion of Stewardship from a Company Law Perspective: Re-defined and Re-assessed in Light of the Recent Financial Crisis?' (2011) 18 *Journal of Financial Crime* 126.

[114] Financial Reporting Council, The UK Stewardship Code (July 2010), Preface, available at https://www.frc.org.uk/getattachment/d67933f9-ca38-4233-b603-3d24b2f62c5f/UK-Stewardship-Code-(September-2012).pdf.

[115] A. Reisberg, note 113 above, at p. 127.

[116] B. Masters and K. Burgess 'Investors Raise Fears on Stewardship Code' *The Financial Times*, 15 April 2010.

[117] *Ibid.*

In his November 2009 report on governance at UK financial institutions, Sir David Walker included a proposal that shareholders should sign up to a new Stewardship Code to be overseen by the FRC, much the same way that it oversaw the UK's Combined Code on Corporate Governance.[118] It was expected that shareholders would have to sign up to several principles of responsible ownership of UK companies. They would then have to comply or explain why they did not adhere to it. Sir David said: '*There is a need for better engagement between fund managers acting on behalf of their clients as beneficial owners, and the boards of investee companies.*'[119] Sir David recommended that the FRC develop and encourage adherence to principles of best practice in stewardship by institutional investors and fund managers. The principles, Walker suggested, would draw from the Institutional Shareholders' Committee (ISC)[120] November 2009 'Code on the Responsibilities of Institutional Investors' and would apply on a 'comply or explain' basis, akin to the market's Combined Code on Corporate Governance for issuers. After a lot of pressure, the ISC dusted down the principles in 2009.[121] The 'Code on the Responsibilities of Institutional Investors', issued on 16 November 2009, states simply that:

> . . . the Code aims to enhance the quality of the dialogue of institutional investors with companies to help improve long-term returns to shareholders, reduce the risk of catastrophic outcomes due to bad strategic decisions, and help with the efficient exercise of governance responsibilities.
>
> The Code sets out best practice for institutional investors that choose to engage with the companies in which they invest. The Code does not constitute an obligation to micro-manage the affairs of investee companies or preclude a decision to sell a holding, where this is considered the most effective response to concerns.

## B The FRC consultation on the UK Stewardship Code principles

As mentioned above, following Sir David Walker's report on the corporate governance of banks and other financial institutions in November 2009, the FRC, at the request of the Government, agreed to take on responsibility of oversight of the proposed code. In January 2010 the FRC launched a consultation on the proposed Stewardship Code,[122] seeking feedback on the content, operation and oversight of such code, including: (i) whether it should in fact be based on the ISC's Code; (ii) what information investors should disclose regarding engagement policies and practices; (iii) how adoption of the standards in the code by UK and foreign investors can be encouraged; and (iv) what arrangements should be put in

---

[118] Available at http://webarchive.nationalarchives.gov.uk/+/http:/www.hm-treasury.gov.uk/d/walker_review_261109.pdf.

[119] *Ibid.*

[120] The Institutional Shareholders' Committee (ISC) is a forum that allows the UK's institutional shareholding community to exchange views and, on occasion, coordinate their activities in support of the interests of UK investors. Its constituent members are: the Association of British Insurers (ABI), the Association of Investment Companies (AIC), the Investment Management Association (IMA) and the National Association of Pension Funds (NAPF): http://www.institutionalshareholderscommittee.org.uk/.

[121] B. Masters and K. Burgess 'Investors Raise Fears on Stewardship Code' *The Financial Times*, 15 April 2010.

[122] Financial Reporting Council, Consultation on a Stewardship Code for Institutional Investors (January 2010), available at http://www.ecgi.org/codes/documents/frc_stewardship_code_consultation_jan2010.pdf.

place to monitor how the code is applied. The consultation period closed on 16 April 2010. Announcing the consultation, Sir Christopher Hodge of the FRC, said:[123]

> The benefits of a code which can help to bring about more effective engagement between companies and shareholders are potentially significant. They should lead to sustainable and enduring improvements in the governance and performance of UK listed companies and greater clarity in the respective responsibilities of asset managers and asset owners, which will assist the ultimate owners to hold to account those acting on their behalf.
>
> To deliver those benefits the code must set standards of stewardship to which mainstream institutional investors should aspire, and maintain the credibility and quality of these standards. It must foster a proper sense of ownership amongst institutional investors in the interests of their clients, and its success should be based on more effective communication between shareholders and the boards of the companies in which they invest.

It is clear then that the aim was to enhance the quality of engagement between institutional investors and companies to help improve long-term returns to shareholders and the efficient exercise of governance responsibility. 'Engagement' is expressed as meaning the pursuit of purposeful dialogue on strategy, performance and the management of risk, as well as on issues that are the subject of votes at general meetings. This does not, therefore, require any dialogue between the shareholders and any other stakeholders. This was very different to the approach taken in, for instance, South Africa, where relationships and dialogue between all stakeholders is required. This is reflected in the South African King III Corporate Governance Code. The Code recognises the importance of stakeholder relationships, in particular in Chapter 8 which, amongst other things, requires management to develop a strategy and formulate policies for the management of relationships with each stakeholder grouping.[124]

## C  Responses to the FRC consultation on the UK Stewardship Code principles

Unsurprisingly, the responses to the consultation underscored that approaches to engagement[125] were mixed. Asset managers subject to short-term performance pressures were less likely to engage than those with a long-term investment horizon. As one respondent noted, short-term investors are more likely to devote money and human capital to stock picking and equity trading than to engagement. Such funds may choose to benefit as a 'free rider'

---

[123] As cited in A. Reisberg 'The Notion of Stewardship from a Company Law Perspective: Re-defined and Re-assessed in Light of the Recent Financial Crisis?' (2011) 18 *Journal of Financial Crime* 126.

[124] This type of provision is not included in any code in the UK, although of course s. 172 (1) (c) of the Companies Act 2006 requires directors to have regard, in carrying out their duties, to the need to foster the company's business relationships with suppliers, customers and others.

[125] It is noteworthy that effective engagement between companies and shareholders was also one of the four key objectives of the Companies Act 2006, i.e. to enhance shareholder engagement and a long-term investment culture. See *Company Law Reform* (Cm 6456). See https://www.frc.org.uk/getattachment/730a755d-f6af-4be8-8339-7a35e82986bc/Feedback-Statement-UK-Stewardship-Code-September-2012.pdf and *The Company Act 2006: Regulatory Impact Assessment* (January 2007). On whether this aim has been met, see A. Reisberg 'Corporate Law in the UK after Recent Reforms: The Good, the Bad and the Ugly' in (2010) *Current Legal Problems* (Oxford: Oxford University Press, 2011) 315 available at http://papers.ssrn.com/sol3/papers.cfm?abstract_id=1635732.

from the engagement of long-only investors. How, observers question, will the FRC address this? Concerns over engagement costs, such as through increased administration or other fees, was common in many responses, with some questioning whether investors bearing such costs would be at a competitive disadvantage compared with rivals who choose not to engage.[126] One respondent proposed financial incentives as a means of mitigating these concerns. Incentives could include enhanced dividends or long-term tax benefits for good stewards. A means for raising funds to reward good stewards could be a market-based levy on listed companies or a transaction levy on shares traded, the respondent noted. The benefit of such an approach, the respondent argued, is that the fees would be spread across all investors.[127]

Another imperative question raised by many respondents concerned how to treat non-UK investors who collectively hold upwards of 40% of the country's equity market. Would they voluntarily adhere to a stewardship code, and, if not, how relevant or effective would the code be? And would adoption of the code result in a non-UK investor being subject to any FRC rules?[128]

Another area of uncertainty centered on the practice of stock lending by institutions, which the code does not address. Many respondents suggest that asset managers should disclose policies related to lending, and the recalling of loaned shares for purposes of voting, as a practice of good stewardship.[129] Some of the respondents worried that adopting the code on a 'comply or explain' basis would pressure some investors to get involved, even if active engagement was not in the best interest of their shareholders.[130] Liz Murrall, director of corporate governance and reporting for the Investment Management Association (at the time 32 of its 180 members already adhered to the Code), noted that: 'A manager may be very passive because that is the way it keeps costs down.'[131] But investors who already engage say the key would be broadening the group of activists to include foreign and smaller investors. Marc Joplin of the Association of British Insurers observed that: 'To be effective the code needs to continue to be investor-led so that it can evolve to reflect the needs of their customers.'[132]

## D The UK Stewardship Code principles and guidance

In the end, the Stewardship Code was significantly watered down in the face of fierce protests from some parts of the asset management industry, which protested at the

---

[126] S. Mishar 'Questions Remain on UK Stewardship Code', blog from 4 May 2010 at https://www.frc.org.uk/getattachment/730a755d-f6af-4be8-8339-7a35e82986bc/Feedback-Statement-UK-Stewardship-Code-September-2012.pdf.
[127] *Ibid.*
[128] S. Mishar, above n. 126.
[129] For example, in its consultation response, the UK's Institute of Directors proposed that the code include a number of principles to address concerns over lending. Other respondents suggest that the code call for institutions to adopt the ICGN's principles on lending. Responses to the consultation can be found at https://www.frc.org.uk/getattachment/730a755d-f6af-4be8-8339-7a35e82986bc/Feedback-Statement-UK-Stewardship-Code-September-2012.pdf.
[130] B. Masters and K. Burgess 'Investors Raise Fears on Stewardship Code' *The Financial Times*, 15 April 2010.
[131] *Ibid.*
[132] *Ibid.*

significant costs of the new requirements (as highlighted above).[133] The ISC Code (discussed above) contained seven principles, which now form the basis for the Stewardship Code and the principles were adopted with only minor amendments. The FRC has made minor amendments to incorporate the guidance for institutional investors which was previously set out in Section E of the Combined Code (now the UK Corporate Governance Code), and to align the Stewardship Code with the current provisions on engagement in the UK Corporate Governance Code. Strangely, there is no definition of stewardship in the new Stewardship Code.[134] As will be seen below, there is simply a requirement on companies to disclose their policy on how they will discharge their stewardship responsibilities. A clearer recognition that stewardship involves responsibility by shareholders, as owners of the company's shares, to promote the long-term sustainable operation of the company for the benefit of all stakeholders would go some way to ensuring that shareholders recognise that holding shares with a view to receiving financial return should carry some duty to others who rely on the company for their well-being and to society in general. This broader recognition of responsibility is not reflected in the Code. Instead, the Stewardship Code contains seven main principles and associated guidance. The seven main principles are as follows:[135]

(1) Institutional investors should publicly disclose their policy on how they will discharge their stewardship responsibilities. The guidance to principle 1 provides that disclosures should include, *inter alia*, how investee companies will be monitored, the strategy of intervention, the policy on voting and the policy on considering explanations made in relation to the UK Corporate Governance Code.

(2) Institutional investors should have a robust policy on managing conflicts of interest in relation to stewardship and this policy should be publicly disclosed. The guidance to principle 2 emphasises that it is an institutional investor's duty to act in the interests of all clients and/or beneficiaries when considering matters such as engagement and voting. It notes that conflicts of interest will inevitably arise and a policy should be put in place for their management.

(3) Institutional investors should monitor their investee companies.[136] The guidance to principle 3 provides that as part of the regular monitoring, institutional investors should:

- satisfy themselves that the investee company's board and committees are effective and that independent directors provide appropriate oversight by meeting the chair and, where appropriate, other board members;

---

[133] *Ibid.*

[134] *Tomorrow's Company* defines it as '. . . the active and responsible management of entrusted resources now and in the longer term, so as to hand them on in better condition.' Tomorrow's Owners – Defining, Differentiating and Rewarding Stewardship (*Tomorrow's Company*) p. 3, available at https://tomorrowscompany.com/wpcontent/uploads/2016/05/Tomorrow_s_Owners___Defining__Differentiating_and_Rewarding_Scholarship__52ef86c12aa78.pdf.

[135] Financial Reporting Council, The UK Stewardship Code (July 2010), pp. 5–9, available at https://www.frc.org.uk/getattachment/e223e152-5515-4cdc-a951-da33e093eb28/UK-Stewardship-Code-July-2010.pdf.

[136] The minor amendments mentioned above made by the FRC to incorporate the guidance for institutional investors which was previously set out in Section E of the Combined Code (now the UK Corporate Governance Code), and to align the Stewardship Code with the current provisions on engagement in the UK Corporate Governance Code, relate to this principle.

- maintain a clear audit trail including records of private meetings held with companies and of votes cast; and
- attend the general meetings of companies in which they have a major holding, where appropriate and practicable.

It is also stated that institutional investors should consider carefully departures from the UK Corporate Governance Code and make reasoned judgments in each case. They should give a timely explanation to the company and be prepared to enter into a dialogue if they do not accept the company's position.

(4) Institutional investors should establish clear guidelines on when and how they will escalate their activities as a method of protecting and enhancing shareholder value. The guidance to principle 4 provides that institutional investors should set out the circumstances when they will actively intervene. Instances when institutional investors may want to intervene include when they have concerns about the company's strategy, its governance or its approach to risk arising from social or environmental matters. The guidance sets out various ways in which institutional investors may wish to escalate their action.

(5) Institutional investors should be willing to act collectively with other investors where appropriate. The guidance to principle 5 explains that this may be most appropriate at times of significant corporate or wider economic stress, or when the risks posed threaten the ability of the company to continue. Institutional investors should disclose their policy on collective engagement.

(6) Institutional investors should have a clear policy on voting and disclosure of voting activity. The guidance to principle 6 provides that institutional investors should seek to vote all shares held and should not automatically support the board. Institutional investors should disclose publicly their voting records and if they do not, they should explain why.

(7) Institutional investors should report periodically on their stewardship and voting activities. The guidance to principle 7 provides that those who act as agents should regularly report to their clients details as to how they have discharged their responsibilities and those who act as principles, or represent the interests of the end investor, should report at least annually to those to whom they are accountable. The guidance emphasises that investors should consider an independent audit opinion on their engagement and voting processes.[137]

## E The scope and application of the UK Stewardship Code

The Stewardship Code came into effect immediately after its publication in July 2010 and is to be applied on a 'comply or explain' basis. A major issue arises over the authority of shareholders to carry out any stewardship role. Institutions generally invest in order to achieve a financial return for the underlying capital provider. There is no, or only a very tenuous, link between those whose capital is being invested (the capital providers) and the

---

[137] Financial Reporting Council, The UK Stewardship Code (September 2012), available at https://www.frc.org.uk/getattachment/d67933f9-ca38-4233-b603-3d24b2f62c5f/UK-Stewardship-Code-(September-2012).pdf.

fund manager who manages and invests the funds. Instructions (if any) are given generally on the basis of high, medium or low financial risk and not on the basis of sustainable growth, social capital or how a company promotes relational operations. Wong calls this 'the lengthening share ownership chain'.[138]

The Code partially acknowledges this shortcoming, in that it states that it is 'addressed in the first instance to firms who manage assets on behalf of institutional shareholders such as pension funds, insurance companies, investment trusts, and other collective vehicles'.[139] The FRC has expected such firms to disclose on their websites how they have applied the Code or to explain why it has not been complied with. However, it has been pointed out that it is not the responsibility of fund managers alone to monitor company performance 'as pension fund trustees and other owners can also do so either directly or indirectly through the mandates given to fund managers'.[140] Therefore the FRC encourages all institutional investors to report whether, and how, they have complied with the Code.

The FRC also issued an Implementation Guide[141], to assist companies to comply with the Code by the end of September 2010 and to include, by that date, a statement on their website of the extent to which they have complied with the Code, and to notify the FRC when they have done so. From October 2010 the FRC has listed on its website all investors who have published a statement indicating the extent to which they have complied with the Code.[142]

## F What is *not* addressed in the UK Stewardship Code

The code does not address the question as to who is to benefit from the exercise of the stewardship role. It is arguable that the duty of shareholders as stewards should not just simply be to themselves and those on whose behalf they invest funds, but it should be a duty to maintain sustainable value for the benefit of all stakeholders, including the local community where the company operates and society in general.[143] In addition, the FRC pointed out that there are a number of significant issues, which were raised during the consultation phase, which are not addressed in the Code.[144] These include disclosure by institutional investors of their policies in relation to stock lending; arrangements for voting

---

[138] That is, increasing use of intermediaries – investment consultants, 'funds of funds', external asset managers, and others – in investment management has lengthened the ownership chain of companies and, in the process, lessened the sense of accountability between ultimate investor and investee company. S. Wong 'Why Stewardship is Proving Elusive for Institutional Investors' (July/August 2010) *Butterworths Journal of International Banking and Financial Law* pp. 407–408. Electronic copy available at https://papers.ssrn.com/sol3/papers.cfm?abstract_id=1635662. Another term for this might be the lengthening of the 'capital supply chain'.

[139] Financial Reporting Council, The UK Stewardship Code (September-2012), Preface, available at https://www.frc.org.uk/getattachment/d67933f9-ca38-4233-b603-3d24b2f62c5f/UK-Stewardship-Code-(September-2012).pdf.

[140] *Ibid*.

[141] Available at https://www.frc.org.uk/getattachment/34d58dbd-5e54-412e-9cdb-cb30f21d5074/Implementation-of-Stewardship-Code-July-2010.pdf.

[142] Financial Reporting Council, The UK Stewardship Code (July 2010), Preface, available at https://www.frc.org.uk/getattachment/e223e152-5515-4cdc-a951-da33e093eb28/UK-Stewardship-Code-July-2010.pdf.

[143] See s. 172 Companies Act 2006 (discussed in Chapter 8 above) with respect of the duty to promote the success of the company imposed on directors.

[144] *Ibid*.

pooled funds; and the information to be disclosed in relation to voting records. It was expected the FRC would undertake additional work in relation to these areas.[145]

## G Adherence to the Stewardship Code

In 2011 Baroness Hogg, chairman of the FRC, spoke at the National Association of Pension Funds (NAPF) conference and took the opportunity to provide an update regarding the Code.[146] There had been, she noted, 147 signatories to the Code, including some from outside the UK, and the concept of stewardship was being considered at the EU level by the European Fund And Asset Management Association (EFAMA) and globally by the Organisation for Economic Cooperation and Development (OECD). Baroness Hogg also noted that the FRC had been working to promote the Code with overseas investors as well as with sovereign wealth funds. Internationalisation of the debate, she observed, was important.

In June 2011, the IMA published a survey looking at activities by a mix of asset managers, asset owners and service providers that support commitment to the Code.[147] The key findings of the survey were that:

- over 90% of major institutional investors vote all or the great majority of their shares in UK companies;
- nearly two-thirds of institutional investors publish their voting records; and
- at the time the survey was conducted, 43 out of 50 respondents had published a statement on adherence to the Code. A further six did so afterwards.

The survey also included case studies showing how institutional shareholders had dealt with a number of controversial topics.[148] The IMA stated that all the cases involved high levels of investor engagement with the relevant companies, including meetings at a senior board level and consultation with other investors. It emphasised that the survey reveals a real long-term commitment to achieving value for shareholders. Liz Murrall, author of the survey and Director of Corporate Governance and Reporting of the IMA, stated that it shows 'real and productive engagement which ultimately improved the governance of major UK companies'. However, the survey also documented what the sample group thought were the biggest obstacles to stewardship. The most quoted issues were the resources required to be effective and that the small size of holdings can mean that they have insufficient influence over the companies concerned.

## 10.9 The EU corporate governance Green Paper

On 5 April 2011, the EU Commission published a Green Paper on the EU corporate governance framework aiming at assessing the need for improvement of the corporate governance

---

[145] *Ibid.*
[146] https://www.frc.org.uk/getattachment/17d771e8-6dd6-4154-a48c-b14ae934f140/Speech-by-Baroness-Hogg-at-NAPF-Corporate-Governance-Conference-November-2012.pdf.
[147] Available at https://www.theinvestmentassociation.org/assets//files/Stewardship_report_FINAL.pdf.
[148] The case studies were: Marks & Spencer Group plc – combined roles of chairman and chief executive; Tesco plc – remuneration; Barclays plc – board re-election following refinancing; Lloyds Banking Group plc – acquisition of HBOS; Royal Dutch Shell plc – the environmental impact of the Canadian oil sands projects; and Prudential plc – the acquisition of AIG's Asian operation.

in European listed companies.[149] The objective of the Green Paper was to have a broad debate on the issues raised and allow all interested parties to see which areas the Commission has identified as relevant in the field of corporate governance.

In essence, the Green Paper sets out a new corporate governance action plan for the years to come. It addresses three core issues: the composition and effectiveness of the board of directors, shareholders and how to encourage greater engagement and a focus on sustainable, longer-term performance rather than short-term profit and how to improve the effectiveness of the 'comply or explain' approach. In preparing the Green Paper, the EU Commission conducted interviews with a sample of listed companies of different sizes, with different shareholder structures, across different sectors and from different member states as well as other interested parties in order to identify the issues most relevant to good corporate governance in the EU. The UK response to the Green Paper was published in July 2011.[150]

Following the Green Paper, on 12 December 2012, the European Commission published an Action Plan with initiatives it intended to undertake in the fields of EU company law and corporate governance.[151] For instance, in April 2014 a proposal[152] for the revision of the Shareholder Rights Directive[153] was subsequently published to tackle corporate governance shortcomings related to the behaviour of companies and their boards, shareholders, intermediaries and proxy advisors. It was not until 2017 that the Shareholder Rights Directive was finally amended by Directive (EU) 2017/828, which aims to encourage shareholder engagement, in particular in the long-term. It has introduced requirements in relation to identification of shareholders, transmission of information, facilitation of exercise of shareholders rights, transparency of accounts of institutional investors, asset managers and proxy advisors, remuneration of directors and related party transactions.

It is also worth noting that on 3 December 2015, the European Commission adopted another proposal to codify and merge a number of existing company law Directives with the aim of making EU company law more reader-friendly and to reduce the risk of future inconsistencies, without any change to legal substance. While the proposal has been considered by the European Parliament and the Council, no action has been taken to date.

---

[149] COM(2011) 164. See also the Q&A on the Green Paper at http://europa.eu/rapid/pressReleases Action.do?reference=MEMO/11/218&format=HTML&aged=0&language=EN&guiLanguage=en. The consultation launched with this Green Paper is part of a wider review of corporate governance in Europe initiated by the consultation on corporate governance and remuneration policies for financial institutions of June 2010 (COM (2010) 284 final). The EU Commission acknowledges, however, that although some of the issues addressed by the Green Paper 2010 are also of relevance for listed companies, financial institutions generally face a different set of challenges. Thus, some of the solutions foreseen by the Green Paper 2010 may not apply for listed companies.

[150] http://www.bis.gov.uk/assets/biscore/europe/docs/u/11-1097-uk-government-response-eu-corporate-governance-framework. See also the FRC response to the Green Paper, particularly about the 'comply or explain' provision and the benefits of the codes: https://www.frc.org.uk/getattachment/2d694942-dd93-4e82-8d80-18c254a02cdb/FRC-response-to-EU-Green-Paper-FINAL1.pdf.

[151] See EC Communication – Action Plan: European company law and corporate governance – a modern legal framework for more engaged shareholders and sustainable companies, available at http://eur-lex.europa.eu/legal-content/EN/ALL/?uri=CELEX:52012DC0740.

[152] See Proposal for a Directive of the European Parliament and of the Council amending Directive 2007/36/EC as regards the encouragement of long-term shareholder engagement and Directive 2013/34/EU as regards certain elements of the corporate governance statement.

[153] Directive 2007/36/EC set certain rights for shareholders in listed companies.

## 10.10 The 'profession' of director?

The Cadbury Report took the view that it was highly desirable that all directors should undertake some form of internal or external training, most particularly those board members who had no previous board experience. In addition, new board members should be entitled to expect an induction into the company's affairs.[154] The report made reference to plans then afoot to set up a course covering the full range of directors' responsibilities and suggested that the successor committee keep the matter under review.[155] Subsequent reports have taken a less radical stance. However, in June 1999 the Institute of Directors (IOD) launched a new professional qualification for directors, the certificate of Chartered Director (C. Dir.). It involves a three-hour examination and requires directors to subscribe to a code of professional conduct and to undertake ongoing training.[156] This looks like a worthwhile development towards establishing company directors as professionals even though it will probably only be available to a few hundred candidates a year.[157]

## 10.11 Consultations 2015–17

Between 2015 and 2017 several major consultations relating to corporate governance in the UK took place, culminating in the following reports:

**The FRC Culture Report**

The FRC's work on culture and, in particular, its publication 'Corporate Culture and the Role of Boards – Report of Observations' released in 2016 revealed that a healthy corporate culture, which derives from a clear understanding of the company's purpose and strategy, can enhance confidence and trust in the business and as such it can be a vital ingredient in delivering long-term sustainable good performance. Moreover, it also found that boards could play a significant role in shaping, monitoring and overseeing culture.[158]

**The UK Government Green and White Papers on Corporate Governance Reform**

In November 2016 the Department for Business, Energy & Industrial Strategy (BEIS) published a Green Paper inviting views on a range of options proposing to improve and strengthen the UK's corporate governance framework, since '*the behaviour of a limited few has damaged the reputation of many*'.[159] In August 2017 BEIS published the Government's response to the Green Paper, the White Paper,[160] which sets out nine headline proposals for reform across the following three specific aspects of corporate governance on which BEIS consulted: executive pay; strengthening the employee,

---

[154] Cadbury Report, para. 4.19.
[155] *Ibid*. para. 4.20.
[156] The IOD has offered a Company Direction Programme since 1983 leading to an IOD Diploma in Company Direction.
[157] There are over three million directors in the UK.
[158] Available at https://www.frc.org.uk/getattachment/3851b9c5-92d3-4695-aeb2-87c9052dc8c1/Corporate-Culture-and-the-Role-of-Boards-Report-of-Observations.pdf.
[159] Under the reference BEIS/16/56, the Green Paper is available at https://www.gov.uk/government/uploads/system/uploads/attachment_data/file/584013/corporate-governance-reform-green-paper.pdf.
[160] https://www.gov.uk/government/uploads/system/uploads/attachment_data/file/640470/corporate-governance-reform-government-response.pdf.

customer and supplier voice; and corporate governance in large privately-held businesses. While many of the more controversial proposals were finally dropped, including annual binding votes, caps on pay and changes to directors' duties – at least for now, none of the remaining proposals will require primary legislation. Instead, the FRC and other key bodies have been mandated to develop codes and guidance. There are nevertheless a number of changes of which companies will need to be aware. At the time of writing, the intention was to bring the reforms into effect by June 2018 to apply to company reporting years commencing on or after that time (although some of the proposals may be implemented earlier).

**The House of Commons' Business, Energy and Industrial Strategy Committee's Report on Corporate Governance**

This inquiry into corporate governance reflected on the evidence that the Committee found of major corporate governance failings at BHS and Sports Direct™ in 2016, with a particular focus on executive pay, directors' duties, and board composition.[161] Whilst supporting the 'comply or explain' basis of the Code, the Report published in April 2017 made a series of recommendations to help embed the behaviours of good governance. In particular, it proposed a series of reforms designed to require directors to take more seriously their duties under the Code, in particular, more specific and accurate reporting, better engagement with shareholders, and increasing accountability on the part of NEDs. On the other hand, it recommended a wide expansion in the role and powers of the FRC, in order to enable it to call out poor practice and engage with companies to improve performance.

**Developments in Corporate Governance and Stewardship 2016**

In January 2017 the FRC™ published a report entitled *Developments in Corporate Governance and Stewardship 2016* on the occasion of the 25th anniversary of the Code.[162] While it concluded that compliance with the Code remained high, the provision for at least half the board, excluding the chair, to be independent NEDs, was the one most frequently not complied with. It generally reduced investor support for remuneration resolutions, noting concern about lack of transparency about the link between executive pay and performance. The FRC undertook an exercise to encourage signatories to improve their reporting against the seven principles of the UK Stewardship Code. The outcome of this exercise was announced in November 2017, with signatories being tiered according to the FRC's assessment of their reporting. The quality of signatory statements has improved substantially as a result and the FRC reported it was pleased with the constructive approach taken by signatories.

## 10.12 The revised UK Corporate Governance Code

In December 2017, the FRC published for further consultation a new proposed revised Code, which, at the time of writing, is expected to apply for reporting years beginning on

---

[161] Available at https://publications.parliament.uk/pa/cm201617/cmselect/cmbeis/702/702.pdf.
[162] Available at http://frc.org.uk/getattachment/ca1d9909-7e32-4894-b2a7-b971b4406130/Developments-in-Corporate-Governance-and-Stewardship-2016.pdf.

or after 1 January 2019. This revised Code is a substantial re-write and a considerable simplification. While the focus remains on the company's approach to governance through the application of principles, it also incorporates elements of the Government's corporate governance reform agenda and proposes the removal of exemptions currently available for smaller listed companies (those outside the FTSE 350).

## A New principles

The new principles include the alignment of company purpose, strategy, values and corporate culture; the responsibilities of the board to the workforce and other stakeholders; demonstrating independent and objective judgment from the chair; and alignment of remuneration and workforce policies to the long-term success of the company and its values.

## B New provisions

A number of new provisions are set out in the revised Code. First, the board is entrusted with the role of monitoring and assessing culture and reporting on how stakeholder interests, and other matters set out in s. 172, may have influenced their decision-making process. Secondly, new mechanisms are set out to gather the views of the workforce and resolve board conflicts of interest. Thirdly, the chief executive has the responsibility for strategy and board information. Other provisions relate to succession planning and board member contribution; diversity and inclusion; holding periods for long-term incentive schemes; and pension arrangements. The proposed Code is divided into the following sections:

## 1 *Culture*

The proposed revisions to the Code include many of the findings from the FRC Culture Report, in particular, the need to demonstrate openness and accountability throughout the entire organisation and the fact that the company's values should be evident in the manner in which it conducts its business and engages with stakeholders.

## 2 *Stakeholders*

The revised Code includes a key issue highlighted in the FRC Culture Report, namely the board's responsibility for considering the need and views of a wide range of stakeholders. This new stakeholder focus also complements the Government's proposed reforms to ensure greater transparency around reporting how directors have discharged their duty under s. 172 of the Companies Act 2006 by the insertion of a provision requiring the board to explain in the annual report how it has engaged with the workforce and other stakeholders, and how their interests and the matters set out in s. 172 influenced the board's decision-making.

    The revised Code also specifically addresses the Government's request as set out in its response to the Green Paper that the FRC develops a new principle to improve board level engagement with employees and other stakeholders and a new provision requiring listed companies to adopt, on a 'comply or explain' basis, a method for gathering employee views which it is envisaged would normally be through a director appointed from the workforce, a formal workforce advisory panel or a designated non-executive director. The FRC specifically applies its proposals to the 'workforce' more generally to ensure a wider reach than just those with formal contracts of employment.

## 3 *Succession and evaluation*

The revised Code aims to ensure that appointment and succession-planning practices are designed to promote diversity of gender, social and ethnic backgrounds, in line with the recommendations of the Hampton-Alexander Review[163] and the Parker Review.[164] Proposals also encourage the building of diversity across the workforce, particularly in the executive pipeline, with oversight and enhanced reporting from the nomination committee. The FRC also proposes that listed companies should disclose in their annual reports the gender balance of those in senior management (i.e. in the first layer of management below the board) and their direct reports.[165]

## 4 *Board composition*

Greater focus on the importance of NED independence is given with proposals to strengthen the independence provisions which, as discussed above, are consistently rated as the lowest in terms of compliance. Specifically, a NED will only be considered independent if he or she does meet the 'independence' criteria (although companies will still have the option to 'explain' non-compliance). The revised Code also proposes clarifying the role of the chair as an independent director at all times (not just on appointment), and allowing the chair to be counted for the purpose of meeting committee composition recommendations. The revised Code also removes current exemptions in the Code for listed companies outside the FTSE 350, not only those that relate to independent director representation on boards and committees, but also those that relate to external board evaluation and annual director re-election. Finally, it also seeks to clarify the role of the chief executive in proposing and delivering strategy and reinforces the link between strategy and culture.

## 5 *Remuneration*

The importance of the role of incentives and reward in driving behaviours that support a healthy corporate culture and, ultimately, long-term success is noted. Incentives and workforce policies should be aligned with purpose, strategy and values. It also gives remuneration committees a broader role for overseeing pay and incentives as well as workforce policies across companies including for senior management and the employees as a whole.

---

[163] This review on gender balance in FTSE leadership is available at https://www.gov.uk/government/publications/ftse-women-leaders-hampton-alexander-review.

[164] This review on ethnic diversity on UK boards is available at https://www.gov.uk/government/publications/ethnic-diversity-of-uk-boards-the-parker-review.

[165] This proposal aims to bring an end to inconsistent disclosure caused by the various interpretations of the term 'senior manager' in s. 414 C (8) (c )(ii) of the Companies Act 2006 as well as implementing one of the recommendations from the Hampton-Alexander Review.

The accompanying revised guidance on board effectiveness envisages that the term 'work-force policies and practices' – a wide term encompassing the full range of HR policies – captures policies that have an impact on the experience of the workforce and drive behaviours, including recruitment and retention, promotion and progression, performance management, training and development, reskilling and flexible working. It is proposed that this responsibility could be delegated to another committee with relevant responsibilities, e.g. a sustainability committee or corporate responsibility committee, which will need to adopt an integrated approach to ensure that the oversight piece feeds into the remuneration committee's consideration of executive remuneration. The annual report should describe the work of the remuneration committee including the company's approach to investing in, developing and rewarding the workforce, and what engagement has taken place with the workforce to explain how executive remuneration aligns with wider company policy. Remuneration committee chairs should be independent and have served for at least 12 months on a remuneration committee before becoming chair. The need for 12 months' previous experience provision was expected and was heralded by the Government response. However, if the committee is given the broader oversight role, there may be some sense in allowing a person with broader relevant experience (in HR or compensation) to become the chair. The revised Code states that remuneration schemes and policies should provide boards with the discretion to override formulaic outcomes and should allow the company to apply clawback and malus to awards, where appropriate. In particular, it lists the items the remuneration committee should address when determining executive director remuneration policy and practices, which is broken down by key themes: (i) clarity, (ii) simplicity, (iii) predictability, (iv) proportionality and reward for individual performance, and (v) alignment to culture. The requirements for clarity, simplicity and predictability are presumably designed to encourage remuneration committees to veer away from complex long-term incentive plan ('LTIP') structures – a move suggested by the White Paper – in favour of simpler incentive structures using restricted shares.

## 6 Significant votes against

To improve transparency, the revised Code proposes that a company should explain, when announcing voting results, what actions it intends to take to understand the reasons behind any vote of more than 20 per cent against a resolution. The threshold is aligned with that which will also trigger inclusion on the Investment Association's public register of shareholder dissent. The Code also proposes an interim action that no later than six months after the vote, companies should publish an update on actions taken before a final summary is provided in the next annual report or in the explanatory notes to the resolutions at the next AGM. These proposals implement the Government's request that the FRC addresses concerns that some companies are not responding adequately when they encounter significant shareholder opposition, particularly to levels of executive pay.

## 7 BEIS Select Committee proposals

While the FRC notes that its review of the Code also took account of issues raised by the BEIS House of Commons Select Committee Inquiry, as discussed above, none of these are being taken forward in the revised Code. These include a number of additional recommendations such as that that the FRC should establish a corporate governance ratings system under which companies would be required to disclose their ranking and that the Code should require a binding vote on executive pay if there is a significant minority of opposition to pay awards in the previous year.

The FRC's proposals for the new Governance Code involve a radical re-writing of the form of the Code. The key question is, to what extent will the form affect the substance in practice? It was already noted that the substantive changes are less radical and rather than a change of direction 'are a turning up of the dial on a range of familiar topics. Most of the new requirements reflect the recommendations and topics covered by the Government's response to the corporate governance Green Paper and many of the changes are an attempt to drive better behaviour through transparency, for example in relation to stakeholders, the workforce and executive remuneration.'[166] Others, nonetheless, believe that the Revised Code contains quite a few nuances, and, in fact '. . . regard the Revised Code as a fundamental development in corporate governance and hence one which will materially impact directors' duties'. The FRC is clear in its approach; they say, 'we are retaining those elements of the current Code that are still relevant today, and adapting others to reflect the changing economic and social climate to ensure that UK-listed companies achieve the high standards of governance.' The FRC are to be complimented for the way in which they have sought to do so in the Revised Code, but the significance of the changes should not be underestimated.[167] Time will tell which view will prevail. That said, whatever the case may be, it is nonetheless clear that for smaller companies, 'the change to a single Code with no concessions will be significant. For all companies perhaps the most significant additional area of change is the new approach to the independence test, particularly as this is the area where there is already the highest level of non-compliance with the current Code.'[168]

## 10.13 Conclusions

For the larger companies,[169] the self-regulatory input of the 1990s will undoubtedly have caused major changes. Many, of course, already had good practice in corporate governance and for them the codes would not have required too much upheaval. Others would have had more work to do, in order to be able to claim that they were in line with the requirements. The UK's surge in interest in corporate governance during the 1990s coincided with a growth in interest worldwide, and people in many countries have followed the work of the UK committees on corporate governance with interest.[170]

---

[166] Herbert Smith Freehill, 'Corporate Governance Briefing: Reshaping the UK Governance Code: The Key Proposals', December 2017, 10.
[167] C. Mayo, 'People Get Ready! The Proposed New UK Corporate Governance Code' (22 December 2017), available at http://www.elexica.com/en/legal-topics/corporate-governance-and-compliance/221217-the-proposed-new-uk-corporate-governance-code.
[168] Note 166, above.
[169] Technically the UK Corporate Governance Code only applies to listed companies, but it is intended, as was the Cadbury Report, to set standards which would have an impact on companies generally.
[170] See generally A. Dignam 'Exporting Corporate Governance: UK Regulatory Systems in a Global Economy' (2000) 21 Co Law 70; for the OECD principles of corporate governance, see the website: http://www.oecd.org/dataoecd/32/18/31557724.pdf; for information on the European scene, see the website of the European Corporate Governance Institute.

The global financial crisis sharpened focus on the need for investors to do more, and engagement between asset owners and corporate managers has been seen by many as a critical component to those efforts.[171] The UK Stewardship Code has been the most detailed attempt to date to give institutional and regulatory form to the belief that shareholders are part of the solution, not part of the problem, and that they have not just a right, but a duty, to engage with the companies in which they invest.[172] In particular, the Code is a timely opportunity for pension trustees to finally get to grips with their role as institutional shareholders. If they do, it will be up to fund managers to demonstrate their own expertise in this area or risk losing business.[173] Given the UK market's role as a governance paragon, the success or failure of the Code is critical to practices of good stewardship taking root globally. Whatever the case may be, in the long run, it is only an important first step. In terms of codes evolution, it represents a new phase albeit at an embryonic stage.[174] Arguably, the steps taken so far do seem to fall short of real engagement by shareholders and their taking some responsibility for the actions of the directors and the company's impact on all stakeholders, in particular employees, suppliers, customers and the local community, but also society generally. Ownership of shares in a company carries certain privileges and powers, and therefore should involve an element of responsibility.

Three related major concerns have remained critical for the success of the Code.[175] First, concerns over engagement costs, such as through increased administration or other fees. Secondly, the FRC need to take stock of the fact that non-UK investors collectively now hold some 40% of the country's equity market. It therefore follows that the FRC needs to respond to these changing social realities. It is no longer possible to dismiss 'overseas investors' as a term of reference, but rather accept that they pose greater challenges in terms of making them engaged in the affairs of UK companies. Perhaps it is time to consider how to tackle these engagement costs, by developing mechanisms to reward good stewardship, preferably with financial incentives. Incentives could include, for example, enhanced dividends or long-term tax benefits for good stewards, or by putting in place arrangements to reward long-term holding of shares and encouragement for shareholders to have closer relationships and understanding with the board and other stakeholders. Finally, it is imperative that side by side with the Code, the deficiencies that make genuine stewardship challenging for institutional investors are tackled head on and remedied.[176]

While there is some merit to the FRC endeavouring to maintain reform momentum by enacting the Stewardship Code expeditiously, this approach presents a substantial risk that

---

[171] C. Mallin, blog from 6 July 2010 at http://corporategovernanceoup.wordpress.com/2010/07/ (visited 11 August 2010).
[172] *Ibid.*
[173] B. Campion 'Managers on Alert to Comply or Explain' *The Financial Times*, 5 July 2010.
[174] See further A. Reisberg 'The Notion of Stewardship from a Company Law Perspective: Re-defined and Re-assessed in light of the Recent Financial Crisis?' (2011) 18 *Journal of Financial Crime* 126.
[175] *Ibid.*
[176] Above under 10.8 and S. Wong 'Why Stewardship is Proving Elusive for Institutional Investors' (July/August 2010) *Butterworths Journal of International Banking and Financial Law*. Electronic copy available at: http://ssrn.com/abstract=1635662.

once a standard is established, inertia will set in and future reforms will be much more incremental.[177] Beyond the contents of the Stewardship Code, policymakers, asset owners, and the investment industry must also tackle investment management practices that impede good stewardship, such as financial arrangements that excessively encourage trading and attainment of short-term returns and increasing intermediation in the share ownership chain, which tends to weaken an 'ownership' mindset.[178] But at the end, one should not forget that legal principles or codes applied to directors or shareholders are founded upon trust.[179]

Although the activity in this field since the financial crisis has been intense, and the advent of the UK Stewardship Code alongside the UK Corporate Governance Code heralds a more settled future in corporate governance, recent developments have also impacted on the UK corporate governance rules. First, EC Directives implemented in the UK continue to impact on corporate governance rules.[180] By s. 1269 of the Companies Act 2006 (which introduces a new section into the Financial Services and Markets Act 2000), the FCA has been given power to make rules about corporate governance.[181] Statute law now, therefore, contains, for the first time, a definition of corporate governance.[182] Secondly, the FRC's proposals to re-write and re-shape the Governance Code, whilst involving a radical re-writing of the form of the Code, do not point, at the time of writing, to a change in the direction of travel of the UK corporate governance rules.

---

[177] B. Campion 'Managers on Alert to Comply or Explain' *The Financial Times*, 5 July 2010; https://www.ft.com/content/25b35772-8600-11df-bc22-00144feabdc0.

[178] S. Wong 'The UK Stewardship Code: A missed opportunity for higher standards' (13 July 2010) available at https://www.ft.com/content/25b35772-8600-11df-bc22-00144feabdc0.

[179] For instance, the preamble to the 2006 version of the Combined Code stated: '7. Whilst recognising that directors are appointed by shareholders who are the owners of companies, it is important that those concerned with the evaluation of governance should do so with common sense in order to promote partnership and *trust*, based on mutual understanding' (emphasis added). In May 2010 the FRC issued a new edition of the Code which applies to financial years beginning on or after 29 June 2010. It also makes reference to '. . . scope for an increase of *trust* which could generate a virtuous upward spiral in attitudes to the Code and its constructive use' (emphasis added).

[180] For example, Directive 2006/46/EC on Company Reporting requires a statement in the annual report and accounts about corporate governance. Member states were required to implement the provisions in the Directive by September 2008. In order to meet this requirement, accounting requirements of the Directive were implemented through regulations on the form and content of accounts to be made under Part 15 of the Companies Act 2006.

[181] By s. 1273 the Secretary of State is also given power to make regulations on the same topic. This power is to enable Community obligations to be met.

[182] According to s. 1269 (2) it includes:
  (a) the nature, constitution or functions of the organs of the issuer;
  (b) the manner in which organs of the issuer conduct themselves;
  (c) the requirements imposed on organs of the issuer;
  (d) the relationship between the different organs of the issuer;
  (e) the relationship between the organs of the issuer and the members of the issuer or holders of the issuer's securities.

## Further reading

B. Cheffins 'The Stewardship Code's Achilles' Heel' (2010) 73 *MLR* 1004.

A. Reisberg 'The Notion of Stewardship from a Company Law Perspective: Re-defined and Re-assessed in Light of the Recent Financial Crisis?' (2011) 18 *Journal of Financial Crime* 126.

A. Reisberg, 'The UK Stewardship Code: On the Road to Nowhere?' (2015) 15 *JCLS* 217.

# 11

# Shareholder litigation: the derivative claim

## 11.1 Introduction: shareholder litigation generally

The possibility that shareholders might sue the directors for breach of duty was mentioned in Chapter 8 as one of the many constraints on the activities of directors.[1] The discussion of the mechanisms involved was postponed until this chapter on account of the length and complexity of the subject.

One thing needs to be made clear at the outset. As we have seen,[2] directors owe their duties to the company; this is the rule in *Percival* v *Wright*,[3] now given statutory force by virtue of s. 170 of the Companies Act 2006.[4] The result is that the cause of action for breach of duty accrues to the company. The company therefore may bring an action for breach of duty against the directors. Normally, of course, it will not, because the directors will not allow the company to bring proceedings against themselves. But in certain situations, control of the company will pass to others, perhaps to a liquidator in a liquidation, or to a new board elected by a successful takeover bidder. Such circumstances sometimes provide rare examples of litigation by the company itself against the directors. We have already looked closely at the litigation in *Regal (Hastings) Ltd* v *Gulliver*[5] and seen how the company there turned on its former directors once they had sold control to a purchaser and the purchaser had elected a new board. The board of directors control the use of the company's name in litigation[6] and the new Regal board instigated the company's action against the former directors. But that is not shareholder litigation; it is litigation by the company. As such, it is relatively problem free. The circumstances in which shareholders may launch litigation discussed below are far more problematic. Because of the size of this topic and the widely differing approaches, the derivative claim will be considered in this chapter, leaving litigation by means of winding up and the popular remedy of unfair prejudice to Chapter 12.

The genesis of the current law in this area can be traced back to the period between 1995 and 1997 when the English Law Commission conducted an extensive inquiry into shareholder remedies.[7] This inquiry led to proposed reforms, which were further appraised

---

[1] See Chapter 8, 8.1 above.
[2] See Chapter 8, 8.1 above.
[3] [1902] 2 Ch 421.
[4] See Chapter 8, 8.1 above.
[5] [1967] 2 AC 134, [1942] 1 All ER 378; and see Chapter 8, 8E 2 above.
[6] By virtue of their general powers of management in art. 70 of Table A (to the Companies Act 1985).
[7] Law Commission *Shareholder Remedies* (Consultation Paper No. 142, 1996) (hereafter 'Consultation Paper'); Law Commission *Shareholder Remedies* (Law Com Report No. 246, 1997) (hereafter 'Report').

and amplified through the deliberations of the Company Law Review Steering Group between 1998 and 2001.[8] It was then endorsed by the Government[9] and finally implemented by the Companies Act 2006, Part 11,[10] not before being modified at almost each stage of its passage. To appreciate the scope of the new statutory derivative claim, it is useful to consider first the complex and often obscure common law that preceded it. This is for two main reasons. First, it will help clarify why a change in the law had become highly desirable. Secondly, and more important, this case law is still material because the conditions laid down for obtaining the courts' permission to continue the statutory derivative claim are rooted in the common law requirements.[11] Consequently, it is safe to assume that the relevant common law principles may well serve to inform the judges on how they exercise their discretion under Part 11.

## 11.2 The old common law

### A Doctrine of *Foss* v *Harbottle*

The starting point for understanding this area is the doctrine of *Foss* v *Harbottle*,[12] which was well stated by Lord Davey in *Burland* v *Earle*[13] (more clearly than in *Foss* itself) where he said:

> It is an elementary principle of the law relating to joint stock companies that the Court will not interfere with the internal management of companies acting within their powers, and in fact has no jurisdiction to do so. Again it is clear law that in order to redress a wrong done to the company, or to recover money or damages alleged to be due to the company, the action should prima facie be brought by the company itself. These cardinal principles are laid down in the well-known cases of *Foss* v *Harbottle* and *Mozley* v *Alston* (1847) 1 Ph 790.[14]

There are really two separate rules here. The second of them is often elevated to the status of being 'the rule' in *Foss* v *Harbottle*; such an approach produces boundless scope for confusion, as will be seen below when we consider the 'exceptions' to *Foss* v *Harbottle*.[15]

The first of the two rules is the very broad statement that the courts will not interfere in the internal management of companies. On the face of it, it has the consequence that a

---

[8] See especially Company Law Review Steering Group, 'Modern Company Law for a Competitive Economy: Final Report' (July 2001) URN 01/942 (CLR *Final Report*) at paras 7.46–7.51.

[9] See especially Department for Trade and Industry, 'Modernising Company Law' (White Paper) (Cm 5553-I, 2002) (which was surprisingly reticent on the matter) and Department for Trade and Industry, 'Company Law Reform' (White Paper) (Cm 6456, 2005), para. 3.4.

[10] Following the Company Law Reform HL Bill (2005) 34. It was renamed the Companies Bill on 20 July 2006. It received Royal Assent on 8 November 2006.

[11] As will be seen below, the government reaffirmed the purpose behind the rule in *Foss* and made it clear that it did not in any way seek to repeal it: 'The sections in Part 11 *do not* (emphasis added) formulate a substantive rule to replace the rule in *Foss* v *Harbottle*, but rather a new procedure for bringing such an action which set down criteria for the court distilled from the *Foss* v *Harbottle* jurisprudence.' See Explanatory Notes on the Companies Act 2006, para. 491.

[12] (1843) 2 Hare 461.

[13] [1902] AC 83, PC.

[14] *Ibid.* at p. 93.

[15] It is also simpler in some ways, but involves drawing the exceptions differently; e.g. the personal rights exception referred to below ceases to be an exception at all, the rule simply does not apply to it. See further C below.

minority shareholder who wishes to complain about the way something has been done will find that he is barred from litigating the matter. There are two ideas behind this policy. One is that there will be an unmanageable deluge of litigation if matters occurring within a company can become the subject of litigation (the 'floodgates' argument). The other probably is that the courts dislike interfering in business decisions reached by a company and regard the shareholders as far better placed to decide what should be done than the judge is.

The second of the two rules is that for wrongs done to the company, the proper claimant is the company itself; sometimes abbreviated to the 'proper claimant' rule. This rule is the embodiment of several technical ideas. First, it incorporates the rule in *Percival* v *Wright*[16] (now enshrined in s. 170 of the Companies Act 2006) that directors' duties are owed to the company and not to the shareholders. Secondly, it embodies the *Salomon* doctrine, that the company is a separate entity from the shareholders and thus has its own assets, its own rights to sue. And so the right to sue is vested and remains vested in the company, and does not flow through to the shareholders. The full significance of this 'proper claimant' rule is only apparent when it is considered how its operation is affected by the principle of majority rule.

## B  The principle of majority rule

It has been seen that the shareholders in a general meeting are the residual source of authority in the company.[17] The courts have evolved the principle that, in the event of disagreements between the shareholders, this authority can be exercised by a bare majority vote.[18] It has also been decided that the shareholders are entitled to vote selfishly, in their own interests, and that they do not owe a fiduciary duty to the other shareholders or to the company to vote 'bona fide'.[19] The authority usually cited for this doctrine is *North-West Transportation Ltd* v *Beatty*[20] which, although only a Privy Council case, has usually been applied generally ever since. The doctrine was well expressed by Baggallay J:

> Unless some provision to the contrary is to be found in the charter or other instrument by which the company is incorporated, the resolution of a majority of the shareholders, duly convened, upon any question with which the company is legally competent to deal, is binding upon the minority, and consequently upon the company, and every shareholder has a perfect right to vote upon any such question, although he may have a personal interest in the subject matter opposed to, or different from, the general or particular interests of the company.[21]

The majority rule doctrine has great significance for the 'proper claimant' part of the *Foss* doctrine, because the ultimate expression of the will of the company as to whether it will sue or not is the majority of shareholders in general meeting. Thus when a shareholder

---

[16] [1902] 2 Ch 421, see Chapter 8, 8.1 above.
[17] See Chapter 7, 7.3 above.
[18] An ordinary resolution; unless the company's constitution or the legislation requires some special majority in the circumstances.
[19] But, if the articles are being altered, or they are voting in a class meeting, the position is different; see Chapter 4, 4C above.
[20] (1887) 12 AC 589, but see now s. 239 of the Companies Act 2006 and *Franbar Holdings Ltd* v *Patel and others* [2008] EWHC 1534 (Ch), discussed below.
[21] *Ibid.* at p. 595.

seeks to get the company to use its name to litigate some matter concerning it, the courts tend to concentrate on what the majority have decided. Lord Davey, in *Burland* v *Earle*[22] said:

> . . . It should be added that no mere formality or irregularity which can be remedied by the majority will entitle the minority to sue, if the act when done regularly would be within the powers of the company and the intention of the majority of shareholders is clear.

Similar sentiments were expressed by Mellish LJ in *McDougall* v *Gardiner*:[23]

> In my opinion, if a thing complained of is a thing which in substance the majority of the company are entitled to do, or if something has been done irregularly which the majority of the company are entitled to do regularly, or if something has been done illegally which the majority of the company are entitled to do legally, there can be no use in having litigation about it, the ultimate end of which is only that a meeting has to be called, and then ultimately the majority gets its wishes.

## C The 'exceptions' to *Foss* v *Harbottle*

It is clear that an unrestrained principle of majority rule or a total fetter on litigation by shareholders could often work injustice. For instance, the majority of the shareholders could vote to divide the assets of the company among themselves, leaving the minority with nothing and with no remedy. That would be absurd and so the courts have developed exceptions. Partly due to the influence of academic writers over the years[24] an orthodoxy has grown up over the way this is presented and the exceptions are usually grouped under various headings. These are:

(1) *Ultra vires* and illegality: it has long been held that where the act is *ultra vires* or illegal by statute, the individual cannot be prevented from litigating the matter merely by an ordinary resolution in general meeting.[25] The standing given to the member by the case law in circumstances of *ultra vires* was preserved by s. 35 (3) of the Companies Act 1985, although the Companies Act 2006 has done much to reduce the impact of the doctrine.[26]

(2) Special majorities: this heading refers to the situation where the constitution of the company requires, say, a special resolution as necessary to do some act. Then, if the company tries to do it by ordinary resolution, the individual minority shareholder can litigate it.[27]

(3) Personal rights: sometimes the articles of association give the shareholders rights which they can enforce against the company. These cannot be taken away by ordinary

---

[22] [1902] AC 83 at p. 93.
[23] (1875) 1 Ch D 13 at p. 18.
[24] See e.g. *Gower's Principles of Modern Company Law* 4th ed. (London: Stevens, 1979) at pp. 644–645. The traditional list of exceptions had its roots in the case law; see e.g. *Edwards* v *Halliwell* [1950] WN 537 at p. 538, *per* Jenkins LJ (although not including the general 'personal rights' category).
[25] See *Hutton* v *West Cork Railway Co. Ltd* (1883) 23 Ch D 654 (*ultra vires*); and *Ooregum Gold Mining Co.* v *Roper* [1892] AC 125 (illegal issue of shares at a discount).
[26] As discussed above in Chapter 5, 5.3.
[27] See *Edwards* v *Halliwell* [1950] 2 All ER 1064 at p. 1067.

resolution. The case *Wood v Odessa Waterworks Co.* has already been seen to be an example of the supremacy of rights in the articles over an ordinary resolution in general meeting.[28] It is probable that not all the provisions in the articles can be enforced in this way.[29]

(4) Fraud on a minority: this is a general concept, difficult to define, and is discussed further below. Not all breaches of duty by directors will amount to a fraud on a minority.[30] If the majority of the shareholders were to divide the assets of the company amongst themselves, to the exclusion of the minority, as mentioned above, then it is clear on the case law that this would amount to a fraud on a minority. This is what the directors and majority shareholders were doing in *Cook v Deeks*[31] and it was held that an ordinary resolution of the shareholders could not deprive the minority of the ability to maintain an action against the directors.[32]

The above four categories of exception have the potential to confuse. This is because they are presented as exceptions to the rule in *Foss v Harbottle*, whereas, as we have seen, the doctrine really involves two rules. Consider the fourth exception, fraud on a minority; it is actually an exception to both rules in *the Foss v Harbottle* doctrine. The first was that the courts would not interfere in the internal management of companies. Clearly, in *Cook v Deeks* they were doing just that, so fraud on a minority is an exception to that first rule. But it is also an exception to the second rule, the proper claimant rule, since there, the wrongs were done to the company (they were breaches of directors' duty owed to the company), and yet the minority shareholders were able to litigate. This is not problematic.

However, the third head of exception, personal rights, is capable of causing some confusion, for whilst the enforcement of a personal right by a shareholder can readily be seen to be an exception to the first rule, that the courts will not interfere in the internal management, it does not seem to be any sort of exception to the second rule, the 'proper claimant' rule. The denial of a personal right is a wrong done to the shareholder in his capacity as such; it is not a wrong done to the company, and the company is not the proper claimant. The proper claimant rule does not 'bite' on the situation at all. This is more than just a semantic subtlety[33] because, as will be seen below, whether a shareholder action is founded on a personal right of the shareholder, or on a right of the company, will produce crucial differences to the procedural and substantive law governing that action.

What about the illegality part of the first exception? Is illegality an improper action by the company which gives the shareholder a personal right to require the company to abstain from the illegality, or is it a wrong perpetrated on the company by its directors and giving the company a cause of action against them? The case law does not give a definitive answer to this. In *Smith v Croft (No. 2)*,[34] Knox J took the view that it depended on whether the illegality had taken place or not; a shareholder had a personal right to restrain the

---

[28] See Chapter 4, 4.2 above.
[29] See the discussion of the insider/outsider doctrine at Chapter 4, 4.2 above.
[33] Or lack of subtlety, perhaps.
[30] It is sometimes called 'fraud on *the* minority'; nothing turns on this.
[31] [1916] AC 554.
[32] The ability of a shareholder to maintain an action for fraud on a minority was subject to further limitations, but as will be seen below, this has changed under the statutory procedure in Part 11. See 11.5 below.
[34] [1987] 3 All ER 909 at p. 945.

commission of a threatened illegality, but thereafter, the company had a right to recover damages against those who had caused it to commit an illegal act.

All this goes to show that a simple and orthodox statement of the *Foss* v *Harbottle* doctrine and its list of exceptions conceals some deep waters,[35] the effect of a jumble of case law spanning more than 150 years.

## D The striking out of derivative actions

### 1 *Introduction*

As suggested earlier, as a result of comparatively recent decisions, the fraud on the minority concept has another layer of doctrine imposed on it. The consequence of this is to restrict further the circumstances in which a shareholder can bring litigation. The whole area is closely bound up with procedural considerations and these will be dealt with as and when appropriate. First, it is necessary to look more closely at the types of litigation which a minority shareholder might bring.

### 2 *Types of action and costs*

It has been seen, with reference to the *Regal* case,[36] that if an action is brought in the name of the company, then that is not shareholder litigation,[37] it is an action in the name of the company, a corporate action, brought by the company at the behest of the board.[38] The vast majority of actions brought every day in the name of the company are brought against other companies for commercial reasons and in no way concern internal disputes with shareholders or directors. *Regal* was a rare example of litigation in the name of the company concerning internal matters.

Shareholder litigation brought under the exceptions to *Foss* v *Harbottle* falls into two categories: the personal action and the derivative action.[39] These actions are not merely procedurally different; the underlying theory of the substantive law is different. The action is called a personal action when the shareholder is claiming that some personal right of his has been infringed which gives him a right to sue. The most obvious example of this is the litigation in *Wood* v *Odessa Waterworks Company*,[40] where the shareholder was claiming that he had a personal right to have a particular clause of the articles enforced against the

---

[35] One aspect of the deep water that has caused controversy is the difficult question that arises when a minority shareholder argues that because a director has broken a fiduciary duty and caused damage to the company, he personally has a right to recover damages for the consequent diminution in the value of his shareholding. This will not be allowed where his loss is merely reflective of the company's loss which is recoverable by derivative action. Only if the shareholder's loss is separate and distinct from the loss suffered by the company will he be permitted to make a personal claim. See *Johnson* v *Gore Wood & Co (No. 1)* [2001] BCLC 313, HL; *Walker* v *Stones* [2001] BCC 757, CA; *Giles* v *Rhind* [2001] 2 BCLC 582; *Day* v *Cook* [2002] BCLC 1, CA.

[36] At 11.1 above.

[37] Although it might have started as shareholder litigation and been adopted later by the company; see *Prudential Assurance Co. Ltd* v *Newman Industries Ltd and others (No. 2)* [1982] Ch 204 whereby the time the shareholder's action reached the Court of Appeal, the company had adopted it.

[38] Or conceivably, the general meeting.

[39] Both the personal and the derivative action are often brought in the representative form.

[40] (1889) 42 Ch D 636.

company. In such cases, the company is a substantive defendant, and damages may be awarded against it, or an injunction may be granted against it. It may also have to pay the shareholder's costs. The action will be a personal action only where the shareholder can be seen to have some cause of action vested in him personally. It has been seen that this can happen as regards parts of the constitution as a result of s. 33 of the Companies Act 2006.[41] But he cannot bring a personal action where there is no cause of action vested in him. Given the rule that directors owe their duties to the company and not to the shareholders,[42] then it is clear that the shareholder will not be able to bring a personal action for breach of duty by directors. Since in practice, most matters which a shareholder would want to litigate in fact arise from a breach of duty by one or more of the directors, the availability of a personal action is often not going to be an effective solution.

To deal with this problem, the courts have developed what is called the 'derivative' action.[43] The derivative action enables the shareholder to enforce the right which is vested in the company to sue its directors for breach of duty. It gets its name from the idea that the shareholder's right to sue is *derived from* the company's right. In a sense, the shareholder is suing as agent of the company, on behalf of the company. Any damages recovered will go to the company. This last point, of course, raises the question of why the shareholder would want to bother bringing such an action if he obtains no personal benefit from it and is at risk of paying the costs if he loses. Often he will not bother, and that is one of the reasons why there has been so little shareholder litigation at common law since the development of the *Foss* v *Harbottle* doctrine. A shareholder will, indirectly, get a pro rata benefit from any damages which swell the assets of the company, and it has to be realised that people will sometimes litigate things in order to make a point of principle which has become important to them.[44]

To mitigate the costs problem with derivative actions, the courts have developed a process known as '*Wallersteiner* orders'. First conceived by Lord Denning MR in *Wallersteiner* v *Moir (No. 2)*,[45] it is basically a system under which the minority shareholder who is bringing the action can obtain from the company an indemnity for costs he may become liable for. In the case in question, Moir had been bringing litigation as a minority shareholder, against one of the directors. Moir had run out of money. In Lord Denning's immortal style, the problem was as follows:

> The only way he has been able to have his complaint investigated is by action in these courts. And here he has come to the end of his tether. He has fought this case for over 10 years on his own [. . .] has expended all his financial resources on it and all his time and labour [. . .]. In this situation he appeals to this court for help in respect of the future costs of this litigation. If no help is forthcoming [. . .], Mr Moir will have to give up the struggle exhausted in mind, body and estate.[46]

---

[41] See Chapter 4, 4.2 above and the discussion in the context of the exceptions to the *Foss* v *Harbottle* doctrine at C above.

[42] See Chapter 8, 8.1 above.

[43] While it has been referred to as a 'minority shareholders' action', a '*Foss* v *Harbottle* action' or even a 'fraud on the minority action', the adoption by the Law Commission of the term 'derivative action' (or 'derivative claim' in Part 11 of the Companies Act 2006) can be taken to have settled the matter.

[44] See *e.g. Wallersteiner* v *Moir (No. 2)* [1975] QB 373, where Moir seems to have been struggling for many years for issues of principle.

[45] [1975] QB 373.

[46] *Ibid.* at p. 380.

That was in 1975. Eventually, *Wallersteiner* orders came to be seen as having the potential for being oppressive. They were usually made without notice to the other side, shortly after the beginning of proceedings, and on affidavit evidence. The result would be that the company would thereafter find itself paying for an action, which it almost invariably did not want brought, and which would usually put the whole management under intense pressure. It would often then later be discovered that the shareholder's complaints were groundless, with the result that the whole matter had been an expensive waste of time. These kinds of factors were present in *Smith* v *Croft (No. 1)*[47] and Walton J took the opportunity to redirect the judicial approach. On the facts he took the view that an independent board of directors would not want the action to go ahead and he struck out the *Wallersteiner* order. Part of the claim was that the directors had taken excessive remuneration and on this, the learned judge felt that they were 'entitled to stand astonished at their own moderation, as Lord Clive once said'.[48]

## 3 Striking out derivative actions

As mentioned earlier, there is another layer of doctrine superimposed on the orthodox list of the exceptions to *Foss* v *Harbottle*. The seeds of it were sown by the Court of Appeal in *Prudential Assurance Co. Ltd* v *Newman Industries Ltd and others (No. 2)*[49] but the ideas in that case were taken up and developed by Knox J in *Smith* v *Croft (No. 2)*.[50]

The *Prudential* case is chiefly[51] remembered for its insistence that there is no fifth category of exception to *Foss* v *Harbottle* and that it was necessary for the claimant to establish a *prima facie* case that the company was entitled to the relief claimed and that the action fell within 'the proper boundaries[52] to the rule in *Foss* v *Harbottle*'.[53] At first instance, Vinelott J had based his approach on a general 'interests of justice' exception, as it was not clear whether the conduct complained of fell within any of the normally recognised exceptions to the *Foss* v *Harbottle* doctrine. On this basis, the first instance trial lasted 72 days. The matter went to the Court of Appeal, who were less than happy with the approach which had been taken by Vinelott J. It had become apparent by then that some of the allegations made by the minority shareholder were only partly substantiated. It had also become clear that the rule in *Foss* v *Harbottle* had ceased to be of much relevance because the company[54] had decided to adopt the judgment in its favour made by Vinelott J; this technically made the Court of Appeal's comments *obiter dicta*, but they have generally been regarded as binding authority ever since.[55]

---

[47] [1986] 2 All ER 551.
[48] *Ibid.* at p. 561. The facts appear in more detail below, in the discussion of the subsequent litigation in *Smith* v *Croft (No. 2)* [1987] 3 All ER 909.
[49] [1982] Ch 204.
[50] [1987] 3 All ER 909.
[51] There are many points of importance in it. In particular, the Court of Appeal took the view that the claimant needed to show that the defendants were in control of the company. This point and others are taken up in the discussion of *Smith* v *Croft (No. 2)* below.
[52] Meaning, the orthodox list of exceptions; see C above.
[53] [1982] 1 Ch 204 at pp. 221–222.
[54] Newman Industries Ltd.
[55] Megarry J tried to apply the Court of Appeal's reasoning in *Estmanco* and Knox J clearly felt bound by *Prudential* in *Smith* v *Croft (No. 2)*.

In *Smith* v *Croft (No. 2)*, Knox J's careful reading of the *Prudential* case became apparent and he developed and applied other aspects of the Court of Appeal's comments. It has already been seen how in *Smith* v *Croft (No. 1)* Walton J had struck out the *Wallersteiner* order. No doubt heartened by this success, the directors decided to try to get the derivative action struck out as well. The facts were complicated, but can be simplified. A minority shareholder was bringing a derivative action which had two different claims in it. The first was that, in breach of fiduciary duty, the directors of the company had used their power to pay themselves wholly excessive remuneration, that the excess was an *ultra vires* gift, and a fraud on the minority. The second was a claim to recover compensation on behalf of the company arising out of payments made allegedly in breach of s. 151 of the Companies Act 1985[56] and therefore illegal and *ultra vires*. The directors had commissioned the accountancy firm Peat Marwick to investigate the allegations and produce a report. The report had concluded that the remuneration was not excessive but that there were some technical breaches of s. 151.

The Court of Appeal in *Prudential* had made it clear that a judge faced with a derivative action should ask himself the question 'ought I to be trying a derivative action?' and had suggested that the matter be dealt with as a preliminary issue.[57] Knox J abstracted the essence of the decision in *Prudential* which he felt required a judge, faced with the prospect of trying a derivative action, to address his mind to two questions. One is to ask whether the claimants have established a *prima facie* case that the company is entitled to the relief claimed.[58] The other is to ask 'whether . . . the action falls within the proper boundaries of the exception to the rule in *Foss* v *Harbottle*'.[59]

The idea in the first of these questions is to hold a sort of mini-trial to see if the evidence of wrongdoing is likely to be sufficient to enable the minority to win the case. Here, the judge would look at the pleadings and the affidavits and try to make up his mind. In this context, it should be remembered that this approach originated in the Court of Appeal in *Prudential*, where to a considerable extent the bold claims made by the minority shareholder were not substantiated once the matter was looked into. In essence, the court is being asked to try to form a view as to whether the action is going to be a good one, or not. The idea in the second of the questions is that at the outset the judge (and the parties) must get the theory of the derivative action right. And the theory is basically the exceptions in *Foss* v *Harbottle*. In other words, the claim must be formulated to and actually fit within the straightjacket of the orthodox statement of the exceptions to the rule in *Foss* v *Harbottle*.

Thus far, there is nothing radical in the analysis and it seemed to be a normal working out of the *Prudential* ideas. However, at this point, the expected conclusion would be that

---

[56] Now s. 678 of the Companies Act 2006. See further Chapter 15 below.
[57] Megarry J in *Estmanco (Kilner House) Ltd* v *GLC* [1982] 1 All ER 437 had been the first judge to struggle with implementing the Court of Appeal's sentiments: 'It is clear from the decision of the Court of Appeal in [*Prudential*] that it is right that a *Foss* v *Harbottle* point should where possible be decided as a preliminary issue and not left for determination at the trial. On such an application the court has to do the best it can on the evidence and other material which the parties have chosen to put before it, even though further evidence and other material may well be put forward later, and perhaps lead to other conclusions': *ibid.* at p. 447.
[58] [1987] 3 All ER 909 at pp. 922, 937.
[59] *Ibid.* at p. 914.

the action could go ahead, because, having established a *prima facie* case, and having established that the claim was for fraud on the minority and therefore lay within 'the proper boundaries of the exceptions to the rule in *Foss* v *Harbottle*', the minority shareholder would have an indefeasible right to go ahead and litigate. But this was not the conclusion Knox J reached. Knox J decided that one could look at the views of the 'independent shareholders', the 'views of the majority inside a minority', what he referred to as the 'secondary counting of heads'. An example might help: if 60 % of the shareholders were the alleged wrongdoers, one would inquire what the majority of the remaining 40 % wanted. If more than half of these (i.e. more than 21 % of the total shareholding) wanted the action to go ahead, then it would. It involves regarding the 40 % minority as a sort of untainted organ of the company which represents the true company and which thus retains the power and the ability to take decisions on behalf of the company.

Knox J stated:

> Ultimately the question which has to be answered in order to determine whether the rule in *Foss* v *Harbottle* applies to prevent a minority shareholder seeking relief as plaintiff for the benefit of the company is, 'Is the plaintiff being improperly prevented from bringing these proceedings on behalf of the company?' If it is an expression of the corporate will of the company by an appropriate independent organ that is preventing the plaintiff from prosecuting the action he is not improperly but properly prevented and so the answer to the question is 'No'.[60]

On the facts, it was clear here how the votes would be cast, and so there was no need to call a meeting of the independent shareholders. They did not want the derivative action and Knox J struck it out. Knox J's ideas were firmly rooted in the tenor of the judgment in *Prudential*.

Elsewhere, across the Atlantic, the same conclusions had already been reached in dealing with similar problems.[61] In *Zapata Corp* v *Maldonado*,[62] the minority shareholder was bringing a properly founded derivative action but the board of directors had formed an independent sub-committee of the board to make proper inquiries into the allegations which formed the substance of the derivative suit. The company brought a pre-trial motion to dismiss the derivative suit and succeeded. The Delaware Supreme Court held that the shareholder did not have an indefeasible right to bring the action and had regard to the conclusions reached by the sub-committee of the board. The action was struck out.

The *Zapata* case goes a little further than *Smith* v *Croft (No. 2)* because it identified the sub-committee of the board as being the appropriate independent organ of the company which could properly reach a conclusion on behalf of the company as to the desirability of derivative litigation. But the expression 'appropriate independent organ' used in *Smith* v

---

[60] [1987] 3 All ER 909 at 942 (first sentence) and 955–956 *passim*.
[61] See further, A. Reisberg *Derivative Actions and Corporate Governance: Theory & Operation* (Oxford: OUP, 2007), Chapter 2. Care needs to be taken when making direct comparisons with shareholder litigation in the US because most states have not developed a rigid form of the rule in *Foss* v *Harbottle*. However, the US legal system has nevertheless had to address the problem of opening the floodgates, and has had resort to various restrictive rules, some of which have similar theoretical suppositions to the English common law; thus, a ratification will sometimes shut down a derivative action. Other rules are technical bars designed to discourage derivative suits, such as the requirement for a minority derivative litigant to post a bond (i.e. give security).
[62] 30 A 2d 779 (1981).

*Croft*[63] and *Prudential*[64] would be sufficient in an appropriate case to extend the idea in England also, to a board sub-committee rather than the independent shareholders.[65] It would be an effective tactic for a board faced with what it saw as inappropriate derivative litigation to form a sub-committee to look into the matter. If the sub-committee commissioned a firm of accountants to look into it, and their report exonerated the defendants, the sub-committee could resolve to terminate the derivative action. It may well be that the sub-committee would then be held to be an appropriate independent organ within the *Smith* v *Croft* doctrine. This extension of the doctrine is probably necessary if it is to work in the long run, because in a large company the practicalities of identifying the independent group among thousands of shareholders would probably prove insurmountable.

Is *Smith* v *Croft (No. 2)* a development which is dangerous for minority shareholders? The point has been made that there were already many disincentives to bringing a derivative action. The decision makes it clear that a minority shareholder no longer has an indefeasible right to bring a derivative action for acts which would normally be categorised as fraud on the minority. The would-be litigant now had to be able to persuade more than half the independent shareholders that the action should be brought. There is perhaps no good reason why an adapted version of the doctrine of majority rule should suddenly spring up at this juncture and be used to stifle litigation.

Subsequent to these developments, the court procedure was amended to ensure that the questions of whether there is a *prima facie* case (the mini-trial) and whether the action falls within the exceptions to the rule in *Foss* v *Harbottle* were dealt with at a very early stage of the proceedings. First, under RSC Ord. 15, r. 12A, it was made clear that a derivative action was to stop once the defendant has given notice of intention to defend. If the claimant wanted it to continue he needed to seek the leave of the court, the idea being that *Foss* v *Harbottle* matters would be dealt with at that application for leave.[66] The claimant was permitted to include in his application a request 'for an indemnity out of the assets of the company in respect of costs incurred or to be incurred.'[67] Thus the question of whether a *Wallersteiner* order[68] should be made would normally be dealt with then also.[69] With the coming into force of the Civil Procedure Rules (CPR)[70] on 26 April 1999, implementing the Woolf reforms contained in the *Access to Justice, Final Report*, derivative claims were governed by r. 19.9 of those rules.[71]

---

[63] [1987] 3 All ER 909 at p. 915.
[64] [1982] Ch 204 at p. 222.
[65] The phrase used.
[66] RSC Ord. 15, r. 12A (2).
[67] *Ibid.* r. 12A (13).
[68] For an unsuccessful attempt to obtain a *Wallersteiner* order see *Halle* v *Trax BW Ltd* [2000] BCC 1,020.
[69] And that led to some unwanted effects as discussed in A. Reisberg 'Funding Derivative Actions: A Re-examination of Costs and Fees as Incentives to Commence Litigation' (2004) 4 *Journal of Corporate Law Studies* 345.
[70] SI 1998 No. 3132.
[71] This provided (in para. 3) that: 'After the claim form has been issued the claimant must apply to the court for permission to continue the claim and may not take any other step in the proceedings – except [. . .] where the court gives permission.' As will be seen in 11.4 below, when Part 11 of the 2006 Act came into force these rules were amended by the Civil Procedure (Amendment) Rules 2007 SI 2204/2007 with effect from 1 October 2007.

## 11.3 Deficiencies in the common law and the approach to reform[72]

To appreciate the scope of the new statutory derivative claim, it is useful to consider briefly the process that led to its reform and to outline the role which its architects had in mind for it. As the Law Commission acknowledged, in an age of increasing globalisation of investment and growing interest in corporate governance, greater transparency in the requirements for a derivative claim is highly desirable.[73] It considered therefore that the derivative procedure should be rationalised and modernised.[74] The extensive inquiry by the English Law Commission resulted in recommendations to abolish the rule in *Foss* v *Harbottle*[75] (hereafter '*Foss*') and its exceptions,[76] at least in part, and to replace the existing derivative procedure with a new form of derivative procedure 'with more modern, flexible, and accessible criteria for determining whether a shareholder can pursue the action.'[77] The aspiration was to provide speedy, fair, and cost-effective mechanisms for resolving disputes between minority shareholders and those running companies without disturbing the balance of power between members and managers.[78] It is evident then that the Law Commission was conscious of the need to achieve a balance between the ability of the company to function effectively on a day-to-day basis, without the unnecessary interference of challenges from shareholders, and the need to protect minority shareholders and enhance shareholder confidence by providing shareholders with a route for redress in certain circumstances.[79] However, it is also clear that the Law Commission favoured the balance being in favour of management,[80] since its clear policy is that derivative actions should be 'exceptional'[81] and be subject to 'tight judicial control at all stages',[82] however permissive the language of the recommendations might appear.[83]

---

[72] For a comprehensive overview of Part 11, see A. Reisberg *Derivative Actions and Corporate Governance: Theory & Operation* (Oxford: OUP, 2007), Chapter 4 and more recently, A. Reisberg 'Derivative Claims under the Companies Act 2006: Much Ado About Nothing?' in J. Armour and J. Payne (eds) *Rationality in Company Law: Essays in Honour of D D Prentice* (Oxford: Hart Publishing, 2009), 17.

[73] Report, para. 6.9.

[74] *Ibid.*, para. 6.12.

[75] (1843) 2 Hare 461; 67 ER 189.

[76] The Law Commission formed the view that, in certain respects, the rule in *Foss* and its exceptions are inflexible and outmoded: Consultation Paper, para. 14.1.

[77] Report, para. 6.15. As Sealy rightly notes there is a problem with formulations (such as 'modern', 'flexible' and 'accessible') that are very short on specifics and loaded with terms that are devoid of any real meaning. This is a common problem with many company law reform programmes: L. Sealy [2006] Sweet & Maxwell's Company Law Newsletter 18, 1.

[78] This is enshrined in the six guiding principles for the proposals in relation to the reform of the law. See Report para. 1.9.

[79] J. Poole and P. Roberts 'Shareholder Remedies – Corporate Wrongs and the Derivative Action' (1999) JBL 99, 101.

[80] Consultation Paper, para. 14.10 expresses the wish not 'to disturb unduly the balance of power between directors and shareholders'.

[81] Consultation Paper, para. 4.6; Report, para. 6.4.

[82] Report, para. 6.6.

[83] Poole and Roberts, n. 79, 101.

In terms of procedure, it was envisaged that the new derivation claim would be governed by the rules of the court but the basis of the claim would be spelt out in a new statutory provision to be included in any future Companies Act.[84] The Report opposed any definitive criteria for granting leave on the basis that there is a danger that they would be incomplete and would not fit the circumstances of each case.[85] Instead, it concluded that the court should take into account *all* the relevant circumstances *without limit*.[86] Put simply, these criteria are merely factors to be considered alongside several others, not a mandatory requirement as in Canada. This list illustrates well how procedurally, and substantively, English law has developed to provide disincentives to prospective claimants.[87] As the Law Commission itself admitted at the time, this approach could easily be seen as maintaining a policy of not favouring derivative claims and as a signal of an over-restrictive approach to shareholders which would over-deter them.[88]

Broadly speaking, the Company Law Review Steering Group ('CLRSG'), the body established to manage the Department of Trade and Industry ('DTI')'s review, endorsed the recommendations of the Law Commission.[89] The CLRSG agreed that the derivative claim should be put on a statutory basis, restricted to breaches of directors' duties, including the duty of care and skill, and should not be confined to cases of self-serving negligence or worse (i.e. fraud).[90] Interestingly, the CLRSG was of the view that the law on ratification should be modernised and simplified.[91] It was proposed that the new companies' legislation would provide that the validity of a decision by the members of the company to ratify a wrong to the company by the directors, or by the board or of the company not to pursue such a wrong, should depend on whether the necessary majority had been reached without the need to rely upon the votes of the wrongdoers, or of those who were substantially under their influence, or who had a personal interest in the condoning of the wrong.[92] Where a wrong had not been lawfully ratified, nor a decision not to sue lawfully taken, the court will have a discretion

---

[84] This means placing the new claim on a similar footing to the unfair prejudice remedy under Companies Act 1985, s. 459, restated as Companies Act 2006, s. 994. All statutory references herein are to the Companies Act 2006, unless otherwise specified.

[85] Report paras 6.74, 6.76, 6.79.

[86] *Ibid.*, para. 6.70.

[87] A. Reisberg 'Theoretical Reflections on Derivative Actions: The Representative Problem' (2006) 3 *European Company and Financial Law Review* 69.

[88] Consultation Paper, para. 16.43.

[89] Company Law Review Steering Group, 'Modern Company Law for a Competitive Economy: Developing the Framework' (Consultation Document) (March 2000) URN 00/656 (CLR *Developing the Framework*) 4.132 and CLR *Final Report*, para. 7.46.

[90] CLR *Developing the Framework*, para. 4.127; CLR *Final Report*, n. 2, para. 7.46.

[91] Company Law Review Steering Group, 'Modern Company Law for a Competitive Economy: Completing the Structure' (Consultation Document) (November 2000) URN 00/1335 (CLR *Completing the Structure*), para. 5.84.

[92] *Ibid.* para. 5.85 and CLR *Final Report* para. 7.46. This is now enshrined in s. 239 of the Companies Act 2006. It was rightly noted that it is unclear whether this approach will help clarify the law on ratification: B. Hannigan *Company Law* (Butterworths: London, 2003) 464–465 and below.

to consider all the circumstances in determining whether a derivative claim should proceed.[93]

While the 2002 White Paper, *Modernising Company Law*, was somewhat equivocal on these reforms, preferring to see 'if a workable scheme can be devised', the DTI in *Company Law Flexibility and Accessibility: A Consultative Document* favoured putting the derivative claim on a statutory footing and the March 2005 consultative document, *Company Law Reform*, confirmed that would be the case.[94] It was eventually implemented by the Companies Act 2006 when it received Royal Assent on 8 November 2006.

## 11.4 The derivative claim under the Companies Act 2006

### A Introduction

As we have seen, there was never any doubt that the new Companies Act 2006 (the Act) would contain a reform of derivative claims, and that following developments in numerous jurisdictions,[95] these claims are now on a statutory footing for the first time.[96]

There are two initial points to consider. First, although the sections under discussion apply to Northern Ireland,[97] separate, but comparable, provision is made for the pursuit of derivative claims in Scotland.[98] The sections relating to proceedings in England and Wales and Northern Ireland use the term a derivative 'claim' rather than 'action'.[99] Consistent with this approach, we shall use the term 'claim' rather than 'action' in this section. The

---

[93] In exercising this discretion, it was envisaged that the court will pay particular regard to the issue of whether it is in the best interests of the company in accordance with the criterion set out in the principles on directors' duties, and in that context to pay particular regard to the views of the majority of members who are not party to and have no personal interest in the wrong complained of. CLR *Completing the Structure*, paras 5.86–5.87; CLR *Final Report*, paras 7.48–7.49.

[94] Department of Enterprise, Trade and Investment, 'Company Law Flexibility and Accessibility' (Consultation Document) (04/994, 2004) available at http://webarchive.nationalarchives.gov.uk/+/http:/www.dti.gov.uk/cld/pdfs/powerscondoc_final.pdf.

[95] New Zealand and Singapore introduced the statutory derivative action in 1993. Australia and Israel followed suit in 2000 after nearly a decade of study and deliberation. The statutory derivative action has been around for some time in Canada and South Africa. In the US, the derivative action is seen as a regulator of corporate management and one of the most effective means of enforcing the management's duties and obligations under the law. In fact, shareholder-initiated actions are now being accommodated in countries that had previously rendered them ineffective. Germany recently enacted the *Gesetz zur Unternehmensintegritt und Modernisierung des Anfechtungsrechts (UMAG)* altering the relevant provisions of the German Act on public companies. In a highly publicised attempt to develop private enforcement as a tool to influence companies' corporate governance, the Consolidated Financial Services Act (CFSA) introduced in 1998 derivative actions into Italian law (CFSA art. 129). Many problems affected that system, which was introduced further to a wide reform of Italian company law as a standard rule also in the general law of joint-stock companies (Italian Civil Code, art. 2393-bis). See generally, A. De Nicola *Soci di Minoranza e Amministratori: Un Rapporto Difficile* (il Mulino: Bologna 2005).

[96] Part 11 ss. 260–269. In principle, the new provisions should be used for all claims brought on or after 1 October 2007.

[97] S. 260 (1).

[98] Ss. 265–9, where the nomenclature is 'derivative proceedings'.

[99] The Scottish action is called a derivative 'action' rather than a 'claim'. This is deemed to be appropriate because the sections confer the right to raise an action; that is, they confer the right to bring the proceedings in the first place, and then regulate the proceedings. By contrast, the sections relating to proceedings in England and Wales and Northern Ireland assume that there is already a right to bring such proceedings in England and Wales and Northern Ireland; they therefore regulate the proceedings rather than confer the right to bring them. See the Explanatory Notes on the Companies Act 2006, http://www.opsi.gov.uk/ para. 506.

second point is that although Part 11 follows the recommendations discussed above in general terms, there are a number of important differences in style, form and, more important, in content. Essentially, the intention was to create a new statutory procedure with criteria for leave based on the Law Commission's recommendations, differing from the common law in some key respects.[100]

First, the Government did not want the claimant to have to show 'wrongdoer control', as that may make it impossible for a derivative claim to be brought successfully by a member of a widely-held company.[101] Secondly, the Government did want it to be possible to bring a claim in cases of negligence, even if it cannot be shown that the directors have profited from the negligence. Thirdly, the Government was keen to achieve a proper balance between the ability of directors to take business decisions in good faith and shareholders' rights, so that shareholders could bring meritorious claims against directors on behalf of the company where appropriate. At the same time, the Government wanted unmeritorious claims to be dismissed by the courts at the earliest possible opportunity and without involving companies. As will be seen, the Act's provisions try to achieve these principles, for example by providing that the courts should be able to throw out unmeritorious claims at an early stage without involving companies. However, as will be seen, whether the Act succeeds in steering a middle course between judicial recourse for the shareholders, and unreasonable interference in the affairs of the company on the other hand, is open to question.

## B General principles

The starting point for considering the statutory derivative claims is through the interaction with the new sections on directors' duties in Part 10 of the Act. Section 170[102] provides that directors' general duties are owed to the company rather than to individual members.[103] It follows that only the company can enforce them.

In line with this, the sections in Part 11 *do not* formulate a substantive rule to replace the rule in *Foss*, but rather a new procedure for bringing actions based on the existing rules. In other words, the sections *do not* seek to overturn these well-established principles.[104] Instead, they implement the recommendation of the Law Commission that there should be a 'new derivative procedure with more modern, flexible, and accessible criteria for determining whether a shareholder can pursue an action'.[105] It is noteworthy that these sections are supplemented by amendments to the CPR.[106]

---

[100] Hansard HL vol. 681, col. GC883 (9 May 2006) (Lord Goldsmith).
[101] *Prudential Assurance Co Ltd v Newman Industries Ltd (No. 2)* [1982] Ch 204, 211.
[102] See Chapter 8, 8.1 above.
[103] S. 170 (1) restates the common law position that the duties of directors are owed to the company: *Percival v Wright* [1902] 2 Ch 241; in special circumstances, directors may owe duties to individual shareholders: *Peskin v Anderson* [2001] 1 BCLC 372. See Chapter 8, 8.1 above.
[104] Explanatory Notes on the Companies Act 2006, para. 491.
[105] Report, para. 6.15.
[106] The Civil Procedure (Amendment) Rules 2007 (SI 20007/2204) provides a new CPR r. 19.9 and rr. 19.9A–F, which replace former r. 19.9 with effect from 1 October 2007. In addition there is a new Practice Direction 19C which offers further details on claim form and other procedural requirements (hearing, discontinuance etc.).

## C Scope of application

### 1 *The three key elements*

The key aspects of a derivative claim are set out in s. 260.[107] A derivative claim is defined in section 260 (1). There are three elements:

(a) the action is brought by a member of the company;[108]
(b) the cause of action is vested in the company; and
(c) relief is sought on the company's behalf.[109]

Section 260 (5) provides that references to a member in this chapter include a person who is not a member but to whom shares in the company have been transferred or transmitted by operation of law, for example where a Trustee in Bankruptcy or Personal Representative of a deceased member's estate acquires an interest in a share as a result of the bankruptcy or death of a member.

### 2 *Extending the types of breach under which a derivative claim may be brought*

It appears that a derivative claim is no longer barred by the common law requirements under the rule in *Foss* (namely, the 'proper plaintiff' and 'majority principle'), although as will be seen below, these factors will clearly still be very much relevant at a later stage in the proceedings. Instead, there is a presumptive right to claim if the conditions of s. 260 are met and the leave requirement can be satisfied. Section 260 (3) specifies the types of breach of duty under which a derivative claim may be brought. A derivative claim is expressly confined to the enforcement of directors' duties which are specified as 'only in respect of a cause of action arising from an actual or proposed act or omission involving negligence, default, breach of duty or breach of trust by a director of the company'. As such, a derivative claim may be brought in respect of an alleged breach of any of the general duties of directors in Chapter 2 of Part 10 of the 2006 Act, including the duty to exercise reasonable care, skill, and diligence. The inclusion of negligence means that any instance of a director's breach of his duty of care and skill can *prima facie*, even if capable of being ratified (subject to s. 239) form the basis for a derivative claim, thereby avoiding the complex distinction under the 'fraud on the minority' exception at common law

---

[107] There is also a special procedure for the pursuit of claims against directors brought by authorised members on behalf of the company in respect of improper political donations under Part 14 ss. 370–372. The Companies Act 2006 s. 370 reproduces the effect of s. 347I of the Companies Act 1985, except that, in a case where liability is owed by directors of a holding company in relation to a donation made by a subsidiary, the action may be brought by shareholders of the subsidiary or of the holding company. This is an approach to allocation of litigation rights which is used in German law (the new § 148 of the German *Aktiengesetz* introduced by Art. 1 Nr 15 *UMAG* now gives a minority holding 1% of the overall shares or EUR 100,000 in nominal capital the right to induce a pre-procedure for shareholder suits). Interestingly, s. 372 enables advance indemnity orders and the court has full discretion to grant such an indemnity on such terms as it thinks fit.

[108] A 'member' is defined in s. 112 but see s. 260 (5) which adds to that.

[109] S. 260 (2) provides further that the claim may only be brought either under this chapter or in pursuance of an order of the court in proceedings under the Companies Act 2006 s. 994 (formerly the Companies Act 1985 s. 459) discussed in Chapter 12.

between negligence *per se* (which was not defined as 'fraud' and which did not therefore qualify as an exception to *Foss*)[110] and negligence benefiting the wrongdoer (which did qualify as 'fraud').[111]

The decision to outline the instances when the statutory claim is available is an interesting one since, for example, there are no express sections under the applicable Canadian, Israeli or New Zealand legislative sections as to the causes of action for which the derivative claim is to be available.[112] Such an outline should be helpful to the courts and to those advising shareholders on whether to pursue a derivative claim. At the same time, if this action is to have the width of application proposed, it will be essential that the courts follow the tenor of these proposals and interpret breaches of the company's constitution, which previously operated as exceptions to *Foss*, as falling within this definition, e.g. causing the company to enter into an *ultra vires* act or to enter into an act on the authority of an ordinary resolution when a special majority is required.[113]

It also appears that the new regime will potentially allow a broader range of claims to be brought more easily than was the case at common law. For example, an employee or an environmental group holding shares could potentially bring an action under the new provisions alleging that the directors are in breach of their duty by not taking into account their interests as required by the new statement of directors' duties.[114] This opening up of derivative claims, by reason of s. 260 (3), might be regarded as a welcome liberalisation of the rules governing derivative claims and therefore a potentially beneficial development in terms of general corporate accountability. At the same time, some worry that there is a danger that it will serve to increase the already heightened fears of directors, and, in particular, non-executive directors.[115] The latter was described by Lord Hodgson during the Grand Committee Stage as a 'double whammy'.[116] The argument was that this risks enlarging the scope of such derivative claims, and that s. 260 , rather than mirroring the

---

[110] *Pavlides* v *Jensen* [1956] Ch 565.

[111] *Daniels* v *Daniels* [1978] Ch 406.

[112] For example, under Companies Act 1999 s. 1 (Israel), derivative action is 'an action brought by a claimant on behalf of a company for a wrong done to the company.' Compare this with Companies Code 1963 s. 210 (Ghana) where the action is only available for breaches of duty set out in the statute (ss. 203–205). See also Companies Act No. 61 of 1973 s. 266 (South Africa) which sets out the circumstances when the shareholder can bring the statutory derivative as being instances where loss has been caused to the company 'by a wrong, breach of trust or breach of faith committed by a director, officer, or former director or officer of that company whilst in office . . .'

[113] The special majorities exception gives rise to the possibility of bringing either a derivative action or a personal action. Since personal actions are not covered by the derivative action, a personal action alleging that a special majority has not been obtained in breach of s. 14 (restated in s. 33 Companies Act 2006) can still be pursued by an individual shareholder. See Report paras 6.56–6.57 and J. Poole and P. Roberts n. 79, 103. Indeed, s. 263 (3) (f) states that in considering whether to give permission (or leave) the court must take into account, in particular, whether the act or omission in respect of which the claim is brought gives rise to a cause of action that the member could pursue in his own right rather than on behalf of the company.

[114] Under s. 172, however, whether this will be allowed in practice will depend on how the courts approach their task under the ensuing sections, which require the claimant to seek permission or leave from the court to continue a derivative claim. See Chapter 8, 8.2B above.

[115] L. Roach 'An Equitable Solution for Non-Executive Directors' (2006) 17 *International Company and Commercial Law Review* 117, 119.

[116] That is the double-whammy effect of codifying directors' duties and at the same time creating a statutory basis for members to bring a claim against company directors thus making it easier for shareholders to commence actions against directors. Hansard HL Vol. 679 (Official Report) (27 February 2006) col GC2.

common law as the Government claims, in fact goes further.[117] Obviously, the word 'proposed' does invite possible extra legal actions and so the potential exposure of directors to risk is broadened. The question, however, is whether the safeguards in the rest of the provisions prevent abuse. It has been further argued that this codification will have a minimal positive benefit of clarifying a rarely used piece of law, while having the damaging and far more significant effect of increasing shareholder litigation and reducing the number of people willing to take directorships.[118]

The then Attorney-General, Lord Goldsmith, put forward a number of points in response.[119] First, he clarified that the Act does not introduce any major change of principle to the law in this area. Although, the derivative claim is not at the moment frequently invoked, it is a well-established mechanism by which shareholders can, in certain circumstances, bring an action in the name of the company. Secondly, it is a fail-safe mechanism rather than a weapon of first resort. It is important to remember that damages are paid not to individual shareholders but to the company itself, and yet it is the shareholder, who brings the action, who may be required to bear heavy legal costs. Thirdly, and importantly, there will continue to be tight judicial control of cases brought under the new procedure. Fourthly, a derivative claim is not and will not be the same thing as an American-style shareholder class action brought in the name of a group of shareholders. Under the reforms of directors' liabilities, introduced by the Companies (Audit, Investigations and Community Enterprise) Act 2004, companies may already indemnify directors against any liability incurred in respect of such actions, even if judgment is given against the director.[120] Lord Goldsmith was at pains to make it clear that it is not expected there will be a significant increase in the number of derivative claims as a result of putting derivative claims on a statutory footing,[121] and the Law Commission did not expect that either. As will be further explained below, this seems a reasonable prediction.

## 3 *Derivative claims against third parties*

A derivative claim can also be brought against third parties who acted as accessories to the director for dishonest assistance in connection with a director's breach of fiduciary duty.

---

[117] *Ibid.*
[118] *Ibid* col GC3.
[119] *Ibid.* Cols GC4–5.
[120] *Ibid.* See now the Companies Act 2006 Chapter 7 Part 10 (Directors' Liabilities).
[121] As there will continue to be tight judicial control of such cases and more importantly: 'We would expect the judiciary to be circumspect when reaching decisions about applications; in particular, we would expect the judiciary to continue to take the view that a disagreement between members should usually be resolved under the company's constitution without recourse to the courts. The procedure that we have set out provides proper safeguards in that respect. We also expect the courts to respect commercial judgments; the procedure that we impose will ensure that. It goes without saying – and this is what the Law Commission wanted – that there should be greater clarity about how a shareholder may bring a derivative action. The existing tests have been widely criticised and we firmly believe that they need to be replaced. May there be cases where courts give permission for cases to continue which might not have been able to previously? Yes, there may be, but in cases where proper claims were improperly being frustrated, that would in general be a welcome development. Certainly I would not expect this to result in opening the floodgates or any other of the horrendous spectacles that I have seen mentioned in some places. We have to strike a careful balance between protecting directors from vexatious and frivolous claims and protecting the rights of shareholders. It would be dangerous to move too far against either of those interests.' Cols GC4–5.

There is no requirement to show that the wrongdoer benefited from the breach in question. Section 260 (3) provides that the cause of action may be against the director or against a third party, or both. Following the Law Commission's proposal it is expected that derivative claims against third parties will be permitted only in very few cases, where the damage suffered by the company arose from an act involving a breach of duty etc. on the part of the director.[122] However, the claim under this head should be allowed only if there has been a breach of duty by the director.[123]

Lord Goldsmith identified a couple of useful examples to show why it is desirable that a claim against third parties should be possible in certain circumstances. One concerns circumstances where, by reason of a breach of duty by the director, a third party has come into possession of property of the company which it should be required to hand back (e.g. the property has been transferred in breach of trust or the individual has been giving knowing assistance). In those circumstances, it should be possible for a derivative claim to proceed against both the director and the third party.[124] Lord Goldsmith added that it needs to be clear whether it would be standard for the shareholders to want to proceed, against both the director and the third party.[125] There may be cases of wrongdoing by a director against whom proceedings could have been brought by the derivative process. For example, he could have acted in cahoots with a third party, or there may simply be a conspiracy between the third party and the director. The provision would enable proceedings to be brought against both or either as appropriate. That would certainly meet the justice of the case and there would not be any advantage in restricting, limiting or barring that derivative process against the third-party conspirator who, on this hypothesis, is not a director of the company.[126]

## 4 Can the applicant bring a derivative claim in respect of wrongs committed prior to his becoming a member (or after he leaves the company)?

Section 260 (4) provides that a derivative claim may be brought by a member in respect of wrongs committed prior to his becoming a member. This may have appeared as a revelation to certain Opposition spokespersons during the Committees Stage who were concerned about individuals joining companies simply in order to generate litigation.[127] However, historically, this has also been the position under the common law.[128] Essentially, it reflects

---

[122] E.g. for knowing receipt of money or property transferred in breach of trust or for knowing assistance in a breach of trust. See Explanatory Notes on the Companies Act 2006, para. 494.
[123] Col GC10 (Lord Goldsmith).
[124] Another example concerns a profitable company that is the victim of a tort by a third party. The directors might decide that they do not want to bring that claim against the third party. These directors, although otherwise committed to the well-being of the company, on this occasion do not wish, for bad reason and ulterior motive, to enforce the remedy for tort. They would in those circumstances be in breach of duty, but that breach of duty would not have given rise to the claim; in the words of the Act, the claim is not 'arising from an actual or proposed act or omission [. . .] by a director'. So it would not be possible in those circumstances for a member to bring a derivative claim against the third party. *Ibid.*
[125] *Ibid.*
[126] Col GC11 (Lord Grabiner).
[127] *Ibid.*, cols GC12–3.
[128] *Seaton* v *Grant* (1867) LR 2 Ch App 459. The claimant must be a shareholder when the action is brought *Birch* v *Sullivan* [1957] 1 WLR 1247.

the fact that the rights being enforced are those of the company rather than those of the member.[129] Also, incoming shareholders tend to get the benefit of successful management actions and, quite naturally, will suffer from past mistakes that affect the company adversely, and therefore they have a legitimate right in principle to initiate derivative proceedings.[130] As such, the point in time at which the member became a member is immaterial. If problems develop with regard to pressure group shareholders initiating opportunistic litigation which is more concerned with political objectives than protecting the interests of the company, it appears that the rules on permission outlined in s. 263 discussed below at E will come into play.[131]

During the Grand Committee Stage, Baroness Goudie moved an unsuccessful amendment to leave out s. 260 (4) directed towards a legitimate concern, namely, the risk of proliferation of vexatious or near-vexatious litigation resulting in making the UK more litigious.[132] It is usually said that that would damage commercial activity. Companies will need to seek more legal advice as the likelihood of litigation increases, management will be diverted from normal management activities and UK businesses will become more risk-averse and less profitable.[133]

Lord Goldsmith replied by rightly pointing out that it should not matter whether one became a member before or after the claim came into existence.[134] Company law works on

---

[129] Lord Grabiner suggested, rightly it is submitted, that it is not right that only past or previous shareholders should be allowed the complaint, because you can buy and sell shares in the company on a daily basis. Once you buy shares, you are party to a changing contract and you derive all the benefits and rights associated with that contract. The fact that you arrive later rather than earlier on the scene should not in principle deprive you of the entitlement of that contractual bargain. Col GC13.

[130] See also D. Milman [2006] Sweet & Maxwell's Company Law Newsletter 13, 2.

[131] Although it is essentially true that an activist could join the company simply in order to litigate, it is a very different question whether the court would grant leave to continue in such a case, and another one whether the litigant will be able to clear all the monumental hurdles awaiting him in s. 263. See also D. Milman *ibid.*

[132] Lord MacGregor argued that there is a real risk of US-style derivative claims coming to the UK on a much greater scale. For example, one case in respect of a major reconstruction of a UK company was mentioned. It was difficult to sort out, not least because the company was under siege from its creditors. Hedge funds were becoming involved by pursuing their own ends in trying to upset the deal and encourage corporate raiders. The view expressed was that, if dissident shareholder groups' rights were considerably enhanced, new directors would not take on the task of reconstructing companies because they would be put in a difficult situation. There was the argument not only about disincentives to take it on, but about there being considerable uncertainties about how those new directors would see their way through if they were subject to a large number of derivative actions, too, particularly from hedge funds. Col GC12. Also, it was said that US law firms are keen to take advantage of the proposed provisions: Col GC13. On the distinctive position of US lawyers in derivative action litigation see A. Reisberg 'Funding Derivative Actions: A Re-examination of Costs and Fees as Incentives to Commence Litigation' (2004) 4 *Journal of Corporate Law Studies* 345. It should be noted that in the US 'a bought out action' does not normally bar a member from taking action.

[133] Col GC12. Lord Hodgson, in support, explained that *ex ante* claims, where people who were not members of the company at the time seek to buy a single share and build a case against the directors, are an invitation for all sorts of activities. An example would be environmental claims, or animal rights activists who might take advantage of this by finding a company which had previously done something, buying a share and building a claim along these lines: *ibid.* col GC12. Another example is a venture fund, working in cahoots with the rough equivalent of the ambulance-chasing solicitor, buying a few shares in a targeted company and then bringing a derivative claim, alleging that its rights as a minority shareholder have been abused by the controllers of the company: *ibid.* col GC13 (Lord Grabiner). Lord Grabiner further explained that there might be an additional incentive for such persons to make such claims because it is possible for the court to make an order that indemnity costs can be paid, so that the claimant can claim his costs out of the company and be indemnified fully in respect of those costs; however, as the writer explained elsewhere, this is not entirely supported by the way these costs orders operate: A. Reisberg *ibid.*

[134] Col GC15.

the basis that, when one acquires shares, one gets all the bad and all the good that go with them and sometimes perhaps a bit of both. Furthermore, it is now clear that former members cannot bring a derivative claim in the name of the company.[135]

At first blush, this last point seems compelling. First, former shareholders are more likely to be acting in their own interests rather than in the company's interests, given that they are no longer directly associated with the company. Secondly, it may not be appropriate to allow a person to become a claimant where he is no longer entitled to receive a share (even indirectly) in a possible future compensation. On the other hand, allowing former members to pursue the action acknowledges the fact that these former members may have been compelled to leave the company in view of the potential dispute leading to a court battle on behalf of the company.[136] Although the other prerequisites to the bringing of the action should take care of the obviously unmeritorious cases, some may slip through the net – more vigilant supervision of the conduct of the proceedings will be required in such cases. This question may be more theoretical than practical. First, even in jurisdictions which allow for wider classes of claimants, evidence suggests that the vast majority of derivative claims are invoked by current shareholders.[137] Secondly, in Canada, where the applications were made by former shareholders[138] these were denied primarily because the court felt that such applicants lacked 'sufficient interest' in the outcome of the derivative claim. This was notwithstanding the fact that these classes of applicants have a *prima facie* right conferred by legislation to bring the application.[139]

## 5 *Derivative claims against a former director and a shadow director*

Section 260 (5) makes it clear that the reference to a director in Part 11 includes a former director and that a shadow director is treated as a director.[140] This means that a shadow director is liable in the same way as a fully paid-up registered director of a company and can be the subject of proceedings in a derivative claim by shareholders. This was also challenged during the Grand Committee Stage on the grounds that it might discourage people from providing their services to a UK plc. Lord Hodgson argued that given the nature of shadow directors some limitations should be imposed and as their name implies, they have ill-defined roles.[141] The argument was that it is not reasonable or desirable to burden shadow directors with the full brunt of responsibility for everything that occurs in

---

[135] This seems to reiterate the common law position in cases such as *Birch* v *Sullivan* [1957] 1 WLR 1247.
[136] Certainly, there is justification for not granting standing to debenture holders as arguably they did not bargain for it, and it may provide them with the means to interfere with management.
[137] This is clearly evident in Canada and in Israel. For Canada see B.R. Cheffins 'Reforming the Derivative Action: The Canadian Experience and British Prospects' [1997] 2 CFILR 227, 239 and the cases cited therein; for Israel see A. Reisberg 'Promoting the Use of Derivative Actions' (2003) 24 *Company Lawyer* 250, 251.
[138] *Jacobs Farms Ltd* v *Jacobs* (1992) OJ No. 813 (Ont Gen Div).
[139] In *Jacobs Farm Ltd ibid.* Blair J opined that 'it could not have been the intention of the Legislature [. . .] to clothe every former shareholder and every former director with the status of a complainant for the purposes of bringing a derivative action'. In *Schafer* v *International Capital Corporation* [1997] 5 WWR 99 (Sask QB), 104 (Baynton J) explained the 'sufficient interest rule' on the grounds that such a rule is required to distinguish between applicants who have a bona fide potential financial stake through the corporation in the outcome of the derivative action, and applicants who seek leave for an improper purpose.
[140] For the meaning of 'director' and 'shadow director' see s. 250 and s. 251 respectively. See also *Ultraframe (UK) Ltd* v *Fielding* [2005] EWHC 1638.
[141] Hansard HL vol. 678 (Official Report) (6 February 2006) col. GC16.

a company in the same way as a director is burdened and that one such issue would be the question of derivative claims.[142] Lord Goldsmith responded that s. 170 provides that the general duties apply to shadow directors when, and to the extent that, the corresponding common law rules or equitable principles so apply.[143] That was a way in which to say that the scope of those general duties is unclear, so it was best left open to the law to develop.[144] The provision in s. 260 (5) is thus simply a consequential effect of that.

## D Procedural requirements

### 1 *General principles*

The application for leave procedure is the subject of s. 261. In principle, s. 261 provides that the courts determine whether an action for a corporate wrong should proceed, taking account of the matters specified in s. 263. Section 261 requires permission to continue the claim. When deciding whether to grant permission two levels of test have to be applied. First, permission must be refused if a *prima facie* case is not disclosed on the evidence filed with the application.[145] Second, s. 263 reinforces this absolute bar by requiring the court to refuse permission if directors acting in accordance with the duty to promote the success of the company (s. 172) would not have pursued it. Moreover, where the matter complained of was authorised in advance or ratified the court must refuse permission. In other cases the grant or refusal of permission becomes a matter of judicial discretion governed by the criteria laid down in s. 263 (3) and (4), both of which are discussed below. That discretion must be exercised judicially and to that end certain factors are identified as relevant.

It is noteworthy that this is regarded by some as a change in emphasis away from control of corporate litigation by management in favour of judicial control.[146] However, the reality is that there was a requirement to apply for leave under CPR Rule 19.9 (3), which expressly required the court's approval for the continuance of a derivative claim.[147] In a

---

[142] Lord Hodgson conceded at the same time that shadow directors should not always be able to evade responsibly no matter what the facts are. They could be intimately involved in a matter that gave rise to a derivative claim, n. 141 col. GC17.

[143] The term 'director' is defined in s. 233 and the duties extend to both de facto directors and shadow directors by reason of s. 170 (5). For the definition of the term 'shadow director' see s. 251.

[144] N. 141 col. GC17.

[145] S. 261 (2).

[146] Report, Draft r. 50.6.

[147] It has been held that the mandatory requirement for permission under CPR r. 19.9 (replaced by CPR, r. 19.9 (4), with no changes, with effect from 1 October 2007) cannot be dismissed as a mere technicality and reflects the real and important principles that the Court of Appeal re-affirmed in *Barrett* v *Duckett* [1995] 1 BCLC 243 and underlines the need for the court to retain control over all the stages of a derivative action. See *Portfolios of Distinction Ltd* v *Laird* [2004] EWHC 2071; *Jafari-Fini* v *Skillglass Ltd* [2005] EWCA Civ 356; *Harley Street Capital Ltd* v *Tchigirinsky* [2006] BCC 209. In *Roberts* v *Gill & Co. and another* [2008] EWCA Civ 803 the Court of Appeal decided that while the old CPR did not deal expressly with a derivative claim by the beneficiary of an estate, it did contain detailed provisions dealing with derivative actions brought by members of a company, body corporate or trade union. In those cases, CPR 19.9 (3) specifically provided that the company, body corporate or trade union should be joined as a defendant. That did not mean that the company, body corporate or trade union would have to take an active part in the proceedings. On the contrary, because the claimant was the driving force in the litigation, it would only be a nominal defendant. The principal reason for joinder was to bind those persons so there could be no further claim based on the same cause of action. The Court of Appeal therefore decided that there was no reason to distinguish that situation from the situation where a beneficiary under a will sought to bring a derivative claim.

similar fashion, s. 261 provides that, once proceedings have been brought, the member is required to apply to the court for permission to continue the claim. Under s. 261 (2), the court is given power to make consequential orders on dismissal of the application. This would presumably relate to costs. The amendments to the CPR made when Part 11 came into effect did not introduce any changes to the spirit of CPR Rule 19.9.[148] Interestingly, under s. 261 (3), if the application is not dismissed under sub-section (2), the court may give directions as to the evidence to be provided by the company, and may adjourn the proceedings to enable the evidence to be obtained. Time will tell whether these powers granted to the court will be enough to address the thorny issue of disclosure and information asymmetries which exist between management and shareholders or between large and small shareholders.[149] Case law generally confers on shareholders only scant corporate rights to 'internal' company documents[150] so it will be interesting to see whether this provision will provide a point for departure from this, or whether litigants will still face up to the traditional suspicion of the English courts towards derivative claims. Finally, under s. 261 (4) the court has discretion to grant permission, to refuse permission and dismiss the claim, or adjourn the proceedings and give such directions as it thinks fit.

## 2 Permission to continue a claim as a derivative claim

Sections 262 and 264 address explicitly the possibility that, where a company or a member has brought a derivative claim, the manner in which the company or the member commenced or continued the claim may be inappropriate. First, under s. 262, where a company has brought a claim and the cause of action on which the claim is based could be pursued by a member as a derivative claim, the manner in which the company commenced or continued the claim may amount to an abuse of the court,[151] or the company may fail to prosecute the claim diligently or it may be appropriate for a member to continue the claim as a derivative claim. In these circumstances, a member may apply to the court to continue the claim as a derivative claim. As with s. 261 (4), under s. 262 (3) the court can respond to the application in a variety of ways.

It is interesting to note that at the Report Stage the need to show a *prima facie* case under s. 262 (3) was added to enable the court to make a speedy decision to dismiss.[152] It appears that prosecuting a claim diligently under s. 262 (2) (b) would mean that a company

---

[148] This rule, while expressly authorising the court to give the claimant an indemnity against costs out of the assets of the company on such terms as it thinks appropriate (CPR r. 19.9E), also expressly requires the court's approval for the continuance of a derivative action. See CPR r. 19.9F ('Where the court has given permission to continue a derivative claim, the court may order that the claim may not be discontinued or settled without the permission of the court').

[149] Information asymmetries accompany managerial misconduct: directors know the frequency and amount of harm caused by their misconduct, whereas shareholders do not. See Reisberg n. 71, Chapters 3 and 5.

[150] *Arrow Trading and Investments* v *Edwardian Group Ltd* [2004] EWHC 1319; *Re DPR Futures Ltd* [1989] BCLC 634.

[151] Abuse of the court would be, for example, if a company brought a claim to prevent a member from bringing a derivative claim and to frustrate that member. Hansard HL (Standing Committee D) (Official Report) (13 July 2006) col. 674 (the Solicitor-General).

[152] *Ibid.*, col. 885.

would have to pursue the claim in a reasonable way.[153] The issue is whether a reasonable amount of diligence is used and whether the company is willing to take action.[154]

Similarly, s. 264 addresses the possibility that, where the court has already decided that there is an appropriate case for a derivative claim (and a member has commenced a claim) another member may apply to the court to continue the claim. This will be possible if (i) the manner in which the member commenced or continued the claim may amount to an abuse of the court[155] (ii) the member may fail to prosecute the claim diligently, or (iii) it is appropriate for another member to continue the claim.[156] Presumably, these will all be rare cases.[157] Likewise, as with s. 261 (4) and s. 262 (3), under s. 265 (5) the court can respond to the application in a variety of ways.

### 3 *An assessment of the procedural requirements*

At first blush it appears that the above procedural rules will achieve greater clarity and rationality;[158] however, their practical operation is unlikely to be simpler or more efficient than the former procedural rules under CPR Rule 19.9 (3).[159] In order to obtain leave under CPR Rule 19.9 (3), it was necessary to establish both a *prima facie* case that the company is entitled to the relief sought and that the action falls within an exception to *Foss*.[160] This has resulted in lengthy hearings and extensive pleadings at the leave stage. Indeed, it has been held that the mandatory requirement for permission under CPR Rule 19.9 cannot be dismissed as a mere technicality and both reflects the real and important principles that the Court of Appeal reaffirmed in *Barrett* v *Duckett*[161] and underlines the need for the court to retain control over all the stages of a derivative claim.[162]

The Law Commission's view was that reform 'will give courts the flexibility to allow cases to proceed in appropriate circumstances, while giving advisers and shareholders the necessary guidance on the matters which the court will take into account in deciding

---

[153] If somebody were merely to issue a writ and then take no further action to serve subsequent pleadings, or were to delay unduly the serving of pleadings with a view to frustrating someone else's capacity to bring a claim, there would clearly have been a lack of due diligence. A member would then be able to seek consent, but would have to show that there had been such a lack of due diligence. If he failed to do that, the court would take the view that the member could not take action n. 151 col. 674 (the Solicitor-General).

[154] In the words of the Solicitor-General: 'If a company acts in a way that enables someone to say, "You are not being diligent. You are not being reasonable about this. You are deliberately taking the view that you will not pursue this claim", that person will be able to seek a derivative claim instead.' *Ibid.*

[155] E.g. the member brought the claim with a view to preventing another member from bringing the claim.

[156] E.g. because the member who brought the claim has become very ill.

[157] As with s. 262 (3) the need to show a *prima facie* case under s. 264 (3) was added to enable the court to make a speedy decision to dismiss n. 151 col. 885.

[158] Report para. 6.14.

[159] Replaced with no changes by CPR r. 19.9 (4) with effect from 1 October 2007.

[160] *Prudential Assurance Co. Ltd* v *Newman Industries Ltd (No. 2)* [1982] Ch 204. See now s. 261 (2) of the Companies Act 2006.

[161] [1995] 1 BCLC 243.

[162] *Portfolios of Distinction Ltd* v *Laird* [2004] EWHC 2071 discussed in A. Reisberg 'Judicial Control of Derivative Actions' (2005) 8 ICCLR 335. See also *Jafari-Fini* v *Skillglass Ltd* [2005] EWCA Civ 356; *Harley Street Capital Ltd* v *Tchigirinsky* [2006] BCC 209; *Airey* v *Cordell* [2006] EWHC 2728 (Ch).

whether to grant leave.'[163] It is true that the real difference between the previous position and the new section is that what needs to be established is set out with greater precision. However, it will still be necessary to satisfy the criteria for the granting of leave under s. 263. And, as will be seen, cases where the wrong in question has been ratified will be surrounded with the same arguments relating to whether the ratification is valid since s. 263 clearly suggests that leave should not be granted if the wrong has been ratified. This means that in many instances the effectiveness of a purported ratification will dominate the hearing for leave and it is therefore unlikely to result in change of emphasis.[164]

## E Criteria for the grant of leave

### 1 *Background*

We arrive now at the core of the statutory procedure. Section 263 sets out the criteria which must be taken into account by the court in considering whether to give permission to continue a derivative claim.[165] The first striking point to note is that the content of this important section is somewhat different from the previous drafts discussed in Part II above. There are a number of additions and, in some cases, some arguably important omissions.[166]

In response to concerns raised that the court should be able to throw out unmeritorious claims at an early stage without involving companies (or perhaps in response to massive political lobbying) and recognising that the Act's provisions could do more to achieve this, the Government tabled a package of amendments in May 2006.[167] First, the amendments introduced a two-stage procedure for permission to continue a derivative claim. At the first stage, the applicant would be required to make a *prima facie* case.[168] The court would be required to consider the issue on the basis of the claimant's evidence (which raises the question of where the shareholder will get the necessary information without discovery), without requiring any evidence from the defendant.[169] The courts must dismiss the application at this stage if it does not show a good case.[170] This should ensure the prompt dismissal of claims that are obviously frivolous, both as regards the underlying merits and, perhaps more significantly, where the applicant should not be bringing the claim on behalf of the

---

[163] Report para. 6.14. The Law Commission clearly regarded one of the failings of the common law as being the uncertainty over the scope of the exception to *Foss* and considers 'greater transparency in the requirements for a derivative action' to be highly desirable. *Ibid.* para. 6.9.

[164] See also Poole and Roberts, n. 79, 104.

[165] Readers are advised to read the detailed s. 263 before proceeding further.

[166] Recall that the subject of derivative claims proved to be rather controversial during the Grand Committee Stage discussions, due largely to companies' fear that the new rules would make it easier for activist shareholders and special interest groups to take actions against directors.

[167] N. 151, cols 883–4.

[168] This follows *Prudential Assurance Co Ltd v Newman Industries Ltd (No. 2)* [1982] Ch 204, 221–222 where the Court of Appeal held that 'the plaintiff ought at least to be required before proceeding with his action to establish a *prima facie* case (i) that the company is entitled to the relief claimed, and (ii) that the action falls within the proper boundaries to the rule in *Foss v Harbottle*'. This case was heavily criticised by the Law Commission as 'this can result in a mini trial which increases the length and cost of the litigation'. Consultation Paper, 14.1.

[169] The applicant must also notify the company of the claim and permission application by sending to the company as soon as reasonably practicable after the claim form is issued, *inter alia*, a notice form and a copy of the evidence filed by the claimant. See CPR r. 19.9A with effect from 1 October 2007.

[170] S. 261 (2) and s. 263 (4).

company. However, it will be rare for a claim to be so poorly compiled that it cannot withstand this initial scrutiny. At the second stage, but still before the substantive action begins, the court should consider if the decision of the directors was one which the company could reasonably and independently have taken.[171]

Secondly, these amendments make it clear that the court may make any consequential order it considers appropriate, for example, a cost order or a civil restraint order against the applicant.[172] That gives the court explicit power to adjourn the permission application, either for a specific event, such as a general meeting of the company and other soundings, or more generally, so that it can revisit the question of permission at a later stage.[173] Finally, the factors which the court must take into account under s. 263 are amended so that they include, 'any evidence . . . as to the views of members of the company who have no personal interest, direct or indirect, in the matter'.[174] It was thought that this would help to address concerns that it would not be practical or desirable for major quoted companies to ask shareholders formally to approve directors' commercial decisions.

Lord Goldsmith believed that this carefully considered package of measures both delivered the Government's objectives in Part 11 and addressed concerns that the derivative procedure should not be abused.[175] It remains to be seen whether this will indeed be the case. It was already noted that if anything, the cumulative effect of these amendments will be stiffening, or even stifling, the procedure by which such claims might be made.[176] And in any case, one may wonder how moving from a one to a two-stage procedure, including a much criticised[177] *'prima facie* case' requirement, sits with the ambitions to have 'more accessible', 'speedy, fair and cost-effective mechanisms'[178] to deal with derivative claims.

## 2 *The new framework*

As noted above, the Law Commission canvassed views on whether there should be a threshold test on the merits of the case,[179] and expressed concern that an express test would increase the risk of a detailed and time-consuming investigation into the merits at the permission stage. The Law Commission accepted that some consideration of merits is necessary to filter hopeless cases, but in this respect, Lord Goldsmith explained that the

---

[171] S. 263 (4). In *Airey* v *Cordell* [2006] EWHC 2728 (Ch) Warren J held that the question that a court should consider in determining whether to permit a shareholder to continue with its derivative action is whether an independent board of the relevant company would sanction the pursuit of the claim. In considering this matter, it is not for the court to assert its own view of what it would do if it was the board; it must rather decide on the view of a hypothetical and independent board. Warren J did not, however, provide any practical guidance as to how the court would assume the mind of an independent board.

[172] S. 261 (2). Arguably, these powers were already available under CPR 19.9.

[173] Ss. 261 (4)–(5).

[174] S. 263 (4).

[175] N. 151, col. 884. In Lord Goldsmith's own words: 'we have put forward a package that strikes the right balance between a degree of long-stop accountability for the directors – which is what derivative action is, not a first resort but the last – and freedom from frivolous claims.' N. 151, col. 887.

[176] N. 151, col. 885 (Lord Sharman). Historically, most claims have been struck out at this stage. Between 2004 and 2006 there have only been seven reported cases on derivative claims, and in the only one of these where permission was granted the company did not oppose the application.

[177] Consultation Paper, 14.1.

[178] Report, para. 1.9.

[179] See 11.3 above.

CPR already give the court the power to dismiss a claim at an early stage if the claim has no realistic prospect of success.

The Law Commission's view was that it would be undesirable to encourage the parties to bring evidence to show that the case met a particular merits test.[180] The Government's view was that there would be a real risk that a threshold test would lead to fine distinctions being drawn about whether the facts of an individual case fell on one side or another of an individual test. Therefore, the Government preferred to leave, as s. 263 (3) does, a much broader set of requirements, which the court must take into account in deciding in its discretion whether to allow the case to proceed. Whether the court, when it develops its principled approach, decides to include some statement about a merits test generally to be reached or always to be reached would be for the court to develop. But, following the Law Commission's line, it is clear that the Government was not disposed to build another threshold test into the statute.[181]

The first of the two-limb process for consideration by the court of whether or not to permit a claim to be continued (permission hearing) is set out in s. 263 (2). In general terms, s. 263 (2) provides that the court *must* refuse leave to continue a derivative claim if any of the *three* conditions identified in this sub-section are present. So, if it is satisfied that either a person acting in accordance with the general duty of directors to promote the success of the company[182] would not seek to continue the claim;[183] or alternatively, the act or omission giving rise to the cause of action has been authorised or ratified by the company, then leave must be refused.

At the second stage, s. 263 (3) sets out the criteria which the court must, in particular, take into account in considering whether or not to grant permission for the derivative claim to be continued (see below). The permission hearing at stage two is likely to be where most derivative claims will fail, given the difficulty of meeting the factors listed below. These criteria (set out below) illustrate how procedurally and substantively English law has developed to provide disincentives to prospective plaintiffs. Imagine a bona fide shareholder who genuinely contemplates taking an action and reads through this (non-exhaustive, it should be stressed) list.[184] Faced with these complexities, the average shareholder will often give up in despair at this early stage.

On top of this, s. 263 (4) further directs the court to have *particular regard* to any evidence before it as to the views of members of the company who have no personal interest, direct or indirect, in the matter. It is noteworthy that the reference here is to the views of *members* without a personal interest rather than to independent directors.[185] Does the fact that s. 263 (4) is separated from the list of factors provided in s. 263 (3) indicate that the views of members

---

[180] There is a real risk of satellite litigation, which can balloon out of all proportion to the significance of what one is doing, if one adopts that approach. Most respondents to the consultation agreed with that view.

[181] Hansard HL vol. 681, col. GC22 (9 May 2006).

[182] S. 172.

[183] Interestingly, the provision uses 'would not' (as opposed to, say, 'might not'), so there is arguably a difference between establishing at a preliminary stage that a hypothetical person 'might not' pursue the claim and satisfying the court that he 'would not'. See further, J. Palmer and G. Milner-Moore 'Derivative Actions: A Step Too Far?' available at http://corporate.practicallaw.com/9-202-0407.

[184] It is no surprise, as the Law Commission itself has admitted, that 'a list may appear to be a set of hurdles which applicants have to overcome and which would deter them. It could easily be seen as maintaining a policy of not favouring derivative actions and as a signal of an over-restrictive approach to shareholders which would over deter them.' Consultation Paper, para. 16.43.

of the company who have no personal interest should have more or less influence than the other factors on the court's decision? Is it significant that the court 'shall have particular regard' to these views, whereas in considering whether to give permission the court 'must take into account in particular' the factors set out in s. 263 (3)? Arguably, s. 263 (4) may be seen as the most important of the criteria because of the added emphasis given to it ('the court shall have particular regard')[186] and the fact that it is separated from the other criteria in s. 263 (3).[187] But equally, 'shall have particular regard' seems weaker than the expression 'must take into account in particular' where there is little discretion left for the court.

One may wonder whether this use of different terminology was done intentionally. Lord Goldsmith anticipates that it is for courts to decide but if, for example, the courts knew that there was a substantial and highly respectable institutional investor who knew what the circumstances were and thought that the directors were doing the right thing in not pursuing the claim, then that would be influential with the court.[188] This may well prove to be a difficult factor to apply in practice. For instance, how would the court ascertain that this institutional investor is not pursuing his *own* agenda? This appears to be a rather subjective point. And why should the court prefer the views of this particular shareholder to, say, that of someone with less substantial holding in the company? Is it simply because of the size of his holdings in the company? Although Lord Goldsmith believed that this factor will help to address concerns that it is not practicable or desirable for major quoted companies to ask shareholders formally to approve directors' commercial decisions,[189] it is doubtful whether this is a welcome addition.[190]

Finally, s. 263 (5) confers on the Secretary of State a power to make regulations with regard to the criteria to which the court must have regard in determining whether to grant leave to continue a derivative claim and where leave of the court must be refused.[191]

---

[185] The decision of a company to embark on litigation is usually a matter for the directors not for the shareholders.
[186] Particular regard is to be had to those views, they are not merely a factor to be 'taken into account' as is the case with the others factors in s. 263 (3). This emphasis may have some consequence if all other factors are finely balanced. See also *Gore-Browne on Companies Act 2006* (Jordans, Special Release, March 2007) Ch SR13 [11].
[187] S. 263 (4) was a late amendment to the factors which the court must take into account.
[188] Hansard HL vol. 681, col. GC888 (9 May 2006). It also appears to be the case that if a decision not to pursue a claim was the decision of the general meeting acting independently of any views of interested parties, that would be regarded as the view of an independent organ and is likely therefore to be decisive. *Gore-Browne on Companies Act 2006*, n. 186.
[189] *Ibid.* col. 884.
[190] The problem lies with the fact that it is clearly putting into statutory form the arguably unwelcome effect of the decision in *Smith* v *Croft (No. 2)* [1988] Ch 114 where the views of a substantial so-called 'independent' shareholder were the critical factor in refusing to allow a derivative action to proceed. The Report recommended that the court should take account of the views of an independent organ that for commercial reasons the action should or should not be pursued (Draft Rule 50.7 (2) (e)). It conceded, however, that since the law in this area is still in a state of development by the courts, the views of an independent organ should *not* be conclusive on the issue whether or not leave should be granted. For a summary of the problems with the concept and practicality of 'independent organ' see A. Reisberg, n. 71. See also, *Airey* v *Cordell* [2006] EWHC 2728 (Ch).
[191] This means that the Secretary of State will keep a watching brief on developments and is empowered by s. 263 (5) to change the criteria governing permission: see s. 263 (7). For the affirmative resolution procedure see s. 1290. In practice, this means that the regulations or order must not be made unless a draft of the statutory instrument containing them has been laid before Parliament and approved by a resolution of each House of Parliament. Lord Goldsmith explained that this provision is simply there due to a requirement for the affirmative resolution procedure. To allow a degree of flexibility to take account of changing circumstances without the need for new primary legislation seems a sensible balance to strike. See n. 181 col. GC32. Note also that s. 263 (6) provides that before making any such regulations, the Secretary of State must consult with such persons and organisations as he considers appropriate. The power reflects the Law Commission's recommendation in the Consultation Paper n. 3.

## 3 *The specific criteria*

Let us examine now in more detail the specific criteria under which the permission (or leave) *must* be refused under s. 263 (2).[192]

### Section 263 (2) (a)[193]

The requirement that a person acting in accordance with the general duty of directors to promote the success of the company under s. 172[194] appears to replace the former requirement of 'interests of the company'[195] in the Draft Rule.[196] Not only is this specified as being a factor to be taken into account in determining the issue of leave, but in accordance with the desires of those responding to the Consultation Paper, it is now a *prerequisite*, which accords with its standing in Canada and New Zealand.[197]

A major concern in relation to s. 263 (2) (a) is that the inclusion of specific matters to have regard to in fulfilling a director's duty may lead to increased activity, or at the very least attempted activity, on the part of activists or disgruntled shareholders.[198] For example, animal rights activist shareholders in a pharmaceutical company may seek to rely on s. 172 (1) (e), which refers to 'maintaining a reputation for high standards of business conduct', or another sort of activist shareholder may seek to rely on s. 172 (1) (d), which refers to 'the impact of the company's operations on the community and the environment'. The fear is that this hits the directors twice, first by making them liable for more things, in Part 10, and secondly by then giving a greater opportunity for disgruntled shareholders to bring claims against them.[199]

Responding to these fears, Lord Goldsmith explained that the Government prefers to use the formulation put forward by the CLR because it answers the question of in whose interests companies should be run.[200] That answer may not be quite the same in relation to a company that is purely profit-making, as opposed to a company that has different public interest measures in mind. This phrase appears twice.[201] The Government believes this to

---

[192] See the following specific criteria under Business Corporations Act 1985 s. 239 (2) (Canada), which was cited as a model for the Law Commission's proposed framework.

[193] Namely 'that a person acting in accordance with s. 172 (duty to promote the success of the company) would not seek to continue the claim.'

[194] This duty, which codifies the current law, enshrines in statute what is commonly referred to as the principle of 'enlightened shareholder value'. The duty requires a director to act in the way he or she considers, in good faith, would be most likely to promote the success of the company for the benefit of its members as a whole and, in doing so, have regard to the factors listed. This list is not exhaustive, but highlights areas of particular importance which reflect wider expectations of responsible business behaviour, such as the interests of the company's employees and the impact of the company's operations on the community and the environment. The decision as to what will promote the success of the company, and what constitutes such success, is one for the director's good faith judgment. This ensures that business decisions on, for example, strategy and tactics are for the directors, and not subject to decision by the courts, subject to good faith. See the Explanatory Notes on the Companies Act 2006 paras 325–332 and *Annotated Companies Acts* (Oxford University Press, looseleaf) under 10.172.01-8.

[195] On the grounds that 'it is surely important that cl 172 and pt 11 use consistent wording', Hansard, HL vol. 681, col. GC679 (9 May 2006) (Lord Goldsmith).

[196] Draft Rule 50.8 (3) provides that: 'The court must refuse leave and dismiss the derivative claim if it is satisfied that the claim is not in the interests of the company.'

[197] Report, paras 6.78–6.79 and Draft Rule 50.8 (3) *ibid.*

[198] N. 181, col. GC23.

[199] *Ibid.*

[200] *Ibid.*

[201] S. 263 (2) (a) and (b).

be a very proper thing to do. As long as the duty in s. 172 remains as it is, that duty should be the test for determining whether the claim should be stopped.[202]

Arguably, this requirement is likely to result in a restrictive approach to the grant of leave. The court is expressly required to have regard to all the elements in s. 172. The duty requires a director to act in the way he or she considers, in good faith, would be most likely to promote the success of the company for the benefit of its members as a whole and, in doing so, have regard to the factors listed in s. 172 (1) (a)–(f). This list is not exhaustive, but highlights areas of particular importance which reflect wider expectations of responsible business behaviour, such as the interests of the company's employees and the impact of the company's operations on the community and the environment. The decision as to what will promote the success of the company, and what constitutes such success, is one for the director's good faith judgment. This ensures that business decisions on, for example, strategy and tactics are for the directors, and not subject to decision by the courts, subject to good faith. It appears that this requirement is an application of business judgment,[203] but it can also operate to abrogate the court's discretion in favour of that of the company's management, who could effectively scupper any derivative claim.[204] Directors might well argue that they did have regard for all of the matters mentioned in s. 172 (1) (a)–(f) and simply believed that what they did promoted the success of the company for the benefit of the members.[205] If so, it might well be difficult for a member to challenge such an assertion successfully, and to establish that the directors did not have regard to the relevant matters.[206]

It should be noted that in most other jurisdictions this specific reference to the views of the directors is *not* included. The danger must surely be that the courts will give too much weight to the views of those who may be involved in the wrongdoing and as such the courts must be encouraged to question the background to the views of directors.[207] However, the business judgment principle provides that the court cannot question the judgment of the directors who are in the best position to make such decisions. As the Consultation Paper argues, if the directors are the wrongdoers their decisions on whether action is in the interests of the company will not normally be made in good faith.[208]

### Section 263 (2) (b) and (c)[209]

The second factor that *must* be taken into account is whether the breach of duty in question either has been approved by the company in general meeting or may so be approved.

---

[202] N. 181, col. GC24.

[203] And accords with guiding principle (iii) 'commercial decision': Consultation Paper, para. 14.11. This is akin to the business judgment rule and is expressed in terms that the courts should not substitute their decisions for what appear to be reasonable decisions of directors made in good faith.

[204] Poole and Roberts, n. 79, 109.

[205] A. Keay, 'Section 172 (1) of the Companies Act: An Interpretation and Assessment' (2007) 28 *Company Lawyer* 106, 110.

[206] *Ibid.*

[207] *Ibid.*

[208] And in any case now subject to s. 239, which prohibits self-interested members from participating in the ratification vote, thereby reversing *North-West Transportation Co. Ltd* v *Beatty* (1887) 12 App Cas 589.

[209] The section reads as follows: '(b) where the cause of action arises from an act or omission that is yet to occur, that the act or omission has been authorised by the company, or (c) where the cause of action arises from an act or omission that has already occurred, that the act or omission – (i) was authorised by the company before it occurred or (ii) has been ratified by the company since it occurred.'

Arguably, these provisions appear to contain the problem that the alleged wrongdoers are themselves in a position to authorise or ratify their wrongdoing.[210] Under s. 263 (2) (b)–(c) where such ratification or authorisation has occurred, the claim must be discontinued. Similarly, s. 263 (3) allows the court to give consideration as to whether this would be likely to occur. In this regard, it has been argued that there is a danger of this undermining the whole purpose of Part 11.[211] What is to stop an unscrupulous director ratifying his own action and so preventing a claim against him and his colleagues on behalf of the company? The answer lies elsewhere. Section 180 (4) preserves any rule of law enabling the company to give authority for anything that would otherwise be a breach of duty. Section 239 preserves the current law on ratification of acts of directors, but with one significant change. The intention is that any decision by a company to ratify conduct by a director amounting to negligence, default, breach of duty or breach of trust in relation to the company must be taken by the members, and without reliance on the votes of those members with a personal interest in the ratification.[212] This is a difficult and controversial issue, which the Report acknowledges,[213] concluding that there ought to be no change to the law on ratification so that no leave should be granted where 'effective' ratification has occurred.[214] This means that the question of whether a ratification is 'effective' will have to be addressed at the permission stage and there is a danger that it will reintroduce pleadings similar to those necessary under the common law to establish fraud by wrongdoers in control, contrary to the Law Commission's (and the Government's) wishes to get away from difficult questions such as the meaning of 'control'.[215]

This position will not, of course, prevent a shareholder from commencing a derivative claim and obtaining leave if the wrong in question is capable of ratification but not yet ratified. There is, nevertheless, a continuing risk that the action will be struck out if ratification should occur: for example, under s. 263 (3) (b) and s. 263 (4) (c) the court has the power to adjourn the derivative claim for a meeting to be held (at which the wrong could be ratified). It must be questioned whether this is a cost effective way of proceeding. It is certainly arguable that, having been given the opportunity to take action via the notice requirement,[216] if the company chooses not to do so at this initial stage, it ought not to be given the opportunity at a later stage in the proceedings unless there are exceptional circumstances.[217] It might also be simpler to provide that, having been given notice, if the

---

[210] Hansard HL vol. 679 (Official Report) (27 February 2006) col. GC24.

[211] *Ibid.*

[212] *Ibid.* col. GC25 (Lord Goldsmith). Recall that s. 239 prohibits self-interested members from participating in the ratification vote, thereby reversing *North-West Transportation Co. Ltd* v *Beatty* (1887) 12 App Cas 589. It is noteworthy, however, that s. 239 (4) does not prevent the director or any such member from attending, being counted towards the quorum and taking part in the proceedings at any meeting at which the decision is considered. One may wonder what impact this may have on how other members cast their votes.

[213] 'There is a danger that our desire to simplify the derivative action could be undermined by the complexities which arise where it is claimed that the relevant breach of duty has been (or may be) ratified.' The Report, para. 6.81.

[214] This expression is used in the recommendation (para. 6.86) but not in the Draft Rule 50.8 (4).

[215] As Boyle puts it: 'There is the further danger that the case law on ratifiable and non-ratifiable directors' duties would once more dominate the new statutory derivative action.' A.J. Boyle 'The New Derivative Action' (1997) 18 *Company Lawyer* 256, 258. See also S. Friedman 'Ratification of Directors' Breaches' (1992) 10 *Company and Securities Law Journal* 252.

company does not ratify the wrong it ought to pursue the action to redress the corporate wrong. Similarly, if the company considers that it is not in the interests of the company to pursue the matter, it ought to ratify and cure the defect.[218] In any event, there is a continuing danger that although ratification has not taken place at the time of the application for leave, the court will be concerned with this when determining leave, especially when it is considered that the policy is only exceptionally to allow derivative claims.

In other jurisdictions, this approach has been rejected as ratification is not fatal to the derivative claim.[219] The fundamental problem with the ratification issue is that it requires a thorough assessment of the complexities of the law on ratification in the context of directors' duties and this was considered to be outside the remit of the Law Commission as being concerned with rights rather than remedies: the Law Commission therefore preferred to preserve the status quo on the effect of ratification,[220] although later the CLR tackled this issue head on.[221] Unfortunately, the two are interdependent and it is not possible to make any truly effective recommendations on shareholders' remedies without first rationalising the effect of ratification.[222] In addition, as noted above, cases where the wrong in question has been ratified will be surrounded with the same arguments relating to whether the ratification is valid. This means that in many instances the effectiveness of a purported ratification will dominate the hearing for leave and there will be no change of emphasis in favour of a broad judicial discretion.[223]

The Report also considered that in determining the question of leave the court should take account of any resolution by the company in general meeting not to pursue the breach of duty.[224] Although this is not the same as ratification, it is affected by the same difficulties, namely the question of whether that decision was obtained after shareholders had been presented with the full facts and whether there was any control by the wrongdoers. Arguably it is for these reasons that this is not a factor that has concerned legislators in other jurisdictions.

## 4 Matters that the court must take into account when considering an application for permission to proceed with a derivative claim

Let us look now at the specific issues which the court *must* take into account under s. 263 (3) in considering whether or not to grant permission for the derivative claim to be continued. If the shareholder cannot show a *prima facie* case the court must dismiss the

---

[216] CPR r. 19.9A with effect from 1 October 2007.

[217] Poole and Roberts, n. 79, 108.

[218] *Ibid*. This would retain control with the company itself and would accord with guiding principles (iii) and (v) in Consultation Paper, para. 14.11, by leaving decisions on litigation with the company and preventing unwelcome shareholder interference.

[219] E.g. Business Corporations Act 1985 s. 263 (Canada) which provides that the action shall not be stayed or dismissed on the basis that the wrong has been ratified, but ratification can be taken into account by the court when deciding on an appropriate remedial order.

[220] Report, para. 6.85.

[221] See 11.3 above. This is now enshrined in s. 239.

[222] Poole and Roberts, n. 79, 110.

[223] *Ibid*. 104.

[224] Report, para. 6.87 and Draft Rule 50.7 (2) (d).

application. Similarly, the court must refuse permission to continue with a derivative claim if (i) a person acting in accordance with the duty to promote the success of the company under s. 172 of the Companies Act 2006 would not seek to continue the claim; or the proposed or past act or omission for which the member wants to bring a derivative claim had been authorised by the company before it occurred or has been ratified since it occurred. While the discretion to grant or withhold permission is exercised regarding all relevant matters, the court must take into account: (i) whether the member is acting in good faith; (ii) the importance which a person acting in accordance with the duty to promote the success of the company would accord to the proposed claim; (iii) whether a proposed or past act or omission would be likely to be authorised or ratified by the company; (iv) whether the company has decided not to pursue the claim; (v) whether the member has a cause of action that he or she may pursue in his or her own right rather than on behalf of the company; and (vi) the views of the members of the company who have no personal direct or indirect interest in the matter.

Arguably, it rehearses the criteria set out in s. 263 (2) and therefore does not sit well with the purpose of having a 'cost-effective', 'speedy' and 'clear' procedure.[225] Lord Goldsmith explained that the formulation here is somewhat different.[226] The Government believed it is better to set out the requirements which the court must have regard to under s. 263 (3).[227] They include a number of matters, one being that the company has decided not to pursue the claim; in such circumstances the court will want to look at why it decided that.[228] Another important factor listed in s. 263 (3) is the significance that a person acting in accordance with s. 172 (duty to promote the success of the company) would attach to continuing it.[229]

During the Grand Committee Stage, Lord Hodgson argued that the courts might be confused about how to apply the six important but different factors. In particular, clarification was sought on whether the list is in order of importance or whether each factor must be given equal weight by the court. One of the issues is the mixture of subjective and objective facts in the list. For example, is it more important that the member is acting in good faith or that the company has decided not to pursue the claim?

Lord Goldsmith expected the court, in exercising its discretion, to take into account *all* the factors set out. They are a mixture of the objective and the factual and it is expected that the court will consider them together.[230] It would not be a question of taking it step by step in a particular order. The test of whether a claim is a sensible one to bring, which is what s. 263 (3) (b) deals with, is objective, since, by definition, what is at issue is whether the director has acted properly. It is coupled with a series of tests which are designed to

---

[225] See Report para. 1.9.

[226] Hansard HL vol. 679 (Official Report) (27 February 2006) col. GC24.

[227] *Ibid.* GC8.

[228] There are a number of possibilities. One would be that it had made a bona fide decision that the claim ought not to be pursued. Such a decision would be very influential with the court, which may decide not to allow the claim to go ahead. Alternatively, the company may have decided not to pursue the claim for reasons that the court finds unsatisfactory, which might have the opposite effect. It would be for the court to determine. See *Official Report*, 27/2/2006; col .GC8 *ibid*.

[229] S. 263 (3) (b). See also *Airey* v *Cordell* [2006] EWHC 2728 (Ch) where it was held that the appropriate test for permission was the view of a hypothetical and independent board of directors. The court made clear in that case that its task was not to assert its own view but merely to be satisfied that such a board could take the decision that the minority shareholder applying for permission to proceed would like it to take.

[230] N. 165, col. GC26.

look at what the company actually wants rather than what an abstract company would want. It has a sense of reality about it. How important each factor is in any particular case would be for the court to determine on the facts of the case, having regard to all the circumstances and all the factors that are set out.[231] But the danger must still be that because the factors are not weighted, the discretion is so open that the case law will provide little guidance because invariably each case will turn on its own facts.

An interesting question is whether the effect of s. 263 (2) and 263 (3) combined is to make it necessary for the court to review any decision by the board *not* to pursue a claim? Lord Goldsmith suggested that under s. 263 (2) (a) the court would look at the question of whether a person acting in accordance with the duty to promote the success of the company would not seek to continue the claim. If the court is satisfied that such a person would not seek to continue the claim, that would be an end to the derivative claim. When it comes to the discretionary element under s. 263 (3) (e), the court would look to see whether the company had decided not to pursue the claim. If it had, that would be a powerful factor, but it would not be conclusive. Looking at all the circumstances, the court might see that there were ulterior reasons for doing so, or even that it was an obviously bad decision.[232] It appears then that the court will need to look at the circumstances and independence of decisions reached, but it is impossible to predict what weight will be given to them. There is certainly no suggestion that they would operate as an absolute bar and much will depend on how the case law develops.[233]

Another interesting question relates to the fact that arguably claimants may pursue a derivative claim where there has been no loss to the company:[234] this issue is not mentioned in the list of matters for the court to consider, nor is it included in the factors that trigger automatic refusal of permission by the court given in sub-section (2). However, Lord Goldsmith thought it unnecessary to state this as a particular factor for the court to take into account. The general discretion and the absolute bars are better dealt with by the procedures set out in sub-sections (2)–(3).[235]

Section 263 (3) (d) requires that 'where the cause of action arises from an act or omission that has already occurred, whether the act or omission could be, and in the circumstances would be likely to be, ratified by the company.' It appears then that the new law will depend on a factual enquiry into whether the breach is 'likely to be ratified' and even then this is simply a factor for the court. Adjournment of the permission hearing for ratification is one possible solution and is, as some suspect, likely to be adopted increasingly by the courts.[236] This may also mean an additional administrative burden. For some companies, this will be an expensive formality giving leverage to minorities.[237]

---

[231] *Ibid.*
[232] *Ibid.* col. GC29.
[233] See also J. Palmer and G. Milner-Moore 'Derivative Actions: A Step Too Far?' available at XXXXXXX
[234] N. 55, col. GC30 (Lord Hodgson). This relates to the 'reflective loss' rule. Painting with a broad brush, this rule proscribes a shareholder from recovering for damage which is merely a reflection of the company's damage: *Prudential Assurance Co. Ltd* v *Newman Industries Ltd (No. 2)* [1982] 1 Ch 204, 222–3 followed or distinguished in various cases until it was reconsidered and endorsed by the House of Lords in *Johnson* v *Gore Wood* [2002] 2 AC 1.
[235] Hansard HL vol. 679 (Official Report) (27 February 2006) col. GC30.
[236] See Palmer and Milner-Moore, n. 183.
[237] *Ibid.*

With respect to the requirement to examine whether the member is acting in good faith in seeking to continue the claim (s. 263 (3) (a)), as explained elsewhere,[238] this is a problematic test. In most cases, the term 'good faith' functions as a rhetorical device rather than a substantive standard. It is an open-textured term, which operates as a speech-act, as opposed to a structured mode of analysis.[239] It is interesting that in considering whether to give permission (or leave) the court *must* take into account whether the member is acting in good faith in seeking to continue the claim.[240] It is likely that it must have more weight than the Law Commission accepted since it is impossible to countenance the court granting leave to an applicant exhibiting bad faith.[241] The Law Commission has deliberately decided that 'good faith' should not be defined in the rules of court, on the assumption that there is no great debate on this matter since the meaning of good faith is 'generally readily recognisable'. That may be true, but it lends itself to subjective interpretation and might lead to differences of opinion and hence to complexity of case law.[242] On the other hand, the Report does indicate that the Law Commission favours a test of whether the applicant is acting 'honestly' and 'without ulterior motive'.[243]

One final point should be made in relation to s. 263 (3) (f).[244] This is potentially an important criterion and an interesting addition. It ought to have received a more detailed evaluation during the Grand Committee Stage. The special majorities exception[245] gives rise to the possibility of bringing either a derivative claim or a personal action. Since personal actions are not covered by the derivative claim, a personal action, alleging that a special majority has not been obtained in breach of the so-called 'company's contract' (s. 14 of the Companies Act 1985 restated in s. 33 of the Companies Act 2006), can arguably still be pursued by an individual shareholder.[246]

---

[238] A. Reisberg 'Theoretical Reflections on Derivative Actions: The Representative Problem' (2006) 3 *European Company and Financial Law Review* 69, 101–103.

[239] S.J. Griffith 'Good Faith Business Judgment: A Theory of Rhetoric in Corporate Law Jurisprudence' (2005) 55 *Duke Law Journal* 1, http://ssrn.com/abstract=728431; B.R. Cheffins 'Reforming the Derivative Action: The Canadian Experience and British Prospects' [1997] 2 CFILR 227, 248 and the evidence therein. For an illuminating discussion on the duty of good faith in American corporate law in the context of directors' duties, see M.A. Eisenberg 'The Duty of Good Faith in American Corporate Law' (2006) 3 *European Company and Financial Law Review* 1.

[240] The Law Commission specifically considered that this should *not* be a prerequisite for leave as in Canada, but rather a relevant factor to be taken into account, so it must be of importance that this more strict approach was eventually preferred.

[241] Poole and Roberts n. 79, 107.

[242] Even the Consultation Paper, 163 admits that 'its express presence could encourage litigation as to its meaning in this context.' This point is well illustrated by Canadian case law. See B.R. Cheffins 'Reforming the Derivative Action: The Canadian Experience and British Prospects' [1997] 2 CFILR 227, 248 and the cases cited therein.

[243] It gives as an example a situation where the applicant would benefit financially from a successful derivative claim (and thus have an ulterior motive) but, if acting honestly, the court might still grant leave. Report, paras 6.75–6.76. It will be interesting to see whether this interpretation will be preferred under the more strict approach prevailing in s. 263 (3) (a).

[244] Which reads as follows: 'whether the act or omission in respect of which the claim is brought gives rise to a cause of action that the member could pursue in his own right rather than on behalf of the company.'

[245] n. 51.

[246] Report, paras 6.56–6.57.

## 5 *What is not there?*

Two arguably important omissions from Part 11 should be briefly highlighted. First, recall that the final criteria in the Report required that before granting leave the court should take account of any alternative remedy to that available in a derivative claim.[247] Whilst the Law Commission clearly has in mind the alternative of winding up,[248] this might also include the unfair prejudice remedy[249] since, in principle, a corporate remedy is obtainable if specifically sought. Although the availability of an alternative remedy is not conclusive on the issue of leave, if s. 994 were to be considered an alternative, it would mean that leave for the derivative claim might be refused and the applicant would have to start again by issuing a s. 994 petition.[250] Thankfully then, this factor is not contained in Part 11.[251]

Secondly, and regrettably, there is no mention of 'multiple' derivative claims.[252] However, the need to expose fraud and serious abuse in groups of companies would seem to require a more realistic approach. This means that the particular needs of groups of companies should be considered and catered for.[253] Indeed, Lord Millett in *Waddington Ltd v Chan Ho Thomas*,[254] a decision of the Final Appeal Court of Hong Kong, rightly opened the door for such actions and subsequent developments, discussed next, suggest that this is the way forward. First, it should be noted that the statutory provision made with regard to derivative claims by members has not, however, abolished the common law double, or multiple, derivative claim,.[255]

In *Universal Project Management Services Ltd v Fort Gilkicker Ltd & Ors* [2013] EWHC 348 (Ch) (26), the High Court had to decide whether common law recognises the concept of double derivative actions and if so, whether they survived the coming into force of the Companies Act 2006. The trial judge, Briggs J., observed at para. [26]:

> the common law procedural device called the derivative action was . . . clearly sufficiently flexible to accommodate as the legal champion or representative of a company in wrongdoer control a would-be claimant who was either (and usually) a member of that company or (exceptionally) a

---

[247] Draft Rule 50.7 (2) (f). See Report n. 2, Draft Rule on Derivative Claims Appendix B.

[248] Consultation Paper, para. 16.4.

[249] Under CA 1985 s. 459 restated in CA 2006 s. 994.

[250] *Barrett v Duckett* [1995] 1 BCLC 243.

[251] Although as will be seen below under 11.6, recent case law suggests that the court uses 263 (3) (f) to factor this in. Interestingly, the Law Society insisted that this additional general factor needed to be included in the list specified in s. 260 (3). See Parliamentary Brief of 25 May 2006, prepared for the Second Reading, House of Commons in June 2006, www.lawsociety.org.uk.

[252] An action by a shareholder of a parent company on behalf of a subsidiary is called a 'double' derivative action and, if on behalf of a 'second tier' subsidiary, it would be called a 'triple' derivative action. It is therefore easier to refer to all these actions as 'multiple' derivative actions. See Consultation Paper paras 9.9–9.13.

[253] See A. Reisberg n. 72, Chapter 5; A. Reisberg and D. Prentice 'Multiple Derivative Actions' (2009) 125 LQR 20. D. Lightman believes such actions can be brought under the Companies Act 2006; see 'Two Aspects of the Statutory Derivative Claim' [2011] LMCLQ 142.

[254] [2009] 2 BCLC 82, discussed in A. Reisberg and D. Prentice, *ibid.*

[255] See *Universal Project Management Services Ltd v Fort Gilkicker Ltd* [2013] EWHC 348 (Ch), [2013] Ch 551, [2013] 3 All ER 546 (adopting *Waddington Ltd v Chan Chun Hoo Thomas* [2008] HKCU 1381, [2009] 2 BCLC 82); applied in *Abouraya v Sigmund* [2014] EWHC 277 (Ch) at [12]–[14], [2014] All ER (D) 208 (Feb); *Bhullar v Bhullar* [2015] EWHC 1943 (Ch), 165 NLJ 7662, [2015] All ER (D) 130 (Jul). See also the Guernsey Royal Court (Ordinary Division) decision in March 2013 in *Jackson v Dear and others* (10/2013), in which the judge accepted that Guernsey customary law permitted the bringing of double derivative actions. This is believed to be the first derivative action placed on the court rôle of the Royal Court. See http://corporatelawandgovernance. blogspot.co.uk/search?q=Guernsey:+Royal+Court+considers+law+on+the+derivative+action.

member of its parent company where that parent company was in the same wrongdoer control. I would not describe that flexibility in terms of separate derivative action, whether headed 'ordinary', 'multiple' or 'double'. Rather it was a single piece of procedural ingenuity designed to serve the interests of justice in appropriate cases calling for the identification of an exception to the rule in *Foss* v *Harbottle*.

At paras. [44]–[46]:

I have come on balance to the conclusion that the 2006 Act did not do away with the multiple derivative action. My reasons follow. First, there was before 2006 a common law procedural device called the derivative action by which the court could permit a person or persons with the closest sufficient interest to litigate on behalf of a company by seeking for the company relief in respect of a cause of action vested in it. Those persons would usually be a minority of the company's members, but might, if the company was wholly owned by another company, be a minority of the holding company's members. These were not separate derivative actions, but simply examples of the efficient application of the procedural device, designed to avoid injustice, to different factual circumstances.

In 2006 Parliament identified the main version of that device, namely where *locus standi* is accorded to the wronged company's members, labelled it a 'derivative claim' and enacted a comprehensive statutory code in relation to it. As a matter of language, section 260 applied Chapter 1 of Part 11 only to that part of the old common law device thus labelled, leaving other instances of its application unaffected.

In *Bhullar* v *Bhullar*,[256] the High Court further underlined the rights of shareholders to challenge wrongdoing, regardless of the precise nature of the overall corporate structure. In deciding whether to grant permission to pursue a derivative claim the court will consider the strength of the case but will not resolve factual disputes. Having sufficient evidence even at an early stage of the proceedings is essential. It is also interesting to note that the courts tend to refuse permission to continue a derivative claim where an unfair prejudice petition is available;[257] Morgan J took the most pragmatic approach by preferring the course most likely to result in overall settlement.

In the light of the above case law, while Parliament has only codified the single derivative action, the Companies Act 2006 does *not* restrict multiple derivative actions, of which double derivative actions is a sub-species. Therefore, the latter continue to be available to shareholders when the shareholders themselves cannot take action for wrongs done to companies further down the chain. Whether or not one agrees with the court's analysis, it is clearly quite logical that derivative claims should be available to shareholders in those cases. Directors should be no more free to exploit subsidiaries for their own gain than to exploit holding companies. Otherwise, in the words of Lord Denning in *Wallersteiner*, 'Injustice would be done without redress'. If the judgment is followed, it would, presumably, by extension, permit derivative actions by members of corporate entities formed outside the UK in respect of directors of UK companies in which those entities hold shares. Depending on the precise circumstances, shareholders in a company that is deprived of a business opportunity may be able to pursue alternative claims against 'wrongdoing' directors in their own names for unfair prejudice under s. 994 of the Companies Act 2006.

---

[256] *Bhullar* v *Bhullar* [2015] EWHC 1943 (Ch).
[257] See, for instance, *Franbar Holdings* v *Patel* [2008] EWHC 1534 (Ch) and *Kleanthous* v *Paphitis* [2011] EWHC 2287 (Ch).

However, actions of this kind may be unnecessary where a more formal joint venture or shareholders' agreement governs what opportunities parties may and may not pursue on their own account. In those cases, ordinary contractual remedies should normally suffice. The *Bhullar* v *Bhullar* case is also of note as the court departed from the ordinary principle of making a pre-emptive order granting a costs indemnity to a claimant with permission to pursue a derivative action. Instead, as the derivative proceedings were viewed as a stepping stone towards the negotiation of a formal split or for an unfair prejudice petition, the court held that all parties should be on risk as to costs.

### F Shareholders' double derivative suits in other jurisdictions

In Japan, an amendment to the Companies Act came into effect in 2015. Until then, while a shareholder of a company could claim against the directors for any breach of directors' duties that resulted in damage to the company by way of a shareholders' derivative suit, shareholders of a parent company who were not also shareholders of its subsidiary had no redress against directors of the subsidiary even if the acts of the directors of the subsidiary resulted in damage to the whole corporate group. From 1 April 2015, a new cause of action called 'lawsuits for claims for specified liability' or the 'shareholders' double-derivative suit' allows shareholders holding 1% or more of outstanding shares in a parent company to bring an action against directors of its significant subsidiaries for any breach of directors' duties. It is expected that this additional category of potential claims will encourage directors to exercise their directors' duties with even greater diligence.[258] The procedure for shareholders' double-derivative suits is similar to the procedure for derivative suits.[259]

In the US, in *Sneed* v *Webre*,[260] the Texan Supreme Court concluded that a shareholder of a parent corporation, as the beneficial owner of the corporation's assets, has also equitable ownership of a subsidiary corporation and could maintain a double-derivative action on behalf of a subsidiary by virtue of his ownership in the parent corporation. 'Thus, in the closely held corporation context, the derivative plaintiff is not required to be a shareholder of the corporation he is bringing suit on behalf of, and the definition of a shareholder does not exclude those with a beneficial or equitable interest in a subsidiary.'[261] '[. . .] [O]therwise,

---

[258] A double-derivative suit may only be brought by shareholders who (i) are the only shareholders of a parent company, which owns all the shares in its subsidiary and is itself not a wholly-owned subsidiary of another company. Consequently, in the case of a multi-tiered companies group (e.g. parent – subsidiary – sub-subsidiary), only shareholders of the parent company at the top of the group may bring the suit; (ii) hold 1% or more of the voting rights of the ultimate parent company, or (iii) own 1% or more of the outstanding shares (excluding treasury shares) in the ultimate parent company; The suit may only be brought against directors of a significant subsidiary of a parent company, the value of which accounts for 20% or more of the total assets of the ultimate parent company as at the date of such act giving rise to liability by the director.

[259] In essence, the shareholder who intends to claim against a director of a subsidiary is first required to request that the target subsidiary bring a lawsuit against such director. If the subsidiary does not bring a lawsuit against the director within 60 days of the date of the request, such shareholder may then bring a shareholders' double-derivative suit on behalf of the subsidiary. As it is the case with current derivative suits, claims for improper purposes are prohibited. Also, shareholders may not bring a double-derivative suit if no damage is incurred by the ultimate parent company. The transfer by a parent company of shares in its subsidiary which account for 20% or more of the total assets of the parent company, as would be required in a business transfer, will now have to be approved by a special majority of shareholders at a shareholders' meeting.

[260] *Sneed* v *Webre*, No. 12–0045, 2015 WL 3451653 (Tex. 29 May 29,2015).

[261] *Ibid.*

the directors of a closely held holding corporation could create a wholly owned subsidiary to circumvent the Legislature's intent to make it easier for shareholders to assert derivative proceedings on behalf of closely held corporations.'[262]

## G Derivative claims in English limited partnerships

While the decision in *Henderson*[263] in 2012 does not present any new case law, it is a useful clarification of an area of law where cases are few and that many have previously considered uncertain. Mr Justice Cooke concluded that there was no room for a derivative claim on the part of the Limited Partners ('LPs') against the General Partner ('GP'). He found that a potential claim against the GP was that of the individual LPs and was not a partnership asset for the following reasons: first, each LP had its own contractual or fiduciary claim for its own loss. The GP could be sued by any LP in respect of its liabilities under the partnership agreement. Secondly, the partnership, which consisted of the LPs and GP together, had no form of joint right or claim against the GP. None of the provisions of the partnership agreement provided for the GP to be liable to the partnership as a whole, even if that was possible under the general law. The claim against the Managing Partner ('MP') was held to be a partnership asset and could not be pursued by any of the LPs individually. If the claim was to be pursued against the MP for breach of the duties governed by the management deed, either the GP had to sue in the name of the partnership, or be replaced by a new GP who would sue, or a derivative action had to be permitted. Having found that a derivative claim could be brought against the MP, the court then considered the potential liabilities that the LPs might incur in doing so. If the LPs pursued a derivative claim against the MP they would be acting in the management of the partnership business within s. 6(1) of theLimited Partnerships Act 1907 and liable accordingly.

## 11.5 An assessment of Part 11

Although it is still early days and one cannot predict with any degree of accuracy how things will develop (see the new case law discussed below under 11.6), the first interesting question is whether Part 11 provides an opportunity to harass company directors, a concern frequently raised in the Parliamentary debates. At one level, there should be no great change because the purpose of the reform is essentially procedural.[264] However, tucked away in the minutiae of the new framework are provisions that are capable of making some dramatic impact, for example by extending directors' exposure to risk.[265] Section 260 (3) suggests that a director can be made the subject of a derivative claim for acts of pure negligence,[266] and indeed this seems to be the intention here. It could be argued that the

---

[262] *Ibid.*

[263] *Henderson PFI Secondary Fund II LLP (a Firm) v (1) Henderson PFI Secondary Fund II LP (a Firm) (2) Henderson Equity Partners Limited (3) Henderson Equity Partners (GP) Limited* [2012] EWHC 3259 (Comm).

[264] Milman n. 130, 2.

[265] *Ibid.*

[266] Recall that at common law a director cannot be made the subject of a derivative action for acts of pure negligence. What is required at common law is negligence coupled with some other element such as personal profit accruing to the alleged wrongdoer: *Pavlides v Jensen* [1956] Ch 565, *cf Daniels v Daniels* [1978] Ch 406.

opening up of derivative claims, by reason of s. 260 (3), is a potentially beneficial development in terms of general corporate accountability on the grounds that it holds out the possibility of greater levels of enforcement of directors' duties, especially breaches of their duty of care, excluded from the scope of the common law derivative action.[267] On the other hand, this very fact may serve as a disincentive to men and women of quality and experience to serve on the boards of public companies. Potentially, in extending the conduct in respect of which shareholders can complain, there is a risk that the new provisions may be abused by disgruntled or activist shareholders.[268] In turn, this could lead to a rise in directors' and officers' (D&O) premiums.[269]

In addition to the possibility of claims for negligence, the ability to claim for breach of duty would allow a shareholder to bring a claim for breach of any of the new general statutory duties as well as regulatory obligations, such as environmental or health and safety obligations, of which there are many. Potentially, shareholders in quoted companies could bring claims for matters such as breaches of the listing rules or the disclosure rules.[270] The new statutory right might provide another tool for use by activist shareholders to push for change at under-performing companies. If it does, then some may argue that this cannot be in the interests of UK plcs.[271] Whether the potential for extending directors' exposure to risk will be realised will depend, to a large extent, on how the courts discharge the wide discretion entrusted to them. We are of the view that members who buy shares simply in order to bring derivative claims will find a hostile judiciary. A complex body of case law has developed regarding the limits of the derivative claim.[272] These precedents are not at all favourable towards shareholders taking an action on behalf of the company. This is problematic, because if it is the case that the Government's intention is not just to put such actions on a statutory footing but also to remove many of the barriers to appropriate cases being brought, the danger might be that in the absence of a more substantial codification and clarification of the regime, the discretion afforded to the courts may continue to impose the same barriers to derivative claims as previously existed.

There is also a concern with the breadth of this discretion. For example, the process is likely, in practice, to involve consideration of the merits of the underlying claim even though the applicant has not yet been given the right to proceed.[273] The danger must be that the judiciary will adopt an overly restrictive approach to Part 11 in order to give effect to

---

[267] *Pavlides* v *Jensen* n. 257, *cf Daniels* v *Daniels* [1978] Ch 406.

[268] Although it should be remembered that even activist shareholders are still likely to be discouraged from bringing such claims by the fact that any damages recovered will go to the company, and not the shareholder personally. See discussion on the financial problems in A. Reisberg n. 72, Chapters 6 and 7 and 'Derivative Actions and the Funding Problem: The Way Forward' (2006) *Journal of Business Law* 445.

[269] It seems likely that insurers would seek to increase rates as the derivative claim could, in theory at least, increase the scope of negligence claims.

[270] In any event, it would be wise for companies to review the wording of their D&O insurance policies to ensure that defending derivative claims is covered.

[271] Hansard HL vol. 681, col. GC886 (9 May 2006) (Lord Hodgson).

[272] Recall that the Law Commission formed the view that the law in this area is inflexible and outmoded. Consultation Paper, para. 14.1.

[273] Thus reintroducing in the back door all the concerns raised by the Law Commission with respect to the common law (that standing has to be established as a preliminary issue by evidence which shows a *prima facie* case on the merits). Without effective case management, however, this can result in a mini-trial which increases the length and cost of the litigation: Consultation Paper, para. 14.1.

the perceived exceptional nature of derivative claims.[274] And as will be seen below under 11.6, this is precisely what is already happening. Therefore, the true test of the effectiveness of this action will be whether the complexity surrounding the ability to pursue a derivative claim will continue to act as a deterrent to potential actions when compared with the broad scope of s. 994.[275]

Furthermore, the Law Commission itself evidently approves of the policies which underline the former restrictive standing rules for individual shareholders.[276] The Government argued that the new legislation does not result in a major change in the law.[277] It insisted that the new provisions provide sufficient safeguards against the development of a litigation culture, as the aim was to prevent a pressure-group level of litigation against particular companies.[278] It is indeed unlikely that the change will significantly affect the number of cases brought.[279] The number of such cases is low and the impact on the courts likely to be negligible.[280] Although focusing on the infrequency of proceedings may portray an overall misleading picture,[281] this may, nonetheless, have a chilling effect on the judiciary. The problem remains that if the courts simply transfer those policies from the common law to their interpretation of the discretion conferred upon them,[282] then the changes brought about by the reform will be very limited indeed.[283] Likewise, if the courts are effective in weeding out cases where the derivative claim is brought to further the personal interests of the individual shareholder, one may wonder what incentive the shareholder will have to seek the court's leave to sue on behalf of the company.[284]

---

[274] As was apparent during the Standing Committee Stage, it is the view of many law firms that the form of Part 11 does not address concerns about the court having an unlimited discretion in deciding whether to allow derivative claims to proceed.

[275] Formerly Companies Act 1985 s. 459. It may also be the case that unless the derivative claim is seen as the only way to achieve the desired remedy, the procedure and potential hurdles in the way of applicants will deter most potential derivative actions. See 11.6 below.

[276] The Report is quite telling: 'We do not accept that the proposals will make significant changes to the availability of the action. In some respects, the availability may be slightly wider; in others it may be slightly narrower. But in all cases the new procedure will be subject to tight judicial control' (para. 6.13).

[277] Secretary of State for Trade and Industry, 'Letter to the Editor', *Financial Times* (London, 9 November 2005): 'It should not give rise to concern on the part of the millions of directors in this country who have high standards of conduct and make such an important contribution to Britain's economy.' This view was followed through in Committee when he said: 'I can say now that we do not see any reason why those provisions should increase litigation' Hansard HL vol. 679 (Official Report) (27 February 2006) col GC2.

[278] Hansard HL vol. 450 (Official Report) (17 October 2006) col. 832 (the Solicitor-General).

[279] The recent experience in Australia may shed some light on this. Although based on a different leave criteria (and thus direct comparison is hard) the statutory derivative action has yielded only 31 cases in the period between March 2000 (when it was introduced) and August 2005, a modest number by any estimate. More important, the statutory derivative action is not resulting in a greater number of judgments than the common law derivative action which it replaced when a similar period of years is examined (1995–9 for *Foss* v *Harbottle*). I. Ramsay and B. Saunders 'Litigation by Shareholders and Directors: An Empirical Study of the Statutory Derivative Action' (2006) 6 JCLS 397, 417.

[280] The Government's Regulatory Impact Assessment published in November 2005 together with the Company Law Reform Bill state that the number of occasions on which these sections are used, and hence the direct financial benefit of clarifying them, is small.

[281] For a number of reasons, it is not necessarily a flaw that few cases brought under the derivative action jurisdiction as this is in line with the very nature of the derivative action. See Reisberg n. 72, Chapter 5.

[282] And this seems to have already happened (below, under 11.6). Recall that the court is reminded it 'must dismiss the application' (or that 'permission (or leave) must be refused') no less than *four* times in ss. 261–264.

[283] P.L. Davies *Introduction to Company Law* (Oxford: Oxford University Press, 2002) 250–251.

[284] The company may be ordered to pay the costs of the litigation but that does not in itself produce a positive incentive to sue. If the individual has only a small shareholding in the company, that may not act as a big enough positive incentive either. See A. Reisberg n. 72, Chapter 6.

This means that the success of any replacement to the common law action would best be judged *not* by the quantity of the case law generated under the new procedure, but by whether the rules governing the circumstances in which such an action may be brought are made more *comprehensible* and *accessible* so that, in exceptional circumstances, the commencement of a derivative claim will be regarded as a remedy worth pursuing instead of being ruled out at an early stage of a dispute as being far too difficult even to contemplate.[285] And on this account, the new procedure fails miserably. A major flaw in the new procedure is that although the Government has tried to put to rest some old (and troubling) demons,[286] it has not pursued this policy all the way through. One salient example is the difficulties associated with ratification. At first blush, the current bar to derivative claims for ratifiable wrongs may be diluted because the possibilities for ratification have been tightened up by s. 239, which prohibits self-interested members from participating in the ratification vote,[287] thereby undermining old case law.[288] However, as explained above,[289] cases where the wrong in question has been ratified will be surrounded with established arguments relating to whether the ratification is valid since s. 263 clearly suggests that leave should not be granted if the wrong has been ratified. This means that in many instances the effectiveness of a purported ratification will dominate the hearing for leave and it is therefore unlikely to result in change of emphasis in favour of a broad judicial discretion. This is a difficult and controversial issue, which is unlikely to be resolved with the new procedure.

Another obstacle can be found in s. 263 (4), which is exclusively directed at an important point of procedure.[290] However, in light of past experience, this might subsequently require some amendment or revision without the need to return to primary legislation, with all the complications and expense associated with it. Indeed, in the areas where 'leave must be refused', practitioners may be concerned that it will be some years before one quite knows how s. 263 will work.[291]

It appears that the success of the new procedure may also depend upon the precise parameters of directors' duties under the new regime. Most of the uncertainty surrounds

---

[285] See 11.3 above. See also S. Deakin, E. Ferran and R. Nolan 'Shareholders' Rights and Remedies: An Overview' [1997] 2 CFILR 162, 165.

[286] The claimant does not need to show 'wrongdoer control' – that is, to show that the company is controlled by the directors whom the claimant believes to have acted in breach of their duties – as that might make it impossible for a derivative claim to be brought successfully by a member of a widely-held company, including almost all major quoted companies. That said, there is some recent authority to suggest that the Companies Act 2006 preserves the need to show 'wrongdoers' control,'12 although there is no such requirement under Part 11. See *Cinematic Finance Ltd* v *Ryder* [2012] BCC 797, [2010] All ER (D) 283 (Oct). See also *Bamford* v *Harvey* [2012] EWHC 2858 (Ch), [2013] Bus LR 590, [2012] All ER (D) 182 (Oct).

[287] This section preserves the previous law on the ratification of acts of directors, but with one significant change. Any decision by a company to ratify conduct by a director amounting to negligence, default, breach of duty or breach of trust in relation to the company must be taken by the members, and without reliance on the votes of those members with a personal interest in the ratification.

[288] *North-West Transportation Co Ltd* v *Beatty* (1887) 12 App. Cas. 589.

[289] See 11.4 above.

[290] See 11.4 above.

[291] Hansard HL vol. 681, col. GC889 (9 May 2006) (Lord Hodgson). Of course, this is the case with any new legislation.

the exact scope of s. 172 (duty to promote the success of the company) and it is apparent that it will take some time until its precise scope will be clarified in practice.[292] But even if duties of directors are sufficiently clarified, as the new legislation does not replicate existing case law, a body of case law will be slow to develop. Although of persuasive nature, the previous rules in *Foss* and other cases will not be directly relevant in determining whether the provisions of the legislation have been applied.[293] That will create uncertainty for some period as to the extent of the provisions, and the burden of that will largely fall on the company. Although the effect of this statutory form of derivative claim has probably been exaggerated, there is little doubt that there is more potential for *tactical proceedings* to be brought by shareholders against an incumbent board, and faith must therefore be placed in the willingness of the courts to exercise restraint in stifling such claims at an early stage. Furthermore, if cases pass the initial scrutiny (i.e. the need to show a *prima facie* case at the first stage) one may wonder what would be the effect of this on the company's reputation,[294] or whether passing this first stage would not by itself provide shareholders with a potent weapon.[295]

A related difficulty is illustrated by the Canadian experience, namely, that the derivative claim will be perceived as the more procedurally complex and less favourable form of action without some limit being placed upon the *scope* of the unfairly prejudicial conduct action.[296] Regrettably, there is also no mention of 'multiple' derivative claims in Part 11. However, the need to expose fraud and serious abuse in groups of companies would seem

---

[292] *Annotated Companies Acts* (Oxford University Press, looseleaf) under 10.172.01–08. See J. Lowry 'The Duty of Loyalty of Company Directors: Bridging the Accountability Gap Through Efficient Disclosure' [2009] CLJ 607.

[293] Although the courts will still be referring to it, and the Government indeed reaffirmed the purpose behind the rule in *Foss* which it did not in any way seek to repeal: 'The sections in Part 11 *do not* (emphasis added) formulate a substantive rule to replace the rule in *Foss* v *Harbottle*, but rather a new procedure for bringing such an action which set down criteria for the court distilled from the *Foss* v *Harbottle* jurisprudence.' Explanatory Notes on the Companies Act 2006, para. 491. However, there is no direct reference to the rule in the new legislation nor does the statute state its purpose. The problem with such an approach is obvious: if the old rule still permeates the new rule, will there ever be an effective change?

[294] E.g. if a claim passes the first stage, the media may be quick to report on the legal proceedings against the company, detrimentally affecting the company's share price and/or future prospects. See A. Reisberg n. 72, 47–50.

[295] A somewhat overlooked benefit of the deterrence aspect of the derivative action relates to the impact it may have internally on the company subject to the litigation. US case law has recognised that when the derivative action is dismissed (for whatever reason), the claimant may have nonetheless conferred a benefit on the company. Such a benefit can arise when internal remedies or reforms are instituted following the litigation. This may include the departure of key personnel who may have been involved in alleged wrongdoing, or structural reforms such as non-cosmetic organisational reform, provision for a review of compensation practices, or modifications of compensation plans. See discussion in Reisberg n. 72, 189–91. If so, it is reasonable to expect an enhanced opportunity to launch derivative claims, even if the chances of passing the second stage are slim.

[296] This is the position despite the fact that shareholders bringing such action face potential liability for costs. See A. Reisberg *ibid.* Chapter 8 (where the inter-relationship and interaction between the remedy of unfair prejudice and the derivative action is examined) and B.R. Cheffins 'Reforming the Derivative Action: The Canadian Experience and British Prospects' [1997] 2 CFILR 227, 259; B.R. Cheffins and J. Dine 'Shareholder Remedies: Lessons from Canada' (1992) 13 *Company Lawyer* 89; J.G. MacIntosh 'The Oppression Remedy: Personal or Derivative?' (1991) 70 *Canada Bar Review* 29. This appears to be at variance with the experience in Australia. See Ramsay and Saunders n. 270, Table 8.

to require a more realistic approach. This means that the particular needs of groups of companies should be considered and catered for.[297]

Another critical issue that will determine the accessibility of the new procedure is access to information. Given the difficulty of obtaining, in advance of litigation, adequate evidence to support alleged wrongdoing (even where this is strongly suspected), the effort to streamline litigation must address the thorny issue of disclosure and information asymmetries between management and shareholders, or between large and small shareholders.[298] Time will tell whether the powers granted to the court under s. 261 (3) will be enough in this respect.[299] Current case law generally confers on shareholders scant corporate rights to 'internal' company documents[300] so it will be interesting to watch whether this provision will provide a point for departure from this or whether litigants will still face up to the traditional suspicion of the English courts towards derivative claims.

## 11.6 The new derivative claim procedure in action: shadows of the past?

Since the new derivative claim procedure became operative in October 2007, it has been considered by a number of cases. But, as will be seen in this section, two underlying themes seem to characterise the early stream of cases. First, although the cases shed some light on the new procedure, in many respects, they actually confuse rather than clarify the operation of the new procedure. Secondly, litigants must still face up to the traditional suspicion of the English courts towards such claims, albeit this time courts are 'armed' with a very restrictive legislation to 'justify' their attitudes. Regrettably then, shadows from the common law derivative action seem to be still very much present and alive in the way in which the courts have been, to date, stifling the operation of Part 11.

An early demonstration of the new statutory procedure in action was provided in *Mission Capital plc* v *Sinclair*,[301] where the two-stage permission procedure set out in s. 261 and s. 262 was put to the test. Mission Capital plc had two executive directors, Mr Ronald Sinclair and his daughter, Emma. They were in a minority on the board of the company, there being three non-executive directors. The contracts under which the Sinclairs were employed contained a provision which allowed the board to terminate their employment with immediate effect if they engaged in conduct that was unacceptable in the reasonable opinion of the board. At a board meeting the board purported to terminate their employment on the basis of such alleged conduct. The company sought injunctive relief to exclude the Sinclairs from the company's premises and to deliver up certain documents. The Sinclairs countered this by challenging the decision to terminate their employment,

---

[297] See Reisberg n. 72, Chapter 5; A. Reisberg and D. Prentice 'Multiple Derivative Actions' (2009) 125 LQR 20. Lightman, in a minority view, believes such actions can be brought under the Companies Act 2006. See, D. Lightman 'Two aspects of the Statutory Derivative Claim' [2011] LMCLQ 142.

[298] See 11.4D 1 above.

[299] Under s. 261 (3) if the application is not dismissed under sub-section (2), the court may give directions as to the evidence to be provided by the company, and may adjourn the proceedings pending this evidence.

[300] See cases cited at n. 150.

[301] [2008] EWHC 1339 (Ch).

disputing the allegations of improper conduct. They also sought permission of the Court to bring a derivative claim on behalf of the company against the non-executive directors, the newly appointed executive director and the company. The Companies Act 2006, as explained above, provides for a two-stage process in relation to permission. The first stage is where the Court considers on paper whether there is a *prima facie* case for permission to be given,[302] leading to a second stage hearing on notice to the company, if the Court concludes at the first stage that the matter can go forward.[303] Interestingly, in this case, however, the parties agreed to combine the two parts of the process. The judge refused permission to pursue the derivative claim on the basis of two of the above factors. First, he felt that a notional director, promoting the success of the company (under s. 172), would not attach much importance to continuing the action. Second, he was not satisfied that there was anything that the Sinclairs were seeking which could not be recovered by means of a Section 994 unfair prejudice petition.[304] In this case, the two-stage filter process (combined, here, into a single stage therefore demonstrating flexibility in this area) worked to prevent the claim from moving forward. It will be interesting to see whether this is a general trend such that the Attorney General's prediction that the new statutory procedure would not open the floodgates will prove to be accurate.[305]

The second interesting case to shed some light on the operation of the statutory derivative claim is *Franbar Holdings Ltd* v *Patel and others*.[306] Like *Sinclair*, it provides some insights concerning the relationship between the new statutory derivative claim and the unfair prejudice remedy in s. 994. Recall that s. 263 (3)[307] specifies several factors to be considered when determining whether permission should be given, including under (f): 'whether the act or omission in respect of which the claim is brought gives rise to a cause of action that the member could pursue in his own right rather than on behalf of the company.' The trial judge observed that where an act or omission gives rise to a claim for unfair prejudice under s. 994 against a member and a claim for breach of duty against a director, s. 263 (3) (f) is engaged. He also held that the adequacy of the remedy in (f) was a relevant consideration. It was decided that permission should not be given for the derivative claim to proceed. Although he found that there was substance in some of the complaints made, further work was needed to establish a clear claim of breach of duty. For this reason it was open to a hypothetical director to decline to proceed with the derivative claim. Most important, the judge attached significant weight to the fact that the shareholder bringing the derivative claim would be able to gain what it wanted through its separate Section 994 petition and shareholder claim. For the reasons mentioned above,[308] this is unfortunate.

*Franbar* also provides some clarification with respect to the operation of s. 263 (2) and the difficult issue of ratification, In *Franbar*, the judge had before him several applications

---

[302] Section 261 (1). On s. 260 (3) and s. 261 see also *Langley Ward Ltd.* v. *Trevor* [2011] ALL ER (D) 78 (Jul).
[303] Section 262.
[304] Section 994 is discussed in Chapter 12.
[305] Note 267 above.
[306] [2008] EWHC 1534 (Ch). This was not a full trial of the various claims, but the trial judge's decision (William Trower QC, sitting as a Deputy Judge of the High Court) merits close attention.
[307] See 11.4 above.
[308] Under 11.4 above.

including a petition under s. 994 and an application to continue a derivative claim. Recall that s. 263 (2)[309] provides that permission must be refused if the court is satisfied:

(a) that a person acting in accordance with s. 172 (duty to promote the success of the company) would not seek to continue the claim, **or**
(b) where the cause of action arises from an act or omission that is yet to occur, that the act or omission has been authorised by the company, **or**
(c) where the cause of action arises from an act or omission that has already occurred, that the act or omission – (i) was authorised by the company before it occurred, or (ii) has been ratified by the company since it occurred.

The judge did not consider sub-section (b) as the allegations concerned past conduct. With respect to sub-section (a), referring to the duty imposed on company directors under s. 172, the trial judge identified several factors which the hypothetical director would take into account including the prospects of success, the disruption which would result if the proceedings continued, the cost of the proceedings and damage to the company's reputation and business if the action failed. This provides a useful guidance for future cases. With regard to sub-section (c), namely, authorisation or ratification, the trial judge considered s. 239 which governs ratification by the shareholders of a director's acts. Section 239 provides that a resolution proposed at a meeting will only be passed if the necessary majority is obtained excluding the votes of the director (if a shareholder) and any shareholder connected with him. It was argued that s. 239 had replaced the principle that directors' acts cannot be ratified where they constitute a fraud on the minority and the wrongdoers are in control of the company. The trial judge rejected this argument, relying upon s. 239 (7) which provides that the framework for ratification in s. 239 'does not affect any other enactment or rule of law imposing additional requirements for valid ratification or any rule of law as to acts that are incapable of being ratified by the company'.[310] In the judge's words:[311]

> [. . .] the [following] words of Sir Richard Baggalay [. . .] in *North-West Transportation* v *Beatty* (1887) 12 App Cas 589, 594, describing the circumstances in which a company cannot ratify breaches of duty by its directors, remain good law:
> '[. . .]provided such affirmance or adoption is not brought about by unfair or improper means, and is not illegal or fraudulent or oppressive towards those shareholders who oppose it.'

It follows that, where the question of ratification arises in the context of an application to continue a derivative claim, the question which the court must still ask itself is whether the ratification has the effect that the claimant is being improperly prevented from bringing the claim on behalf of the company [. . .]That may still be the case where the new connected person provisions are not satisfied, but there is still actual wrongdoer control pursuant to which there has been a diversion of assets to persons associated with the wrongdoer, albeit

---

[309] See 11.4 above.
[310] Indeed, there is some recent authority to suggest that the Companies Act 2006 preserves the need to show 'wrongdoers' control', although, as explained above, there is no such requirement under Part 11. See *Cinematic Finance Ltd* v *Ryder* [2012] BCC 797, [2010] All ER (D) 283 (Oct). See also *Bamford* v *Harvey* [2012] EWHC 2858 (Ch), [2013] Bus LR 590, [2012] All ER (D) 182 (Oct) and below.
[311] *Ibid.* at para. [45].

not connected in the sense for which provision is made by section 239 (4). In *Bamford* v *Harvey*,[312] Roth J accepted that wrongdoer control is not an absolute condition for a derivative claim, and decided to follow the Scottish decision in *Wishart* v *Castlecroft Securities*,[313] stating that it was clearly desirable that the interpretation of the statutory provisions (or their equivalents) should be the same in England as in Scotland, but went on to state that he did not see anything in *Wishart* to suggest that the potential for the company itself to commence proceedings is not a relevant consideration in the exercise of the court's discretion.

An even stricter approach than that taken by the court in *Franbar Holding* to the standard to be applied generally under s. 263 (the first stage) was subsequently delivered in *Iesini* v *Westrip Holdings Ltd*.[314] Lewison J held that something more than simply a *prima facie* case that the company has a good cause of action and that it arose out of a director's breach must be needed since that forms the first stage of the procedure and that while it would be wrong to embark on a mini-trial, the court must form a view on the strength of the claim, albeit on a provisional basis.[315] That may have been true under the common law (namely, the decision of the Court of Appeal in *Prudential Assurance Co. Ltd* v *Newman Industries Ltd*,[316] but later, the Scottish court in *Wishart*[317] correctly observed that Lewison J had adopted a wrong approach to the matter.

On a more positive side, Lewison J usefully noted some of the factors which a director, acting in accordance with s. 172, would take into account in reaching his or her decision:[318]

> They include: the size of the claim; the strength of the claim; the cost of the proceedings; the company's ability to fund the proceedings; the ability of the potential defendants to satisfy a judgment; the impact on the company if it lost the claim and had to pay not only its own costs but the defendant's as well; any disruption to the company's activities while the claim is pursued; whether the prosecution of the claim would damage the company in other ways (e.g. by losing the services of a valuable employee or alienating a key supplier or customer) and so on. The weighing of all these considerations is essentially a commercial decision, which the court is ill-equipped to take, except in a clear case.

Lewison J also held that the mandatory bar in s. 263 (2) (a) will apply 'only where the court is satisfied that *no* director acting in accordance with section 172 would seek to continue the claim. If some directors would, and others would not, seek to continue the claim the case is one for the application of section 263 (3) (b). Many of the same considerations would apply to that paragraph too.'[319]

In the fourth consecutive case in which permission was refused, *Stimpson* v *Southern Landlords Association*,[320] the applicant's motives played a deciding factor in not granting leave. HHJ Pelling QC found that the claimant had brought the action in order to retain control of the company and because he did not want it to lose its identity through a merger.

[312] [2012] EWHC 2858 (Ch).
[313] [2009] CSIH 65.
[314] [2009] EWHC 2526 (Ch).
[315] *Ibid.* at [79].
[316] [1982] Ch. 204.
[317] *Wishart* v *Castlecroft Securities Ltd* [2009] CSIH 65.
[318] [2009] EWHC 2526 (Ch) at [85].
[319] *Ibid.* at [86], followed later in *Stainer* v *Lee* [2010] EWHC 1539 (Ch).
[320] [2009] EWHC 2072 (Ch).

As rightly noted,[321] at common law, using the derivative action for the first purpose demonstrated a lack of good faith.[322] Confusingly, however, the judge was not prepared to rule clearly on whether this motive did go to good faith.[323] He considered this unnecessary since the list of factors contained in s. 263 (3) were not exhaustive, and it was open to the courts to take account of other factors.[324] While it is true that it cannot be helpful to allow the factors which the courts will take into account in deciding whether to grant permission to proliferate unnecessarily[325] (this can prolong proceedings, create uncertainty and result in the unprincipled development of the jurisdiction), the list of factors contained in s. 263 (3) are clearly not exhaustive (the words 'in particular' suggest that there may well be other factors not listed in the provision that are relevant).

So far, we have seen that the first four cases continue to reflect the stance established by the case law predating the Companies Act 2006. No surprise then that in all four permission was refused under the Part 11 procedure. However, in the next couple of cases the courts adopted a less stringent approach. First, in *Kiani* v *Cooper*,[326] permission was granted, although limited to continuing the claim down to disclosure. The application by Kiani, K, both a director and shareholder of the company, was founded upon allegations of breaches of fiduciary duty by Cooper, C, his co-director and shareholder in the company. K also sought to restrain the presentation of winding up petitions threatened by C and the third defendant, DPM Property Services Ltd ('DPM'), a company in which C was both a director and the majority shareholder. Proudman J, examining the framing of s. 263 (3), noted as key factors the requirement of good faith, the availability of an alternative remedy, and, in particular, the attitude of a person acting in accordance with the duties imposed by s. 172 of the Companies Act 2006. The judge drew upon Lewison J's detailed consideration of the statutory procedure in *Lesini* v *Westrip Holdings Ltd*[327] (recall that Lewison J observed that there are a range of factors that a director, acting in accordance with s. 172, would consider in reaching his decision, in particular, the importance of the derivative action being based on an act or omission involving negligence, default or breach of duty by a director. As the directors had followed the advice of eminent professionals, the judge considered that they had not been negligent or breached their duties. The strength of the claim against the board was so weak that no director, acting in accordance with s. 172, would pursue the claim). Proudman J found that K was acting in good faith and that a notional director acting in accordance with his duties under s. 172 would pursue the action given the strength of the evidence in favour of the case advanced by K. Turning to the availability of an alternative remedy, i.e. the argument that an unfair prejudice petition was the appropriate redress available to K, the judge thought this was only one of the factors to be taken into account and as such it was not to be regarded as determinative of the issue.

---

[321] A. Keay and J. Loughrey 'Derivative Proceedings in a Brave New World for Company Management and Shareholders' (2010) 3 *Journal of Business Law* 151, 168.
[322] *Konamaneni* v *Rolls-Royce Industrial Power (India) Ltd* [2002] 1 WLR 1269 Ch D.
[323] *Ibid.*
[324] *Ibid.*
[325] A. Keay and J. Loughrey 'Derivative Proceedings in a Brave New World for Company Management and Shareholders' (2010) 3 *Journal of Business Law* 151, 168.
[326] [2010] EWHC 577 (Ch).
[327] *Iesini* v *Westrip Holdings Ltd* [2009] EWHC 2526 (Ch).

Then in June 2010, the court in *Stainer* v *Lee*[328] granted permission to continue a derivative action, subject to various conditions, including one relating to costs. The permission given was limited to the conclusion of disclosure on the basis that by that stage, the facts and strength of the case would be much clearer. With respect to s. 263, the trial judge made some interesting observations:

> I consider that section 263 (3) and (4) do not prescribe a particular standard of proof that has to be satisfied but rather require consideration of a range of factors to reach an overall view. In particular, under section 263 (3) (b), as regards the hypothetical director acting in accordance with the section 172 duty, if the case seems very strong, it may be appropriate to continue it even if the likely level of recovery is not so large, since such a claim stands a good chance of provoking an early settlement or may indeed qualify for summary judgment. On the other hand, it may be in the interests of the Company to continue even a less strong case if the amount of potential recovery is very large.[329]

And in relation to the claimant's costs, the judge observed:

> The Applicant seeks an indemnity for his costs, relying on *Wallersteiner* v *Moir (No. 2)* . . . I think that is clear authority that a shareholder who receives the sanction of the court to proceed with a derivative action should normally be indemnified as to his reasonable costs by the company for the benefit of which the action would accrue. But where the amount of likely recovery is presently uncertain, there is concern that his costs could become disproportionate. Accordingly, I place a ceiling on the costs for which I grant an indemnity for the future . . . There will be liberty to apply to extend the scope of that indemnity.[330]

But if one thought that hope is on the horizon and some order has been restored, the decision in *Cinematic Finance Ltd* v *Ryder and Others*[331] quickly cast that aside. The case, in which permission to continue with the derivative claims was refused, provides a further illustration of the cautious approach being taken by the courts towards the new regime. Cinematic Finance ('CF') Ltd granted loans to several investment companies. When these were not repaid, CF Ltd took recourse and became the sole and majority shareholder of those companies. It sought permission to pursue a derivative action against the former directors of the investment companies for alleged breaches of their fiduciary duties. At the time, CF Ltd was having difficulties gaining access to the companies' books and records, but had not disclosed to the court that it was the sole and majority shareholder. The court held that as the sole and majority shareholder of the investment companies, CF Ltd had complete control over them and so a derivative action was neither necessary nor appropriate. Although the court did not go so far as to say that permission would never be granted to a majority shareholder, it confirmed that permission would only be granted in exceptional circumstances. However, it is difficult to envisage what such exceptional circumstances might be, since a majority shareholder has control of the company and so should be able to either ensure that the company itself pursues the action, or remove the directors who are refusing to act on the majority shareholder's instructions to do so.

---

[328] [2010] EWHC 1539 (Ch).
[329] At [29]. See also *Kleanthous* v *Paphitis* [2011] EWHC 2287 (CL).
[330] At [56].
[331] [2010] EWC 3387 (Ch).

While this may be of little significance in practice, more troubling was the fact that the court insisted that the new statutory code in the 2006 Act preserved the existing law relating to the need to show 'wrongdoer control'. As the court explained, although s. 263 (2) did not state that permission was to be refused where the applicant had *control* of the company, it would only be in exceptional circumstances that such an application would be allowed to continue. The instant circumstances were not viewed as exceptional.[332] But as we explained above,[333] the Government did not want the claimant to have to show 'wrongdoer control', because that may make it impossible for a derivative claim to be brought successfully by a member of a widely-held company. So, one may wonder, why has it resurfaced, and why is it to be brought to bear albeit via the back door?

## 11.7 The future of derivative claims: much ado about nothing?

There is no denying the fact that the new statutory restatement of the derivative claim broadens the circumstances in which, at least in theory, it may be brought. In practice, however, it may be doubted whether this will result in any significant extension of the circumstances in which such claims are allowed. Concerns that this would fuel the development of US-style litigation have proven, so far, to be far off the mark. A number of reasons combine to ensure that this may continue to be the case. First, the courts still retain a wide discretion over whether a derivative claim may proceed. Litigants must therefore still face up to the traditional suspicion of the English judges towards such claims, although this time the courts are 'armed' with a very restrictive legislative regime to 'justify' their restrictive attitudes.[334] The early case law on the new procedure considered above suggests this is already happening. Not only have the cases to date not been clear or consistent regarding what exactly the first and the second stage of the process requires, but taken together, they also appear to set the bar far higher than would have been envisaged.[335] Secondly, permission to continue a derivative claim will in any event be refused in respect of a claim against a director based upon an act or omission that could be authorised or ratified by the company. In practice, this is likely to exclude the possibility of such claims in respect of ordinary negligence by directors. Thirdly, the issue of availability of an alternative remedy continues to form a dark cloud over the future of derivative claims. For example, although Proudman J in *Kiani* permitted the continuation of the derivative claim notwithstanding the fact that it was possible for an unfair prejudice petition to be presented by the shareholder (clearly a correct interpretation of the language of Part 11), the decisions in *Franbar* and *Iesini* seem to make the availability of an alternative remedy a compelling reason for withholding permission. This is so notwithstanding that in the latter case Lewison J did say that the existence of an alternative remedy was not an

---

[332] The court concluded that evidence indicated that one of the principal reasons for the use of a derivative action procedure was to save the cost of pursuing the remedy through the insolvency procedure. That was not a sufficient reason to allow a derivative action to proceed.

[333] See above under 11.4.

[334] Recall that the court is reminded it 'must dismiss the application' (or that 'leave must be refused') no less than *four* times in ss. 261–264.

[335] See also A. Keay and J. Loughrey 'Derivative Proceedings in a Brave New World for Company Management and Shareholders' (2010) 3 JBL 151 at p. 156.

absolute bar to permission being granted. Finally, and most importantly, the practicalities of financing shareholder litigation will remain a major obstacle. There is nothing in the new procedure that will convince a rational shareholder he will be better off litigating the case on behalf of the company rather than selling his shares.[336] Regrettably, the common law position on costs of derivative claims has not changed.[337] Costs and fees rules need to be re-evaluated if any real change is to occur.[338] In the final analysis, whether the preference in Part 11 of the Companies Act 2006 for detailed and largely inaccessible criteria supported by wide discretion provided to the judiciary strikes the right balance between managerial freedom and investor protection is seriously open to question. Since the introduction of the statutory regime, most particularly in recent years, the courts have sought to limit statutory derivative claims or at least keep them within measured bounds. For instance, in the light of the cases reported in this chapter, the courts are unlikely to grant permission to continue a derivative claim where there is an alternative, typically an unfair prejudice petition. Derivative claims are therefore proving to be a remedy of last resource.

## Further reading

A. Reisberg *Derivative Actions and Corporate Governance: Theory & Operation* (Oxford: OUP, 2007).

A. Reisberg and D. Prentice 'Multiple Derivative Actions' (2009) 125 *LQR* 20.

J. Lowry 'The Duty of Loyalty of Company Directors: Bridging the Accountability Gap Through Efficient Disclosure' [2009] *CLJ* 607.

D. Lightman 'Two Aspects of the Statutory Derivative Claim' [2011] *LMCLQ* 142.

---

[336] On the lack of proper incentives to take on an action on behalf of the company, see Reisberg n. 72, Chapters 6–7.

[337] Advance indemnities, along the lines of those supported in *Wallersteiner v Moir (No. 2)* [1975] QB 373 (and CPR r. 19.9 (7) replaced with no changes by CPR r. 19.9E), where the company may reimburse the shareholder for bringing the action if the court grants leave to continue, will be difficult to obtain as the statutory reforms fail to induce the courts to rethink their cautious position here. See Milman n. 130, 3.

[338] Amendments to the Companies Act 1999 (Amendment No. 3 to the Companies Act 1999, March 2005) s. 199 (Israel) illustrate this point. They allow for a wider discretion for the court in relation to costs in the course of conducting a derivative claim, including lifting some of the burden in financing the claim from the claimant already at an early stage of the proceeding. This is an interesting development as the Israeli Act is already rather liberal in relation to the thorny issue of costs. See e.g. the Companies Act 1999 (Israel) s. 201 under which the court has discretion to award successful plaintiffs part of the proceeds of a successful derivative action beyond their indirect recovery, so that the plaintiff can benefit directly in monetary terms (discussed in Reisberg n. 72, 355). However, in spite of the above and the liberal approach of the court towards derivative litigants, the legislator has felt the need to intervene as derivative claims have been far and few between since the introduction of the new Act in 2000.

# 12

# Shareholder litigation: winding up on just and equitable grounds and the unfair prejudice remedy

## 12.1 Introduction

Part 30 of the Companies Act 2006 (ss. 994–999) enables a shareholder in a company who is being treated in an 'unfairly prejudicial' way to seek relief from the court. Typically, these cases involve companies with relatively small numbers of shareholders.

Those shareholders are usually also directors and may be the only directors of the company. The shareholders/directors will generally have fallen out with each other. Such falling out is often as a result of an exclusion of one shareholder/director by another from the affairs of the company. On other occasions, they may have fallen out because of the misappropriation by one shareholder/director of property belonging to the company or of a business opportunity that might have been enjoyed by the company. Part 30 gives the court very wide powers to control the conduct of the affairs of the company and its shareholders/directors. Such proceedings regularly result in the court ordering that one shareholder/director should purchase the shares of another at a value determined by the court to be fair in the circumstances.[1]

In order to understand fully the nature and scope of the unfair prejudice remedy, it is helpful to know something of its history. As we shall see, the remedy was introduced to give the courts more flexibility and as an alternative to winding up a company on just and equitable grounds.[2] Nevertheless, the relationship between winding up under s. 122 (1) (g) of the Insolvency Act 1986 and the unfair prejudice remedy remains important for two main reasons. First, it is common for s. 122 (1) (g) to be pleaded in the alternative to s. 994.[3] Secondly, the principles developed by the courts in construing the meaning of 'just and equitable' in this context have, to a certain extent, been imported into their consideration of the requirements of s. 994.

---

[1] S. 996 (2) 1(e).
[2] Under s. 122 (1) (g) of the Insolvency Act 1986.
[3] But see *Re Sunrise Radio Ltd* [2009] EWHC 2893 (Ch); [2010] 1 BCLC 367, where the court stated, at [303]: 'Given that possible alternative, the Court should not in general put a shareholder in a worse position than would be the case in a winding-up, if the facts would otherwise justify invocation of the "just and equitable" jurisdiction. That does not mean, however, that winding-up should routinely be sought as an alternative in section 994 cases. Rather, the potential availability of relief through the winding-up process should in an appropriate case be taken into account in fashioning the remedy, including the determination of the price, under section 996.'

## 12.2 Winding up on just and equitable grounds

By analogy with their ancient equitable jurisdiction to dissolve partnerships where the partners had lost their close bonds of trust and good faith, the courts have developed a jurisdiction to wind up companies in similar circumstances. It is based on s. 122 (1) (g) of the Insolvency Act 1986, which provides that the court may wind up a company if it is 'just and equitable that the company should be wound up'. The winding up is available in various circumstances where the company is of the type where it could be described as an incorporated partnership[4] and the necessary bonds of trust and cooperation have broken down.[5] The usual situation where it is invoked in practice these days is where there is a company, which we might call Paradigm Ltd, which has, say, three members with equal shareholdings who are also directors. There is an understanding between them that they will all participate in management and share equally in the profits of the business. They choose not to pay dividends and instead take any profits as directors' fees. The members quarrel and two of them combine their votes to dismiss the third from his directorship under s. 168 of the Companies Act 2006. He thus no longer has any managerial role and, because there are no dividends, receives no return on his capital investment in the company. To make matters worse, his capital investment is locked in because, being a small private company, the shares are not publicly quoted on any market, and in the circumstances, even a private buyer is not going to want to pay much for the shares for more or less the same reasons that the director wants to get shot of them: they give no income, no control and no management participation.[6] In such circumstances,[7] the courts will often grant a winding-up order.[8]

In many ways it is an unsatisfactory remedy, particularly if the company has made its profits mainly out of its 'know-how' and business contacts, for on a winding up there may be very little in the way of assets left over for distribution to the shareholders.[9] Because of this, there is a major restriction on the 'just and equitable' jurisdiction. Section 125 (2) of the Insolvency Act 1986 provides in effect that the court may not make a winding-up order on the just and equitable ground if the court is of the opinion both that some other remedy is available and the petitioners are acting unreasonably in seeking to have the company wound up rather than pursue the other remedy. In practice, a fair offer to purchase the

---

[4] 'Quasi-partnership' is the expression often used.

[5] The leading authoritative summary of the circumstances in which the jurisdiction will be exercised is the speech of Lord Wilberforce in *Ebrahimi* v *Westbourne Galleries Ltd* [1973] AC 360 at p. 379.

[6] If the articles of association give the directors the power to refuse to register a transfer, there will be additional difficulties; see generally Chapter 13, 13.3F below.

[7] Other examples include 'deadlock', see *Re Yenidje Tobacco Ltd* [1916] 2 Ch 426; and 'justifiable lack of confidence in the management of the affairs of the company', see *Loch* v *John Blackwood Ltd* [1924] AC 783, PC.

[8] There is another unrelated set of circumstances where the courts have traditionally wound up under s. 122 (1) (g) of the 1986 Act or its forerunners. The courts will wind up where the 'substratum' has failed. That is, where the objects clause in the memorandum of association stipulates a particular purpose of incorporation and that purpose has failed or been achieved so that, either way, the company no longer has any reason for existence, and its substratum has gone; see generally *Re German Date Coffee Company* (1882) 20 Ch D 169, *Re Perfectair Ltd* (1989) 5 BCC 837. Invocation of this doctrine is extremely rare and, in view of the usual broadly drafted objects clauses and flexibility of alteration, it is not currently of great importance.

[9] Although if there will be none at all, then winding up on this ground will not be available, because the petitioner must show a *prima facie* case that there will be a surplus of assets over liabilities: *Re Rica Gold Washing Co. Ltd* (1879) LR 11 Ch D 36.

shares of the petitioner, made by the other side, the respondents to the petition, will often disentitle him from pursuing the winding up under s. 122 (1) (g).[10] Also, the possibility of an unfair prejudice petition will sometimes produce this result, but not always.[11]

## 12.3 Unfair prejudice

### A The alternative remedy failure

In response to influential calls for reform, Parliament enacted s. 210 of the Companies Act 1948 as an 'alternative remedy' to the jurisdiction to wind up on the just and equitable ground. The intention was to vest in the courts a discretion to make an order which was appropriate to the circumstances. The section required that the petitioner could show that there had been conduct which was oppressive.[12] In the event, there were very few successful reported petitions.[13] One which showed what imaginative use might be made of the new jurisdiction was *Re Harmer Ltd*.[14] Harmer was a small family company involved in a stamp-dealing business. The father was very old and his sons, themselves in their sixties, were finding their father very difficult to get on with. The father had founded a branch of the business in the US without consulting the sons and there were other matters of contention. The sons sought some way of controlling their father and petitioned the court. Harman J made a sensitive order, under which the old man would be president for life of the company, but without any powers.

The judges developed a rule which effectively killed off the jurisdiction in the circumstances in which it was most needed. In the sort of situation discussed above,[15] in the example with Paradigm Ltd, it was held that the director who had been dismissed under what is now s. 169 of the Companies Act 2006 had been oppressed in his capacity as a director, and not in his capacity as a member, as the statute impliedly required.[16] His membership (i.e. shareholder) rights were said to be unaffected by his dismissal as director and loss of directors' fees. Thus the s. 210 jurisdiction was a failure. The courts seemed reluctant to take the steps necessary to put the situation right and preferred to wind up the companies instead.

### B Unfair prejudice

#### 1 *Section 459 replaces s. 210 and restated in the 2006 Act*

In 1980, Parliament tried again.[17] It repealed s. 210 of the 1948 Act and replaced it with a new remedy based on a new concept: unfair prejudice. The provisions were contained in

---

[10] See *Re a Company* 002567/82 (1983) 1 BCC 98,931.
[11] See further 12.3, B 3 below. On the interaction between the just and equitable jurisdiction and the unfair prejudice remedy, see 12.3, B 8 below.
[12] It was also necessary to show that the facts would otherwise justify the making of a winding-up petition on the just and equitable ground.
[13] Three: *SCWS* v *Meyer* [1959] AC 324; *Re Harmer Ltd* [1959] 1 WLR 62 (see below); and *Re Stewarts* [1985] BCLC 4 (although this was a preliminary application).
[14] [1959] 1 WLR 62.
[15] At 12.1.
[16] See *Re Lundie Bros Ltd* [1965] 1 WLR 1051.
[17] This time on the recommendation of the Jenkins Committee.

ss. 459–461 of the Companies Act 1985 and were slightly amended in 1989. Part 30 of the Companies Act 2006 (ss. 994–999) represents a restructured unfair prejudice regime with no real change in substance.[18]

By virtue of s. 994 (1):[19]

(1)  A member of a company may apply to the court by petition for an order under this Part on the ground –

(a)  that the company's affairs are being or have been conducted in a manner that is unfairly prejudicial to the interests of members generally or of some part of its members (including at least himself), or

(b)  that an actual or proposed act or omission of the company (including an act or omission on its behalf) is or would be so prejudicial.

The remainder of s. 994 and ss. 995–996[20] contain further provisions relating to the basic idea in s. 994 (1) and, in particular, provide that the court, if satisfied that the petition is well founded, may make 'such order as it thinks fit for giving relief in respect of the matters complained of'.[21]

Parliament's second attempt was successful. So successful, in fact, that the floodgates of litigation, firmly shut for so long by *Foss* v *Harbottle*, were well and truly thrown open. The judges were flexible and innovative in their use of the new jurisdiction. By the late 1980s there were dozens of reported cases. These represented only the tip of the iceberg, for many cases were settled before getting into court, the petition having served its usefulness as a mechanism for bringing the other side to the bargaining table. Gradually, it was realised that the availability of the new remedy was capable of being oppressive towards respondents and some of the judges sought to develop ways of restricting the number of cases.[22] The reform proposals in the Report of the Law Commission on *Shareholder Remedies* reflect the concern that the availability of litigation to an aggrieved shareholder can bring problems as well as advantages, but we shall leave this for later.[23]

## 2 *Scope of s. 994 (formerly s. 459 of the 1985 Act)*

As we saw above, s. 994 restates s. 459 of the Companies Act 1985 without any substantive changes. It follows that although some of the case law and articles below are concerned with ss. 459–461 of 1985 Act, the doctrinal and practical learning of the jurisprudence and academic literature surrounding the earlier provision remains relevant. Likewise, some of the case law on s. 210 of the Companies Act 1948 (the initial provision, also known as 'the oppression remedy') is still considered influential.

There are no hard and fast rules for deciding whether conduct can amount to unfair prejudice, although certain general principles have emerged. There are two main areas of

---

[18] The statutory restatement is designed to provide a more user-friendly framework.

[19] This should be read in conjunction with the Companies (Unfair Prejudice Applications) Proceedings Rules 2009 (SI 2009/2469) which bring the procedure into line with the Companies Act 2006, including the removal of the requirement for the petitioner to state the objects of the company. These rules also take account of changes in the Civil Procedure Rules since 1986.

[20] Ss. 997–999 contain 'supplementary provisions'.

[21] Companies Act 2006, s. 996 (1).

[22] See the following section.

[23] See 12.3, 9 below.

development. The first is that the judges have made various general statements about how the jurisdiction should be exercised.[24] The second is that quite a lot of case law has developed around the problem of where to draw the line between the shareholders' private matters (which cannot form the substance of an unfair prejudice petition) and matters which can properly be seen as conduct of the company's affairs and which unfairly prejudice some of the members.

The early cases contained various attempts by judges to elaborate in a general way on the idea of 'unfairness' and 'prejudice' in the context of the running of commercial companies. It was decided very early on that the test of unfairness was objective in the sense that the respondents need not have acted as they did in the conscious knowledge that it was unfair to the petitioner, or be in bad faith and that the test was 'whether a reasonable bystander observing the consequences of the conduct would regard it as having unfairly prejudiced the petitioner's interests'.[25] The overall approach came to be reviewed by the Court of Appeal in *Re Saul Harrison plc*.[26] The petition had been struck out by the judge, and the petitioner appealed. The gist of the petitioner's main complaint was that the company had some valuable assets but poor business prospects and that by carrying on its business the directors were dissipating those assets, and any reasonable board would have closed the company down and distributed the assets to the shareholders. In a landmark judgment, Hoffmann LJ reviewed the development of the case law on unfair prejudice, holding that a petitioner would only be entitled to a remedy if she could establish that the powers of management had been used for an unlawful purpose or the articles otherwise infringed. The exception to this would be where she had been able to show that the circumstances were such that because of the personal relationship between her and those who controlled the company, there was a 'legitimate expectation' that the board and the general meeting would not exercise whatever powers they were given by the articles of association. But she would have to show that the relationship was not purely a commercial one, and that there was 'something more' so that the letter of the articles did not fully reflect the understandings upon which the shareholders were associated. In the circumstances she failed to show that there was 'something more' and moreover failed to show any bad faith on the part of the directors in the exercise of their powers.

*Re Saul Harrison* also contained what looked like an attempt to restrict the circumstances in which a remedy under s. 459 (of the 1985 Act) would be granted, to those

---

[24] For example, in *Re Grandactual Ltd; Hough v Hardcastle* [2005] EWHC 1415 (Ch), the court stressed that although s. 459 (now s. 994) was not subject to any formal limitation period, the greater the delay on the part of the petitioner, the more likely that relief will be denied. In this case a nine-year delay led the court to strike out the petition.

[25] *Per* Slade J in the unreported case of *Re Bovey Hotel Ventures Ltd*; approved and cited by Nourse J (as he then was) in *Re RA Noble and Sons (Clothing) Ltd* [1983] BCLC 273. Nourse J took the view in *Re RA Noble and Sons* that a petitioner who had behaved badly himself would not get a remedy, but in a later case, *Re London School of Electronics Ltd* (1985) 1 BCC 99,394, he seemed to retract this in favour of the approach that although he need not come to the court with clean hands, his own conduct could affect the remedy which he received. See J. Lowry 'Stretching the Ambit of section 459 of the Companies Act 1985: The Elasticity of Unfair Prejudice' [1995] LMCLQ 337.

[26] [1994] BCC 475.

circumstances in which it had already been granted. Hoffmann LJ recalled the objective reasonable bystander test[27] and, while accepting that the test was objective, he stressed that the standard of fairness must necessarily be laid down by the court and that it was more useful to examine the factors which the law actually took into account in setting the standard, rather than appealing to the views of an imaginary 'company watcher'. Whether Hoffmann LJ intended his approach to be restrictive or not, very soon after, a judge of the Chancery Division put down a marker that this was not the last word on the matter and that it was not open to the Court of Appeal to limit the general words of the statute:

> [I]n my judgment, it is not the effect of *Re Saul Harrison* that a remedy under section 459 [of the Companies Act 1985] can be given only if the directors have acted in breach of duty or if the company has breached the terms of its articles or some other relevant agreement. These matters constitute in most cases the basis for deciding what conduct is unfair. But the words of the section are wide and general and, save where the circumstances are governed by the judgments in *Re Saul Harrison*, the categories of unfair prejudice are not closed.[28]

*Re Saul Harrison* was an example of the courts being concerned as to the possible oppressive effects of the opening of the floodgates of litigation and it was not the first time that Hoffmann LJ had attempted to stem the tide.[29] As will be seen below, *Re Saul Harrison* has now largely been superseded by the House of Lords' decision in *O'Neill* v *Phillips*, but since *O'Neill* v *Phillips* also deals with various other ideas and developments which have not yet been explained here, it is necessary to consider these in their historical context before turning to an analysis of *O'Neill* v *Phillips*.

The second area of development has been in respect of the '*qua* member' idea encountered in the example of Paradigm Ltd discussed above,[30] and the related matter of whether the acts complained of amount to conduct of the company's affairs as opposed to the member's private affairs. Given the devastation wrought on the old s. 210 of the 1948 Act by the judicial doctrine that the dismissal of a director in a quasi-partnership company was not oppression '*qua* member' as the statute was said to require, it became very important to see what the judges would do with that problem under the new unfair prejudice provisions in the 1980 Act. The wording was similar and so there was nothing on the face of the statute to require a different approach. The judges of the Chancery Division of the 1980s made a point of circumventing the problem by admitting the principle that the prejudice had to be *qua* member but taking a wide view of what membership rights

---

[27] See *Re Bovey Hotel Ventures Ltd*, n. 25 above.
[28] *Re BSB Holdings (No. 2)* [1996] 1 BCLC 155, *per* Arden J at p. 243.
[29] See below.
[30] At 12.1. In *Gamlestaden Fastigheter AB* v *Baltic Partner Ltd* [2007] UKPC 26; (2007) BCC 272, where a member had provided a loan to the company in order to inject working capital. The issue was whether the member's petition should be struck out in circumstances where the company was insolvent and the relief sought (payment of compensation by the directors to the company) would confer no financial benefit on the petitioner *qua* member. The Privy Council took the view that 'interests' may extend to cover those of a member *qua* creditor where, in the circumstances, the distinction becomes artificial. In *Re Phoenix Contracts (Leicester) Ltd*, [2010] EWHC 2375 (Ch) the court confirmed that the requirement that prejudice must be suffered as a member is not to be too narrowly construed. See also *Re Woven Rugs Ltd*, [2010] EWHC 230 (Ch).

entailed in a quasi-partnership company. The matter was put well by Hoffmann J (as he then was) in *Re a Company (No. 00477 of 1986)*:[31]

> In principle I accept [the] proposition [that the section must be limited to conduct which is unfairly prejudicial to the interest of the members as members. It cannot extend to conduct which is prejudicial to other interests of persons who happen to be members] . . . but its application must take into account that the interests of a member are not necessarily limited to his strict legal rights under the constitution of the company. The use of the word 'unfairly' in section 459 [of the 1985 Act], like the use of the words 'just and equitable' in [s. 122 (1) (g)], enables the court to have regard to wider equitable considerations . . . Thus in the case of a managing director of a large public company who is also the owner of a small holding in the company's shares, it is easy to see the distinction between his interests as a managing director employed under a service contract and his interests as a member. In the case of a small private company in which two or three members have invested their capital by subscribing for shares on the footing that dividends are unlikely but that each will earn his living by working for the company as a director, the distinction may be more elusive. The member's interests as a member who has ventured his capital in the company's business may include a legitimate expectation that he will continue to be employed as a director and his dismissal from that office and exclusion from the management of the company may therefore be unfairly prejudicial to his interests as a member.

Thus a new chapter in company law was born; a remedy was available in the kind of situations where previously only a winding up on the just and equitable ground would have been granted.[32] But the genie was out of the bottle, and within a few years the judges were trying to develop ways of restricting the jurisdiction.

The related matter of whether the acts complained of amount to conduct of the company's affairs as opposed to the member's private affairs has received attention in several cases. The difficulty stems from the fact that in small private companies, the shareholders may be interacting with each other in various ways: as members, obviously, but perhaps also as father and son, or as sisters, and perhaps also as joint owners of a piece of land leased to the company, or as participants in a huge family business involving several companies. In these kinds of situations, when faced with an unfair prejudice petition, the court finds that it has to sort out which matters constitute conduct of the company's affairs, and which therefore fall to be taken into account in judging the petition, and which matters constitute conduct of private matters between the members themselves and which are therefore irrelevant to the petition.

---

[31] (1986) 2 BCC 99,171 at p. 99,174. The same judge took a similar approach in *Re a Company 008699 of 1985* (1986) 2 BCC 99,024. As did Nourse J (as he then was) in *Re RA Noble and Sons (Clothing) Ltd* [1983] BCLC 273 and Vinelott J in *Re a Company 002567 of 1982* [1983] 2 All ER 854, and in *Re Blue Arrow plc* [1987] BCLC 585. An earlier narrow decision of Lord Grantchester QC in *Re a Company* [1983] Ch 178 was not followed.
[32] More recently, in *Strahan v Wilcock* [2006] EWCA Civ 13, it was held that exclusion from management will justify a pro rata buyout where the relationship between the parties is that of a quasi-partnership. Where this is the case, equitable considerations require the petitioner to be bought out on a non-discounted basis. See also *Re Zetnet Ltd* [2011] EWHC 1518 (Ch).

*Re Unisoft Ltd (No. 2)*[33] was a case which also shows judicial concern with the way in which s. 459 (of the 1985 Act) can become oppressive to the respondents,[34] and perhaps also to the petitioners. The case was estimated to last three months:

> Petitions under section 459 [of the Companies Act 1985] have become notorious to the judges of this court – and I think also to the Bar – for their length, their unpredictability of management, and the enormous and appalling costs which are incurred upon them particularly by reason of the volume of documents liable to be produced. By way of example, on this petition there are before me upwards of thirty lever-arch files of documents. In those circumstances it befits the court, in my view, to be extremely careful to ensure that oppression is not caused to parties, respondents to such petitions, indeed, petitioners to such petitions, by allowing the parties to trawl through facts which have given rise to grievances but which are not relevant conduct within even the very wide words of the section.[35]

This was a case where there were the normal allegations of exclusion of a director and removal from office. However, there were also various complaints about dealings between the shareholders themselves, relating to sales of shares, and shareholder agreements. These matters were struck out as they were about their private position as shareholders and not about unfair conduct of the company's business.[36] It is clear that this is an area which will lead the courts into making some subtle distinctions in future cases.[37]

## 3 *Share purchase orders*

We have seen that the courts are prepared, in appropriate cases, to give a remedy to the shareholder director who is dismissed from a quasi-partnership company. This kind of situation is by far the most common which comes before the courts. The remedy usually sought and granted in such cases is an order that the respondents purchase the shares of the petitioner, although such an order is by no means confined to these situations, and it will be seen later that unfair prejudice proceedings are used to remedy a wide range of problems.[38]

---

[33] [1994] BCC 766.

[34] More recently, in *Richardson v Blackmore* [2005] EWCA Civ 1356, the link between a petitioner's misbehaviour and the matters alleged to be unfairly prejudicial was relevant. The Court of Appeal confirmed that there is no formal 'clean hands' bar (unlike the common law derivative action, see Chapter 11), but inappropriate behaviour by the petitioner might affect prospects of success and/or the nature of any relief granted. This proposition is now well established: see *Amin v Amin* [2009] EWHC 3356 (Ch) (in the context of partnerships).

[35] *Ibid.* at p. 767, *per* Harman J.

[36] Similar points arose in *Re JE Cade Ltd* [1991] BCC 360. The argument was raised in *R & H Electric Ltd v Haden Bill Electrical Ltd* [1995] BCC 958, but failed.

[37] Such as, for example, in *Re Belfield Furnishings Ltd* [2006] EWHC 183 (Ch), [2006] 2 BCLC 705, where the court explained that the answer to the question as to whether it was an abuse of process to bring a Section 459 (or now 994) petition where the parties had agreed in advance a valuation procedure in the event of breakdown of relationship, depended on whether it was an even-sided breakdown or whether there was evidence of misconduct on one side. If the latter was the case, or if genuine concerns existed with regard to the valuation process, then an unfair prejudice petition might be allowed to proceed.

[38] See 4 below.

The share purchase order almost invariably requires a majority to buy out a minority. An order the other way around is likely to be an extremely rare event. Hoffmann J[39] expressed the view in *Re a Company 006834/88*[40] that it would be:

> . . . very unusual for the court to order a majority shareholder actively concerned in the management of the company to sell his shares to a minority shareholder when he is willing and able to buy out the minority shareholder at a fair price.

But, sooner or later, rare events occur and there has been at least one case where the situation was so unusual that a majority shareholder was ordered to sell out to a minority petitioner.[41]

The question of how the shares are to be valued has given rise to a number of issues, as well as the fairly complex matter of how the valuation is to be arrived at.[42]

These cannot be considered in detail here,[43] but one point which has cropped up in many important recent cases needs to be explained. In *Re Bird Precision Bellows Ltd*,[44] the judge at first instance had valued the shares on a pro rata basis, without any discount for the fact that they were a minority holding. The Court of Appeal held that this was fair in the circumstances and ever since then, valuation without discount has generally been regarded as the *prima facie* norm in unfair prejudice cases.[45] The idea is of great benefit to the minority shareholder. If the share value is discounted to reflect the fact that the petitioner's shares are a minority holding, then it will produce a much lower value than a pro rata valuation. A pro rata valuation would fix a value for the whole company, and then give 40% of that figure to someone who had a 40% holding of the shares in the company. A discounted valuation would be done on the assumption that the 40% holding was really worth a lot less than 40% of the total value of the company. The reasons why this might be are obvious: the minority holding carries no control, can vote no director on to the board, can remove no director, and is dependent on the majority for any dividends.

In *Re Sunrise Radio Ltd*,[46] it was held that a petitioner had been unfairly prejudiced by an allotment of shares and an increase in share capital in circumstances where the directors had failed (*inter alia*) in the fulfilment of the requirement of fairness and even-handedness, to give proper consideration to the price that should have been extracted from those willing and able to subscribe for the shares. The court ordered that the petitioner's shares be purchased by the respondents, but refused to apply a discount to the valuation of those shares and instead required them to be valued on a pro rata basis. This is particularly noteworthy because the case did not concern a quasi-partnership which is the usual circumstance in

---

[39] As he then was.
[40] (1989) 5 BCC 294, CA.
[41] *Re a Company 00789 of 1987* (1989) 5 BCC 792, [1991] BCC 44. See also the proceedings in *Re Copeland Ltd* [1997] BCC 294, CA.
[42] And the date of valuation; for the principles as to this see *Profinance Trust SA v Gladstone* [2002] 1 BCLC 141, CA. In *Re Abbington Hotel Ltd CD* [2011] EWHC 635 the court stated, at [123], that 'The starting point for the date of valuation of shares for a buy-out order under s. 996 is the date of judgment, but the court is free to choose such date as is most appropriate and just in the circumstances of the case. In particular, the date should be that which best remedies the unfair prejudice held to be established.'
[43] See e.g. *Re OC Transport Services Ltd* [1984] BCLC 251; *Re Cumana Ltd* [1986] BCLC 430.
[44] [1984] Ch 419, [1986] Ch 658, CA.
[45] But there are rare exceptions; see, for instance, *Elliott v Planet Organic Ltd* [2000] BCC 610.
[46] [2010] 1 BCLC 367.

which the court will refuse to apply a discount. Relying on decisions such as *Re Bird Precision Bellows Ltd* (to the effect that the Court must do what is just and equitable as between the parties) the judge said that there is no inflexible rule excluding an undiscounted valuation in a non-quasi-partnership relationship. To support his decision not to allow a discount to be applied, the judge set out ten reasons including the fact that the business to date had been conducted with a view to capital growth rather than the payment of dividends and the fact that the respondents stood to be unjustly enriched as a result of a buyout on a discounted basis, given that the discount could be as high as 80% in that case.[47]

The main developments in this field have centred around trying to find an answer to one specific question: where a petitioner is seeking an order that the respondents purchase his shares, what effect does it have on that petition if the respondents make an offer to purchase the petitioner's shares? There can be no definitive answer to cover every situation, but a number of dominant ideas have developed steadily over 25 years. We have already seen that in the closely related situation of a winding up on the just and equitable ground the existence of s. 125 (2) of the Insolvency Act 1986 can mean that, in some circumstances, an offer to purchase can terminate the petition.[48] In the early 1980s, it was soon established that the same might be true for an unfair prejudice petition, on the basis that whatever harm the petitioner had suffered at the hands of the respondents, a proper offer from them to purchase his shares made the situation no longer unfair and so it would often be appropriate to accede to the respondent's motion to strike out the petition. But the doctrine acquired a sharp edge in the hands of Hoffmann J, for at that time he and a number of the other judges of the Chancery Division seemed concerned to find a fair way of restricting the number of petitions. The learned judge expounded and applied his striking-out doctrine in cases where the articles of association of the companies contained mechanisms designed to govern the valuation of shares in certain circumstances.[49] Strictly speaking, those circumstances had not always arisen and so the approach involved an element of extension of the provisions of the articles.[50] The provisions usually provided for valuation by an accountant acting as an expert, the practical consequence of which was that the valuer would not have to give reasons for his valuation and nor would it be possible to ensure that he did not apply a discount to the valuation because the shares were a minority holding. Hoffmann J set out the background and rationale for his approach:

> This is an ordinary case of breakdown of confidence between the parties.[51] In such circumstances, fairness requires that the minority shareholder should not have to maintain his investment in a

---

[47] *Ibid*. at pp. 442–443.

[48] *Re a Company 002567/82* (1983) 1 BCC 98,931; see further 12.1 above.

[49] These were usually share transfer or expropriation provisions in common form; see *Re a Company 004377 of 1986* (1986) 2 BCC 99,520 (also called *Re XYZ Ltd* in some reports), *Re a Company 007623 of 1984* (1986) 2 BCC 99,191 and *Re a Company 006834 of 1988* (1989) 5 BCC 218.

[50] See e.g. *Re a Company 006834 of 1988* (1989) 5 BCC 218, where it really could not be said that the articles actually covered the situation that had arisen.

[51] But see *Re Jayflex Construction Ltd, McKee v O'Reilly* [2003] EWHC 2008 (Ch), [2004] 2 BCLC 145, ChD, where a breakdown in the relationship of trust and confidence in a quasi-partnership was not enough here to amount to unfairly prejudicial confidence. Both shareholders had unjustifiably charged personal expenses to the company and therefore the mutuality of the behaviour precluded either party relying on it for the purposes of s. 459. Likewise, in *Re Baumler (UK) Ltd* [2005] BCC 181, the court stressed the need for the petitioner to demonstrate that the respondent behaved in such a way as to cause a loss of confidence and that were relief to be denied, the petitioner, in being compelled to remain as part of a quasi-partnership, would be unfairly prejudiced.

company managed by the majority with whom he has fallen out. But the unfairness disappears if the minority shareholder is offered a fair price for his shares. In such a case, section 459 [of the Companies Act 1985] was not intended to enable the court to preside over a protracted and expensive contest of virtue between the shareholders and award the company to the winner.[52]

In general . . . if a petitioner is complaining of conduct which would be unfairly prejudicial only if accompanied by a refusal on the part of the majority to buy his shares at a fair price, and the articles provide a mechanism for determining such a price, he should not be entitled to petition . . . until he has invoked or offered to invoke that mechanism and the majority have refused to buy at the price so determined.[53]

This approach quickly ran into trouble. Hoffmann J struck out the petition in *Re Abbey Leisure Ltd*[54] but the petitioner appealed. The respondents had offered to purchase his shares at a price fixed by an accountant and the petitioner was worried that the accountant would discount the price because the petitioner had a 40% minority holding. The Court of Appeal reinstated the petition, holding that, in the circumstances, it was not fair to expect the petitioner to run the risk that the accountant would apply a discount.[55] For a time, this put a stopper on the striking-out process. The effect of *Re Abbey Leisure Ltd* was described by Harman J in a later case:

. . . The decision . . . was one which in my judgment plainly changed the whole approach of the court to petitions under sections 459 and 461 [of the Companies Act 1985] . . . What [the passage in the case] says is that a petitioner is entitled to refuse to accept a risk – any risk – in an accountant's valuation of his interest if such a risk can be seen to be one that would depreciate in any way the valuation.[56]

However, the striking-out process did not die. It is apparent from subsequent litigation that if the offer really is a fair one in all the circumstances, then the court may well take the view that there is nothing to be gained from litigation. The offer in *Re a Company 00836 of 1995*[57] was a clever one in the sense that it took account of most of the objections that were being raised to offers in previous cases. Although it is also clear that the judge was not imbued with a sense that the litigation here was essential:

This is the latest instalment in a long running[58] feud between father and son. The feud has been conducted through the medium of the Companies Court . . . It has cost, I am told, so far at least £1m, and possibly nearer £2m, for both sides. In one corner is [the father] . . . He is 85 . . . In the other corner is his younger son . . . who fell out with his father in the late 1980s . . .[59]

Both had petitioned against the other and both applied to strike out the other's petition. The son, the majority shareholder, made an offer to purchase his father's shares. The offer had been drafted to avoid most of the points that might be taken against it and so it was a pro rata offer – the price for the minority holding to be the proportion of the net asset value

---

[52] *Re a Company 006834 of 1988* (1989) 5 BCC 218 at p. 221.

[53] *Re a Company 007623 of 1984* (1986) 2 BCC 99, 191 at p. 99,199.

[54] [1990] BCC 60.

[55] The case largely concerned a petition for winding up (although there was also a petition for unfair prejudice) but the principles were felt to be the same as in unfair prejudice cases.

[56] *Re a Company 00330 of 1991, ex parte Holden* [1991] BCC 241 at p. 245.

[57] [1996] BCC 432.

[58] There had been earlier litigation, reported as *Re Macro Ltd* [1994] BCC 781.

[59] [1996] BCC 432 at p. 433, *per* Judge Weeks QC.

of the company that those shares bore to the whole of the issued share capital, both sides could have their own accountants make written representations to the expert valuer, and the valuer had to give reasons for the figure to be produced. The judge took the view that:

> [T]here is no substance in the objection [that the petitioner is entitled to his day or week or month in court, and that it is inappropriate to have these matters effectively decided by an accountant rather than the court] . . . and an independent accountant can perfectly well, with the assistance of a solicitor, if he thinks it desirable, make the valuation which he is required to do under the terms of that offer, and that way of proceeding is as good as the method of proceeding before the court with cross-examination, valuers on both sides, and a protracted hearing . . .[60]

More recently, in *Irvine* v *Irvine*[61] the High Court decided that, for the purposes of a buyout ordered following a successful petition, a shareholding of 49.96% was to be valued as any other minority holding, and that no premium should be attached to the shares simply because the buyer was the majority shareholder who would gain control of the whole of the issued share capital. The court also held that where the parties had agreed a method for valuing the shares that made no distinction between the various assets of the company, the valuation of the cash surplus held by the company was also to be subject to the minority discount, and was not to be treated as having been notionally distributed to the shareholders prior to the buyout order. Although the court's jurisdiction to strike out is one that must be exercised sparingly,[62] it is clear that a fair offer followed by striking-out proceedings will remain an important and sometimes successful tactic in future unfair prejudice cases.

In an interesting development in *Atlasview Ltd* v *Brightview Ltd*,[63] the court took the view that rather than seeking relief under the Companies Act 1985, s. 461 (now s. 996 of the 2006 Act) in the form of 'damages' the court may award the remedy sought as financial, equitable or statutory compensation, although this may be rare.

In *Arbuthnott* v *Bonnyman*,[64] the Court of Appeal considered the fairness and validity of a share purchase effected to release retiring founding members from a business. The appellant, along with others, was a founder shareholder of a company governed by a shareholders' agreement, whose terms established that, in the event of an agreed exit by a founder majority, the shareholder would agree to sell his shares on the same terms as those offered to the other shareholders. When the appellant and other members of the original team approached retirement, members intending to continue with the business offered to purchase all of the shares in the company. All retiring members accepted, except the appellant, who considered the company valuation, and the share price offered, to be too low. When the remaining members altered the company's articles of association

---

[60] *Ibid.* at p. 441. The judge also made the point that *Re Abbey Leisure* was a case of a winding-up petition and that this diminished its authority. It is respectfully suggested that this is not necessarily a strong criticism because since the early 1980s the courts have assimilated their approach to striking out summonses whether under s. 125 (2) of the Insolvency Act 1986 on the ground that the offer is a reasonable alternative which makes pursuing the petition unreasonable, or under s. 459 of the Companies Act 1985 (now s. 999 of the 2006 Act) on the ground that the unfairness has ceased. Furthermore, it is clear from the passage quoted above from the judgment of Harman J in *Re a Company 00330 of 1991, ex parte Holden* that he felt bound by *Re Abbey Leisure Ltd* in the proceedings that were before him even though they were in respect of alleged unfair prejudice.
[61] [2006] EWHC 1875 (Ch).
[62] See *Re Copeland Ltd* [1997] BCC 294, CA.
[63] [2004] BCC 542. See also *Re Home & Office Fire Extinguishers Ltd* [2012] EWHC 917 (Ch).

to enable the buyout to proceed without the appellant's consent, he presented an unfair prejudice petition. The Court of Appeal held, on the facts, that amendments to the articles were no more than a tidying-up exercise with no evidence of bad faith or improper motive and that the amendment to allow the buyout to proceed was not inconsistent with original arrangements between the founding members and that it made 'commercial common sense'. Furthermore, the shareholders' agreement provided that the appellant would be bound by the price with which the founder majority was content. Interestingly, the court confirmed that a term could be implied that, as sophisticated financial professionals, the founder majority would not accept a price which they did not honestly consider to be fair and reasonable.

In *Thomas v Dawson*,[65] the Court of Appeal upheld the first instance decision confirming that courts have absolute discretion to make awards in unfair prejudice petitions under s. 994. The Court at first instance found that the petition under s. 994 was successful. The order given under s. 996 was the grant of an option to Mr Thomas to purchase Ms Dawson's share in Invicta™ for £50,000. In calculating this figure, the judge considered the amount of income Ms Dawson would have received had she remained a shareholder and the liability outstanding on the order made against Ms Dawson for the repayment of the director loan. Mr Thomas appealed the decision, stating that the judge had not followed procedure and had veered away from the results of the valuation, which indicated the share should have had a nominal value, due to the balance sheet insolvency. Section 996 of the Companies Act 2006 states that the judge has absolute discretion in making orders. It was for the judge to decide what value to put on Ms Dawson's share. The decision illustrates again how wide the discretion is under a Section 994 petition in that the parties cannot not be sure of the order the court will make.

## 4 *The era of O'Neill v Phillips*

Many of the doctrines and ideas discussed above arose again in the landmark case of *O'Neill* v *Phillips*.[66] The House of Lords account of the rationale of this area of law is the sole House of Lords decision in this area to date and is worth studying at length. Phillips (the respondent) owned the share capital of the company which consisted of 100 £1 shares. The company operated a business in the construction industry. O'Neill (the petitioner) was originally employed as a manual worker, but later he was promoted and then eventually was given 25 shares and made a director. Phillips told O'Neill that he hoped that O'Neill would eventually take over the day-to-day running of the business and would then have 50% of the profits. Phillips then retired and O'Neill ran the company as de facto managing director. The profits were shared 50/50 thereafter and bonus shares were issued pro rata to existing holdings. O'Neill guaranteed the company's bank account. There were discussions about the allotment of more shares, to take O'Neill to a 50% holding when certain asset targets were reached. But this never happened due to a recession and Phillips resumed control of the company. Meanwhile, O'Neill ran the operations abroad. There

---

[64] *Charterhouse Capital Ltd Geoffrey Arbuthnott* v *James Gordon Bonnyman & 18 others* [2015] EWCA Civ 536.
[65] *Thomas* v *Dawson & Anor* [2015] EWCA Civ 706.
[66] [1999] BCC 600.

was an acrimonious meeting, when Phillips told O'Neill that he would no longer receive 50% profits and would only get salary and any dividends on his 25% holding. O'Neill then terminated the guarantee and set up a competing business abroad. O'Neill petitioned, alleging unfair prejudice by reason of Phillips' terminating the equal profit sharing, and repudiation of an alleged agreement to allot more shares.

At first instance the petition was dismissed on the basis that no concluded agreement for profit sharing had been reached, and refusal to allot more shares was not prejudice to O'Neill in his capacity as a member. The Court of Appeal (reported as *Re Pectel Ltd*) allowed the petition, on the basis that although there was no concluded agreement for more shares, O'Neill had a legitimate expectation that he would get them when the targets were reached and a legitimate expectation of 50% of profits. In the House of Lords, the petition was dismissed. Lord Hoffmann's speech[67] reviewed many of the ideas which had been developing and can be taken as clearly settling the approach to be adopted in future cases. It is also a state-of-the-art account of the rationale of this area of law and so is worth quoting at length:[68]

> In section 459 [s. 994 of the 2006 Act] Parliament has chosen fairness as the criterion by which the court must decide whether it has jurisdiction to grant relief . . . [content of fairness] will depend upon the context in which it is being used . . . and background.
>
> In the case of section 459, the background has the following two features. First, a company is an association of persons for an economic purpose, usually entered into with legal advice and some degree of formality. The terms of the association are contained in the articles of association and sometimes in collateral agreements between the shareholders. Thus the manner in which the affairs of the company may be conducted is closely regulated by rules to which the shareholders have agreed. Secondly, company law has developed seamlessly from the law of partnership, which was treated by equity, like the Roman *societas*, as a contract of good faith. One of the traditional roles of equity, as a separate jurisdiction, was to restrain the exercise of strict legal rights in certain relationships in which it considered that this would be contrary to good faith. These principles have, with appropriate modification, been carried over into company law.
>
> The first of these two features leads to the conclusion that a member of a company will not ordinarily be entitled to complain of unfairness unless there has been some breach of the terms on which he agreed that the affairs of the company should be conducted. But the second leads to the conclusion that there will be cases in which equitable considerations make it unfair for those conducting the affairs of the company to rely upon their strict legal powers. Thus unfairness may consist in a breach of the rules or in using the rules in a manner which equity would regard as contrary to good faith.
>
> This approach to the concept of unfairness in section 459 runs parallel to that which your Lordships' House in *Re Westbourne Galleries Ltd* [1973] AC 360, adopted in giving content to the concept of 'just and equitable' as a ground for winding up . . .
>
> . . . So I agree with Jonathan Parker J when he said in *Re Astec (BSR) plc* [1999] BCC 59 at p. 86H: 'in order to give rise to an equitable constraint based on "legitimate expectation" what is required is a personal relationship or personal dealings of some kind between the party seeking to exercise the legal right and the party seeking to restrain such exercise, such as will affect the conscience of the former . . .'

---

[67] With which the other Lords of Appeal concurred.
[68] [1999] BCC 600, pp. 603–613 *passim*.

In *Re Saul Harrison* . . . I used the term 'legitimate expectation', borrowed from public law . . . It was probably a mistake to use this term, as it usually is when one introduces a new label to describe a concept which is already sufficiently defined in other terms . . . The concept of legitimate expectation should not be allowed to lead a life of its own, capable of giving rise to equitable constraints in circumstances to which the traditional principles have no application. This is what seems to have happened in this case.

The Court of Appeal found that by 1991 the company had the characteristics identified by Lord Wilberforce in *Re Westbourne Galleries* . . . as commonly giving rise to constraints upon the exercise of powers under the articles. They were (1) an association formed or continued on the basis of a personal relationship involving mutual confidence, (2) an understanding that all, or some, of the shareholders shall participate in the conduct of the business and (3) restrictions on the transfer of shares, so that a member cannot take out his stake and go elsewhere. I agree. It follows that it would have been unfair of Mr Phillips to use his voting powers under the articles to remove Mr O'Neill from participation in the conduct of the business without giving him an opportunity to sell his interest in the company at a fair price. Although it does not matter, I should say that I do not think that this was the position when Mr O'Neill first acquired his shares . . . He received them as a gift and an incentive and I do not think that in making that gift Mr Phillips could be taken to have surrendered his right to dismiss Mr O'Neill from the management without making him an offer for the shares. But over the following years the relationship changed . . . [worked in business, guaranteed overdraft] . . .

The difficulty for Mr O'Neill is that Mr Phillips did not remove him from participation in the management of the business . . . he remained a director and continued to earn his salary as manager of the business in Germany . . . [as regards whether Mr O'Neill] had a legitimate expectation of being allotted more shares when the targets were met . . . Mr Phillips never agreed to give them . . . there is no basis consistent with established principles of equity, for a court to hold that Mr Phillips was behaving unfairly in withdrawing from the negotiation . . . Where, as here, parties enter into negotiations with a view to a transfer of shares on professional advice and subject to a condition that they are not bound until a formal document has been executed, I do not think it is possible to say that an obligation has arisen in fairness or equity at an earlier stage.

The same reasoning applies to the sharing of profits . . . Mr Phillips had made no promise to share the profits equally in [the circumstances when he had come back to running the business] . . . and it was therefore not inequitable or unfair for him to refuse to carry on doing so.

The judge, it will be recalled, gave as one of his reasons for dismissing the petition the fact that any prejudice suffered by Mr O'Neill was in his capacity as an employee rather than as a shareholder . . . [A]ssuming there had been [unfair prejudice] I would not exclude the possibility that prejudice suffered from the breach of that obligation could be suffered in the capacity of shareholder . . . As cases . . . [have shown] . . . the requirement that prejudice must be suffered as a member should not be too narrowly or technically construed. But the point does not arise because no promise was made.

Lord Hoffmann went on to consider the consequences of the fact that the respondent had made an offer to purchase the petitioner's shares at a fair price. Although his Lordship's comments were strictly *obiter* (since it had been held that there was no unfair prejudice), he nevertheless felt that the matter should be considered, because of the practical importance of the effect of an offer by a respondent to purchase the shares of the petitioner.[69] On the facts of *O'Neill* v *Phillips* it was said that the petitioner was justified in rejecting the offer because it did not provide for his costs which had been accumulating in

---

[69] See the discussion at 12.3B, 3 above.

the almost three years since the presentation of the petition. Nevertheless, Lord Hoffmann's general observations are important guidelines:[70]

> If the respondent to a petition has plainly made a reasonable offer, then the exclusion as such will not be unfairly prejudicial and he will be entitled to have the petition struck out. It is therefore very important that participants in such companies should be able to know what counts as a reasonable offer.
>
> In the first place, the offer must be to purchase the shares at a fair value. This will ordinarily be a value representing an equivalent proportion of the total issued share capital, that is, without a discount for its being a minority holding . . . This is not to say that there may not be cases in which it will be fair to take a discounted value . . .
>
> Secondly, the value, if not agreed, should be determined by a competent expert . . .
>
> Thirdly, the offer should be to have the value determined by an expert as an expert. I do not think that the offer should provide for the full machinery of an arbitration or the half-way house of an expert who gives reasons. The objective should be economy and expedition, even if this carries the possibility of a rough edge for one side or the other (and both parties in this respect take the same risk) compared with a more elaborate procedure . . .
>
> Fourthly, the offer should, as in this case, provide for equality of arms between the parties. Both should have the same right of access to information about the company which bears upon the value of the shares and both should have the right to make submissions to the expert, though the form (written or oral) which these submissions may take should be left to the discretion of the expert himself.
>
> Fifthly, there is the question of costs . . . [p]ayment of costs need not always be offered . . . the majority shareholder should be given a reasonable opportunity to make an offer . . . before he becomes obliged to pay costs . . .

It is fitting that Lord Hoffmann, who played such a major judicial role in the development of the unfair prejudice remedy from the early 1980s onward, should ultimately have been in a position to expound and clarify these important concepts. *O'Neill* v *Phillips* did much to provide guidance to future litigants.[71]

More recently, in *Re Phoenix Contracts (Leicester) Ltd*,[72] the court found that the petitioner, S, had been unfairly excluded from the management of the company and ordered the respondent, W, to purchase the petitioner's shares. At the relevant time, the company operated as a quasi-partnership with S and W being the only shareholders and executive directors. Proudman J held that S had been unfairly excluded from the management of the company when W suspended him as a director (after he had made a protected disclosure about the company being involved in anti-competitive practices) when W had no right to do so. Since the date of the petitioner's exclusion, the value of the company, PC(L) Ltd, had fallen. This was partly due to the general fall in the market but had also occurred whilst PC(L) Ltd was under the sole control of W. Although W had made various offers to purchase the petitioner's shares, these could not be regarded as 'fair offers'. By the time of the hearing PC(L) Ltd had been placed into administration by way of a pre-pack sale (allegedly at an undervalue), to a new company controlled by senior employees of

---

[70] [1999] BCC 600 at pp. 613–615.
[71] The principles in *O'Neill* are being applied in many cases; see for instance *Re G H Marshall Ltd* [2001] BCC 152; *Re Phoenix Office Supplies Ltd* [2003] 1 BCLC 76, CA.
[72] [2010] EWHC 2375 (Ch) (Ch D).

PC(L) Ltd. W had known about this; S did not. These were all factors which led the court to conclude that the correct date for valuation of the petitioner's shares was the date of his exclusion, rather than the date of the order.

The factors which were relevant to the court's conclusion that the offers by W to purchase S's shares were not 'fair' included the fact that there was no equality of arms between the two parties. At the time of the offer, S was still suspended, was denied access to the company's management accounts and the minutes and papers of management meetings, and a bonus which had been allocated to him had remained unpaid. The court found that it was unfair to expect S to take the risk of a valuation at current values without knowledge of what had happened whilst he had been suspended. Other factors which were relevant to the court's finding that the offers by W to purchase S's shares were unfair included the fact that no provision had been made for costs and no provision had been made for the payment of the bonus owing to S, and the fact that under the terms of the offer, W reserved the right to reject the independent valuer's valuation and place the company into liquidation instead.[73] The court therefore held that it would not strike out the proceedings on the basis that these offers had not been accepted by S.

### 5 *The parent–subsidiary relationship*

In considering the role of the unfair prejudice remedy in the context of corporate groups, the issue of parent company control over subsidiaries has attracted most comment. Indeed, it is now accepted following *Nicholas* v *Soundcraft*[74] and the earlier House of Lords decision in *Scottish Co-Operative Wholesale Society Ltd* v *Meyer*,[75] that the unfair prejudice remedy has the potential to perform a valuable function in this context. For example, Joffe contends that '[t]he acts or omissions of a parent company in relation to a subsidiary in which it has a majority shareholding are capable of amounting to conduct of the subsidiary's affairs'.[76]

One particular type of situation has given rise to difficulty. The issue here is whether conduct of the affairs of a parent company as majority shareholder in a subsidiary can be conduct in the affairs of the subsidiary. This appears to be of particular relevance where the subsidiary contains an independent minority of shareholders. It clearly has implications in certain limited circumstances for the freedom of the parent company to run its affairs. In *Gross* v *Rackind*,[77] the main question was whether the court had power to order relief on a company when in fact it is the affairs of that company's subsidiary that had been conducted in an unfairly prejudicial manner. Judge Weeks, citing *Nicholas* v *Soundcraft Electronics Ltd*,[78] took the view that 'in the right circumstances acts in the

---

[73] See also *Maidment* v *Attwood* [2012] EWCA Civ 998 in which it was held that if company is in insolvent liquidation the petitioner must first show that, but for the alleged wrongdoing, his shares would have had value. It was also held that the fact the company was now insolvent was a complicating factor but courts take a wide view of prejudice suffered by shareholders and take a flexible approach to do what is necessary to achieve a just and fair result.

[74] [1993] BCLC 360 (CA).

[75] [1959] AC 324 (HL).

[76] V. Joffe *Minority Shareholders: Law, Practice and Procedure* (London: Butterworths, 2000), p. 152.

[77] [2004] EWCA Civ 815.

[78] [1993] BCLC 360.

conduct of a subsidiary's affairs can also be acts in the conduct of the holding company's affairs'. He could 'see no logical reason for protecting shareholders of a trading company by s. 459 [s. 994] but not shareholders in a holding company.' The facts were that the shares in the holding company, Citybranch Group Ltd, were held in equal shares by the Gross and Rackind families. The holding company had been incorporated in 2001 in order to acquire two companies, Citybranch Ltd and Blaneland Ltd. The shares in these companies had been held by two families. The relationship between the families broke down and Mr Rackind (R), a director and shareholder of the holding company, decided to wind it up. The Gross family petitioned under s. 994 on the basis that R was in breach of fiduciary duty to Blaneland Ltd and had misappropriated funds belonging to Citybranch Ltd. They argued that R's conduct with respect to the subsidiaries amounted to conduct in relation to the affairs of the parent company. R's application to strike out the petition on the basis that, *inter alia*, it alleged unfairly prejudicial conduct in relation to the subsidiaries rather than the company itself was dismissed. His appeal to the Court of Appeal failed. Sir Martin Nourse, who delivered the only reasoned judgment, endorsed the views of the trial judge that conduct taking place in relation to a subsidiary could fall within the affairs of the holding company. He agreed with Judge Weeks that the decision in *Nicholas* could support such a conclusion on the basis that it is in line with the views expressed by Phillimore J in *R* v *Board of Trade, ex p St Martins Preserving Co Ltd*:[79]

> The observations of Phillimore J demonstrate that the expression 'the affairs of the company' is one of the widest import which can include the affairs of a subsidiary. Equally, I would hold that the affairs of a subsidiary can also be the affairs of its holding company, especially where, as here, the directors of the holding company, which necessarily controls the affairs of the subsidiary, also represent a majority of the directors of the subsidiary. (In the case of Blaneland they are identical.)

Sir Martin Nourse also felt that this approach is entirely consistent with Commonwealth authorities, notably *Re Norvabron Pty Ltd*[80] and *Re Dernacourt Investments Pty Ltd*[81] where petitions were brought under equivalent provisions to s. 994. In finding that R, as a director of the company, knew very well what was happening in Citybranch and Blaneland given that he was the person involved, the judge was particularly persuaded by the summing up in the notion of the 'company's affairs' which was made in *Re Dernacourt Investments Pty Ltd* (which followed the decision in *Re Norvabron*). Powell J made two broad statements:[82]

> (a)  The words 'affairs of a company' are extremely wide and should be construed liberally: (a) in determining the ambit of the 'affairs' of a parent company for the purposes of s. 320, the court looks at the business realities of a situation and does not confine them to a narrow legalistic view; (b) 'affairs' of a company encompass all matters which may come before its board for consideration; (c) conduct of the 'affairs' of a parent company includes refraining

---

[79] [1965] 1 QB 603.
[80] *(No. 2)* [1986] 11 ACLR 279.
[81] [1990] 2 ASCR 553.
[82] Cited in [2004] EWCA Civ 815, para. 29.

from procuring a subsidiary to do something or condoning by inaction an act of a subsidiary, particularly when the directors of the parent and the subsidiary are the same.[83]

(b) The proposition that the business or 'affairs' of a parent company include the business of its wholly owned subsidiary for the purposes of s. 320 is consistent with a general tendency in modern cases for the courts to ignore, where justice and commonsense so require, the separate legal identities of various companies within a group and look instead at the economic entity of the whole group.[84]

Looking back at *Gross* v *Rackind*, Sir Martin Nourse concluded that:[85]

In my judgment none of the three further authorities can be said to diminish the persuasive value of the decisions in Norvabron and Dernacourt. Those were considered judgments of judges of the Supreme Courts of Queensland and New South Wales respectively and they are directly in point. I would follow them accordingly.

Although there are English first instance decisions (not considered by Sir Martin Nourse) which took a contrary view,[86] the Court of Appeal's approach leaves a number of questions unanswered.[87] Must the subsidiary company be wholly owned in order for its affairs to fall within those of the parent company? Must the subsidiary company's directors also be directors of the parent company? Thus uncertainty still remains, notwithstanding *Nicholas*, with regard to the issue of whether parent company actions can be regarded as falling within subsidiary company affairs.[88] Whatever the case may be, using s. 994 to address problems arising within corporate groups will often involve a difficult choice between the consequences of preserving the separate legal identity of group companies and acceding to the call for enhanced protection of shareholders.[89]

In *Oak Investment Partners XII Ltd Partnership* v *Boughtwood & Ors*,[90] Sales J provided a rather broad interpretation of the concept of the company's affairs. While stressing that the provision was concerned with the practical reality in relation to the conduct of a company's affairs, Sales J observed that:

The precise distribution of management decision-making authority in any particular company may be a matter of chance. In some companies, the board itself may take a wider range of day-to-day

---

[83] In *Hawkes* v *Cuddy* [2009] EWCA Civ 291; [2010] BCC 597, the Court of Appeal accepted these propositions but with some qualification. Stanley Burnton LJ stated, at [50], that: '(b) may extend to matters which are capable of coming before the board for its consideration, and may not be limited to those that actually come before the board: I do not accept that matters that are not considered by the board are not capable of being part of its affairs. Nonetheless, like the judge, I am unable to see how it can be said that the affairs of Neath and of Osprey were so intermingled that all of the affairs of the latter were the affairs of the former. It would, for example, be quite irrational to suggest that Mr Blyth, when acting as a director of Osprey, was conducting the affairs of Neath.'

[84] This is the position in Australia. However, recall that in *Adams* v *Cape Industries plc* the idea that a court was free to disregard *Salomon* merely because it considered that justice so required was firmly rejected by the court. See Chapter 2, 2.1B.

[85] *Ibid.* para. 32.

[86] For example *Re Leeds United Holdings plc* [1996] 2 BCLC 545 and *Reiner* v *Gershinson* [2004] EWHC 76 (Ch); [2004] 2 BCLC 376.

[87] For an analysis of these issues in light of *Gross* v *Rackind*, see B. Taylor 'Implications for the Corporate Veil Principle: *Gross* v *Rackind*' (2005) 26 *Business Law Review* 2; R. Goddard and H.C. Hirt 'Section 459 and Corporate Groups' (2005) JBL 247.

[88] As a general rule the separate personality of companies that are not in a group relationship must be respected. See *Re Grandactual Ltd; Hough* v *Hartland* [2005] EWHC 1415 (Ch) on this point.

[89] Goddard and Hirt, n. 84, 252.

[90] [2009] EWHC 176 (Ch).

management decisions than in others, where greater scope is left to the directors or employed managers acting alone. It is difficult to see why the application of section 994 should turn upon such fortuitous matters: the jurisdiction under that provision is above all a jurisdiction concerned with substance rather than form. In my view, conduct of a shareholder/director who acted in breach of fiduciary duty in the carrying on of his company's affairs (but not through use of any company organ) would be conduct capable, in principle, of attracting relief under section 994. There is often a very fine line between duties of employees engaged as senior managers of a company and the fiduciary duty of skill and care owed by a director of a company carrying out similar tasks. I can see no reason in principle why, in an appropriate case, conduct by a person employed as a senior manager in a business, even if not a director, should not be relevant to the grant of relief under section 994. Moreover, the cases on mismanagement of a company's affairs . . . contemplate that complaint may be made under section 994 even if the mismanagement is not the product of business decisions taken by the board of a company, but by individual directors or others.

[Counsel] submitted that there is a distinction between conduct of the affairs of a company falling within section 994 and conduct which does not. He referred to an example given by Harman J of a director who steals from a safe, in *Re a Company (1761 of 1986)* [1987] BCLC 141, at 148. In broad terms, I accept the distinction (although I would wish to reserve my position in relation to the particular example given by Harman J; it seems to me a great deal may depend on the facts: if mismanagement by a director in breach of his duty of skill and care may found a petition under section 994, I have difficulty in seeing why a director's theft from his company in breach of his fiduciary duty may not). Conduct of anyone involved in a company may be so far removed from actually carrying on the affairs of the company that it does not amount to the conduct of the company's affairs for the purposes of section 994. But in my view, section 994 is concerned with the practical reality which obtains on the ground in relation to the conduct of a company's affairs, and there is no sound reason to exclude the possibility that what someone does in exercising or purporting to exercise managerial powers as a director or senior employee should not in principle qualify as conduct of the affairs of a company for the purposes of that provision.[91]

More recently, in *F&C Alternative Investments (Holdings) Ltd v Barthelemy*,[92] the judge considered the scope of the fiduciary duties owed by board members of a limited liability partnership (F&C Partners LLP) and allegations of unfairly prejudicial conduct under s. 994. One of the LLP's partners was a company, F&C Alternative Investments (Holdings) Limited, which was in turn wholly owned by F&C Asset Management plc. The judge found both of these companies liable under s. 994, observing that the former was in reality a cipher for the latter:

Although F&C plc may perhaps be said to be at one further remove from the active conduct of the affairs of the LLP (in that it was not a party to the Agreement), I also have no hesitation in concluding that it also should be held liable under section 994 for the same pattern of unfairly prejudicial conduct of the affairs of the LLP. In truth, there is no clear distinction to be drawn between Holdings and F&C plc in this regard. Holdings was in reality a cipher for the F&C Group, and F&C plc in particular. There were no Board meetings of Holdings. Mr Ribeiro was authorised by its directors (Mr Grisay and F&C plc) to conduct its affairs, reporting back to Mr Grisay and F&C plc as he thought appropriate. F&C plc, acting by Execom, was informed about Mr Ribeiro's strategy of trying to remove decision-making in the LLP to the Members' meeting and in substance endorsed his approach and authorised him to proceed . . . Thereafter, F&C plc continued to be happy to leave Mr Ribeiro to handle the detailed conduct of the dispute, trusting

---

[91] *Ibid.* at [14]–[15].
[92] [2011] EWHC 1731 (Ch).

him to promote F&C's interests, without making any attempt to intervene to control his actions. There was thus, in a broad sense, authorisation from F&C plc to Mr Ribeiro and the F&C representatives to proceed in acting as they did . . .[93]

In addition, the same points as in para [1097(x) to (xii)] above apply with equal force in relation to F&C plc as in relation to Holdings. Indeed, in my view, they apply with greater force, since (because of the cipher-like nature of Holdings) when thinking about the interests of F&C and in understanding how they might be advanced by action against the interests of the Defendants, the individuals concerned tended in reality to think about F&C plc (and the F&C Group, of which F&C plc was the head company) rather than Holdings. The practical benefits for F&C derived from the pattern of unfairly prejudicial conduct also flowed, in reality, to F&C plc, which (rather than Holdings) had the ultimate commercial interest in controlling the LLP's affairs.[94]

In *Re BC&G Care Homes Ltd*,[95] the Chancery Division, Companies Court held that the removal of the petitioner Mr Crowley's right to be involved in the management of a quasi-partnership was an unfair, disproportionate and unjustifiable response to allegations of misconduct in the absence of a fair offer to acquire his shares in the company. Despite incorporation of the Company as a limited company, evidence suggested that the shareholders' relationship broadly continued under the former partnership agreement. Therefore, the exercise of rights in the Company's articles to remove Mr Crowley as a director was subject to equitable constraint. The court decided that this was contrary to the 'quasi-partnership' basis of the Company, which had been formed as a result of the original partnership agreement. It was decided that irrespective of any misconduct, his removal as director and employee, without an offer to purchase his shares, amounted to unfair prejudice. In other words, it was 'clearly prejudicial' to his interests as a shareholder as he no longer had employment or a position on the board to monitor the care homes, the companies and his own investment. Such removal in breach of the agreements and understandings underlying his position as a shareholder, whereby he could expect to be a director and employee, was also considered to be unfair, notwithstanding the petitioner's conduct, as none of the allegations justified 'his exclusion while leaving him locked into the Company'. Whilst it is clear that a 'useful test is always to ask whether the exercise of the power or rights in question would involve a breach of an agreement or understanding between the parties . . . [s]uch agreements do not have to be contractually binding in order to found the equity.' Failure to buy out shares of a sacked director in a quasi-partnership company was unfair. Consequently, company directors and shareholders proposing to remove a director should consider whether the company is a 'quasi-partnership' and are, therefore, required to make a fair offer to buy out the director's shares.

While the courts have displayed a slightly greater willingness to entertain actions initiated by majority shareholders in unfair prejudice petitions, it still remains exceptional. This is unsurprising as a majority shareholder will generally have control over the composition of the board of directors and should be able to put right any prejudice that may have

---

[93] *Ibid.* at [1099]–[1100].
[94] *Ibid.* at [1101].
[95] *Re BC&G Care Homes Ltd; subnom Crowley v Bessell and others* [2015] All ER (D) 115; *Re BC&G Care Homes Ltd; subnom Crowley v Bessell and Others* [2015] EWHC 1518 (Ch).

been suffered. That said, although rare, it is possible that there may be more complex situations, for example where a majority shareholder does not control board appointments because of provisions in the articles of association, and it is possible that an action by the majority shareholder could proceed.

## 6 *Examples of situations remedied*

The discussion thus far has largely[96] centred on cases where a share purchase order has been sought, and where the core of the matters complained of relate to exclusion of a shareholder director from management in a quasi-partnership company.

But unfair prejudice proceedings have been used to remedy a wide variety of abuses and the judges have taken seriously the jurisdiction of the court to make, in the words of the statute, 'such order as it thinks fit'.[97] However, in spite of this wide discretion, petitioners are expected to state the nature of the relief they seek, and not simply pour out a list of grievances and then leave it up to the court to do something appropriate.[98]

Cases in the early years of the jurisdiction showed it being used to maintain the status quo, pending, say, the holding of a meeting.[99] It has been used successfully to complain of failures to run a company properly such as ignoring the need to hold meetings or produce accounts.[100] A wide variety of abusive share issues or share watering situations have triggered successful petitions.[101] In some circumstances it is possible that failure to declare dividends could be unfairly prejudicial conduct.[102] It has even been held possible for a court to make a buyout order against a third party.[103] In the early days after 1980, lawyers eagerly discussed whether negligence could ever form the substance of a successful petition.[104] Derivative litigation by a minority had not generally been permitted since it was a ratifiable breach.[105] Would it be 'prejudice' but not 'unfair'? Arguably, it was a commercial risk that you accepted by risking your capital when buying into a company. If a person

---

[96] Though not exclusively.

[97] Companies Act 2006, s. 996 (1).

[98] See Companies (Unfair Prejudice Applications) Proceedings Rules 1986 (SI 1986 No. 2000).

[99] *Whyte, Petitioner* (1984) 1 BCC 99,044; *Re a Company 002612 of 1984* (1984) 1 BCC 99,262.

[100] *Re a Company 00789 of 1987* (1989) 5 BCC 792, and [1991] BCC 44, CA.

[101] Examples are: *Re a Company 007623 of 1984* (1986) 2 BCC 99,191; *Re a Company 005134 of 1986* (1989) BCLC 383.

[102] *Re Sam Weller Ltd* (1989) 5 BCC 810. But the argument failed on the facts in *Re Saul Harrison Ltd* [1994] BCC 475.

[103] This occurred in *Re Little Olympian Each-Ways Ltd (No. 3)* [1995] 1 BCLC 636, where the petitioner complained that the company's business had been transferred at an undervalue to another company under the same control as the transferor, and it was held that the court had jurisdiction under s. 461 of the Companies Act 1985 to make the buyout order against that other company. Relief against a third party was similarly granted in *Re Fahey Ltd* [1996] BCC 320. Some aspects of the proceedings in this case had the substance of a derivative action and yet, curiously, it was held that legal aid was available to the petitioner. It was clear that legal aid would not have been available for a derivative action. It remains to be seen whether this is an isolated example, or whether it represents a softening of the rule against aiding corporate claimants in these kinds of cases.

[104] There was also a technical problem connected with the wording of s. 459 of the Companies Act 1985 which was remedied by amendment in the Companies Act 1989. The words 'or members generally' were added to obviate the argument that certain wrongs, like negligence, damaged the whole company, and not merely the petitioner and so were not within the section; see A.J. Boyle 'The Judicial Interpretation of Part XVII of the Companies Act 1985' in B. Pettet (ed.) *Company Law in Change* (London: Stevens, 1987) pp. 23–27.

[105] *Pavlides v Jensen* [1956] Ch 656, but see now s. 260 (3) of the Companies Act 2006 discussed in Chapter 11, 11.4C.

chooses to invest in a company run by fools then that was a bad investment decision, and for the law to interfere with that was to cut across the principle of sanctity of bargain in the making of contracts and relieve a party of the consequences of a bad bargain freely made. These considerations have not won the day and the courts have recently made it clear that they are prepared to regard negligence or mismanagement as a matter which could form the subject of a successful petition if it is sufficiently serious.[106]

A useful illustration of the power of the unfair prejudice jurisdiction occurred in the *Windward Islands* saga,[107] which is a rare example of the unfair prejudice jurisdiction being used to overturn directly the effect of a statutory provision. The Companies Act 1948, s. 132[108] contained an important minority shareholders' power whereby members holding 10% or more of the voting shares could require the directors of the company to requisition a meeting. The obvious purpose of it was to enable a minority to get a forum within the company to discuss and resolve matters of dispute. The section provided that: 'The directors of a company . . . shall . . . on the requisition of members . . . forthwith proceed duly to convene . . . [a meeting].' On 13 April 1982, the minority deposited a requisition with the company with the aim of having a meeting to remove two of the directors and 16 days later the directors sent out a notice convening the meeting. It was going to be held several months later, at lunchtime, on Sunday 22 August. Nourse J carried out an impeccable clinical analysis of the statutory provisions and correctly held that this was lawful. The distinction between *convening* a meeting and *holding* one was there in the statutory provisions.[109] It was an old trick and, as the judge pointed out, had been criticised 20 years earlier by the Jenkins Committee[110] but the recommendations had not been implemented. It was, as he said, 'An oddity, in regard to a section whose evident purpose was to protect minorities . . .'[111] However, once the statutory provisions were put under the scrutiny of the unfair prejudice jurisdiction, the result was astonishingly different. In *McGuinness, Petitioners*[112] some of the shareholders deposited their requisition with the company on 4 November 1987 and 'forthwith' on 23 November, their Glasgow-based company convened the meeting, to be held, in London, the following June. The Court of Session affirmed the analysis of Nourse J in *Windward Islands* but held that the shareholders were entitled to expect that the meeting would be held within a reasonable period and that in the circumstances this was unfairly prejudicial to their interests. Thus, when applied head-on against a statutory anomaly, s. 994 can simply reverse the result.[113]

---

[106] *Re Elgindata (No. 1) Ltd* [1991] BCLC 959; *Re Macro Ltd* [1994] BCC 781.
[107] *Re Windward Islands Ltd* (1988) 4 BCC 158.
[108] Later s. 368 of the Companies Act 1985, now s. 303 of the Companies Act 2006 (changed).
[109] See Companies Act 1948, s. 132 (3), which incorporated the distinction between 'convened' and 'held': 'If the directors do not within twenty-one days from the date of the deposit of the requisition proceed duly to convene a meeting, the requisitionists . . . may themselves convene a meeting, but any meeting so convened shall not be held after the expiration of three months from the said date.'
[110] Cmnd 1749, 1962, para. 458.
[111] *Ibid.* para. 161.
[112] (1988) 4 BCC 161.
[113] This problem has later been resolved by s. 368 (8) of the Companies Act 1985 which provided: 'The directors are deemed not to have duly convened a meeting if they convene a meeting for a date more than 28 days after the date of the notice convening the meeting': inserted by the Companies Act 1989, Sch. 19, para. 9. See now s. 304 of the Companies Act 2006.

In *Fulham Football Club (1987) Ltd* v *Richards*,[114] the judge, faced with conflicting authorities in *Re Vocam Europe Ltd* [1998] BCC 396 and *Exeter City Association Football Club Ltd* v *Football Conference Ltd* [2004] EWHC 831 (Ch), granted an application under s. 9 of the Arbitration Act 1996 to stay a petition brought under s. 994, in circumstances where rules had been agreed under which disputes would be referred to and resolved by arbitration. On appeal it was argued that the petition should not have been stayed and that the trial judge should have followed *Exeter City* in which HHJ Weeks QC held that the shareholder's right to petition for relief under (what is now) s. 994 was inalienable and could not be 'diminished or removed by contract or otherwise'.[115] The Court of Appeal[116] unanimously rejected this argument and upheld the trial judge's decision to stay the petition. Patten LJ, delivering the leading judgment, held that *Exeter City* had been wrongly decided and observed, amongst other things, that s. 994 gave shareholders 'an optional right to invoke the assistance of the court in cases of unfair prejudice . . . there is nothing in the scheme of these provisions which, in my view, makes the resolution of the underlying dispute inherently unsuitable for determination by arbitration on grounds of public policy'.[117]

More recently in *Re McCarthy Surfacing Limited*,[118] the failure of the board of directors to consider declaring a dividend, or taking excessive director's remuneration,[119] were both held to be sufficient grounds for an order that the petitioners had been unfairly prejudiced.[120] In *Rahman* v *Malik*,[121] it was held that a quasi-partnership agreement between two brothers endured for the benefit of the son of one of them and what was fair as between the parties was determined by reference *inter alia* to cultural perceptions within the Bangladeshi community. In other words, the cultural setting can be an important factor for the purposes of determining the existence of unfair prejudice. And in *Holman* v *Adams Securities Ltd*[122] the court held that unfair prejudice may be established by a number of incidents, none of which on their own constitutes unfair prejudice, but if taken together could be considered to do so.

As to standing to bring the petition, in *Harris* v *Jones*[123] the High Court held that a person not yet registered as a member but to whom shares have been transferred or transmitted by operation of law *may* petition under s. 994 (2).

Any mismanagement for unfair prejudice purposes must also be connected to the affairs of the company rather than the affairs of another shareholder. The most high profile dispute on this point remains the *McKillen* v *Misland*[124] case, in which the Court of Appeal

---

[114] [2010] EWHC 3111 (Ch).
[115] At [23].
[116] [2011] EWCA Civ 855.
[117] At [78].
[118] [2009] 1 BCLC 622.
[119] See *Re Tobian Properties Ltd* [2012] EWVA Civ 998.
[120] However, the petitioners' shares were ordered to be bought out on a discounted as opposed to a pro rata basis because the company had ceased to operate as a quasi-partnership at the relevant time, the petitioners having withdrawn from the company following an earlier, unsuccessful petition. That was because they themselves destroyed the quasi-partnership by their own acts in bringing the previous proceedings. See also *Sikorski* v *Sikorski* [2012] EWHC 1613 (Ch).
[121] [2008] 2 BCLC 403.
[122] [2010] EWHC 2421 (Ch).
[123] [2011] EWHC 1518.
[124] *McKillen* v *Misland (Cyprus) Investments Ltd and Others* [2011] EWHC 3466 (Ch).

confirmed that the breach of a pre-emption clause in a shareholders' agreement or articles is unlikely to result in s. 994 relief, as the breach relates to a dispute amongst shareholders rather than the conduct of the company's affairs. While prejudice is a wide concept and unfairness is fairly elastic, the conduct must still relate to company management, rather than the actions of shareholders in their capacity as such.

## 7 Relationship with derivative claims[125]

An obvious problem for analysis is to consider the relationship which the unfair prejudice action has with the statutory derivative claim. Does the would-be litigant sometimes have the choice of bringing either a derivative claim or, alternatively, unfair prejudice proceedings? If so, which is the most advantageous procedure? Or will it depend on the circumstances?

The old case law on the common law derivative action and s. 459 of the Companies Act 1985[126] make it clear that a complaint by a minority shareholder, which is in substance derivative, in the sense that he is seeking to litigate a breach by a director of a duty owed to the company, can be the substance of unfair prejudice proceedings. For instance, in *Re Fahey Ltd*[127] the unfairly prejudicial conduct involved the diversion of company funds, and it was held that the petitioner was entitled to seek an order against members and directors involved in the unlawful diversion, for payment to the company itself.[128] Indeed, shareholders, even in situations whereby they are adversely affected by the breach of the directors' duties, are more inclined to pursue the unfair prejudice remedy. In many ways, this is a more flexible and useful remedy for the minority shareholder than derivative actions. The presence of this remedy and the unclear interaction between the two remedies projects an uneasy shadow, which in turn affects the viability of derivative actions.

First, with the exception of situations where only the company would have an action, a shareholder would be better off to rely upon 'unfair prejudice' since there is no need to go through the expense and uncertainty of a preliminary costs orders application. In addition, there is no requirement to make an application for leave to bring the unfair prejudice remedy. Secondly, two recent decisions indicate that the unfair prejudice remedy could substantially replace the derivative action.[129] Even in situations where the relief sought is claimed under s. 996 of the Companies Act 2006,[130] but is sought for the benefit of the

---

[125] For a comprehensive overview of this area see A. Reisberg *Derivative Actions and Corporate Governance: Theory and Operation* (Oxford: OUP, 2007), Chapter 8 and by the same author, 'Shareholders' Remedies: In Search of Consistency of Principle in English Law' (2005) 5 *European Business Law Review* 1063. See also, B. Hannigan, 'Drawing Boundaries Between Derivative Claims and Unfairly Prejudicial Petitions' (2009) 6 JBL 606 and L Yap 'Authorising Derivative Actions on Unfair Prejudice Petitions' (2011) 32 Comp Law 150. See also the recent cases on the statutory derivative procedure discussed in Chapter 11, 11.6 above.

[126] The early technical worry that the wording of s. 459 of the Companies Act 1985 precluded a complaint about a breach of duty owed to the company was eradicated by an amendment in the Companies Act 1989. It had been held that a breach of duty which affected all members equally was not within the section; see *Re Carrington Viyella plc* (1983) 1 BCC 98,951 at p. 98, 959, *per* Vinelott J.

[127] [1996] BCC 320. See also *Re Sherbourne Park Residents Co. Ltd* (1986) 2 BCC 99, 528 (where the point was *obiter*), *Re a Company 005287 of 1985* (1985) 1 BCC 99,586, and more recently *O'Donnell v Shanahan & Anor* [2009] EWCA Civ 751, discussed in Chapter 8 above under 8.2E 2.

[128] Also against a third party company.

[129] *Bhullar v Bhullar* [2003] EWCA Civ 424 taken together with *Clark v Cutland* [2003] EWCA Civ 810, see below.

[130] Formerly s. 461 of the Companies Act 1985.

company, it is still open for a shareholder to seek a recovery order against the company for payment to him of any cost incurred by him.[131] This is likely, in turn, as we explain below, to make (perhaps unintentionally) derivative claims even less attractive than they already are. Thirdly, proving unfair prejudice may be easier than proving a breach of corporate rights or proving that the derivative action is 'likely to promote the success of the company'.[132] Finally, in most cases, the applicant personally receives the benefit of the relief provided under the unfair prejudice remedy whereas the benefit of any recovery under the derivative action accrues to the company directly and only indirectly to the applicant. The fact that recovery is the right of the company in derivative claim means that a successful litigant will not be better off than fellow shareholders who made no effort to support the proceedings.[133]

Against this backdrop, the popularity of the unfair prejudice remedy is not surprising. The experience in Canada indeed illustrates that the derivative claim will be perceived as more procedurally complex and the less favourable form of action without some limit being placed upon the *scope* of the unfairly prejudicial conduct action.[134] And the decisions in *Mission Capital plc* v *Sinclair*,[135] *Franbar Holdings Ltd* v *Patel and others*[136] and *Cinematic Finance Ltd* v *Ryder and Others*[137] discussed in the Chapter 11[138] will do very little to change this.

To add to this, a number of other recent decisions have reaffirmed the view that the unfair prejudice remedy could substantially replace the derivative claim.[139] Arden LJ gives no reasons for her expansion of the role of the unfair prejudice remedy in *Cutland*. However, some strong arguments do exist to support this decision. First, the pre-*Cutland*

---

[131] *Clark* v *Cutland*, para. 35. On the issue of costs, in *Re Southern Counties Fresh Foods Ltd* [2011] EWHC 1370 (Ch) Warren J said that costs flowing from an unfair prejudice petition did not attract any special principles: the starting point was the general rule in CPR r. 44.3 (2) (a) that the unsuccessful party will be ordered to pay the costs of the successful party. However, an unsuccessful party did not bear an onus to demonstrate that adopting the general rule would be unjust: it was for the court to consider what departures from the general rule were appropriate in light of all the circumstances of the case. In this case, the costs order had to reflect the fact that although C was successful in obtaining the relief sought, its success was qualified as it had failed to establish many of its allegations of unfair prejudice. There was no way of sensibly apportioning the overall costs between general costs and costs of specific issues without engaging in a disproportionate detailed analysis of the transcripts or expending a great deal of time and expense. Accordingly, it was necessary to do the best one could do on the material available.

[132] *Smith* v *Croft (No. 2)* [1988] Ch 114 and see Chapter 11, 11.6 above.

[133] See Chapter 11, 11.2D and 11.7 above.

[134] This is the position despite the fact that when bringing such action shareholders face potential liability for costs. B.R. Cheffins 'Reforming the Derivative Action: The Canadian Experience and British Prospects' [1997] 2 CFILR 227, 259; B.R. Cheffins and J. Dine 'Shareholder Remedies: Lessons from Canada' (1992) 13 *Company Lawyer* 89; J.G. MacIntosh 'The Oppression Remedy: Personal or Derivative?' (1991) 70 *Canada Bar Review* 29. This appears to be at variance with the experience in Australia. See I. Ramsay and B. Saunders 'Litigation by Shareholders and Directors: An Empirical Study of the Statutory Derivative Action' (2006) 6 JCLS 397, Table 8.

[135] [2008] EWHC 1339 (Ch).

[136] [2008] EWHC 1534 (Ch).

[137] [2010] EWC 3387 (Ch).

[138] See 11.7 above.

[139] *Bhullar* v *Bhullar* [2003] EWCA Civ 424; *Clark* v *Cutland* [2003] EWCA Civ 810 considered in A. Reisberg 'Indemnity Costs Orders under S. 459 Petition?' (2004) 25 Co Law 118. But see *Stainer* v *Lee* [2010] EWHC 1539 (Ch), where the trial judge observed that 'I consider that given what is at the heart of the present case, a derivative action is entirely appropriate and therefore the theoretical availability to the Applicant of proceedings by way of an unfair prejudice petition is not a reason to refuse permission' (para. 52).

line drawn by the judges allowed the unfair prejudice remedy to be brought where a wrong is done to the company but only in order to support a claim for personal relief for the petitioner.[140] However, this approach is not necessitated by the terms of s. 994 and there is nothing within the legislation to prevent Arden LJ's approach.[141] Indeed s. 996 (2) (c) provides that a corporate remedy may be awarded by the courts, albeit via the commencement of a new piece of litigation in the company's name. In circumstances where a wrong is done to the company and corporate relief is sought by a petitioner, it is difficult to see why the cost and inconvenience of two sets of proceedings should be preferable to the court awarding corporate relief directly under s. 996.[142] The chances of a petitioning shareholder wishing to undertake a second piece of litigation are also extremely unlikely given the fact that in most circumstances they are seeking to exit the company by obtaining a buyout order. Unsurprisingly, s. 996 (2) (c) has been little used in practice and few reported cases exist in which such an order has been made.[143]

Why, then, has it taken the courts so long to make use of the unfair prejudice remedy to provide a substantive remedy to the company in relation to corporate wrongs, and why was the assimilation of these two remedies actively resisted by the Law Commission when it investigated the issue of shareholders' remedies? As is explained elsewhere,[144] there are very compelling reasons for this resistance.

## 8 Relationship with just and equitable winding up

In the early years of the judicial development of the unfair prejudice jurisdiction, it was common for an unfair prejudice petition to include, as an alternative, a claim for winding up on the just and equitable ground.[145] This often also had an *in terrorem* element, since a winding-up order would kill off the company and perhaps the inclusion of it would help to coerce the respondents into making the offer to buy out the petitioner. The practice has been less common since the 1990 *Practice Direction*,[146] which required that a claim for winding up must not be made as a matter of course, and should only be included if winding up is the remedy which is preferred or if it is thought that it might be the only relief

---

[140] See e.g. *Re Charnley Davies Ltd (No. 2)* [1990] BCLC 760, 784 *per* Millett J. These cases undoubtedly blur the classic distinction between personal wrongs and corporate wrongs, and raise some potentially difficult questions about the ability of shareholders to recover reflective loss, but they do not infringe the principle of collective enforcement of directors' wrongs because of the personal nature of the remedy involved. H. Hirt 'In What Circumstances Should Breaches of Directors' Duties Give Rise to a Remedy Under Ss. 459–461 of the Companies Act 1985?' (2003) 24 *Company Lawyer* 100, 109.

[141] J. Payne 'Shareholders' Remedies Reassessed' (2004) 67 MLR 500, 501–502.

[142] See e.g. *Re a Company* (No. 005287 of 1985) [1986] 1 WLR 281; Consultation Paper para. 10.9.

[143] One example is *Re Cyplon Developments Ltd* (Court of Appeal, 3 March 1982). L. Kosmin 'Minority Shareholders' Remedies: A Practitioner Perspective' [1997] 2 CFILR 201, 213 ('If ever an example were sought of an impractical remedy which exists only in the minds of the parliamentary draftsman, this is it').

[144] See A. Reisberg *Derivative Actions and Corporate Governance: Theory and Operation* (Oxford: OUP, 2007) Chapter 8 and 'Shareholders' Remedies: In Search of Consistency of Principle in English Law' (2005) 5 *European Business Law Review* 1063.

[145] As to which, see the cases referred to under 12.2 above.

[146] [1990] 1 WLR 490. Practice Direction: Order under s. 127 of the Insolvency Act 1986 [2007] BCC 839 repeats the undesirability of asking as a matter of course for a winding-up order as an alternative to an order against unfairly prejudicial conduct because of the freezing effect of s. 127 of the 1986 Act.

available.[147] If no winding-up claim is made but the court concludes that the share purchase order sought in respect of unfair prejudice is an inappropriate remedy, it seems that the court has no power under s. 996 to make a winding-up order instead. In such circumstances a court told the petitioner to present a winding-up petition.[148]

The effect of s. 125 (2) of the Insolvency Act 1986 has already been noted[149] but it is worth alluding to again in this context because the availability of an unfair prejudice remedy might, in some circumstances, be held to disentitle the petitioner to wind up.[150] It would be a different remedy and in some circumstances the court might take the view that the petitioner was being unreasonable in not pursuing that remedy. For example, in *Hawkes* v *Cuddy*,[151] the Court of Appeal took the opportunity to reassert the distinctiveness of the unfair prejudice remedy from the just and equitable winding up remedy. It rejected the observations of in *Re Guidezone*[152] by Jonathan Parker J that conduct which is not sufficient to found an unfair prejudice petition is necessarily insufficient to found a winding-up petition based on the 'just and equitable' ground.[153] The Court of Appeal also rejected a converse submission of Robin Hollington QC that a breakdown of trust and confidence, resulting in deadlock and the inability of the company to conduct its business in the manner originally contemplated, was sufficient to found an order under s. 994 of the Companies Act 2006. The Court held that there must be unfairness based on established equitable principles.

Finally, it is worth noting that in *Amin* v *Amin*[154] Warren J found the petitioners' allegations of unfair prejudice unfounded but nevertheless recognised that the circumstances may well have founded a successful petition for just and equitable winding up, although the petitioners had not sought this.[155] Interestingly, Warren J also observed, *obiter*, that:[156]

> If the facts are such that a winding up petition on the 'just and equitable' ground would succeed but the majority refuse to agree to a winding up out of court, that conduct might amount to unfair prejudice, the unfairness being to compel the minority to continue to participate in the company when the court would, on this hypothesis, wind it up.

---

[147] Though facts which fall short of achieving an unfair prejudice remedy will also often fail to achieve a just and equitable winding up because the basic ideas behind these two remedies are similar; see, for instance, *Re Guidezone Ltd* [2000] 2 BCLC 321.

[148] *Re Full Cup Ltd* [1995] BCC 682.

[149] See 12.1 above.

[150] See *Re a Company 002567 of 1982* [1983] 2 All ER 854; *Re a Company 003843 of 1986* [1987] BCLC 562; *Coulon Sanderson and Ward Ltd* v *Ward* (1986) 2 BCC 99,207, CA; *Re a Company 001363 of 1988* (1989) 5 BCC 18; *Re Abbey Leisure Ltd* [1990] BCC 60, CA.

[151] [2009] EWCA Civ 291. The decision is also known as *Re Neath Rugby* [2009] 2 BCLC 427.

[152] [2000] 2 BCLC 321.

[153] Indeed, in *Fulham Football Club (1987) Ltd* v *Richards* [2011] EWCA Civ 855 (para. 56) the court held that s. 994 will usually provide the source of a satisfactory alternative remedy such as a buy-out order so that winding up under s. 122 (1) (g) is therefore a last resort and an exceptional remedy to grant in the context of disputes between shareholders. The court stated that this is confirmed by the terms of the current Practice Direction 49B which draws attention to the undesirability of asking, as a matter of course, for a winding-up order as an alternative to an order under s. 994. See also *Dineshkumar Jeshang Shah* v *Mahendra Jeshang Shah* [2010] EWHC 313 (Ch) 38.

[154] [2009] EWHC 3356 (Ch).

[155] See [613].

[156] At [584].

## 9 *Law reform proposals*

The Law Commission's Consultation Paper No. 142 (1996) and its ensuing Report No. 246 in 1997, which were considered in Chapter 11 in relation to reforming the derivative claim,[157] also encompassed consideration of the unfair prejudice remedy. Although these reforms were not eventually implemented in the Companies Act 2006, they shed some light on the problems brought forward by the success of the unfair prejudice remedy.

The Law Commission, in its reform proposals,[158] was concerned to deal both with the excessive length and cost of unfair prejudice petitions and also to try to reduce the amount of litigation.[159] The Law Commission proposed that the problems of excessive length and cost should be dealt with primarily by active case management to be dealt with in the context of the Woolf rules of court. These would involve techniques such as greater use of the power to direct that preliminary issues be heard, giving the court power to dismiss parts of a case which had no realistic prospect of success, adjournment to facilitate alternative dispute resolution, and increased flexibility on costs orders.

There were also several proposals which would have the effect both of reducing the amount of litigation being brought in the first place and also shorten it up if it was brought. The Law Commission recommended that in certain circumstances[160] there should be a legislative presumption that unfair prejudice will be presumed where the shareholder has been excluded from participation in the management of a private company. This would no doubt act as a major deterrent to litigation in many cases, since it will put considerable pressure on the respondent to settle, as he otherwise faces an uphill task. However, if litigation nevertheless occurs and the presumption is not rebutted, then a second presumption arises, namely that if the court feels that a share purchase order is the appropriate remedy, then that order should be on a pro rata basis.[161] The other Law Commission suggestion which was aimed to prevent litigation arising is that appropriate provisions should be included in Table A of the Companies Act 1985 to encourage parties to sort out areas of potential dispute. In particular here, they recommend that Table A contains what they call an 'exit article', the broad effect of which is that the shareholder will have a right to be bought out if he is removed as director.[162]

Later, the Company Law Review considered the recommendations of the Law Commission in the light of the responses to the DTI's subsequent consultation. The

---

[157] See 12.3 above.

[158] Law Com. Report No. 246 (Cm. 3769, 1997); and see further Chapter 11, 11.3 above. See also J. Lowry 'Mapping the Boundaries of Unfair Prejudice' in J. de Lacey (ed.) *The Reform of Company Law* (London: Cavendish, 2002).

[159] There were also various technical recommendations relating to other matters, including the operation of the winding-up remedy. As regards this, the Law Commission recommended *inter alia* that winding up should be added to the list of remedies available to a petitioner in unfair prejudice proceedings, that leave should be required before a petitioner under s. 994 could apply for winding up, and, most significantly, leave should be required before a petitioner could apply for winding up in conjunction with an unfair prejudice petition.

[160] The conditions are, broadly, that: the company is a private company limited by shares; that the petitioner has been removed as director or has been prevented from carrying out all or substantially all of his functions as a director; that all or substantially all the members were directors; that immediately before the exclusion the petitioner held shares giving him 10% of the voting rights; see further Law Com. Report No. 246 (Cm. 3769, 1997) para. 8.4.

[161] *Ibid.* paras 8.5–8.6.

[162] *Ibid.* para. 8.9.

Review strongly supported the proposal for stronger case management (although this is already in operation under the Civil Procedure Rules 1998). However, it was felt that the exit article would not be used in practice owing to its inflexibility; it was impossible to prescribe in advance what would be a fair exit regime.[163] Other matters were also considered (including the desirability of the decision in *O'Neill* v *Phillips*), although the view was expressed that winding up should not be included as a remedy under s. 996.[164] In the Final Report, the Review came down in favour of not reversing *O'Neill*.[165]

## Further reading

J. Lowry 'Stretching the Ambit of section 459 of the Companies Act 1985: The Elasticity of Unfair Prejudice' [1995] *LMCLQ* 337.

J. Lowry 'Mapping the Boundaries of Unfair Prejudice' in J. de Lacey (ed.) *The Reform of Company Law* (London: Cavendish, 2002).

A. Reisberg 'Shareholders' Remedies: In Search of Consistency of Principle in English Law' (2005) 5 *European Business Law Review* 1063.

A. Reisberg *Derivative Actions and Corporate Governance: Theory & Operation* (Oxford: OUP, 2007), Chapter 8.

B. Hannigan 'Drawing Boundaries Between Derivative Claims and Unfairly Prejudicial Petitions' (2009) 6 *JBL* 606.

---

[163] DTI Consultation Document (March 2000) *Developing the Framework*, para. 4.103.
[164] *Ibid.* paras 4.104–4.111.
[165] *Modern Company Law for a Competitive Economy Final Report* (London: DTI, 2001), paras 7.41–7.45.

# Part IV
# Corporate finance law

# 13

# Techniques of corporate finance

## 13.1 Some basic concepts of corporate finance

### A Assets and capital

In order to perform a trading or manufacturing activity a company will need assets. What exactly is needed will depend on the type, size and complexity of the business operations to be conducted, but one could imagine that it might need to take a lease of premises, perhaps a factory, install machinery, acquire office furniture, computers and communications equipment, storage facilities and hire staff. Decisions will have to be made about the acquisition of each of these items and once the company is up and running, decisions will continue to have to be made about the purchase of further assets, even if this is simply confined to replacing existing assets which have become worn out or have been used up. Each of these decisions is an investment decision, and the financial success or failure of the company will depend, in large measure, on these decisions being well made. They are of course, decisions about how the company's money is to be invested.

Which brings us to the next[1] question: 'Where does the money come from?' The broad answer is that companies sell claims against them in return for money, for capital. That capital can then be used to finance the company's investment decisions. The claims that they sell will fall into one or other of two categories; equity or debt. The term 'equity' can mean different things in different contexts, but here it means the risk bearing shares, usually[2] what are called 'ordinary shares'. A purchaser of an ordinary share will usually be purchasing a package of rights which can be described as 'residual' in the sense that he or she and the other ordinary shareholders, in proportion to their shareholdings, will lay claim to what remains of the assets[3] of the company after those with fixed money sum claims (i.e. the creditors) have been paid. The term 'debt' denotes a claim against the company for the payment at a future date of a fixed money sum, usually with interest accruing pending repayment of the principal sum. Thus, a company will raise the money it needs to

---

[1] 'Next' for the purposes of this account. In a practical sense, answering it and taking effective action on it is a prerequisite to the company's being able to put into effect any investment decisions.

[2] The position is complicated by hybrid types of shares such as participating preference shares, particularly where the participation is as to capital; see e.g. *Bannatyne* v *Direct Spanish Telegraph Co.* (1886) 34 Ch D 287. In some situations, preference capital can turn into equity in the sense of becoming residual owners as a result of a rationalisation of loss of capital; see *Re Floating Dock* [1895] 1 Ch 691. These cases are discussed below.

[3] Obviously under the *Salomon* doctrine, they are not, *qua* shareholders, entitled to the assets of the company; but behind this legal doctrine lies the financial reality that in a liquidation, the ordinary shareholders are the residual owners of the assets of the company.

finance its investment decisions by issuing equity securities, or by borrowing, either by obtaining loans from banks or by issuing debt securities.[4] In order to operate efficiently the company will need to raise the capital as cheaply as possible, by issuing its shares for the highest prices possible and issuing debt securities at the lowest interest rates possible.[5]

## B The aims of the company

In modern corporate finance doctrine, the aims of the company will normally be to maximise shareholder wealth or as it is often called, 'shareholder value'.[6] Maximising shareholder wealth/value is not the same as maximising profits, although in the long term the latter will have much bearing on the former. Profits are an accountancy-based concept which depend upon measuring net gains according to accountancy practice over a defined period of time, usually a year. Shareholder wealth is concerned with the flow of dividends to the shareholder over a long period of time. The current share price on the market will reflect the expected future dividend flow and so the current share price is taken as the measure of shareholder wealth. Thus the basic financial goal for the board of directors will be to get and keep the share price as high as possible.[7]

## C Cash flows and capital raising

Much of the work of the finance director with overall responsibility for the financial well-being of the company is taken up with the management of cash flows and hence a considerable portion of corporate finance theory is concerned with cash flow. One of the basic problems that confronts a company is that there is a time gap between its outgoing cash flow when it purchases assets and the incoming cash flow when it sells a product or service which it has created out of those assets. Developing techniques to bridge these gaps is a fundamental part of corporate finance theory.

In order to create shareholder value, a firm needs to generate more cash flow than it uses, by buying assets that generate more cash than they use, and selling financial instruments in order to raise cash.[8] Seen in terms of cash flow, shareholder value will have been created where the cash flows out of the firm to the shareholders (and loan creditors) are higher than the cash flows which they put into it.[9]

---

[4] On the different types of equity and debt securities, see below.
[5] See generally S. Ross *et al. Corporate Finance* 5th edn (Boston, MA: Irwin McGraw-Hill, 1997) pp. 1–5.
[6] This of course assumes that the company has not decided to operate in a way which elevates some other aim above the pursuit of maximum shareholder wealth. As has been seen (Chapter 3) some aspects of stakeholder philosophy might appear to require this, although as has also been argued, if stakeholder policies result in efficiency gains, then there may be no conflict with the principle of maximising shareholder wealth. Aside from stakeholder doctrine, some companies sometimes make the decision to operate on a broader basis than profit motive, such as co-operative societies. See the discussion of s. 172 of the 2006 Act in Chapter 8.
[7] See generally G. Arnold *Corporate Financial Management* (London: Financial Times Management, 1998) pp. 4–14.
[8] See Ross *et al.*, n. 5 above, at p. 5.
[9] *Ibid.*

The techniques of managing cash flows[10] are very much the province of specialist books on corporate finance.[11] These books also deal in detail with the techniques of capital raising; and here there is an overlap with the study of company law. Since a considerable part of company law is concerned with the law relating to how companies finance themselves, it is useful to examine briefly the techniques which companies employ to raise the finance needed to fund their activities.

## 13.2 Financing the company

### A Initial finance

In the first instance, for most companies, the initial source of finance comes from cash provided by the entrepreneur promoters themselves, or by a bank. Typically, the promoters will utilise their savings, raise personal loans (e.g. by remortgaging their houses), or persuade relatives to let them have money.[12] Wherever it comes from, the promoters will use the money to subscribe for equity shares in the company.[13] They could endeavour to persuade others to take shares, but of course, this may mean diluting their control and they may be reluctant to do this. Quite often a person can be found, perhaps through business contacts such as the firm's accountant, who will be prepared to take a small equity stake in the company and give advice to the promoters. In modern jargon such persons are referred to as 'business angels'[14] but the type is not new.[15]

Many companies will also rely on bank finance to provide initial capital. This will not always be forthcoming, owing to the very high risk of failure of the business at this stage and the bank will usually require a floating charge over the company's assets[16] and security over the promoter's own assets and/or personal guarantees from him and any others whom he can persuade to support him. In an attempt to overcome this problem, the government operates a small firms' loans guarantee scheme.[17] In some circumstances, other sources of financial help might be available such as hire purchase, credit sale and leasing agreements.

---

[10] And many other aspects of corporate finance techniques.

[11] See Arnold, n. 7 above, at pp. 49–133; Ross *et al.*, n. 5 above, at pp. 5–41. See also E. Ferran *Principles of Corporate Finance Law* (Oxford, OUP, 2008); L. Gullifer and J. Payne *Corporate Finance Law: Principles and Policy* (Oxford, Hart Publishing, 2011); and *Capital Markets and Company Law* edited by K.J. Hopt and E. Wymeersch (Oxford, OUP, 2003).

[12] The members will not always wish to bring their capital to the company in the form of money. It is possible to make contributions in kind (although subject to the rules on share discounts discussed below) and a particularly common form of this is where the promoter is already operating some form of small business either as a sole trader (or in partnership with others) and desires to incorporate that business. He will sell and transfer the business he owns to the company and in return receives an allotment of fully paid-up shares in the company.

[13] Instead of taking equity shares, a promoter may wish to form a company with only one £1 issued share but finance its business activities by making a loan from himself to the company. If the loan is secured by a floating charge it will give him priority over the trade creditors in a subsequent liquidation. The *Salomon* case (Chapter 2) is a striking example of the effectiveness of this.

[14] See further 'Venture capital financing' below.

[15] The person who provided the debenture to Mr Salomon's new company (Mr Broderip) could perhaps be described as a 'business angel'; see Chapter 2.

[16] Obviously in priority to any taken by the promoter.

[17] See the Business Support section in the DBEIS website: https://www.gov.uk/government/policies/business-enterprise.

If the company's initial capital requirements are well beyond what can be raised through any of the above sources, then it will need to turn to the venture capital industry for initial financing, or, in rare cases of initial financing, make an offer of shares to the public and seek a stock exchange quotation.[18]

## B Venture capital financing

Venture capital[19] is most commonly seen as a middle stage of finance suitable for companies which are growing in size but which are not yet ready to make a public offering of shares and seek a stock market quotation.[20] However, as has been suggested above, it is sometimes available for companies which have not yet started trading. Entrepreneurs seeking venture capital will usually be concerned to ensure that they do not part with control of the company on a permanent basis. For this reason, redeemable securities are often used, or other arrangements which enable the entrepreneurs to free themselves from the venture capitalist within, say, a five-year period.

The venture capital industry has seen enormous growth since the early 1980s, and since 1984 has invested more than £50bn in around 22,000 companies. In 2016, around 728 UK companies received a total of £7.1bn in venture capital financing; the worldwide figure was £21.4bn. By 2007 the figure for UK companies had almost doubled to £12.6bn and by 2010, notwithstanding the worst global recession since the 1930s, the worldwide figure was £20.4bn.[21] Venture capital comes from two main sources: 'business angels' and venture capital firms. The former are often high net worth individuals who have expertise in entrepreneurial activity and who invest their own money, either alone or with others, directly in unquoted businesses. Business angels usually invest between £50,000 and £500,000 in a company in the form of equity finance in the expectation of achieving a significant financial return.[22] In 2009–10, the overall deal size ranged from less than £25,000 to over £1m. However, most deals were in the £50,000–£500,000 range, with fewer than 10% being over £1m or more.[23] Business angels are an important source of finance for entrepreneurial businesses, especially at their start-up and early growth stages where the sums required are too small to be economic for venture capital funds to invest. Venture capital firms obtain their capital from various sources, principally from institutions such as pension funds, but also from banks and individuals. They usually target firms which are seeking an investment of over £100,000. In 2009 the average deal size was around £2.5m.[24] Recent years have seen an internationalisation of venture capital, especially in continental Europe as UK and US venture capital companies seek to find new

---

[18] As happened with the financing of the Channel Tunnel, for which the initial equity finance (of £976m) needed to be raised by an international placing and offers for sale in the UK and France. Without such public offerings, the project would not even have seemed viable at the outset; see further T. Stocks *Corporate Finance: Law and Practice* (London: Longman, 1992) pp. 55–72. Additionally, there was £5,000m of debt finance from banks.
[19] Or 'private equity' as it is often called.
[20] Or a placing; see Chapter 19.
[21] Statistics from BVCA Private Equity and Venture Capital Report on Investment Activity 2016; see the British Venture Capital Association (BVCA) website: http://www.bvca.co.uk.
[22] See Business Angel Finance 2009–10, on the BVCA website; *ibid.*
[23] *Ibid.*
[24] *Ibid.*

investment opportunities; for instance, 3i Group plc[25] reports having multiple offices or portfolio operations across the globe.[26]

The venture capital industry broadly categorises the investment stages of a company's life into: seed capital (to finance the development of a business idea, prior to trading); start-up (further developments prior to trading); early stage (finance for the commencement of trading); expansion (finance for a successful company, to enable further growth);[27] management buyouts (MBOs, where the managers buy the business); and management buy-ins (MBIs, where a group of managers from outside the company buy the business).[28] Owing to the high risks involved with new companies, most venture capital firms will confine their inputs to expansion, MBOs and MBIs, leaving the business angels to provide seed, start-up and early-stage finance. The venture capital provider will usually make her money out of the capital gain arising on the equity shares or other investments which she took in return for the capital which she provided. Various methods of realising the gain are employed: selling the shares to another company in the sector which needs the business,[29] share repurchase by the company or its management, refinancing,[30] or, in the very successful cases, a flotation of the company on the Stock Exchange or some other market which will provide liquidity. Where a company seeks very large sums of capital, it will usually make an offering of shares to the public and arrange to have the shares quoted on a stock exchange. This is considered in more detail in Chapter 19. We now turn to consider the means by which a company can raise capital through secured borrowing together with the law relating to share capital.

## C Raising capital through debt

As commented on above, companies also raise capital through debt.[31] Debt finance comes from two main sources, bank lending and the capital markets, although only the very large companies will use the capital markets to finance their borrowings. Bank lending usually takes the form of short-term overdraft facilities, or medium-term loans where the borrowed sum and interest is repaid in instalments throughout the term,[32] or by the supply of revolving credit facilities. The bank will often seek security.[33] In the case of a very large loan, a syndicate of banks will each contribute a portion of it.

Companies wishing to raise debt finance from the capital markets will usually do so by issuing bonds or other securities. Bonds (or debentures)[34] are documents which acknowledge

---

[25] The UK's oldest and largest venture capital organisation.

[26] https://www.3i.com/about-us/global-reach/europe/.

[27] Although it perhaps should be emphasised that much of the finance which is available to companies for growth comes from retained profits; equity and debt finance (and various other sources) provide the remainder.

[28] Venture capital also has a role to play in 'rescue situations' when the company has got into difficulties.

[29] Trade sale.

[30] I.e. selling the shares to another venture capital company.

[31] Detailed analysis of this is beyond the scope of this text. For an excellent account of the role of debt in corporate finance and the legal aspects see E. Ferran *Corporate Finance Law* (Oxford: OUP, 2008) Chapters 11 and 12; L. Gullifer (ed.) *Goode on Legal Problems of Credit and Security* (London: Sweet & Maxwell, 2009). See also E. Ferran 'Creditors' Interests and "Core" Company Law' (1999) 20 Co Law 314; and D. Prentice and A. Reisberg (eds) *Corporate Finance Law in the UK and the EU* (Oxford: OUP, 2011), Chapters 8–13.

[32] Sometimes called 'term loans'.

[33] For the effect of this in liquidation, see Chapter 22 below.

[34] If the bond is secured it will usually these days be referred to as a 'debenture'. Debentures are considered further below.

a debt (owed by the company to the lender).[35] They are usually long-term finance in the sense that the principal sum is often expressed to be repayable up to a decade in the future. Shorter-term arrangements are often referred to as loan notes or commercial paper. In addition there are many other forms of debt financing, in particular the Eurobond market which falls outside the control of the UK regulatory authorities.[36]

A company which chooses to have debt as part of its capital structure in addition to equity shares will find that it may make the market share price more volatile and the ratio of debt to equity which a company chooses is a fundamental decision that may affect its financial well-being or survival. The debt/equity ratio is known as gearing; a company which has a lot of debt compared to equity is described as highly geared. High gearing can make the share price volatile by creating a business in which the equity shareholders have provided only a small part of the overall working capital. Since they are the residual owners of the company, when the company is doing well they will be entitled to all the profits of the largely debt-financed business after the interest on the debt has been paid; thus the profits are shared among a relatively small group of people. Conversely, if the company's fortunes change, it will quickly find that the profits are eaten up in servicing the debts with the result that there will be little or nothing remaining for the equity shares.

## 1 *Debentures*

The companies legislation offers little assistance in seeking a definition of the term 'debenture'.[37] In essence, as we noted above, it is merely a document which acknowledges the existence of a debt. As such, it will generally contain the terms of the contract between the debtor-company and the creditor and, if the debt is secured on an asset of the company, the terms of the mortgagor–mortgagee relationship. Given the lack of any statutory definition, perhaps not surprisingly there have been numerous attempts by the judges at defining the term. For example, Lindley LJ in *British India Steam Navigation Co* v *IRC*:[38]

> Now, what the correct meaning of 'debenture' is I do not know. I do not find anywhere any precise definition of it. We know that there are various kinds of instruments commonly called debentures. You may have mortgage debentures, which are charges of some kind on property. You may have debentures which are bonds; and, if this instrument were under seal, it would be a debenture of that kind. You may have a debenture which is nothing more than an acknowledgement of indebtedness. And you may have [as on the facts] . . . a statement by two directors that the company will pay a certain sum of money on a given day, and will also pay interest half-yearly at certain times and at a certain place, upon production of certain coupons by the holder of the instrument. I think any of these things which I have referred to may be debentures within the Act.[39]

---

[35] In practice debt securities which are traded are generally referred to as 'bonds' or 'notes'. However, since the term 'debenture' is the one traditionally used by corporate lawyers and is the one adopted by the companies legislation, it will be used in this chapter.

[36] Although it is subject to forms of self-regulation.

[37] Section 738 of the Companies Act 2006 merely states that 'debenture' includes debenture stock, bonds and any other securities of a company, whether or not constituting a charge on the assets of the company. See also s. 29 (2) of the Insolvency Act 1986.

[38] (1881) 7 QBD 165.

[39] *Ibid.* at p. 172. See also *Levy* v *Abercorris Slate & Slab Co.* (1887) 37 Ch 260 at p. 264, in which Chitty J observed, rather too broadly, that: 'a debenture means a document which either creates a debt or acknowledges it . . .' See further *Lemon* v *Austin Friars Trust* [1926] Ch 1 at p. 17, *per* Warrington LJ.

Whatever the difficulties of formulating a comprehensive and precise definition of the term, this has caused relatively few problems in the marketplace and, given the paucity of case law on the issue, does not seem to have caused major problems for the courts.

It is noteworthy at this juncture that loan capital can be an attractive alternative to shares as a means of raising finance, especially for larger companies which can look to the loan capital markets as a source of funds.[40] As with shares, investments in loan capital are classified as 'securities' but the risk is very different. For example, where a company is wound up the claims of creditors must be met before any surplus funds are returned to shareholders. In this regard, the nature of the relationship that shareholders and investment creditors have with the company is very different. Simply put, shareholders have rights in the company, while creditors have rights against the company. And, if a loan is secured over an asset of the debtor-company, the creditor will have rights in the company's property. Further, unlike share capital which, particularly in relation to public companies, is subject to a strict regime aimed at protecting the fund against, for example, unlawful distributions and reductions, loan capital is treated fairly flexibly. Thus, interest can be paid out of capital and the fund is not subject to the rules relating to (share) capital maintenance.[41]

## 2 Debenture stock

As noted above, the reference made in s. 738 of the Companies Act 2006[42] to debentures includes the term 'debenture stock'. There are practical distinctions between the two. Whereas debentures can only be transferred as whole or complete units, debenture stock, on the other hand, is a loan fund that has generally been aggregated and advanced to the company by trustees. Investors in the fund subscribe for such amounts as each chooses and, as with shareholders in a public company, each subscriber is free to sell a part or the whole of their stock holding.[43] While the fund is sourced from different lenders (debenture-holders) the terms of the loan are nevertheless the same. Thus, the rights of the debenture-holders are generally set out in a trust deed and the trustees,[44] in practice usually a financial institution, represent their interests, as a group, with the company. The practical advantage to the company is that its contract is only with the trustees rather than having separate contracts with a dispersed group of debenture-holders. Further, a charge can be executed in favour of the trustees who will hold it on trust for the debenture-holders. As a consequence, a specific legal charge over the company's real estate together with an equitable floating charge over its assets can be created.[45]

---

[40] As compared to share allotments, the allotment of debentures, where there is no public offer, is largely unregulated by the Companies Act 2006. There are administrative requirements, however, such as s. 741 which introduced the requirement that the issuing company must register an allotment of debentures (as is the case with shares), within two months of the allotment, with the Registrar of Companies. There is no requirement that the company itself maintain a register of debenture-holders. For public offers see Chapter 19.

[41] See Chapter 14.

[42] See n. 37 above.

[43] Subject to the terms of the trust deed.

[44] Nowadays the trust device is also adopted when a company issues a series of debentures.

[45] This is an obvious practical advantage since it is not possible to vest a legal interest (and title deeds) in a disparate group of debenture-holders. The trustees stand between the debenture-holders and the company. As such, they can be liable to the debenture-holders for breach of duty, for example in failing to protect properly their interests. See *Concord Trust* v *Law Debenture Trust Corp plc* [2006] 1 BCLC 616, HL.

## 13.3 The law relating to shares

### A Definitions of share capital

As we saw in Chapter 2, one of the requirements for registering a company with a share capital is that the application must contain a statement of capital and initial shareholdings.[46] It will be recalled that under the 1985 Act it was a requirement that the memorandum of association would state the amount of the company's 'authorised' share capital. The 'authorised' capital bore virtually no relationship to the actual money that was being put into the company when it was first formed and it simply meant the amount of share capital which the company was allowed to issue without needing to alter the capital clause in the memorandum to sanction the issue of more. Following the recommendations of the CLR, the Companies Act 2006 abolished the requirement of authorised share capital. By s. 10 (2) the statement of capital must declare, amongst other things, the total number of shares of the company to be taken on formation by the subscribers to the memorandum together with the aggregate nominal value of those shares and the prescribed particulars of the rights attached to them.[47] Thus, it might state, for example, 'Three shares of £1.00 each taken by the three founding directors, John Lowry, Arad Reisberg and Anna Donovan'. Once more shares are issued, similar information has to be delivered to the Registrar of Companies in a 'return of allotments'.[48]

While the requirement to have authorised share capital is now redundant, s. 763 (1) nonetheless requires public limited companies to have an 'authorised minimum' in relation to the 'nominal' value of their allotted share capital (currently set at £50,000) or prescribed euro equivalent (set at £65,000). As was the case before the 2006 Act, no minimum capital is required for private companies. Crucially, a public company that does not meet the minimum requirement will not be issued with a trading certificate by the Registrar of Companies and cannot do business or exercise any borrowing powers until such a certificate has been issued.[49] With respect to the so-called 'nominal' or par value of shares (i.e. fixing a monetary value to the shares), it is noteworthy that for some considerable time Company Law Reform committees have recommended that companies should be permitted to issue shares having no nominal value.[50] No action has ever been taken on this; probably because people are used to operating under the present system and there has been little advantage seen in any change. In any case, public companies are required to have a nominal value for their shares[51] and the CLR's consultation process revealed little support for forcing private companies to have shares with no nominal value.[52]

[46] Section 9 (4) of the Companies Act 2006.
[47] Prescribed particulars are the right to vote, to receive a distribution (either by way of dividend or capital) and provisions concerning redemption; the Companies (Shares and Share Capital) Order 2009.
[48] Section 555 of the Companies Act 2006.
[49] Section 761.
[50] See e.g. the Gedge Committee, in 1954, Cmd 9112 and the Jenkins Committee, in 1962, Cmnd. 1749. The CLR expressed the view in *The Strategic Framework* that 'the requirement that shares should have a nominal value has become an anachronism'.
[51] See the EC Second Company Law Directive.
[52] *Completing The Structure*, para. 7.3.

As commented on above, while the 2006 Act mandates a minimum capital requirement for public companies that must be satisfied before a trading certificate will be issued by the Registrar,[53] a company is free to denominate shares in such currency as it chooses. In this regard, s. 542 (3) gives statutory effect to the decision in *Re Scandanavian Bank Group plc.*[54] The company was intending to have a share capital of £30m, US$30m, SFr30m, and DM30m. Each of these four classes of shares were to be divided into 300 million shares of, respectively, 10 pence each, 10 US cents each, 10 Swiss centimes each and 10 German pfennigs each. Harman J held that this was permissible and was within the relevant provisions contained in the Companies Act 1985.

It is common practice to issue shares on the basis that the allottee need not pay, for the time being, the whole nominal value of the shares. If a share of a nominal value of £1 is issued on terms that only 75 pence needs to be paid up, then that 75 pence is referred to as the 'paid up' share capital and the £1 share is said to be 'partly paid'. The remaining 25 pence will be made payable at a future date, possibly only on the occurrence of a certain contingency such as liquidation. With a public company, s. 586 of the 2006 Act provides that its share must be 'paid up at least as to one-quarter of its nominal value and the whole of any premium'.

Certain provisions in the Companies Act 2006 mention or relate to called-up share capital[55] and for the sake of clarity s. 547 gives a definition of called-up share capital. In essence, the Act provides that the called-up share capital means the total of capital already paid up, together with any share capital which must be paid on a specified future date by virtue of provisions contained in the articles, the terms of allotment or other arrangements relating to payment.

## B Authority to issue share capital

Section 549 of the Companies Act 2006 limits the power of the directors to issue shares.[56] Where a private company has only one class of shares, s. 550 empowers the directors to allot shares of that class unless they are prohibited from doing so by the company's articles of association. Therefore, the former requirement under s. 80 of the 1985 Act that a share issue be authorised by ordinary resolution or by the articles is dispensed with. Thus, directors of a private company that does not have different classes of shares are now free to issue new shares without the need for an ordinary resolution of the members in general meeting. This is part of the overall policy of deregulation which underpins the 2006 Act, as is also the case with the abolition of the requirement for authorised share capital.[57] However, it should be noted that in exercising this power directors are subject to the duties codified in Part 10 of the Companies Act 2006.[58] Where a private company has more than one class of shares or where the company in question is a public company, the position under the 1985 Act is essentially restated by s. 551, which requires prior authorisation by the articles or by an ordinary resolution of the members. The authorisation must specify

---

[53] Section 761.
[54] (1987) 3 BCC 93.
[55] E.g. Companies Act 2006, ss. 92 (1)–(3) and 831 (1)–(3).
[56] With certain exceptions.
[57] See above.
[58] See Chapter 8; particularly ss. 171 and 172 of the 2006 Act.

the maximum amount of share capital to which it relates and its expiry date (the maximum duration is five years).[59]

## C Preferential (pre-emption) subscription rights

The legislation provides existing equity shareholders of the company with preferential subscription rights in the event of an issue of further shares.[60] The highly complex provisions are contained in Part 17, Chapter 3 of the 2006 Act. Briefly, the position is as follows: a company proposing to allot 'equity securities'[61] must not allot them to anybody unless it has first made an offer of allotment to the existing holders of either 'relevant shares' or 'relevant employee shares'.[62] The offer must be on the same or more favourable terms and in more or less the same proportion to the size of the shareholder's existing stake in the company.[63] The offer must remain open for at least 21 days and in the meantime the company may not allot any of the securities, unless it has earlier received notice of the acceptance or refusal of every offer.[64] Allotments under an employee share scheme are exempt[65] as are allotments of equity securities which are to be wholly or partly paid up otherwise than in cash.[66] Special provisions apply,[67] sometimes enabling a modified form of offer to be made, where the company has more than one class of equity share in existence.[68]

In some circumstances the preferential rights given by s. 561 can be disapplied. Private companies may exclude them in their articles.[69] Public and private companies may sometimes disapply the preferential rights under s. 570 (1) which provides that where the directors are given authorisation under s. 551 (to allot shares) they may be given power by the articles, or by special resolution of the company, to allot equity securities pursuant to that authority as if s. 561 did not apply, or as if it applied with the modifications chosen by the directors. Various procedures are set out in ss. 570, 571 and 573. In the case of public companies which are also quoted on the Stock Exchange, the FCA listing rules contain further requirements.

## D Nature of shares and membership

The most helpful judicial definition of a share is to be found in *Borland's Trustee* v *Steel Bros & Co. Ltd*,[70] where Farwell J said:

A share is the interest of the shareholder in the company measured by a sum of money, for the purpose of liability in the first place, and of interest in the second, but also consisting of a series of mutual covenants entered into by all the shareholders in accordance with [section 33 of the Companies Act 2006].

---

[59] Section 551 (3).
[60] See above for a discussion of this in relation to rights issues.
[61] Defined in s. 560 so as to exclude subscriber shares, bonus shares, employee shares and certain preference shares but so as to include certain convertible debentures and warrants.
[62] Defined in s. 560 so as to exclude some types of preference shares.
[63] Companies Act 2006, s. 561 (1).
[64] *Ibid.* ss. 561 (1) and 562 (5).
[65] *Ibid.* s. 566.
[66] *Ibid.* ss. 561 (2) and 565.
[67] *Ibid.* s. 568 (1) and (2).
[68] *Ibid.* s. 562 makes detailed provisions as to the method of making the s. 561 offer and ss. 563 and 568 (4)–(5) govern the consequences of contravening the various provisions.
[69] *Ibid.* s. 567.
[70] [1901] 1 Ch 279 at p. 288.

The reference to liabilities in the definition is, in the case of a company limited by shares, mainly a reference to the member's liability to pay any amount on his shares which is not yet paid up. There may also be liability for the company's debts in some circumstances. In addition to the points made in the definition, it should be noticed that a share is also a piece of property which can be bought and sold, mortgaged, charged and left by will. It is classified as 'personal' property rather than 'real' property.[71] Ownership of shares gives ownership of the company (in proportion to the share) but not of course of any assets in the company.[72] As commented on above, it is this concept of being an owner of the company, a proprietor, which distinguishes a share from a debenture or bond, for debentures give rights against the company and not in it; a debenture-holder or bond-holder is a creditor.

When the company is first formed the subscribers to the memorandum are deemed to have agreed to become members, and are accordingly entered in the register of members.[73] In every other case, membership is acquired in accordance with s. 112 (2), which requires, first, an agreement to become a member and, secondly, entry of name on the share register. Companies are required to keep a share register that is made available for inspection, save that as of 30 June 2016 private companies can choose to send this information to the Registrar of Companies to be kept on the public register rather than maintain their own registers.[74] It should be noted that in two situations it is possible as a matter of technicality, for a person to be a shareholder and not a member: (1) where renounceable letters of allotment are used during the course of an offer for sale, the holder of the allotment letter will be a shareholder and yet not a member, since he is not yet entered on the share register; (2) where share warrants are issued, the warrant holder is a shareholder but since his name will not be on the share register he is not a member (although sometimes the articles will deem him to be a member).[75]

At present, the law usually requires that a shareholder is given a share certificate in respect of his shares within two months of allotment or lodgement with the company of an instrument of transfer.[76] The share certificate is *prima facie* evidence of the member's title to the shares[77] and the certificate is intended to facilitate commercial dealings with the shares by the member, so that, for instance, he can transfer them, or create an equitable mortgage of the shares merely by deposit of the certificate.[78] There is a considerable body of case law (most of it fairly old) concerned with the situation where the share certificate is stolen by a thief and then used to help represent (falsely) to a purchaser that he is the owner of the shares. In this, and other similar circumstances, the company can become liable for damages by virtue of the representation contained in s. 768.[79] Problems in this area are rare these days, presumably because company secretaries, aware of the dangers,

---

[71] Companies Act 2006, s. 541.
[72] See Chapter 2 above. In particular, see *Macaura* v *Northern Assurance Co.* [1925] AC 619.
[73] Companies Act 2006, s. 112 (1).
[74] *Ibid.* ss. 113–114.
[75] See further below.
[76] Companies Act 2006, s. 769.
[77] *Ibid.* s. 768.
[78] See below.
[79] See e.g. *Re Bahia and San Francisco Railway Co.* (1868) LR 3 QB 584; *Balkis Consolidated Ltd* v *Tomkinson* [1893] AC 396.

are more careful when registering transfers. In the case of a Stock Exchange transfer under CREST the requirement for a share certificate is dispensed with by statutory instrument.

## E Classes and types of shares

### 1 *Ordinary shares*

*Prima facie* all shares rank equally.[80] Thus if nothing is stated in the terms of issue or the articles, then the shares will have equal rights to dividend, return of capital in a winding up, and voting. Such shares are usually referred to as 'ordinary' shares, although sometimes these days the American expression 'common' share is used. However, companies often issue other classes of shares. In the absence of some express restriction, a company will have the right to issue shares which carry rights which are preferential to the ordinary shares already issued.[81]

### 2 *Preference shares*

Most preference shares carry preferential rights to a fixed preference dividend while the company is a going concern and prior return of capital on a winding up. They are thus a comparatively safe form of investment and when issued by the larger plcs they are often similar in quality to debenture stock or government bonds in that the capital is expected to be mainly secure and the rate of preference dividend is fixed and will bear a close relationship to the interest rates prevailing at the time of issue. Often preference shares are issued as redeemable preference shares, redeemable either at the option of the company or sometimes the shareholder, or as is more usual 'convertible' preference shares, giving the holder the right to convert them into ordinary shares in certain circumstances. Preference shares are usually expressed to have no voting rights, or to have voting rights which are restricted to certain circumstances such as a right to vote on whether the company goes into liquidation or not.

Not all preference shares follow the usual pattern of giving a preference as to fixed dividend and return of capital on a winding up. Hybrid versions are encountered, which perhaps give a right to a fixed preference dividend and then an entitlement to share profits rateably with the ordinary shareholders, with similar[82] provisions on a winding up. Such shares are usually known as 'participating' preference shares. Such 'participating' rights will need to be spelled out very clearly in the articles or terms of issue, for if the terms provide for a fixed dividend and prior return of capital on a winding up, it will not be open for the shareholder to argue that he is also entitled to share in profits, rateably with the ordinary shareholders, nor will it be possible for him to contend that, if the terms give him a right to a prior return of capital on a winding up, he can also share in surplus assets.[83] Nor will it help him, when seeking to imply participating rights as to capital, to point to his express rights to participating dividend rights.[84]

---

[80] *Birch* v *Cropper* (1889) 14 AC 525, HL.
[81] *Andrews* v *Gas Meter Co.* [1897] 1 Ch 361.
[82] I.e. prior return of capital and then rateable share in surplus assets.
[83] *Will* v *United Lankat Plantations* [1914] AC 11.
[84] *Scottish Insurance Corporation* v *Wilson and Clyde Coal Co.* [1949] AC 462; *Re Isle of Thanet Electricity Co.* [1950] Ch 161.

## 3 *Deferred shares*

Deferred shares are shares which have rights that are deferred to the ordinary shares. As such, they will only receive a dividend after a specified minimum has been paid to the ordinary shareholders and, as regards return of capital on a winding up, they similarly rank behind the ordinary shares (which in turn will be ranking behind any preference shares). Deferred shares are sometimes known as 'founders' shares' because it used to be the practice that promoters would agree to take founders' shares to demonstrate their confidence in the company's ability to pay dividends. Founders' shares fell into disrepute because they would often give the promoters a large share of the profit if the business was successful and they were usually structured with enhanced voting rights so as to permit retention of control. Deferred shares are now a rare phenomenon.

## 4 *Non-voting and multiple voting shares*

Sometimes non-voting ordinary shares are issued, usually to enable the present controlling group to retain their control and at the same time raise more capital without resorting to issuing preference shares. Such non-voting shares are sometimes given the label 'A' shares to distinguish them from the normal ordinary shares.

Another device used by a controlling group to acquire or maintain control is to issue shares which have an enhanced voting strength. These can produce the situation where a management group lock themselves in to the company so that although an outsider owns more than 51% of the market value of the company's shares he or she nevertheless has no control over the company. A good example of this was the long-running saga of the attempt by Trust House Forte to take over the Savoy Hotel. The takeover battle began in the 1950s and ended in the late 1980s when Trust House Forte finally abandoned its attempt.[85]

## 5 *Share warrants*

The term 'warrant' is used in two senses in modern parlance. In its non-technical sense, it is used to describe a form of call option which gives the holder a right to call for a share at a fixed price at a future date if he or she so chooses. Such 'warrants' are often offered to the target company's shareholders by a takeover bidder as part of his or her offer package, which often consists of shares in the bidder itself, cash and warrants.

The second and more technical meaning of 'share warrant' refers to bearer shares. The Companies Act 2006 historically provided[86] that a company could, if authorised by its articles, issue with respect to any fully paid shares a warrant stating that the bearer of the warrant is entitled to the shares specified in it. The holder of the warrant was not technically a member of the company[87] and on the issue of the share warrant the company was required to strike out of its register of members the name of the member then entered in it

---

[85] The story is outlined in *Re Savoy Hotel Ltd* [1981] 3 WLR 441.
[86] Companies Act 2006, s. 779.
[87] Unless the articles deem him to be a member of the company, although this is subject to the Companies Act 2006 s. 122 (3).

as if he or she had ceased to be a member. In place of the member's name must be entered the fact that the warrant had been issued, a statement of the shares included in the warrant and date of issue of the warrant.[88] However, s. 84 of the Small Business, Enterprise and Employment Act 2015 abolished the issue of share warrants and amended s. 779 of the Companies Act 2006 accordingly. As such, with effect from 26 May 2015 a company can no longer issue share warrants and Sch. 4 of the Small Business, Enterprise and Employment Act 2015 makes provision for, *inter alia*, the conversion into shares of those warrants already in issue at that date.

## 6 *Depositary receipts*

Depositary receipts, usually issued by a bank, are negotiable receipts certifying that a stated number of securities of an issuer have been deposited on behalf of the holder in a financial institution. Increasing numbers of depositary receipts are being listed on the London Stock Exchange.

Depositary receipts are often used to enable a company in a country which has an undeveloped economy to make its shares attractive to overseas investors by, in effect, attaching a different currency and regulatory package to the shares. Thus with American Depositary Receipts (ADRs), for example, the ADRs will be issued by a US Depositary Bank,[89] and the shares will be deposited in a branch of the bank in the issuer's home country. Dividends are collected from the company by the branch and remitted to the bank in the US and will be paid to the holder of the receipt in US dollars. The US regulatory system will apply to the ADRs.

## F Transfer of and transactions in shares

### 1 *Transfers on sale*

Once a contract for the sale of shares[90] has come into existence,[91] then provided that it is specifically enforceable (and it will be, in the absence of some vitiating factor), the equitable interest in those shares will pass to the purchaser; on the principle that 'equity regards that done which ought to be done'.[92] Thus the vendor remains legal (though not equitable) owner and in effect is holding the shares on trust for the purchaser, subject to receipt of purchase money. The purchaser will not become the full legal owner until his name is entered on the share register of the company. To get that to happen, the following procedures need to be complied with.

---

[88] Companies Act 2006, s. 122 (1).

[89] Usually Citibank, JP Morgan or the Bank of New York.

[90] Different procedures apply to the transfer of shares on the death of a shareholder; see the 1985 Table A, articles 31–32; the model articles for private and public companies, articles 27–29 and 65–68 respectively; and the Companies Act 2006, s. 773.

[91] There are special procedures for the transfer of shares which are the result of a sale on the Stock Exchange; see above, 13.2, C.

[92] *Wood Preservation Ltd* v *Prior* [1969] 1 WLR 1977. On the difficult question of voting rights in this situation see *Michaels* v *Harley House (Marylebone) Ltd* [1999] 1 All ER 356, CA.

Sections 544 (1)–(2) of the Companies Act 2006 provides that the shares[93] of any member are 'transferable in accordance with the company's articles but subject to the Stock Transfer Act 1963'. In the 1985 Table A, articles 23–28 deal with transfer of shares; in the model articles for private and public companies, article 26 (private companies) and articles 63–64 (public companies) deal with share transfers. Articles 26 (private companies) and 63 (public companies) of the model articles (and article 23 of the 1985 Table A articles) are particularly relevant in this context since they provide that the instrument of transfer may be in 'any usual form' or in any other form approved by the directors. In practice the form adopted will usually be that set out in the Stock Transfer Act 1963 which provides that the form need be executed by the transferor only, and need not be attested but it must specify the particulars of the consideration, describe the shares and give the numbers or amounts of shares, details of the transfer and name and address of the transferee. The Stock Transfer Act does not apply to partly paid shares but will normally be followed. Whatever form is used, it must be one which it is possible to regard as a 'proper instrument of transfer' within s. 770 (1) for it is unlawful for a company to register a transfer unless such a 'proper instrument' has been delivered to it.[94]

The normal procedure is for the transferor to hand over the transfer instrument and share certificate to the transferee who then sends them to the company for registration. Assuming that the registration is not liable to be refused,[95] the transferee's name will be entered on the share register and he will then be sent a certificate in respect of the shares. If the transferor is selling only part of the holding to which his certificate relates, a procedure known as 'certification of transfer' is followed (to avoid fraud) whereby the transferor sends the share certificate and instrument of transfer to the company to be endorsed by the company secretary to the effect that there has been produced to the company a certificate in respect of the transfer.[96] This certification procedure is needed because the vendor would be unwilling to hand over a certificate for 1,000 shares to the transferee if, for instance, he has only sold and been paid for 200.

## 2 Security interests in shares

Shares are an important item of wealth and over the years the law has developed ways in which the wealth locked up in a share can be used as collateral for borrowing. There are three types of security interest commonly granted over shares: mortgages, charges and liens.

Mortgages of shares are usually 'equitable' mortgages, meaning that the mortgagor remains on the share register as 'legal' owner but holds his shares subject to the equitable interest of the mortgagee. Legal mortgages are uncommon because if the mortgagee's name is entered on the share register he will be personally liable for any calls on the

---

[93] Or other interest.
[94] Although there are exceptions for transfers of government stock and other similar securities which are dealt with on a computerised basis under the provisions of the Stock Transfer Act 1982 and other exceptions where the shares are transmitted by 'operation of law' (e.g. bankruptcy of member) or by a personal representative (death of member); see Companies Act 2006, ss. 770 (1)–(2) and 773.
[95] See below.
[96] Companies Act 2006, s. 775.

shares.[97] An equitable mortgage of shares is usually created by deposit of the share certificate. Alternatively, an equitable charge on shares will come into existence provided that the parties have agreed that those shares should stand as security for the satisfaction of a debt.[98] A lien is a form of equitable charge which is security for the payment of money. It is quite common for the articles of association of companies to provide that the company shall have a lien on the shares of a member in respect of any debts owed by him to the company.[99] Since 1980, and now contained in the Companies Act 2006, public companies can only have liens over their own shares in certain circumstances.[100]

## 3 *Restrictions on transfer*

Public or private companies may contain provisions in their constitutions restricting the transferability of shares, although a public company which is seeking a Stock Exchange quotation or a dealing arrangement on AIM will find that this is unacceptable. Many private companies have restrictions on transfer, usually with a view to keeping control within the family or other small group of individuals. Such restrictions are commonly of two types, usually both being present: directors' discretion to refuse transfer, and pre-emption clauses. A power for the directors to refuse to register a transfer is commonly contained in the articles of association of private companies. The clause will read something like: 'The directors may, in their absolute discretion and without assigning any reason therefore, decline to register the transfer of any share, whether or not it is a fully paid share.' The 1985 Table A contains what looks deceptively like a similar clause but which in reality has a very restricted ambit since it mainly only applies to shares which are not fully paid.[101] Article 26 (5) of the model articles for private companies states in more straightforward terms that: 'The directors may refuse to register the transfer of a share, and if they do so, the instrument of transfer must be returned to the transferee with the notice of refusal unless they suspect that the proposed transfer may be fraudulent.' Over the years, the courts have established the principle that the shareholder has a basic right of transfer of his shares and so unless there is an effective and proper exercise of the directors' power of refusal, the transfer right will remain intact.[102] Like all directors' powers, the power of refusal must be exercised '. . . bona fide in what they consider – not what a court may consider – is in the interests of the company and not for any collateral purpose'.[103] Generally, if the clause gives an unfettered discretion, the directors are not required to give reasons for their decision but it appears that if they do give reasons then the court may review them.[104] If the clause gives a right of refusal on certain grounds, it seems that as long as they state the grounds of refusal they similarly need not give reasons.[105]

---

[97] *Re Land Credit Company of Ireland* (1873) 8 Ch App 831.
[98] *Swiss Bank Corp* v *Lloyds Bank* [1982] AC 584.
[99] Article 8 of Table A gives a lien over partly paid shares in respect of moneys due on that share. Article 52 of the model articles for public companies is in similar terms to art. 8 of Table A (for private companies, art. 21 states that all shares are to be fully paid up).
[100] Companies Act 2006, s. 670.
[101] Table A, art. 24.
[102] *Re Copal Varnish* [1917] 2 Ch 349.
[103] *Re Smith & Fawcett* [1942] Ch 304 at p. 306, *per* Lord Greene MR. See now, s. 171 of the 2006 Act, discussed in Chapter 8.
[104] *Re Bell Bros* (1891) 65 LT 245.
[105] *Re Coalport China* [1895] 2 Ch 404.

Pre-emption clauses are often contained in the articles of private companies; long and elaborate, they are designed to give the directors or members the right to buy the shares of any member who wishes to sell his shares.[106] Poor drafting of the clauses, perhaps combined with a lack of efficiency in carrying out the prescribed procedures, can lead to complex litigation and difficult priority problems if third party rights intervene.[107]

## 4 Disclosure of interests in shares

The Companies Act 2006, Part 22 contains provisions relating to the right of public companies to require shareholders to disclose their interests in shares, thus enabling the company to investigate the ownership of its shares.[108] A company may wish to investigate who are the 'real' owners of the company's shares, for often shares are held by nominees on trust for the real holders. By issuing a s. 793 notice the company can require the registered holder to state for whom he holds on trust. A series of s. 793 notices can be used if a chain of trustees has been used to try to avoid the investigation. Breach of the provisions attracts criminal penalties.[109] A favourite avoidance device is to take the chain out of the jurisdiction so that the company comes up against a nominee who simply ignores the s. 793 notice. In practice, this is very effectively dealt with by the company applying to the UK court for an order under s. 794 applying restrictions to the shares in question. Furthermore, the courts require a very speedy response to the s. 793 notice; in one case, *Lonrho plc* v *Edelman*,[110] two clear days was the maximum allowed for a recipient of the notice abroad, and it was said that even less time is available for a UK recipient. Companies are required to keep a register of interests in shares that must be open for public inspection (recall that a private company may elect for the register of members to be held by the Registrar as part of the public register). Section 808 therefore provides that the information received by the company as a result of the requirement imposed under s. 793 must be entered on a public register against the name of the present holder of the shares. Companies must now also maintain a register of persons with significant control and file this information with Companies House. Broadly defined, this generally means those individuals who hold more than 25% of the shares (or voting rights) in the company or who can appoint or remove the majority of the board of directors.

The Companies Act 1985 also contained provisions requiring directors to disclose shareholdings in their company.[111] One of the policy considerations here was the prevention of insider dealing. They also operated as a barometer of the directors' levels of confidence in the company so that if they had just sold most of their holdings, their assertions of confidence in the company's future could be judged in that light.[112] The Companies Act 2006

---

[106] See e.g. *Borland's Trustee* v *Steel Bros & Co. Ltd* [1901] 1 Ch 279.
[107] *Tett* v *Phoenix Ltd* (1986) 2 BCC 99,140.
[108] Companies Act 2006, s. 793 (notice by company requiring information about interests in its shares).
[109] Section 795.
[110] (1989) 5 BCC 68.
[111] Companies Act 1985, ss. 324–326, 328–329.
[112] The Law Commissions noted that: 'the interests which a director has in his company and his acquisitions and disposals of such interests convey information about the financial incentives that a director has to improve his company's performance and accordingly these provisions form part of the system put in place by the Companies Acts to enable shareholders to monitor the directors' stewardship of the company.' See the Law Commission and the Scottish Law Commissions, *Company Directors: Regulating Conflicts of Interest and Formulating a Statement of Duties: A Joint Consultation Paper* (1998), para. 5.2.

does not, however, contain these rules for directors. Rather, following the Market Abuse Directive,[113] the disclosure requirements in this respect are to be found in the FCA regime.[114]

Overall, the disclosure provisions are ostensibly designed to ensure that information is available to the market so that buyers and sellers of a company's shares are in a position to know who controls it and who is building a stake in it. In fact, the provisions are also very useful to incumbent management who are sometimes able to obtain early warning of a potential takeover bidder before he or she manages to build a sizeable stake in the company from which to launch their bid.

## 13.4 The legal nature of debentures (and bonds)

### A The definition of a debenture and the distinction between a fixed and a floating charge

The important role of loan capital in corporate finance has already been discussed.[115] It is necessary to consider briefly some of the legal aspects of debt finance. It has already been observed that a debenture-holder is not a member of the company and he has rights against the company, as a creditor, rather than rights in it. A debenture is, essentially, a document which acknowledges a debt, but the notion usually also connotes some degree of permanence, or absence of short-term quality.

As we have seen,[116] a debenture is defined in s. 738 of the Companies Act 2006 as including 'debenture stock, bonds and any other securities of a company, whether or not constituting a charge on the assets of the company'. Thus, it is important to realise that although the commercial world draws a rough distinction between a debenture and a bond based mainly on the idea that the former is secured, the Companies Act will regard a bond as a 'debenture' for the purposes of the Act's provisions.

A debenture will sometimes specify a repayment date, or it may be reserved to the company to choose when to pay it off, with no fixed date, or it may be made irredeemable. Usually a debenture will be repayable if the company defaults on its payment of interest. A common feature of modern corporate finance is debentures which contain provisions enabling them to be converted into shares in certain circumstances; these are usually referred to as 'convertible debentures'.

A debenture (as opposed to a bond) will usually be secured by fixed and floating charges.[117] If the charge is fixed, the chargee's rights attach to the property which is the subject of the security, e.g. a warehouse. If it is floating, the chargee's rights attach to a 'shifting fund of assets'[118] such as receivables or stock in trade. Unlike a floating charge,

---

[113] Directive 2003/6/EC on insider trading and market manipulation. See further, Chapter 20.
[114] See Chapter 20.
[115] See above, 13.2.
[116] See 13.2C 1 above.
[117] If the charge is to be valid it will need to be registered in accordance with s. 860. Detailed consideration of these matters is beyond the scope of this text, but see E. Ferran *Principles of Corporate Finance Law* (Oxford: OUP, 2008), Chapter 12.
[118] *Re Cimex Tissues Ltd* [1994] BCC 626. In *Spectrum Plus Ltd, Re* [2005] 2 AC 680, at [111], Lord Scott observed: 'In my opinion, the essential characteristic of a floating charge, the characteristic that distinguishes it from a fixed charge, is that the asset subject to the charge is not finally appropriated as a security for the payment of the debt until the occurrence of some future event. In the meantime the chargor is left free to use the charged asset and to remove it from the security.' See also *Gray v G-T-P Group Ltd* [2010] EWHC 1772 (Ch).

therefore, a fixed charge will restrict the company's freedom to deal with the charged property without first obtaining the chargee's permission. The conceptual basis underlying the distinction between the two types of charge has generated considerable debate among the judges and commentators.[119] Categorising a particular charge as either fixed or floating is not a straightforward exercise, though it is a question of law whether a charge is one or the other. As Lord Millett explained in *Agnew v IRC (Brumark Re)*:[120]

> In deciding whether a charge is a fixed or a floating charge, the Court is engaged in a two-stage process. At the first stage it must construe the instrument of charge and seek to gather the intentions of the parties from the language they have used. But the object at this stage of the process is not to discover whether the parties intended to create a fixed or a floating charge. It is to ascertain the nature of the rights and obligations which the parties intended to grant each other in respect of the charged assets. Once these have been ascertained, the Court can then embark on the second stage of the process, which is one of categorization. This is a matter of law. It does not depend on the intention of the parties. If their intention, properly gathered from the language of the instrument, is to grant the company rights in respect of the charged assets which are inconsistent with the nature of a fixed charge, then the charge cannot be a fixed charge however they may have chosen to describe it.[121]

Lord Millett's reasoning has been approved by the House of Lords in *Spectrum Plus Ltd, Re*,[122] in which emphasis was given to the freedom of the company to deal with the assets in the ordinary course of business rather than the nature of the assets in question.[123]

The distinction between the two types of charge has recently come to the fore in relation to charges over book debts. Put simply, if the charge holder, typically a bank, does not have complete control over how the chargor-company uses the proceeds of its book debts, the charge will be classified as floating. On the other hand, if its control is absolute, the charge will be fixed. Thus in *Re Keenan Bros Ltd*,[124] the company was required to pay the proceeds of its book debts into a special account over which the chargee-bank had an absolute discretion in deciding to allow the company to transfer moneys to its working account. The Supreme Court of Ireland, finding that the bank's control over the special account was such as to deprive the company of its freedom to use the proceeds, held that a fixed charge had been created. However, the English courts had in the past taken a less

---

[119] For a thorough review of this debate, and of secured charges generally, see E. Ferran *Principles of Corporate Finance Law* (Oxford: OUP, 2008), Chapter 12; and L. Gullifer (ed.) *Goode on Legal Problems of Credit and Security* (London: Sweet & Maxwell, 2009).
[120] [2001] 2 AC 710, PC.
[121] *Ibid.* at para. [32].
[122] [2005] 2 AC 680.
[123] Lord Phillips MR in the Court of Appeal decision in *National Westminster Bank plc v Spectrum Plus Ltd* [2004] EWCA Civ 670, explained that: 'Initially it was not difficult to distinguish between a fixed and a floating charge. A fixed charge arose where the chargor agreed that he would no longer have the right of free disposal of the assets charged, but that they should stand as security for the discharge of obligations owed to the chargee. A floating charge was normally granted by a company which wished to be free to acquire and dispose of assets in the normal course of its business, but nonetheless to make its assets available as security to the chargee in priority to other creditors should it cease to trade. The hallmark of the floating charge was the agreement that the chargor should be free to dispose of his assets in the normal course of business unless and until the chargee intervened. Up to that moment the charge "floated".' Lord Millett's approach reflects the view expressed by Romer LJ in *Re Yorkshire Woolcombers Association Ltd* [1903] 2 Ch 284 at p. 295, to the effect that a charge is floating if the company is free to continue to deal with the assets so charged in the ordinary course of its business.
[124] [1986] BCLC 242.

strict approach. In *Siebe Gorman & Co Ltd* v *Barclays Bank Ltd*,[125] the company granted a debenture in favour of Barclays Bank described as a 'first fixed charge' over all present and future book debts. The debenture required the company to pay the proceeds of its book debts into a designated account which it held with the bank and it prohibited the company from charging or assigning its book debts without obtaining the bank's consent, although the company was free to use the funds in that account. Slade J held that the charge was fixed. The judge reasoned that the restrictions placed on the company's power to deal with the proceeds of the debts gave the bank a degree of control which was inconsistent with a floating charge. In *Re New Bullas Trading Ltd*,[126] the Court of Appeal held that a fixed and floating charge could be combined. The debenture provided for a fixed charge over the company's uncollected book debts, but once the proceeds were collected and credited to a designated account, a floating charge took effect. Both *Siebe Gorman* and *New Bullas* were overruled by the House of Lords in *Spectrum*. Lord Scott, delivering the leading speech, explained that where the chargor is free to deal with the charged assets or their proceeds without first obtaining the chargee's permission, the charge must be floating. On the facts before the House, he reasoned:

> The bank's debenture placed no restrictions on the use that Spectrum could make of the balance on the account available to be drawn by Spectrum. Slade J in [*Siebe Gorman*] thought that it might make a difference whether the account were in credit or in debit. I must respectfully disagree. The critical question, in my opinion, is whether the chargor can draw on the account. If the chargor's bank account were in debit and the chargor had no right to draw on it, the account would have become, and would remain until the drawing rights were restored, a blocked account. The situation would be as it was in *Re Keenan Bros Ltd* [above]. But so long as the charger can draw on the account, and whether the account is in credit or debit, the money paid in is not being appropriated to the repayment of the debt owing to the debenture holder but is being made available for drawings on the account by the charger.[127]

The decision in *Spectrum* adds certainty to the law. For a charge to be fixed the chargee must restrict totally the chargor's freedom to deal with the assets so charged,[128] thereby maintaining them for the benefit of the chargee.

## B Registration requirements for charges

### 1 *Why register charges?*

It is generally agreed that it is important that there be a public record of charges created by companies over their property. The Law Commission,[129] drawing on the review conducted by Professor Diamond,[130] noted:[131]

> Apart from the objective of providing information for persons proposing to deal with the company so that they, or credit reference agencies on their behalf, can assess its creditworthiness,

---

[125] [1979] 2 Lloyd's Rep 142.
[126] [1994] 1 BCLC 485.
[127] [2005] 2 AC 680, at [117]. See also *Re Harmony Care Homes Ltd* [2010] BCC 358.
[128] As in *Re Keenan Bros Ltd*, above.
[129] Law Com (No. 296, 2002).
[130] *A Review of Security Interests in Property* (1989) (the Diamond Report), para 11.1.5.
[131] Law Com (No. 296, 2002), para. 1.3.

persons considering whether to provide secured credit can find out whether the proposed security is already the subject of a charge; by the same token, a registration system benefits the company itself if it is enabled to give some sort of assurance to a prospective secured creditor that the property it is offering as security is unencumbered.

Registration can also ease the task of a receiver or liquidator in knowing whether to acknowledge the validity of an alleged mortgage or charge, and does away with the risk of fraud by inventing a security only when a receiver is appointed or the company goes into liquidation.

One can also recognise that, in addition to the use of information by financial analysts and persons considering whether to invest in a company, there is today a general climate of opinion in favour of public disclosure of companies' financial activities.

It is also important that the law should set out clear rules to resolve disputes when two or more parties lay claim to the same property. This may occur, for example, when the same asset has been charged to two separate lenders, and where charged property has been sold to an innocent buyer. Priority disputes may arise rarely but the rules have a significant impact on the steps that potential secured lenders and buyers of company property have to take to safeguard their interests.[132]

The Law Commission then explained the problems with the current law in the following terms:[133]

Despite its importance, the current law on company security interests has been severely criticised for many years. The scheme for registering company charges dates back to 1900 and is now inappropriate to modern needs. It is particularly inefficient in two ways.

First, it requires charge documents to be submitted in paper form, although the register of company charges maintained at Companies House is electronic.

Secondly, registry staff must check the particulars submitted against lengthy legal documents before the registrar issues a conclusive certificate of registration. This requires a significant number of staff and is, in our view, unnecessary and impossible to justify. A system of electronic on-line registration, with the party filing being responsible for ensuring that the information registered is accurate, would be far more efficient.

## 2 *Current registration requirements*

The current registration requirements are found in Companies Act 2006, Part 25, which has been amended by the Companies Act 2006 (Amendment of Part 25) Regulations 2013. Importantly the 2013 amendments require, amongst other things, that all charges granted by a company registered in the UK must now be registered at Companies House unless they fall within a specific exclusion.[134] Notwithstanding this clear improvement, the amended regime does not fully achieve the goals discussed immediately above. First, although it is primarily the responsibility of the company to register prescribed particulars of any charge, it is the chargee who will suffer if the charge is not registered or if it is registered late. Secondly, according to ss. 859 A and 859 B the period allowed for registration of the charge created by a company is 21 days, which means that there is no certainty that searching the register will discover all and/or existing charges, i.e. the so-called 21-day invisibility period.

---

[132] *Ibid.* para 1.4.
[133] *Ibid.* para 1.5.
[134] Formerly the Companies Act 1985, Part XII – ss. 395, 396 *et seq.*

Finally, ss. 859 P–859 Q state that a company has to keep its own register of all charges at its registered office. However, a charge is not rendered void if not entered on this register.

## 3 Registration of charges: basic rules

Let us briefly go through the basic rules of registration. The Registrar of Companies is required to maintain a register of charges that is available for public inspection. When a company gives security for its obligations, the prescribed particulars of any charge must be registered at Companies House.[135] The particulars must be duly completed and filed, together with the original charging document within 21 days of the creation of the charge.

If the charge is not registered at Companies House within this timescale it is *void* against an administrator or liquidator of the company and against any person who, for value, acquires an interest in or a right over the property that is charged. Any debt owed by the company to the lender still remains outstanding but it ranks as an unsecured debt in the event of the company's insolvency. The existence of a negative pledge in a floating charge is not a prescribed particular, but it is common practice to include it – thereby it becomes known to anyone searching the register.

The registrar checks that all requirements have been complied with and if so satisfied issues a certificate of registration stating the amount secured by the charge. Importantly, s. 859 I stipulates that the certificate is *conclusive evidence* that the requirements for registration under Part 25 of the Companies Act 2006 have been complied with. Although it is primarily the responsibility of the company to register prescribed particulars of any charge, it is the chargee who will suffer if the charge is not registered or if it is registered late. Due to this, it is common for the chargee to arrange for the registration. If the 21-day registration period is missed, then the court has the power to order an extension of time but this remedy is far from automatic. Details of any charge created by the company should also be kept in the company's own register of charges at its registered office.

Section 859 D of the Companies Act 2006 sets out the information to be provided to the Registrar of Companies on the registration of a charge under Part 25 of the Companies Act 2006. When a company registered in England and Wales or Northern Ireland creates a charge of a kind specified in ss. 859 A or 859 B of the 2006 Act it must deliver to the registrar the following particulars of charge (amongst others set out in s. 859 D): the date of the creation of the charge; a description of the instrument creating or evidencing the charge; the amount secured by the charge; the name and address of the person entitled to the charge; and short particulars of the property charged.

If the charge is not registered in accordance with Part 25 then the charge is void against a liquidator, administrator and creditor of the company.[136]

---

[135] These are set out in s. 859 D of the Companies Act 2006.
[136] Section 859 H of the Companies Act 2006.

## Further reading

E. Ferran and L. Chan Hoo *Principles of Corporate Finance Law* (Oxford: OUP, 2nd edition, 2014).

L. Gullifer and J. Payne *Corporate Finance Law: Principles and Policy* (Oxford: Hart Publishing, 2nd edition, 2015).

L. Gullifer (ed.) *Goode on Legal Problems of Credit and Security* (London: Sweet & Maxwell, 2009). 6 edition (2017).

E. Ferran 'Creditors' interests and "core" company law' (1999) 20 Co Law 314.

D. Prentice and A. Reisberg (eds) *Corporate Finance Law in the UK and the EU* (Oxford: OUP, 2011), Chapters 8–13.

# 14

# Raising and maintenance of capital

## 14.1 Introduction

This chapter is concerned with principles that were, primarily, developed and settled by the courts towards the end of the nineteenth century and relate to the raising and maintenance of corporate capital. As a result of the need to comply with the EC Second Harmonisation Directive,[1] some of the principles can now be found in the companies legislation in a codified form.[2] The broad principle which infuses this field is that of creditor protection,[3] and in this context this idea leads to some very fundamental rules that are designed to regulate the way in which the company's capital is dealt with (both as to the raising and, thereafter, maintenance of capital). Whether these rules actually serve any useful purpose, or could be replaced by something better, is open to question.[4]

## 14.2 The raising of capital – discounts and premiums

### A Introduction

It has been seen[5] how in English company law, when shares are issued they have to be given a nominal (or 'par') value, such as £1. This has enabled the development of two

---

[1] 77/91/EEC, implemented by the Companies Act 1980. Directive 2006/68/EC amends Directive 77/91 in the following areas: (1) Articles 10 and 11 – Valuation of non-cash consideration for the allotment of shares/acquisition of assets from those involved in the formation of a company: removes the requirement for independent valuation of assets in certain circumstances. (2) Article 19 – Acquisition by a company of its own shares: aims to make more flexible the circumstances in which a company can purchase and hold in 'treasury' its own shares. (3) Article 23 – Financial assistance: prescribes rules allowing the company to provide financial assistance to third parties for the purchase of its own shares (in general terms, financial assistance is presently prohibited by the Directive). (4) Article 32 – Safeguards for creditors in the case of a reduction in subscribed capital: places an express burden on creditors to 'credibly demonstrate' that their 'claim is at stake' when objecting to a proposed reduction in the capital of a company. Many of the changes are optional for member states to adopt within the limits and circumstances specified in the Directive.

[2] It will be seen that the input of the European Commission here has sometimes been to open up differences between the regime applicable to public companies and that applicable to private companies, since the requirements of the Second Directive apply only to 'public limited liability companies'.

[3] See *In Re National Funds Assurance* (1878) 10 Ch D 118, 125 (Jessel MR): 'capital . . . is to be applied to purposes to which capital is properly applicable, namely, payment of the debts, obligations and liabilities of the company.'

[4] See e.g. E. Ferran *Principles of Corporate Finance Law* (Oxford: OUP, 2008), 180–184 for a review of the major arguments in favour and against these rules; see also J. Armour 'Legal Capital: An Outdated Concept?' (2006) 7 *European Business Organization Law Review* 5; L. Enriques and J. Macey 'Creditors versus Capital Formation: The Case against the European Legal Capital rules' (2001) 86 *Cornell Law Review* 1165; J. Vella and D. Prentice 'Some Aspects of Capital Maintenance Law in the UK' in M. Tison *et al.* (eds) *Perspectives in Company Law and Financial Regulation* (Cambridge: CUP, 2009).

[5] See Chapter 13, at 13.3.

rules. The first is designed to regulate the situation where the company receives (and purportedly is only ever entitled to receive),[6] less than the nominal value for the share (which is then said to be issued at a 'discount'), the second applies (conversely), where more than the nominal value of the share is received (when the share is said to be issued at a 'premium').

## B Discounts

A discount occurs where a share of, say, £1 nominal value is issued in return for, say, 80 pence. The discount is 20 pence. It was firmly settled at the end of the nineteenth century in *Ooregum Gold Mining Co* v *Roper*[7] that the issue of shares at a discount is illegal. The rationale for the rule is that without it, the company could easily give a false impression that at some stage in its past, a certain sum of money had been raised for its venture, when, if the shares had been issued at a discount, a much smaller sum had in fact been raised. This might mislead people who were at a later date considering whether to give credit to the company, or to invest in shares in it. As part of the UK's obligations under the EC Second Directive[8] the rule was effectively codified and is now to be found in s. 580 (1) of the Companies Act 2006. If shares are allotted in contravention of the prohibition, the allottee is liable to pay an amount equal to the discount.[9]

If shares are allotted for cash then obviously a share discount is relatively easy to spot and the scope for avoidance of the legislation is limited. However, once it is seen that shares could be allotted in return for a non-cash consideration, then it can be imagined that it would not be difficult to avoid the rule. As a result of the implementation of the EC Second Directive,[10] public companies are subjected to various statutory prohibitions and procedures, designed to ensure that the share capital is properly paid for and also to avoid hidden discounts. The regime applicable to private companies is less onerous.

The basic position as regards payment for shares is that[11] shares allotted by a company, and any premium on them, may be paid up in money or money's worth (including goodwill and know-how).[12] That said, a public company may not accept, in payment for shares, an undertaking given by any person that he or another should do work or perform services for the company or any other person.[13] Nor should a public company allot shares (otherwise than in cash) if the consideration for the allotment is or includes an

---

[6] In this way shares issued at a discount (which is impermissible) can be contrasted with shares that are issued as partly paid, which is permissible (s. 581 of the Companies Act 2006) subject to certain conditions. See, for example, s. 586 of the Companies Act 2006.

[7] [1892] AC 125, HL.

[8] EC Second Directive, art. 8, as amended. According to the amended Directive, member states should be able to permit public limited liability companies to allot shares for consideration other than in cash without requiring them to obtain a special expert valuation in cases in which there is a clear point of reference for the valuation of such consideration. Nonetheless, the right of minority shareholders to require such valuation should be guaranteed.

[9] Plus interest (Companies Act 2006, s. 580 (2)).

[10] As amended.

[11] Subject to what appears hereafter.

[12] Companies Act 2006, s. 582 (1) and (3); EC Second Directive, art. 7.

[13] Companies Act 2006, s. 585 (1); EC Second Directive, art. 7.

undertaking which is to be, or may be, performed more than five years from the date of the allotment.[14]

Of particular relevance to the prevention of discounts are the rules contained in Part 17, Chapter 6 of the 2006 Act that prevent a public company from allotting shares in return for a non-cash consideration unless the consideration has been independently valued.[15] These provisions are not applicable to private companies and so these continue to be governed by the common law as set out in *Re Wragg Ltd*.[16] The facts illustrate quite well the operation of the discount principle in circumstances where a non-cash consideration is given for the allotment and also provide us with another example of the manoeuvre which is extremely common in company law, whereby an existing business is incorporated by being sold to a newly formed shell company in return for shares and other consideration.[17] Wragg and Martin carried on a coach business in partnership. After some years they decided to turn it into a limited company, which they did by forming a company and then selling the assets of the partnership to it at a price fixed at £46,300. In return, they received cash, debentures, and shares. Soon afterwards, the company went into insolvent liquidation and the liquidator argued that when one looked at the actual values of the assets which had been sold to the company, it was clear that the shares had been issued at a discount. Therefore, it was argued that Wragg and Martin were still liable to the company for the discount. The Court of Appeal refused to accept this and held that directors (of a private company) were under a duty to make a bona fide valuation of the asset but in the absence of any evidence showing bad faith, the court will not substitute a valuation of its own.

## C Premiums

Shares are issued at a premium if, say, a share of £1 nominal value is issued in return for £1.30. The 30 pence is the premium. Prior to 1948, the premium was not treated as share capital. This meant that the premium was free of the legal restrictions which normally apply to share capital. As will be seen,[18] one of the main restrictions is that the company cannot use share capital to pay a dividend to the shareholders. In 1937 in *Drown* v *Gaumont Picture Corp Ltd*,[19] it was confirmed that a company could use a premium to pay a dividend to shareholders. However, the Companies Act 1948 contained a provision[20] which required the premium to be credited to a share premium account on the balance sheet which means, in effect, that it was largely to be treated, for legal purposes, as if it were share capital.

---

[14] Companies Act 2006, s. 587; EC Second Directive, art. 9 (2). There are also provisions which restrict subscribers to the memorandum from transferring non-cash assets to a public company in return for shares unless the assets have been independently valued (see Part 17, Chapter 6 of the Companies Act 2006 and s. 599 in particular) and prohibitions from giving anything other than cash for shares taken pursuant to an undertaking in the memorandum (s. 584).

[15] See Companies Act 2006, Part 17, Chapter 6, particularly s. 593, which prescribe various conditions. Mergers by share exchange are excluded from the ambit of these provisions; see *ibid.* s. 595 and Second Directive, art. 10 (according to the new Directive member states may decide not to apply article 10.

[16] [1897] 1 Ch 796.

[17] The example of how Salomon did this has already been considered at Chapter 2, 2.1 above.

[18] See further 14.3D below.

[19] [1937] Ch 402.

[20] Section 56.

The statutory requirement for the share premium account is now contained in s. 610 of the Companies Act 2006. It provides that if a company issues shares at a premium, whether for cash or otherwise, a sum equal to the aggregate amount or value of the premiums must be transferred to an account called 'the share premium account'.[21] The share premium account must be treated as paid up capital,[22] so that, for instance, the rules on reduction of capital[23] apply just as if the share premium were capital. The basic rationale of this is that if a company issues shares at a premium, then the actual capital which has been raised is the full consideration received, including the premium, and the balance sheet has to reflect this. The rule is the direct result of the concept of the nominal (or par) value of shares.

Shortly after the 1948 Act was passed, the effect of the new legislation became clear in *Henry Head & Co Ltd* v *Ropner Holdings Ltd*.[24] Here the defendant company had entered a sum on to its balance sheet in what was called a share premium account. For reasons which will gradually become apparent, the claimant thought that this produced very undesirable consequences and sought an injunction restraining the defendant from doing this. In effect, the claimant was challenging what was then a new statutory requirement, and hoping that it was not really as compulsory as it seemed. The background to the case indicates that the various participants had not realised what the effect of the new section on their transaction would be.[25] The circumstances concerned an amalgamation of two shipping companies that were being carried on separately, but under the same management. The amalgamation was to be carried out by forming a shell company (the defendant Ropner Holdings Ltd) and then getting the shareholders in the two shipping companies to sell their shares to it, in exchange for shares in it. By the time the amalgamation was carried out, various steps had been taken to ensure that the shares in each of the shipping companies were worth the same, and so it was fair, and made financial sense, for the amalgamation to be carried out by 'a pound-for-pound capitalisation – that is to say, a pound of the new company's shares for a pounds worth, nominal, of the constituent company's shares'.[26] Thus the shareholders in the shipping companies were getting a £1 share in Ropner Holdings Ltd in return for the handing over of each of their £1 shares in the shipping company. In all, in this way, Ropner Holdings Ltd issued shares having a nominal value of £1,759,606. However, the actual value of the assets in the shipping companies was about £5m more than that. So, in a sense, Ropner Holdings Ltd was getting a premium of about £5m when it issued its shares to the shareholders of the shipping companies. And that £5m was entered in a share premium account on the balance sheet. In essence, what

---

[21] *Ibid.* s. 610 (1).

[22] *Ibid.* s. 610 (4). This is subject to exceptions in respect of using the share premium account to issue bonus shares to the members and writing off the company's preliminary expenses (or expenses or commissions etc. allowed on any issue of shares) or it may be used to pay up new shares to be allotted to members as fully paid bonus shares (s. 610 (2) and (3)).

[23] See further 14.3B below.

[24] [1952] 1 Ch 124.

[25] The judge referred to the 'sense of shock' in some quarters ([1952] 1 Ch 124 at p. 127). It is not uncommon for practitioners to find that the technicalities of company law legislation largely ruin the effect of a well-intentioned reconstruction carried out for bona fide commercial reasons. The operation of s. 678 of the Companies Act 2006 (formerly s. 151 of the Companies Act 1985) is well known for causing these problems; see further Chapter 15, at 15.1.

[26] [1952] 1 Ch 124 at p. 126, *per* Harman J.

the claimant objected to was the entry of the £5m in a share premium account, as the statute seemed to require that this had the effect that the £5m was treated as capital. This greatly restricted the way in which the company's assets could be used. As Harman J said:

> [I]t fixes an unfortunate kind of rigidity on the structure of the company, having regard to the fact that an account kept under that name, namely, the Share Premium Account, can only have anything paid out of it by means of a transaction analogous to a reduction of capital. It is in effect, as if the company had originally been capitalised at approximately £7,000,000 instead of £1,750,000.[27]

It is not clear exactly what particular aspect of the rigidity was worrying the claimant company in this case. It is probable that it was upset at the prospect of £5m becoming 'undistributable' in the sense that after the amalgamation it could no longer be used to pay a dividend to shareholders because it was share capital, whereas prior to the amalgamation, it would have been a 'distributable' reserve, which could have been used to pay dividends because it was merely accumulated profits and not share capital. The claimant failed to get an injunction. Its argument that the statute only applied to a cash premium and not, as here, a premium thrown up by the asset values on the balance sheet, failed. The statute clearly said 'whether for cash or otherwise' and so Harman J held that the sum of £5m had been correctly shown in the share premium account.

The share premium account problem also arose in the similar context of a takeover by share exchange. Thus, for instance, when the bidder issued shares (in itself) to the shareholders of the target company, in return for its shares in the target, there was a potential for a share premium to arise. City practitioners tried to minimise the effects of this by ensuring that there was nothing to upset the assumptions made by the parties involved that the value of the shares received by the bidder was equal to the nominal value of the shares issued by it, and hence, no premium. Then in 1980, Walton J in *Shearer* v *Bercain Ltd*[28] made it clear that a proper valuation needed to be made of what the bidder was getting. This was then likely to throw up a share premium and the legislation would then require the establishment of a share premium account which would often have the effect that pre-acquisition distributable reserves would become undistributable after the takeover. The Conservative government of the time responded very quickly to City pressure and the Companies Act 1981 contained provisions designed to provide some relief from the requirement to establish a share premium account in a takeover situation. These 'merger accounting' provisions are now contained in ss. 611–615 of the Companies Act 2006.[29]

---

[27] *Ibid.* at p. 127. The judge was rounding the figures somewhat. On reduction of capital see further 14.3D below.
[28] [1980] 3 All ER 295. For a detailed account of this saga see the article by R. Pennington 'The Companies Act 1981 (2)' (1982) 3 Co Law 66.
[29] The main provision as regards takeovers and mergers is ss. 612–613 which will apply where the company which issues the shares (i.e. the bidder) had secured at least a 90% equity holding in another company (the target) in pursuance of an arrangement providing for the allotment of equity shares in the issuing company on terms that the consideration for the shares allotted is to be provided either by the issue or transfer to the issuing company of equity shares in the other company (the target) or by the cancellation of any such shares not held by the issuing company (bidder); see s. 612 (1). It is then provided that a premium arising on the issuing company's shares is exempt from the section requirement to establish a share premium account s. 612 (2). There is also provision for relief from share premium accounts in situations involving group reconstructions where a company in the group issues shares to another in the group in return for non-cash assets (s. 611).

## 14.3 The maintenance of capital

### A The meaning of the doctrine

In a series of leading cases towards the end of the nineteenth century, the courts[30] estab-lished the capital maintenance doctrine,[31] which requires that the share capital of a company[32] must be maintained as a fund of last resort for the creditors of the company to look to. Put in this form, the maintenance doctrine makes little sense because companies often go into insolvent liquidation and the creditors frequently then get little or nothing back. The idea of the capital being maintained as a fund of last resort is, at best, a rather general concept and there are a number of important qualifications to it. First, the capital needs to be maintained only so far as the ordinary risks of business allow. If a company is capital-ised with 1,000 £1 shares and loses this capital through bad luck or negligent trading, that is not a breach of the maintenance of capital rule and the rule provides no remedy in that situation.[33] Secondly, there is no requirement that the debt which a company takes on should bear any relationship to its share capital in the sense of there being a fixed ratio. Thus, it is possible to form an English company with 100 £1 shares and a loan from the bank of £1m.[34] Thirdly, there is no basic requirement in English law that a company be adequately capitalised.[35] In other words, if it is formed with a share capital of 1,000 £1 shares, then there is no fundamental legal doctrine which lays down limits as to the size of the business that it undertakes. However, it is possible that case law on wrongful trading may have indirectly introduced a form of capitalisation requirement; this is discussed above.[36] In effect then, the maintenance of capital doctrine is heavily qualified, and really amounts to a group of rules which restrict the circumstances in which capital can be given to, or back to, the shareholders.

---

[30] As a result of the implementation of the EC Second Directive, much of the case law has (since 1980) been codified in the Companies Act 1985, and more recently in the Companies Act 2006; see EC Second Directive, articles 15–22.

[31] The doctrine relates only to 'capital' in the strict sense of *share* capital. The term 'capital' is often used in common parlance to refer to all the funds which are available to the company to operate its business, whether arising from the issue of shares (equity capital) or from debt (loan capital).

[32] Including any quasi-capital funds such as share premium account.

[33] *Trevor* v *Whitworth* (1887) 12 AC 409, 423: 'Paid up capital may be diminished or lost in the course of the company's trading; that is a result which no legislation can prevent; but [creditors] . . . naturally rely upon the fact that the company is trading with a certain amount of capital already paid . . . and they are entitled to assume that no part of the capital which has been paid into the coffers of the company has been subsequently paid out, except in the legitimate course of its business . . .' There may be other remedies, such as an unfair prejudice petition.

[34] Other jurisdictions have different rules and it is not uncommon to find a prescribed debt/equity ratio in com-pany legislation.

[35] This can be contrasted with specific requirements that apply to banks and other financial institutions.

[36] At Chapter 2, 2.2C above. A public company will need to have an issued share capital of at least the authorised minimum, S. 761 of the Companies Act 2006 (currently set at £50,000 or the prescribed euro equivalent, s. 763), but this is a fixed amount and not a concept of capital adequacy; see Chapter 1, 1.8A, above. Further to art. 28 of the Companies Act 2006 (Consequential Amendments and Transitional Provisions) Order 2011, SI 2011/1265 (made on 11 May 2011), s. 766(1) now gives the Secretary of State power to make regulations which specify how the authorised minimum test would apply where all of the shares of a public company are denominated in a currency other than sterling or euros. Subsection (1a) previously granted the Secretary of State the power in relation only to companies that had shares denominated in more than one currency. See Companies (Authorised Minimum) Regulations 2009, SI 2009/2424 which was initially used on 12 March 2008 and came into force on 6 April 2008.

There are three areas that can be clearly viewed as capital maintenance problems. First, and perhaps most obviously, is when a company wishes to reduce its capital. Here, the company is often seeking to return money to the shareholders in some way and to reduce the share capital on the company's balance sheet. Secondly, and again a clear capital maintenance concern, is the purchase by a company of its own shares. This involves a very similar mechanism to some reductions, in that the company gives the shareholder money and then removes the corresponding shares from the balance sheet. The third area, the payment of dividends, involves a payment of money by the company to its shareholders. Dividends are periodic (but not guaranteed) payments to shareholders and the capital maintenance regime makes clear that unless the company has made profits at least equal to the amount of the dividend, then the distribution to the shareholder will diminish the assets available to the creditors and constitute an unlawful return of capital.[37] Hence the courts developed the rule that dividends can only be paid out of 'distributable reserves'.

There is a fourth area which is often seen as an example of the maintenance of capital principle.[38] It is the problem of a public company giving financial assistance for the acquisition of its own shares (or those of its holding company, regardless of whether that holding company is a private or public company).[39] Note that a private company is also prohibited from providing financial assistance for the acquisition of shares in its holding company, when that holding company is a public company.[40] The prohibition is usually simply referred to as 'financial assistance'. Such an activity less obviously involves a breach of the maintenance principle, for no diminution of the undistributable elements on the balance sheet occurs, nor is there necessarily any payment made to the shareholders. It might perhaps tentatively be argued that it represents an example of a broader maintenance principle which forbids any payment or arrangement made other than for the legitimate purposes of the company's business or objects. However, there are two problems with this argument. First, is that it is highly doubtful whether the case law on maintenance really justifies this view. Secondly, if it was really possible to see the financial assistance problem as covered by the maintenance principle then it would not have been necessary to introduce special legislation in 1929 to deal with it.[41] Financial assistance is more properly seen as a discrete problem that is (or should be) largely unrelated to the maintenance principle, and for this and other reasons, financial assistance forms a chapter of its own in this text.[42]

---

[37] Although it is also clear that no diminution in the share capital as stated on the balance sheet is being contemplated.

[38] See e.g. the DTI Consultation Document (February 1999) *The Strategic Framework* para. 5.4.20: '[ss. 151–158] . . . normally regarded as part of the capital maintenance regime'.

[39] See ss. 677–680 Companies Act 2006. To be carefully distinguished from the situation where a company purchases its own shares.

[40] Section 678 of the Companies Act 2006.

[41] See s. 45 of the Companies Act 1929. The present much-modified provisions are contained in the Companies Act 2006 ss. 677–683; see Chapter 15 of this text. As will be seen, the prohibition on financial assistance by private companies for the acquisition of shares in themselves or other private companies (including the whitewash procedure) has been repealed from 1 October 2008. Part 18, Chapter 2 of the 2006 Act (financial assistance for purchase of own shares) preserves the financial prohibition for public companies and which came into force on 1 October 2009.

[42] Chapter 15 below. For a similar view, see W. Knight 'Capital Maintenance' in F. Patfield (ed.) *Perspectives on Company Law: 1* (London: Kluwer, 1995) p. 49.

## B The Company Law Review and the reforms of the Companies Act 2006

One of the 'key issues' selected by the Company Law Review[43] in *The Strategic Framework*[44] was 'capital maintenance'. Subsequently, in *Company Formation and Capital Maintenance*,[45] the recommendations were set out and consultation began. The Steering Group noted that many major creditors attached little importance to the company's nominal capital and looked to other indicators of creditworthiness.

A range of reforms were proposed, the main ones being: first, to abolish par (i.e. nominal) value for private companies[46] so that a share would then merely represent a proportion of the company's value.[47] This would mean that the concept of the share premium account would become redundant and would be replaced by a requirement that on the issue of new shares the undistributable reserves on the balance sheet would be increased by the net proceeds of the shares.[48] Secondly, it was proposed to relax the rules regulating reductions of capital and to abolish the burdensome requirement of an application to the court for confirmation of the reduction.[49] For public companies, in order to comply with the Second Directive, creditors would be given a right to apply to the court to cancel the reduction. In a subsequent DTI (the name by which the DBEIS was then known) Consultation Document *Capital Maintenance: Other Issues*,[50] and in the light of various criticisms raised by consultees, the Steering Group expressed the view that the merits of the proposals concerning par value and the related concepts of share premium and share discounts remained uncertain.

Eventually, the Final Report of the Company Law Review favoured retaining the capital maintenance regime, but recommended certain relaxations for private companies. The concept of par (i.e. nominal) value was to be retained. This is to be welcomed, since it was always highly questionable whether creating a separate regime for private companies and public companies on such fundamental matters as par value and undistributable reserves is a reform, which looking at company law as a whole, is necessarily to be seen as an improvement, particularly in view of the fact that the Second Directive has sought to harmonise the position. However, it recommended the abolition of the requirement for companies to have an 'authorised share capital' so that in effect the company no longer need have a ceiling on the amount of capital it can issue. Also, capital reduction requirements for private companies were streamlined so as to reduce the number of situations in which reduction needs confirmation by the court.[51]

By the time the document *Company Law: Flexibility and Accessibility: A Consultative Document* (London: DTI, 2004) was published, it became clear that a number of statutory

---

[43] See generally Chapter 11, at 11.10.
[44] DTI Consultation Document (February 1999).
[45] DTI Consultation Document (October 1999).
[46] The public company position is constrained by the Second Directive, as amended by Directive 2006/68/EC.
[47] DTI Consultation Document (October 1999) *Company Formation and Capital Maintenance* para. 3.8.
[48] *Ibid*. para. 3.18.
[49] *Ibid*. paras 3.27 *et seq.*
[50] June 2000. The document seeks consultation on further matters, especially on clarifying the concepts of 'distribution' and 'realised losses'.
[51] *Modern Company Law for a Competitive Economy Final Report* (London: DTI, June 2001) paras. 4.4–4.5, 10.1–10.7.

changes were likely in this area. The Companies Act 2006 indeed made some important reforms, at the heart of which was a move towards greater reliance on solvency standards. Some of these reforms have already been considered above, and some of the more important aspects of these reforms will be considered in detail in the reminder of the chapter. In relation to the proposals mentioned above the following reforms have been introduced into the law. First, the 2006 Act abolishes the requirement to have authorised share capital for private and public companies, but in line with the Final Report of the Company Law Review shares must still have a nominal value (s. 542). Secondly, as was recommended by the Company Law Review, under the 2006 Act the maximum ceiling for authorised share capital requirement was abolished, though a statement of capital will still have to be registered on formation (s. 10).[52] Moreover, as various transactions affecting share capital are implemented, an updated statement of the state of the company's issued share capital will be required. Share capital is still capable of being altered by an ordinary resolution (s. 617–618). Thirdly, directors of private companies will not require any authority to allot shares where the company has one class of shares, unless the articles provide otherwise (s. 550). Finally, under ss. 761–767 public companies are still required to have an allotted share capital of not less than the 'authorised minimum' (currently £50,000), but the 2006 Act allows this to be satisfied either by reference to sterling or by euros,[53] but not partly in sterling and partly in euros. The Government has power to prescribe the amounts of sterling and euros to be treated as equivalent for this purpose.[54] The Act sets out a new procedure for redenominating share capital from one currency into another, which has caused uncertainty in the past. It permits redenomination by ordinary resolution, establishes the rate at which redenomination is to be effected and sets out steps for calculating the new nominal value of each share.

## C Statements of capital

As we saw in the previous section, the Companies Act 2006 introduced, from 1 October 2009, a requirement for a company to produce a statement of capital in certain circumstances. Prior to implementation of the 2006 Act, information on this subject was provided in the memorandum of association; nonetheless, since the demise of the memorandum the information is provided in the application form for registration and at various stages of a company's life cycle (namely when changes to the company's capital have been made). Difficulties have arisen in practice in relation to preparing statements of capital, in particular as regards the details required about share rights and share premium. In response,

---

[52] The Companies (Shares and Share Capital) Order 2009/0388 prescribes the particulars required in statements of capital, some returns of allotments and permissible capital payments (payments out of capital for the redemption or purchase of own shares by a private company).
[53] The amount in euros that is to be treated as equivalent to the sterling amount(s) is €57,100. See the Companies (Authorised Minimum) Regulations 2009, SI 2009/2425 reg. 2. This figure replaces from 1 October 2009 the higher amount of €65,600 fixed previously by the Companies (Authorised Minimum) Regulations 2008, SI 2008/729 art. 2.
[54] Section 761 (1) of the Companies Act 2006. The power granted under sub-section (1) (a) to the Secretary of State to make regulations as to the application of the authorised minimum in relation to a public company that has shares denominated in more than one currency has been used in the Companies (Authorised Minimum) Regulations 2009, SI 2009/2425.

Companies House produced some FAQs on statements of capital which are available on the Companies House website.[55] Furthermore, the Government has considered the scope to simplify the financial information requirements in Companies Act statements of capital and these were the subject of a consultation that closed in January 2011.[56] For example, DBIS (now DBEIS) suggested that only the aggregate value of the share premium account be included, instead of the more detailed breakdown currently required. In filing a statement of capital, the company must report the following information: the total number of shares of the company; the aggregate nominal value of those shares; the aggregate amount unpaid on those shares (whether on account of nominal value of the shares or by way of premium); the total number of shares in each class; the aggregate nominal value of shares in each class; the aggregate amount unpaid on shares in each class (whether on account of nominal value of the shares or by way of premium). After the initial statement of capital is filed, provided there have been no changes to the share capital in a given year, a company can simply file its annual confirmation statement indicating this. If changes to capital have been made, the company must file an updated statement of capital together with its confirmation statement.

## D Reduction of capital

### 1 *Statutory procedure*

Reductions of capital essentially involve a diminution in the company's share capital[57] on the balance sheet. Under the capital maintenance doctrine this entails a threat to the interests of creditors and, as such, the courts and the legislature have adopted a policy that allows reductions to take place only under strict safeguards designed to protect the interests of those who might otherwise be adversely affected by it.[58] Prior to the Companies Act 2006, all companies (both public and private) that wished to reduce their capital were required to make an application to court, with the result that capital reductions were a time-consuming and expensive process.[59] Alternatively, private limited companies could re-register as unlimited companies to undertake a reduction without reference to the court supported by, *inter alia*, a special resolution of the members and provided the articles of association permitted this.

The Companies Act 2006 introduced a significant relaxation to the capital reduction regime with regard to private companies. As a result of this reform a private company does

---

[55] In particular, the FAQs state that when describing the rights attached to the shares in a statement of capital: a cross reference to the rights as set out in the articles is not sufficient; for a company with one class of shares with simple voting rights, such as a company with the 2006 Act model form articles, the voting rights may be described as 'one vote for each share' and 'right to dividends'; and in an annual return, the only rights that have to be described are the voting rights: there is no need to include information on the right to participate in a winding up or distribution.

[56] The DBIS consultation paper is available on the DBIS website at: http://www.bis.gov.uk/Consultations/companies-act-2006-statements-of-capital-consultation.

[57] 'Share capital' in its broadest sense, including quasi-capital funds such as the share premium account.

[58] As will be seen below (under D 3) it is not only the creditors who need protection because where there are different classes of shares there will be complicated issues between them.

[59] In limited circumstances, if the reduction is returning capital to the shareholders and the company is a private company, then the procedure can be simplified if the transaction is carried out via a purchase by the company of its own shares; see further D 3 below.

not need to have a reduction confirmed by the court[60] (although it retains the right, but not the obligation, to do so if it wishes).[61] Part 17, Chapter 10 of the Companies Act 2006 contains the statutory regime governing reductions of capital. The main provision is s. 641 which provides that:[62]

> A limited company having a share capital may reduce its share capital –
>
> (a) in the case of a private company limited by shares, by special resolution supported by a solvency statement . . .
> (b) in any case, by special resolution confirmed by the court.

Crucially, the solvency statement must be signed by each director of the company (no more than 15 days before the date of the resolution).[63] In signing the solvency statement, each director is attesting to the fact that she has formed the opinion that on the date of the statement (and, effectively, for 12 months thereafter) there is no basis on which the company could be found unable to pay (or discharge) its debts.[64] Further, that if the company was to be wound up within 12 months that the company could pay its debts within 12 months of the winding up.[65] It is an offence, punishable by a fine or imprisonment (or both), to make a solvency statement without reasonable grounds to do so.[66] Thus, by shifting the responsibility of this assertion to the board (rather than the scrutiny and certainty of a court process) it becomes clear why directors of private companies might still prefer to exercise the right to submit the reduction to the court for approval.[67] Companies no longer need authority in their articles for a reduction, although they are able to restrict or prohibit it if they wish according to s. 641 (6). If a company adopts the court reduction regime, creditors are protected by ss. 645–648 which require the notification of creditors and give them, in some circumstances, the right to object to the reduction at the court proceedings for confirmation and also make their consent necessary.[68]

## 2 *Examples of reduction*

Reductions often fall into two main categories: those where the company has more capital than it needs or wants and thus the reduction involves paying back capital to the shareholders;

---

[60] Section 642 of the Companies Act 2006.
[61] Section 641 of the Companies Act 2006. For an examination of the effect of this, see D. Kershaw 'The Decline of Legal Capital: An Exploration of the Consequences of Board Solvency Based Capital Reductions', Chapter 2 in A. Reisberg and D. Prentice (eds), *Corporate Finance Law in the UK and US* (Oxford: OUP, 2011).
[62] Without prejudice to the generality of the section, according to s. 641 (3) (subject to s. 641 (2)), a company may reduce its share capital under this section in any way. Sub-section (4) goes on to give examples of the types of reduction most commonly desired.
[63] Sections 642–643 of the Companies Act 2006.
[64] Section 643 of the Companies Act 2006.
[65] Section 643 of the Companies Act 2006.
[66] Section 643 (4) of the Companies Act 2006.
[67] The Company Law Committee of the City of London Law Society has published a short memorandum concerning the reduction of share capital by private companies where the directors make a solvency statement. The memorandum records some consensus views of members of the Committee regarding the practical steps that directors can take before making a solvency statement in order to reduce the risk of committing an offence under s. 643 (4) of the Companies Act (2006).
[68] As an alternative to getting their consent, the court may order the company to secure the debt (s. 648 (2)). Section 646(1) (B) was inserted by the Companies (Share Capital and Acquisition by a Company of its Own Shares) Regulations 2009, SI 2009/2022.

and those where no capital is being returned to the shareholders but, instead, the reduction involves a write-off against share capital.

An example of the former type of reduction occurred in *Re Chatterley-Whitfield Collieries Ltd*[69] where the company was engaged in coal mining. After the coal mines were nationalised in 1948, the company decided to carry on mining in Ireland though it obviously needed less capital than before. Hence it returned capital to the shareholders. It was returning the preference share capital in this case, which was expensive in the sense that, with a reduction in profits flowing from the reduced scale of operations, little or nothing would be left for the ordinary shareholders after the preference shares had been serviced (as the preference shares had been entitled to a dividend in priority to the ordinary shareholders). In other cases, preference capital is returned because the preference shares have rights to a fixed preference dividend of say 14%, issued at a time when interest rates were around that figure. Later, when rates have dropped to 7%, that capital is expensive and the company may want to pay off the preference shares in a reduction and either issue some more at a lower dividend or obtain finance in some other way.

A good example of the second type of reduction, the 'write-off' against share capital, occurred in *Re Floating Dock Ltd*.[70] Over many years some promoters were, through the companies which they formed from time to time, engaged in constructing and operating a floating dock on St Thomas in the West Indies.[71] It was an 'iron and wooden structure' and cost £100,000 to build. From time to time storms came, the dock sank and was duly raised again. The progress of the companies mirrored those of the dock and they were periodically wound up. Eventually, in 1878, the company which was the subject matter of the petition was formed. It had a capital of £20,800 as ordinary shares and £70,994 as first preference shares and £71,823 as second preference shares. But the storms came again – and then it was eventually found that modern steamers were too big for the dock. The upshot was that by 1894 the assets of the company were only worth £50,000, but the company had a total issued share capital of £163,618. This would have produced the dilemma (among others) that it was difficult to raise any further capital by the issue of shares since any shares issued would immediately be worth less than their nominal value[72] and an issue at less than nominal value was not feasible as it would involve an illegal discount. Hence, a reduction by cancellation of capital was necessary to bring the share capital into line with the available assets.[73]

## 3 *Exercise of the judicial power to confirm reductions*

The classic statement of the judicial approach to reaching a decision as to whether to confirm a reduction or not was made by Evershed LJ in *Re Chatterley-Whitfield Collieries Ltd*[74]

---

[69] [1949] AC 512, HL, [1948] 3 All ER 593, CA.

[70] [1895] 1 Ch 691.

[71] As Chitty J ([1895] 1 Ch 691 at p. 695) put it: 'The circumstances connected with this floating dock [were] somewhat remarkable', although the fact that for 30 years the dock behaved more like a submarine than a pontoon must have been a source of continuing dismay to the incorporators.

[72] An option here might have been the creation of a new class of preference shares ranking in priority to any of those already issued.

[73] Other aspects of this seminal case are dealt with at D 4 below.

when he said that: '[T]he court must be satisfied not only of the formal validity of the steps taken by the . . . company, but also that the reduction proposed is one that is fair and equitable to the shareholders or classes of shareholders affected.' At first sight, this looks straightforward enough. However, where there is more than one class of shares in existence in the company, the application of these basic principles has given rise to disputes and a large number of hard-fought cases. The test 'fair and equitable' to the classes of shareholders is applied and interpreted to mean that the reduction will usually satisfy the test, provided that the shareholders are being treated in accordance with their rights on a winding up as set out in the company's constitution or terms of issue of the shares. This seems a strange proposition. Why should the rights of the shareholders who are being unwillingly paid off in a reduction be judicially equated with what their rights would have been had the company been in liquidation? The answer lies in the realisation that to some extent, a reduction is a mini winding up, a winding up *pro tanto*, because, in the reduction, the shareholder is being pushed out of the company, to the extent that his shareholder rights are being reduced. Thus, it makes some sense, and produces a type of fairness, to draw the analogy with a winding up. The 'rights' which the courts are primarily having regard to in this context are therefore their rights to a return of capital. It will be seen that the cases turn on such matters as: whether the shares have a prior[75] right to repayment on a winding up, and whether the shares have a right to participation in surplus assets on a winding up.[76]

It is often said that in a reduction of capital, the rule is that the preference shareholders are first to be paid off. Indeed, authorities can be found where that is clearly what is happening.[77] It is argued that preference shareholders cannot complain as they know when they take their shares that this is part of the bargain.[78]

But there is a two-part problem with this approach if it becomes a substitute for thinking through the principles and appropriateness of what is happening in each case. The first aspect of the problem is that preference shares do not always carry the same kinds of rights. Most do have a prior right to a return of capital on a winding up. But some shares, which would still broadly be referred to as preference shares,[79] have a prior right to a dividend while the company is a going concern, but rank equally (*pari passu*) with ordinary shares

---

[74] When the case was in the Court of Appeal, see [1948] 2 All ER 593 at p. 604. See also at D 2 above.

[75] 'Prior' meaning that they rank in priority to other classes of shares such as ordinary shares.

[76] Where there is only one class of shares, the 'fair and equitable' test will normally require equal treatment of the shareholders, although in unusual circumstances a different result might be reached; see *British and American Trustee Corporation* v *Couper* [1894] AC 399.

[77] *Re Chatterley-Whitfield Collieries Ltd* (above) and *House of Fraser plc* v *ACGE Investments Ltd* (1987) 3 BCC 201.

[78] *Per* Lord Greene MR in *Re Chatterley-Whitfield Collieries* [1949] AC 512 at p. 596. The repayment in such a reduction is at par, i.e. they get the nominal value, since this is all they would have been entitled to in a winding up. If interest rates have fallen since the shares were issued it is likely that they will stand at a premium to the nominal value. It is usual these days for the terms of issue to mitigate the possibility of a repayment reduction by including a clause which ties the repayment on a reduction to the market price. The preference shares in *House of Fraser plc* v *ACGE Investments Ltd* (1987) 3 BCC 201 contained a detailed version of such a clause (at p. 204) which is sometimes referred to as a 'Spens formula'. Another way of protecting the preference shareholders is to include a provision in the articles to the effect that a reduction of capital is deemed to be a variation of class rights. This will trigger the procedure in s. 630; see *Re Northern Engineering Co. Ltd* [1994] BCC 618 and D 4 below.

[79] There is no definition; see Chapter 13, at 13.3F.

on a winding up.[80] In such circumstances, it is patently wrong to rely on the rule of thumb that the preference shareholders 'go first'; they do not. On a winding up, they rank equally with the ordinary shares and must be treated in the same way. In order to satisfy the test of 'fair and equitable to the . . . classes of shareholders', the reduction would need to bear equally on all the shareholders, preference and ordinary.[81] The second aspect of the problem is that if the reduction involves, for example, a cancellation of capital rather than a repayment of capital, then the application of the 'fair and equitable' test will produce a result which is the converse of the idea that 'preference shareholders go first'.[82] Thus, in *Re Floating Dock Ltd*[83] although the (first) preference shareholders had a priority to a return of capital on a winding up, they did not go first in the reduction. They were the last to be cancelled.[84] This is because in a cancellation reduction the whole theory of what is happening is different from the repayment reduction. The cancellation reduction is about bearing losses of capital. In *Floating Dock*, the first preference shares were the class which under the articles had the highest priority to a return of capital in a winding up, and so they were the last to be reduced in the cancellation reduction.

Has the judicial approach to reaching a decision as to whether to confirm a reduction changed under the Companies Act 2006 jurisdiction? A couple of interesting cases shed some light on this. In the first, the High Court in *Re Liberty International Plc*[85] confirmed a reduction of capital carried out under s. 641 (1) (b) of the Companies Act 2006. In the course of its decision, the court held that a theoretical pensions claim, which was dependent on the Pensions Regulator exercising its discretion to make either a contribution notice or a financial support direction (followed by a contribution notice), was not admissible in proof and so did not need to be taken into account by the court for the purposes of determining which creditors were entitled to object to the reduction under s. 646 of the 2006 Act. The court also ruled that the rateable part of a merger reserve did not have to be added to the amount shown as paid up on each share by way of premium for the purposes of a statement of capital to be filed under s. 649 of the 2006 Act.

In the second case, interestingly, the Scottish Court of Session in *Royal Scottish Assurance*[86] approved a reduction of share capital by a long-term insurer regulated by the UK FSA (as it was) without requiring any form of creditor protection. In reaching this decision, the court had regard to factors including that the FSA regulatory regime is

---

[80] See e.g. the reduction in *Bannatyne* v *Direct Spanish Telegraph Ltd* (1886) 34 Ch D 287 where, in the words of Cotton LJ, the preference shares 'were constituted without any preference as regards capital, though they had a preference as regards dividend'. But it is important to be aware, in reading this case, that it is not a repayment reduction but is instead a cancellation reduction. It is therefore also an example of the second aspect of the problem referred to in the text above.

[81] Sometimes referred to as an 'all round reduction'.

[82] Unless the first aspect of the problem is also operative, as it was in *Bannatyne* v *Direct Spanish Telegraph Ltd* (n. 72 above).

[83] The facts are given at D 2 above.

[84] They were partially cancelled; by £1 per share of a nominal value of £3.10. The ordinary shareholders and the second preference shareholders were wiped out entirely by the cancellation. In effect, as a result of the elimination of the other classes, the first preference shares were recognised to be the residual owners of the company; in a sense they had become 'equity' shares.

[85] [2010] EWHC 1060 (Ch); [2010] 2 BCLC 665.

[86] [2011] CSOH 2; 2011 SLT 264.

likely to provide a reliable test of a company's ability to meet its debts as and when they fall due:

> In general terms, it has become the practice of the Court of Session in Scotland and, as I understand it, *also of the Companies Court in London* [emphasis added], to dispense with settlement of a list of creditors if the court can be satisfied that there is no realistic possibility of any creditor being put at risk by the reduction (by a consideration of the value of the company's realisable assets, or a variant of that approach: c.f. *Re Martin Currie Ltd* 2006 CSOH 17) or if one or more of certain accepted methods of creditor protection are adopted. The principal methods are: (a) obtaining the consent of creditors and, where only some of the creditors consent, subordinating the claims of consenting creditors to those of non-consenting creditors; (b) setting aside cash in a blocked account in an amount sufficient to discharge the claims of non-consenting creditors; (c) the provision by a bank or other third party with a sound credit covenant of a guarantee in an amount sufficient to cover the claims of non-consenting creditors; and (d) the giving of an appropriately worded undertaking, the effect of which is to ensure that any distribution consequent upon the reduction being confirmed by the court does not reduce the net assets of the company below a figure sufficient to ensure that the claims of non-consenting creditors will be paid as they fall due. No doubt other methods have been used from time to time.[87]

The decision follows that in *Re Liberty International plc.* Prior to that decision, the courts assumed that all creditors of the company at the time of the reduction needed to have consented to the reduction or to be protected in some other way (e.g. by way of guarantee). In this case, the creditors were holders of long-term policies with claim payments not due for many years and the court could see no realistic possibility that any creditor would be able to persuade it that the reduction of capital proposed would result in a real likelihood that its debt would not be discharged.

## 4 *Variation of class rights*

What happens if the reduction is not in conformity with the 'fair and equitable' test? The basic result is that the proposed reduction is a variation of class rights. It can still be confirmed by the court, provided that the procedures in s. 630 for variation of class rights are complied with. As with the comparable area of company law, schemes of arrangement, it is possible to find that conflicts of interest problems can make it difficult to hold meetings which can satisfy the court that they were an adequate safeguard of class rights.[88] This occurred in *Re Holders Investment Trust Ltd.*[89] The redeemable preference shares carried a right to a 5% fixed preference dividend while the company was a going concern and a prior right to a return of capital on a winding up. The reduction proposed to cancel the preference shares and in return substitute loan stock which carried 6% but which had a later redemption date. It was common ground that the reduction involved a variation of class rights and after the company had passed the special resolution to reduce the capital as proposed, a class meeting of the preference shares was convened and held, at which an

---

[87] *Ibid.* at [8].
[88] See the discussion of *Re United Provident Assurance Ltd* at Chapter 4, 4.5F 2 above.
[89] [1971] 1 WLR 583. This case is also important for showing that members of a class have a duty, in class meetings, to vote bona fide for the benefit of the class.

extraordinary resolution[90] of the class was passed, consenting to the reduction. At the hearing of the petition for confirmation, Megarry J refused to sanction the reduction. It had become clear that 90% of the preference shares were vested in trustees who also held 52% of the ordinary shares. The ordinary shares stood to gain from the reduction. The trustees admitted that they had voted in the class meeting on the basis of what was for the benefit of the trust as a whole, not bona fide that they were acting in the interests of the general body of members of that class. Megarry J held that there was therefore 'no effectual sanction for the modification of class rights'[91] and that it was therefore incumbent on those proposing the reduction to prove that it was fair;[92] on the evidence, he held that it was unfair.

## E Company purchase of own shares

### 1 *Mischief*

In 1887 the House of Lords took the decision to prohibit companies from buying their own shares. The case which gave rise to this opportunity was *Trevor* v *Whitworth*.[93] The insolvent company was in liquidation and was faced with a claim from the executor of a deceased shareholder for the balance of the purchase price of shares which the shareholder had sold to the company.[94] The articles of association provided that: '[A]ny share may be purchased by the company from any person willing to sell it, and at such price, not exceeding the marketable value thereof, as the board think reasonable.'[95] The decision largely proceeded on the technical basis that the purchases were *ultra vires* the company as being neither 'in respect of or as incidental to any of the objects specified in the memorandum'.[96] But it is clear that their Lordships felt that the practice was thoroughly undesirable and unlawful for reasons other than being beyond the powers of the company as defined in the memorandum – indeed, Lord Macnaghten went so far as to say that even 'if the power to purchase its own shares were found in the memorandum of association . . . it would necessarily be void'.[97]

The main thrust of the rationale against allowing share purchase was expressed in the form that a proponent of the practice was on 'the horns of a dilemma'[98] (and a dilemma which was made 'perfect'),[99] namely that if the shares purchased by the company were going to be resold, then this was 'trafficking' in shares and if they were not, then it was a reduction of capital which was unlawful because it fell outside the statutory provisions

---

[90] It should be noted that these types of resolution have been abolished by the Companies Act 2006. See Chapter 7, 7.3B.

[91] [1971] 1 WLR 583 at p. 589.

[92] A difficult burden to discharge once it is agreed that the proposal is a variation of class rights.

[93] (1887) 12 AC 409.

[94] There was an issue as to whether the shares were being purchased by a director on his own account but it was held that the purchase was in fact made by him on behalf of the company: (1887) 12 AC 409 at p. 413.

[95] Article 179. By art. 181 it was provided that: 'Shares so purchased may at the discretion of the board be sold or disposed of by them or be absolutely extinguished, as they deem most advantageous to the company.'

[96] (1887) 12 AC 409 at p. 416, *per* Lord Herschell.

[97] *Ibid.* at p. 436.

[98] *Ibid.* at p. 425, *per* Lord Watson citing James LJ in *Hope* v *International Society* (1876) 4 Ch D 335.

[99] (1887) 12 AC 409 at p. 419, *per* Lord Herschell citing Brett JA in *Hope* v *International Society* above.

regulating reductions.[100] The need for careful regulation of reductions in accordance with the maintenance of capital principle was stressed:

> The creditors of the company which is being wound up . . . find coming into competition with them persons, who, in respect only of their having been, and having ceased to be shareholders in the company, claim that the company shall pay to them a part of that capital . . . The capital may, no doubt, be diminished by expenditure upon and reasonably incidental to all the objects specified. A part of it may be lost in carrying on the business operations authorised. Of this all persons trusting the company are aware and take the risk. But I think they have a right to rely, and were intended by the legislature to have a right to rely, on the capital remaining undiminished by any expenditure outside these limits, or by the return of any part of it to the shareholders.[101]

Although the courts developed a few marginal exceptions,[102] *Trevor* v *Whitworth* remained the main source of authority until the legislature intervened in the early 1980s.

## 2 *A residual prohibition*

The Companies Act 1980 contained provisions codifying the basic common law rule on company purchase of own shares.[103] While this legislation was passing through Parliament, moves were afoot to consider the possibility of extending the exceptions to the legislation, to the extent permitted by the EC Second Directive.[104] The DTI (as DBEIS was known then) issued a consultative document[105] and in due course the Companies Act 1981 brought in the wider exceptions. The 2006/68/EC EC Directive prescribes that public limited liability companies should be allowed to acquire their own shares up to the limit of the company's distributable reserves and the period for which such an acquisition may be authorised by the general meeting should be increased so as to enhance flexibility and reduce the administrative burden for companies which have to react promptly to market developments affecting the price of their shares.

All the relevant legislation is now contained in ss. 658–659 of the Companies Act 2006. The basic prohibition is contained in s. 658 which provides that: 'A limited company must not acquire its own shares, whether by purchase, subscription or otherwise, except in accordance with the provisions of this Part.' The sanctions are contained in s. 658 (2) and (3) which provides for a fine for the company and fines or imprisonment for the officers in default. The purported acquisition is void. It has been held in *Acatos & Hutcheson plc* v *Watson*[106] that s. 143 of the Companies Act 1985 (now s. 658 of the Companies Act 2006) was not contravened when a company acquired another company which held shares in it.

---

[100] Then contained in the Companies Act 1867, ss. 9–13 (now Part 17, Chapter 10 of the Companies Act 2006). 'When Parliament sanctions the doing of a thing under certain conditions and with certain restrictions, it must be taken that the thing is prohibited unless the prescribed conditions and restrictions are observed': (1887) 12 AC 409 at pp. 437–438, *per* Lord Macnaghten.

[101] *Ibid.* at pp. 414–415, *per* Lord Herschell. On the facts it seemed fairly clear that a systematic breach of the maintenance principle was being perpetrated despite the argument that the purchases were being carried out to facilitate the retention of family control.

[102] See *Kirby* v *Wilkins* [1929] 2 Ch 444; *Re Castiglione's Will Trusts* [1958] Ch 549.

[103] Companies Act 1980, ss. 35–37.

[104] Mainly arts 19–22, 24 and also art. 39 (redeemable shares).

[105] *The Purchase by a Company of its Own Shares: A Consultative Document* (Cmnd 7944, 1980) paras 15–16. The document was written by Professor Gower.

[106] [1995] 1 BCLC 218.

The exceptions are set out in a list contained in s. 659 and by sub-section (2) (a) the prohibition is expressed not to apply to 'the acquisition of shares in a reduction of capital duly made'.[107] Section 690 then provides: 'A limited company having a share capital may purchase its own shares (including any redeemable shares) subject to (a) the following provision of this chapter and (b) any restriction or prohibition in the company's articles.'[108] According to s. 690 (2) a limited company may not purchase its own shares if, as a result of the purchase, there would no longer be any issues shares of the company other than redeemable shares or shares held as treasury shares. Shares purchased are normally treated as cancelled[109] although, as a result of recent reform, it is now possible in some situations[110] for companies to hold the shares 'in treasury'. The DTI (as DBEIS was known then) felt that the facility of using treasury shares might come to be seen as a less cumbersome and less expensive process than a conventional buy-back and fresh issue.[111] It is also possible that it might enable companies to take advantage of capital growth in their own shares by selling small numbers of treasury shares opportunistically.[112]

The procedure required for a company to purchase its own shares depends on whether the share purchase is an 'off-market'[113] purchase or a 'market'[114] purchase. The main examples in practice of market purchases are those made of shares listed on the London Stock Exchange or quoted on the Alternative Investment Market ('AIM'). With off-market purchases the company may only make the purchase if the contract is approved in advance.[115] Obviously this would not be possible in the case of a market purchase and so the legislation here requires merely prior authorisation in general meeting.[116] The provisions

---

[107] Companies Act 2006, s. 659 (2) is mainly a gathering together list of exceptions which already exist or are already dotted about in other parts of the Act. Section 659 (1) also makes it clear that a company may acquire any of its own fully paid shares 'otherwise than for valuable consideration' such as by way of gift. In ss. 660–669 there are complex provisions dealing with companies having beneficial interests in their own shares and designed to prevent circumvention of the prohibition in s. 658.

[108] The necessary authority is normally supplied by art. 35 of Table A of the Companies Act 1985. Also of importance are the amendments made by Companies (Tables A to F)(Amendments) (No. 2) Regulations 2007 to art. 35 which state that: 'Subject to the provisions of the Act, the company may purchase its own shares (including any redeemable shares) and, if it is a private company, make a payment in respect of the redemption or purchase of its own shares otherwise than out of distributable profits of the company or the proceeds of a fresh issue of shares.'

[109] Companies Act 2006, ss. 688 and 706 and 691–692.

[110] See generally ss. 724–732 of the Companies Act 2006. There are various conditions, such as that the shares need to be those which are traded on a regulated market. See generally the Companies (Acquisition of Own Shares) (Treasury Shares) Regulations 2003 (SI 2003, No. 1116); there have been subsequent amendments. For example, the Companies (Share Capital and Acquisition by a Company of its Own Shares) Regulations 2009 removed the 10% limit on number of shares that may be held in treasury – a company listed on the Official List or traded on AIM can now, when it purchases its own shares out of distributable profits, hold those shares in treasury instead of cancelling them. Previously, a company can only hold 10% of its shares in treasury. From 1 October 2009 there is thus no limit in the 2006 Act on the number of shares that can be held in treasury.

[111] DTI Consultative Document (May 1998) *Share Buybacks*, which raised the question of whether companies should be allowed to hold their repurchased shares 'in treasury' for resale at some later date.

[112] Possibly a dangerous procedure; see Chapter 20 on insider dealing and market abuse.

[113] The 2006 Act provides a complex definition of 'off-market' in s. 693 (2) and (3).

[114] Defined in Companies Act 2006 s. 693 (4) as '. . . made on a recognised investment exchange and is not an off-market purchase by virtue of subsection 2(b)'.

[115] The terms of the proposed contract must be authorised by special resolution before the contract is entered into (ss. 693, 694). Note that the period prescribed under s. 694 (5) was substituted by the Companies (Share Capital and Acquisition of Own Shares) Regulations to 5 years (previously it was 18 months). Not surprisingly, the owner of the shares is effectively barred from voting on the resolution (s. 695 and there are various other conditions and extensions (see Part 18, Chapter 4)).

[116] Companies Act 2006, ss. 693 (1), 701 (1). Various conditions are laid down in s. 701 (2)–(8).

make various other specifications applying to share purchases, so that the shares must be fully paid up,[117] there may be no purchase if as a result of the purchase there would no longer be any member of the company holding shares other than redeemable shares[118] and there is a requirement for disclosure by delivery of particulars to the Registrar of Companies.[119]

## 3 *Payment for the shares*

It is in the provisions concerning the payment for the shares that Parliament meets some of the challenges posed by the rationale of *Trevor* v *Whitworth*. One of the main objections was that such a purchase would operate as an unlawful reduction of capital:

> The shareholders receive back the moneys subscribed, and there passes into their pockets what before existed in the form of cash in the coffers of the company, or of buildings, machinery, or stock available to meet the demands of the creditors.[120]

Subject to the relaxations for private companies introduced by the 2013 and 2015 reforms identified below, this problem is avoided by specifying that the shares can only be purchased out of the proceeds of a fresh issue of shares made for the purpose or out of distributable profits of the company. The drafting by which this is achieved is convoluted to say the least. The approach adopted is to effectively import these rules (by s. 692) from the provisions governing the redemption of redeemable shares (s. 687) where the underlying principles concerning maintenance of capital are identical. On the other hand, also applicable here, but standing alone, are the provisions of s. 733 which require the establishment of a capital redemption reserve to the extent that the payment for the purchase[121] of the shares is out of distributable profits. The capital redemption reserve effectively makes those profits undistributable and so preserves the capital.

With private companies, it is possible in some circumstances to reduce capital to redeem or purchase the company's own shares. Where various conditions set out in Part 18, Chapter 5 of the Companies Act 2006 are satisfied (effectively a procedure similar to a solvency statement reduction of capital, but with additional publicity requirements)[122] the Act permits the use of capital to the extent of what is called 'the permissible capital payment'.[123] The *Trevor* v *Whitworth* objection is met to a large extent by the existence of numerous safeguards such as the need for directors' declarations as to solvency and enhanced protection for creditors.

In 2013[124] and 2015[125] important reforms were introduced that relaxed the restrictions that applied as to the funding of a share buy-back by private companies. In particular, a

[117] *Ibid.* ss. 686, 691 and 692.
[118] *Ibid.* s. 690 (2).
[119] Respectively *ibid.* ss. 707, 708. Other matters are dealt with in s. 704 (assignment) and s. 735 (effect of failure to purchase).
[120] *Trevor* v *Whitworth* (1887) 12 AC 409 at p. 416, *per* Lord Herschell.
[121] Or redeemable shares redeemed under Companies Act 2006 Part 18, Chapter 3.
[122] Section 713 of the Companies Act 2006.
[123] Section 692 (1) of the Companies Act 2006; the permissible capital payment is defined in s. 710.
[124] The Companies Act 2006 (Amendment of Part 18) Regulations 2013.
[125] The Companies Act 2006 (Amendment of Part 18) Regulations 2015.

private company purchasing shares for the purpose of an employees' share scheme can now pay for such shares by instalments.[126] Moreover, and effectively introducing a *de minimis* exception, a private company can purchase its own shares out of capital *otherwise* than in accordance with Chapter 5 of the Companies Act 2006, up to an amount not exceeding the lower of £15,000 or the nominal value of 5% of the company's fully paid share capital.[127]

The other main objection emanating from *Trevor* v *Whitworth* was that a purchase of own shares would enable the company to traffic in its own shares, i.e. buy and sell for profit. This is effectively prevented by provisions that the shares purchased are treated as cancelled.[128] There is an additional safeguard in the background here. If the company were to buy its own shares in an effort to force up or support the market price the directors and the company itself could face liability under the Financial Services and Markets Act 2000.[129]

## 4 *Commercial uses of share buy-backs*

In recent years, the statutory facility permitting companies to purchase their own shares has become popular. It has even acquired a popular name: share 'buy-backs'. Listed public companies have been setting up share buy-backs in a variety of circumstances. In 1995–96, a total of £1.4bn worth of share buy-backs were conducted in the UK market.[130] Share buy-backs have become an essential component of the finance director's armoury in the battle to manage the company's capital flexibly and efficiently.

Many different commercial reasons can lie behind the decision of a company to set up a buy-back. One of the reasons for the current frequency of buy-backs is that during the early 1990s favourable economic conditions left many plcs with very substantial earnings. Companies which have cash which is surplus to their current needs will sometimes find that this dilutes their average earnings per share. This is because they get a higher return on their trading and acquisition activities than they can by investing the money. If this is the situation, a share buy-back will enhance the future earnings per share of the remaining shares. This will tend to make the shares more attractive and thus bolster the market price.[131] Earnings per share might also be enhanced by a buy-back in other situations such as where the cancelled share capital was to be replaced by a cheaper source of funding. Another example of commercial use has been occurring where the situation is that the traded price of the shares of the company is thought by the directors to be undervaluing its assets. Assuming that the directors' view of the situation is correct, a buy-back will provide a method of increasing the value of the remaining shares and so wipe out or reduce the discount in the traded price.[132]

---

[126] Section 691 (3) of the Companies Act 2006.

[127] Section 692 (1) (as amended by regulation 4 of the Companies Act 2006 (Amendment of Part 18) Regulations 2013).

[128] See *ibid* ss. 688, 706.

[129] See Chapter 20.

[130] *Financial Times*, 25 March 1996. Although in 2016–2017 we are starting to witness a decline in the hitherto steady increase in buy-backs: see R. Wigglesworth and A. Samson 'Buyback Outlook Darkens for US Stocks' *Financial Times*, 21 June 2017.

[131] A reason suggested by S. Edge 'Do We Have an Imputation System or Not?' (1996) 375 *Tax Journal* 2.

[132] A reason advanced by H. Nowlan and I. Abrahams 'Share Buy-Backs' (1994) 278 *Tax Journal* 10.

## F Dividends and distributions

Unless the company is making profits out of which dividends can be paid, the payment of dividends will gradually reduce the stock of assets that are available to creditors. It will not diminish the amount of share capital entered on the balance sheet as such, and in this important sense, the problem differs from those so far examined, which have been concerned with reduction of capital and share purchases that essentially involve striking out capital from the balance sheet and thereby decreasing the undistributable reserves of the company. As such, the payment of dividends represents a less overt threat to the maintenance of capital doctrine. Nevertheless, the rule was established in *Re Exchange Banking Co., Flitcroft's Case*[133] that dividends could only be paid out of profits.

Thereafter, the way that the rules were developed and applied over many years produced a situation where the legal rules were considerably less stringent than those which would normally have been applied by prudent businessmen or accountants. An example of this can be seen in *Ammonia Soda Co.* v *Chamberlain*,[134] where it was made clear that trading losses occurring in previous accounting periods could be ignored in such a way that the trading periods in the accounts became separate from each other. This threw the losses on to capital, in the sense, at least, that the assets of the company would be diminished by the amount of the dividend. Suppose, for instance, that in its first year of trading, the company made a trading loss of £1,000, and in its second year a £1,200 profit. A distribution of the second year's profit as dividend would mean that, taking a two-year perspective, the company's assets available to creditors was still £1,000 less than when it started.

In 1980, in fulfilment of the UK's obligations under the EC Second Directive, the case law rules were replaced by statutory provisions that are more in line with normal business and accountancy practice. These provisions were contained in ss. 263–281 of the Companies Act 1985 and now can be found in ss. 830–853 of the Companies Act 2006.[135] The basic prohibition is contained in s. 830, which provides that a company may not make a distribution except out of profits available for the purpose. 'Distribution' is defined as meaning every description of distribution of a company's assets to its members, whether in cash or otherwise,[136] thereby including so-called 'disguised' distributions.[137] As such, the court will look to the substance of a transaction, rather than its form, to determine whether it should properly be classified as a distribution.[138] In this way, remuneration payments in excess of a director's entitlement[139] and a transfer of land at an

---

[133] (1882) 21 Ch D 519. See also M. Finn and S. Young in *Accountancy* (2009) 143(1387), 60–61 where they explore the reasons for the fall off in share buy-backs in 2008 and consider this against the flexibility they offer for companies seeking to redistribute surplus cash or increase their earnings per share.

[134] [1918] 1 Ch 266.

[135] For a critique of the rules determining when companies may make distributions to shareholders and why they are in dire need of reform see D. Kershaw 'Involuntary Creditors and the Case for Accounting-Based Distribution Regulation' (2009) 2 *Journal of Business Law* 140.

[136] Companies Act 2006, s. 829 (1). However, distribution does not include an issue of bonus shares, redemption or purchase of the company's own shares out of capital (including the proceeds of any fresh issue of shares) or out of unrealised profits. Nor does it include certain reductions of share capital or distributions of assets to members of the company on its winding up; s. 829 (2). That is, the definition of 'distribution' for this part excludes those transactions that are already governed by capital maintenance protection mechanisms.

[137] *Aveling Barford Ltd* v *Perion Ltd* (1989) 5 BCC 677.

[138] *Progress Property Co Ltd* v *Moorgrath Group Ltd* [2010] UKSC 55.

[139] *Re Halt Garage (1964) Ltd* (1982) 3 All ER 1016.

undervalue[140] have been found to be distributions that, in the absence of the requisite distributable reserves, were *ultra vires*.

Crucially, the profits available for distribution are defined in s. 830 (2) as follows:

> ... [A] company's profits available for distribution are its accumulated, realised profits, so far as not previously utilised by distribution or capitalisation, less its accumulated, realised losses, so far as not previously written off in a reduction or reorganisation of capital duly made.

The wording contains some subtle effects. For instance, the use of the word 'accumulated' reverses the *Ammonia Soda Case* because it shows that the profit and loss account is to be treated as a continuum, in that it may not be split up into artificial and isolated trading periods. Similarly, the presence of the word 'realised' ends another earlier dispute between the cases on whether unrealised profits[141] could be used to pay dividends. It is now clear that unrealised profits cannot be so used, although an unrealised profit can be used to pay up bonus shares, since these are not a 'distribution' within s. 829 (2).[142] Whether or not distribution may lawfully be made is to be determined by reference to the company's accounts.[143] It should be noted that although there is no definition of 'realised' some useful guidance on the determination of realised profits and losses in the context of distributions under the Companies Act 2006 is provided in the publication by the Institute of Chartered Accountants in England and Wales (ICAEW) TECH 02/17.[144] For example, it suggests that profits arising from re-measurement of acquired liabilities prior to settlement should only be treated as realised when that profit is readily convertible to cash and that goodwill written off to reserves should follow the principles of the accounting framework used to prepare the financial statements.

Public companies are subjected to further conditions before a distribution can be made. It is necessary that at the time of the distribution the amount of the public company's net assets is not less than the aggregate of its called up share capital and undistributable reserves and that the distribution does not then reduce the net assets below that aggregate.[145] The 'undistributable reserves' referred to means, broadly, the share premium account, capital redemption reserve, the amount by which the accumulated unrealised profits exceed its accumulated unrealised losses (unless the profits or losses have, respectively, already been

---

[140] *Aveling Barford Ltd* v *Perion Ltd* (1989) 5 BCC 677, 683: '. . . it was a sale at a gross undervalue for the purpose of enabling a profit to be realised by an entity controlled . . . by its sole beneficial shareholder. This was as much a dressed-up distribution as . . . excessive remuneration in *Halt Garage*.' Section 845 of the Companies Act 2006 has now codified how to value distributions in kind to determine the amount of distributable reserves that are required.

[141] In other words, those arising merely from a revaluation of assets in the books of the company rather than an actual sale. For the earlier case law dispute, see *Dimbula Valley (Ceylon) Tea Co.* v *Laurie* [1961] Ch 353; *Westburn Sugar Refineries Ltd* v *IRC* 1960 SLT 297, 1960 TR 105. In *Re Loquitur Ltd, Inland Revenue Commissioners* v *Richmond* [2003] EWHC 999 (Ch), [2003] 2 BCLC 442, ChD, the court dealt with a dividend that had been declared based on incorrect interim accounts, deciding that the dividend was unlawful.

[142] Companies Act 2006, s. 829 (2) (a). 'Realised' loss may in some circumstances within s. 844 include development costs.

[143] The relevant accounts are either, the company's last annual accounts (s. 836 (2)) or interim accounts (s. 836 (2) (a)). As to the accounting provisions more generally, see Part 23, Chapter 2, ss. 836–840.

[144] Issued in April 2017, its purpose is to identify, interpret and apply the principles relating to the determination of realised profits and losses for the purposes of making distributions under the 2006 Act. It is based on the guidance originally issued as TECH 01/09 in June 2009 (as updated by, for example, TECH 02/11) but includes some significant additional material. This technical release is 173 pages long (compared with 23 pages in the original release in 2003) which reflects the growth of accounting standards that apply today.

[145] *Ibid*. s. 831 (1). By s. 831 (2) the term 'net assets' means here the aggregate of the company's assets less the aggregate of its liabilities. Further relevant provisions are contained in s. 831 (4).

capitalised, or written off).[146] What this provision is actually doing is requiring that a public company keep its share capital intact, before it can pay a dividend, even in respect of unrealised capital losses. Thus if the fixed assets of the company have fallen in value, this will reduce its net assets in the balance sheet and so the company will be unable to pay a dividend unless this shortfall is made good. A private company is not troubled by such a downwards revaluation because it is not a 'realised loss' within s. 830 (2).

Distributions made in breach of the legislation are dealt with by s. 847, which provides that a member is liable to repay a distribution if at the time of the distribution, the member knows, or has reasonable grounds for believing, that it is made in breach of the provisions.[147] Section 847 (2) preserves any case law obligation to repay.

Over the years, the judicial method of requiring a recipient to repay a sum or asset received in breach of the doctrine of maintenance of capital has been to hold that it is *ultra vires*.[148] The link with *ultra vires* has enabled the court to move speedily to the conclusion that the money could be recovered by the imposition of a constructive trust. Although since the 1989 reforms *ultra vires* acts can be ratified by special resolution, and the doctrine now is largely academic in the light of s. 31 of the 2006 Act,[149] in *Revenue and Customs Commissioners* v *Holland*,[150] the Court of Appeal, nonetheless, stated:

> Mr Knox contends that there are three grounds on which, even assuming that Mr Holland was a de facto director, he should not have been found liable for misfeasance in effecting the distribution of the dividends. First, he contended that since the payments were in the best interests of the composite companies, since they would otherwise have had to cease trading with significant potential contractual liabilities, they should not be treated as unlawful at all. That argument is wholly unsustainable if the payments are properly to be treated as the payments of dividends, as they undoubtedly are. It is *ultra vires* for the company to make payments to shareholders out of undistributable profits; it is forbidden both at common law and under statute (see section 263 of the Companies Act 1985) and since it is illegal it cannot be done even with the consent of all the members: see e.g. *Aveling Barford Ltd* v *Perion Ltd* [1989] BCLC 626. So the fact that the directors may consider the payment to be in the company's best interests cannot conceivably be a defence, at least if the officer appreciates that the payment, properly characterised, is the return of undistributed profits by way of dividend.[151]

Directors who authorise payments in breach of the provisions may find themselves liable for breach of fiduciary duty and liable to restore any loss to the company.[152] In *It's a Wrap*

---

[146] And also any other reserve which the company is prohibited from distributing by any other enactment or by its articles; see generally s. 831 (4) (d).

[147] See also *It's A Wrap (UK) Ltd* v *Gula* [2006] EWCA Civ 544.

[148] See *Re Precision Dippings Ltd* (1985) 1 BCC 99,539; *Aveling Barford Ltd* v *Perion Ltd* (1989) 5 BCC 677 (discussed at Chapter 5, 5.3C). The idea was also very much present in *Trevor* v *Whitworth* (D 3 above).

[149] See discussion in Chapter 4, 4.2. Unless a company's articles of association say otherwise, a company's objects are unrestricted. This means that what currently remains of the *ultra vires* doctrine will be practically all but abolished and all companies will have unlimited capacity unless their articles say otherwise. So, unless a company's articles specifically restrict its objects, neither the company's capacity nor the authority of its directors to bind the company will be limited. This change applies to all companies (although restrictions will still be needed for companies registered as charities).

[150] [2009] EWCA Civ 625.

[151] *Ibid.* at [121].

[152] *Bairstow* v *Queens Moat Houses plc* [2002] BCC 91, CA. See also the relevant Model Articles on dividends. For private companies see, Model Articles for Private Companies, Part 3: Procedure for declaring dividends (article 30); Payment of dividends and other distributions (article 31); No interest on distributions (article 32); Unclaimed distributions (article 33); Non-cash distributions (article 34) and Waiver of distributions (article 35). For public companies see, Model Articles for Public Companies, Part 4: Procedure for declaring dividends (article 70); Calculation of dividends (article 71); Payment of dividends and other distributions (article 72); Deductions from distributions in respect of sums owed to the company (article 73); No interest on distributions (article 74); Unclaimed distributions (article 75); Non-cash distributions (article 76) and Waiver of distributions (article 77).

*(UK) Ltd* v *Gula*,[153] the liquidator sought repayment of dividends paid to the defendants who were the sole shareholders and directors of the company. During a two-year period in which there were no profits available for distribution, the company's accounts showed that dividends had nevertheless been paid to the defendants. When the company went into insolvent liquidation, the liquidator claimed that the dividends had been paid in contravention of s. 263 (1) (now s. 830 (1) of the Companies Act 2006) and were therefore recoverable under s. 277 (now s. 847 of the Companies Act 2006). The defendants argued that the sums in question were paid to them as remuneration and only appeared in the accounts as 'dividends' because they had been advised that this was tax efficient. The trial court dismissed the liquidator's claim on the basis that it was clear that the defendants had sought to gain a proper tax advantage and had not deliberately set out to contravene the Act. The judge found that the phrase 'is so made' contained in s. 277 (1) of the Companies Act 1985 required that the defendants knew or had reasonable grounds to believe not just the facts giving rise to the contravention but also the legal result of the contravention. However, the Court of Appeal reversed the judge's decision and held that the defendants' ignorance of the law was no defence. Arden LJ stated that s. 277 had to be interpreted in a manner consistent with art. 16 of the Second Company Law Harmonisation Directive which it is designed to implement. Arden LJ concluded that s. 277 must be interpreted as meaning that the shareholder cannot claim that he is not liable to return a distribution because he did not know of the restrictions in the Act on the making of distributions. He will be liable if he knew or ought reasonably to have known of the facts which mean that the distribution contravened the requirements of the Act.

## Further reading

J. Armour 'Legal Capital: An Outdated Concept?' (2006) 7 *European Business Organization Law Review* 5.

J. Vella and D. Prentice 'Some Aspects of Capital Maintenance Law in the UK' in M. Tison *et al.* (ed.) *Perspectives in Company Law and Financial Regulation* (Cambridge: CUP, 2009).

D. Kershaw 'The Decline of Legal Capital: An Exploration of the Consequences of Board Solvency Based Capital Reductions' in A. Reisberg and D. Prentice (eds) *Corporate Finance Law in the UK and US* (Oxford: OUP, 2011).

---

[153] [2006] EWCA Civ 544.

# 15

# Financial assistance for the acquisition of shares

## 15.1 Background and development of the present law

This chapter is concerned with an area of statute and the case law that has sprung from it, which has a long history of failure.[1] Failure, in the sense of not preventing the abuses it was designed to prevent, and failure in the sense of preventing or vitiating transactions that have been carried out for bona fide commercial reasons. Dating from 1929,[2] and notwithstanding undeniably important reforms introduced by the Companies Act 2006, the financial assistance prohibition continues to engage practitioners on a daily basis, providing a fruitful source of income for the Chancery Bar who are frequently asked to provide opinions on an area almost unrivalled for its ability to cause trouble.[3]

Broadly speaking, s. 678 of the Companies Act 2006 penalises the provision of financial assistance by a public company (or its subsidiary, whether public or private) for the acquisition of its own shares by another. Section 679 extends the prohibition so as to prevent a public company providing such assistance for the acquisition of shares in its private parent company. Sections 677–683 of the Companies Act 2006 originated in 1981,[4] when the Government embarked on a radical restructuring of the existing provisions then contained in s. 54 of the 1948 Act. The mischief that the provisions were originally designed to prohibit was clearly described by the Greene Committee[5] in 1926:

> A practice has made its appearance in recent years which we consider to be highly improper. A syndicate agrees to purchase from the existing shareholders sufficient shares to control a company, the purchase money is provided by a temporary loan from a bank for a day or two, the syndicate's nominees are appointed directors in place of the old board and immediately proceed to lend to the syndicate out of the company's funds (often without security) the money required to pay off the bank . . . Thus in effect the company provides money for the purchase of its own shares.

Later, in *Re VGM Holdings Ltd* [1942] Ch 235 at 239 Lord Greene MR observed:

> Those whose memories enable them to recall what had been happening for several years after the last war will remember that a very common form of transaction in connection with companies

---

[1] Chief among the criticisms directed at this area arises from its complexity and fitness for purpose. See J. Lowry 'The Prohibition Against Financial Assistance Constructing a Rational Response', Chapter 1 in D. Prentice and A. Reisberg (eds) *Corporate Finance in the UK and EU* (Oxford: OUP, 2011).
[2] Companies Act 1929, s. 45.
[3] It nevertheless found its way into the Second EC Company Law Directive (79/91/EEC) from where it continues to dismay our European partners; art. 23 provides: 'A [public] company may not advance funds, nor make loans, nor provide security, with a view to the acquisition of shares by a third party.'
[4] First enacted as ss. 42–44 of the Companies Act 1982 and then consolidated in the 1985 Act, ss. 151–158.
[5] Cmnd 2657, 1926, para. 30.

was one by which persons – call them financiers, speculators, or what you will – finding a company with a substantial cash balance or easily realisable assets, such as war loan, bought up the whole, or the greater part, of the shares of the company for cash, and so arranged matters that the purchase money which they then became bound to provide was advanced to them by the company whose shares they were acquiring, either out of its cash balance or by realisation of its liquid investments. That type of transaction was a common one, and it gave rise to great dissatisfaction and, in some cases, great scandals.

Sixty years later Arden LJ in *Chaston* v *SWP Group plc* confirmed that: 'The general mischief . . . remains the same, namely that the resources of the target company and its subsidiaries should not be used directly or indirectly to assist the purchaser financially to make the acquisition.'[6] In *Wallersteiner* v *Moir* Lord Denning MR summed up the abuse succinctly, describing it simply as a 'cheat'.[7] In terms of the class of persons protected by the prohibition in *Wallersteiner* v *Moir*, Scarman LJ explained that it was 'to protect company funds and the interests of shareholders as well as creditors'.[8] Similarly, Arden LJ, in *Chaston* stated: 'This may prejudice the interests of the creditors of the target or its groups, and the interests of shareholders who do not accept the offer to acquire their shares or to whom the offer is not made.'[9]

That the statutory provisions were not very successful in the prevention of this type of abuse became well known[10] and was illustrated by the glaring examples of it in *Selangor United Rubber Estates Ltd* v *Cradock (No. 3)*[11] and *Wallersteiner* v *Moir*.[12] The penalty of £100 fine in s. 54 of the 1948 Act was hardly a realistic deterrent. It was not until 1980 that breach of the provisions could carry up to two years' imprisonment.[13]

On the other hand, for all its feebleness, s. 54 was seen by others as a thorough nuisance, capable of penalising and preventing many desirable commercial transactions. Lord Seebohm said (in the debates on the 1981 reforms): 'I joined Barclays Bank in 1929 the year in which section [45] of the Companies Act [1929] came into force. Ever since that time it has been a plague for those operating in the banking field.'[14] This sentiment is understandable given the penalties for breach. The Act imposed both criminal and civil sanctions; whilst the former were rarely imposed the civil consequences[15] were (although sometimes uncertain) far-reaching and draconian. A security or other financial assistance given in breach of the section was void;[16] the sale of the shares was liable to be set aside unless it could be severed from the illegal parts of the transaction; directors who participated in breaches were liable to the company for any loss suffered; and worst of all, from

---

[6] [2003] 1 BCLC 675, at [31].
[7] [1974] 3 All ER 217, CA, at p. 222.
[8] [1974] 3 All ER 217, CA, at p. 255.
[9] Above, n. 6, at [31].
[10] Section 54 was described by Neville Faulks QC in the Board of Trade Investigation into the Affairs of H. Jasper and Company Ltd as 'honoured more in the breach than in the observance' (London: HMSO, 1961) para. 161 (B).
[11] [1968] 1 WLR 1555.
[12] [1974] 1 WLR 991.
[13] Companies Act 1980, s. 80, Sch. 2, then Companies Act 1985, s. 730, Sch. 24, but see now ss. 1121, 1124 and 1125 of the Companies Act 2006.
[14] *Hansard*, HL, vol. 418, col. 973.
[15] The current position is examined in detail below.
[16] Probably; see further 15.7 below.

the point of view of the business community in general, *Selangor United Rubber Estates Ltd* v *Cradock (No. 3)* established a wide constructive trust liability for banks and others who unintentionally became participants in complex schemes which were in breach of the section.

Two situations in particular had been seen to give difficulty. The first was the kind of situation where the small private company was owned by, say, a 65-year-old managing director[17] who wanted to retire and had found a buyer for his shares. The buyer needed a loan from a bank in order to help him fund the purchase. The bank was prepared to lend but wanted security. The purchaser's house was already second-mortgaged and had no security to give. Could the company help out by giving a floating charge over its undertaking? If the bank lent on this basis it would find that its security, the floating charge was illegal and void, since the company had given financial assistance for the purchase of its shares.

The second situation was where company A buys an asset from company B at a fair price. The asset is one that company A genuinely wants for bona fide commercial reasons. Because the purchase money passes to company B, the transaction also has the incidental effect of putting company B in funds to buy shares in company A. When discussing this situation in the Court of Appeal case of *Belmont Finance Corporation Ltd* v *Williams Furniture Ltd (No. 2)*,[18] Buckley LJ expressed the view that where the sole purpose was to put B in funds to acquire the shares, this clearly contravened the legislation, but, somewhat alarmingly, he suggested that it might also have contravened it where putting B in funds was merely one of a number of purposes.

In 1962, the Jenkins Committee[19] recommended reform on the basis that: 'From the evidence we have received, we are satisfied that s. 54, as it is now framed, has proved to be an occasional embarrassment[20] to the honest without being a serious inconvenience to the unscrupulous.' Thus, by 1981, the time was long due for major reform of the section, the previous year having seen two cases which further demonstrated both the vagueness of the section and its undesirably wide ambit.[21] But it was not until November 1992 that the Department of Trade and Industry (now DBEIS) finally set up a working party of business people, members of the accountancy and legal professions and DTI officials to examine the law regulating financial assistance for the acquisition of shares. This led in October 1993 to the publication of a consultation document[22] setting out three main approaches[23] to the reform of the law affecting public companies: (1) to amend ss. 151–154 of the Companies Act 1985; (2) to reproduce art. 23 of the EC Second Directive;[24] or (3) to restructure ss. 151–154 of the Companies Act 1985. As they observed in the consultation

---

[17] Some versions of this example could contravene the directors' loan provisions (Companies Act 2006, ss. 197 *et seq.*).

[18] [1980] 1 All ER 393 at p. 401 d–h.

[19] Cmnd 1749, 1962, paras 176, 170–187.

[20] This was in 1962. After *Selangor* (1968) this became something of an understatement.

[21] One of these was the *Belmont Finance* case (discussed in the text above), the other was *Armour Hick Northern Ltd* v *Whitehouse* [1980] 1 WLR 1520.

[22] DTI Consultative Document (October 1993) *Proposals for Reform of Sections 151–158 of the Companies Act 1985*.

[23] *Ibid.* para. 4.

[24] 77/91/EEC.

document, the third of these possibilities appeared to offer the greatest scope for improvement of the existing legislation. In a subsequent paper in September 1994 the DTI set out proposals for future reform of the area, opting for a substantial restructuring of the legislation to take account of the various criticisms which have been levelled at it over the years, in particular those consequent on the *Brady* case.[25] The Company Law Review then took the matter in hand. The area was considered in the consultation document of February 1999, *The Strategic Framework*, and in more detail in the later consultation document of October 1999, *Company Formation and Capital Maintenance*. The kind of issues that were raised for consultation were whether the ban on financial assistance should be removed entirely for private companies (the Second Company Law Directive prohibiting such removal with regard to public companies), and whether the 'principal purpose' exception could be satisfactorily redrafted. In addition, many small technical changes were considered.[26] Subsequently, in the consultation document *Completing the Structure*,[27] it seemed that the view had been reached that ss. 151–158 of the Companies Act 1985 should be amended so as to apply only to public companies and therefore the s. 155 whitewash procedure for private companies would no longer be needed.[28] The *Company Law Review Final Report* largely endorsed this.[29] Eventually, the application of these provisions has been significantly *relaxed* by the Companies Act 2006, under which the provisions *do not* apply to the giving of financial assistance by private companies for the acquisition of their own shares.[30] That said, the Companies Act 2006 makes very few amendments in respect of public companies, and so, as will be seen below, many of the difficulties and uncertainties that emerged in relation to the Companies Act 1985 provisions continue to affect the law. This also means that although much of the case law considered below is concerned with ss. 151–158 of the Companies Act 1985, the doctrinal and practical learning of these decisions remains relevant and must clearly still be considered influential. It should also be noted that although leveraged buyouts ('LBOs'),[31] as a mode of acquisition of companies, are becoming increasingly popular,[32] the special issues that arise in the context of LBOs were not envisaged at the time of framing of the laws on financial assistance. For example, the law on financial assistance does not take into account the highly leveraged nature of LBOs and so the current legal framework is ill-equipped to deal with them.[33]

Finally, it should be noted that Article 23 of the Second Company Law Directive (EEC 77/91) was amended by Directive 2006/68/EC in 2006. As part of this, it prescribes rules allowing (on an optional basis for member states) the company to provide financial assistance to third parties for the purchase of its own shares (although in general terms, financial assistance is presently prohibited by the Directive). But when the detail of this

---

[25] Discussed below 15.4.
[26] DTI consultation document (October 1999) *Company Formation and Capital Maintenance* paras 3.41 *et seq.*
[27] Paragraph 7.12 *et seq.*
[28] Discussed below 15.5.
[29] See n. 26 above, paras 4.4 and 10.6.
[30] See 15.5 below.
[31] A leveraged buyout is a type of takeover where a substantial proportion of the acquisition price is financed by borrowings, using the target company's own assets as collateral. See L. Rabinowitz *et al.* (eds) *Weinberg and Blank on Takeovers and Mergers* (5th edn, London, Sweet & Maxwell, 2005), 1024.
[32] For an examination of the mechanics of LBOs and the legal issues that arise in their financing see S. Singhal 'Financing of Leveraged Buy-outs' (2008) 29 Comp Lawyer 355.
[33] *Ibid.*

amendment is examined, it has been argued that it delivers only a 'modest concession' in favour of financial assistance.[34] It appears that the Government has no intention, at the moment, to allow for this.[35]

## 15.2 The modern scope of the prohibition

The general prohibition is contained in s. 678 of the Companies Act 2006, which makes the key difference between the prohibition set out in the Companies Act 2006 and that of its predecessors, namely the relaxation for private companies, immediately clear. Section 678 (1) provides that:

> . . . Where a person is acquiring or is proposing to acquire shares in a public company, it is not lawful for that company, or a company that is a subsidiary of that company, to give financial assistance directly or indirectly for the purpose of the acquisition before or at the same time as the acquisition takes place . . .

Thus, s. 678 (1) relates only to what might be termed '*pre*-acquisition assistance'. However, s. 678 (3) extends the prohibition to a situation that might be termed '*post*-acquisition' assistance. In this regard, s. 678 (3) provides that:

> . . . Where – (a) a person has acquired shares in a company, and (b) a liability[36] has been incurred (by that or another person) for the purpose of the acquisition, it is not lawful for that company, or a company that is a subsidiary of that company, to give financial assistance directly or indirectly for the purpose of reducing or discharging the liability if, at the time the assistance is given, the company in which the shares were acquired is a public company.

It is generally thought that ss. 678 (1) and 678 (3) give separate treatment to *pre*- and *post*-acquisition assistance in order to prevent problems arising in the kind of situation where a parent company (H Co.) gives a debenture (to D Bank) which requires all its assets and those of its subsidiaries to be charged by way of floating charges, and H Co. later acquires a new subsidiary (S Co.) by purchasing S Co.'s shares (from V Co.). A floating charge given on the assets of the new subsidiary would possibly have been in breach of the old s. 54 provisions[37] since it was arguably given (in a loose sense) '. . . in connection with a purchase . . . of . . . shares . . .'. Now, however (i.e. since 1981), there is clearly no breach of s. 678, for s. 678 (1) is inapplicable and under s. 678 (3) the issue is whether assistance is given for the purpose of reducing or discharging a liability incurred (with V Co.) for the purpose of the acquisition (and the charge in favour of D Bank is clearly not being given to discharge a liability incurred for the purpose of the acquisition).[38]

---

[34] *Ibid.* 308.

[35] *Ibid.* 309.

[36] By s. 683 (2) (a), this is expressed to include 'changing his financial position by making an agreement or arrangement (whether enforceable or unenforceable, and whether made on his own account or with any other person) or by any other means . . .'

[37] Section 54 of the Companies Act 1948 provided: 'Subject as provided in this section, it shall not be lawful for a company to give, whether directly or indirectly, and whether by means of a loan, guarantee, the provision of security or otherwise, any financial assistance for the purpose of or in connection with a purchase or subscription made or to be made by any person of or for any shares in the company, or, where the company is a subsidiary company in its holding company.' The legislation contained exceptions.

[38] See Standing Committee A, 30 June 1981, col. 298 and also *Hansard*, HC, vol. 10, cols 206–207.

Another significant difference between s. 678 and the old s. 54 is that, for the prohibition under s. 678 to apply, the financial assistance needs to be given '*for the purpose of*[39] that acquisition' which is considerably narrower[40] in ambit than the words 'in connection with' in the old s. 54. In view of the emphasis laid on the concept of 'purpose' in the legislative exceptions which are discussed below, it is worth emphasising this threshold test of purpose.

It is clear from s. 678 that the giving of assistance by a subsidiary can be within the prohibition where the target company is a public company (thus we see that private companies are not entirely excluded from the ambit of the prohibition). Section 679 further extends the prohibition to the giving of financial assistance by a public company for the acquisition of shares in its private holding company. The question of whether the giving of financial assistance by a subsidiary that is registered in a different jurisdiction also constituted the giving of financial assistance by its parent was examined by Millett J in *Arab Bank plc v Mercantile Holdings Ltd*,[41] a case which illustrates the complexity of companies legislation. Mercantile Holdings Ltd[42] had given a charge over some of its property in favour of Arab Bank plc in order to secure a loan facility which the bank had given another company to enable that other company to acquire the shares of the parent company of Mercantile Holdings Ltd. The bank wished to realise its security by selling the property and to prevent this happening, Mercantile Holdings Ltd sought to argue that the security had been given in breach of s. 151 of the Companies Act 1985 (now s. 678 of the Companies Act 2006) and was therefore void. Without more, the parties were agreed that the giving of the charge was a breach of s. 151. However, Mercantile Holdings Ltd had been incorporated in Gibraltar and had received legal advice at the time it created the charge that because it was a foreign subsidiary the transaction was not caught by the section; in reliance on that advice the company entered into the transaction honestly and in good faith. However, it now suited the company to maintain that the transaction was in fact unlawful.

The first question that Millett J addressed was whether the mere giving of financial assistance by the subsidiary[43] *ipso facto* also constituted the giving of such assistance by the parent company. The answer to this was:

[P]lainly 'no'. The statutory prohibition is, and always has been, directed to the assisting company, not to its parent company. If the giving of financial assistance by a subsidiary for the acquisition of shares in its holding company necessarily also constituted the giving of financial assistance by the holding company, s. 73 of the 1947 Act would not have been necessary.[44]

---

[39] Emphasis added.

[40] This also helps to produce the result in the example given above.

[41] [1993] BCC 816.

[42] The name is confusing. Although called 'Holdings', in fact Mercantile Holdings Ltd was the subsidiary here.

[43] For the definition of 'subsidiary' under Companies Act 2006 see *Farstad Supply A/S v Enviroco Limited* [2011] UKSC 16 (although for the purposes of that dispute the relevant provisions were found in the Companies Act 1985, identical provisions are re-enacted by the Companies Act 2006).

[44] The point being that s. 45 of the Companies Act 1929 first introduced the prohibition on a company from giving financial assistance in connection with the purchase of its own shares and it was s. 73 of the Companies Act 1947 which extended it to the giving of financial assistance in connection with the purchase of shares in the company's holding company. It did this by enacting that s. 45 of the 1929 Act should apply to shares in a company's holding company as it applied to shares in the company itself.

> Moreover, ss. 153–158 of the 1985 Act [Sections 677–683 of the Companies Act 2006] are clearly predicated on the assumption that it is the conduct of the subsidiary alone which needs statutory authorisation.[45]

On the other hand, if a parent company were to procure the unlawful acts of the subsidiary, then this would be an offence (assuming those acts were actually unlawful). Also, there clearly may be situations where a parent company's conduct might make it liable for the indirect provision of financial assistance even if the act of the subsidiary itself was not unlawful. The example given[46] by Millett J was that of an English company which hives down an asset to a foreign subsidiary in order for it to be made available to finance a contemplated acquisition of shares of the English company.

The second question that arose was whether s. 151 (s. 678 of the Companies Act 2006) made it unlawful for a foreign subsidiary of an English parent company to give financial assistance for the purpose of the acquisition of shares of its parent company. Millett J observed that if read literally, s. 151 did make the assistance unlawful and, in the circumstances, Mercantile Holdings Ltd was certainly a 'subsidiary'[47] within the meaning of the Companies Act 1985, for s. 736 (now s. 1159 of the Companies Act 2006) sets out the circumstances in which one company may be deemed to be a subsidiary of another. In it, the word 'company' includes any 'body corporate'.[48] The term 'body corporate' is defined by s. 740 (now s. 1173 of the Companies Act 2006) to include a company incorporated elsewhere than in Great Britain. This position differed from that which pertained under the previous version of the legislation[49] and was attributed to a change in drafting style rather than any parliamentary intention to change the law.[50] It explains Millett J's opening remarks in the case which, in the current maelstrom of reform of company law, may perhaps be seen as a timely warning about disturbing settled law in complex areas:

> The case illustrates the dangers which are inherent in any attempt to recast statutory language in more modern and direct form for no better reason than to make it shorter, simpler and more easily intelligible.[51]

The judge reached the conclusion that: '"any of its subsidiaries" in s. 151[52] must be construed as limited to those subsidiaries which are subsidiary companies, that is to say English companies.'[53] Such a departure from the literal meaning of a statute needs strong justification, and so, perhaps with this in mind, Millett J listed no fewer than 10 reasons

---

[45] [1993] BCC 816 at p. 819.
[46] *Ibid.* at pp. 819–820. The example is predicated on the basis (as was later held) that s. 151 did not make unlawful the conduct of the foreign subsidiary itself.
[47] Although it was not a 'company' within the Companies Act 1985, because s. 735 (1) (a) (now s. 1 (1) of the Companies Act 2006) defines a company as 'a company formed and registered under this Act'. Having an established place of business in Great Britain, it was in fact an 'oversea company' (s. 744) (now s. 1044 of the Companies Act 2006 (changed)).
[48] Companies Act 1985, s. 736 (3) now s. 1159 (4) of the Companies Act 2006.
[49] I.e. 'old' s. 54.
[50] [1993] BCC 816 at p. 819.
[51] *Ibid.* at p. 816.
[52] S. 678 (3) of the Companies Act 2006 now uses a slightly different wording, namely, 'or a company that is a subsidiary of that company'.
[53] *Ibid.* at p. 821.

for his decision.[54] For the purposes of the general law, the most significant of these were probably the private international law considerations, namely:

(a) There is a presumption that in the absence of a contrary intention expressed or implied, UK legislation does not apply to foreign persons or corporations outside the UK whose acts are performed outside the UK. Some limitation of the general words of s. 151 is necessary in order to avoid imputing to Parliament an intention to create an exhorbitant jurisdiction which is contrary to generally accepted principles of international law . . .

(b) The capacity of a corporation, the regulation of its conduct, the maintenance of its capital and the protection of its creditors and shareholders are all matters for the law of the place of its incorporation, not the law of the place of incorporation of its parent company.[55]

The obvious criticism to be levelled at this decision is that in some circumstances it may make it possible to evade the statutory provisions by arranging things so that when financial assistance is needed, and is not going to be within any of the legitimate statutory exceptions, then it is given by a foreign subsidiary. However, as suggested earlier, this may in any event make the parent company liable for providing indirect assistance[56] although the prosecution will often find it difficult to show that the parent was sufficiently involved with the structuring of the subsidiary and the use of its assets. Overall, it is clear that Millett J reached the right conclusions in law as to the scope of the statute, and to the extent that it exists, the danger of evasion is the result of unstated legislative policy or defective legislating.

## 15.3 Meaning of financial assistance

The scope of the prohibition on giving 'financial assistance' in s. 678 is circumscribed by s. 677 that deals in considerable detail with what is meant by 'financial assistance'. The 'old' s. 54 of the Companies Act 1948 also used the expression 'financial assistance' but without much elaboration as to its meaning, beyond the addition of the phrase 'whether by means of a loan, guarantee, the provision of security or otherwise'. Indeed, the case law acknowledged that 'though s. 151(1)(a) [of the 1985 Act, now s. 677 of the 2006 Act] purports to define "financial assistance" it does not do so because in the purported definitions it repeats the word financial'.[57]

In *Charterhouse Investment Trust Ltd* v *Tempest Diesels Ltd*,[58] Hoffmann J (as he then was) took the view that:

One must examine the commercial realities of the transaction and decide whether it can properly be described as the giving of financial assistance by the company, bearing in mind that the section is a penal one and should not be stretched to cover transactions which are not fairly within it.

[54] *Ibid.* at pp. 821–822.
[55] *Ibid.*
[56] Although not for procuring, since the foreign subsidiary is not in breach of s. 151 (or s. 678 of the Companies Act 2006) and is therefore doing nothing unlawful.
[57] *AMG Global Nominees (private) Ltd* v *Africa Resources Ltd* [2009] 1 BCLC 281, at [22] per Sir Andrew Morritt. In *Chaston* v *SWP Group Plc* [2003] 1 BCLC 675, at [55]–[57], Ward LJ summarised the problem: 'Without the benefit of any authority to clarify the meaning of "financial assistance", ordinary enough words, I would have had no trouble in concluding this was indeed financial assistance . . . When, however, Mr Todd QC took me to [s. 677] and the singularly unhelpful definition of financial assistance, I began to worry whether it was as simple as it appeared.'
[58] [1986] BCLC 1 at p. 10.

It is clear then that 'the words "financial assistance" have no technical meaning and their frame of reference . . . is the language of ordinary commerce',[59] that is to say, it is a commercial, not a legal, concept. This was a decision on the Companies Act 1948 but it has since been held that a similar approach must be taken when construing s. 152 of the Companies Act 1985,[60] and probably is still the case under s. 677 of the Companies Act 2006. So, for example, an agreement for a target company to make payments to the vendor were found not to be 'financial assistance' (in a commercial sense) where the target owed such payments to the purchaser under a secured obligation. Here, the court held that the transaction was financially neutral and reflected a mere 'shortcut' to enforcement by the purchaser.[61] As to the meaning of 'assistance', it involves something in the nature of aid or help.[62] It cannot exist in vacuum; it must be given to someone.[63]

The nature of financial assistance as a means of providing aid or help was considered in the English High Court decision of *ParOs Plc* v *Worldlink Group Plc*,[64] where a break fee was held to amount to unlawful financial assistance. The break fee was set out in Heads of Terms concerning a possible reverse takeover of Worldlink™ by ParOs™, an AIM listed shell company. If discussions ended due to Worldlink™ refusing to proceed, Worldlink™ agreed to bear ParOs's costs at the rate of £12,500 per week between signing and re-registering Worldlink™ as a private company (to which the prohibition against financial assistance did not apply), with a cap of £150,000.

Although proposed investors had assumed a post-transaction value of £20m, Worldlink™ had very limited liquid assets. The judge considered that the break fee amounted to financial assistance under the terms of the UK legislation because it would materially reduce the net assets of Worldlink™, given they were negative at the time. It was financial assistance because it would 'smooth the path' toward the acquisition of shares.[65] His Honour also noted that it was not clear that a break fee is always financial assistance, referring to *dicta* suggesting that in some circumstances it may be an 'inducement' rather than 'assistance'.

Ultimately, the Heads of Terms were varied to provide for the acquisition of assets rather than shares (meaning that the prohibition against financial assistance did not apply) and the court found that the fact that it contravened the prohibition when given did not make it unenforceable.

Some commentators have argued that break fees cannot give rise to financial assistance because the fee is only payable if the transaction does not proceed, and accordingly the

---

[59] *Ibid.* at p. 40.
[60] See *British & Commonwealth Holdings plc* v *Barclays Bank plc* [1996] 1 BCLC 1 at 38, CA; *Chaston* v *SWP Group plc* [2003] 1 BCLC 675, CA, considered later by Peter Smith J in *Anglo Petroleum Ltd* v *TFB (Mortgages) Ltd* [2006] EWHC 258 (Ch); *MT Realisations Ltd (In Liquidation)* v *Digital Equipment Co. Ltd* [2003] 2 BCLC 117, CA.
[61] *MT Realisations Ltd* v *Digital Equipment Ltd* [2003] EWCA Civ 494, [2003] 2 BCLC 117, CA. See also H. Hirt 'The Scope of Prohibited Financial Assistance After *MT Realisations Ltd* v *Digital Equipment Co Ltd*' (2004) 25 Company Lawyer 9.
[62] *Ibid.*
[63] See J. Birds *Annotated Companies Legislation* (ed.) (Oxford: OUP, 2010), 802 and *obiter* remarks of HHJ Christopher Nugee QC in *Makram Barsoum Estafnous* v *London & Leeds Buisness Centres Limited* [2009] EWHC 1308 (Ch), at [80].
[64] [2012] EWHC 394 (Comm).
[65] *Chaston* v *SWP Group plc* [2002] EWCA Civ 1999; [2003] BCC 140, [31].

company's financial resources will only be diminished where there is no acquisition of shares. The *ParOs* decision implicitly rejects that argument, taking the view that a break fee 'smooths the path' for an acquisition because it allows an acquirer to incur costs to progress an acquisition secure in the knowledge that it will be reimbursed if the transaction fails.

Section 677 (1) includes both a list of specific types of transaction (s. 677 (1) (a)–(c), and a residual category of 'any other financial assistance . . . where the net assets of the company are reduced to a material extent by the giving of the assistance' (s. 677 (1) (d)). With respect to the former, the categories of financial assistance listed in them are applied strictly, they are prohibited whether or not there is any diminution in net assets and thus can be contrasted with the final 'catch all' provision set out in s. 677 (1) (d).[66]

Let us look at the specific types of transaction more closely. First is a 'gift' (s. 677 (1) (a)). It has been held that undervalue transactions may in substance be 'gifts' or part of the consideration.[67] Secondly, s. 677 (1) (b) mentions 'Guarantee, Security, Indemnity . . . etc.' It has been held that 'Guarantee' and 'Indemnity' are legal terms of art, notwithstanding that the general words of 'financial assistance' are not. 'Guarantee' is a contract to answer for the debt, default or miscarriage of another who is principally liable to the promisee. 'Indemnity', on the other hand, is a contract where A promises to keep B harmless against loss.[68] Finally, s. 677 (1) (c) (i) deals with a 'loan or any other agreement under which any of the obligations of the person giving the assistance are to be fulfilled at a time when in accordance with the agreement any obligation of another party to the agreement remains unfulfilled', whereas s. 677 (1) (c) (ii) deals with 'novation of, or the assignment (in Scotland, assignation) of rights arising under, a loan or such other agreement'. In *Chaston* v *SWP Group Ltd*[69] it was held that a loan need not reduce the company's net assets. On the other hand, a loan, or other transaction in which the company's consideration passes first, can nevertheless 'assist' by putting the counterparty in funds to pay for the shares.[70]

Turning to the residual head (other financial assistance), which is found in s. 677 (1) (d) and is concerned with financial assistance of a kind not specifically mentioned in ss. 677 (1) (a)–(c). This is only prohibited if it either materially reduces the company's net assets, or if the company has no net assets. Under this head the concept of 'financial assistance' is *not* limited by specific words.[71] With respect to the expression 'material extent', it appears that 'materiality' excludes *de minimis* transactions and the test will depend on the size of a company's net assets.[72] Later, in *Makram*, the court emphasised that the issue in 'material' is not whether the acquisition as a whole causes the material reduction, but

---

[66] An observation made by Arden LJ in *Chaston* v *SWP Group plc* [2003] BCC 140, 152.

[67] *Plaut* v *Steiner* (1989) 5 BCC 352, at 363–5; *British & Commonwealth Holdings plc* v *Barclays Bank plc* [1996] 1 BCLC 1 at 40 *per* Aldous LJ.

[68] *Yeoman Credit Ltd* v *Latter* [1961] 2 All ER 294 at 296, adopted by CA in *British & Commonwealth Holdings plc* v *Barclays Bank plc* [1996] 1 BCLC 1 at 38–39.

[69] [2002] EWCA Civ 1999, [2003] 1 BCLC 675 at [41] *per* Arden LJ.

[70] *Charterhouse Investments Ltd* v *Tempest Diesels Ltd* [1986] BCLC 1.

[71] For example, paying for the company's accountants to perform the purchaser's due diligence is 'financial assistance'. See *Chaston* v *SWP Group plc* [2002] EWCA Civ 1999, [2003] 1 BCLC 675; or agreements for services under which the company is obliged to pay, and the counterparty either not obliged to do any work (*Diamond* v *Foo* [2002] EWHC 1450), or compensation is excessive (*Parlett* v *Guppys (Bridport) Ltd* [1996] BCC 299).

[72] *Chaston* v *SWP Group plc*, *ibid.* at [35].

whether the financial assistance itself does so.[73] While showing a reduction in a company's net assets to a material extent is necessary to qualify the company as a possible provider of financial assistance, this alone is insufficient because it remains necessary to identify the disposition of assets or assumption of liabilities by the company which are to count as the giving of financial assistance by the company.[74]

## 15.4 Principal/larger purpose exceptions

A salient and problematic feature of the current legislation is the inclusion of a general purpose based exception to the prohibitions, partly as a result of the recommendations earlier made by the Jenkins Committee and partly in response to the observations of the Court of Appeal in the *Belmont Finance* case.[75]

The relevant provisions are ss. 678 (2) and (4)[76] which, like the corresponding provisions in s. 678 to which they provide exception, give separate treatment to *pre-* and *post-*acquisition assistance. Thus s. 678 (2) provides that:

> Subsection (1) does not prohibit a company from giving financial assistance for the acquisition of shares in it or its holding company if –
>
> (a) the company's principal purpose in giving the assistance is not to give it for the purpose of any such acquisition, or
> (b) the giving of the assistance for that purpose is only an incidental part of some larger purpose of the company, and the assistance is given in good faith in the interests of the company.

In similar terms, s. 678 (4) is designed to provide exception in circumstances of post-acquisition assistance:

> Subsection (3) does not prohibit a company from giving financial assistance if –
>
> (a) the company's principal purpose[77] in giving the assistance is not to reduce or discharge any liability incurred by a person for the purpose of the acquisition of shares in the company or its holding company, or
> (b) the reduction or discharge of any such liability is only an incidental part of some larger purpose of the company, and the assistance is given in good faith in the interests of the company.

To help understand these provisions we need to consider a House of Lords decision that, since 1988, has overshadowed the effect of s. 153 of the Companies Act 1985 (now s. 678 of the Companies Act 2006). That is, the somewhat complicated case *Brady* v *Brady*.[78] Two

---

[73] *Makram Barsoum Estafnous* v *London & Leeds Buisness Centres Limited* [2009] EWHC 1308 (Ch), at [82].
[74] *AMG Global Nominees (Private) Ltd* v *Africa Resources Ltd* [2009] 1 BCLC 281, at [22] *per* Sir Andrew Morritt.
[75] See 15.1 above.
[76] S. 679 (2) and (4) is concerned with assistance by public company for acquisition of shares in its private holding company, but largely uses the same wording as in s. 678.
[77] Something is 'a purpose' of a transaction between A and B if it is understood that it will enable B to bring about that result: see *Re Hill and Tyler Ltd* [2005] 1 BCLC 41 at 18 [24]–[32] (secured loan by bank to target, which bank understood would be used to provide 'on-loan' to purchaser to finance acquisition). However, it must be understood by *both* parties as being for that purpose: see *Dyment* v *Boyden* [2005] 1 WLR 792 at [34].
[78] [1988] BCLC 579.

brothers, Jack and Bob, ran the company T. Brady & Sons Ltd ('Brady') and relations between the brothers had broken down. A complex scheme was proposed and agreed upon which would enable the brothers to separate their activities, each with different parts of the business, whilst nevertheless keeping the company alive and trading. The brothers reached a contractual agreement to reconstruct the company along certain lines but Bob, feeling that he was not getting a fair deal, refused to go ahead with the arrangements. Jack brought an action for specific performance. Bob responded by arguing that specific performance should not be awarded because the scheme was illegal under s. 151 (2) (now ss. 678 (3) and 679 (3) of the Companies Act 2006).

The illegality problem arose because at one stage of the elaborate scheme prepared by the professional advisers to the parties, a company called Motoreal Ltd purchased the shares of Brady and in doing so incurred a liability. At a later stage in the scheme, Motoreal Ltd caused Brady to transfer half its assets to another company (Actavista Ltd) to discharge the liability that Motoreal Ltd had incurred in the purchase of the shares. All the parties accepted that this transaction was in breach of s. 151 (2) (now ss. 678 (3) and 679 (3) of the Companies Act 2006), and the main issue[79] that confronted the House of Lords was whether it was saved by the principal purpose exception enshrined in s. 153 (2) (now ss. 678 (4) and 679 (4) of the Companies Act 2006). The judgment of the House of Lords was delivered by Lord Oliver. It was held that the scheme, as proposed, contravened s. 151 (2) and that it was not saved by s. 153 (2). Whereas the majority of the Court of Appeal[80] had felt that the difficulty with the scheme lay in para. (b) of s. 153 (2) (assistance being given in good faith in the interests of the company), the House of Lords felt that the difficulty with the scheme lay with para. (a), namely the principal purpose exception.[81] The House of Lords' analysis is set out at length in a difficult passage in the speech of Lord Oliver.[82] He held that s. 153 (2) (a) contemplates two alternative situations:

> . . . The first envisages a principal and, by implication, a subsidiary purpose. The inquiry here is whether the assistance was given principally in order to relieve the purchaser of shares in the company of his indebtedness resulting from the acquisition or whether it was principally for some other purpose – for instance the acquisition from the purchase of some asset which the company requires for its business. That is the situation envisaged by Buckley LJ in the course his judgment in the *Belmont Finance* case as giving rise to doubts. That is not this case, for the purpose of the assistance here was simply and solely to reduce the indebtedness incurred by Motoreal . . .

Lord Oliver went on to say that the second alternative situation in s. 153 (2) (a) (now ss. 678 (4) (a) and (b), and 679 (4) (a) and (b) of the Companies Act 2006), was where:

> . . . [I]t is not suggested that the financial assistance was intended to achieve any other object than the reduction or discharge of the indebtedness but where that result (that is, the reduction or discharge) is merely incidental to some larger purpose of the company. These last three words are

---

[79] It was also argued *inter alia* that the scheme was *ultra vires*. This contention had succeeded in the Court of Appeal but ultimately failed in the House of Lords.
[80] [1988] BCLC 20 at pp. 26–27, 41.
[81] Of s. 153 (2) (b) (now ss. 678 (4) and 679 (4) of the Companies Act 2006), it was said: 'The words "in good faith in the interests of the company" form, I think, a single composite expression and postulate a requirement that those responsible for procuring the company to provide the assistance act in the genuine belief that it is being done in the company's interest': [1988] BCLC 579 at p. 597.
[82] Lords Keith, Havers, Templeman and Griffiths concurring.

important. What has to be sought is some larger overall purpose in which the resultant reduction or discharge is merely incidental . . . [P]urpose is, in some contexts, a word of wide content but in construing it in the context of the fasciculus of sections regulating the provision of finance by the company in connection with the purchase of its own shares there has always to be borne in mind the mischief against which s. 151 is aimed. In particular, if the section is not, effectively, to be deprived of any useful application, it is important to distinguish between a purpose and the reason why a purpose is formed. The ultimate reason for forming the purpose of financing an acquisition may, and in most cases probably will be more important to those making the decision than the immediate transaction itself. But 'larger' is not the same thing as 'more important' nor is 'reason' the same as 'purpose'. If one postulates the case of a bidder for control of a public company financing his bid from the company's own funds – the obvious mischief at which the section is aimed – the immediate purpose which it is sought to achieve is that of completing the purchase and vesting control of the company in the bidder. The reasons why that course is considered desirable may be many and varied . . . It may . . . be thought . . . that the business of the company would be more profitable under his management than it was heretofore. There may be excellent reasons but they cannot, in my judgment, constitute a 'larger purpose' of which the provision of assistance is merely an incident. The purpose and the only purpose of the financial assistance is and remains that of enabling the shares to be acquired[83] and the financial or commercial advantages flowing from the acquisition, whilst they may form the reasons for forming the purpose of providing the assistance, are a by-product of it rather than an independent purpose of which the assistance can properly be considered to be an incident.

This reasoning was then applied to the facts of the *Brady* case itself with the result that the only 'purpose' of the scheme was said to be the acquisition of the shares and the wider benefits such as freedom from management deadlock were merely the 'reasons' for doing it. In an unexpected ending to the case, it was held that the exception for private companies contained in ss. 155–158 of the Companies Act 1985 (now repealed by the Companies Act 2006, see below) could still be utilised, because the contractual obligation to reconstruct was still subsisting and was sufficiently broadly drawn to permit different ways of performing the contract. So, ultimately, the parties were required to use that method and accordingly, subject to compliance with those sections,[84] the scheme was not illegal under s. 151.

The House of Lords thus adopted a very narrow construction of s. 153 (2), which would have had the effect in *Brady* (absent the s. 155 point) of allowing s. 151 (2) to prohibit what was a completely normal commercial transaction. Lord Oliver's policy in adopting the narrow approach was so as not to provide a 'blank cheque for avoiding the effective application of s. 151 in every case'.[85] It is arguable that this approach does not give enough consideration to the fact that the principal/larger purpose concept is only the first stage in a carefully drafted two-stage gateway. Paragraph (b) in s. 153 (1) and (2) (now ss. 678 (4) and 679 (4) of the Companies Act 2006), requires that 'the assistance is given in good faith in the interests of the company' and this might often close the gate on undesirable or improper transactions.

---

[83] Here, Lord Oliver is referring to s. 153 (1) (now s. 678 (1) of the Companies Act 2006) by way of example, rather than s. 153 (2) (now ss. 678 (4) and 679 (4) of the Companies Act 2006).
[84] And subject to the right of the respondents to raise certain points which they had agreed not to raise earlier in the litigation.
[85] [1988] 2 All ER 617 at p. 633.

Soon afterwards, *Plaut v Steiner*[86] provided a further demonstration of the vulnerability of business reconstructions and that post-*Brady*, the exemption provisions in ss. 153 (1) and (2) were going to be of limited practical utility. The case was concerned with a complex agreement designed to separate family businesses that had become 'commercially integrated'. The splitting was necessary due to friction between the personalities involved and increasing deadlock. The agreement was designed to enable the families to exchange certain shareholdings in the companies. It arose out of a 'reversible offer' from the Steiners containing two packages described as options with provisions designed to make either option equally attractive. Before the agreement was fully executed, various external circumstances changed, and the Steiners felt that the deal had gone badly and wished to turn the clock back. The Plauts sought specific performance. The hearing of the action was postponed to await the decision of the House of Lords in *Brady*. When the case was heard, it was held that certain elements of the agreement amounted to financial assistance within s. 152 (now s. 677 of the Companies Act 2006). The main issue was whether the financial assistance was given 'for the purpose' of the acquisition within s. 151 (now ss. 678 (1) and (3) and 679 (1) and (3) of the Companies Act 2006), and if so, whether the prohibition was removed or excepted by s. 153 (1) (now ss. 678 (2) and 679 (2) of the Companies Act 2006). No doubt with the need to avoid *Brady* in mind, it was argued that the purpose of the companies was to effect a division of the commercially integrated business and while the reason or motive for that purpose may have been to enable the families to exchange their shareholdings, such reason or motive was irrelevant. Morritt J rejected this as 'ingenious' but wrong; the financial assistance was not necessitated by the division of the integrated business between the companies. In the circumstances the financial assistance was:

> [D]irected entirely to the need to make each option equally attractive. There was no need to make the options equally attractive to the companies, only to the shareholders in those companies . . . [I]t is plain that the financial assistance was to be given for the purpose of the acquisition by the Steiners of the Plauts' shares . . . and by the Plauts of the Steiners' shares . . .[87]

Morritt J then used the logic of this to reject the contention based on s. 153 that the principal or larger purpose of the companies was to effect a division of the commercially integrated business between the companies (so that the purpose of the financial assistance either was not the principal purpose or was an incidental part of that larger purpose):

> As I have already said in relation to section 151 (1) [ss. 678 (1) and 679 (1) of the Companies Act 2006], the financial assistance had nothing to do with the division of the business between the companies; therefore the principal purpose in giving that assistance cannot have been and was not to effect that division. Likewise the giving of the assistance cannot have been and was not an incidental part of the larger purpose of effecting the division. The division of the business between the companies could have been effected without the financial assistance.[88]

The learned judge went on to hold that s. 153 (1) (b) (now ss. 678 (2) and 679 (2) of the Companies Act 2006) was not satisfied here either, mainly because the giving of the assistance would have rendered insolvent one of the companies providing it. Nor was it

---

[86] [1989] 5 BCC 352.
[87] *Ibid.* at p. 369.
[88] *Ibid.*

possible lawfully to perform the agreement in some other way, for alternative performance had to be within the framework of what had been agreed, and in the circumstances, it was not. Further, none of the ways suggested within the framework were lawful; in particular (and unlike in *Brady*) owing to the financial position of the companies involved, s. 155 of the Companies Act 1985 (now repealed) could not be used.[89] Thus, the claim for specific performance was dismissed; the defence of illegality had succeeded.

It should be noted that although over the years there have been calls to reform the purpose exception due to its very narrow scope as a result of *Brady*, this opportunity was not taken by the those drafting the Companies Act 2006.[90] As a result, case law such as *Chaston v SWP Group plc*,[91] and *Brady v Brady*,[92] have created difficulties for transactions that would otherwise involve an element of financial assistance, by restricting the prohibition's ordinary interpretation and access to its statutory exceptions. Thus, non-detrimental transactions that could operate for the benefit – and even survival – of the company giving the financial assistance have been impeded. However, the pension debt-for-equity swap,[93] which was approved by the High Court in *Re Uniq plc*,[94] provides an interesting illustration of how financial assistance may be permitted for the acquisition of shares as part of a court-approved scheme of arrangement.[95] At a time when companies with defined benefit pension schemes are facing substantial contributions to clear billion-pound deficits, *Re Uniq plc* provides a way for companies to give financial assistance for the purpose, and even with the intention of, assisting an acquisition of shares that would otherwise be prohibited.[96]

The applicant company (U) applied under s. 899 of the Companies Act 2006 for the court sanction of a scheme of arrangement between it and its members.[97] The scheme, which involved a complex business restructure, was presented as the only viable way for U to avoid insolvency. The financial assistance proposed by the scheme potentially contravened s. 678 (1) of the Act. Specifically, elements of the proposal fell within the categories of financial assistance set out in s. 677 (1), but David Richards J found that it was clear on the evidence that the principal purpose of the payments satisfied the requirements of s. 678 (2) and it was therefore appropriate to approve them. Interestingly, the judge thought it was important to note that the court's power under s. 681 (2) (e) to sanction financial assistance as part of a scheme was not qualified by reference to particular criteria. For example, satisfaction by analogy of the conditions set out in s. 155 of the Companies Act 1985 had never been a necessary precondition to the exercise of the power. There was no particular test; a general approach would emerge on a case-by-case basis.[98]

---

[89] *Ibid.* at pp. 371–376 *passim*.

[90] As Ferran reports, this was not because the government had changed its mind on the desirability of reversing the effects of *Brady*, but rather felt it had yet hit upon a form of words that would achieve the desired effect! See further, E. Ferran *Principles of Corporate Finance Law* (Oxford: OUP, 2008), 295.

[91] [2003] BCLC 140.

[92] [1989] AC 755.

[93] Debt-for-equity swaps are increasingly common in restructuring transactions and involve the issue of equity instruments in settlement of debts. See, for example, the debt-for-equity swap agreed between the Bank of Ireland and its junior bondholders (see K.B. Doyle 'Bank of Ireland Cuts Rights Issue After Debt-For-Equity Swap' in *The Independent*, 10 May 2011).

[94] *Re Uniq plc* [2011] EWHC 749 (judgment of David Richards J).

[95] K.J. Leivesley 'Financial Assistance: Why a Uniq Approach May Overcome Chaston' [2011] JBL 725.

[96] *Ibid.*

[97] Schemes of arrangement are discussed in Chapter 4 under F.

[98] *Re Uniq plc* [2011] EWHC 749, at [45–46].

The approach in *Re Uniq plc* of accepting individual components of a scheme of arrangement as a complete package through which the ultimate purpose of the scheme permeates, even where it is known or intended that some of those components will directly or indirectly assist a third party share acquisition, is a positive development in the financial assistance jurisprudence and restructuring practices.[99]

## 15.5 Private company exception

One of the main defects of s. 54 of the Companies Act 1948 had been the obstacles that it created in the situation of a management buyout. Often the management would need a loan to enable them to purchase the shares. It was usually necessary for the loan to be secured and the financial assistance prohibition would prevent the company itself from charging its own assets as security (as s. 54 would render the charge void).[100] In this context, the 1981 legislation (later contained in ss. 155–158 of the Companies Act 1985, now repealed) introduced the significant innovation of permitting private companies to give financial assistance provided that the procedures prescribed are followed (the so-called 'whitewash procedure'). This made institutional finance more readily available and was one of the factors behind the increase in management buyouts in the early 1980s.[101]

The 2005 White Paper, in line with the *Company Law Review Final Report*, stated that private companies should no longer be prevented from providing financial assistance for the purchase of their own shares. It endorsed the view expressed by the Steering Group that creditors have other safeguards, such as the wrongful trading provision in the Insolvency Act 1986,[102] which render the 'elaborate safeguards specifically directed at financial assistance' superfluous. Thus, a major change introduced by the Companies Act 2006, and one described by BERR (now DBEIS) 'as one of the key benefits of the Act for private companies',[103] is that private companies are no longer prohibited from giving financial assistance for the purpose of acquiring their own shares or those of their private company parent. In terms of transaction costs, it has been estimated that this freedom will save private companies some £20 million per year.[104] This repeal of the so-called 'whitewash procedure' came into force on 1 October 2008. Despite the changes under the Companies Act 2006, there are still a number of issues companies should consider. First, although the Companies Act 2006 does not prohibit a private company from giving financial assistance for the acquisition of its own shares, if it has a subsidiary which is a public company, the public company may not assist the acquisition of shares in the private holding company.[105] Further, a private company

---

[99] K.J. Leivesley 'Financial Assistance: Why a Uniq Approach May Overcome Chaston' [2011] JBL 725.
[100] As described at 15.1 above.
[101] See M. Wright, J. Coyne and A. Mills *Spicer and Pegler's Management Buy-outs* (1987) pp. 3–4 and D. Sterling 'Financial Assistance by a Company for the Purchase of its Shares' (1987) 8 Co Law 99.
[102] See Chapter 2, 2.2C.
[103] See BERR 'Companies Act 2006: Major Business Benefits', available on the BERR website (an archive page).
[104] *Ibid.* and see also *The Strategic Framework* (1999). According to an early evaluation of the Companies Act 2006 commissioned by DBIS, published in December 2010, six out of eight respondents agreed that there had been cost savings from the relaxation of the prohibition on financial assistance. See http://www.bis.gov.uk/policies/business-law/company-and-partnership-law/evaluation%20of%20companies%20act%202006.
[105] Section 679 of the Companies Act 2006.

cannot provide financial assistance for the acquisition of shares in its public company parent.[106] Secondly, other general company law principles continue to apply. For instance, the transaction must promote the success of the company (see s. 172 of the Companies Act 2006, discussed in Chapter 8 above). It follows that it would still be prudent for private companies to draft board minutes identifying the corporate benefit and solvency of entering into (previously prohibited) transactions as well as obtaining shareholder approval for those transactions. Thirdly, the transaction must not breach the rules on distributions or constitute an illegal reduction of capital (Part 23, Companies Act 2006 discussed in Chapter 14 above). Finally, the transaction must not be an under-value (see s. 238 of the Insolvency Act 1986).

## 15.6 Other exceptions

In addition to the above exceptions, s. 681 (unconditional exceptions) contains a list of specific transactions that are expressed not to be prohibited by ss. 678–679. Section 681 (2) (a) refers to a 'distribution[107] of a company's assets by way of dividend lawfully made or a distribution made in the course of the company's winding up.' The Jenkins Committee[108] had felt that the payment of a dividend was unobjectionable in principle (although probably in breach of old s. 54 of the 1948 Act) even in the situation where 'A borrows the money to buy control of company B and then causes company B to pay a dividend, which company B can properly do, and uses the dividend to repay the loan'. The reasons given were that: 'the payment of a dividend properly declared is no more than the discharge of a liability and we cannot see why the discharge by a company of a lawful liability should be regarded as giving financial assistance to the creditor. Such a payment cannot prejudice the rights of creditors, while minority shareholders will directly benefit from it.' It is arguable that the Jenkins Committee was unwise to view this situation as unobjectionable. The potential difficulties were pointed out by Lord Mackay of Clashfern in debate in the House of Lords where he said: 'Permitting other-wise lawful dividends would for example, allow a predator to borrow sufficient funds to acquire control of a cash-rich company, in the knowledge that he could then declare a lawful, substantial dividend from the assets of the company and repay funds borrowed from this dividend.'[109] This warning went unheeded, for the Government felt[110] that Part III of the Companies Act 1980[111] (which was new at that time), with its provisions that dividends could only be paid out of profits, was sufficient to protect the minority share-holder and creditor. The Government's view was that prior to 1980, the real danger was that the company could declare an unusually large dividend which was clearly an objectionable practice but which by 1981 had already been foreclosed by the provisions in the 1980 Act, hence no further protection was needed from s. 151 of the Companies Act 1985

---

[106] Section 678 (1) of the Companies Act 2006.
[107] According to s. 683 'distribution' has the same meaning as in Part 23 (distributions) of the Companies Act 2006 (see s. 829).
[108] Cmnd 1749, 1962, at para. 175.
[109] *Hansard*, HL, vol. 419, col. 1298.
[110] In committee; see Standing Committee A, 30 June 1981, col. 300.
[111] Now Part 15 of the Companies Act 2006; see Chapter 14, 14.3D above.

(now ss. 678 and 679 of the Companies Act 2006). However, the Government did acknowledge that in exempting lawful dividends from s. 151 they were 'widening the scope for a company's liquid funds to be extracted from it'. But this is precisely one of the main dangers that is exacerbated where there is a distribution made in a winding up, which s. 681 (2) (a) also permits. Sections 678 and 679 of the Companies Act 2006 (formerly s. 151 of the Companies Act 1985) were passed for the wider purpose of preventing objectionable schemes whereby a company's shares are purchased using its own assets and ss. 678 and 679 may often fail to prevent that, to the extent that a scheme utilises either limb of s. 681 (2) (a).[112]

The remainder of s. 681 (2)[113] exempts from ss. 678 and 679 the allotment of bonus shares,[114] and then various transactions that are already regulated by statute elsewhere.[115] Section 682 (2) contains further exceptions, namely the lending of money where this is part of the ordinary business of the company and the lending is in the ordinary course of the business; the provision by the company in accordance with an employees' share scheme of money for the acquisition of fully paid shares in the company or its holding company; the making of loans to persons (other than directors) employed in good faith by the company, with a view to enabling those persons to acquire fully paid shares in the company to be held by them by way of beneficial ownership.[116]

## 15.7 The consequences of breach

### A Criminal sanctions

According to s. 680 of the Companies Act 2006 the company, and every officer in default, commits a criminal offence. Section 680 (2) adds that a person guilty of an offence under this section is liable to imprisonment for a term not exceeding two years or a fine (or both). The effect of this is to make the transaction unlawful which can affect the enforceability of the underlying agreement, as will be seen next.

### B Civil consequences

The civil effects of breaches of s. 54 of the Companies Act 1948 were not defined in the statute itself and it fell to the courts to work these out. The provisions in ss. 678 (1) and 679 (1) of the 2006 Act use substantially the same words[117] as s. 54, namely '. . . it is not

---

[112] The *Brady* case also illustrates the curious results produced by this exception since it was pointed out there that the scheme, unlawful under s. 151 (now ss. 678–679 of the Companies Act 2006), and not saved by s. 153 (2) (now ss. 678 (2) and 679 (2) of the Companies Act 2006), could nevertheless be carried out lawfully by using the dividend exception: [1988] BCLC 579 at p. 582.

[113] Companies Act 2006, s. 681 (2) (b).

[114] It is possible that this too is unwise and may be open to abuse, particularly in view of the fact that safeguards in the Companies Act 2006, ss. 829 *et seq.* do not apply to distributions made by way of bonus shares; see s. 829 (2) (a).

[115] See s. 681 (2) (c)–(g).

[116] But for public companies, s. 681 (1) and (2) of the Companies Act 2006 authorises the giving of financial assistance only if the company has net assets which are not thereby reduced, or if they are reduced, then only out of distributable profits; see s. 682 (1), s. 682 (3) and (4) and s. 840 (4) and (5).

[117] Section of the Companies Act 1948 had '. . . it shall not be lawful . . .'

lawful . . .' and it is reasonable to assume therefore that the pre-existing case law applies to ss. 678 (1) and 679 (1) of the 2006 Act also. A number of questions arise: What is the validity of a security (or other assistance) given in breach of the section? The result reached by Fisher J in *Heald* v *O'Connor*[118] was that a security given in breach of the section was void. Vitiating the security in these circumstances benefits the company and serves to protect the company from having its assets misused (since the security is unenforceable). Where, however, the company makes a loan in breach of the section, this outcome is not such an attractive result since *prima facie* the company cannot recover its loan[119] under the void contract and would have been in a better position if the transaction had been voidable at the option of the company, or even valid. However, the position is not without doubt and an earlier case[120] regarded security given in breach of the section as valid and enforceable.

Another question which arises is, 'what is the effect on the actual contract to purchase the shares if the scheme or transaction as a whole involves a breach of ss. 678 and 679 because it contains illegal financial assistance?' The main English authority on this is the Court of Appeal decision in *Lawlor* v *Gray*,[121] where it was said that a vendor of shares owed a statutory duty to the company and a contractual duty to the purchaser to perform the agreement without any breach of the section,[122] but on the facts of this particular case it was possible for the sale of the shares to have been carried out lawfully. In other cases, this might not be the position. A subsequent Privy Council case has taken this further. In *Carney* v *Herbert*,[123] the transaction for the purchase of the shares involved sales agreements, a guarantee and mortgages in a composite transaction. It was held that the mortgages were illegal since they amounted to provision by a subsidiary company of financial assistance in connection with the purchase of shares in the holding company[124] but that the remainder of the transaction could be enforced if the mortgages were severable from it. Here the mortgages were severable as they were ancillary to the basic sale contract (in that they did not go to the heart of the transaction) and the elimination of the mortgage would leave unchanged the subject matter of the contract and the primary obligations of the vendors and the purchaser. There was also no public policy objection to the enforcement of the contract from which the mortgage had been divorced.

The liability of directors and others who deliberately breach the section is well settled: the directors themselves are liable for breach of fiduciary duty if they misapply assets of

---

[118] [1971] 1 WLR 497.
[119] It is clear from *Selangor* (above) that in some circumstances the company may recover by way of constructive trust and the illegality created by the section will not prevent this. It is also possible that since the illegality was created for the protection of one of the parties to the transaction (i.e. the company), then the innocent party may recover; see *Wallersteiner* v *Moir* [1974] 1 WLR 991 at p. 1014, *per* Lord Denning MR; *Hughes* v *Liverpool Victoria Friendly Society* [1916] 2 KB 482.
[120] See *Victor Battery Co. Ltd* v *Currys Ltd* [1946] Ch 242.
[121] An unreported Court of Appeal decision but noted in (1980) 130 New LJ 31. Also in *Brady*, the House of Lords adopted a comparable approach.
[122] A similar approach (in a slightly different context) was adopted by the Privy Council in *Motor and General Insurance Co. Ltd* v *Gobin* [1987] 3 BCC 61.
[123] [1985] AC 301.
[124] Contrary to s. 67 of the Companies Act 1961 (New South Wales).

the company in this way;[125] and so also are nominee (or shadow) directors in some circumstances.[126] As an alternative, there may be liability for the tort of conspiracy whereby the company can recover the loss which is reasonably foreseeable as flowing from the unlawful transaction.[127]

A significant civil effect of breach of the section is the wide constructive trust liability applied in *Selangor United Rubber Estates Ltd* v *Cradock (No. 3)*,[128] where the District Bank Ltd became involved in a circular cheque transaction in breach of s. 54 of the Companies Act 1948. The bank's officers had acted in good faith but due to their inexperience had failed to realise the significance of what was happening. The bank was held liable because it had knowledge of the circumstances which made the transaction a breach of trust and a dishonest intention on its part was unnecessary. There then followed a series of cases in which the courts either followed this approach,[129] or swung towards ameliorating the position of third parties by requiring something amounting to dishonesty before a constructive trust could be imposed.[130] The very full discussion in the Privy Council case of *Royal Brunei Airlines Sdn Bhd* v *Tan*[131] has settled[132] the matter. An insolvent company called Borneo Leisure Travel owed money to an airline. The company had been a general travel agent for the airline for the sale of passenger and cargo transportation. It was required to account to the airline for all amounts received from sales of tickets and it was common ground that the effect of the agreement of appointment was to constitute the company a trustee of the ticket money for the airline. In practice the money received by the company was not paid into a separate account but into its ordinary current

---

[125] *Wallersteiner* v *Moir* [1974] 1 WLR 991; *Belmont Finance Corporation Ltd* v *Williams Furniture Ltd (No. 2)* [1980] 1 All ER 393; *Re In a Flap Envelope Ltd* [2004] 1 BCLC 64. In the Scottish Court of Session (Outer House) case, *Fowler* v *Gruber* [2009] CSOH 36; [2010] 1 BCLC 563, it was held that taking a loan from the company in order to acquire a majority shareholding in the company apart from being clearly contrary to the provisions of ss. 151 and 330 of the Companies Act 1985, is also conduct of the company's affairs which was unfairly prejudicial to the interests of the petitioner and the other shareholders, and only in the interests of the respondent himself. On unfair prejudice (s. 994) see above Chapter 12.

[126] See *Selangor United Rubber Estates Ltd* v *Cradock (No. 3)* [1968] 1 WLR 1555.

[127] For example, in *Starglade Properties Ltd* v *Roland Nash* [2010] EWCA Civ 1314 the Court of Appeal considered the test for dishonest assistance in a commercial context. Relying on the Privy Council's interpretation in *Barlow Clowes* v *Eurotrust Ltd* [2006] 1 WLR 1476 of the House of Lords' finding in *Twinsectra Ltd* v *Yardley* [2002] 2 AC 164, the Court of Appeal described it as a single standard of honesty, objectively determined by the court. The standard is applied to the specific conduct of a specific individual possessing the knowledge and qualities he actually enjoyed. The relevant standard is the ordinary standard of honest behaviour. The subjective understanding of the person concerned as to whether his conduct is dishonest is irrelevant. It is also irrelevant that there may be a body of opinion which regards the ordinary standard of honest behaviour as being set too high. *Starglade*, at [32].

[128] [1968] 1 WLR 1555.

[129] *Karak Rubber Co. Ltd* v *Burden (No. 2)* [1972] 1 WLR 602; *Baden* v *Société Générale* [1992] 4 All ER 161.

[130] See e.g. *Belmont Finance Ltd* v *Williams Furniture Ltd* [1979] Ch 250 at pp. 267 and 274; *Re Montagu's Settlement Trusts* [1987] Ch 264 at p. 285; *Agip* v *Jackson* [1990] Ch 265 at p. 293; *Eagle Trust plc* v *SBC Ltd* [1992] 4 All ER 488 at p. 499; *Polly Peck International plc* v *Nadir (No. 2)* [1992] 4 All ER 769 at p. 777.

[131] [1995] 3 All ER 97.

[132] Probably. In theory, since it is only a Privy Council case, of persuasive rather than binding authority, the dispute could restart at some future date. This seems unlikely, however, particularly in the light of the endorsement of the subjective approach by the House of Lords in *Twinsectra Ltd* v *Yardley* [2002] 2 All ER 377, where it was held that there could be liability as accessory only where it was established that the conduct had been dishonest by the ordinary standards of reasonable and honest people *and* that the defendant himself had realised that by those standards his conduct was dishonest. However, other views continue, and Lord Millett delivered a strong dissenting speech.

account. The company was poorly run with heavy overhead expenses and the money was lost in the ordinary course of business. The airline sued Tan who was the company's principal director and shareholder. The claim against Tan was that he was liable as constructive trustee for assisting with knowledge in a dishonest and fraudulent design on the part of the trustees.

Their Lordships began by changing the 'shorthand' terminology often used in this field as a result of the existing judicial distinction between 'knowing receipt' and 'knowing assistance'.[133] 'Knowing receipt' was referred to as being 'concerned with the liability of a person as a recipient of trust property or its traceable proceeds'. 'Knowing assistance' is concerned with the 'liability of an accessory to a trustee's breach of trust'.[134] In the context of ss. 151–158 of the 1985 Companies Act (now ss. 677–683 of the Companies Act 2006) the chief interest in the lengthy judgments in this case lies in what was said about the role and nature of dishonesty in 'accessory liability'. First, it was made clear that 'dishonesty' is a necessary ingredient of accessory liability[135] and that:

> [I]n the context of the accessory liability principle acting dishonestly . . . means simply not acting as an honest person would in the circumstances . . . Honesty . . . [has] . . . a strong subjective element[136] in that it is a description of a type of conduct assessed in the light of what a person actually knew at the time, as distinct from what a reasonable person would have known or appreciated . . . Unless there is a very good and compelling reason, an honest person does not participate in a transaction if he knows it involves a misapplication of trust assets . . . Nor does an honest person in such a case deliberately close his eyes and ears, or deliberately not ask questions, lest he learn something he would rather not know, and then proceed regardless.[137]

Ultimately, Tan was held liable. The company had committed a breach of trust by using the money in its business instead of simply deducting its commission and holding the money intact until it paid the airline, and Tan's conduct, by causing or permitting his company to apply the money in a way he knew was not authorised by the trust of which the company was trustee, was dishonest. It was also held 'for good measure' that the company also acted dishonestly in that Tan was the company and his state of mind was to be imputed to the company. Overall, the decision should have provided some relief for banks and others whose commercial functions put them at risk from this type of liability. However, any sense of relief should perhaps be tempered with the reflection that the notion of dishonesty set out in the judgment is of a very robust quality. It does not give a general exemption from making inquiries, for in some circumstances an honest person would have made them.

---

[133] The liability of third parties was set out by Lord Selborne in *Barnes v Addy* (1874) 9 Ch App 244 at p. 251: '[S]trangers are not to be made constructive trustees . . . unless [they] receive and become chargeable with some part of the trust property, or unless they assist with knowledge in a dishonest and fraudulent design on the part of the trustees.'
[134] [1995] 3 All ER 97 at p. 99.
[135] *Ibid.* at p. 105.
[136] It was also said to be an objective standard in the sense that 'if a person knowingly appropriates another's property, he will not escape a finding of dishonesty simply because he sees nothing wrong in such behaviour'.
[137] [1995] 3 All ER 97 at pp. 105–107 *passim*.

## Further reading

J. Armour 'Share Capital and Creditor Protection: Efficient Rules for a Modern Company Law' (2000) *MLR* 355.

E. Ferran 'Corporate Transactions and Financial Assistance: Shifting Policy Perceptions But Static Law' *The Cambridge Law Journal* (2004) 63(1), 225.

K.J. Leivesley 'Financial Assistance: Why a Uniq Approach May Overcome Chaston' [2011] *JBL* 725.

J. Lowry 'The prohibition against financial assistance constructing a rational response' Chapter 1 in D. Prentice and A. Reisberg (eds) *Corporate Finance in the UK and EU* (Oxford: OUP, 2011).

S. Mercouris 'The Prohibition on Financial Assistance: The Case for a Commercially Pragmatic Interpretation' (2014) *Company Lawyer* 321.

# Part V
# Securities regulation

# 16

# Theory and regulation of the capital markets law

## 16.1 The relationship between traditional company law and securities regulation

One of the main aims of this text is to move the study of securities regulation (or 'capital markets law')[1] closer to traditional company law. Securities regulation is concerned with the way in which the marketing of shares and other financial products is regulated, either by the state or by the financial services industry itself.

Thus it will involve rules regulating the offer of shares[2] to the public; it will involve rules covering the way in which the secondary market for trading in those shares is run, by supervision of the market participants and by rules about how the market itself must be conducted, such as rules against insider dealing. Takeovers essentially involve the buying and selling of shares, but since corporate control is usually at stake, there will be extra rules to ensure fairness and other matters; so takeover regulation forms part of securities regulation. Many of these are matters which would feature in one way or another in a book on mainstream company law: public offerings of shares, insider dealing, takeovers, are all the stuff of traditional company law.

There is a fundamental difference between the law relating to securities (including public offerings, takeovers and insider dealing) and the more mainstream type of company law. The former is largely a matter of public law with clear investor protection objectives whereas the latter is more concerned with private law and takes a more facilitative approach in its provision of legal structures businesses need to be created and to run efficiently. Within securities regulation the *laissez-faire* culture of company law is replaced by an environment in which the state claims (and will enforce) the right to regulate in minute detail exactly how each bargain is to be struck – the regulation including authorisation requirements for industry participants, fitness requirements, prudential rules for the structure of firms, conduct of business rules requiring, for example, suitable advice to be given.

To be sure, all these arguments can be partially reversed. Does mainstream company law not have areas of state regulation in the form of competition law, or DBEIS investigations? Why confine the idea of efficient business structures to company law; is not the goal of securities regulation also efficiency in the sense of providing efficient primary and secondary markets which facilitate capital raising and economic growth? But these counter observations merely indicate that the distinction is one of degree or emphasis rather than of unbridgeable principle.

---

[1] Capital markets law is the European term for securities regulation.
[2] And other securities.

This leads on to the next point. The boundaries between what falls within traditional company law and what forms part of securities regulation are fluid, and in recent years it is common knowledge that there have been examples of migration from company law to securities regulation. To take one example:[3] insider dealing has its theoretical origins in the idea that insiders are breaching a fiduciary duty of confidentiality owed to the company whose securities are being traded, and in the US and the UK the law has reflected that. However, within the EU, that principle has taken a back seat since the adoption of the Directive on insider dealing.[4] The Directive is based on the securities regulation policy of ensuring a fair market and not on the company law fiduciary concept. Hence, since the implementation in the UK of the Directive in 1993, UK law on insider dealing largely follows EU capital markets law and its theoretical basis is the securities regulation concept of market egalitarianism.[5] The existence of this migration process makes it increasingly difficult to justify the study of mainstream company law without also securities regulation.

## 16.2 The birth of securities regulation

Modern securities regulation in a systematic and sophisticated form began in the US in 1933 with the passing of the Securities Act,[6] which set up an elaborate federal system of regulation of public offerings of securities, in other words, of the primary market.

In the following year, the Securities Exchange Act put in place regulation of the secondary market, the brokers, dealers, exchanges and other matters. Also with this Act, Congress established the Securities and Exchange Commission,[7] the SEC, which became and has remained globally a name which evokes an image of rigorous and comprehensive securities enforcement.

The events which had led to these Acts had been cataclysmic. The Wall Street crash of 1929 had produced an economic depression and shattered public confidence in the banking system and capital markets.[8] The supply of capital to industry had consequently dried up. The Roosevelt Government of 1933 brought in a series of 'New Deal' reforms aimed at restoring confidence in capitalism. The Securities Act and the Exchange Act were fundamental to this, along with important legislation on the structure of banking.[9]

As suggested above, the 1933 and 1934 Acts can reasonably be regarded as the birth of 'modern' securities regulation in the sense that they laid down in a comprehensive way policies and formats which are largely followed and copied throughout the world. But elements of partial (and not very effective) systems of securities regulation were in existence prior to

---

[3] For another example, see Chapter 19, 19.1 below.
[4] See Chapter 20, 20.3B below.
[5] For a more detailed account of this, see Chapter 20, 20.3B 2 below.
[6] This and other federal securities legislation can be found in the 'Securities Lawyer's Deskbook' at https://lawblogs.uc.edu/sld/.
[7] The 1933 Act was administered by the Federal Trade Commission until the creation of the SEC.
[8] These events have served as a paradigm for the securities regulation concept of 'systemic risk' which is the risk that the collapse of one bank or financial institution within a system will trigger a series of collapses in others that are not structured with sufficient capital to be able to absorb the damage caused by the initial failure.
[9] The so called 'Glass–Steagall' Act, after the Members of the Congress who were involved in drafting it. It required the separation of deposit-taking banking business from investment banking (i.e. business related to dealing in securities). The Act was repealed in 1999. Consequently, the distinction between commercial banks and brokerage firms has blurred.

that. In the US, securities frauds and stock market crashes of the first decade of the twentieth century invoked a response at state government level in the form of state legislation which required disclosure and, often also, compliance with standards of fairness.[10] The first of these[11] statutes was enacted in Kansas in 1911 and state legislation remains a feature of US securities regulation at the present day,[12] the most recent example being the Dodd–Frank Act.[13]

In the UK, securities regulation can be traced to the early provisions for the licensing of brokers who acted as agents and who were required to take an oath of good behaviour.[14] And so already there were two basic techniques of securities regulation operating: registration of market participants and, albeit very basic, an early version of conduct of business rules. Further licensing provisions were enacted in 1697. And then there was that ultimate blunt tool of securities regulation: the Bubble Act 1720. The story of this has been told many times[15] but it is worth emphasising that the securities regulation technique being used was, in effect, *suppression* of the securities activity rather than regulation of it because the 1720 Act tended towards prohibiting the creation of the companies themselves and prohibiting the issuance of transferable stock. The importance of the Joint Stock Companies Act 1844 has been noted with regard to its setting up of the system of incorporation by registration, but it also had significance for securities regulation, for it introduced a requirement for registration of a prospectus when shares were issued to the public.[16]

Despite this and many subsequent developments, such as the introduction of legislation against insider dealing in 1980,[17] it is fair to say that the UK had no comprehensive system of securities regulation until the Financial Services Act 1986 under which the Securities and Investments Board ('SIB') was set up. By then, the Barlow Clowes affair had revealed both the inadequacy of the system of Department of Trade and Industry ('DTI')[18] regulation of share dealers required by the Prevention of Fraud (Investments) Act 1958 and the inadequacy of the response by the various City regulators which involved a feast of buckpassing between them.[19] As will be seen below, even the SIB system was not considered

---

[10] Usually referred to as a 'merit' test.

[11] State public utility regulation pre-dated even this.

[12] State legislation on public offerings of securities is known as 'blue sky law' after the story that the legislation was aimed at promoters who 'would sell building lots in the blue sky in fee simple'; see L. Loss *Fundamentals of Securities Regulation* (Boston, MA: Little, Brown, 1988) p. 8. Similarly, going through the processes of making sure that a public offering complies with state law is known as 'blue skying' an issue.

[13] Or in its full name, the Dodd–Frank Wall Street Reform and Consumer Protection Act (Pub. L. 111–203, H.R. 4173) signed into law by President Obama on 21 July 2010. The Act tries to restructure US regulation to force regulators to consider institutions in the light of what they do, rather than what they nominally are. Institutions that are not banks but are designated as 'systemically significant' face tougher risk-based standards forcing them to set more capital against proprietary trading as well as large derivatives or securitisation operations. A new Consumer Financial Protection Bureau is one of the key innovations of the Act. For an interesting review of the background to the Act see http://topics.nytimes.com/topics/reference/timestopics/subjects/c/credit_crisis/financial_regulatory_reform/index.html.

[14] A Statute of Edward I in 1285. See generally B. Rider, C. Abrams and M. Ashe *Guide to Financial Services Regulation* 3rd edn (Bicester: CCH, 1997) pp. 3–4; G. Gilligan 'The City of London and the Development of English Financial Services Law' in B. Rider (ed.) *The Corporate Dimension* (Bristol: Jordans, 1998) at p. 3.

[15] See for instance Loss, n. 12 above, at p. 2.

[16] Joint Stock Companies Act 1844, s. 4.

[17] See Chapter 20, 20.3. below.

[18] Now the Department for Business, Energy and Industrial Strategy.

[19] See generally L. Lever *The Barlow Clowes Affair* (London: Macmillan, 1992). Ultimately it led to the DTI (as it was known at the time) agreeing to pay compensation to the investors for the Government's role in handling the matter.

sufficiently comprehensive, and events have now moved on with the passing of the Financial Services and Markets Act 2000.

## 16.3 The SEC

A major feature of systems of securities regulation is the high profile presence of the state, in the form of the regulatory authority. Historically, nowhere has this been clearer than in the US with the federal government making itself felt through the agency of the Securities and Exchange Commission. The SEC has its headquarters in Washington, DC and is comprised of five commissioners, appointed by the President in consultation with the Senate.[20] They have five-year terms, with one expiring each year. There is a support staff of around 4,600, made up of lawyers, accountants, economists, computer experts and administrators.

The Securities Act 1933 and the Securities Exchange Act 1934 together provide the core of the legislation which the SEC is responsible for administering. In addition there are six other statutes which, together with the 1933 and 1934 Acts, make up what are often referred to as 'the SEC statutes'. They are the Trust Indenture Act 1939, which supplements the 1933 Act where a distribution consists of debt securities; the Investment Company Act 1940, which regulates collective investment schemes; the Investment Advisers Act 1940, which requires the registration of investment advisers; the Sarbanes–Oxley Act 2002, which oversees the auditing profession, enhances corporate responsibility and disclosure and combats fraud; the Dodd–Frank Wall Street Reform and Consumer Protection Act 2010, regulating consumer protection, credit rating, financial products and corporate governance; and Jumpstart Our Business Startups Act 2012, helping businesses raise funds on the capital markets. While these statutes provide a solid background of legislation, in practice much of the day-to-day regulation by the SEC is carried out under its rule-making powers which legislative provisions delegate to it. Key to the statutory development here has been the dramatic corporate scandals that have rocked corporate America in recent years, such as Enron, which culminated in the passing of the Sarbanes–Oxley Act of 2002 referred to above. It makes widespread changes to US corporate governance, such as requiring all listed companies to have fully independent audit committees. Notably, it fixes the Chief Executive Officer ('CEO') and the Chief Finance Officer ('CFO') with liability for the financial statements of the company.[21] The near-collapse of the world financial system in 2008 and the global credit crisis that followed gave rise to widespread calls for changes in the regulatory system. A year and a half later, in July 2010, Congress passed a statute, which, as seen above, later became the Dodd–Frank Act,[22] which expanded the federal government's role in the markets, reflecting a renewed mistrust of financial markets.

---

[20] Not more than three may be members of the same political party.
[21] For interesting discussions of the effects of this on US corporate governance and the market reaction to the Act see L. Ribstein 'Raising the Rent on US Law: Implications of the Sarbanes–Oxley Act 2002' (2003) 3 JCLS 132; D.A. Cohen, A. Dey and T.Z. Lys 'The Sarbanes–Oxley Act of 2002: Implications for Compensation Structure and Risk-Taking Incentives of CEOs' (July 2004) available at http://leeds-faculty.colorado.edu/Bhagat/SOX-CEO-Compensation-Investment.pdf; Z. Rezaee and P.K. Jain 'The Sarbanes–Oxley Act of 2002 and Security Market Behavior: Early Evidence' (May 2005) available at http://ssrn.com/abstract=498083; L. Zingales 'The Future of Securities Regulation' (29 January 2009) Chicago Booth School of Business Research Paper No. 08-27; FEEM Working Paper No. 7.2009, available at http://ssrn.com/abstract=1319648.
[22] See n. 13 above.

The above-mentioned power to make rules and regulations has enabled the SEC to put flesh on the bones of the statutory provisions, to meet new developments, or to clarify matters. Such delegated legislation is usually the result of a three-stage procedure involving a concept release seeking public views on how to approach the problem, then a rule proposal, also for public consultation before, finally, rule adoption. A visit to the SEC website shows that this process is very much ongoing.[23]

Much can be learned from the SEC's enforcement processes,[24] and indeed, as will be seen below, the UK regulator has adopted some of the SEC's techniques.[25] The SEC itself has no powers to begin criminal proceedings. However, if the facts found by the SEC are sufficiently serious that it is felt that the public interest would be served by criminal proceedings being brought, then the matter will be brought to the attention of the US Department of Justice which will work with the SEC in setting up the criminal processes.[26] In spite of this, the SEC is an extremely effective enforcement agency.[27] Enforcement is carried out through an array of civil processes, which, coupled with the SEC's formidable reputation (which usually causes targets to settle actions by the SEC against them) provide effective sanctions.[28] Broadly, there are two types of process used: civil injunctive actions and SEC administrative proceedings.

Civil injunctive actions are a frequently used mechanism and a variety of remedies are available to the SEC under these proceedings if it appears that any person is engaged or is about to engage in violation of the Securities Acts or rules made under them.[29] The civil burden of proof makes it an easier remedy to obtain than any criminal penalty would be, and the courts are empowered to give a range of ancillary relief such as rescission, restitution and civil monetary penalties.[30] Several hundred civil actions are brought annually and most are settled.[31] The settlement process is greatly helped by the device of the consent decree[32] under

---

[23] http://www.sec.gov. According to the SEC 2017 budget request, the SEC's plans involve increasing examination of investment advisers, improving SEC technology to keep pace with regulated entities and markets, expanding their enforcement programme and bolstering their risk analysis functions.
[24] For an excellent analysis of this and other aspects of enforcement from a comparative perspective, see J. Fishman 'A Comparison of Enforcement of Securities Law Violations in the UK and US' (1993) 14 Co Law 163; J.D. Cox and R.S. Thomas 'Mapping the American Shareholder Litigation Experience: A Survey of Empirical Studies of the Enforcement of the US Securities Law' (2009) 6 *European Company and Financial Law Review* 164; and L. Zingales 'The Future of Securities Regulation' (29 January 2009) Chicago Booth School of Business Research Paper No. 08-27; FEEM Working Paper No. 7.2009, available at http://ssrn.com/abstract=1319648.
[25] E.g. the adoption of civil (as opposed to criminal) processes for combatting insider dealing and other forms of market abuse.
[26] According to the *SEC Annual Report* 2010 there were 139 such cases in 2010: http://www.sec.gov/about/secpar/secpar2010.pdf.
[27] E.g. in 2015 the SEC obtained orders for $4.2bn in penalties and disgorgements over 807 enforcement actions; see *SEC Annual Report* 2015 p. 16.
[28] Prior to an enforcement process, the SEC will mount an investigation and it has wide-ranging powers to require the production of documents and the giving of information. Quite often, the SEC will feel that all that is necessary is a private cautionary letter which will advise the recipient of violations of the securities laws or the likelihood of violation in the circumstances.
[29] Securities Exchange Act 1934, s. 21, as amended.
[30] *Ibid*. Also available under s. 21 are bars against persons acting as officers or directors.
[31] For example in 2015 the figure was 507; see *SEC Annual Report* 2015.
[32] See J. Fishman 'A Comparison of Enforcement of Securities Law Violations in the UK and US' (1993) 14 Co Law 163 at p. 166.

which the person accused agrees not to repeat his conduct, agrees to pay a money penalty but does not need to admit wrongdoing. Most enforcement actions are settled in this way.

SEC administrative proceedings are available in many situations and are often used.[33] They are available where a person is registered with the SEC under the 1934 Act or has registered securities with it[34] and that person appears to have violated one of the provisions of the Act or rules or regulations made under it.[35] The proceeding is in effect a trial conducted by an SEC official. On a finding that the person has broken a rule the official can impose sanctions which may include censure or restriction of his activities, revocation of registration, civil money penalties, disgorgement of profits, or a 'cease and desist order'.[36] Often the matter is settled. The SEC occasionally then uses the rulings which are made in administrative proceedings to create a kind of 'judicial' precedent as regards the interpretation of its rules and regulations.[37] More recently, under changes brought about by the Dodd–Frank Act,[38] the SEC's new whistleblower programme was introduced. The Act provided the SEC with the authority to pay financial rewards to whistleblowers who provide new and timely information about any securities law violation.[39] Among other things, to be eligible, the whistleblower's information must lead to a successful SEC enforcement action with more than $1 million in monetary sanctions. The SEC launched a new webpage for people to report a violation of the federal securities laws and apply for a financial award.[40] Prior to the enactment of the Act, the SEC only had authority to reward whistleblowers in insider trading cases.

This brief look at the SEC has given a glimpse of some of the techniques used by the world's leading regulator; many of the ideas have found their way into other regulatory systems and sure enough, when we look at the UK's Financial Conduct Authority, its powers and methods of operation, much of it will seem familiar.

---

[33] In 2007 the figure was 394; see *SEC Annual Report* 2007.

[34] See Securities Exchange Act 1934, s. 12.

[35] Securities Exchange Act 1934, s. 15 (c) (4).

[36] *Ibid.* ss. 21 B, 21 C.

[37] See e.g. the importance of the SEC decision in the *Cady, Roberts* case, discussed at Chapter 20, 20.2 below.

[38] On the Act see n. 13 above. Under the Act the SEC is responsible for implementing a series of regulatory initiatives required (see http://www.sec.gov/spotlight/dodd-frank.shtml), which expanded the SEC mandate including creating five new offices. The SEC 2011 study 'Organizational Study and Reform' (March 2011) provides a detailed account of these and other changes: http://www.sec.gov/news/studies/2011/967study.pdf.

[39] According to a 2011 SEC Press Release (see http://sec.gov/news/press/2011/2011-167.htm) the SEC's new whistleblower programme strengthens the SEC's ability to protect investors in several ways: (1) better tips: the SEC has seen an increase in the quality of tips that it has been receiving from individuals since Congress created the program; (2) timely tips: potential whistleblowers are incentivised to come forward sooner rather than later with 'timely' information not yet known to the SEC; (3) maximises outside resources: with fewer than 4,000 employees to regulate more than 35,000 entities, the SEC cannot be everywhere at all times. With a robust whistleblower programme, the SEC is more likely to find and deter wrongdoing at firms it may not have otherwise uncovered; (4) new protections against retaliation: employees who come forward are provided with new tools to protect themselves against employers who retaliate; (5) bolsters internal compliance: the new rules provide significant incentives for employees to report any wrongdoing to their company's internal compliance department before coming to the SEC. Therefore, companies that would prefer their employees report internally first are incentivised to a have credible, effective compliance programme in place.

[40] The SEC's webpage at www.sec.gov/whistleblower includes information on eligibility requirements, directions on how to submit a tip or complaint, instructions on how to apply for an award, and answers to frequently asked questions.

## 16.4 From the Financial Services Authority to the Prudential Regulation Authority and the Financial Conduct Authority

### A The self-regulation era – the SIB and FSA

Some of the events which led up to the Financial Services Act 1986 and the establishment of the Securities and Investments Board ('SIB') have already been alluded to;[41] the technical aspects have not. Towards the end of the 1970s the DTI asked Professor Jim Gower to look into ways of improving investor protection in the UK.[42] This ultimately led to the publication of his *Review of Investor Protection – A Discussion Document*[43] and, subsequently, a *Review of Investor Protection – Part 1*[44] and *Part 2*.[45] The Government set out its views in the White Paper *Financial Services in the United Kingdom: A New Framework for Investor Protection*,[46] emphasising that improvements in the system should come about primarily through self-regulatory mechanisms. Although it wanted to appear to be firm with the City, the Government had no stomach for the setting up of a tough SEC-style public regulator[47] and the City itself wanted regulation to be left largely in its own hands. The resulting compromise was the Financial Services Act 1986 and various subsequent Orders. In effect, the UK's first general system of investor protection was to be characterised as a feature of the private sector rather than state regulation; investor protection was to remain company law, rather than become securities regulation. In fact, as soon emerged, the self-regulatory aspect of it was probably a good deal less in evidence than the City lobby had expected, as Gower observed in his lecture at the London School of Economics in 1987 when he expressed the view that the Government's description of the system in their White Paper as 'self-regulation within a statutory framework' was more accurately expressed as 'statutory regulation monitored by self-regulatory organisations recognised by, and under the surveillance of, a self-standing Commission'.[48]

In essence it worked as follows: the Act set up the SIB[49] with the role of overseeing the carrying on of investment business in the UK. In order to carry on such business it was usually necessary to get 'authorised', and the main way of doing this was by joining a self-regulating organisation ('SRO'). There were originally nine of these but by the time the regime reached its final phase, as a result of mergers, there remained only three: the

---

[41] E.g. the Barlow Clowes scandal, 16.2 above. Other events include: one of the periodic Lloyd's debacles had helped to undermine confidence in the City during the late 1970s; see further J. Gower '"Big Bang" and City Regulation' (1988) 51 MLR 1. The setting up of the SIB coincided (in 1986) with major changes in Stock Exchange practice which became known as the 'Big Bang'.

[42] See the detailed and racy account of this by B. Rider in B. Rider, C. Abrams and M. Ashe *Guide to Financial Services Regulation* 3rd edn (Bicester: CCH, 1997) pp. 13–22.

[43] London: DTI, 1982.

[44] Cmnd 9125, 1984.

[45] London: DTI, 1985. Part 2 was published after the Government's White Paper referred to in the next note; it reflected differences of opinion between Gower and the DTI.

[46] Cmnd 9432, 1985.

[47] The SEC's unpopularity in the City of London probably owed much to the fierce stance it took on its jurisdictional reach, which often threatened to ensnare UK business activities in the requirements of the US Securities Acts; see e.g. *Manley v Schoenbaum* 395 US 906 (1968). Recent years have seen a moderation of the position.

[48] J. Gower '"Big Bang" and City Regulation' (1988) 51 MLR 1 at p. 11.

[49] In fact in a technical sense the Act did not set this up because it merely gave power to the DTI to transfer powers to a designated agency; when the powers were transferred, the agency was the SIB; see Financial Services Act 1986, s. 114 (1)–(2).

Securities and Futures Authority ('SFA'), the Investment Managers Regulatory Organisation ('IMRO') and the Personal Investment Authority ('PIA'). The SROs were organisations designed to regulate certain sectors of the financial services industry while at the same time ensuring that the business interests of the participants in those industries were properly taken account of in the process of deciding what regulatory burdens to impose. In the early years some firms obtained their authorisation direct from the SIB but as time went by this became increasingly rare and the role of the SIB became more focused on regulating the SROs themselves since they were, what it termed, the 'front-line regulators'.

In the years immediately following the passing of the Act, the SIB concentrated on producing a model rulebook containing detailed prescription as to how various types of investment business should be operated. The SROs, feeling bound by what the SIB had thought was needed, tended to transmute these rules largely unaltered into their own rulebooks. This was widely felt to have produced over-heavy regulation and led to the reforms contained in the Companies Act 1989. These reforms, dubbed the 'New Settlement',[50] brought in some softer regulatory techniques, such as the laying down of broad principles.[51]

By the mid-1990s, it began to be apparent that the writing was on the wall for this system. It does not really seem to be the case that the regulation was ineffective or weak. On the contrary, SRO disciplinary proceedings were clearly capable of imposing high levels of fines on their own members and it will be seen that their widespread practice of both expelling a member (thus shutting down his business) and giving him a hefty money penalty has been discontinued in the new legislation.[52] Nor were the SROs really seen as failing organisations; in many ways they were confident and hard-hitting.[53] A combination of reasons lay behind the decision for change: there were overlaps in the self-regulatory system, so that multi-function financial services institutions had to join more than one SRO; there were doubts about the need for the 'two-tier' system with the SIB supervising the SROs and it began to seem to make more sense to roll the SROs into one regulator; furthermore, the pensions mis-selling scandal had exacerbated tensions between the SIB and the SROs; there were also strong arguments for widening the scope of the powers of the regulatory authority so that it would cover areas of finance and business which were currently covered by a variety of other regulators, such as Lloyd's, the building societies and the Bank of England. Ultimately, although the pressure for change was building before the Labour Government came to power in 1997, there may have been simply a political aspect: that the self-regulatory system should be replaced with a system which more overtly derived its authority from the state.

The transition from the 1986 Act's regime to the new system under the Financial Services and Markets Act 2000 ('FSMA 2000') was a work[54] of thoughtful legal and administrative creativity. The SIB changed its name to the Financial Services Authority ('FSA'), which was the name it wanted to have under the system to be brought in, although in legal terms

---

[50] Note the cultural links being made with Roosevelt's 'New Deal' and the big brother regulator, the SEC.
[51] For an excellent account of this see A. Whittaker 'Legal Technique in City Regulation' (1990) 43 *Current Legal Problems* 35.
[52] They were staffed by professionals with expertise in law and finance.
[53] Under the then FSA chairmanship of Sir Howard Davies.
[54] Although most of the banking regulatory functions of the Bank of England were transferred to it by the Bank of England Act 1998.

it broadly remained the same old SIB.[55] Then the SROs were rolled into the FSA by co-locating their staff and arranging for the staff of the SROs to become employed by the FSA which then leased them back to the SROs to enable the SROs to continue to perform their functions. In substance the organisation began to function as one entity, almost as the future FSA would function when the Financial Services and Markets Bill became law, while legally the old system remained, with the SROs as the front-line regulators carrying out their usual authorisation and disciplinary functions, and the SIB (now the FCA) monitoring their functions, and preparing the policy documents for the new regime. The system risked challenge, perhaps on the basis that in substance the FSA and the SROs were one organisation and that accordingly the FSA was exceeding its powers and illegally purporting to regulate members of SROs. In the event, there seems not to have been great difficulty.

So marked the end of an era. In the 14 years between 1986 and 2000 regulatory policy in the UK had undergone a marked shift. In 1986, all that seemed politically acceptable and therefore possible[56] was a beefed-up version of the self-regulatory approach to investor protection which owed more to company law, with its emphasis on private law and minimal state interference, than to anything else. By 2000 the UK had acquired a statutory commitment to an SEC-style regulator,[57] the state in human form, with responsibilities ranging across almost the entire spectrum of financial activity; and widespread powers of enforcement. US-style[58] securities regulation had reached the UK.

## B Statutory securities regulation: accountability issues

The FSMA 2000 provided that the former FSA was to have the functions conferred on it by the Act.[59] The detail of its statutory functions and enforcement powers fall to be discussed below.[60] At this point it is useful to consider the extent to which the FSA was made accountable, as the problem of controlling the regulator is a fundamental policy consideration in the field of securities regulation.

---

[55] It seems that the Conservative Government of the time was not willing to upset City interests by a wholesale departure from a tradition of self-regulation.
[56] See generally FSMA 2000 and Chapter 18 below.
[57] See generally FSMA 2000 and Chapter 18 below. Since 2006 the SEC and the FSA established a Strategic Dialogue to collaborate on matters affecting the US and UK capital markets. In 2010 the SEC and FSA agreed to expand their supervisory cooperation and review the existing memorandum of understanding between the two regulators.
[58] Although in some respects the remit of the FSA (now the FCA) is even broader than that of the SEC.
[59] Section 1. Its current form is the merged form described above and consists of an organisation of around 3,000 staff (about the same size as the SEC) with a similarly wide range of skills, located mainly on one site in Canary Wharf. For details of the organisation and other matters the reader is referred to the website: http://www.fsa.gov.uk. Interestingly, figures obtained under the UK's Freedom of Information Act and published in February 2008 by UK satirical magazine *Private Eye* revealed that the number of supervisory staff at the FSA fell 14% to 695 from 807, while the percentage decline in enforcement staff numbers was twice as extreme. The FSA employed 175 enforcement staff by the end of 2007, down from 243. The combined number of enforcement and supervisory staff has fallen 17% since 2005. See *FT*, 8 February 2008. Following the financial crisis, under the Supervisory Enhancement Programme, the FSA has significantly increased the number and quality of its supervisory staff and has adopted a more 'intensive and intrusive' approach to supervision. See http://www.fsa.gov.uk/pubs/other/enhancement.pdf. For details of FSA enforcement in 2010, see the figures provided in the briefing paper at http://www.freshfields.com/publications/pdfs/2010/feb10/27415. According to the FSA Business Plan 2010/11 during 2010/2011 the FSA hired 478 full-time staff and a further 246 full-time staff in its supervisory sector. See http://www.fsa.gov.uk/pages/Library/Corporate/Plan/bp2010.shtml.
[60] See under 16.5C below and the Chapter 17.

Schedule 1 sets out the constitution of the FCA, providing checks and balances both internally in terms of procedures and structures and externally in terms of monitoring by outsiders. As regards the internal controls, it is provided that the constitution of the FCA must continue to provide for it to have a chair and a governing body (i.e. a board) and that the board must have a majority of members who are non-executives (i.e. outsiders who are not involved in the day-to-day functioning of the FCA).[61] This last provision is perhaps of considerable theoretical significance, for it requires the FCA board to act in such a way as to be able to carry the support of the informed public. Also to be part of the constitution is a 'non-executive committee', which has the role of monitoring the FCA as to its efficient use of resources, its financial controls and as to the remuneration of the chair and executive members of the governing body.[62] Additionally, the FCA is required to have regard to such generally accepted principles of corporate governance as it is reasonable to regard as applicable to it.[63]

An important external monitoring input comes from the role of the Treasury, which is of course of constitutional significance, since it represents input from a democratically elected government. The Treasury has significant powers over the FCA. It has power to appoint and remove the chair and members of the board.[64] An annual report to the Treasury is required[65] which Treasury ministers will lay before Parliament where it will probably come under the scrutiny of the Treasury Select Committee of the House of Commons. If past practice is anything to go by, the Treasury Select Committee will periodically summon the chair for public questioning. The Treasury can commission a 'value for money' audit of the FCA's operations[66] under which a person independent of the FCA conducts a review of the economy, efficiency and effectiveness with which the FCA has used its resources in discharging its functions. A major inquiry can be ordered by the Treasury where there has been an occurrence of what might be described as a regulatory 'meltdown'; i.e. where something has gone very fundamentally wrong in such a way that it could precipitate systemic failure, and the regulatory system has seriously failed in relation to it. Inquiries may also arise where there has been fraud or failure in relation to a collective investment scheme, failure or misbehaviour of persons which posed a grave risk to the financial system,[67] or failures in relation to listed securities or issuers, and these events might not have occurred or the risk or damage might have been reduced, but for a serious failure in the regulatory system.[68] Thus, overall there are significant opportunities for the representatives of the electorate to exercise influence over the FCA.

In addition, there are other constraints on the FCA. It has been clear for some time that the FCA and its predecessor, the SIB,[69] are subject to judicial review.[70] However, since

---

[61] Financial Services and Markets Act 2000, Sch. 1, paras 2 and 3.
[62] *Ibid.* Sch. 1, paras 3 (1) (b), 4.
[63] *Ibid.* s. 7.
[64] *Ibid.* Sch. 1, para. 2 (3).
[65] *Ibid.* Sch. 1, para. 10
[66] *Ibid.* s. 12.
[67] For example, the collapse of Barings Bank.
[68] Financial Services and Markets Act 2000, ss. 14–18.
[69] And indeed the SROs; IMRO was held to be subject to judicial review in *Governor and Company of the Bank of Scotland, Petitioners* [1989] BCLC 700.
[70] See e.g. *R* v *Securities and Investments Board, ex parte IFAA* [1995] 2 BCLC 76; *R (British Bankers Association)* v *Financial Services Authority* [2011] EWHC 999 (Admin) (judicial review dismissed in May 2011).

judicial review is a remedy of last resort, in that statutory remedies have to be used up first, then, in view of the existence of mechanisms such as the complaints procedure discussed above, it is likely that resort to judicial review will be rare.[71] More likely to make appearances in this field is the European Convention on Human Rights, which was incorporated into UK law by the Human Rights Act 1998 in October 2000. The likely impact of this is discussed in Chapter 17, in the context of FCA enforcement powers, where of course, there is potential for the oppressive use of powers.

It is clear that the FCA is subject to considerable constraints and that care has been taken to build some powerful checks and balances into the structure.[72]

## C The Prudential Regulation Authority and the Financial Conduct Authority

### 1 *From FSA to PRA and FCA*

In April 2013, the FSA was replaced by two new regulatory bodies. The first is the Prudential Regulation Authority ('PRA'), and the second is the Financial Conduct Authority ('FCA').[73] The reforms were thought necessary because, according to the Financial Secretary to the Treasury: 'Britain's system of financial regulation failed to identify the risks posed by a rapid and unsustainable rise in debt, and when the crunch came no one knew who was in charge. Reform was essential to avoid a repeat of the financial crisis.'[74]

Prior to the unveiling of the FCA and the PRA, the Government had more complex intentions. Intitially, the plan was to create four new regulatory bodies:

(1) An independent Financial Policy Committee ('FPC') at the Bank of England, to look across the economy at the macro issues that may threaten economic and financial stability and take effective action in response.
(2) A new regulator, the Prudential Regulatory Authority ('PRA'), to operate as a subsidiary of the Bank of England, and carry out the prudential regulation of financial firms, including banks, investment banks, building societies and insurance companies.
(3) A new Consumer Protection and Markets Authority ('CPMA') to protect consumers, oversee conduct of business, market regulation, the Financial Ombudsman Service and the Financial Services Compensation Scheme.
(4) A Serious Crime Authority ('SCA') to take over the roles of various government departments and agencies, including the Serious Fraud Office ('SFO').

---

[71] Other rare possibilities include actions for misfeasance in public office; see generally *Three Rivers District Council* v *Bank of England (No. 3)* [2003] 2 AC 1, HL.
[72] For a thoughtful analysis of striking the balance, see E. Lomnicka 'Making the Financial Services Authority Accountable' [2000] JBL 65.
[73] Ferran suggests that there was not a clear-cut case for outright abolition of the FSA. Fixing it was a solid option in principle and it was politics that dictated a different result. Since all institutional models for financial market supervision have pros and cons, Ferran argues that flaws must be expected in the objectives-oriented institutional model that the UK has now chosen to adopt in place of the integrated approach. See E. Ferran 'The Break-Up of the Financial Services Authority' University of Cambridge Faculty of Law Research Paper Series No. 10/04 (11 October 2010) at https://papers.ssrn.com/sol3/papers.cfm?abstract_id=1690523.
[74] M. Hoban 'The Right Path for British Financial Regulation', *The Financial Times*, 17 November 2010.

This early pronouncement was followed by two detailed consultations by the Treasury.[75] Then, on 16 June 2011, the Treasury published a White Paper, *A New Approach to Financial Regulation: The Blueprint for Reform.*[76] It made it clear that the Government did not intend to repeal and replace the FSMA 2000 but rather to amend it.[77] Consequently, the Financial Services Act 2012 ('FSA 2012') came into force on 19 December 2012.

## 2 *Roles and powers of the new regulators*

### Prudential Regulation Authority

The PRA is responsible for promoting the stable and prudent operation of the financial system through the regulation of all deposit-taking institutions (banks, building societies and credit unions), insurers and the major investment firms (together, PRA-authorised persons). The PRA's general objective is to promote the safety and soundness of PRA-authorised persons. To advance that objective, the PRA will seek to ensure that the business of PRA-authorised persons is carried on in a way which avoids any adverse effect on the stability of the UK financial system. It will also seek to minimise the adverse effect that the failure of a PRA-authorised person could be expected to have on the stability of the UK financial system. Additionally, commensurate with its responsibility for regulating insurers, the PRA has an insurance objective: to contribute to the securing of an appropriate degree of protection for those who are or may become policyholders.

In discharging its general functions, the PRA is to have regard to the regulatory principles applicable to both the PRA and the FCA and also to the need to minimise any adverse effect on competition in the relevant markets. The FSMA 2012 also made provision for the setting of further objectives.

### The Financial Conduct Authority

The FCA is responsible for regulation of conduct in retail, as well as wholesale, financial markets and the infrastructure that supports those markets. The FCA also has responsibility for the prudential regulation of firms that do not fall under the PRA's scope. The FCA's strategic objective is to ensure that the relevant markets function well. Its operational objectives are: to secure an appropriate degree of protection for consumers; to protect and enhance the integrity of the UK financial system; and to promote effective competition in the interests of consumers in the markets for regulated financial services

---

[75] The first, '*A New Approach to Financial Regulation: Judgement, Focus and Stability*'" (26 July 2010), (see http://www.hm-treasury.gov.uk/d/consult_financial_regulation_condoc.pdf) which encapsulated the above proposals and also made proposals regarding the future of the UKLA (which were unpopular and thus dropped). On 17 February 2011 the Government launched the second consultation, "*A New Approach to Financial Regulation: Building a Stronger System*', (see http://www.hm-treasury.gov.uk/d/consult_newfinancial_regulation170211.pdf) which provided further detail on its proposals for reforming the framework of financial regulation in the UK.

[76] See https://www.gov.uk/government/uploads/system/uploads/attachment_data/file/81403/consult_finreg__new_approach_blueprint.pdf.

[77] This approach was apparently widely supported by respondents to the above consultations and should, in theory at least, minimise the extent to which regulated firms and other users of FSMA 2000 have to deal with legislative change.

or services provided by a recognised investment exchange in carrying on exempt regulated activities. The FCA is tasked with maintaining arrangements for supervising authorised persons, monitoring compliance and taking enforcement action. For all this the FCA has wide-ranging rule-making powers, which in some cases go beyond the powers enjoyed by the FSA.[78]

## Coordination and cooperation

The PRA and the FCA have a duty to coordinate the exercise of their functions. In certain circumstances the PRA may, if it considers it necessary, direct the FCA to refrain from exercising its regulatory or insolvency powers in relation to PRA-authorised persons if the PRA is of the opinion that the exercise of the powers in the manner proposed may threaten the stability of the UK financial system or result in the failure of a PRA-authorised person in a way that would adversely affect the UK financial system.

Both the FCA and the PRA must take appropriate steps to cooperate with the Bank of England in connection with, among other things, the Bank's pursuit of its financial stability objective.

## The Financial Policy Committee

The FPC is a sub-committee of the Court of Directors of the Bank of England, consisting of the Governor of the Bank, the Deputy Governor of the Bank, the Chief Executive of the FCA, a member appointed by the Governor of the Bank after consultation with the Chancellor of the Exchequer, four members appointed by the Chancellor of the Exchequer and a representative of the Treasury.

The FPC is primarily responsible for contributing to the achievement by the Bank of its financial stability objective (the FPC also has a role in supporting the economic policy of the Government, including its objectives for growth and employment). To this end, the FPC will identify, monitor and take action to remove or reduce systemic risks with a view to protecting and enhancing the resilience of the UK financial system.[79]

The FPC may give directions to the FCA or the PRA requiring them to exercise their functions so as to ensure the implementation of a macro-prudential measure (prescribed by the Treasury by order) described in the direction. In addition, the FPC may make recommendations within the Bank, including as to the provision by the Bank of financial assistance to financial institutions and the exercise by the Bank of its functions in relation to payment systems, settlement systems and clearing houses.

---

[78] For example, the FCA has the power to make product intervention rules, prohibiting authorised persons from entering into specified agreements if the FCA considers it to be necessary or expedient for the purposes of advancing the consumer protection objective or the competition objective (the Treasury may by order extend this to include also the integrity objective). Contravention of a product intervention rule could lead to the relevant agreement or obligation being unenforceable against any person or specified person, and to the recovery paid or property transferred and to the payment of compensation.

[79] Those risks include systemic risks attributable to structural features of financial markets, such as connections between financial institutions, systemic risks attributable to the distribution of risk within the financial sector, and unsustainable levels of leverage, debt or credit growth.

Prior to the FCA coming into effect, hopes were high regarding what the new regulatory environment would bring. In introducing a document outlining the plans of the FCA, Hector Sants, then the FSA Chief Executive, stated that:[80]

> Trust in the financial services sector is at an all-time low and the new regulatory arrangements provide the opportunity to restore confidence in an industry which has generated in excess of £15bn detriment over the last two decades.
>
> For the FCA to be successful it must have the support of society and Parliament, and its objectives and approach must be clearly understood by all.
>
> [One of the] the key questions to be resolved, [. . .] includes finding the right balance between the benefits of early intervention and the consequent risks of reducing choice and raising costs, and also clarity regarding the balance of responsibilities between consumers and industry.
>
> The FCA's proposed approach moves the calibration of these questions in favour of more intervention but the question which needs to be answered is whether society is happy to accept the resultant costs and potential reduction in individual freedom.

Margaret Cole, interim Managing Director of the Conduct Business Unit, added that:[81]

> I am confident that, if implemented, this approach will deliver significantly higher levels of protection than consumers have enjoyed over the last 20 years.

## 16.5 Legal theory in securities regulation

### A Aims of securities regulation

In considering what are the aims of securities regulation we find ourselves confronted with a series of rather basic underlying questions. Why do we have securities regulation at all? Why do we have markets?[82] Some rudimentary answers are necessary before a discussion of the aims of securities regulation can be attempted.

Markets exist because of the general increase in social welfare which results from specialisation facilitated by the exchange process. Our ancient ancestors, prior to the existence of markets of any kind, had, each one, to be self-sufficient; then the practice grew up of swapping goods and resources; exchange was born, and a hunter who has killed two rabbits could swop one of them for some vegetables to make himself a more nourishing stew than would otherwise be the case; presumably also the recipient of the rabbit felt enriched by his market exchange. In the modern world, all this is taken for granted and we all are daily surrounded by goods and services which are the products of specialisation and then exchange on countless markets.

Markets channel scarce resources into various sectors of the economy. If the man who produces the vegetables finds that no one wants them, he may well decide to channel his scarce resource (of labour) into pursuing the rabbits; absent demand for a product and the supplier will find that his choice of specialisation may need to be reassessed. Modern day capital markets perform this function of channelling scarce resources (i.e. capital) into the

---

[80] See FSA/PN/059/2011 of 27 June 2011 entitled 'FSA Launches FCA Approach Document', available at http://www.fsa.gov.uk/pubs/events/fca_approach.pdf.

[81] *Ibid.*

[82] For discussion of the related question of why we have companies, see Chapter 1.

various sectors of the economy. This is particularly obvious as regards markets for new issues of shares (the primary markets). An efficient-looking company in a rising sector of the economy will be able to raise new capital easily, whereas one operating in a dying sector will not. The subsequent trading of those shares on the market supports the primary market by making the initial share investment highly liquid and therefore more attractive.[83]

This process of allocation of scarce resources on the markets is a fundamental feature of capitalist systems. Without it, it becomes necessary to make some sort of administrative allocation of labour and raw materials to manufacturing organisations. However, in order for the capitalist system to function reasonably well, it is necessary for the allocation to be accurate. If the allocative process is distorted by, for instance, the dissemination of false information, then the allocative function of the market will become inefficient. Thus 'allocative efficiency' is an important goal of capital markets.

It is now possible to consider the goals of securities regulation. The SEC's position in the US is that the primary purpose of securities laws is the protection of investors, and that investors can best be protected by making certain that they all trade on the basis of equal[84] information; this is often referred to as 'market egalitarianism'. This leads to the two main principles which govern the SEC's position:[85]

(1) There is a need for mandatory disclosure of information; in other words, information that is deemed useful in evaluating securities must be disclosed publicly by issuers of shares so that it will be equally available to all investors.[86]

(2) There is a need for regulation of insider dealing so that information not equally available to all investors through this egalitarian disclosure mechanism cannot be used unfairly to earn excessive profits.[87]

The SEC's approach to securities regulation came to be challenged by the development of a theory known as the efficient capital markets hypothesis ('ECMH'). The broad thrust of the theory is this:[88] that capital markets are efficient, which means that security prices fully reflect all available information and adjust to new information almost instantaneously; and that prices move randomly, so that traders will not be able to spot patterns so as to enable them to beat the market.[89] Arguments were made along the lines that, since investors cannot be cheated in an efficient market, the SEC should encourage the use of all sources of

---

[83] And obviously if the securities are getting a rough time on the secondary market this diminishes the ability of the company to raise more capital (attract more scarce resources) by a fresh issue of securities.

[84] Roughly equal.

[85] For a recent reassessment of these in light of the financial crisis see L.A. Aguilar 'Exemplifying Fundamentals–Back to Basics in Securities Regulation' (12 April 2011) at https://corpgov.law.harvard.edu/2011/04/.

[86] In pinning its colours to the mast of adequate disclosure or, as it has been called, 'truth in securities' law, the SEC turned away from the 'merit' approach to securities regulation operated by some state blue sky law systems under which there would be an evaluation of the fairness of the offer, and instead put its faith in the disclosure mechanisms themselves as being sufficient to create an adequate level of investor protection. Thus the primacy of freedom of contract is preserved, so that the investor is free to make a bad bargain, but the disclosure should ensure that the bargaining game is played 'on a level playing field'.

[87] See generally C. Saari 'The Efficient Capital Markets Hypothesis, Economic Theory and the Regulation of the Securities Industry' (1977) 29 Stan LR 1031 at pp. 1032–1033.

[88] See generally the excellent account in G. Arnold *Corporate Financial Management* (London: Financial Times Management, 1998) pp. 595–633.

[89] *Ibid.* at 596.

information rather than trying to ensure that information passes through its narrow disclosure mechanisms before reaching the public.[90] In due course counter-arguments supportive of the SEC's position were developed[91] and the SEC's policy remains unchanged.[92]

For a clear and comprehensive statement of the objectives of securities regulation, reference may be made to the statement contained in the influential International Organization of Securities Commissions ('IOSCO')[93] document *Objectives and Principles of Securities Regulation*.[94] The document argues that there are three objectives upon which 38 securities regulations are based and that, although there are differences in market structures, they form a foundation for an effective system of securities regulation, and these are protecting investors, ensuring the markets are fair, efficient and transparent, and reducing systemic risk.[95]

It is clear that none of this is particularly new and they can all, one way or another, be traced to the New Deal legislation (passed in an effort to stabilise the economy following the US stock market crash of 1929) and its subsequent interpretation by the SEC. On the other hand, it is useful to find a statement of these fundamental ideas at the highest level of international cooperation.

## B Techniques of securities regulation

There are a variety of techniques utilised in securities regulatory systems with varying success. The main techniques have already been discussed above but will also be described individually below. Readers will find many examples of these techniques in operation throughout Part V of this text. Disclosure is obviously the mainstay of the US system and it will be seen[96] that this is true of the UK also. Disclosure can operate in a number of ways[97] but in securities

---

[90] See e.g. C. Saari 'The Efficient Capital Markets Hypothesis, Economic Theory and the Regulation of the Securities Industry' 29 Stan LR 1031 (1977).

[91] See e.g. J. Coffee 'Market Failure and the Economic Case for a Mandatory Disclosure System' 70 Vir LR 717 (1984); see also V. Brudney and W. Bratton *Corporate Finance* 4th edn (Westbury, NY: Foundation Press, 1993) pp. 128–147.

[92] Although, challenges continue to appear; see e.g. R. Romano 'Empowering Investors: A Market Approach to Securities Regulation' in K.J. Hopt, H. Kanda, M.J. Roe, E. Wymeersch and S. Prigge (eds) *Comparative Corporate Governance – The State of the Art and Emerging Research* (Oxford: OUP, 1998) p. 143, advocating a system under which securities issuers could choose a federal or state regime to govern their securities, thus creating competition between regimes and so ensuring a greater alignment of securities laws with investor interests. See also, F. Easterbrook and D. Fischel 'Mandatory Disclosure and the Protection of Investors' (1984) 70 *Virginia Law Review* 669; M. Fox 'Retaining Mandatory Disclosure: Why Issuer Choice is not Investor Empowerment' (1999) 85 *Virginia Law Review* 1335; A. Kraakman 'Disclosure and Corporate Governance: An Overview Essay' in Ferrarini *et al. Reforming Company and Takeover Law in Europe* (OUP: 2004).

[93] The nature and functions of IOSCO are discussed below in 16.5D.

[94] June 2010. Available on the IOSCO website at http://www.iosco.org. An excellent account can also be found at R. Kraakman, P.L. Davies *et al. The Anatomy of Corporate Law: A Comparative and Functional Approach* 2nd edn (Oxford: OUP, 2009) Chapter 8.

[95] IOSCO *Objectives and Principles of Securities Regulation*, p. 1.

[96] In Chapter 18.

[97] These are: (1) the 'enforcement effect', where disclosure is being used as an aid to the enforcement of a law which contains a substantive prohibition of conduct and the disclosure requirement helps to draw attention to the violation; (2) the 'public disapproval' effect, where disclosure merely draws attention to what is happening and then public reaction makes some kind of adverse input on the perpetrator; (3) the 'informative effect' where disclosure informs people and enables them to act so as to protect their own interests; see the note entitled 'Disclosure as a Legislative Device' (1963) 76 Harv LR 1273. See also R. Kraakman, P.L. Davies *et al. The Anatomy of Corporate Law: A Comparative and Functional Approach* 2nd edn (Oxford: OUP, 2009) Chapter 8, under 8.2.

regulation its main *modus operandi* is informative, being designed to make sufficient information available to the investor to empower him when making his investment decisions.

Regulation and registration of market participants is another mainstay regulatory technique which has ancient origins.[98] It can be found almost everywhere from the US
Exchange Act's requirement for the registration of brokers or dealers[99] to the basic requirement for authorisation of persons carrying on regulated activities contained in the FSMA
2000. This kind of registration will usually encompass a screening process as to whether
the person is fit and proper and the application of general principles thereafter.

Conduct of business rules are rules which regulate both in general and in detail how
business is to be conducted by the market participants. They may involve general principles of conduct such as honesty and fair dealing and detailed principles of conduct such as
the duty to give appropriate advice to a client who is considering buying a product.

Prudential regulation and supervision are techniques used to ensure that the structure
and financial standing of financial services firms is suitable to the activities they are carrying on. It will often require the firm to have sufficient capital to withstand the knocks that
are likely to come to it in the business in which it is engaged. Prudential regulation is one
of the major ways of reducing systemic risk.

Rescue systems are a technique used to deal with systemic risk. They occur mainly in
banking regulation[100] and involve national or international structures which are able to
support a bank which has got into difficulties before that bank collapses and possibly
causes a wave of failures throughout the system.

Investor compensation schemes are an important method of investor protection used to
meet the situation when all the other regulatory techniques have failed and the firm which
owes its clients money has become insolvent. Compensation schemes are a kind of insurance mechanism under which either the state or other firms in the industry are required to
contribute towards paying compensation to the investors who have lost out.

Rules against insider dealing and other forms of market abuse are important methods of
ensuring that markets are fair and efficient in the sense that they are able to perform their
function of allocation of scarce resources.

Separation of function is used in different situations to create safeguards or prevent
abuses which would otherwise be likely to arise. The paradigm example of this was the
US Glass–Steagall Act, which required the separation of deposit taking from investment
banking.[101]

Suppression of the activity is a securities regulation technique of last resort. Mention
has already been made of the UK's Bubble Act in this regard[102] although this is an extreme
example. A softer option, containing prohibitions on an activity for certain periods of time,
might be seen in the Stock Exchange's Model Code for Transactions in Securities by
Directors etc., which puts a ban on share dealings by directors for a period, in certain
circumstances.[103]

---

[98] See 16.2 above.
[99] Securities Exchange Act 1934, s. 15 (1) (a).
[100] Which is largely outside the scope of this text.
[101] See n. 13 above.
[102] See 16.3 above.
[103] See generally, FSA Listing Rules, Chapter 16, Appendix.

## C The statutory objectives of the Financial Services and Markets Act 2000, the Financial Services Act 2012 and the Bank of England and Financial Services Act 2016

It is interesting to consider the regulatory objectives which are set out in the FSMA 2000, the Financial Services Act 2012 ('FSA 2012') and the most recent Bank of England and Financial Services Act 2016. These represent a modern and sophisticated statement of the objectives of securities regulation. Of particular interest is the way in which they capture the dilemmas which face the regulatory authority; for instance, its need to balance investor protection against the need not to stifle the financial services industry with unnecessary burdens.

### 1 FSMA 2000

With this in mind, the strategic objective of the FCA is to ensure the relevant markets are functioning well.[104] In working towards its strategic objective, the FCA must be advancing one or more of its operational objectives which are:

(1) Consumer protection. Whilst consumer protection remains key to the remit of the FCA, the scope of consumer protection has been expanded (see s. 1 C (2)a–h FSMA 2000).
(2) Protection of the integrity of the UK financial system. Here there has been a conflation of the FSMA 2000 requirements to reduce financial crime and ensure financial stability.[105] The integrity requirement not only requires the FCA to ensure the soundness, stability and resilience of the financial systems, it must also ensure the financial systems are not being used in connection with financial crime.[106] In addition, the FCA must ensure the financial system:[107]
   - is not being affected by behaviour that amounts to market abuse;
   - is operating in an orderly manner; and
   - has a transparent price formation process.
(3) Promotion of effective competition (see s. 1 E (2)a–e FSMA 2000).

These provisions represent a moderate departure from the original drafting of the FSMA 2000, when the regulatory objectives were market confidence, the promotion of public understanding, the protection of consumers, the reduction of financial crime and financial stability.

The statutory provision as drafted makes the point that the public are expected to become aware of the risks so that they can take responsibility for the bargain which they are making. Securities regulation systems are perhaps often prone to creating the impression that the investor should be immersed in a cocoon of rules designed to protect him from invariably unscrupulous suppliers of financial products. There is, however, a balance

---

[104] Section 1 B (2) of the FSMA 2000 as amended by the FSA 2012.
[105] Section 2 (2) (d) (e) of the FSMA 2000 as amended by the FSA 2012.
[106] Section 1 D (2) (a) (b) of the FSMA 2000 as amended by the FSA 2012.
[107] Section 1 D (2) (e) of the FSMA 2000 as amended by the FSA 2012.

to be struck and it is clear that the underlying principle of sanctity of bargain has not changed under the new legislation.

The FSMA 2000 also lays down the FCA's general functions. Not surprisingly, in discharging its general functions it has to try to meet its operational objectives.[108] The general functions are delineated as:[109]

(a) its function of making rules (considered as a whole);
(b) its function of preparing and issuing codes under this Act (considered as a whole);
(c) its functions in relation to the giving of general guidance (considered as a whole); and
(d) its function of determining the general policy and principles by reference to which it performs particular functions.

The FSMA 2000 t seeks to build into the FCA's *modus operandi* a wide range of policies. It is provided that:

In discharging its general functions the Authority must have regard to:[110]

(a) the regulatory principles in section 3B FSMA 2000 which include (but are not limited to):
    (a) the need to use resources efficiently;
    (b) the importance of acting to minimise the possibility that businesses are carried on by authorised persons for a purpose connected with financial crime;
    (c) the principle that a burden should be proportionate to its benefits;
    (d) the sustainability of growth of the UK economy;
    (e) the principle that consumers should take responsibility for their decisions.

The provision that the FCA must 'have regard' to these matters shows that the balance and mix of these policies is in the hands of the regulator. This is clearly an important list of considerations; in particular the principle of proportionality in relation to benefits and burdens of regulation (in para. (c)) is part of several measures designed to ensure that the regulatory environment is not unnecessarily heavy.[111]

## 2 The FSA 2012 and the Banking Reform Act 2013

These are the two major pieces of legislation that the Coalition Government took through Parliament to fundamentally reform the financial sector. With the previous 'tripartite system' developed by Prime Minister Gordon Brown tested and ultimately found to be lacking in effectiveness and governance, the FSA 2012 dismantled the failed system, putting the Bank of England at the centre of a new framework of financial regulation. Later on, the Banking Reform Act 2013 adopted the recommendations of the Independent Commission on Banking and the Parliamentary Commission on Banking Standards, to put in place strict new rules on bank ring-fencing and make sweeping changes to enhance individual accountability and raise standards in banking.

---

[108] Thus it is provided that 'the Authority must, so far as is reasonably possible, act in a way (a) which is compatible with the regulatory objectives; and (b) which the Authority considers the most appropriate for the purpose of meeting those objectives': FSMA 2000, s. 2.
[109] Section 1 B (6) of the FSMA 2000 as amended by the FSA 2012.
[110] Section 1 B (6) of the FSMA 2000 as amended by the FSA 2012.
[111] See also, e.g., s. 155 (2) (a) of the FSMA 2000, which requires a cost benefit analysis of proposed new rules.

## 3 *The Bank of England and Financial Services Act 2016*

### Background

Passed by Parliament on 4 May 2016, the Bank of England and Financial Services Act 2016 ('the Act') was the third major piece of legislation to complete the reform of the financial sector.[112] The new Conservative Government completed the overhaul of the regulatory system and put the Bank of England ('the Bank') back at the heart of financial stability. The Act contains a range of legislative provisions for the UK regulatory framework. At its heart are measures to provide the Bank with the authority and tools to oversee and ensure financial stability in the UK and implement Governor Mark Carney's 'One Bank' reforms to broaden its range of responsibilities.[113]

### Measures

One of the key features of the Act is its ending of the subsidiary of the PRA by bringing micro-prudential regulation of financial institutions into the scope of the Bank of England through the establishment of a new Prudential Regulation Committee ('PRC').

The Act strengthens the governance and accountability of the Bank, by allowing the National Audit Office to undertake value for money reviews of the Bank for the first time. As well as bringing prudential policy into the Bank's expanded remit, the Act provides a number of measures which cement the Bank's position at the centre of the UK's financial regulatory regime. The changes to the statutory basis of the Financial Policy Committee ('FCP') (first established in 2011) will mean that the setting of the Bank's financial stability strategy is transferred from the Court of Directors to the Bank itself. This puts the FPC in line with the Bank's Monetary Policy Committee and the new PRC and is aimed at helping to harmonise the conflicts around monetary policy and financial stability.

The Act extends the Senior Managers and Certification Regime to all financial services firms, and implements a fairer system by introducing a 'duty of responsibility' for senior managers in all authorised firms, superseding the 'reverse burden of proof' that would have applied in the banking sector. This ensures that senior managers across the financial services industry can be held to account for failings that occur on their watch. It also gives the Treasury a new power to provide financial assistance to illegal money lending teams tasked with tackling loan sharks and supports the Government's aims to have a robust and proportionate anti-money laundering and counter-terrorist financing regime, with resources focused on higher-risk areas and individuals in line with accepted practice and makes technical changes to the Scottish and Northern Irish Banknote issuance regime to facilitate group restructuring.

The Act takes further steps to protect taxpayers from firm failure, by updating resolution planning and crisis management of institutions in distress arrangements between the Bank and Treasury.

---

[112] http://www.legislation.gov.uk/ukpga/2016/14/pdfs/ukpga_20160014_en.pdf.

[113] The 'One Mission, One Bank' strategy was launched in March 2014 by the Bank of England's Governor Carney to bring all parts of the Bank's responsibilities under one shared vision and culture. See further https://www.bankofengland.co.uk/speech/2015/one-bank-research-agenda-launch-conference. In June 2017 the strategy was hailed for being 'well thought through' by the National Audit Office, which, however, noted that reforms to the Bank's IT systems had suffered delays and more was needed to meet its targets on diversity.

The Act also makes further important reforms to help consumers by extending the scope of the Pension Wise service;[114] giving the Treasury new powers to help tackle illegal money lending; and taking further steps to promote diversity and competition in the banking sector, by ensuring that regulators take into account different business models as part of their competition objectives. This ensures that consumers with a higher value annuity receive appropriate financial advice before making the decision to sell their annuity income stream.

### Conclusion

Under the new system, the Bank is a more powerful regulator than ever before. It follows that questions about its accountability and governance are likely to be an important part of public debate going forward.

## D IOSCO and global convergence

Recent years have seen the increasing internationalisation[115] of securities markets, not just in the sense of markets for dealings in shares, but generally as regards the marketing of investment products. These kinds of developments pose challenges for securities regulators, in terms of detection of fraud or improper practices, and as a result of the existence of weak national regimes of securities regulation which can provide a haven for unscrupulous activity.[116] Securities commissions have sought various ways of meeting these challenges.[117]

Probably of paramount importance here is the existence of the IOSCO, currently based in Madrid. The objectives of the securities commissions which are members of the IOSCO are to cooperate in the development, implementation, promotion and enforcement of internationally recognised standards of regulation, to enhance investor protection and confidence in the securities markets, and to exchange information in order to help with the strengthening and development of markets.[118] As part of this, the IOSCO published a report offering suggestions on how regulators could enhance cross-border cooperation with a view to better supervision of regulated entities.[119] Additionally, the Technical Committee of the IOSCO published a final report containing principles designed to provide guidance to securities regulators who are developing or reviewing their regulatory disclosure regimes for public offerings and listings of asset-backed securities ('ABS').[120]

---

[114] Pensioners who, from April 2017, are able to sell their annuity income can access free, impartial guidance.

[115] Internationalisation of securities markets has been enhanced by the recent financial crisis. See D.C. Langevoort 'Global Securities Regulation after the Financial Crisis' (2010) *Journal of International Economic Law* 799.

[116] Some types of criminal activity which sometimes have a bearing on securities and corporate frauds will fall to be dealt with by ICPO-Interpol or by Europol.

[117] For a full account, see H. Baum 'Globalizing Capital Markets and Possible Regulatory Responses' in J. Basedow and T. Kono (eds) *Legal Aspects of Globalization: Conflict of Laws, Internet Capital Markets and Insolvency in a Global Economy* (The Hague: Kluwer, 2000) p. 77.

[118] See the IOSCO website, http://www.iosco.org.

[119] The final report from May 2010 entitled 'Principles Regarding Cross-Border Supervisory Cooperation Final Report' is available online at: http://www.iosco.org/library/pubdocs/pdf/IOSCOPD322.pdf.

[120] The report from April 2010 *Disclosure Principles for Public Offerings and Listings of Asset Backed Securities (ABS Disclosure Principles)* is available online at: http://www.iosco.org/library/pubdocs/pdf/IOSCOPD318.pdf.

It should be noted that the IOSCO is not a securities regulator as it has no power over the nationals of any state. On the other hand, its role in providing a forum for discussion of problems, and formulating principles[121] for the guidance of the world's regulators is an important one. In the long run, it seems possible that through its influence, the world's securities regulation regimes will increasingly take on similarities.[122]

In 1985 the SEC and the UK's SIB signed what was probably the first major memorandum of understanding ('MOU') between securities regulators.[123] MOUs are declarations of intent by which, in a non-legal way, regulators agree to cooperate with each other.[124] They involve an exchange of information about the regulators and the systems in operation in their respective countries and agreements for the exchange of information in certain circumstances. There are several hundred MOUs[125] in existence and they perform an important role in combatting the difficulties presented by internationalisation.[126]

## E Financial market integration in the EU

### 1 The internal market in financial services

Within the EU, securities regulation has become inseparably bound up with the creation of the European Single Market.[127] The basic mechanisms for many areas of creation of the internal market were the Treaty of Rome provisions coupled with the case law of the European Court of Justice ('ECJ'). In the field of financial services this would have been theoretically possible by use of the relevant Treaty provisions.[128] Article 43[129] gives a right of establishment.[130]

---

[121] Its major publication, *Objectives and Principles of Securities Regulation*, sets out 30 principles of securities regulation, which are based upon three objectives of securities regulation. These are: the protection of investors; ensuring that markets are fair, efficient and transparent; and the reduction of systemic risk. It is amended periodically. It was last revised in 2010 to include eight new principles. See http://www.aciforex.org/docs/market-topics/20100611_IOSCO.pdf. As of 2018 there were 117 signatories to the MMOU (mulitinational memorandum of understanding) which represents a common understanding regarding consultation, cooperation and exchange information for the purpose of regulatory enforcement.. See http://www.iosco.org/news/pdf/IOSCONEWS204.pdf; https://www.iosco.org/library/pubdocs/pdf/IOSCOPD323.pdf. See also the IMF Country Report on the UK (July 2011) which provides a useful overview of the implementation of IOSCO principles in the UK securities market at: http://www.imf.org/external/pubs/ft/scr/2011/cr11232.pdf.

[122] For an interesting exploration of the idea of a World Financial Authority, see J. Eatwell and L. Taylor 'New Issues in International Financial Regulation' in E. Ferran and C. Goodhart (eds) *Regulating Financial Services and Markets in the 21st Century* (Oxford: Hart Publishing, 2001) p. 35.

[123] For a description of the FCA's relations with the international regulatory community see https://www.fca.org.uk/about/international-standards-regulations.

[124] S. Bergstrasser 'Cooperation between Supervisors' in G. Ferrarini (ed.) *European Securities Markets: The Investment Services Directive and Beyond* (London: Kluwer, 1998) p. 373.

[125] *Ibid.* p. 376, suggesting 200.

[126] IOSCO has recently been developing a Multilateral MOU for Securities Regulators; see https://www.iosco.org/about/?subsection=mmou.

[127] See generally P. Clarotti 'The Completion of the Internal Financial Market: Current Position and Outlook' in M. Andenas and S. Kenyon-Slade (eds) *EC Financial Market Regulation and Company Law* (London: Sweet & Maxwell, 1993) p. 1; L. Garzaniti and D. Pope 'Single Market-Making: EC Regulation of Securities Markets' (1993) 14 Co Law 43; E. Lomnicka 'The Single European Passport in Financial Services' in B. Rider and M. Andenas (eds) *Developments in European Company Law* (Deventer: Kluwer, 1996) p. 181.

[128] See Lomnicka, ibid at p. 182 and references cited there.

[129] Its pre-Amsterdam Treaty numbering was art. 52.

[130] '. . . restrictions on the freedom of establishment of nationals of a member state in the territory of another member state shall be abolished by progressive stages . . . Such progressive abolition shall also apply to restrictions on the setting up of agencies, branches or subsidiaries by nationals of any member state established in the territory of any member state.'

Article 49[131] gives a freedom to provide services on a cross-border basis.[132] The case law of the ECJ has established that articles 43 and 49 are directly applicable[133] and so, for instance, in the financial services field could be used to bring about recognition of the rights of establishment of a financial services firm in another member state and the right to offer cross-border financial services.[134] However, in the field of financial services law, it was felt that what was needed was something more detailed than the Treaty provisions.[135] The approach which was finally adopted was set out in the European Commission's White Paper *Completing the Internal Market*[136] involving the use of Directives which required minimal coordination of rules.[137] The key concept employed was the European 'passport', which would give EC-wide recognition to the authorisation by each member state of its own firms. To illustrate this it is useful to consider the 1993 Investment Services Directive ('ISD'),[138] which contains the fundamental techniques, many of which survive into the 2004 Directive which has replaced it.

[131] Article 59, pre-Amsterdam.

[132] '[R]estrictions on freedom to provide services within the Community shall be progressively abolished [. . .] in respect of nationals of member states who are established in a State of the Community other than that of the person for whom the services are intended.'

[133] See, on articles 43 and 49 respectively, Case 2/74 *Reyners* v *Belgian State* [1974] ECR 631; Case 33/74 *Van Binsbergen* v *Bedrijfsvereniging Metaalnijverheid* [1974] 1 ECR 1229.

[134] For use in the financial services field, see Case C-101/94 *EC Commission* v *Italy (Re Restrictions on Foreign Securities Dealers)* [1996] 3 CMLR 754.

[135] See Lomnicka, n. 127 above, at p. 182.

[136] COM (85) 310.

[137] The main Capital Markets Directives, both prior and subsequent to the Commission's 1985 White Paper, are listed below. Many have been amended and the current amended versions can be found on the European Union's website, http://europa.eu/. Most of these Directives are discussed in this and in Chapters 17–21 of this text. Directive 79/279/EEC coordinating the conditions for the admission of securities to official stock exchange listing (the 'Admissions Directive'); Directive 1980/390/EEC coordinating the requirements for the drawing up, scrutiny and distribution of the listing particulars to be published for the admission of securities to official stock exchange listing (the 'Listing Particulars Directive'); Directive 82/121/EEC on information to be published on a regular basis by companies the shares of which have been admitted to official stock exchange listing (the 'Interim Reports Directive'); Directive 85/345/EEC (the 'Second Banking Co-ordination Directive') – later repealed; Directive 85/611/EEC on EC Undertakings for Collective Investment in Transferable Securities (the 'UCITS Directive'); Directive 87/345/EEC on the mutual recognition of listing particulars (the 'Mutual Recognition Directive'); Directive 88/627/EEC on the information to be published when a major holding in a listed company is acquired or disposed of (the 'Major Shareholdings Directive'); Directive 89/298/EEC coordinating the requirements for the drawing-up, scrutiny and distribution of the prospectus to be published when transferable securities are offered to the public (the 'Prospectus Directive'); Directive 89/592/EEC coordinating regulations on Insider Dealing (the 'Insider Dealing Directive'); Directive 91/308/EEC (the 'Money Laundering Directive'); Directive 93/6/EEC (the 'Capital Adequacy Directive') – later repealed; Directive 93/22/EEC on investment services in the securities field (the 'Investment Services Directive') – later repealed; Directive 97/9/EC on investor compensation schemes; Directive 2000/12/EC relating to the taking up and pursuit of the business of credit institutions. In recent years, following the impetus created by the Financial Services Action Plan, the pace of EC legislation has increased, and it defies listing in totality here. And as will be seen in appropriate parts of this text, many of the above have been replaced, although in many cases it will be some years before the replacement legislation comes into force. For instance, the first three above have been consolidated into Directive 2001/34/EC, there is a new Prospectus Directive 2010/73/EU, a Directive on Takeover Bids 2004/25/EC, a Directive on Insider Dealing and Market Manipulation (Market Abuse) 2003/6/EC, and a replacement for the Investment Services Directive called the Directive on Markets in Financial Instruments 2004/39/EC (MiFID).

[138] Directive 93/22/EEC on investment services in the securities field. See generally G. Ferrarini (ed.) *European Securities Markets: The Investment Services Directive and Beyond* (London: Kluwer, 1998). The Investment Services Directive was implemented in the UK by the Investment Services Regulations 1995 (SI 1995 No. 3275). Also of general relevance to investment firms, but not examined here, is the Capital Adequacy Directive (93/6/EEC), which seeks to impose capital requirements on investment firms with a view to ensuring that they have adequate capital to meet business risks. The Directive has been subsequently amended.

## 2 1993 Investment Services Directive

The ISD is expressed to apply to all 'investment firms'.[139] An investment firm is defined so as to mean 'any legal person the regular occupation or business of which is the provision of investment services for third parties on a professional basis'.[140] 'Investment service' is defined as meaning 'any of the services listed in section A of the Annex relating to any of the instruments listed in section B of the Annex that are provided for a third party'. Section A of the Annex then lists various services which broadly speaking can be said to cover the activities carried out by brokers, dealers, investment managers and underwriters. Section B of the Annex lists the instruments such as 'transferable securities'. Interestingly, there is also a section C list of non-core services which can only be carried out under the passport if an activity in section A has been authorised.[141] The giving of investment advice or matters such as advising companies about takeovers are section C activities.[142] Behind this lies the background that in some EU member states, these activities are not subjected to authorisation or regulation requirements and it would therefore not have been appropriate to subject them to the authorisation requirements of the ISD.[143]

The basic principle of 'home state' authorisation is contained in art. 3, which requires that:

> Each Member State shall make access to the business of investment firms subject to authorisation for investment firms of which it is the Home Member State.'[144] Article 14 gives effect to the passport[145] by providing that: 'member states shall ensure that investment services . . . may be provided within their territories . . . either by the establishment of a branch or under the freedom to provide services . . .

These passport rights are subject to notification provisions[146] under which a firm wishing to use its passport abroad must notify its own competent authorities who will then require information from it which will be communicated by them to the host state's competent authorities.

One of the most problematic aspects of the ISD is the division of functions between the home and host states with regard to the rules which investment firms have to observe. The basic idea is that a passporting firm must observe two sets of rules, 'prudential rules' and 'rules of conduct', the former relating mainly to organisation and structure of the firm and

---

[139] Article 2 (1).

[140] Article 1 (2). This would obviously exclude UK partnerships and so there are special rules for these and other business organisations which are not legal persons. There are also various exclusions from the definition of investment firm, e.g. members of professions (such as solicitors and accountants) conducting investment services incidentally to the practice of their profession; see generally art. 2 (2).

[141] Article 3 (1).

[142] Section C, paras 6 and 4.

[143] See G. Ferrarini 'Towards a European Law of Investment Services and Institutions' (1994) 31 *Common Market Law Review* 1283 at p. 1289.

[144] It is further provided (art. 3) that: '[. . .] such authorisation shall be granted by the Home Member State's competent authorities [. . . .]. The authorisation shall specify the investment services referred to in Section A of the Annex which the undertaking is authorised to provide. The authorisation may also cover one or more of the non-core services referred to in Section C of the Annex.'

[145] See also art. 15, which gives a right to passporting firms to have access to or become members of securities exchanges of member states.

[146] In arts 17 and 18.

the latter pertaining to the way in which it carries out its business transactions. But it must observe the prudential rules which emanate from its home state, and the rules of conduct which emanate from the host state.[147] The prudential rules are set out in art. 10, which states that: 'Each Home Member State shall draw up prudential rules which investment firms shall observe at all times.'[148] They involve, for instance, having sound administrative and accounting procedures, making adequate arrangements for the safeguarding of the funds belonging to investors, arranging for records of transactions to be kept, and being structured so as to avoid conflicts of interest.

Rules of conduct are covered by art. 11, which requires Member States[149] to 'draw up rules of conduct which investment firms shall observe at all times'. The rules must implement the principles set out, such as ensuring that an investment firm acts 'honestly and fairly in conducting its business activities in the best interests of its clients and the integrity of the market' and 'acts with due skill, care and diligence . . .' and 'makes adequate disclosure of relevant material information in its dealings with its clients'. Also, and significantly, it is required to comply with 'all regulatory requirements applicable to the conduct of its business activities so as to promote the best interests of its clients and the integrity of the market'.[150] It is possible that the power of member states to draw up rules of conduct is limited by a requirement that the rules must be such that they can only be justified by reference to the ECJ concept of the 'general good'.[151] This limitation does not appear from the wording of art. 11, but other parts of the ISD arguably proceed on the basis that art. 11 is so limited.[152]

## 3 *The Financial Services Action Plan (FSAP)*

As the end of the 1990s approached, it became apparent that the success of the ISD and the other Capital Markets Directives had been limited. The Commission communication entitled *Financial Services: Implementing the Framework for Financial Markets – Action Plan*[153] assessed the situation as follows:

A single market for financial services has been under construction since 1973. Important strides have been made towards providing a secure prudential environment in which financial institutions can trade in other Member States. Yet, the Union's financial markets remain segmented and business and consumers continue to be deprived of direct access to cross-border financial institutions [. . .][154]

---

[147] Articles 10 and 11.

[148] Although, whatever the content of these rules, there are some fundamental requirements imposed by art. 8 (1), (2) and (3); capital adequacy and fitness. Article 8 (3) makes it clear that the prudential supervision of an investment firm is the responsibility of the home member state, although this is expressed to be 'without prejudice to those provisions of this Directive which give responsibility to the authorities of the Host Member State'.

[149] The host member state is given responsibility for implementation and supervision of compliance; see art. 11 (2).

[150] There is also art. 13, which enables host member states to make rules about advertising (these are not specifically mentioned in art. 11), although the power to do this is limited by the concept of the general good; for discussion of this see the text.

[151] Which perhaps broadly 'translates' as 'public interest'.

[152] See further Lomnicka, n. 127 above, at pp. 198–199.

[153] COM (1999) 232, 11 May 1999.

[154] *Ibid*. p. 3.

The document went on to say that the introduction of the euro provided an opportunity for further action and then set out detailed proposals for future action. These ideas were endorsed at the Lisbon European Council in March 2000, and thereafter the progress towards carrying out this FSAP gathered pace. By June 2004, a total of 39 measures had been produced, many of them major pieces of EC legislation in the form of Directive or regulation, others Commission communications. Many of the most important ones are dealt with in appropriate places in this text.[155] All this has presented an awesome challenge to the securities commissions of the member states.

Alongside this revolution in the substantive law and rules of EU securities regulation, events have occurred which have in themselves changed forever the shape of securities regulation across Europe. In 2001 the Lamfalussy Report on the Regulation of European Securities Markets was published.[156] The Report's perspective on the malaise in the progress towards an integrated EU securities market was that the legislative system was not working. Its processes were too slow to enable it to mould the regulatory structure appropriate to markets where the pace of change was accelerating, and the use of Directives meant that there were considerable divergences between member states on how they were implemented. They recommended a four-level legislative structure, making use of the comitology procedures which had been developed many years earlier for use in other areas of the internal market. The four levels have been restated and re-explained by various institutional sources ever since, and it may well be that the concept of four 'levels', whilst having a user-friendly feel to it, does not really get to grips with the detail of what is happening in legal legislative terms, but nevertheless, using that format, the approach is broadly as follows:

*Level 1*: This consists of a Directive (or EC regulation) setting out broad principles. So, for instance, in the field of market conduct, we have had the enactment of the Directive on Insider Dealing and Market Manipulation (Market Abuse or 'MAD').[157] The principles are kept at a high level of generality so that member states can easily agree to them. The detail will come later.

*Level 2*: Here come the details, which are needed to properly implement the broad principles of level 1. At level 2, the European Commission makes legislation, known as 'implementing measures', in conjunction with the ESC.[158] In fact, the European Commission in doing this will have had the benefit of detailed thought, research and advice from the ESMA (the then CESR),[159] an independent committee made up of the

---

[155] For ananalysis of the FSAP's impact on corporate finance, see H. McVea 'The EU Financial Services Action Plan and its Impact on Corporate Finance', Chapter 14 in D. Prentice and A. Reisberg (eds) *Corporate Finance in the UK and EU* (Oxford: Oxford University Press, 2011).

[156] Final Report of the Committee of Wise Men on the Regulation of European Securities Markets (The Lamfalussy Report), Brussels 15/2/2001.

[157] 2003/6/EC, OJ 2003, L 96/16. On this generally, see Chapter 21 below.

[158] The ESC, a committee consisting of high-level government representatives from each member state, fulfils a constitutional function in the enactment of the 'implementing measures' rather than making any input of expertise. Although needed for constitutional and legal aspects of the comitology process, its role in the four-level picture is very much in the background. The ESC website contains details of its meetings, members etc. See https://ec.europa.eu/info/business-economy-euro/banking-and-finance/financial-reforms-and-their-progress/regulatory-process-financial-services/expert-groups-comitology-and-other-committees/european-securities-committee_en.

[159] In January 2011 the CESR became the ESMA (European Securities and Markets Authority). See immediately below.

heads of the Securities Commissions[160] of Europe's member states, and based in Paris. It replaces the earlier CESR and the less formal grouping known as FESCO[161] and takes over its functions and agreements which under the four-level classification mainly starts at level 3, although its non-constitutional advisory role in the background of level 2 is crucial. So, for instance, in relation to MAD, the European Commission made a series of formal technical requests (mandates)[162] to the then CESR for advice on what was needed to fill in the detail of some of the broad principles in MAD. After various working documents and consultations, the comitology process then led to three implementing measures on really detailed and complex matters: one on the question of defining (and disclosing) inside information and defining market abuse,[163] another on presentation of investment recommendations and disclosure of conflicts of interest,[164] and a third on exemptions for buy-back programmes and stabilisation of financial instruments.[165]

*Level 3*: At this level we find the ESMA (the then CESR). As we have seen, it operates as an advisory group to the Commission in the preparation of implementing measures, and in advising the Commission generally on the development of the EU's regulation of securities. It also has the function of ensuring a consistent day-to-day implementation of the legislation, and will work towards enhanced cooperation between the states. It will produce guidance and codes. Perhaps in this body we can see the beginning of the development of true pan-European securities regulation; it is indeed an interesting development.[166] Already, its ability to speak effectively for the whole of Europe is bringing a new dimension to global securities regulation for it has already led to an agreement on enhanced collaboration between the SEC and the EU.[167]

*Level 4*: This seems to be an exhortation to the European Commission to strengthen its enforcement powers. It is clear that this will involve liaison between all the bodies involved in this process.

## 4 *The new CESR 2 is called ESMA*[168]

The ESMA, one of the three new European Supervisory Authorities, along with the European Banking Authority and the European Insurance and Occupational Pensions

---

[160] More technically, 'the heads of the national public authorities competent in the field of securities.' The CESR regularly published updated frequently asked questions (FAQs) regarding prospectuses, setting out common positions agreed by CESR members. This is now published by the ESMA.

[161] Forum of European Securities Commissions.

[162] EC Commission Mandate of 27 March 2002, and EC Commission Mandate of 31 January 2003 (Ref: MARKT/G2 D (2003), leading to CESR's Advice on Level 2 Implementing Measures for the proposed Market Abuse Directive (Ref: CESR/02.089d).

[163] Commission Directive 2003/124/EC, OJ 2003, L 339/70.

[164] Commission Directive 2003/125/EC, OJ 2003, L 339/73.

[165] Commission Regulation (EC) No 2273/2003, OJ 2003, L 336/33.

[166] ESMA have an informative website: https://www.esma.europa.eu/.

[167] Press Release, CESR 11-04, 4 June 2004.

[168] For a helpful analysis of ESMA's structure and powers compared to CESR, see N. Moloney 'Reform or Revolution? The Financial Crisis, EU Financial Markets Law, and the European Securities and Markets Authority' (2011) 60 *International and Comparative Law Quarterly* 521.

Authority, was established in January 2011[169] following a recommendation by the de Larosiere Report,[170] issued on 25 February 2009.[171] The ESMA, which, like the CESR, is based in Paris, is 'an independent EU authority that contributes to safeguarding the stability of the European Union's financial system by ensuring the integrity, transparency, efficiency and orderly functioning of securities markets, as well as enhancing investor protection'.[172] Its objective is to 'protect the public interest by contributing to the short, medium, and long-term stability and effectiveness of the financial system, for the Union economy, its citizens and businesses.'[173] To that end, it is charged with contributing to a range of outcomes, including improving the functioning of the internal market, ensuring the integrity, transparency, efficiency and orderly functioning of financial markets, strengthening international supervisory coordination, preventing regulatory arbitrage and promoting equal conditions of competition, ensuring the taking of investment and other risks is appropriately regulated and supervised, and enhancing consumer protection.[174] It is conferred with a legal personality,[175] enjoys an independence guarantee,[176] and has a sound (if limited)[177] funding basis based on obligatory contributions from member state competent authorities, an EU subsidy, and any fees paid to the ESMA.[178] It is composed of a Board of Supervisors;[179] a Management Board; a Chairperson; an Executive Director; and a Board of Appeals, reflecting the ESMA's power to make decisions with third party effects.[180] By contrast, and notwithstanding the exponential growth in its influence and range of activities, the CESR's founding Commission decision established it simply as 'an independent advisory group on securities' and, for most of its life, the CESR employed a troublesome consensus-driven approach to decision making and rested on an insecure funding basis.[181] The ESMA thus represents a significant move beyond the harmonisation techniques and unstable convergence structures previously adopted in EU financial market regulation.[182]

The ESMA has a range of quasi-rule-making and supervisory powers. The most significant of these are its power to propose 'binding technical standards' ('BTSs'), which

---

[169] For background on the ESMA and the intensification of EU intervention in financial markets and European business since the financial crisis, see N. Moloney 'The European Securities and Markets Authority and Institutional Design for the EU Financial Market – A Tale of Two Competences: Part 1: Rule-Making' (2011) *Business Organization Law Review* 43.

[170] See http://ec.europa.eu/internal_market/finances/docs/de_larosiere_report_en.pdf.

[171] See https://www.esma.europa.eu/.

[172] ESMA website, *ibid.*

[173] ESMA Regulation, article 1(5).

[174] *Ibid.*

[175] Article 5.

[176] Article 1.

[177] Moloney, n. 168 above.

[178] Article 62. The breakdown is a mixture of Union (40%) and member state (60%) funding. See ESMA Impact Assessment, SEC (2009) 1234, at pp. 35–36. This funding model is designed to support its independence. See ESMA Regulation, recital 59.

[179] As Moloney usefully explains, the constituent member state Board of Supervisors injects a strong intergovernmental dynamic into the new body as the board is responsible for ESMA decision making and operates under a simple majority vote, save with respect to its quasi-rule-making activities when a qualified majority vote applies. Moloney, n. 168 above.

[180] Article 6.

[181] Moloney, n. 168 above.

[182] *Ibid.*

acquire legal effect as a form of delegated article 290/291 TFEU[183] measure, through subsequent endorsement by the Commission (arts 10–15). BTSs can take the form of regulatory technical standards ('RTSs') (where the measure has a quasi-rule quality, and so represents a delegation from the legislative institutions under art. 290 TFEU), or implementing technical standards ('ITSs') (where the measure has a more operational, implementing quality, and so represents a delegation from the member states under art. 291 TFEU).[184] Specific delegations for BTS adoption are set out in relevant legislative measure: the first group of delegations from earlier FSAP measures has been adopted in the form of the Omnibus I Directive 2010. Different forms of institutional oversight by the Council and European Parliament apply to RTS and ITS adoption, reflecting the post-Lisbon Treaty comitology settlement, but the Commission's powers to endorse, and to revise or reject, the ESMA's draft BTSs is common to both. The same applies to its power to propose BTSs where the ESMA does not act. Like the CESR, the ESMA is also empowered to adopt guidance,[185] although by contrast with the CESR model, a range of techniques apply to harden the ESMA's guidance, including the obligation for competent authorities and financial market participants to 'make every effort' to comply.[186]

The ESMA has extensive supervisory powers and these fall into three categories: the controversial powers[187] to impose decisions directly on market participants and competent authorities (i.e., overrule competent authorities) in three horizontal situations; specific powers with respect to particular legislative measures; and an array of softer coordination and convergence powers. With respect to the first category, the ESMA is empowered to investigate breaches of EU law by a competent authority, make related recommendations to the authority and, exceptionally and subject to an array of conditions,[188] impose decisions on market participants in cases of continuing breach.[189] In emergency situations, the ESMA can, subject again to an array of conditions, impose decisions on competent authorities and market participants.[190] It can also do so in cases where it is empowered or requested to mediate between competent authorities and mediation fails.[191] With respect to the second category of supervisory powers, the ESMA is empowered, under art. 9, to prohibit certain products or services in an art. 18 emergency situation, or where the relevant power to do so has been conferred. With respect to the third, the ESMA has a range of supervisory coordination powers, including with respect to participation in and coordination of colleges of supervisors,[192] the identification and management of systemic risk

---

[183] The Treaty of Rome was renamed the Treaty on the Functioning of the European Union (TFEU) after the Treaty of Lisbon was signed in 13 December 2007 and entered into force on 1 December 2009.
[184] *Ibid.*
[185] Article 16.
[186] Moloney, n. 168 above.
[187] As Moloney rightly describes them. See N. Moloney 'The European Securities and Markets Authority and institutional Design for the EU Financial Market – A Tale of Two Competences: Part 2: Rule-Making in Action' (2011) *Business Organization Law Review* 178, at p. 198.
[188] Including the delivery of a Commission 'formal opinion' given the Commission's Treaty pre-eminence with respect to enforcement.
[189] Article 17.
[190] Article 18.
[191] Article 19.
[192] Article 21.

and the development of resolution structures, in cooperation with the ESRB,[193] the promotion of a common supervisory culture,[194] peer review,[195] supervisory coordination,[196] market assessment,[197] and information-gathering.[198]

As Moloney notes,[199] the potential for, and the desirability of, a single EU regulator (in terms of rule-making and/or supervision) for EU financial markets has been a hardy perennial of the scholarly debate for years,[200] but political support has been limited. The financial crisis, however, delivered the dramatic resetting of the political, market and institutional environment on which any centralisation was dependent.[201] Severe weaknesses were revealed in the EU's rule-book and in pan-EU supervisory coordination[202] and the fiscal risks to member states from poor coordination and management of cross-border risk transmission in an integrated market were laid bare.[203] With the ESMA, a significant redesign of the institutional structure supporting EU financial market regulation has been achieved.[204]

The ECA can also hold the ESMA to account with respect to its performance. On the basis of art. 287 (4), second sub-paragraph, of the Treaty on the Functioning of the European Union ('TFEU'),[205] ECA may at any time submit observations on specific questions, particularly in the form of special reports and may deliver opinions at the request of one of the other institutions of the EU. The ECA published the first report of this kind on 1 February 2016 on the ESMA's role as the single supervisor of credit rating agencies ('CRAs') in the EU. This audit was a performance audit with the aim of establishing whether or not the ESMA had succeeded in establishing itself as the CRA watchdog in the EU. It found that the ESMA has laid down good foundations for supervising CRAs in a short period of time, but that there was still room for improvement.

Only time will tell whether restructuring will lead to a radical change in the intensity of the EU's intervention in financial markets.

---

[193] The new European Systemic Risk Board. See arts 22–27.
[194] Article 29.
[195] Article 30.
[196] Article 31.
[197] Article 32.
[198] Article 25.
[199] Moloney, n. 168 above, at p. 45.
[200] See, e.g., E. Wymeersch 'The Structure of Financial Supervision in Europe: About Single Financial Supervisors, Twin Peaks and Multiple Financial Supervisors', (2007) 8 *European Business Organization Law Review* 237; P.M. Boury 'Does the European Union Need a Securities and Exchange Commission?' (2006) 1 *Capital Markets Law Journal* 184; D. Langevoort 'Structuring Securities Regulation in the European Union: Lessons from the US Experience', in G. Ferrarini and E. Wymeersch (eds) *Investor Protection in Europe: Corporate Law Making, the MiFID and Beyond* (Oxford: OUP 2006) p. 485; G. Hertig and R. Lee 'Four Predictions about the Future of EU Securities Regulation', (2003) 3 *Journal of Corporate Law Studies* 359.
[201] Moloney, n. 168 above, at p. 45.
[202] See, e.g., N. Moloney 'EU Financial Market Regulation after the Financial Crisis: "More Europe" or More Risks?' (2010) 47 *Common Market Law Review* p. 1317.
[203] Fiscal consequences were a frequent feature of the policy debate on the ESAMs. E.g., N. Tait and B. Masters 'Big Promises Fail to Dispel Prosaic Doubts', *The Financial Times*, 24 September 2009, p. 6, quoting Commission President Barroso.
[204] Moloney, n. 201 above, at p. 46.
[205] See the consolidated version of the Treaty on the Functioning of the European Union, OJ C 326, 26.10.2012, p. 47–390, available at: http://eur-lex.europa.eu/legal-content/EN/TXT/?uri=celex%3A12012E%2FTXT.

## 5 *The new ISD 2 was called MiFID*

The 1999 FSAP, among all the other ideas, criticised the ISD as being:

> [I]n urgent need of upgrading if it is to serve as the cornerstone of an integrated securities market . . . host country authorities are unwavering in applying their conduct of business rules. However, there may ultimately be a need to reconsider the extent to which host country application of conduct of business rules – which is the basic premise of the ISD – is in keeping with the needs of an integrated securities market.[206]

In the subsequent years, many drafts and consultations on the proposal for the ISD 2 followed. At a comparatively late stage of gestation the proposal underwent a name change, and the Directive which was ultimately adopted on 21 April 2004[207] was called the Directive on Markets in Financial Instruments ('MiFID').[208] The Lamfalussy process moved on to produce the level 2 implementing legislation, and as of its effective date, 1 November 2007, the repeal of the old ISD[209] took effect.

MiFID carried forward many of the basic ideas in the ISD, such as home state authorisation and prudential supervision. It sought to avoid the problem of host state imposition of conduct of business rules on incoming firms, by including a large measure of harmonisation of the principles contained in COB rules. For example, with respect to mutual recognition within the EC, MiFID further improved the passport for investment firms: the cross-border right to do business in other states[210] and to establish branches in other member states[211] without going through a separate authorisation process. In this way it sought to ensure that the passport did actually enable firms to do business in other member states without interference by the regulatory authorities of those host states, and in particular by the host authorities imposing their own COB rules. Under MiFID the powers of the host state were relatively limited, usually extending only to monitoring compliance with COB rules.[212]

Notwithstanding that MiFID had the same basic purpose as the ISD, it made significant changes to the regulatory framework to reflect developments in financial services and markets since the ISD was implemented.[213] In particular, MiFID widened the scope or range of 'core' investment services and activities that firms can passport and in addition to the services covered by the ISD. The key issues of MiFID were:[214]

(1) Extension of the scope of the passport to cover commodity derivatives, credit derivatives and financial contracts for differences. It is important to note, however, that not all firms trading commodity derivatives are covered by the Directive.[215]

---

[206] *Ibid.* at p. 5. In this regard, the document focuses on the possibility of developing the concept of letting 'sophisticated investors' choose the conduct of business regime which will apply to their contract.
[207] Directive 2004/39/EC, OJ 2004, L 145/1 amended by 2006/31/EC.
[208] As subsequently amended by Directive 2008/10/EC.
[209] Directive 93/22/EC.
[210] Article 31 MiFID.
[211] Article 32 MiFID.
[212] E.g. arts 32 (7) and 61–62.
[213] The former FSA's publication 'The Overall Impact of the MiFID' (November 2006) outlines some of the more important changes introduced by MiFID that affect investment (especially equity) markets and clearing operations.
[214] See further, J.D. Haines 'The Markets in Financial Instruments Directive (MiFID): Investor Protection Enhanced by Suitability Requirements' (2007) Comp Law 344.
[215] Guidance on this exemption is contained in FSA Guidance note 06/09, 'Organisational Systems and Controls: Common Platform for Firms'.

(2) Introduction of an operating multilateral trading facility ('MTF') as a new core invest-ment service covered by the passport. MiFID improved the passport for investment firms by clearly defining how the FCA would allocate responsibility between home state and host state passported branches. Therefore, the home state continued to be responsible for conduct of business and organisational issues.[216] For example, if a mat-ter is not carried out on a cross-border basis, but through a branch, then the host state's conduct of business rules will apply.

(3) Adapting to the advice that a personal recommendation to a core investment service can be passported on a standalone basis.

MiFID also had a potential impact on the detection of market abuse by introducing more extensive transaction reporting requirements, both pre- and post-trade.[217] All of this meant a great deal of work in at level 2, and in the securities commissions of member states implementing it in their own legislation and regulatory rules.[218] It has likewise become clear that post-MiFiD the EU securities market landscape has changed significantly. Some believe it represents a revolution in European securities markets that is likely to lead to deep and long-lasting structural changes.[219]

## 6 MiFID II and MiFIR

Due to the global financial crisis which revolved around over the counter ('OTC') derivative exposure and trade scandals such as the FX Fix and LIBOR,[220] the EU moved to create an enhanced version of MiFID. In 2011 the European Commission adopted a legislative proposal for its revision, which took the form of a revised Directive and a new Regulation. After more than two years of debate, the Directive on Markets in Financial Instruments repealing Directive 2004/39/EC and the new Regulation on Markets in Financial Instruments, commonly referred to as MiFID II[221]

---

[216] At the same time, the MiFID has also increased powers of enforcement of host state and increased cooperation between member states generally re enforcement. See arts 56–62 MiFID introducing new s. 194A FSMA 2000.

[217] Articles 27–28 MiFID. For a summary of the changes introduced see FSA, 'Implementing MiFID for Firms and Markets' (CP 06, 14 July 2006) Chapter 17 (Transaction Reporting) available at: www.fsa.gov.uk/pubs/cp/cp06_14.pdf.

[218] In the UK, the Financial Services and Markets Act 2000 (Markets in Financial Instruments) Regulations 2007 were introduced in January 2007. These regulations implement in part Directive 2004/39/EC ('MiFID'). MiFID is also implemented by other statutory instruments including the Financial Services and Markets Act 2000 (Regulated Activities) (Amendment No. 3) Order (S.I. 2006/3384) (now SI 2011/133), the Financial Services and Markets Act 2000 (Exemption) (Amendment) Order 2007 (SI 2007/125) (now SI 2011/1626), the Financial Services and Markets Act 2000 (Recognition Requirements for Investment Exchanges and Clearing Houses) (Amendment) Regulations 2006 (SI 2006/3386) and the Financial Services and Markets Act 2000 (EEA Passport Rights) (Amendment) Regulations 2006 (SI 2006/3385), and by the FSA using powers under FSMA 2000.

[219] For interesting predictions about the likely impact of MiFID on market structures, and the likely strategic responses of financial services firms, see J.P. Casey and K. Lannoo 'The MiFID Revolution' ECMI Policy Brief (No. 3, November 2006). See also an interesting speech by David Lawton, Head of Markets Infrastructure and Policy at the FSA from April 2011, on the current and future strategy for securities markets regulation: http://www.fsa.gov.uk/pages/Library/Communication/Speeches/2011/0318_dl.shtml.

[220] The scandal involved bankers from various financial institutions fraudulently providing information on the interest rates they would use to calculate the London Interbank Offer Rate (LIBOR). See further https://www.investopedia.com/terms/l/libor-scandal.asp.

[221] Directive 2014/65/EU of the European Parliament and of the Council of 23 July 2014 amending Directive 2009/65/EC on the coordination of laws, regulations and administrative provisions relating to undertakings for col-lective investment in transferable securities ('UCITS') as regards depositary functions, remuneration policies and sanctions, available at http://eur-lex.europa.eu/legal-content/EN/TXT/PDF/?uri=CELEX:32014L0091&from=ES.

and MiFIR,[222] were adopted by the European Parliament and the Council of the European Union and published in the EU Official Journal on 12 June 2014.

Many of the obligations under MiFID II and MiFIR have been further specified in the Commission Delegated Directive and two Commission Delegated Regulations, as well as regulatory and implementing technical standards developed by ESMA. MiFID II and MiFIR, together with the Commission delegated acts as well as regulatory and implementing technical standards, have been applicable across the EU from 3 January 2018.

## MiFID II

Created in 2014, and going into effect in 2018, MiFID II replaces MiFID I, the 2004 version discussed above. It is a much wider ranging legislation, including 97 articlesas as opposed to 73 for MiFID I. MiFID II applies to certain persons in circumstances where they are otherwise exempt from being authorised. These include, for example, those dealing on their own account in commodity derivatives, or providing non-algorithmic investment services in commodity derivatives as an ancillary activity to their main (non-investment) business. The Directive also applies some of its investor protection requirements to firms when they sell, or advise clients in relation to structured deposits.

MiFID II expands the status of what is considered an organised trading venue, and their accompanying supervisory rules. In particular, the Directive creates organised trading facilities ('OTFs'), a new category of trading venue, which, like regulated markets and multilateral trading facilities, are a type of multilateral system in which multiple buying and selling interests can interact in a way that results in contracts. However, OTFs can only facilitate the trading of non-equity financial instruments on a discretionary basis. Investment firms and market operators operating OTFs are permitted to conduct matched principal trading in bonds, structured financed products, emission allowances and certain derivatives where a client has consented to the process, and to deal on their own account other than matched principal trading in sovereign bonds where they do not have a liquid market.[223]

In terms of trade reporting, MiFID II provides a wider scope than its predecessor. More than just equities and bonds, commodities, currencies and credit products and their derivatives are now under its scope.

Many of the ambiguities that existed with MiFID I are being clarified under MiFID II in order for financial regulators to be more unified in their supervision. MiFID II requires that national competent authorities ('NCAs') establish the maximum size of net position that a person may hold in commodity derivatives traded on trading venues and economically equivalent OTC contracts according to a methodology set out in the Regulatory

---

[222] Regulation (EU) No. 600/2014 of the European Parliament and of the Council of 15 May 2014 on markets in financial instruments and amending Regulation (EU) No. 648/2012, available at http://eur-lex.europa.eu/legal-content/EN/TXT/PDF/?uri=CELEX:32014R0600&from=ES.

[223] Binary options are a form of financial contract which typically pays a fixed sum if the option is exercised or expires in the money, or nothing at all if the option is exercised or expires out of the money. Discussing the scope of the existing MiFID, the Commission said that some binary options are financial instruments. At the time of writing, the FCA has confirmed in its website at www.fca.org.uk/consumers/binary-options that given the growth of the binary options market and concerns about consumer protection it is appropriate to treat binary options relating to certain underlyings as MiFID financial instruments. This will bring them within the UK regulatory perimeter and ensure that investor protections that apply for similar derivative contracts also apply to these contracts.

Technical Standards ('RTS') relating to position limits.[224] MiFID II also requires that NCAs have the power to remove a person from the management board of an investment firm or market operator.

In terms of corporate governance, MiFID II puts in place stricter policies to protect and make more transparent the handling of client funds, executing on their behalf and account onboarding.

### MiFIR

MiFIR regulates the implementation of MiFID II over 55 articles of its own. The main focus of MiFIR is related to rules for net position limits and reporting requirements of executions of positions in derivatives and securities products.[225] The trading venue transparency rules regard information that trading venues need to publish, volume allowances of trading members and what products need to be traded on a trading venue. The trade reporting rules are trade transparency rules applicable to investment firms and systematic internalisers. This part of MiFIR requires basic details of trades to be reported to an Approved Publication Arrangement in near real-time. The transaction reporting rules are a set of rules regarding reporting of trade details on the transaction date plus one additional day to an Approved Reporting Mechanism ('ARM'). Information is much more in-depth than trade report requirements and includes details of who the buyer and seller are and how the trade was executed.

## Further reading

L. Zingales 'The Future of Securities Regulation' (29 January 2009) Chicago Booth School of Business Research Paper No. 08-27; FEEM Working Paper No. 7.2009, available at http://ssrn.com/abstract=1319648.

E. Ferran, 'The Break-Up of the Financial Services Authority', University of Cambridge Faculty of Law Research Paper Series No. 10/04 (11 October 2010), available at: http://ssrn.com/abstract=1690523.

FCA, Markets in Financial Instruments Directive II Implementation – Policy Statement II, Policy Statement PS17/14 July 2017, available at https://www.fca.org.uk/publication/policy/ps17-14.pdf.

---

[224] Positions held by non-financial entities in order to reduce risks directly relating to their commercial activity may be excluded from these limits.

[225] MiFID II/MiFIR post-trade reporting requirements is available at https://www.afme.eu/globalassets/downloads/publications/afme-mifidii-mifir-post-trade-reporting-requirements.pdf.

# 17

# Credit rating agencies and their role in capital markets

## 17.1 Introduction

This chapter discusses the uses of credit rating agencies ('CRAs') in contemporary financial markets, with a focus on the more theoretical issues at play here.[1] Whilst a particular emphasis is given to the UK market, a discussion of CRAs cannot confine itself to this market alone.[2] In the last 15 years or so the activities of CRAs have come under scrutiny. The intense scrutiny is, in many ways, a reflection of the prominent role these agencies play in the capital/securities markets. Back in 1996, Thomas Friedman, the influential *New York Times* columnist, described their significance in the following terms: '. . . there are two superpowers in the world today in my opinion. There's the [US] and there's Moody's Bond Rating Services [Moody's].'[3] But more recently, their inability to predict corporate scandals like Enron in the US and Parmalat in Italy and to adequately assess the risk associated with securities backed by sub-prime mortgages that caused the financial crisis of 2007–2008 and downgrade them quickly enough has certainly intensified the debate about their merits.[4] The growing demand for rating services, which has been driven partly by new debt issues and the advent of new structured finance products, has also contributed to

---

[1] In this chapter references to credit rating agencies shall be taken as references to the three main credit rating agencies: Moody's Investor Service, S&P [Standard & Poor's] Rating Services and Fitch Ratings (together the 'Big Three'). For an in-depth anyalsis of the issues raised in this chapter, see A. Reisberg 'The Future Role of Credit Rating Agencies in Contemporary Financial Markets – A Theoretical Perspective', Chapter 7 in D. Prentice and A. Reisberg (eds) *Corporate Finance in the UK and EU* (Oxford: OUP, 2011).

[2] Most of the issues discussed in this chapter have a European or global dimension. The European Securities and Markets Authority (ESMA) regulates CRAs and most of the debate on the future of CRAs takes place at EU level. It should be noted that although this chapter touches on the latest regulatory proposals in the light of policy documents drafted in the wake of or during the recent financial crisis, a comprehensive, even if concise, account of the factors that contributed to this crisis is beyond the scope of this chapter. For a recent account of these see e.g. D. Ramos Muñoz *The Law of Transnational Securitization* (Oxford: OUP, 2010), paras. 1.40–1.61, at pp. 13–27. Also beyond the scope of this chapter are issues relating to the role of CRAs in rating sovereign debts such as S&P decision in August 2011 to downgrade the AAA rating of the US to AA+ with a negative outlook, citing concerns about budget deficits.

[3] *New York Times*, 13 February 1996.

[4] In the US, the drive comes after a series of high profile hearings, such as those chaired by Mr Levin and Mr Angelides, which have highlighted the mortgage security failings and potential conflicts in the ratings model. The Securities and Exchange Commission ('SEC') in June 2010 introduced new rules requiring much more disclosure of the information used to rate securitised deals in the hope of encouraging others to analyse it too – called Rule 17g-5. In addition, new laws that could have two significant effects are being considered. One would increase the liability of CRAs, opening them up to lawsuits from issuers and investors. The second will, if adopted, change the way ratings are allocated, with the proposal suggesting the SEC should assign raters to deals. See A. Van Duyn 'Dilemmas of Reforming the Rating Agencies', *Financial Times*, 11 June 2010.

the CRAs move under the spotlight. Numerous stakeholders have looked into ways to increase the accountability of the agencies and to lessen dependence on them. As will be discussed below, European Union ('EU') institutions and the UK Government have introduced new measures aimed at increasing the regulation of the activities of CRAs.[5] But the problem with regulation is convoluted by the fact that regulators use credit ratings as well, or permit ratings to be used for regulatory purposes. And so there is an interesting discussion about reducing the dependency of the regulatory system on ratings. For instance, under the Basel II agreement of the Basel Committee on Banking Supervision,[6] banking regulators can allow banks to use credit ratings from certain approved CRAs (called 'External Credit Assessment Institutions' – 'ECAIs') when calculating their net capital reserve requirements. The Basel capital framework (including several components of the recent Basel III agreement) continues to incorporate credit ratings in material ways. Such reliance gives CRAs their power. If that reliance was not on ratings, would this not reduce the dependency?[7] In the US, the SEC permits investment banks and broker-dealers to use credit ratings from Nationally Recognized Statistical Rating Organizations ('NRSROs') for similar purposes. And so, notwithstanding the criticism, ratings continue to be widely used by investors to evaluate whether to purchase securities.[8] Additionally, regulators continue to favour credit ratings over more idiosyncratic, subjective standards when needing to classify debt instruments for regulatory purposes.

## 17.2 Credit rating agencies: the basics

### A The credit rating agencies industry

Out of the approximately 150 CRAs at a global, regional and industry level, only three major CRAs dominate the market, namely Moody's, established by John Moody in 1909 to rate US railway bonds; Standard & Poor's (S&P), the merged entity resulting from the 1941 merger of Standard and Poor's, which were established in 1919 and 1922 respectively;, and Fitch Ratings Services (Fitch), which has been in operation since 1924 (all together referred to as the 'Big Three'). Side by side with the growth and expansion of the financial markets in the 1980s, CRAs saw great expansion overseas during that time. Crucially, most CRAs are either private independent companies or owned by non-financial companies. Historically, CRAs used to offer public ratings free of charge for the issuer. Their financing came exclusively through the sale of publications and related material. Today, CRAs charge the issuers approximately 80% of revenues depending on the size

---

[5] See discussion below under 17.5. In Europe, the impact of ratings during the Greek debt crisis – and other controversial decisions such as the downgrades of Greece and Spain – have also highlighted just how influential CRAs are.

[6] For the Basel Committee, see http://www.bis.org/about/factbcbs.htm.

[7] Admittedly, this may be a US problem (more so than an EU problem) and the EU may not have much ability to grapple with this point. On the issue of how to reduce rating agency dependence (by, for example, reducing the 'privilege' enjoyed by rated securities *vis-à-vis* banking and financial regulations), see discussion in D. Ramos Muñoz *The Law of Transnational Securitization* (Oxford: OUP, 2010) paras 7.2–7.13, p. 342 *et seq.*

[8] For example, according to the US Financial Crisis Inquiry Commission, which investigated the causes of the financial crisis, Moody's alone rated $4,700bn of residential mortgage-backed securities ('MBSs') between 2000 and 2007, and $736bn of collateral debt obligations ('CDOs') (on the latter, see below under 17.4). See A. Van Duyn 'Dilemmas of Reforming the Rating Agencies', *Financial Times*, 11 June 2010.

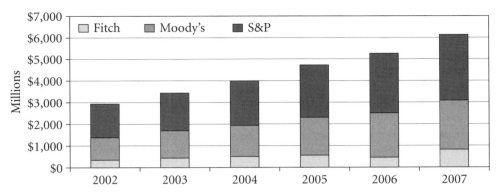

**Figure 17.1** Revenue of Big Three credit rating agencies 2002–2007

*Source:* www.thismatter.com/money.

and type of issue (approximately 2–3 basis points of the principal). We will explain this in more detail later in this chapter. If one wonders why they are usually referred to as an 'industry' on its own, then a quick look at the figures provided by www.thismatter.com shows how large a business they have become (see Figure 17.1).

As of 2015, of the 26 CRAs established in the EU, only 9 offer ratings on Structured Finance Instruments ('SFIs'). Moreover, as of 2014, the Big Three still held almost 95% of the market share in SFI ratings, due to a lead in expertise and reputation. In particular, as of 31 December 2012, S&P and Moody's continued to be the two CRAs with the highest number of ratings reported to be outstanding, accounting for about 45.6% and 36.9% respectively, of all outstanding ratings. On the other hand, Fitch reported having the third highest number of outstanding ratings, accounting for about 14% of all outstanding ratings. In total, these three CRAs issued about 96.5% of all the ratings that were reported to be outstanding.[9]

In terms of revenue, for instance, Moody's 2Q17 revenue of $1.0bn was up 8% from 2Q16. Its 2Q17 operating income of $457.5m was also up 12% from 2Q16. For the financial year 2017, diluted earnings per share guidance range was $5.69–$5.84; adjusted diluted EPS guidance range was $5.35–$5.50.[10]

## B Defining credit ratings

In order to assess properly the role that CRAs have in the capital markets it is important to try to establish a working definition of CRAs. Trying to find a worldwide accepted definition of credit rating or trade association of CRAs can be a surprisingly difficult task.[11] What is a credit rating and what do raters actually do?

[9] Marioara (Orheian) Oana Mihaelajméno 'Credit Rating Agency Performance in Terms of Profit' *Procedia Economics and Finance* (2015) Vol. 30, 631–642.
[10] See Moody's Corporation Reports Results for Second Quarter 2017, available at http://ir.moodys.com/news-and-financials/press-releases/press-release-details/2017/Moodys-Corporation-Reports-Results-for-Second-Quarter-2017/default.aspx.
[11] H.M. Lagohr and P.T. Laghor *The Rating Agencies and their Credit Ratings* (Chichester: John Wiley and Sons, 2008), 23.

The following definitions give a comprehensive picture of the essential ingredients of a credit rating. According to the International Organization of Securities Commissions ('IOSCO'), 'a "credit rating" is an opinion regarding the creditworthiness of an entity, a credit commitment, a debt or debt-like security or an issuer of such obligations, expressed using an established and defined ranking system [. . .] credit ratings are not recommendations to purchase, sell, or hold any security.'[12] For IOSCO, the term 'CRA' refers to 'those entities whose business is the issuance of credit ratings for the purposes of evaluating the credit risk of issuers of debt and debt-like securities.'[13] The European Commission explained that CRAs 'issue opinions on the creditworthiness of a particular issuer or financial instrument. In other words, they assess the likelihood that an issuer will default either on its financial obligations generally (issuer rating) or on a particular debt or fixed income security (instrument rating).'[14]

It should also be pointed out that through self-marketing, CRAs have also managed to establish a widely accepted definition of credit ratings of their own. S&P [Standard & Poor's] 'Guide to Credit Rating Essentials' defines a credit rating as an 'opinion about credit risk [. . .] about the ability and willingness of an issuer, such as a corporation or state or city government, to meet its financial obligations in full and on time.'[15] In its written evidence to the UK House of Commons Treasury Select Committee,[16] S&P explained that its business is to provide financial market intelligence and that a credit rating is an opinion on the creditworthiness of particular issuers or financial obligations. Creditworthiness is taken to mean the likelihood that a particular obligor or financial obligation will pay, on time, the principal amount of the debt and interest owed. Ratings therefore *do not* constitute recommendations as to whether investors should '*buy*', '*sell*' or '*hold*' rated securities, but rather they more simply address the likelihood of timely repayment. Similarly, Fitch also defines a credit rating as 'an opinion on the relative ability of an entity to meet financial commitments, such as interest, preferred dividends, repayment of principal, insurance claims or counterparty obligations.' Finally, Moody's states that 'a credit rating is an independent opinion about credit risk. It is an assessment about the ability and willingness of an issuer of fixed-income securities to make full and timely payment of amounts due on the security over its life.'[17] As will be seen below, these definitions will prove critical in assessing the legal immunity of the CRAs.

---

[12] Technical Committee of International Organisation Securities Commission, May 2008, Revised Code of Conduct Fundamentals for Rating Agencies, 4. The Code of Conduct Fundamentals for Rating Agencies was first published by the IOSCO Committee in September 2003 and then revisited in May 2008.
[13] *Ibid.*
[14] Commission of the European Communities, 2005, Communication from the Commission on Credit Rating Agencies (2006/C 59/02).
[15] S&P 'Guide to Credit Rating Essentials', 3. Accessed at https://jpn.up.pt/pdf//rating.pdf. The usual disclaimer that is printed at the bottom of S&P credit ratings states: '. . . any user of the information contained herein should not rely on any credit rating or other opinion contained herein in making any investment decision.'
[16] On 13 November 2007 S&P senior representatives alongside other major rating agencies addressed the UK House of Commons Treasury Select Committee as part of an ongoing inquiry into financial stability and transparency. The questions addressed concerned the role, record and regulation of CRAs as well as providing information in relation to Northern Rock.
[17] Moody's Investor Service, 2004, 'Guide to Moody's Ratings, Ratings Process, and Rating Practices'.

## C The use of credit ratings made by market participants

As financial intermediaries, CRAs maintain a complex set of relationships with a wide range of market participants in the UK. We briefly highlight here their relationship with three key stakeholders, namely, issuers of corporate securities, investors and investment banks.

(1) Issuers of corporate securities resort to CRAs to gain access to capital markets. In fact, by obtaining a credit rating on their securities, they make these more marketable. This is because where investors believe that uncertainties or broader information asymmetries exist they are unlikely to invest without first being reassured by a positive rating or before being compensated for the risks they take. In the case of fixed income securities, this compensation usually mean that investors expect to be rewarded by higher interest rates, which will in turn increase the cost of capital for the issuers of such securities. CRAs can thereby provide a service to both investors and issuers by redressing some of the informational asymmetry while ensuring that issuers avoid incurring extra unnecessary costs when issuing securities.

(2) Investors are primary users of rating information. They represent a relatively heterogeneous group ranging from small investors with limited analysis skill to highly-sophisticated bond investors.[18] The CESR Report emphasises how, due to the complexities and the rising interest of larger categories of investors, which often do not have the resources, time or expertise for a thorough analysis of the risk of the available securities, the market has come to heavily rely on credit ratings.[19] According to a report prepared by the Bank for International Settlement ('BIS'), reliance by investors on credit ratings is somewhat higher in the structured finance market than in the other traditional bond markets.[20] Nonetheless, the report goes on to note how investors do not actually appear to be overly reliant on ratings in making structured finance investment decisions, suggesting that they view ratings as just one part of an informed investment decision.[21]

Investors face three types of risk when investing in bonds. The first is interest rate risk, i.e. the risk that interest rates could rise. The second is purchasing power risk, i.e. the risk that inflation will rise and thereby erode the value of bonds. The third is credit risk, i.e. the (default) risk that a bond issuer will become unable to meet its debt obligations. Credit ratings are essentially rankings of a company's ability to repay their debts and resist various types of financial and economic stress compared to that of other companies. They are intended to help provide forward-looking opinions on a company's ability and willingness to pay interest and repay principal as scheduled.[22]

---

[18] A. Duff 'The Credit Rating Agencies and Stakeholder Relations: Issues for Regulators' (2009) 24 *Journal of International Banking and Financial Law*.
[19] The Committee of European Securities Regulator's (hereinafter 'CESR') second report to the EU Commission on the compliance of credit rating agencies with the IOSCO code and the role of credit rating agencies in structured finance (May 2008). On 25 May 2009 the CESR published a second report on compliance with the 2008 IOSCO code. This can be accessed at http://www.cesr-eu.org/index.php?page=contenu_groups&id=43&docmore=1.
[20] See BIS 'The Role of Ratings in Structured Finance: Issues and Implications' (2005) available at http://www.bis.org/publ/cgfs23.pdf?noframes=1.
[21] *Ibid*.
[22] The same general principles apply to government debt (e.g. for sovereign bonds), municipal debt and other fixed income securities, but these are not the subject of this chapter.

(3) Banks make extensive use of ratings for capital adequacy purposes. Since the introduction of Basel II[23], their internal rating scales broadly reflect the CRA ratings. Banks usually calibrate their internal ratings using Moody's KMV, which is a rating system that applies forward-looking equity market measures to assess the ratio of asset market value to liabilities.[24]

From an economics perspective, CRAs contribute to solving principal–agent problems by helping lenders. They reduce information asymmetry between lenders and investors on the one hand, and issuers on the other hand. At the same time, there are informational issues that may cause problems such as frictions in the securitisation process, adverse selection, moral hazard behaviour and the issue that CRAs, while being private parties, perform a semi-public role. We return to these issues in more detail below.

## D Credit risk models

The processes and methods that are used to establish credit ratings vary widely among the CRAs. The two key measures are the probability of default ('PD') and the recovery rate ('RE'). S&P ratings seek to capture only the forward-looking probability of the occurrence of default. No assessment is provided on the expected time of default or mode of default resolution and recovery values. Fitch's ratings also focus on both PD and RE. They have a more explicitly hybrid character in that analysts are also reminded to be forward looking and to be alert to possible discontinuities between past track records and future trends. By contrast, Moody's ratings focus on the expected loss ('EL'), which is a function of both PD and the expected RE. Thus $EL = PD (1 - RE)$. In light of the above considerations, there is no surprise, therefore, that these alternative methodologies lead to rating disagreements, in particular in the ratings of speculative-grade bonds.

The ratings lie on a spectrum ranging between highest credit quality at one end and default and 'junk' at the other. Long-term credit ratings are denoted with a letter: a triple A ('AAA') is the highest credit quality, and C or D (depending on the agency issuing the rating) is the lowest quality. Within this spectrum there are different degrees of each rating, which are, depending on the agency, sometimes denoted by a plus or negative sign or a number. For example, for Fitch, a 'AAA' rating signifies the highest investment grade and very low credit risk. 'AA' represents very high credit quality; 'A' means high credit quality, and 'BBB' is good credit quality. All these ratings are considered to be investment grade, which means that the security or the entity being rated carries a level of quality that many institutions require when considering overseas investments. By contrast, ratings that fall under 'BBB' are considered to be speculative or junk. So, for example, for Moody's, a 'Ba2' is a speculative grade rating while for S&P, a 'D' denotes default of junk bond status. Table 17.1 gives an overview of the different ratings symbols that both Moody's and S&P issue.[25]

---

[23] Basel II is the second of the Basel Accords, which are recommendations on banking laws and regulations issued by the Basel Committee on Banking Supervision. The purpose of Basel II, which was initially published in June 2004, is to create an international standard that banking regulators can use when creating regulations about how much capital banks need to put aside to guard against the types of financial and operational risks banks face.

[24] A. Duff 'The Credit Rating Agencies and Stakeholder Relations: Issues for Regulators' (2009) 24 *Journal of International Banking and Financial Law* 11.

[25] Source: http://www.investopedia.com/articles/03/102203.asp#ixzz1V7FnxER4.

**Table 17.1** CRA bond rating systems

| Moody's | S&P | Grade | Risk |
|---------|-----|-------|------|
| Aaa | AAA | Investment | Lowest risk |
| Aa | AA | Investment | Low risk |
| A | A | Investment | Low risk |
| Baa | BBB | Investment | Medium risk |
| Ba, B | BB, B | Junk | High risk |
| Caa/Ca/C | CCC/CC/C | Junk | Highest risk |
| C | D | Junk | In default |

## E Distinguishing credit rating agencies from other rating agencies

CRAs are a unique type of agency offering rating services across all sectors of the economy. Coffee usefully explains that the basis to differentiate CRAs from other agencies offering ratings services is by reference to the market. The market for CRAs is apparently distinctive from other markets for information in three critical respects.[26] The first way in which one can differentiate the market for CRAs is by reference to its concentration. Since the beginning of the twentieth century, Moody's[27] and S&P[28] have effectively been exercising a duopoly over the market for credit ratings. Fitch[29] has only recently been able to acquire a more meaningful market share by entering some specialised submarkets (e.g. financial services). It is this high level of market concentration that is leading some authors to argue that CRAs could actually be breaching EC competition law.[30]

The second way in which the market is different is because CRAs suffer from internal conflicts of interest. As we will see in the next section, these conflicts are generated most specially in the area of structured finance products. Broadly speaking, this happens because CRAs are paid by the issuer whose securities they rate as opposed to being paid by the investors. If CRAs were to be paid by investors (i.e. they would be subject to normal contractual relationships), their ratings would not be a public good, as they are now. CRAs provide information universally (though of course there is an asymmetry of information), and this benefits many who otherwise would not have had the time, money or skill to invest in obtaining this information. It is perhaps worth bearing this in mind when we

[26] J.C. Coffee *Gatekeepers: The Professions and Corporate Governance* (Oxford: OUP, 2006) 284.
[27] Moody'sis a public company listed on the New York Stock Exchange. It performs financial research and analysis on commercial and government entities and ranks the creditworthiness of borrowers using a standardised rating scale. The company has a 40% share on the world credit market. Its corporate headquarters are located in New York. Its holding company is Moody's Corporation.
[28] S&P operates as a financial services company. Its product and services include credit ratings for both public and private organisations. Its corporate headquarters are also located in New York. Its holding company is McGraw Inc., a large publicly-owned publishing group. Source: http://www.standardandpoors.com/home/en/us.
[29] Fitch is a global CRA with headquarters in both New York and London and is part of the Fitch Group, which is a majority-owned subsidiary of a French conglomerate, FIMALC SA. As discussed above, Fitch is the smallest of the 'Big Three', covering a smaller market share than S&P and Moody's, though it has grown with acquisitions and frequently positions itself as a 'tie-breaker' when S&P and Moody's have similar but not equal ratings.
[30] For an argument that increased competition might actually produce lower quality ratings, see B. Becker and T. Milbourn, 'Reputation and Competition: Evidence from the Credit Rating Industry', Harvard Business School Working Paper 09-051 (21 June 2009).

discuss reforms below. As Coffee rightly points out, even securities analysts do not generally accept direct payment for their ratings from the issuers they rate. But CRAs do.[31] In 1999 approximately 95% of the annual revenues generated by CRAs were coming from issuers' fees, typically two to three basis points of a bond's face amount.[32]

The third aspect in which one can differentiate the market for CRAs regards the complex role that CRAs assume. According to Coffee, in order to minimise the costs of capital, debt issuers have an incentive to disclose information that show the superior quality of their debt securities.[33] By disclosing confidential information to CRAs, debt issuers use them as 'reputational intermediaries'. CRAs send a signal to the market that the issuer's securities are of above average quality and, in turn, the issuers do not have to pay higher interest rates on the securities they issue.[34] Partnoy disputes the above reputational view of CRAs.[35] He views the theory by which CRAs can be seen as granting a 'regulatory license' to issuers as a better description of the role that the CRAs have in the financial markets. According to this view, ratings are valuable not because they are accurate and credible but because they are key to reducing costs associated with regulation.[36] Absent the regulation which governs the issue of ratings, CRAs would survive due to their 'ability to accumulate and retain reputational capital'.[37] However, once regulation incorporating the ratings is passed, the CRAs begin to sell not only information but also the more valuable property rights associated with compliance with such regulation.[38] As we will see below, when this happens, the capital markets also become less vigilant about CRAs' business activity, and in some cases, this has proven to be most unfortunate.[39]

## 17.3 The criticisms advanced against credit rating agencies

### A General criticism

In recent years, particularly as a result of the financial crisis of 2007–2008, various flaws in the operation of CRAs have been identified and raised for public analysis and debate. Prior to the collapse of Enron in 2001, the prevailing view among market participants was that CRAs were sound enough. For instance, Schwarcz indicated that CRAs had a

---

[31] J.C. Coffee *Gatekeepers: The Professions and Corporate Governance* (Oxford: OUP, 2006) 286.
[32] F. Partnoy 'The Siskel and Ebert of Financial Markets? Two Thumbs Down for the Credit Rating Agencies', (1999) 77 *Washington University Law Quarterly* 652.
[33] Coffee, above, n. 31, 287.
[34] For a brief discussion regarding the fact that issuers resort to CRAs to increase the marketability of their securities see the next section.
[35] Above n. 31, 681. For a study that suggests that there are a number of reasons why CRAs may not serve financial markets well in the capacity of informational intermediaries see H.M. Morgan 'Credit Rating Agencies and Regulatory Reform: The Case of Moody's Investors Services' (2011) *Journal of International Banking Law and Regulation* 389.
[36] Above n. 31, 681.
[37] Above n. 31, 682.
[38] *Ibid.*
[39] A detailed account of the role of CRAs as 'reputational intermediaries', the problems associated with this view and a discussion of the regulatory licence view goes beyond the scope of this chapter. For a detailed account of these issues see F. Patrnoy 'The Siskel and Ebert of Financial Markets? Two Thumbs Down for the Credit Rating Agencies' (1999) 77 *Washington University Law Quarterly* 652. See also by the same author, 'How and Why Credit Rating Agencies are Not Like Other Gatekeepers' in Y. Fuchita and R.E. Litan *Financial Gatekeepers: Can they Protect Investors?* (Baltimore: Brookings Institute Press, 2006).

remarkable track record of success in their ratings, pointing to only one company with an investment grade by Moody's defaulting on long-term debt.[40] He referred to an article in *The Economist* which back in 1991 cited:

> In 20 years only one company with an investment grade rating from Moody's has defaulted on long term debt – Manville, a single A company that went bankrupt voluntarily to protect itself from asbestosis lawsuits.[41]

In explaining why government regulation would neither reduce costs nor improve reliability, Schwarcz indicated that the reliability in the ratings could be explained by reference to the theory of reputational costs: inaccurate ratings will impair, if not destroy, a CRA's reputation.[42] CRAs therefore have an incentive to issue accurate ratings in the interest of avoiding losing the confidence of the market participants on the one hand, and retaining their client base on the other. But then, why is it that CRAs have failed so miserably with Enron in the US, Parmalat in Europe and more recently in recognising the dangers concealed behind complex structured financial products?

As far as the Enron case goes, it has been argued that it is plausible to believe that for CRAs to get it so significantly wrong, both massive fraud and complexity were necessary and that neither of these factors alone was sufficient.[43] In terms of the recent financial crisis, to explain why things went so wrong, it is probably useful to start our discussion by looking briefly, first of all, at the general criticisms which were advanced against the CRAs even before the recent economic meltdown. In short, the main charges include the following:

(1) *Imperfect competition: oligopoly viewpoint.* The US financial regulatory system incorporates ratings issued by CRAs that benefit from the Government status of a nationally recognized statistical rating organization ('NRSRO'). While the SEC recognises at least 10 NRSROs, the Big Three enjoy over 95% market share. Furthermore, a rise in the number of CRAs increases the likelihood that marginal borrowers meet minimum ratings thresholds.

(2) *Timeliness of rating changes.* CRAs have been too slow in adjusting their ratings to changes in corporate creditworthiness. For example, on 2 December 2001 Enron filed for bankruptcy just a couple of days after the major CRAs confirmed its investment grade status.

(3) *Accountability gap.* There is a widespread use of credit ratings as instruments of market regulation (rating-dependent regulation). The CRAs set a standard of creditworthiness that is enforced by public authorities. In other words, large influence is conferred to CRAs without assigning any responsibility.

(4) *Regulation is being privatised.* With the credit rating market itself having been effectively under-regulated, CRAs have functioned as de facto market regulators.

(5) *Lack of independence.* At the same time that CRAs sell ratings to rated firms, they advise them . Reliability of ratings is critical.

---

[40] S.A. Schwarcz 'Private Ordering of Public Markets: The Rating Agency Paradox' (2002) 2 *University of Illinois Law Review* 13.
[41] 'Credit Rating Agencies: Beyond the Second Opinion', *The Economist*, 30 March 1991, 80.
[42] Schwarcz, above n. 40, 14.
[43] See C.A. Hill, 'Why Did Anyone Listen to the Rating Agencies After Enron?' (2009) (4) *Journal of Business and Technology Law* 283, 284.

## B Criticisms in light of the financial crisis of 2007–2008

Following the financial crisis, CRAs have been largely criticised.[44] In April 2010, at a US Senate hearing to determine the extent of their role in the housing crisis, CRAs' internal emails were publicly discussed. One of the emails of April 2006 by an S&P employee revealed what many suspected: 'We rate every deal. It could be structured by cows and we would rate it.' For ease of reference, the criticisms discussed next have been divided into the following separate categories:[45]

### 1 *Conflicts of interest*

First of all, as we have already seen, CRAs currently operate an 'issuer pays' business model. They are paid by the issuer whose securities they rate as opposed to being paid by the investors. This system has created an obvious conflict of interest, as CRAs have the incentive to issue higher ratings simply not to displease their clients. Secondly, CRAs have usually acted as consultants to the issuer both in relation to the structuring phase of the securities and the underwriting process. As such, CRAs have found themselves in conflict if during the underwriting process they had to give a lower rating than that expected by the issuer following the advice received during the structuring phase. Thirdly, CRAs have been likely to be retained by the same issuer in the future and as such they were incentivised to keep their client pleased by offering a high rating. Finally, CRA employees were too close to the companies whose securities they were rating. Perhaps the best case to illustrate this relates to Goldman Sachs, which is explored next. The US SEC civil fraud case against Goldman Sachs is an interesting example of the effect that CRAs can have on financial markets. The SEC alleged that Goldman misled investors, a German Bank, IKB, and a US financial services firm, ACA, about the role played by the hedge fund Paulson & Co. in the construction of a CDO called Abacus 2007, whilst also concealing that Paulson's was, through separate transactions with Goldman, betting against Abacus 2007. According to Goldman, as of 15 July 2010, the firm agreed to a settlement with the SEC which was subject to the approval of the US Court for the Southern District of New York. It has done so 'without admitting or denying the SEC's allegation.' However, they acknowledge that:[46]

> [. . .] the marketing materials for the ABACUS 2007-ACI transaction contained incomplete information. In particular, it was a mistake for the Goldman marketing materials to state that the reference portfolio was 'selected by' ACA Management LLC without disclosing the role of Paulson & Co. Inc. In the portfolio selection process and that Paulson's economic interests were adverse to CDO investors. Goldman regrets that the marketing materials did not contain that disclosure.

---

[44] See further, T. Hurst 'The Role of Credit Rating Agencies in the Current Worldwide Financial Crisis' (2009) 30 Comp Lawyer 61–64.
[45] These do not include the sub-prime crisis concerns in the US, which are beyond the scope of this chapter. These focused on three main charges. First, that CRAs assigned too favourable ratings, especially for sub-prime residential mortgage-backed securities. Secondly, that they failed to adjust those ratings sooner as the performance of the underlying assets deteriorated. And finally, that they did not maintain appropriate independence from the issuers and underwriters of those securities.
[46] *Ibid.*

When these allegations were first made in April 2010, an inquiry was conducted by the Senate sub-committee following 16 months of a separate investigations by the SEC. Goldman always denied any wrongdoing. This case is relevant to our discussion because of the role that both S&P and Moody's played in the matter. The record of emails over a period of 16 months running up to the hearing gathered by the SEC showed that both CRAs were pressurised into giving Abacus 2007 and other such toxic complex credit instruments a much higher rating than they knew they actually deserved. Goldman sold these ostensibly AAA securities to investors, and the results were disastrous. Carl Levin, the Democrat Senator who headed the sub-committee, gave Goldman a damning verdict:

> They bundled toxic mortgages into complex financial instruments, got the credit rating agencies to label them as AAA securities, and sold them to investors, magnifying and spreading the risk throughout the financial system, and all too often betting against the instruments they sold and profiting at the expense of their clients.[47]

The email trail presented as documentary evidence during the SEC hearing gives an insight into the relationship between Goldman and the two CRAs during the 16 months running up to the hearing. In 2007, one Moody's managing director admitted that its 'behaviour in terms of handing out triple A ratings for, say, mortgage bonds made it either incompetent at credit analysis, or like we sold our soul to the devil'.[48] One S&P official emailed a colleague comparing the organisation to the Nixon White House.[49] Evidently, then, it appears that CRAs were fully aware of what they were doing, and of the existing conflict of interest. Ultimately, as suggested above, it is bankers who pay their fees, so it is hardly surprising that CRAs sometimes serve their interests, rather than those of investors. And surely, this is particularly true for an investment bank as large and powerful as Goldman. A senior managing director at Moody's is reported to have said: 'There has always been pressure from banks, and it is quite common for banks to ask for analysts to be removed.'[50]

So, can investors today, in 2018, really continue to rely on CRAs? In the case of Goldman, Abacus 2007 was AAA rated, which was apparently enough to invest without any more questions asked. At the hearing, Goldman's defence was *caveat emptor* – buyer beware. It argued that investors were 'sophisticated', and should therefore have been assumed to be able to protect their own interests. Rather surprisingly, Warren Buffet came out in support of Goldman, saying, '. . . if you care who's on another side of the trade, you shouldn't be in the business of insuring bonds.'[51] However, even if Goldman can be exempted from any responsibility, and that is arguable, is the same true for the CRAs involved? Presumably even the most sophisticated investors rely on CRAs to a certain extent, and in this case, both S&P and Moody's gave a very clear signal that Abacus 2007 was not at all a risky investment. At the very least, CRAs contribute to shape investors' beliefs about the market. This may explain why investors are taking the view that CRAs should be held accountable, a position increasingly shared by lawmakers and judges.

---

[47] S. Kirchgaessner 'Goldman Profited on Shorts', *Financial Times*, 24 April 2010.
[48] G. Tett 'E-mails Throw Light on Murky World of Credit', *Financial Times*, 25 April 2010.
[49] *Ibid.*
[50] S. Kirchgaessner and K. Sieff 'Moody's Chief Admits Failure over Crisis', *Financial Times*, 23 April 2010.
[51] 'The Sage's verdict on Goldman Sachs', *The Times*, 3 May 2010.

On 7 May 2010, Moody's revealed that the SEC was considering bringing an enforcement action against the company, and 'judges had allowed four separate investor lawsuits against the [CRAs] into the evidence gathering stage'.[52] The SEC had warned in a 'Wells notice' that it was moving towards filing charges that Moody's ratings procedures were false and misleading. 'The allegations stem from a 2008 revelation by the *Financial Times* that Moody's awarded incorrect triple A ratings to billions of dollars in European constant proportion debt obligation because of a modelling error.'[53] Within two weeks running up to Moody's statement, judges in New York and California refused to dismiss lawsuits brought by pension funds against Moody's, as well as its main competitors, S&P and Fitch. In these cases, the investors argued that the agencies 'committed either fraud or gross negligence in granting high rating to structured products that later went sour'.[54] 'The victories stand in stark contrast to the failed efforts to hold the agencies accountable in the 2001 collapse of Enron.'[55]

## 2 *Failure to downgrade the securities*

A second charge against CRAs is that they have very often been slow in recognising the decline of the creditworthiness of issuers.[56] As a result, CRAs have been downgrading the securities only after the market had already recognised that the issuers' finances had deteriorated.[57] This contributed to huge losses for private investors and to write downs at both large banks and investment firms.

## 3 *Underestimating the risks involved in novel structured finance securities*

Critics also contend that CRAs have made serious errors of judgment in rating structured finance products, especially securities linked to sub-prime residential mortgages. They have been faulted for initially assigning ratings that were too high; for failing to adjust those ratings sooner as the performance of the underlying assets deteriorated; and for not maintaining appropriate independence from the issuers and underwriters of those securities. As we will see below, to re-address the weaknesses of the CRAs within the current oversight regime in the structured finance market, several recommendations for reform have been advanced. Some of these recommendations include reducing the liability exemptions for certain structured finance rating practices and requiring agencies to form independent statistical staffs to develop, test, implement and review their rating models.[58] Prior to discussing these reform proposals in some detail, it is important to discuss what role CRAs assumed in the structured finance market. The following section turns to explore this thorny issue.

---

[52] B. Masters 'Moody's and Rating Agency Peers Face Legal and Regulatory Pitfalls', *Financial Times*, 10 May 2010.
[53] *Ibid.*
[54] *Ibid.*
[55] *Ibid.*
[56] Hurst, above n. 44, 61–64.
[57] *Ibid.*
[58] J. Rosner 'Toward an Understanding: NRSRO Failings in Structured Ratings and Discreet Recommendations to Address Agency Conflicts' (2009) 14 (4) *The Journal of Structured Finance*, 7–22.

## 17.4 The relationship between CRAs and the structured finance market

### A Background

This section focuses on the relationship between CRAs and the structured finance market in the UK. The recent credit crisis has its origins in the loosening of the lending standards which occurred in the US at the beginning of the new millennium. The loans were made by a variety of banking institutions and affiliates of other major financial institutions. With the help of CRAs these loans were wrapped up in securities and sold to various institutional investors in the form of financial products. By then concentrating various residential mortgage backed securities ('RMBS') into CDOs and by making combinations with derivative products such as credit default swaps in order to imitate the achievements of RMBS these financial products became more complex.[59] Critics contend that CRAs, by assigning AAA ratings to CDOs, have made a serious error of judgment. Examining why this has happened requires an explanation of certain structured finance terminology first.

### B Asset securitisation

According to a study undertaken at a leading English law firm, until the middle of 2007 the securitisation market in the UK was both active and well developed.[60] Nowadays, despite a clear 'reduction in the level of activity new issuances have not completely stopped, although activity has been concentrated on assisting originators in a difficult market, using securitisation in an innovative way to refinance existing debt or to provide liquidity.'[61] In the asset backed securities ('ABS') sector, the UK securitisation market in 2008 saw the BAA infrastructure issue, which refinanced the acquisition debt raised by Ferrovial in 2006.[62]

According to the legal criteria adopted by S&P, most structured financing consists of assets securitisation where the investors' central credit risk lies in the assets that have been securitised. A key risk in many of the asset securitisations is represented by the fact that the underlying obligor actually defaults on its payment, such as when the homeowner fails to make his mortgage repayment. CRAs try to model the likelihood of such an event to determine the appropriate rating. In addition CRAs usually try to evaluate whether there are legal issues which could result in the holders of the rated notes suffering a loss.[63]

---

[59] D. Coskun 'Supervision of Rating Agencies: The Role of Credit Rating Agencies in Finance Decisions' (2009) *Journal of International Banking Law and Regulation* 7.
[60] G. O'Keefe and G. Belsey (Slaughter & May), *Structured Finance and Securitisation, the Law in Key Jurisdictions* (2009/10) (London: Practical Law Company), 147.
[61] *Ibid.*
[62] In June 2006 BAA (British Airports Authority) was bought by a consortium led by Ferrovial, the Spanish construction company, and in August BAA officially delisted from the London Stock Exchange. Ferrovial is one of the world's leading infrastructure companies, with 104,000 employees and operations in 43 countries in a range of sectors including construction, airport, toll road, and car park management and maintenance, and municipal services. The company leveraged construction, its original business, to finance expansion into other sectors that are more profitable and capable of generating growing cash flow in the long term. See further: http://www.heathrowairport.com.
[63] Structured Finance Rating, European Legal Criteria 2005 (S&P) 7, 8.

The initial structuring consideration in an asset securitisation transaction normally focuses on how the assets can be isolated under local law. By transferring the assets by means of a 'true sale' to a 'bankruptcy-remote' special purpose vehicle ('SPV'), the bankruptcy or corporate reorganisation of the originator of the assets does not adversely affect the payment of principal and interest by the SPV on the rated securities.

The SPV's only function is that of owning the assets backing the securities and it typically has no other assets, liabilities or employees. In assessing whether the SPV is actually bankruptcy remote, CRAs consider the insolvency regimes that would govern a bankruptcy of the SPV. CRAs have also developed other specific criteria to assess whether an SPV is sufficiently protected against both voluntary and involuntary insolvency risks.[64]

Asset securitisation transactions are also structured to have internal credit enhancement. According to Krishna Prasad, former employee at Lehman Brothers, 'one of the great innovations of the securitised market has been the realisation that different investors have different needs'.[65] To meet these needs the SPVs have been issuing a variety of bonds attracting 'different ratings, different average lives and different levels of exposure to prepayments, defaults, interest rates'[66] backed by the same pool of assets. One way in which this was achieved was by subordinating some categories of bonds (tranches) to others, with the best protected bonds called senior bonds and the least protected being labelled as subordinate.

As we have seen, the issuer of asset backed securities in structured finance transactions is usually an SPV. These securities are normally categorised as mortgage backed securities ('MBS'), ABS or CDOs. As mentioned above, critics contend that CRAs, by assigning AAA ratings to CDOs, made a serious error of judgment. Accordingly, the later focus of this section will be on CDOs. MBS and CDOs were the most popular. Yet normally in CDOs the asset pool was formed in turn by other asset backed securities; which often turned CDOs into a mechanism of re-securitisation.[67]

## C Collateralised debt obligations

A broad range of financial instruments owe their existence to the credit derivatives market and, in particular, the expansion in the market for credit default swaps agreements ('CDS'). According to Moore, this is the case for the CDO market which, at least in its synthetic form, is supported by the underlying CDS market.[68]

In the UK, one of the most notable CDO transactions was in the insurance sector where the Merlin CDO saw an innovative synthetic CDO of insurance and reinsurance risk.

---

[64] S&P adopted the following 'SPV criteria' to determine the insolvency risk of an SPV: restriction on objects and powers; debt limitations; independent director; no merger or reorganisation etc.; separateness covenants; and security interests over assets. These elements are usually addressed in the relevant organisational and or transaction documents. An analysis of the rationales for adopting these criteria is, however, beyond the scope of this text. See S&P Structured Finance Ratings, European Legal Criteria 2005, 11.
[65] R. Watson and J. Carter *Asset Securitisation and Synthetic Structures, Innovations in the European Credit Market* (Euromoney Institutional Investors: London, 2006), 5.
[66] *Ibid.*
[67] See D. Ramos Muñoz *The Law of Transnational Securitization* (Oxford: OUP, 2010) para 1.24, 8.
[68] P. Moore *The New ABC of CDO, The Credit Guide to Collateralised Debt Obligations* (Sean O'Callaghan, 2005), 8–10.

Following the credit crisis, volumes in respect of CDO transactions have dropped significantly compared to, say, the 2007 levels.[69] Analysts and investors such as Warren Buffett and the IMF former chief economist Raghuram Rajan had anticipated that CDOs and other ABS spread risk and uncertainty about the value of the underlying assets more widely, rather than reducing the risk through diversification.[70] In the aftermath of the credit crisis this view has gained substantial credibility. Assessing why CRAs have failed to adequately account for large risks (such as the collapse of the prices in the housing market in the US) when rating CDOs requires a brief investigation into the particular nature of CDO transactions. CDOs are a type of asset backed security whose value and payments derives from an underlying portfolio of fixed income assets. As with ABS, they are divided into different tranches with the 'senior' tranches considered to be the safest securities. The payment of principal and interest on the 'tranches' are made depending on the order of seniority. The lower tranches attract higher interest rates so as to compensate for the additional risk of default. CDOs can be classified in different ways. The most common classifications have been developed according to the following criteria:

(1) *Origin of the underlying assets: static v dynamic*
   (i) Static: where the assets from the originator are designed at the outset.
   (ii) Dynamic: where the assets are also designed from the outset but the originator/arranger is given the right to substitute the assets in its sole discretion within contractually specified criteria.[71]
(2) *Source of funds: cash flow v market value*
   (i) Cash flow: when the cash flow is generated by the CDOs assets. Cash flow CDOs' main focus is to manage the credit quality of the underlying portfolio.
   (ii) Market value: 'A market value CDO is one where the performance of the CDO tranches is primarily a marked-to-market performance, i.e. all securities in the collateral are marked to market with high frequency.'[72]
(3) *Underlying motivation: arbitrage v balance sheet*
   (i) Arbitrage transactions:[73] these are organised to profit from market anomalies. The aim of arbitrage CDOs is to capture the arbitrage opportunity that exists in the credit spread differential between the high yield collateral and the highly rated notes.[74]

   It is interesting to note that prior to the economic meltdown, S&P considered their key legal feature to be represented by the fact that the securitised assets were being purchased in the open market from a variety of market sellers unconnected with the rated transaction.[75]

---

[69] G. O'Keefe and G. Belsey, above n. 66, 147. It should be noted that securitisation fulfils different purposes in the (re)insurance market and the mortgage market. Also, a thorny legal/regulatory issue is whether CDSs are insurance contracts (and should therefore be subject to insurance regulation).

[70] R. Hunter 'Sustainability. Economics. Public policy', 3 March 2009: http://rosshunter.wordpress.com/2009/03/.

[71] Muñoz divides the structures into static, revolving (where by their nature some assets have to be replaced, such as credit card receivables, lines of credit etc.) and dynamic. D Ramos Muñoz *The Law of Transnational Securitization* (Oxford, OUP, 2010) para. 1.22, p. 7 *et seq.*

[72] D. Picone 'Collateralised Debt Obligations' (2002) Working Paper, City University Business School, London and Royal Bank of Scotland.

[73] Arbitrage transactions are classified as either cash flow or market value transactions. Prior to the economic crisis about 85% of the CDO market was arbitrage motivated..

[74] R. Watson and J. Carter, above n. 71, 4.

[75] G. O'Keefe and G. Belsey, above n. 69, 147.

(ii) Balance sheet transaction: primarily motivated by the issuing institution capital, accounting or regulatory requirements. A bank may, for instance, wish to offload some of its credit risk in order to reduce its balance sheet's credit risk.

(4) *Funding: cash v synthetic*

(i) Cash CDOs: where the ownership of the underlying assets such as loans, corporate bonds or ABS is transferred to the SPV which then issues the CDO tranches.

(ii) Synthetic CDOs: here the underlying credit ownership of the underlying pool remains in the originator's book and the credit risk is transferred to the SPV through a credit default swap agreement[76] (about 8.5% of the market in 2006).[77] As we will see in the section dedicated to issues of reform, one of the great challenges at the moment consists in regulating the underlying credit default swap market.

(iii) Hybrid CDOs: represent an intermediate instrument between cash CDOs and synthetic CDOs. The portfolio of assets includes both cash assets as well as swaps that give the CDO credit exposure to additional assets.

(iv) Sub-participation: a technique used mostly by bankers to allow several other banks to share the risks and the returns of financial transactions, including the funding of the transaction. The principal contract between the originating bank and the borrower remains unaffected, the sub-participation: a contract between the participating banks and the originating bank. If the sub-participants also provide funding to the originating bank, it is funded risk participation. If the sub-participant bank undertakes the credit risk but does not fund the transaction, it is unfunded risk participation.

In a CDO, the securities are typically backed by a pool of assets consisting of a mixed pool of mortgage loans and/or other receivables owned by the SPV.

Figure 17.2 illustrates a typical CDO structure. The main steps of a typical CDO transaction can be summarised as follows:

(1) The assets are transferred to the SPV. The SPV funds these assets from cash proceeds of the notes it has issued.

(2) The CDO structure allocates interest income and principal repayment from a pool of different assets to a prioritised collection of securities notes called tranches.

(3) Senior notes are paid before mezzanine and lower rated notes. Any residual cash flow is paid to the equity.

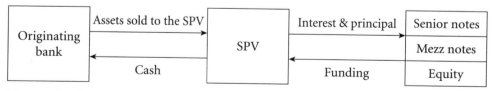

**Figure 17.2** A typical CDO structure[78]

---

[76] R. Watson and J. Carter, above n. 65, 11.
[77] S.K. Henderson 'Regulation of Credit Derivatives: To What Effect and For Whose Benefit?' (2009) 24 (3) *Journal of International Banking and Finance Law* 147, 148.
[78] R. Watson and J. Carter, above n. 65, 1.

The role of CRAs with these types of transactions broadly consists of three main issues: approving the legal and credit structure of the CDO, performing due diligence on the assets manager and the trustee and, thirdly, rating the various seniorities of debt issued by the SPV.[79] The asset manager in an arbitrage CDO selects the initial portfolio of assets and manages them according to prescribed guidelines. The trustees, on the other hand, generally hold the CDO assets for the benefit of debt and equity holders, monitor and report on collateral performance and disburse cash to debt and equity investors according to set rules. As such, their role also encompasses that of collateral custodian and CDO paying agent.[80]

With respect to the rating of the various seniorities of debt, CRAs base their rating on the SPV's ability to service debt with the cash flows generated by the underlying assets. The debt service depends on the collateral diversification and quality guidelines, subordination and structural protection (credit enhancement and liquidity protection). As we move down the CDO's capital structure, the level of risk increases.[81] In CDOs, like other classes of securitised transactions, CRAs have been rating more highly the classes of these securities than the quality of the underlying receivables. For example, senior securities were usually rated AAA even if the underlying receivables consisted of sub-prime mortgages.[82] Apparently, the CRAs based such rating on the belief that separating such securities into 'tranches', with the highest rated 'tranche' having the first priority on receiving payments from the underlying assets, was enough to justify an AAA rating for such securities.[83] Also, the diversification of assets and the credit enhancement mechanisms by highly rated institutions played a role.

The almost universal demand by investors for CRAs meant that investors worldwide were influenced by the ratings assigned and this led many of them to invest in securities which later turned out to be worthless. In fact, when in the US the home loan market crashed, the adjustable rate mortgage ('ARM') interest rate rose to unprecedented levels. This brought many borrowers to default on their mortgage repayments. As the mortgage loans represented the class of assets supporting a significant portion of the CDO market, the equity and mezzanine tranches, and in many cases the senior tranches too, were wiped out. Investors in these securities lost billions, creating a general loss of confidence in the financial markets[84] and as a result the world economy entered into a recession.

## 17.5 The regulation of credit rating agencies

### A Introduction

To what extent are CRAs really to blame for the recent financial crisis? Are they the main culprits or were they only assisting a larger structural deficiency of structured finance in

---

[79] D.J. Lucas, L.S. Goodman and F.J. Fabozzi 'Collateralized Debt Obligations and Credit Risk Transfer', Yale ICF Working Paper No. 07-06, 7.
[80] *Ibid.*
[81] R. Watson and J. Carter, above n. 65, 2.
[82] S.L. Schwarcz *Structured Finance, A Guide to the Principles of Asset Securitization* 3rd edn (New York: Practising Law Institute, 2008), 13–18.
[83] Hurst, above n. 44, 61–64.
[84] Schwarcz, above n. 82, 13:1.2.

the mortgage context? The picture that emerges from our discussion so far is that CRAs should shoulder some responsibility, although, unsurprisingly, they were not solely responsible for the catastrophic collapse of the financial markets.[85] To believe that for the CRAs to get it so significantly wrong, both other factors operating at the same time and the complexity of the financial markets, as well as the financial products (and the interdependence of all these factors on each other) were necessary and that neither was sufficient. And so when we consider the appropriate reform efforts, it should be remembered that fiscal, operational and macroeconomic factors rather than CRAs on their own should form part of the debate on the right way forward.[86] But whilst reform of CRAs on their own may be relatively insignificant, the package of regulatory reform initiatives should, at least, take into account the various flaws identified above.

It has been contended by several policy makers that CRAs are the constituency that actually control their ratings. But is this really the case? Calomiris[87] explains that it is more accurate to conclude that ratings which exaggerated the quality of securitised debts were demanded by the buy side of the market, i.e. by institutional investors.[88] One can immediately see the force in this argument. Ratings that understate risk are helpful to institutional investors because they reduce the amount of capital institutions have to maintain against their investments while increasing institutional investors' flexibility in investing. Once one recognises that the core constituency for exaggerating the quality of the ratings is the buy side of the securitised debt market, that will carry important implications for reform. Any solution to the problem must therefore make it profitable for CRAs to issue non-inflated ratings notwithstanding the demand for inflated ratings by institutional investors. One way to accomplish this is by linking the fees earned by CRAs to their performance.[89]

Interestingly, and in contrast to other areas of the financial services industry where reform efforts have dragged on and on, some meaningful steps have been taken to improve the functioning of the CRA industry in the recent past. In the US, for example, reform efforts at the federal level are taking place.[90] When Congress passed the Sarbanes–Oxley Act of 2002, it included a provision requiring the Securities and Exchange Commission to prepare a report on CRAs and include suggestions for possible legislative reform. As a result, in June 2003, the SEC published a 'Concept Release' discussing possible reforms. Several years later, in June 2008, the SEC issued proposed rules. The rules would, among other steps: (1) prohibit a CRA from using a rating on a structured product unless

---

[85] Although this section touches on the latest regulatory proposals in the wake of or during the recent financial crisis, a comprehensive, even if concise, account of the factors that contributed to this crisis, are beyond the scope of this chapter. For a recent account of these see e.g. D. Ramos Muñoz *The Law of Transnational Securitization* (Oxford: OUP, 2010) paras 1.40–1.61, pp. 13–27.

[86] Wood, for example, lists about 100 measures or proposals following the financial crisis. These are divided into the following sets: measures taken during the crisis, such as government bail-outs and central bank financing; post-crisis regulatory proposals, such as those relating to bank capital and liquidity and to securitisations; current and future proposals regarding insolvency law in relation to banks, corporates and sovereign states. See P.R. Wood 'Legal Impact of the Financial Crisis: A Brief List' (2009) 4 *Capital Markets Law Journal* 436.

[87] Charles Calomiris is the Henry Kaufman Professor of Financial Institutions at Columbia Business School. See C. Calomiris 'A Recipe for Ratings Reform' *The Economist Voice* (November 2009).

[88] C. Calomiris, *ibid.*

[89] *Ibid.* How this would be done is unclear; it raises perverse incentives: as fees are paid by banks, who may encourage CRAs to get it wrong by giving them higher ratings than deserved.

[90] See further, Hurst, above n. 44, 63.

information on the underlying assets was made available for review; (2) prohibit CRAs from rating products which they had played a role in creating; (3) require CRAs to make all rating actions publicly available, including those that were not included by an issuer in a public offering; (4) require elaborate disclosure provisions designed to increase transparency and minimise conflicts of interest. Then, in May 2011 the SEC voted unanimously to propose new rules and amendments intended to increase transparency and improve the integrity of CRAs.[91] Under the SEC's proposal, NRSROs would be required to: report on internal controls, protect against conflicts of interest, establish professional standards for credit analysts, publicly provide – along with the publication of the credit rating – disclosure about the credit rating and the methodology used to determine it and enhance their public disclosures about the performance of their credit ratings. The SEC's proposal also requires disclosure concerning third-party due diligence reports for asset backed securities.

Some US commentators argue that the three largest CRAs, S&P, Moody's Investor Service and Fitch, exploited their privileged regulatory status to profit from the booming sub-prime mortgage market at the expense of homeowners.[92] These CRAs boosted their own bottom lines and assisted predatory lenders by effectively vetoing state consumer protection initiatives. And so, while regulators have identified enhanced investor protection regulation of CRAs as a priority, future regulation must ensure that the systemic biases of the rating agency industry are no longer permitted to trump legitimate state consumer protection initiatives.[93]

## B The IOSCO model

In explaining why government regulation is needed one should consider first why self-regulation would neither reduce costs nor improve reliability. Self-regulation has in the past failed to effectively regulate CRAs.[94] It seems then that further regulation is necessary and has long been overdue. At the EU level, with the passing of the CRA Regulation at the beginning of May 2009, there has certainly been a move in that direction. Whether enough is being done to avoid a future crisis of this type is still open for debate.

The IOSCO model, i.e. its voluntary code of practice, is perhaps the most prominent example of self-regulation of CRAs. It was published by the IOSCO in December 2004 and a number of CRAs, including S&P, Moody's and Fitch, have since adhered to it.[95] The code seeks to deal with issues of integrity, independence and transparency, without, however, addressing the issue of enforcement. Following publication of the IOSCO Code of Conduct Fundamentals ('IOSCO Code'), the Committee of European Securities Regulators ('CESR') was asked to prepare a Technical Advice on possible future regulatory measures for CRAs. It considered six different options, ranging from full-scale registration of CRAs and integration of the IOSCO Code within EU legislation (option 1) to self-regulation and 'wait and see' (option 6). It was the latter option that was finally endorsed by the Commission, as it wished

---

[91] http://www.sec.gov/news/press/2011/2011-113.htm.
[92] D.J. Reiss 'Rating Agencies: Facilitators of Predatory Lending in the Subprime Market' (27 July 2009). Available at http://ssrn.com/abstract=1439748.
[93] *Ibid.*
[94] See failures of the IOSCO model, discussed further below.
[95] IOSCO Code of Conduct Fundamentals for Credit Rating Agencies (23 December 2004): http://www.iosco.org/library/pubdocs/pdf/IOSCOPD271.pdf.

to see whether the industry would embrace the IOSCO Code, and whether the Code would prove a worthy surrogate for direct regulation.'[96] The IOSCO model was strengthened in May 2008, when IOSCO published an updated revised version of the Code.[97] This included changes arising out of the financial crisis, including requiring CRAs to ensure the quality and integrity of the ratings process, e.g. by prohibiting analysts from making recommendations on structuring; be independent and avoid conflicts of interests; act responsibly towards investors and issuers, e.g. by differentiating structured finance ratings; and disclose codes of conduct, rating methodologies and historic performance data in a prominent position on its website. But will this prove to be sufficient?

In March 2009, the IOSCO Task Force published a report reviewing implementation by CRAs of the revised code.[98] It concluded that Fitch, Moody's and S&P had also substantially implemented the revised Code but that 14 other CRAs reviewed had not addressed the revisions. This indicates that amongst the smaller rating agencies there is still substantial work to be done in getting CRAs universally to adopt practices based on the revised Code. Of course, any such agencies wishing to obtain registration in the EU will now need to comply with the regulation.

Since the onset of the credit crisis there have been a number of proposed regulatory and industry reforms from the international regulators and industry bodies.[99] These proposed reforms have generally been founded on a principles-based approach, focusing largely on conflicts of interest and greater transparency and disclosure. Two, in particular, are worth highlighting next.

## C The Financial Stability Forum

In its 'Report of the Financial Stability Forum on Enhancing Market and Institutional Resilience'[100] published on 7 April 2008, the Financial Stability Forum ('FSF') set out various recommendations relating to the quality of the rating processes within CRAs, issues particular to structured products, the assessment of underlying data quality by CRAs and the use of ratings by investors and regulators. These measures involved requiring greater transparency relating to rating practices, including the publication of historical performance data. It also recommended a separate rating scale or additional rating symbol for structured products. The Report urged investors to reconsider how they use credit ratings in their investment guidelines and mandates and for risk management and valuation. It also stated that supervisory authorities need to check the roles they allocate to ratings in regulations and that supervisory rules are consistent with the objectives of investors making independent judgment or risks and carrying out their own due diligence, and do not induce uncritical reliance on credit ratings as a substitute for such independent evaluation.

---

[96] P. Maris 'The Regulation of Credit Rating Agencies in the US and Europe: Historical Analysis and Thoughts on the Road Ahead' (15 July 2009). Available at http://ssrn.com/abstract=1434504.
[97] See Annex A to the IOSCO Technical Committee's Final Report on The Role of Credit Rating Agencies in Structured Finance Markets (revised May 2008): http://www.iosco.org/library/ pubdocs/pdf/IOSCOPD270.pdf.
[98] The latest report on the regulatory implementation of the Statement of Principles by the Technical Committee of IOSCO was issued in February 2011. See http://www.fsa.go.jp/inter/ios/20110302/01.pdf.
[99] See further, P. Green and J.C. Jennings-Mares 'United Kingdom: The EU Rating Agency Regulation', Morrison & Foertser client alert: 'The EU Rating Agency Regulation' (28 April 2009).
[100] http://www.fsb.org/wp-content/uploads/r_0804.pdf?page_moved=1.

At the G20 summit in London in March 2009, the working group on enhancing sound regulation and strengthening transparency noted the fact that the IOSCO Code lacks legal authority and that any enforcement of the Code rests with national regulators. It noted that the FSF is following national and regional initiatives relating to such regulation including in the US, the EU and Japan.

## D SIFMA

On 31 July 2008, the Securities Industry and Financial Markets Association ('SIFMA') issued global recommendations for CRAs which were developed by the SIFMA Task Force.[101] The recommendations included encouraging CRAs to provide clear standardised disclosure of rating methodologies; disclose the results of due diligence and other information relied upon; provide access to performance of ratings to allow comparison among agencies; address conflicts of interest, being sensitive in particular towards the difference between core ratings services and consulting services; work towards a global regulatory framework; and disclose CRA fees.

The SIFMA Task Force has also urged legislators, regulators and law enforcement agencies to coordinate more closely in addressing the global issues surrounding CRAs. It has been keen, in particular, to avoid 'counter-productive, piecemeal, inconsistent attempts at remediation'.[102] The Task Force recommended that a SIFMA global advisory board of industry participants should be established to advise regulators and lawmakers on ratings issues.

## E The Turner Review in the UK

Although most of the recent debate on the future of CRAs has taken place at EU level, it is still, nonetheless, worth looking briefly at the UK level to examine to what extent the view in the UK reflects or diverges from the wider global and EU initiatives.[103]

The Turner Report was published in the UK by the chairman of the then FSA with a series of recommendations required to create a stable and effective banking system.[104] The Report had a much larger remit than just looking at CRAs. As such it addressed the need for banks to increase their capital requirements to protect themselves against risks, demanded a clampdown on the excessive remuneration system and, most importantly for the purpose of the present discussion, called for closer supervision of CRAs. The Report identified three underlying causes to the current financial crisis. First, the macro-economic imbalances, which were driven by the very high savings rates in oil exporting countries,

---

[101] See: https://circabc.europa.eu/webdav/CircaBC/FISMA/markt_consultations/Library/financial_services/credit_agencies/citizens/SIFMA-CRA-Recommendations.pdf.

[102] *Ibid.*

[103] It should be noted that the Turner Review predates the initiatives to further regulate CRAs, and belongs perhaps more to the group of policy statements; together with the G20 statements and IOSCO Reports (global level), or the Larosiere Report (at EU level) that created a consensus, and helped to set the stage for further regulatory initiatives.

[104] The Turner Review: 'A Regulatory Response to the Global Banking Crisis' was published by Lord Turner in his capacity as chairman of the Financial Services Authority in March 2009 and is accessible at http://www.fsa.gov.uk/pubs/other/turner_review.pdf (hereinafter 'the Report').

like China. Secondly, financial market innovation of securitised trading instruments, which occurred unlinked to genuine economic growth. The third cause of the financial crisis was linked to the deficiencies in the bank capital and liquidity regulation. The key recommendations set out in the Report included the following:[105]

(1) Increasing the quantity and the quality of the overall capital in the global banking system.
(2) Recognising the liquidity regulation as of equal importance to the capital regulation.
(3) Regulating the 'shadow banking' activities: supervisory coverage to follow the principle of economic substance rather than legal form. The authorities should have the power to gather information on all significant unregulated financial institutions (like hedge funds) to allow an objective assessment of the overall system-wide risk.
(4) Registration and supervision of CRAs to ensure good corporate governance and the management of the conflicts of interest.[106]
(5) Reform of the remuneration policies both at the national and the international level to avoid future incentives for undue risk taking.
(6) Development of clearing and central counterparty systems to cover the standardised CDS market, used to support synthetic CDOs.
(7) Shifting the supervisory approach of the FSA with a broader focus encompassing system-wide risks.
(8) Creating a new European institution (to replace the Lamfalussy's committees) with regulatory powers and significantly involved in macro-prudential analysis.

All in all, as far as CRAs are concerned, the Turner Report seems to reflect the wider global and EU initiatives (discussed below under F). With respect to methodologies and key rating assumptions (see art. 8 of the EU Regulation) the FCA (then the FSA) has made it clear that any attempts by regulators to supervise CRAs' methodologies would pose a number of complex challenges and the FSA does not see a case for pursuing this form of intervention.[107] The FSA believed there is no evidence to suggest that regulators would be more accurate in assessing the appropriateness of methodologies than the CRAs. It also expressed concerns that regulation of methodologies would shift the reputational risk for rating inaccuracy further from the rating agencies.[108]

## F The EU regulation on CRAs[109]

It is sometimes argued that the state's involvement in the regulatory process would entail a number of difficulties.[110] First, political manipulations in view of the interests associated with

---

[105] The Turner Report recommends actions required to create a stable and effective banking system, 7–9.
[106] This appears to be in line with the requirement for registration contained in art. 14 of the EU Regulation, discussed below.
[107] FSA Discussion Paper, 'A Regulatory Response to the Global Banking Crisis', March 2009, 171.
[108] *Ibid.*
[109] Regulation (EC) (No. 1060/2009) and the new Regulation on Credit Rating Agencies (No. 513/2011).
[110] See, for example, P. Maris 'The Regulation of Credit Rating Agencies in the US and Europe: Historical Analysis and Thoughts on the Road Ahead' (July 15, 2009): http://ssrn.com/abstract=1434504.

credit ratings.[111] But, of course, this is not unique to CRAs. This may be true in most cases where the state is called in to regulate. Secondly, there are inherent discrepancies in allowing the state to regulate CRAs as the former is a major client of the latter and therefore the governments also faces a conflict of interest.[112] Although there is some force in this argument, when it comes to regulating issues of government bonds, one could still opt for self-regulation. Thirdly, how could the state possibly assess the rating methodologies of complex financial instruments? This would involve the state becoming a better rating agent than CRAs themselves. And, of course, this would require much expertise, time, costs and public money. But such a sceptical assessment only suggests the need to be vigilant, not abandon the reform process altogether. How this might be done is explained below, but the following comments serve as a useful bridge between the arguments in this section and those still to come.

In June 2008, Mr McCreevy, then the European Commissioner for Internal Markets and Services, referred to the revised IOSCO Code as a 'toothless wonder' and stated that he did not believe the recommendations set out in the Code were enforceable in a meaningful way. Following on from these comments, on 31 July 2008, the European Commission published two consultation papers on CRAs. The first paper sought views on proposals to introduce a Directive or regulation relating to the authorisation, operation and supervision of CRAs, including the introduction of an authorisation and external oversight regime for CRAs active in the EU based on a home state principle. The stated rationale for these proposals was to reform CRAs' corporate and internal governance, including appropriate

---

[111] This is well-illustrated by the decision of China's leading CRA to strip the US, Britain, Germany and France of their AAA ratings, accusing Anglo-Saxon competitors of ideological bias in favour of the West. Dagong Global Credit Rating Co. used its first foray into sovereign debt to paint a revolutionary picture of creditworthiness around the world, giving much greater weight to 'wealth creating capacity' and foreign reserves than Fitch, S&P or Moody's. The US falls to AA, while Britain and France slither down to AA−. Belgium, Spain and Italy are ranked at A− along with Malaysia. Meanwhile, China rises to AA+ with Germany, the Netherlands and Canada, reflecting its a2.4 trillion (£2 trillion) reserves and a blistering growth rate of 8% to 10% a year. Chinese president Hu Jintao said in April 2010 that the world needs 'an objective, fair, and reasonable standard' for rating sovereign debt. Dagong appears to have stepped into the role, saying its objective was to assess countries using methods that would 'not be affected by ideology'. The agency, known in China for rating companies, said its goal is to 'correct the defects' of the existing system and offer a counterweight to Western agencies. Dagong appears to base growth potential on past performance but this can be misleading, especially in states enjoying technology catch-up. Japan was a high-flyer in 1970s and 1980s before stalling when the Nikkei bubble burst. It has been trapped in near perma-slump ever since. China may start to face some of Japan's demographic problems by the middle of this decade when the working age population peaks. The Western rating agencies put a high value on a long-established rule of law and government institutions that have proved resilient over many decades, or even centuries. China's political system may appear strong − as did the Soviet Union's − but only time will tell whether its foundations are brittle. The violent upheavals of the Cultural Revolution are still a very fresh memory. See A. Evans-Pritchard 'Chinese Rating Agency Strips Western Nations of AAA Status', *The Daily Telegraph*, 12 July 2010.

[112] The most obvious recent example is the S&P decision in August 2011 to downgrade the United States' top-notch AAA rating by one notch to AA+ with a negative outlook, citing concerns about budget deficits. The downgrade is a major embarrassment for the administration of President Barack Obama and could raise the cost of US Government borrowing as it is already struggling with huge debts, unemployment of 9.1% and fears of a possible double-dip recession. Another example is the news that S&P warned Britain remains at risk of a rating downgrade despite the tough measures unveiled in the Budget to rein in the national debt. See P. Aldrick 'UK Dealt Rating Blow as Economic Growth Fears Mount', *The Daily Telegraph*, 13 July 2010. Interestingly, S&P was the only leading ratings agency to have had the UK under review. Both Moody's and Fitch have confirmed Britain's AAA rating as stable. S&P said Britain's top-notch credit rating was the result of its wealthy and diversified economy, coupled with its policy flexibility. 'However, in our view, a number of large and politically challenging spending decisions are still to be made, and S&P's medium-term economic forecasts for the UK are less optimistic than the assumptions underlying the budget. We therefore believe there is still a material risk that the UK's net general government debt burden may approach a level incompatible with the triple-A rating.' *Ibid.* One wonders what effect such statements do to the appetite of the Government to regulate CRAs.

management of conflicts of interest and to increase transparency of CRAs' activities. The second paper was aimed at tackling the problem of excessive reliance on credit ratings, including requiring greater health warnings and requiring regulated and sophisticated investors to rely more on their risk analysis.

The reaction to the EU proposals was mixed and included criticism from many market participants and trade bodies. On 5 September 2008, the SIFMA Task Force published a response to the EU consultation papers noting its reservations about the nature and scope of the proposed measures. In particular, it was concerned that the EU proposal suggested a pre-scriptive regime favouring rigid rules over principles and did not form part of a coordinated international approach. It also felt that the lack of confidence in the IOSCO Code was over-stated. Particular concerns raised included the potential extra territorial scope of the proposals and the scope for the relevant authorities to unduly interfere in ratings decisions. Concerns were also raised that the proposals could give rise to market disruption and raise barriers to entry. While ESMA (then CESR) also responded acknowledging the drivers behind the EU approach, it considered its 2008 annual report was the most appropriate and proportional way of dealing with the issue. It also reiterated the need for a coordinated international response to the challenges, noting that the EU proposal was not aligned with the US regulations and the IOSCO Code, and that the Commission should not take any measures that might result in anti-competitive consequences. It also shared SIFMA's view that the proposed rules were too rigid and detailed and conveyed its preference for a principles-based approach.

On 12 November 2008, the European Commission published its draft CRA regulation, which sought to address some of the issues raised in response to its consultation papers. It stated that the financial crisis had revealed weaknesses in the methods and models used by CRAs, partially because theys operate in an oligopolistic market that offers limited incen-tives to compete on the quality of the ratings produced. It also stated that whilst it considers the IOSCO Code of Conduct to be the global benchmark, some of its rules were quite abstract and generic and needed to be more specific and consolidated, to make them easier to apply in practice and more efficient. Most importantly, it stated that the Code lacked teeth and is fatally weakened as a result. It further stated that it believes it is important to take a globally focused approach and create a regulatory framework in the EU comparable to that applied in the US and based on the same principles. Although the draft regulation sought to address some of the issues raised in response to its consultation papers, criticisms were raised that the provisions still provided an overly prescriptive approach and were not sufficiently coordinated with other global initiatives on CRAs. Following further consultation and nego-tiation with the EU Parliament and the Council of Ministers, the regulation was approved on 23 April 2009. Member states had 6 months to give effect to its provisions, although provi-sions relating to the recognition of rated products for regulatory purposes would not come into effect for another 12 months.[113] The regulation contains detailed provisions dealing with:

- the mechanism for registration and surveillance of CRAs, seeking to avoid 'forum shopping' among EU jurisdictions;

[113] On 2 June 2010 the EU Commission adopted proposals to amend Regulation (EC) No. 1060/2009 of the European Parliament and of the Council on credit rating agencies. It proposed improved EU supervision of CRAs and launched a debate on corporate governance in financial institutions. The Commission's proposal has now passed to the EU Council of Ministers and the European Parliament for consideration. See further immediately below.

- the effect of ratings issues by CRAs registered under the regulation (and the effect of those issued by CRAs that are not registered);
- rules seeking to ensure that CRAs are independent and avoid conflicts of interest in the rating process (or at least manage them adequately);
- transparency of ratings by setting disclosure obligations for CRAs; and
- the imposition of organisational and operational requirements.

It is clear then that the regulation aims to set behavioural standards for CRAs, such as increasing transparency and improving their standards of corporate governance.[114] The regulation also puts in place a regime for registering and regulating CRAs and subjecting them to supervision. The aim is that ratings will be qualitatively better than under current standards.

Later, and after a period of consultation, the new Regulation on Credit Rating Agencies (No. 513/2011), part of Europe's response to commitments made to the G20 group of nations, was published in the *Official Journal of the European Union* in May 2011.[115] The Regulation established an effective supervisory framework for CRAs. The appointment of the new European Securities and Markets Authority ('ESMA'), discussed in Chapter 16 above, as the single supervisory authority responsible for the registration and supervision of CRAs is designed to bring consistency to the application of the rules. The list of CRAs that are registered in accordance with the CRA regulation is set out on the European Commission's website and ESMA is also planning to publish the list on its website.[116]

So, is the Regulation likely to make any difference? It seeks to be consistent with the revised IOSCO Code. The Regulation, however, contains detailed prescriptive rules and some market participants have questioned whether these are appropriate.[117] Although the European Parliament has sought to address a number of concerns raised by various stakeholders including trading bodies, concerns remain in some quarters that the provisions are overly prescriptive in some respects, particularly in relation to corporate governance.[118] S&P, whilst welcoming greater transparency and accountability for CRAs, highlighted the need for consistent application of the rules across the EU.[119] But while the creation of the single supervisory authority responsible for the registration and supervision of CRAs assists in ensuring a greater degree of cooperation and consistency of approach, there are those who believe that the problem is a different one altogether, requiring a radically different solution. They suggest that CRAs have too much power and influence and obtain access to information that other market participants do not.[120] Attempting to tie them even more tightly into the regulatory system may in fact exacerbate these contradictions by

---

[114] See generally, http://www.mondaq.com/article.asp?articleid=78634.

[115] Available at http://eur-lex.europa.eu/LexUriServ/LexUriServ.do?uri=OJ:L:2011: 145:0030:0056:EN:PDF. In the UK they have been implemented by the Credit Rating Agencies (Amendment) Regulations 2011 (SI 2011/1435) in force from 1 July 2011. The regulation transfers responsibility for regulating CRAs from national authorities to the ESMA. See: http://www.legislation.gov.uk/uksi/2011/1435/pdfs/uksiem_20111435_en.pdf.

[116] On 6 July 2011 the European Commission held an interesting roundtable to gather views from various shareholders in order to shape future policy in the field of CRAs complementing existing EU regulation. For a summary of the points raised, see http://ec.europa.eu/internal_market/securities/docs/agencies/roundtable_en.pdf.

[117] See, for example, views expressed in Morrison/Foertser, News Bulletin, 'The EU Rating Agency Regulation' (28 April 2009).

[118] *Ibid.*

[119] House of Lords, European Union Committee, 14th Report of Session 2008–09. Ordered to be printed 9 June 2009 and published 17 June 2009.

[120] Morrison/Foertser, News Bulletin, 'The EU Rating Agency Regulation' (28 April 2009).

raising barriers to new entrants and making CRAs appear even less fallible. An alternative approach is to instead have less regulation, permit more competition and require bond issuers to publicly release any information which they provide to CRAs. Investors would then be required to make credit judgments of their own, the absence of which is potentially the greatest single factor behind the credit crisis. It is, however, clear that this approach does not hold favour with most regulators and legislators, very much like the previous attempts for voluntary regulation of CRAs discussed above (in particular the IOSCO Code). A greater regulatory oversight for CRAs is therefore now a reality.

From the point of view of CRAs, the Regulation imposed an increased administrative, disclosure and supervisory burden, although for CRAs that already comply with the IOSCO Code, the transition required to be regulations-compliant may be less than the changes that they have already undertaken. For third-country CRAs looking to do business within the EU, and for EU credit institutions looking to buy securities rated only by third-country CRAs, the impact of the regulation may be considerably harsher.[121]

With the new regulations in force there were a number of important issues that remained unanswered. Although there were new disclosure requirements on CRAs, it was still difficult for ESMA to assess quality of ratings because of informational asymmetry. The reform had also not addressed competition issues within this area, with S&P, Moody's and Fitch dominating the CRA market.

In May 2011 the Regulation was amended to adapt it to the creation of the ESMA, which has held all supervisory powers over agencies since July 2011. Another regulatory package entered into force in June 2013 to reinforce the rules on CRAs and address weaknesses related to sovereign debt credit ratings. This new regulatory framework, focused on enhancing competition in the credit rating market, consists of a new regulation (Regulation No. 462/2013)[122] and a new directive (Directive 2013/14/EU).[123] It has included rules aimed at reducing over-reliance on credit ratings, improving the quality of sovereign debt ratings, enhancing disclosure on SFIs, making CRAs more accountable for their actions and further mitigating potential conflicts of interest. The most significant provisions in the Regulation aimed at reaching these objectives were as follows:

(1) *Policy to reduce regulatory references to ratings (Articles 5b–5c).* Articles 5b–5c aim to reduce over-reliance on credit ratings by reducing the use of credit ratings for regulatory purposes. Under Article 5b, the European Supervisory Authorities (European Banking Authority ('EBA'), European Insurance and Occupational Pensions Authority 'EIOPA'), and the ESMA) may not refer to credit ratings in guidelines, recommendations and draft technical standards if they have the potential to trigger 'sole or mechanistic reliance' on ratings. Under Article 5c, references to credit ratings in EU law have to be deleted if there are appropriate alternatives available. In practice, removing references to ratings is difficult, especially because appropriate alternatives to credit ratings are not always easily available. Although efforts have been made, references to ratings can still be found in important pieces of EU legislation such as the Capital Requirements Directive ('CRD IV') and the Capital Requirements Regulation ('CRR') for the

---

[121] Mayer Brown 'EU Regulation of Credit Rating Agencies Approved' (29 April 2009).
[122] http://eur-lex.europa.eu/legal-content/EN/TXT/PDF/?uri=CELEX:32013R0462&from=EN.
[123] *Ibid.*

banking sector and the Solvency II Directive and its Delegated Regulation for the insurance sector, so that market participants may continue to have to rely on credit ratings.

(2) *Rotation-provision (Article 6b).* The rotation-provision (Article 6b) prescribes that the CRA that enters into a contract to attach ratings to re-securitisations (repackaged securitised products) shall not issue ratings on new re-securitisations with underlying assets from the same originator for a period exceeding four years. It primarily aims to decrease potential conflicts of interest that occur due to the fact most CRAs are paid by the very issuers of debt instruments they are supposed to impartially rate (issuer-pays model), which creates an incentive to inflate ratings, as discussed above.

(3) *Double rating-provision (Articles 8c–8d).* Under Article 8d, where issuers or related third parties intend to use two or more CRAs, they should consider appointing one CRA with less than a 10% market share. Otherwise, they must document their decision. In order to assist with this assessment and allocation, each year the ESMA is required to publish a list of registered CRAs and the types of credit ratings they issue, together with a calculation of market shares, which are assessed using CRAs' revenues from credit rating activities and ancillary services at group level. This provision aims to stimulate competition in the credit rating industry. At the time of writing, however, it has failed to do so to a large extent. It is believed that the level of market concentration has been left unsolved by Article 8d, as issuers can deviate and seem to have done so frequently when they can convincingly explain such a decision, because the reputation of small CRAs is often considered insufficient.

## 1 *International cooperation*

Under the Regulation, it is possible for a CRA established outside the EU to have its rating recognised and used for regulatory purposes in the EU. This can happen in one of two ways:

(1) *Equivalence certification.* CRAs established and supervised outside the EU that have no presence or affiliation in the EU can be certified by the ESMA under this regime, which applies to CRAs that are not systemically important for the stability or integrity of EU financial markets. The regime allows financial entities and instruments established or issued in non-EU countries to be rated. The European Commission has made a number of equivalence decisions attesting that the regulatory and supervisory regimes of several non-EU countries meet the requirements of the CRA regulation. The relevant certification requires a cooperation arrangement to be established between the ESMA and the relevant countries' authority.

(2) *Endorsement.* The endorsement regime applies to CRAs that are established outside the EU and affiliated or work closely with EU-registered CRAs. It requires these to comply with certain legal requirements, which must be as stringent as the ones set out in the Regulation and be subject to effective supervision. This assessment is made by the ESMA, which establishes the list of non-EU countries whose regulatory regimes are equivalent to the EU standards.

## 2 *The regulatory technical standards*

In September 2014, the European Commission strengthened regulatory control of CRAs by adopting a package of measures designed to apply 'stricter new rules' for the regulation of

CRAs. Three regulatory technical standards ('RTS') set out disclosure requirements for issuers, originators and sponsors of SFIs, the reporting requirements applicable to CRAs for the purpose of the European Rating Platform ('ERP') and reporting requirements applicable to CRAs over fees to help the supervisory work of the ESMA. The RTS were published in the *Official Journal of the European Union* on 6 January 2015. In respect of SFIs, the RTS specified the content, frequency and presentation of the information that issuers, originators and sponsors of SFIs established in the EU will jointly need to disclose on a website launched by the ESMA. This has improved investors' ability to make an informed assessment of the risks related to such complex financial instruments. The disclosure obligation is aimed in particular at reducing investors' dependence and reliance on credit ratings and reinforcing competition between agencies.

The RTS relating to the ERP, set up by the ESMA, allow investors to consult and easily compare all available credit ratings for all rated instruments. This RTS streamlines the data reported by CRAs in order to allow for more efficient data reporting to the ESMA. It also integrates the existing reporting requirements for the purpose of historical performance data, available in the central repository established by the ESMA, and for the purpose of ongoing supervision by the ESMA.

On reporting fees charged by CRAs, the European Commission has stated that the RTS sets out the content and format of data on fees charged to CRA clients to be periodically reported to the ESMA. Information collected allows the ESMA to verify whether pricing practices are discriminatory and facilitate fair competition and mitigate conflicts of interest. Enhanced disclosure on SFIs including full availability of credit ratings issued by authorised CRAs should enable investors to make better-informed investment decisions on these products. Reporting by CRAs on their pricing practices allows the ESMA to ensure that they act in a non-discriminatory manner.

Ever since the ESMA has been working on developing the ERP (or 'the SFIs website' as it is referred to in the relevant RTS), the new platform for the collection of individual rating data to which issuers of SFIs must submit information on an ongoing basis. Having created additional reporting burdens for the industry by significantly expanding the information that CRAs are required to provide to the ESMA, further changes to the CRA III framework are likely to be resisted at this stage.

Under the RTS, the disclosure requirements apply to all types of securitisations, regardless of whether the transaction involves listed and/or rated securities, meaning that private and bilateral transactions are also within its scope. Separately from the information required to be submitted to the ESMA under the RTS, CRAs must also make periodic submissions to the ESMA, covering a wide range of matters such as financial revenues and costs, headcount and staff turnover, complaints and compliance, internal audit and risk management and IT strategy. A new set of Guidelines published by the ESMA provides the information that CRAs should submit to the ESMA in their quarterly and semi-annual reports.

## G Policy studies

### 1 *IOSCO Code of Conduct Fundamentals for Credit Rating Agencies*[124]

In 2015, the IOSCO issued a revised Code for CRAs to ensure it remains relevant in the context of, and operates in harmony with, the latest CRA legislation. In particular, it

[124] https://www.iosco.org/library/pubdocs/pdf/IOSCOPD271.pdf.

introduces strengthened provisions on conflicts of interest, transparency, governance, training and risk management measures, and improves clarity around key terminology and definitions. The Code reflects an international standard for CRA self-governance and, although it is not explicitly stated, compliance with the Code (on a voluntary basis) has been required ever since.

## 2 *EC Study on the Feasibility of Alternatives to Credit Ratings*[125]

Published also in 2015, this Study mapped the various alternatives to external credit ratings that are currently being issued by market participants across the EU. Most importantly, it then assessed the feasibility of implementing the identified alternatives in an EU context based on consideration of criteria such as costs, market accessibility, accuracy and reliability, comparability, and suitability for regulatory purposes. Under arts 39 (4) and 39 (5) of the Directive, the ESMA, both corporate and sovereign issuers, the CRAs themselves and investors all provided the European Commission with Technical Advice on Competition[126] to establish whether existing provisions in the Directive have met their objectives,[127] and whether new rules could be necessary in other areas, such as requiring additional disclosures beyond those introduced for SFIs and measures to stimulate competition.[128]

## 3 *EC Study on the State of the Credit rating market*[129]

The aim of this Study published by the European Commission in January 2016 was to take stock of the current situation and recent developments in the EU-wide credit rating market, and assess the impact and effectiveness of a range of measures contained in the Regulation in achieving their overarching objectives. The work also identified potential additional measures or amendments in relation to selected areas and assessed the potential impacts and feasibility of these. The analysis did not show any trend toward decreasing concentration. While their fieldwork showed that since 2010 stakeholders have noticed an increase in the number of CRAs within the corporate bond rating and structured finance instrument rating markets, the impact of market entry on competition was limited. Barriers to entry[130] may act to inhibit further competition. The Study considered three scenarios for the possible future impact of the Regulation measures on competition and concentration. Based on these, it concluded that the likely evolution through to 2020 is as follows: for the low and medium-impact scenarios, in SFI, market shares between the Big Three and the rest are likely stable. No change is anticipated in other markets (e.g. bonds, re-securitisation). For the high-impact scenario, in SFI, market share held by the Big Three may see a small-scale decline

---

[125] https://ec.europa.eu/info/system/files/alternatives-to-credit-rating-study-01122015_en.pdf.
[126] Technical Advice on Competition, Choice and Conflicts of Interest in the Credit Rating Industry.
[127] For instance, provisions such as the rule requiring at least two CRAs to be appointed in structured finance transactions and the requirement for mandatory CRA rotation in re-securitisations.
[128] The ESMA stated that the market share calculation carried out for the purposes of art. 8d should be used with caution as evidence suggested that there are separate markets for credit ratings of different categories issued in different national markets within the EU, as well as international markets used by global issuers and investors.
[129] https://ec.europa.eu/info/system/files/state-of-credit-rating-market-study-01012016_en.pdf
[130] In particular, insufficient demand for additional rating agencies, high switching costs for issuers, and administrative / regulatory barriers.

(up to 1–2%). The Study also identified several ways to foster competition: developing a track record score for CRAs, making amendments to the ECB's selection of approved CRAs rating SFIs, and appointing CRAs by means of some form of competitive tender.

These recently published studies above have served an important purpose. In addition to showing that achieving significant changes in the credit rating sector takes time and effort, they also show that the sector continues to have fundamental structural problems–for instance, market concentration and conflicts of interest – that need to be addressed on an ongoing basis. Therefore, in order to preclude history from repeating itself, the credit rating industry is very likely to remain a centre of attention of the EU legislature and supervisors so that in the long term, conflicts of interest can be further addressed and disclosure on SFIs can be further enhanced.

## 4 ESMA Reports

In 2015, the ESMA published a Consultation Paper considering the specific issues highlighted from collected information from market participants about the approach to disclosure for SFIs originated and/or traded on a private and/or bilateral basis.[131]

In the Report *Competition and Choice in the Credit Rating Industry*,[132] published in December 2016, the ESMA provided information about CRAs' shares of supply of issued credit ratings at both an EU level and also within the five largest markets by issuance volume. At the time of writing, the ESMA intends to use data from the ERP to present CRAs' shares of supply of credit ratings with next year's market share calculation in order to improve the comparability of data across different categories. The ESMA encourages issuers and related third parties to consider the information provided in this market share calculation as a part of the due diligence they carry out before appointing CRAs.

## 5 House of Commons Briefing Credit Ratings Agencies Regulation[133]

Published in 2016, this Briefing sets out the development of regulation covering CRAs since the financial crisis of 2007–2008.

## 17.6 Towards liability for credit rating agencies

### A Credit ratings: just an opinion?

There is one important issue this chapter has yet to deal with. As CRAs become more and more regulated will that also mean they will be more accountable for their decisions in terms of liability?

As it may have become apparent by now, a key word or concept employed by the various definitions of credit ratings is *'opinion'*. In fact, a review of the definition of credit ratings by various academics and regulatory agencies illustrates how successful the CRAs

---

[131] See: https://www.esma.europa.eu/

[132] Market share calculation required by Article 8d of Regulation 1060/2009 on Credit Rating Agencies as amended, available at https://www.esma.europa.eu/sites/default/files/library/2016-1662_cra_market_share_calculation.pdf.

[133] http://researchbriefings.files.parliament.uk/documents/SN05603/SN05603.pdf.

have been in establishing their definition of credit ratings as 'opinions'. For instance, Hurst,[134] Fight[135] and Langohr[136] all accept the CRAs' assertion that they provide opinions although Fight does not accept the fact that providing opinions necessarily means exemption from any responsibilities. Langohr goes further and provides a list of definitions of credit ratings by regulatory agencies which nearly all refer to ratings as 'opinions'. Partnoy notes that CRAs are 'unique amongst gatekeepers in their ability to argue that their function is merely to provide "opinions"'.[137] As noted above, the IOSCO Committee and the EU Commission accept that credit ratings reflect the opinions of CRAs.

The fact that credit ratings come as 'opinions' should perhaps come as no surprise. After all, ratings are forward looking statements which represent the rater's judgment of the creditworthiness of an entity, to use part of the definition employed by the IOSCO Committee. As forward looking statements, 'ratings are not performance guarantees; they are beliefs about the downside risks surrounding promised future outcomes. Because the future cannot be known, credit ratings are, by nature, opinions, and necessarily come with various degrees of uncertainty.'[138] Finally, the fact that credit ratings are not regarded as investment advice within the meaning of the Directive on Insider Dealing and Market Manipulation (Market Abuse) ('MAD')[139] or the Directive on Markets in Financial Instruments (known as 'MiFID')[140] also helps to support the conclusion that credit ratings can be seen as 'mere' opinions. And so, 'however non-controversial these characterisations may seem, they have deep implications about immunity.'[141]

## B  The traditional approach on liability in the US, EU and the UK

In the US, the traditional position of the CRAs regarding their legal responsibility has been that since they are expressing an opinion to the public about the creditworthiness of a borrower they are acting in a journalistic capacity and as such they should be protected by the principles of freedom of the press under the First Amendment of the US Constitution. This claim has been tested and upheld in the US courts.[142] In other words, the fact that CRAs are not giving investment advice or recommendations but rather are expressing an opinion on the creditworthiness of an entity has so far provided them with a defence against liability for loss arising from detrimental reliance on their ratings. However, an order issued at

---

[134] T. Hurst 'The Role of Credit Rating Agencies in the Current Worldwide Financial Crisis' (2009) 30 Comp Lawyer, 61.
[135] A. Fight *The Ratings Game* (Chichester: John Wiley and Sons Ltd, 2001), 3.
[136] H.M. Lagohr and P.T. Laghor *The Rating Agencies and their Credit Ratings* (Chichester: John Wiley and Sons, 2008) 24.
[137] F. Partnoy 'How and Why Credit Rating Agencies are Not Like Other Gatekeepers' in Y. Fuchita and R.E. Litan (eds) *Financial Gatekeepers: Can They Protect Investors*? (Baltimore: Brookings Institute Press, 2006), 84.
[138] Lagohr and Laghor, above n. 136, 85. An interesting comparison can be drawn with the type of information which a public company must disclose when issuing new securities. In some jurisdictions the management of a public company must in fact disclose information which is 'soft', 'projective', or 'forward looking.' This information can prove essential for valuing the firm as a going concern since it permits an investor to estimate future changes in a firm's cash flow. See further, R. Kraakman, P. Davies, H. Hansmann (*et al.*) *The Anatomy of Corporate Law, A Comparative and Functional Approach* 2nd edn (Oxford: OUP, 2009), 284.
[139] Directive 2003/6/EC, OJ 2003, L 96/16.
[140] As subsequently amended by Directive 2008/10/EC.
[141] Lagohr and Laghor, above n. 136, 85.
[142] *Ibid*.

the beginning of September 2009 by a US district court in Manhattan might be changing the approach in the US towards CRAs. Judge Shira Scheindlin, in *Abu Dhabi Commercial Bank* v *Morgan Stanley*,[143] stated that 'ratings on notes sold privately to a "select" group of investors were not "matters of public concern" deserving of traditionally broad protection under the First Amendment of the US Constitution'. As a result 'the plaintiffs were allowed to pursue fraud claims accusing Moody's, Standard & Poor's and Morgan Stanley, which marketed the notes, of making false and misleading statements about the notes.' What must be pointed out is that if no longer found to have protection under the First Amendment, CRAs can still point to the fact that they have no direct privity of contract with the investors to attempt to avoid liability.[144] In fact, CRAs are appointed and compensated by the companies whose securities they rate and not by the investors themselves. As a result the privity of contract for the service is between the CRAs and the companies that initially sell the securities.[145] This point will also have to be taken into consideration when addressing the issue of whether the CRAs are bound by a duty of care in the UK.[146]

Moving to the EU, in the past, the EU legislator concluded that the freedom of the press argument could not be applied by analogy to the opinions issued by the CRAs since an investment grade rating is a prerequisite for being able to place one's bond with institutional investors.[147] Therefore, as the rating of a bond affects its regulatory eligibility for certain institutional portfolios, negligently maintaining too high a rating would cause losses for the portfolio beneficiaries that the ratings based regulation were supposed to protect.[148] There is force in this argument. If it is accepted that press articles are generally opinions on matters of public concern, credit ratings, on the contrary, are issued so that investors with limited time and skill can rely on their accuracy. This does not mean that CRAs should be seen as providing 'investment advice'. There is plenty of room for variation between a recommendation to invest and an opinion. CRAs should bear some degree of responsibility for their ratings, and, to some extent, they should be held accountable for their 'opinions'.

In the UK, the English tort of negligence adopts a generally exclusionary rule towards pure economic losses. However, in the leading case of *Hedley Byrne*[149] it was established that a duty of care against such losses might arise if the defendant voluntarily assumed responsibility for the claimant's economic welfare.[150] Of particular interest to our discussion are two cases, both involving auditors. The first, *Candler* v *Crane, Christmas*

---

[143] *Abu Dhabi Commercial Bank* v *Morgan Stanley*, US District Court, Southern District of New York (Manhattan), No. 08-7508.
[144] K.C. Kettering 'Securitisation and its Discontents: The Dynamics of Financial Product Development' (2008) 29 *Cardozo Law Review* 1553, 1668. Surely then liability will turn to tort (i.e. is there a duty of care?), as discussed below.
[145] *Ibid*, 1680.
[146] A discussion about the liability of the CRAs in the UK is below.
[147] G. Katiforis 'Report on Role and Methods of Rating Agencies', European Parliament, 29 January 2004, Sessions document A5-0040/2004, 10. This report was presented to the EU Parliament and later adopted in a resolution.
[148] Lagohr and Laghor, above n. 136, 85.
[149] *Hedley Byrne & Co. Ltd* v *Heller & Partners Ltd* [1964] AC 465.
[150] M. Lunney and K. Oliphant *Tort Law, Text and Materials* (Oxford: OUP, 2008), 375.

& *Co*[151] concerned negligent statements by an accountant about the financial position of a company. The recipient of the statements was a potential investor, and the accountant was fully aware that his statements would be relied on in making the decision on whether to invest or not. A majority of the Court of Appeal held that no duty arose: there was no general duty of care for statements. Denning LJ dissented. For him, a duty was owed by accountants, valuers and analysts both to their employers and to third parties to whom either they or their employers showed their reports, knowing that the purpose was to prompt an investment decision. Whilst the Court of Appeal in *Hedley Byrne* was bound by the majority's decision, the House of Lords was able to approve Lord Denning's dissent.

In the second case, *Caparo Industries plc* v *Dickman*[152] (*'Caparo'*), the defendant company, Caparo, owned shares in another company, Fidelity. Shortly before the publication of Fidelity's audited accounts Caparo started buying shares in the company. Once the accounts (which had shown a £ 1.2m profit) were made public, Caparo proceeded to make a successful takeover bid. It was later discovered that Fidelity had not made a profit during that tax year but that actually it had incurred losses of £400,000. Caparo then decided to initiate proceedings against Fidelity's auditors for the loss caused for having paid an excessive price for Fidelity's shares.[153] The court held that the auditors of a public company owe no duty of care to members of the public who have relied on the company's accounts in deciding to buy its shares. The court stated:[154]

> [. . .] where a statement [that of the auditors] is put into more or less general circulation and may foreseeably be relied upon by strangers to the maker of the statement for any one of a variety of different purposes which the maker of the statement has no specific reason to anticipate. To hold the maker of the statement to be under a duty of care in respect of the accuracy of the statement to all and sundry for any purposes for which they may choose to rely on it is not only to subject him, in the classic words of Cardozo CJ, to 'liability in an indeterminate amount for an indeterminate time to an indeterminate class' (in *Ultramares Corp* v *Trouche* (1931) 255 NY 170 at 179) it is also to confer on the world at large a quite unwarranted entitlement to appropriate for their own purposes the benefit of the expert knowledge or professional expertise attributed to the maker of the statement.

Is it therefore reasonable for us to assume that since in *Caparo* the auditors were not held accountable for having produced defective statements which were relied upon, the same conclusion could be reached with regards to the rates given by the CRAs? In *Caparo* the auditors carried out the audits to comply with a statutory duty arising under the Companies Act 1985. The reason for this requirement was represented by the need to provide shareholders with information about the company's performance so that, if the shareholders thought it necessary, action could be taken against those responsible for its management, i.e. the board of directors.[155] They were not provided to give potential investors information on which to make an investment decision, as in the case of CRAs. One of the most

---

[151] [1951] 2 KB 164 (CA).
[152] [1990] 2 AC 605. The most recent detailed House of Lords consideration of *Caparo* was in *Customs and Excise Commissioners* v *Barclays Bank plc* [2007] 1 AC 171. See further below.
[153] M. Lunney and K. Oliphant, above n. 160, 421.
[154] *Caparo Industries plc* v *Dickman* [1990] 2 AC 605, at p. 620.
[155] Lunney and Oliphant, above n. 160, 426.

recent detailed House of Lords (now the Supreme Court) considerations of *Caparo* was in *Customs and Excise Commissioners* v *Barclays Bank plc*.[156] The House of Lords established what is known as the 'three-fold test', which is that for one party to owe a duty of care to another, the following factors must be established:

- harm must be a 'reasonably foreseeable' result of the defendant's conduct;
- a relationship of 'proximity' between the defendant and the claimant;
- it must be 'fair, just and reasonable' to impose liability.

So, where does this leave us as to whether the CRAs are bound by a duty of care in the UK?[157]

The first question that must be addressed in order to assess the potential liability of the CRAs is whether there is a contract between the CRAs and the issuer, or the investors. In such a case, 'the issue of liability would turn on whether the liability sought to be established was allowed or excluded under the contract.'[158] Should there be no contract, then the question of liability would depend upon the identity of the person with whom the CRAs were in business. For instance, one could argue that it would be foreseeable to the rater that potential investors in the securities being rated may rely to their detriment upon a negligent rating. However, such a scenario would probably border on what Chief Justice Cardozo had called a liability in an indeterminate amount for an indeterminate time to an indeterminate class.[159] It therefore seems most unlikely that a duty of care could be found to exist between the CRAs and potential purchasers of the securities. With regards to the liability of CRAs towards the rated companies some distinctions must be drawn. For Ebenroth, in the case of unsolicited ratings damaging a company, any imposition of a duty of care would be foreclosed by the proximity requirement developed in *Hedley Byrne*.[160] Different considerations might apply in the event that the rated company was receiving advice from the CRAs on how to structure its credit or on how to enter into particular financing techniques. In such a circumstance, where reliance on the advice is foreseeable, the CRA has voluntarily assumed responsibility to the claimant and the claimant relies on the assumption of responsibility,[161] a sufficient degree of proximity can be found and the CRAs could consequently be held in breach of their duty of care.

---

[156] [2007] 1 AC 171.

[157] The analysis that follows does not touch on the standard of care to be followed to appraise negligence. The IOSCO Code of Conduct discussed above focuses on rating agency methodology, conflicts of interest etc. and formulates several substantive rules that have been followed by regulations in the US and the EU.

[158] C.E. Ebenroth and T.J. Dillon 'The International Rating Game: An Analysis of the Liability of Rating Agencies in Europe, England, and the United States' (1993) 24 *Law and Policy of International Business* 783, at p. 799. In the US, Nelson analyses the liability of CRAs under both contract and tort theories. Specifically, the potential liability is analysed under the doctrine of promissory estoppel in contracts and under an extension of negligence and products liability theories in torts. See K.W. Nelson 'Rough Waters for the Ratings Companies: Should the Securities Ratings Companies Be Held Liable for Investor Reliance in the Wake of the Real Estate Meltdown of 2007–2008?' (2009) 63 *University of Miami Law Review*. Available at http://ssrn.com/abstract=1430552.

[159] Ebenroth and Dillon, *ibid*.

[160] Ebenroth and Dillon, *ibid*, 801.

[161] See *Caparo Industries*, above n. 154 at p. 620.

## C Policy considerations

To assess whether it is correct or not to hold the CRAs liable for the losses suffered by investors one should also explore the relevant policy considerations. One, in particular, deserves attention. As mentioned above, ratings are issued so that investors with limited time and skill can rely on them. CRAs could therefore argue that they provide an integral service to market investors in rating the securities and companies[162] (although, of course, the fact that investors have limited time and skill makes them more reliant, not less, on CRAs). Should CRAs be found liable to pay investors' losses, the argument goes, some CRAs would not be able to pay the damages and therefore would no longer rate the companies or their securities. At the same time, CRAs that survive could be hesitant to continue to rate companies in the light of the new legal liability.[163] Without the ratings, investors would either have to choose investments based on insufficient or expensive data, or more likely seek other types of investments.[164] This scenario would lead to information inequality which, in a market system, could lead to large gains to the few who have the resources and losses by those who do not possess the resources to accurately assess the risks of the securities and the companies.[165]

## D Is imposing liability on credit rating agencies just a matter of time?

In the US, a number of developments point to the relative immunity CRAs enjoy in their place of birth. First, in 2011 the three major US CRAs won the dismissal of substantial lawsuits in relation to the collapse of Lehman Brothers seeking to hold them liable as 'under-writers' for helping banks structure securities transactions to achieve desired ratings.[166] A second development that favoured CRAs then took place in 2011. Rule 436

---

[162] See Kettering, above n. 144, pp. 1671–1680.

[163] K.W. Nelson 'Rough Waters for the Rating Companies: Should the Securities Rating Companies Be Held Liable for Investor Reliance in the Wake of the Real Estate Meltdown of 2007–2008?' (2009) 63 *University of Miami Law Review*, available at http://ssrn.com/abstract=1430552.

[164] *Ibid*, 22.

[165] *Ibid*, 22. Muñoz argues that, from the perspective of the 'reliance' requirement, investors cannot reasonably rely exclusively on the rating agency's assessment, but should perform an independent analysis. The exception would be in those cases where a rating agency has been deeply involved in a transaction, which creates a basis for such reliance. See D. Ramos Muñoz *The Law of Transnational Securitization* (Oxford: OUP, 2010) para 6.55, p. 263 *et seq*., especially paras 6.72–6.78, pp. 269–270; and by the same author, 'SEC v Goldman Sachs and the New Wave of Asset-backed Securities Litigation. What are the Arguments? What is at Stake?' [2010] *Law and Financial Markets Review* 413.

[166] The case is *In re Lehman Brothers Mortgage-Backed Securities Litigation*, 10-0712-cv; 10-0898-cv; 10-1288-cv. The plaintiffs, including a group of unions, said they bought $155bn in mortgage backed securities. Many of the securities were given top-notch ratings by the agencies but declined in value when the agencies downgraded them during the 2008 mortgage crisis. The plaintiffs claimed the agencies 'exceeded their traditional roles by actively aiding in the structuring and securitization process' to achieve higher ratings. The agencies should be considered 'underwriters' under the Securities Act of 1933, the plaintiffs argued. Under s. 11 of the statute, underwriters who make material misstatements and omissions in registration statements filed with the Securities and Exchange Commission are strictly liable. The court held that the rating agencies did not qualify as underwriters because they did not directly participate in the distribution of the securities, but simply enabled others to do so through their ratings. Judge Raggi (at p. 19) stated: 'Nothing in the statute's text supports expanding the definition of underwriter to reach persons not themselves participating in such purchases, offers, or sales, but whose actions may facilitate the participation of others in such undertakings.' The decision is available at http://newsandinsight.thomsonreuters.com/uploadedFiles/National_Litigation/News/2011/05_-_May/credit%20rating%20agencies%20opinion.pdf.

(g) of The Securities Act of 1933 originally exempted CRAs from 'expert' liability when they issue credit ratings on asset backed securities. However, the Dodd–Frank Act[167] had repealed 436 (g) in the summer of 2010[168] until the SEC issued a temporary no-action letter effectively exempting CRAs from liability.[169] Then the House Financial Services Committee voted to approve legislation that would repeal the provision of the Dodd–Frank legislation from 2010 which made CRAs liable for increased lawsuit exposure.[170] With the exemption for credit ratings removed, CRAs had feared exposure to the same degree of expert liability under the Securities Act of 1933 as accountants and other parties that participate in bond sales. Therefore, in July 2010, S&P, Moody's and Fitch refused to give their consent to allow their ratings to appear in prospectuses and registration statements.

In stark contrast to the developments in the US, in the EU CRAs do not seem to have enjoyed the same fortunes. In 2011 MEPs voted on a non-legislative resolution, drafted by Dr Wolf Klinz,[171] that looks at ways to hold CRAs to account for the advice that they give. They recommended that CRAs should be liable in civil law for their ratings. Most importantly, the text has called on the European Commission to identify ways in which CRAs could be held liable under member states' civil law. The resolution also suggests that all registered CRAs should assess the accuracy of their past credit ratings and make these assessments available to supervisors, and that ESMA should be empowered to conduct unannounced checks on these assessments. In addition, MEPs called for the creation of a European CRA as a counterweight to the three largest CRAs – Moody's, S&P and Fitch – which were felt to be too dominant on the European scene. The resolution calls on the European Commission to carry out a detailed assessment for a fully independent credit rating foundation, with start-up funding covering the first five years at most. Left-of-centre groups would have preferred a public CRA which could tap subsistence funding for a more open period. The non-legislative resolution comes some weeks before the EU Commission is to table legislative proposals to further regulate CRAs on an issue that has split political groups. Some hints as to what may come were provided earlier in 2011, at the Select Committee on the European Union of the House of Lords, when Dr Wolf Klinz stated:[172]

> Rating agencies should be held accountable to develop the rating in a professional manner and if there is negligence then there should be liability . . . If you look at the sub-prime crisis, agencies developed ratings too hastily so in that particular case I would have held them liable.

---

[167] The Dodd–Frank Wall Street Reform and Consumer Protection Act (Pub.L. 111–203, HR 4173), signed into law by President Barack Obama on 21 July 2010.

[168] On the liability that was imposed by the Dodd–Frank legislation, see http://www.pwc.com/us/en/financial-services/regulatory-services/publications/assets/closer-look-credit-rating-agencies.pdf.

[169] The SEC no-action letter was meant to last for six months, but the SEC later extended the disclosure exemption indefinitely, avoiding a potential shutdown of the securitisation market.

[170] The Asset-Backed Market Stabilization Act of 2011 (HR 1539).

[171] An MEP and Chairman of the Special Committee on the Financial, Economic and Social Crisis (CRIS) of the European Parliament.

[172] See the full text from the 8 June 2011 unrevised transcript of evidence taken before the UK House of Lords Select Committee on the European Union Economic and Financial Affairs and International Trade (Sub-Committee A) Inquiry on CRAs at http://www.parliament.uk/documents/lords-committees/eu-sub-com-a/Creditrating/ucEUA08062011ev4.pdf.

## 17.7 Final matters

CRAs have been very much in the eye of the storm of the sub-prime crisis and ongoing turmoil in the financial markets, in which they have been heavily implicated. A greater regulatory oversight for CRAs is therefore not only inevitable but is a matter of fact.[173] In retrospect, CRAs badly underestimated the risk of newly developed structured investment vehicles and were too quick to give these vehicles their highest investment grade ratings. As discussed above, the built-in conflict of interest created by the business model, whereby the agencies compete for the business of, and are compensated by, the issuers of such securities, creates undesirable incentives for the CRAs to bend to their clients' wishes. As we have seen, legal commentators seem to agree on the fact that there is little that is structurally wrong about how structured finance works in the mortgage sector. The CRAs' models are rather to blame in that they failed to take into account the dramatic changes in the level of risks created by innovative financing techniques. CRAs should ensure a greater lead time before rating new products so that the default characteristics of such products can more assuredly be measured, and therefore commented upon.

Like many complex situations, there is no easy solution to the issues discussed above. Reducing conflicts of interest, increasing reporting requirements and duties to inform as well as effective public supervision of CRAs are important steps in the rating process that should benefit all concerned. However, they are only important first steps.[174] They have to be buttressed by defining more precisely the possible conflicts of interest and the necessary measures to avoid them.[175] Perhaps the next concrete efforts should focus on finding different funding models (such as transaction levy) to mitigate these conflicts.[176] Improvements in rating technology can also provide further safeguards. These issues so far have not been addressed with the necessary determination. In addition, the problem subsists that the CRA market is dominated by three powerful CRAs. Effective sanctions are necessary but remain extremely uncertain, and to date there has been no successful claim for damages against a CRA.[177] Some in the US have been calling for an establishment of a public CRA that would, arguably, be able to offer a counterforce to the perverse incentive system

---

[173] On both sides of the Atlantic, the debate about how to reform CRAs has taken on renewed zeal and fervour. Such is the magnitude of the changes being considered that, it is reported, since the beginning of April 2010, billions of dollars have been knocked off the stock market values of Moody's and S&P. See A. Van Duyn 'Dilemmas of Reforming the Rating Agencies', *Financial Times*, 11 June 2010.

[174] T.J. Mollers 'Regulating Credit Rating Agencies: The new US and EU law – Important Steps or Much Ado About Nothing?' [2009] *Capital Markets Law Journal* 24.

[175] It is clear that particular emphasis should be made on the conflicts of interest issue. The discussion should focus on whether this is a matter to be resolved by substantive rules on the standard of conduct; or, rather, by reforms affecting the market structure; and, if so, what should be their content. Likewise, more thought should be devoted not just to *whether* provisions on conflict of interest should be included (clearly, yes) but *how* conflict of interest can be avoided in a situation that intrinsically involves it.

[176] For example, there was a US proposal for CRAs not to be paid by issuers, but be selected by regulators.

[177] Readers are advised to follow the resolution of *Abu Dhabi Commercial Bank* v *Morgan Stanley*, US District Court, Southern District of New York (Manhattan), No. 08-7508, discussed above and which, at the time of writing, is not yet concluded.

facing private agencies.[178] And so as we have moved swiftly towards a more regulatory environment, the question arises as to what would be the price for more regulation? It is inevitable that enhanced regulation has come with its own costs and problems, as follows.

First, confronted with a globally concentrated industry, can the EU act alone? CRAs are global organisations providing global benchmarks. As such, efforts should be made to ensure that global consistency in regulation becomes a priority. The result of doing otherwise would be a competitive disadvantage to those who implement new regulatory requirements. The European Commission noted this crucial factor and that it is important for EU rules to be similar to those in the US. In the UK the FCA is working to achieve this through IOSCO, whose work has created a solid basis for the further harmonisation of securities laws. That said, there are still major differences in approach to some issues between the US and the EU,[179] and as we saw above, there is certainly much more appetite in the EU to move towards liability for CRAs than there is in the US.

Second, will increased regulation actually encourage rather than discourage over-reliance on ratings?[180] The Association of British Insurers ('ABI') warned that regulation itself could contribute to the problem of over-reliance in ratings if it is seen as giving a 'seal of quality' to a particular CRA. There is a clear need for a regulatory framework that is capable of stabilising markets and channelling financial resources away from the speculative casino. But, of course, this is easier said than done.

Third, comparing the substance and style of the IOSCO Code (before and after 2008), the US Rating Agency Act 2006, and the new EU Regulation indicates that the aftermath of the crisis involves more detail and prescription, but *not* necessarily better solutions. For example, the rules that might have a more significant impact on CRAs could be not the rules on rating agencies, but the rules on the use of ratings by credit institutions under the new reformed framework for banking supervision (so-called Basel III Framework), which continues to incorporate credit ratings in material ways.

---

[178] Susan K. Schroeder in *Public Credit Rating Agencies* (Palgrave Macmillan, 2015) argues for the creation of national public CRAs, offering the first in-depth discussion of their implied role and function operating alongside private agencies. In addition to providing an up-to-date overview of the ratings industry and the government bodies that monitor its activities, Schroeder suggests that the proper implementation of public CRAs will promote the stability of lending, further development and adaptation of new technology, and increase labour productivity and the profitability of new investment in businesses. Other relevant literature includes M. Ahmed Diomande *et al*. 'Why US Financial Markets Need a Public Credit Rating Agency' *The Economist Voice* (June 2009). Others in the USA conclude that ongoing efforts to reform the regulation of the CRAs fail to address their systemic bias against the public interest. As their regulators seek to tighten oversight of these important players in the financial markets, it is argued that it is important to ensure that future regulation provides additional protection for consumers as well. See D.J. Reiss 'Ratings Failure: The Need for a Consumer Protection Agenda in Rating Agency Regulation' (12 June 2009) Banking and Financial Services Policy Report, 2009, Brooklyn Law School, Legal Studies Paper No. 154. Available at http://ssrn.com/abstract=1418549. See also the Wall Street Reform and Consumer Protection Act, signed into law on 21 July 2010 by President Obama, which is designed to ensure that the US economy works for consumers, investors and financial institutions and described as 'the most sweeping overhaul of Wall Street regulations since the 1930s, less than two years after the collapse of Lehman Brothers'. See E. Luce and J. Politi 'Obama Signs Bill to Overhaul Wall Street', *Financial Times*, 21 July 2010.

[179] T.J. Mollers, above n. 174.

[180] The CRAs claim that they cannot be blamed for the way ratings are used. Avinash Persaud has sympathy with this: '. . . it reminds me of what the gun manufacturers say after each mass shooting in the US. What puts the smoking gun in the hand of ratings agencies, according to many, is the business model. When markets are under stress, investors question the veracity of ratings. The fact that ratings are paid for by issuers undermines confidence at this critical juncture and contributes to the market freezing up, with dire results.' See A. Persaud 'The Right Direction for Credit Ratings Agencies', *Financial Times Online*, 18 October 2007: http://www.ft.com/cms/s/0/de994db4-7d8e-11dc-9f47-0000779fd2ac.html.

Fourth, to date, the efforts have presumed that CRAs are involved *before* the day the transaction is closed and the securities are issued. The truth is that, quite often, they are also consulted *during* the life of the transaction, in case a restructuring needs to be made, to see if it will affect the rating given by the agency. These are the so-called rating agency confirmations ('RACs'), and were very common in structured transactions. Such RACs can potentially enhance flexibility if a transaction needs to be adjusted to avoid default and the agency refuses to confirm; but, on a broader basis, this may hinder the agency's ability to remain independent (how can an agency downgrade after having confirmed that the adjustment will not impair the transaction's rating?).[181]

Fifth, what is the right balance between liability and regulation? In particular, what should be the balance between prevention and punishment? Could substantive rules serve as a basis for liability actions by private investors? If so, how do such enforcement actions fit within the existing framework that limits liability on the basis of privity and freedom of speech? Should those limits be secondary in cases of breach of regulatory rules on standards of conduct? From the perspective of enforcement, it is not obvious how the new substantive rules will be applied by the ESMA.[182]

Sixth, as seen above, although there are more calls in recent times, reforms have not yet addressed competition issues within this area, with S&P, Moody's and, more recently, Fitch dominating the CRA market.[183] Regulatory changes may encourage new entrants to the business. There are a handful trying to break in or expand their market share. Some, such as DBRS, the Toronto-based CRA, have been on the sidelines for years, though DBRS has more recently picked up greater market share.[184] With legislation heading in the other direction, managing the urge to grab more market share will be vital, not least to restore investor confidence in ratings.[185]

Finally, as touched upon under s. 17.4 above, one of the recent challenges consists in regulating the underlying derivatives market itself. But is this being done? Industry participants have delivered and are delivering on a series of reforms which focus predominately on the CDS market.[186] These major steps include greater consistency of trading terms; clarity on settlement processes; central counterparty clearing; enhanced transparency; reduction in national amounts outstanding; inclusion of the views of the full

---

[181] See further, D. Ramos Muñoz 'In Praise of Small Things. Securitization and Governance Structure' (2010) 5 *Capital Markets Law Journal* 363.

[182] For example, the ESMA regulation does not specify how ESMA decisions addressed to market participants are to be enforced in national courts.

[183] 'The lack of competition [between CRAs] is of particular concern,' said José Manuel Barroso, the former EC president, as cited in A. Van Duyn 'Dilemmas of Reforming the Rating Agencies', *Financial Times*, 11 June 2010.

[184] 'There is much more interest [among investors] in looking for other opinions,' said Daniel Curry, former president of DBRS's US operations. 'It gives us a chance to go in and in effect sell ourselves.' Others are complete newcomers that have not yet acquired the rating agency status needed in the US, such as K2 Global Partners set up by Jules Kroll. Others, such as consultancy Pricewaterhouse Coopers, are eyeing the sector. 'There are efforts on the part of legislators to reduce the power of the rating agency oligopoly,' says Mr Kroll. 'These efforts could give alternative approaches more of a chance.' As cited in A. Van Duyn 'Dilemmas of Reforming the Rating Agencies', *Financial Times*, 11 June 2010.

[185] A. Van Duyn, *ibid*.

[186] P. Augustin, M.G. Subrahmanyam, D.Y. Tang and S.Q. Wang 'Credit Default Swaps: Past, Present, and Future' in *The Annual Review of Financial Economics* 2016, 8:10.1–10.22, available at http://people.stern.nyu.edu/msubrahm/papers/ARFE.pdf.

spectrum of market participants; and exploration of new markets and new products. All of these measures combined should impact on the environment in which CRAs operate. But as Hurst noted, in the end perhaps the greatest incentive for reform lies in the CRAs' own self-interest in preserving their reputations for impartiality and due diligence in the ratings process. If the public loses confidence in the integrity of CRAs, their value will almost certainly decline.[187]

## Further reading

A. Reisberg 'The Future Role of Credit Rating Agencies in Contemporary Financial Markets– A Theoretical Perspective', Chapter 7 in D. Prentice and A. Reisberg (eds) *Corporate Finance in the UK and EU* (Oxford: OUP, 2011).

H.M. Lagohr and P.T. Laghor *The Rating Agencies and their Credit Ratings* (Chichester: John Wiley and Sons, 2008).

A. Duff 'The Credit Rating Agencies and Stakeholder Relations: Issues for Regulators' (2009) 24 *Journal of International Banking and Financial Law* 11.

[187] Hurst, above n. 134, 64.

# 18

# The regulatory machinery of the Financial Services and Markets Act 2000 (FSMA 2000)

## 18.1 Introduction

Having considered the theory and background to securities regulation it is now necessary to provide an account of the complex system of regulation established by the Financial Services and Markets Act 2000 ('FSMA 2000'), the Financial Services Act 2012 ('FSA 2012') and The Bank of England and Financial Services and Markets Act 2016. It will be seen that many aspects of the regime established by the FSMA 2000 relate to what are often termed 'intermediated securities'. These are products which are formed out of securities originally issued by companies to large financial institutions, or purchased by them, but which have been fashioned by those intermediaries into a product which is suitable for domestic consumers.[1] An example would be a collective investment scheme ('CIS'), such as a unit trust, operated by an investment bank intermediary. Such an intermediated product is attractive to domestic consumers because it spreads risk and is available in small amounts. These intermediated products are economically very important because they ensure that domestic capital[2] forms part of the overall picture of corporate finance. As will be seen, the effect that they have on the regulatory structure is that the regulator feels obliged to establish a high degree of consumer protection,[3] which would probably have been unnecessary had the transaction merely taken place between the intermediary and the company or secondary market where the shares were being traded.[4]

---

[1] In an economic sense, holders of intermediated products are still shareholders, although in technical terms, within traditional company law, this is not the case and shareholder rights will fall to be exercised by the intermediary.

[2] I.e. that part of a householder's income which she or he has decided should, for whatever reasons, be set aside as savings.

[3] For recent examples of the FCA civil proceedings, see http://www.fca.org.uk/your-fca/documents/final-notices/2015/threadneedle-asset-management-limited; and http://www.fca.org.uk/your-fca/documents/final-notices/2016/shay-jacob-reches.

[4] Note that the FSMA 2000 was amended by SI 2011/1613 (The Undertakings for Collective Investment in Transferable Securities Regulations 2011), available at http://www.legislation.gov.uk/uksi/2011/1613/pdfs/uksi_20111613_en.pdf.

## 18.2 Scope of the FSMA 2000

### A The general prohibition

The most fundamental provision of the Act is s. 19, which provides:

> (1) No person may carry on a regulated activity in the United Kingdom, or purport to do so, unless he is:
> (a) an authorised person;
> (b) or an exempt person.
> (2) The prohibition is referred to in this Act as the general prohibition.

A person who contravenes this is guilty of a criminal offence[5] and enforceability of agreements may be affected.[6]

Thus, people wanting to carry on a regulated activity have to get authorised, or be exempt.

### B Regulated activities

#### 1 Relationship between the Act and the Order

The legislature has adopted a two-stage approach to defining 'regulated activities'. There is a very general provision in the Act and then detailed but fundamental provisions in a statutory instrument, the Financial Services and Markets Act (Regulated Activities) Order.[7] The rationale behind this approach is that the Order can easily be adjusted as necessary to cope with market developments. It is a recognition of the fact that commercial practice is fast changing and the law needs to be as well. To amend an Act takes valuable parliamentary time, but it is comparatively simple to amend a statutory instrument.

The general provisions of s. 22 of the FSMA 2000 specify various requirements for an activity to qualify as a regulated activity. However, relying on the FSMA itself to establish whether an activity is regulated has not proven very helpful as it refers to the Order containing multiple chapters stipulating different types of regulated activity.

The Regulated Activities Order (RAO) 2015 is not an easy document to construe and the account which follows is not an exhaustive analysis but instead provides an introduction to some of its more important aspects. The first point is that the Order seems to ignore comprehensively Sch. 2 of the Act, which relates to regulated activities, in the sense that it imposes many detailed conditions and exceptions and ignores the layout of the Schedule. Secondly, Part II of the Order lists specified activities, Part III lists specified investments, Part III A lists specified activities in relation to information and Part V refers to unauthorised persons carrying on insurance mediation activities.

---

[5] Subject to a penalty of up to two years' imprisonment (s. 23 (1)). It appears that no *mens rea* is required unless perhaps something can be implied from the words 'carry on'. See also s. 24 (1), which contains criminal penalties for making false claims to be authorised or exempt. It is necessary to distinguish s. 20, the effect of which is dealt with in the context of the 'permissions' regime at 18.3 below.

[6] See generally ss. 26–28, under which agreements made by or through unauthorised persons become unenforceable against the other party.

[7] Financial Services and Markets Act 2000 (Regulated Activities) Order 2001 (SI 2001, No. 544). It is frequently amended. The most recent, at the time of writing, is the Financial Services and Markets Act 2000 (Regulated Activities) (Amendment) (No. 3) Order 2015, SI 2015/1863.

## 2 The 'business' test

There is a fundamental condition which usually needs to be fulfilled before the activity counts as a regulated activity for the purposes of s. 22 of the FSMA 2000. This is what is called the 'business' test (or business requirement). In other words, a person will only be regarded as engaging in an activity within s. 22 if it is carried on by way of business. There is no general definition of 'carried on by way of business'.[8] Various questions spring to mind. Do the words 'carry on' add much? Do they import a requirement that there must be a degree of repetition and continuity in the activity[9] and that an isolated occasion would not be sufficient? On the other hand, a one-off transaction might be very large and of great commercial significance.[10] Although not discussed at length here, the judgment in *Morgan Grenfell* v *Welwyn Hatfield DC*[11] under the previous regime can give useful guidance in this regard. It was held there that for the purposes of the words 'by way of business' in s. 63 of the Financial Services Act 1986 ('FSA 1986'), the test is whether:

> [I]n ordinary parlance [it] would be described as a business transaction, as opposed to something personal or casual . . . As regards the test of the frequency with which the relevant type of transaction is entered into, this can be no more than a guide. Regularly entering into a certain type of transaction for the purpose of profit is a good indication that the party doing so is doing so by way of business. But it is equally possible that the very first time it enters into such a contract it is doing so by way of business because it is doing so as part of its overall business activities.[12]

Most recently in *Helden* v *Strathmore Ltd*[13] it was held that under certain circumstances lending and charges can be classified as 'an activity carried on by way of business' under s. 22 (1) of the FSMA 2000.

## C Examples of prescribed 'activities' and 'investments'

The wide scope of the regulatory power wielded by the Financial Conduct Authority ('FCA') is apparent from a perusal of the Regulated Activities Order ('RAO'). In some circumstances[14] the following[15] will be specified activities: accepting deposits; effecting contracts of insurance; establishing a collective investment scheme; dealing in investments; managing investments; issuing electronic money; safeguarding and administering

---

[8] Although in some circumstances exemptions and definitions are applied by the FSMA 2000 (Carrying on Regulated Activities by Way of Business) Order 2001 (SI 2001 No. 1177), frequently amended, the most recent being FSMA 2000 (Carrying on Regulated Activities By Way of Business) (Amendment) Order 2014 SI2014/3340. See, in particular, art. 3, which provides that in relation to a range of activities relating to investments: 'A person is not to be regarded as carrying on by way of business an activity to which this article applies, unless he carries on the business of engaging in one or more such activities.' See also the FSMA 2000 (Carrying on Regulated Activities by Way of Business) (Amendment) Order 2011, available at http://www.legislation.gov.uk/ukdsi/2011/9780111513088/contents.
[9] Some support for this interpretation can be gained from the judgment in *Lloyd* v *Poperly and another* [2000] BCC 338 (case decided on similar words in the FSA 1986).
[10] The FCA guidance on the business element can be found in PERG 2.3.
[11] [1995] 1 All ER 1.
[12] *Ibid.* at pp. 13–14, *per* Hobhouse J.
[13] [2011] EWCA Civ 542.
[14] The actual wording of the RAO needs to be looked at carefully as there are many conditions, definitions and exceptions in it.
[15] This list is not exhaustive.

investments; managing investments; advising on investments; various activities at Lloyd's; and agreeing to carry on certain activities. These are only examples, and it is thus clear that this regime covers a very wide range of financial services.[16]

The following are some examples of what in some circumstances will be prescribed investments: deposits; electronic money; contracts of insurance; shares etc.; instruments creating or acknowledging indebtedness; sukuk (shariah-compliant debt instruments); government and public securities; instruments giving entitlement to investments; certificates representing certain securities; units in a collective investment scheme; options; futures; contracts for differences etc.; Lloyd's syndicate capacity and syndicate membership; regulated mortgage contracts; rights to or interests in investments. As above, this list is not exhaustive.

## D  Territorial scope of the general prohibition

The territorial scope of the general prohibition is stated simply in s. 19 (1), which contains a prohibition on carrying on a 'regulated activity in the [UK]'. This relatively simple statement is then supplemented and altered, in effect, by provisions which regulate 'inward' and 'outward' scope. Inward scope is dealt with in art. 72 of the RAO and creates exemptions for people overseas in some circumstances. Outward scope is dealt with in s. 418 of the FSMA 2000, which, broadly, is dealing with the question of how far jurisdiction can be claimed over people who are located in the UK but do business abroad. The purpose of the section is to enable the UK to claim jurisdiction to regulate financial services which are being offered from the UK because if they are unregulated it could damage international confidence in the UK as a place to invest and do business. It is not unusual for countries to be concerned about their image as a fair market and the idea is broadly in line with the tenor of the European Court of Justice ('ECJ')'s approach in *Alpine Investments*,[17] where it was held that concern for the reputation of Dutch securities markets was a valid reason for the imposition of controls on Dutch securities traders who were based in Holland but selling their securities out of the country. The provisions also give effect to the rights and obligations of passporting firms under the Capital Markets Directives.

## E  The financial promotion regime[18]

It has been seen that the key to avoiding contravention of the general prohibition in s. 19 is by becoming authorised, or by being exempt. These matters are dealt with later. It is necessary here to consider the effect of the financial promotion regime which is set out in s. 21 of the FSMA 2000 and in the Financial Services and Markets Act 2000 (Financial Promotion)

---

[16] To this one should add the Capital Requirements Directive, comprising Directive 2006/48/EC and Directive 2006/49/EC which was published on 30 June 2006 and came into force in January 2007. The objective of the capital requirements is to have in place a comprehensive and risk-sensitive framework and to foster enhanced risk management amongst financial institutions. It was hoped this will maximise the effectiveness of the capital rules in ensuring continuing financial stability, maintaining confidence in financial institutions and protecting consumers. See now 2010/76 – The Third Capital Requirements Directive: http://eur-lex.europa.eu/LexUriServ/LexUriServ.do?uri=OJ:L:2010:329:0003:0035:EN:PDF.

[17] Case C–384/93 *Alpine Investments BV* v *Minister van Financien* [1995] ECR 1–1141.

[18] See https://www.handbook.fca.org.uk/handbook/PERG/8.pdf.

Order 2005.[19] It should be noted that the drafting of the Financial Promotion Order is complex and in some places considerably alters the effects of the primary legislation.

Obviously, most promotional activity is carried out by *authorised* persons operating within the financial services sector by way of business. And they will be authorised by the FCA in order to carry on those businesses. Their promotional activities will be regulated by the Conduct of Business Sourcebook issued by the FCA.[20] Also, authorised persons will have to comply with the FCA's Principles for Businesses which apply to authorised persons generally.[21] Thus, in particular, Principle 7 requires that 'a firm must pay due regard to the information needs of its clients, and communicate information to them in a way which is clear, fair and not misleading'.[22] So, for authorised persons engaging in financial promotion, the system makes detailed provision.

FSMA 2000 provides definitions of financial promotion and the Financial Promotion Order provides various exemptions. None of this is very remarkable (though the legislation is complex). However, the legislation also seeks to do one further thing; it seeks to extend the regime to promotions by unauthorised persons by requiring them to get the content of the financial promotion approved by an authorised person.[23]

All these matters are clearly reflected in section 21 of the Act, which provides:

(1) A person ('A') must not, in the course of business, communicate[24] an invitation or inducement to engage in investment[25] activity.

(2) But subsection (1) does not apply if:

    (a) A is an authorised person; or

    (b) the content of the communication is approved[26] for the purposes of this section by an authorised person.

A deceptively simple definition of 'engaging in investment activity' is given in s. 21 (8), but in fact, because of the link made there to the concept of 'controlled activity', the legislature is using the definition to fine-tune the scope of the regime. This is because, behind s. 21 (8), lies some complex subordinate legislation by statutory instrument. Section 21 (8) provides:

'Engaging in investment activity' means –

    (a) entering or offering to enter into an agreement the making or performance of which by either party constitutes a controlled activity; or

    (b) exercising any rights conferred by an investment to acquire, dispose of, underwrite or convert an investment.

---

[19] This has been amended and updated multiple times, most recently by the Financial Services and Markets Act 2000 (Misc Provisions) Order 2015 SI 2015/853. The FCA has provided detailed guidance on financial promotion in its 'PERG' Module (PERG 8) as part of its Handbook (available from its website). See further, FCA Handbook, PERG 8.

[20] These are in the FCA Handbook of Rules and Guidance, COBS Chapter 4.

[21] See 18.5 below.

[22] Also relevant is Principle 6 (customers' interests).

[23] See *Financial Services Authority* v *Fox Hayes (A Firm)* [2009] EWCA Civ 76, in which the FSA challenged the finding of the Financial Services and Markets Tribunal on the question of whether solicitors' firm had contravened the financial promotion regime. See also *Atlantic Law LLP* v *Financial Services Authority*, Financial Services and Markets Tribunal, 1 March 2010, at http://www.fsa.gov.uk/pages/Library/Communication/PR/2010/079.shtml.

[24] By s. 21 (13), '"Communicate" includes causing a communication to be made'.

[25] By s. 21 (14), '"Investment" includes any asset, right or interest'.

[26] In deciding whether to give approval, authorised persons will be required to have regard to the rules mentioned above, e.g. the FCA COBS and FCA Principles for Businesses.

The concept of 'controlled activity' and hence, largely, the scope of the financial promotion regime depends on Treasury 'specification'.[27] The relevant provisions are contained in the Financial Services and Markets Act (Financial Promotion) Order.[28] Schedule 1 to the Order defines 'controlled activity'. It lists the controlled activities and specifies the investments to which they relate. Other parts of the Financial Promotion Order contain many exotically worded exemptions, such as where shares are offered around to rich or sophisticated persons.[29]

The territorial scope of the financial promotion regime is dealt with by s. 21 (3), which provides that: 'in the case of a communication originating outside the United Kingdom, subsection (1) applies only if the communication is capable of having an effect in the United Kingdom.' This is a very broad territorial claim. However, as with much of the legislation in the FSMA 2000, the effect of the provision in the primary legislation is substantially altered by the subordinate legislation, and there are many provisions in the Financial Promotion Order which narrow the effect of this.[30]

## 18.3 Authorisation and exemption

### A Methods of authorisation

It has been seen that, by virtue of s. 19, in order to avoid the 'general prohibition', a person engaging or purporting to engage in a regulated activity in the UK must be authorised or an exempt person in relation to that activity. Section 31 provides four categories of authorised person.

First, and most importantly for UK business, s. 31 (1) (a) refers to authorisation by the FCA from within the UK. Authorisation by the FCA is the primary route from within the UK. This is examined in detail below under the heading 'Part 4 A permissions'.

Secondly, EEA firms qualifying for authorisation under Sch. 3 are what are generally referred to as 'passporting firms'. As has been seen, under the Capital Markets Directives, such as the Investment Services Directive ('ISD'),[31] it is possible for a person to obtain a passport to enable them to provide investment services in another member state without needing to get authorised there. Broadly, the idea is that a firm can get authorised in its home state, and this gives it a passport. It can then do business throughout the EEA, thus giving substance to the EU concept of a single market in financial services.[32]

Thirdly, treaty firms are persons established in other member states of the EU who, by virtue of being authorised or permitted to carry on certain other activities in their home state, have rights to carry on regulated business in the UK which go beyond the rights referred to by the Capital Markets Directives.

Finally, s. 31 (1) (d), on persons 'otherwise authorised . . .' in fact refers to operators or trustees of collective investment schemes which are undertakings for collective investment

---

[27] Section 21 (9), (15).
[28] See n. 19 above. As commented on above, these are subject to the amendment in the Regulated Activities Order 2011 and amendment to the order 2010/905.
[29] Thus providing an exemption for business angels; see arts 48–50.
[30] See e.g. art. 12.
[31] See further MiFID, 2008/10/EC.
[32] Although it may need to comply with e.g. conduct of business rules of the host state; see ss. 193–202.

in transferable securities (within the meaning of the Undertakings for Collective Investment in Transferable Securities ('UCITS') Directive).[33]

## B Part 4 A permissions

Getting a Part 4 A permission is in fact the primary way of getting authorised and, as a description of being authorised, the wording of s. 31 (1) (a) is thus somewhat backhanded.[34] Nevertheless, the effect is clear. A person intending to carry on a regulated activity in the UK must apply to the FCA for a permission (or the Prudential Regulation Authority ('PRA') in relation to PRA regulated activities).[35] If he or she gets it, he or she is 'authorised'.

The permissions regime is set out, unsurprisingly, in Part 4 A of the Act.[36] The essence and effect of it is that being an authorised person does not mean being in a position to carry out each and every type of regulated activity. A person will be in a position to carry out the regulated activities for which permission has been given, and it is the intention of the legislature that that person will not get permission for activities which he or she is not suited for. This is achieved by imposing on the FCA a requirement that it must specify the permitted regulatory activity or activities.[37]

It is provided that, in relation to its permission, the FCA must ensure that the person concerned 'will satisfy and continue to satisfy, in relation to all of the regulated activities for which the person has or will have permission, the threshold conditions for which the regulator is responsible'.[38] These 'threshold conditions' are set out in Sch. 6 and impose requirements such as adequate resources and suitability. The FCA has set out its policies on how it intends to approach this and other threshold conditions.[39]

Obviously, over the years, the business direction of a firm carrying on regulated activities might well change. The Act makes provision for this by enabling the FCA to vary the permission by, for instance, adding a regulated activity to those for which it gives permission, or removing an activity.[40] If a firm exceeds its Part 4 A permissions it has contravened the general prohibition in s. 19.[41]

> The consequences of contravention can include conviction and/or a fine.[42] In addition, the agreement may be unenforceable and compensation may be payable to the party sustaining loss.[43] In specified circumstances there may also be an action for breach of statutory duty.[44]

---

[33] See further 18.6 below. For revision of this directive, see https://ec.europa.eu/info/business-economy-euro/growth-and-investment/investment-funds_en.

[34] The sections fit together in this way: s. 19 introduces the term 'authorised person' by prohibiting the carrying on of a regulated activity (etc.) unless he is an 'authorised person . . . [or . . .]'. The term 'authorised person' is defined in s. 31 (2) as 'a person who is authorised for the purposes of this Act'. And then s. 31 (1) gives the list of those persons who are 'authorised for the purposes of this Act', the first in the list of these being 'a person who has a Part IV permission . . .'.

[35] The word 'person' used here has the broad meaning ascribed by s. 55 A which provides that: 'An application for permission to carry on one or more regulated activities may be made to the appropriate authority by: (a) an individual; (b) a body corporate; (c) a partnership; (d) an unincorporated association.' Neither of the last two categories (in England) would usually be regarded as legal persons.

[36] Sections 40–55.

[37] Section 55 E (4).

[38] Section 55 B (3).

[39] FCA Handbook of Rules and Guidance, Threshold Conditions, COND.

[40] Sections 44–50. Under these sections the FCA may also cancel permissions in certain circumstances.

[41] Section 20 of the FSMA 2000.

[42] Section 23 of the FSMA 2000.

[43] Section 26 of the FSMA 2000.

[44] Section 20 (3).

## C The register

Section 347 requires the FCA to maintain a public record containing certain details about all authorised firms, including a description of the regulated activities they are permitted to undertake. It is available on the FCA website[45] and constitutes an important plank in the FCA's consumer protection objective.

## 18.4 Exempt persons and exemption of appointed representatives

It will be recalled that the general prohibition in s. 19 makes it clear that in order to avoid committing a criminal offence, a person who carries on, or purports to carry on, a regulated activity in the UK must be an authorised person or an exempt person in relation to that activity. It is now necessary to examine the concept of 'exempt person'.

Section 38 gives power to the Treasury to make an exemption order and under this power it has made the Financial Services and Markets Act (Exemption) Order.[46] The Order makes various official bodies exempt, such as the Bank of England and the central banks of other EU member states.

Of more complexity is the provision in s. 39 which provides:

(1) If a person –
    (a) is a party to a contract with an authorised person (his 'principal') which:
        (i) permits or requires him to carry on business of a prescribed[47] description, and
        (ii) complies with such requirements as may be prescribed,[48] and
    (b) is someone for whose activities in carrying on the whole or part of that business his principal has accepted responsibility in writing,

he is an exempt person in relation to any regulated activity comprised in the carrying on of that business for which his principal has accepted responsibility.[49]

A person who is exempt under the section is called an appointed representative.[50] The exemption is designed to deal with the fact that self-employed sales representatives often work under the auspices of an 'umbrella' organisation which takes responsibility for what they do. The idea of the system is that the principal needs to be authorised and needs to accept responsibility for the acts of his appointed representative. If so, then the appointed representative does not need to get authorised himself. However, it is clear from *Re Noble Warren Investments Ltd*[51] that the system must be seen to work in fact. In that case the principals lost their authorisation because *inter alia* they had failed to train or supervise the appointed representatives.[52]

---

[45] http://www.fca.org.uk/register.

[46] SI 2001, No. 1201. This instrument has been amended on multiple occasions, most recently by the FSMA 2000 (Exemption) (Amendment) Order 2015 SI 2015/447.

[47] Certain businesses are prescribed by FSMA 2000 (Appointed Representatives) Regulations 2001 (SI 2001, No. 1217) as amended; see art. 2.

[48] See art. 3 of the regulations referred to in the previous footnote.

[49] There are further provisions which deal with the responsibility of the principal, and other matters; see s. 39 (3)–(6).

[50] Section 39 (2). See also s. 39 A which deals with certain tied agents operating outside the UK.

[51] Noted by E. Lomnicka [1989] JBL 421.

[52] This case was subject to the 1986 Act but the relevant provisions are were largely the same.

## 18.5 Conduct of business

### A Textures of regulation

As the law developed, from 1986 to 1999, various different techniques of regulation were tried out, giving rise to what has been described as 'textures' of regulation.[53] At one stage, in 1989, a three-tiered structure was introduced as part of the so-called 'New Settlement', which was designed to restore industry confidence in a regulator who had come to be perceived as unnecessarily heavy handed and rule orientated. It produced three tiers of rules, including both general rules applying to all authorised persons and rules which were more industry specific, as tailored by the SROs.

Under the system brought in by the FSMA 2000, some aspects of this 'textured' approach remain. Gone, of course, are the SROs. The FCA now regulates those areas formerly covered by the SROs. However, we can still see different textures. There are high-level standards which are applicable throughout the financial services industry. And there are detailed rules, not of general application, but applying to particular sectors of the industry, tailor-made to cover widely different situations.

As discussed in Chapter 16 above, the FSA 2012, which came into force on 1 April 2013, set out a clear and coherent regulatory framework, replacing the uncertainty and inadequacy of the failed tripartite system.[54] The Act provides regulators with comprehensive powers to counter future risks to financial stability and to ensure that consumers are treated fairly. It also takes important steps to focus the regulators on rebuilding competition in a banking sector that has become too concentrated. In particular, the Act: (i) gave the Bank of England responsibility for protecting and enhancing financial stability, bringing together macro and micro prudential regulation; (ii) abolished the FSA and created a strengthened regulatory architecture consisting of the Financial Policy Committee ('FPC'), the PRA and the FCA; and (iii) empowered authorities to look beyond 'tick-box' compliance and foster a regulatory culture of judgment, expertise and proactive supervision.

From 1 April 2013, the FSA was replaced by the FCA and the PRA. A kind of texturing can be seen in the different types of rule-making power which the Act gives to the FCA. Section 137 A gives the FCA a wide enabling power to make *rules*. As subordinate legislation these rules will have the force of law, and they will be capable of imposing binding obligations upon authorised persons.[55] This section was substituted by the FSA 2012.[56] There is also power for the FCA to issue *guidance* on its rules and other regulatory matters. Guidance will not be legally binding but will be a way of putting flesh on principles or rules to bring out their bearing on a particular problem or situation. The FCA has now issued guidance on many matters and it is clear that this is a major feature in the regime.[57]

---

[53] The term was used by A. Whittaker in 'Legal Technique in City Regulation' (1990) 43 *Current Legal Problems* 35.
[54] http://www.legislation.gov.uk/ukpga/2012/21/contents/enacted?view=plain.
[55] In contrast to the position under the previous regime, there is no separate power to state 'principles' and it is intended that the general rule-making power in s. 137 A will enable the FCA to lay down requirements anywhere along the spectrum from broad principle to detailed requirement. (There are also more specific rule-making powers in Part X.) There is also a power (in s. 148) for the FCA to give *waivers*; i.e. to disapply its rules on a case by case basis.
[56] As a result of this section, the FCA's rule-making powers will be exercisable for the purpose of advancing one or more of its operational objectives.
[57] See generally the FCA Handbook of Rules and Guidance.

## B The FCA Handbook of Rules and Guidance

The former FSA Handbook was split into the FCA Handbook and the PRA Handbook. Between 2013 and 2016, the PRA Handbook was fully rewritten into its current form in clear and concise language and restructured under the sector format, the PRA Rulebook.[58] All guidance was deleted but retained, where applicable, in relevant PRA supervisory statements and webpages. While all regulated firms must comply with the rules set out in the FCA Handbook, dual-regulated firms will need to consider both FCA and PRA rules. In November 2015 the FCA published a 'Reader's Guide: An Introduction to the Handbook',[59] which provides an introduction to the structure and contents and its related materials, explaining how the different modules fit together, and how to interpret and use the Handbook.

The FCA Handbook of Rules and Guidance lies at the heart of the regulatory structure established by the FSMA 2000. Much of it is familiar material in the sense that it is the progeny of the SIB/FSA and SRO rulebooks from the previous regime. Change has been made where circumstances have made it necessary, but much of the old wisdom and ways of doing things are reflected in its current format. Over the years, it can be expected that there will be further redrafting and rationalisation. Its early format owed much to the need to get the new regime up and running within the tight time frame which was available but its current state reveals that much work is being done on it to rationalise and clarify.

In *David Anderson v Openwork Ltd*,[60] the County Court found that the common law duty of care in tort is in addition to existing statutory duties under the FSMA 2000 and the FCA's COB Rules. In particular, it dismissed an appeal against an earlier decision, finding that where a financial adviser provides advice (rather than just information) to their client in circumstances where there is no statutory duty of care, he or she owes their client a common law duty of care. In considering the extent of this duty, the County Court held that consideration should be given to the standards imposed by the relevant regulatory regime, in this case the rules in the FCA's COB Sourcebook ('COBS') in the FCA Handbook.

## C The FCA Principles for Businesses

The aim[61] of the FCA Principles for Businesses, of which there are currently 11, is to formulate succinct high-level precepts stating the fundamental obligations of regulated businesses.[62] Firms would then have a basic standard to guide their behaviour. The Principles apply to all authorised persons. It is intended that the existence of these principles will mean that the regulatory system need never be completely silent on an issue, even if rapid changes in the business environment have meant that gaps have appeared in the more detailed COBS. Furthermore, often the detailed COBS will flesh out the more basic ideas in the Principles, but the COBS will not exhaust the effect of the general Principle which will still be there to plug any gaps. It is clear that some of the Principles overlap, but the FCA have expressed the view that this is inevitable when drafting at this level of generality.

---

[58] http://www.prarulebook.co.uk.
[59] https://www.fca.org.uk/publication/handbook/readers-guide.pdf.
[60] *David Anderson v Openwork Ltd* [2015] EW Misc B14 (18 June 2015).
[61] The former FSA's policy behind the Principles was set out in various places in *Consultation Paper 13* (September 1998) and in *Response on Consultation Paper 13* (October 1999).
[62] *Consultation Paper 13* (September 1998) p. 5.

It is fundamental that breach of FCA rules such as detailed COB rules will give rise to the possibility of FCA disciplinary action against the authorised person concerned. However, interestingly, the FCA has made it clear that it is possible to imagine a situation where breach of a Principle would, of itself, be the cause for initiating disciplinary action.[63] Such cases are likely to be rare, but the possibility adds a significant dimension to the regulatory armoury and will probably do much to raise the profile of the Principles in day-to-day conduct.[64]

The Principles give quite a comprehensive picture of the spectrum of situations which frequently need to be addressed by the regulator and it is worth setting them out in full. At the time of writing, the current version[65] is as follows:

(1) Integrity
A firm must conduct its business with integrity.
(2) Skill, care and diligence
A firm must conduct its business with due skill, care and diligence.
(3) Management and control
A firm must take reasonable care to organise and control its affairs responsibly and effectively, with adequate risk management systems.
(4) Financial prudence
A firm must maintain adequate financial resources.
(5) Market conduct
A firm must observe proper standards of market conduct.
(6) Customers' interests
A firm must pay due regard to the interests of its customers and treat them fairly.
(7) Communications with clients
A firm must pay due regard to the information needs of its clients, and communicate information to them in a way which is clear, fair and not misleading.
(8) Conflicts of interest
A firm must manage conflicts of interest fairly, both between itself and its customers and between a customer and another client.
(9) Customers: relationships of trust
A firm must take reasonable care to ensure the suitability of its advice and discretionary decisions for any customer who is entitled to rely on its judgment.
(10) Clients' assets
A firm must arrange adequate protection for clients' assets when it is responsible for them.
(11) Relations with regulators

A firm must deal with its regulators in an open and cooperative way, and must disclose to the appropriate regulator anything relating to the firm of which the FCA would reasonably expect notice.

---

[63] *Response to Consultation Paper 13* (October 1999) p. 7. It was not envisaged by the FSA that breach of the Principles alone would give rise to civil liability under s. 150 in the way that breach of the rules may do. The Principles have been devised as a statement of regulatory expectations, not as a set of legal rights at large. Nor would such breach give an entitlement to payments under the Compensation Scheme, since the general principles are not designed to create rights or liabilities in civil law; see generally *Consultation Paper 13* (September 1998) p. 11.
[64] It is reported that during the 2010 calendar year, the then FSA levied fines totalling a staggering £89.3m compared to £35m imposed during 2009, a year-on-year increase of 155%. Not only are these figures staggering, but this figure of £89m represents almost 40% of the £225.8m in total fines the FSA has imposed between 2002 and 2010. See G. Stephenson 'Why 2011 is the Year to Beware of the FSA's Fines', at http://www.ftadviser.com/.
[65] March 2016, FCA Handbook of Rules and Guidance, Principles for Businesses, PRIN.

In ensuring that firms adhere to these Principles, the FCA must itself adhere to Principles of good regulation, of which the Handbook provides eight. These are: economy and efficiency, proportionality, sustainable growth, consumer responsibility, senior management responsibility, recognition of the differences in the businesses carried on by different regulated persons, openness and disclosure and transparency.

## D Ancillary regimes

The FSMA 2000 contains a number of provisions relating to conduct of business and designed to extend regulatory reach beyond merely authorised persons. These relate to approval of special categories of employee, controllers of authorised persons, and employment of prohibited persons.

We have already seen that the regulatory framework focuses primarily on those businesses which will require authorisation by the FCA. However, where the authorised person is a firm (as opposed to a sole trader), it has been decided that the FCA should also have regulatory powers which it can use against certain of the employees of those firms, namely the significant ones like the senior managers and also salespersons who have direct contact with the customers. The Act accordingly contains provisions[66] which make the appointment of the special categories[67] of employee subject to FCA approval before they take up their employment, with the aim of ensuring that they are fit and proper to occupy the post in question. Thereafter, they become subject to the FCA Principles for Businesses.

A similar regime[68] exists in relation to persons who have control over authorised persons. Controllers of firms such as major shareholders and 'shadow' directors can have significant influence over how the firms operate, for often it is they who will choose the board and the senior managers. The provisions require that any person who acquires influence or additional influence over a regulated firm has to notify and be cleared by the FCA who will need to be satisfied that the applicant is fit and proper to exercise the relevant degree of influence, so that the interests of consumers would not be threatened.

Lastly, the FCA is given power[69] to make a 'prohibition order' against any person where it considers that that person is not fit and proper to perform a function or type of function in relation to certain regulated activities. Authorised persons then come under a duty to take care that they do not employ prohibited persons. This provision is similar to the above two regimes in that it is designed to operate against people who are not authorised, but who have managed to become involved in regulated activities by, for instance, being employees or owners of a business.

---

[66] Sections 59–63.
[67] Which categories of job need to be subject to the approval regime will be kept under review by the FCA.
[68] Sections 178–192. Note that s. 178 was substituted by the FSMA 2000 (Controllers) Regulations 2009 (SI 2009/534) in order to give effect to Directive 2007/44/EC ('the Acquisitions Directive').
[69] Sections 56–58.

## 18.6 Collective investment schemes

### A Background

Before the present regulatory structure relating to CISs is examined, it is useful to gain some idea of the purpose and nature of such schemes, and the regulatory background. Obviously investments carry risk and a pooling of investments might help to reduce that risk. Thus, a fund of 60 different shares is likely to remain largely intact even if a few of the companies selected underperform or collapse altogether. However, sharing in a fund of shares has other advantages than just spreading the portfolio, since it can be arranged that the fund can be invested by expert managers and they will be able to achieve economies of scale. Historically, the UK has seen three main[70] types of pooling of investment capital.

The oldest type is the investment (trust) company. These companies date from the middle of the nineteenth century. In business form they are merely companies registered under the Companies Act 1985.[71] They are not based on trust law and the use of the word 'trust' in the name is inappropriate. The basic aim of investment (trust) companies is to make profits by trading in the shares of other companies. Investors in the companies buy and sell their shares in the ordinary way, through the stock market. This raises a problem, since the price investors get for their shares will not necessarily depend on the actual asset value of the investments which the investment (trust) company holds. Market factors will have an influence on the price and this has tended to make them unpopular as investment vehicles. The recurrent problem seems to be that the shares of the company trade at a discount of 10–20% to the net asset value. This is perhaps because there is an excess of supply in the market which depresses the price. The lack of demand may be partly due to their being unpopular with investment fund managers. In recent years one way of mitigating this has been for the company to buy back its shares on the open market. This increases the underlying value of the remaining shares[72] and helps to mop up excess supply and so increases the market price.

During the 1930s an alternative investment vehicle, the unit trust became popular, and its popularity has remained ever since. The investors here pool their capital. The resultant fund is held and invested by trustees, acting on the advice of managers, who are expert in the fields in which they are investing. There is no corporate structure involved and the assets are held by the trustees for the benefit of investors who get certificates stating that they hold units in the fund. They are popular with investors because they are bought and sold by the trust itself; no 'complicated' stock exchange mechanisms are involved. The price paid reflects the value of the assets held by the fund. There is usually a 6% spread between the bid to offer price[73] which is a kind of premium the investor pays for joining the fund, to cover administrative costs etc. and to discourage people from trading in and out very frequently, and including 5% for the manager's initial charge. Additionally, the managers take 1% a year for their fees and administration. Many different types of unit trust have grown up, some offering high income at the expense of capital growth, some

---

[70] These are the main ones, but there are many other schemes and ideas in operation.
[71] And its predecessors.
[72] Since the market price of 100 shares is less than the actual proportion of the net asset value that 100 shares represents and the excess accrues to the remaining shares, in proportion.
[73] 'Bid' means the price the trust will pay the investor for his units, 'offer' means the price at which units are offered to the public.

offering capital growth at the expense of high income, some specialising in the shares of smaller companies, some in European shares, some in Japan, some in the US. Unit trusts have been permitted to move to a single pricing system, having a single unit price based on a mid-market valuation.

The third main type of mechanism for the pooling of capital[74] is the open-ended investment company ('OEIC').[75] These are a form of collective investment vehicle which has only recently become allowed in the UK. Indeed, these companies are more popular in continental countries where the UK unit trust, based on antiquated rules of trust law, is regarded as a strange creature. Difficulties in marketing the unit trust in Europe mean that there is a need to offer OEICs to compete successfully there. The name comes from the feature that OEICs can issue shares to investors and buy them back again. They are open-ended, as opposed to closed-ended companies, which cannot buy back their shares. For many years the formation of OEICs was illegal in the UK. It became possible after 1981 when the Companies Act of that year permitted companies to purchase their own shares. However, the complex rules on maintenance of capital made such companies inappropriate vehicles for the formation of investment companies and, once it was decided that the UK needed OEICs, a special sort of company, tailor-made for the purpose, was created by legislation. OEICs have a single pricing structure and the FCA has considered making this compulsory for unit trusts since it is confusing to have two price structures operating side by side. But in reality many OEICs charge an initial fee of 5% on entry which is what the dual-pricing structure was about anyway. Some have argued that concern over dual pricing is exaggerated, that the two-price system is readily understood by the public and is similar to the system operating when foreign exchange is bought at a bank or travel agent. The pricing of an OEIC, like the pricing of a unit trust, is based on the net asset value per share and so unlike investment trusts, OEICs will not trade at a discount or premium to net asset value per share. In recent years many investment trust companies have converted to OEICs; the conversion removes the discount and the possibility of marketing in Europe is attractive. Similarly, many unit trusts have converted.

From the regulatory point of view, CISs pose high risks. They involve very large sums of money which come under the control of the operators and the opportunity for fraud on a grand scale is significant. The FSA 1986 introduced a regulatory regime for the regulation of collective investment schemes. The existing scheme was regarded as working well and so with a few minor changes it was re-enacted in Part XVII of the FSMA 2000. To some extent, the background to these new provisions is the UCITS Directive[76] which sought to harmonise the laws of the member states with regard to UCITS, to ensure equivalent protection for unit-holders, so that the conditions of competition are not distorted, and overall to help bring about a European capital market. The Directive

---

[74] Unit trusts, OEICs and investment trust companies are the main three. However, various other arrangements, such as limited partnerships or informal pools operated by stockbrokers, are sometimes used to create collective investment schemes in land, metals and minerals.

[75] For a detailed account, see E. Lomnicka 'Open-Ended Investment Companies – A New Bottle for Old Wine' in B. Rider (ed.) *The Corporate Dimension* (Bristol: Jordans, 1998) p. 47.

[76] Directive 85/611/EEC on EC Undertakings for Collective Investment in Transferable Securities. This was frequently amended until 18 March 2016 when UCITS V came into force (Directive 2014/91/EU), amending Directive 2009/65/EC. For an account of the provisions of the older Directive see F. Wooldridge 'The EEC Directive on Collective Investment Undertakings' [1987] JBL 329.

requires that UCITS cannot carry on activities unless they have been authorised by the competent authorities of the member state in which they are situated[77] and lays down many other structural and regulatory details, such as disclosure requirements.[78]

It is interesting to note that the old investment trust companies did not fall within either the Directive or the UK legislation.[79] They were not CISs. This is still the case; the FSMA 2000 provided that the Treasury could make regulations specifying that certain arrangements do not amount to collective investment schemes, and the regulations they made exclude investment trust companies.[80] Investment trust companies, while not falling within the regulatory regime applicable to collective investment schemes, nevertheless attract a considerable amount of regulation under the FCA listing rules,[81] and if, as is common, they appoint a separate investment management company to manage the funds, that company will need normal FCA authorisation (i.e. Part IV Permission), otherwise it will breach the general prohibition in s. 19 of the FSMA 2000. Additionally, if FCA-authorised intermediaries are involved in selling the securities of investment trust companies, they will need to comply with any relevant COB rules.[82]

## B The basic regulatory position

The basic regulatory position is that the FSMA 2000 defines a collective investment scheme, and then, broadly, requires persons involved in running such things to be FCA authorised under Part 4 A, as follows:

235 – (1) In this Part 'collective investment scheme' means any arrangements with respect to property of any description, including money, the purpose or effect of which is to enable persons taking part in the arrangements (whether by becoming owners of the property or any part of it or otherwise) to participate in or receive profits or income arising from the acquisition, holding, management or disposal of the property or sums paid out of such profits or income.

(2) The arrangements must be such that the persons who are to participate ('participants') do not have day-to-day control over the management of the property, whether or not they have the right to be consulted or give directions.

(3) The arrangements must also have either or both of the following characteristics:
(a) the contributions of the participants and the profits or income out of which payments are to be made to them are pooled;
(b) the property is managed as a whole by or on behalf of the operator of the scheme.[83]

---

[77] UCITS Directive, art. 4.

[78] For implementation of the UCITS Directive in the UK, see the Implementation of the UCITS V Directive P516/2. In addition, the FCA has published the UCITS V Directive Instrument.

[79] *Ibid.* art. 2 (1) and the FSA 1986, s. 75 (7).

[80] FSMA 2000, s. 235 (5), and FSMA 2000 (Collective Investment Schemes) Order 2001 (SI 2001, No. 1062), art. 3 and Sch., para. 21.

[81] Chapter 20.

[82] The former FSA developed enhanced COB rules to deal with problems relating to 'split-capital' investment trusts. See http://www.fsa.gov.uk/Pages/consumerinformation/product_news/saving_investments/split_capital_investment__/index.shtml.

[83] Financial Services and Markets Act 2000, s. 235 (4) further provides: 'If arrangements provide for such pooling as is mentioned in subsection 3 (a) in relation to separate parts of the property, the arrangements are not to be regarded as constituting a single collective investment scheme unless the participants are entitled to exchange rights in one part for rights in another.'

This basic definition is complemented by a range of exemptions contained in the FSMA 2000 (Collective Investment Schemes) Order[84] covering for instance 'schemes not operated by way of business'[85] and the situation where 'the predominant purpose of the arrangements is to enable the participants to share in the use or enjoyment of property, or to make its use or enjoyment available gratuitously to others'.[86] The definition of 'collective investment scheme' in s. 235 of the FSMA 2000 was considered in *Financial Services Authority* v *Fradley*.[87] The Court of Appeal held that a scheme will be a CIS even if not all participants have transferred day-to-day control of the management of their money to the operators of the scheme so long as some participants have done so, since the provisions of s. 235 (2) of the FSMA 2000 would be satisfied in respect of them.[88] The Court has also found that an unauthorised CIS scheme will be classed as being carried on in the UK for the purposes of the FSMA if activities carried on in the UK form a significant part of the business activities of running the scheme.

Having thus defined what is meant by the term 'collective investment scheme' the legislation requires, in effect, the persons running it to become authorised, otherwise they will break the general prohibition in s. 19. This is largely achieved by art. 51 Z A–51 Z B of the RAO, which removes the word 'scheme' from the name, largely referring to them as UCITS and defining the specified activity in relation to the UCITS Directive. The result is that such persons will of course have to comply with the FCA Handbook of Rules and Guidance, and in particular COBS, and COLL (the CIS Sourcebook).[89]

## C The marketing of collective investment schemes: restricted

Section 238 of the FSMA 2000 imposes a special restriction on the marketing of collective investment schemes. Section 238 (1) prohibits authorised[90] persons from promoting collective investment schemes. However, various exemptions have been made in relation to, for instance, marketing between investment professionals.[91]

However, there is a more general exemption from the restriction. This is contained in s. 238 (4), which provides that: 'Subsection (1) does not apply in relation to – (a) an authorised unit trust scheme; (b) a scheme constituted by an authorised open-ended investment company.'[92] The upshot of this is to prevent generally the marketing of collective investment schemes in the UK unless they are unit trusts or OEICs where the schemes themselves have been given an *authorisation order* by the FCA.[93] It will be seen in the following two paragraphs that getting that order will involve compliance with detailed rules.

---

[84] SI 2001, No. 1062 (variously amended, most recently by the FSMA 2000 (Collective Investment Scheme) (Amendment) Order 2015 2015/2061.
[85] Article 4.
[86] Article 14.
[87] [2004] All ER (D) 297 & (on appeal) [2005] EWCA Civ 1183 CA: *The Times*, 1 December 2005.
[88] Following *Russell Cooke Trust Co. Ltd* v *Elliott* (2001) WL 753378; [2001] 1 All ER (D); [2007] EWHC 1443 (Ch); [2007] 2 BCLC 637.
[89] See 'The CIS Information Guide', available at https://www.handbook.fca.org.uk/handbook/COLLG.pdf.
[90] Unauthorised persons who do this would anyway be in breach of ss. 19 and/or 21.
[91] See the FSMA 2000 (Promotion of Collective Investment Schemes) (Exemptions) Order 2001 (SI 2001, No. 1060), available at https://www.legislation.gov.uk/uksi/2001/1060/contents/made.
[92] Note that s. 238 (4) (c) refers to a third category which is permitted, namely certain overseas schemes, confusingly referred to as 'a recognised scheme'. See under F below.
[93] See further s. 237 (3).

# D Authorised unit trust schemes

The FSMA 2000 contains various provisions which set out fundamental rules about authorisation[94] of the scheme and its organisation. One of the main protection mechanisms against fraud is the provision for separate roles for the scheme manager and the holder of the assets, the trustee. Either the manager or the trustee has to apply for authorisation of the scheme.[95] They must be corporate bodies[96] and they must be different persons.[97] Participants must be entitled to have their units redeemed in accordance with the scheme at a price related to the net value of the property to which the units relate, or if arrangements are made for sale on an investment exchange at a similar price.[98]

In addition to these provisions in the Act, many other aspects are regulated by the complex provisions in the FSA Handbook of Rules and Guidance and COLL (the Collective Investment Schemes Sourcebook) which replaced CIS, the previous sourcebook on CIS in 2007. These cover organisational structure, pricing and dealing, investment powers and duties of the managers and trustees.

# E Open-ended investment companies

The basic legal existence and nature of OEICs[99] is set up by the Open-Ended Investment Companies Regulations 2001.[100] An OEIC is formed by the act of the FCA making an 'authorisation order'.[101] Again, as with the unit trusts, there is provision for a split between the holding of the property and the management of it. Thus, the property must be looked after by a depositary.[102] There is to be authorisation by the FCA.[103] In addition, the Regulations set up a new company law code, a 'corporate code' setting out a set of company law rules specially for OEICs.[104] These are broadly similar to normal company law, but specially tailored for OEICs.

There is also a whole range of matters provided for by the FCA Handbook, the Perimeter Guidance Manual.[105] This guidance covers in detail such matters as prospectus, pricing and dealing and generally have the effect of making OEICs similar to unit trusts. Of particular note is the fact they make provision for the existence of an authorised corporate director, who basically acts as manager.[106]

---

[94] If they fall within the scope of the UCITS Directive, the product will get the passport. There are in existence some non-UCITS authorised unit trusts, but these are only a small part of the market. In other words, they are authorised by the FSA for the purposes of UK law, but are investing in products which the Directive does not extend to, so they do not get the passport.

[95] *Ibid.* s. 242. Both must themselves be authorised persons, see s. 243 (7).

[96] *Ibid.* s. 242 (5).

[97] *Ibid.* s. 242 (2).

[98] *Ibid.* s. 243 (10), (11).

[99] Often these days referred to as ICVCs (Investment Companies with Variable Capital).

[100] SI 2001, No. 1228 as amended by SI 2009, No. 553. See http://www.legislation.gov.uk/uksi/2009/553/pdfs/uksi_20090553_en.pdf.

[101] *Ibid.* reg. 3.

[102] *Ibid.* reg. 5.

[103] *Ibid.* reg. 9.

[104] *Ibid.* regs. 28–64.

[105] The Perimeter Guidance Manual. See https://www.handbook.fca.org.uk/handbook/PERG.pdf.

[106] If they fall within the scope of the UCITS Directive, then, as with Authorised Unit Trusts, they will get passporting rights.

## F Overseas collective investment schemes

Sections 264–283 of the FSMA 2000 make provision for the recognition of overseas CISs which are then regarded as 'recognised[107] schemes' and may be marketed to the public in the UK.[108] Section 264 gives automatic recognition to UCITS schemes constituted in another EEA state. Under s. 270, certain schemes in designated countries can be recognised and under s. 272 the FCA can recognise foreign schemes on an individual basis.

## G Case law

In *Financial Conduct Authority* v *Capital Alternatives Limited*,[109] the court provides important elucidation as to the meaning of what constitutes a CIS, in particular (1) the meaning of 'pooling' of income; (2) what 'property' is relevant for the purposes of s. 235 and (3) what is entailed by the concept of 'property' being 'managed as a whole by or on behalf of the operator of the scheme'. *Capital Alternatives* concerned two types of scheme, viz. the African Land Scheme and Carbon Credit Schemes. The former related to some 3,000 acres of rice farming land in Sierra Leone (called 'Yoni Farm') which was sub-let to investors in plots allocated to each sub-tenant for a sub-lease premium of £1,250. The rice harvests from each plot were counted so as to ensure that each 'plot sub-tenant' received 40% of the profit arising from their individual holding. This artificial accounting method was operated deliberately in an attempt to avoid the arrangement constituting a CIS:

> Section 235 is concerned with an arrangement with respect to property, the purpose or effect of which is to enable investors ('whether by becoming owners of the property or any part of it or otherwise') to participate in or receive profits or income arising from, inter alia, the management of the property. In that context 'the property' (which the section does not require to be owned by any investor) is perfectly apt to cover a farm from the management of which, including the buildings, roads etc., the investor, who becomes the owner of part of the property, is to receive the share of profit attributable to the proceeds of his plot.[110]

In *Brown* v *InnovatorOne Plc*,[111] it was noted that care must be taken when documenting the structure of limited liability partnerships arrangements in order to prevent them from being treated as a CIS. It may be advisable to ensure that all participants should have day-to-day control over the management of the LLP. It is not enough for participants merely to have a legal right to exercise control over the property, but rather that they actually exercise that right sufficiently to be regarded as being in effective control. Accordingly it is necessary to look beyond any documents which may provide for 'day-to-day control' and consider how the arrangements are designed to operate in practice.

The decision of the Supreme Court in *Asset Land*[112] follows a similar judgment in February 2014, which also made clear that the FCA's approach was sound. Investors were

---

[107] A name which seems unnecessarily confusing.
[108] Subject to the amendments in Undertakings for Collective Investment in Transferable Securities Regulations 2011/1613, available at http://www.legislation.gov.uk/uksi/2011/1613/pdfs/uksi_20111613_en.pdf.
[109] *Financial Conduct Authority* v *Capital Alternatives Limited 5* [2014] EWHC 144; [2015] EWCA Civ 284.
[110] *Ibid*, at para 50.
[111] *Brown* v *InnovatorOne Plc* [2012] EWHC 1321 (Comm).
[112] *Asset Land Investment Plc and another (Appellants)* v *The Financial Conduct Authority (Respondent)*, 20 Apr 2016 [2016] UKSC 17 UKSC 2014/0150.

persuaded by Asset Land to buy individual plots of land for between £7,500 and £24,000 with the promise that the land would increase in value if it got planning permission or was re-zoned. In February 2013 the then FSA had won its case against Asset Land in the High Court when it found that David Banner-Eve, Start Cohen, Asset Land Investments plc and Asset L.I. Inc. ran an illegal land bank by operating a CIS without authorisation. Asset Land and David Banner-Eve appealed to the Court of Appeal, which confirmed in April 2014 that Asset Land was operating a CIS. The Supreme Court confirmed that Asset Land had been operating an unauthorised CIS in the course of operating a land bank, which involved the selling of small plots of land to investors at hugely inflated prices. It found that, although investors were the legal owners of their individual plots of land, in reality the arrangements of the scheme were that investors did not have control over their investment and Asset Land was the central operator of the scheme.

The judgment provides further protection to consumers by confirming that it is necessary to consider the substance of the arrangements put in place by the operator when assessing if they are operating a CIS. Operators of such schemes will not be able to benefit by providing purely illusory rights to investors. Operators need to ensure that investors have genuine control over their investments to avoid being found to have operated a CIS.

## 18.7 Enforcement

### A 'Policing the perimeter'

Persons who carry on[113] a regulated activity in the UK without being authorised[114] fall outside the perimeter fence of the FCA's now vast domain, within which it wields disciplinary powers over its authorised disciples who are bound by the 'Eleven Commandments' and other FCA rules. They face criminal penalties.[115] Over the years the FCA (and the former FSA and SIB) have adopted a flexible hard/soft approach to what it has called 'policing the perimeter', i.e. dealing with those who are discovered to have contravened the authorisation requirement. Annually it has been investigating several hundred cases, most of whom were unaware that they were in breach of the statutory requirements and who would usually merely receive a warning letter from the FCA, requiring compliance with the authorisation procedures or cessation of the activity. However, recalcitrance or calculated infringement has elicited a tougher response.

### B Disciplinary measures

Trouble for authorised persons suspected of committing infringements of the FCA's rules usually starts by the exercise of the FCA's wide powers to call for information. If they have queries about specific matters, the FCA can require by notice in writing, an authorised person to provide specified information or documents.[116] If they have general concerns about a firm

---

[113] Or purport to carry on.
[114] Or exempt persons in relation to that activity.
[115] See the analysis of the effect of s. 19 at 18.2 above and the financial promotion regime at 18.2E. Note that the effect of exceeding a Pt IV permission by an authorised person falls within 'the perimeter' and is to be dealt with as an FCA disciplinary matter; see s. 20 and 18.4B above.
[116] The FSMA 2000, s. 165 (1) – Authority's power to require information [authorised persons etc.] – the word inserted by the FSA 2010, Sch. 2 (1) para. 15.

but there are no circumstances suggesting any specific breach they may start an investigation into the matter if there is 'good reason'.[117] The investigators then have wide powers to require the person to attend for questioning or otherwise provide information or documents.[118]

The provisions in ss. 205–211 of the FSMA2000[119] are the core of the FCA's enforcement machinery. It is these provisions which replace the contractual powers of the SROs to levy money penalties for breach of their rules.[120] The centrepiece is s. 206, which authorises the FCA to impose a penalty of such amount as it considers appropriate, if it considers that an authorised person has contravened a requirement imposed on him by or under the Act. Additionally, the FCA may cancel a person's Part IV permission,[121] which has the effect of removing their authorisation; effectively shutting down their business, at least in so far as it involves regulated activities. Obviously it is likely that this sanction will be reserved only for the more severe cases.[122] There is also the possibility of public censure.[123] Court orders are available to restrain a likely contravention of the Act or the FCA's rules, or to restrain the continuance or repetition of a contravention.[124]

During the long and stormy passage through Parliament of the FSMA2000, the disciplinary structure which the FCA was proposing to adopt came under attack on human rights grounds, mainly on the basis that the hearing process in disciplinary proceedings was vitiated by being too closely linked with the rest of the FCA and therefore in breach of art. 6 of the European Convention on Human Rights. With this in mind the FCA has carefully developed internal mechanisms which are designed to minimise the risk of human rights breaches. Disciplinary matters which are likely to be contentious[125] are dealt with by a Regulatory Decisions Committee ('RDC'),[126] which is a body outside the FCA's

---

[117] Under *ibid.* s. 167.

[118] *Ibid.* s. 171. There are restrictions on the extent to which and manner in which the answers given can be used against the person in subsequent criminal proceedings; broadly, only where the accused during the criminal proceedings has made reference to the answers which he gave in the earlier proceedings (s. 174). The need for this narrow gateway came about after the decision of the European Court of Human Rights in *Saunders* v *United Kingdom* [1997] BCC 872, where statements made to DTI inspectors operating under powers in the Companies Act 1985 were used to help secure a conviction in subsequent criminal proceedings. It was held that this deprived the defendant of a fair hearing, contrary to art. 6 of the European Convention on Human Rights.

[119] Subject to the amendments made by the Undertakings for Collective Investment in Transferable Securities Regulations 2011/1613 and the FSA 2010. Note also s. 206 A added by the FSA 2010 suspending permission to carry on regulated activities etc.

[120] The SROs found that they had extremely effective powers to exact money penalties. In order to get authorised under the FSA 1986, it was necessary for a person to join an SRO (unless he was directly authorised by the SIB/FSA, which became very rare). By joining the SRO, a person became contractually bound to comply with its rules and also contractually bound to pay up if its disciplinary procedures required a money penalty from him. Towards the end of the FSA 1986 regime, penalties in excess of £250,000 were being exacted by the SROs.

[121] Under the power in ss. 33 and 54 of the FSMA 2000.

[122] Section 206 (2) makes it clear that the FCA is not empowered both to withdraw authorisation *and* make the person pay a money penalty. This is designed to reverse the practice of the SROs whereby they would order a person to be expelled from the SRO (thus withdrawing their authorisation under the 1986 Act) and also impose a money penalty as a parting shot.

[123] The FSMA2000, s. 205.

[124] *Ibid.* s. 380. By s. 381 these powers also apply to cases of market abuse, on which, see Chapter 20 below. For discussion of the authorities on this section see *Financial Services Authority* v *Anderson* [2010] EWHC 1547 (Ch).

[125] Such as restricting regulated activities, making prohibition orders, imposing financial penalties. Matters not likely to be contentious (e.g. requiring a firm to send in more reports or a business plan) are dealt with by Executive Procedures, meaning by members of FCA staff of appropriate seniority.

[126] On all this, see generally the FCA Handbook Enforcement Guide, available at https://www.handbook.fca.org.uk/handbook/document/EG_Full_20140401.pdf and also the Decision Procedure and Penalties Manual (DEPP), available at https://www.handbook.fca.org.uk/handbook/DEPP.pdf.

management structure, where, apart from the chair, none of the members is an FCA employee. The RDC will have a matter referred to it by the FCA staff member investigating it and the RDC will then decide whether or not to take the matter further by taking disciplinary action against the authorised person. The trump card in terms of fending off human rights cases lies in the fact that if that person is not content to accept the penalty imposed on them, they have the right to refer the matter[127] to the Financial Services and Markets Tribunal, which is a tribunal independent of the FCA.[128] They will hear the matter *de novo*. It is likely that this will usually be sufficient to avoid successful human rights challenges.[129]

The FSA 2010[130] gave the FCA new enforcement powers to publish decision notices and to impose (i) suspensions or restrictions on authorised and approved persons and (ii) financial penalties on persons who perform controlled functions without approval and who breach short selling prohibition rules or short selling disclosure requirements. The restriction on imposing a financial penalty including withdrawing a person's authorisation previously contained in s. 206(2) of the FSMA 2002 has been removed. Moreover, the time for taking action against an approved person for misconduct contained in s. 66(4) of the FSMA 2000 has been extended from two to three years.

The former FSA explained how it intended to implement these changes in practice in para. 18 of the Enforcement Annual Performance Account 2010/11:[131]

'Our approach is to achieve credible deterrence in respect of our [FSMA] mandate. We focus on cases where we think we can make a real difference to consumers and markets, using enforcement strategically as a tool to change behaviour in the financial services industry. We have a range of sanctions available – criminal, civil and administrative – and we use these sanctions to deliver strong, visible enforcement outcomes. To achieve credible deterrence, wrongdoers must not only realise that they face a real and tangible risk of being held to account, but must also expect to face a significant penalty.

- We consider the threat of custodial sentence to be a significant deterrent to market misconduct. We are committed to bringing appropriate criminal prosecutions against those who abuse the markets. In 2010/11 guilty verdicts were returned in the prosecutions of five individuals for insider dealing, resulting in custodial sentences of between 12 months and three years and four months.
- We published Final Notices imposing a record £98.5m in financial penalties during the year.

---

[127] See *ibid.* s. 208 (4).
[128] See generally *ibid.* ss. 132–137, and Sch. 13. Section 132 was repealed by Transfer of Tribunal Functions Order 2010/22 Sch. 2 para. 44 (6 April 2010). Section 133 was substituted by the Transfer of Tribunal Functions Order 2010 (SI 2010/22). The Explanatory Note to that Order explains that the Order is made under the Tribunals, Courts and Enforcement Act 2007 ('the 2007 Act'). Part 1 of the 2007 Act creates a new two-tier tribunal structure; the First-tier Tribunal and the Upper Tribunal are established under s. 3 of the 2007 Act. Order-making powers are provided under Part 1 of the 2007 Act to enable existing tribunals to be transferred into the new structure. This Order effects the transfer into the new structure of various tribunal functions. Finally, note that s. 137 was also repealed by Transfer of Tribunal Functions Order 2010/22 Sch. 2 para. 46 (6 April 6 2010).
[129] In the first reported case, the Court of Appeal made it clear that the courts would allow judicial review only in the most exceptional circumstances. Thus, normally the aggrieved person's right to go to the FSM Tribunal and then (on a point of law) to the Court of Appeal, would be a sufficient remedy. See: *R (Davies and others)* v *Financial Services Authority* [2003] 4 All ER 1196.
[130] See http://www.legislation.gov.uk/ukpga/2010/28/pdfs/ukpga_20100028_en.pdf. For an excellent assessment of the changes made by the FSA 2010 see: N. Willmott *et al.* 'Equipping the Modern Regulator: Assessing the New Regulatory Powers under the Financial Services Act 2010' (2010) 78 *Compliance Officer Bulletin* 1.
[131] See http://www.fsa.gov.uk/pubs/annual/ar10_11/enforcement_report.pdf.

- We consider that action against individuals has a greater deterrent effect than action against firms and we are committed to holding senior managers to account for competency and integrity failings. In 2010/11 we published prohibitions of 71 individuals.
- We consider it appropriate to use our range of civil and criminal powers to protect consumers from the risks posed by businesses offering financial services without authorisation to do so. Proceedings were commenced last year in ten cases relating to unauthorised business valued at approximately £100m.

While the [then] FSA was given the new power to publish Decision Notices last year . . . A new approach to financial regulation: building a stronger system, the government set out its proposal to allow the Prudential Regulation Authority and the Financial Conduct Authority to publish a summary of a Warning Notice once it is issued. This summary would include the grounds on which the action is being taken. The FSA welcomes this proposal and considers that it will provide increased transparency of enforcement action as well as allowing the new regulators to highlight relevant issues to consumers and the industry at an earlier stage 'after stage'.

Responding to criticism of its 'light touch' approach to regulation deployed during the financial boom prior to the global credit crisis, the FCA embarked on a programme of more intrusive supervision from 2010 that sought to judge the outcomes of regulated firms' compliance arrangements as opposed to merely checking that systems are in place.[132] In recent years, the general trend in the FCA's enforcement policy has shown a steady increase in the level of civil penalties, and during 2010 it levied two of its largest. In May 2010, the then FSA imposed its largest ever financial penalty against an individual by fining Simon Eagle £2.8 million in connection with market abuse. In June 2010, it fined JP Morgan Securities Ltd £33.32 million for failing to protect client money by segregating it appropriately. Finally, in September 2010 it fined Goldman Sachs International (Goldman) £17.5 million for weaknesses in controls resulting in a failure to provide the FSA with appropriate information regarding the US SEC investigation into a collateral debt obligation structured by Goldman' US affiliate.

Further, in a controversial move, the FCA has been publishing Decision Notices.[133] Until 6 March 2011, the only notice that had been published was the Final Notice which was produced after the case has been settled or been determined by the Tribunal. The initial proposal appeared to be to publish decision notices in all cases. This was an issue which raised concerns during the FSA consultation and the FSA has recognised that it needs to consider this question on a case-by-case basis. But concern remains, however, that even if a Decision Notice is successfully challenged, if it has been published it will remain on the FSA's website indefinitely or until a party successfully requests its removal.[134] Furthermore, publication of Warning Notices is also a possibility.[135] The Government has legislated to allow for publication of the fact that a Warning Notice has been issued and of a summary of the Warning Notice. This new power applies to both the PRA and FCA.

---

[132] See further, S. Bazley 'FSA Enforcement Activity, Reflections on 2010 and the Challenges of Regulatory Change' (2011) 32 Comp Lawyer 1.

[133] Former FSA's Business Plan for 2011/12 (22 March 2011), available at http://www.fsa.gov.uk/pubs/plan/pb2011_12.pdf.

[134] C. Burnett and A. Chakrabarti The FSA 2011/12 Business Plan and Risk Outlooks, at http://www.allenovery.com/AOWEB/AreasOfExpertise/Editorial.aspx?contentTypeID=1&itemID=60748&prefLangID=410.

[135] See Chapter 6 Warning and decision notices of the FCA Handbook in relation to regulated covered bonds, available at https://www.handbook.fca.org.uk/handbook/RCB/6.pdf.

On 14 September 2016, the FCA published a Decision Notice in respect of Mr Andrew Tinney, formerly Chief Operating Officer of Barclays Wealth and Investment Management, setting out the FCA's finding that Mr Tinney should be publicly censured and banned from carrying out any senior management or Significant Influence Functions in any regulated financial service provider.[136]

## C Restitution, private actions for damages and insolvency

The FCA may apply to the court for a restitution order if a person has contravened the Act or rules,[137] or been knowingly concerned in the contravention, and profits have been made or loss sustained as a result, or an adverse effect. The court has power to order the person to pay to the FCA such sum as appears just, having regard to the profits or loss.[138]

With regard to private actions for damages, the FSMA 2000 provides that a contravention by an authorised person of a rule is actionable at the suit of a private person who suffers loss as a result of the contravention.[139] This is a rather important provision. The legislation is in effect giving an action in tort for breach of statutory duty. It is limited to actions by private persons. This is done with a view to preventing large firms from suing each other for technical breaches of the rules. However, exceptions can be made for certain rules if the FCA wishes, thus opening the way for it to use the threat of civil actions by powerful firms as an additional way of securing compliance with certain rules; an interesting regulatory technique.[140]

The FCA has been given a number of rights, enabling it to participate in insolvency proceedings.[141] For instance, if there is a voluntary arrangement being entered into by a firm and its creditors, the FCA might consider it necessary to become involved in certain circumstances. Of particular importance is the provision that the FCA can present a petition for winding up of a body or partnership which has been an authorised person, or appointed representative, or carrying on a regulated activity in contravention of the general prohibition.[142] Similarly, it can petition for a bankruptcy order in respect of an individual.[143]

## 18.8 Investor compensation

Investor compensation schemes ('ICS') are an important part of the mechanisms used to achieve one of the basic goals of securities regulation: investor protection. They operate as a kind of enforced insurance mechanism whereby investors are to some extent insured against the insolvency or bankruptcy of financial services suppliers. If the scheme is funded by a levy on the financial services industry, then ICS can also have the effect of operating as an encouragement on the industry as a whole to monitor the other players.

---

[136] See https://www.fca.org.uk/publication/decision-notices/andrew-tinney.pdf.
[137] The FSMA2000, s. 382.
[138] For market abuse (as to which see Chapter 20 below) there are similar restitution possibilities, but here, the FCA can require it, without the intervention of the court; see *ibid*. ss. 383–384.
[139] *Ibid*. s. 150.
[140] For definitions and conditions see the FSMA 2000 (Rights of Action) Regulations 2001 (SI 2001, No. 2256), available at https://www.legislation.gov.uk/uksi/2001/2256/contents/made.
[141] *Ibid*. ss. 355–379.
[142] *Ibid*. s. 367.
[143] *Ibid*. s. 372.

This is an area which is particularly circumscribed by part of the EU legislation designed to bring about the internal market in financial services. The ICS Directive[144] requires that member states shall ensure that a scheme or schemes are operative and that no investment firm can carry on investment business unless it belongs to such a scheme.[145] The cover must not be less than €20,000. Member states can provide that the investor will get only 90% of his claim.[146] This is with a view to diminishing the tendency of an investor to cease to act carefully in his choice of investment firm. The Directive keys in to the ISD[147] so that an investor who deals with a passporting firm knows that there are at least minimum provisions for compensation in force in the member state which that firm comes from. The matters in respect of which claims can be made are limited, so that they will usually only involve getting money or investments back[148] and the ability to make claims only arises where the competent authority has decided that the firm is not going to be able to meet its financial commitments or a court has made an order which has the effect of suspending investors' ability to make claims against it.[149]

The UK's implementation of the ICS Directive is contained in the FSMA 2000.[150] This sets up a single scheme of compensation to replace the five schemes previously in existence and in particular to replace the ICS established under s. 54 of the FSA 1986. The new scheme, called the FSMA Compensation Scheme, is a separate organisation from the FCA, but accountable to it. It is a limited company, and will carry out the functions cast upon the 'scheme manager' by the Act. The FCA sets the maximum levels of compensation to be offered and makes rules on the circumstances in which it is to be paid,[151] although it is clear[152] that it is a scheme for compensating persons where the investment firm is unable or likely to be unable to satisfy claims made against it. The scheme is funded by levies on the industry[153] but the cost of paying compensation will fall on firms in the same area[154] of financial services business; so that defaults will affect their contribution levels rather than those of unrelated firms.[155]

On 12 July 2010, the European Commission adopted a proposal to amend the ICS Directive. Indeed in some EU countries, ICS did not have sufficient funds to pay out claims or there were lengthy delays in payouts. The proposal includes increasing the compensation limit in each member state to €50,000 (member states will not be permitted to exceed this limit). It also requires compensation schemes to provide partial payment if final payment has not been made within nine months of a formal determination that the

---

[144] Directive 97/9/EEC. On 12 July 2010 the EU Commission adopted a proposal to amend the Directive. Discussed below. The proposals were anticipated to come into effect by the end of 2012; see below.

[145] *Ibid.* art. 2.

[146] *Ibid.* art. 4.

[147] See Chapter 16, 16.5 above.

[148] Directive 97/9/EEC, art. 2 (2).

[149] E.g. a winding-up order.

[150] Ss. 212–224, subject to the amendments made by the FSA 2010 and the Collective Schemes Regulations.

[151] Compensation limits changed in December 2010. See https://www.fscs.org.uk/what-we-cover/compensation-limits/.

[152] From s. 213 (1) of the FSMA 2000.

[153] Full details of the funding rules for the FSCS are in the former FSA's Handbook under Redress, Compensation withthe main rules relating to funding set out in FEES 6. See http://www.fsa.gov.uk/pages/About/What/International/pdf/ICSD.pdf.

[154] This helps to enhance the monitoring effect described above.

[155] On all this see FSA Handbook of Rules and Guidance, Compensation Sourcebook (COMP).

firm is 'in default', requiring member states to establish an ex ante fund (the Commission and Parliament each propose a different percentage on which to base the calculation of the pre-fund), introducing a mandatory mutual borrowing facility between investor compensation schemes in different member states. Other noticeable proposals include extending compensation to investors who incur a loss due to the financial failure of third party custodians, UCITS depositaries and UCITS sub-custodians and increasing the requirements for investment firms to disclose information about the compensation available under the terms of the Directive. Any changes may ultimately require changes in the Compensation Sourcebook (COMP) and FEES 6 which will require amendment. As the proposal was not endorsed at EU level, the Commission decided to withdraw it in March 2015.

In 2012 UK authorised banks, building societies and credit unions were required to display information about FSCS protection in branch and online (this included posters and window stickers). This action followed the introduction of new rules obliging deposit takers to display information about FSCS protection available to consumers. The UK branches of EEA banks have had to specify that their customers would not be covered by FSCS and clearly state which national scheme provides protection. On 14 January 2013 FSCS launched a consumer awareness programme, aiming to reassure consumers and boost confidence, thereby aiding financial stability. It follows on from the disclosure requirements which use protection to engage with the consumers and highlight the safety FSCS provides to savings and deposits. The advertising programme is run in the national press, radio, online and by digital means.

## 18.9 The Financial Ombudsman Service

Prior to the regime under the FSMA 2000, there were eight ombudsman schemes in existence which enabled consumers to pursue a complaint about a financial services provider. The former FSA put forward proposals[156] for the new scheme, which is a single financial services ombudsman scheme. Membership of that scheme is compulsory for firms that are UK authorised. The legislature has preferred the ombudsman approach rather than arbitration because one of the main differences between the two processes is that an ombudsman can bind the firm whilst leaving complainants free to pursue their claim before the courts if they wished, whereas an arbitration can only take place where both parties agree in advance to be bound by the arbitrator's decision. The ombudsman has power to direct a firm to take remedial steps to pay compensation for financial loss and for distress and inconvenience.[157] In May 2011, the FSA confirmed new complaints-handling rules for the businesses it regulated and increased the maximum compensation the ombudsman can require businesses to pay from £100,000 to £150,000 (for complaints the ombudsman receives from 1 January 2012).[158]

The Financial Ombudsman Service (FOS), the UK's official expert in sorting out problems with financial services, was set up by Parliament to resolve individual complaints between financial businesses and their customers. The FOS can look into problems involving most types of money matters, from payday loans to pensions, pet insurance to PPI. If they decide someone has been treated unfairly, they have legal powers to put things right.

---

[156] In Consultation Paper 4 *Consumer Complaints*.
[157] See generally ss. 225–234 and the FOS website at http://www.financial-ombudsman.org.uk.
[158] See details at http://www.fsa.gov.uk/pages/Library/Communication/PR/2011/046.shtml.

## 18.10 Regulation of investment exchanges and clearing houses

The FSMA 2000[159] largely continues the 1986 Act's regime in relation to recognised investment exchanges ('RIEs') and recognised clearing houses ('RCHs').[160] Broadly speaking, the system is that the FCA issues a recognition order in respect of, say, the LSE[161] which then becomes exempt from the general prohibition[162] as respects any regulated activity which is carried on as part of the Stock Exchange's business as an investment exchange or which is carried on for the purposes of, or in connection with, the provision of any clearing services by it.[163] In order to be recognised, an exchange will need to meet certain conditions as thereafter be subject to the FCA's supervision.[164] However, such market infrastructure providers have a choice between being recognised as an RIE or just authorised as firms.[165] The over-the-counter ('OTC') markets such as the multilateral trading facility ('MTF')[166] of broking firms have largely opted for authorisation rather than RIE status, and in that context the FSA has developed a light-touch regulatory regime in certain respects.[167] A major difference between the recognised body regime (RIE) and the authorised regime is that recognised bodies are themselves regulators who establish rules governing the conduct of their members or participants and are required to have an in-house regulatory resource to monitor and enforce compliance with those rules,[168] subject to oversight by the FCA. Thus, in a very real sense they are an important manifestation of the survival of self-regulation in some areas of the regulatory scene. On the other hand, being an RIE will give greater flexibility in the regulatory regime (the FCA cannot make rules for recognised bodies) and some tax advantages.

The Financial Services and Markets Act 2000 (Recognition Requirements for Investment Exchanges and Clearing Houses) Regulations 2001[169] (sometimes known as the 'Recognition Requirements Regulations'), Chapter 2 of the FCA Handbook, contain the recognition requirements for UK RIEs (other than Regulatory Accounting Principles) and sets out guidance on those requirements.[170]

The Investment Exchanges and Clearing Houses Act 2006[171] has conferred power on the FCA to disallow excessive regulatory provision RIEs and clearing houses, and for connected purposes. The Act came into force in December 2006 and gave the regulator powers under the FSMA 2000 to review the rules and other regulatory provisions made by recognised bodies and to prevent them from making excessive regulatory provisions. Since the Act came into force, the former FSA and subsequently the FCA have put

---

[159] See ss. 285–301.
[160] Subject to amendments to the Recognised Investment Exchanges and Recognised Clearing Houses Sourcebook (REC) made by the Consequential Amendments (Financial Services Act 2010) Instrument 2010.
[161] Section 285 (1) (a).
[162] Section 19.
[163] Section 285 (2).
[164] Sections 286, 293, 296.
[165] See *The FSA's Approach to Regulation of the Market Infrastructure* (Financial Services Authority, January 2000) pp. 7–8.
[166] When the MiFID came into effect on 1 November 2007 and replaced the ISD.
[167] See FCA Handbook of Rules and Guidance, Market Conduct.
[168] Thus they have their own disciplinary proceedings.
[169] https://www.legislation.gov.uk/uksi/2001/995/contents/made?view=plain.
[170] https://www.handbook.fca.org.uk/handbook/REC/2.pdf.
[171] https://www.legislation.gov.uk/ukpga/2006/55/contents?view=plain.

temporary waivers in place to relieve recognised bodies from the notification obligation in certain cases. The implementation of the Act resulted in changes to the RIEs and Recognised Clearing Houses Sourcebook and related definitions in the FCA's Glossary. The new rules and guidance covered the extent of the notification duty on recognised bodies and the information that should accompany notifications.[172]

## 18.11 Final matters

The account in this chapter has provided an overview of the theory of securities regulation as well as the main,[173] concepts and mechanisms being employed by the Financial Services and Markets Act 2000 and the FSA 2012 in the regulation of financial services activity in the UK. The UK has been through a prolonged period of radical change to its financial services regulation. Firms are now seeking to adapt to the new powers recently bestowed upon the FCA as well as to life under a new regime. What is clear is that the risk and compliance burden on firms will continue to grow as they gear up for dealing with multiple regulators who wield an expanding selection of supervisory and enforcement tools, and who can be expected to use those tools aggressively to pursue their potentially inconsistent regulatory objectives.[174]

## Further reading

The Financial Conduct Authority, *Principles of Good Regulation*, available at https://www.fca.org.uk/about/principles-good-regulation.

S. Bazley 'FSA Enforcement Activity, Reflections on 2010 and the Challenges of Regulatory Change' (2011) 32 Comp Lawyer 1.

FCA Enforcement Information Guide, at https://www.fca.org.uk/publication/corporate/enforcement-information-guide.pdf.

NERA Trends in Regulatory Enforcement in UK Financial Markets 2016/2017, at http://www.nera.com/content/dam/nera/publications/at-a-glance/PUB_UK_Regulatory_Trends_FCA%201116-MY%202016-17.pdf.

---

[172] Notifications Obligations under the Investment Exchanges and Clearing Houses Act 2006, available at http://www.fsa.gov.uk/pubs/policy/ps07_21_newsletter.pdf.

[173] Certain matters have not been covered, such as the regulation of Lloyd's (ss. 314–324) and of professionals who engage in financial services activities as ancillary to their main profession (ss. 325–333). However, some further aspects of the FSMA 2000 are considered below. For a full account of the effect of the 2000 Act and the rules, see A. Whittaker (ed.) *Butterworths Financial Services Law and Practice* (London: Butterworths, looseleaf).

[174] N. Willmott *et al.* 'Equipping the Modern Regulator: Assessing the New Regulatory Powers under the Financial Services Act 2010' (2010) 78 *Compliance Officer Bulletin* 1, at p. 27.

# 19

# The regulation of public offerings of shares

## 19.1 Migration into capital markets law

### A Background

The regulation of public offerings of shares is dealt with in this Part of the text on Securities Regulation because it is another of those areas of mainstream company law which arguably have migrated into capital markets law. This migration, which is well known among European scholars, had become fairly apparent, at least by 1986, when some of the provisions governing public offerings of shares were included in the statute which set up the UK's first comprehensive system of securities regulation, namely the Financial Services Act 1986. More recently there has been a graphic confirmation of it when the functions of the London Stock Exchange ('LSE') as the competent authority under the Listing Directives[1] were transferred to the Financial Services Authority ('FSA'), mainly because it was felt that there was a conflict of interest between the money-making functions of the LSE as a private body and its public functions as competent authority.[2] Thus, the final vestiges of the company law aspects of the public regulation of public offerings of shares had literally[3] decamped into securities regulation. The commercial functioning of the LSE and its role in facilitating corporate finance are clearly still part of mainstream company law and in this book have been dealt with accordingly.[4]

### B Public offerings of securities

### 1 *Effects on management*

When a company needs very large amounts of capital to enable it to expand to the size which the directors think would be economically beneficial, it will usually need to make an offering of shares to the public and arrange to have the shares publicly quoted on a stock exchange. Usually in this situation, the company will have a long and successful trading record and will have grown to its present size as a result of inputs of venture capital. However, this is not always the case and sometimes, although rarely, a company will not have started trading prior to making a public offering, as happened, for example, with Eurotunnel which needed to raise large sums of money before it could see its way ahead sufficiently to commence the vast project.[5]

---

[1] See below.
[2] See further below.
[3] In Chapter 13. In view of the consequent staff transfers between the LSE and the FSA.
[4] In Chapter 13.
[5] See n. 18, Chapter 13 above.

Seen from the point of view of managers seeking to expand their company there are three main advantages of a public offering:

(1) Assuming that the company is financially attractive, they will be in a position to raise almost unlimited amounts of capital over a long period of time, in the initial offering and in later offerings.
(2) The shares will be made more attractive to buyers (with the effect that the cost of the capital to the company will be lower) because they are liquid investments by virtue of the fact that there will be a ready market which will enable shareholders to 'exit' whenever they wish.
(3) With publicly quoted shares the company will be in a position to grow by making share for share takeover bids for other companies.

For the management, these advantages come at a price. The stock exchange quotation will bring pressures on them through increased monitoring by the financial press, through continuing obligations to maintain the quotation,[6] and through increased self-regulatory burdens such as the UK Corporate Governance Code. They will also become subject to market disciplines, because with a public offering will come dispersed ownership of the shares making the company potentially subject to a hostile takeover bid. The risk of this will increase if the company is seen to be underperforming as compared to other companies in that sector of industry. Very often, a public offering will mean that the entrepreneurs who founded the company will find that their controlling shareholding in the company is massively diluted after flotation. They may not like the loss of influence and control which this brings, nor perhaps fully appreciate the consequences of it in advance.[7] Very occasionally, a company which has gone public in this way will be taken private again by its former entrepreneur, who, for whatever reasons, has become disenchanted with the new situation.

## 2 *The London Stock Exchange – initial public offerings and flotation*

The LSE plays an important role in the facilitation of UK corporate finance mainly by providing the mechanisms of the market for the trading of shares which have been issued to the public. In addition to complying with the Stock Exchange's rules for admission to trading,[8] a company seeking access to the market will also have to comply with the listing rules issued by the FCA as the UK Listing Authority ('UKLA').[9] Before the securities can be admitted to the market, they will need to be sufficiently widely held by the public that their marketability when listed can be assumed. Thus a company coming to the market for the first time will normally make an initial public offering ('IPO') by one of the methods approved by the Stock Exchange.[10] Closely coordinated, there will then be a second stage[11]

---

[6] See further below.
[7] See e.g. *Re Blue Arrow plc* discussed in Chapter 12 B 2 above.
[8] *The Admission and Disclosure Standards*; see 19.5 below.
[9] See below on the transfer of responsibilities from the FSA.
[10] And UKLA; see further below.
[11] These two stages are sometimes loosely referred to as the primary market and the secondary market.

to the overall process, generally called 'flotation',[12] in which the securities of the company are admitted to the market and trading in them begins.[13] Prior to flotation its shares will have been relatively closely held by management and other private individuals, venture capital companies and possibly by a few other financial institutions. After making an IPO and subsequent flotation on the LSE, its share ownership will be widely spread among very many financial institutions and private individuals worldwide. Its shares will be traded on a daily basis and thereafter its reputation and fortunes will largely depend on its current share price in the market.

The LSE currently operates four markets for the trading of shares which have been issued to the public: the Main Market,[14] a regulated market aimed at larger, more established companies;[15] a smaller market for younger 'fledgling' companies, called the Alternative Investment Market ('AIM').[16] The regulatory criteria for AIM are less onerous than for the Main Market and so securities marketed on AIM are generally a riskier investment.[17] The Main Market is home to over 2,600 companies from 60 countries, and since its launch in 1995 some 2,500 companies have joined;[18] the Professional Securities Market ('PSM'): an unregulated market for the listing of specialist securities including debt and depository receipts to professional investors;[19] and the Specialist Funds Market: a regulated market for specialist investment funds targeting institutional, professional and highly knowledgeable investors.[20]

Although the LSE is not the world's biggest market for domestic securities,[21] it has the largest volume of non-domestic trading. For many years trading on the Main Market has been based on a system of competing market makers, under which the market makers throughout the trading day[22] offer buying and selling prices in the shares for which they are registered as market makers and for which are committed to quoting buy and sell prices, making their living from the margin (i.e. difference) between the buying and selling price. Market makers deal with financial institutions direct, whereas members of the public need to go through a broker/dealer.[23] In recent years, the trading systems have been subjected to a rolling programme of modernisation. Buying and selling prices are displayed

---

[12] The word 'flotation' is not really a term of art and both stages together, seen as a unified whole are quite often referred to as 'flotation'.

[13] The LSE is not the only secondary market in the UK but in terms of trading volume and capitalisation it is by far the most significant.

[14] This used to be called the 'Listed Market' but since the transfer of the LSE's functions under the Listing Directives to the FCA as the UKLA that name has been dropped; see further 19.3 below.

[15] www.londonstockexchange.com/companies-and-advisors/main-market/main-market/home.htm.

[16] www.londonstockexchange.com/companies-and-advisors/aim/aim/aim.htm.

[17] However, the term 'market' is fluid, and it should also be mentioned that there is also a facility called techMARK which is available for innovative technology companies which have been admitted to the Main Market; in effect it is a market grouping, or market within a market. On similar lines there is also techMARK Mediscience, and landMARK (regional groupings). For international securities there is the International Order Book and the International Bulletin Board.

[18] See the LSE website at http://www.londonstockexchange.com.

[19] www.londonstockexchange.com/companies-and-advisors/psm/home/psm.htm.

[20] https://www.lseg.com/sites/default/files/content/documents/sfm-factsheet.pdf.

[21] The New York Stock Exchange and the Tokyo Stock Exchange are bigger.

[22] I.e. during the mandatory quote period, which runs from 08.00hrs to 16.30hrs.

[23] I.e. stockbroker.

on an automated price information system, called SEAQ[24] This ensures that information about available prices and volume of trading is readily available throughout the market. Actual trading is done by telephone, although the process is becoming computerised. Settlement[25] of trades is mainly done through a paperless securities settlement system called CREST,[26] which enables shareholders to hold their shares in a CREST account in a manner similar in some ways to a bank account, rather than by holding paper share certificates. CREST is a UK-based central securities depository that holds UK equities and UK gilts, as well as Irish equities and other international securities, and has been owned and operated by Euroclear since 2002. For the trading constituents of the FTSE All Share Index,[27] in which there is a very high volume of daily trading, a fully computerised trading system called SETS[28] has been implemented. The SETS service permits an alternative to market making trading by allowing brokers to place on-screen offers to buy and sell only those blocks of shares which they wish to trade at that moment. This 'order-driven' system aims to give investors a better deal since it cuts out the market makers and their profit. It is also intended that it will make the LSE more competitive as an international exchange.

As an institution, the LSE has been going through upheavals as great as at any time in its history.[29] The main impetus for this has been the internationalisation of capital markets[30] and the consequent competition from securities exchanges in other countries. Developments have occurred, all of which can be attributed, at least in part, to the relentless pressure on the Stock Exchange to modernise and become more commercially orientated in order to compete successfully with other international exchanges. First, the LSE has demutualised. Its former status was as a 'mutual',[31] owned by the member firms; its status as a public limited company is intended to enable it to raise the capital needed in future times to maintain or improve its position in the world league.

The second development has been the transfer of the regulatory and monitoring functions required by the EC Directives on Listing to the FCA acting as the UKLA. These

---

[24] Stock Exchange Automated Quotation system. It is a continuously updated electronic noticeboard. SETSqx (Stock Exchange Electronic Trading Service – quotes and crosses) was introduced by the LSE in 2007 as a trading platform for less liquid securities. Since October 2007, all Main Market and EUROM AIM equity securities not traded on a full order book are traded on SETSqx. They joined the Main Market and AIM securities with less than two market makers which were added on 18 June 2007 following the replacement of SEATS Plus (Stock Exchange Alternative Trading Service). From 14 February 2011 the LSE's UK cash markets have migrated to a new ultra-low-latency trading platform – Millennium Exchange. Developed by the LSE Group's leading trading technology business MillenniumIT, Millennium Exchange is a highly scalable, multi-asset class trading platform, offering the Exchange's clients superior technical performance, ultra-low-latency and enhanced functionality.

[25] I.e. transfer of shares from seller to buyer and corresponding payment.

[26] Replacing the older and only partially computerised system called TALISMAN. CREST functions on the basis of ss. 784–790 of the Companies Act 2006.

[27] Including Exchange Traded Funds, Exchange Traded Commodities and some 180 of the most traded AIM and Irish securities.

[28] Stock Exchange Electronic Trading Service. Also called the 'order book'. There is also a hybrid system called SETSmm. As well as significant improvements in latency, the switch of the trading system to Millennium Exchange (see n. 24 above) saw the launch of new order types Stop Loss and Stop Limit.

[29] Save perhaps the great changes which occurred in the 1986 'Big Bang', which permitted firms which were not members of the Stock Exchange to take ownership stakes in member firms, thus opening the way for foreign (mainly US) firms to establish a presence in the City of London, and increased competition by abolishing minimum commissions.

[30] One feature of this is that companies have sometimes found it worth their while to seek an additional listing in another country; for further discussion of the implications of this phenomenon see Chapter 3, 3.4 above.

[31] I.e. an unincorporated association usually regarded as being owned by the members from time to time.

matters are discussed in further detail in Chapter 20 and the reasons for the transfer are explored there. However, it is important to observe here that although a company wishing to list in the UK will need to comply with the Listing Rules in order to be admitted to the Official List by UKLA, it will also have to comply with the LSE's Admission and Disclosure Standards.[32]

Thirdly, as trading on Europe's securities markets becomes ever more internationalised and the markets themselves become less easy to identify with particular territorial bases, then the LSE has been facing increased competition from other markets and trading platforms such as Euronext.[33] Indeed, in Feburary 2011, the LSE chief Xavier Rolet predicted that following the merger of NYSE Euronext and Deutsche Börse further stock exchange consolidation is expected, and this rash of mergers between the world's largest stock exchanges would eventually lead to the creation of just three or four international markets.[34] The growth in alternative trading systems ('ATSs') operated by investment firms has also provided a source of competition.[35] However, in March 2017 the European Commission blocked the anticipated £21bn merger between the LSE and its German rival, Deutsche Börse, on competition grounds as the new merged entity would have created a de facto monopoly in the crucial area of fixed income instruments.[36]

## 3 *Methods of flotation*

There are currently five main methods by which a company that is coming to the Main Market for the first time can make an IPO: an offer for sale, offer for subscription, a placing, an intermediaries offer, or by book-building.

Historically, the offer for sale has often been used for large flotations partly because the Listing Rules have limited the size of placings to raising £15m.[37] This limit has been lifted and so placings are currently being used for much larger flotations than was formerly the case. The legal mechanism of an offer for sale involves the company allotting the shares to an investment bank which will then offer[38] the shares to the public. From the company's point of view the issue is effectively underwritten because if the bank cannot sell the shares it will be left with them, unless it has made its own arrangements for other banks to

---

[32] These are designed to run in parallel with the listing rules to avoid unnecessary duplication.

[33] Euronext was formed as a result of the merger of the stock exchanges of Amsterdam, Brussels, Paris and Lisbon. It also took over the London International Financial Futures and Options Exchange (LIFFE); see http://www.euronext.com. Other markets providing elements of competition are Virt-x (formed by a merger between Tradepoint and SWX) which in 2008 changed its name to SWX Europe. However, it ceased trading and all its business was transferred to SIX Swiss Exchange. The LSE has recently opened a European market called EUROSETS, and a derivatives market called EDX London.

[34] H. Wilson 'LSE Chief Xavier Rolet Predicts Further Stock Exchange Consolidation', *The Telegraph*, 24 February 2011.

[35] The traditional stock exchanges in the US have faced similar competition from the development of their over-the-counter markets such as the National Association of Securities Dealers Automated Quotation (NASDAQ), which specialises in high growth technology stocks.

[36] See http://ec.europa.eu/competition/elojade/isef/case_details.cfm?proc_code=2_M_7995 including http://europa.eu/rapid/press-release_IP-17-789_en.htm.

[37] Or £30m if the intermediaries offer mechanism was used, which would result in the shares being more widely disseminated than under a normal placing.

[38] In technical legal terms the offer is actually made when members of the public respond to the advertisement and offering to buy the shares; see *Re Metropolitan Fire Insurance Co.* [1900] 2 Ch 671.

underwrite the issue. If the issue is very large then a syndicate of banks will jointly offer the shares for sale. As well as getting the public to purchase the shares, the process of flotation involves ensuring that the shares become listed on the Stock Exchange. This aspect of it will also be handled by the investment bank in their capacity as sponsors.[39] It is they who will prepare the company for listing by UKLA and admission to the LSE Main Market.[40] In addition, a flotation will require an accountant who will be required to carry out a thorough investigation into the company's affairs and to produce financial information or a report of audited accounts.[41] Solicitors will be needed to advise the parties and to draft much of the necessary documentation. It will also be necessary to appoint a firm of registrars to handle the huge volume of applications.

An 'offer for subscription' is a variant of the offer for sale, where the shares are not allotted to the investment bank but instead the bank makes the offer on behalf of the company which then allots the shares to the applicants. It is sometimes combined with an offer for sale. Underwriting will also normally be arranged.

A 'placing' involves the company allotting shares[42] to the investment bank which will then 'place' the shares with its institutional investor clients. It does not involve an offer to the general public and avoids the expense of advertising and other matters associated with an offer for sale or offer for subscription. Coupled with the placing will be an arrangement for the shares to be admitted to the Main Market.

An 'intermediaries offer' is similar to a placing but the shares are offered to other intermediaries (i.e. investment banks) for them to allocate to their own clients.

In recent years a technique called 'book-building', originally developed in the US, has come to be used in European IPOs, particularly by US investment banks operating in Europe. In the UK, versions of it were used by the Treasury in many of the major privatisations to enable them to compile a picture of the strength of institutional demand over a range of prices. It involves an investment bank seeking information from institutional investors about how many shares they are willing to take at particular prices. When all the information is compiled it enables the bank to determine the appropriate offer price.

This brief account thus far has dealt with the specificities of a flotation on the Main Market. An AIM flotation will be subject to the AIM *Rules for Companies*, which are generally more relaxed than the FCA Listing Rules and the LSE Admission and Disclosure Standards, although the latter do require the company to have a nominated adviser ('NOMAD'), a firm or company which has been approved by the LSE as a nominated adviser for AIM and whose name has been placed on the register of nominated advisers published by the LSE.[43] This role is equivalent to that of sponsor in a Main Market flotation and will normally be filled by an investment bank. An IPO on AIM is normally carried out by a placing.

---

[39] The FCA Listing Rules require the appointment of a sponsor if an application for premium listing is being made; FCA Listing Rules, 8.2.1 R.
[40] The obligation to publish a prospectus and similar matters are dealt with below.
[41] FCA Listing Rules, 6.1.3 R.
[42] Or agreeing to allot.
[43] AIM *Rules for Companies*, July 2016 - AIM Notice 45 r. 1. See https://www.londonstockexchange.com/companies-and-advisors/aim/advisers/aim-notices/aimrulesforcompaniesjan16.pdf.

## 4 *Subsequent capital raising – rights issues*

At some stage after flotation, a company will often find that it needs further capital. It will often seek to obtain this by way of a 'rights issue', which is an offer of shares to the existing shareholders of the company in proportion to the size of their existing holdings. Rights issues have been very much part of the culture of the City and additionally Part 17, Chapter 3 of the Companies Act 2006 requires an offer of equity shares to be made to existing shareholders[44] although the provisions can be disapplied. The offer is usually made attractive to the shareholders by making it at a discount of 10–15% to the quoted price of the existing shares; occasionally a deep discount technique of around 50% is employed.[45] The terms of the offer will ensure that the rights can only be taken up within a short period of time. Quite often, the rights issue is of the type known as an open offer, under which the rights cannot be subsequently traded; this is sometimes thought to have the effect of increasing the pressure on the existing shareholders to take up the offer.

## 19.2 Pre-EC Directives

Prior to EC legislation dating from 1979, listing of shares on the LSE[46] was mainly governed by the detailed requirements of the Stock Exchange Regulations on Admission of Securities to Listing. However, by virtue of a provision in the then prevailing Companies Act,[47] an offer of shares to the public was prohibited unless accompanied by a 'prospectus' which complied with the requirements set out in Sch. 4 to that Act. The original requirement for a prospectus can be traced back to the Joint Stock Companies Act 1844.[48]

Thus before any EC intervention, the regulation of public offerings of shares was governed largely by the twin devices of control by the LSE over listing and, whether or not the shares were to be listed,[49] legislative requirements on disclosure in a prospectus of details relating to the securities being offered. In addition, the common law background to this area provided important contractual doctrines and tortious remedies.[50] Broadly speaking, this twin approach, of regulating the trading of shares and the offering of shares to the public, continues at the present day although the legal mechanisms governing both listing and prospectus requirements have been subjected to EU legislation that has brought changes.

## 19.3 The Listing Directives and the Prospectus Directive

As has already been observed, the former EU Directives in the securities regulation field were adopted with a view to establishing a European capital market. In the field of public

---

[44] See, in particular, s. 561 of the Companies Act 2006. See further Chapter 14 above. Further requirements are contained in the listing rules, see, e.g. LR 9.3 R.
[45] The shareholders are initially given 'letters of right' which they can sell if they do not wish to take up the offer themselves.
[46] Its predecessor having been the International Stock Exchange of the UK and Northern Ireland.
[47] Companies Act 1948, s. 38 (3).
[48] Section 4. Although not in this form.
[49] Technically, listing is not a prerequisite for a public offering of shares, as long as the prospectus rules are complied with, although if it is to have much chance of success, a public offering will need to have made arrangements for listing (or these days a quotation on AIM) and for the issue to be underwritten; see further above.
[50] See 19.8 below. Cases are rare, but practitioners need to be mindful of the common law here.

offerings of shares, a series of Directives were issued governing trading of securities and public offerings of securities.

The Listing Directives aimed to regulate the listing of securities on exchanges. Historically, there were three of them, which were later consolidated into one single directive. The first was the Directive coordinating the conditions for the admission of securities to official stock exchange listing,[51] in 1979, usually known as the 'Admissions Directive'. It set out minimum conditions for what it called 'official listing' on a stock exchange in a member state and which requires the process of listing to be overseen by a 'competent authority' designated by each member state. This Admissions Directive was followed, in 1980, by the Directive coordinating the requirements for the drawing up, scrutiny and distribution of the listing particulars to be published for the admission of securities to official stock exchange listing;[52] usually known as the 'Listing Particulars Directive'.[53] Lastly, the Directive known as the 'Interim Reports Directive'[54] supplemented the reporting requirements in the Admissions Directive by requiring half-yearly reports on their activities in the first six months of each financial year. This area was first governed by a consolidating Directive,[55] and then the Prospectus Directive,[56] which sets out the initial disclosure obligations for issuers of securities that are offered to the public or admitted to trading on a regulated market in the EU, and now the Prospectus Regulation. It provides a passport for issuers that enables them to raise capital across the EU on the basis of a single prospectus. This is dealt with below.[57] In December 2010 Directive 2010/73/EU amending the Prospectus Directive came into force.[58] The most important changes related to the summary of the prospectus and the withdrawal rights in connection with prospectus supplements and included a new reduced disclosure regime for rights offerings. In addition, a number of changes were made to the offer and admission exemptions, including an increase of wholesale debt denominations.

---

[51] 79/279/EEC, OJ 1979 L66/21.

[52] 80/390/EEC, OJ 1980 L100/1.

[53] The principles of mutual recognition and home state control were added by an amending Directive in 1987; see the Directive on the Mutual Recognition of Listing Particulars (87/345/EEC).

[54] Directive on information to be published on a regular basis by companies the shares of which have been admitted to official stock exchange listing; 82/121/EEC, OJ 1978, L222/11.

[55] Directive on the Admission of Securities to Official Stock Exchange Listing and on information to be published on those securities; 2001/34/EC, OJ 2001, L 184/1. This Directive is sometimes referred to as the Consolidated Admissions and Reporting Directive ('CARD'). The CARD was repealed on 1 July 2005 by a number of Directives: Directive 2003/71/EC on the prospectus to be published when securities are offered to the public or admitted to trading (sometimes referred to as the Prospectus Directive); Directive 2004/109/EC on the harmonisation of transparency in relation to information about issuers whose securities are admitted to trading on a regulated market (sometimes referred to as the Transparency Directive); and Directive 2005/1/EC.

[56] Directive 2003/71/EC on the prospectus to be published when securities are offered to the public or admitted to trading (sometimes referred to as the Prospectus Directive). In the case of unlisted securities mutual recognition will only be accorded after compliance with the regime in s. 87 of the FSMA 2000 (see below the changes with regards to unlisted securities in 19.6: briefly, the Prospectus Directive requires offerors including AIM issuers to prepare a prospectus when undertaking a public offer of securities. Historically, there has been no requirement for AIM issuers to submit their documents to the UKLA for approval. But from 1 July 2005 this changed – see UKLA publications list, issue no. 11 – September 2005).

[57] Unless they are already officially listed; see further 19.4B below.

[58] The Herbert Smith Briefing on the Prospectus Directive provides a useful summary of all the changes, see https://www.herbertsmithfreehills.com/.

## 19.4 UK implementation

### A The 'competent authority'

The implementation of the above Directives in the UK had a very complex history which need not be investigated here.[59] The requirements for official listing are dealt with in Part VI of the FSMA 2000.[60] The Act provides that the FCA is to be the 'competent authority'[61] to carry out the functions conferred on it by this Part of the Act.[62] Previously, the LSE was the competent authority and the transfer of this function to the FCA was actually made under the pre-existing legislative regime.[63] The reasons for this structural reform were that the demutualisation of the LSE might have led to conflicts of interest between its role as a regulator and its new status as a profit seeker. Also, there was dissent from other competing stock exchanges at that time, about the LSE's wide powers of regulation which could sometimes extend over shares marketed on their exchanges.

Today, the LSE continues to function as a commercial enterprise providing quotation and dealing facilities,[64] but has lost its functions under the Directives. Rather than perpetuate the term 'competent authority', the FCA has adopted what it calls the UKLA. Thus the position is that the FCA is acting as the UKLA. Under the FSMA 2000 the UKLA has the role of maintaining the 'Official List' and in accordance with the Directives (and the listing rules) will decide upon which securities can be admitted to the Official List and thus traded on the Main Market.[65] Compliance with the LSE's own admission rules remains necessary.[66] Listed companies have to comply with the Listing Rules, which are detailed requirements for listing which help to implement the Directives as well as embodying the LSE procedures which have grown up over many years.[67] Failure to comply with the listing rules has traditionally attracted censure or, very rarely, delisting. UKLA has the power to fine for breaches of the listing rules.[68]

### B Prospectuses and listing particulars

As has been discussed above, apart from setting up a regulatory structure for listing, the Directives regulate the documentation to be completed when shares are issued to the public. In some circumstances a document called a 'prospectus' is required, in other, rarer circumstances, a document called 'listing particulars' is required. The starting point for an understanding of this area is the Prospectus Directive.[69]

---

[59] For the review of the PD and its implementation across the EU, see www.esma.europa.eu.
[60] As amended by the Prospectus Regulations 2005/1433.
[61] Section 72, also see Prospectus Rules (PR) 1.1.2.
[62] Section 72(3) states: 'But provision is made by Sch. 8 allowing some or all of those functions to be transferred by the treasury so as to be exercisable by another person.'
[63] See the Official Listing of Securities (Change of Competent Authority) Regulations 2000 (SI 2000 No. 968).
[64] See Chapter 13, 13.2C 2 above.
[65] The FSMA 2000, ss. 74–75. On the markets see Chapter 13, 13.2C 2 above.
[66] See Listing Rules, R. 2.2.3: 'Other than in regard to securities to which LR 4 applies, to be listed, equity shares must be admitted to trading on a regulated market for listed securities operated by a RIE. All other securities must be admitted to trading on a RIE's market for listed securities.' RIE is a recognised investment exchange. According to the FCA Register this is not only the LSE but other exchanges such as PLUS Markets plc. See http://www.fsa.gov.uk/register/exchanges.do.
[67] The listing rules (and the guidance) are available on the FCA website: https://www.handbook.fca.org.uk/handbook/LR.pdf.
[68] See s. 91 of the FSMA2000. See also ss. 87K, 87L, 87M and 97 of the FSMA 2000.
[69] Subject to the recent amendments from December 2010 – Directive 2010/73.

Over the last few years the Prospectus Directive has required that a prospectus is produced whenever there is a public offer of securities or where securities are admitted to trading on a regulated market.[70] The Directive specifies the content of the prospectus and requires that they are approved by the relevant competent authority. Article 1 states: 'the purpose of this directive is to harmonise requirements for drawing up, approval and distribution of the prospectus to be published when securities are offered to the public or admitted to trading on a regulated market situated or operating within a member state.'[71]

Section 85 (1) of the FSMA 2000 provides that 'it is unlawful for transferable securities to which this subsection applies to be offered to the public in the [UK] unless an approved prospectus has been made available to the public before the offer is made.'[72] Sometimes, as has been seen, a prospectus is not required, for example, in relation to qualified investors.[73]

## 19.5 Listed securities

### A Introduction

The FSMA 2000 provides that admission to the Official List may be granted only on an application to the UKLA in such manner as may be required by listing rules.[74] As well as admitting securities to the List, the UKLA has power to discontinue or suspend the listing in some circumstances[75] which it will exercise when it is necessary to protect investors and ensure the smooth operation of the market.[76]

What follows is a brief outline of the main structure of the rules governing a new listing of an issue of equity shares by a UK company, although the length of the listing rules is

---

[70] Article 4 of the Prospectus Directive deals with exemptions from the obligation to publish a prospectus. Broadly, these exemptions apply by reference to the amount of capital being sought (offers of less than €5 million fall outside its scope), the number of investors to whom the offer is made (offers directed at fewer than 150 people per member state), the nature of the investors to whom the offer is made (offers to non-retail investors are exempted), or the minimum purchase price of the securities. See art. 1 and art. 3 (2) (b) of Directive 2010/73, at http://eur-lex.europa.eu/LexUriServ/LexUriServ.do?uri=OJ:L:2010:327:0001:0012:EN:PDF.

[71] See art. 3 – when the obligation to publish a prospectus does not apply. On 12 October 2004 AIM ceased to be an EU regulated market and became an Exchange regulated market. This means the companies do not have to produce a full prospectus on admission to the AIM unless an offer of securities is being made to the public as part of the company's admission.

[72] Section 85 (7) further provides that 'approved prospectus means, in relation to transferable securities' to which this section applies, a prospectus approved by the competent authority of the home state in relation to the issuer of securities. For transferable securities see s. 102 A and Sch. 11 A. The 'offer of transferable securities to the public' is defined in s. 102 B.

[73] See arts 2 and 3 of the Prospectus Directive. Under the amending Directive 2010/73 'qualified investors' are defined as those persons that are classified as professional clients or eligible counterparties in accordance with Annex 2 of MiFID (see art. 2 (1) (e). See also s. 86 of the FSMA 2000 as amended by Prospectus Regulations 2011/1668 reg. 2 (2) (31 July 31 2011) ('In section 86(1)(b) of the Financial Services and Markets Act 2000(c) (exempt offers to the public), for "100 persons" substitute "150 persons"'). With regards to listing particulars see s. 79 of the FSMA.

[74] In ss. 74–76.

[75] The FSMA 2000, ss. 77–78. In addition, s. 78A of the FSMA 2000 was added by Regulatory Reform (FSMA 2000) Order 2007/1973 art. 7. It refers to cases where a decision to discontinue or suspend listing is made by the FCA on its own initiative. However, where the issuer is requesting the discontinuance or suspension of listing the Order introduced a separate set of procedures in s. 78 A. Listing rules were amended accordingly (LR 5). The section came into force on 12 July 2007.

[76] LR 5.5 (dealing with suspension). But note that according to LR 5.2, the FCA may cancel the listing of securities if it is satisfied that there are special circumstances that preclude normal regular dealings in them.

such that very many details are necessarily omitted. It should also be made clear that not every applicant will necessarily be a normal public company; for instance, an issuer of Government bonds will usually be a nation state. It is also important to realise that since the transfer of the LSE's functions as competent authority to UKLA, there is now a two-stage process for admission to the Official List, and compliance with the LSE's Admission and Disclosure Standards[77] and consequent admission to trading is also necessary.[78] Finally, it is worth bearing in mind that since June 2010 there is a different admission criteria for each listing route, namely, Premium or Standard listing.[79] A Premium listing means that a company must meet standards that are over and above (often described as 'super-equivalent') those set forth in the EU legislation, including the UK's Corporate Governance Code.[80] Investors trust the super-equivalent standards as they provide them with additional protections. By virtue of these higher standards, companies may have access to a broader range of investors and may enjoy a lower cost of capital owing to heightened shareholder confidence. A Premium listing is only available to equity shares issued by commercial trading companies. With a Standard listing, a company has to meet the requirements laid down by EU legislation. This means that their overall compliance burden will be lighter, both in terms of preparing for listing and on an ongoing basis. Standard listings cover the issuance of shares and depositary receipts ('DRs') as well as a range of other securities, including fixed-income. Large companies from emerging markets may wish to list their DRs, thus attracting investment from the significant international pool of capital available in London.[81]

## B Background conditions

The company applying for a listing must comply with a number of basic conditions if its application is to be successful. The UKLA ensures that the company complies with the listing rules but it may make admission subject to any special condition if this is considered appropriate.[82] In any event, it is made clear that mere compliance with the listing rules will not necessarily ensure admission to the Official List, and the UKLA may refuse an application for listing if it considers that the applicant's situation is such that admission of the securities would be detrimental to the interests of investors or for securities already listed in another EEA state, the issuer has failed to comply with any obligations under that listing.[83] It is interesting to speculate as to the way UKLA will exercise its discretion here.

---

[77] See http://www.londonstockexchange.com/home/homepage.htm.
[78] See also 19.4 above, and LR 2.2.3: 'To be listed, securities must be admitted to trading on an RIE's market for listed securities.'
[79] For the April 2010 changes see the UKLA publication from June 2010, at http://www.fsa.gov.uk/pages/Doing/UKLA/pdf/listing_regime_faqs.pdf. See the LSE website at http://www.londonstockexchange.com/home/homepage.htm. Each type of listing has different requirements. It might be that admission to listing and admission to trading are parallel as in the case of listing debt or in the case of listing DRs (depository receipts) the company's prospectus should first be approved by the UKLA.
[80] Discussed in Chapter 10 above.
[81] For the key differences between a Premium Listing and a Standard Listing, see http://www.londonstockexchange.com/home/guide-to-listing.pdf.
[82] LR 2.1.2 and 2.1.4.
[83] LR 2.1.3.

It is likely that refusal on those grounds will be rare and will not develop into the kind of procedures employed in some US states which have a merit test[84] in their 'blue sky' laws, in which they make an assessment of aspects of the commercial desirability of the security rather than merely check compliance with disclosure standards.

It is provided that the company must be duly incorporated under the law of the place where it is incorporated and obviously it must be a public company.[85] It is also made clear that the securities must comply with the law of the place where the applicant is incorporated, be duly authorised according to the requirements of the company's constitution and have any necessary statutory or other consents.[86] Also any necessary authorisations (such as those required under the Companies Act 2006, ss. 549 or 551) must have been given and there must be compliance with the preferential subscription rights provisions.[87]

The applicant must also have published or filed audited accounts covering a period of three years preceding the listing application although in some circumstances the UKLA will accept a shorter period if that is desirable in the interests of the company or investors and provided that the investors will have the necessary information available to arrive at an informed judgment on the company and the equity shares for which listing is sought.[88] Further requirements relate to transferability of securities,[89] nature and duration of business activities,[90] sufficient working capital,[91] and many other matters. According to LR 3.2.6, the FCA when considering the application may impose any additional conditions on the applicant as the FCA considers appropriate. The Listing Rules, in Chapter 8, make it clear that, in certain circumstances, for premium listing the company will need to appoint a sponsor who will normally be corporate brokers or an investment bank but may also be certain other professional advisers.[92]

The minimum market value of the securities for which initial listing is sought is £700,000 (less for debt securities) although securities of a lower value can be admitted provided that the UKLA is satisfied that adequate marketability is expected. Further issues of shares of a class already listed are not subject to these limits.[93]

---

[84] See Chapter 16, 16.2 above.

[85] LR 2.2.1. A private company may not issue shares to the public; Companies Act 2006, s. 755.

[86] LR 2.2.2.

[87] *Ibid.* LR 3.3 as amended in April 2010. See Chapter 13, 13.3D above.

[88] In LR 6 as amended in April 2010 – additional requirements for listing for equity securities, LR 6.1.3 requires accounts, LR 6.1.13 – FSA may modify accounts requirement.

[89] LR 2.2.4.

[90] For equity shares this requirement can be found in LR 6.1.4.

[91] LR 6.1.16.

[92] The new rules which came into effect in July 2005 increased the circumstances in which a sponsor has to be appointed as well as the sponsor's role. Likewise, the relationship between the sponsor and the FCA has been widened. The responsibilities of a sponsor is to provide assurance to the FCA where required that the responsibilities of the listed company or applicant under the listing rules have been met, and guide the listed company or applicant in understanding and meeting its responsibilities under the listing rules and disclosure rules and transparency rules. See LR 8.3.1. Amendments to the listing rule requirements for sponsors to listed companies came into effect on 6 February 2009. The changes clarify and, to a certain extent, relax the previous rules and reflect a move away from specific rules to a principles-based regime. For an example of enforcement against a sponsor, see http://www.fsa.gov.uk/pages/Library/Communication/PR/2011/047.shtml. For an example of enforcement on grounds of listing rules breaches, see https://www.fca.org.uk/news/press-releases/financial-conduct-authority-censures-co-operative-bank-listing-rules-breaches.

[93] LR 2.2.7.

## C Methods of issue

The main methods of issue have been discussed above.[94] Here it is sufficient to recall that applicants without equity shares already listed may bring securities to listing by any of the following methods: offer for sale to the public by a third party; direct offer to the public for subscription; a placing; an intermediaries offer where the shares are offered to intermediaries for them to allocate to their own clients; an introduction; or in some circumstances other methods will be permitted.[95]

## D Application procedures

When an issuer applies for admission to the list of its securities which are to be offered to the public in the UK for the first time before admission, a document called a 'prospectus' must be submitted to and approved by the FCA in its role as the UKLA. The technical legal background to this has been described above and as has been seen, sometimes the prospectus rules will provide rules governing the submission, approval, publication and contents of the prospectus/listing particulars.[96] In the following account, the term 'prospectus' will be used.

There is a requirement for publication of the prospectus in accordance with the detailed requirements in prospectus rules ('PR') 3.2. A prospectus should be published either in one or more newspapers or in a printed form available free of charge to the public or on the issuer's website or on the regulated market website where admission to trading is sought. In some circumstances, advertisements are needed.[97] However, the prospectus must *not* be published until it has been formally approved by the UKLA.[98] PR 3.1 requires that 10 working days before the intended approval date of the prospectus, information must be submitted to the FCA.[99] With effect from 1 July 2005, prospectuses and listing particulars are no longer required to be registered at Companies House.

The application for admission of the securities for listing must then be submitted at least 48 hours (two *business* days) before the hearing of the application for listing by the UKLA, accompanied by various documents including the prospectus.[100] Other documents must be submitted on the day itself, or later. Assuming that the application for admission to the Official List is granted, the date for the commencement of dealings which is requested by the applicant will usually also be approved at the hearing of the application. Admission of securities only becomes effective when the decision of the UKLA to admit the securities to listing has been announced in accordance with para. LR 3.2.7 (usually by being disseminated by the electronic system used by the UKLA for communication with the public (a Regulated Information Service or 'RIS')).[101]

---

[94] At 18.2.
[95] The Document titled 'A Practical Guide to Listing', available at www.londonstockexchange.com provides a useful summary of these methods.
[96] See also Rule 2.2.10 of the listing rules. In accordance with PR 3.2 and 3.3. For document viewing facility see LR 17.3.1.
[97] In accordance with PR 3.2 and 3.3. For document viewing facility see LR 17.3.1.
[98] PR 3.1.10 and for timing of publication see 3.2.2.
[99] PR 3.1.3.
[100] LR 3.3.2.
[101] On RIS see http://www.fsa.gov.uk/Pages/Doing/UKLA/ris/index.shtml.

# E Contents of the prospectus

Much of the prospectus rules is taken up with extremely detailed requirements as to the precise form and contents of the prospectus, but before briefly considering these it is necessary to allude to a more general disclosure requirement contained in s. 80 of the FSMA 2000 which provides:

(1) Listing Particulars [i.e. prospectus][102] submitted to the competent authority under section 79 must contain all such information as investors and their professional advisers would reasonably require, and reasonably expect to find there, for the purpose of making an informed assessment of (a) the assets and liabilities, financial position, profits and losses, and prospects of the issuer of the securities; and (b) the rights attaching to those securities.

(2) That information is required in addition to any information required by:
  (a) listing rules, or
  (b) the competent authority, as a condition of the admission of the securities to the official list.

(3) Subsection (1) applies only to information:
  (a) within the knowledge of any person responsible for the listing particulars; or
  (b) which it would be reasonable for him to obtain by making enquiries.

(4) In determining what information subsection (1) requires to be included in listing particulars by virtue of this section, regard shall be had (in particular) to:
  (a) the nature of the securities and their issuer;
  (b) the nature of the persons likely to consider acquiring them;
  (c) the fact that certain matters may reasonably be expected to be within the knowledge of professional advisers of a kind which persons likely to acquire the securities may reasonably be expected to consult; and
  (d) any information available to investors or their professional advisers as a result of requirements imposed on the issuer of the securities by a recognised investment exchange, listing rules or under any other enactment.

Section 80 thus puts significant pressure on issuers and their advisers to give very careful consideration to the contents of their prospectus. The requirements for the contents of the prospectus for the admission of shares are set out mainly in Chapter 2 of the Prospectus Rules.[103] Sections 87A (2), (3) and (4) of the Act provide for the general contents of a prospectus:[104]

(1) The necessary information is the information necessary to enable investors to make an informed assessment of –
  (a) the assets and liabilities, financial position, profits and losses, and prospects of the issuer of the transferable securities and of any guarantor; and
  (b) the rights attaching to the transferable securities.

(2) The necessary information must be presented in a form which is comprehensible and easy to analyse.

(3) The necessary information must be prepared having regard to the particular nature of the transferable securities and their issuer.

---

[102] This section was substituted by Prospectus Regulations 2005/1433 Sch. 1 para. 5.
[103] PR 2.1.1.
[104] See also PR 2.3 which deals with minimum information to be included in a prospectus.

These matters are supplemented by accountants' reports (see LR 6.1 with regards to equity shares to premium listing and publishing accounts) and financial information which is found in the disclosure rules and transparency rules ('DTR').

It should finally be noted here that if at any time after the preparation of the prospectus for submission to the UKLA and before dealings begin there is any significant change or new matter affecting the prospectus, then a supplementary prospectus will need to be submitted as soon as possible, approved and published.[105]

## F Continuing obligations

Once the formalities connected with the listing have been complied with, matters do not end there, for the listing rules, in Chapter 9, set out what are referred to as 'continuing obligations', that is to say obligations which a listed company is required to observe once any of its securities have been admitted to listing.[106]

Broadly speaking, Chapter 9 requires notification of information about changes affecting the company.[107] Other continuing obligations are set out in other chapters, namely: significant transactions: Premium listing (Chapter 10); transactions with related parties: Premium listing (Chapter 11); dealing in own securities and treasury shares: Premium listing (Chapter 2); contents of circulars: Premium listing (Chapter 13).

## G Other provisions

Chapter 14 contains provisions dealing with Standard listing.[108] Chapters 15–19 deal with special situations: closed-ended investments funds (Premium listing), open-ended investment companies (Premium listing), debt and specialist securities (Standard listing), certificates representing certain securities (Standard listing) and securitised derivatives (Standard listing).

## 19.6 Unlisted securities

As has been described above,[109] the offer to the public of shares which are *not* listed on the LSE pursuant to Part VI of the FSMA 2000 (i.e. s. 85 (1)) is governed by the prospectus rules. There are then various exemptions so that, for example, a person does not contravene s. 85 (1) if the offer is made to or directed at qualified investors or the offer is made to or directed at fewer than 150 persons, other than qualified investors, per EEA state.[110]

---

[105] PR 3.4 and see the FSMA2000, ss. 81 (for listing particulars) and 87G.
[106] For changes made to this chapter in April 2010, see http://www.fsa.gov.uk/pubs/hb-releases/rel100/rel100lr. pdf and http://www.fsa.gov.uk/pages/Doing/UKLA/pdf/listing_regime_faqs.pdf. A useful speech made on 21 November 2007 highlighted recent trends in the FSA's Continuing Obligations Regime. See http://www.fsa.gov. uk/pages/Library/Communication/Speeches/2007/1121_mk.shtml and Chapter 9 of the Listing Rules on Continuing Obligations at https://www.handbook.fca.org.uk/handbook/LR/9.pdf.
[107] The former FSA inserted a specific continuing obligation requirement for a listed company that has equity shares listed to have control of the majority of its assets and carry on an independent business as its main activity (LR 9.2.2.A). This took effect from 6 August 2007.
[108] As amended in April 2010. See http://fsahandbook.info/FSA/html/handbook/LR/14/1.
[109] See 19.4B above.
[110] The FSMA, s. 86 as substituted by Prospectus Regulations 2011/1668 reg. 2 (2) (31 July 2011).

A security which falls outside the regime will sometimes then fall within the rules relating to financial promotion.[111]

The prospectus must contain all such information necessary to enable investors to make an informed assessment of the assets and liabilities, financial position, profits and losses and prospects of the issuer and of a guarantor and the rights attaching to the securities.[112] This is in addition to the detailed list of information required by the PR.[113] The information must be presented in a form that is easy to analyse and comprehend.[114]

## A The Alternative Investment Market (AIM)

AIM exists as the lightly regulated alternative to the Main Market, for younger companies.[115] Evidence suggests that the AIM has been playing an important role in promoting IPO activity.[116] Since its launch in 1995, more than 3,600 companies have joined AIM, raising over £100bn to fund their growth.[117] New companies that floated on AIM raised an average of £30m in 2017. Entry to AIM is governed by the conditions set out in the LSE's AIM rules. These are similar to the provisions in the listing rules although much less detailed and onerous. An AIM company which makes a public offering of shares will usually need to comply with the prospectus requirements of the Prospectus Rules unless the offer falls within the exemptions. Also as noted before, there is no need for prospectus if an AIM company is not making a public offer, as AIM is not 'a regulated market'.[118] In that case an admission document will be required under the requirements in the AIM rules themselves. Further recent ramifications in relation to AIM's new status are considered in 19.7C below.

## 19.7 The Prospectus Directive

## A Background

With effect from 1 July 2005 the Prospectus Directive was repealed and replaced by the *new* Prospectus Directive,[119] as amended by Directive 2010/73/EC.[120] Along with the

---

[111] On the financial promotion regime, see Chapter 18, 18.2E above. Note changes to the requirements for investment financial promotions from 1 November 2007 (COBS replaced COB).

[112] PR 2.1.1.

[113] PR 2.3.

[114] PR 2.11.

[115] See above.

[116] Price WaterhouseCoopers reports that there had been 325 IPOs raising a 3,618m in 2006 and 220 IPOs raising a 9,537m in 2007. See IPO Watch Europe – Review of the Year 2007. Since the financial crisis there have been far fewer IPOs, but London still dominates the EU IPO market. See Price WaterhouseCoopers' Report from March 2011.

[117] See http://www.londonstockexchange.com/companies-and-advisors/aim/publications/documents/a-guide-to-aim.pdf.

[118] The LSE decided to change AIM's status as an EU regulated market in an effort to minimise the effect of the new changes required by pan-European securities laws on prospectus and period disclosure on AIM (i.e. to ease the regulatory burden and maintain AIM's competitive position). However, as will be seen in the next section, amendments have had to be made to AIM rules.

[119] Directive on the Prospectus to be Published when Securities are Offered to the Public or Admitted to Trading, 2003/71/EC, OJ 2003, L 345/64.

[120] Of 24 November 2010. See http://eur-lex.europa.eu/legal-content/EN/TXT/?uri=CELEX:32010L0073.

Transparency Directive[121] and the Market Abuse Directive,[122] the Directive has prompted the FCA to carry out a thorough review of the listing regime, as discussed above.

The *new* Prospectus Directive is intended to improve the framework for raising capital on an EU-wide basis. There were many different practices within the EU regarding the content and layout of prospectuses, and the mutual recognition system has not succeeded in providing a single passport for issuers. The new Directive introduces a system of notification, whereby the competent authority of the issuer's member state will merely have to notify their counterparts in other member states in order for the prospectus to be accepted in those host states; thus the host states will no longer have the right to request additional information to be included in the prospectus. There is also a new language regime under which, if the prospectus is drafted in a language customary in international finance (normally English) then the host state will have to accept that, and can request only a summary of the prospectus in their own language. The financial disclosure content of the prospectus will be on the basis of a single set of accounting standards as a result of the recent requirement that consolidated accounts be prepared in accordance with International Accounting Standards ('IAS'). Various formats of prospectus will be permitted, in particular one designed for fast-track new issues for frequent issuers whereby the prospectus is in two parts. One part will be a registration statement containing details about the issuer, the other will be a securities note containing details of the securities being issued and admitted to trading. As with the other recent Capital Markets Directives developed under the Financial Services Action Plan, many of the details will be worked out under the comitology procedures recommended by the Lamfalussy Report; they can also be kept under review so as to cope with developments in market conditions.

In the context of implementing these Directives, the then FSA inaugurated a general review of the listing regime[123] which was to be implemented by changes to the rules in accordance with the timetable mentioned above. The review also aimed to modernise the listing regime and proposed a range of reforms such as the introduction of a set of high-level listing principles. The Directive was implemented in the UK by the revision of Part VI of the FSMA and the FCA rules. As a piece of framework legislation, it does not specify the detailed form and contents of a prospectus – instead this is achieved by an EU regulation.[124] From 1 July 2005, all prospectuses required to be published in the UK need to be approved by the FCA acting as the UKLA. Even prospectuses prepared by AIM, Ofex and unquoted public companies now need to be vetted by UKLA. Despite steps taken by the LSE to minimise the effect of the new changes on AIM, amendments have had to be made to the AIM Rules.

---

[121] Directive 2004/109/EC on the harmonisation of transparency in relation to information about issuers whose securities are admitted to trading on a regulated market. It amends and upgrades provisions of the Consolidated Admissions Directive 2001/34/EC with regard to the information which companies are required to supply to investors. It also improves the dissemination of the information by, for instance, requiring companies to make it available on their websites. The European Parliament, by a legislative resolution of 17 June 2010, adopted a Commission proposal to make consequential amendments to Directive 2004/109/EC (the 'Transparency Directive'). The Amending Directive was published in the EU's Official Journal on 11 December 2010 and entered into force on 31 December 2010. These changes made by the Amending Directive must be implemented by member states by 01 July 2012.

[122] See Chapter 20 below.

[123] See https://www.treasurers.org/ACTmedia/dp08_01.pdf.

[124] EC/809/2004 (PD Regulation) which is directly applicable in all member states.

Finally, it should be noted that further review of the structure of the listing regime has been completed recently. Back in January 2008, the FSA published a Discussion Paper reviewing the structure of the UK listing regime.[125] The Paper discussed ways to re-label the Primary and Secondary listing segments to help participants in the markets understand better the obligations on issuers of the various types of listed securities. The Paper set out a new structure for the regime in which securities subject to higher standards are more clearly separated from directive minimum standards.[126]

On 28 February 2017 the FCA launched a review of the UK listing regime. In particular, it published a Discussion Paper on the effectiveness of the existing regime[127] and a Consultation Paper on some more detailed changes to the Listing Rules regarding eligibility for premium listing and the application of the class tests.[128] Subsequently, on 3 November 2017, the FCA released a Policy Statement setting out enhancements to the regime as part of its review of the UK's primary markets.[129] The final rules set out are, therefore, in line with the proposals contained in the Discussion Paper. A few minor amendments were made to reflect feedback received. These new rules have taken effect from 1 January 2018. Companies seeking admission to premium listing after 1 January 2018 need to prepare their submission based on these new requirements.

## 1 *Eligibility requirements for premium listed companies (LR 6)*

An applicant must demonstrate that (i) it carries on an independent business as its main activity (New LR 6.4.1R); (ii) it is able to carry on an independent business as its main activity if it has a controlling shareholder (New LR 6.5.1R); and (iii) it exercises operational control over the business it carries on as its main activity (New LR 6.6.1R). New UKLA Technical Notes cover the independent business requirements for companies applying for premium listing with the three-year financial track record requirements being clarified[130] and guidance on the financial information and track record requirements of LR 6, noting that an applicant should be able to demonstrate a track record that puts prospective investors in a position to make an informed assessment of the business that is to be listed (LR 6.3.1R).[131] In some cases an applicant can have three years of financial information which does not properly reflect the applicant's business, as the information does not demonstrate a revenue earning record that is representative of the business to be listed. In such cases the applicant does not have a compliant financial track record. References in LR 6 to the FCA's ability to waive the requirement for a clean working capital statement and the financial track record requirement have been deleted.

---

[125] DP08/1: 'A Review of the Structure of the Listing Regime' can be found on the former FSA website. The paper asked for comments by 14 April 2008.
[126] Premium and Standard.
[127] The FCA Discussion Paper DP 17/02 on the review of the effectiveness of the listing regime is available at https://www.fca.org.uk/publication/discussion/dp17-02.pdf.
[128] The FCA Consultation Paper CP17/04 on changes to the listing rules is available at https://www.fca.org.uk/publication/consultation/cp17-04.pdf.
[129] PS17/22 'Review of the Effectiveness of Primary Markets: Enhancements to the Listing Regime'
[130] UKLA/TN/103.1.
[131] UKLA/TN/102.1.

## 2 *New concessionary route to premium listing for property companies*

The new concession for certain property companies from the revenue earning track record requirements in LR 6.3.1R adds to the existing 'concessionary routes' to premium listing which exempt them from the general rule, under which commercial companies which apply for premium listing are required to have a three-year revenue earning track record. This new concession is meant to allow property companies to demonstrate maturity in other ways than through three years of revenue generation.

Two types of property companies could be eligible for a new concessionary route: (i) property companies which have been established for less than three years, but which predominantly hold mature, let assets that generate revenue; and (ii) property companies which develop assets, and have done so for three years, but which focus on long-term projects. The concessionary route focuses on the property valuation report rather than on the issuer's financial track record.[132]

## 3 *Changes to the profits test used by premium listed issuers (LR 10)*

The following changes have been made to the profits test:

(1) Anomalous results: if all of the following conditions are met, an issuer which has a premium listing can disregard the profits test for the purposes of classifying the transaction without consulting the FCA: (i) the calculation under the profits test produces a percentage ratio of 25 per% or more and this result is anomalous; (ii) the transaction is not a related party transaction; and (iii) each of the other applicable percentage ratios are less than 5%.

(2) Adjustments to the figures used in the profits test: if all of the following conditions are met, an issuer which has a premium listing can make certain amendments to the figures used in the profits test without consulting the FCA: (i) the calculation under the profits test produces a percentage ratio of 25% or more and this result is anomalous; and (ii) the transaction is not a related party transaction.

The new rules will be contained in LR 10 Annex 1 at paras 12R–15G. Class 2 transactions are not affected by these changes. Although some stakeholders suggested that the proposals could apply to Class 2 transactions (where the anomalous profit test result is between 5% and 25% and the other class test results are below 5%), the FCA has decided to keep the existing FCA consultation requirement. The new rules do not apply to standard listed issuers. Issuers should note that they are still required to obtain the guidance of a sponsor in accordance with LR 8.2.2R.[133]

## 4 *Suspension of listing for reverse takeovers: a new approach*

The presumption of suspension has been removed for listed issuers unless the issuer is a shell company.[134] LR 5.6 has been amended accordingly. This reflects the FCA's view that

---

[132] Further guidance on the concessionary route is contained in a new UKLA Technical Note (UKLA/TN/426.1).
[133] Further guidance is contained in a new UKLA Technical Note (UKLA/TN/302.2): Classification tests.
[134] As defined in the Listing Rules.

proper price formation can take place based on the information disclosed as part of issuers' obligations under MAR and the market can operate smoothly without the presumption of suspension.

## B The new format of prospectuses

The new requirements on the format for, and contents of, prospectuses are laid down in the UKLA's Prospectus Rules. With certain limited exceptions, all prospectuses have to include a summary of the core provisions of the securities offer to make it easier for investors to understand the terms. It is also now possible to draw up prospectuses in several parts. Issuers contemplating a rolling programme of public offers will be able to file a registration document which will be valid for 12 months. When they make a public offer and/or an application for the admission of the securities to trading on a regulated market, they need then only to file a smaller security note containing information on the securities that are the subject of the offer.

## C Review of the effectiveness of the Prospectus Directive

Under art. 31 of the Prospectus Directive,[135] which stipulates when and how a prospectus must be published when securities are offered to the public or admitted to trading on a regulated market, the European Commission was required to undertake a review of the effectiveness of the Prospectus Directive five years after its entry into force. Following a review in 2009, the Commission's assessment found that the prospectus regime was broadly operating well and that the quality and appropriateness of information given to investors had improved. However, the review identified a need to increase legal clarity and the overall efficiency of the prospectus framework, as well as an opportunity to simplify the regime for the benefit of issuers, without compromising investor protection. An issue of duplication was also identified and examined.

Consequently, an Updated Prospectus Directive[136] made changes to both the Prospectus and Transparency Directives to ensure that issuers were not required to duplicate their disclosures under the two regimes and to ensure the two regimes are aligned. Implementation of the modifications to the Transparency Directive, to be set out in the Disclosure and Transparency Rules ('DTRs'), is the responsibility of the FCA and considered in Chapter 3. In brief, the key changes that were made to the Prospectus Directive fall into the following categories:

(1) Proportionate disclosure regime: this was introduced for small companies admitted to trading on a regulated market; pre-emptive offers of equities; and for offers of debt securities by lenders (totalling up to €75m per year). The requirements of the proportionate disclosure regime have been set out in Level 2 legislation developed by technical work conducted by the ESMA at Level 2.

---

[135] Directive 2003/71/EC of the European Parliament and of the Council of 4 November 2003 on the prospectus to be published when securities are offered to the public or admitted to trading.
[136] Directive 2010/73/EU of the European Parliament and of the Council of 24 November 2010 amending Directives 2003/71/EC on the prospectus to be published when securities are offered to the public or admitted to trading and 2004/109/EC on the harmonisation of transparency requirements in relation to information about issuers whose securities are admitted to trading on a regulated market.

(2) Prospectus summaries: improvements have been made to strengthen the format, content and comparability of the prospectus summary. The extent to which liability ought to attach to the prospectus summary has also been clarified. Further work is being undertaken at Level 2 to determine the specific contents and format of a summary.

(3) Final Terms and Supplementary Prospectuses: the Amending Directive clarifies that final terms to a base prospectus should only contain information which is specific to the issuance. The specific demarcation of information between final terms and a supplementary prospectus is being undertaken at Level 2.

(4) Exemptions and thresholds: revisions have been made as to the scope of provisions and exemptions which determine when the Prospectus Directive applies and whether a prospectus is needed. These generally involve increases in the threshold and exemption amounts. The Amending Directive also extends the current exemptions from producing a prospectus for employee share schemes to benefit non-EEA companies with employees in the EEA.

(5) Retail cascades: the exemption from the obligation to publish a prospectus for subsequent resales of securities through intermediaries (known as the 'retail cascade') has been formalised.

(6) Supplementary prospectuses and withdrawal of rights: clarification is provided as to the period for which a supplement must be produced. Additionally, the rights of investors to withdraw from an offer have been clarified.

(7) Alignment with other EU regulation: disclosure requirements which overlap with the Transparency Directive have been repealed. Additionally, the definition of a 'qualified investor' has been brought into line with the MiFID definition.

(8) Finally, the Prospectus Regulations 2012 amended a number of provisions of the FSMA 2000, in order to transpose into domestic law the provisions of the Updated Prospectus Directive.

## D The impact on AIM[137]

### 1 The AIM changed status

While the Prospectus Directive has the laudable goal of harmonising rules across the EU, it has resulted in a more complicated regulatory structure than was previously the case and had a detrimental impact on the existing flexibility of the AIM regime – the principal factor which sets it apart from the LSE's main market and other stock exchanges.

The LSE has therefore taken steps to minimise the impact of the changes. As mentioned above, it changed its regulatory status from a regulated market to an exchange regulated market so that in effect it became self-regulated from an EU point of view.[138] An application for the admission of securities to AIM will therefore not require the production of a prospectus unless securities are also being offered to the public at the same time. This should not cause a problem in practice as the majority of AIM IPOs are effected through

---

[137] See *The Prospectus Directive and AIM companies.*
[138] AIM is not a regulated market but instead falls within the classification of a multilateral trading facility (MTF) as defined under MiFID I.

a private placing to a limited number of investors. AIM companies have however been required to produce a full prospectus complying with the Prospectus Directive where any secondary issue of shares exceeds the €5.0m limits and 150 non-qualified investors.[139]

It is worth noting that the 2011/1668 Financial Services and Markets Prospectus Regulations 2011: Regulation 1 (2) increases the number of persons to whom an offer may be directed before it ceases to be an exempt offer from 100 to 150 persons. Regulation 1 (3) increases from €2.5 to €5 million the limit for the total consideration of the offer in the EU below which it is not unlawful to offer transferable securities to the public without an approved prospectus first having been made available to the public. A prospectus may be required, for example, in the following circumstances: rights issues;[140] open offers;[141] take-overs where the company's securities are being offered as consideration; and where shares are offered under employee share option schemes.[142]

## 2 New standard for AIM admission documents

Following the repeal of the Public Offers of Securities Regulations 1995 ('POS Regulations'),[143] the LSE had to adopt a new standard of information required for admission documents. The latter is now based on UKLA's new prospectus rules.[144] However, the LSE considers that certain types of information required by the Prospectus Directive are inappropriate for AIM. The AIM Rules were amended with effect from 1 July 2005 so as to adopt the contents requirements of the Prospectus Directive but with certain carve-outs from the information required by the prospectus rules (although the information referred to in the carve-outs may be included at the nominated adviser's discretion). The minimum standard of information required under the amended rules is intended to be broadly equivalent with the standard of information currently required by the POS Regulations. The carve-outs will not apply and the prospectus rules will need to be followed in full if there is an offer to the public and a prospectus is required.

While potentially increasing the burden on AIM companies undertaking fund raisings the Prospectus Directive had a number of benefits.[145] First, it changed the current definition

---

[139] As amended by Prospectus Regulations 2011/1668.

[140] Note that the Prospectus Directive 2010/73/EC allowed reduced disclosure requirements for pre-emptive offers, by the introduction of a 'proportionate disclosure regime' or 'PDR'.

[141] *Ibid.*

[142] Subject to exemptions. The new amending Propectus Directive 2010/73/EC extended the employee share exemption to include issuers that do not already have their shares admitted to trading on a regulated market. This extends the exemption to companies with their shares admitted to trading on AIM, the PLUS-quoted market and companies listed outside the European Economic Area (e.g. on the New York Stock Exchange) provided that the company's head office or registered office is in the EU. The amending Directive amends the employee share schemes exemption so that: all companies with their head office or registered office in the EU can benefit from the employee share schemes exemption; and companies with their head office or registered office outside the EU can benefit from the employee share schemes exemption if they have securities traded on a regulated market in the EU or they have securities traded on a market in a country outside the EU and certain other requirements are met. See amending Article 4, at http://eur-lex.europa.eu/LexUriServ/LexUriServ.do?uri=OJ:L:2010:327:0001:0 012:EN:PDF.

[143] Before 1 July 2005 the Public Offers of Securities Regulations 1995 (SI 1995/1537) applied whenever unlisted securities were offered to the public in the UK for the first time. They were repealed by the Prospectus Regulations 2005 (SI 2005/1433).

[144] Prospectus Rules (Miscellaneous Amendments) Instrument 2017, FCA 2017/40, available at https://www.handbook.fca.org.uk/instrument/2017/FCA_2017_40.pdf.

[145] See *The Prospectus Directive and AIM companies*: https://www.pinsentmasons.com/mediafiles/225081526.pdf.

of an offer to the public from 50 people to 100 people.[146] Secondly, by introducing the concept of shelf registration, it opened the possibility of cost savings for AIM companies likely to make share offers on a regular basis. Its principal goal was to allow an AIM company which has prepared a prospectus approved by UKLA to market that securities offering across the EEA (and thereby to access capital in places like Paris and Frankfurt) without the need for further documentation. On the other hand, the greatest impact has been on secondary issues where it is more likely that a prospectus is required. The need for ULKA approval and the consequent impact on timetable and increased cost will need to be factored into future transactions. It may well be that there is an increase in non-pre-emptive placings by issuers as they move away from traditional rights issues and open offers in order to avoid delay and cost.

## 19.8 New Prospectus Regulation 2017

The Prospectus Directive has been much criticised over the years. For some, the exemption regime was too restrictive. Others thought that the content requirements for prospectuses were too onerous, particularly for smaller firms, and there was not sufficient proportionality built into the regime. A few thought that the content requirements were burdensome and had led to overly long prospectuses, which were of little value to investors, with required prospectus summaries often running to many pages. As part of the European Commission's Capital Markets Union ('CMU') Action Plan,[147] which is aimed at reinvigorating the European Capital Markets, the European Commission published a legislative proposal in November 2015 for a new Prospectus Regulation to repeal and replace the Prospectus Directive and its implementing measures. The provisions of the draft Regulation were extensively debated during the legislative process and the trialogue between the European Commission, the EU Council of Ministers and the European Parliament, and various amendments were proposed.

The Regulation, which finally came into force on 20 July 2017, sets out a new framework of rules which govern when a prospectus is required, what information must be included and how it must be approved.[148] The Regulation replaced and repealed the Prospectus Directive and its corresponding measures and tasked the European Commission and the ESMA with developing implementing rules and standards. It is hoped, in particular, that it will make it easier and cheaper for small to medium enterprise ('SMEs') to access capital markets and generally simplify the process for all companies wishing to offer debt securities or shares to the public within the EU. Except for the few specific provisions below which took immediate effect and became effective on 20 July 2017, most of the provisions will apply from 21 July 2019.

---

[146] Note that the amending Propectus Directive 2010/73/EC reduced the disclosure requirements for rights issue prospectuses (provided the issuer has not disapplied pre-emption rights) which will apply to both companies listed on the Official List and quoted on AIM.
[147] http://ec.europa.eu/finance/capital-markets-union/docs/building-cmu-action-plan_en.pdf.
[148] Regulation (EU) 2017/1129 of the European Parliament and of the Council of 14 June 2017 on the prospectus to be published when securities are offered to the public or admitted to trading on a regulated market, and repealing Directive 2003/71/EC, available at http://eur-lex.europa.eu/legal-content/EN/TXT/PDF/?uri=CELEX%3A3 2017R1129&from=EN.

## A Provisions enforced with inmediate effect

### 1 *Increased threshold for exempting additional issuance of less than 20% of existing listed securities*

The threshold and the scope of the exemption from the requirement to publish a prospectus have increased and expanded respectively. Issuers with existing securities admitted to trading on a regulated market can now take advantage of a wider exemption from the requirement to publish a prospectus in connection with the issuance of new securities that are fungible with securities already admitted to trading on the same regulated market, if the new securities represent less than 20% of the existing listed securities for a 12-month period. This is an increase from the prior threshold of 10%. Moreover, the exemption now applies to all types of listed securities, not just shares. This wider scope is expected to facilitate more efficient capital raising by listed companies, through accelerated bookbuild offerings and tap issuances. However, even if no prospectus is required, follow-on securities offerings may still be subject to other legal requirements, such as the need to obtain shareholder or bondholder approval or pre-emptive rights, and other timing constraints.

### 2 *New 20% cap on shares issued on conversion of convertible or exchangeable securities*

The Regulation imposes a 20% cap on the exemption available for shares resulting from the conversion or exchange of other securities, which previously had no such limit. As a result, a new prospectus is not required for the admission to trading of shares resulting from conversion or exchange of securities if the resulting shares represent, over a period of 12 months, less than 20% of the same class already admitted to trading on the same regulated market. This new cap has not affected convertible securities offered pursuant to an approved prospectus; issued before 20 July 2017; where the shares qualify as Common Equity Tier 1 items that result from the conversion of Additional Tier 1 instruments; or where the shares are certain eligible own funds or eligible basic own funds. In the case of shares, with effect from 21 July 2019, these two exemptions cannot be combined. Thus, if this 20% threshold is exceeded by a combination of a fresh issue of shares and the issue of shares upon the conversion or exchange of other securities in a 12-month period, a prospectus will be required.[149]

## B Provisions effective from 21 July 2018

### *Public offer of securities with total EU consideration less than €1 million*

No prospectus is required for an offer of securities with a total consideration in the EU of less than €1m over a period of 12 months. Additionally, individual members states may exempt offers of securities to the public where the total consideration of each offer in the

---

[149] The European Commission has already mandated ESMA to start preparing recommendations and a draft for a separate Regulation with more detailed 'Level 2' requirements (e.g. on disclosure requirements).

EU over a period of 12 months is between €1m and €8mn. This compares to the current disapplication of the Prospectus Directive to offers below €5m (in total over a period of 12 months). However, these exempted offers do not benefit from the passporting regime under the New Prospectus Regulation. Also, these exemptions only apply to public offers of securities. If the securities are also to be admitted to trading on a regulated market, a prospectus is still required unless any of the exemptions applicable to such admissions apply. As a result, and also given the small offering size, exemption may be of limited use in cross-border transactions.

## C  Provisions effective from 21 July 2019

### 1  *Exception to the offer and admission of non-equity securities by credit institutions for total consideration of less than €75 million*

From this date the Regulation will provide for a new exemption for the offer or admission of non-equity securities issued in a continuous or repeated manner by a credit institution, where the total aggregated consideration in the EU is less than €75m calculated over a period of 12 months, provided that those securities: (i) are not subordinated, convertible or exchangeable; and (ii) do not give a right to subscribe for or acquire other types of securities and are not linked to a derivative instrument.

### 2  *Universal registration document*

For issuers whose securities are admitted to trading on a regulated market or a multilateral trading facility ('MTF'), there will be a new form of shelf-registration type mechanism, under which frequent issuers can benefit from faster access to the capital markets and more streamlined financial reporting. If the issuer has had a universal registration document ('URD') approved by a competent authority for two consecutive years, subsequent URDs can be filed or amended without prior approval (but subject to *ex post* review), and a prospectus using such URDs benefits from a faster approval process (within five working days as opposed to the typical ten business days). Furthermore, the URDs can be used in lieu of annual financial reports (if published within four months after the end of the year) or half-yearly financial reports (if published within three months after the end of the first six months of the year) required under the Transparency Directive. This allows frequent issuers to use a single annual disclosure document and save the cost and time of having to make duplicative public disclosures to the market.

### 3  *New simplified disclosure regime for secondary issuances*

The Regulation will relax disclosure requirements for follow-on issuances by issuers with existing listings. Issuers that have had securities already admitted to trading on a regulated market or an SME growth market continuously for at least the last 18 months will be able to benefit from a short form disclosure regime for secondary issuances. This could be particularly beneficial for the issuance of debt securities, or additional shares, by issuers that have had equity securities already admitted to trading for the requisite period, especially if the securities are not intended to be offered in the US, where more fulsome disclosure standards will still be applicable.

### 4 *EU growth prospectus*

Provided they do not have securities admitted to trading on a regulated market, SMEs and certain other issuers that either (i) have an average market capitalisation of less than €500m over three calendar years with securities traded on an SME growth market or (ii) are offering securities with a total EU consideration of less than €20m over a 12-month period and do not have securities traded on an MTF, will be able to use a standardised EU Growth prospectus in order to gain easier and more cost-efficient access to capital markets financing. Simplified contents requirements will apply to such prospectuses, including information on the issuer's organisational structure, the company's strategy and objectives related to its development and future performance, the company's management and business operations, financial statements and key performance indicators, and shareholders' information.[150]

### 5 *Changes to prospectus disclosure requirements*

The Regulation makes some important changes to the current requirement for a prospectus to include a key information summary. Any such summary will now be made up of the following four sections: (i) an introduction with prescribed warnings and key information on (ii) the issuer, including its key financial information, (iii) the securities and any guarantors and (iv) the offer to the public and/or admission to trading. The length of the summary will be limited to seven A4-size pages (reduced from the current limit of 15 pages and 7% of prospectus). No summary will be required for prospectuses relating to the admission to trading on a regulated market of non-equity securities that are accessible only by qualified investors or with a per unit denomination of at least €100,000.

### 6 *Changes to the content and format of risk factor analysis*

The required content and format of risk factors will also change. The Regulation limits the risk factors to only those specific to the issuer and/or the securities and which are material to investors. They will need to be presented in a limited number of categories depending on their nature and each category must list them in order of materiality. Among others, risk factors resulting from the level of subordination of a security, the impact on the expected size or timing of payments to holders of the securities in the event of bankruptcy and, if there is a guarantee, risk factors pertaining to the guarantor's ability to fulfil its commitment under the guarantee must all be included.

---

[150] For this purpose, 'SMEs' means companies which either: meet at least two of the following three criteria, based on their last annual or consolidated accounts: an average number of employees during the financial year of fewer than 250, a total balance sheet not exceeding €43m, and/or an annual net turnover not exceeding €50m; or had an average market capitalisation of less than €200m on the basis of end-year quotes for the previous three calendar years.

## 7 Accountant's/auditor's report for profit forecasts or estimates

The ESMA has proposed to remove the requirement that profit forecasts or estimates included in a prospectus be accompanied by a report by an independent accountant or auditor. Because profit estimates are based on the issuer's most recent financial analysis and will in due course be published as part of the issuer's annual report and accounts, the EMSA considers such a report requirement to be unnecessarily onerous and costly. As for the profit forecasts, which are forward-looking statements, the ESMA considers an auditor's report to be of limited value and has proposed to allow such forecasts be included in a prospectus without an auditor's report so long as the issuer provides clear, unambiguous forecasts in an explicit manner with full assumptions.

Although the Regulation makes some important changes to the former regime, it is far from the radical overhaul that many were advocating. While on 6 July 2017 the ESMA already published three consultation papers containing draft technical advice on the format and content of the prospectus, the content and format of the new EU Growth prospectus, and the criteria for scrutiny and procedures for approval and filing of the prospectus, with a view to delivering technical advice to the Commission by 31 March 2018, it may still be some time before it is known whether the length and complexity of many existing prospectuses are likely to be reduced in the future. Indeed, concerns have been raised by market participants as to how quickly the new rules will be finalised to give issuers sufficient time to prepare to comply with the new regime. Although many of the amendments made by the Regulation – including the new provisions relating to simplified prospectuses for secondary issuances, the EU Growth prospectus for SMEs and other smaller issuers, and the introduction of the URD – are likely to be regarded as welcome by issuers, some of the changes could be problematic. In particular, concerned have been raised about having to rank risk factors in prospectuses and in limiting the number of risk factors in the summary to 15 factors.

## 19.9 Remedies for investors

### A General

Part VI of the FSMA 2000 contains provisions giving legal remedies to investors in a number of circumstances. The main provisions relevant to prospectuses/listing particulars are contained in s. 90.[151] Persons responsible[152] for listing particulars are liable to pay compensation to any person who has acquired any of the securities and suffered loss in respect of them as a result of any untrue or misleading statement in the particulars (or omission from them of matters required to be included). However, there is no liability if the person responsible satisfies the court that at the time when the prospectus was submitted to UKLA he reasonably believed (having made whatever inquiries he should reasonably have made) that

---

[151] As substituted by Prospectus Regulations 2005/1433. Section 90 applies in relation to a prospectus as it applies to listing particulars with some modification. See s. 90 (1). Other relevant provisions are found in Sch. 10 to the FSMA 2000 and ss. 90A and 90B of the FSMA inserted by the Companies Act 2006, discussed below.

[152] Regulations have been made to cover this; see s. 79 (3) and the FSMA 2000 (Official Listing of Securities) Regulations 2001 (SI 2001 No. 2956) as amended (2001/3439). Thus, for instance, in some cases, directors are responsible for listing particulars.

the statement was true and not misleading or that the matter whose omission caused the loss was properly omitted. It is also necessary for him to show that he continued in that belief until the time when the securities were acquired.[153] There are various other situations where a defence is available, such as:[154] where the statement is made by or on the authority of an expert and various conditions (similar to the above) are satisfied;[155] or where the defendant has published or tried to publish a correction;[156] or where the statement is made by a public official;[157] or that he reasonably believed that a change or new matter was not sufficient to require the issue of a supplementary prospectus.[158] Obviously, also, there is no liability if the person suffering the loss knew of the falsity or omission.[159]

There are also rules and doctrines developed by the case law (occasionally modified by statute) which may be of relevance in a situation where a person suffers loss as a result of relying on prospectuses *or* other documents published in connection with share issues. In brief, the types of such common law remedies which may become available are: rescission of the contract for misrepresentation,[160] damages for misrepresentation (whether fraudulently made or not),[161] damages for common law deceit, or for negligent misstatement. There has been a steady trickle of case law over a long period of time on the question of when the prospectus becomes 'spent' in the sense that it is no longer reasonable to regard it as a representation. It has been held that a person cannot rely on the prospectus if he subsequently buys shares in the secondary market,[162] or similarly where the prospectus was addressed to the claimant for a particular purpose, such as a rights issue, then he could not rely on it for another purpose, namely the purchase of shares on the market.[163] On the other hand, if the circumstances are such that the prospectus can be treated as a continuing representation then it can sometimes be relied on.[164]

In *Hall* v *Cable and Wireless plc*,[165] it was held that FSMA 2000 does not give investors a private action for market abuse or breach of the listing rules. Four former shareholders in Cable and Wireless claimed damages for market abuse, breach of the listing rules, misrepresentation, and negligence, in respect of Cable and Wireless' failure to disclose the ratings clause to the market before 6 December 2002. The court found that the variety of

---

[153] Or that they were acquired before it was reasonably practicable to bring a correction to the attention of persons likely to acquire the securities in question, *or* that before the securities were acquired he had taken all such steps as it was reasonable for him to have taken to secure that a correction was brought to the attention of those persons, *or* that he continued in that belief until after the commencement of dealings in the securities following their admission to the Official List and that the securities were acquired after such a lapse of time that he ought in the circumstances to be reasonably excused (the FSMA 2000, s. 90 (2) and Sch. 10).
[154] See, generally, the FSMA 2000, Sch. 10.
[155] *Ibid.* Sch. 10, para. 2.
[156] *Ibid.* Sch. 10, para. 3.
[157] *Ibid.* Sch. 10, para. 5.
[158] *Ibid.* Sch. 10, para. 7.
[159] *Ibid.* Sch. 10, para. 6.
[160] Or damages in lieu of rescission under s. 2 (2) of the Misrepresentation Act 1967.
[161] Under s. 2 (1) of the Misrepresentation Act 1967.
[162] *Peek* v *Gurney* (1873) LR 6 HL 377.
[163] *Al Nakib Ltd* v *Longcroft* [1990] BCC 517.
[164] See *Andrews* v *Mockford* [1896] 1 QB 372 where false information had been published in a newspaper to revive interest in the prospectus; similarly in *Possfund* v *Diamond* [1996] 2 BCLC 665 it was held that the defendants intended to inform and encourage after-market purchasers. On measure of damages, see *Smith New Court* v *Scrimgeour Vickers (Asset Management) Ltd* [1997] AC 254, HL.
[165] [2009] EWHC 1793 (Comm); [2010] 1 BCLC 95.

enforcement provisions in the FSMA 2000 indicate that Parliament expressly considered which of the duties or obligations imposed by the statute would give rise to a cause of action at the suit of a private person.[166] Parliament did not provide that market abuse or a breach of the listing rules (as they then were) would give rise to a cause of action at the suit of a shareholder. The FSMA 2000 ss. 91, 123, 382, 383 and 384 provide for other remedies and penalties. Teare J observed that this was a clear indication that Parliament did not intend that market abuse or a breach of the listing rules would give rise to a cause of action at the suit of a private person. To hold otherwise would interfere with the scheme and modes of enforcement provided by the FSMA 2000.[167] The judge concluded that the former shareholders did not have a cause of action for breach of statutory duty and also rejected the claims under the Misrepresentation Act 1967 ('the 1967 Act'). If the former shareholders had suffered loss, it was as a result of entering into a contract of purchase for the shares, not as a result of entering into a contract with Cable and Wireless, as required by s. 2(1) of the 1967 Act.[168] However, Teare J allowed the negligence claim to proceed on the basis that it was at least arguable that a duty of care arose when Cable and Wireless issued its accounts, by reason of its failure to disclose the ratings clause in 1999. The judge acknowledged this might enable the claimant shareholders to circumvent the principle laid down in *Caparo Industries plc* v *Dickman* that statutory accounts are not provided for any parties, members or otherwise, to make personal business decisions as to whether to buy or sell shares.[169]

Teare J's decision has made it clear then that many investors (both large and small) will have to rely on the FSA to take action if they are to be compensated for the effects of market abuse or a breach of the Part VI rules.[170] The non-actionability of s. 118 and the Part VI rules is in contrast to equivalent legislation in the US, where private suits for losses caused by short-selling shares or disseminating deceptive information are common. In the wake of *Cable and Wireless*, shareholders or former shareholders who consider they have suffered loss as a consequence of market abuse or breach of the Part VI rules will either have to find an alternative cause of action to breach of statutory duty, or rely on the FCA to make or apply for a restitution order, if they are to obtain any compensation.[171] The difficulty with the former is that currently there is no obvious action for damages caused by market abuse or a breach of the Part VI rules in English law. Unless an investor traded directly with the person alleged to have abused the market or breached Part VI rules (for instance, in a rights issue), they will lack the contractual nexus necessary for a claim for breach of contract or misrepresentation under the 1967 Act.[172] In that situation, the shareholder is also likely to struggle to establish the duty of care or special relationship necessary to bring a claim for negligence or negligent misstatement. However, if an investor can show that a statement was addressed to him or to a section of the public to which he belongs, and the defendant knowingly or recklessly made a false statement intending to

---

[166] *Ibid.* at [16].
[167] *Ibid.*
[168] *Ibid.*, at [25].
[169] *Ibid.* paras [26]–[29].
[170] H. Jones-Fenleigh 'No Private Action for Market Abuse or Breach of the Listing Rules', available at http://www.inhouselawyer.co.uk/.
[171] *Ibid.*
[172] *Ibid.*

induce him to act, he may have a cause of action in deceit.[173] It is notable that claims both in negligence and deceit will require the investor to show reliance. Although not directly considered in *Cable and Wireless*, establishing such reliance, particularly as a private investor, is likely to be a difficult obstacle to overcome.[174]

## B A new statutory liability regime for periodic financial information

As a part of the implementation of the Transparency Obligations Directive, a new statutory liability regime for periodic financial information issued under the transparency rules (and preliminary results) was introduced from 20 January 2007. It was introduced in the form of a new s. 90A of the FSMA 2000 inserted by s. 1270 of the Companies Act 2006. Under new s. 90A of the FSMA 2000, only the issuer is liable to compensate an investor who acquires securities and suffers loss as a result of an untrue or misleading statement or omission in a periodic financial report required by the Transparency Directive or in a preliminary statement. An issuer will then only be liable to investors where a director knew or was reckless as to whether the statement was untrue or misleading or knew that the omission was a dishonest concealment of a material fact.

As a part of the s. 90A consultation process, the Government considered whether the proposed statutory liability regime should be extended to cover other types of disclosure. It concluded that the complex question of extending its scope could not be properly considered within the time frame for finalisation of the Companies Act 2006. Instead it decided that it would include a power in the 2006 Act to amend and extend the s. 90A provision[175] and would carry out a further review of the issue. In October 2006, in an effort to deepen its understanding of the complex issues related to issuer liability, the Government appointed Professor Paul Davies to carry out a formal review. The Final Report by Professor Davies on 'Issuer Liability for Misstatements to the Market', following up a March 2007 Discussion Paper, was published on Monday 4 June 2007.[176] The Report recommended that the Treasury should use its power in s. 90B of the FSMA 2000 to extend the statutory liability regime in s. 90A to liability for corporate misstatements to the market. More specifically, the report recommended (1) that fraud be maintained as the standard of liability; (2) that the statutory regime should apply to all ad hoc disclosures and RIS announcements; (3) that the regime should extend to disclosure by issuers with securities traded on exchange-regulated markets (including AIM and Plus market) and all multilateral trading facilities; (4) that there should be liability for dishonest delay in making RIS statements; and (5) that rights should be conferred on buyers and sellers.

Following the Davies Review, in July 2008 HM Treasury published a paper outlining proposed changes to the regime, as set out in draft regulations.[177] The draft regulations

---

[173] *Ibid.*
[174] *Ibid.*
[175] Contained in s. 90B of the FSMA 2000 (inserted by s. 1270 of the Companies Act 2006).
[176] The Report, and copies of the submissions on the points raised in the Discussion Paper, are available at http://webarchive.nationalarchives.gov.uk/+/hm-treasury.gov.uk/independent_reviews/davies_review/davies_review_index.cfm.
[177] HM Treasury, *Extension of the Statutory Regime for Issuer Liability* (July 2008).

containing the revised regime inserted into the main legislation a (revised) s. 90A and Sch. 10 A extended the original version in a variety of directions, including:

(1) applying it to issuers with securities admitted to trading on any UK multilateral trading facility as well as those admitted to regulated markets;
(2) covering a broader range of disclosures;
(3) permitting recovery in respect of losses caused by dishonest delay; and
(4) giving sellers as well as purchasers a right to sue.

At HM Treasury's first publication of the draft proposals in September 2008, companies were told that the new proposals would also bring 3,500 more companies within the regime which previously ovnly applied to main market companies, meaning AIM and Plus market companies face an increased reporting liability risk. The aim in enacting a statutory liability regime was to provide certainty in an area where it was unclear whether any common law duty was owed by issuers and their directors to investors.[178] Resolution of that uncertainty had become an issue because the Transparency Obligations Directive imposes an obligation on member states to have in their national laws a liability regime in respect of periodic disclosures.[179] The first version of the regime did not go far beyond the minimum that the Government felt that it needed to do to discharge Community obligations. The revised version of the regime has been deliberately designed to be more comprehensive in its scope. Indeed, the Revised Transparency Directive[180] aims to ensure transparency of information for investors through a regular flow of disclosure of periodic and ongoing regulated information and the dissemination of such information to the public. Regulated information consists of financial reports, information on major holdings of voting rights and information disclosed pursuant to the Market Abuse Directive. The Directive lays down three major requirements with respect to individual pricing and reimbursement decisions: these must be made within a specific timeframe (90 to 180 days); they must be communicated to the applicant and contain a statement of reasons based on objective and verifiable criteria; and they must be open to judicial appeal at national level. In particular, art. 10 establishes a consultative committee, called the 'Transparency Committee', which is responsible for discussing issues relating to the implementation of the Directive, includes representatives of all EU countries and is chaired by the European Commission.[181]

---

[178] Companies Act 2006 Explanatory Notes (TSO, 2006), paras 1636–1653.
[179] Transparency Obligations Directive, art. 7.
[180] Directive 2013/50/EU of the European Parliament and of the Council of 22 October 2013 amending Directive 2004/109/EC of the European Parliament and of the Council on the harmonisation of transparency requirements in relation to information about issuers whose securities are admitted to trading on a regulated market, Directive 2003/71/EC of the European Parliament and of the Council on the prospectus to be published when securities are offered to the public or admitted to trading and Commission Directive 2007/14/EC laying down detailed rules for the implementation of certain provisions of Directive 2004/109/EC. Text with EEA relevance available at http://eur-lex.europa.eu/legal-content/EN/TXT/PDF/?uri=CELEX:32013L0050&from=EN.
[181] See Implementation of the Transparency Directive Amending Directive (2013/50/ EU) and other Disclosure Rule and Transparency Rule Changes including feedback on CP15/11 and final rules, November 2015, at https://www.fca.org.uk/publication/policy/ps15-26.pdf.

Under s. 90A an issuer of securities traded in the UK, or which has the UK as its home state, will be liable to pay compensation to a person who:

- acquires, continues to hold or disposes of the securities in reliance on published information; and
- suffers loss in respect of the securities as a result of:
  - any untrue or misleading statement in that information; or
  - the omission from that information of any matter required to be included in it.[182]

As was the case before, liability only arises where a person discharging managerial responsibilities within the issuer ('PDMR') knew the statement to be untrue or misleading or was reckless as to that fact, or, in respect of the omission of information, knew the omission was a dishonest concealment of a material fact. However, from 1 October 2010 liability also arises where a person acquires, continues to hold or disposes of the securities and suffers loss as a result of a delay by the issuer in publishing information.[183] The issuer is then liable only if a PDMR acted dishonestly in delaying the publication of the information. Conduct will, in this respect, only be regarded as dishonest if it is regarded as dishonest by persons who trade on the market in question and the person was aware (or must be taken to have been aware) that it was so regarded. There will be times where the disclosure of information is delayed for good reason, for example to confirm facts before publication. That of itself will not be dishonest behaviour and will not give rise to a claim. All information published on or after 1 October 2010 is subject to the new regime. Any information published before that date is subject to the previous regime.

Section 90A applies to issuers of securities admitted to trading on any securities market (whether regulated or unregulated) where either the market is situated or operating in the UK, or the UK is the issuer's home state.[184] In contrast to the previous position, this catches multilateral trading facilities (e.g. AIM or PLUS markets) and not just regulated markets such as the main market of the LSE. The substantial extra-territorial reach of s. 90A (it could, for example, catch a UK issuer with shares admitted to trading on the Hong Kong Stock Exchange) may be more apparent than real. HM Treasury confirmed this in its consultation response, where it commented that, in practice, a right of compensation will only arise where English law is found to be the applicable law of the forum in which a claim was brought with the relevant courts determining which law applies. In its view, the number of cases where the courts would apply English law outside the UK and EEA is likely to be small, but it did not see this, or the fact that most overseas listings are in jurisdictions with well-developed securities regimes, as a reason to exclude the relevant investors from the potential scope of the regime.

The regime applies to transferable securities as defined in s. 102A (3) of the FSMA 2000. It is therefore very wide and includes derivative securities as well as shares. In the case of depositary receipts, derivative instruments or other financial instruments representing securities, provided that it has consented to the admission to trading of the secondary securities, the issuer that is liable to pay compensation is the issuer of the underlying

[182] Para. 3(1) of sch. 10A.
[183] Para. 5 of sch. 10A.
[184] Paragraph 1 of sch. 10 A.

securities. Where, however, the issuer has not consented to their admission, and for all other derivative instruments, the issuer of the depositary receipts or other secondary securities will be the one liable to pay compensation under the regime. For this purpose, an issuer that has accepted responsibility for a document prepared for the purpose of admission of securities to trading on a securities market will be taken to have consented to their admission to that market.

The new regime applies to all information published by, or the availability of which is announced by, 'recognised means'[185] For UK listed companies, 'recognised means' includes a regulated information service ('RIS'), or other means required or authorised to be used when an RIS is unavailable. This is very different to the previous regime which only applied to periodic financial disclosures. An issuer will then be liable irrespective of whether the claimant obtains the relevant information from an RIS or from another source. The key point is that the information was published on an RIS. The breadth of the definition of 'information' means that extensive range of disclosures will fall within it (though note also the comments below about the basis of any claim). For example, it will catch a business plan appended to a joint venture agreement that is identified in an announcement as being on display and where an announcement refers to annual accounts being made available, the entire contents of those accounts will fall within the regime. Prospectuses and listing particulars are treated differently to other types of publication as they are already subject to a specific compensation regime in s. 90 of the FSMA. Whilst information contained within a prospectus or listing particulars will potentially be within the s. 90 A regime, an issuer will not be liable to pay compensation in respect of such information if it is liable to pay compensation under s. 90.[186]

Fraud continues to be the basis of liability. The term is used in its civil sense, i.e. for an issuer to be liable under s. 90A there needs to be knowledge, recklessness or dishonesty on the part of the relevant PDMR. The fraud standard, it is hoped, will avoid reporting which is made over-defensive through fear of litigation. The fraud standard sets a high evidential burden for anybody wishing to bring a s. 90A action. It will therefore be difficult for a claimant, on whom the burden of proof lies, to allege fraud in the absence of sufficient evidence and such a claim would be susceptible to strike-out. Arguably, this will deter unmeritorious claims and help avoid the settlement pressures that tend to surround civil litigation. However, as Professor Davies points out in his report, the bringing of a s. 90A claim may in some respects be easier than bringing a common law deceit claim. Nevertheless, given the high threshold set by the fraud standard, the UK is not expected to see a flood of speculative s. 90A claims.

The new regime does not formulate statutory rules for the assessment of damages. Instead, the power of decision making in this regard has been reserved to the courts. Professor Davies's view was that it would be difficult to formulate effective rules which do not tie the hands of the courts in an undesirable way. The measure of liability under s. 90A has not yet been the subject of any judicial decision. However, Professor Davies's clear recommendation is that damages should, in most cases, be assessed by reference to the loss caused by the reliance on the statement rather than the loss caused by its falsity.

---

[185] Paragraph 2 of sch. 10 A, FSMA.
[186] Paragraph 4 of sch. 10 A, FSMA.

Under s. 90A, claims for misstatement are able to be brought not only by buyers of securities but also by sellers and holders of securities. This represents a significant extension to the previous regime which only applied to buyers of securities. An issuer, however, is only liable under the regime if the claimant acquired, continued to hold or disposed of the relevant securities in reliance on the information in question at a time when, and in circumstances in which, it was reasonable for him to do so. On this basis, a claimant may not succeed under s. 90A if he has an available means of checking the information but chooses not to do so. The maker of the statement does not have to have intended the recipient to rely on the information. This arguably makes the bringing of a s. 90A claim easier than at common law.[187] However, as outlined above, fraud is a very high threshold for a claimant to satisfy. Furthermore, with regard to claims by holders of securities there is a clear distinction between a passive and an active holder: unless a holder of securities can show that he or she consciously decided to continue to hold the securities in reliance on the misstatement (e.g. by cancelling an order with a stockbroker to sell the securities) it will be difficult for that claimant to bring a s. 90A action.

Section 90A liability continues to attach to issuers only. The general principle is that an issuer is then not subject to any other form of liability for the specific losses covered by the s. 90A regime. There are, however, a number of exceptions to this safe harbour which are listed in para. 7 of Sch. 10 A . In particular, liability arising from a person having assumed 'responsibility to a particular person for a particular purpose' is preserved. This is important as it preserves the common law on misstatement as decided in *Caparo* v *Dickman*[188] and subsequent cases.

Whilst a director of an issuer to which the s. 90A regime applies will not, at least under English law, be subject to any direct liability to shareholders under the regime (para. 7 of Sch. 10 A of the FSMA 2000), a director is nonetheless at risk where any s. 90A liability claim succeeds against the company. The director at fault may be liable to the company for breach of duty. In a situation where, following a successful action against a company by an investor, that company decided not to take action against the director, shareholders may seek to pursue a derivative claim against the director; albeit that they would have significant procedural hurdles to overcome to do so.

It is not clear from the legislation whether by giving responsibility statements in reports and accounts directors will inadvertently be regarded as making a representation to a particular person for a particular purpose of the accuracy or completeness of the information concerned. However, the minutes of the Parliamentary committee at which this issue was discussed helpfully confirm that such responsibility statements would not, in and of themselves, be regarded as constituting such a representation.

---

[187] Where broadly the maker of the statement is liable only if it had intended that the recipient rely on it.

[188] *Caparo Industries plc* v *Dickman* [1990] 2 AC 605. The most recent detailed House of Lords consideration of *Caparo* was in *Customs and Excise Commissioners* v *Barclays Bank plc* [2007] 1 AC 171, in light of which *Caparo* must now be viewed. The House of Lords established what is known as the 'three-fold test' (a series of three factors), which is that for one party to owe a duty of care to another, the following must be established:
• harm must be a 'reasonably foreseeable' result of the defendant's conduct;
• a relationship of 'proximity' between the defendant and the claimant;
• it must be 'fair, just and reasonable' to impose liability.

The Government decided against expanding the regime to encompass direct actions by investors against auditors. As mentioned above, the s. 90A action itself continues to be against the issuer only. It is, however, possible for an issuer that is a defendant to a s. 90A action to join its auditors as a third party and claim a contribution or an indemnity in respect of any liability imposed on the issuer in that action, where the auditors did some work on the statement to the market on which the action is based. So, for example, if the action is based on an alleged misstatement in the audited accounts the issuer may join its auditors on the basis that they should have detected the misstatement in the course of their audit work. This highlights the importance for auditors of carefully defining the scope of each task they are asked to perform by an issuer and not being drawn into, for example, approving ad hoc announcements which will now be caught by the regime unless they have documented the basis on which such work is being done. Finally, the safe harbour provisions have been amended to make it clear that where liability may attach to an audit report, for example by virtue of an assumption of responsibility (i.e. where it is provided to a particular person in the knowledge that that person is going to rely on it for a particular purpose), such liability is not affected by this regime.

Given the discussion above, it is no surprise that it was suggested that s. 90A/Sch. 10 A may prove to be more fertile territory for investor litigation than s. 90.[189] The new s. 90A has set the threshold at a high level. Future case law will, no doubt, assist in settling the precise boundaries of certain concepts used in s. 90A. However, given the importance of the factual matrix in determining the extent of any liability imposed, it may be difficult for the common law to evolve a generic set of standards or a test that will apply to all scenarios.

From an enforcement perspective, the new regime gives a wide range of persons the chance to privately enforce the continuing disclosure obligations to which listed issuers in the UK are subject and which previously have only really been dealt with by way of public enforcement.[190] Whilst the high threshold required to establish liability under s. 90A demonstrates a Government preference for public rather than private enforcement, it will be interesting to see what impact, if any, private enforcement has on our securities laws and on issuers' behaviour. However, it may be some time before there are enough claims to have any discernible impact. Finally, when those claims do arise, the subordination of investor claims may be an issue. The previous position was that in the event of an issuer's insolvency, investors' claims under the statutory liability regime rank alongside those of other unsecured creditors and ahead of those of shareholders. Professor Davies stated that this was an area which needed further consideration, but the Government felt that resolution of this issue should not delay the introduction of these changes. The Government has meanwhile acknowledged that this important issue needs further consideration.

Looking at the new UK regime from a wider perspective, it is worth asking how it compares when viewed against the background of the positions in, say, Ontario (Canada),

---

[189] For in-depth analysis, see E. Ferran 'Are US-Style Investor Suits Coming to the UK?' (2009) 9 *Journal of Corporate Law Studies* 315, at p. 319.
[190] Given the impact of the new regime, companies have been advised to review their D&O insurance for the increased risk of an action being brought against the directors following a successful s. 90A action.

Australia, and the recent US debate.[191] In overall terms, the new UK regime looks rather limited in scope when compared to these jurisdictions.[192] Looking at it from the perspective of an investor who might be thinking of bringing a claim: issuer-only liability, fraud and dishonesty liability standards, no legal presumptions with regard to transaction or loss causation, exclusion of possible common law liabilities, the absence of class actions, and a loser pays, costs-shifting rule. The feature that is potentially most favourable to investors is the generous fraud basis for the assessment of damages, but set against the number of hurdles that an investor would have to clear in order to obtain judgment in their favour, this does not seem likely to be the trigger for an explosion of investor claims.[193]

## Further reading

E. Ferran 'Are US-Style Investor Suits Coming to the UK?' (2009) 9 *JCLS* 315.

A. Casale *et al.* 'The New Prospectus Regulation: A Missed Opportunity?' available at https://www.law.ox.ac.uk/business-law-blog/blog/2017/03/new-prospectus-regulation-missed-opportunity.

---

[191] The UK, like Australia and Canadian provinces, has built upon common law foundations in the design of its statutory liability regime. As Professor Ferran rightly notes, historically, investor actions have not featured significantly as an actively used compliance-promoting tool in British securities regulation. While investor suits may become more common as a result of the adoption of the new statutory regime, there seems little immediate prospect of an explosion of securities litigation that could threaten the international competitiveness of the UK capital markets. As such, the British situation is very different from that in the US. Nevertheless, the US's unrivalled experience of making extensive use of civil enforcement in securities regulation makes it an obvious jurisdiction for other countries to look to for guidance on issues that need careful consideration in designing a civil liability regime. E. Ferran 'Are US-Style Investor Suits Coming to the UK?' (2009) 9 *Journal of Corporate Law Studies* 315, p. 317.

[192] E. Ferran, *ibid.*, at p. 342.

[193] *Ibid.*

# 20

# The regulation of insider dealing and market abuse

## 20.1 Regulation of market conduct

Until fairly recently, the regulation of market conduct has emphasised the way in which particular markets attempt to regulate the problem of insider dealing. Other methods of regulation, such as the prohibition of misleading statements designed to affect investment decisions and create a false market, while historically sometimes predating insider dealing regulation have nevertheless maintained a lower profile in securities regulation. For this reason, this chapter will approach the topic of the regulation of market conduct by first looking at the development of regulation of insider dealing. However, it will then be necessary to have regard to the wider picture, both at European level and in the UK. For at European level we have the Market Abuse Directive([1] (MAD), which was implemented in the UK through the Financial Services and Markets Act 2000 (Market Abuse) Regulations 2005[2] and through changes to the FSA's Code of Market Conduct.[3] These amendments came into force on 1 July 2005 (apart from some provisions which came into force on 17 March 2005) some nine months after the deadline set in MAD for implementation. On 28 June 2010 the EU Commission launched a public consultation on the review of MAD.[4] Concerns of market distortion arising through regulatory arbitrage have led to the introduction of new harmonising measures in the form of an updated EU rulebook against insider dealing and market manipulation, which consists of the Market Abuse Regulation[5] and the new Market Abuse Directive.[6] This new regime, which will be discussed in 20.6 below, strengthens and replaces those existing EU rules on market integrity and investor protection, first adopted in 2003.[7]

## 20.2 Insider dealing and market egalitarianism

It will be seen that case law and legislative systems of insider dealing regulation have produced some very subtle concepts of what amounts to insider dealing. However, for the sake of this introductory discussion, the facts of *SEC v Texas Gulf Sulphur Co.*[8] can give

---

[1] Directive 2003/6/EC, OJ 2003, L 96/16 on Insider Dealing and Market Manipulation.
[2] SI 2005 No. 381.
[3] Pursuant to s. 119 of FSMA 2000 to provide guidelines as to what behaviour the FCA will regard as market abuse.
[4] http://ec.europa.eu/finance/consultations/2010/mad/index_en.htm. The deadline for responses was 23 July 2010.
[5] Regulation (EU) No. 596/2014 on Market Abuse.
[6] Directive on Criminal Sanctions for Market Abuse.
[7] In particular, the new Regulation repeals Directive 2003/06EC of the European Parliament and of the Council, Commission Directives 2003/124/EC, 2003/125/EC and 2004/72/EC.
[8] 401 F 2d 833, 394 US 976, 89 S Ct 1454, 22 L Ed 2d 756 (1969).

a basic idea. The directors of a company learned that huge deposits of copper and zinc had been discovered under land owned by the company. Some of them purchased more shares[9] and later, when the discovery had become common knowledge and the market price had risen, they sold their shares at a profit. The SEC brought a civil action for violation of r. 10b-5[10] by 'insider dealing'.

The regulatory stance against insider dealing toughened from the 1960s. In the US in 1961 there was the landmark case of *Cady, Roberts & Co.*,[11] which for the first time held that insider dealing could violate the general anti-fraud provision of r. 10b-5.[12]

In 1980 the UK passed legislation which was a complicated and detailed attempt at comprehensive regulation of insider dealing.[13] In 1989 the European Community adopted a Directive 'Coordinating regulations on insider dealing'[14] designed to bring about a high level of coordination of regulation and to combat the problem that many member states had no legislation at all against insider dealing.[15]

As a backdrop to this decisive regulatory activity, a debate has simmered[16] as to whether there should be regulation against insider dealing. The arguments which have been ranged against regulation proceed along the lines that it is compensation for entrepreneurial activity, and that no one is harmed by it.[17] The pro-regulatory block has mounted various responses, which have often been mirrored in the jurisprudence of the case and statute law. Arguments for regulation are that insider dealing is wrong because it involves a breach of fiduciary duty by the director or insider, or that it involves a misappropriation of confidential information, or that it is contrary to basic notions of market fairness.[18] This last view is dominant in Europe, since market fairness is the rationale adopted by the relevant Directive. In practical terms, the battle has been won and the International Organization of Securities Commissions ('IOSCO') and other regulatory authorities have generally taken the view that regulation against insider dealing is an essential part of any system of securities regulation.

---

[9] There were other significant facts concerning their denial of a rumour about the discovery of the zinc, but these have been omitted for present purposes.

[10] On this, see 20.3 A below.

[11] 40 SEC 907 (1961). See further 20.3 A below.

[12] In effect this meant that, thereafter, the SEC could take action against insider dealing. Until *Cady, Roberts* the main US regulatory plank against insider dealing was s. 16 (b) of the Securities Exchange Act 1934, which sought to prevent directors and other corporate insiders and certain shareholders from making profits from e.g., purchase and resale of shares within a six-month period. It was certainly designed with insider dealing in mind: 'For the purpose of preventing the unfair use of information which may have been obtained by [a director . . .] by reason of his relationship with the issuer.' However, it has never been or become a general proscription of insider dealing.

[13] Companies Act 1980, ss. 68–73. Provisions prohibiting directors from dealing in options were first contained in the Companies Act 1967, it then being felt that this was the most likely area where directors could abuse insider knowledge. They were then contained in the Companies Act 1985, ss. 323, 327, but now repealed by the Companies Act 2006.

[14] 89/592/EEC.

[15] On implementation, see J. Black 'Audacious But Not Successful? A Comparative Analysis of the Implementation of Insider Dealing Regulation in EU Member States' [1998] CFILR 1.

[16] It is still current: see H. McVea 'What's Wrong with Insider Dealing?' (1995) 15 *Legal Studies* 390; D. Campbell 'Note: What *Is* Wrong with Insider Dealing?' (1996) 16 *Legal Studies* 185.

[17] See generally H. Manne *Insider Trading and the Stock Market* (New York: Free Press, 1966).

[18] Sometimes called 'market egalitarianism'.

## 20.3 Development of regulation against insider dealing

### A The cradle: SEC r. 10b-5

Systematic regulation against insider dealing is the result of SEC administrative and judicial interpretation in the US. It came about as a result of interpretation of a general anti-fraud provision. Rule 10b-5 was promulgated by the SEC in 1942 under s. 10 (b) of the Securities Exchange Act 1934. It was not intended to apply to insider dealing[19] and its wording was not apposite to do so:

> It shall be unlawful for any person, directly or indirectly, by the use of any mails or instrumentality of interstate commerce, or of the mails, or any facility of any national securities exchange,[20]
> (a) to employ any device, scheme, or artifice to defraud,
> (b) to make any untrue statement of a material fact or omit to state a material fact necessary in order to make the statements made, in the light of the circumstances under which they were made, not misleading, or
> (c) to engage in any act, practice or course of business which operates or would operate as a fraud or deceit upon any person,
> in connection with the purchase or sale of any security.

Since basic insider dealing simply involves buying or selling shares on a market (albeit with some special insider knowledge), none of this looks very promising as a basis for proscribing it. However, in *Cady, Roberts & Co.*[21] the SEC held that insider dealing does violate para. (c) of r. 10b-5.[22] On the face of it, it does not look as though para. (c) could be breached by insider dealing activity, because the act which operates as a fraud or deceit is 'keeping quiet' (i.e. not revealing that inside knowledge) and does not seem to be covered by the wording in para. (c). However, it was held that persons who are seeking to deal in shares and have inside knowledge are under a fiduciary duty to disclose to the counterparty that they have the knowledge,[23] or to abstain from dealing. The existence of this positive duty is the judicial device which then enables insider dealing to fall under para. (c).[24] This approach, founded on the insider's fiduciary duty, became known as the 'classical' theory of liability.

The limitations of r. 10b-5 soon became apparent. The legal system was forced to confront the question of whether someone to whom insider knowledge was passed and who then made use of it to deal and make a profit or avoid a loss could be liable. Persons in that kind of position have colloquially been referred to as 'tippees'.[25] The difficulties which the

---

[19] It had been introduced to deal specifically with the problem of directors who had been dishonestly telling their shareholders that the company was doing badly (when it was not) and then buying their shares at a reduced price.
[20] By the inclusion of these technical words, Congress was signalling that it was claiming federal application for its new law.
[21] 40 SEC 907 (1961). This was an SEC administrative action.
[22] Confirmed in later cases; see e.g. *Chiarella v US* 445 US 222 (1980).
[23] Since it would affect his investment judgment. The duty arises from (1) the existence of a relationship affording access to inside information intended to be available only for a corporate purpose, and (2) the unfairness of allowing a corporate insider to take advantage of that information by trading without disclosure. See *Chiarella v US* 445 US 222 (1980) at p. 227.
[24] It was later held that r. 10b-5 could not be breached by negligent conduct. '*Scienter*' was required (i.e. dishonesty); see *Ernst and Ernst v Hochfelder* 425 US 185 (1976).
[25] Someone in receipt of a 'tip'.

classical theory faced in extending liability to tippees became apparent in *Chiarella* v *US*.[26] Chiarella was a printer who was involved in printing documents for takeover bids and although the names of the parties were omitted, he managed to work out who was involved. He purchased shares in the targets and when the bids were announced and the market price went up, he took his profit. He was indicted for violating r. 10b-5 and convicted but the conviction was reversed by the US Supreme Court. It was held, in accordance with the *Cady, Roberts* approach, that his use of the information was not a fraud under r. 10b-5 unless he was subject to an affirmative duty to disclose it before trading. Here, there was no such duty: he was not a corporate insider and received no confidential information from the target company, and the information upon which he relied related only to the plans of the acquiring company. *Chiarella* produced an uncomfortable result and later cases have been at pains to point out that a tippee will be under a fiduciary duty to the shareholders of a corporation not to trade on material non-public information if (1) the insider has breached his fiduciary duty to the shareholders by disclosing the information to the tippee and (2) the tippee knows or should know that there has been a breach.[27]

*Chiarella* was revisited in *US* v *O'Hagan*.[28] O'Hagan was a partner in a law firm which was representing the bidder in a takeover bid. Although he was not involved in the bid himself, O'Hagan learned who the parties were by overhearing it being discussed at lunch, and bought stock and options out of which he in due course made a profit. Here again, the limitations of the classical theory became apparent. As a 'lawyer'[29] to the bidder, he owed no fiduciary duty to the target or its shareholders in the market to disclose the information or refrain from dealing. The Supreme Court felt the need for something more than the classical theory and adopted a doctrine, additional to the classical theory, which had been set out in Burger J's dissenting judgment in *Chiarella* and which is generally referred to as the 'misappropriation theory'. Burger J put it in this way:

> . . . A person who has misappropriated nonpublic information has an absolute duty to disclose that information or to refrain from trading . . . The evidence shows beyond all doubt that Chiarella, working literally in the shadows of the warning signs in the printshop, misappropriated . . . valuable nonpublic information entrusted to him in the utmost confidence. He then exploited his ill-gotten informational advantage by purchasing securities in the market. In my view, such conduct plainly . . . violates Rule 10(b)-5.[30]

One final recent development should be mentioned. Under changes brought about by the Dodd–Frank Act,[31] the SEC's whistleblower programme was introduced. The Act pro-

---

[26] 445 US 222 (1980).
[27] See e.g. *Dirks* v *SEC* 463 US 646 (1983) at p. 660.
[28] 117 S Ct 2199 (1997). See further K. McCoy 'Supreme Court Affirms Second Theory of Liability for Insider Trading' (1997) 18 Co Law 335.
[29] I.e. member of the law firm which was acting for the bidder.
[30] 445 US 222 (1980) at p. 245. Further amendments to Sec r. 10b-5 were made in 2000 by adopting new rules 10b5-1 (Trading 'On the Basis Of' Material Nonpublic Information) and 10b5-2 (Duties of Trust or Confidence in Misappropriation Insider Trading Cases). This has been thought to be necessary to resolve issues on which various courts disagreed: http://www.sec.gov/answers/insider.htm.
[31] On the Act see Chapter 16 above under 16.3. Under the Act the SEC is responsible for implementing a series of regulatory initiatives required (see http://www.sec.gov/spotlight/dodd-frank.shtml), which expanded the SEC mandate including creating five new offices. The SEC 2011 study 'Organizational Study and Reform' (March 2011) provides a detailed account of these and other changes: http://www.sec.gov/news/studies/2011/967study.pdf.

vides the SEC with the authority to pay financial rewards to whistleblowers who provide new and timely information about any securities law violation.[32]

## B UK legislation

### 1 *The 1980 legislation*

The UK's early attempt to construct a regime against insider dealing was permeated with a theory of liability based broadly on the US classical theory. Thus, the statute laid stress on the need for the 'individual knowingly connected with a company' (i.e. the insider) to have information which 'it would be reasonable to expect a person and in the position by virtue of which he is so connected not to disclose except for the proper performance of the functions attaching to that position . . . '[33] Here lies the theoretical emphasis on his position, and the confidentiality and limitations on use arising from that position; in other words, the fiduciary duty of the insider to the company.

With tippee liability, the 1980 Act adopted the kind of structure seen in the US law above, of making the tippee liable where the insider has breached his fiduciary duty to the company by giving it to the tippee in the first place, and, where the tippee knows or should know that there has been a breach of fiduciary duty and so is affected by the same trusts as the insider. This is reflected in the provisions of the 1980 Act which deal with tippee liability. The tippee was liable if he dealt in circumstances where he had:

> [I]nformation which he knowingly obtained . . . from another individual who is connected with a particular company . . . and who the former individual knows or has reasonable cause to believe held the information by virtue of being so connected; and . . . the former individual knows or has reasonable cause to believe that, because of the latter's connection and position, it would be reasonable to expect him not to disclose the information except for the proper performance of the functions attaching to that position.[34]

Thus, the theoretical building blocks of the 1980 UK law were closely linked to the case law concepts being developed in the US.[35] In the 1985 consolidation, the insider dealing provisions of the Companies Act 1980 were re-enacted in the Company Securities (Insider Dealing) Act 1985. This Act was then repealed and replaced by the Criminal Justice Act

---

[32] See, Chapter 16 above, 16.3. According to a 2011 SEC Press Release (see http://sec.gov/news/press/2011/2011-167.htm) the SEC's whistleblower programme strengthens the SEC's ability to protect investors in several ways: (1) Better tips: the SEC has seen an increase in the quality of tips that it has been receiving from individuals since Congress created the program; (2) Timely tips: potential whistleblowers are incentivised to come forward sooner rather than later with 'timely' information not yet known to the SEC; (3) Maximises outside resources: with around 4,600 employees to regulate more than 35,000 entities, the SEC cannot be everywhere at all times. With a robust whistleblower programme, the SEC is more likely to find and deter wrongdoing at firms it may not have otherwise uncovered; (4) New protections against retaliation: employees who come forward are provided with new tools to protect themselves against employers who retaliate; (5) Bolsters internal compliance: the new rules provide significant incentives for employees to report any wrongdoing to their company's internal compliance department before coming to the SEC. Therefore, companies that would prefer their employees report internally first are incentivised to a have credible, effective compliance programme in place.
[33] Companies Act 1980, s. 68 (1) *passim.*
[34] *Ibid.* s. 68 (3) *passim.*
[35] For this view, see B. Rider, C. Abrams and M. Ashe *Guide to Financial Services Regulation* 3rd edn (Bicester: CCH, 1998) at p. 222.

('CJA') 1993. What had happened in the meantime was the adoption of the 1989 Directive[36] on insider dealing and this produced some subtle changes.

## 2 *The Directive and the shift to 'market egalitarianism'*

By the time the EC Directive 'Coordinating regulations on insider dealing'[37] was adopted,[38] the European Commission's programme of creating the EC-wide capital market was well advanced and it seemed possible to take some bold steps with insider dealing policy. As ever, the Preamble to the Directive reflects the policy background and it traces the link between the basic need to create the structure of the internal market and a small plank in that structure, insider dealing regulation:

> Whereas . . . the Treaty states that the Council shall adopt the measures for the approximation of the provisions laid down by law, regulation or administrative action in Member States which have as their object the establishment and functioning of the internal market;
>   Whereas the secondary market in transferable securities plays an important role in the financing of economic agents;
>   Whereas, for that market to be able to play its role effectively, every measure should be taken to ensure that market operates smoothly;
>   Whereas the smooth operation of the market depends to a large extent on the confidence it inspires in investors;
>   Whereas the factors on which such confidence depends include the assurance afforded to investors that they are placed on an equal footing and that they will be protected against the improper use of inside information;
>   Whereas, by benefiting certain investors as compared with others, insider dealing is likely to undermine that confidence and may therefore prejudice the smooth operation of the market;
>   Whereas the necessary measures should therefore be taken to combat insider dealing . . .

Gone is the Anglo/US company law basis for insider dealing regulation, with its emphasis on breach of duty by fiduciaries. In its place stands capital markets law. Company law has here migrated into capital markets law; company law has become capital markets law.[39] This is discernible in the current UK legislation.

## 3 *UK enactment of the 1989 Directive – the current law relating to criminal offences*

The detail of the current UK provisions reflects the policy shift. Liability is no longer based on having received information as a result of a breach of fiduciary duty by a corporate insider. Instead, liability is based on knowing that you have inside information, and it

---

[36] Subsequently this has been replaced by the Directive on Insider Dealing and Market Manipulation (Market Abuse), which will usher in further changes in the law. This is dealt with in more detail at para. 20.6 below. This Directive did not change the UK's criminal provisions on insider dealing contained in the CJA 1993, which will thus continue to reflect the influence of the 1989 Directive; see further 20.6 below.
[37] 89/592/EEC.
[38] I.e. 1989.
[39] For this idea generally see P. Davies 'The European Community's Directive on Insider Dealing: From Company Law to Securities Markets Regulation' (1991) 11 OJLS 92.

does not matter much how you acquired it; it does not have to come through an official who is acting in breach of duty.[40]

The offences and defences to them are set out in ss. 52 and 53 of the CJA 1993. There are basically three ways of committing the offence of insider dealing: (1) dealing in securities; (2) encouraging another person to deal and (3) disclosing information. These are now examined in more detail.

### (a) Dealing in securities

The main elements are set out in s. 52 (1) which provides:

> An individual who has information as an insider is guilty of insider dealing if, in the circumstances mentioned in subsection (3),[41] he deals in securities that are price-affected securities in relation to the information.

The legislation contains various definitions of the terminology being used. 'Securities' is defined widely[42] so that it includes not only certain shares and debt securities, but also, for instance, certain options and futures. 'Dealing' is also given a wide definition:[43]

Section 57 sets out the concept of 'insiders':

> (1) . . . a person has information as an insider if and only if:
>    (a) it is, and he knows that it is, inside information, and
>    (b) he has it, and knows that he has it, from an inside source.
> (2) For the purposes of subsection (1), a person has information from an inside source if and only if:
>    (a) he has it through:
>       (i) being a director, employee or shareholder of an issuer of securities; or
>       (ii) having access to the information by virtue of his employment, office or profession; or
>    (b) the direct or indirect source of his information is a person within paragraph (a).

This needs to be read in the light of s. 56, which provides further definitions.[44]

---

[40] See Rider, Abrams and Ashe, n. 35 above, at pp. 222–223.

[41] Criminal Justice Act 1993, s. 52 (3) provides that: 'The circumstances . . . are that the acquisition or disposal in question occurs on a regulated market, or that the person dealing relies on a professional intermediary or is himself acting as a professional intermediary.'

[42] In Criminal Justice Act 1993, s. 54 and Sch. 2. The actual definition is complicated by the detailed extra conditions imposed by arts 4–8 of the Insider Dealing (Securities and Regulated Markets) (Amendment) Order 2002 (SI 2002 No. 1874). The order made changes to the list of 'regulated markets' in the 1994 Order. This Order is also of relevance for the definition of 'regulated market' in s. 52 (3) above. Section 62 deals with the fairly complex territorial scope of the provisions.

[43] In Criminal Justice Act 1993, s. 55.

[44] Section 56 of the Criminal Justice Act 1993 states:

(1) For the purposes of this section and section 57, 'inside information' means information which – (a) relates to particular securities or to a particular issuer of securities or particular issuers of securities and not to securities generally or to issuers of securities generally; (b) is specific or precise; (c) has not been made public; and (d) if it were made public would be likely to have a significant effect on the price of any securities.

(2) For the purposes of [ss. 52–64], securities are 'price-affected securities' in relation to inside information, and inside information is 'price-sensitive information' in relation to securities, if and only if the information would, if made public, be likely to have a significant effect on the price of the securities.

(3) For the purposes of this section 'price' includes value.

There are then further definitions of 'made public', 'professional intermediary' and various other terms; see generally ss. 58–60.

It can be seen from ss. 52 and 57 that the essence of the offence under the CJA 1993 is, broadly, knowing that you have information as an insider and then dealing. This represents a subtle shift from the theoretical basis of liability under the previous legislation, which was predicated on the basis of a breach of fiduciary duty along the lines of the US classical theory. However, in fact, the insider dealer will usually be in breach of a fiduciary duty of confidentiality.

The same shift of emphasis is apparent as regards the basis of tippee liability within ss. 52 and 57. A tippee will be caught by the offence in s. 52 in circumstances where it can be said that he '. . . has information as an insider . . .' within that section and within the definition of those words in s. 57. It is clear that s. 57 (2) needs to be satisfied in order for s. 57 (1) to be satisfied. The part of s. 57 (2) which relates to tippees is s. 57 (2) (b)[45] 'the direct or indirect source of his information is a person within paragraph (a)'. Therefore, although the person giving the tippee the information will often in fact be in breach of a fiduciary duty of confidentiality, the statute does not require this as a precondition of liability.

The offence is however subject to the defences set out in s. 53 (1) which provides that:

An individual is not guilty of insider dealing by virtue of dealing in securities if he shows:

(a) that he did not at the time expect the dealing to result in a profit attributable to the fact that the information in question was price-sensitive information in relation to the securities,[46] or

(b) that at the time he believed on reasonable grounds that the information had been disclosed widely enough to ensure that none of those taking part in the dealing would be prejudiced by not having the information, or

(c) that he would have done what he did even if he had not had the information.[47]

As regards these defences, para. (a) seems to be importing a kind of intent requirement into the offence, although the burden of proof is the reverse of the normal situation where the prosecution has to prove the mental intention as part of the elements of the offence. Paragraph (b) is an important provision since it is often not going to be clear to someone who deals on the basis of information whether or not the information has been made public.[48] Paragraph (c) is designed to prevent injustice in what will probably be quite rare cases where there are overlapping causes of the events. Thus, for instance, if a person is planning to sell shares on Wednesday to pay for his daughter's wedding taking place on Saturday, even if the prosecution can make out the elements of the offence in s. 52 (1), it is clear that they are not an operative cause of the actions being taken.

All in all, even taking into account the availability of these defences, these provisions are quite tough. They have a tendency to reverse the burden of proof so that the prosecution has

---

[45] It could be argued that a tippee might fall within s. 57 (2) (a) in some circumstances. Consider the example of *O'Hagan* (20.3A above) who, although not himself involved with the takeover bid, heard the information over lunch. Could he be said to fall within s. 57 (2) (a) (ii) as having the information 'by virtue of his employment, office or profession'? He was, after all, in the building and at the lunch table by virtue of some or all of those things. Perhaps the better view is that para. (a) is only meant to apply to the situation where the information comes to the person in the course of him exercising functions in relation to the employment, office or profession; the words 'has it through' in para. (a) might help this construction. Thus, *O'Hagan* would perhaps more properly fall under para. (b).

[46] By s. 53 (6) 'profit' here includes avoidance of loss.

[47] Also by s. 53 (4) there are various exemptions for market makers and by s. 63 (1) for individuals acting on behalf of public sector bodies in pursuit of monetary policies.

[48] If it has, it is no longer 'inside information' within s. 56 (1) (c).

to prove only some matters related to the concept of 'insiders'. The prosecution does not have to prove intention to make a profit, nor does it have to prove a breach of fiduciary duty of confidentiality. On the other hand, as will be seen below, it is notoriously difficult to detect insider dealing and then manage to bring a successful prosecution and so perhaps there is no real element of overkill in the statutory provisions.[49]

### (b) Encouraging another person to deal

The main elements of the second way of committing the offence of insider dealing are set out in s. 52 (2) (a), which provides:

> An individual who has information as an insider is also guilty of insider dealing if:

> (a) he encourages another person to deal in securities that are (whether or not that other knows) price-affected securities in relation to the information, knowing or having reasonable cause to believe that the dealing would take place in the circumstances mentioned in subsection (3) . . .

The defences to this are set out in s. 53 (2) and are broadly similar to those which pertain to the offence under s. 52 (1). There are then various definitions; these have been mentioned in more detail under (a) above.

### (c) Disclosing information

The main elements of the third way of committing the offence of insider dealing are set out in s. 52 (2) (b), which provides:

> An individual who has information as an insider is also guilty of insider dealing if: . . .

> (a) he discloses the information, otherwise than in the proper performance of the functions of his employment, office or profession, to another person.

The defences to this are set out in s. 53 (3) and are similar to the ones already discussed except that they omit the third defence contained in s. 53 (1) (c) and (2) (c), which would clearly be inappropriate in the circumstances covered by s. 52 (2) (b).

## 20.4 Enforcement

Given the internationalisation of the world's securities markets during the 1980s, insider dealing has become an international problem and this is reflected in the increasing co-operation between countries.[50]

---

[49] Listed companies are required to comply with the Stock Exchange's Model Code for Securities Transactions contained in the LR9 Annex 1. The Code imposes restrictions on dealing in the securities of a listed company beyond those imposed by law. Its purpose is to ensure that persons discharging managerial responsibilities and employees do not abuse and do not place themselves under suspicion of abusing inside information that they may be thought to have, especially in periods leading up to an announcement of the company's results. Nothing in this Code sanctions a breach of s. 188 (Market Abuse) of FSMA 2000, the insider dealing provisions of the Criminal Justice Act or any other relevant legal or regulatory requirement. The Code provides that there are circumstances when it would be undesirable for a director and certain employees to buy or sell their company's securities, even though this would not of itself amount to a breach of the insider dealing legislation.
[50] On global efforts to combat insider dealing, see http://knowledge.wharton.upenn.edu/article.cfm?articleid=2776; on international cooperation, see para. 29 in the report at http://www.fsa.gov.uk/pubs/annual/ar10_11/enforcement_report.pdf; on how technology and social networks have changed the access to confidential information, see http://knowledge.wharton.upenn.edu/article.cfm?articleid=2776.

In the US, insider dealing will in most instances be dealt with by the SEC bringing a civil action[51] for disgorgement of profit, a monetary penalty,[52] and an injunction against future violations. The action will then usually be settled. Over the years, this has provided a cheap and expeditious means of dealing with insider dealing.[53] In the more serious cases, the SEC civil action will be put on hold pending the outcome of a criminal indictment brought by the District Attorney in the District Court. For detection of the insider dealing violation, the SEC relies on its own computer monitoring of the market and denouncements by private individuals.[54] Many a UK visitor to the SEC website[55] will be bemused to find it using the old 'Wild West' technique of offering 'bounty' to people who supply it with information of insider dealing violations. As we have seen in Chapter 16, under changes brought about by the Dodd–Frank Act the SEC's new whistleblower programme was introduced. The SEC launched a new webpage for people to report a violation of the federal securities laws and apply for a financial award.[56] In 2010 the SEC unveiled a new Market Abuse Unit which aims to identify large-scale insider trading networks and rings. The unit aims 'to be proactive by identifying patterns, connections and relationships among traders and institutions at the outset of investigations', rather than waiting for tips from informants or referrals from stock exchanges about unusual trading.[57]

It is settled in the US that insiders trading on the basis of material non-public information may violate the federal securities laws, regardless of whether the trading nets a profit. However, as a result of the Second Circuit Court of Appeal's ruling in *SEC* v *Rosenthal*,[58] it appears that unsuccessful insider traders can escape monetary penalties in SEC enforcement actions. The court ruled that the SEC may not obtain civil money penalties when insider trading results in no monetary gain (profit or loss avoided) to the defendants. In other words, traders who trade on inside information, but do not obtain a monetary benefit, are not subject to penalties.

---

[51] See Chapter 16 above, 16.3.
[52] Normally about the same amount as the profit. The power to impose a civil monetary penalty was first granted in the Insider Trading Sanctions Act 1984 and is now contained in the Insider Trading and Securities Fraud Enforcement Act 1988 which amended and codified the 1984 Act. As a result of the 1988 Act there is also the possibility of a private right of action under s. 20 A of the Securities Exchange Act 1934, although damages are limited to profits gained or loss avoided and are subject to reduction for amounts paid in actions brought by the SEC. There is also a possibility of action at common law, based on fiduciary duties; see *Diamond* v *Oreamuno* 24 NY 2d 494 (1969) NY Ct App.
[53] See further J. Fishman 'A Comparison of Enforcement of Securities Law Violations in the UK and US' (1993) 14 Co Law 163.
[54] The SEC market abuse unit currently consists of a staff of 50 and 2–3 specialists and support staff across eight regional offices and its home office. Ten of the staff are in New York, nine in Washington, with the rest spread between Los Angeles, Denver, Chicago, Philadelphia, San Francisco and Boston. More recently, the SEC's market abuse unit has been using new approaches to better identify insider trading and abusive conduct by market professionals. Unit Chief Daniel M Hawke said the SEC is using a trader-based approach to look for patterns across groups of people, such as related trades across different products and markets by a single trader or connected group of traders. The new approach has given the SEC a greater ability to detect relationships among traders, and bring cases against large trading networks. See http://blogs.reuters.com/financial-regulatory-forum/2011/02/22/sec-market-abuse-chief-takes-trader-based-approach/.
[55] http://www.sec.gov.
[56] The SEC's Office of the Whistleblower was established to administer the SEC's whistleblower program. Its webpage at www.sec.gov/whistleblower includes information on eligibility requirements, directions on how to submit a tip or complaint, instructions on how to apply for an award, and answers to frequently asked questions.
[57] See 'SEC Names New Specialized Unit Chiefs and Head of New Office of Market Intelligence' 13 January 2010, at http://www.sec.gov/news/press/2010/2010-5.htm.
[58] 2d Cir. June 9, 2011. See http://www.crowell.com/files/SEC-v-Rosenthal-No-10-1204-2d-Cir-June-9-2011.pdf.

In the UK, criminal proceedings in respect of alleged insider dealing may only be brought by or with the consent of the Secretary of State or the Director of Public Prosecutions or the FCA.[59] Many cases of suspected insider dealing are referred to the Department for Business, Energy and Industrial Strategy (BEIS)[60] from the London Stock Exchange ('LSE'), which has its own insider dealing monitoring department with one of the most advanced artificial intelligence systems in the world, called 'IMAS'.[61] For instance, back in 1998 this system highlighted over 10,000 significant price movements and the LSE carried out 1,150 subsequent inquiries, resulting in 28 referrals. However, the number of prosecutions has remained fixed at only one or two a year.[62] These have increasingly resulted in prison sentences[63] and many of those convicted have been minor offenders. In view of this, it is perhaps not surprising that the FCA has pioneered the inclusion in the Financial Services and Markets Act 2000 ('FSMA 2000') of civil monetary penalties for market abuse.[64]

The CJA 1993 makes no provision for any civil remedy and it is certainly arguable that directors who deal in their company's securities using insider knowledge commit a breach of fiduciary duty so that the company could recover their profit.[65] Similar liability might even apply to people who are not directors but who can be shown to have received confidential information and made a profit out of it.[66] So far there has been no reported litigation in the UK along these lines, but it is possible that some encouragement might have been given by the litigation in *Chase Manhattan Equities Ltd* v *Goodman*,[67] a first instance case decided under the previous legislation, which established that, despite the wording of s. 8 (3) of the Company Securities (Insider Dealing) Act 1985, in some circumstances a transaction by an insider dealer could be set aside for illegality. The sale was by a director of the company (via nominees) to Chase Manhattan Equities in circumstances where the director was using unpublished price-sensitive information to avoid a loss. The transaction was not fully carried out on the LSE and just before the transaction would have been delivered into the TALISMAN system.[68] Chase sought to rescind the sale agreement. It was held *inter alia* that the agreement was tainted by the illegal insider dealing and was therefore unenforceable. This was so, in spite of s. 8 (3), which provided that 'No transaction is void or voidable by reason only that it was entered into . . .' in contravention of the insider dealing prohibitions. The judge took the view that s. 8 (3) was enacted for the purpose of preventing the disruption and unwinding of completed LSE transactions and

---

[59] Criminal Justice Act 1993, s. 61; the FSMA 2000, s. 402 (1) (a).
[60] Until July 2016 BEIS was formerly called the Department for Business, Innovation and Skills (DBIS) and prior to that the Department for Business, Enterprise and Regulatory Reform (BERR), having changed from the Department of Trade and Industry (DTI).
[61] Integrated Monitoring and Surveillance System.
[62] For the period of 1981–1993 it was reported that 51 people were charged. Only 23 were convicted, mostly because they pleaded guilty. See news.independent.co.uk/business/analysis_and features/article285783.ece. In 2010–2011 there were five guilty verdicts against five individuals resulting in sentences between 12 months and three years and four months. See http://www.fsa.gov.uk/pubs/annual/ar10_11/enforcement_report.pdf.
[63] The maximum prison sentence was increased from two years to seven years by the Criminal Justice Act 1987.
[64] See 20.5 below.
[65] See discussion in Chapter 8 above.
[66] See e.g. *Seager* v *Copydex* [1967] 2 All ER 415.
[67] [1991] BCC 308.
[68] The Stock Exchange's settlement system at that time, now mainly replaced by CREST.

did not cover the present case because the transaction had not been put through the LSE completion machinery and only the parties to the original dealing were involved. Section 8 (3) is now replaced by s. 63 (2) of the 1993 Act, which provides that 'No contract shall be void or unenforceable by reason only of section 52'. It is possible that the new word 'unenforceable' has overturned this case, although this is far from clear.

In January 2008 the FCA (then the FSA), for the first time, prosecuted someone for insider dealing under the CJA 1993.[69] Former General Counsel of TTP Communications, Christopher McQuoid and James William Melbourne, appeared at City of London Magistrates' Court on a charge of insider dealing contrary to s. 52 of the CJA 1993. They were charged that on the 30 May 2006, having inside information which related to a proposed cash offer from Motorola Incorporated for the entire issued share capital of TTP Communications PLC, they acquired 153,824 shares in TTP Communication PLC. The defendants indicated a plea of not guilty. The court convicted both, sentencing them to 8 months in prison, suspended for 12 months in the case of Melbourne. Later on the Court of Appeal rejected an appeal against the sentence stating that insider dealing undermines public confidence in the financial system. As a result, public prosecutions and jail sentences were appropriate. This case signalled a major change for the FCA, which until then pursued civil cases rather than criminal charges. The potential fines for individuals found guilty on criminal charges are heavier and there is also the possibility of a prison sentence. Indeed,FCA shortly afterwards, Matthew Uberoi and his father, Neel Uberoi, were found guilty of 12 counts of insider dealing at Southwark Crown Court. They were sentenced to 12 and 24 months in prison respectively. In 2006, Matthew Uberoi, whilst working as an intern at a corporate broking firm, obtained insider information in relation to three takeover deals and subsequently passed on this information to his father. As a result, his father purchased shares in those companies and made profits of approximately £110,000. Passing sentence, the judge said:

> This offence is cheating and it is important for economic and social wellbeing to have clean markets. The public rightly recoils from the idea of people with inside information having a licence to print money.[70]

In 2010 Malcolm Calvert, a former partner at stockbroker Cazenove, was sentenced to 21 months in prison for insider dealing. He was found guilty of five counts of insider dealing after making £103,883 profit. The FCA spent four years bringing Calvert to trial. If it had lost it would have backed off on other cases that were pending. Instead, the FCA have gone down the criminal route to send a very clear signal to the City that this sort of behaviour will not be tolerated. Indeed, by February 2011 the FCA secured convictions in nine cases, including that of banker Christian Littlewood, who was jailed for 40 months for insider dealing (the longest jail sentence so far) and his wife, who was given a 12-month suspended sentence. Their third accomplice, Helmy Omar Sa'aid, was sentenced to two years in jail. Interestingly, before sentencing at Southwark Crown Court, the FCA released details of the Littlewood case and, for the first time, how it detects, investigates and

---

[69] See http://www.fsa.gov.uk/pages/Library/Communication/PR/2008/006.shtml.
[70] *R v Neel and Matthew Uberoi* (2009) (not reported). See also http://www.fsa.gov.uk/pages/Library/Communication/PR/2009/149.shtml.

prosecutes insider dealing.[71] The two-year investigation crossed continents, involved thousands of hours' work and resulted in 1,700 gigabytes of information.[72]

In 2011, the FCA called on the Government to introduce tougher sentences for insider dealing, raising the maximum sentence from seven to ten years. Margaret Cole, then the FCA's head of enforcement, said in an interview with the *Financial Times*, 'a longer sentence is important because a lot of enforcement work is about sending messages that this is serious to disincentivise people from doing it'. She went on to add that 'we would welcome an increase in the maximum sentence as well as a clearer and more effective application of the discount for guilty pleas.' The *Financial Times* quoted a spokesman for Dominic Grieve, then the attorney-general, as saying he 'agrees that it is essential that the sentencing framework for fraud is right', and that he planned to raise the issue with the Justice Secretary. The call for increased sentencing for insider dealing indicates that the FCA was hoping that some of its current cases could break new ground in terms of the length of the jail sentences handed down. According to accountants BDO, the average sentence for insider dealing is just 18 months.[73] As we saw above, the toughest sentence, of three years and four months, was handed down to banker Christian Littlewood in February 2011.

In 2016, in a case brought by the FCA and following a three-month trial at Southwark Crown Court, two defendants – Martyn Dodgson, a senior investment banker, and Andrew Hind, a chartered accountant – were convicted of conspiring to insider deal between November 2006 and March 2010.[74] They were subsequently sentenced to four and a half and three and a half years' imprisonment respectively, with Dodgson's sentence being the longest ever handed down for insider dealing in the UK.[75]

In 2017, under a prosecution brought by the FCA, Manjeet Mohal, a former employee of Logica Plc, was sentenced to ten months' imprisonment suspended for two years in respect of two counts of insider dealing. He was also ordered to undertake 180 hours of community work. Reshim Birk, Mr Mohal's neighbour, was sentenced to 16 months' imprisonment suspended for two years in respect of one count of insider dealing. He was ordered to undertake 200 hours of community work.[76]

Since Mark Steward was appointed as Director of Enforcement and Market Oversight for the FCA in October 2015 there has been a noticeable upturn in the number of investigations into insider dealing, including the first cross-jurisdictional prosecution of insider dealing. Information obtained from the FCA shows that, prior to Steward's appointment, a relatively small number of investigations had been opened – reaching a low point in 2010 and 2011 with a combined total of only six new investigations. In contrast, in 2016 the FCA commenced 70 investigations into insider trading – at the time of writing final figures for 2017 are on target to equal, if not exceed, that number. The FCA is using increasingly sophisticated methods to identify and investigate insider dealing.

---

[71] See further http://www.telegraph.co.uk/finance/financial-crime/8517581/Inside-deal-cases-may-smash-sentencing-records.html.
[72] See http://www.fsa.gov.uk/pages/Library/Communication/PR/2011/002.shtml.
[73] http://www.telegraph.co.uk/finance/financial-crime/8517581/Inside-deal-cases-may-smash-sentencing-records.html.
[74] https://www.fca.org.uk/news/press-releases/two-convicted-insider-dealing-operation-tabernula-trial.
[75] https://www.fca.org.uk/news/press-releases/insider-dealers-sentenced-operation-tabernula-trial.
[76] https://www.fca.org.uk/news/press-releases/two-sentenced-insider-dealing-case.

## 20.5 UK regulation against market abuse

### A The criminal law background

Apart from some early common law offences, the first major legislation occurred in the Prevention of Fraud (Investments) Act 1939, largely re-enacted in 1958. This, broadly, made it a criminal offence to induce an investment transaction, by making a false statement either dishonestly or recklessly, or by dishonestly concealing a material fact.[77] These 'misleading statements' provisions are now contained in s. 397 of the FSMA 2000, where there are various amplifications and defences. A common example of the kind of offence which these provisions are aimed at is what the Americans refer to as 'pump and dump' such as where a person puts out false information about a company in which he holds shares, in order to boost the share price; when the share price rises he sells out.

In 1986 the regulatory armoury was augmented by legislation[78] against 'market manipulation', which is also now contained in s. 397.[79] In essence, the provisions are aimed at engaging in an act or course of conduct which creates a false or misleading impression as to the market in an investment or price or value of it. The example often given of this is what the Americans refer to as a 'boiler house' operation, in which fraudsters buy and sell shares to each other, thus misleading investors into thinking that there is a lively market in the shares. The FCA currently has power to prosecute for all these offences, as well as offences under the Money Laundering Regulations. Criminal provisions relating to insider dealing have been dealt with above.

The first criminal market abuse case taken under s. 397 by the FCA was in 2005 in the case of *R* v *Rigby, Bailey and Rowley*.[80] The first two defendants, both directors of call-centre software firm AIT, had issued a statement to the market saying that the turnover and profit of the company were in line with the expectations. The turnover and profit took account of contracts that did not exist. Both were convicted of recklessly making a misleading statement to the market under the FSMA 2000 and received custodial sentences of 18 months and 9 months respectively (reduced on appeal). In June 2011, in *Serious Fraud Office (SFO)* v *Pearson*,[81] Stuart Pearson, former chief executive of AIM-listed investment services company Crown Corporation Limited (later named Langbar International), was found guilty of three counts of making misleading statements under s. 397 of the FSMA 2000.[82] He falsely claimed that the company had assets held by Banco do Brasil and also that some assets were being transferred to the company. These claims, made through official London Stock Market announcements in 2005 and personally to investors, were designed to describe the company as an attractive investment and to increase its share price. He was sentenced to 12 months' imprisonment and disqualified from acting as a director of a company for five years.

---

[77] Section 13(1).
[78] Financial Services Act 1986, s. 47 (2).
[79] There are detailed provisions and various defences.
[80] [2005] EWCA Crim 3487. See also the FSA website for the press release from 8 August 2005: http://www.fsa.gov.uk/pages/Library/Communication/PR/2005/091.shtml.
[81] See *R* v *Pearson Southwark Crown Court,* 20 June 2011, at https://www.sfo.gov.uk/.
[82] On how the much under-used s. 397 could have a role to play in many activities that amount to market abuse involving making communications, see A. Haynes 'Misleading Communications – The Unnoticed Danger' (2010) 31 Comp Lawyer 229.

## B Civil penalties for market abuse

This section outlines the civil penalties that can be imposed by the FCA in relation to market abuse cases. Experience has shown that it has been difficult to bring successful prosecutions under the criminal legislation and perhaps having cast a few longing glances at the SEC's very effective civil enforcement remedies in respect of insider dealing, the FCA ensured that the FSMA 2000 gave it additional tools in the fight against insider dealing and other forms of market abuse. The new tools are civil penalties,[83] and it is probable that infringements will be readily settled by firms on the receiving end of the FCA's investigations.

The Act provides that the FCA will have power to impose a financial penalty for market abuse,[84] both where a person is or has engaged in market abuse, or by taking or refraining from any action has required or encouraged another person to engage in behaviour which [if he had done it] would amount to market abuse.[85] An appeal lies to the Financial Services and Markets Tribunal if the person does not accept the findings and the penalty. The power applies generally and may therefore be used against not only authorised persons, but also non-authorised persons (in other words, against anyone who happens to be trading on the market). Instead of a penalty, the FCA may issue a statement of censure. The FCA's policy as to how it intends to use these new provisions, and elaborate and detailed guidance, is set out in its Code of Market Conduct.[86]

Market abuse is defined in s. 118.[87] Although this definition is very similar to that found in s. 57 (1) of the CJA,[88] there is one crucial difference: as this is a civil penalty regime there is no need to prove *mens rea*. By way of defences, it is provided that the FCA may not impose a penalty if there are 'reasonable grounds for it to be satisfied that (a) he believed, on reasonable grounds that his behaviour did not [amount to market abuse], or (b) that he took all reasonable precautions and exercised all due diligence to avoid behaving in a way which [amounted to market abuse]'.[89] It is also clear that the Code will itself in many circumstances provide defences and safe harbours.[90]

By August 2004 there had been three market abuse cases completed under the new regime which had resulted in the imposition of civil money penalties. The first two were separate examples of the misuse of unpublished confidential information involving individuals who had traded in shares for personal profit. Both were separately fined £15,000.[91]

---

[83] Often referred to as 'administrative' enforcement in some jurisdictions.

[84] The FSMA 2000, ss. 118, 123–131. In some circumstances (injunctions and restitution orders) the court may order a penalty (s. 129). On injunctions, see http://www.fsa.gov.uk/pages/Library/Communication/PR/2011/077.shtml.

[85] It is worth noting that in April 2010 the Financial Services Act 2010 amended s. 391 of the FSMA 2000, giving the FCA the power to publish decision notices. This power was then activated in October 2010. The FCA's approach to publishing decision notices is explained in Policy Statement 11/3, published in January 2011.

[86] Available on the FCA website, in the FCA Handbook of Rules and Guidance, MAR 1. Detailed examination of these complex provisions is outside the scope of this text.

[87] See 20.6 below for the revised text of s. 118 following the implementation of the EC Market Abuse Directive. See generally *ibid.* ss. 118, 118A, 188B, 188C and 119–131.

[88] See 20.3B 3 above.

[89] Section 123 of the Act.

[90] On the effect of the Code, see s. 122. Also relevant in the context of defences is s. 118 A (5).

[91] FSA Market Watch; issue 10, July 2004.

The third case was at the other end of the size spectrum, involving the giant petroleum company Shell™,[92] which had made false or misleading announcements in relation to its hydrocarbon reserves and reserves replacement ratios between 1998 and 2003. For this market abuse behaviour consisting of misleading statements and impressions,[93] the FCA levied the unprecedented fine of £17 million.[94] By 2007, the FCA has issued final notices against eight firms and 15 individuals for market conduct related offences.[95] According to the Enforcement Annual Performance Account of the FCA for 2006–2007 published on the FCA's website, the record for market abuse in 2006–2007 was three (two in favour of the applicant and one case withdrawn).

In August 2006, the FCA issued the largest fine by then against an individual for market abuse and breaching FCA principles in *FCA* v *Jabre*.[96] Philippe Jabre, a senior trader at the hedge fund manager GLG Partners, was 'well crossed' as part of the pre-marketing for a new issue of convertible preference shares by a bank. He was given confidential information and was restricted from dealing in that bank's securities until the new issue was announced. Jabre ignored this restriction by short-selling $16m (£7.68m) of the bank's ordinary shares. When the new issue was announced Jabre made a substantial profit for a GLG fund. Jabre and GLG were fined £750,000 each. Jabre was found to have committed market abuse for the purposes of s. 118 of FSMA and also breached Principle 2 (Due skill, care and diligence) and Principle 3 (Market conduct) of the FCA's Statement of Principles. This case demonstrated how enforcement cases that involve individuals tend to be harder fought, less likely to settle and take longer to resolve than those against firms alone, despite the legal costs involved.[97] In 2010–2011, the FCA issued financial penalties of over £8.3m on 15 individuals for market abuse.[98] This included the highest fine on an individual for market abuse to date, against Simone Eagle, of £2.8m. These penalties comprise a disgorgement of benefit element, to strip wrongdoers of their profits, as well as involving a significant deterrent element. The FCA also prohibited nine individuals from trading as a result of market abuse. On 31 August 2011, the FCA published a decision notice for Swift Trade Inc. (Swift Trade) indicating that it had decided to fine Swift Trade £8m for market abuse.[99]

---

[92] Shell™ Transport and Trading Company, Royal Dutch Petroleum Company, and the Royal Dutch/Shell™ Group of Companies.

[93] There were also breaches of the listing rules.

[94] See FSA Press Release of 24 August 2004. The FSA also perhaps felt constrained to point out that: 'Financial penalties are not treated as income by the FSA. They are applied for the benefit of authorised persons . . . as appropriate, and so given back to the industry in subsequent years.'

[95] See the speech by Margaret Cole, director of Enforcement FSA, 29 June 2007: www.fsa.gov.uk/pages/library/communication/speeches/2007/0629_mc.shtml.

[96] FSA/PN/077/2006 (1 August 2006): http://www.fsa.gov.uk/pages/Library/Communication/PR/2006/077.shtml.

[97] See the detailed account of this case, at https://www.gov.uk/tax-and-chancery-tribunal-decisions/philippe-jabre-v-financial-services-authority-fin-2006-0006-jurisdiction.

[98] See para. 32 in the Enforcement Report from 2010/11: http://www.fsa.gov.uk/pubs/annual/ar10_11/enforcement_report.pdf.

[99] http://www.fsa.gov.uk/pages/Library/Communication/PR/2011/075.shtml.

## 20.6 The new EU Market Abuse Regulation and the new Market Abuse Directive

### A Background: the Market Abuse Directive 2003 and successive amendments and corrections

As part of the Financial Services Action Plan, the European Commission (then the EC Commission) developed a Directive in the field of insider dealing and market abuse, with a view to a more detailed harmonisation Europe-wide of regulation in this area. The old Directive on Insider Dealing and Market Manipulation (Market Abuse)[100] was a framework 'principles' Directive operating at level 1 under the Lamfalussy processes. Below that, at level 2, the comitology procedure of the Committee of European Securities Regulators ('CESR') assisted by the European Securities Committee ('ESC')[101]developed detailed legislation in certain areas covered by the Directive.[102] In July 2007, the CESR published the second set of guidance and information on the common operation of the Directive to the market.[103]

While much of the UK regime on insider dealing and market abuse prior to the formal implementation deadline was already in line with the new Directive, changes were needed in a number of areas to upgrade the provisions. In other areas the FCA left our more wide-ranging provisions in force, so that in some respects the UK regime went beyond that required by the Directive. In particular, certain defences which were available under the 'regular user test' have not been available under the Directive and the legislation has changed to reflect that. The territorial scope changed with the result that the regime has a wider effect in some circumstances than was reflected by UK law; also there is a wider definition of investment instruments covered. Since the Directive is only concerned with establishing a civil (administrative) regime for insider dealing and market abuse, the UK's current criminal provisions in this regard did not change significantly.[104] The Directive was implemented by changes to UK legislation, in particular by producing a new s. 118 of the FSMA 2000.[105] The wording of the amended section is as follows:[106]

**118 Market abuse**
(1) For the purposes of this Act, market abuse is behaviour (whether by one person alone or by two or more persons jointly or in concert) which –
    (a) occurs in relation to –
        (i) qualifying investments admitted to trading on a prescribed market,

---

[100] For reference see n. 1 above.
[101] For an explanation of these acronyms and the processes which they give rise to see Chapter 17, 17.5.
[102] Commission Directive 2004/72/EC, Commission Directive 2003/124/EC, Commission Directive 2003/125/EC and Commission Regulation (EC)2273/2003.
[103] CESR members will apply the guidance on a voluntary basis. The guidance deals with the following issues: what constitutes inside information? When is it legitimate to delay disclosure of inside information? When does information relating to a client's pending orders constitute inside information and insider lists in multiple jurisdictions? See also (2007) 28 Company Lawyer 374–375 on the Guidance of Market Abuse Directive.
[104] See above for changes. See generally the joint FSA/Treasury consultation document of June 2004: UK Implementation of the EU Market Abuse Directive (Directive 2003/6/EC). See also Comparative Implementation of EU Directives – Insider Dealing and Market Abuse, The British Institute of International and Comparative Law, December 2005. For an excellent summary on the implementation in the UK and other countries of the Directive see the report on Administrative Measures and Sanctions available in member states under the Market Abuse Directive published by the CESR on 22 November 2007; 'Review Panel Report' March 2010.
[105] Excerpts from Annex A of the consultation document mentioned in the previous note.
[106] Certain parts and words are omitted.

       (ii)  qualifying investments in respect of which a request for admission to trading on such a market has been made, or

       (iii)  in the case of subsection (2) or (3) behaviour, investments which are related investments in relation to such qualifying investments, and

   (b)  falls within any one or more of the types of behaviour set out in subsections (2) to (8).

(2)  The first type of behaviour is where an insider deals, or attempts to deal, in a qualifying investment or related investment on the basis of inside information relating to the investment in question.

(3)  The second is where an insider discloses inside information to another person otherwise than in the proper course of the exercise of his employment, profession or duties.

(4)  The third is where the behaviour (not falling within subsection (2) or (3)) –

   (a)  is based on information which is not generally available to those using the market but which, if available to a regular user of the market, would be, or would be likely to be, regarded by him as relevant when deciding the terms on which transactions in qualifying investments should be effected, and

   (b)  is likely to be regarded by a regular user of the market as a failure on the part of the person concerned to observe the standard of behaviour reasonably expected of a person in his position in relation to the market.

(5)  The fourth is where the behaviour consists of effecting transactions or orders to trade (otherwise than for legitimate reasons and in conformity with accepted market practices on the relevant market) which –

   (a)  give, or are likely to give, a false or misleading impression as to the supply of, or demand for, or as to the price of, one or more qualifying investments, or

   (b)  secure the price of one or more such investments at an abnormal or artificial level.

(6)  The fifth is where the behaviour consists of effecting transactions or orders to trade which employ fictitious devices or any other form of deception or contrivance.

(7)  The sixth is where the behaviour consists of the dissemination of information by any means which gives, or is likely to give, a false or misleading impression as to a qualifying investment by a person who knew or could reasonably be expected to have known that the information was false or misleading.

(8)  The seventh is where the behaviour (not falling within subsection (5), (6) or (7)) –

   (a)  is likely to give a regular user of the market a false or misleading impression as to the supply of, demand for or price or value of, qualifying investments, or

   (b)  would be, or would be likely to be, regarded by a regular user of the market as behaviour that would distort, or would be likely to distort, the market in such an investment, and the behaviour is likely to be regarded by a regular user of the market as a failure on the part of the person concerned to observe the standard of behaviour reasonably expected of a person in his position in relation to the market.

(9)  Subsections (4) and (8) and the definition of 'regular user' in section 130A(3) cease to have effect on 31 December 2011[107] and subsection (1) (b) is then to be read as no longer referring to those subsections.

On the test to be applied under s. 118, a decision of the Court of Appeal in *Winterflood Securities Ltd* v *The Financial Services Authority*,[108] held that:

Section 118 defines market abuse in terms of behaviour which is either likely to have a certain effect (the creation of a false or misleading impression) or which would be regarded by a regular user as likely to have a certain effect (distortion of the market). As such the test is wholly

---

[107] Words substituted by the FSMA 2000 (Market Abuse) Regulations 2009/3128 reg. 2 (2) (31 December 2009).
[108] [2010] EWCA Civ 423.

objective; it does not require any particular state of mind on the part of the person whose behaviour is under consideration. However, Mr. Flint is right in saying that section 118 of the Act forms only one part of a regulatory regime which includes sections 119 and 122 and the Code itself. The Code is an integral part of the regime. In so far as it describes behaviour which, in the FSA's opinion, does not amount to market abuse, that is conclusive. However, section 122(2) also provides that the Code may be relied on in so far as it indicates whether behaviour of a certain kind does or does not amount to market abuse. In principle it is possible that the identification of a particular kind of behaviour as constituting market abuse could amount to a statement that, in the absence of one or more constituent elements, there would be no market abuse. However, that would be the case only if there was a true dichotomy, so that it followed as a necessary and inevitable conclusion . . .[109]

The legislation then goes on to set out provisions in relation to a range of related matters, such as territorial scope, safe harbours, definitions of insider and inside information.[110] The FCA's Code of Market Conduct ('COMC')[111], which gives guidance on the market abuse offence, has also been amended to clarify its application to disclosure of information in relation to block trades.[112] No offence of market abuse is committed if the information is disclosed in the proper course of a person's employment, profession or duties. The amendments to the COMC set out the circumstances when the disclosure of inside information in the course of a block trade will not amount to market abuse.

In February 2008, the Treasury issued a consultation document reviewing the appropriate scope for the civil market abuse regime under FSMA 2000.[113] The review is concerned solely with ss. 118 (4) (misuse of information) and 118(8) (behaviour that is likely to give rise to a false or misleading impression or to market distortion) of the FSMA 2000. These sections are commonly referred to as the 'super-equivalent provisions', which prohibit a wider range of market abuse behaviour than under MAD.[114] The Treasury reviewed the regime's scope to assess whether this broader definition remains justified as there were mixed views as to the merits of a super-equivalent regime.[115] The consultation paper also discussed whether the super-equivalent provisions have had any effect in deterring market abuse.[116] The consultation paper noted that the FSA has indicated that it will be making greater use of its

---

[109] *Ibid*, at [25].

[110] See ss. 118A, 118B and 118C.

[111] See https://www.handbook.fca.org.uk/handbook/MAR/.

[112] The amended COMC is available from the FSA website, at http://fsahandbook.info/FSA/html/handbook/MAR.

[113] HM Treasury, *FSMA Market Abuse Regime: A Review of the Sunset Clauses*, February 2008. The consultation paper together with the summary of responses to it are available at https://www.lexology.com/library/detail.aspx?g=26a6d941-7e69-427d-a271-f3a20b6a36cf.

[114] These provisions were initially the subject of a three-year 'sunset clause', which meant that they would have automatically lapsed on 30 June 2008, unless new legislation is adopted to allow them to remain in force. These 'super-equivalent' provisions are under a sunset clause and were due to expire on 31 December 2011.

[115] This is balanced against the need to ensure market integrity; maintaining investor confidence in the financial markets; ensuring proper application of the principles of better regulation; and maintaining efficiency in the financial system. See further, S. Sheikh 'FSMA Market Abuse Regime: A Review of the Sunset Clauses' (2008) 19 *International Company and Commercial Law Review* 234.

[116] This was hard to measure given that the FSA has not brought a successful enforcement action under the two super-equivalent provisions to date. Although the consultation paper noted that this could be seen as evidence that MAD requirements alone were comprehensive enough to cover all types of behaviour that amount to market abuse it concluded that this was unlikely as market abuse cases have been considered by the FSA under both super-equivalent provisions but those cases have not been further pursued for evidentiary reasons.

enforcement powers to deal with insider dealing and market abuse, and it is possible that there may be cases in the future based on either, or both, of the two super-equivalent provisions. The consultation paper recommended, and the majority of responses to the consultation supported, a short-term extension of the sunset date of the super-equivalent provisions to 31 December 2009, which was later extended until 31 December 2011, pending the outcome of the European Commission review of MAD.[117] This approach was sensible given that the European Commission review of MAD, discussed below under B, led to changes in MAD. If the Treasury had allowed the super-equivalent provisions to expire or entrenched the super-equivalent provisions indefinitely, it is possible that the UK would have had to go through two sets of changes to its market abuse regime in order to implement MAD.[118]

In January 2010, the European Court of Justice ('ECJ') handed down judgment in the case of *Spector Photo Group and Van Raemdonck* v *Commissie voor het Bank, Financie en Assurantiewezen*.[119] The case reached a number of significant conclusions about MAD and its interpretation.[120] In particular, the ECJ held that if a person deals while in possession of inside information, there will be a rebuttable presumption that the inside information was used. The ECJ was required to consider, *inter alia*, whether making use of information for the purposes of art. 2 would be satisfied by the mere fact that a person in possession of inside information, acquires or disposes of, or tries to acquire or dispose of, for his own account or for the account of a third party, financial instruments to which that inside information relates. The ECJ found that this would amount to the use of inside information but recognised the right to rebut the presumption. In reaching this position, the ECJ made clear that before it was:

> The question whether that person has infringed the prohibition on insider dealing must be analysed in the light of the purpose of that directive, which is to protect the integrity of the financial markets and to enhance investor confidence, which is based, in particular, on the assurance that investors will be placed on an equal footing and protected from the misuse of inside information.[121]

In light of the ECJ's decision, the FCA proposed to amend the COMC.[122] MAR 1.3.4 currently sets out the FCA's opinion that if any inside information was the reason for, or a material influence on, the decision to deal, this indicates that the person's behaviour is 'on the basis of' inside information. This evidential provision suggests that, in order to prove insider dealing, the FCA would need evidence of a person's intention. The FCA believes that, following the *Spector Photo* decision, MAR 1.3.4 should be deleted from the COMC as it is not necessary to provide evidence of a person's intention to prove insider dealing.

---

[117] By virtue of the FSMA 2000 (Market Abuse) Regulations 2008 (SI 2008/1439), which extended the sunset clauses until 31 December 2009. It was initially decided to extend the sunset clauses until 31 December 2009 until the outcome of the EU's review of the Market Abuse Directive became known. The EU's review of the Market Abuse Directive was subsequently delayed. The call for evidence was only launched on 20 April 2009
[118] See T. Dolan and D. Park 'United Kingdom: Extension of Sunset for Sunset Clauses' 14 August 2008, available at http://www.mondaq.com/article.asp?articleid=63482.
[119] Case C-45/08. See, http://eur-lex.europa.eu/LexUriServ/LexUriServ.do?uri=CELEX:62008J0045:EN:HTML.
[120] For a discussion of these see J.L. Hansen 'Insider Dealing After the Market Abuse Directive' ch. 4 in D. Prentice, A. Reisberg (eds) *Corporate Finance in the UK and EU* (Oxford: OUP, 2011).
[121] Case C-45/08, at [62].
[122] The proposals are contained in Consultation Paper CP10/22 which is available at http://www.fsa.gov.uk/pubs/cp/cp10_22.pdf.

The proposed change is significant because it reverses the burden of proof. It will be for the defence to prove that the inside information was not the basis of the trade or attempted trade, rather than for the FCA to establish that it was.

In July 2011, the ECJ handed down judgment in *IMC Securities BV* v *Stichting Autoriteit Financiële Markten*.[123] The case concerned a reference for a preliminary ruling from the College van Beroep voor het bedrijfsleven (Netherlands) with regard to interpretation of art. 1 (2) (a), second indent, of MAD. Article 1 (2) provides definitions of market manipulation, including, in subsection (a), transactions or orders to trade which – to quote directly from the Directive – 'give, or are likely to give, false or misleading signals as to the supply of, demand for or price of financial instruments [*the first indent*], or which secure, by a person, or persons acting in collaboration, the price of one or several financial instruments at an abnormal or artificial level [*the second indent*], unless the person who entered into the transactions or issued the orders to trade establishes that his reasons for so doing are legitimate and that these transactions or orders to trade conform to accepted market practices on the regulated market concerned.' In answer to the referred question, the ECJ stated that the second indent must be interpreted as not requiring, in order for the price of one or more financial instruments to be considered to have been fixed at an abnormal or artificial level, that that price must maintain an abnormal or artificial level for more than a certain duration.

## B The European Commission review of MAD

Following its call for evidence in April 2009 and CESR's review of how the different member states use the options and discretions granted under the MAD regime, the Commission published in June 2010 a consultation paper seeking views and its proposals to amend MAD. Amongst the questions asked were: Should MAD be extended to cover attempts to manipulate the market? How can the powers of competent authorities to investigate market abuse be enhanced? To what extent need the sanction regimes be harmonised at the EU level in order to prevent market abuse? How can the system of cooperation among national and third country competent authorities be enhanced? And what should the role of the European Securities and Markets Authority be in this regard? The Commission proposals included the following:[124]

- *Delay in disclosure* – It proposes making it compulsory for listed issuers to inform their regulator as and when they decide to delay disclosure of inside information. Currently, under the MAD regime (and DTR 2) issuers may delay the public disclosure of inside information provided that they have a legitimate interest in doing so; that this delay would not be likely to mislead the public, and that the information can be kept confidential. Member states have the option of requiring issuers to inform the regulator of their intention to delay disclosure. The CESR review found that 16 member states already require notification to the regulator should the issuer decide to delay the publication of such information, while 11 – including the UK – do not.

---

[123] Case C-445/09.
[124] See http://ec.europa.eu/internal_market/consultations/docs/2009/market_abuse/call_for_evidence.pdf. See also, http://www.fsa.gov.uk/pages/About/What/International/pdf/MAD%20(PL).pdf.

- *Emergency funding disclosure* – If an issuer requires emergency assistance from a government or public body to remain viable, the Commission proposes that the national competent authority ('NCA') (rather than the issuer) should decide whether or not the obligation to disclose inside information should apply to information about the assistance. In order to permit non-disclosure, the NCA would need to be satisfied that the entity is systemically important; that not disclosing the information would be in the public interest; and that confidentiality can be ensured.
- *Market manipulation* – An extension of the existing MAD provisions is also proposed to prohibit 'attempts' to manipulate the market in the same way that 'attempts' at insider dealing are currently prohibited.
- *Use of telephone/email evidence* – The Commission proposes enhancing the powers of competent authorities to investigate market abuse by clarifying that the E-privacy Directive (Directive 2002/58/EC) does not preclude regulators from obtaining telephone and data traffic records when investigating market abuse and includes the right to request authorisation from a judicial authority to enter private premises and/or seize documents.

Following the consultation, the European Commission's draft for a Directive amending MAD was published in October 2011. Given that the UK (and Denmark) did not opt in to the Directive on Criminal Sanctions for Market Abuse ('CSMAD')[125], it is not discussed in any detail here.[126] Participating member states were required to transpose it into national law by 3 July 2016. Prior to CSMAD, EU countries were only required to adopt administrative sanctions which were 'effective, proportionate and dissuasive' but were allowed to elect whether or not to impose criminal sanctions. This led to divergent market abuse and insider dealing penalties from country to country in the EU, as well as difficulties for regulators and enforcement agencies in coordinating and enforcing such rules. This new framework should give certainty to the rules in force across all 28 countries of the EU and allow regulators and enforcement agencies to effectively work together to fight financial crime. The European Commission intends that the CSMAD should work with the Market Abuse Regulation ('MAR') to create a stronger market abuse regulatory framework with harmonised sanctions throughout the EU, with minimum rules on criminal offences and criminal sanctions for anybody conducting market abuse anywhere within the EU or on EU markets.

## C The Market Abuse Regulation

MAR came into effect on 3 July 2016 with the aim of establishing a common regulatory framework on insider dealing, the unlawful disclosure of inside information and market manipulation. In addition, it introduces some measures to prevent market abuse.

The new framework strengthens the fight against market abuse across commodity and related derivative markets, explicitly bans the manipulation of benchmarks, such as

---

[125] Directive 2014/57/EU of the European Parliament and of the Council of 16 April 2014 on criminal sanctions for market abuse (the Updated Market Abuse Directive)
[126] D. Kirk 'Enforcement of Criminal Sanctions for Market Abuse: Practicalities, Problem Solving and Pitfalls' in *ERA Forum*, September 2016, vol. 17, issue 3, pp 311–322.

LIBOR, and reinforces the investigative and sanctioning powers of regulators. Administrative authorities now have greater powers to investigate market abuse and to impose significant fines, while those found guilty of market abuse will be deterred by the prospect of facing jail. This new regime will increase investor protection and confidence by allowing deeper and more integrated financial markets, and contribute to the creation of the Capital Markets Union. The Regulation also ensures that rules keep pace with market developments, such as new trading platforms, as well as new technologies, such as high frequency trading ('HFT').

## 1 *Definitions*

This section has been modified. The precise nature of inside information has been defined, harmonising the definition related to commodity derivatives with the definition related to referred issuers and financial instruments, as follows:

> . . . information of a precise nature, which has not been made public, relating, directly or indirectly, to one or more issuers or to one or more financial instruments, and which, if it were made public, would be likely to have a significant effect on the prices of those financial instruments or on the price of related derivative financial instruments.

Inside information operations are defined as those carried out by a person in possession of this information and who uses it not only to acquire or dispose of financial instruments referred to in said information, but also to cancel or modify an order issued before the person became aware of the inside information. It also includes anyone who uses recommendations or inducements to engage in insider dealings when they use or disclose the recommendation or inducement knowing, or having the obligation of knowing, that it is based on inside information. A new definition of inside information in connection with emission allowances is introduced.

Behaviour amounting to attempted market manipulation, which is now prohibited under MAR, is defined as any attempt to engage in any of the activities amounting to market manipulation. Such an attempt may include situations where the activity is started but is not completed, for example as a result of a technical failure or an instruction to trade that is not acted upon.

## 2 *Scope/offences*

Issuers have an obligation to disclose to the public all inside information relating to them as soon as possible. MAR provides that it is an offence to: (i) engage or attempt to engage in insider dealing; (ii) recommend that another person engage in insider dealing or induce another person to engage in insider dealing; (iii) unlawfully disclose inside information; or (iv) engage in or attempt to engage in 'market manipulation'.

The regime is extended beyond regulated markets to cover (i) financial instruments traded on multilateral trading facilities ('MTFs') or other organised trading facilities ('OTFs') as well as spot commodity contracts not related to wholesale energy products and derivatives and certain over-the-counter activities (including derivatives and credit default swaps), both within and outside the EU in relation to instruments admitted to trading on

an EU trading venue. This extra-territorial reach could potentially have sweeping consequences: for example, abusive trading by a New York-based hedge fund with a US bank
as counterparty in a US-listed security would apparently be subject to the MAR regime if
that US security were traded on a single European OTF. MAR's market manipulation
offence includes the manipulation of benchmarks. Under s. 91 of the Financial Services
Act 2012, it is already a criminal offence in the UK to make false or misleading statements
relating to benchmarks or to engage in a course of conduct that creates a false or misleading impression that may affect the setting of a benchmark. Since the current UK criminal
offence has a lower threshold than the new MAR offence, as the current offence can be
committed by a person either knowing that it is false or misleading or simply being reckless as to whether it is so, we do not expect that MAR will materially change the UK
offences in relation to benchmarks.

### 'Market soundings'

The Regulation describes in depth different situations of unlawful disclosure of inside
information. These take place when someone in possession of inside information discloses
it to a third party within a market sounding, unless the disclosure takes place under normal
work or professional circumstances or in the exercise of their duties. MAR introduces a
new 'market soundings' safe harbour to the offence of unlawfully disclosing inside information. Market soundings (also known as 'pre-marketing') comprise the communication
of information, before the announcement of a transaction, to one or more potential investors in order to gauge their interest in a possible transaction and the conditions relating to
it, such as its potential size or pricing. The market sounding safe harbour applies provided
certain disclosure and record-keeping conditions are met. For example, before conducting
a market sounding, the issuer must specifically assess whether the market sounding will
involve the disclosure of inside information. Before disclosing such inside information,
the issuer must also: (i) obtain the consent of the person to whom the disclosure is made
to receive inside information; and (ii) inform that person that they will be restricted by
MAR from trading or acting on that information and that they will be obliged to keep the
information confidential. Issuers must put in place procedures to provide certain information to the person receiving a market sounding. This prescribed information must be provided in a pre-determined sequence. There is also a requirement to inform the recipient as
soon as possible once the information disclosed in the course of a market sounding ceases
to be inside information. A record of all information given to the person receiving the
market sounding should be maintained, including the prescribed information given and the
identity of the potential investors to whom the information has been disclosed. All records
must be kept for five years. Issuers wishing to conduct market soundings on or after 3 July
2016 should ensure that their policies and procedures are consistent with the relevant provisions of MAR so as to ensure that those soundings benefit from the safe harbour.
Appropriate training should also be given to all individuals involved in market sounding
exercises.

### 'Legitimate behaviour' and 'accepted market practices'

MAR identifies certain categories of behaviour wherein the possession of inside information will not give rise to a presumption of insider dealing. A number of behaviours are

identified, some of which are, in principle, considered legitimate. For instance, when someone uses inside information that has been obtained during a public takeover or a merger. These safe harbours for 'legitimate behaviour' and 'accepted market practices' mirror the existing MAD provisions. Examples of legitimate behaviour include instances where a person has established, implemented and maintained adequate and effective internal arrangements and procedures (i.e. Chinese walls) and the decision to deal is taken by individuals not in possession of inside information, or where a person has obtained inside information in the conduct of a public takeover or merger with a company and uses that inside information solely for the purpose of proceeding with that merger or public takeover (provided that at the point of approval of the merger or acceptance of the offer by the shareholders of that company, any inside information has been made public or has otherwise ceased to constitute inside information). However, MAR provides that the safe harbour will not apply if the NCA establishes that there was an illegitimate reason for the relevant behaviour, transaction or order to trade. As under the former MAD regime, accepted market practices may be established by national regulators, provided certain criteria and conditions set out in MAR are met. Accepted market practices must be notified to and approved by the ESMA. There are currently no accepted market practices in the UK and the FCA has not indicated whether it will seek to establish any under the new regime.

New market manipulation situations have been identified. In addition to transactions and instructions to trade, other activities and behaviours that have a real impact on the demand or price of a financial instrument are included.

### Insider lists

MAR, as with MAD, provides that issuers must draw up a list of persons working for them who have access to inside information. These insider lists must include the identity of any person having access to inside information; the reason for including that person in the insider list; the date and time at which that person obtained access to inside information; and the date on which the insider list was drawn up. To harmonise insider list requirements across the EU, the MAR regime includes a detailed template of information that must be included in insider lists. The requirements are similar to those already set out in the FCA's template insider list. Issuers will need to review and update their inside information policies and procedures in order to align them with the MAR regime, particularly the new requirements: to prepare and retain written records of the details of any decision to delay disclosure and the justification for the delay; to notify the FCA that disclosure was delayed at the time such information is subsequently disclosed; and relating to the content of insider lists.

A common rule is established to notify any transactions carried out by persons with management responsibilities, as well as anyone closely associated with them. They must notify the issuer and the NCA of any transactions conducted on their own account relating to the shares or financial instruments linked to them, no later than three working days after the date of such a transaction. Additionally, thresholds are set out below which said notification is not needed. Any person discharging management responsibilities within an issuer shall not be able to conduct any transactions during a period of 30 calendar days before the announcement of an interim financial report or a year-end report, unless otherwise provided.

## Delays

The Regulation homogenises the disclosure of the inside information delay system. As a general rule, the MAR regime continues to permit issuers, on their own responsibility, to delay disclosure if the following conditions are satisfied: (i) disclosure is likely to prejudice the legitimate interests of the issuer; and (ii) delay of disclosure is not likely to mislead the public; and the issuer can ensure the confidentiality of that information.

MAR has introduced a new requirement for issuers to inform the NCA that the disclosure was delayed. This notification should take place immediately after the delayed inside information has been publicly disclosed. MAR also requires issuers to provide national competent authorities with a written explanation of how the above-listed regulatory conditions were satisfied in respect of the delay of a particular piece of inside information, although in the UK it is proposed that such an explanation will only be required if the FCA requests it. Where an issuer delays the public disclosure of inside information, it must keep a record of the circumstances of the delay. The technical standards produced by the ESMA set out the details of the information that must be recorded.

### Administrative sanctions

The Regulation introduces some basic rules concerning administrative sanctions. One of the new sanctions shall be the disgorgement of the profits gained or losses avoided due to the infringement, if these can be determined. In the event of repeated infringement, the Regulation establishes a permanent ban from discharging managerial responsibilities in investment firms.

For the first time, it takes care of the person reporting an infringement to the competent authorities. Member states must establish effective mechanisms and suitable protection measures that shall allow reporting of any potential or real infractions to the competent authorities.

## 20.7 The new regulatory system in the UK: responsibility of FCA for market abuse

As discussed above,[127] from 2013, the FCA has been responsible for dealing with financial crime within the new regulatory framework. It is the competent authority specified for the purposes of the money laundering regulations and also retains the former FSA's powers of criminal prosecution for insider dealing and market manipulation.[128] The FCA is also the body that maintains the key links with the other stakeholders in this area, including the Police, the SFO, the Serious Organised Crime Agency, the National Fraud Authority, the Economic Crime Agency and the National Crime Agency.

One area in which the FCA has been given increased powers is in relation to the early publication of warning notices. Previously, the regulator could only publish information about enforcement proceedings at a later stage in the enforcement process, once it had decided to take action. In 2012, the Financial Services Act 2012 gave the FCA the power to publicise warning notices, which is now set out in the FSMA 2000. In 2013, the FCA

---

[127] Chapter 16 under 16.4.
[128] http://www.fsa.gov.uk/pubs/events/fca_approach.pdf.

consulted on their proposed policy for using this power[129] and set out their final policy in a Policy Statement, which will result in earlier transparency of enforcement proceedings.[130] With the introduction of the early publication of information about warning notices, the FCA has looked set to increase its impact in this area in a move that would take it closer to the current approach in the US. At the start of 2018, it is still not clear how the FCA's use of this new power has helped to 'promote early transparency of enforcement proceedings' and enabled the industry to better 'understand the types of behaviour that [the FCA] consider unacceptable at an earlier stage'.[131]

It also seems likely that there will be increased enforcement action against individuals, as opposed to simply focusing on firms, signalling the FCA's key emphasis on deterrence. Further, as we saw above, the FCA has now increasingly been pursuing criminal prosecutions and this is a trend that it is likely to continue and develop.

## Further reading

A. Haynes 'Misleading Communications – The Unnoticed Danger' (2010) 31 Comp Lawyer 229.

J.L. Hansen 'Insider Dealing After the Market Abuse Directive,' Chapter 4 in D. Prentice and A. Reisberg (eds) *Corporate Finance in the UK and EU* (Oxford: OUP, 2011).

M. Ventoruzzo and S. Mock (eds) *Market Abuse Regulation* (Oxford: OUP, 2017).

---

[129] See FSA CP13/8, at https://www.fca.org.uk/publication/consultation/cp13-8.pdf
[130] https://www.fca.org.uk/publication/policy/ps13-9.pdf.
[131] For the period 2013–2015, the FCA published information about 18 warning notices it had issued: all but one of these warning notice statements concerned individuals; none of the subjects of the warning notices were named in the warning notice statements (despite the FCA having the discretion to do so); and half of the warning notice statements published by the FCA concerned individuals being investigated in relation to alleged LIBOR-related misconduct.

# 21

# The regulation of takeovers

## 21.1 Takeover battles

A hostile takeover bid[1] is a phenomenon that has a long history in both the UK and the US,[2] and has gradually been extended to other countries.[3] In the UK, it will usually take the form of a predator company making an offer to the shareholders of the target company to buy its shares at a price which is a premium to the market price.[4] The offer will remain open for a specific period of time, during which the target shareholders will consider whether to accept the offer. Played out in the full glare of the financial press, the management of the target company is subjected to whirlwind pressure over a period of weeks. The word 'battle' has been coined and it is not an exaggeration. The management teams of the target and the bidder will spend most of that time locked in frantic conference with their investment bank and legal advisers. Both sides become tempted to 'bend the rules', for the stakes are high; the target management team who lose will be at the mercy of a successful bidder and will usually lose their jobs; with them will go reputation and large measures of self-esteem. The newspapers will carry pictures of the losers with exhaustion and the

---

[1] Interestingly, only about 9% of UK bids would be classified as hostile; see statistics on p. 24 of The Takeover Panel 2006–07 Report, showing that during that year there were 143 takeover or merger proposals that reached the stage where formal documents were sent to shareholders and that 13 offers remained unrecommended at the end of the offer period. There are many types of agreed takeover and a full account is beyond the scope of this book. See the 2011 statistics on p. 15 of The Takeover Panel 2010–11 report showing that during the year ended 31 March 2010 there were 93 takeover or merger proposals that reached the stage where formal documents were sent to shareholders and that 16 offers remained unrecommended at the end of the offer period: http://www. thetakeoverpanel.org.uk/wp-content/uploads/2008/11/report2011.pdf. For the statistics for 2014–15 which show a similar trend to that in 2006–07 see pp. 18–19 of The Takeover Panel 2014–15 report, at http://www.thetake-overpanel.org.uk/wp-content/uploads/2008/11/935766_TakeOver-AR_web-version1.pdf. See L. Rabinowitz (ed.) *Weinberg and Blank on Takeovers and Mergers* 5th edn (London: Sweet & Maxwell, 1989, looseleaf).

[2] US takeovers rules have different provisions for the players but some of the outcomes are similar.

[3] See generally T. Ogowewo 'The Underlying Themes of Tender Offer Regulation in the United Kingdom and the United States of America' [1996] JBL 463; G. Barboutis 'Takeover Defence Tactics part I: The General Legal Framework on Takeovers' (1999) 20 Co Law 14; and part II: (1999) 20 Co Law 40; and J. Armour, J.B. Jacobs and C.J. Milhaupt 'The Evolution of Hostile Takeover Regimes in Developed and Emerging Markets: An Analytical Framework' (2011) 52 *Harvard International Law Journal* 221 (http://www.harvardilj.org/wp-content/uploads/2011/02/HILJ_52-1_Armour_Jacobs_Milhaupt.pdf).

[4] There is another form of hostile takeover where the predator does not attempt to gain more than a small percentage of shares in the target company, but as an insurgent within the company wages a campaign designed to 'win the hearts and minds' of the target shareholders so that they then vote in a new management team who are nominees of the predator. Called a 'proxy battle' because it involves getting the target shareholders to complete their proxy forms in favour of the insurgents this form is more common in the US although it is by no means unknown in the UK. Although it is relatively cheap, it has the obvious disadvantage that without voting control the influence obtained could be transitory if the company is either subjected to a full bid or the voters change their minds again. See further, L. Bebchuk and O. Hart 'Takeover Bids Versus Proxy Fights in Contests for Corporate Control' (November 2001). CEPR Discussion Paper No. 3073: http://ssrn.com/abstract=292883.

shock of defeat etched in their faces, juxtaposed to ecstatic winners drunk on adrenalin. In takeover battles the winners really do win; and the losers lose heavily.[5]

## 21.2 Disciplining management – the market for corporate control

The appearance and rapid growth of hostile takeovers in the US and UK in the 1960s quickly led to the beginning of systematic regulation in both jurisdictions. In the US, in 1968, it was public regulation (primarily federal legislation) in the form of the Williams Act 1969.[6] In the UK, in 1968, it was self-regulation in the form of the City Code on Takeovers and Mergers ('Takeover Code') promulgated and administered by the Takeover Panel ('Panel'). The hostile takeover phenomenon and the appearance of regulation were the catalysts for a long-lasting academic and political debate. Economists engaged themselves in precise monitoring of the effects of takeovers on share prices; the effects of the bid, the effects of defences and subsequent developments.[7] The desirability of takeovers was put under scrutiny. To some extent, it can be said that they have survived the scrutiny process in that regulatory authorities have not decided to ban them totally. Given the amount of positive evidence which has emerged about their economic and societal effects and their role, this is not surprising.[8]

Four main functions or economic benefits of takeovers can be identified. First, the possibility of hostile takeovers is often seen as a way of disciplining corporate managers to use the assets of the company in an efficient (and therefore socially optimal) way.[9] The second function of takeovers, which is broader, in the sense that it is not mainly related to hostile takeovers but will relate to the whole range of agreed takeovers and mergers, is that the bidder will often make gains from the resulting business combination.[10] Indeed, in industries with extremely high R&D costs (which can ultimately amount to fixed costs), takeovers can provide tremendous returns and gains because the bidder is benefiting from a product's success without having invested the time and expense in R&D and commercialisation. Nowhere is this more aptly exemplified than in the pharmaceuticals industry.[11]

Thirdly, there exists considerable empirical evidence about the positive effect of takeovers on shareholders' wealth, particularly the shareholders of the target company.[12]

---

[5] For a cogent overview of the challenges for merger and acquisition in today's era of investor activism, see: http://corpgov.law.harvard.edu/2015/10/27/deal-activism/#more-71922.

[6] Amending ss. 13 and 14 of the Securities Exchange Act 1934. US public regulation of takeovers has been further enhanced by state takeover statutes and a substantial case law on directors' duties.

[7] See *e.g.* Chapter 3, 3.4A above.

[8] See generally: H. Manne 'Mergers and the Market for Corporate Control' (1965) 73 *Journal of Political Economy* 110; M. Jensen and R. Ruback 'The Market for Corporate Control' (1983) 11 *Journal of Financial Economics* 5; J.A. Tanassov 'Do Hostile Takeovers Stifle Innovation? Evidence from Antitakeover Legislation and Corporate Patenting' (April 26, 2012): http://ssrn.com/abstract=967421.

[9] See M. Mandelbaum 'Economic Aspects of Takeover Regulation with Particular Reference to New Zealand' in J. Farrar (ed.) *Takeovers, Institutional Investors and the Modernization of Corporate Laws* (Auckland: OUP, 1993) pp. 203, 206.

[10] *Ibid.* at p. 207.

[11] For a recent illustration in the US context see: http://www.bloomberg.com/news/articles/2015-10-30/merck-ceo-says-drug-price-debate-doesn-t-account-for-r-d-risks.

[12] See the summary in F. Easterbrook and D. Fishel *The Economic Structure of Corporate Law* (Cambridge, MA: Harvard University Press, 1991) p. 171, and more recently W. Drobetz, and P. Momtaz 'Bidder Wealth Effects in European M&As After the Fifth Takeover Wave: Institutional Determinants and Corporate Governance Convergence Through Cross-Border Acquisitions' (11 August, 2015): http://ssrn.com/abstract=2642487.

Finally, takeovers allow for quick and efficient product and market diversification as well as entry into new geographical markets.

## 21.3 Goals of takeover regulation

### A The struggle for a Europe-wide regulatory policy

It is obviously necessary to consider why we regulate takeovers and what the goals of that regulation are. Apart from US law, UK experience and ideas on the fundamentals of take-over regulation have the oldest pedigree in the world, and many of these ideas are to be found in the new European (partial) consensus[13] on regulatory techniques and goals. The story of the EU Takeover Directive[14] is an amazing 15-year saga, which eventually seemed to catch the imagination of all member states ; it was as if the mere idea of exciting take-over battles had spilled over into the discussion about the regulation of them, so that the regulatory scene itself became a battleground.

The first draft proposal[15] on what became the 13th Directive on Takeovers had been put forward in 1989. It was amended in 1990 but there was no agreement between the member states on the first proposal so negotiations were finally suspended in 1991. It became apparent that detailed harmonisation was not going to be the way forward, at least at that early stage, and an amended proposal, a streamlined 'framework' Directive, was presented by the Commission in 1996.[16] However, this too met opposition. An amended proposal was put forward in 1997 which made better progress and on 21 June 1999 the EU's Council of Internal Market Ministers reached political agreement on this amended pro-posal, subject only to settling a dispute with Spain concerning Gibraltar. Although the proposal was subsequently redrafted and renumbered to some extent, it remained unchanged in substance and the Common Position on this proposed Directive was eventu-ally reached on 19 June 2000. Subsequently, the European Parliament proposed amend-ments which the Council did not approve of and eventually an agreement was reached within the Conciliation Committee on 6 June 2001. On 4 July the European Parliament rejected the compromise text in unusual circumstances; a historic tied vote of 373 each side. Undaunted, the Commission decided to construct a new proposal for a Directive, aimed at meeting the concerns of the European Parliament but without departing unneces-sarily from the basic principles approved unanimously in the Council's common position of 19 June 2000. The Commission established the High-Level Group of Experts in Company Law under the chairmanship of the Dutch lawyer, Professor Jaap Winter, asking them to find a way of resolving the matters which had been causing concern to the European Parliament.

The 'Winter Report'[17] was published on 10 January 2002. It argued that there were two distinct stages of a bid: the first stage commences when the bid is announced and the sec-ond is the stage commencing after the successful completion of the bid. The Report

---

[13] A broad consensus, with some divergences, as will be seen.
[14] Directive on Takeover Bids, 2004/25/EC, OJ 2004, L 142/12.
[15] COM (88) 823 final – SYN 186; 16 February 1989.
[16] COM (95) 655 final; 95/0341 (COD) 7 February 1996.
[17] For the Report of the High-Level Group of Company Law Experts on Issues Related to Takeover Bids, see http://ec.europa.eu/internal_market/company/docs/takeoverbids/2002-01-hlg-pressrelease_en.pdf.

focused[18] on the desirability of implementing two main principles in both stages of the bid: (i) that in the event of a takeover bid, the ultimate decision must be with the shareholders; (ii) that there should be proportionality between risk-bearing and control, so that only risk-bearing capital should carry control rights, in proportion to the risk carried.

With respect to the first stage of a bid, the Directive would require the board of the offeree to be 'neutral'[19] after the bid has been announced (a revolutionary proposal in some European countries). As regards the second stage, a bidder who acquires 75% should be allowed to 'break through' mechanisms and structures in the constitution of the company which would otherwise frustrate the bid by denying control (another revolutionary proposal). Neither of these ideas can have been popular among industrialists in some of the Nordic countries, particularly Germany and the Netherlands, where elaborate devices are often in place to protect incumbent management from a hostile bidder. On a wide spectrum of human ingenuity, these range from the simple concept of shares with voting uplift to the esoteric legally robotic devices of the Netherlands whereby a kind of guardian foundation offshore will automatically react to defend a target against the bid by, for instance, issuing a steady trickle of shares to supporters of the management.

On 2 October 2002, the European Commission published its renewed proposal for a Directive[20] stating that it had taken 'broad account' of the recommendations in the Winter Report but making it clear that they were not taking up all the recommendations. Thhis proposal had a rough ride thereafter and underwent many amendments. By 28 April 2003, the proposal had acquired the title 'the Revised Presidency Compromise Proposal'.[21] Throughout the summer of 2003 the fortunes of the proposal waxed and waned in various committees and meetings, sustained by what became known as the 'Portuguese option' whereby versions of the controversial breakthrough rights were made optional for member states, in effect creating a two-track regulatory policy for Europe. In November 2003, agreement was finally reached and the Directive formally adopted on 21 April 2004, coming into force at the end of that month. Article 21 of the Directive makes it clear that member states have until 20 May 2006 to bring the Directive into force in their own lands. By the start of 2006, it was clear that the UK Company Law Reform Bill (later to be re-named the Companies Bill) would not have completed the Parliamentary process by 20 May 2006 and so the UK Government decided that regulations would be enacted under powers of the European Communities Act 1972 to implement the Directive on an interim basis in time to meet the implementation deadline.[22] On 2 May 2006, the Government published the Takeovers Directive (Interim Implementation) Regulations 2006 (and Explanatory Memorandum thereon). These regulations came into force on 20 May 2006 and placed the Panel on a statutory footing for certain offers on an interim basis pending implementation of the takeover provisions in the Companies Act 2006. As will be seen below,[23] since then, the Directive has been implemented in the UK by means of a combination of statutory

---

[18] It also dealt with other matters which had become contentious.

[19] Sometimes referred to as 'board passivity' in European circles.

[20] Proposal for a Directive on Takeover Bids (COM) (2002) 534 final.

[21] Interinstitutional File 2002/0240 (COD).

[22] On 21 April 2006, the Panel issued a Response Statement on the amendments to the Takeover Code in order to implement the Takeovers Directive (RS2005/5).

[23] 21.4 below.

provisions in part 28 of the Companies Act 2006 (ss. 942–992) and amendments to the Takeover Code. The Companies Act (Unregistered Companies) Regulations 2007 extended certain provisions of the Act concerning takeover to unregistered companies.

## B The ideas in the Takeovers Directive

An examination of the stated objectives of the Directive can be a useful summary of the aims which a regime of takeover regulation might usefully seek to achieve. The 1st and 3rd Recitals to the Preamble to the Directive contain the policy of EU-wide coordination of regulation. The 2nd Recital refers to the need to 'protect the interests of holders of securities of companies '. . . when those companies are the subject of takeover bids or of changes of control and at least some of their securities are admitted to trading on a regulated market', making explicit the main thrust of the takeover policy, which is to protect shareholders of the target companies. There is also perhaps a hint of protecting the reputation of the capital markets.[24] Recital 9 contains the policy for the mandatory offer: 'Whereas Member States should take the necessary steps in order to protect holders of securities having minority holdings after the purchase of the control of their company . . .' Recital 5 contains the idea that member states must have a supervisory authority. Recitals 13, 14 and 16 contain extra provisions with regard to proper information in offer documents, time limits for the bid, and prohibition of frustrating action.[25]

Thus, the outlines[26] of the basic model of a regulatory system emerge: takeovers in the EU are to be subject to regulation by a supervisory authority, subject to timetables, transparency requirements and sharing of the control premium. This last point needs some further explanation.[27] The control premium arises because in an unregulated system, a purchaser seeking to acquire control of a target company will normally need to acquire around only 30% of the shares and for the last few blocks of shares which take his holding of say 25% up to 30% will be prepared to pay a price which is above the prevailing market price. This premium price is being paid because the purchaser knows that those shares are very valuable to him, because they will give him control over the company. From the regulatory standpoint the problem with this is that most of the shareholders do not get a chance to get a share of the premium that is being paid when control passes and thus some system of ensuring that they do share is needed. The UK system and that to some extent adopted in the Directive is to have a requirement that the purchaser who has acquired control must extend his offer to all the shareholders of the company. An underlying policy may also be that a company should not be able to take over a target merely by acquiring around 30% of its shares and it should be a company with sufficient means to buy the whole of the target issued share capital.

---

[24] The 12th Recital, aiming to 'reduce the scope for insider dealing . . .' contains a more overt protection of capital markets provision.
[25] Overall, the Preamble is curiously thin on economic rationale, unlike most of the other Capital Markets Directives. There is no mention of other recognised goals of takeover regulation, such as encouraging efficient allocation of resources, encouraging competition for corporate control and monitoring management, although these must surely underlie the Directive, even if they are unstated; of course, the statement of such objectives might have been politically difficult.
[26] The Directive also deals with many other matters.
[27] The prohibition on frustrating action is examined below in connection with defences.

What does the Directive say about the much debated 'breakthrough rights'? As heralded above, there is an option. Article 12 is headed 'Optional Arrangements' and provides that member states 'may reserve the right not to require companies [. . .], which have their registered offices within their territories to apply Article 9(2) and (3) and/or Article 11'. And in those articles we find enshrined the essence of an open market for corporate control: prohibition on frustrating action by the board in circumstances of a bid (art. 9),[28] and restrictions on arrangements designed to deny control to a successful bidder (art. 11).[29] On this crucial policy issue the Directive thus creates a two-track regulatory environment across the EU.[30]

A full review of the Directive[31] was expected to take place in 2011 but was finally delayed until 2012 due to other European financial regulation issues arising from the banking and the credit crises of 2007–2008. The External Study on the application of the Directive was carried out, on behalf of the Commission, by Marccus Partners, in cooperation with the Centre for European Policy Studies.[32] Their Assessment Report concluded that the Directive had been transposed in all of the 22 member states they considered and that no substantial compliance issues had emerged. For instance, as far as the Board Neutrality Rule (art. 9) and the Breakthrough Rule (art. 11) are concerned, their analysis found that, as of 2012, 19 member states applied the Board Neutrality Rule (i.e. had not opted out of art. 9), and that only Estonia applied the Breakthrough Rule in full.

In its subsequent Report[33] to the European Parliament and the European Council dated 26 June 2012, the European Commission advised that 'the operation of the [Directive] show[ed] that, generally, the regime created by the Directive [was] working satisfactory. No structural compliance issues ha[d] emerged in relation to the application of the legal framework in the Member States.'[34] At the same time, it noted that 'there [were] areas where the rules of the [Directive] could merit some clarification in order to improve legal certainty for the parties concerned and the effective exercise of (minority) shareholder rights.'[35] Other areas that, in the view of the European Commission, may need further consideration included: the concept of 'acting in concert'; whether provisions are needed to ensure better engagement with employee representatives; any possible improvements to the provisions regarding takeover defences; and whether steps should be taken to discourage bidders from circumventing the mandatory offer rule. As far as the Board Neutrality and the Breakthrough Rules are concerned, no changes to the opt-out arrangements were envisaged

---

[28] This has been implemented in the UK in the Takeover Code (r. 21, subject to amendments in the new Code).
[29] This has been implemented in the UK in the Companies Act 2006 ss. 966–972. Companies with voting shares traded on a regulated market may opt in to these breakthrough provisions should they wish to do so.
[30] For further commentary on this and other aspects of the Directive, see 21.6 below.
[31] For an examination of how the implementation of the Directive changed the takeover rules applicable to European companies see, P.L. Davies, E.P. Schuster and E. Van de Walle de Ghelcke 'The Takeover Directive as a Protectionist Tool?' (17 February 2010), ECGI – Law Working Paper No. 141/2010, at http://ssrn.com/abstract=1554616.
[32] http://ec.europa.eu/internal_market/company/docs/takeoverbids/study/study_en.pdf
[33] The Report from the European Commission on the application of the Takeover Directive is available at http://ec.europa.eu/internal_market/company/docs/takeoverbids/COM2012_347_en.pdf.
[34] See http://ec.europa.eu/internal_market/company/docs/takeoverbids/COM2012_347_en.pdf, para 21. See also, G. Tsagas, 'The Revision of the EU Takeover Directive in Light of the 2011 UK Takeover Law Reform: Regulation and Supervision of Takeovers in an EU in Crisis *International and Comparative Corporate Law Journal* (3 July, 2012) vol. 10, no. 1, 2013: http://ssrn.com/abstract=2098938.
[35] *Ibid.*, at para 22.

by the European Commission. However, some authors still maintain that this needs to be re-thought because there are strong arguments in favour of making the rule mandatory.[36]

## 21.4 The UK system

### A The Takeover Panel

Following implementation of the Takeover Directive in the UK, the Takeover Code has gained statutory effect.[37] It is issued and enforced by the Panel, which compromises a select body of representatives mainly from those financial institutions primarily engaged in the business of takeovers and certain other relevant bodies. The Panel's statutory functions are set out under Chapter 1 of Part 28 of the Companies Act 2006.[38]

### B The Panel's main powers[39]

First, the Panel makes rules giving effect to certain articles of the Directive and may make other provisions for or in connection with the regulation of takeover bids (ss. 942–943). Likewise, it gives rulings on interpretation, application or effect of the City Code (s. 945) as well as directions (s. 946). The Code Committee carries out the rule-making functions of the Panel and is responsible for keeping the Code under review and issuing amendments to those parts. To perform its duties, the Panel has the power to require documents and information (ss. 947–949). It is also responsible for enforcing the rules contained in the Code. The Panel has power to order compensation in circumstances where a rule requiring the payment of money has been breached (s. 954) and to apply to the court to enforce its rulings and directions (s. 955). It can also impose a range of sanctions upon persons who breach its rules, including reporting conduct to other regulatory authorities such as the Financial Conduct Authority ('FCA').

In the past, the practically binding but non-legal effect of the Takeover Code enabled the Panel to operate with great flexibility. It was available to the parties for consultation on the applicability and meaning of the Takeover Code and, in making speedy decisions, gave effect to the spirit rather than the letter of the rules.[40] However, even at the time when

---

[36] See K.J. Hopt, 'Takeover Defenses in Europe: A Comparative, Theoretical and Policy Analysis' *Columbia Journal of European Law* (2014) vol. 20.2, 249–282. For a more general discussion, see B. Clarke 'The Takeover Directive: Is a Little Regulation Better Than No Regulation?' *European Law Journal* (2009) vol. 15.

[37] Thus, changing its historical position which had no statutory or other legal authority.

[38] As mentioned above under 21.3A, the Panel had statutory powers since 20 May 2006. Part 28 extended the Panel's statutory powers to cover all takeovers, rather than only those within the scope of the Takeover Directive. For a review of Part 28 see T. Matthews 'Part 28 of the Companies Act 2006' (2007) 28 Comp Lawyer 40.

[39] Further details if required can be found on www.thetakeoverpanel.org.uk.

[40] The importance and meaning of the Panel's 'flexible' approach has been usefully summarised by Amour and Skeel as follows: '[T]he flexibility of the Panel's approach means that it is able to adjust its regulatory responses both to the particular parties before it, and to the changing dynamics of business within the City of London. Takeover participants are expected to comply with the "spirit" as well as the letter of the Code, on which they are expected to seek guidance from the Panel. Because they are actively engaged with the parties, the Panel's Executive are able to tailor the regulatory requirements (outlining compliance conditions or waiving rules, as appropriate) to the circumstances of a particular case. Moreover, the Panel's Code Committee is charged with regular and proactive updating of the Code's provisions to reflect changes in the marketplace.' See J. Amour and D.A. Skeel 'Who Writes the Rules for Hostile Takeovers, and Why? – The Peculiar Divergence of US and UK Takeover Regulation' (2007) 95 *Georgetown Law Journal* 1727, 1745.

the Takeover Code was self-regulatory in the sense that those engaged in the takeover industry were by and large the people who had an input into the content and operation of the Code, it has nevertheless not been voluntary. There have been considerable practical pressures which have made compliance with the Code essential.

Historically (until the transfer of its 'competent authority' functions to the then FSA (now the FCA) as the UKLA in 2000), the London Stock Exchange lent its support to the Panel, and the Takeover Code, even to the extent of suspending the listing of a company.[41]

Before the relevant sections in the Companies Act 2006 came into effect, the courts generally expressed approval of the City Code and its administration and even though judicial review of Panel decisions was possible, it was done in such a way as not to undermine the Panel's authority in the particular case, merely being declaratory of the position for the future. With the aim of not interfering with the outcome of the bid, the relationship of the courts with the Panel has been expressed to be 'historic rather than contemporaneous'.[42] The result of this attitude was that takeover battles in the UK were largely immune from tactical litigation designed to thwart the bid, and thus were left open for the outcome to be freely determined by market forces and the economics of the situation. The experience of the US with its public systems of legal regulation of takeovers has been that the outcome of takeovers is often in the hands of the lawyers rather than the shareholders.[43] In 1986, a new form of support for the self-regulatory regime emerged. Under the partially self-regulatory system established by the Financial Services Act 1986, support was given to the Panel and the Takeover Code. For instance, in the Securities and Futures Authority's ('SFA') conduct of business ('COB') rules, there was one rule[44] in a section headed 'Market Integrity, Support of the Takeover Panel's Functions'. Breach of that rule could lead to an SFA disciplinary hearing, with possible expulsion from the SFA and consequent withdrawal of authorisation to conduct investment business. The FSA 1986 has now been replaced by the FSMA 2000 which has ushered in a new version of this kind of support for the Panel, containing a redefinition of the relationship which the statutory regulator, then the FSA, now the FCA, has with the Panel.

The new relationship is set out in a number of places. First, the FCA Handbook.[45] Secondly, s. 354 of the FSMA 2000 states that the FCA must take such steps as it considers appropriate to cooperate with 'other persons . . . who have functions . . . similar to those of the Authority' (i.e. the Panel). Indeed, cooperation and an information sharing relationship seem to characterise the new relationship between the FCA and the Panel. For

---

[41] See the account of the St Piran saga by G. Morse 'Attempting to Enforce a Mandatory Bid' [1980] JBL 358.

[42] *R v Panel on Takeovers and Mergers, ex parte Datafin* (1987) 3 BCC 10; *R v Panel on Takeovers and Mergers, ex p Guinness plc* [1990] 1 QB 146, [1989] 1 All ER 509, CA; *R v Panel on Takeover and Mergers, ex p Fayed* [1992] BCLC 938, CA.

[43] See, e.g., Langevoort's analysis of board duties in a takeover situation and his account of associated litigation, in 'The Law's Influence on Managers' Behaviour in Control Transactions: An American Perspective' in K. Hopt and E. Wymeersch (eds) *European Takeovers – Law and Practice* (London: Butterworths, 1992) at p. 255.

[44] Rule 48 provided: '(1) A firm must not act or continue to act for a specified person . . . in connection with a takeover . . . unless it has the consent of the Takeover Panel. (2) Subject to the provisions of the Takeover Code, a firm must (a) provide . . . such information as the Takeover Panel requests . . . and (b) otherwise render all such assistance as the firm is reasonably able to provide to enable the Takeover Panel to perform its functions.'

[45] Market Conduct, MAR 4: Support of the Takeover Panel's Functions. See https://www.handbook.fca.org.uk/handbook/MAR/4/3.html. It should be noted that since 05/02/2007 the endorsement section itself is not in force anymore; nonetheless, the sections regarding the support of the Panel's functions are in force.

example, under s. 950 of the Companies Act 2006 the Panel must, to the extent it has the power to do so, take such steps as it considers appropriate to cooperate with the FCA, other supervisory authorities designated for the purposes of the Directive and regulators outside the UK having functions similar to the FCA or to the Panel.[46]

## C The operation of the Takeover Code

The Takeover Code applies to offers for all public companies (listed or unlisted) resident in the UK.[47] It also applies to offers for certain resident private companies which have in some way been involved in public markets, but only where certain requirements are also satisfied.[48] It is made clear that 'offer' in this context includes partial offers, offers by a parent for shares in its subsidiary and certain other transactions where control of a company is to be obtained or consolidated (s. 3 (b), Introduction to the Code). The Takeover Code comprises six general principles and 38 detailed rules with notes, together with an introduction, definitions and appendices. The overall aim is to ensure that all shareholders are treated fairly and equally in relation to takeovers and are not denied an opportunity to decide on the merits of a takeover.[49] Part of the mechanism for doing this lies in the orderly framework and timetable which the Code lays down, designed to prevent shareholders from being panicked into accepting an offer without time to consult their financial advisers. Great emphasis is laid on equality and high standards of information, both in offer documents and in advertisements and announcements.

One of the striking features of the Takeover Code is the acceptance condition, which is contained in rule 10. Rule 10 regulates what the Code refers to as the 'voluntary offer', that is to say, the normal case,[50] such as where a company wishes to make a full takeover bid for the target company and has gone ahead and done so. Rule 10 imposes an acceptance condition. It provides that it must be a condition of an offer[51] which 'if accepted in full,

---

[46] See also s. 12 of the Introduction to the Takeover Code. Further, there are Operation Guidelines agreed between the FCA and the Panel. These Guidelines are intended to assist the FCA and the Panel when considering cases of possible market misconduct which are, or could be, of mutual interest to the FCA and the Panel. See http://www.fca.org.uk/static/documents/operating-guidelines-takeover-panel.pdf.

[47] And in some cases outside the UK (i.e. applies to a limited extent to European Economic Area ('EEA') countries), 'residence' to be determined by the Panel; see Takeover Code, Introduction, s. 3.

[48] See generally Takeover Code, Introduction, s. 3 (a). Offers for private companies falling outside the definitions there are not wholly unregulated and in some circumstances an offer document may fall within the financial promotion regime; see Chapter 18, 18.2E above. Post the Directive, the Panel's jurisdiction has been extended to both companies and transactions covered by the Directive and to other companies and transactions not covered by the Directive which the Panel previously regulated. All companies that have their registered office in the UK, the Channel Islands or the Isle of Man and which have any of their securities admitted to trading on a regulated market in the UK or on a stock exchange in the Channel Islands or the Isle of Man, are subject to the Panel's jurisdiction. Previously, the Panel only had jurisdiction over these companies if their central place of management was also in the UK, the Channel Islands or the Isle of Man. The Panel has jurisdiction over companies which satisfy the residency test, but the Directive also contains complicated rules for shared jurisdiction over the regulation of an offer where the target company has its registered office in one EEA state but has its securities admitted to trading on the regulated markets of one or more other EEA states.

[49] Section 2 (a) of the Introduction to the Code.

[50] The term 'voluntary offer' is used to distinguish the 'mandatory offer' which is discussed below. Although an actual mandatory offer is a rare event, this fact should not be allowed to obscure the importance of the existence of the provisions which require the mandatory offer in certain circumstances.

[51] For other transferable securities carrying voting rights. The Panel may waive the rule in certain circumstances.

would result in the offeror holding shares carrying over 50 per cent of the voting rights of the offeree company[52] that the offer will not become or be declared unconditional as to acceptances, unless the offeror has acquired or agreed to acquire[53] . . . shares carrying over 50 per cent of the voting rights . . .' What this means, in effect, is that the offeror not only has a get-out if the bid has failed to win him *de jure* control[54] of the company, but also that there is a requirement that he give up and admit defeat. This is only clear in the light of some further explanation. The basic mechanism of the voluntary bid is that the offeror will make an offer to the shareholders of the target. Under the terms of the Takeover Code, the offer must remain open for at least 21 days.[55] During that period the target shareholders will send in their indications to the offeror's receiving agents as to whether they wish to accept or not. The offeror makes the contract binding once he announces that the offer is 'unconditional as to acceptances', meaning that his acceptance of the tenders is no longer subject to any condition.[56] By this rule 10 mechanism, the Takeover Code seeks to ensure both that the offeror is not stuck with a bid which has failed, in the sense that it has left him with 45%, and also that he is not permitted to try to run the company from that position. Perhaps an equally important feature of the Takeover Code, and certainly the one for which it is most famous internationally, is the mandatory bid requirement. The policy which lies behind this has already been explained.[57] A mandatory offer will be required in two situations:[58] (1) where any person acquires[59] shares which[60] carry 30% or more of the voting rights of a company; (2) where any person[61] holding not less than 30% but not more than 50% of the voting rights acquires[62] additional shares which increase his percentage of the voting rights.[63] The details of the mandatory offer are set out in rule 9. In essence, an offer must be made to the shareholders,[64] and it must be in cash[65] at not less than the highest price paid by the offeror[66] for shares of that class during the offer period and within 12 months prior to its commencement.[67]

---

[52] I.e. it is not a bid for a small block of shares.

[53] Either pursuant to the offer or otherwise.

[54] I.e. more than 50% of the votes.

[55] Rule 31.1.

[56] I.e. as to his getting 50.1% of the votes. Although if the 90% acceptance condition is satisfied, the offeror is not required to make a declaration.

[57] See 21.3B above.

[58] Takeover Code, r. 9.1.

[59] Whether by a series of transactions over a period of time or not.

[60] Taken together with shares held or acquired by persons acting in concert with him; for a discussion of 'acting in concert', see r. 9.1, note.

[61] Together with persons acting in concert with him.

[62] Such acquisition may be by the person or any person acting in concert with him.

[63] This is for the July 2000 version of the Code, and subsequent versions. Earlier versions permitted a 'creeping' increase in the holding.

[64] Various classes: equity shares voting or non-voting, and voting non-equity shares; see Takeover Code, r. 9.1.

[65] Or accompanied by a cash alternative; see r. 9.5.

[66] Or any person acting in concert with it.

[67] There are various other conditions, including a rule about the circumstances in which the offer must become unconditional as to acceptances; see City Code, rule 9.3. On the merits and demerits of the mandatory bid, see S. Sepe, 'Private Sale of Corporate Control: Why the European Mandatory Bid Rule is Inefficient' (13 August 2010) Arizona Legal Studies Discussion Paper No. 10–29, available at SSRN http://ssrn.com/abstract=1086321; E.P. Schuster, 'The Mandatory Bid Rule: Efficient, After All?' (2013) 76 MLR 529.

## D Other provisions applying to takeovers

In addition to the disclosure requirements under rule 8 of the Code, the requirements of the UKLA rules may also be relevant.[68] Companies subject to the Listing Rules will need to comply with its detailed provisions regarding takeovers.[69] The Code defines the UKLA rules as including not only the listing rules but also the disclosure and transparency rules and the prospectus rules of the FCA (or any of them as the context may require).[70] Under the Enterprise and Regulatory Reform Act 2013, a merger is liable to be referred to the Competition and Markets Authority (CMA)[71] if certain conditions are satisfied, and it will then be for the CMA to decide whether there is a substantial lessening of competition.[72] Certain large mergers above the prescribed financial thresholds and having a 'Community Dimension' are required to be notified to the European Commission which will have exclusive jurisdiction and which may then eventually prohibit such mergers.[73] Rule 12 of the Takeover Code recognises the significance to certain takeovers of these reference and notification requirements since it provides that it must be a term of an offer that it will lapse if there is a reference to the CMA or if the European Commission initiates proceedings (or takes certain other actions).

Various legislative provisions may have significance for certain takeovers, not necessarily applying only to takeovers which fall under the scope of the Takeover Code. Most of these have been considered in detail elsewhere and are merely listed here. Sections 611–613 of the Companies Act 2006 provide relief for share premium accounts in certain takeover situations.[74] Sections 678–683 of the Companies Act 2006 prohibit financial assistance for the acquisition of shares, which may sometimes have relevance in the takeover context. Part 22 of the Companies Act 2006 relates to disclosure of interests in shares.[75] Sections 215–225 of the Companies Act 2006 (Part 10, Payments for loss of office) will apply to payments made to directors in some takeover situations.[76] Insider dealing legislation will often be relevant. If the offeror company is allotting shares as part of the takeover, this will of itself activate various legal considerations; e.g. ss. 595(1) and (2) of the Companies Act 2006. Finally, reference should be made here to the complex provisions in ss. 974–991 of the Companies Act 2006 (Part 28, Chapter 3, 'Squeeze out' and 'Sell out'), under which in some circumstances an offeror who acquires 90% of shares to which the offer relates and 90% of the voting rights carried by those shares (this is a slightly different test (dual test) to that under the previous regime), may compulsorily buy out or be required to buy out the remaining 10%.[77]

---

[68] Note 13 on rule 8 of the Code.
[69] In particular, Chapter 10.
[70] See https://www.handbook.fca.org.uk/handbook/DTR.pdf.
[71] See the CMA Guidance on Mergers, at https://www.gov.uk/government/uploads/system/uploads/attachment_data/file/384055/CMA2__Mergers__Guidance.pdf.
[72] The test is now one of competition, i.e. 'significantly impeded effective competition' and not 'public interest', the latter is broader and less clear cut. Quite helpfully, the CMA publishes online all the mergers it has reviewed since its inception. See https://www.gov.uk/topic/competition/mergers.
[73] European Community Merger Regulation, Council Regulation No. 139/2004.
[74] See further Chapter 13, 13.3 above.
[75] See Chapter 13, 13.F 2 and 4 above.
[76] See Chapter 9 above.
[77] There are further technical changes from the previous regime, for instance, the timing for the giving of a squeeze-out notice has changed.

Although litigation is rare in the context of UK takeovers, the courts have occasionally become involved in making pronouncements about various aspects of takeover regulation and so a small body of law has grown up. Some aspects of this have already been mentioned; e.g. judicial review of the decisions of the Panel. However, many aspects of company law have sometimes been relevant in takeover situations. In particular, the courts have had to consider the duties owed by directors of the target company in the context of, for instance, conflicting or competing bids.[78]

## E Defences

Takeover defences in the UK are heavily circumscribed by what seems to be a prevailing attitude among financial institutions and business that hostile bids are beneficial and even if not actually encouraged, they should not be stifled.[79] Some of the economic arguments on this topic have already been alluded to.[80] The salient fact is that the bid will be at a price which is higher than the current market price for the shares and the feeling is that the shareholders should not be deprived of an opportunity of taking up the offer.

Prior to the bid being made, boards of directors no doubt consider various possibilities for putting themselves into the best possible position (1) to discourage a predator from mounting a bid and (2) to win the takeover battle if it starts. Whatever they choose to do will obviously have to comply with their general duties (under Part 10 of the Companies Act 2006).[81] This has usually been thought to rule out devices like 'poison pills' which have been a recurrent feature of US takeover battles. A poison pill is an arrangement which becomes financially damaging once a company is taken over. The predator, who has taken over the company, will therefore have swallowed the pill. As an anti-takeover device it is obviously necessary for the predator to be aware of the pill's existence prior to making a bid so that he decides not to go ahead. A typical poison pill would be a warrant issued to target shareholders which gives them rights to subscribe for further shares in the target at half the prevailing market price if any predator company gets a controlling stake in the target.[82] Although this is primarily a post-bid defence, the preparation for it, possibly involving restructuring[83] so as to make it difficult for a particular likely predator to avoid a merger reference, is a pre-bid defence mechanism.

---

[78] See *Heron International Ltd v Lord Grade* [1983] BCLC 244; *Re a Company 008699/85* (1986) 2 BCC 99,024; *Dawson plc v Coats Patons* (1988) 4 BCC 305 and generally *Gething v Kilner* [1972] 1 All ER 1166.

[79] For an examination of the North American position, see J. Lowry 'Monitoring Defensive Tactics Against Takeover Bids – The Role of the Ontario Securities Commission' [1994] JBL 99; J. Lowry 'Poison Pills in U.S. Corporations – A Re-examination' [1992] JBL 337 and A. Seretakis 'Hostile Takeovers and Defensive Mechanisms in the United Kingdom and the United States: A Case Against the United States Regime' (26 October 2013) *The Ohio State Entrepreneurial Business Law Journal*, vol. 8, no. 2, 2013, available at SSRN: http://ssrn.com/abstract=2345718.

[80] See 21.2 above.

[81] For a fascinating (and rare) example of UK litigation on the legality of poison pills, see *Criterion Properties plc v Stratford UK Properties LLC* [2002] 2 BCLC 151, [2003] BCC 50, CA, [2004] BCC 570, HL.

[82] It should be questioned whether under s. 51 of the Enterprise Act 2002, where the statutory deadline for merger inquiries is now 24 weeks (also, an extension of up to 8 weeks is available in special circumstances), this is still possible.

[83] I.e. if a particular predator is identified, a target company could take on a subsidiary business which would put the predator in danger of a reference, were it to mount a bid.

It is the orthodox view that the most effective method of preventing a bid is a well-run company with a high share price. The economics of this make it relatively difficult for the bidder to come up with a higher offer price, or to want to. The corollary of this is the painful fact that if the share price is low and the company appears not to be well run, then there may well not be a great deal which can be done.

After the bid has been made, the position of the target board is governed by general principle 3 and rule 21 of the Takeover Code, which prevent activities that can generally be described as frustrating action. Additionally, it can usually be said that the timetable under the Takeover Code leaves very little time to mount much by way of defence unless preparations have been made beforehand. Often the most that a target board can do at this stage is to issue reports and interim accounts showing how things are going to improve in the near future. But the tone and quality of such documents is controlled by the Takeover Code, rule 19. And usually the fact will remain that, faced with an offer at a significant premium to the current share price, the target board faces an unbridgeable credibility gap; the predator has effectively said to target shareholders that the target management is no good and that the company's share price is depressed as a result, and has backed its statement with its offer.

In October 2010, the Panel Executive publicly criticised Kraft Foods Inc. ('Kraft') for its failure to meet the standard required under rule 19.1 of the Takeover Code in respect of statements made during its takeover bid for Cadbury plc ('Cadbury').[84] Public criticism is one of the disciplinary measures available to the Panel; a public criticism had last been issued in 2007. Rule 19.1 provides that 'Each document, announcement or other information published, or statement made, during the course of an offer must be prepared with the highest standards of care and accuracy.'

During its bid for Cadbury, Kraft had stated, on the basis of an honest and genuine belief, that it could keep operational one of Cadbury's factories located in Somerdale. In its statement, the Executive observed that rule 19.1 was of 'great importance' and 'fundamental to ensuring the orderly conduct of takeovers'[85] and that where a party to an offer makes a statement of belief of the kind made by Kraft, rule 19.1 required 'not only that the party concerned honestly and genuinely holds that belief (a subjective test) but also that it has a reasonable basis for so holding that belief (an objective test)'.[86] The Executive accepted that Kraft held an honest and genuine belief that it could keep Somerdale operational. However, the Panel found that Kraft did not have a reasonable basis for holding this view because it did not know the details of Cadbury's phased closure of Somerdale.[87] Moreover, Kraft did not seek further information, or take the opportunity to take mitigating action in respect of its statements when it learned, from Cadbury representatives, that the phased closure of Somerdale was well advanced.[88] Following these affairs DBIS published a report on the takeover of Cadbury by Kraft,[89] and launched a formal consultation in October 2010, discussed next.

---

[84] The course of events before and during the bid are usefully summarised in B. Clarke 'Reviewing Takeover Regulation in the Wake of the Cadbury Requisition – Regulation in a Twirl' (2011) JBL 299.
[85] http://www.thetakeoverpanel.org.uk/wp-content/uploads/2009/12/2010-14.pdf, p. 3.
[86] *Ibid*, p. 4.
[87] *Ibid.*
[88] *Ibid.*, pp. 4–5.
[89] Business, Innovation and Skills Committee – Ninth Report, Mergers, Acquisitions and Takeovers: the takeover of Cadbury by Kraft (October 2000), at http://www.publications.parliament.uk/pa/cm200910/cmselect/cmbis/234/23402.htm.

## F The aftermath of the Kraft takeover and recent review and amendments to the Takeover Code

### 1 *The Panel's Code Committee review*

Kraft's takeover of Cadbury in 2009–2010 triggered significant public debate in the UK, in particular about whether the regulatory regime meant that it was too easy for a hostile bidder to gain control of a UK target.[90] In June 2010, the Code Committee of the Takeover Panel ('the Code Committee') issued a preliminary consultation paper on key aspects of the regulation of UK takeovers.[91] The radical proposals on which it sought views included raising the minimum acceptance threshold to 66% and disenfranchising holders of shares purchased during an offer period. In October 2010, the Panel rejected these specific proposals in a public statement,[92] but set out a number of significant proposed changes to the Takeover Code relating to virtual bids, deal protection measures, increased disclosure of fees and financing arrangements, and greater rights for employees. This was followed by the issue in March 2011 of a consultation paper[93] which sought comments on the detail of the proposed Code changes. The consultation paper did not contain any changes of principle from the proposals set out in the October 2010 statement. The response statement,[94] published in July 2011, contained the final form of the changes to the Code in force from 19 September 2011.[95] Again, there have been no fundamental changes to the proposals made in the March consultation paper although there have been more changes in the detail. In its response the Panel stated that it received a number of responses from the pension fund industry suggesting that target company pension scheme trustees should be entitled to receive information on a potential bid and be permitted to circulate their opinion about the bid. The Panel said that these suggestions were outside the scope of its consultation process but it intended to consider them in due course. The Panel also noted that, given the significance of the changes, it intended to review the operation of the amendments not less than 12 months after implementation, subject to the level of bid activity.[96]

### 2 *Recent review and amendments to the Takeover Code*

On 19 September 2011, the Panel implemented amendments to the Takeover Code adopted by the Code Committee following its review in 2010 of certain aspects of the regulation of

---

[90] That was reflected in the national press. See, for example, http://www.bbc.co.uk/news/business-13498203; and http://www.telegraph.co.uk/finance/comment/tracycorrigan/7029357/Krafts-takeover-leaves-a-bitter-taste-in-the-mouth.html.
[91] PCP 2010/2 issues on 1 June 2010: http://www.thetakeoverpanel.org.uk/wp-content/uploads/2008/11/PCP201002.pdf.
[92] PS 2010/22 at: http://www.thetakeoverpanel.org.uk/wp-content/uploads/2009/12/2010-221.pdf.
[93] See Public Consultation Paper PCP 2011/1, available at http://www.thetakeoverpanel.org.uk/wp-content/uploads/2008/11/PCP201101.pdf.
[94] See http://www.thetakeoverpanel.org.uk/wp-content/uploads/2008/11/RS201101.pdf.
[95] These additions to the Code are available at http://www.thetakeoverpanel.org.uk/; for implementation and transitional arrangements see http://www.thetakeoverpanel.org.uk/wp-content/uploads/2008/11/transitionalarrangements.pdf.
[96] *Ibid.* para. 1.13.

takeover bids.[97] There were four major objectives behind the 2011 Amendments:[98] (a) to increase the protection for offeree companies (i.e. targets) against protracted 'virtual bid' periods by requiring potential offerors (i.e. bidders): (i) to be identified in the announcement which commences an offer period; and (ii) to announce either a firm intention to make an offer or that they do not intend to make an offer by the 28th day following the date on which they are first identified (or by any extended deadline); (b) to strengthen the position of the offeree company by: (i) prohibiting deal protection measures and inducement fees, other than in certain limited cases; and (ii) clarifying that offeree company boards are not limited in the factors that they may take into account in giving their opinion on an offer; (c) to increase transparency and improve the quality of disclosure by: (i) requiring the disclosure of offer-related fees; and (ii) requiring the disclosure of the same financial information in relation to an offeror and the financing of an offer irrespective of the nature of the offer; and (d) to provide greater recognition of the interests of offeree company employees by: (i) improving the quality of disclosure by offerors and offeree companies in relation to the offeror's intentions regarding the offeree company and its employees; and (ii) improving the ability of employee representatives to make their views known.

Another amendment was the introduction into the Code of a new 'put up or shut up' ('PUSU') deadline, bidder naming and anti-break fee rules in order to strengthen the position of targets and increase the protection for targets against protracted 'virtual bid' periods.[99] At the same time, certain dispensations would allow a target that wished to conduct an auction for its own shares by way of a formal sale process ('FSP') to (i) do so without the participants being required to be publicly named and being subject to a PUSU deadline, and (ii) to agree to pay the eventual FSP 'winner' a break fee in certain circumstances (FSP dispensations).

Since September 2011, traditional break fees (i.e. payable from a target to a bidder) and all other forms of deal protection which impose obligations on a target in the UK have also been subject to a general prohibition under the Takeover Code. Such deal related arrangements are only permitted, with the consent of the Panel, in certain very limited circumstances, such as when a target company is seeking to encourage a competing offer following receipt of a hostile bid or in a formal sale process.[100]

In November 2012, the Panel reviewed its 2011 amendments and concluded that it '*[did] not intend to propose any immediate changes*' to the rules and will instead keep a number of provisions under review.[101] According to the report, the number of 'virtual bid'

---

[97] The final form of the 2011 Amendments was confirmed in Response Statement 2011/1 ('RS 2011/1') on 21 July 2011, available at http://www.thetakeoverpanel.org.uk/wp-content/uploads/2012/01/2012-8.pdf.
[98] See http://www.thetakeoverpanel.org.uk/wp-content/uploads/2012/01/2012-8.pdf , pp. 1–2.
[99] The PUSU deadline means that companies planning a takeover must make a firm offer within 28 days after expressing their interest in a target company. Bidding companies must be identified in the announcement which begins any offer period, while financial information about the bidder and its plans for the bid must also be disclosed.
[100] For further analysis of reverse break fees in UK public takeovers, see G. Fairfield, 'Reverse Break Fees in UK Public Takeovers', Herbert Smith Freehills LLP (6 February 2016).
[101] The Takeover Panel, *Review of the 2011 Amendments to the Takeover Code* (2012/8, November 2012), para 9.2. For an assessment by a law firm a year after the reform took place, see Clifford Chance 'Impact of the UK Takeover Code Reform: One Year On' (18 September 2012), at http://www.cliffordchance.com/briefings/2012/09/impact_of_uk_takeovercodereformoneyearon.html.

periods involving market rumours, speculation or share price fluctuations had fallen since the new regime came into force, while the number of offer periods that began with a firm offer announcement rose over the same period.[102] The new requirement for the identity of potential bidders to be disclosed had resulted in a decrease in the amount of leaks of such information, while at the same time the Panel did not see any 'significant reduction' in activity over the year despite concerns that bidders might be put off from approaching target companies by the disclosure requirements.[103] The Panel said that the introduction of PUSU periods had successfully allowed target companies to control the period of 'uncertainty and disruption' leading up to a formal takeover announcement.[104]

Target companies may apply to the Panel for an extension of the deadline where necessary. According to its figures, the Panel extended deadlines following such a request on 15 occasions over the review period.[105] It did not refuse a request for a deadline extension by the board of a target company during this period.[106] The new general ban on 'deal protection measures',[107] inducement fees and any other arrangements between a bidder and the target company during or immediately before an offer period had also generally achieved its objectives, the report said.[108] The ban was intended to reduce the tactical advantages that bidding companies were able to obtain over target companies. However, the Panel noted several examples of scenarios in which parties and their advisers had used 'cooperation agreements' to go beyond narrow exceptions contained in the revised Takeover Code, such as restrictions on the target company's ability to make announcements or communicate with shareholders in relation to the offer, or commitments by the target company not to publish documentation without the bidder's approval.[109] The Panel also noted that in a number of cases, shareholders of the target company who were also company directors had entered into agreements that went beyond agreements to accept or vote in favour of an offer, contrary to the Takeover Code.[110] In some cases these included agreements not to solicit competing offers, to recommend the offer to other shareholders and undertakings to notify the bidder if the director became aware of a possible competing offer.[111] The Panel noted a 'general improvement' in the quality of bidding companies' disclosures in relation to the future of a target company's employees in accordance with the new rules.[112] However, it noted that some of these had not been specific enough or instead referred to their need to 'undertake a review of the offeree company's business' following completion of the takeover. It reiterated that general statements were 'unlikely to be acceptable' where a bidding company had had the opportunity to fully consider its plans for the target company, and that if mass redundancies or similar actions took place after the takeover without disclosure beforehand this could be a 'serious breach' of the Code.[113]

---

[102] *Ibid*, para. 2.2.
[103] *Ibid*, para. 7.2.
[104] See note 98, para. 2.10.
[105] See note 98, para. 2.11.
[106] *Ibid*.
[107] Deal protection measures and inducement fees are now banned other than in certain limited cases, while offer-related fees must be disclosed.
[108] See note 98, s. 3.
[109] See note 98, para. 3.4.
[110] See note 98, para. 3.5.
[111] *Ibid*.
[112] *Ibid*, para. 3.7.
[113] *Ibid*.

With effect from 30 September 2013, the 'residency test' no longer applies for companies incorporated in the UK, the Channel Islands or the Isle of Man whose shares are admitted to trading on AIM. Therefore the Takeover Code now applies to (i) all UK public companies whose shares are traded on AIM, or any other multilateral trading facility ('MTF') including the ISDX Growth Market, regardless of whether they have their central management and control overseas, and (ii) private companies where during the relevant prior period of ten years they have (a) had any of their securities traded on a regulated market, MTF or a stock exchange in the Channel Islands or Isle of Man; or (b) publicly filed a prospectus for the offer, admission to trading or issue of securities with the registrar of companies or any other relevant authority.

On 12 September 2016, the Panel published the 12th edition of the Takeover Code, replacing in its entirety the previous edition published in September 2011 in the wake of Kraft's takeover of Cadbury. This latest edition consolidated rule changes and guidance relating to, among other things, profit forecasts and quantified financial benefits statements, post-offer undertakings and intention statements and the communication and distribution of information during an offer. Since then, there have been a number of additional developments relating to the Code and its interpretation, as follows.

On 13 April 2017, the Panel published an amended Practice Statement ('PS') No. 20.[114] This clarifies that the requirement to consult the Panel before more than six parties are approached about an offer or possible offer continues to apply during an offer period in relation to a possible offer by any potential offeror which has not been identified. If a shareholder or other relevant person is approached before the commencement of an offer period and the relevant meeting relates to a possible offer, such meeting needs to be attended by a financial adviser or corporate broker.

On 7 July 2017 the Panel published PS No. 31, which describes how and when the Executive could grant FSP dispensations and explains the way in which the Executive normally interprets and applies certain aspects of the Takeover Code in the context of FSPs or a strategic review that may result in a sale.[115] The key rules of the Code affected were rule 2 (secrecy and announcements), rule 21.2 (deal protection measures) and rule 21.3 (equality of information between bidders). The Executive intends to be more prescriptive about the application of the Code to auctions conducted by the target company.

On 19 September 2017, the Panel launched a Public Consultation on proposed amendments to rules 2.7, 19.5, 19.6, 24 and 25 of the Code. If these are finally introduced, an offeror, when making statements of intention with regard to the business, employees and pension schemes of the offeree company (and, where appropriate, of the offeror itself), would be required to make specific statements of intention with regard to the company's research and development functions, the balance of the skills and functions of the company's employees and management, and the location of the company's headquarters and headquarters' functions. In addition, the requirement for an offeror to make statements of intention would be brought forward to the time of the announcement of its firm intention

---

[114] Rule 2 – secrecy, possible offer announcements and preannouncement responsibilities.
[115] The full text of PS No. 31 is available at http://www.thetakeoverpanel.org.uk/wp-content/uploads/2008/11/PDF-of-Practice-Statement-No.31.pdf. For a full analysis of PS No. 31, see Cleary Gottlieb Steen & Hamilton 'UK Takeover Code Update: Panel Publishes Practice Statement 31: Strategic Reviews and Formal Sale Processes, 2017'.

to make an offer. While offerors and offeree companies would be required to publish reports on post-offer undertakings and post-offer intention statements given during the course of an offer, offerors must not publish an offer document for 14 days from the announcement of its firm intention to make an offer without the consent of the board of the offeree company.[116] At the time of writing the Panel is considering the responses to the formal consultation.

## 21.5 The future in the EU under the Directive

It is interesting to consider whether the implementation of the Directive, which has changed the status of the Panel, the rules and principles of the Takeover Code, will give rise to US-style litigation in the UK. These matters have been on the minds of various negotiators in Brussels ever since 1989 and a number of solutions have been built into the proposals over the years to accommodate the UK. And, indeed, versions of these are now in the Directive,[117] and in the new legislation.[118] How these will work out in practice remains to be seen, although it would be ironic if the legacy of the Directive in the UK was to increase takeover-related litigation.[119]

It is also interesting to consider what the future under the Directive might hold for Europe.[120] As has been seen, it is largely modelled on the UK's market for corporate control which, unusually for the EU, is open and competitive. Companies, even very large ones, are open to the discipline of a takeover bid. Already in recent years we have seen the opening up of the German takeover market. The hostile takeover of the German company Mannesmann™ by the UK's Vodafone, apart from being an epic battle, was a watershed

---

[116] PCP 2017/2 'The Takeover Panel' Consultation Paper issued by the Code Committee of the Panel, Statements of Intention and Related Matter (19 September 2017).

[117] For example, Recital 7 'Self-regulatory bodies should be able to exercise supervision' and art. 4.1; Recital 8 '. . . Member States should be left to determine whether rights are to be made available which may be asserted . . . in proceedings between parties to a bid' and art. 4.6.

[118] For example, the Panel retains considerable autonomy to provide for its own constitution and appointment procedures. See Explanatory Notes of the Companies Act 2006, para. 1175. In addition, ss. 945, 951, 955, 956 and 961 of the Act are intended to limit litigation by: (a) channelling parties to seek decisions of the Panel (including the Panel's Hearings Committee and the independent Takeover Appeal Board) before having recourse to the courts; (b) excluding new rights of action for breach of statutory duty; (c) protecting concluded transactions from challenge for breach of the Panel's rules; and (d) exempting the Panel and its individual members, officers and staff from liability in damages for things done in, or in connection with, the discharge of the regulatory functions of the Panel. *Ibid.* para. 1177.

[119] One of the many policy themes behind the Directive is to avoid battles in court. See T. Matthews 'Part 28 of the Companies Act 2006' 28 (2007) Comp Lawyer 240, at p. 242.

[120] A recent report on the implementation into national law of the Directive has revealed strong reluctance on the part of many member states to lift takeover barriers, with an unexpectedly large number of jurisdictions implementing the Directive in a seemingly protectionist way. The Report shows that widespread use has been made of provisions in the Directive allowing states to opt out of certain key provisions and to exempt companies from those provisions if the bidder is not subject to the same obligations. Furthermore, although the transposition deadline for the Directive expired on 20 May 2006, eight member states have not yet fully aligned their domestic legislation accordingly (Belgium, Cyprus, the Czech Republic, Estonia, Italy, the Netherlands, Poland and Spain). See *Report on Implementation of the Directive on Takeover Bids – Commission of the European Communities* SEC (2007) 268 (21 February 2007). See also 28 (2007) Comp Lawyer 179–180.

for the German corporate world. Until then, the Germans referred to their industrial set-up as 'Deutschland AG',[121] indicating that it was organised in such a way as to be impervious to hostile takeovers. The main features of this were: (1) the fact that the German banks hold large stakes in major companies and are traditionally not willing to sell to hostile bidders; (2) the secrecy of the share registers; and (3) that shares are often in the form of warrants held by the banks which will vote the shares in favour of the status quo unless instructed otherwise. The Mannesmann™ takeover revealed that the German banks were prepared to sell out to the higher offer mounted by Vodafone.[122]

It is arguable that the art. 12 option, creating as it does a two-track regulatory environment for takeovers, has made the Directive pointless.[123] This can be overstated as there are many other less controversial features of the Directive which will help to bring about a level playing field for takeovers in Europe. In the course of time it may even be seen that the art. 12 option has the effect of drawing attention to the international capital markets that the management of companies in certain countries are not willing to submit themselves to the market discipline inherent in the open takeover regime. Economic theory would then have it that because their corporate governance mechanisms are softer on them, they will find it harder (i.e. more expensive) to raise capital, and thus be 'punished in the market'. In the long run, the Directive will probably be seen as having made it harder for countries to resist an open market for corporate control.

Lastly, some features of the Directive might need to be revised.[124] But it is a Lamfalussy Directive[125] and the necessary ideas can be brought forward by the European Commission under the comitology procedures, developed by member states through the Committee of European Securities Regulators[126] and the European Securities Committee. The Takeover Directive has a long history of painstaking negotiation behind it, and in a Union which has many different corporate cultures and economic structures, it may well now be some time before it can be seen to bear any fruit, if at all.

---

[121] Deutschland Aktien Gesellschaft (i.e. Deutschland Corporation).

[122] For a critique of the German legal approach to takeovers, see G. Deipenbrock, 'The Takeover Directive and German Takeover Law – Some Fundamentals from a Market and Sustainable Development Perspective' (5 March 2013) University of Oslo Faculty of Law Research Paper No. 2013-06, available at SSRN: http://ssrn.com/abstract=2228649.

[123] According to the Implementation Report, a mere 1% of listed companies in the EU will apply the rule of breakthrough on a mandatory basis. Most member states have not imposed (or are unlikely to impose) this rule but instead have made it optional for companies.

[124] In view of the potentially negative effects of the Directive, the European Commission has monitored closely the way its rules are being applied and worked in practice. See *Report on Implementation of the Directive on Takeover Bids – Commission of the European Communities* SEC (2007) 268 (21 February 2007). See also, DTI, *Implementation of the EU Directive on Takeover Bids – Guidance on Changes to Rules on Company Takeovers*, February 2007, URN 07/659. However, it has been delayed as a consequence of the many other issues for European financial regulation arising from the banking and the credit crisis. See the Takeover Report 2011, p. 10, available at http://www.thetakeoverpanel.org.uk/wp-content/uploads/2008/11/report2011.pdf.

[125] Article 18.

[126] It should be noted that the informal network of European takeover regulators, set up under the aegis of the CESR, continues under the auspices of the ESMA. See the Takeover Report 2011, p. 10, available at http://www.thetakeoverpanel.org.uk/wp-content/uploads/2008/11/report2011.pdf.

## Further reading

J. Amour and D.A. Skeel 'Who Writes the Rules for Hostile Takeovers, and Why? – The Peculiar Divergence of US and UK Takeover Regulation' (2007) 95 *Georgetown Law Journal* 1727.

J. Armour, J.B. Jacobs and C.J. Milhaupt 'The Evolution of Hostile Takeover Regimes in Developed and Emerging Markets: An Analytical Framework' (2011) 52 *Harvard International Law Journal* 221.

# Part VI
# Insolvency and liquidation

# 22

# Insolvency and liquidation procedures

## 22.1 The development of corporate insolvency law

The decision taken by Parliament in 1844 to enact the Joint Stock Companies Act and enable the creation of companies by registration also led to the systematic development of a regime for the winding up of companies. The same year saw the passing of an Act for 'Winding up the Affairs of Joint Stock Companies unable to meet their Pecuniary Engagements' and in the years leading up to the passing of the Companies Act 1862 there were various enactments relating to the development of corporate insolvency law.[1] The Companies Act 1862 provided that a company could be wound up voluntarily where the members had resolved that it could not by reason of its liabilities continue its business and that it was advisable to wind up, and made provision for the appointment of a liquidator by the members.[2] The Act also provided that a company might be wound up by the court in certain circumstances, such as where the company was unable to pay its debts, and made provision for the appointment of an official liquidator to administer the proceedings. The Companies (Winding-up) Act 1890 provided, *inter alia*, that in the case of a winding up by the court, the Official Receiver automatically became the provisional liquidator and that he was responsible for investigating the affairs of the company and acting as liquidator with responsibility for getting in the assets and distributing the proceeds.[3] The Companies Act 1929 introduced a distinction between two types of voluntary liquidation so that if the company was expected to be unable to pay its debts in full, then there would be a creditors' voluntary winding up (rather than a members' voluntary winding up) in which the creditors would be in control of matters such as the appointment of the liquidator.[4] One of the other major innovations in the 1929 Act was the provision against fraudulent trading. Subsequently, the Companies Acts 1947 and 1948 and the Insolvency Act 1976 introduced further reforms.

In 1977, a committee was appointed by the Secretary of State for Trade under the chairmanship of Mr Kenneth Cork[5] to carry out a fundamental and exhaustive reappraisal of all aspects of the insolvency laws of England and Wales. The Report was presented to Parliament in 1982 and recommended wide-ranging reforms.[6] As a consequence, the DTI (now DBEIS) set out its policy in the White Paper, *A Revised Framework for Insolvency Law*.[7] Its fundamental objectives were stated to be to encourage, and to assist and ensure

---

[1] See generally *Insolvency Law and Practice. Report of the Review Committee* (London: HMSO, Cmnd 8558, 1982) paras 74–99.
[2] Such a voluntary winding up might later be made subject to the supervision of the court if the court so ordered.
[3] Cmnd 8558, 1982, para. 79.
[4] *Ibid.* paras 76, 89.
[5] Later Sir Kenneth Cork.
[6] See n. 1 above.
[7] Cmnd 9175, 1984.

the proper regulation of trade, industry and commerce and to promote a climate conducive to growth and the national production of wealth.[8]

In pursuing those objectives, the principal role of the insolvency legislation was said to be to establish effective and straightforward procedures for dealing with and settling the affairs of corporate (and personal) insolvents in the interests of their creditors; to provide a statutory framework to encourage companies to pay careful attention to their financial circumstances so as to recognise difficulties at an early stage and before the interests of creditors were seriously prejudiced; to deter and penalise irresponsible behaviour and malpractice on the part of those who manage a company's affairs; to ensure that those who act in cases of insolvency are competent to do so and conduct themselves in a proper manner; to facilitate the reorganisation of companies in difficulties to minimise unnecessary loss to creditors and to the economy when insolvency occurs.[9]

It was stressed that the main task in furthering the DTI's (as DBEIS was then known) objectives was to ensure that action is taken at an early stage in insolvencies under the control of the court to protect the assets of the insolvent, in the interests of creditors, and to investigate the affairs of insolvents where it appears that the cause of the liquidation or bankruptcy has been malpractice rather than misfortune, so that undesirable commercial or individual conduct is sufficiently deterred.[10] In 1985, legislation now in the form of the Insolvency Act 1986[11] produced the most thoroughgoing reforms in insolvency law for over 100 years.[12]

## 22.2 Pre-insolvency remedies

### A  Corporate rescue

One of the main aims of the reforms of 1985 was to make it easier for companies in financial difficulties to rescue themselves or be rescued, so as to prevent if possible, the onset of

---

[8] *Ibid.* para. 2.

[9] *Ibid.* It is beyond the scope of the short account in this chapter to consider the theoretical debates which have taken place as to the proper role of insolvency law. For an excellent summary and critique of the leading theories, see R. Goode *Principles of Corporate Insolvency Law* 4th edn (London: Sweet & Maxwell, 2011) Chapter 2. See further V. Finch and D. Milman *Corporate Insolvency Law: Perspectives and Principles* 3rd edn (Cambridge: CUP, 2017); and J. Bhandari and L. Weiss (eds) *Corporate Bankruptcy: Economic and Legal Perspectives* (Cambridge: CUP, 2008).

[10] Cmnd 9175, 1984.

[11] And its accompanying Insolvency Rules 1986 (SI 1986 No. 1925), which have since been amended to make them compatible with the Civil Procedure Rules 1998; generally, the effect of the amendments is that the Civil Procedure Rules do not apply to insolvency proceedings, although they will apply to the extent that they are not inconsistent with them. There have also been many other subsequent amendments to the 1986 rules, e.g. the Insolvency (Amendment) Rules 2008 (SI 2008/737), the Insolvency (Amendment) Rules 2010 (SI 2010/686) and, most recently, the Insolvency (England and Wales) Rules 2016 (SI 2016/1024), which came into force on 6 April 2017 (see also text to note 12 below).

[12] Subsequently amendments to various areas have been made by the Insolvency Act 2000, and by the Enterprise Act 2002. The EC Regulation on Insolvency Proceedings EC 1346/2000 came into force in May 2002 and is designed to regulate cross-border insolvency proceedings. It is noteworthy that the Insolvency Service has now completed a rewrite of the Insolvency Rules 1986 (as amended). The new Rules replace, rather than a consolidate, the 1986 Rules (as amended) and are enshrined in the Insolvency (England and Wales) Rules 2016 (SI 2016/1024). This was a significant phase in the Insolvency Rules modernisation project, following on from the April 2010 amendments under the Insolvency (Amendment) Rules 2010, *ibid.*, the Insolvency (Amendment No. 2) Rules 2010 (SI 2010/734), the Legislative Reform (Insolvency) (Miscellaneous Provisions) Order 2010 (SI 2010/18) and the Insolvency (Amendment) Regulations 2011 (SI 2011/2203). The new Rules came into force on 6 April 2017.

insolvency. To this end, two new procedures were introduced, both of which have been in frequent use. The company voluntary arrangement ('CVA') mechanism was introduced to make it easier for companies to enter into arrangements with their creditors without, for instance, having to go through the more formal mechanisms contained in ss. 895–901 of the Companies Act 2006.[13] The CVA is discussed below.[14] The other major innovation was the administration order which was designed to vest the powers of management of the company in an 'administrator' (usually an insolvency expert from one of the leading firms of accountants or insolvency specialists). It is then hoped that the administrator will have the necessary expertise and detachment that will enable her to make the tough decisions necessary to restructure and revive the company, or at least save some part of it. The administration regime has recently been completely overhauled by the Enterprise Act 2002.

## B Administration

The purpose of administration is apparent from the statutory duty which is cast[15] upon the administrator who:

'... must perform his functions with the objective of:

(a) rescuing the company as a going concern, or

(b) achieving a better result for the company's creditors as a whole than would be likely if the company were wound up . . .[16] or

(c) realising the property in order to make a distribution to one or more secure or preferential creditors.'

The legislation then makes further prescription about the duties of the administrator.[17]

A person may be appointed as administrator by order of the court,[18] by the holder of a floating charge,[19] or by the company or its directors.[20] The circumstances and conditions vary according to which of those circumstances of appointment is being adopted. The onset of administration has many legal effects designed to give the administrator a chance to carry out her objectives, so for instance, there is a moratorium on insolvency proceedings and other legal process.[21] The administrator has a broad range of powers, for it is provided that she may 'do anything necessary or expedient for the management of the affairs, business, and property of the company', although without prejudice to the generality of this, some are specified, such as removing and appointing directors.[22] The process of

---

[13] See further, Chapter 4.
[14] At 22.2D, below.
[15] By s. 8 of and para. 3 (1) of Sch. B1 to the Insolvency Act 1986, as substituted by the Enterprise Act 2002, s. 248.
[16] '. . . (Without first being in administration).'
[17] *Ibid.* paras 3–4, 67–69 of Sch. B 1. An administrator must be a qualified insolvency practitioner, and there are other restrictions; see paras 6–9.
[18] Paragraph 10. See, *Bank of Scotland plc* v *Targetfollow Properties Holdings Ltd* [2010] EWHC 3606 (Ch) (Ch D).
[19] Paragraph 14.
[20] Paragraph 22.
[21] Paragraphs 40–45.
[22] Paragraphs 59–66.

administration is set out in the legislation and, broadly, involves the administrator making a proposal about what she intends to do, and obtaining the approval of the creditors.[23]

## C Pre-pack administration

Pre-pack administration is the process of selling the assets of a company immediately after it has entered into administration. In essence, the business of an insolvent company is prepared for sale by the administrator to a selected buyer, i.e. 'pre-packaged', prior to the company's entry into formal insolvency proceedings.[24] This has the advantage of rescuing the viable parts of the business before the company is visibly in difficulties. Although the purchaser may be an outsider, more generally the sale of the business is to the existing management.[25] Pre-pack sales have attracted considerable critical comment because, for example, unsecured creditors are given little or no say in the process.[26] This clearly goes against one of the key aims of administration, which is to give them greater involvement in the procedure so that creditors have the opportunity to influence events. It has also been suggested that 'pre-packs' are but a facet of the 'phoenix' syndrome.[27] As a response to the mounting criticisms of the procedure, the Association of Business Recovery Professionals ('R3') issued the Statement of Insolvency Practice, 'SIP 16', which came into force in January 2009 and has since been amended (most recently to take into account the recommendations of the Graham Report, discussed below).[28] This is highly prescriptive in terms of the detailed information that must be disclosed to creditors and, as such, its policy is directed towards increasing the transparency of the pre-pack administration process. Thus, for example, paras 16 and 17 of SIP 16 provide that:

DISCLOSURE
(16) An administrator should provide creditors with a detailed narrative explanation and justification [the SIP 16 statement] of why a pre-packaged sale was undertaken and all alternatives considered, to demonstrate that the administrator has acted with due regard for their interests. The information disclosure requirements in the appendix should be included in the SIP 16 statement unless there are exceptional circumstances, in which case the administrator

---

[23] Paragraphs 46–58.

[24] Examples include the British School of Motoring, EMI and Jane Norman.

[25] The sale of the business to the directors when a company is in administration does not require shareholder approval as a substantial property transaction: see s. 193(1) of the Companies Act 2006. Further, in a series of decisions the courts have held that, where the circumstances of the case warrant it, an administrator has the power to sell assets without the prior approval of the creditors or the permission of the court; see *T&D Industries plc* [2001] 1 WLR 646; *Transbus International Ltd* [2004] EWHC 932 (Ch), [2004] All ER 911; and *DKLL Solicitors* [2007] EWHC 2067 (Ch). However, s. 129 of the Small Business, Enterprise and Employment Act 2015 grants a reserve power to the Secretary of State to introduce regulations prohibiting (or imposing requirements or conditions for) pre-pack sales by an administrator to connected parties.

[26] See, for example, V. Finch 'Pre-packaged Administrations: Bargains in the Shadow of Insolvency or Shadowy Bargains' [2006] JBL 568. See further, S. Frisby 'Report to the Association of Business Recovery Professionals, A Preliminary Analysis of Pre-Packaged Administrations' (2007) at < https://www.iiiglobal.org/sites/default/files/sandrafrisbyprelim.pdf. See the judgment of HHJ David Cooke in *Re Kayley Vending Ltd* [2009] EWHC 904 (Ch), in which he provides a comprehensive summary of the criticisms directed against pre-packs.

[27] See V. Finch, *ibid*. See further, S. McMahon 'Pre-Pack Sales by Administrators: The Implications of SIP 16' [2009] *Corporate Rescue and Insolvency* 51.

[28] Version 3 of SIP 16 is effective from 1 November 2015, see https://www.r3.org.uk/media/documents/technical_library/SIPS/SIP%2016%20Version%203%203%20Nov%202015.pdf.>

should explain why the information has not been provided. In any sale involving a connected party, it is very unlikely that commercial confidentiality alone would outweigh the need for creditors to be provided with this information.

(17) The explanation of the pre-packaged sale in the SIP 16 statement should be provided with the first notification to creditors and in any event within seven calendar days of the transaction. If the administrator has been unable to meet this requirement, the administrator will provide a reasonable explanation for the delay. The SIP 16 statement should be included in the administrator's statement of proposals filed at Companies House.[29]

Notwithstanding the arguments against pre-pack administration, the underlying policy of the process is founded upon rescue and, as such, it is an economically efficient mechanism. Procedurally it is fast and, therefore, cost effective and it prevents the loss of goodwill value and customer confidence and can result in job preservation.[30] However, bearing in mind the concerns that creditors are in a vulnerable position in pre-pack sales, in 2013 the then Government commissioned Teresa Graham CBE to undertake a review of pre-pack administrations as part of its 'transparency and trust agenda'.[31] The Graham Report did not propose further regulation but set out six recommendations that were designed to address a number of the legitimate concerns that pre-packs give rise to. These are:

> *Key recommendation 1:* Pre-pack Pool. On a voluntary basis, connected parties approach a 'pre-pack pool' before the sale and disclose details of the deal, for the pool member to opine on.
> *Key recommendation 2:* Viability Review. On a voluntary basis, the connected party complete a 'viability review' on the new company.
> *Recommendation 3:* SIP 16: that the Joint Insolvency Committee considers, at the earliest opportunity, the redrafted SIP16 in Annex A.
> *Recommendation 4:* Marketing: that all marketing of businesses that pre-pack comply with six principles of good marketing and that any deviation from these principles be brought to creditors' attention.
> *Recommendation 5:* Valuations: SIP16 be amended to the effect that valuations must be carried out by a valuer who holds professional indemnity insurance.
> *Recommendation 6:* SIP 16: that the Insolvency Service withdraws from monitoring SIP16 statements and that monitoring be picked up by the Recognised Professional Bodies.[32]

Following the release of the Graham Report the Government discontinued (for the time being) plans to regulate pre-packs, instead endorsing the adoption by insolvency practitioners of Graham's six principles (SIP 16 has already been amended accordingly). Nevertheless, should this approach fail, the Small Business, Enterprise and Employment Act 2015 (which received royal assent shortly after the release of the Graham Report) includes a reserve power effectively enabling the Secretary of State to regulate pre-packs if necessary.

---

[29] *Ibid.*
[30] See S. Frisby 'A Preponderance of Pre-Packs' [2008] *JIBFL* 23; and S. Frisby 'The Pre-Pack Progression: Latest Empirical Findings' [2008] *Insolv Int* 157. See also, M. Ellis 'The Thin Line in the Sand – Pre-Packs and Phoenixes' (2006, Spring Issue) *Recovery* 3; and C. Greenhalgh 'Corporate Rescue: An Assessment of the "Pre-Packaged" Administration' [2011] *ICR* 1 (Special Issue).
[31] Vince Cable's foreword to Teresa Graham CBE '*Graham Review into Pre-Pack Administration, Report to the Rt Hon Vince Cable MP*' (June 2014).
[32] Teresa Graham CBE '*Graham Review into Pre-Pack Administration, Report to the Rt Hon Vince Cable MP*' (June 2014) Part 4, p.10.

## D Administrative receivers

Prior to the Enterprise Act 2002, a situation similar to administration could often come about as a result of the appointment of a receiver. If a company created a floating charge to secure a debenture, the terms of the debenture would almost always give the debenture holder power to appoint a receiver. Such a receiver would usually have been a receiver and manager so that he could not only take possession of the company's assets with a view to speedily realising them for the benefit of the debenture holders but also manage the business of the company and keep it going while the assets are being realised. A receiver under a floating charge would usually have been deemed to be an 'administrative receiver' within the terms of the Insolvency Act 1986,[33] with the result that, in addition to any powers set out in the debenture or trust deed, he would have had wide powers of management of the company. However, it had been found that this in practice meant that any administration procedure (discussed above) needed the concurrence of the institutional lenders, the banks, for their loans, almost invariably secured by floating charges, and would have entitled them to block the appointment of an administrator by appointing an administrative receiver.[34] The Enterprise Act 2002 deals with this by removing the right of a floating charge holder to appoint an administrative receiver,[35] so that only in rare and exceptional cases will appointment of an administrative receiver be possible.[36]

## E Company voluntary arrangement or other reconstruction

Sections 1–7 of the Insolvency Act 1986[37] contain provisions designed to produce a method by which the company can reach a legally binding agreement with its creditors without the need to use the fairly cumbersome and elaborate mechanism of ss. 895–901, 902–903 of the Companies Act 2006.[38] In practice the CVA is used only in situations involving smaller companies, because it binds only those creditors who 'in accordance with the rules had notice of' the meeting. In a large company with many creditors, one may be overlooked, and he or she will then be in a position to upset the arrangement by, for instance, putting the company into liquidation. In such situations it will sometimes be preferable to proceed by a scheme of arrangement under the Companies Act 2006 because that will bind all creditors whether they had notice or not, provided that the scheme has been duly advertised in accordance with the directions of the court.[39]

Broadly, the CVA mechanism is that the directors[40] make a 'proposal' to the company and its creditors for a 'voluntary arrangement'.[41] The term 'voluntary arrangement' means

---

[33] See s. 29 (2).
[34] Under the former ss. 9–10 of the Insolvency Act 1986.
[35] Enterprise Act 2002, s. 250, inserting new ss. 72A–H into the Insolvency Act 1986.
[36] Instead, as mentioned in the previous section, the floating charge holder may in some circumstances appoint or secure the appointment of an administrator; see Insolvency Act 1986, s. 8 and Sch. B1, paras 14–21, 35–39.
[37] As augmented by Part I of the Insolvency Rules 1986 (SI 1986 No. 1925) as amended.
[38] For this and other methods of reconstruction see the discussion in Chapter 4, 4.4.
[39] It was envisaged by the Cork Report, n. 1 above, at paras 400–430, that CVAs would provide a user-friendly, cost-effective and quick-acting vehicle to enable a company to conclude a binding arrangement with its creditors.
[40] When the company is in liquidation or subject to an administration order, then the directors are not empowered to make a proposal, and the liquidator or administrator may make the proposal instead of the directors and the procedures differ slightly; Insolvency Act 1986, s. 1 (1). These situations are not dealt with here.
[41] *Ibid.* s. 1 (1).

a composition in satisfaction of its debts or a scheme of arrangement of its affairs.[42] A 'proposal' is defined as one which provides for some person, who is called the nominee, to act in relation to the voluntary arrangement either as trustee or otherwise for the purpose of supervising its implementation.[43] The procedure is that a report is submitted to the court by the nominee.[44] Assuming that the nominee thinks that the proposal should go ahead, the report will state that meetings of the company and of creditors should be summoned to consider the proposal. The approval of the meeting binds everybody who was entitled to vote at it.[45]

Protection for minorities is covered by provisions that the court may direct that the meetings shall be summoned,[46] and that the results of the meetings are reported to the court.[47] Also, aggrieved parties can apply to the court in certain circumstances on the ground that the voluntary arrangement approved at the meetings unfairly prejudices the interests of a creditor, member or contributory and/or that there has been some material irregularity at or in relation to either of the meetings.[48]

The CVA procedure had been seen to have defects mainly because there was no provision for a moratorium on enforcement by creditors pending the adoption of the CVA so that unless the company was already in liquidation or administration, the proposal could have been upset by one or more of the creditors.[49] Proposals for change were duly made[50] and the Insolvency Act 2000 provides a mechanism for a moratorium.[51]

## 22.3 Types of winding up and grounds

### A Voluntary winding up

Section 84 of the Insolvency Act 1986 sets out the circumstances in which a company[52] may be wound up voluntarily:

A company may be wound up voluntarily:

(a) when the period (if any) fixed for the duration of the company by the articles expires, or the event (if any) occurs, on the occurrence of which the articles provide that the company is to be dissolved, and the company in general meeting has passed a resolution requiring it to be wound up voluntarily;

(b) if the company resolves by special resolution that it be wound up voluntarily; . . .

---

[42] *Ibid.*

[43] *Ibid.* s. 1 (2); the nominee must be a person who is qualified to act as an insolvency practitioner in relation to the company.

[44] *Ibid.* s. 2.

[45] *Ibid.* ss. 3–5. It is noteworthy that s. 5 (2) (b), substituted by the Insolvency Act 2000, eliminates the need for creditors to have had notice of the meeting before they can be bound.

[46] *Ibid.* s. 3 (1).

[47] *Ibid.* s. 4 (6).

[48] *Ibid.* s. 6.

[49] As to the position of secured or preferential creditors, see s. 4 (3), (4).

[50] See Insolvency Service, Revised Proposals for a New Company Voluntary Arrangement Procedure, April 1995, and DTI Company Voluntary Arrangements Press Notice P/95/839, November 1995.

[51] Section 1 inserts a new s. 1A and Sch. A1 into the Insolvency Act 1986.

[52] As regards the meaning of 'company' in s. 84 and which companies may be wound up voluntarily, see below.

There are requirements for disclosure and publicity. A copy of the resolution must be sent to the Registrar of Companies and there must be an advertisement in the *Gazette*.[53]

A voluntary winding up commenced under s. 84 will be one of two types. It may be a members' voluntary winding up or a creditors' voluntary winding up, the basic difference being (as the names suggest) that in the former type the members are in control of the winding up, whereas this vests in the creditors in the latter type. In order for it to be a members' voluntary winding up, it will be necessary for the directors to make a declaration of solvency, for otherwise the winding up will automatically be a creditors' voluntary winding up.[54] The declaration of solvency is a declaration to the effect that the directors have made a full inquiry into the company's affairs and that they have formed the opinion that the company will be able to pay its debts in full (together with interest) within such period (not exceeding 12 months) from the commencement of the winding up as may be specified in the declaration.[55] The legislation further prescribes a timetable, disclosure requirements and tough penalties (imprisonment) for making a false declaration without reasonable grounds. Furthermore, if it turns out that the company cannot pay its debts, there is a rebuttable presumption that the directors did not have reasonable grounds for their opinion.[56]

## B Winding up by the court

Section 122 (1) of the Insolvency Act 1986 sets out the circumstances in which companies may be wound up by the court:

A company may be wound up by the court if:

(a) the company has by special resolution resolved that the company be wound up by the court,

(b) being a public company which was registered as such on its original incorporation, the company has not been issued with a trading certificate under section 761 of the Companies Act 2006 (requirement as to minimum share capital) and more than a year has expired since it was so registered,

(c) it is an old public company within the meaning of the Sch. 3 to the Companies Act 2006 (Consequential Amendments, Transitional Provisions and Savings) Order 2009,

(d) the company does not commence its business within a year from its incorporation or suspends its business for a whole year,

(e) . . .[57]

(f) the company is unable to pay its debts,

(fa) at the time at which a moratorium for the company under section 1A comes to an end, no voluntary arrangement approved under Part I has effect in relation to the company

(g) the court is of the opinion that it is just and equitable that the company should be wound up.

Most of the above categories are self-explanatory but, with the exception of paras (f), (fa) and (g), are fairly rare. Winding up litigation under para. (g) is an important remedy for

---

[53] Insolvency Act 1986, ss. 84 (3) and 85.
[54] *Ibid.* s. 90.
[55] *Ibid.* s. 89.
[56] *Ibid.* s. 89 (2)–(6).
[57] Section 122 (e) omitted pursuant to art. 6 (4) of the Companies 2006 (Consequential Amendments and Transitional Provisions) Order 2011 (SI 2011/1265).

the minority shareholder in a small company.[58] Paragraph (f) is the unsecured creditor's basic remedy of last resort and is frequently used. Inability to pay debts is defined extensively in s. 123. A company will be deemed unable to pay its debts where a written demand (in the prescribed form) has been served on the company by a creditor owed more than £750 and the money is not paid within three weeks;[59] also where it is proved that the company is unable to pay its debts as they fall due or where it is proved that the value of the company's assets is less than the amount of its liabilities.[60]

In *BNY Corporate Trustee Service Ltd* v *Eurosail-UK 2007-3BL plc*,[61] the Supreme Court considered the meaning of when a company is 'unable to pay its debts' under s. 123 of the Insolvency Act 1986. Lord Walker stressed that the burden of proof is on the person claiming that the company is insolvent on a balance-sheet basis, for which prospective and contingent liabilities must be taken into account, as discounted (it is noteworthy that some of the loan notes in this case were not repayable for over 30 years). Depending on the circumstances of the business, the cash-flow test is not concerned simply with the petitioner's own due debt, but requires reasonably near future debts to be taken into account.

## C Procedure and scope

An application for winding up by the court must be by petition presented by the company, or directors, creditors (including contingent or prospective creditors), 'contributories,' or by a liquidator within the meaning of art. 2 (b) of EC Regulation No. 1346/2000.[62] The term 'contributory' has the broad technical meaning of 'every person liable to contribute to the assets of a company in the event of its being wound up'[63] and these persons are[64] 'every present and past member', although the legislation goes on to make it clear that not all those who are technically called contributories will in fact actually have to contribute anything, so that, for instance, in the case of a company limited by shares, no contribution is required from any member which would exceed the amount (if any) unpaid on his shares (or former shares).[65]

Both the voluntary winding up provisions[66] and winding up by the court[67] apply to 'a company'. This is defined in s. 1 (1) of the Companies Act 2006[68] as follows: '"company" means a company formed and registered after the commencement of this Part', or an 'existing company.' In essence an 'existing company' is defined so as to include companies formed under earlier Companies Acts. However, the provisions for winding up by the

---

[58] See further Chapter 13.
[59] Insolvency Act 1986, s. 123 (1).
[60] *Ibid.* s. 123 (1), (2). If the carrying out of a court order for payment fails to produce sufficient money, then the company will be deemed unable to pay its debts; s. 123 (1) (b).
[61] [2013] UKSC 28.
[62] *Ibid.* s. 124.
[63] *Ibid.* s. 79 (1).
[64] By *ibid.* s. 74.
[65] *Ibid.* s. 74 (2) (d). The right of contributories to petition for winding up is restricted in various ways; ss. 124 (2), (3). Various others are also entitled to petition; ss. 124 (1), (4), (5), 124 A. Other statutes, such as the Financial Services and Markets Act 2000, also sometimes give a right to petition; see Financial Services and Markets Act 2000, s. 367.
[66] Insolvency Act 1986, s. 84.
[67] *Ibid.* s. 122.
[68] Imported into the Insolvency Act 1986 by s. 73 thereof.

court also apply (with certain exceptions and modifications) to overseas companies and certain other 'unregistered' companies.[69]

## 22.4 Effects of winding up, purpose and procedure

### A Immediate effects of winding up

In a voluntary winding up the company must, from the commencement of the winding up,[70] cease to carry on its business, except so far as may be required for the beneficial winding up.[71] Furthermore, any transfer of shares, unless made with the sanction of the liquidator, and any alteration in the status of the company's members, made after the commencement of the winding up, is void.

In the case of a winding up by the court, the effects are more extensive, for it is provided that any disposition of the company's property and any transfer of shares or alteration in the status of the company's members, made after the commencement of the winding up, is void, unless the court otherwise orders.[72] With a winding up by the court, the commencement of the winding up is deemed to be at the time of the presentation of the petition for winding up (although in some circumstances it will be the time of passing the resolution for the voluntary winding up if such an earlier resolution had been passed).[73] Except with leave of the court, no action or proceeding may be proceeded with or commenced against the company or its property.[74] Various enforcement proceedings put in force after the commencement of the winding up are also void.[75] Carrying on of business by the liquidator is possible 'so far as may be necessary for its beneficial winding up' but the sanction of the court (or sometimes liquidation committee)[76] is necessary.[77]

### B Aims and purpose of liquidation

Although there may be many different reasons for commencing a winding up, once it has started, the overall policy and purpose is the same: to ensure that the creditors (if any) are treated equally (*pari passu*) and, subject to that, the property of the company is to be distributed to the members in accordance with their various rights.[78] However, the principle of equal treatment of creditors is subject to a number of inroads.[79] Sometimes (but rarely) the liquidation process is being used as a technical step in certain types of reconstruction.[80]

---

[69] Insolvency Act 1986, ss. 221, 225 and generally 220–229. The expression 'unregistered company' includes 'any association and any company' but it excludes statutory railway companies.
[70] Which by Insolvency Act 1986, s. 86, is the date of the passing of the resolution for winding up.
[71] *Ibid*. s. 87.
[72] *Ibid*. s. 127. There are exemptions in respect of administration.
[73] *Ibid*. s. 129.
[74] *Ibid*. s. 130 (2).
[75] *Ibid*. s. 128.
[76] As to which see further below.
[77] Insolvency Act 1986, ss. 167 (1) (a), 168, and Sch. 4, Part II.
[78] *Ibid*. s. 107.
[79] These are discussed below.
[80] Insolvency Act 1986, s. 110. This is discussed in Chapter 4.

# C Procedure[81]

## 1 *Appointment of liquidator*

In a members' voluntary winding up, the liquidator is appointed by the general meeting 'for the purpose of winding up the company's affairs and distributing its assets', and on his appointment the powers of the directors cease (unless the liquidator or general meeting otherwise decide).[82]

In a creditors' voluntary winding up the liquidator is normally appointed by the creditors' meeting which takes place within 14 days of the resolution to wind up.[83] During the interim the directors have very reduced and limited powers over the company's assets and they must prepare a 'statement of affairs' of the company to lay before the creditors' meeting.[84] The meeting may also appoint a 'liquidation committee' to assist the liquidator.[85] Once the liquidator is appointed, all the powers of the directors cease (unless the liquidation committee or creditors otherwise decide).[86]

Where the winding up is by the court, the official receiver automatically becomes liquidator[87] and continues as such unless he decides to summon meetings of the creditors and contributories to choose a 'private sector' liquidator.[88] Sometimes, if it is necessary to preserve the assets of the company prior to the hearing of the winding-up petition, the court will appoint a liquidator provisionally.[89]

Any liquidator must be properly qualified. The Insolvency Act 1986 regulates anyone who 'acts as an insolvency practitioner', which phrase includes acting as a liquidator.[90] The person must be an 'individual' (i.e. not a corporate body).[91] She must be authorised to act as an insolvency practitioner, either by membership of a specified professional body (such as the institutes of accountants) and compliance with its rules, or by a direct authorisation granted by the Secretary of State or other 'competent authority'.[92]

## 2 *Collection and distribution of assets*

Normally the assets of the company remain its property[93] and the liquidator's function is to 'get in' the assets by taking them under her control, then to realise the assets and then

---

[81] Insolvency law procedure is complex, and in addition to many sections of the Insolvency Act 1986, there are detailed rules set out in the Insolvency Rules 2016. What follows here is a brief outline of the remaining main steps in the liquidation process.

[82] Insolvency Act 1986, s. 91.

[83] *Ibid.* ss. 98–100.

[84] *Ibid.* ss. 99, 114.

[85] *Ibid.* s. 101.

[86] *Ibid.* s. 103.

[87] Unless the court appoints a former administrator under s. 140 of the Insolvency Act 1986.

[88] Insolvency Act 1986, s. 136. Alternatively, he can apply to the Secretary of State for the appointment of a liquidator under s. 137.

[89] *Ibid.* s. 135.

[90] *Ibid.* ss. 388–398. It also includes, in relation to companies, acting as provisional liquidator, administrator or administrative receiver.

[91] The person must also satisfy s. 390 (3) of the Insolvency Act 1986 and the Insolvency Practitioners Regulations 1990 (SI 1990 No. 439) (as amended) which require a security for the proper performance of his functions, up to a maximum of £5m. There are also certain disabilities listed in s. 390 (4) (e.g. disqualification order, mental patient).

[92] Insolvency Act 1986, ss. 390–393.

[93] Except where an order under s. 145 of the 1986 Act is made.

distribute them to those entitled.[94] Liquidators have very wide powers, some exercisable subject (in various circumstances) to permission given by the members, the liquidation committee, creditors or the court, while other powers are exercisable without such restrictions.[95] Powers may also be delegated to the liquidator by virtue of s. 160. Additionally, there are various other powers scattered throughout the Insolvency Act, such as the power to apply to the court for directions in relation to any particular matter arising in the winding up,[96] the power to apply to have the winding up stayed, and the power to disclaim onerous property.[97]

Creditors are entitled to submit their claims to be paid to the liquidator, technically referred to as 'proving for his debt'.[98] The procedures for proof of debts[99] differ slightly as to which type of liquidation is being conducted. In some cases the liquidator will need to estimate the value of a claim that does not bear a fixed or certain value.[100] If the liquidator feels that the claim is unfounded, she may reject the proof, a process that then sometimes leads to litigation.[101] This is especially so if the law is unclear as to whether the claim can be admitted to proof or not.[102]

Before dealing with the rules as regards priority of payments, it is worth observing that where the liquidation is not an insolvent liquidation, then little turns on the order in which the debts are repaid since everybody is going to get paid and any surplus will be paid to the shareholders. Where the assets are insufficient to pay everybody in full, then the question of priority becomes important.

It is also important to realise that various legal principles exist which will either swell or reduce the assets available to the creditors in the liquidation. Those that tend to swell the assets are discussed below. As regards diminishing or reducing the assets, there are two main principles of common law that will have this effect. The first is the concept of security, under which assets that are charged may be appropriated by the creditor to the satisfaction of his debts in priority to the unsecured creditors.[103] The second is the doctrine of set-off, under which a creditor who owes, say, £1,000 to the company, but who himself is owed, say, £300 by the company, may deduct the money owed by the company to him, leaving him with a debt of only £700. As regards the £300 here owed to him by the company, the effect of the set-off is that he is, in a sense, paid in full. It should also be mentioned that various other legal grounds exist for claiming that certain assets should not be regarded as assets in the liquidation and thus not available for the creditors. Goods supplied subject to a retention of title clause are sometimes in this category,[104] and trust doctrines may sometimes produce this result.[105]

---

[94] Insolvency Act 1986, ss. 107, 143–144, 148, and Insolvency Rules 2016 r. 14.27.
[95] Insolvency Act 1986, ss. 165–168 and Sch. 4.
[96] *Ibid.* ss. 168 (3), 112 (1).
[97] *Ibid.* ss. 178–182. Investigatory powers are discussed below at 22.4D 1.
[98] Insolvency Rules 2016, r. 14.3.
[99] Set out in Insolvency Rules 2016, rr. 14.2–14.25.
[100] Insolvency Rules 2016, r. 14.14.
[101] *Ibid.* rr. 14.7–14.9.
[102] See e.g., the discussion of the litigation in *Re Introductions Ltd* in Chapter 5 above.
[103] In certain circumstances the order of priority produced by the normal operation of the legal principles of security and property is set aside. Section 175 (2) of the Insolvency Act 1986 operates to produce a statutory restriction of the normal priority given to the floating chargee as against 'preferential' creditors. For the meaning of 'preferential creditors' see below.
[104] See *Aluminium Industrie Vaassen BV v Romalpa* [1976] 2 All ER 552 and subsequent vast case law.
[105] See *Re Kayford* [1975] 1 WLR 279.

Subject to the operation of the principles discussed above, the order of priority for the payment of claims will be as follows:

(1) Expenses of the winding up.
(2) Preferential debts.
(3) Section 176 creditors.
(4) General (unsecured) creditors.
(5) Deferred debts.
(6) Shareholders.

These categories need further explanation:

'Expenses of the winding up' basically refers to the liquidator's expenses and remuneration. There are different types of these and they are subject to detailed priority rules set out in the Insolvency Rules 1986[106] and may be varied by the court in some circumstances.[107]

'Preferential debts' are those debts that Parliament has decided should have priority. These relate mainly to certain employee wages set out in s. 386 of and Sch. 6 to the 1986 Act. Prior to the Enterprise Act 2002 certain 'crown debts' were also deemed preferential, but with a view to improving the lot of the general unsecured creditors, the preference was discontinued.[108]

'Section 176 creditors' are creditors who have distrained on goods of the company in the period of three months ending with the date of the winding-up order. The goods (or proceeds) are subject to a charge for meeting the preferential claims to the extent that these are otherwise unsatisfied. To the extent that the distraining creditor makes payments under such charge, he is subrogated to the rights of the preference creditors and thus becomes in effect entitled to the same priority as they had as against other creditors.[109]

'General creditors' refers to the ordinary trade or other creditors who have no special priority of deferral.

'Deferred debts' are those that are postponed to the other classes of creditor by virtue of some statutory provision. Certain payments of interest on proved debts are thus postponed.[110] Debts due to any member in his capacity as such (e.g. dividends declared but not paid) are deferred.[111]

'Shareholders' means that any surplus remaining should be distributed among the shareholders in accordance with their rights as set out in the memorandum, articles, or terms of issue of the shares.

The process of actually paying the creditors is sometimes a protracted one and often a 'dividend' (i.e. distribution) is paid as soon as it is clear that it can be distributed, with the

---

[106] In *Re Leyland Daf Ltd* [2004] UKHL 9, the House of Lords established that liquidation expenses are not payable out of assets subject to a floating charge. Perhaps not surprisingly the decision generated considerable controversy and s. 1282 of the Companies Act 2006 (which inserts s. 176 Z A into the Insolvency Act 1986) reversed it by allowing assets subject to a floating charge to be available to fund general expenses of a liquidation: see also the Insolvency (England and Wales) Rules 2016 (SI 2016/1024), r. 6.42. See R. Mokal 'Liquidation Expenses and Floating Charges – The Separate Funds Fallacy' [2004] LMCLQ 387–404.
[107] Insolvency Act 1986, s. 156.
[108] Enterprise Act 2002, s. 251. This account assumes that this legislation is in force.
[109] See *ibid*. s. 176.
[110] *Ibid*. s. 189 (2).
[111] *Ibid*. s. 74 (2) (f).

possibility of a further final dividend in the future. In the past, it has often been the case that unsecured creditors end up with little or nothing since the lion's share of the assets are taken by floating charge holders. With a view to amelioration of the position of unsecured creditors, the Enterprise Act 2002 has introduced a concept under which a 'prescribed part of the company's net property' is to be made available for the satisfaction of unsecured debts.[112] The policy underpinning the creation of the 'prescribed part' is aimed at offering unsecured creditors at least some recovery from an insolvency situation rather than receiving nothing at all. All too often, however, the prescribed part is of little real value, especially where there is a high number of unsecured creditors. Section 176 A (2) of the Insolvency Act 1986, introduced by the Enterprise Act 2002, enables insolvency practitioners to seek court authority to disapply the prescribed part. Such an application can be made where the costs of making the distribution to unsecured creditors would be disproportionate to its benefit. The burden of proof is high. In *Re International Sections Ltd,*[113] the liquidators applied where the prescribed part was £6,731; unsecured claims amounted to £230,613; the estimated costs of distribution was £3,332; and the estimated dividend was 1.48p in the pound. The court agreed that the dividend was an 'admittedly small benefit', but that 'it would not be right to deprive the unsecured creditors of what remained' and that disapplication 'should be the exception, and not the rule'.[114]

## 3 *Dissolution of the company*

As soon as the company's affairs are fully wound up, the liquidator[115] must prepare an account thereof and present this to meetings of members (in the case of a members' voluntary winding up) or of members and of creditors (in every other case).[116] It is up to these final meetings to decide whether or not the liquidator should 'have his release', that is to say, that he is 'discharged from all liability both in respect of acts or omissions of his in winding up and otherwise in relation to his conduct as liquidator'.[117] After the meetings, the liquidator must submit a report to the Registrar of Companies.[118]

Within three months of the day on which the report is registered by the Registrar, the company is deemed dissolved.[119] The company thus ceases to exist, it no longer has legal personality. It is possible for the liquidator to apply for 'early dissolution' in cases where the company is hopelessly insolvent and the assets will not even cover the expenses of winding up.[120]

---

[112] Enterprise Act 2002, s. 252 inserting a new s. 176 A into the Insolvency Act 1986. It was held in *Kelly* v *Inflexion Fund 2 Ltd* [2011] BCC 93 (Ch D) that there is nothing in s.176 A to exclude a floating charge holder who has surrendered his entire security from participating in the prescribed part.

[113] [2009] EWHC 137 (Ch). For a case which fell on the other side of the line, see *Stephen* v *QMD Hotels Limited* [2010] CSOH 168, in which the court offered some guidance by noting that where the dividend is likely to be less than 1p in the pound, liquidators are quite right to consider applying for an order to disapply the prescribed part.

[114] *Ibid.* at [15].

[115] Not being the Official Receiver.

[116] Insolvency Act 1986, ss. 94, 106, 146.

[117] *Ibid.* ss. 173 (4), 174 (6). Such release is, however, subject to the courts' powers in relation to any misfeasance by him under s. 212.

[118] *Ibid.* ss. 94 (3), 106 (3), 172 (8).

[119] *Ibid.* ss. 201 (2), 205.

[120] *Ibid.* ss. 202–203.

Quite often in practice, particularly with small private companies and where the company is solvent, the whole of the liquidation process is by-passed; it is simply never started. Instead, the directors cause it to stop trading, pay off the creditors, and then pay any surplus to the shareholders. The practice has then often been to invite the Registrar of Companies to exercise his powers under s. 1000 of the Companies Act 2006 to strike the name of the now defunct company off the register; the Registrar will usually assent to this. However, the dissolution does not discontinue the liability of the directors and members, and it may also be subjected to formal winding-up proceedings later, if necessary. The general s. 1000 powers, of course, continue, but since the amendments made by the Deregulation and Contracting Out Act 1994, new provisions were inserted into the Companies Act 1985, now replaced by ss. 1003–1009 of the 2006 Act, which set out a procedure under which the directors of a private company which has not been active for three months, other than paying its debts, may apply to the Registrar to have the company's name removed from the register.

## D Misconduct, malpractice and adjustment of pre-liquidation (or pre-administration) transactions

### 1 Investigation

There are a variety of investigatory powers. A winding up by the court inevitably involves some degree of investigation by the Official Receiver, for by s. 132 of the Insolvency Act 1986, it is the duty of the Official Receiver to investigate the causes of failure of the company (if it has failed) and, generally, the promotion, formation, business, dealings and affairs of the company, and then to report to the court if he thinks fit. He has power to apply to the court for public examinations of officers and others.[121] This is in practice rare, although the powers of the court to order a private examination are widely used. These powers[122] are not restricted to the Official Receiver but can also be requested by any liquidator, administrator, administrative receiver or provisional liquidator[123] and apply to voluntary liquidations as well as winding up by the court. They are used in attempts to obtain explanations from former directors as to their conduct. Obviously, matters discovered in the course of a winding up might also trigger full-scale investigations by the DBEIS, the Serious Fraud Office, or the Director of Public Prosecutions. Indeed, s. 218 requires liquidators who have discovered criminal malpractice to submit a report to the Secretary of State.

### 2 Remedies

Once misconduct has been discovered, the Insolvency Act 1986 makes available a wide range of remedies and penalties to deal with it: fraudulent trading;[124] wrongful trading;[125]

---

[121] The Insolvency Act 1986, s. 133.
[122] Contained in *ibid*. s. 236.
[123] *Ibid*. ss. 236, 234.
[124] *Ibid*. s. 213; and see Chapter 2 above.
[125] *Ibid*. s. 214 and see Chapter 2 above.

misfeasance proceedings;[126] fraud in anticipation of winding up;[127] falsification of the company's books;[128] omissions from statement of affairs;[129] false representations to creditors.[130] There are also restrictions[131] designed to prevent the name of the wound-up company from being used again within a five-year period. The provisions relating to disqualification of directors often become relevant in the context of liquidation.[132]

The Insolvency Act 1986 contains a number of provisions designed to adjust or set aside transactions effected prior to a liquidation or administration. Briefly, these are as follows: certain transactions at an undervalue may be set aside under ss. 238 and 340–341. Also certain preferences may be set aside (ss. 239, 240–241). Extortionate credit transactions may be set aside or restructured under s. 244. Under s. 245 certain floating charges can be declared invalid to the extent that the company did not get consideration for them.[133]

## Further reading

V. Finch 'Pre-packaged Administrations: Bargains in the Shadow of Insolvency or Shadowy Bargains' [2006] *JBL* 568.

S. McMahon 'Pre-Pack Sales by Administrators: The Implications of SIP 16' [2009] *Corporate Rescue and Insolvency* 51.

S. Frisby 'A Preponderance of Pre-Packs' [2008] *JIBFL* 23.

S. Frisby 'The Pre-Pack Progression: Latest Empirical Findings' [2008] *Insolv. Int.* 157.

C. Greenhalgh 'Corporate Rescue: An Assessment of the "Pre-Packaged" Administration' [2011] *ICR* 1 (Special Issue).

R. Mokal 'Liquidation Expenses and Floating Charges – The Separate Funds Fallacy' [2004] *LMCLQ* 387.

---

[126] *Ibid.* s. 212.
[127] *Ibid.* s. 208.
[128] *Ibid.* s. 209.
[129] *Ibid.* s. 210.
[130] *Ibid.* s. 211.
[131] In *ibid.* ss. 216–217.
[132] See further Chapter 23.
[133] For further explanation of these matters, see I. Fletcher *Law of Insolvency* 5th edn (London: Sweet & Maxwell, 2017).

# 23

# Disqualification of directors

## 23.1 Background

The provisions for the disqualification of directors introduced by the Insolvency Act 1985 were not a wholly new phenomenon in that the Companies Act 1948[1] had provided for the disqualification of directors who were guilty of fraud, breach of duty or liquidation offences. Subsequently, the jurisdiction was steadily extended by legislation over the years until the Insolvency Act 1985[2] produced its current form, now contained in the Company Directors Disqualification Act 1986.[3] As a result of this legislation and changes of policy within the DBEIS, the number of disqualifications has increased drastically in recent years. In 1983–84, a total of 89 were made,[4] in 1987–88, 197 orders were made, in 1994–95, 493 orders were made but by 1999–2000 the annual total had risen to 1,509.[5] In the year 2015–16, a total of 1,366 disqualifications orders were notified to the Secretary of State, of which 989 were undertakings (as discussed below).[6] This number has the potential to further increase following reforms introduced by the Small Business, Enterprise and Employment Act 2015 that amends the Company Directors Disqualification Act 1986 ('CDDA 1986').[7] These reforms include, *inter alia*, the extension of the disqualification regime to those persons who exercise 'the requisite amount of influence' over a director who has been disqualified[8] whilst also allowing the court to take into account a director's conduct with regard to overseas companies.

[1] Section 188.
[2] The expansion of the jurisdiction in the Insolvency Act 1985 was largely the result of recommendations contained in the Cork Report (Cmnd 8558, 1982) and the White Paper, *A Revised Framework for Insolvency Law* (Cmnd 9175, 1984).
[3] There are accompanying rules governing the procedure: Insolvent Companies (Disqualification of Unfit Directors) Proceedings Rules 1987 (SI 1987 No. 2023). These have been subsequently amended to make them compatible with the Civil Procedure Rules 1998, although broadly the position is that the Civil Procedure Rules do not apply to the Disqualification Rules, except to the extent that they are not inconsistent with them.
[4] Mainly under the Companies Act 1948, s. 188.
[5] See *Companies in 1998–99* (London: DTI, 1999) p. 36 and earlier editions. For analysis of the decision-making mechanisms relating to the bringing of disqualification proceedings, see S. Wheeler 'Directors' Disqualification: Insolvency Practitioners and the Decision-making Process' (1995) 15 *Legal Studies* 283.
[6] See *Companies House Management Information Tables 2016/2017* (Companies House, 2017), available at https://www.gov.uk/government/statistical-data-sets/companies-house-management-information-tables-2016-17.
[7] For a discussion of the amendments introduced by the Small Business, Enterprise and Employment Act 2015 to the CDDA 1986, see S. Lawson 'Power to the IP? Latest Corporate Insolvency Amendments in SBEEA 2015 and their Impact on IPs in Practice' (2015) 8(6) *Corporate Rescue and Insolvency* 249.
[8] Section 8 Z A of the Company Directors Disqualification Act 1986.

## 23.2 The disqualification order

The CDDA 1986 consolidated various prior enactments under which the court[9] could disqualify persons from acting as directors (and holding other positions). Section 1 (1) of the CDDA 1986 provides that a disqualification order is an order that provides that an individual shall not (for a period specified in the order):

(a) . . . be a director of a company, act as receiver of a company's property or in any way, whether directly or indirectly, be concerned or take part in the promotion, formation or management of a company unless (in each case) he has the leave of the court, and

(b) he shall not act as an insolvency practitioner.[10]

The order need not be a total disqualification and the director can be allowed to act in relation to certain companies subject to conditions, while being disqualified from acting for any others.[11] Furthermore, even once disqualified, the legislation effectively enables a director to later apply for leave to act in relation to certain companies.[12]

Although disqualification proceedings are a civil proceeding,[13] it is clear that they may also involve matters in respect of which criminal proceedings are sometimes brought and acting in breach of a disqualification order is a criminal offence as well as giving rise to personal liability for the debts of the company.[14] The disqualification is widely construed and in *R* v *Campbell*[15] it was held that a management consultant who advised on the financial management and restructuring of a company was in breach of the order, in particular, the words in the statute that he should not 'be concerned in' the 'management of a company'. It is clear from *Re Sevenoaks Ltd*[16] that the director cannot be disqualified on the basis of charges which were not formally made against him, but which happened to be made out once the evidence had been given in court.[17]

The jurisdiction is available against 'persons'; the first case against a corporate director was *Official Receiver* v *Brady*[18] where Jacob J said:

As a matter of practice there may be a useful purpose in being able to disqualify companies as well as the individuals behind them. It means that one of the tools used by people who are unfit to be company directors can themselves be attacked. There may be a host of . . . advantages. You may not be able to find the individuals behind the controlling director.[19]

---

[9] It also contains two outright prohibitions on persons acting as directors: undischarged bankrupts, s. 11 (see e.g. *R* v *Brockley* [1994] BCC 131) and (hardly of general application) s. 12.

[10] For practice procedures, see *Civil Procedure Rules, Practice Direction: Directors Disqualification Proceedings*.

[11] See *Re Lo-Line Ltd* (1988) 4 BCC 415.

[12] CDDA 1986, s. 17. See e.g. *Secretary of State for Trade and Industry* v *Rosenfield* [1999] Ch 413, where it was held that if the applicant was not acting as director, the companies would suffer, with severe consequences for the employees, and so subject to conditions, leave was granted. In *Secretary of State for Trade and Industry* v *Griffiths* [1998] BCC 836 the Court of Appeal set out detailed guidance on the manner in which s. 17 applications should be dealt with.

[13] *Re Churchill Hotel Ltd* (1988) 4 BCC 112.

[14] CDDA 1986, ss. 1 (4), 13, 15.

[15] [1984] BCLC 83 (a case under s. 188 of Companies Act 1948).

[16] [1990] BCC 765, CA.

[17] Similarly, the disqualification period should be fixed by reference only to the matters properly alleged.

[18] [1999] BCC 258.

[19] *Ibid.* at p. 259.

One of the most frequently disputed issues in disqualification proceedings is the question of whether a person can, in the circumstances, be regarded as a shadow director, or as a de facto director, so as to make him liable.[20] In *Re Kaytech International plc,*[21] the Court of Appeal discussed various judicial observations on the matter but declined to lay down a firm test for determining de facto directorship other than to pass the fairly general observation that 'the crucial issue is whether the individual in question has assumed the status and functions of a company director so as to make himself responsible under the 1986 Act as if he were a de jure director'.[22]

Lastly here, it could be observed that the cases under the CDDA 1986 provided scant comfort for non-executive directors that they might be under a lower standard of duty than ordinary full-time directors. In *Re Continental Assurance Co. of London plc,*[23] one of the directors held a senior position at the bank which had financed the company and was effectively a non-executive director with the company appointed to the board to protect the bank's interest. The judge accepted that the facts showed that he did not know what was going on, but that he should have known.[24]

## 23.3 Grounds – unfitness and insolvency

### A The s. 6 ground

There are numerous grounds for disqualification.[25] The most commonly used is s. 6, which provides that it is the duty of the court to disqualify where it is satisfied that an individual:

> [I]s or has been a director[26] of a company which has at any time become insolvent (whether while he was a director or subsequently) and . . . that his conduct as a director of that company (either taken alone or taken together with his conduct as a director of any other company or companies) makes him unfit to be concerned in the management of a company.

Under this ground[27] the minimum period of disqualification is two years, the maximum is 15 years. The term 'becomes insolvent' is defined very broadly, so it will embrace both voluntary and involuntary liquidation. It covers 'going into liquidation at a time when its assets are insufficient for the payment of its debts and other liabilities and the expenses of the winding up'[28] and also where an administration order is made or an administrative receiver is appointed. The case law has given a wide meaning to the term 'director' so that acting as a director is sufficient, even if there has never been any formal appointment.[29]

---

[20] See e.g. *Re Richborough Furniture Ltd* [1996] BCC 155 and *Secretary of State for Trade and Industry* v *Tjolle* [1998] BCC 282, where on the facts the respondents were held not to be de facto directors. Different conclusions were reached in *Secretary of State for Trade and Industry* v *Jones* [1999] BCC 336 and *Re Kaytech International plc* [1999] BCC 390, CA.

[21] [1999] BCC 390, CA.

[22] *Ibid.* at p. 402, *per* Robert Walker LJ.

[23] [1996] BCC 888.

[24] A similar attitude towards non-executives was expressed in *Re Wimbledon Village Restaurant Ltd* [1994] BCC 753 although on the facts, the circumstances were not sufficient to establish unfitness.

[25] The others are dealt with below.

[26] Director in ss. 6–9 of the CDDA 1986 includes shadow director; see ss. 22 (4) and 22 (5).

[27] Other grounds sometimes attract different maximums and there are no minimum periods; see 23.4 below.

[28] CDDA 1986, s. 6 (2).

[29] *Re Lo-Line Ltd* (1988) 4 BCC 415.

The proceedings can only be invoked by the DBEIS in accordance with s. 7, which empowers them in some circumstances to direct the Official Receiver to bring proceedings. There are also time limits governing the commencement of proceedings, for it is provided[30] that an application for the making under s. 6 of a disqualification order 'shall not be made after the end of the period of 3 years beginning with the day on which the company . . . became insolvent'[31] except where the leave of the court has been granted to do so.

## B Unfitness

### 1 *Statutory provisions*

Guidance on whether a director is unfit or not is given in s. 12 C and Sch. 1 of the CDDA 1986. Schedule 1, paras 1–4 set out the matters that the court must take into account in all cases. These include: the extent to which the individual was responsible for the causes of any material legislative contravention by the company; the extent to which the individual was responsible for the causes of the company's insolvency; the frequency of any such conduct; and the nature and extent of any loss or harm caused (or potentially caused) as a result of the individual's conduct.

Paragraphs 5–7 of Sch. 1 apply additionally in those cases where the individual is, or has been, a director (recall that s. 105 of the Small Business, Enterprise and Employment Act 2015 extended the CDDA 1986 to those persons instructing an unfit director). These relate to any misfeasance or breach of fiduciary duty by the director, any material breach of any legislative or other obligation of the director that applies as a result of being a director and the frequency of any such conduct. In *Re AG (Manchester) Ltd (in liquidation); Official Receiver v Watson*,[32] the Official Receiver sought disqualification orders against two former directors, L and W, of the company which had gone into compulsory liquidation with a deficiency of £81.2 million. W was its financial director and CEO. Among the allegations brought against him was the claim that, together with L's husband and another director (H), he had formed an inner group of directors that had usurped the functions of the company's full board and made all strategic and financial decisions, including setting up an offshore trust for the benefit of all the directors and their families and paying dividends of £11.2 million, without notice to, or the consent of, the other directors. It was also alleged that some of the dividends were unlawful insofar as the company's distributable reserves were insufficient and that W had provided misleading information to the company's auditors. Patten J explained that the duty of a finance director is to assess properly a company's ability to pay dividends and to inform the board, and through it the company's members, of any concerns about the proposals. It was a dereliction of duty to acquiesce in inappropriate dividend decisions without ensuring that the company operated on a solvent basis in accordance with the companies' legislation. Although, on the evidence, the court concluded that W had not been dishonest in his dealings with the auditors, he was grossly negligent in his communications with them. It was also clear that the dividends to L and

---

[30] CDDA 1986, s. 7 (2).

[31] Note that this period was extended from two to three years by s. 108 of the Small Business, Enterprise and Employment Act 2015. On the interpretation of this, see *Re Tasbian Ltd* [1990] BCC 318, where it was held that the time limit in s. 7 (2) ran from the happening of the first of the events mentioned in s. 6 (2).

[32] [2008] 1 BCLC 321.

her husband and to the trust were in no way responsible for the collapse in the company's fortunes. During this period the company appeared to be fully solvent. However, W was in breach of his standard of care in presiding over a system of corporate governance, which permitted a trust to be set up and dividends to be paid which were illegal. He had allowed his personal profit incentive to blind him to his duty to challenge these arrangements. L was also unfit because she had abdicated her responsibilities as director to the inner group. At a further hearing, W was disqualified for six years and L for four years.

## 2 Commercial morality

In addition to these statutory indicators, the courts have developed a concept of 'commercial morality' in which they try to balance the need to protect the public from those who abuse the privilege of limited liability with the need to be careful not to make it so strict that it stultifies enterprise and with the need to be fair to the directors themselves. Hoffmann J (as he then was) set out the balance in *Re Ipcon Fashions Ltd*[33] where he said:

> The public is entitled to be protected not only against the activities of those guilty of the more obvious breaches of commercial morality, but also against someone who has shown in his conduct . . . a failure to appreciate or observe the duties attendant on the privilege of conducting business with the protection of limited liability.

Thus, limited liability is seen as a privilege that must not be abused. On the other hand, this policy of protecting the public from abusers of limited liability does not stand on its own and, as commented above, it has been made clear that it has to be balanced against the need not to 'stultify all enterprise'.[34] It was also stressed that there was a need to be fair to the directors themselves:

> Looking at it from the point of view of the director on the receiving end of such an application, I think that justice requires that he should have some grounds for feeling that he has not simply been picked on. There must, I think be something about the case, some conduct which if not dishonest is at any rate in breach of standards of commercial morality, or some really gross incompetence which persuades the court that it would be a danger to the public if he were allowed to continue to be involved in the management of companies.[35]

It is useful to look at the facts of some of the cases falling either side of the line; first, cases where there was held to be a contravention of the principle of commercial morality.

In *Re Ipcon Fashions Ltd*,[36] the director knew the company was insolvent and he siphoned off its business to another company with a view to resurrecting it. During all this, the old company was used to incur liability. A five-year period of disqualification was imposed. In *Re McNulty's Interchange Ltd*,[37] the main problem was that the director had no new ideas which might have improved the business of the company and he simply went on incurring debts; disqualification for 18 months.

---

[33] (1989) 5 BCC 733 at p. 776. See also, *Re Lo-Line Electric Motors Ltd* [1988] Ch 477.
[34] See e.g. Harman J in *Re Douglas Construction Ltd* (1988) 4 BCC 553 at p. 557 (a case on the similar jurisdiction in the predecessor to the CDDA 1986, namely, s. 300 of the Companies Act 1985).
[35] *Per* Hoffmann J in *Re Dawson Print Ltd* (1987) 3 BCC 322 at p. 324 (the Companies Act 1985, s. 300); followed by Browne-Wilkinson J in *Re McNulty's Interchange Ltd* (1988) 4 BCC 533 at p. 536 (the Companies 1985, s. 300).
[36] (1989) 5 BCC 733. See also, *Secretary of State for Trade and Industry v Blunt* [2005] 2 BCLC 463.
[37] (1988) 4 BCC 533.

Secondly, there are cases where the conduct was held to be within the boundaries of commercial morality. In *Re Douglas Construction*,[38] the director had put a lot of his own money into the company in order to keep it going. In view of this it was held that it was difficult to say he was abusing the concept of limited liability. In *Re Dawson Print Ltd,* there was a very young entrepreneur who was only about 20 years old when he started his first companies. He had had some bad luck and some problems with employees. No disqualification was imposed. Hoffmann J made the memorable statement: '. . . [H]aving seen him in the witness box I thought that he was a great deal more intelligent than many directors of successful companies that I have come across.'[39] An interesting issue that arose in this case concerned the relevance of the use by the director of moneys that represented Crown debts. In other words, what weight does the court attach to the fact that the directors have used PAYE and NI money collected from employees to finance the company in its dying days, instead of handing it over to the Inland Revenue or other appropriate authority? Some judges had taken the view that the director was a 'quasi-trustee' of these moneys and that use of these to finance the business was more culpable than failure to pay commercial debts.[40] In the *Dawson* case, the assets realised £3,855 and debts were £111,179 of which about £40,000 represented unpaid PAYE, NI, VAT and rates. Hoffmann J was not prepared to regard the use of these Crown moneys as being especially culpable:

> The fact is that . . . the Exchequer and the Commissioners of Customs and Excise have chosen to appoint traders to be tax collectors on their behalf with the attendant risk. That risk is to some extent compensated by the preference which they have on insolvency. There is as yet no obligation upon traders to keep such moneys in a separate account as there might be if they were really trust moneys, they are simply a debt owed by the company. I cannot accept that failure to pay these debts is regarded in the commercial world generally as such a breach of commercial morality that it requires in itself a conclusion that the directors concerned are unfit to be involved in the management of a company.[41]

This passage was subsequently approved by the Court of Appeal in *Re Sevenoaks Ltd*[42] and they made it clear that non-payment of Crown debts was not to be treated automatically as evidence of unfitness and it was necessary to look closely at each case to determine the significance of non-payment.[43]

These then are merely examples of cases falling on either side of the line. It is clear that each case will fall to be decided very much on its own facts and that the judges are having to perform some quite subjective assessments of the conduct of individuals.[44]

---

[38] (1988) 4 BCC 553.

[39] (1987) 3 BCC 322 at p. 324.

[40] See e.g. *Re Lo-Line Ltd* (1988) 4 BCC 415 and earlier cases.

[41] (1987) 3 BCC 322 at p. 325. See also, *Secretary of State for Trade and Industry* v *TC Stephenson* [2000] 2 BCLC 614.

[42] [1990] BCC 765 at p. 777.

[43] On the other hand, it is often a failure to pay Crown debts which causes the s. 6 proceedings to be brought and was the ground upon which the Court of Appeal upheld the disqualification order in *Sevenoaks* itself; see *Re Verby Print for Advertising Ltd* [1998] BCC 656, *per* Neuberger J. In *Secretary of State for Trade and Industry* v *Thornbury* [2008] BCC 768, the director was disqualified because his culpable failure to make proper enquiries led to the company continuing to trade to the detriment of the Crown.

[44] For a case involving the disqualification of a non-executive director, see *Secretary of State for Trade and Industry* v *Swan (No. 2)* [2005] EWHC 2479; see J. Lowry 'The Whistle-Blower and the Non-Executive Director' [2006] *Journal of Corporate Law Studies* 249.

### 3 *Reference to other companies*

The courts have been required to form a view about whether the respondent is able to refer to his subsequent or contemporaneous conduct of other companies by way of mitigation. In *Re Matthews (DJ) (joinery design)*[45] companies had been wound up insolvent in 1981 and 1984 but the respondent argued that the current position was what mattered, that he had learned from his mistakes, and was now running a third company successfully. It was held that although this later company could be some mitigation, it could not entirely wipe out the past. Peter Gibson J put it thus:

> It was submitted that . . . just as there is joy in heaven over a sinner that repenteth, so this court ought to be glad that a director who has been grossly in dereliction of his duties, now wishes to follow the path of righteousness. But I must take account of the misconduct that has occurred in the past, and give effect to the public interest that required such misconduct to be recognised.[46]

In a later case,[47] the same judge took the view that the wording of s. 6 (1) (b): 'did not enable the court to look at the respondent's conduct in relation to any company whatsoever. The attention of the court is focused on the conduct of the respondent as a director of one or more companies as specified in that subsection.'[48] Subsequently, in *Re Country Farms Inns Ltd,*[49] it has been observed that there is a 'lead company' concept built into s. 6 (1) (b), which is the necessary consequence of the words 'either taken alone or taken together with it', to the effect that conduct relating to the collateral company alone could not justify a finding of unfitness sufficient to lead to a disqualification order under that section. In that case, the issue arose of whether the conduct in relation to the 'collateral' company (or companies) in s. 6 (1) (b) should be the same as or similar to that relied on in relation to the 'lead' company. The Court of Appeal held that there was no requirement for this.[50]

### 4 *Appropriate periods of disqualification*

In *Re Sevenoaks Ltd,*[51] the Court of Appeal laid down guidelines as to the appropriate periods of disqualification:

> I would for my part endorse the division of the potential 15-year disqualification period into three brackets . . .
>
> (1) The top bracket of disqualification for periods over ten years should be reserved for particularly serious cases. These may include cases where a director who has already had one period of disqualification imposed on him falls to be disqualified yet again.

---

[45] (1988) 4 BCC 513 (Companies Act 1985, s. 300).
[46] *Ibid.* at p. 518.
[47] *Re Bath Glass* (1988) 4 BCC 130.
[48] *Ibid.* at p. 132.
[49] [1997] BCC 801 at p. 808, *per* Morritt LJ.
[50] *Ibid.* departing from statements to the contrary in earlier cases.
[51] [1990] BCC 765 at pp. 771–772, *per* Dillon LJ.

(2) The minimum bracket of two to five years' disqualification should be applied where, though disqualification is mandatory, the case is, relatively, not very serious.

(3) The middle bracket of disqualification for from six to ten years should apply for serious cases which do not merit the top bracket.

In the later case of *Secretary of State for Trade and Industry* v *Griffiths*,[52] the Court of Appeal gave further general guidance on the process of deciding upon the appropriate period of disqualification. In particular it took the view that it is something that ought to be dealt with comparatively briefly and without elaborate reasoning. The Court of Appeal also made it clear that in view of the very large number of cases which have now appeared in the law reports, it would not usually be appropriate for the judge to be taken through the facts of previous cases in order to guide him as to the course he should take in the case before him.[53]

## 5 Disqualification undertakings: the Carecraft procedure and its displacement under the Insolvency Act 2000

In *Re Carecraft Construction Ltd*,[54] the court was asked to follow a summary procedure in view of the circumstances that there was no dispute about the material facts and no dispute about the period of disqualification. The procedure comprised a schedule of agreed facts. The directors accepted that the court would be likely to find that their conduct made them unfit to be concerned in the management of a company. On that basis, the Official Receiver agreed that it was not necessary for other comparatively unimportant disputes about the facts to be settled and accepted that he would not seek more than the minimum period of disqualification. The court held that it had jurisdiction to proceed in this way.

Subsequently, many cases have been decided in this way under what has become known as the *Carecraft* procedure.[55] The details of the rationale behind it were recently summarised by Jonathan Parker J in *Official Receiver* v *Cooper*:[56]

[T]he public interest in relation to proceedings under [section 6] lies in the protection of the public against persons acting as directors or shadow directors of companies who are unfit to do so. That in turn involves ensuring, so far as possible, that disqualification orders of appropriate length are made in all cases which merit such orders and that they are made as speedily and economically as is reasonably practicable . . . The Carecraft procedure represents, in my judgment, an important means of advancing that public interest. In the first place, it avoids the need for a contested hearing, with the attendant delays and inevitably substantial costs. Not only does this benefit the taxpayer, who ultimately bears the burden of the Secretary of State's costs (in so far as they are not recovered from the respondent) and of the costs of a legally aided respondent,

---

[52] [1998] BCC 836.
[53] *Ibid.* at pp. 845–846.
[54] [1993] BCC 336.
[55] A director who is unwilling to become involved in the *Carecraft* procedure is not able to prevent the bringing of full disqualification proceedings by offering undertakings to the court not to act as a director; see *Re Blackspur Group plc* [1998] BCC 11, CA.
[56] [1999] 1 BCC 115. It was held here that the respondent could make the admissions and concessions for the purpose of *Carecraft* proceedings only, and without prejudice to other proceedings.

it also avoids the situation where a non-legally aided respondent against whom an order for costs is made is in effect buried under an avalanche of costs, causing his financial ruin in addition to any disqualification order made against him . . . In the second place, the Carecraft procedure discourages respondents from requiring the Secretary of State to prove at a contested hearing allegations which the respondent knows to be true. In the third place, the Carecraft procedure encourages respondents to recognise their wrong doing and to face the consequences of it.[57]

The judge in *Carecraft* proceedings is not bound to make a disqualification order, and is not bound by the length of period of disqualification that the parties have agreed is appropriate. On the other hand, the case comes before him on agreed facts and those are the only facts on which he can base his judgment.[58]

The Insolvency Act 2000 established a regime[59] under which the Secretary of State can accept a 'disqualification undertaking' from a director. The aim of this new administrative procedure was to avoid the need to use the *Carecraft* procedure which although a summary procedure nevertheless involves, to some extent, the expense of a court process. The basic rules on disqualification undertakings are set out in s. 1 A of the CDDA 1986.[60] Statistically it is looking as though disqualification undertakings are replacing *Carecraft* in most situations in which in the past *Carecraft* would have been used. For instance, in 2003–2004 disqualifications under s. 6 by court order numbered 213, whereas disqualifications under s. 6 by means of disqualification undertakings numbered 1,154.[61] In contrast, in the last year prior to the coming into use of disqualification undertakings, there were 1,548 disqualifications under s. 6 by court order.[62]

## 23.4 Other grounds

### A Disqualification after investigation

Section 8 (1) provides in effect that if it appears to the Secretary of State from a report made by inspectors under various enactments (or from information or documents obtained under certain enactments) that it is expedient in the public interest that a disqualification order should be made against any person who is (or has been) a director,[63] he may apply to the court for an order. The court may make the order where it is satisfied that his conduct in relation to the company makes him unfit to be concerned in the management of a company.[64] Under these provisions the test of unfitness is similarly to be applied by reference to the matters set out in Sch. 1 (as applicable), and the case law.[65] Under this ground the maximum period of disqualification is 15 years.

---

[57] [1999] 1 BCC 115 at p. 117.
[58] *Secretary of State for Trade and Industry* v *Rogers* [1997] BCC 155, CA.
[59] Insolvency Act 2000, ss. 6–8 amending the CDDA 1986.
[60] And ss. 7 and 8.
[61] *Companies in 2003–04* (DTI: London, 2004) p. 44.
[62]*Ibid.*
[63] Or shadow director of any company. See also the CDDA 1986, s. 22 (4) and (5).
[64] *Ibid.* s. 8 (2). See, for example, *Secretary of State for Business, Enterprise and Regulatory Reform* v *Sullman* [2008] EWHC 3179 (Ch).
[65] *Ibid.* s. 12 (C).

## B Disqualification on conviction of an indictable offence

The court[66] has power to make a disqualification order against a person convicted of an indictable offence[67] in connection with the 'promotion, formation, management, liquidation or striking off of a company, or with the receivership or management of a company's property'.[68] Following amendments introduced by the Small Business, Enterprise and Employment Act 2015 this power has been extended to similar offences that an individual has committed overseas.[69] An example of this occurred in *R v Georgiou*.[70] The defendant was convicted of carrying on insurance business without the necessary authorisation under the Insurance Companies Act 1982. He was also disqualified from being a director for five years.[71] His argument that the court had no jurisdiction to disqualify him because he had not used the company as a vehicle for the commission of the offence and so the misconduct was not 'in connection with management' was rejected by the Court of Appeal; carrying on insurance business through a limited company was sufficiently a function of management.

## C Disqualification for persistent breaches of the companies legislation

Here, the ground for disqualification is where it 'appears to the court that [the person] has been persistently in default in relation to the provisions of the companies legislation requiring any return, account or other document' to be sent to the Registrar of Companies.[72] If the respondent has been found guilty[73] of three or more such defaults within the five years ending with the date of the Secretary of State's application for disqualification, it is treated as conclusive proof of persistent default.[74] The maximum period of disqualification is five years.

## D Disqualification for fraud in a winding up

It is provided that the court[75] may make a disqualification order against a person if, in the course of a winding up, it appears that he:

(a) has been guilty of an offence for which he is liable (whether he has been convicted or not) under section 993 of the Companies Act 2006 (fraudulent trading), or

(b) has otherwise been guilty, while an officer or liquidator of the company, receiver of the company's property or administrative receiver of the company, of any fraud in relation to the company or of any breach of his duty as such officer, liquidator, receiver or administrative receiver.[76]

Here, the maximum period of disqualification is 15 years.

---

[66] Defined so as to include certain criminal courts; *ibid*. s. 2 (2).
[67] Whether on indictment or summarily.
[68] CDDA 1986, s. 2 (1). The offence need not relate to the actual management of the company but must be committed in connection with its management: *R v Creggy* [2008] EWCA Crim 394.
[69] Section 5 A of the CDDA 1986.
[70] (1988) 4 BCC 322.
[71] Under the CDDA 1986, s. 2.
[72] *Ibid*. s. 3 (1).
[73] Technically, the CDDA 1986, s. 3 (3) applies here.
[74] *Ibid*. s. 3 (2).
[75] Defined in the CDDA 1986, s. 4 (2).
[76] *Ibid*. s. 4 (1).

## E Disqualification on summary conviction

This provision permits disqualification in certain circumstances where a person is convicted of certain offences. Broadly, it relates to convictions for failures to comply with companies legislation relating to returns, accounts and similar matters to be sent to the Registrar of Companies.[77] If there have been three of these within the five years ending with the date of the current proceedings[78] then the court may disqualify him for a period of up to five years.[79]

## F Disqualification for fraudulent or wrongful trading

Section 10 of the CDDA 1986 fits with the fraudulent and wrongful trading provisions[80] by giving the court power to disqualify in addition to any other order that is being made under those provisions.[81] As many of the facts that give rise to a disqualification order under s. 6 (i.e. unfitness and insolvency) may also trigger liability for fraudulent or (more usually) wrongful trading, this additional power of the court makes sense.

## G Disqualification for breach of competition law

Sections 9 A–9 E of the CDDA 1986 (inserted by s. 204 of the Enterprise Act 2002) place the court under a duty to make a disqualification order against a director of a company which commits a breach of competition law, provided the court is satisfied that the director's conduct is such as to make him unfit to be concerned in the management of the company. The maximum period for disqualification is 15 years. The Office of Fair Trading[82] and other specified regulators such as, for example, the Rail Regulator, may apply for a disqualification order against a director on this ground. There is also a scheme for competition disqualification undertakings under s. 9 B of the 1986 Act.

## H Disqualification of persons instructing an unfit director

Section 8 Z A of the CDDA 1986 (inserted by s. 105 of the Small Business, Enterprise and Employment Act 2015) provides that the court may make a disqualification order against a person (P) if the court is satisfied that: (i) a disqualification order under s. 6 of the CDDA 1986 has been made against a person who is or was a director or that such a person has given a disqualification undertaking; and (ii) that P exercised the requisite amount of undue influence over the director.[83] The requisite amount of influence test is satisfied where the conduct that gave rise to the director's disqualification was the result of that director acting in accordance with P's directions or instructions.[84]

---

[77] See the CDDA 1986, s. 5 (1).
[78] Including those proceedings.
[79] See the CDDA 1986, s. 5 (2)–(5). There are marked similarities between this and the s. 3 provisions but the main point is that s. 5 applies only where criminal proceedings are ongoing.
[80] See Chapter 2, 2.2C above.
[81] See e.g. *Re Brian D Pierson (Contractors) Ltd* [1999] BCC 26.
[82] See *Director Disqualification Orders in Competition Cases: An OFT Guidance Document* (2010), available at http://www.oft.gov.uk/shared_oft/business_leaflets/enterprise_act/oft510.pdf.
[83] Section 8 Z A (1) of the CDDA 1986.
[84] Section 8 Z A (2) of the CDDA 1986.

Here the minimum period of disqualification is two years, subject to a maximum of 15 years.[85]

## I Compensation awards

Section 15 A of the CDDA 1986 (inserted by s. 105 of the Small Business, Enterprise and Employment Act 2015) makes a significant change to the previous disqualification regime. Here, the court is allowed to make a compensation order against an individual director[86] where:

(a) the person is subject to a disqualification order or disqualification undertaking under this Act, and

(b) conduct for which the person is subject to the order or undertaking has caused loss to one or more creditors of an insolvent company of which the person has at any time been a director.[87]

The ability to impose a compensation order applies to both directors and those instructing a director and serves to provide an important mechanism for compensation to be paid directly (and personally) from an individual director to creditors. The Secretary of State may apply for a compensation order to be made up to two years from the date the disqualification order was made (or the disqualification undertaking accepted).[88]

## 23.5 Human rights challenges

It is possible that proceedings under the CDDA 1986 are challenged on the basis that in some way or other, they have infringed the European Convention on Human Rights which was incorporated into UK law by the Human Rights Act 1998 and came into force on 2 October 2000.[89] Whilst we have not seen significant attempts in this regard, even prior to October 2000 it has made its appearance in the cases.[90] In *Hinchliffe* v *Secretary of State for Trade and Industry,*[91] the director wished to argue that various aspects of the disqualification proceedings infringed art. 6 of the Convention and sought, as the judge put it: 'whatever . . . adjournment of the disqualification proceedings is necessary to ensure that they will not be heard before the passage into law of the Bill presently before Parliament for incorporation of the European Convention on Human Rights into English law, so as to give the English court the power and duty to apply the provisions of that Convention.'[92] The director's argument failed, mainly on the ground that it was held that the court could not embark on the speculative course of whether a Bill before Parliament would be passed into law in its then form.

---

[85] Section 8 Z A (4) of the CDDA 1986.
[86] Section 15 A (1) of the CDDA 1986.
[87] Section 15 A (3) of the CDDA 1986.
[88] Section 15 A (5) of the CDDA 1986.
[89] Disqualification cases involving human rights arguments will probably come to be regarded as the exact opposite of the *Carecraft* procedure.
[90] Arguments based on art. 6 have also arisen in judicial review proceedings connected with disqualification; see *R* v *Secretary of State for Trade and Industry, ex parte McCormick* [1998] BCC 379.
[91] [1999] BCC 226.
[92] *Ibid.* at p. 227, *per* Rattee J.

In *EDC* v *United Kingdom,*[93] the former director applied to the European Commission of Human Rights against the UK Government alleging that there had been unreasonable delays in the disqualification proceedings that constituted a violation of art. 6 of the Convention. The relevant part of art. 6 provided that 'in the determination of his civil rights and obligations . . . everyone is entitled to a . . . hearing within a reasonable time.' The proceedings had begun in 1991 and ended in 1996 and in all the circumstances of the case had failed to meet the reasonable time requirement in art. 6 (1).[94]

## 23.6 Concluding remarks

This chapter has covered the disqualification of directors. The penalty of disqualification in effect makes a public statement that disqualified directors should, for a time at least, no longer be part of the corporate world; that they are not fit to be doing what they have done in the past; that in respect of their efforts at work, the nation is better off without them.

As a final thought, it is worth raising the question whether the Government has achieved the right balance. Here we are concerned not only with the balance as regards the operation of the area of law concerned with disqualification, but also as regards all the regulatory aspects of mainstream company law, and as regards the regulation that is imposed on the capital markets, by (for the moment at least) the EU and UK regulatory authorities.

Disqualifications are now averaging a figure of about 1,400 per year. The process involves the public imposition of very high levels of disapproval by the judicial system, the heavy arm of the machinery of the state. It is cast upon people who were in the main running small businesses, trying their best to earn a living, and usually providing employment for others in the process. The vast majority will have got into difficulties, not through planned fraud, but by struggling on, trying to pretend to their employees and to their families that they were on top of the problems; hoping that things would turn out for the best. Many will have also suffered personal insolvency as a result of the collapse of their business, or come very close to insolvency. The Company Law Review expressed the view that the evidence suggests that small firms are the main job creators.[95]

Almost without exception, the agencies of government responsible for setting levels of regulation, and enforcing them, are operated by salaried employees, whose work environments will be very different, and will involve relatively high levels of certainty, of reward, and advancement; certainties which are no part of the life of an entrepreneur. There is a danger that over the years the government agencies will misjudge the balance. If so, in due course, it may be found that fewer able people will choose to make their living through

---

[93] Application No. 24433/94 [1998] BCC 370.
[94] Subsequent cases are less encouraging for directors; see e.g. *DC, HS and AD* v *United Kingdom* [2000] BCC 710; *WGS and MSLS* v *United Kingdom* [2000] BCC 719; *Re Westminster Property Management Ltd* [2001] BCC 121, CA. In *Re Stakefield (Midlands) Ltd* [2010] EWHC 2518 (Ch), Newey J said, at [21], 'I take the view that neither article 6 of the European Convention on Human Rights, nor the Secretary of State's duty to act fairly, will normally extend to requiring the Secretary of State to obtain evidence or to ensure that investigations are undertaken . . .'
[95] In the sense of new jobs. Thus the example is given of statistics available to the DBIS which show that between 1989 and 1991 over 90% of additional jobs created were in firms with fewer than ten employees even though they accounted for only 18% of total employment in 1989; see DTI Consultation Document (February 1999) *The Strategic Framework*, para. 2.19.

entrepreneurial activity. Arguably, this is happening in other areas of life in the UK, where high levels of regulation and relatively poor rewards are making essential jobs increasingly unattractive; and then it is found that there are shortages.

Although company law has many areas where the rules are permissive, left largely in the hands of business people, the ultimate fact is that if the state acting on behalf of the general populace wants to intervene and make new rules, it will. Company law is, in essence, public regulation of the organisational structures through which production takes place, and of the capital markets through which money is raised to finance the production process. The agencies of the state know that they bear the responsibility for ensuring a stable yet vital commercial environment by means of an unbiased approach to both *laissez-faire* and regulation. If they get the balance wrong, the economy will suffer. It is not an easy balance to strike and there is no panacea.

## Further reading

White Paper, *A Revised Framework for Insolvency Law* (Cmnd 9175, 1984).

J. Lowry 'The Whistle-Blower and the Non-Executive Director' [2006] *JCLS* 249.

# Index